The Winn L. Rosch Hardware Bible, Third Edition

Winn L. Rosch

MONTEREY COUNTY FREE LIBRARIES

MARINA CALIFORNIA

SAMS
PUBLISHING

201 West 103rd Street
Indianapolis, Indiana 46290

Copyright © 1994 by Sams Publishing

All rights reserved. No part of this book shall be reproduced, stored in a retrieval system, or transmitted by any means, electronic, mechanical, photocopying, recording, or otherwise, without written permission from the publisher. No patent liability is assumed with respect to the use of the information contained herein. Although every precaution has been taken in the preparation of this book, the publisher and author assume no responsibility for errors or omissions. Neither is any liability assumed for damages resulting from the use of the information contained herein. For information, address Sams Publishing, 201 W. 103rd St., Indianapolis, IN 46290.

International Standard Book Number: 1-56686-127-6

Library of Congress Catalog Card Number: 93-075014

97   96   95   4

Interpretation of the printing code: the rightmost double-digit number is the year of the book's printing; the rightmost single-digit, the number of the book's printing. For example, a printing code of 94-1 shows that the first printing of the book occurred in 1994.

Composed in Agaramond and MCPdigital by Macmillan Computer Publishing

Printed in the United States of America

Trademarks: All terms mentioned in this book that are known to be trademarks or service marks have been appropriately capitalized. Sams Publishing cannot attest to the accuracy of this information. Use of a term in this book should not be regarded as affecting the validity of any trademark or service mark.

Publisher
Richard K. Swadley

Acquisitions Manager
Greg Wiegand

Managing Editor
Cindy Morrow

Acquisitions Editor
Sarah Browning

Development Editor
Sunthar Visuvalingam

Production Editor
Tim Cox

Copy Editors
Jo Anna Arnott
Geneil Breeze
Howard Jones
Melinda Taylor

Editorial Coordinator
Bill Whitmer

Editorial Assistants
Carol Ackerman
Sharon Cox
Lynette Quinn

Marketing Manager
Gregg Bushyeager

Cover Designer
Jay Corpus

Book Designer
Alyssa Yesh

**Director of Production
and Manufacturing**
Jeff Valler

Imprint Manager
Juli Cook

**Manufacturing
Coordinator**
Paul Gilchrist

Production Analysts
Angela Bannon
Dennis Clay Hager
Mary Beth Wakefield

Production
JoAnna Arnott
Don Brown
Mona Brown
Michael Brumitt
Cheryl Cameron
Mary Ann Cosby
Terri Edwards
Dennis Clay Hager
Donna Harbin
Aleata Howard
Deb Kincaid
Ayanna Lacey
Shawn MacDonald
Liz Peterson
Brian-Kent Proffitt
Chad Poore
Susan Shepard
SA Springer
Marcella Thompson
Scott Tullis
Suzanne Tully
Dennis K. Wesner
Holly Wittenberg

Indexer
Bront Davis

Overview

Contents

Preface to the Third Edition

Times change, and so has the personal computer. After more than a dozen years, technology has pushed the PC in two directions: up in power and down in price. Although neither move is surprising, the rate of travel has been unprecedented.

Today's most powerful PC whips through everyday tasks more than 100 times faster than the first desktop machines. Even today's entry-level machines are 20 to 50 times faster than the original PC. Not only is that power available, it's also necessary because modern software demands every bit of performance (and every byte of memory) a PC can deliver.

The rewards are great: you can do more with a PC than might even have been imagined with the first machines. Every screen is a graphic slate for drawing or composing page-perfect text. An up-to-date PC can generate a cacophony of sounds or control a symphony of instruments. Where once PCs were machines of words and numbers, now they work with images, even morphing faces right before your eyes. Almost anything you can imagine you can call up on your monitor screen. And the stuff that you can't imagine you can look up in your CD-ROM library.

Yet prices have plummeted. Today, anyone can afford a PC. Machines using the latest, more powerful microprocessors now cost less than a decent television set. Price is no longer a reason for not putting a PC on every office desk or in every home.

These changes in PCs and the PC industry have been marked by two technological break-throughs that separate PCs into three distinct generations. In the years since the first real PC was introduced, we have already seen two generations pass by, and we're well on our way through the third. Although some people define computer generation by the numbers stamped on top of particular microprocessors, the better definition derives from how PCs are used and what they can do.

The first generation began before the introduction of IBM's original PC. The earliest PCs were marked by an orientation to characters—text and numbers. These machines substituted for word processors, bookkeeping machines, and file systems and added electronic speed, accuracy, and repeatability.

This first generation was also dominated by IBM. The IBM PC brought wide notice to what a personal computer was and what it could do. This generation, this technology, and IBM's dominance of the industry all reached a peak with the IBM AT and its 286 microprocessor. IBM set the standard and the world followed.

The second generation broke free from IBM with the acceptance of new concepts: graphics and multitasking. The dominant player shifted dramatically, from hardware-vendor IBM to software-seller Microsoft. Microsoft's Windows, an idea born in 1984, finally blossomed with the power and versatility of the 386 microprocessor, first introduced in personal computers by Compaq Computer Corporation in 1987. With the next flowering of the Intel microprocessor family, the 486, PCs finally broke through their old barriers and opened the graphical world of windowed multitasking to everyone.

The new (and current) generation of PCs splits from all the limits of the past. This generation brings the promise of platform-independent personal computing. That is, what's inside your box doesn't matter as much as what you do with it. We're stepping into a strange new world where you can pick and choose the microprocessor inside your PC not just from the Intel family or its clones, but from a variety of high-performance chips with entirely different architectures—new chips that look ahead at ever-higher performance instead of backward at the need for carrying the heavy baggage of backward compatibility.

Although Intel holds the strongest card to dominate this generation with its Pentium microprocessors, half a dozen other companies offer competing chips that can serve as alternatives. One may even break free and become the new dominant architecture. Odds are, however, all will stick around and give you choices you have never had before. You can choose your chip for its own particular advantages: speed, price, or versatility. With competition on a new level, the promise is more power for a lower price than ever before, more opportunity, and more options to sort through.

This third edition of the *Hardware Bible* reflects this major change in the way personal computers will develop over the next few years. Instead of concentrating solely on Intel chips, this edition looks at all the major families of microprocessors and compares them. Chapter 3, "Microprocessors," has been substantially revised to reflect the growing influence of RISC technology. When the first edition of this book was published, fewer than 40 percent of the workstations sold had RISC pretentions; now nearly 90 percent do. This same RISC influence is now infiltrating the world of the personal computer. Chapter 3 now integrates RISC with the mainstream of microprocessor design and helps you sort through all the new chip architectures (RISC and CISC) from Alpha to SPARC. In-depth treatment is given both to Intel's Pentium and the new PowerPC chips from IBM and Motorola.

Bus designs, too, are changing. In consequence, Chapter 6, "The Expansion Bus," has been greatly expanded to cover the new, high-speed local buses that you will want to demand in your next PC: VL Bus and PCI. ISA coverage has been expanded to include its connection with the new Plug-and-Play standard. Reflecting the growing influence of notebook and low-power (Green) PCs, PCMCIA's PC card standards up through the latest hardware and software revisions are covered in full detail.

Chapter 7, "The Basic Input/Output System," takes an in-depth look at the setup options offered by today's most popular BIOS systems so that you can better sort through your options in optimizing the performance of your PC. Coverage has also been extended to reflect the needs of Plug-and-Play technology that soon will let you expand your system with nary a concern or DIP switch.

Video systems have undergone a revolution in the last few years. Now, performance is defined by the graphic accelerator chip your system uses. Consequently, Chapter 13, "Display Adapters," now includes an in-depth look at graphics acceleration as well as a head-to-head comparison of all the major graphics accelerator chips.

But there are more changes in store for the PC industry. Sound was once the realm of a tiny speaker (better termed a "squeaker") inside the PC that did little more than beep and chirp. Now PCs are able to generate and manipulate digital-quality audio. A sound board makes any PC into a synthesizer for making music, sound effects, or just dramatic narration for presentations. A MIDI connection puts the PC in control of almost any imaginable combination of electronic instruments. A new chapter (Chapter 15, "Audio") covers sound boards, standards, and MIDI matters.

In the Audio chapter you also find background on a new technology that's popping up everywhere from synthesizers to modems: Digital Signal Processors.

Multimedia and other data-intensive technologies have made a CD ROM a mandatory peripheral for all PCs, so this edition gives the subject its own chapter (Chapter 24, "Compact Discs"). In that chapter, you find everything you want to know, not just about data disks, but also about audio CDs and Kodak's PhotoCD system.

With most businesses and many homes having more than one PC, connecting them is more a necessity than a convenience. Chapter 20, "Networking," another new chapter, covers connectivity basics to help you understand and sort through the alternatives.

Other changes you will find in this third edition are more evolutionary. Modem coverage now includes the latest V.34 (once known as V.Fast) technology and extended command sets. Chapter 16, "Printers and Plotters," shifts greater emphasis to lasers and the latest languages for them (emphasizing PCL used by the overwhelming majority of new machines).

The emphasis in Chapter 22, "Hard Disks," has shifted to today's important interfaces—SCSI and AT Attachment (IDE)—while keeping older designs in historical perspective. You will find information about the most recent revisions to the ATA standard and details about the next incarnation of SCSI.

To keep things more readable in this ever-growing book, technologies that have proven themselves out of the mainstream (for example, WORM drives) have been moved into the appendixes along with regulatory issues and material regarding older PCs that still can be of help in keeping veteran hardware running.

This book has always served two purposes: It's an introductory text to help anyone get up to speed on PCs and how they work. But once you know what's going on inside, it continues to serve as the ultimate PC reference.

In keeping with the latter role, this edition now incorporates a more detailed history of the PC, and more charts and illustrations than ever before. For example, the drive parameter table is the largest, most detailed we have ever published. You also will find memory charts and new microprocessor comparisons. In other words, if you need an answer about PCs, how they work, how to make them work, or when they began to work, you will find it answered here, definitively.

About the Author

Winn L. Rosch has written about personal computers since 1981 and has penned nearly 1,000 published articles about them—a mixture of reviews, how-to guides, and background pieces explaining new technologies. One of these was selected by The Computer Press Association as the best feature article of the year for 1987; another was runner-up for the same award in 1990. He has written other books about computers, the most recent of which are *Winn L. Rosch's Your Old PC* and *The Winn L. Rosch Hardware Bible,* Second Edition. At present, he is a contributing editor to *PC Magazine, PC Week, PC Sources,* and *Computer Shopper.* His books and articles have been reprinted in several languages (French, Italian, German, Greek, and Portuguese).

Besides writing, Rosch is an attorney licensed to practice in Ohio and holds a Juris Doctor degree. He was appointed to and currently serves on the Ohio State Bar Association's Computer Law Committee.

In other lifetimes, Rosch has worked as a photojournalist, electronic journalist, and broadcast engineer. For 10 years, he wrote regular columns about stereo and video equipment for *The Cleveland Plain Dealer,* Ohio's largest daily newspaper, and regularly contributed lifestyle features and photographs. In Cleveland, where he still holds out, he has served as a chief engineer for several radio stations. He also has worked on electronic journalism projects for the NBC and CBS networks.

In his spare time, Rosch conducts experiments on spontaneous generation in his refrigerator and is researching a definitive study of Precambrian literature.

Introduction

Tools define our culture. We aren't so much what we make as what we use to make it. Even barbarians can make holes with a bow and shaft; we have drill presses, hydraulic punches, and lasers. More importantly, the development of tools defines civilization. No culture is considered civilized unless it uses the latest tools. The PC is the tool that defines today's current age and culture.

Once a tool only for initiates and specialists, today the PC has become as common as, well, all those monitors sitting on office desks and overweight attaché cases bulging with keyboard-screen-and-battery combinations. The influence and infiltration of the PC stretch beyond comparison with any other modern tool, even beyond the reach of common metaphors. No office machine is as common; none so well used; none so revered—and so often reviled. Unlike the now-nearly forgotten typewriter that was restricted to secretaries and stenographic pools, the PC resides resplendently on once-bare drafting tables, executive desks, and kitchen counters. Unlike fax machines, calculators, and television sets, the PC doesn't do just one thing but meddles in nearly everything you do at work and at home. Unlike your telephone, pager, or microwave oven, the PC isn't something that you use and take for granted; it's something you wonder about, something you want to improve and expand, perhaps even something that you would like to understand.

Indeed, to use any tool effectively you have to understand it—what it can do, how it works, how you can use it most effectively. Making the most of your PC demands that you know more than how to rip through the packing tape on the box without lacerating your palms. You cannot just drop it on your desk, stand back, and expect knowledge to pour out like you have tapped into a direct line to a fortune cookie factory.

Unfortunately, despite the popularity of the PC, the machine remains a mystery to too many people. For most people, the only one more baffling than programming a VCR. Everyone knows that something happens between the time your fingers press down on the keys and a letter pops up on the screen, or a page curls out of the printer, or a sound never heard before by human ears shatters the cone of your multimedia loudspeakers. Something happens, but that something seems beyond human comprehension.

It's not. The personal computer is the most logical of modern machines. Its most complex thoughts are no more difficult to understand than the function of a light switch. Its power comes from combinations—a confluence of ideas, circuits, and functional blocks—each of which is easy to understand in itself. The mystery arises only when your vision is blocked by the steel wall of the computer case that blinds you to the simplicity fitted inside.

This book is designed to be both X-ray vision and explanation. It lets you see what's inside your PC, helps you understand how it works, and lets you master this masterpiece of modern technology. Moreover, you learn what you can do to make your PC better, how you can use it more effectively, how you can match the right components to make it better suit what you want to do, and how you can get the most speed, the most quality, the most satisfaction from today's technology.

In home and workplace, the personal computer is today's most technically advanced tool. With a PC, you can get yourself and your office organized, you can tackle jobs that would otherwise be too time-consuming to try, you can extend your imagination to see forms your mind cannot make, and you can relieve yourself of the tedium of repetitive, busy work.

For some, tools or the technologies behind them define the ages of man. Humankind started in the Stone Age. The apes that came before (and still persist in a few places where civilization has bowed to nature) pounded with rocks. Our ancestors went further, shaping rocks to better suit their needs: hammers, points, and knives. The story of civilization has been much the same during the passing millennia. As we have progressed from stone to bronze to iron, the aim has been the same: making the tool that best suits the task at hand, one that's sharper, stronger, and better fits the hand and job.

The story of the PC fits this same pattern. When the PC was introduced, it was like the rock in the raw. You grabbed it because you could. It was the right size to get your hands on, clumsy to use, and accomplished a job without any particular elegance. You sort of pounded away on the thing and hoped for the best.

The coming of metal meant that tools could be molded to their purpose. In the Bronze Age, then the Iron Age, work was faster and more precise. The modern PC offers the same kind of malleability. It's a machine made to be molded to your exact needs. Fortunately you don't need a forge to fit your PC to the function you desire. The physical part of the change is simple; the hard work is all mental—you have to know your PC to use it. You have to understand this most modern of tools.

Only a poor workman blames his tools when his job goes awry. But what kind of workman doesn't understand his tools at all, doesn't know how they work, and cannot even tell a good tool from a bad one? Certainly you wouldn't trust such a workman on an important job, one critical to your business, one that might affect your income or budget, or take control of your leisure pursuits. Yet far too many people profess ignorance about the PC, a tool vital to their businesses, their hobbies, or their households.

The familiar PC is the most important business tool to emerge from electronic technology. It is vital to organizing, auditing, even controlling, most contemporary businesses. In fact, anywhere there is work to do, you likely will find a PC at work. If you don't understand this modern tool, you will do worse than a bad job. Soon, you may have no job at all.

Unlike a hammer or screwdriver, however, the personal computer is a tool that frightens those uninitiated into its obscure cabala. Tinkering with a personal computer is held in the same awe as open-heart surgery, except that cardiovascular surgeons, too, are as apprehensive as the rest of us about tweaking around the insides of a computer. But computers are merely machines, made by people, meant to be used by people, and capable of being understood by people.

As with other tools, they are unapproachable only by those inexperienced with them. An automobile mechanic may reel at the sight of a sewing machine. The seamstress or tailor may throw up his hands at the thought of tuning his car. The computer is no different. In fact, today's personal computer is purposely designed to be easy to take apart and put back together, easy to change and modify, and generally invincible except at the hands of the foolish or purposely destructive. As machines go, the personal computer is sturdy and trouble-free. Changing a card in a computer is safer and more certain of success than fixing a simple home appliance such as a toaster or changing the oil in your car.

Times change, and so has the personal computer. After its first decade, it has become more complex and more affordable. New software such as the latest versions of Windows and OS/2 means that your PC is easier to use than ever. New developments promise to make your next PC easier to set up, too. A far-reaching new standard called Plug-and-Play can make upgrading your system as easy as plugging in new components—no adjustments, no configuration, no brains necessary. But even these innovations don't mean that you can take full advantage of your investment in your PC without understanding it and the underlying technology.

If anything puts people off from trying to understand PCs, it is the computer mystique. After all, the computer is a thinking machine, and that one word implies all sorts of preposterous non-sense. The thinking machine could be a devious machine, one hatching plots against you as it sits upon your desk, thinking of evil deeds that will cause you endless frustration. Although you might attribute satanic motivation to the machine that swallows up a day's work the instant your lights flicker, you would be equally justified in attributing evil intent to the bar of soap that makes you slip in the shower.

Even if you don't put your PC in a pentacle and light candles around it, the image of a thinking machine can mislead you. A thinking machine has a brain, therefore opening it up and working inside is brain surgery, and the electronic patient is just as likely to suffer irreversible damage at the hands of an unskilled operator as a human. A thinking machine must work the same unfathomable way as does the human mind—something so complicated that in thousands of years of attempts by the best geniuses no one has yet satisfactorily explained.

But computers think only in the way a filing cabinet or adding machine thinks—hardly in the same way as you do or Albert Einstein did. The computer has no emotions or motivations. It does nothing on its own, without explicit instructions that specify each step it must take. Moreover, the PC has no brain waves. The impulses traveling through the computer are no odd mixture of chemicals and electrical activity, of activation and repression. The computer deals in simple pulses of electricity, well understood and carefully controlled. The intimate workings of the computer are probably better understood than the seemingly simple flame that inhabits the internal combustion engine inside your car. Nothing mysterious lurks inside the thinking machine called the computer.

Computers are thought fearsome because they are based on electrical circuits. Electricity can be dangerous, as the ashes of anyone struck by lightning will attest. But inside the computer, the danger is low. At its worst, it measures 12 volts, which makes the inside of a computer as safe as playing with an electric train—even safer because you cannot trip over a PC's tracks (they're safely ensconced in the PC's disk drive). In fact, nothing that's readily accessible inside the computer will shock you, straighten your hair, or shorten your life. The personal computer is designed that way. It's made for tinkering, adding in accessories, and taking them out.

Computers are thought delicate because they are built from supposedly delicate electronic circuits. So delicate that their manufacturers warn you to ground yourself to a cold water pipe before touching them. So delicate that, even though they cost $500 each, they can be destroyed by an evil glance. In truth, even the most susceptible of these circuits, the one variety of electronic component that's really delicate, requires extreme protection only when it's not installed where it belongs. Although pulses of static electricity can damage circuits, the circuitry in which the component is installed naturally keeps the static under control. (Although static pulses are a million times smaller than lightning bolts, the circuits inside semiconductor chips are a million times smaller and more delicate than you are.) Certainly a bolt of lightning or a good spark of static can still do harm, but the risk of either can be minimized simply. In most situations and workplaces, you should have little fear of damaging the circuits inside your computer.

Most people don't want to deal with the insides of their computers because the machines are complex and confusing. In truth they are and they aren't. It all depends on how you look at them. Watching a movie on videotape is hardly a mental challenge, but understanding the whirring heads inside the machine and how the image is synchronized and the hi-fi sound is recorded is something that will spin your brain for hours. Similarly, changing a board or adding a disk drive to a computer is simple. It's designing the board and understanding the Boolean logic that controls the digital gates on it that take an engineering degree.

As operating systems get more complicated, computers are becoming easier to use. Grab a mouse and point the cursor at an on-screen window, and you can be a skilled computer operator in minutes. That may be enough to content you. But you will be shortchanging yourself and your potential. Without knowing more about your system, you probably won't tap all the power of the PC. You won't be able to add to it and make it more powerful. You may not even know how to use everything that's there. You definitely won't know whether you have the best computer for your purposes or some overpriced machine that cannot do what simpler models excel at.

In other words, although you don't need skill or an in-depth knowledge of computer or data processing theory, you do need to know what you want to accomplish and what you can accomplish, the how and why of working with, expanding, even building a personal computer system.

And that's the purpose of this book, to help you understand your present or future personal computer so that you can use rather than fear it. This text is designed to give you an overview of what makes up a computer system. It will give you enough grounding in how the machine works so that you can understand what you're doing if you want to dig in and expand or upgrade your system.

At the same time, the charts and tables provide you with the reference materials you need to put that knowledge in perspective and to put it to work. Not only can you pin down the basic dates of achievements in technology, find the connections you need to link a printer or modem, and learn the meaning of every buzzword, this book also will help you understand the general concept of your personal computer and give you the information you need to choose a computer and its peripherals. As you become more familiar with your system, this book will serve as a guide. It will even help you craft your own adapters and cables, if you choose to get your hands dirty.

The computer is nothing to fear, and it need not be a mystery. It is a machine, and a straightforward one at that. One that you can master in the few hours it takes to read this book.

Chapter 1
Background

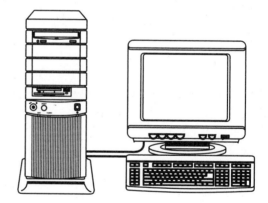

What is a PC? Where did it come from? And why should you care? The answers are already cloudy and the questions may one day become the mystery of the ages. But the PC's origins are not obscure; its definition is malleable but manageable, and your involvement is, well, personal but promising.

Archaeologists poring through the ruins of prehistory will one day discover that a sudden shift came in human culture, some cataclysm that forever changed the human social fabric. Examined over the span of centuries, the shift would appear abrupt, like some great body fell and polluted the planet or a great rift grew in the surface with an eruption that spewed a hitherto unknown substance over the surface. When, through a final stroke of luck, the last of the primitive carbon-based markings hidden in the vast cellulose energy storage mounds are decoded through an exhaustive search of the "Great Database," this enigmatic fallout will be identified by the simple code, "PC." The mystery of the ages will shift to understanding the origins of this strange substance.

Today we're closer to the cause of this social shift, if not in the midst of it. We don't need to dig through newspapers in the dump to see what's going on, as interesting as that might be, or wonder whether the landfill might by coming generations be seen as an energy storage mound. Already the mystery is here. The PCs on desktops and dealers' shelves appear to have sprung into existence in final form, a complete machine capable of processing and managing most of the information we deal with throughout our lives. They may just as well have been dropped from alien spaceships, exploded out of volcanoes, or flooded into society by some secret government organization intent on bending our thoughts and our lives to fit their plans. Already the history of the PC is becoming cloudy, ever more so as the current machines shake free from their roots and head into new generations.

But if you really want to understand what a PC is, how it works, and what it can do for you, you need more than a description of the gadgets you can buy today. After all, if a description were enough, you could get all the answers you need just by looking at what you have or what you want to buy. To really master the technology and the tool that is the PC, however, you need to know more—what makes a PC a PC? What are the ideas and concepts it encapsulates? Where did it and those underlying ideas come from?

Defining a PC

Before you can talk about PCs at all, you need to know what you're talking about. The question is simple: What is a PC?

Giving an exact definition of a personal computer is a task that seems amazingly straightforward until you're charged to actually do it. When you take the challenge, the term transforms itself into a strange cross-mating between amoeba and chameleon (biologists alone should shudder even at the thought of that one).

Yet PCs have been around long enough that the only folks likely not to recognize one by sight have vague notions that mankind may someday harness the mystery of fire.

The words should be self-defining—a personal computer could be a machine that's meant to be used by one person instead of shared among a number of operators. But that definition includes such things as the expensive graphic workstation and the humble dedicated word processor.

You could try to define personal computer by price, but that, too, would be frustrated by reality. The price range has changed so quickly that moving-target metaphors cannot even keep up. The price of the most powerful personal computers fell by a factor of five in little more than a year at the beginning of the 1990s as competing computer vendors took aim at one another. Where once the top of the line meant spending nearly $10,000, a year later the same power cost about $2,000. Machines with all the characteristics of a classic personal computer cost well under $1,000 today.

Another way would be to define personal computer by reference to the machine that first put the term into public parlance, the original IBM Personal Computer. But most people staring at personal computer monitor screens today may never have even seen an original IBM PC. In fact, soon the only places to catch a glance of such vintage hardware will be a computer museum or the local antique store.

Moreover, the term "personal computer" is becoming redundant in itself. Not only is it becoming impossible to draw the line between different classes of thinking machines, finding anything but a personal computer has become like looking for hay in a needle-stack—not only is the task not one to be taken lightly (or without heavy gloves) but the quest is pointless. Where once a personal computer was one that lacked the computational horsepower of a mainframe or minicomputer, power alone no longer distinguishes machines. The quickest of today's personal computers easily outruns most minicomputers and overlaps the low end of what diehards insist are mainframe machines. Like furry little mammals, PCs are pressing the lumbering dinosaurs to extinction. Even workstations, an eternally rising star in the hardware business, are falling prey to the onslaught of the PC. Today you can buy personal computers with the same microprocessors inside them that run in engineering workstations, at a fraction of the cost.

Like so much of the modern world, a personal computer is something that's easy to recognize and difficult to define. In truth, the personal computer is not defined by its parts (because the same components are common across the entire range of computers from pocket calculators to super-computing vector processors) but by how it is used. Every computer has a central processing unit and memory, and the chips used by PCs are used by just about every size of machine. Most computers also have the same mass storage systems and similar display systems to those of the PC. Although you'll find some variety in keyboards and connecting ports, at the signal level all have much in common, including the electrical components used to build them.

But in operation, you use your PC in an entirely different manner from any other type of computer. The way you work and the way the PC works with you are the best definition of the PC. Among the many defining characteristics of the personal computer, you find that:

➤ A PC is interactive. That is, you work with it, and it responds to what you do. You press a key and it responds—sort of like a rat in a Skinner box pressing a lever for a food pellet.

Although that kind of give-and-take, stimulus-and-response relationship may seem natural to you, that's not the way computers have always been. Most of the first three decades that computers were used commercially, they worked on the batch system. You had to determine what you wanted to do ahead of time, punch out a stack of cards, and dump them on the desk to the computer operator who, when he finished his crossword puzzle, would submit your cards to processing. The next day, after a 16-hour overnight wait, your program, which took only seconds to run, generated results that you would get on a pile of paper big enough to push a paper company into profitability and wipe out a small section of the Pacific Northwest. And odds are (if your job was your first stab at solving a particular problem) the paper would be replete with error messages, basically guaranteeing you lifelong tenure at your job because that's how long it would take to get the stupid program to run without error flags.

➤ A personal computer is dedicated. Like a dog with one master, the PC responds only to you—if only because it's sitting on your desk and has only one keyboard. Although the PC may be connected to other machines and people through modems and telephone wires or through a network, the link-up is for your convenience. In general, you use the remote connection for individual purposes, such as storing your own files, digging out data, and sending and receiving messages meant for your eyes (and those of the recipient) alone.

In effect, the PC is an extension of yourself. It increases your potential and abilities. Although it may not help you actually think faster, it will answer questions for you, store information (be it numeric, graphic, or audible), and manage your time and records. By helping you get organized, it cuts through the normal clutter of the work day and helps you streamline what you do.

➤ A personal computer also is versatile. Its tasks are not defined by its design, just its limitations. Within its capabilities, a PC can do almost anything. Its function is determined by programs, which are the software applications that you buy and load. The same hardware can serve as a word processor, file system, or presentation display.

➤ A personal computer is cooperative, meaning that it is connected and communicative. It can work with other computer systems no matter their power. A computer is equally adept at linking to hand-held Personal Digital Assistants and supercomputers to exchange information, even to take control. Through hard-wire or modem connections, a personal computer can tie into the world-wide information infrastructure, probing into other computers and their databases no matter their location.

One favored variety of connection brings together multiple personal computers to form a network or workgroup. These machines can cooperate together continuously, sharing expensive resources, such as high-speed printers and huge storage systems. Through this cooperation, the individual power of the personal computer is multiplied by the array of new options and capabilities available to it.

➤ A personal computer also is accessible. That is, you can get at one when you need it. It's either on your desk at work, tucked into a corner of your home office, or in your kid's bedroom.

The PC is so accessible, even ubiquitous, because it is affordable. Save your lunch money for a few weeks, and you can buy a respectable PC. Solid starter machines cost about the same as a decent television or mediocre stereo system.

More importantly, when you need to use a PC, you can. Today's software is nearly all designed so that you can use it intuitively. Graphic operating systems, on-line help, consistent commands, and enlightened programmers have turned the arcana of computer control into something feared only by those foolish enough not to try their hands on a keyboard.

A PC brings together those five qualities to help you do your work or extend your enjoyment. You could call your personal computer your interactive, dedicated, versatile, cooperative, and accessible problem-solver, but the acronym PC is much easier to remember; besides, that's what everyone else is calling the contraption anyway.

PC Prehistory

In the great scheme of things, the personal computer is just the flowering of hundreds of years of development, the coming together of diverse ideas, inspiration, technology, and tinkering. In retrospect, the PC was inevitable. In prospect, however, today's discount-store wonders were inconceivable. The groundwork was laid without any conception of where it would eventually lead.

Hardware Evolution

If any single inspiration for the development of computers exists, it was the simple principle that mathematicians don't like to do math problems either. With the coming of the mechanical age in the 17th Century, mathematicians looked for ways of mechanizing the busy work of making their calculations. They had better things to do than cramp their hands on pencils and overheat their brains adding numbers. Rather than calculate pages of tables, mathematicians would rather be developing numbers theories, classifying fauna, and visiting the public house to quaff a few beers.

Mechanical Computers

William Schickard is believed to have been the first of these lazy number workers to think of giving the work of calculating to a machine. However, he was overshadowed by the French philosopher Blaise Pascal, who was favored by modern-day computer language developer Nicolas

Wirth when Wirth was looking for a name for his procedural programming language. Among Pascal's achievements that led to his selection for that singular honor was the creation of the first mechanical calculator in 1642.

Pascal actually built several calculating machines that successfully carried out simple arithmetic, but they over-reached 17th Century technology. Although they were robust enough that several still survive, at the time they were regarded as unreliable.

Nearly two centuries passed before manufacturing technology caught up with the concept of mechanical calculations. The *Arithmometer,* invented by Thomas de Colmar in 1820, is generally regarded as the first commercially successful mechanical calculator.

While the mathematicians were tinkering away with their impractical calculators, an independent group of inventors tangled with what today we regard as an immensely more complicated problem: programming. This work, too, was based on a fundamental human drive: getting someone or (better still) something to do the work that you find too boring, too tiring, or too much trouble to bother with. One solution was long known. When the work is simply methodical, you can teach a servant, slave, serf, or graduate assistant to carry it out for you. Better still, give the task to a machine that won't complain, come in late for work, or run away and start a competing business.

Most boring jobs can be broken down into a series of simple steps. With a little incentive, (say the promise of an evening meal or a long enough whip), a servant can be taught to carry out each step in turn. Inventors saw that machines, dim-witted as they were at the time, could be made to master the same step-by-step tasks. The steps taken together make up what today we call a program.

The origins of the idea of a program of clearly defined steps for carrying out a complex task are lost in obscurity. But as early as the 16th Century, a form of programming had been developed and successfully commercialized, one that not only worked but sounded good. Music boxes were probably the first truly programmed machines. Using an arrangement of pegs on a rotating drum, the music box then (and now) can select the proper notes to play in a long sequence to make recognizable (or nearly so) melodies.

By 1725, the French inventor Bouchon came up with the idea of using a similar method for programming a weaving machine. The idea was perfected when it was combined with Edmund Cartwright's 1785 power loom and put to work in 1804 by Joseph Marie Jacquard. The final creation is generally regarded as the first truly programmable machine, the Jacquard loom. Using a belt of linked punched cards, the Jacquard loom could be programmed to produce any of an infinite variety of woven patterns in cloth.

These two streams of development, mechanical calculating and programming, came together in the work of Charles Babbage, who designed what many regard as the first computer, the Analytical Engine. Babbage believed that the most complex mathematical problems of the time could be solved by his machines. After all, the questions to which he sought answers required nothing but repetitive, mechanical calculations carried out again and again; for example, finding square roots by repeated approximation using division and multiplication—the same monotonous calculating that has inspired inventors over the ages.

Babbage first created his own mechanical calculator, Difference Engine Number 1, in 1822. He started work on a more ambitious calculator (Difference Engine Number 2) but never built the machine. Instead, he abandoned that project in 1834 in favor of a more flexible, versatile design that could tackle more complex problems. His insight was to combine his mechanical calculators with the programming facility of the Jacquard loom.

Many of Babbage's ideas foreshadowed the work of other inventors. For example, Babbage imagined using punched cards to create a machine to step through complex calculations at the turn of a crank. This idea would later independently occur to other inventors. Herman Hollerith, for instance, used punched cards for the tabulating machines in 1890. Hollerith himself is notable because the company he founded merged with two others to become the Computing-Tabulating-Recording Company. In 1924, that company changed its name to International Business Machines.

Babbage anticipated many of the concepts embodied in modern computers, including the capability to jump from one point in a program to another. He even added a printer so that his Analytical Engine could crank out (literally) answers as hard copy.

His design called for a collection of cams, gears, and pulleys more complex than any machine ever before created. In fact, the Analytical Engine proved too complex and never got off paper. Although a few others were inspired by Babbage's work, those who built the first successful mechanical computer were unaware of his work. For the most part, Babbage resurfaced only after the success of electronic computers caused historians to poke into the darker crannies of the 19th century.

Perhaps the most notable direct influence of Babbage is an interesting footnote in the history of computing. Babbage inspired Augusta Ada Byron, Countess of Lovelace (more commonly addressed as Lady Lovelace), to develop a nearly complete program that would have enabled the Analytical Engine to compute Bernoulli (fluid-flow) equations. For this work (and being the first to describe what today are regarded as program subroutines), Lady Lovelace is regarded as the first computer programmer. The short-lived Ada programming language of 1979 was named after her.

Nearly a century passed before technology had once again caught up with the ideas of the theorists. In 1937, work began on what is regarded as the first (and last) truly successful mechanical computer, the Automatic Sequence Controlled Calculator. Credited to Howard Aiken, this machine is most often called Harvard Mark I because of Aiken's affiliation with Harvard University, although it was actually financed by IBM and built at IBM Development Laboratories in Endicott, Massachusetts.

Essentially completed in 1943, the Mark I first performed calculations in August 1944, using rotating shafts, gears, and cams like the Analytical Engine. The differences reflected only changes in technology, not the underlying concepts. The Harvard Mark I was electrically powered instead of hand-cranked, and it was programmed using punched paper tape instead of punched cards. The working machine could add two numbers in 0.3 seconds (the time it took its shafts to rotate once around—200 RPM) and was capable of multiplying two 23-digit numbers in about six seconds.

Another mechanical program-controlled calculator, the Z3, was built by Konrad Zuse. Operational before Harvard Mark I in 1941, its existence was not known outside Germany until after World War II, so it does not figure in the mainstream development of computers.

Relay Computers

Even in the 40s the primary speed limit on these rudimentary computers was mechanical, so developers looked to other technologies to build their computers. Bell Telephone Laboratories began work on relay-based computers in 1938. A *relay* is an electrically controlled switch—one source of electricity activates an electromagnet which operates a switch that, in turn, alters the electrical flow in another circuit. Relays are a hybrid technology, electro-mechanical. Their mechanical side performs physical work while their electrical nature makes them very flexible. One relay can control others almost unlimited in number and distance. The gears and levers of purely mechanical calculators are limited in reach in both regards.

The choice of relay technology was a natural one for the telephone company. After all, the telephone switching systems of the time made extensive use of relays—rooms and rooms filled with them.

Bell Lab's first successful machine, Bell Model V, began work at the end of 1946. Although it was no faster than Harvard Mark I at addition, multiplication took the Bell machine only one second.

The speed of relay technology also intrigued Aiken, and in September 1948, he had his own relay-based machine, Harvard Mark II operating. By 1950, several other relay-based machines were running in Europe.

Electronic Computers

Early in the development of the computer, designers recognized the speed advantages of a totally electronic machine. After all, electronic signals could switch thousands or millions of times faster than mechanical cams or electrical relays.

Several inventors made initial stabs at the challenge of electronic computers. John Atansoff and Clifford Berry designed an electronic digital calculator at Iowa State College in 1938 but abandoned their work in 1942. They had the arithmetic unit of their machine working successfully but had not completed work on its input/output unit. In Germany, Zuse proposed a vacuum tube-based computer in 1939, but its design was rejected by the Nationalist-Socialist government.

The first successful electronic machine was secretly developed as part of the British cryptoanalysis program at Bletchley Park during World War II. There, T. H. Flowers created an electronic machine known as Colossus for comparing cipher texts. Colossus, first tested in December 1943, pioneered the concept of electronic clocked logic (with a clock speed of 0.005MHz) and used 1,500 vacuum tubes.

Although Colossus was a programmable machine, neither it nor the succeeding generations of cryptographic machines developed at Bletchley Park were designed to handle decimal multiplication. Moreover, the development of Colossus and its kin was kept secret until long after the war, so it did not in itself contribute to the development of the computer. In fact, many details of the Bletchley Park operation are still secret more than forty years later.

The most notable contributions to computing came from another member of the Bletchley Park operation, Alan M. Turing. Although not one of the principle developers of Colossus, his theoretical work explored the limits of what a computer can do. He conceptualized a mechanism now called a Turing Machine, the ultimate reductionist computer that broke the task of computing into elemental steps. Given enough time, the Turing Machine could compute anything computable. Turing also explored the realm of artificial intelligence—and, by definition, anything that it could not compute was not computable. His Turing Test is regarded as the measurement of success of an artificial intelligence system. The test requires that the responses of a computer be indistinguishable from those of a human given any set of questions.

The seminal machine in the history of the computer is generally regarded as ENIAC, the Electronic Numerical Integrator and Computer, developed at the Moore School of the University of Pennsylvania in Philadelphia by a team led by John Mauchly and J. Presper Eckert, Jr. Proposed in 1943, it was officially inaugurated in February 1946. The most complex vacuum-tube machine ever built, ENIAC occupied a 30-by-50 foot room (at 1,500 square feet, that's the size of a small house), weighed 30 tons, and required 200 kilowatts of electricity. It used 18,000 vacuum tubes and was based on a clocked logic design.

When operating at its design clock speed of 0.1MHz, ENIAC required a mere 200 microseconds for addition and 2.6 milliseconds for multiplication. At about 5,000 arithmetic operations per second, it was approximately 1,000 times faster than the Harvard Mark I.

The design goal of ENIAC was to calculate ballistic trajectories, and the machine succeeded well. It was able to compute the path of a 16-inch artillery shell in less than real time—that is, it could predict about where a shell would fall after it was fired but before it hit.

In late 1946, ENIAC was disassembled, moved to Aberdeen Proving Ground in Maryland, and reactivated. It served there until October 2, 1955. Portions of ENIAC survive in the Smithsonian Institution.

The next step in the development of the computer and PC was EDVAC, the Electronic Discrete Variable Automatic Computer. Unlike the decimal-based ENIAC, EDVAC was designed as a binary computer. Information to EDVAC was encoded in its most essential form—the presence or absence of a code symbol— which could be represented by a voltage. This binary basis is the essence of today's digital logic upon which nearly all current computers are based.

EDVAC was also the first stored-program computer; it held its binary instructions in memory exactly as it stored its binary data, a concept based on the ideas of John von Neumann, one of its developers.

The new EDVAC design resulted in vacuum-tube economy. Only 4,000 tubes (and 10,000 crystal diodes) were required to build it. It was delivered in 1949 to the Ballistic Research Laboratories at Aberdeen Proving Ground and became operational in 1951. It remained in service until December 1962.

During the development of EDVAC, Eckard and Mauchly of ENIAC fame left the Moore School to form the Eckert-Mauchly Computer Corporation in 1948. There they developed the first commercial electronic computer, UNIVAC (the Universal Automatic Computer). After the first UNIVAC was completed in 1951, another 45 were made throughout the next seven years. (Eckert-Mauchly Computer Corporation was acquired by Remington Rand Inc., which merged with Sperry Corporation to form Sperry Rand Corporation in 1955. Sperry later merged with Burroughs Corporation to form Unisys.)

UNIVAC had an internal clock rate of 2.25MHz and about 12K of RAM in the form of mercury delay lines. It could add or subtract in 0.525 milliseconds and multiply in 2.15 milliseconds.

With UNIVAC, the basic operating principles of the computer were in place. Further developments have come in the refinement of the technology used to make computer circuits. Switching from tubes to transistors increased reliability and allowed designs to become both more complex (mainframes) and smaller (minicomputers). Memory shifted from mercury delay lines and cathode ray tubes to magnetic core, and finally to solid-state transistors. Integrated circuits continued this trend and made possible microprocessors and RAM chips, which, in turn, led to the circuits that formed the basis of the first personal computers.

Software Evolution

The first giant computers were by no means personal, nor were any of the machines of the 1950s and 60s. You couldn't put one on your desk unless your desk was large enough to shame even the most profligate CEO. You probably couldn't afford the price tag that reached into the millions. Moreover, you would need a small squad to keep the blessed things running—someone to load tapes, another to type commands at the console, several to wring their hands when something went wrong, and half a day's work evaporated into a glitch. In fact, the idea of a personal computer was foreign to the people who worked on these machines. Most of the software was homegrown and designed for specific business chores such as billing you for your electrical use. Few people had use for a machine that did its best work mailing monthly bills to a million utility customers.

Personal Information Managers

But even as vacuum tubes were straining the power grid, the ideas behind the personal computer were simmering on the back burner in computer science classes. In 1945, *Atlantic Monthly* magazine ran an article by eminent M.I.T researcher Vannevar Bush in which he described his vision of the computer of the future. It wasn't a personal computer because that word hadn't yet been coined. Bush instead made up the term "memex" to identify his vision of a machine that would store the records and correspondence of a person and be able to retrieve any information with lightning speed. The memex would be an enhancement to the human memory, which Bush saw as becoming unable to keep up with the vast outpouring of information in nearly every field.

In Bush's mind, the memex would be controlled by a keyboard, knobs, and levers and would use photographic processes like microfilm for storing information. But the machine would not simply store information, it would keep it indexed, link information together, and even allow annotation. The machine would not fit on a desktop, but take the place of the desk itself.

Bush's conception of the computer of the future inspired Douglas C. Englebart at Stanford Research Institute to explore the potentials of information technology. Englebart saw the computer as more than memory. Besides augmenting a single individual, it could link many people together. The computer could be the basis of a communication system to the extent of forming a workgroup. In his explorations, Englebart's group invented many concepts now factual in PCs, such things as What-You-See-Is-What-You-Get (WYSIWYG) word processing, on-screen windows to look into multiple applications running simultaneously or multiple messages in a communication session, electronic meeting rooms, and the mouse as a pointing device to control everything. Englebart published his ideas as early as October 1962, but again these ideas outpaced the technology of the time.

Interactive Computing

The computer first became interactive at M.I.T. in the 1950s. Jay Forrester developed a computer he called Whirlwind, which was able to process telemetry data in real time and interact with an operator running the machine at a console. The entire machine would be devoted to a single task under the control of a single individual.

Only at the university could such single-user interactive computing work. In the real world, the expensive computer could not be squandered on a single person. But interactive computing could be brought into the realm of affordability by dividing the time of a large computer among several people. This concept, now termed "time-sharing" was first described in 1959 by Christopher Strachey who saw the potential of a single large computer acting as several smaller (slower), separate machines for individual users. He realized that to make this vision possible, he needed new operating mechanisms. This included prioritized interrupts, so that individual users (or their applications) could gain immediate (if brief) system control when their job needed immediate attention, and memory protection to keep the work of multiple operators (multiple computing sessions or tasks) from interfering with one another. These concepts are a fundamental part of today's personal computers. The first application of these concepts was the Simulated Air-Ground Environment (SAGE) air defense system, a project that evolved out of M.I.T.'s Whirlwind system.

Graphic User Interface

The first computers were about as accessible as a medieval alchemical text. They responded only to programs that resembled mathematical formulas more than the product of a normal human mind. The first step on the long road to the graphic user interface used by today's most powerful personal computer operating systems was a demonstration program called *Sketchpad*, first formally described by its creator, Ivan Sutherland, in 1963. Sketchpad enabled the user to push a lightpen across a monitor screen to make engineering drawings. Sketchpad introduced many of the concepts basic to today's most powerful software, including windows and the graphic cursor.

Workgroup Computing

The groundwork for computer cooperation was laid in the first time-sharing systems. In these systems, the users exchanged data in the sense that by sharing a single computer they were all connected to the same system and resources. The backbone of today's world wide computer link-up was first organized in 1969 by the Advanced Research Projects Agency of the Department of Defense (ARPA). Initially, four systems were linked together to form a network that was termed ARPAnet. In the late 1980s, the system was renamed Internet, in part because it had by then already reached far beyond the Defense Department.

Workgroup computing can trace its beginnings to Xerox Corporation's Palo Alto Research Center (PARC) where researchers developed an experimental single-user computer called Alto. To tie together the individual systems so that they could cooperate, the systems were linked into an Ethernet network. Some histories list the Alto as the first true personal computer, but it lacked the accessibility that characterizes the modern machine. The honor of being first must go to a more personal effort.

Personal Computers

By the middle of the 1970s, most of the software concepts underlying what would become the personal computer had been developed. What the world lacked was an affordable means of bringing that software to life. Just as the ideas in Babbage's Analytical Engine outpaced the available technology, the software concepts of the 1950s and 1960s far exceeded the capability of hardware accessible to the people for whom it was designed.

The necessary hardware breakthrough was the microprocessor. Originally designed for hand held calculators (see Chapter 3), the microprocessor was a fully programmable electronic circuit. Its programmability, however, was limited to hardware engineers who took advantage of it to quickly build machines more modest than computers. They used programmability as a design tool that saved much of the effort of designing electrical circuits. Complex electrical logic designs could be reduced to microprocessor programs hard-wired into read-only memory (now more familiar as ROM).

The creation of a true personal computer was delayed because microprocessors lacked a convenient way of being programmed. In general, programmers used a large computer as a development system to emulate the microprocessor and write programs step by step while monitoring their progress. Once all the code was finished, it would be recorded into read-only memory, packaged with the microprocessor and sold as a unit along with all the peripherals the machine was to use.

This situation arose from necessity. Programming languages required huge amounts of memory, and microcomputers had little. The IMP-16C, for example, had 256 bytes of RAM and 512 bytes of ROM. A few lines of mainframe computer program source code would fill the entire memory of the machine, leaving no room for compiling or running the program.

Altair

In late 1974, Ed Roberts brought together all the elements necessary for launching the personal computer. Roberts worked in the laser division of the Air Force weapons lab in Albuquerque, New Mexico. Together with some partners, he founded a company called Micro Instrumentation Telemetry Systems, now better known by its acronym, MITS. The original intent of the company was to sell model rocketry equipment. Roberts, however, believed he could do better selling a calculator kit, so he bought out his partners. The product he designed earned fame as a feature on the cover of *Popular Electronics*, a magazine read by electronic hobbyists and experimenters, and proved successful for a while. Then, an influx of mass-produced calculators from across the Pacific ignited price wars that made the MITS's product unprofitable.

Roberts decided to take the next step; he would make a true computer. Using a $65,000 loan, he developed what he called the PE-8. He also arranged for *Popular Electronics* to run a story about the machine (which appeared on the cover of the January 1975 issue). The magazine was anxious for a computer story, having been scooped by *Radio Electronics* magazine, that had run a construction project story about the Mark-8 computer designed by Jonathan Titus around Intel's 8008 microprocessor.

The editors of *Popular Electronics* renamed Roberts' PE-8 something they thought catchier, the Altair 8080. According to legend, a daughter of one of the magazine's editors suggested Altair, which was the name of a planet on an early episode of the television program Star Trek. The 8080 was the model designation of the Intel microprocessor that powered it.

The original Altair 8080 cost $397 in kit form and included an attractive (at least to the hobbyist's eye) painted tin box with front panel switches and lights (to impress the nonbelievers and incidentally program the thing) as well as 256 bytes of memory.

Besides being a challenge to build, the Altair was a misery to operate. It had no other storage except its RAM, so everything you did was lost as soon as you switched it off. Worse than the lack of storage was the shortage of software. The Altair came with none, not even a programming language.

This omission was obvious even to the most dedicated computer hobbyists. Most put up with the shortfall. They were happy just to have a computer with which to experiment. Some even got a thrill from the challenge (or ordeal) of stringing numbers of machine language together. But two teenagers from Washington state, Paul Allen and William "Bill" Gates, had a better idea: a compact version of the BASIC programming language that would actually run on the minimal resources of the Altair. They offered MITS their language, and Roberts gladly accepted, not knowing that their version of BASIC was closer to conception than completion. The twosome moved to Albuquerque, and Allen became director of software for MITS. Later, they formed their own software company that proved even more successful than the Altair. They called it Microsoft.

Not only is the Altair considered the first PC, it also spawned the first expansion bus standard (the Altair bus, which evolved into the S-100 standard) and the first compatible computer or clone, the *Imsai* made by IMS Associates. This and other machines based on the Altair design proved useful for both hobbyists and, when coupled with a standardized operating system, the first small business computers. The Altair itself, however, faded from the scene after Roberts sold MITS to a company called Pertec in May 1977, leaving the electronics industry for medicine. Not long afterward, Pertec abandoned the Altair name and, eventually, the PC industry.

CP/M

Although the original Altair was too limited to take advantage of the operating system that eventually brought small computers into small businesses, other machines using the same microprocessor and basic bus design were not. This operating system, called CP/M (Control Program for Microcomputers), was developed by Gary Kildall. CP/M linked the very popular and powerful 8080 and Z80 microprocessors and up to 64K of memory with floppy disk drives for mass storage. The new operating system led Kildall to launch his own company, initially called Intergalactic Digital Research, which he started in his home in 1974. The corporate name soon was shortened to Digital Research.

The combination of microprocessor and operating system yielded enough power to handle many business chores, from word processing to bookkeeping. It was exactly what was needed in business. Consequently, CP/M computers emerged as the business standard among desktop machines. In the early 1980s, more business-oriented software—which often consisted of little more than a few dozen lines of BASIC code— was available for CP/M than any other computer operating environment.

CP/M survived into the PC age, and a few holdouts still use it—just as a few men still use a brush and mug to lather their faces before shaving.

At one time, IBM offered a version of CP/M for the PC called CP/M 86. Note, however, that programs written for CP/M and CP/M 86 are not compatible.

Legend holds that, in 1981 when IBM was looking for an operating system for its new PC, CP/M 86 was the company's first choice. When IBM's negotiators went to California to arrange a deal, however, Digital Research head Kildall was unavailable, so the IBM negotiators instead flew to Washington state and licensed MS-DOS (Microsoft Disk Operating System) from Microsoft. Depending on the version of the legend you believe, Kildall was racing his Maserati, flying his plane, or off in the Orient. Kildall, who passed away in 1994, liked to keep the tale shrouded in mystery. However, at one time he admitted he actually took the interview with IBM while pressed for time before a two-week vacation. The negotiations were chilly, noted one meeting participant, because Kildall arrived late and IBM would not sign a reciprocal non-disclosure agreement with Digital Research. Nevertheless, after the meeting Kildall believed he had struck a deal with IBM, only to find out later that the company had agreed to a license with Microsoft. Although IBM offered both MS-DOS and CP/M 86, it priced the Microsoft product $200 cheaper ($40 for MS-DOS versus $240 for CP/M).

The Microsoft that IBM visited in lieu of Kildall was the same upstart company that developed the BASIC language for the Altair. (The company moved from Arizona to Washington in part, legend holds, to avoid speeding tickets liberally acquired by one founder.) Microsoft actually had bought rights to the original MS-DOS from Seattle Computing—after striking the deal with IBM—although it later developed and improved on the original.

This price difference as well as a slightly easier-to-use syntax helped MS-DOS quickly develop a huge base of applications. In a few years the Microsoft operating system had left CP/M 86 in the dust. Nevertheless, CP/M persevered and evolved into one of the first multitasking systems for PCs: Concurrent DOS.

Digital Research much later developed an operating system compatible with standard MS-DOS called DR DOS (Digital Research DOS, but often called Doctor DOS). The first DR DOS, version 3.3, was released in May 1988, followed by two revisions (version 3.40, released in January 1989, and version 3.41 in June 1989). DR DOS 5.0 was introduced in 1990, followed by DR DOS 6.0 in 1991. In 1992, Digital Research was acquired by Novell, and the offspring of the DR DOS product is now sold as Novell DOS.

Apple Computer

An alternative to the bus-oriented Altair design was the single-board microcomputer like the IMP-16C. Miniaturization made it possible to put a small computer comprised of a microprocessor, memory, and support circuitry on a single (although large) circuit board. Such a single-board design is economical because it saves the expense of the bus connector and redundant circuitry on supplemental circuit boards.

Two hobbyists, Steve Jobs and Steve Wozniak, experimented with this approach and, in 1976, built boards they called the Apple Computer. But, even back then, the market for products aimed at people born with soldering irons in hand was limited, and the original Apple circuit-board computer is now regarded as a curiosity, an interesting antique for computer collectors.

But the next attempt by Jobs and Wozniak proved a hit. In 1977, the twosome combined an innovative ready-made computer and professional marketing. The result was the Apple II, the longest lived of all small computer models. The Apple II blazed a path as the best of both worlds, combining a single board for consistency, efficiency, and economy with a dedicated expansion bus into which accessories (and some necessities) could be attached.

The Apple II was based on a single microprocessor and was a single-board computer because everything needed to make it work (at least in the most rudimentary way) was built onto a single glass-epoxy printed circuit board. Its expansion bus provided a way of connecting additional printed circuit boards almost directly to the microprocessor. Even the keyboard was combined into the attractively designed plastic case that housed all the electronicsa simple, practical, and cost-effective approach.

The central processing unit of the Apple II was its microprocessor, the 6502 made by Motorola. At the time, this was a respectable chip choice. It could perform eight-bit calculations at an operating speed of about one million cycles per second (megahertz).

Compared to the personal computers of today, the Apple II was rudimentary. The straightforward original design of the Apple II made no provision for lowercase letters, could put only 40 columns of text across the screen, and could be bought with as little as 8K of memory. For more permanent storage, it could route data from its electronic memory onto magnetic tape using a conventional audio cassette machine. Compared to what came before, however, it was groundbreaking. You could buy an Apple II, pull it from its box, plug it in, and have a working computer. Previous small computers universally required at least a moderate degree of technical knowledge, a great deal of patience to withstand the tedious process of assembling parts not necessarily meant to work together, and an overriding faith that they would, in fact, work.

Later, Apple added features to bring the Apple II up to par with other PCs, including lowercase characters in 80 columns, bit-mapped graphics, and disk storage controlled by Apple DOS. But in the early 1980s Apple's development attention shifted to the Macintosh, a more powerful architecture based on the Motorola MC68000 microprocessor. The Macintosh was introduced in January 1984. The original Apple II design was adapted through several models, which later found their primary application in elementary schools. The last models in the Apple II product line were discontinued in 1993.

Commodore

The first large manufacturer to announce a personal computer was Commodore International. Its first effort was the Pet, announced in 1977. Designed around the 6502 microprocessor as a business machine, it had all the hardware characteristics of a modern PC including expansion slots, a dedicated monitor, and floppy disk drives. Its software, however, was proprietary. Despite its early entry into the world of personal computing, Commodore was unable to establish its Pet as a standard, and the line faded from the scene after 1981. In 1994, Commodore International itself went into liquidation.

Tandy/Radio Shack

The second pre-PC small computer design camp rallied under the Radio Shack flag. The familiar corner store vendor of everything from batteries and toys to watches and telephones added small computers to its wide range of offerings by producing a number of machines based on different technologies, microprocessors, and operating systems.

The first machine offered was the TRS-80, which earned its name from its Z80 microprocessor (rather than the year). The TRS-80 was a desktop computer that combined monitor, keyboard, and electronics into a single silver-grey plastic box that was styled to make Buck Rogers feel homesick. Both cassette and floppy disk storage was available, the latter using TRS-DOS (widely known as Trash DOS to both its friends and detractors).

When the success of IBM's PC pushed the TRS-80 line out of the limelight, Tandy slowly adapted to the challenge. It first offered a machine that ran MS-DOS but was not compatible with the PC (the Model 5000 in 1982). Then, Tandy began building successful PC-compatibles under the Tandy name. As part of corporate restructuring, Tandy sold its computer manufacturing operation to AST Research in 1993.

IBM

This book would not exist, nor would the personal computer industry in its present form, were it not for a number of seemingly arbitrary but, at heart, practical decisions made at the IBM Corporation Entry Systems Division in Boca Raton, Florida, just as the 1980s were dawning. The culmination of that decision making came on August 12, 1981, with the introduction of the IBM PC.

Far from idealists intent on starting a revolution, the PC was created as a machine for a limited number of people. Some sources inside IBM have stated that expectations were that about 100,000 Personal Computers would be sold, machines that would appeal primarily to hobbyists intent on exploring what computers could do. (But, of course, who would probably never do anything useful on the electronic curiosities. After all, useful computing work remained in the realm of the mainframe computer.) At the time, hobbyists were already exploring programming with other small computers. The IBM Personal Computer was seen as just another of these—perhaps a toehold in the hobbyist market, perhaps an exploration into a new technological area, or perhaps just something that some anxious engineers at IBM wanted to play with (with official sanction, of course).

With such a market in mind, one design influence on the original Personal Computer can be understood. It was a machine of compromises, designed to keep costs down, designed without any particular purpose in mind. In retrospect, that almost accidental element of the Personal Computer design may have been IBM's masterstroke. It allowed the simple creation to grow into a variety of fields, to serve many masters, to be a true general-purpose computing instrument.

IBM was as surprised as the rest of the world when even in the initial months of its release, demand for the PC far outran supply, resulting in shortages and an unbelievable windfall to authorized IBM dealers who found that a little silicon could be worth its weight in gold.

The true motivations and design decisions underlying that first PC are forever the secret of IBM. The best guess that can be made is that the success of the PC stemmed from equal measures of serendipity and hard-nosed, bottom-line-oriented decision making. IBM wanted to cash in on the success that small computers were having among hobbyists and, increasingly, small businesses. The desktop computer presented a tremendous opportunity; an opportunity that IBM did not want to miss, as it had with minicomputers. (Most industry analysts attribute the astounding success of Digital Equipment Corporation (DEC) in the 1970s and 1980s to IBM's failure to move into the minicomputer field fast enough.)

To create IBM's first true desktop machine, the company's engineers carefully pruned and grafted the ideas embodied in other small computers on the market with a scattering of minor changes and innovations to make their new product stand out. The engineers put together a computer mostly made from parts and components crafted by other manufacturers, so that if the product misfired, losses would not be great, and IBM could go on to other products in its bread-and-butter mainframe line. They borrowed design concepts from the machines that hobbyists were toying with, engineered around semiconductor parts widely available on the market that required no exotic proprietary design work, and exploited an operating system based on the most popular of those used in small business computers.

This environment provided IBM with the incentive for creating the PC. By then, the small computer market had grown to tens of thousands of machines per year, clearly too large to ignore, particularly when much of the growing base was among business users.

Developing its own machine was not quite so far fetched. IBM had already made small computers in the guise of its transportable (by a stretch of the imagination and arm) Model 5100. Built without benefit of such innovations as miniature (5.25-inch) floppy disk drives, the 5100 primarily found use inside IBM but never did well as a commercial product.

There could be no doubt the IBM machine would be based on a microprocessor. The smart chips were what had originally made small computers practical and the industry possible. The question was which chip to use.

IBM chose Intel's 8088. The choice was a compromise between performance, cost, compatibility, and marketability. Because the 8088 had 16-bit internal registers, IBM could (and did) market its PC as a 16-bit computer, more powerful than the older 8-bit Apple, CP/M, and Radio Shack machines.

Although IBM could have made the PC a true 16-bit machine (16-bit microprocessors were available even before the 8088 had been offered), the company had one good reason for foregoing full 16-bit power: cost. In the early 1980s, the price of microprocessor support chips and memory was much higher than today, and 16-bit components were substantially more expensive than the 8-bit variety.

Because the PC was built without a true idea of what the machine would be used for, IBM hedged its bets. It allowed for 64K of memory in the system—the same capability as Apple and CP/M machines—but took advantage of the 8088 and allowed for adding up to 448K using expansion boards. (A second model pushed total capacity to 640K.) In addition to floppy disk drives (each floppy held 160K, about double other machines), IBM also hedged by including a cassette port as part of the first PC. Instead of buying a $500 floppy disk drive, you could use your $20 portable tape recorder to record programs and data and exchange files with your friends. But the keyboard and monitor quality of the PC was on a par with IBM's business machines so that the PC could do real work.

IBM steadily added power to its PC, but was careful not to add too much so that its traditional customers wouldn't abandon the profitable mainframe and minicomputers in favor of PCs. First IBM added a hard disk drive as standard equipment to the PC, creating the XT in 1982. In 1984, IBM attempted to broaden the PC market by adding a low-end home machine, the PCjr, and a high-end 286-based powerhouse, the AT. The PCjr proved to be an expensive failure. The AT machine set the architectural standard for more than a decade.

In 1987, IBM's PC influence and stock price peaked almost concurrently with what the company hoped would set the standard for the next generation of personal computers, the PS/2. Instead of being the new industry standard, however, the PS/2 line became a mere design alternative. A PC-compatible industry had arisen, and it was steadily eating into IBM's share of the computer market. Few compatible makers chose to follow the new standard.

Compatible PCs

The PC gave the world what it had been waiting for: a standard for personal computers.

Many large companies launched their own PCs. Some (for example, the Xerox 820) relied on proven CP/M. Some pursued MS-DOS. A few (for example, the DEC Rainbow 100) tried it both ways. Their goal was to achieve the same success as IBM, and with true corporate hubris, they tried to set their own standards, all of which have been left by the wayside.

Smaller, often start-up, companies chose to cash in on IBM's success rather than challenge it. They immediately started to create their own products that would match the IBM standard, hoping to duplicate the fortunes of plug-compatible companies that copied IBM's mainframe products.

(These companies made mainframe computers that would "plug in" in place of IBM's own machines, identical in operation and able to run the same software.)

At first, the going was slow as these small companies tried to figure out exactly what was necessary for compatibility. The first few attempts at building compatibles (Columbia Data Systems and Corona) didn't go far enough. These machines were supposedly software-compatible, but they didn't duplicate IBM's complete hardware design. Unfortunately, many programmers didn't follow IBM's rules, and they expected all computers to be built identically to the PC. Their software didn't work on these first compatibles, and the machines failed to win acceptance.

The first company to truly duplicate both the PC hardware and the firmware—the programs stored in read-only memory that gave the machine its electronic identity (see Chapter 7, "The Basic Input/Output System")—was Compaq Computer Corporation. Besides running all IBM software, the new Compaq computer had a gimmick: it was portable. At least it had a handle and was entirely self contained, despite its 40-pound bulk. In itself, portability was not revolutionary (Osborne and Kaypro had earlier offered similar portables based on CP/M), but the combination with PC-compatibility proved a winner.

IBM published the essential blueprint of the PC, a complete schematic diagram, so the hardware of the system was no challenge for designers. It also published its essential-for-compatibility BIOS. But the BIOS was copyrighted and couldn't be copied. Compaq led the way by writing a compatible BIOS without copying. But writing a BIOS was too time-consuming, challenging, and fraught with legal pitfalls for most start-up companies to afford. Moreover, the results weren't always completely compatible with IBM software. But there was no choice because neither IBM nor Compaq would license their BIOSs.

The breakthrough came when Phoenix Technologies wrote its own very compatible BIOS with the explicit intention of licensing it to computer makers. Compatibility worries vanished, and a new industry grew. By 1985, anyone could buy off-the-shelf parts and build a PC compatible. The PC revolution was complete.

Chapter 2
The Motherboard

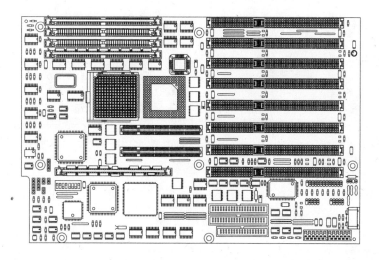

Traditionally, the centerpiece of most personal computers is the motherboard. It is the physical and logical backbone of the entire system. The circuitry located on the motherboard defines the computer, its capabilities, limitations, and personality.

Nearly all PCs and compatible computers share one common feature: they are built with a single, large printed circuit board as their foundation. This big board holds the most vital components that define the system: its microprocessor, support circuitry, and memory. Additions to the system plug into this central board. Without this board, there would be no computer.

This design is not inevitable. Rather, its roots reach back to the original engineering choice made by early small computer makers. Most manufacturers, including Apple, Commodore, and Tandy, found building their products with a single, large motherboard to be most economical. Then the manufacturers added sockets into which you could plug additional circuits to add capabilities to the computer. When IBM drafted its first personal computer, it followed the same pattern, ensuring that it would be the basis of nearly all desktop computers.

Small Computer Designs

The basic PC design is a combination and compromise between two diametrically opposed design philosophies. One group aimed at diversity, adaptability, and expandability by putting the individual functional elements (microprocessor, memory, and input/output circuitry) on separate boards that plugged into connectors that linked them together through a circuit bus. Such machines are known as *bus-oriented computers.* The other design camp concentrated on economy and simplicity by uniting all the essential components of the computer on a large board, as in the PC. The result was the true *single-board computer.* Each of these designs has its strengths.

Bus-Oriented Computers

At the time the PC was developed, the bus-oriented design was the conservative approach. The bus gets its name because, like a Greyhound, all the signals of the bus travel together and make the same stops at the same connectors along the way. The most popular small business computers of that era were built around the S-100 bus standard (the name indicated that the bus comprised 100 connections). Most larger computers used the bus-oriented design as well. The bus approach enabled each computer to be custom configured for its particular purpose and business. Larger, more powerful processors, even multiple processors, could be added to the machine as needed. The modular design enabled the system to expand as business needs expanded. It also allowed for easier service. Any individual board that failed could be quickly removed and replaced without circuit-level surgery.

Actually, the bus-oriented design originated as a matter of necessity simply because all the components required to make a computer would not fit on a circuit board of practical size. The overflowing circuitry spread among multiple boards, and the bus was the easiest way to link them all.

Single-Board Computers

The advent of integrated circuits, microprocessors, and miniaturized assemblies that put multiple electronic circuit components into a single package often as small as a fingernail greatly reduced the amount of circuit board required for building a computer. By the end of the 1970s, putting an entire digital computer on a single circuit board became practical. It was desirable for a number of reasons. Primary among them was cost. Fewer boards means less fabrication expense and less materials cost. Not only can the board be made smaller, but the circuitry that's necessary to match each board to the bus can be eliminated. Moreover, single-board computers have an advantage in reliability. Connectors are the most failure-prone part of any computer system. The single-board design eliminates the bus connectors as a potential source for system failure.

On the downside, however, the single-board computer design is decidedly less flexible than the bus-oriented approach. The single board has its capabilities forever fixed the moment it is soldered together at the factory. It can never become more powerful or transcend its original design. It cannot adapt to new technological developments.

Although the shortcomings of the single-board computer make it an undesirable (but not unused) approach for desktop computers, the design works well for many laptop and notebook computers. The compactness of the single-board approach is a perfect match for the space- and weight-conscious laptop design, and the lack of expandability is not a serious drawback. In fact, the laptop design attempts to shoehorn as many functions as possible into the small cases of the machines, leaving little, if any, room for expansion.

The PC Compromise

Rather than strictly following either the single-board or bus-oriented approach, the companies that made the first mass-market small computers brought the two philosophies together, mixing the best features of the single-board computer and the bus-oriented design in one box. In IBM's initial implementation of this design (the first PC model), one large board hosts the essential circuitry that defines the computer and slots that are available for expansion and adaptability.

The flexibility of the bus-oriented design presupposes that you have a wide selection of plug-in boards available to you. After all, a slot that you can plug but one board into offers no advantage over having all the circuitry in one assembly. Consequently, the desirability of bus-oriented computers depends on the acceptance of the bus design as a standard. *Proprietary buses*, designs for which only a single manufacturer builds boards (often because the manufacturer refuses to reveal the technical workings of the bus to others), fall short of the full flexibility of standardized buses. In effect, they offer little (if any) advantage over single-board designs.

The history of the PC has been one of moving closer to the single-board computer design. As manufacturers introduce new models, they inevitably add an increasing number of functions to the central circuit board. The original IBM PC, for example, required separate expansion boards for its display system, mass storage, input/output ports, and system clock. (If you wanted a decent amount of memory, you needed to add it with another expansion board.) As IBM introduced new models, however, the company moved the clock, ports, display system, mass storage control, and prodigious amounts of memory onto the main circuit board.

At least three motivations underlie this migration: expectations, cost, and capability. As the power and potential of personal computers have increased, people expect more from their PCs. The basic requirements for a personal computer have risen so that features that were once options and afterthoughts are now required. To broaden the market for personal computers, manufacturers have striven to push prices down. Putting the basics required in a computer on the main circuit board lowers the overall cost of the system for exactly the same reasons that a single-board computer is cheaper to make than the equivalent bus-oriented machine. Moreover, using the most modern technologies, manufacturers simply can fit more features on a single circuit board. The original PC had hardly a spare square inch for additional functions. Today, all the features of a PC nearly 100 times more powerful than the original fit onto a circuit board half the size of that inside an original PC.

Notebook computers show the essence of the single-board design. Created to be completely self-contained while minimizing mass and volume, notebook machines cram as much as possible onto their circuit boards. In a quest for compactness, some of the biggest savings come from shaving away ordinary expansion slots. But notebook machines also illustrate the shortcomings of the pure single-board design and why slots survive and will continue to flourish. Computer technology changes fast, but innovations in different areas arrive independently. A notebook PC that's otherwise in tune with the times may fall short in one particular area of operation. You may, for example, buy a fast notebook PC only to find that a new kind of high-speed modem becomes affordable a few months later. A single-board system with a built-in modem would be forever stuck with older, slower modem designs. With expansion slots, however, you can adapt your system to new standards and technologies as they arrive.

As with any trend, however, aberrant countertrends in PC design appear and disappear occasionally. Some system designers have chosen to complicate their systems to make them explicitly upgradeable by pulling essential features, such as the microprocessor, off the main board. The rationale underlying this more modular design is that it gives the manufacturer (and your dealer) more flexibility. The PC maker can introduce new models as fast as he can slide a new expansion board into a box—motherboard support circuitry need not be re-engineered. Dealers can minimize their inventories. Instead of stocking several models, the dealer (and manufacturer) need only keep a single box on the shelf, shuffling the appropriate microprocessor module into it as the demand increases. For you, as the computer purchaser, these modular systems also promise upgradability, which is a concept that's desirable in the abstract (your PC need never become obsolete) but often impractical (upgrading is rarely a cost-effective strategy).

The compromise of a big board and slots will continue to be popular as long as PCs need to be expandable and adaptable. In the long term, however, you can expect single-board systems to appear again in the form of products dedicated to a purpose, for example, a dedicated multimedia playback machine (an intelligent entertainment engine, essentially a VCR with a college education).

Circuit Board Nomenclature

You may hear a variety of names bandied about when those in the know (or those who think they are) discuss those big printed circuit boards around which their PCs are built. They will speak of motherboards, system boards, planar boards, and backplanes as if they all were the same. Although the terms are used interchangeably in common parlance, the concepts underlying them are subtly different.

Mother and Daughterboards

Long before the 1991 Gulf War was proclaimed the "Mother of All Battles" by Saddam Hussein, the biggest circuit assembly in any PC was colloquially known as the *motherboard*. In a way, this circuit assembly is the "mother of all boards," but not in the way Hussein intended to refer to the preeminence of the expected engagement. Rather, the term hints at the function of the board and its relationship to boards that plug into it, which are termed *daughterboards*. Drawing a direct analogy begets some strange images: you may imagine the smaller boards sucking from the larger one or the archaic concept of daughters clinging to their mother. Better to just think of the terms referring to the relative importance of the boards—mother is preeminent (mother knows best). There's no more sexism in the terms than there is in the Spanish language assigning the female gender to a table radio. (After all, sex and language gender are entirely different concepts, and anyone doubting that must have missed one of the more important high school health classes.) Besides, the term "daughterboard" is more mellifluous than alternatives such as "sonboard" or the more generic "offspringboard."

The motherboard-daughterboard relationship has nothing to do with size. Just as daughters can grow up to be taller than their mothers, daughterboards can be larger than the motherboards they plug into. In fact, the defining characteristic of the motherboard is not size or the circuitry it holds but the linkage it provides for expanding the system. Connectors rather than active circuitry are the essential element of the motherboard. PCs can be (and have been) built with no components except expansion connectors and the electrical links between them (which means little more than wires) on the motherboard.

System Board

IBM developed its own name, the *system board*, for the board that held the principal circuitry of its entire line of personal computers, from the original IBM PC through its successors XT and AT. The name is apt because the board (or more correctly, the circuitry on the board) defines the entire computer system. And, yes, one reason for using the term was to create a gender-neutral term. IBM didn't want to take sides in the war between the sexes.

Planar Boards

Another gender-neutral term promoted by IBM for the motherboard, which first came into common parlance with the introduction of the Personal System/2 line of machines, was *planar board*. In conversation, IBM engineers often shorten the term to the simple adjective, planar. Like most gender-neutral neologisms, planar board is less descriptive than the terms it is meant to replace. At face value, the term could not be more vague or all-embracing. All printed circuit boards are planar—that is, flat—except, perhaps, for a few special-purpose flexible assemblies like those folded into cameras. Even the term *system board* is more precise in that it at least describes the function of the circuit assembly.

Expansion Boards

The gender-neutral term for daughterboard that matches the system board nomenclature is *expansion board*. The term seems apt in that these plug-in boards enable you to expand your system. But many PCs require that you plug in expansion boards just to get the thing to work; even an unexpanded PC requires some way of connecting a monitor, after all. Nevertheless, expansion board is the accepted term, and the boards plug into connectors called *expansion slots* on the system board.

Logic Board

IBM has no monopoly on vague, gender-neutral terms. In the realm of the Apple Macintosh, the main circuit board inside a computer is often called a *logic board*. Of course, every circuit board inside a computer is based on digital logic, so the term could hardly be less specific.

Backplanes

Another name sometimes used to describe the motherboard in PCs is *backplane*. The term is a carry-over from bus-oriented computers. In early bus-oriented design, all the expansion connectors in the machine were linked by a single circuit board. The expansion boards slid through the front panel of the computer and plugged into the expansion connectors in the motherboard at the rear. Because the board was necessarily planar and at the rear of the computer, the term backplane was perfectly descriptive. With later designs, the backplane found itself lining the bottom of the computer case.

Backplanes are described as *active* if, as in the PC design, they hold active logic circuitry. A *passive backplane* is nothing more than expansion connectors linked by wires or printed circuitry. The system boards of most personal computers can be described as active backplanes, though most engineers reserve the term backplane for bus-oriented computers in which the microprocessor plugs into the backplane rather than residing on it. The active circuitry on an active backplane under such a limited definition would comprise bus control logic that facilitates the communication between boards.

Printed Circuit Technology

The "board" part of the motherboard name refers to the assembly being a *printed circuit board*. The term is sometimes confusingly shortened to "PC board" even when the board is part of some other, non-computer device. Today, printed circuit boards are the standard from which nearly all electronic devices are made.

The old alternative was point-to-point hand wiring. Actual physical wires connected circuit elements, each end soldered in place by hand. This was a workable if not particularly cost-effective technology in the days of tubes when even a simple circuit spanned a few inches of physical space. Today point-to-point wiring is virtually inconceivable because a PC crams the equivalent of half a million tube circuits into a few square inches of space. Connecting them with old-fashioned wiring would take a careful hand and some very fine wire. The time required to cut, strip, and solder each wire into place would make building a single PC a lifetime endeavor.

Printed circuits allow all the wiring for an entire circuit assembly to be fabricated together in a quick process that can be entirely mechanized. The wires themselves are reduced to copper *traces*, a pattern of copper foil bonded to the substrate that makes up the support structure of the printed circuit board. In computers, this substrate is usually green composite material called *glass-epoxy* because it has a woven glass fiber base that's filled and reinforced with an epoxy plastic. Less critical (read "cheap") electronic devices substitute a simple brownish substrate of phenolic plastic for the glass-epoxy.

The simplest circuit boards start life as a sheet of thin copper foil bonded to a substrate. The copper is coated with a compound called *photo-resist*, a light-sensitive material. When exposed to light, the photo-resist becomes resistant to the effects of compounds, such as nitric acid, which strongly react with copper. A negative image of the desired final circuit pattern is placed over the photo-resist covered copper and exposed to a strong light source. The board is then immersed in an *etchant*, one of those nasty compounds that etch or eat away the copper that is not protected by the light-exposed photo-resist. The result is a pattern of copper on the substrate corresponding to the photographic original. The copper traces can then be used to connect the various electronic components that will make up the final circuit. All the wiring on a circuit board is thus fabricated in a single step.

When the electronic design on a printed circuit board is too complex to be successfully fabricated on one side of the substrate, engineers can switch to a slightly more complex technology to make two-sided boards. The traces on each side are separately exposed but etched during the same bath in etchant. In general, the circuit traces on one side of the board run parallel in one direction, and the traces on the other side run generally perpendicular. The two sides get connected together by components inserted through the board or through *plated-through holes:* holes drilled through the board and then filled with solder.

To accommodate even more complex designs, engineers can use *multi-layer circuit boards.* These are essentially two or more thin double-sided boards tightly glued together into a single assembly. Most PC system boards use multi-layer technology. Sometimes a layer is left nearly covered with copper to shield the signal in the layers from interacting with one another. These shields are typically held at ground potential and are consequently called *ground planes.*

The biggest problem with the multi-layer design (besides the difficulty in fabrication) is difficulty in repair. Abnormally flexing a multi-layer board can break one of the traces hidden in the center of the board. No reasonable amount of work can repair such damage.

Two technologies are in wide use for attaching components to the printed circuit board. The older technology is called *pin-in-hole.* Electric drills bore holes in the circuit board at the points where the electronic components are to attach. Machines (usually) push the leads (wires that come out of the electronic components) into and through the circuit board holes and bend them slightly so that they hold firmly in place. A conveyer belt slides the entire board over a pool of molten solder (a tin and lead alloy), and a wave on the solder pool extends up to the board, coating the leads and the circuit traces. The solder holds all the components firmly in place after it cools.

Workers can also push pin-in-hole components into circuit boards and solder them individually in place by hand. Although hand fabrication is time-consuming and expensive, it can be effective when only small quantities need to be made. Automatic machinery cuts labor costs and speeds production on long runs; assembly workers typically make prototypes and small production runs or provide the sole means of assembly for tiny companies that can afford neither automatic machinery or farming out their circuit board work.

The newer method of attaching components, *surface-mount technology,* promises greater miniaturization and lower costs than pin-in-hole. Instead of holes to secure them, surface-mount components are glued to circuit boards using solder paste, which temporarily holds them in place. After all the components are affixed to a circuit board, the entire board assembly runs through a temperature-controlled oven, which melts the solder paste and firmly solders each component to the board.

Surface-mount components are smaller than their pin-in-hole kin because they don't need leads. Packaging is simplified and miniaturized. More electronic components fit in a given space with surface-mount technology.

On the downside, surface-mount fabrication doesn't lend itself to small production runs or prototyping. It can also be a headache for repair workers. They need to squint and peer at components that are often too small to be handled without tweezers and a lot of luck.

Standard Dimensions

Although all motherboards aren't exactly interchangeable, some share physical characteristics that enable them to fit the same physical constraints. As a result, a computer maker that designs his products to accept a particular size of motherboard has his choice of products to screw in. Two major standards exist for the physical size of motherboards. These standards follow the pattern set by IBM when it was the major force in the realm of personal computers. These standards follow IBM's original designs for its motherboards.

The motherboards of the original IBM Personal Computer measured about 8-1/2 by 11 inches and had five expansion slots spaced one inch apart in the left rear corner of the board (see fig. 2.1).

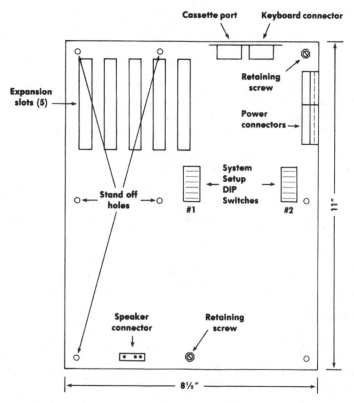

FIGURE 2.1. PC system board and screw placement.

Although the general layout of this board became part of the emerging standard, its size and slot spacing did not. More satisfactory to most motherboard makers was the original IBM XT design. The XT motherboard measured 8-1/2 by 12 inches. Eight expansion slots, spaced at 0.8-inch intervals, were provided as in Figure 2.2.

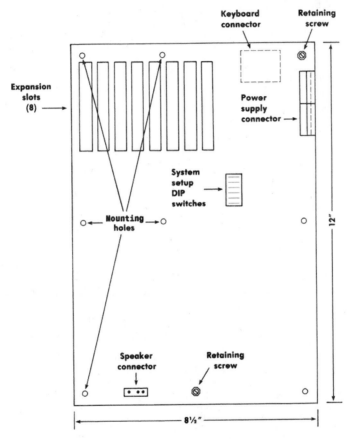

FIGURE 2.2. XT system board and screw placement.

The next IBM motherboard design accepted as an industry standard was that of the AT. Manufacturers prefer the AT layout when they require more space for more circuitry. The AT motherboard measured 12 by 13-1/2 inches. As with the XT layout, the AT motherboard design allows for eight expansion slots spaced at 0.8-inch increments as shown in Figure 2.3.

After the introduction of the AT, IBM lost its role as the setter of motherboard standards. When it supplanted the AT with its line of PS/2 models, most manufacturers continued to use the older XT and AT layouts for their systems. Although larger manufacturers like AST, Compaq, and Dell have developed their own motherboard layouts and dimensions, none of these have achieved the wide acceptance of the early IBM designs.

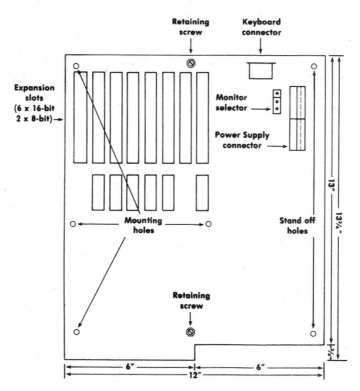

FIGURE 2.3. AT system board and screw placement.

Some motherboard makers have taken advantage of the miniaturization possible with the latest integrated circuit technologies to create products even more compact than the XT design. Manufacturers that aim their products to the replacement market tailor their motherboards to match the XT and AT expansion slot layout (eight slots with 0.8-inch spacing) but reduce the overall size of the board.

Makers of small-footprint PCs, machines designed with smaller dimensions to cover less of your desktop, often build their motherboards in sizes that vary widely from the IBM standards. These machines compromise expansion by reducing the number of expansion slots and drive bays to gain their more modest measurements. Any motherboard layout that does not conform to the XT or AT standard tends to tie you (as purchaser) closer to the board's manufacturer. Because the motherboard is not a standard dimension, if it fails or you want to upgrade it, you're stuck having to rely on the original manufacturer of the system or motherboard. With standard-size motherboards, you have your choice of aftermarket motherboards to repair or upgrade your PC.

Makers versus Suppliers

Because the motherboard defines each computer's functions and capabilities and because every computer is different, it only stands to reason that every motherboard is different, too. Not exactly. Many different computers have the same motherboard designs inside. Oftentimes a single computer model may have any of several different motherboards depending on when it came down the production line (and what motherboard the manufacturer got the best deal on).

OEMs

Although this variability of PCs and their motherboards may seem strange, it arises from a fact of marketing life long present in manufacturing. Brand names and manufacturers often have no closer association than the glue that holds on the nameplate. The brand name is owned by the company marketing a product at the wholesale or retail level. The company doing the marketing can handle the manufacturing itself, hire (contract or subcontract) another company to do the manufacturing for it, or simply buy parts or whole products made by someone else.

Companies that supply the marketing organizations and oftentimes the marketing organizations themselves that follow this last strategy are known as *Original Equipment Manufacturers* or *OEMs*. The term, which has become almost meaningless through overuse and generalization, is now even accepted as a verb. An equipment maker OEMs to the marketing organization and the marketing organization OEMs from the manufacturer.

OEM relationships often are as confusing as the terminology. Some manufacturing OEMs may market products under their own names, and marketing OEMs may build products other than those that they OEM. Sometimes the source of supply shifts. For example, Digital Equipment Corporation OEMed its first PCs from Tandy Corporation, then later began to manufacture some of its own products without any outward indication of the different origins.

One rationalization of this approach is that the marketing company, the brand name, stands behind the product that it sells. You depend on the warranty applied to the brand name (notwithstanding that the marketing company may merely send the product back to the original manufacturer for repair).

Integrators and VARs

The relationship between manufacturer and marketer can be tenuous. Some marketing organizations may invest as little time and effort as putting a nameplate on a finished product made by someone else. Others incorporate subassemblies into more powerful products, combine them with software, and submit them to thorough testing. Because they bring together components from different sources and integrate them, these latter companies are often termed *system integrators*. Because they take the original product and add more features or powers to it such as equipping a computer with a vertical software package (one designed for a particular industry), these organizations are sometimes called *value-added remarketers* (sometimes value-added retailers) or *VARs*.

The difference between the OEM and the company that entirely makes its own products is that you're likely to find that same system board inside many computers bearing the names of different OEMs. In many instances, you'll find nothing to distinguish them but the case or the label. Such computers are essentially interchangeable, termed by economists as *commodities*. As with all commodities, the best of these look-alike-inside off-the-shelf computers is the one with the lowest price.

Motherboard Components

The motherboard of any computer that follows the IBM design scheme performs several major functions. At the most basic level, it is the physical foundation of the computer. It holds all the expansion boards in place, provides firm territory to attach connections to external circuit elements, and provides the base of support for the central electronics of the computer. Electrically, the circuitry etched on it includes the brain of the computer and the most important elements required to nourish that brain. This circuitry determines the entire personality of the computer: how it functions, how it reacts to your every keystroke, what it does.

No one part of the system board completely defines a computer's personality. Its essence is spread throughout the circuit traces and components. Among these, the most important include the following:

➤ **The microprocessor.** It does the actual thinking inside the computer. Which microprocessor of the dozens currently available determines not only the processing power of the computer but also what software language it understands (and thus what programs it can run).

➤ **Coprocessors.** An adjunct to the microprocessor in some older computers, the coprocessor permits a computer to carry out certain operations much faster. A coprocessor can make a computer run 5 to 10 times faster in some operations.

➤ **Memory.** Required by the microprocessor to carry out its calculations, the amount and architecture of the memory of a system determines how it can be programmed and, to some extent, the level of complexity of the problems that it can work on.

➤ **BIOS.** The Basic Input/Output System or BIOS of a computer is a set of permanently recorded program routines that give the system its fundamental operational characteristics. The BIOS also includes instructions telling the computer how to test itself every time it is turned on. In older PCs, the BIOS determines what the computer can do without loading a program from disk and how the computer reacts to specific instructions that are part of those disk-based programs. Newer PCs may contain simpler or more complex BIOSs. A BIOS can be as simple as a bit of code telling the PC how to load the personality it needs from disk. Some newer BIOSs also include a system to help the machine determine what options you have installed and how to get them to work best together.

➤ **Expansion slots.** These are portals that enable new signals to enter the computer and directly react with its circuitry. Expansion slots enable new features and enhancements to be added to the system as well as allow the quick and easy alteration of certain computer prerequisites, such as video adapters.

➤ **Support circuitry.** A microprocessor, although the essence of a computer, is not a computer in itself (if it were, it would be called something else, such as a computer). The microprocessor requires additional circuits to bring it to life: clocks, controllers, and signal converters. Each of these support circuits has its own way of reacting to programs, and thus helps determine how the computer works.

Each of these are discussed fully in its own chapter.

Newer PCs also include additional functions on their motherboards, functions that once were reserved to expansion boards. These include:

➤ **Display electronics.** A means to tell you what your PC is thinking, display electronics generate the image that appears on-screen. Many PCs now include at least a rudimentary form of display electronics on their system boards.

➤ **Input/Output ports.** Every PC needs some way of acquiring information and putting it to work. Input/output ports are the primary route for this information exchange. Most PCs now include at least one serial port and one parallel port in their motherboard circuitry.

➤ **Mass storage interfaces.** Computers need a way to store the huge amounts of programs and data that they work with every day. The repository for this information is the mass storage system. A mass storage interface links the storage system to the rest of the PC. In modern PCs, two or more interfaces may be integrated into the motherboard. These include connections for floppy disk drives, hard disk drives, and CD-ROM players.

Each of these aspects of the motherboard and, thus, the entire PC, is addressed individually in the chapters that follow.

Chapter 3
Microprocessors

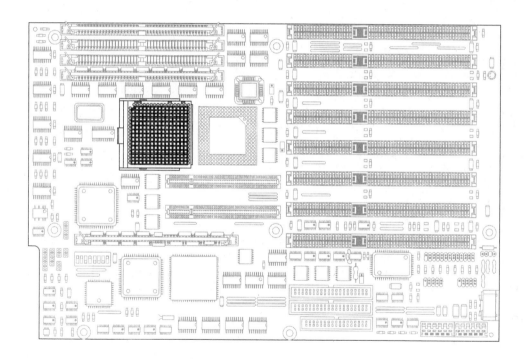

The microprocessor is the heart and brain inside every personal computer. This tiny chip of silicon determines the speed and power of the entire computer by handling most, if not all, the data processing in the machine.

All personal computers and a growing number of more powerful machines are based on a special type of electronic circuit called the microprocessor. Often termed "a computer on a chip," today's microprocessor is a masterpiece of high-tech black magic. It starts as silicon that has been carefully grown as an extremely pure crystal. The silicon is sliced thin with great precision, and then the chips are heinously polluted by baking in hot ovens containing gaseous mixtures of impurities that defuse into the silicon and change its electrical properties. This alchemy turns sand to gold, creating an electronic brain as capable as that of, say, your average arthropod.

As with insects and crustaceans, your PC can react, learn, and remember. Unlike higher organisms bordering on true consciousness (for example, your next door neighbors with the plastic fauna in their front yard), the microprocessor doesn't reason. Nor is it self-aware. Although computers are often labeled as "thinking machines," what goes through their microprocessor minds is far from your thought processes and stream of consciousness. Or maybe not. Some theoreticians believe your mind and a computer work fundamentally the same way, although no one knows exactly how the human mind actually works.

The operating principals of the microprocessor, on the other hand, are well understood. After all, microprocessor hardware was designed to carry out a specific function, and silicon semiconductor technology was simply harnessed to implement those functions. Nothing about what the microprocessor does is magic.

In fact, a microprocessor need not be made from silicon (scientists are toying with advanced semiconducting materials that promise higher speeds) nor need it be based on electronics. A series of gears, cams, and levers or a series of pipes, valves, and pans could carry out all the logical functions exactly the same way. Mechanical and hydraulic computers have, in fact, been built.

The advantage of electronics and the microprocessor is speed. Electrical signals travel at the speed of light; microprocessors carry out their instructions at rates up to several million per second. Without that speed, elaborate programs would never have been written. Executing such a program with a steam-driven computing engine might have taken lifetimes. The speed of the microprocessor makes it into the miracle that it is.

The advantage of silicon is familiarity. An entire industry has arisen to work with silicon. The technology is mature. Fabricating silicon circuits is routine and the results are predictable. Familiarity also breeds economy. Billions of silicon chips are made each year. Although the processes involved are precise and exotic, the needed equipment and materials are readily available.

Operating Principles

Reduced to its fundamental principles, the workings of a modern silicon-based microprocessor are not difficult to understand. They are simply the electronic equivalent of a knee-jerk. Every time you hit the microprocessor with an electronic hammer blow (the proper digital input), it reacts by doing something specific, always the same thing for the same input, kicking out the same function.

The complexity of the microprocessor and what it does arises from the wealth of inputs it can react to and the interaction between successive inputs. Although the microprocessor's function is precisely defined by its input, the output from that function varies with what the microprocessor had to work on, and that depends on previous inputs. For example, the result of you carrying out a specific command—"Simon says lift your left leg"—will differ dramatically depending on whether the previous command was "Simon says sit down" or "Simon says lift your right leg."

Getting an electrical device to respond in knee-jerk fashion rates as one of the greatest breakthroughs in technology. The first application was to extend the human reach beyond what could be immediately touched, beyond the span of the proverbial 10-foot pole. The simple telegraph is perhaps the best example. Closing a switch (pressing down on the telegraph key) sends a current down the wire that activates an electromagnet, causing the rattle at the other end that yields a message to a distant telegrapher. This grand invention underlies all of modern computer technology. It puts one electrical circuit in control of another circuit a great or small distance away.

Logic Gates

From these simple beginnings, you can build a computer. Everything that a computer does involves one of two operations: decision-making and memory, or in other words, reacting and remembering. The capability to control one signal with another signal enables you to carry out both operations with simple electrical circuits.

Suppose that you start with that same remote mechanical of the telegraph but couple it with a light switch so that the arm of the telegraph pulls down the switch and flashes a light. Certainly the electricity could be used to directly light the bulb, but there are other possibilities. You could, for example, pair two telegraph arms so that their joint effort would be required to throw the switch to turn on the light. Or you could link the two telegraphs so that a signal on either one would switch on the light. Or you could install the switch backwards so that when the telegraph activated, the light would go out.

These three telegraph-based design examples actually provide the basis for three different types of computer circuits called *logic gates* (the AND, OR, and NOT gates respectively). As electrical circuits, they are called "gates" because they regulate the flow of electricity, allowing it to pass through or cutting it off, much as a gate in a fence allows or impedes your own progress. These logic gates endow the electrical assembly with decision-making power. In the light example, the decision is necessarily simple: when to switch on the light. But these same simple gates can be formed into elaborate combinations that make up a computer that can make complex logical decisions.

The concept of applying the rigorous approach of algebra to logical decision-making was first proposed by English mathematician George Boole. In 1847, Boole founded the system of modern symbolic logic that we now term Boolean logic (alternately, Boolean algebra). In his system, Boole reduced propositions to symbols and formal operators that followed the strict rules of mathematics. Using his rigorous approach, logical propositions could be proved with the same certainty as the mathematical.

The three logic gates can perform the function of all of the operators in Boolean logic. They form the basis of the decision-making capabilities of the computer as well as other logic circuitry.

These same gates also can be arranged to form memory. If the voltage controlled by a switch is fed back so that it, too, can energize and activate the switch, the gate will latch in its on state. That is, once you supply voltage to the gate, it will switch on and supply voltage to itself, keeping itself on. Even when you discontinue providing the remote voltage, the switch will stay on, powered by its own output. In effect, it remembers after it has been turned on.

This basic form of memory has one shortcoming: how to make the switch forget so that you can start over. Turning it off requires switching off both the control voltage and the main voltage source.

A more useful form of memory takes two control signals; one switches it on, the other switches it off. In simplest form, each cell of this kind of memory is made from two latches connected at cross purposes so that switching one latch on cuts the other off. Because one signal sets this memory to hold data and the other one resets it, this circuit is sometimes called *set-reset memory*. A more common term is *flip-flop* because it alternately flips between its two states.

Instruction Sets

Real computers have more than one gate and memory cell: they have thousands or millions of them. But like their elemental circuits, they are controlled by electrical signals. The signals are more complicated, reflecting the more elaborate nature of the computer. With today's microprocessors, each microprocessor command is coded as the presence or absence of an electrical signal at one of the pins of the microprocessor's package. These signals, each representing a digital information bit that can be coded as a zero or one, make up a bit pattern.

Certain bit patterns are given specific meanings by the designers of a microprocessor and thus become a microprocessor instruction. The bit pattern 0010110, for example, is the instruction that tells an Intel 8086-family microprocessor to subtract in a very explicit manner. Other instructions tell the microprocessor to add, multiply, divide, move bits or bytes around, change individual bits, or just wait around for another instruction. Microprocessor designers can add instructions to do just about anything from matrix calculations to back flips—if the designers wanted to, if the instruction actually did something useful, and if they had unlimited time and resources to engineer the chip. Practical concerns like keeping the design work and the chip manageable constrain the range of commands given to a microprocessor.

The entire repertoire of commands that a given microprocessor model understands and can react to is called that microprocessor's *instruction set* or its *command set*. Different microprocessor designs recognize different instruction sets, just as different board games have different rules.

Despite their pragmatic limits, microprocessor instruction sets can be incredibly rich and diverse, and the individual instructions incredibly specific. The designers of the 8086-style microprocessor, for example, felt that a simple command to subtract was not enough by itself. They believed that the microprocessor also needed to know what to subtract from what and what it should do with the result. Consequently, they added a rich variety of subtraction instructions to the 8086 family of chips. Each different subtraction instruction tells the microprocessor to take numbers from different places and find the difference in a slightly different manner.

Some microprocessor instructions require a series of steps to be carried out. These multistep commands are sometimes called *complex instructions* because of their composite nature. Although the complex instruction looks like a simple command, it may involve much work. A simple instruction would be something like "pound a nail"; a complex instruction may be as far ranging as "frame a house." Simple subtraction or addition of two numbers may actually involve dozens of steps, including the conversion of the numbers from decimal to binary (1's and 0's) notation that the microprocessor understands. For instance, the previous sample subtraction instruction tells one kind of microprocessor that it should subtract a number in memory from another number in the microprocessor's accumulator, a place that's favored for calculations in today's most popular microprocessors.

Everything that the microprocessor does consists of nothing more than a series of these step-by-step instructions. A computer program is simply a list of microprocessor instructions. The instructions are simple, but long and complex computer programs are built from them just as epics and novels are built from the words of the English language. Although writing in English seems natural, programming feels foreign because it requires that you think in a different way—in a different language. You even need to think of jobs, such as adding numbers, typing a letter, or moving a block of graphics, as a long series of tiny steps. In other words, programming is just a different way of looking at problems and expressing the process of solving them.

Registers

Before the microprocessor can work on numbers or any other data, it first must know what numbers to work on. The most straightforward method of giving the chip the variables it needs would seem to be supplying more coded signals at the same time the instruction is given. You could drop in the numbers 6 and 3 along with the subtract instruction, just as you would load laundry detergent along with shirts and sheets into your washing machine. This simple method has its shortcomings, however. Somehow the proper numbers must be routed to the right microprocessor inputs. The microprocessor needs to know whether to subtract 6 from 3 or 3 from 6 (the difference could be significant, particularly when you're balancing your checkbook).

Just as you distinguish the numbers in a subtraction problem by where you put them in the equation (6–3 versus 3–6), a microprocessor distinguishes the numbers on which it works by their position (where they are found). Two memory addresses might suffice were it not for the way most microprocessors are designed. They have only one pathway to memory, so they can effectively "see" only one memory value at a time. A microprocessor loads at least one number to an internal storage area called a *register*. It can then simultaneously reach both the number in memory and the value in its internal register. Alternately (and more commonly today) both values on which the microprocessor is to work are loaded into separate internal registers.

Part of the function of each microprocessor instruction is to tell the chip which registers to use for data and where to put the answers it comes up with. Other instructions tell the chip to load numbers into its registers to be worked on later or to move information from a register to someplace else, for instance to memory or an output port.

A register functions both as memory and a workbench. It holds bit patterns until they can be worked on or output. The register also is connected with the processing circuits of the microprocessor, so that the pan changes ordered by instructions actually appear in the register. Most microprocessors typically have several registers, some dedicated to specific functions (such as remembering which step in a function the chip is currently carrying out; this register is called a *counter* or *instruction pointer*) and some designed for general purposes. At one time, the accumulator was the only register in a microprocessor that could manage calculations. In modern microprocessors, all registers are nearly equal (in some of the latest designs, all registers are equal, even interchangeable), so the accumulator is now little more than a colorful term left over from a bygone era.

Not only do microprocessors have differing numbers of registers, but the registers may be of different sizes. Registers are measured by the number of bits that they can work with at one time. A 16-bit microprocessor, for example, should have one or more registers that each holds 16 bits of data at a time.

Adding more registers to a microprocessor does not make it inherently faster. Because the design of a microprocessor (in older PCs) without advanced pipelining or superscalar technology allowed performing only one operation at a time, more than two registers seemed superfluous. After all, most math operations involve only two numbers at a time (or can be reduced to a series of two-number operations). Even with old-technology microprocessors, however, more registers helped the software writer produce more efficient programs. With more places to put data, information needed to be moved in and out of the microprocessor less often, potentially saving several program steps and clock cycles.

Modern microprocessor designs, particularly those influenced by RISC research, demand more registers. Because microprocessors run much faster than memory, each time the microprocessor has to go to memory, it must slow down. Therefore, minimizing memory accessing helps improve performance. Keeping data in registers instead of memory speeds things up.

On the other hand, having many registers is the equivalent of moving main memory into the microprocessor with all the inherent complexities and shortcomings of memory technology. Research has determined that 32 registers for microprocessors using current technologies work best. Consequently, nearly all of today's RISC processing modules (whether an integer unit or floating-point unit) have 32 registers.

The width of the registers does, however, have a substantial effect on the performance of a microprocessor. The more bits assigned to each register, the more information that can be processed in every microprocessor operation. Consequently, a 64-bit register in one of today's top RISC chips holds the potential of calculating eight times as fast as an 8-bit register of a first generation microprocessor—all else being equal.

The performance advantage of using wider registers, however, depends on the software being run. If, for example, a computer program tells the microprocessor to work on data 16 bits at a time, the full power of 32-bit registers will not be tapped. For this reason, DOS, a 16-bit operating system written with 16-bit instructions, does not take full advantage of today's powerful 32-bit microprocessors. Nor do most programs written to run under DOS. Modern 32-bit operating systems are a better match and consequently deliver better performance.

Clocked Logic

Microprocessors do not carry out instructions as soon as the instruction code signals reach the pins that connect the microprocessor to your computer's circuitry. If chips did react instantly, they would quickly become confused. Electrical signals cannot change state instantly; they must always go through a brief, though measurable, transition period—a period of indeterminate level during which the signals would probably perplex a microprocessor into a crash. Moreover, all signals do not necessarily change at the same rate, so when some signals reach the right values, others may still be at odd values. As a result, a microprocessor must live through long periods of confusion during which its signals are at best meaningless, at worst dangerous.

To prevent the microprocessor from reacting to these invalid signals, the chip waits for an indication that it has a valid command to carry out. It waits until it gets a "Simon says" signal. In today's PCs, this indication is provided by the *system clock*. The microprocessor checks the instructions given to it each time it receives a clock pulse—providing it is not already busy carrying out another instruction.

Except for the latest superscalar, pipelined microprocessors, most chips cannot carry out one instruction every clock cycle. In some older microprocessor designs, a single instruction may involve as many as 100 discrete steps, each of which require a tick of the system clock in which to execute. The number of cycles required to carry out instructions varies with the microprocessor design. Some instructions take a few cycles, others dozens. Moreover, some microprocessors are more efficient than others in carrying out their instructions. The trend today is to minimize and equalize the number of clock cycles needed to carry out a typical instruction.

Some chips go even further in breaking the correspondence between the system clock and the number of instructions that are executed. They deliberately change the external system clock speed internally before it is used by the microprocessor circuitry. In most cases, the system clock frequency is increased by some discrete factor (typically two or three, although some Pentium chips use a factor of 1.5 as a multiplier). Despite the different frequencies inside and outside the chip, the system clock is still used to synchronize logic operations. The microprocessor's logic makes the necessary allowances.

The lack of correspondence between cycles and instruction execution means that clock speed (typically a frequency given in megahertz or MHz) alone does not indicate the relative performance of two microprocessors. If, for example, one microprocessor requires an average of six clock cycles to execute every instruction and another chip needs only two, the first chip will be slower (by 50 percent) than the second even when its clock speed is twice as fast. The only time that clock speed gives a reliable indication of relative performance is when you compare two identical chip designs that operate at different frequencies, say Pentium chips running at 60 and 66 MHz. (The latter Pentium would calculate 10 percent faster.)

The clocked logic circuitry inside the typical microprocessor is divided into three function parts: the input/output unit (I/O unit), the control unit, and the arithmetic-logic unit (ALU). The last two are sometimes jointly called the *central processing unit* (CPU), although the same term often is used as a synonym for the entire microprocessor. Some chip makers further subdivide these units, give them other names, or include more than one of each in a particular microprocessor. In any case, the functions of these three units are an inherent part of any chip.

All three parts of the microprocessor interact together. In all but the simplest microprocessor designs, the I/O unit is under control of the control unit, and the operation of the control unit may be determined by the results of calculations of the arithmetic/logic unit CPU. The combination of the three parts determines the power and performance of the microprocessor.

Each part of the microprocessor also has its own effect on the processing speed of the system. The control unit operates the microprocessor's internal clock, which determines the rate at which the chip operates. The I/O unit determines the bus width of the microprocessor, which influences how quickly data and instructions can be moved in and out of the microprocessor. And the registers in the arithmetic/control unit determine how much data the microprocessor can operate on at one time.

The Input/Output Unit

The input/output unit links the microprocessor to the rest of the circuitry of the computer, passing along program instructions and data to the registers of the control unit and arithmetic /logic unit. The I/O unit matches the signal levels and timing of the microprocessor's internal solid-state circuitry to the requirements of the other components inside the PC. The internal circuits of a microprocessor, for example, are designed to be stingy with electricity so that they can operate faster and cooler. These delicate internal circuits cannot handle the higher currents needed to link to external components. Consequently, each signal leaving the microprocessor goes through a signal buffer in the I/O unit that boosts its current capacity.

The I/O unit can be as simple as a few buffers or it may involve many complex functions. In the latest Intel microprocessors used in some of the most powerful PCs, the I/O unit includes cache memory and clock-doubling logic to match the high operating speed of the microprocessor to slower external memory.

The microprocessors used in IBM-compatible personal computers have two kinds of external connections to their input/output units: those connections that indicate the address of memory locations to or from which the microprocessor will send or receive data or instructions; and those connections that convey the meaning of the data or instructions. The former is called the *address bus* of the microprocessor; the latter, the *data bus*.

The number of bits in the data bus of a microprocessor directly influences how quickly it can move information. The more bits that a chip can use at a time, the faster it is. Microprocessors with 8-, 16-, and 32-bit data buses are all used in various IBM personal computers. The latest microprocessors go all the way to 64 bits.

The number of bits available on the address bus influences how much memory that a microprocessor can address. A microprocessor with 16 address lines, for example, can directly work with 2^{16} addresses; that's 65,536 (or 64K) different memory locations. The different microprocessors used in various PCs span a range of address bus widths from 20 to 32 bits. Some members of the latest generation of chips take the address bus to 64 bits, too.

The Control Unit

The control unit of a microprocessor is a clocked logic circuit that, as its name implies, controls the operation of the entire chip. Unlike more common integrated circuits, whose function is fixed by hardware design, the control unit is more flexible. The control unit follows the instructions contained in an external program and tells the arithmetic/logic unit what to do. The control unit receives instructions from the I/O unit, translates them into a form that can be understood by the arithmetic/logic unit, and keeps track of which step of the program is being executed.

With the increasing complexity of microprocessors, the control unit has become more sophisticated. In the Pentium, for example, the control unit must decide how to route signals between what amounts to two separate processing units. In other advanced microprocessors, the function of the control unit is split among other functional blocks, such as those that specialize in evaluating and handling branches in the stream of instructions.

The Arithmetic/Logic Unit

The arithmetic/logic unit handles all the decision making (the mathematical computations and logic functions) that are performed by the microprocessor. The unit takes the instructions decoded by the control unit and either carries them out directly or executes the appropriate microcode to modify the data contained in its registers. The results are passed back out of the microprocessor through the I/O unit.

Because higher clock speeds make circuit boards and integrated circuits more difficult to design and manufacture, engineers have a strong incentive to get their microprocessors to process more instructions at a given speed. Most modern microprocessor design techniques are aimed at exactly that.

One way to speed up the execution of instructions is to reduce the number of internal steps the microprocessor must take for execution. Step reduction can take two forms: making the microprocessor more complex so that steps can be combined or by making the instructions simpler so that fewer steps are required. Both approaches have been used successfully by microprocessor designers—the former as CISC microprocessors, the latter as RISC.

Another way of trimming cycles required by programs is to operate on more than one instruction simultaneously. Two approaches to processing more instructions at once are pipelining and superscalar architecture.

Pipelining

In older microprocessor designs, a chip works single-mindedly. It reads an instruction from memory, carries it out step by step, and then advances to the next instruction. Pipelining enables a microprocessor to read an instruction, start to process it, and then, before finishing with the first instruction, read another instruction. Because every instruction requires several steps each in a different part of the chip, several instructions can be worked on at once, and passed along through the chip like a bucket brigade. Intel's Pentium chips, for example, have four levels of pipelining. So up to four different instructions may be undergoing different phases of execution at the same time inside the chip.

Pipelining is very powerful, but it is also demanding. The pipeline must be carefully organized, and the parallel paths kept carefully in step. It's like a chorus singing a canon like *Frere Jacques*—one missed beat and the harmony falls apart. If one of the execution streams delays, all the rest delay as well. The demands of pipelining are one factor pushing microprocessor designers to make all instructions execute in the same number of clock cycles. Keeping the pipeline in step is easier this way.

In general, the more stages to a pipeline, the greater acceleration it can offer. But real-world programs conspire against lengthy pipelines. Nearly all programs branch. That is, their execution can take alternate paths down different instruction streams depending on the results of calculations and decision-making. A pipeline can load up with instructions of one program branch before it discovers that another branch is the one the program is supposed to follow. In that case, the entire contents of the pipeline must be dumped, and the whole thing loaded up again. The result is a lot of logical wheel-spinning and wasted time. The bigger the pipeline, the more time wasted. The waste resulting from branching begins to outweigh the benefits of bigger pipelines in the vicinity of five stages.

Today's most powerful microprocessors are adopting a technology called *branch prediction logic* to deal with this problem. The microprocessor makes its best guess at which branch a program will take as it is filling up the pipeline. Such guesses are good enough to make pipelines of five, six, and seven stages beneficial to overall performance.

Superscalar Architectures

The steps in a program normally are listed sequentially but they don't always need to be carried out exactly in order. Just as tough problems can be broken into easier pieces, program code can be divided as well. If, for example, you want to know the larger of two rooms, you need to compute the volume of each, and then make your comparison. If you had two brains, you could compute the two volumes simultaneously. A superscalar microprocessor design does essentially that. By providing two or more execution paths for programs, it can process two or more program parts simultaneously. Of course, the chip needs enough innate intelligence to determine which problems can be split up and how to do it. The Pentium, for example, has two parallel, pipelined execution paths.

The first superscalar computer design was the Control Data Corporation 6600 mainframe, introduced in 1964. Designed specifically for intense scientific applications, the initial 6600 machines were built from eight functional units and were the fastest computers in the world at the time of their introduction.

Superscalar architecture gets its name because it goes beyond the incremental increase in speed made possible by scaling down microprocessor technology. An improvement to the scale of a microprocessor design would reduce the size of the microcircuitry on the silicon chip. The size reduction shortens the distance signals must travel and lowers the amount of heat generated by the circuit (because the elements are smaller and need less current to effect changes). Some microprocessor designs lend themselves to scaling down. Superscalar designs get a more substantial performance increase by incorporating a more dramatic change in circuit complexity.

Using pipelining and superscalar architecture cycle-saving techniques has cut the number of cycles required for the execution of a typical microprocessor instruction dramatically. Early microprocessors needed, on average, several cycles for each instruction. Many of today's chips (both CISC and RISC) actually have average instruction throughputs of less than one cycle per instruction.

Microcode

Instructions are the basic unit for telling a microprocessor what to do. Internally, however, the circuitry of the microprocessor often needs to go through several steps to carry out one instruction. The instruction tells the microprocessor to carry out a list of steps that make up one operation. How these steps are controlled mark the great divide in microprocessor and computer design.

The first electronic computers used a hard-wired design. An instruction simply activated the circuits appropriate for carrying out all the steps required. This design has its advantages. It optimizes the speed of the system because the direct hard-wire connection adds nothing to slow down the system. Simplicity means speed, and the hard-wired approach is the simplest. Moreover, the hard-wired design was the practical and obvious choice. After all, computers were so new that no one had thought up any alternative.

But the hard-wired computer design has a significant drawback. It ties the hardware and software together into a single unit. Any change in the hardware must be reflected in the software. A modification to the computer means that programs need to be modified. A new computer design may require that programs be entirely rewritten from the ground up.

Throughout the history of computing, determining exactly what instructions should make up a machine's instruction set was more an art than a science. IBM's first commercial computers, the 701 and 702, were designed more from intuition than from any study of which instructions programmers would need to use. Each machine was custom tailored to a specific application. The 701 ran instructions thought to serve scientific users; the 702 had instructions aimed at business and commercial applications.

When IBM tried to unite its many application-specific computers into a single, more general-purpose line, these instruction sets were combined so that one machine could satisfy all needs. The result was a wide, varied, and complex set of instructions. The new machine, the IBM 360 (introduced in 1964), was unlike previous computers in that it was created not as hardware but as an architecture. IBM developed specifications and rules for how the machine would operate, but enabled the actual machine to be created from any hardware implementation designers found most expedient. In other words, IBM defined the instructions that the 360 would use but not the circuitry that would carry them out. Previous computers used instructions that directly controlled the underlying hardware. To adapt the instructions defined by the architecture to the actual hardware that made up the machine, IBM adopted an idea originally conceived by Maurice Wilkes at Cambridge University called *microcode.*

Although the additional layer of microcode made machines more complex, it added a great deal of design flexibility. Engineers could incorporate whatever new technologies they wanted inside the computer yet still run the same software with the same instructions originally written for older designs. In other words, microcode enabled new hardware designs and computer systems to have backward compatibility with earlier machines.

Since the introduction of the 360, all mainframe computers have used microcode. When the microprocessors that enabled PCs were created, they followed the same design philosophy as the 360 by using microcode to match instructions to hardware. In effect, the microcode in a microprocessor is a secondary set of instructions that run invisibly inside the chip on a nanoprocessor—essentially a microprocessor within a microprocessor.

This microcode-and-nanoprocessor approach makes creating a complex microprocessor easier. The powerful data processing circuitry of the chip can be designed independently of the instructions it must carry out. The manner in which the chip handles its complex instructions can be fine-tuned even after the architecture of the main circuits are laid into place. Bugs in the design can be fixed relatively quickly by altering the microcode. It's an easy operation compared to the alternative of developing a new design for the whole chip, a task that's not trivial when a million transistors are involved. The rich instruction set fostered by microcode also makes writing software for the microprocessor (and computers built from it) easier, reducing the number of instructions needed for each operation.

Microcode has a big disadvantage, however. It makes computers and microprocessors more complicated. In a microprocessor, the nanoprocessor must go through several of its own microcode instructions to carry out every instruction you send to the microprocessor. More steps means more processing time taken for each instruction. Extra processing time means slower operation. Engineers found that microcode had its own way to compensate for its performance penalty: complex instructions.

Using microcode, computer designers could easily give an architecture a rich repertoire of instructions that carry out elaborate functions. A single, complex instruction might do the job of half a dozen or more simpler instructions. Although each instruction would take longer to execute because of the microcode, programs would need fewer instructions overall. Moreover, adding more instructions could boost speed. One result of this microcode "more is merrier" instruction approach is that typical PC microprocessors have seven different subtraction commands.

In the mainstream of computer and microprocessor design, microcode is not necessary. While system architects were staying up nights concocting ever more powerful and obscure instructions, a counter force was gathering. Starting in the 1970s, the microcode approach came under attack by researchers who claimed it takes a greater toll on performance than its benefits justify.

By eliminating microcode, this design camp believed simpler instructions could be executed at speeds so much higher that no degree of instruction complexity could compensate. By necessity, such hard-wired machines would offer only a few instructions because the complexity of their hard-wired circuitry would increase dramatically with every additional instruction added. Practical designs are best made with small instruction sets.

RISC

John Cocke at IBM's Yorktown Research Laboratory analyzed the usage of instructions by computers and discovered that most of the work done by computers involves relatively few instructions. Given a computer with a set of 200 instructions, for example, two-thirds of its processing involves using as few as 10 of the total instructions. Cocke went on to design a computer that was based on a few instructions that could be executed quickly. He is credited with inventing the Reduced Instruction Set Computer or RISC in 1974. In 1987 Cocke's work on RISC won him the Turing Award (named for computer pioneer Alan M. Turing, known best for this Turing Test definition of artificial intelligence), given by the Association for Computing Machinery as its highest honor for technical contributions to computing.

Note that the RISC concept predated the term, however. The term *RISC* is credited to David Peterson, who used it in a microprocessor design course at the University of California at Berkeley in 1980. The first chip to bear the label and to take advantage of Cocke's discoveries was RISC-I, a laboratory design that was completed in 1982. To distinguish this new design approach from traditional microprocessors, microcode-based systems with large instruction sets have come to be known as Complex Instruction Set Computers or CISC designs.

Cocke's research showed that most of the computing was done by basic instructions, not by the more powerful, complex, and specialized instructions. Further research at Berkeley and Stanford Universities demonstrated that there were even instances in which a sequence of simple instructions could perform a complex task faster than a single complex instruction could. The result of this research is often summarized as the *80/20 Rule*: about 20 percent of a computer's instructions do about 80 percent of the work. The aim of the RISC design is to optimize a computer's performance for that 20 percent of instructions, speeding up their execution as much as possible. The remaining 80 percent of the commands could be duplicated, when necessary, by combinations of the quick 20 percent. Analysis and practical experience has shown that the 20 percent could be made so much faster that the overhead required to emulate the remaining 80 percent was no handicap at all.

In 1979 IBM introduced its model 801, the first machine to take advantage of Cocke's findings. It is credited as the first computer intentionally designed with a reduced instruction set. The 801 was a 32-bit minicomputer with 32 registers that could execute its simple instructions in a single processor cycle. The 801 led to the development of IBM's Personal Computer/RT in 1986, which was refined into the RISC System/6000. The multichip processor in the RS/6000 was consolidated into a single chip that formed the basis of IBM's PowerPC microprocessors (now being jointly developed with Motorola).

The Berkeley line of RISC research led to the RISC-II microprocessor (in 1984) and SOAR. Together, these laboratory designs inspired Sun Microsystems to develop the SPARC line of microprocessors.

RISC philosophy also inspired John Hennesey at Stanford University to found the MIPS project there. Although the MIPS group once said that the acronym was derived from a description of their design goal (Microprocessor without Interlocked Pipeline Stages), more commonly it is held to stand for Millions of Instructions Per Second, a rudimentary yardstick of microprocessor performance. The MIPS project eventually spawned RISC-chip developer MIPS Computer Systems (known as MIPS Technologies since its merger with Silicon Graphics in 1992). The Silicon Graphics R2000, R3000, R4000, R4400, and R6000 chips trace their heritage back to the Stanford line of development.

No sharp edge demarcates the boundaries of what constitutes a reduced or complex instruction set. The DEC Alpha, for example, one of the most recent RISC designs, has a full repertoire of 160 instructions. In contrast, Intel's 486, generally considered to be a CISC microprocessor, features about 150 instructions (depending on how you count). In light of such incongruities, some RISC developers now contend the RISC term has stood for not Reduced Instruction Set but rather Restricted Instruction Set Computer all along.

More important than the nomenclature or number of instructions that a computer or microprocessor understands in characterizing RISC and CISC is how those instructions are realized. Slimming down a computer's instruction set is just one way that engineers go about streamlining its processing. As the instructions are trimmed, all the ragged edges that interfere with its performance are trimmed off, and all that remains is honed and smoothed to offer the least possible resistance to the passage of data. Consequently, RISC designs are best distinguished from CISC not by a single to-be-or-not-to-be rule but whether (and how well) they incorporate a number of characteristics. Some of the important characteristics of RISC include:

Single-cycle or better execution of instructions. Most instructions on a RISC computer will be carried out in a single clock cycle, if not faster, because of pipelining.

Uniformity of instructions. The RISC pipeline operates best if all instructions are the same length (number of bits), require the same syntax, and execute in the same number of cycles. Most RISC systems have instruction sets made up solely of 32-bit commands.

Lack of microcode. RISC computers either entirely lack microcode or have very little of it, relying instead on hard-wired logic. Operations handled by microcode in CISC microprocessors require sequences of simple RISC instructions. Note that if these complex operations are performed repeatedly, the series of RISC instructions will lodge in the high-speed memory cache of the microprocessor. The cache contents then act like microcode that's automatically customized for the running program.

Load-store design. Accessing memory during the execution of an instruction often imposes delays because RAM cannot be accessed as quickly as the microprocessor runs. Consequently, most RISC machines lack immediate instructions and minimize the number of instructions that affect memory. Data must be explicitly loaded into a register before it can be worked on using a separate load instruction. The sequence of instructions in program code can then be organized (by an optimizing compiler) so that the delay on the pipeline is minimized.

The hard work is in the software. The RISC design shifts most of the work in achieving top performance to the software that runs on the system. RISC performance depends on how efficiently the instructions for running the system are arranged. Processing multiple instructions in a single clock cycle requires that the program pipeline be kept full of instructions that are constantly moving. If the pipeline harmony breaks down, the system stalls. RISC systems depend on special language programs called *optimizing compilers* that analyze the instruct steps they generate to see whether rearranging the instructions will better match the needs of the microprocessor pipeline. In effect, RISC programs are analyzed and rewritten for optimum speed before they are used. The extra time spent on preparing the program pays off in increased performance every time it runs. Commercial programs are already compiled when you get them, so you normally don't see the extra effort exerted by the optimizing compiler. You just get quicker results.

Design simplicity. Above all, simplicity is the key to the design of a RISC machine or microprocessors. Although the Intel 80486 microprocessor has the equivalent of about one million transistors inside its package, the RISC-based MIPS M/2000 has only about 120,000, yet the two are comparable in performance. Fewer transistors mean fewer things to go wrong. RISC chips aren't necessarily more reliable, but making them without fabrication errors is easier than with more complex chips.

More important than number of transistors is the amount of space on the silicon chip that needs to be used to make a microprocessor. As the area of a chip increases, the likelihood of fabrication errors increases. During the fabrication process, errors are inevitable. A speck of dust or a bit of semiconductor that doesn't grow or etch properly can prevent the finished circuit from working. A number of such defects are inevitable on any single silicon matrix. The larger and more complex the circuits on the matrix, the more likely any one (or all of them) will be plagued by a defect. Consequently, the yield of usable circuits from a matrix plummets as the circuits become more complex and larger. Moreover, the bigger the design of a chip, the fewer patterns that will fit on a die. That is, the fewer chips that can be grown at a time with given fabrication equipment. Overall, the yield of RISC chips can thus be greater. In more practical terms, it costs more to build more complex microprocessors.

Because they are simpler, RISC chips are easier to design. Fewer transistors means less circuitry to lay out, test, and give engineers nightmares. Just as the blueprints of an igloo would be more manageable than those for a Gothic cathedral, RISC chip designs take less work and can be readied faster.

It's why new microprocessor manufacturers favor RISC. In fact, some people claim that every microprocessor designed since 1985 has been RISC. Like every exaggeration, this one holds more than a grain of truth. RISC ideas have infiltrated every high-performance microprocessor design. The only CISC chips surviving in the high-performance market are those designed by Intel, and even the newest of them incorporate RISC concepts. RISC has become such a big selling point that every chip maker claims to have it. Because no one can pin down exactly what constitutes RISC, who is to say otherwise?

In light of all the advantages of RISC, the survival of any CISC microprocessors may seem odd. In truth, CISC chips in the real world outnumber RISC chips by more than a thousand to one. Fax machines, microwave ovens, hand held calculators, VCRs, even automobiles all have microprocessors inside, and such chips are almost universally CISC chips. The power and performance of RISC is simply unnecessary in such applications. Even in computers, CISC-based systems outsell RISC machines by a factor on the order of 100 to 1.

With the new generation of computers, however, that situation may dramatically change. Macintosh computers based on the PowerPC chip could double the market penetration of RISC in a single year. Once new operating systems catch on among PCs, the RISC potential is even greater.

Very Long Instruction Words

Just as RISC is flowing into the product mainstream, a new idea is sharpening the leading edge. *Very Long Instruction Word* technology at first appears to run against the RISC stream by using long, complex instructions. In reality, VLIW is a refinement of RISC meant to better take advantage of superscalar microprocessors. Each very long instruction word is made from several RISC instructions. In a typical implementation, eight 32-bit RISC instructions combine to make one instruction word.

Ordinarily combining RISC instructions would add little to overall speed. As with RISC, the secret of VLIW technology is in the software—the compiler that produces the final program code. The instructions in the long word are chosen so that they execute at the same time (or as close to it as possible) in parallel processing units in the superscalar microprocessor. The compiler chooses and arranges instructions to match the needs of the superscalar processor as best as possible, essentially taking the optimizing compiler one step further. In essence, the VLIW system takes advantage of pre-processing in the compiler to make the final code and microprocessor more efficient.

VLIW technology also takes advantage of the wider bus connections of the latest generations of microprocessors. Existing chips link to their support circuitry with 64 bit buses. Many have 128-bit internal buses. The 256-bit very long instruction words push a little further yet enable a microprocessor to load several cycles of work in a single memory cycle.

No VLIW microprocessor to systems are currently available. In fact, the only existing VLIW command sets remain experimental. The next generation of microprocessor very likely will see the integration of VLIW concepts.

Construction

The essence of any digital logic system is that one electrical current (or voltage) can control another one. No matter whether a microprocessor is CISC, RISC, something in between, or something out of the mainstream, it depends on this principle of electrical control. Over the years, improving technology has steadily refined the mechanisms for carrying out this action.

The first approach to electrical control of electrical flow evolved from the rattling telegraph key. Instead of just making noise, the solenoid of the telegraph sounder was adapted to closing electrical contacts, making a mechanism now called the *relay*. The basis of Bell Lab's 1946 Mark V computer, the relay is a component that's still used in modern electrical equipment.

The vacuum tube improved on the relay design by eliminating the mechanical part of the remote-action switch. Vacuum tubes harness the power of the attraction of unlike electrical charges and repulsion of like charges, enabling a small charge to control the flow of electrons through the vacuum inside the tube. The advantage of the vacuum tube over the relay is speed. The relay operates at mechanical rates, perhaps a few thousand operations per second. The vacuum tube can switch millions of times per second. The first recognizable computers (like Eniac) were built from thousands of tube-based logic gates.

Analog and Digital Circuits

Tubes also ushered in an entirely new technology. Using a small current to control a larger current (or a small voltage to control a larger voltage) is a process called *amplification*. The large current (or voltage) mimics the controlling current (or voltage) but is stronger or amplified. In that every change in the large signal is exactly analogous to each one in the small signal, devices that amplify in this way are called *analog*. The intensity of the control signal can represent continuously variable information—for example, a sound level in stereo equipment. The electrical signal in this kind of equipment thus is an analogy to the sound that it represents.

The limiting case of amplification occurs when the control signal causes the larger signal to go from its lowest value, 0, to its highest value. In other words, the large signal goes off and on— switches—under control of the smaller signal. The two states of the output signal (on and off) can be used as part of a binary code that represents information. For example, the switch could be used to produce a series of seven pulses to represent the number 7. Because information can be coded as groups of such numbers (digits), electrical devices that use this switching technology are described as *digital*. Note that this switching directly corresponds to the movement of the telegraph key and the switching of a relay. It enables the construction of logic gates, and from them, computers.

Semiconductors

Using tube-based electronics in computers is fraught with problems. First is the space heater effect: tubes have to glow like light bulbs to work and they generate heat along the way, enough to smelt rather than process data. And, like light bulbs, tubes burn out. Large tube-based computers required daily shut-down and maintenance and several technicians on the payroll. In addition, tube circuits are big. The house-sized computers of 1950s vintage science fiction would easily be outclassed in computing power by today's desktop machines. In the typical tube-based computer design, one logic gate required one tube. Consider that a PC may have hundreds of thousands of gates, and you begin to see the size of the problem. Moreover, the bigger the computer, the longer it takes its thoughts to travel through its circuits, and the more slowly it thinks.

Making today's practical PCs took another true breakthrough in electronics: the transistor, which emerged in 1947 at Bell Laboratories. A tiny fleck of germanium (later, silicon) formed into three layers, the transistor was endowed with the capability to let one electrical current applied to one layer alter the flow of another, larger current between the other two layers. Unlike the vacuum tube, because the transistor needed no hot electrons since the current flowed entirely through a solid material—the germanium or silicon; hence, the common name for tubeless technology, solid-state.

Germanium and silicon are special materials (actually, metals) called *semiconductors*. The term describes how these materials resist the flow of electrical currents. They resist more than conductors (like the copper in wires) but not as much as insulators (like the plastic wrapped around the wires).

By itself, being a poor but not awful electrical conductor is as remarkable as lukewarm water. Infusing atoms of impurities into the semiconductor's microscopic lattice structure dramatically alters the electrical characteristics of the material. The process of adding impurities is called *doping*. Some impurities add extra electrons (carriers of negative charges) to the crystal; others leave holes in the lattice where electrons would ordinarily be, and these holes act as positive charge carriers. A semiconductor is often described by the type of impurity that has been added to its structure: *N-type* for those with extra electrons (negative charge carriers) and *P-type* for those with holes (positive charge carriers). Ordinary three-layer transistors, for example, come in two configurations, NPN and PNP, depending on which type of semiconductor is in the middle.

Modern computer circuits mostly rely on a kind of transistor in which the current flow through a narrow channel of semiconductor material is controlled by a voltage applied to a gate (which surrounds the channel) made from metal oxide. The most common variety of these transistors is made from N-type material and results in a technology called NMOS (N-channel Metal Oxide Semiconductor). A related technology combines both N-channel and P-channel devices and is called CMOS (Complementary Metal Oxide Semiconductor) because the N- and P-type materials are complements (opposites) of one another.

The typical microprocessor once was built from NMOS technology. Although NMOS designs are distinguished by their design simplicity and small size (even on a microchip level), they have a severe shortcoming: they constantly use electricity whenever their gates are turned on. Because about half of the tens or hundreds of thousands of gates in a microprocessor are switched on at any given time, an NMOS chip can draw a lot of current. This current flow creates heat and wastes power, making NMOS unsuitable for miniaturized computers (which can be difficult to cool) and battery-operated equipment, such as notebook computers.

Some earlier and most contemporary microprocessors now use CMOS designs. CMOS is inherently more complex than NMOS because each gate requires more transistors, at least one pair per gate. But this complexity brings a benefit. When one transistor in a CMOS gate is turned on, its complementary partner is switched off, minimizing the current flow through the complementary pair that make up the circuit. When a CMOS gate is idle, just maintaining its state, it requires almost no power. During a state change, the current flow is large but brief. Consequently, the faster the CMOS gate changes state, the more current that flows through it and the more heat it generates. In other words, the faster a CMOS circuit operates, the hotter it becomes. This speed-induced temperature rise is one of the limits on the operating speed of many microprocessors.

CMOS technology can duplicate every logic function made with NMOS but with a substantial saving of electricity. On the other hand, manufacturing costs somewhat more because of the added circuit complexity.

Integrated Circuits

The transistor overcomes several of the problems with using tubes to make a computer. Transistors are smaller than tubes and give off less heat because they don't need to glow to work. But every logic gate still requires one or more transistors (as well as several other electronic components) to build. If you allocated a mere square inch to every logic gate, the number of logic gates in a personal computer microprocessor would require a circuit board on the order of 16 square feet.

At the very end of the 1950's, Robert N. Noyce at Fairchild Instrument and Jack S. Kilby independently came up with the same brilliant idea of putting multiple semiconductor devices into a single package. Transistors are typically grown as crystals from thin-cut slices of silicon called *wafers*. Typically thousands of transistors are grown at the same time on the same wafer. Instead of carving the wafer into separate transistors, the engineer linked them together (integrated them) to create a complete electronic circuit all on one wafer. Kilby linked the devices with micro wires; Noyce envisioned fabricating the interconnecting circuits between devices on the silicon itself. The resulting electronic device, for which Noyce applied for a patent on July 30, 1959, became known as the *integrated circuit* or IC. Such devices now are often called *chips* because of their construction from a single small piece of silicon, a chip off the old crystal. Integrated circuit technology has been adapted to both analog and digital circuitry. Their grandest development, however, is the microprocessor.

The IC has several advantages over circuits built from individual (or discrete) transistors, most resulting from miniaturization. Most importantly, integration reduces the amount of packaging. Instead of one metal or plastic transistor case per logic gate, multiple gates (even millions of them) can be combined into one chip package.

Because the current inside the chip need not interact with external circuits, the chips can be made arbitrarily small, enabling the circuits to be made smaller, too. Today, the limit on the size of elements inside an integrated circuit is mostly determined by fabrication technology; internal circuitry is as small as today's manufacturing equipment can make it affordably. The latest Intel microprocessors, which use integrated circuit technology, incorporate the equivalent of more than a million transistors using interconnections that measure about four-tenths of a micron (millionths of a meter) across.

In the past, a hierarchy of names was given to ICs depending on the size of circuit elements. Ordinary ICs were the coarsest in construction. Large-scale integration (LSI) put between 500 and 20,000 circuit elements together; very large scale integration (VLSI) puts more than 20,000 circuit elements onto a single chip. All microprocessors use VLSI technology, although the most recent products have become so complex (Intel's 486, for example, has the equivalent of about 1.2 million transistors inside) that a new term has been coined for them, ultra large scale integration (ULSI).

Thermal Constraints

The tight packing of circuits on chips makes heat a major issue in their design and operation. Heat is the enemy of the semiconductor because it can destroy the delicate crystal structure of a chip. If a chip gets too hot, it will be irrevocably destroyed. Packing circuits tightly concentrates the heat they generate, and the small size of the individual circuit components makes them more vulnerable to damage.

Heat can cause problems more subtle than simple destruction. Because the conductivity of semiconductor circuits also varies with temperature, the effective switching speed of transistors and logic gates also changes when chips get too hot or too cold. Although this temperature-induced speed change does not alter how fast a microprocessor can compute (the chip must stay locked to the system clock at all times), it can affect the relative timing between signals inside the microprocessor. Should the timing get too far off, a microprocessor may make a mistake, with the inevitable result of crashing your system. All chips have rated temperature ranges within which they are guaranteed to operate without such timing errors.

Because chips generate more heat as speed increases, they can produce heat faster than it can radiate away. This heat build up can alter the timing of the internal signals of the chip so drastically that the microprocessor will stop working and—as if you couldn't guess—cause your system to crash. To avoid such problems, computer manufacturers often attach heatsinks to microprocessors and other semiconductor components to aid in their cooling.

A *heatsink* is simply a metal extrusion that increases the surface area from which heat can radiate from a microprocessor or other heat-generating circuit element. Most heatsinks have several fins, rows of pins, or some geometry that increases its surface area. Heatsinks are usually made from aluminum because it is one of the better thermal conductors, enabling the heat from the microprocessor to quickly spread across the heatsink.

Heatsinks provide passive cooling because it requires no power-using mechanism to perform its cooling. Heatsinks work by convection, transferring heat to the air that circulates past the heatsink. Air circulates around the heatsink because the warmed air rises away from the heatsink and cooler air flows in to replace it.

In contrast, active cooling involves some kind of mechanical or electrical assistance in removing heat. The most common form of active cooling is a fan, which blows a greater volume of air past the heatsink than would be possible with convection alone.

As a by-product of a microprocessor's thinking, heat is wasted. The energy that raises the temperature of the microprocessor does no useful work. But it does drain the energy source that's supplying the microprocessor.

Operating Voltages

In desktop computers, overheating rather than excess electrical consumption is the major power concern. Even the most wasteful of microprocessors use far less power than an ordinary light bulb. The most that any PC-compatible microprocessor consumes is about nine watts, hardly more than a night light and of little concern when the power grid supplying your PC has megawatts at its disposal.

If you switch to battery power, however, every last milliwatt is important. The more power used by a PC, the shorter the time its battery can power the system or the heavier the batteries it will need to achieve a given life between charges. Every degree a microprocessor raises its case temperature clips minutes from its battery run-time.

Battery-powered notebooks and sub-notebook computers consequently caused microprocessor engineers to do a quick about-face. Where once they were content to use bigger and bigger heatsinks, fans, and refrigerators to keep their chips cool, today they focus on reducing temperatures and wasted power at the source.

One way to cut power requirements is to make the design elements of a chip smaller. Smaller digital circuits require less power. But shrinking chips is not an option; microprocessors are invariably designed to be as small as possible with the prevailing technology.

To further trim the power required by microprocessors to make them more amendable to battery operation, engineers have come up with two new design twists: low-voltage operation and system management mode. Although founded on separate ideas, both are often used together to minimize microprocessor power consumption. Most new microprocessor designs will likely incorporate both technologies. In fact, some older microprocessor designs have been retrofitted with such power-saving technologies (for example, the SL-Enhanced series of Intel 486DX and 486SX chips).

Since the beginning of the transistor-transistor logic family of digital circuits—the design technology that later blossomed into the microprocessor—digital logic has operated with a supply voltage of five volts. That level is essentially arbitrary. Almost any voltage would work. But five-volt technology offers some practical advantages. It's low enough to be both safe and frugal with power needs but high enough to avoid noise and to enable several *diode drops*.

Every semiconductor junction, which essentially forms a diode, reduces or drops the voltage flowing through it. Silicon junctions impose a diode drop of about 0.7 volts, and there may be one or more such junctions in a logic gate.

But there's nothing magical about five volts. Reducing the voltage used by logic circuits dramatically reduces power consumption because power consumption in electrical circuits increases by the square of the voltage. That is, doubling the voltage of a circuit increases the power it uses by fourfold. Reducing the voltage by one-half reduces power consumption by three-quarters—providing, of course, that the circuit will continue to operate at the lower voltage.

Microprocessor designers have begun to exploit the potential of lower voltage operation by creating new microprocessors that scorn traditional five-volt operation. Advanced Micro Devices developed the first of this new generation of microprocessors in 1992 as a version of the 386 microprocessor that operated at 3.3 volts. Other chip makers followed with their own low-voltage products, nearly all of which are designed for 3.3-volt operation. For example, Intel's fastest chips, the higher-speed Pentiums and the 486DX4 series, are all designed for 3.3-volt power success.

The 3.3-volt level was chosen because its signals remain compatible with those of traditional 5-volt TTL circuits but are low enough to halve power consumption. The new 3.3-volt microprocessors will work with conventional 5-volt support chips (a PC will have to supply 3.3 volts to the microprocessor and 5 volts to the rest of its circuits), but the real energy savings will come when the rest of the circuits in the PC (support chips and memory) also operate at the lower voltage level. As with microprocessors, these semiconductors will need to be entirely redesigned for low-voltage operation, and chip makers have already taken up the challenge.

Power Management

Most microprocessors have been designed to be like the Coast Guard, always prepared (the U.S. Coast Guard motto is *semper paratus*). They kept all of their circuits constantly ready and operating at full potential, whether they were being used or not. From an energy usage viewpoint, that's like burning all the lights in your entire house while you sit quietly in the living room reading a book. You may venture into some other room, so you keep those lights burning—and keep the local electric company in business.

Most people (at least, most frugally minded people) switch on the lights only in the rooms in which they are roaming, keeping other lights off to minimize the waste of electricity. Newer microprocessors are designed to do the same thing, switch off portions of their circuitry and even some of the circuits in your PC external to the microprocessor when they are unneeded. When, for example, you're running a program that's just waiting around for your to press a key, the microprocessor could switch most of its calculating circuits off until it receives an interrupt from the keyboard controller. This use-only-what's-needed feature is called *system management mode*. It was pioneered by Intel's 386SL microprocessor and has become a standard feature of most newer chips.

In addition, many microprocessors are able to operate at a variety of speeds. Slowing a chip down reduces its power consumption (it also reduces performance). Many current chips enable their host computers to force a speed reduction by lowering the clock speed. Microprocessors that use static logic designs are able to stop operating entirely without risking their register contents, enabling a complete system shutdown to save power. Later they can be reactivated without losing a beat (or byte). The electrical charges in ordinary, dynamic designs drain off faster than they get restored if the dynamic circuit slows too much.

Packaging

The working part of a microprocessor is exactly what the nickname "chip" implies: a small flake of a silicon crystal no larger than a postage stamp. Although silicon is a fairly robust material with moderate physical strength, it is sensitive to chemical contamination. After all, semiconductors are grown in precisely controlled atmospheres, the chemical content of which affects the operating properties of the final chip. To prevent oxygen and contaminants in the atmosphere from adversely affecting the precision-engineered silicon, the chip itself must be sealed away. The first semiconductors, transistors, were hermetically sealed in tiny metal cans.

The art and science of semiconductor packaging has advanced since those early days. Modern ICs are often surrounded in epoxy plastic, an inexpensive material that can be easily molded to the proper shape. Unfortunately, microprocessors can get very hot, sometimes too hot for plastics to safely contain. Most powerful modern microprocessors are consequently cased in ceramic materials that are fused together at high temperatures. Older, cooler chips reside in plastic.

The most primitive of microprocessors—that is, those of the early generation that had neither substantial signal nor power requirements—fit in the same style housing popular for other integrated circuits, the infamous *dual in-line pin* or *DIP* package. The only problem chips the DIPs face is getting signals in and out. Even ancient 8-bit chips require more connections than the 14 to 20 that fit on normal-size DIP packages. Consequently, most DIP microprocessors have housings with 40 or more pins.

The typical microprocessor DIP is a black epoxy plastic rectangle about two inches long and half an inch wide. Some more powerful DIP chips use ceramic cases with metal seals over the location where the silicon itself fits. A row of connecting pins line both of the long sides of the chip package like the legs of a centipede.

The most important of these legs is *pin number one*, which helps determine the proper orientation for putting the chip in its socket. The number-one pin of the two rows is the pin that terminates the row of pins that's on the same end of the chip as its orientation notch, on the left row when viewed from the top of the chip (see fig. 3.1).

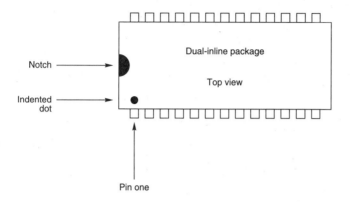

FIGURE 3.1. DIP chip identifying pin one.

The DIP package is far from ideal for a number of reasons. Adding more connections, for example, makes for an ungainly chip. A centipede microprocessor would be a beast measuring a full five inches long. Not only would such a critter be hard to fit onto a reasonably sized circuit board, it would require that signals travel substantially farther to reach the end pins than those in the center. At modern operating frequencies, that difference in distance can amount to a substantial fraction of a clock cycle, potentially putting the pins out of sync.

Modern chip packages are compact squares that avoid these problems. At least four separate styles of packages have been developed to accommodate the needs of the latest microprocessors.

Today, the most common is the *Pin Grid Array* or *PGA*, a square package that varies in size with the number of pins that it must accommodate. Recent microprocessors are about two inches square. Sixteen-bit chips typically have two rows of pins parallel to each edge of the chip and dropping down from its bottom, a total of about 68 pins. Processors with 32-bit bus connections have between 112 and 168 pins arranged similarly but in three rows. Chips with 64-bit connection potential may have nearly 300 pins in four rows arrayed as one square inside another.

In any case, the pins are spaced as if they were laid out on a checker board, all evenly spaced, with the central block of pins (and sometimes those at each of the four corners) eliminated. Again, pin number one is specially marked for orientation purposes. The ferrule through which the pin leaves the ceramic case is often square for pin one and round for the others. In addition, the corner of the chip that corresponds to the location of pin one is typically chopped off (see fig. 3.2).

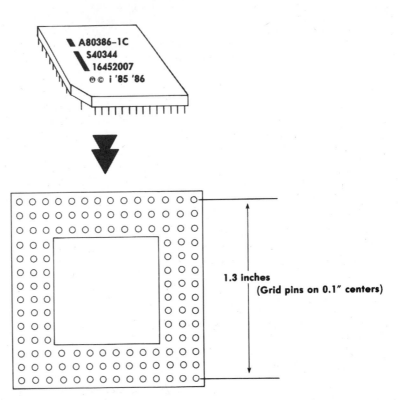

FIGURE 3.2. Pin-grid array socket (with PGA chip).

Pins are prone to damage and relatively expensive to fabricate, so chip makers have developed pinless packages for microprocessors. The first of these to find general use was the Leadless Chip Carrier, or LCC, socket. Instead of pins, this style of package has contact pads on one of its surfaces. The pads are plated with gold to avoid corrosion or oxidation that would impede the flow of the minute electrical signals used by the chip (see fig. 3.3). The pads are designed to contact special spingy mating contacts in a special socket. Once installed, the chip itself may be hidden in the socket, under a heat sink, or perhaps only the top of the chip may be visible, framed by the four sides of the socket.

In an LCC socket, the chip is held in place by a pivoting metal wire. You pull the wire off the chip, and the chip pops up. Hold an LCC chip in your hand and it resembles a small ceramic tile. Its bottom edge is dotted with bright flecks of gold—the chip's contact pads.

PGA and LCC packages are made from a ceramic material because the rigid material provides structural strength needed by the chip. To avoid the higher cost of ceramics, chip makers created an alternate design that could be fabricated from plastic. Called the *Plastic Leaded Chip Carrier*, or PLCC, this package has another advantage besides cost: a special versatility. It can be soldered directly to a printed circuit board using surface-mount techniques. Using this package, the computer manufacturer can save the cost of a socket while improving the reliability of the system. (Remember, connections like those in chip sockets are the least reliable part of a computer system.)

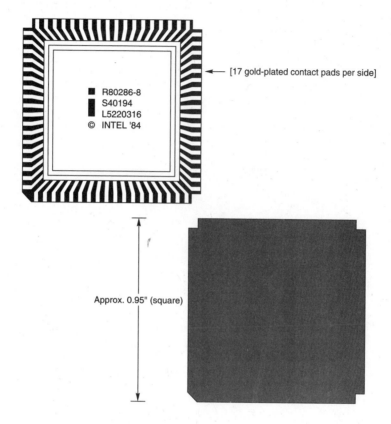

[17 gold-plated contact pads per side]

R80286-8
S40194
L5220316
© INTEL '84

Approx. 0.95" (square)

FIGURE 3.3. Leadless Chip Carrier microprocessor.

The PLCC chip can also be used in a socket. In this case, the socket surrounds the chip. The leads from the chip are bent down around its perimeter and slide against mating contacts inside the inner edge of the socket's perimeter. A PLCC chip is rather easy to press into its socket but difficult to pop out—you must carefully wedge underneath the chip and lever it out.

New microprocessors with low thermal output sometimes use a housing designed to be soldered down, the *Plastic Quad Flat Package* or *PQFP*, sometimes called simply the "quad flat pack" because the chips are flat (they fit flat against the circuit board) and they have four sides (making them a quadrilateral).

Manufacturers like this package because of its low cost and because chips using it can be installed in exactly the same manner as other modern surface-mount components. However, the quad flat pack is suitable only to lower power chips because soldered connections can be stressed by microprocessors that get too hot. As with other chip packages, proper orientation of a quad flat pack is indicated by a notch or depression near pin number one (see fig. 3.4).

Figure 3.4. Plastic Quad Flat Package microprocessor.

The package that the chip is housed in has no effect on its performance. It can, however, be important when you want to replace or upgrade your microprocessor with a new chip or upgrade card. Many of these enhancement products require that you replace your system's microprocessor with a new chip or adapter cable that links to a circuit board. If you want the upgrade or a replacement part to fit on your motherboard, you may have to specify which package your PC uses for its microprocessor.

Location

Ordinarily, you should have no need to see or touch the microprocessor in your PC. As long as your computer works (and considering the reliability that most have demonstrated, that should be a long, long time), you really need have no concern about your microprocessor except to know that it's inside your computer doing its job. However, some modern system upgrades require that you plug a new microprocessor into your system or even replace the one that you have.

Before you can replace your microprocessor, you need to identify which chip it is. That's easy. As a general rule, all you need to look for is the largest integrated circuit chip on your computer's motherboard. Almost invariably it will be the microprocessor. That's only fitting because the microprocessor is also the most important chip in the computer. In modern PCs, the microprocessor uses a large, square package.

If you find several large chips on your system board, odds are that one of them is the microprocessor. Others may be equally big because they have elaborate functions and need to make many connections with the system board, which means they need relatively large packages to accommodate their many leads.

Almost universally, the microprocessor chip will be installed in a socket (which may or may not be visible); most support chips will be soldered directly to the system board. Sometimes the microprocessor will be hidden under a heatsink, which you can identify by its heat-radiating fins.

The appearance of each different microprocessor depends on the package it uses, but all can be identified by their model number emblazoned on top. You'll have to sort through a few lines of numbers to find the key identifying signature, but the model designations of most chips are readily sorted out.

Commercial Models

The history of microprocessor development has been mostly a matter of increasing these numbers. With each new generation of microprocessor, the number and size of its registers increases, and data and address buses become wider. As a result, microprocessors and the personal computers made from them have become increasingly powerful.

Intel Products

Today, Intel Corporation, the largest maker of microprocessors, has moved into the role of the largest independent maker of semiconductors in the world. Depending on your viewpoint, you could credit its dominance of the industry to hard work, astute planning, corporate predation, or cosmic coincidence. But the root of the success is undeniable. Credit for the invention of the microprocessor goes to Intel.

Since the invention of the microprocessor, the company has pushed the limits of technology to keep ahead of its competition. Its designs—all direct descendants of its original creation—are now the only CISC microprocessors used in PCs. And yet, chance has played a role in Intel's fantastic growth as well. The company probably would not be on top of the industry had not a handful of engineers at IBM thought one of Intel's products offered a tenuous marketing advantage over the other chips available (see table 3.1).

TABLE 3.1. Intel Microprocessor Time Line

Chip	Introduction date	Estimated power (MIPS)	Internal register width	External bus width	Number of transistors
4004	Nov-71	0.06	4	4	2300
8008	Apr-72	0.06	8	8	3500
8080	Apr-74	0.64	8	8	6000
8085	Mar-76	0.37	8	8	6500
8086	Jun-78	0.33	16	16	29,000
		0.66	16	16	29,000
		0.75	16	16	29,000
8088	Jun-79	0.33	16	8	29,000
		0.75	16	8	29,000
80286	Feb-82	1.2	16	16	134,000
		1.5	16	16	134,000
		1.66	16	16	134,000
386DX	Nov-85	5.5	32	32	275,000
	Feb-87	6.5	32	32	275,000
	Apr-88	8.5	32	32	275,000
	Apr-89	11.4	32	32	275,000
386SX	Jun-88	2.5	32	16	275,000
	Jan-89	2.5	32	16	275,000
		2.7	32	16	275,000
		2.9	32	16	275,000
386SL	Oct-90	4.2	32	16	855,000
	Sep-91	5.3	32	16	855,000
486DX	Apr-89	20	32	32	1,200,000
	May-90	27	32	32	1,200,000
	Jun-91	41	32	32	1,200,000
486SX	Sep-91	13	32	32	1,185,000
	Sep-91	16.5	32	32	1,185,000
	Sep-91	20	32	32	1,185,000
	Sep-92	27	32	32	900,000
486DX2	Mar-92	41	32	32	1,200,000
	Aug-92	54	32	32	1,200,000
486SL	Nov-92	15.4	32	32	1,400,000
		19	32	32	1,400,000
		25	32	32	1,400,000
486DX4	Mar-94	60	32	32	1,200,000
		81	32	32	1,200,000
Pentium	Mar-93	100	64	32	3,100,000
	Mar-93	112	64	32	3,100,000
	Mar-94	150	64	32	3,100,000

Chip	Tecnology (Microns)	Addressable memory	External Clock Speed (MHz)	Internal Clock Speed (MHz)	Integral Floating Point Unit
4004	10.0	640 bytes	0.108	0.108	NO
8008	10.0	16K	0.2	0.2	NO
8080	6.0	64K	2	2	NO
8085	3.0	64K	5	5	NO
8086	3.0	1MB	5	5	NO
	3.0	1MB	8	8	NO
	3.0	1MB	10	10	NO
8088	3.0	1MB	5	5	NO
	3.0	1MB	8	8	NO
80286	1.5	16MB	8	8	NO
	1.5	16MB	10	10	NO
	1.5	16MB	12	12	NO
386DX	1.5	4GB	16	16	NO
	1.5	4GB	20	20	NO
	1.5	4GB	25	25	NO
	1.5	4GB	33	33	NO
386SX	1.5	4GB	16	16	NO
	1.5	4GB	20	20	NO
	1.5	4GB	25	25	NO
	1.5	4GB	33	33	NO
386SL	1.0	32MB	20	20	NO
	1.0	32MB	25	25	NO
486DX	1.0	4GB	25	25	YES
	1.0	4GB	33	33	YES
	0.8	4GB	50	50	YES
486SX	1.0	4GB	16	16	NO
	1.0	4GB	20	20	NO
	1.0	4GB	25	25	NO
	0.8	4GB	33	33	YES
486DX2	0.8	4GB	25	50	YES
	0.8	4GB	33	66	YES
486SL	0.8	64MB	20	20	YES
	0.8	64MB	25	25	YES
	0.8	64MB	33	33	YES
486DX4	0.6	4GB	25	75	YES
	0.6	4GB	33	100	YES
Pentium	0.8	4GB	60	60	YES
	0.8	4GB	66	66	YES
	0.6	4GB	100	100	YES

The history of the microprocessor stretches back to a 1969 request to Intel by a now-defunct Japanese calculator company, Busicom. The original plan was to build a series of calculators, each one different and each requiring a custom integrated circuit. Using conventional IC technology, the project would have required the design of 12 different chips. The small volumes of each design would have made development costs prohibitive. Intel engineer Mercian E. (Ted) Hoff had a better idea, one that could slash the necessary design work. Instead of a collection of individually tailored circuits, he envisioned creating one general-purpose device that would satisfy the needs of all the calculators. His approach worked. The result was the first general-purpose microprocessor, the Intel 4004.

The chip was a success. Not only did it usher in the age of the low-cost calculators, it also gave designers a single solid-state programmable device for the first time. Instead of designing the digital decision-making circuits in products from scratch, developers could buy an off-the-shelf component and tailor it to their needs simply by writing the appropriate program.

The 4004 Family

The 4004 was first introduced to the marketplace in 1971. As might be deduced from its manufacturer's designation 4004, this ground breaking chip had registers capable of handling four bits at a time through a four-bit bus. Puny by today's standards, those four bits—enough to code 16 symbols including all numbers from zero to nine as well as operators—were just useful enough to make calculations. The chip could add, subtract, and multiply just as capably (but hardly as fast) as the much larger computers of the time. It was designed to run at 108 KHz (that's about 1/10 megahertz).

One major difference divided the capabilities of the 4004 from the brains in real computers. Larger computers worked not only with numbers but also with alphabetic symbols and text. Handling these larger symbol sets was something beyond the ken of the 4004. After all, most alphabets have more than 16 characters. Making the microprocessor into a more general-purpose device required expanding the size of the chip's registers so it could handle representations of all the letters of our alphabet and more.

Although six bits could accommodate all upper- and lowercase letters as well as numbers (26 bits can code 64 symbols), it would leave little room to spare for punctuation marks and such niceties as control codes. In addition, the emergence of the eight-bit byte as the standard measure of digital data resulted in it being chosen as the register size of the next generation of microprocessor, Intel's 8008 introduced in 1972.

The 8008 was at heart just an update of the 4004 with more bits in each register. It used the same technology (which meant the smallest features etched onto the silicon chip measured 10 microns across) and ran a bit faster (200 KHz), but broke no new ground. Overall, the 8008 was an interesting and workable chip, and it found application in some initial stabs at building personal computers. Now, however, it's only a footnote in the history of the PC.

The 8080 Family

Intel continued development (as did other integrated circuit manufacturers) and, in 1974, created a rather more drastic revision, the 8080. Unlike the 8008, it was planned from the start for byte-size data. Intel gave the 8080 a richer command set, one that embraced all the commands of the 8008 but went further. This set a pattern for Intel microprocessors: every increase in power and range of command set enlarged on what had gone before rather than replacing it, ensuring backward compatibility (at least to some degree) of the software. The improvements made to the 8080 made the chip one of the first with the inherent capability to serve as the foundation of a small computer.

A few engineers had even better ideas for improving the 8080, and left Intel to develop these improvements on their own. After forming Zilog Corporation, they unveiled to the world the Z80 microprocessor. In truth, the Z80 was an evolutionary development, an 8080 with more instructions, but it began a revolution by unlocking the power of the first widely accepted standard small computer operating system, CP/M, an acronym for the Control Program for Microcomputers.

An operating system is a special program that links programs, the microprocessor, and its related hardware, such as storage devices. CP/M developed Digital Research and modeled on the operating systems used by larger computers. Though hardly perfect, it worked well enough that it became the standard for many small computers used in business. Its familiarity helped the programmers of larger computers adapt to it, and they threw their support behind it. Although CP/M was designed to run on the 8080, the Z80 chip offered more power, and it became the platform of choice to make the system work.

All the while Intel continued to improve on its eight-bit microprocessor designs. One effort was the 8085, a further elaboration on the 8080, which was designed to use a single five-volt power supply and use fewer peripheral chips than its predecessor. Included in its design were vectored interrupts and a serial input/output port. Alas, the 8085 never won the favor of the small computer industry. A few small computers, now almost entirely forgotten, were designed around it.

The 8086 Family

In 1978, Intel pushed technology forward with its 8086, a microprocessor that doubled the size of its registers again to 16 bits and promised 10 times the performance of the 8080. The 8086 also improved on the 8080 by doubling the size of the data bus to 16 bits to move information in and out twice as fast. It also had a substantially larger address bus (20 bits wide) that enabled the 8086 to directly control over one million bytes—a megabyte—of memory.

As a direct descendent of the 8080 and cousin of the Z80, the 8086 shared much of the command set of the earlier chips. Just as the 8080 elaborated on the commands of the 8008, the 8086 embellished those of the 8080. The registers of the 8086 were cleverly arranged so that they could be manipulated either at their full 16-bit width or as two separate 8-bit registers exactly like those of the 8080.

The memory of the 8086 was also arranged to be a superset of that of the 8080. Instead of being one vast megabyte romping ground for data, it was divided into 16 segments that each contained 64 kilobytes. In effect, the memory of the 8086 was a group of 8080 memories linked together. The 8086 looked at each segment individually and did not permit a single large data structure to span segments—at least not easily.

In some ways, the 8086 was ahead of its time. Small computers were based on eight-bit architectures, memory was expensive (that's why a megabyte seemed like more than enough), and few other chips were designed to handle 16 bits at a time. Using the 8086 forced engineers to design full 16-bit devices which, at the time, were not entirely cost-effective.

8088

Consequently, a year after the introduction of the 8086, Intel introduced the 8088. The 8088 was identical to the 8086 in every way—16-bit registers, 20 address lines, the same command set—except one. Its data bus was reduced to 8 bits, enabling the 8088 to exploit readily available 8-bit support hardware.

As a backward step in chip design, the 8088 might have been lost to history, much like the 8085, had not IBM begun to covertly design its first personal computer around it. IBM's intent was evidently to cash in on the 8088 design. Its 8-bit data bus enabled the use of inexpensive off-the-shelf support chips. Its 16-bit internal design gave the PC an important edge in advertising over the 8-bit small computers already available. And its 8080-based ancestry hinted that the wealth of CP/M programs available at that time might easily be converted to the new hardware. In the long run, of course, these advantages have proven either temporary or illusory. Sixteen-bit support chips are available cheaply, the IBM name proved more valuable than the 16-bit registers of the 8088, and few CP/M program were ever directly adapted for the PC.

What was important is that the lame 8088 microprocessor became the basis of a generation of small computers. The fast track to making compatible computers was paved with 8088s.

The 8086 is potentially twice as fast and almost completely compatible with the 8088. Consequently, manufacturers intent on selling performance engaged in the extra effort to design around the 8086. Even IBM chose the older yet more powerful 8086 to power its low-end PS/2s.

As compatible as they are, the 8088 and 8086 are not interchangeable. The need for eight additional data bits going into the chip requires eight more data lines or leads. The connections made to each of the two chips are thus different. The 8088 and 8086 are not identical pin-for-pin and are not plug-compatible. Computers must be designed for one chip or the other.

80C86 and 80C88

The typical microprocessor requires a few watts of electricity to perform its functions. When the electrical supply is drawn from a wall outlet, the amount of power is almost insignificant. A typical home has 10,000 watts or so at its disposal and an outlet can supply about 2,000. Batteries, however, aren't so munificent. A AA battery cell, for instance, might be expected to deliver 20 milliwatts (thousandths of a watt) or so. Switching to battery power to make a truly portable computer thus requires a drastic downward revision in the amount of power required for running the microprocessor.

The original 8086 and 8088 chips were designed using simple but energy-wasteful NMOS technology. These chips were unsuitable for notebook and sub-notebook computers, for which low power requirements are mandatory. To trim the electrical hunger of these NMOS designs, equivalent microprocessors based on CMOS technology were developed.

Versions of both the 8088 and 8086 are available in CMOS: the 80C88 and 80C86. These low-power microprocessors are logically identical to their NMOS equivalents. They have the same command sets and run the same programs. However, they have different electrical requirements, so computers are designed to use either the CMOS or NMOS circuits. You cannot directly substitute one for the other if you want to reduce the electrical requirements of your PC. (The only time such an exchange would be useful would be in a notebook computer, and these machines almost universally have CMOS microprocessors.)

80186 and 80188

Just as the microprocessor incorporates thousands of discrete logic components on its tiny sliver of silicon, it's possible to build more functions into a single chip. Besides a microprocessor, a number of other special circuits are typically used in building a small computer, such as interrupt controllers, timing generators, and bus controllers. All of these functions can be designed to fit onto the same chip as the microprocessor circuitry.

Normally, all this extra circuitry would not be included because a microprocessor is a general-purpose device, not necessarily committed to becoming the base of a desktop computer system. The additional circuitry might be wasted in something like an industrial process controller.

As the small computer industry grew, however, the market for circuits optimized for that purpose reached the point that Intel felt safe in creating a more complete computer chip that had most of its support circuitry on one substrate. Introduced in 1982 as the 80186, this chip has served as the basis for a number of compatible computers and at least one turbo board. Intel also offers the 80188, essentially an 8088 blessed with more on-chip support, much like the 80186.

Each member of the 8086 family of chips normally uses a standard DIP package. Intel identifies these chips with silk-screened lettering on a black plastic case. A large lowercase "i" indicates that Intel Corporation is the manufacturer. (Advanced Micro Devices, a second-source licensee of the 8086 design, labels its chips with the initials "AMD.") On Intel chips, the top line of the chip label is its designation, often following the letter "P."

The 8086 and 8088 chips are available in 5 MHz and 8 MHz speeds. Chips labeled with just their model designation (for instance, 8088) have the lower speed rating. Chips whose model designations are followed by a "-2" are rated at the higher speed. An 8088-2, for example, is rated to operate at up to 8 MHz.

The second line of the chip designation contains coded manufacturing information, including the week during which the chip was manufactured.

The 80286 Family

The introduction of IBM's Personal Computer AT in 1984 immediately focused attention on another of the Intel microprocessor family, the 80286, which was introduced in 1982. Compared to its immediate forerunner, the 8086, the 80286 was endowed with several features that made it superior for personal computers. The 80286 chip used a full 16-bit data bus with 16-bit internal registers. It was designed to run faster, initially at 6 MHz, which quickly rose to 8 MHz, and then 10 MHz. Versions that operate at 12.5, 16, and even 20 MHz have also become available.

The speed ratings of 80286 chips are plainly marked after the model designation. The figure given is the chip's maximum rated operating speed in MHz. Hence, a chip marked "80286-10" would be rated to operate at 10 MHz.

The 286 also featured redesigned internal circuitry. It functioned more efficiently than the 8086 family, giving it even more of a performance advantage than its faster speed would imply. For instance, although the first run of IBM's 286-equipped ATs ran only 25 percent faster than the PC (6 MHz versus 4.77 MHz), it achieved throughput about five times greater.

Most important of all, at least in the long run, was the superior memory-handling capability of the 80286. Instead of the 20 address lines of the 8088/8086, the 80286 had 24. The four extra lines increased the maximum amount of memory the chip could address by 15 megabytes, up to a total of 16 megabytes.

The 80286 also enabled the use of virtual memory. As the name implies, virtual memory is not made up of real, physical memory chips. Rather, it is information stored in a mass storage system that can be transferred into physical memory when it needs to be worked on. The 80286 has special provisions for distinguishing each memory byte that's in real and virtual memory, although it requires additional circuitry to handle the actual swapping of bytes. The chip can track up to one gigabyte (1,024 megabytes or 1 billion bytes) of total memory (16 megabytes real memory and 1,008 megabytes of virtual memory).

In theory, the upgraded memory handling of the 80286 should have made the 1M addressing barrier faced by earlier Intel microprocessors a thing of the past. In reality, the improvement was not realized.

The problem was partly a matter of compatibility, partly tradition. By the time the 80286 was being readied for the market, the success of the IBM PC had already been ensured. A substantial software base had been built for the 8088 and 8086 microprocessors. Taking advantage of that software would speed the acceptance of the improved chip.

Intel's attempt at a solution to the backward compatibility and memory problem was to give the 286 two different operating modes. One mode provided compatibility, the other enabled the use of more memory.

Real mode mimicked the operation of an 8086 microprocessor and suffered the same limitations. Operating in real mode, the 286 could address only one megabyte of memory, working with it in 64K segments.

In *protected mode*, the 286 could reach all 16M of its addressing range. Moreover, as the name implies, protected mode operation allows the 286 to protect ranges of memory so that when multiple tasks run simultaneously, they do not interfere with each other's memory. The protected mode memory remained segmented, however. The 286 boots up in real mode and switches by software command into protected mode when such operation is wanted.

As a faster 8086 with the capability to handle more memory, the 80286 proved immensely successful. Protected mode did not, however, win favor with programmers very quickly. Almost three years elapsed between the time of the introduction of the AT and the availability of an IBM-endorsed protected mode operating system, OS/2.

Two reasons underlie the slow support of protected mode. For programmers working under the constraints of DOS, the problem was shifting between real mode and protected mode. Intel designed the process to be a one-way affair. After all, once you have experienced 16 megabytes, why would you want to go back to just 1M? Although the 80286 readily shifted gears from real to protected mode (necessary because the chip starts functioning only in real mode) downshifting was not possible. Once in protected mode, the only way to regain real mode control was to reset the microprocessor, which is equivalent to rebooting a computer.

In addition, protected mode was only a partial fulfillment of the dreams of programmers. Although it did enable more memory to be used, it still operated with 64K memory segments. Instead of a free romping ground for their software, programmers had a bunch of little boxes among which they had to shift their numbers.

The problems with mode shifting and the dichotomy between the two modes eventually led to the 286 being labeled "brain dead." The drawbacks of the chip design only became apparent after the introduction of the 286's successor, the 80386. The 286 could not run some of the advanced applications designed for the 386. Because the 80286 cannot run today's latest operating systems (such as Windows versions later than 3.1 and OS/2 version 2.0 and later), it is no longer in the microprocessor mainstream.

The 286 chip is not completely dead, however. It remains useful for running simple DOS applications at moderate speeds. That capability suits a steadily declining number of applications, such as dedicated bookkeeping systems and portable computers designed principally for note-taking. For general-purpose work, particularly if it includes graphics, you don't want a 80286 microprocessor. The only reason to think about buying an 80286 is the rock bottom price of the chip and of the machines that use it. But the low cost of more advanced and more capable microprocessors has made even the cheapest 286 a dubious value.

The 80386 Family

Unlike the 80286, which was seemingly aimed at a brave new world beyond DOS, the next generation of Intel microprocessor opened its arms to DOS and the 16 billion dollar software library built around it. The 386 family, first introduced in 1985, combines the hard lessons learned from the 286 with the needs and dreams of programmers. The 80386 chip brought more speed, more power, and more versatility than ever before available in an Intel microprocessor. It can handle nearly every chore of an 8088, 8086, and 286, yet leap beyond them in features and power.

The enlightenment embodied by the 386 makes the 286 look like a misfire—too late and too bad. Some former Intel employees have explained away the shortcomings of the 286 as a result of its design having been begun earlier than even the 8086. The 286 was the original idea of a chip to follow on the heels of the 8080, but may have proved too ambitious. The 8086 was born from a reappraisal of design objectives. Only later was the original idea marketed as the 286.

The 386 was created in full awareness of the personal computer and microprocessor marketplace. Consequently, it had to accommodate all the features that were making other Intel processors sell. For instance, its instruction set is a superset of that of the 286 so older software will run on the chip without a hitch. At the same time, the 386 had to be designed so that it would be accepted in new designs, maybe even lure engineers away from the microprocessors made by other manufacturers, which did not suffer from the handicap of the segmented memory.

386DX

The first member of the 386 family was introduced simply as the 80386. The chip proved so successful that Intel spread the name around to capitalize on its immediate recognition and the positive regard generally accorded it. Consequently, when the next family member was introduced, Intel gave it the revered name with a distinguishing suffix, the 386SX. The name of the original design was changed to 386DX.

First and foremost, the 386DX was a leap ahead in raw power. It doubled the size of its registers and data buses to a full 32 bits. Information could be moved into the chip and processed twice as fast as with 16-bit chips.

Intel uses the term *double word* for a 32-bit chunk of memory. A 16-bit chunk is a *single word.* Consequently, the nomenclature of the initial two members of the 386 family can be explained as the 386DX handling data externally as double words; the later 386SX (which reverted to a 16-bit data bus) works with single words.

The 80386 was designed from the beginning to be a fast chip, perhaps a product of the speed wars among AT-compatible computers. Using a semiconductor technology called CHMOS, the first 386 chips to be marketed started where the 286 left off. The 386 initially came in two speeds, 12.5 and 16 MHz, but speed-hungry computer designers pretty much ignored the 12.5 MHz chips. Shortly thereafter, a 20 MHz version became available. Then, in 1988, the limit became 25 MHz and, in 1989, 33 MHz. At that point, Intel stopped development of the 386. Other companies, however, have developed microprocessors that functionally duplicate the 386DX and operate at speeds up to 40 MHz.

Complementing the expansion of the data bus of the 386 to 32 bits, the number of available address lines was also increased to 32. By itself, this expansion enables the 386 to directly address up to 4 gigabytes of physical memory. In addition, the chip can handle up to 16 terabytes (that's trillion bytes) of virtual memory. The chip has full facilities for managing all this memory built into its circuitry.

The big breakthrough in the 386 is the way this memory is organized. All memory can be addressed as one contiguous section, equivalent to the great open prairie for programs. Programs or data structures can be as large as the full memory capacity of the chip.

Dividing this memory into segments is possible, but optional. Segments are not, however, arbitrarily limited to 64K in length, but can be virtually any size that's convenient for a program or programmer to work with (as long as it's smaller than 4 gigabytes).

In addition, the 386 incorporates 16 bytes of *pre-fetch cache memory.* This special on-board memory area is used to store the next few instructions of the program the chip is executing. Independently of the calculating portion of the chip, special circuitry loads software code into this memory before it's needed. This small cache helps the 80386 run more smoothly, with less waiting as code is retrieved from system memory.

To maintain compatibility with previous Intel microprocessors, and therefore with the library of DOS programs, the 386 was designed to be as compatible as possible with the 8086 and 286. As a result, the 80386 has a real mode, complete with 1M addressing limit. The chip boots up in this mode and operates as if it were one of its older siblings.

From real mode, the chip can be switched into protected mode which functions like a 286, except that it has more memory at its disposal and has more flexibility in manipulating the memory because of its variable segment size. In contrast with the 286, the 386 can switch modes without being reset by using simple software commands.

An new mode called *virtual 8086 mode* gives the 386 particular freedom in running DOS programs. In this mode, the chip simulates not just one 8086 but an almost unlimited number of 8086s, all at the same time. This mode enables a single 386 microprocessor to divide its memory into many virtual machines, each machine acting like an entirely separate computer equipped with an 8086 microprocessor.

Each of these virtual machines can run its own program, totally isolated from the rest of the virtual computers, which means you can simultaneously run several DOS programs on one computer. Although this kind of multitasking was possible without the exotic architecture of the 80386, most such systems were either complex or shaky, and most required that software was written specially to proprietary standards to effect multitasking operation. The 386, on the other hand, makes multitasking control software simple because all the hard work is done in hardware. Off-the-shelf DOS programs work without modification in most 386-based multitasking environments.

The 386 has suffered more severe teething pains than most microprocessors. Shortly after it was originally released, design errors were found that caused inaccuracies when the chip performed 32-bit mathematical operations. The problem was undiscovered in the first PC-compatible computers to use the chip because DOS uses only 16-bit operations. The random errors occur only when software uses the 386's 32-bit modes.

The problem was quickly discovered and corrected, and 80386 chips manufactured after April, 1987, do not have the problem. According to Intel, all 386 chips manufactured after the correction was made are labeled with a *double-sigma* symbol (see fig. 3.5). Some earlier chips that were recalled but which may exhibit the problem have been stamped "For 16-bit Operations Only." These chips work with all 16-bit versions of DOS (which include all versions up to DOS 6.2) and the initial releases of OS/2 (versions 1.0 and 1.1), which do not use 32-bit mathematics. Because the 16 MHz 80386 was discontinued by Intel and 386 chips rated at speeds faster than 16 MHz never exhibited this math problem, there's no longer a reason to worry about the 32-bit math capabilities of any new 386-based PC.

FIGURE 3.5. Double-sigma mark indicates revised 386 that eliminates problems with 16-bit mathematics.

386SX

Which of the virtues of the 80386 is best depends on what you want to do with the chip. For many, speed's the thing. They want to roar through calculations lickety-split. A second saved on the recalculation of a spreadsheet or the drawing of a blueprint is an extra dollar earned. For these people, 32-bit power is the essence of the 80386.

But other strengths of the 386 make it an exciting chip to people who want to take advantage of its multiuser and multitasking power. The virtual 8086 mode alone is worth the premium price of 386 silicon to them, and the extensive memory handling capabilities of the chip make it all the more valuable. Although the speed of the 80386 may be exciting, for those users it's unnecessary, particularly considering the modest performance increase the 32-bit chip brings to standard 16-bit software, such as DOS and OS/2 versions 1.0 and 1.1.

For exactly this sort of person, Intel created the ultimate compromise, the 386SX, a scaled-down 80386 that loses power but not features. Just as the 8088 was derived from the 8086 to facilitate the use of cheaper 8-bit components, Intel created the 386SX as a little sister to the 386.

Internally, the 386SX is nearly identical to the 386 with full 32-bit registers and all of the same operating modes.

Only two important differences separate the 386DX from the SX. Instead of interfacing to a 32-bit memory bus, the 386SX is designed for a 16-bit bus. Its 32-bit registers must be filled in two steps from a 16-bit I/O channel. Also, the 386SX is cheaper by about $100, a bargain of sorts for those who prefer a more leisurely pace.

But the 386SX is no sluggard. Its initial version operated at a full 16 MHz, almost 33 percent faster than Intel's quickest 80286. Despite its 16-bit I/O channel, the 386SX still races along faster than an 80286 with an equivalent speed rating because it can process instructions twice as fast after they're inside the chip.

In addition, the 386SX understands the same 32-bit instructions as the 386. Just like the 386, it is backward compatible with the 16- and 8-bit instructions of previous Intel microprocessors.

Long before its introduction in June, 1988, the 386SX had been long rumored in the computer industry. Mostly, it was known by its code name P9. The P9 was long rumored to be a plug-compatible upgrade for the 80286. In theory, you could pop out the old chip and pop in 386 power by using the P9. But with the final 386SX design, this direct conversion is not possible.

The 386SX is packaged entirely differently than the 80286, and the two chips do not fit the same sockets. The big reason is that the 80286 multiplexes its bus connections (so that fewer physical wires are needed for a larger number of connections); the connections of the 386SX are not multiplexed. As a result, the 386SX requires simpler interface circuitry than the 80286, facilitating its application in lower-cost computers. A small adapter card with auxiliary multiplexing circuitry can convert the 386SX to an 80286 socket, however. Such an adapter promises to be a low-cost way of adding 386 features to existing computers.

On the other hand, the 386SX does demand a slight price premium over the 80286, and, when operating at its rated speed, it requires faster, more expensive memory. Computers based on the 386SX are likely to be more expensive than their 80286-equipped equivalents. In the long run, however, no compelling reason exists to settle for 80286 technology. As more software requires 80386 features, the 386SX becomes more desirable, and the 80286-based machines become more obsolete.

386SL

The 386SL represents Intel's approach to the needs of notebook computers. The chip combines reduced power consumption with a high degree of integration to enable the construction of small, lightweight computers. The 386SL introduced System Management Mode so that battery-powered systems expends only as much of their energy budgets as each computer job requires, shutting down unused parts of the microprocessor and computer. Although sometimes discussed as a low-power version of the 386SX microprocessor, the 386SL is both more and less than a 386SX.

The 386SL is a member of the Intel 386 family, which means that the chip can run all 386-specific programs requiring protected and virtual 8086 modes. The 386SL has the same internal 32-bit register structure but does not include a built-in floating-point unit. The 386SL, however, is not complete in itself. Rather, it is designed to work with Intel's 82360SL I/O subsystem chip. Together, the microprocessor and I/O subsystem require only memory to make a complete PC.

As with the 386SX, the 386SL chip has limited direct memory-addressing capabilities. Its design enables the PC designers to connect up to 20 megabytes to the chip. While handling that amount of memory would require at least 25 address lines, the 386SL gets by with 11 lines by multiplexing and addressing RAM only in 16-byte lines (therefore the three least significant bits of each address are unnecessary). Multiplexing works by alternately specifying the memory address in rows and columns, first indicating the row address of the location it wants to address, and then indicating the column. The 386SL addressing system is designed to link directly to a PC's memory controller. The circuitry of the 386SL enables the use of either static or dynamic memory. In addition, the 386SL incorporates expanded memory control circuitry for bank-switching up to 32M.

Although no cache memory is built into the 386SL system, most chips have a static RAM cache interface that enables the use of a 16K, 32K, or 64K memory cache. The system designer can choose to configure the cache with direct two-way or four-way set associative organization. Cache control circuitry is standard on all 25 MHz and some 20 MHz versions of the 386SL.

But the 386SL goes further. Like the Intel 80186 series, the 386SL also incorporates many of the functions required by a PC-style computer, which includes full control circuitry for a standard PC expansion bus as well as a high-speed link (which Intel calls a Peripheral Interface Bus or PI bus) similar to local bus systems.

To conserve battery power in notebook computers, the 386SL is designed with facilities for controlling electrical usage. The chip was designed to reduce its power usage by taking advantage of System Management Mode. The power management control circuitry, however, is not part of the chip but is inside the 82360SL I/O Subsystem. In addition, the 386SL is designed to operate at reduced speed. In fact, it can be slowed to clock speeds as low as 0 by altering an internal clock divider; the rest of the PC can be kept at the normal operating speed even when the 386SL is effectively shut down. The chip also incorporates a true suspend mode, during which its complete operating state is preserved in static memory with minimal power consumption.

The power saving is substantial. The 386SL typically consumes about 100 milliamps for every 5 MHz of clock speed at which it operates—at 20 MHz, the chip requires about 400 milliamps (about 2 watts from a 5-volt power supply); at 25 MHz, about 500 milliamps (2.5 watts). When the clock speed is reduced to 0, current consumption drops to 50 milliamps. In suspend mode, the chip needs only 0.3 milliamp to maintain data integrity.

The 82360SL I/O Subsystem adds the rest of the circuitry needed to build a PC-compatible computer from the 386SL microprocessor. All the support chips are part of the 82360SL's silicon. These support chips include two direct memory access controllers, two programmable timers/counters, two interrupt controllers, power for attaching an AT interface (IDE) hard disk drive, a real-time clock with CMOS RAM for preserving system configuration information, two serial port controllers, and one parallel port. The 82360SL I/O Subsystem also enables direct support of a keyboard and floppy disk controller (although it does not incorporate the controllers themselves). The design goal of the 82360SL is economy. It requires a minimum of external circuitry to build a complete PC.

The power-saving features of the 386SL and 82360SL combination don't work automatically. The chips have the capability of reducing their power consumption, but they must be programmed to do so. The system designer selects which component of the system to shut down and when to shut it down. For example, what period of inactivity must elapse before the port circuitry is switched off or under what circumstances to reduce microprocessor speed.

The 80486 Family

Introduced in 1989, the 80486 microprocessor was Intel's better 80386. To smooth over the transition between 386 and 486 technologies, Intel at first called the 486 a member of the 386 family. With the huge popularity won by the newer design, however, Intel has rearranged its family tree. The latest Intel chip, the Pentium, is now classed as part of the 486 family.

No matter which way you look at the generations, the 486 is an improved 386 chip. The 486 (and the members of its family) run all 386 software. In fact, from a software standpoint, the 486 is distinguished from the 386 by one flag, one exception, two page-table entry bits, six instructions, and nine control-register bits. Although that may sound like a lot, none of your programs are likely to be able to see the difference. The commands and controls of the 486 represent nothing more than a superset of the 386—the 486 does everything the 386 does and a little more. Your programs operate as if the 486 is just a faster 386. For running DOS, Windows, or OS/2 applications, the added bits and instructions of the 486 remain unneeded and unused.

That small step is a notable difference from the giant leap between the 286 and 386. Those two chips are qualitatively different from the software standpoint in that the 386 has an additional operating mode and advanced memory management capabilities that are not built into the 286. The Virtual 8086 mode of the 386 is required to run multitasking applications such as Windows 3.0 in its Enhanced Mode and DESQview 386. The memory-management facilities of the 386 chip are crucial to extending the range of DOS beyond its traditional 640K addressing limit. Although the 80486 retains these capabilities of the 386, it brings nothing that will affect which programs you can run.

From a hardware perspective, the 80486 chip retains the principal features of the 80386 that are important for the two chips to be compatible at the software level. Both chips have three operating modes (real, protected, and virtual 8086), and both have full 32-bit data and address buses enabling up to four gigabytes of memory to be directly addressed. Both support virtual memory that extends their addressing to 64 terabytes. Both have built-in memory management units that can remap memory in 4K pages.

But the hardware of the 486 also differs substantially from the 386 (or any previous Intel microprocessor) and the changes mean more speed. Most important of these changes are a streamlined hardware design, tighter silicon design rules (smaller details etched into the actual silicon that make up the chip), an integral math coprocessor, instruction pipelining, and an internal memory cache.

The streamlined hardware design (particularly its pipelining) means that the 486 can think faster than a 386 microprocessor when the two are operating at the same clock speed. Therefore, a 33 MHz 486 is faster than a 33 MHz 386. On most applications, the 486 is about twice as fast as a 386 at the same clock rate, so a 20 MHz 486 delivers about the same program throughput as a 40 MHz 386.

To some people, that seems contradictory because they confuse the processing of instructions with ticks of the clock. In most earlier microprocessors, carrying out a single instruction required multiple clock cycles, the exact number depending on the instruction itself. Some instructions required just one cycle; others could take dozens. Because of its improved internal design, the 486 reduces the number of clock cycles needed for most instructions. Thanks to pipelining and other advances, many of the most common 486 instructions can be carried out in a single clock tick.

Size is the scourge of speed. Computer circuits are becoming so fast that the speed of light (actually the somewhat slower rate that it takes electrons to travel through semiconductors) becomes a factor in limiting the performance of circuits. When signals have to travel long distances, they take a finite time in their traverses. Calculations can occur no quicker than the signals move. By integrating more functions onto a single slab of silicon, signals can be kept within near-microscopic confines instead of needing to travel extra inches to external support chips. In addition, the inevitable delays imposed by forcing signals through buffering and conditioning circuits are avoided by integration. Because of the tighter design rules of the 486, its circuitry could be upgraded to higher speed operation, creating a new line of chips (the DX2, for example, which is discussed later in this chapter) that could operate at speeds of 66 MHz.

Inside the chip, size has a more important influence. The larger a logic circuit element, the more power it can handle, and the more power it takes to make it work. Inside today's microprocessors, the primary limit to speed is heat dissipation. Run a chip too fast and its silicon will heat up until it boils its life away. Smaller circuits require less power, so they generate less heat and can operate faster. The 486 pioneered one-micron design rules, which means that the finest details etched into the chip measure one micron (one millionth of a meter) across. The new 50 MHz 80486 has 0.8 micron design rules, small enough to extend clock speeds to 100 MHz.

Anyone having math-intensive applications, such as a statistical program or graphics package, knows the value of a numeric coprocessor in accelerating system performance. The 80486 incorporates all the necessary coprocessor circuitry on the same slice of silicon (almost an exact duplicate of a 387 chip; see Chapter 4, "Numeric Coprocessors"). The new home for the coprocessor is more than a matter of convenience. Operating at the same clock speed as a 387 that's combined with a 386 microprocessor, the internal coprocessor of the 486 delivers about double the performance.

The difference is the proximity and direct connection between the processor and coprocessor circuitry. Commands and data for the 386 coprocessor need to travel from one chip to another across a printed circuit board, encountering all manners of delays along the way.

The faster a microprocessor operates, the more it suffers from the shortcomings of today's slow DRAM chips. In some systems, microprocessors spend one-third or more of their time waiting for memory to catch up. The 486 helps minimize the effect of this memory slowdown by incorporating its own high-speed memory cache.

The 486 cache is organized as a four-way set associative design which essentially splits up its 8K total size as four smaller 2K caches, an arrangement that further enhances its performance, particularly on multi-threaded applications.

The internal cache uses write-through technology, which puts a higher premium on the integrity of the contents of cache and system memory than it does on eking out the utmost in speed. When the 486 microprocessor wants to read from memory, it first checks the cache. When it writes, however, it updates both the cache and system memory at the same time, which holds the potential of adding delays in waiting for system memory to become ready.

Although the 8K cache is sufficient to match the 486 to commercially available memory chips, it doesn't offer the optimum match. Larger, external caches can further improve the performance of the 486 chip, up to about 30 percent more according to Intel.

The 486 microprocessor is available in a variety of speed ratings, which currently top out at 66 MHz, but may eventually extend to 100 MHz. The faster the chip is operated, the faster it performs in direct proportion to its clock speed. A 50 MHz 486 will compute twice as fast as a 25 MHz 486.

In addition to different speed ratings, the 486 chip comes in two models, the 486DX and the 486SX. The former might be considered the 486 Classic, the chip that was initially introduced and incorporates all the performance-enhancing features already noted. The 486SX is the 486 Lite, a chip stripped of its internal numeric coprocessor. The difference is substantial, particularly when you pay for the chips.

486DX

The standard 486DX comes in a 168-pin ceramic PGA package. The pin-out of the 50 MHz version is subtly different from that of lower speed chips. Four additional signals (test clock, test data input, test data output, and test mode select) are provided on the higher speed chip for use in testing purposes. (These signals are not used during normal operation.)

486SX

As initially conceived, the 486SX was the engine of choice for people who needed performance but didn't require a coprocessor. The best example of such an application is a network server, where the paramount concern is response and the data processing work is simple and no number crunching is necessary. Selecting the 486SX would deliver the high speed of the 486 family without the cost of adding an unnecessary coprocessor section.

Using the 486SX this way presupposes that the chip is available with the same speed potential as the full-blown 486DX. Today, that is not the case. The 486SX is available only in 20 and 25 MHz versions from Intel. In effect, the 486SX is the low end of the 486 line. It essentially replaces the 386DX. The 486SX is available with similar speed ratings as a 386DX and is priced competitively with the older chip. But the 486SX is faster than a 386DX running at the same clock speed because of its internal efficiencies.

The lack of a coprocessor in the 486SX is not a life-long defect. In fact, it makes the 486SX a better value for systems that make little use of math, for example, file servers and machines meant for ordinary office work like word processing.

The 486SX is available in either a 168-pin PGA package or a 196-pin plastic quad flat pack. The pin-out of the PGA chip is subtly different from the 486DX, differing in the assignment of the non-maskable interrupt signal (pin A15 for the 486SX; pin B15 for the 486DX) and the lack of floating-point signals on the 486SX.

Intel offers a coprocessor, the 487SX, to give systems based on the 486SX extra floating-point performance so that you can bring a 486SX system up to the same power level as a 486DX. Better yet, Intel's new OverDrive chips add a coprocessor and extra speed to 486SX systems.

Most PCs that come equipped with a 486SX also have an upgrade socket to accommodate these system-improvement chips. The initial Intel design required that you have your old 486SX and 487SX or OverDrive chips present for the host PC to properly boot. However, many systems now enable you to directly replace the 486SX microprocessor with one of the upgrades or even a 486DX. The 487SX has an extra pin as a key so that it will fit only in the upgrade socket.

486DX2 and OverDrive

With every increase in microprocessor speed, motherboard makers' worries become worse. They have to worry about controlling signals in frequency ranges assigned to television broadcasters and radio telescope operators, signals so quirky that even the slightest shift in a copper trace on a motherboard will stop it from working. They have to worry not only about how signals get from one place to another on the motherboard but also which signals come close to one another, where each component is placed, and even how sharply the foil traces turn. Moving a component a fraction of an inch in a design can totally change the characteristics of the high-speed signals and the operation of the motherboard.

Consequently, motherboard engineers usually greet the arrival of yet another faster microprocessor with the same glee accorded the approach of a tornado.

In 1992, Intel came to the rescue of motherboard makers by introducing two new lines of clock-doubling 486-family microprocessors: the 486DX2 and OverDrive series. Both of these chips are designed for high-speed internal operation while connecting to lower speed external components. They internally double the speed of the clock signal that's supplied to them so that their circuits work at double the normal pace. Interface circuits to external components, however, continue to operate at the normal clock speed supplied to the chip.

In effect, one clock-doubling chip can do twice as much work as it looks like it should. Motherboard makers benefit because they only need to design their products to operate at half the speed that the microprocessor carries out its operations. These lower speed requirements translate into lower costs for the buyer.

On the other hand, lower speed operation means that every external operation that the clock-doubling chip carries out suffers the speed penalty imposed by the lower speed motherboard. The internal circuitry of the chip must wait for the motherboard to catch up. In other words, the clock-doubling chip achieves its high-speed performance only on operations that fully take place inside the chip— heavy-duty calculations. Memory accesses and transfers to and from input/output devices occur at the slower external speed of the chip. The internal cache helps make up for the external slow down, enabling clock-doubling chips to achieve about 80 percent of the overall performance of a full-speed chip (that is, one that operates internally and externally at the higher internal speed of the clock-doubling chip).

The difference between the 486DX2 and OverDrive processors is mostly one of application. The 486DX2 is designed to be the original microprocessor in a PC. OverDrive chips are designed to work as upgrades in systems originally designed for 486SX or 486DX chips. Basically, the difference between the two sub-families is the pin-out. The chips are designed to match different sockets. Although they work similarly with the same internal circuitry, you cannot use one in place of the other because it simply won't fit.

Upgrading with an OverDrive requires that you check whether the microprocessor in your PC is a 486DX or 486SX and whether an OverDrive-compatible socket is available in your system. OverDrive chips for 486SX computers were originally designed to plug into 487SX coprocessor sockets (which Intel dubbed "OverDrive" sockets). OverDrive chips do not fit sockets designed for Weitek coprocessors although both may have the same number of pins.

Outside of the clock-doubling operation, the 486DX2 and OverDrive chips match the 486DX standard, which is 32 address lines, 32 data lines, 8K internal cache, and a built-in floating-point unit. The minimal changes mask the extensive internal reengineering of these chips.

486SL

In 1992, Intel introduced its portable 486 alternative, an altogether formidable chip called the 486SL. Unlike the 386SL (which was essentially a 386SX engineered for power saving), the 486SL doesn't slight on performance. Moreover, it integrates a substantial number of system functions into its silicon.

The foundation for the 486SL is a full 486DX—the 486SL is a true 32-bit chip with internal 32-bit registers and external 32-bit address and data buses. The 486SL also includes its own, built-in floating-point unit, the same as that in the 486. The 486SL also incorporates the same 8K four-way set associative combined instruction and data cache of the 486DX.

To conserve power in portable applications, the semiconductor design of the 486SL was altered to make it fully static. The chip can operate at reduced speed or can even stop without losing the data in its registers. Also built into its circuitry is a full system management mode to enable various chip functions to shut down when they are unused to conserve power.

To make portable computers more compact (and easier to design), the 486SL also includes a built-in DRAM controller and bus interface that supports Industry Standard Architecture. Add the Intel 82360SL I/O chip, which was originally created for use with the 386SL, and you have nearly everything necessary for a sub-notebook computer, including interrupt and DMA control, internal and external power management, system timers, real-time clock, two serial ports, and a parallel port.

The silicon circuitry of the 486SL is also designed to operate in mixed-voltage environments. The microprocessor part of the chip operates from a 3.3-volt supply, but the bus control and memory interfaces can work at 5 or 3.3 volts (at least when there's a 3.3-volt standard for the ISA expansion bus).

The low-voltage and power-saving features of the 486SL put it well ahead of the 386SL with twice the performance level but only half the power needs. The 486SL even comes in the same package as the 386SL, a 196-pin plastic quad flat pack. The pin-out is different, however, because of the extra features in the 486SL and its wider, 32-bit address bus interface. The 486SL is also available in a 208-pin slim quad flat pack (which is smaller than the plastic quad flat pack because the connector leads are more closely spaced). The chip is also available in a 227-pin LGA (Land Grid Array) package.

SL-Enhanced 486

Instead of special low-power microprocessors for portable applications, other chip-makers elected to make their entire product lines more energy frugal. In 1993, Intel changed directions and followed suit, announcing that it would cease further development of the 486SL line and instead move its features into the main 486 series. The process involves a gradual phase-in that is producing what Intel calls its *SL Enhanced Intel 486 Microprocessor Family*. The new SL-enhanced family includes equivalents to the 486DX, 486DX2, 486SX, and 486SX2 chips.

The innovations added to these chips read like the 486SL specification sheet. First and foremost, SL-enhanced 486 microprocessors include a system management mode with a dedicated interrupt and address space for controlling active power management of its host PC. The system management interrupt can stop an SL-enhanced chip—even in the middle of an instruction—and the chip can later be restarted without affecting the executing program or integrity of its data.

All SL-enhanced chips have two low-power states: a Stop Grant State that reduces current consumption to 20 to 55 milliamps while allowing the chip to quickly resume normal-speed operation; and a Stop Clock state during which the microprocessor clock literally stops and chip current consumption falls to 100 to 200 microamps. In addition, all SL-enhanced chips automatically power down to the same level as Stop Grant state upon encountering a halt instruction. Clock-doubled SL-enhanced chips have an auto idle power down mode in which the chips' internal clock speed is cut in half (matching external speed) to reduce power consumption.

486DX4

The next logical step after clock doubling is, of course, clock tripling. Intel took its 486-series the next step in March 1994, with the introduction of its *486DX4*. Obviously the designation did not reflect the integral speed multiple but was Intel's attempt to be coy—and keep the industry guessing. Before rumors of the actual designation escaped Intel, most journalists pegged the name as the DX3. Their speculations about the design of the chip proved far from the mark and Intel, at least by its own accounts, selected the DX4 name so that the public would not confuse the features rumored to be in the new chip with what the company actually delivered.

Those differences were major. Most insiders expected a simple tweak of the internal clock, much as the DX2 is little more than a hyperactive DX. But the DX4 incorporates several innovations that make it stand out from the rest of the 486 family.

The obvious change is the higher internal multiplier. The DX4 operates internally at three times the system clock frequency. The initial release of the DX4 includes two models: a 75MHz version that plugged into 25 MHz system boards and a 100MHz version designed for 33MHz system boards.

Because of the greater disparity between internal and external clocks, Intel added more primary cache to smooth over the differences. The DX4 doubles the standard 486 cache to 16K. Other aspects of the cache remain unchanged from other family members: the four-way set-associative cache uses write-through technology and handles both data and instructions as a single, combined cache.

To keep power consumption down—all else being equal the DX4 would produce 50 percent more heat than a DX2 in the same PC—Intel built the DX4 to use its SL-enhancement features. In addition, the DX4 uses 3.3-volt logic and takes advantage of Intel's 0.6 micron fabrication technology. Because of the voltage difference alone, you cannot replace a 486DX or 486DX2 with a 486DX4. After-market vendors are, however, developing adapter boards to allow you to make such an upgrade.

Apart from those innovations, the 486DX4 maintains full software compatibility with the rest of the 486 family. Its other hardware features match other 486DX-level chips: 32-bit internal registers, 32-bit external data bus, and a 32-bit address bus capable of reaching 4 gigabytes of RAM. It also includes an integral floating-point unit.

The Pentium Family

In 1993, Intel introduced its latest microprocessor. Although long expected to be called the 80586 in keeping with the other chips in the Intel microprocessor family, the company opted for the name Pentium. The unusual name probably stems from a federal court ruling that the 386 numeric designation was generic; that is, it describes a type of product rather than something exclusive to a particular manufacturer. Consequently, Intel strove for a name of its own so that when other companies cloned its new chip they could not use the same name as the original.

Part of the reason for the declining difference with respect to RISC chips is that Intel has incorporated some design elements of RISC into its chips. The falling cost of hardware added impetus to integrate more instructions into the computer's repertoire, resulting in today's dominance of CISC designs. Intel has become so good at designing and manufacturing its CISC microprocessors that for practical purposes the advantage of RISC evaporates. Intel's chips are more complex than RISC chips (they involve more junctions and larger chunks of silicon) but they deliver performance that approaches RISC designs, and they come closer every time Intel increases the clock speeds of its chips.

The effective difference between RISC and CISC systems is that most CISC systems run DOS and most RISC systems use UNIX as their operating system. Windows NT, OS/2, Macintosh, and other new operating systems and DOS emulators stand to substantially change that situation. Tradition more than design architecture accounts for the operating system split. As the new, processor-independent operating systems become more accepted, even this difference between RISC and CISC may disappear.

Pentium breaks with the 386/486 family by sporting a 64-bit interface rather than the 32-bit connections of the older microprocessors. Inside, however, the Pentium still uses 32-bit technology, although in an unusual way. Instead of a single 32-bit central processing unit, the Pentium uses 486 chips linked together with circuitry to divide the work among them.

To help match the Pentium to your PC, Intel has built a 16K internal cache into the chip. This cache is arranged quite differently from that of the 486. It is effectively split in half with 8K of it used for managing program instructions and the other 8K for buffering data. This design is a more efficient way of dividing data for processing by the microprocessor. Combined caches can stall when program requirements don't match cache contents. For example, the cache might fill with program data while executing a loop. When it needs the next instruction, it must reach out of the cache to slow main memory. Separate caches for program instructions and data assure that neither will stall the system. As a result, the caches of the Pentium are much more efficient than those of the 486, even after allowing for its increased size.

The Pentium carries on the Intel tradition of backward compatibility. Despite its revolutionary design, the Pentium will still run all the same programs that execute on the 386 and 486 in exactly the same operating modes. In other words, the Pentium boots up in real mode, then can be switched to (and back from) protected and virtual 8086 modes. The Pentium instruction set includes all the commands used by the 486 and adds new instructions of its own.

The primary (and most interesting from an upgrade perspective) difference between the Pentium and its predecessors is that the Pentium is faster. The initial Pentium chips were supposed to start at about twice the fastest 486 running at the same clock speed with even greater potential with quicker clocks. Although the first Pentium chips operated at a top speed that only matched the internal 66MHz of Intel's quickest clock-doubling 486 chips, it came close to its goal by turning in results about 80 percent faster when running DOS applications. With the introduction of versions operating at 100 MHz, the Pentium pulled far ahead as Intel's quickest microprocessor.

Unfortunately, the Pentium doesn't show its complete prowess when running ordinary DOS applications. Its dual nature requires programs to be optimized to be split between its two processing sections. DOS is a one-thing-at-a-time operating system. Windows and OS/2 have the potential to exploit the power of the Pentium, but for the best effects even they will require changes in application software. (Programs will have to be recompiled for the Pentium by their publishers. Unfortunately, the result may be that programs optimized for the Pentium may not work on older Intel processors.) Considering the slow market acceptance of full 32-bit software (32-bit OS/2 appeared five years after the introduction of the 32-bit 386 chip), new Pentium-optimized programs may be a long way off.

According to Intel, the most powerful enhancement to the Pentium is not in its regular microprocessor circuitry but its internal coprocessor section. Intel claims that the Pentium coprocessor is three to five times faster than the floating-point unit in a 486 running at the same clock speed (MHz). As with other coprocessors, this advanced Pentium feature will come into play only when you run applications that use complex math functions. Oddly, the most popular initial Pentium application as network servers doesn't tap this capability at all.

Pentium chips connect to their computer hosts through a full 64-bit address bus. This wide link-up enables the Pentium to acquire and save data at twice the speed of a chip with 32-bit connections. (Internally, parts of the Pentium are linked with connections as wide as 256 bits!) For reaching memory, the Pentium uses the same 32-bit addressing system as the 386 and 486 family, enabling it to directly reach four gigabytes of system RAM.

The initial Pentium chips released by Intel were available in two speed ratings: 60 MHz and 66 MHz. Each was designed for system boards operating at the rated microprocessor speed. These chips used standard five volt logic.

The second wave of Pentiums, released in March 1994, brought two innovations. They operated at higher speed thanks to an internal clock multiplier. The boost was by a factor of 1.5, which allowed a 100MHz Pentium to plug into a 66MHz system board and a 90MHz Pentium to link to a 60MHz board. The new chips could *not* be used as direct replacements for their forebears because of the second innovation: the new Pentiums used 3.3-volt logic. Outside of those changes, the new Pentiums are identical to the earlier models.

To take full advantage of the higher speed of the newer Pentiums, system board makers must redesign their products to accommodate the lower voltage requirements of the chips. In the interim, however, some companies have developed adapter cards that match the 3.3-volt Pentiums with 5-volt Pentium sockets. These adapters have their own drawbacks—physically they add substantially to the stature of the Pentium and can cause interference with expansion slots. In addition, older Pentium system boards often are not capable of operating at the higher speeds. Although you might adapt a fast Pentium to plug into one of these motherboards, its cache, system memory, and local bus expansion are likely to run at a slower rate. In other words, you get a modest performance increase from the faster chip clock on what stays inside the Pentium cache, but you gain little on applications that make extensive use of input and output instructions.

The Pentium represents the current culmination of Intel's architecture. In little more than a decade, Intel-compatible microprocessors and the PCs built from them have come a long way, from chips capable of delivering about one-third MIPS (million of instructions per second) to those racing through more than 50 million instructions in a second.

Pentium OverDrive

The increased number of connections used by the Pentium has one important implication for upgraders: there's no hope of plugging a current Pentium chip in place of a 486. You cannot just plug an ordinary Pentium into your 486 PC and get Pentium performance.

However, Intel has promised (for late 1994) a version of the Pentium that will work in 486 computers. Code named the P24T, the upgrade chip is not pin-compatible with the 486 chips it supersedes, and it requires a special upgrade socket, one with 268 pins. Most new 486-based PCs built since Intel released the P24T pin-out specification in 1992 have included upgrade sockets. However, as this is written, the general upgradability of these PCs is clouded.

Some manufacturers contend that taking full advantage of all the features of the P24T will require a BIOS upgrade. Interestingly, the same manufacturers making this contention are those who tout PCs with Flash ROM-based BIOSs that can be easily upgraded.

A bigger problem is heat. The initial Pentium chips dissipated about 17 watts of power—on the order of a small light bulb. Because they are based on the same Pentium design, P24T chips probably will dissipate a similar magnitude of power. That heat has to go somewhere—if it doesn't, the result may be a melt down (or at least a system shutdown). A problem may arise in that many so-called Pentium-upgradable PCs with P24T sockets were not designed with cooling in mind. Although these machines may have the necessary socket for a P24T chip, they don't provide the cooling the higher power chip will require. A P24T upgrade in such a system would be doomed to failure. Intel tried to prevent such a problem by publishing the cooling requirements of the P24T, but a number of manufacturers did not heed the Intel guidelines. Intel is working on a solution to the problem; for example, P24T chips with different cooling technologies (such as built-in fans) for different systems and a selection chart to help you pick the right chip for your PC. In any case, Intel hopes to have some means of providing a functional P24T upgrade for all systems that sport a proper socket.

Intel-Compatible Microprocessors

Years of research and development go into the design of every integrated circuit, and microprocessors are among the most complicated (and expensive to design) of ICs. But most of the design and development work can be avoided by simply copying someone else's effort by reverse-engineering, deducing the design from the product. More reputable firms start with the specifications of the chip and its instruction set and design from the ground up a chip that mimics the function of the original. Less reputable sources may merely x-ray a chip to determine the layout of the various silicon layers. To prevent other companies from copying their chip designs, most makers of integrated circuits refuse to disclose any of the inner workings of their products. Moreover, they use patents, copyrights, and secrecy to prevent predatory copying.

On the other hand, when a design is unproved and a company struggling, chip makers will sometimes license other makers to use the masks they have designed to lay down the silicon circuitry of a chip to provide a second source for a product. This licensing or "second-sourcing" earns the original designer a royalty and, often, greater acceptance of the chip because buyers of integrated circuits look askance at any product with a single source of supply. Second sources insulate against labor or manufacturing troubles and can sometimes reduce costs through competition.

Before the success of the PC was proven, Intel licensed its designs to other chip makers. Both the 8086 family and 286 families were offered by second sources. Starting with the 386 series, however, Intel has staunchly refused to license other chip makers, with the exception of IBM. The success of Intel microprocessors has attracted a number of companies to do their best to copy Intel's designs while skirting the company's legal protections.

Either way, a number of Intel-compatible chips have found their way to market at various processor levels. Table 3.2 summarizes the essential characteristics of today's Intel-compatible microprocessors.

TABLE 3.2. Summary of Features of Intel-Compatible Microprocessors

Chip	Manufacturer	Data Bus Width	Address Bus Width	Internal Clock Multiplier	Internal Cache Unit	Integral Floating-Point
386SX	Intel	16	24	1x	No	No
	AMD	16	24	1x	No	No
38600SX	C&T	16	24	1x	No	No
386SLC	IBM	16	24	1x	8K	No
38605SX	C&T	16	24	1x	0.5K	No
386DX	Intel	32	32	1x	No	No
	AMD	32	32	1x	No	No
38600DX	C&T	32	32	1x	No	No
38605DX	C&T	32	32	1x	0.5K	No
486S	Cyrix	32	32	1x	2K	No
486Se	Cyrix	32	32	1x	2K	No
486SL	Intel	32	32	1x	8K	Yes
486SLC	Cyrix	16	24	1x	1K	No
486SLC/E	TI	16	24	1x	1K	No
486SLC2	IBM	32	32	2x	16K	No
486SRx2	Cyrix	32	32	2x	iK	No
486SX	Intel	32	32	1x	8K	No
	Cyrix	32	32	1x	8K	No
	AMD	32	32	1x	8K	No
486SXLV	AMD	32	32	1x	8K	No
486DLC	Cyrix	32	32	1x	1K	No

continues

TABLE 3.2. Continued

Chip	Manufacturer	Data Bus Width	Address Bus Width	Internal Clock Multiplier	Internal Cache Unit	Integral Floating-Point
486DLC/E	TI	32	32	1x	1K	No
486DRx2	Cyrix	32	32	1x	8K	No
486DX	Intel	32	32	1x	8K	Yes
	AMD	32	32	1x	8K	Yes
486DXLV	AMD	32	32	1x	8K	Yes
486DX2	Intel	32	32	2x	8K	Yes
486DX4	Intel	32	32	3x	16K	Yes
Blue Lightning	IBM	32	32	3x	16K	No
Pentium	Intel	64	32	1x or 1.5x	16K	Yes

8088 and 286-Level Chips

Because Intel was a relatively small and struggling chip maker in the early 1980s, many corporate buyers were unwilling to commit to products for which it was the single source of supply. So Intel licensed its designs to a variety of manufacturers. Compatible 8086, 8088, and 80286 chips were sold by a number of different vendors. All, however, were based on Intel's own chip layouts and microcodes. These licensed products were identical to Intel's own and were entirely interchangeable.

NEC V20 and V30

One company, Nippon Electric Company (NEC) was not satisfied with licensing Intel's designs and instead reverse-engineered Intel's chips, improving on them somewhat along the way. The results were NEC's V20 and V30 chips, which are directly interchangeable with Intel's 8088 and 8086. Pin and signal compatible, the V20 can be used to replace a 8088; the V30 replaces the 8086. (NEC offers other microprocessors in this series, but they have not found wide application.) The NEC chips proved so compatible with Intel's own that Intel sued NEC, alleging that the V20 and V30 were not so much reverse engineered as duplicated, in violation of the copyright laws. Intel claimed that NEC used as much as 25 percent of Intel's microcode in the V20 and V30.

Although the NEC chips use the same command set as the Intel devices, they are not identical. Much of their microcode is different (at least 75 percent of it, even if you believe Intel's contentions). Not just different, but more efficient. Because the NEC chips were designed with the benefit of hindsight, their inner workings could be adjusted for greater performance. Replacing an 8088 with a V20 or replacing an 8086 with a V30 can improve overall microprocessor throughput and, thus, the speed of the computer around which it is based from 10 to 30 percent.

As a practical matter, the fast pace of the microprocessor industry has left these issues far behind. You wouldn't want an 8088 or V30 in your PC when today's entry-level machines are 50 times more powerful. Although the NEC chips do work well in place of the Intel products, you probably will want to replace any system based on such old technology.

Chips and Technologies F8680

Just when you thought the 8086 was long dead, someone comes up with a better idea. In 1991, long after the 8088 and 8086 had been left for dead by major chip makers, Chips and Technologies developed a new compatible chip designed specifically for notebook computers. Designated the F8680, the new Chips and Technologies chip combines nearly all the circuitry needed to build a complete PC: the microprocessor, keyboard controller, bus control logic, serial port, and a video controller for an LCD display.

At heart, however, the F8680 is an 8086 microprocessor designed for low-voltage operation with a built-in system management mode to reduce power consumption. It can operate at speeds up to 14 MHz, putting its performance at the low end of the 286-class PCs. Memory is addressed through a 26-bit bus, which enables access to 64M. Unlike 286 microprocessors, however, the F8680 has no protected mode. It addresses memory beyond the one megabyte 8086 addressing limit using bank-switching (for EMS compatibility).

Low power is the essence of the design. Operating with a 3-volt supply (the F8680 tolerates normal 5-volt supplies as well), the chip draws only 20 milliamps during 8 MHz operation. In standby mode, the current consumption of the chip drops to 30 microamps—that's .00009 watt. Some batteries leak more current than the F8680 draws in standby mode.

The F8680 is not directly socket compatible with the 8088, 8086, or any other microprocessor. Taking advantage of the chip requires designing a complete computer around it (not hard, considering that the chip is most of the computer already) and connecting its 160-pin plastic flat pack.

Although the F8680 is intriguing, the technology inside is even more promising—imagine a 486 with the power needs of the F8680. However, Chips and Technology suspended its microprocessor development effort in 1992, leaving the F8680 an orphan, albeit one with potential for light-duty, minimal performance sub-notebook and hand-held computers.

386-Compatible Processors

Once the success of the PC and the microprocessor inside it was proven, Intel no longer needed to have second sources to reassure chip buyers. So Intel decided to keep the entire market for PC-compatible processors to itself after it introduced the 386. Only IBM was licensed to make the new chip in return for other favors, and even IBM was not able to sell the individual chips it made under license. The chips could only be sold as parts in assemblies. The rest of the semiconductor industry was effectively frozen out of the profitable 386 market.

At least until the reverse-engineers began to put on the heat. A number of companies began to develop their own versions of Intel's chips. At the 386 level, Advanced Micro Devices and Chips and Technologies took up the challenge. At the 486 level, Cyrix and Texas Instruments joined in. In the meantime, IBM became more aggressive on the market. Although abiding by the terms of its licensing agreement with Intel, IBM began to sell its versions of the 386 and 486 chips in low-cost motherboard assemblies.

Today you can buy PCs with any of a wide variety of Intel-compatible but not Intel-made microprocessors. These include the AMD 386, Chips and Technologies 386 chips, and IBM's 386SLC.

AMD 386

Without a doubt, the Advanced Micro Devices 386 line is the closest to the Intel original. That's because AMD started with Intel's own microcode, arguing that a technology-sharing agreement with Intel back in the days of the 286 enabled AMD to use the valuable microcode. Although the courts still haven't had the last word on the meaning of the Intel-AMD technology sharing agreement, the chips exist, and you can buy PCs built around them.

AMD was founded in 1969 and first got into the microprocessor business in 1975 when it released a reversed-engineered version of the Intel 8080 chip. Although that product put AMD and Intel into direct competition, the two companies entered into a patent cross-licensing agreement in 1977 so that each could take advantage of the other's designs, giving each company a better chance of success in the then-unproved microprocessor market. The two companies became more closely involved when IBM demanded a second source for Intel's 8088 microprocessor before they would put the chip into its first PCs. IBM wasn't sure that Intel would stay in business and was afraid to build a product with the possibility of not having a chip supplier. Consequently, Intel allowed AMD to second-source the 8088. For much the same reason of giving microprocessor purchasers a greater sense of security, Intel also granted AMD the right to make its 286.

By the time the 386 had been rolled out, however, Intel had a secure place in the semiconductor industry, and the company figured it could cash in on a monopoly on the 386. Consequently, it never directly granted AMD the right to make the 386.

AMD nevertheless developed its own version of the 386 chip using its own hardware design and Intel's microcode. The circuit design underlying the AMD chips is slightly more efficient and uses less power than the Intel chips. Intel promptly sued. According to AMD, contracts between the two companies enabled AMD to use all of Intel's designs and patents through 1995, a right for which AMD paid Intel approximately $350,000 (about 35 percent of its profits in the year the agreement was signed). In the dispute, Intel claimed the 1975 agreement gave AMD the right only to copy Intel's microcode, not to distribute it. (Intel had also claimed the designation "386" as a trademark, but the numbers were ruled generic on March 1, 1991, enabling AMD and other companies to call their clone chips 386's.) Finally, on February 24, 1992, an arbitrator awarded AMD the right to use Intel's 386 microcode without royalty or disputes, but AMD got no more rights to Intel's technology. Recent developments in the case have turned the matter more in Intel's favor.

Despite the legal problems, AMD has developed a full line of 386 microprocessors. The flagship is a 40 MHz 386DX, which is about 20 percent faster than Intel's quickest 386 chip because of its higher clock speed. AMD also offers 386SX chips that operate at 16, 20, 25, and 33 MHz as well as 386DX chips with 20, 25, 33, and 40 MHz ratings. Because all of these microprocessors use Intel microcode, they are the most compatible of the clone microprocessors.

Most notable of the AMD 386 products is its Am386DXLV chip (the final two letters stand for low voltage). This chip was the first Intel-compatible microprocessor designed to operate at supply voltages from 3.3 to 5 volts (at least in its 25 MHz version; a 33 MHz version of the chip requires at least 4.5 volts for proper operation).

The Am386DXLV also includes several other power-saving features. Its normal power consumption is less than Intel or other AMD 386 products. Operating at 20 MHz, the Am386DXLV requires no more than 110 milliamps (that's about three-eighths of a watt); at 25 MHz, it requires 135 milliamps (about two-thirds of a watt).

Because the Am386DXLV is a static design, the chip can operate at any clock speed up to its maximum rating. A PC could reduce the frequency supplied to the chip to reduce its power consumption when processing speed is not required. In addition, the Am386DXLV also has a system management mode that reduces power requirements in standby mode to 0.150 milliamp.

Chips and Technologies 386s

Chips and Technologies, which is best known for their chip sets with which PC makers build their motherboards, also offers clone 386 chips that plug directly into the sockets designed for the Intel products. These chips include a 386SX clone, the 38600SX (available in 20 and 25 MHz speeds), and a 386DX clone, the 38600DX (available in 25, 33, and 40 MHz clock speeds). Unlike the AMD chips, however, the C&T 386 products were developed without benefit of Intel's microcode. The chips are C&T through and through.

In addition, C&T has extended the power of the 386 into its unique improved line of microprocessors, which includes the 38605SX (available in 20 and 25 MHz speeds) and 38605DX (available in 25, 33, and 40 MHz clock speeds). These chips are code compatible but not socket compatible with the 386SX and 386DX, respectively. C&T's primary enhancements to these chips include a 512-byte instruction cache in each, multi-stage memory and instruction pipelines (which enable processing in stages as data travels through the pipeline), and C&T's own SuperState V management system (essentially a super-protected mode that enables system monitoring and control independent of the chip's protected mode operations).

IBM 386SLC

Under license from Intel, IBM is allowed to make its own 386 chips. The license terms allow IBM to use the Intel designs and microcode to develop improved products. In return, Intel gets rights to whatever new creations flow from the minds of IBM's engineers. The first product of this agreement was IBM's 386SLC (first used in two IBM PS/2 computers, the Model 56SLC and Model 57SLC).

The 386SLC is basically a 16-bit 386SX microprocessor, but it is an improved design because it was released in 1991 after Intel produced the 486. In improving on the basic 386 design, IBM added the extra commands the 486 understands while keeping the final product electrically compatible with the 386SX. Both address and data buses match the 386SX specifications, which are 24 address lines enabling direct addressing of 16 megabytes of RAM and 16 address lines, although the internal registers of the 386SLC are the full 32-bits of the rest of the 386 family.

However, IBM made several performance improvements on the 386SLC. The IBM chip executes most of its instructions in far fewer clock cycles than does the Intel 386 design. In addition, IBM added an internal cache, an 8K two-way set associative design. The improvements proved sufficient to make the initial 20 MHz version of the 386SLC quicker than any 386SX on the market, comparable in performance to a full 386DX running up to 25 MHz. The internal cache of the 386SLC compensates for the disadvantage of the narrower data bus. IBM designed 16, 20, and 25 MHz versions of the chip, although all versions have not been used in systems.

As with Intel's 386SL, the 386SLC is designed for low current operation and includes many of the same power management features. At 25 MHz, the 386SLC draws slightly more current than the 386SL, about 590 milliamps. The 386SLC can also reduce its internal operating speed and incorporates its own System Management Mode. Unlike the 386SL, however, the 386SLC handles its power management function within its own confines.

The 386SLC includes two Model Specific Registers, one to control power management features and the other is the internal cache. The chip's instruction set was also enhanced with commands used to control these new registers. Through these registers, the cache can be switched on and off or the microprocessor can be switched into its suspend mode to conserve electricity.

Although electrically compatible with the 386SX, the 386SLC adds six extra control signals to its package. Although pins 27 through 30, 43, and 45 through 47 on the 386SX are not connected, the 386SLC uses them for its own chip-specific control functions. The 386SLC itself is designed to fit a plastic quad flat package. As with an ordinary 386SX, it mates with a 387SX floating-point coprocessor.

Compatibility is not an issue with the 386SLC because it was designed under license from Intel and incorporates Intel microcode. Its incompatibilities with the 386SX appear only where the 386SLC has more features. Because of its superior performance when compared to other low-end Intel chips, the 386SLC would have definite advantages in low-cost computers, but IBM is not permitted to sell the chip to other manufacturers, and Intel has not chosen to do so.

486-Compatible Processors

Intel's strategy for beating the cloners of the 386 was simple: stay ahead. As competitors struggled to build 386-compatible chips, Intel publicized the superiority of its 486. Unfortunately, that strategy only worked for a while. Other companies soon developed their own versions of the 486, some (like the initial Cyrix 486 chips) stretching the 486 definition. Although few of the chips discussed in this section look like Intel's and many are not even socket-compatible, all execute the same instruction set as the 486. At the software level (where it counts) all are true 486 chips.

Cyrix 486SLC and 486DLC

Cyrix Corporation started in the semiconductor business in 1988 and makes its principal business designing chips compatible with Intel products. Its first venture into microprocessors was the 486DLC and 486SLC, a pair of products reverse-engineered to be compatible with Intel's 486.

The Cyrix products earn their name through their recognition of the same instructions as the Intel 486-series of microprocessors. The Cyrix chips, however, differ in significant ways from the Intel products. They are so different, in fact, that they are not socket-compatible. The Cyrix chips resemble the Intel 386 design in that they require a clock that runs at double the speed of the microprocessor; Intel 486 chips operate at the clock speed supplied to them.

As with Intel's 486SX, neither Cyrix chip includes floating-point circuitry. Instead, Cyrix bundles its 387-compatible coprocessors with its products, offering the combination of processor and coprocessor at a slight increase over the processor-alone price (in contrast to Intel, which doubles or triples the price of a processor when including a floating-point unit).

Instead of a floating-point processor, Cyrix includes a hardware multiplier. Instead of relying on microcode to carry out instructions requiring multiplication, the Cyrix chips execute those operations directly using fewer clock cycles than would be required by an Intel chip. Because multiplication instructions are used extensively in graphics, the hardware multipliers earn the Cyrix chips a slight performance advantage in some graphic operations.

The 486DLC and 486SLC are distinguished from one another in that the 486DLC uses a 32-bit external data bus and 32 address lines, so it has the same data-handling and addressing capabilities as the 386DX and 486 series of Intel microprocessors. The 486SLC is patterned after the 386SX, with a 16-bit data bus and 24-bit address bus. The 486SLC is not, however, socket-compatible with the 386SX (in fact, neither chip is likely to use a socket; most are soldered into place, making replacing one chip with another on a motherboard a moot point).

The 486DLC is available in three speeds: 25, 33, and 40 MHz. The 486SLC is available in two speeds: 20 and 25 MHz. The 486DLC is designed solely for 5-volt operation. The 486SLC works at 5 volts, but a special version, the 486SLC-V, will operate at either 5 or 3.3 volts.

As with the Intel 486 chips, the Cyrix 486DLC and 486SLC include an on-chip combined instruction and data cache. The cache on the Cyrix chips is substantially smaller, however, both in size and capacity.

Where the Intel 486 cache occupies about one-third the total silicon space of the chip, the Cyrix cache requires only about one-sixth the chip. Consequently, the piece of silicon making up a Cyrix chip is smaller than that of an Intel chip, which makes the Cyrix products less expensive to manufacture.

The capacity of the Cyrix cache is only 1K, and its operation is effective only during memory read operations (it is a write-through cache). Six special registers on the 486DLC and 486SLC that are not present on Intel chips set up the cache and power management features of the chips. Four registers allow programmers to define four blocks of memory to be excluded from caching. Each register defines one excluded block by location and size, which is programmable from 4 kilobytes to 4 gigabytes. Another register excludes sections of real mode memory for caching. This register can also be used to switch the cache off and on and to configure it as a direct-mapped or two-way set associative cache.

The current consumed by the Cyrix 486DLC chip can be reduced to about 10 milliamps at 40 MHz clock operation (about 0.05 watt) by shifting the chip into its suspend mode. The 486SLC reduces to 5 milliamps at its 25 MHz clock. Both chips will make the switch either by receiving a software instruction (HALT) or through direct hardware signaling on special chip pins. Because the Cyrix chips are designed with static logic, they lose no data when their operation is suspended. If the clock supplied to the chip is also stopped when the chip is suspended, current requirements drop to 0.1 milliamp (that's just 0.0005 watt).

During normal operation, the 486DLC requires about 435 milliamps at 25 MHz and about 560 milliamps at 40 MHz. The 486SLC requires about 380 milliamps at 20 MHz and about 435 milliamps at 25 MHz.

At one time, Cyrix entered into an agreement with Texas Instruments to have its chips manufactured. In return, Texas Instruments received rights to duplicate some Cyrix designs. Unfortunately the relationship between the two companies quickly proved strained, so Cyrix instead had its products manufactured by SGS-Thompson. On April 14, 1994, Cyrix entered yet another manufacturing agreement, this time with IBM. The relationship holds promise for both companies. Not only does Cyrix get a chip foundry, but it also can take advantage of IBM's advanced 0.5-micron design rules. IBM also benefits. It can use the Cyrix designs to manufacture Intel-compatible chips not bound by the earlier agreement made with Intel. A chief benefit is that IBM can sell Cyrix-based chips individually instead of only as parts of assemblies, as the Intel agreement requires.

Cx486DRx^2 and Cx486SRx^2

Cyrix divides its chip business into two parts, OEM products and end-user products. The company made its 486DLC and 486SLC as OEM products. These chips require custom motherboard designs.

Cyrix adapted the same chip design to its first end-user products—a series of chips designed as exact replacements (actually upgrades) for Intel's products. By giving the 486SLC the same pinout as Intel's 386SX, and giving the 486DLC the same pinout as the Intel 386DX, Cyrix gave you a quick, easy means for adding 486 performance to aging 386-based PCs. You can simply pop out your old Intel chip and press in the Cyrix product for a substantial performance increase.

To give you an even better upgrade, Cyrix doubled the internal clock speeds of the upgrade chips the same way Intel sped up its DX2 line. The result was the *Cx486DRx^2* to upgrade 386DX systems and the *486SRx^2* to replace 386SX chips.

A key part of enabling the Cyrix chips to deliver improved performance is the on-board primary cache. As with the 486DLC and 486SLC, the Cyrix upgrade chips also use a 1K cache. They also include extra circuitry to enable the operation of the cache in 386 PCs not designed to accommodate internal microprocessor caching.

The cache is both the strong point and weakness of the Cyrix upgrade chips. The integral cache helps isolate the fast microprocessor logic from the slower base system. Thanks to the integral cache, the Cyrix upgrade chips can give a factor of two or three performance boost to your older PC—at least with software that confines itself to the cache. But when programs reach beyond the integral cache, performance plummets to only 30 percent to 50 percent faster than the base system. The small size of the Cyrix cache aggravates the situation. All things considered, however, the upgrade delivers more than the base system ever could—and it's a faster, easier, and cheaper solution than any alternative offered by Intel (because there aren't any Intel alternatives short of replacing the motherboard or entire PC!).

Cx486S and Cx486Se

In April 1993, Cyrix announced an improved budget microprocessor for system developers: the Cx486S. Although patterned after the Intel 486SX with a full 32-bit design from its bus through its registers, and compatible with the 486 command set, the 486S has unique features of its own.

As with the Intel 486SX, the Cyrix 486S lacks an integral floating-point unit (math coprocessor). But where Intel math upgrade involves replacing the entire chip with what's essentially a 486DX, Cyrix permits a 386-style upgrade. That is, only the coprocessor circuitry needs to be added, in the guise of a Cyrix Cx487S floating-point unit.

To accommodate all the connections required between the main processor and coprocessor, the Cx486S takes advantage of the pins of its 168-pin grid array socket that are not connected in the Intel 486SX pin-out. The chip is also available in a 196-pin Quad Flat Pack. Although the Cx486S fits into an Intel 486SX socket, the use of pins not defined by Intel means that you cannot substitute the Cyrix chip for an Intel one and expect all the chip's features to work. A system designed for an Intel 486SX won't be able to properly control the write-back feature of the cache, nor will you be able to add a Cyrix coprocessor.

Compared to earlier Cyrix chips like the 486SLC, the Cx486S includes an enhanced cache. Instead of 1K of cache, the Cx486S has 2K. Moreover, the Cx486S uses a write-back cache design so that both read and write operations are buffered by the cache.

The core logic of the Cx486S operates at speeds up to 50MHz, and it will run at one or two times the chip's external bus speed. Cyrix offers the Cx486S in 33, 40, and 50MHz versions that operate at full bus speed, and a clock-doubled version (the Cx486S2) that runs at 25MHz externally and 50MHz internally—much like an Intel 486SX/2.

For notebook computers, Cyrix offers the same design in a power-saving version called the *Cx486Se.* The core logic of the Cx486Se is fully static, allowing the chip to stop operating and reduce its power consumption to 0.1 percent of its active power when idle. The Cx486Se incorporates both advanced power management and its own system management mode to control the operating speed of the chip which, in turn, affects power consumption.

For even more frugal PCs, Cyrix offers a 3.3-volt version of the Cx486Se that operate at 25 and 33MHz: the Cx486Se-V25 and Cx486Se-V33. Low-voltage operation cuts the power consumption of these chips by 50 percent compared to their 5-volt kin.

Cx486DX and Cx486SX

To round out its 486 line-up, in late 1993 Cyrix introduced its fully compatible version of Intel's 486DX and 486SX microprocessors. These chips use the same basic internal design as earlier Cyrix chips—a full 486 command set augmented by a hardware integer multiplier. The most significant change over earlier Cyrix chips is the adoption of a full 8K combined instruction and data cache. Moreover, the Cyrix cache uses a true write-back design instead of the write-through technology used in the Intel chip.

The Cyrix nomenclature follows Intel's. The Cyrix 486DX incorporates an internal floating-point processor, patterned after Cyrix's own FasMath chips. The Cyrix 486SX lacks an integral floating-point unit, but the chip will accommodate an external coprocessor.

IBM 486SLC2

With the 386SLC, IBM's engineers worked over the basic 386 architecture to deliver the greatest possible performance from a 16-bit interfaced package compatible with the 386SX. With the 486SLC2, they have been at it again, reworking the 386SLC architecture. In fact, the 486SLC2 is specifically designed to replace IBM's own 386SLC.

IBM's 486SLC2 is the venerable 386SX taken to the extreme with every state-of-the-art microprocessor feature mixed in with its 1.349 million transistors. As with IBM's 386SLC, the new chip recognizes the complete 486 command set. However, it still retains the 16-bit data bus and 16-megabyte addressing limit of the 386SX. Streamlined internal circuitry and an improved cache pushes the performance of the 486SLC2 into the low end of 486 territory.

To enhance the performance of the chip with a 16-bit data bus, IBM grafted the largest internal cache of any available microprocessor into the 486SLC2, a full 16K. Although twice the size, the 486SLC2 cache is arranged much like that of Intel's 486 series. It is a full four-way set associative architecture that buffers only read operations (it is a write-through design).

IBM makes the 486SLC2 chip with three speed ratings: 16, 20, and 25 MHz. In addition, the chip can optionally internally double the clock speed supplied it while maintaining its external connections at the slower original speed. In effect, the chip can carry out internal operations at twice its clock speed without any changes in external circuitry or clocking.

As with most recent microprocessors, the 486SLC2 is designed with a system management mode controlled through a proprietary register, which can suspend the processor's operation to save battery power. At most, the chip draws 2.3 watts (about 460 milliamps from a 5-volt supply), but throttles down to no more than 25 milliamps in suspend mode.

In addition, the 486SLC2 is designed to operate at lower voltages. The 25 MHz version of the chip is designed for a nominal 3.3-volt supply and will operate as low as 3 volts. The clock-doubling 20 and 25 MHz versions of the chip are designed for 3.6-volt operation, although they tolerate supply voltage as low as 3.42 volts.

As with the 386SLC, the 486SLC is present only in IBM's own machines. The company's agreement with Intel prohibits it from selling the 486SLC2 to other computer makers, although Intel can manufacturer the chip (if it chooses) and sell it as its own.

IBM Blue Lightning

In 1993, IBM Technology Products formally unveiled its next generation of enhanced 486 chips called Blue Lightning.

Building from the same processor core and 16K cache as the earlier 486SLC2, the newer chip offers a full 32-bit processor bus in a package that fits a 386DX socket. As with the 486SLC2, the Blue Lightning does not include an internal floating-point unit.

The most important feature of Blue Lightning is that it advances clock-doubling technology to the next step. Blue Lightning runs internally at three times its external clock rate. The initial chips operate at 75 MHz in sockets otherwise designed for 25 MHz chips. Similarly, the 100 MHz version looks externally like a 33 MHz chip.

The IBM design operates at 3.3 volts and consumes substantially less power than standard Intel chips. At 75 MHz, Blue Lightning consumes only 2 watts, compared to the 5 watts needed by Intel's 50 MHz 486DX2. The fabrication technology is the same that IBM used for its PowerPC RISC microprocessors.

Texas Instruments TI486SLC/E and TI486DLC/E

Once a major microprocessor manufacturer of its own, Texas Instruments got back into the mainstream after pairing up with Cyrix Corporation. Texas Instruments provided the foundry which manufactured chips for Cyrix. Later, TI brought out under its own name a line of chips that were derived from the Cyrix products. The results include the TI486SLC/E and TI486DLC/E.

The TI486SLC/E is a 486 code compatible microprocessor that fits the same package, a 100-pin plastic quad flat pack, like many 386SX chips. It uses the same interfaces as a 386SX (a 16-bit data bus and a 24-bit address bus), but it has full 32-bit internal architecture. To augment its performance, the 486SLC/E incorporates a hardware multiplier and a 1K combined instruction-and-data cache with a two-way set associative design. To conserve power in portable applications, the standard 5-volt 486SLC/E offers a system management mode and a fully static logic design that can be slowed or stopped without affecting data integrity. In addition, a 3.3-volt version, the TI486SLC/E-V, is also available. The TI486SLC/E is offered in two speeds: 25 and 33 MHz. The low voltage chip operates only at 25 MHz.

The features of the TI486DLC/E duplicate those of the TI486SLC/E chip with one exception: the TI486DLC/E is designed to be pin compatible with the 386DX. As a result, it uses a full 32-bit external data bus and 32-bit address bus. Otherwise, it boasts the same innovations as its narrow-bus cousin: 486-code compatibility, hardware multiplier, 1K internal cache, static design, and system management mode. The standard 5-volt 486DLC/E uses a 132-pin ceramic pin grid array socket and is offered in 33 and 40 MHz versions. A 3.3-volt version, the 486DLC/E-V, is available in the same package but with 25 or 33 MHz top clock speeds.

Both the TI486SLC/E and TI486DLC/E lack internal floating-point units. Although the 486DLC/E fits the same sockets as the Intel 386DX, it is not a drop-in replacement because cache control requires either a BIOS change or an additional software driver.

Pentium-Level Chips

As soon as Intel introduced the Pentium, you could be sure engineers the world over would start working on a clone of it. Unlike with previous generations of microprocessors, however, the first efforts to duplicate the Pentium did not attempt to reverse-engineer the Intel product or even craft an electrical equivalent. Instead, manufacturers strove to beat Intel at its own game—maintain software compatibility but take advantage of design innovations to deliver performance superior to the Pentium. Where the Pentium requires a program to be recompiled to take best advantage of its superscalar design, these other chip-makers have striven to optimize speed with existing software. Instead of carrying all the baggage of Intel's CISC heritage, some of the new designs start with RISC technology. Others use special hardware techniques to do the work sorting instructions that Intel left to new compilers. Whatever design the new contenders use, their wildly different designs mean these chips can't claim to be Pentium copies or even complete Pentium equivalents. They do claim to deliver Pentium-level power for PCs—in fact, most claim more speed (particularly on existing applications) than the Pentium can deliver at a substantially lower price. This combination of virtues makes them candidates for powering your next PC.

Cyrix M1

Having proven its capability to duplicate the function of Intel's older microprocessors, Cyrix has pushed ahead by combining classical designs with new technologies to go the Pentium one better—at least in Cyrix's own humble view. Where the Pentium requires a new generation of software or at least recompiled applications to take advantage of its superscalar design, Cyrix has shifted to hardware the job of matching today's software to tomorrow's microprocessors. The result is M1 architecture, not a single chip but a plan for a new family of high-performance processors.

At its heart, the M1 architecture is superscalar like the Pentium with two somewhat asymmetrical integer arithmetic units capable of operating in parallel. Each integer unit has its own pipeline, the pair known as the X Pipeline and the Y Pipeline. Where the Pentium is pipelined with four stages, Cyrix calls its design *superpipelined* because it features a full seven stages. These stages are termed prefetch, decode 1, decode 2, address calculation 1, address calculation 2, execute, and write-back.

Processing in each of the pipelines begins with the *prefetch* stage. At this point, the pipeline gathers up to 16 bytes of instructions (typically about four instructions) from an on-chip cache. At this stage, the instructions are first evaluated to determine whether they code any program branches. If a branch is detected, the chip attempts to predict the course the branch will take at this preliminary stage.

Next, processing moves to the *decode 1* stage, which is primarily charged with determining the length of the instruction. The actual decoding of each instruction occurs in the *decode 2* stage. At this point, the chip determines whether a given instruction will travel through the X or Y pipeline. Most instructions can take either path, and the one chosen will be the one that best keeps the twin pipelines full and flowing. Certain instructions, however, must take the X pipeline. These include protected mode segment loads, string instructions, multiply or divide instructions, input and output instructions, far branches, instructions that may require multiple memory accesses, and certain push and pop instructions.

Processing then progresses to the *address calculation 1* stage, in which up to two addresses are calculated per clock cycle. This stage also determines which of the chip's registers will be used for carrying out the instruction.

The *address calculation 2* stage performs the actual memory access, checking the translation lookaside buffer, cache, and register files.

The *execute* stage then carries out any arithmetic or logical instructions, including multiply and divide commands.

The *write-back* stage finishes the execution by writing the resulting data to the register file and write buffers (whence they go to the cache and memory).

The biggest challenges of the M1 design are twofold: dividing the work between two processing chains, and making the additional pipeline stages pay off. Cyrix uses a number of technologies to pull off these tricks. Branch prediction and speculative execution help keep the pipelines full without stalling. According to Cyrix, its four-state branch prediction algorithm achieves 90 percent accuracy. Its speculative execution abilities handle up to four conditional branches or floating-point operations.

To eliminate problems that might arise in parallel execution, Cyrix takes advantage of several novel techniques. *Register renaming* allows each pipeline to work with what it thinks is the same register. The architecture includes 32 registers and allows each physical register to be assigned a logical name equivalent to any of the registers in an Intel microprocessor. For example, two instructions can execute simultaneously even though they both call for manipulating the EAX register. The M1 chip assigns a different hardware register the EAX name in each pipeline. Later it consolidates the results. *Data forwarding* allows the M1 chip to route the results of execution in one pipeline to the other when the operation of one instruction is dependent on the other. Further, the M1 design allows for *out-of-order execution* so that no problem arises when one pipeline completes execution of a simple instruction before the other pipeline finishes a more complex instruction that appears earlier in the program. Out-of-order execution only occurs at the execute stage or later so that memory control (which takes place in the address calculation stages) and faults always occur in the proper order.

As with the Pentium, the M1 design incorporates an integral floating-point unit in addition to its two integer units. The Cyrix floating-point unit operates fully in parallel with the integer units when the instruction stream permits. Floating-point instructions can be executed out of order with related integer instructions, and a set of four write buffers permit speculative execution of floating-point instructions. The floating-point unit itself links to the rest of the M1 processor through a 64-bit internal bus and follows the IEEE 754 standard. It recognizes and executes all standard Intel coprocessor instructions.

The cache design of M1 architecture is unlike that of any other current microprocessor. Its cache has a two-layer structure. To speed loading of instructions, the M1 design uses a special 256-byte primary instruction cache, which Cyrix calls the *microcache*. Another cache, much larger, combines the functions of primary data cache and secondary instruction cache. Although the size of this large unified cache is not set by the architecture's specifications, in initial implementations it will likely be on the order of the 16K cache of the Pentium. The unified cache uses a four-way set-associative design.

Other elements of the hardware design of the M1 are much like the Pentium. It is a full 32-bit chip—all registers are 32 bits wide—that connects to its support circuitry with a 64-bit data path. It uses 32-bit addressing to support up to 4 gigabytes of physical memory. The internal hardware design is optimized for high-speed operation at 100MHz or higher. Sample chips are due out as this is written.

NexGen 586

According to one manufacturer, the first efforts to duplicate the Pentium started well before it was released—even before it was named. NexGen, based in Milpitas, California, traces back the initial design work for its 586 to 1988 when it began its Intel-compatible work. The final design, announced in March 1994, claims to outperform the Pentium without sacrificing software compatibility.

The NexGen chip holds many similarities to the Pentium, but it is a revolutionary design that combines an understanding of the Intel instruction set with the latest ideas in microprocessor design—ideas that relegate the Intel hardware design to dinosaur status.

Justifying its claim of Pentium equivalence, the NexGen 586 boasts five advanced performance features it shares with the Intel chip. These include superscalar execution, separate data and instruction caches, pipelining with branch prediction logic, a 64-bit data bus, and a high-performance floating-point processor. However, important differences separate the Intel and NexGen approaches to these and other features.

As with the Pentium, the NexGen 586 is a superscalar chip. Instead of a single integer unit like Intel chips before the Pentium, the NexGen 586 has twin 32-bit integer units, each capable of processing separately and simultaneously. Each NexGen integer unit can process an instruction in a single clock cycle, giving the chip the ability to handle up to two instructions per clock. NexGen claims that its method of dividing processing chores between the two integer units is superior to Intel's, so it can squeeze more speed from its twin design. This advantage is also a drawback because it may be incompatible with the software compile to take advantage of the Intel superscalar design.

Where the Pentium has a total of 16K of internal cache divided equally between program instructions and data, the NexGen 586 offers separate instruction and data caches of 16K *each*. As with the Pentium, the cache of the NexGen is four-way set associative with full write-back capabilities. In addition, the NexGen 586 incorporates its own secondary cache controller on the chip itself. Not only does this integral cache controller eliminate the need for an external chip, it allows the secondary cache circuitry to be more tightly coupled with the rest of the chip. The integral cache controller operates at full chip speed without the need for critical component layout on the system board.

As with the Pentium, the NexGen 586 incorporates dual pipelines (for its twin integer units) with branch prediction logic. The NexGen chips, however, use a branch prediction algorithm that attempts *speculative execution*. The on-chip logic not only guesses at which branch a program will take, but it also follows that branch's stream of instructions. If it encounters a second branch, it attempts to predict the course the program will take at that juncture and continues to go forward until it encounters a third branch (before resolving the actual path taken on the first branch). When the predictions are successful, the NexGen 586 can race through a many-branched program without the need to flush its cache at each turn. Of course, as with any branch prediction, should the prognostication be in error, all the work done in preparing for the branch not taken will be wasted.

As with the Pentium, the NexGen 586 uses a full 64-bit data bus to allow its twin 32-bit integer units to fill with external data simultaneously. But where the Pentium has one 64-bit external bus, the NexGen 586 has three. One bus connects conventionally to main memory and is used for ordinary data transfers. A second 64-bit bus links the NexGen chip's integral secondary cache controller with external cache memory. A third 64-bit bus provides a link with the NexGen chip's optional external floating-point.

NexGen includes a floating-point processor in its 586 system, but unlike Intel, NexGen makes the circuitry optional. In other words, the NexGen 586 lacks an internal floating-point unit, but its architecture allows an external chip to be tightly integrated to the rest of the chip by using one of the 586's high-speed 64-bit buses. The floating-point chip itself is a thoroughly modern, high-speed design that NexGen puts on par with Intel's fourth-generation Pentium floating-point processor.

The most noteworthy part of the NexGen 586 is not its Intel compatibility but how it achieves that compatibility. The 586 makes no pretenses of copying Intel's complex hardware and microcode; instead, it uses a powerful design based on Reduced Instruction Set Computer (RISC) principles. The core logic of the 586 is optimized for handling instructions and data of a single size. Of course, the rich Intel instruction set includes instructions of a variety of lengths. To cope with the differences, the 586 has a special hardware section called a *Decoder/Scheduler*. Essentially a hardware chip emulator, this circuit first decodes the Intel instruction to determine which RISC instructions correspond to it. Then it schedules which RISC instruction will run on each of the chip's integer units (and floating-point unit, should one be installed). Besides performance, this design offers several benefits. The Decoder/Scheduler determines compatibility, so designers can tinker with the integer units without worrying about causing problems when running software. Because the integer units use the latest RISC designs, as RISC core logic improves, so will the potential of the 586.

Motorola CISC Chips

The only other major CISC microprocessor architecture chosen for building personal computers was the 68000-series of chips from Motorola Corporation, which were chosen by Apple Computer for its Macintosh machines. These chips are not compatible with software written for chips that use the Intel architecture. Table 3.3 summarizes the Motorola family.

TABLE 3.3. Motorola 68000 Family Microprocessor Timeline

Chip	Intro-duction Year	Register Width (Largest in bits)	Bus Interface Width (bits)	Memory Bus Width (bits)	Integral Floating Point Unit	Memory Manage-ment	Caching
68000	1979	32	16	24	No	None	
68010	1982	32	16	24	No	External MMU	3 Instructions
68020	1984	32	32	32	No	External MMU	256 bytes
68030	1987	32	32	32	No	Integral MMU	2X 256 bytes
68040	1989	32	32	32	Yes	2X Integral MMUs	2X 4Kbytes

68000

At the time of the induction of the Mac (January 1984) the original 68000 chip was as much advanced over Intel chips as the original 8088 was over the Z80. It boasted of being a 32-bit chip in the world of 16-bit machines, although the claim was as dubious as the one made by IBM for the "16-bit" 8088. Indeed, the 68000 boasted 32-bit internal construction, but used a

16-bit data bus. Inside, it offered a total of 17 32-bit general-purpose registers in addition to a 32-bit program counter and 16-bit status register. The 68000 also featured a 24-bit address bus that could direct access 16M of RAM.

Although the 68000 might seem an heir to Motorola's earlier 6800 series of 8-bit chips, its designers chose not to burden the 68000 with the heavy load of full backward compatibility as Intel's engineers had done. As a result, the 68000 avoids such handicaps as the segmented memory of the 8088 and multiple operating modes of the 286. Instead, it features two states, user state and supervisor state. The difference between the two states is that a few instructions act only in the supervisor state. This restriction on user state instructions is designed for multiuser environments to prevent the programs from using memory assigned to another program or from otherwise interfering with concurrent programs or the operating system.

The 68000 was first introduced in 1979. In personal computers, it found its primary application in the original Macintosh, Mac Plus, and Mac SE computers.

68010

In 1982, Motorola updated the 68000 to the 68010 by adding virtual memory support using an external memory management unit (MMU) chip. In addition, the 68010 introduced a special "loop mode," which was, effectively, a three instruction cache that enabled the chip to execute a three-instruction loop repeatedly without the need to reread the instructions from memory. This mode can substantially accelerate small subroutines, such as those to move a string of bytes from one memory location to another. For the most part, however, the 68010 did not improve on the 68000 and was not used in any memorable personal computer systems.

68020

The first true 32-bit chip in the Motorola family was the 68020, introduced in 1984. Internally, the 68020 featured 16 32-bit general-purpose registers, five special-purpose control registers, a 32-bit program counter, and a 16-bit status register. The chip connects with external circuitry through a full 32-bit data bus that makes allowances for narrower 8- or 16-bit transfers using a facility Motorola calls "dynamic bus sizing." Instead of loop mode, the 68020 uses a true dedicated instruction cache. Its 256 bytes hold up to 64 full 32-bit instructions. The instruction cache is direct-mapped.

The 68020 can directly access up to 4 gigabytes of RAM using its 32 address lines. An external memory management unit, Motorola's 68851, gives the 68020 virtual memory capabilities. That is, it can then translate physical addresses into different logical addresses. It enables page sizes from 256 bytes to 32K and provides for a variety of page table formats. A floating-point processor, the Motorola 68881, also links to the 68020 to provide full IEEE 754 support. The commands for the 68881's eight 80-bit internal floating-point registers are a superset of the IEEE standard and enable direct execution of trigonometric and transcendental functions. The 68881 was superseded by a compatible chip with improved performance, the 68882 floating-point unit.

The 68020 found its first application in the Apple Macintosh II series of personal computers.

68030

In 1987, Motorola released the 68030. Built on the full 32-bit foundation of the 68020, the new chip incorporated demand-page memory management into the chip itself. The MMU enables the same wide range of page sizes as the external 68851 MMU chip, but a few of its rarely used features were dropped. In addition, a second cache, a 256-byte direct-mapped data cache, was added. The data cache was a write-through design that only accelerated memory read operations. To further improve data exchange with memory, the 68030 also adds a burst transfer mode that takes advantage of the features of static column, page mode, and nibble mode. The 68030 was used in later Mac II-series computers.

68040

Announced early in 1989, Motorola's 68040 appears to be that company's answer to Intel's 486. Both chips are full 32-bit designs that incorporate relatively large caches, pipelining, integral memory management, and on-chip floating-point processors. But the Motorola chip differs substantially in underlying technology.

The cache on the 68040 is divided into separate instruction and data caches like that of the 68030. Each cache has 4K capacity and features a four-way set associative organization. As with the 486, the 68040 supports a demand-paged, virtual memory environment, but the Motorola chip effectively operates with two internal memory management units, one for data and one for instructions so that simultaneous accesses of data and instructions from the separate on-board caches do not interfere with one another.

To further accelerate performance, the 68040 uses a six-stage pipeline for integer operations and a three-stage pipeline for floating-point operations. The integral floating-point unit differs from Motorola's external units in that it lacks the extended support for trigonometric and transcendental functions. By reallocating the circuitry in the chip to handle fundamental operations, Motorola was able to speed up some operations to nearly 14 times the speed of the external floating-point chips. Nevertheless, the 68040 floating-point unit conforms to the IEEE 754 standard.

Apple's Macintosh Quadra computers use Motorola 68040 microprocessors.

After the introduction of the 68040, Motorola continued to work on enhancements to this microprocessor family. In light of the advancements made by RISC technology, however, Motorola decided its CISC family was a dead end, and it discontinued development. In the meantime, the company had developed its own RISC chip, the 88000 series. But after lengthy development and the product's release, Motorola found it not to be competitive. Instead, in 1993, the company shifted to working with IBM and developing the PowerPC line of RISC processors.

RISC Challengers

Where once the dominance of Intel seemed unassailable, the new generation of RISC microprocessors appears posed to steal the mantel. This surprising turn of events is a result of many converging causes.

Most important is the platform independence of the latest operating systems. Once all operating systems were tied to specific hardware; today those bonds are breaking. Software engineers have learned much about operating systems in the last decade, not only what makes one better than another but also how to give a degree of platform independence. Although you still cannot expect code written expressly for one chip to work on another unrelated microprocessor, the new generation of operating systems making moving applications easier. In some cases, the conversion between platforms is merely a matter of recompiling the program, taking the same source code and running it through different compiler programs for each target microprocessor. Because data formats are maintained between platforms, data files are easily interchanged.

Of course, today's powerful operating systems sap the power of any microprocessor. The new software is only possible (or tolerable) thanks to the unbelievable performance of the new microprocessors.

Power, of course, is not enough. Power has always been available, but at a price. If you could afford a supercomputer, you could get all the computer power that technology could provide. But if your budget was insufficient to afford a personal space shuttle, you probably couldn't buy that computer horsepower for your desktop. Today, however, competition and technical development has driven down the price of microprocessor power so far that the mainframe and supercomputer industries have virtually fallen apart. Anything you want will fit on your desktop and at a fraction of the cost of a new car. In fact, most microprocessors are in the price range of a tune-up for your existing jalopy.

There's even an undercurrent of dissatisfaction with the power that is: The Microsoft/Intel PC oligopoly.

The most surprising development came in June 1994, when Intel announced a technology sharing agreement with Hewlett-Packard. The two companies decided to work together to design future microprocessors based on HP's Precision Architecture RISC system. Eventually the Intel microprocessor line would shift its design center to the HP logic core.

In effect, Intel had finally taken the step that most of the microprocessor industry had predicted: a move from its old CISC design to a new RISC engine. Intel had thrown in the towel and admitted that its long advocacy of the CISC design—seemingly against all odds—was futile. The end of Intel architecture had finally come.

Not quite. Pentium is here to stay. And the next chip after the Pentium—the P6 or 686 (depending on your code-name preference—will certainly find its way into PCs. After all, work on the next generation of microprocessor is always well under way when Intel releases a new chip. The P6 will come in late 1995 or 1996 and set yet another high standard for PC performance.

After that, Intel's own projections see the HP alliance coming into bloom—not only a new architecture but a quantum leap in performance. By the next decade, century, and millennium, personal computer performance will leap to a new level as much ahead of today's machines as PCs are ahead of ancient mainframes.

The big worry with any new architecture is software. Programs and operating systems familiar for more than a decade appear destined for demise. People familiar with the half-baked heritage of PC software with its memory problems, hardware conflicts, and primitive interface designs will leap for joy—and land in tears once they realize the investment required to replace the installed base of programs.

Emulations ease the worry. RISC chips have so much performance to spare, they can emulate the Intel environment at speeds comparable to 486 chips. The Intel/HP pairing has a unique advantage. Intel brings the know-how to put emulation in hardware. Future Intel/HP products likely will run today's software at rates many times faster than today's PCs—and their own, native-mode software so fast you'll willingly toss DOS in the trash.

Any coming change in software opens opportunities for other architectures and chip-makers. Once you're willing to sacrifice compatibility with the box of Version 1.0 of Lotus 1-2-3 you keep under your pillow at night, you have a wide choice of chips. In addition to the future outgrowth of HP's Precision Architecture, four major families of fully 64-bit RISC chips are vying for sales, and each holds hope that it will become the next industry standard. Most also have 32-bit kin that can be useful and economical on today's market.

DEC Alpha

One aspect of the design goal of the engineers at Digital Equipment Corporation is plain from the company's claim of "The Fastest Microprocessor on the Planet." The company's highly publicized Alpha microprocessor earned that epithet in the Guiness Book of Records (October

1992) with its fantastic benchmark performance and equally amazing clock speed. Forget the fractions of 100 MHz. Today, the Alpha tears along at 275 MHz and its designers hope to nearly double that.

DEC began its work on Alpha long after the other RISC players were well down the development track. At the time of its conception, industry pundits questioned the need for yet another family of RISC chips. So the DEC engineers had their challenge of making the fastest chip in the world. They started with 1.68 million transistors and a 200 MHz clock speed and built from there, releasing the first version in 1992, the 150 MHz Alpha 21064.

Of course, there's more to Alpha than just speed; and there's less to its speed than the benchmarks would have you believe.

The Alpha project at DEC rose phoenix-like from the ruins of a failed DEC microprocessor project called Prism. At the time the project began, 1989, DEC was a company in trouble. Its major products, VAX minicomputers, were aging and severely penalized by their vintage design. Alpha's charge was to change that and bring to the installed VAX user base state-of-the-art technology with good future potential. One announced design goal was to make the Alpha architecture a suitable foundation for 25 years of development.

One necessity of this approach was that Alpha had to provide a migration path for software meant to run under the VMS operating system used by most VAX computers. In addition, the Alpha was designed to run the UNIX operating system, the choice for VAXs that forego VMS as well as most RISC chips. Glaringly absent is any nod to DOS, although Alpha was one of the first chips for which Windows NT was adapted.

Benefiting from the RISC development work of other designers, Alpha incorporates most of the best features of the technology. The chip is designed with four functional units (input/output, integer unit, EPU, and branch control) and uses a seven stage pipeline. The design is superscalar and handles up to two instructions per clock cycle. It also adds register scoreboarding that tracks and coordinates when the results in one register depend on another.

To accommodate its quarter-century future, the Alpha architecture specifies a full 64-bit design, both in registers and addressing. Because existing software has little need to investigate 16 hexegabytes of RAM, initial Alpha chips have more restricted addressing capabilities, which helps minimize the complexity and power requirements of the chip.

Alpha doesn't sport just 64 address lines, however. DEC felt that the huge memory that the chip was capable of handling required error correction, and not just the main RAM but any cache RAM as well. Because charging memory with its own error-correction would have slowed the performance of part of the system already hard-pressed to keep up with the microprocessor, DEC moved error handling onto the chip itself. Fourteen additional bits for each 64-bit quad word are assigned to error-correction code, so the Alpha bus interface is actually 78 bits wide.

The Alpha thus constantly monitors the accuracy of main and cache memory and corrects errors if they are discovered. The penalty for this approach is that more bits are needed for storage: main and cache memory for the Alpha must have the full 78-bit bus width. Two more bits are used for parity checking of bus transfers.

Alpha instructions are designed for handling both 64-bit and 32-bit data. Smaller data units are handled only with an ungainly (and performance robbing) series of instructions. As a result, although the Alpha is an exemplary performer with software that works with 32 or 64 bits at a time, it stumbles in the 16-bit world. In consequence, it suffers a huge handicap in emulating DOS.

Designing for pure speed has taken its toll in other areas. High speeds means higher currents and more heat. The initial Alpha chips proved to be hot stuff, indeed—a single chip dissipating over 30 watts (even when operating at 3.3 volts!), which is three to five times as much as many Pentium and 486 microprocessors.

Moreover, the high-speed, high-current ECL bus interconnections dominate the chip, stealing space that might have otherwise been used for internal caching. Alpha is designed to link to both standard TTL and high-speed ECL logic systems using a unique (and patented) programmable timing buffer that enables the Alpha to connect with external circuits operating at one-half to one-sixteenth the rate of the chip's internal clock.

The Alpha has only 16K of on-chip cache (compared with the Viking SuperSparc chip, which is the same size but has 36K of cache). The cache is divided into an 8K instruction cache with a two-way set associative design and an 8K data cache. Although the relatively modest cache is obviously no handicap in handling floating-point benchmarks, real world multitasking may fall short of expectations based on such test results.

Hewlett-Packard Precision Architecture

The foundation for the eventual replacement of Intel's CISC architecture was laid in 1985 when Hewlett-Packard introduced its first Precision Architecture computers. Since then the company has developed and improved the hardware design, putting it to work in minicomputers and workstations. The pairing between Intel and Hewlett-Packard appears particularly appropriate because Intel's CISC chips now share many characteristics with RISC chips, and HP's Precision Architecture chips are among the most complex RISC engines.

Precision Architecture with a solid RISC foundation. In fact, many of the engineers who developed it were veterans of IBM's original RISC explorations. Precision Architecture has uniform, fixed-size instructions, consistent instruction formats (with some exceptions), a load-store design, and virtually no microcode. As with most offspring of the original IBM effort, Precision Architecture is based on 32 registers with pipelining to minimize the number of cycles needed to handle each instruction. Although the original Precision Architecture design was essentially scalar with a single instruction path through its Arithmetic-Logic Unit, new implementations include parallel ALUs. The design also boasts an integral floating-point unit that conforms to the IEEE 754 standard and supports single-, double-, and quad-precision math.

Notably different about the Precision Architecture design compared to other RISC chips is its wealth of instructions. Just listing the possible instruction formats takes about four printed pages in the HP reference manual. The variety, according to HP, results from a desire to optimize the instructions to suit the hardware rather than to make an aesthetically pleasing arrangement—function is more important than form.

In some ways, Precision Architecture tip-toes between RISC and CISC. Many of its basic instructions combine two functions in one, for example, compare-and-branch, move-and-branch, shift-and-add, multiply-and-add, and compare-and-clear. This gives the design a speed edge over other RISCs—one instruction (and cycle) can take the place of two. On the other hand, it makes the hardware design of Precision Architecture chips more complicated, particularly in coaxing maximum speed from their more complex circuitry.

One place where Precision Architecture and Intel Architecture find common ground is memory handling. Although HP avoids the term, the addressing range of Precision Architecture is essentially segmented. Memory addresses comprise two parts, a 32-bit *linear offset* and a *space identifier* (essentially a segment, although segments can overlap while spaces are disjointed) that can be either 16, 24, or 32 bits long. Eight space registers store space identifiers, so switching between spaces is as fast as changing pointers. This design permits implementations of Precision Architecture to address up to 18,446,744,073,709,500,000 bytes. Linear addresses, however, are limited to the 4 gigabyte range of the 32-bit linear offset.

Before the announcement of the technology-sharing agreement with Intel, Hewlett-Packard began pushing Precision Architecture into the PC mainstream. For example, its PA-7100LC incorporates audio and video extensions that make it into a multimedia engine. By splitting its 32-bit registers to operate separately on two 16-bit data words, an 80MHz PA-7100LC can process MPEG software in real-time to display near broadcast-quality resolution. Although capable of anchoring a true multimedia system, the chip is currently hampered by a lack of software; ordinary DOS and Windows cannot run on the chip—or on Precision Architecture in general (without emulation).

While Hewlett-Packard will undoubtedly improve and update Precision Architecture to keep its workstations competitive, the final result of the technology merger between Intel and HP likely will be very different from the HP chips of today. It may be a break between both the current Intel and HP designs, a hybrid or half-breed. The capabilities, compatibilities, and performance of such products can only be a source of speculation.

MIPS Family

If you're wary of running with RISC, MIPS should allay your fears. Its processors were used by engineers developing Window NT, so you can be sure the match is a good one. Moreover, MIPS ranks as one of the oldest commercial RISC companies. Its R2000 was the first commercially available RISC chip, and the company is now working on its fourth generation of RISC chips.

As with SPARC, MIPS is a chip designer, not a chip maker. MIPS develops the architecture and software (principally optimizing compilers) to match. Other companies manufacture the chips for MIPS or license the designs for their own products. Currently, the MIPS line up is one of the widest among RISC companies.

R2000 and R3000

The first MIPS design on the market was the R2000, a true RISC chip with 32 full 32-bit general-purpose registers. In addition, it includes a 32-bit program counter and two 32-bit registers to hold the results of multiplication and division operations. But the R2000 is more than a single processor; it's actually two tightly coupled processors in one housing. One of these is the integer unit, which incorporates the general-purpose registers. The other is a system control processor, which not only holds the control and exception registers of the chip but also functions as a memory management unit and translation look-aside buffer. The R2000 is also less than some other microprocessors. Its cache and floating-point units are not an integral part of its circuitry but are added as external components.

The central processing unit of the R2000 is designed to operate with up to four coprocessors. One of these is the integral system control processor. Another has to be an external floating-point unit. The identity and function of the other coprocessors is left to system designers.

The R2000 can address up to four gigabytes of physical memory using its 32 address lines. It can handle individual external primary instruction and data caches with 4K to 64K each, accessing each one in a single clock cycle. Its pipeline has five stages.

One of the few differences between the R2000 and R3000 is the handling of cache misses. The R2000 always reloads the cache with a data block of four bytes (one MIPS word) on a miss. The R3000 refills the cache selectably with 4, 8, 16, or 32 four-byte words.

R4000

MIPS increased the power of its designs by doubling the register size in the R4000. Although this chip follows much the same overall architecture as the R2000, all internal operation has been expanded to 64-bit operation. Its 32 general-purpose registers are all 64 bits wide, although they can also be operated in 32-bit wide mode for backward compatibility. All instructions remain 32 bits wide. A floating-point unit is integrated into the basic chip silicon.

Performance is further enhanced by a longer pipeline (a super pipeline) of eight stages. In addition, the on-chip data and instruction caches can hold 8K to 32K each. Secondary caches from 128K to 4MB are supported. Because it has 36 address lines, the R4000 can also handle more memory, up to 64 gigabytes of physical RAM.

The R4000 family also includes a low-power version for portable applications, the R4200, which nominally requires only 1.5 watts, dropping to 0.4 watts in its reduced power mode. A high performance version of the R4000, the R4400, operates at clock speeds up to 200 MHz.

R6000

The MIPS R6000 follows the basic R2000 pattern. Although truly a full 32-bit RISC processor, its bit width was increased to 36. Each of its 32 registers is 36 bits wide, not for more precise calculations but to provide four parity check bits for 32-bit computations. The address bus was also increased to 36 bits to enable the physical addressing of up to 64 gigabytes of RAM.

The R6000 pipeline has five stages. The primary data cache size is fixed at 16K, and the R6000 instruction cache can vary from 16K to 64K. This chip supports either 512K or 2M secondary caches.

TFP

MIPS's entry into the world of superscalar RISC processing is its TFP processor. Actually, the current implementation of the TFP is a two-chip package that doubles up on power for true superscalar performance. The combination has two integer units, two floating-point units, two load/store pipes, and one branch unit that can process up to four instructions per clock cycle. (The components are not divided evenly; one chip provides the integer units, the other the floating-point units.) The TFP has a five-stage pipeline that has been reorganized for more efficient operation. Primary cache memory for floating-point processing is external, with separate 16K each of internal instruction and data integer caches. It even has twin 64-bit buses for the integer and floating-point units. Each chip uses a 591-pin ceramic pin grid array with 382 signal pins. Although they operate at 3.3 volts, each of the two chips radiates about 15 watts at a clock speed of 75 MHz.

PowerPC

IBM, along with Motorola and Apple Computer, is developing the PowerPC system to operate the next generation of personal computers. Together the three companies have laid out a full family of microprocessors capable of filling any PC niche from notebook PCs through high-usage servers. Apple has used the chips as the basis of its next generation of Macintosh computers, though the PowerPC chips are not limited to making super-performance Macs.

PowerPC is an outgrowth of RISC workstation efforts that began with the Personal Computer RT in 1986, and were refined into the RISC System/6000 system. The PowerPC microprocessors are a refinement of the RS/6000 central processing unit that effectively combines several chips into one.

PowerPC chips are not code compatible with chips that use Intel architecture, although they can run DOS programs using software emulation.

PowerPC earns its name from IBM's name for the architecture, Performance Optimization With Enhanced RISC.

As with all RISC systems, the Power architecture is based on several design concepts. The compact instructions used by the microprocessors are the same bit length, and the encoding system is consistent between them. These instructions are relatively simple with a three-operand format. It uses a load/store architecture using primitive addressing modes with a large, orthogonal register file.

Power pushes RISC forward by incorporating superscalar design. Parallel instruction processing using three independent execution units permits PowerPC microprocessors to complete up to three instructions in the time of a single clock cycle. In addition, Power extends its integral handling of integer functions to floating-point numbers. PowerPC chips include dedicated instructions for floating-point math in addition to integer math, so floating-point operations that might take several (or dozens of) integral instructions can be handled with just one.

In fact, the enhanced RISC of the Power architecture pushes the chip design in the direction of CISC computing by adding compound instructions (that is, operations that take two or more standard-length instructions). These more complex instructions actually improve processing speed by reducing instruction path length.

As originally conceived, the PowerPC family was built on a foundation of four chips: the PowerPC 601; the PowerPC 603, a chip optimized for low-power, portable, and single-user systems; PowerPC 604, a faster, refined and enhanced 603 for general-purpose applications (including those involving multiple processors); and the PowerPC 620, the highest power chip designed for server and calculation-intensive applications.

PowerPC 601

The first implementation of the Power architecture in a single chip, the PowerPC 601 is a full 32-bit RISC-based microprocessor with some 64-bit attributes. It uses a 64-bit data bus connection but, for integer operations, it includes 32 full 32-bit general-purpose registers. For floating-point operations, however, the PowerPC includes 32 special 64-bit registers that are fully compliant with the IEEE-754 floating-point specification for single- and double-precision math.

The PowerPC 601 can carry out three instructions simultaneously through three separate execution units: an integer unit, a branch unit, and a floating-point unit. Most of the processing in the chip is done in the integer unit, so the single integer pipeline is the biggest performance handicap in the chip. Even so, it achieves performance on par with Intel's Pentium, which has two integer units.

To help speed up operation through its integer pipeline, the PowerPC 601 uses several advanced processing techniques including data forwarding and out-of-order execution. Data forwarding allows the chip to rapidly send the results of register updates to subsequent instructions that will execute in the same register—the results of the first instruction are passed simultaneously to the register file and the next instruction, instead of requiring multiple cycles. Out-of-order execution allows the parallel branch and floating-point pipelines to start carrying out instructions occurring later in the instruction stream before the integer unit tackles earlier instructions. The PowerPC 601 sorts through the results from the various execution units and collates them. This out-of-order execution helps keep the branch and floating-point pipelines full.

The PowerPC 601 accesses its memory through a 32-bit address bus (enabling direct connection with up to 4 gigabytes of RAM). Internally, however, the PowerPC 601 can track memory with 52-bit virtual addressing, enough for four petabytes of control—that's 4,503,599,627,370,480 bytes, *peta-* being the prefix indicating a factor of a quintillion, a thousand more than the prefeix tera- (trillion), a million times more than giga- (billion, in the United States).

To link to that memory, the PowerPC 601 uses a 32K combined instruction-and-data cache with an eight-way set associative design. The cache can operate in read-only or write-back modes or be entirely switched off. To maintain cache integrity, the PowerPC uses bus snooping. It also includes built-in secondary cache support.

A memory queue between the cache and external circuitry enables the PowerPC to stack up two entries to read or three to write. The queue connects internally to the cache through a 256-bit bus. The cache also links to the instruction queue and dispatch logic of the chip through a 256-bit bus.

The PowerPC 601 was initially offered at 50 and 66 MHz speeds. Later an 80 MHz version was added. The PowerPC 601 is designed to operate synchronously with an expansion bus running at a sub-multiple of its clock speed.

The PowerPC 601 uses 0.6 micron CMOS technology to fit 2.8 million transistors onto a chip that measures less than half an inch (10.95 mm) square. Designed to operate at 3.6 volts, the chip consumes about seven watts at 66 MHz.

PowerPC 603

For portable implementation of the Power architecture, the PowerPC 603 drops some of the features of the 601 without sacrificing its effective processing power. Like its bigger, older sibling, the 603 is a full 32-bit RISC design that includes many 64-bit attributes. External connections can be through either a 32-bit or 64-bit data bus connection. As with the 601, the 603 includes 32 general-purpose integer registers 32 bits wide and 32 floating-point registers 64 bits wide to conform with the IEEE-754 floating-point specification for single- and double-precision math.

Memory access is identical to the 601. The 603 accesses physical RAM through a 32-bit address bus, but tracks memory internally using 52-bit virtual addressing. The caching and buffering of the 603 is entirely different from the 601. The PowerPC 603 divides its cache between data and instructions, and it assigns 8K to each purpose. Both caches use a two-way set associative design, but only the data cache uses write-back technology.

The PowerPC 603 does not use a memory queue between the cache and external circuitry but, instead, directly connects its bus interface unit with the instruction and data cache through a 64-bit bus. In fact, all signals flow throughout the 603 except those between the integer unit and the load/store unit in 64-bit buses.

The PowerPC 603 is specifically designed for energy conservation and includes dynamic power management that enables unused portions of the chip to be shut down to conserve energy. Moreover, the semiconductor logic used to build the 603 is a static design that enables stopping the processor while preserving its contents.

The PowerPC 603 was initially offered at 66 and 80 MHz speeds. At its designed operating voltage of 3.3 volts and running at 66 MHz, the PowerPC 603 requires only 2.5 watts. That demand increases to 3 watts at 80 MHz.

The smaller cache and more streamlined design enable the PowerPC 603 to be implemented using only 1.6 million transistors. Its 0.5-micron technology fits them all onto a fleck of silicon measuring less than one-quarter by one-half inch (7.4 mm by 11.5 mm).

PowerPC 604

The next generation of single-user PowerPC chips is slated to be the PowerPC 604. Basically an improved version of the 601, its new design promises to more than double the processing throughput of the older chip.

To achieve that greater performance, the PowerPC 604 will be a true superscalar design. Its circuitry will include at least two integer units in addition to the branch and floating-point units included in the 601. To better link with memory, the 604 will include an enhanced cache, divided into separate data and instruction areas like that of the PowerPC 603 but on the scale of that of the 601.

PowerPC 620

The first true 64-bit member of the PowerPC family will be the PowerPC 620. Few details of the design of the 620 have been released, but IBM confirms that it will have 32 64-bit registers in its main integer unit. The chip will likely be a superscalar design with the advanced caching of the 604. It will be the chip of choice in the PowerPC family for multiprocessing in advanced workstations, workgroup servers, and supercomputers.

SPARC

Where most microprocessor architectures are based on the design of a chip, SPARC (an acronym for Scalable Processor ARChitecture) is a specification that chips are designed to meet. Although pioneered by Sun Microsystems, the SPARC specification is governed by the SPARC Architecture Committee of SPARC International, an independent consortium which tests systems for compliance with the definition of the architecture. With more than 250 members and a liberal licensing policy, SPARC is arguably the most open of microprocessor architectures. Chips can be designed from the specification without the need for reverse engineering, and at least six vendors manufacture SPARC-compatible chips. These include Fujitsu Microelectronics (SPARClite MB86932 and MB86933); LSI Logic (L64831, L64811, and L64801); AT&T (NCR NCR89C100, NCR89C105); Ross Technology (hyperSPARC CY7C625); Texas Instruments (MicroSPARC TMS390S10 and SuperSPARC TMS390); and Weitek (W8701).

Despite its independence from hardware implementation, the "scalable" part of the SPARC name refers to chip technology; specifically to the size of the smallest lines on the chip. The simple design of SPARC enables the chip design rules to be tightened easily (making the lines smaller) as fabrication technology improves. The result is a chip with finer details and more compact layout that enables faster operation. More complex microprocessor architectures require substantially more effort to shrink. As a result, SPARC can quickly take advantage of fabrication improvements to augment its speed.

SPARC architecture can trace its heritage back through the RISC family tree, but the strongest influence on its conception were the 1981 RISC and 1986 SOAR designs developed at the University of California at Berkeley. In the period from 1984 to 1987, engineers at Sun Microsystems extended the Berkeley design to be more friendly to future generations of software and to support coprocessor and multiprocessor system designs. From a collection of off-the-shelf semiconductors (a pair of Fujitsu MB86900 20K gate arrays, Weitek floating-point processors, and a 128K cache), the Sun team designed the Sun-4/200 series of workstations. The initial system, operating at 16.67 MHz, was announced on July 8, 1987. Simultaneously Sun released the design specification of the architecture.

In the initial design, the SPARC processor comprised two required parts (an integer unit and a separate floating-point unit) and an optional coprocessor. Each of these had its own set of 32-bit registers. The architecture does not specify how many registers be allocated to each of these units, only how they operate using 55 basic integer and 13 floating-point instructions. Moreover, the SPARC architecture doesn't specify cache or memory architecture, memory management units, or input/output interfaces. Third-party designers and Sun's own engineers were thus free to adapt the basic design while retaining architectural compatibility. The only hitch was that each implementation would require different software compilers to match the underlying differences. Similarly, the original SPARC design did not specify a chip package or even that the processor be a single chip. After all, the original Sun processor was a multi-chip amalgamation. The allure of the SPARC architecture was its flexibility that enabled a single family of machines to share software at the source level while products of individual manufacturers could be readily distinguished.

Perhaps the most innovative part of the SPARC design was its window register design, borrowed from the Berkeley designs. The integer unit of the SPARC system can consist of from 40 to 520 individual 32-bit registers of which only 32 are directly accessible by a program at any given time. The 32 accessible registers make up a window. Individual registers are not permanently assigned to a single window. Rather, which register is in the current window shifts with the needs of the executing program.

Eight of total integer unit registers are defined as global registers, which maintain their identity and integrity in any window. In other words, they are accessible by any window and can be altered by any window. The definition of the other registers shifts with changes in the window.

Beside the eight global registers, each window is assigned eight in registers, eight local registers, and eight out registers. Another eight registers are used as local trap-handler registers, bringing the window total to 40, the SPARC window minimum. When a program shifts from working in one window to the next window, the out registers of the first window (along with their contents) become the in registers of the next window.

The active window is tracked by a 5-bit pointer called the Current Window Pointer. This pointer can be incremented or decremented to move from the current window to the next or back to the previous window.

The shifting register window reduces the need to load registers from memory and to store register contents to memory; that is, the many shifting registers mean that SPARC needs fewer accesses to memory than would otherwise be required. According to Sun, register windows reduce the number of memory accesses from the 30 to 40 percent of executed instructions required by other RISC systems (Sun's figure) to about 20 percent with SPARC.

The SPARC floating-point unit follows the IEEE specification with 32 registers each 32 bits wide.

The SPARC integer and floating-points units are entirely independent from one another. They execute instructions separately, even simultaneously. Moreover, they do not directly communicate. Each has its own direct path to memory, although the integer unit sets the addresses used for memory loading and storing instructions for both itself and the floating-point unit. No instructions allow for shifting the contents of integer unit registers to floating-point registers. When it is not being used by a program, the floating-point unit can be disabled so that its registers don't have to be saved when switching to processes that don't use it.

The SPARC specifications have been revised several times since the initial announcement. The most recent specification is impressive, indeed, specifying a full 64-bit architecture with 64-bit virtual addressing and 64-bit integer data handling. Although previous SPARC designs have been based on traditional RISC technology (one instruction/one clock), Version 9 allows for superscalar designs. It also enables for software enhancements including advanced optimizing compilers and support for advanced operating systems with new privileged registers to simplify the access of control information. To better accommodate software written for other microprocessor families (like Intel), it also enables for Intel-style little-endian byte ordering. The new specification also enhances the SPARC instruction set by adding 64-bit integer multiply and divide instructions, load and store instructions for 128-bit "quad words," branch prediction, and conditional move instructions.

As with many other aspects of its hardware implementation, the SPARC specification does not go so far as to indicate operating speeds, so the performance of SPARC systems ranges over a wide field.

The Version 9 specification is too new, however, for the development of products. Available systems follow the Version 8 specification (with which Version 9 is generally backwardly compatible). Version 8 is a 32-bit specification.

SPARC does not run DOS, Windows, or OS/2 directly. The most popular operating system for the architecture is UNIX (which can emulate the popular PC operating systems, although with reduced performance). Consequently, its preferred language is C. Its instruction set also includes four commands that are designed to benefit operand tags for languages such as LISP and Smalltalk. FORTRAN compilers are also available.

Programming Languages

By itself, a microprocessor does nothing. It needs software, that list of instructions called a program, to make it work. But a program is more than a mere list. It is carefully organized and structured so that the computer can go through the instruction list step by step, executing each command in turn. Each builds on the previous instructions to carry out a complex function. The program is essentially a recipe for a microprocessor.

Microprocessors by themselves only react to patterns of electrical signals. Reduced to its purest form, the computer program is information that finds its final representation as the ever-changing pattern of signals applied to the pins of the microprocessor. That electrical pattern is difficult for most people to think about, so the ideas in the program are traditionally represented in a form more meaningful to human beings. That representation of instructions in human-recognizable form is called a *programming language.*

Because the programming language is a coding scheme, it need not have a one-to-one correspondence between its symbols and the computer's instructions. Just as a microprocessor instruction can have several microcode steps, a single programming language symbol can indicate multiple microprocessor instructions.

Machine Language

The most basic of all coding systems for microprocessor instructions merely documents the bit pattern of each instruction in a form that human being can see and appreciate. This is an exact representation of the instructions that the computer machine understands, so it is termed *machine language.*

The bit pattern of electrical signals in machine language can be expressed directly as a series of ones and zeros, such as 0010110. Note that this pattern directly corresponds to a binary (or base-two) number. As with any binary number, the machine language code of an instruction can be translated into other numerical systems as well. Most commonly, machine language instructions are expressed in hexadecimal form (base-16 number system). For example, the 0010110 subtraction instruction becomes 16(hex).

Assembly Language

People can and do program in machine language. But the pure numbers assigned to each instruction require more than a little getting used to. After weeks or months of machine language programming, you begin to learn which numbers do what.

For human beings, a better representation of machine language codes involves mnemonics rather than strictly numerical codes. Descriptive word fragments can be assigned to each machine language code so that 16(Hex) might translate into SUB (for subtraction). *Assembly language* takes this additional step, enabling programmers to write in more memorable symbols.

Once a program is written in assembly language, it must be converted into the machine language code understood by the microprocessor. A special program, called an *assembler* does the necessary conversion. Most assemblers do even more to make the programmer's life more manageable. For example, they enable blocks of instructions to be linked together into a block called a *subroutine,* which can later be called into action by using its name instead of repeating the same block of instructions again and again.

Most assembly language involves directly operating the microprocessor using the mnemonic equivalents of its machine language instructions. Consequently, programmers must be able to think in the same step-by-step manner as the microprocessor. Every action that the microprocessor does must be handled in its lowest terms. Assembly language is consequently known as a low-level language because programmers write at the most basic level.

High-Level Languages

Just as an assembler can convert the mnemonics and subroutines of assembly language into machine language, a computer program can go one step further, translating more human-like instructions into multiple machine language instructions that would be needed to carry them out. In effect, each language instruction becomes a subroutine in itself.

The breaking of the one-to-one correspondence between language instruction and machine language code puts this kind of programming one level of abstraction farther from the microprocessor. Such languages are called *high-level languages*. Instead of dealing with each movement of a byte of information, high-level languages enable the programmer to deal with problems such as decimal numbers, words, or graphic elements. The language program takes each of these high-level instructions and converts them into a long series of digital code microprocessor commands in machine language.

High-level languages can be classified into two types: interpreted and compiled.

An *interpreted language* is translated from human to machine form each time it is run by a program called an *interpreter*. People who need immediate gratification like interpreted programs because they can be run immediately, without intervening steps. If the computer encounters a programming error, it can be fixed, and the program can be tested again immediately. On the other hand, the computer must make its interpretation each time the program is run, performing the same act again and again. This repetition wastes the computer's time. More importantly, because the computer is doing two things at once, both executing the program and interpreting it at the same time, it runs more slowly. BASIC, an acronym for the Beginner's All-purpose Symbolic Instruction Set, is the most familiar programming language. BASIC, as an interpreted language, has been built into every personal computer IBM has made.

Using an interpreted language typically involves two steps. First, you start the language interpreter program, which gives you a new environment complete with its own system of commands and prompts, and then you execute your program. Although these two steps can be linked together at your point of view (for instance, when you start BASIC by typing the name of a program to run on your DOS command line), your PC still must run the language interpreter before it can deal with your program.

Compiled languages cut the waste of interpreted languages. A program written with a compiled language is translated from high-level symbols into machine language just once. The resulting machine language is then stored and called into action each time you run the program. The act of converting the program from English into machine language is called *compiling* the program;

to do this you use a language program called a *compiler*. The original, English-like version of the program, the words and symbols actually written by the programmer, is called the *source code*. The resulting machine language makes up the program's *object code*.

Compiling a complex program can be a long operation, taking minutes, even hours. Once the program is compiled, however, it runs quickly because the computer needs only to run the resulting machine language instructions instead of having to run a program interpreter at the same time. Most of the time, you run a compiled program directly from the DOS prompt or by clicking on an icon. The operating system loads and executes the program without further ado. Examples of compiled languages include C, COBOL, FORTRAN, and Pascal.

Because of the speed and efficiency of compiled languages, compilers have been written that convert interpreted language source code into object code that can be run like any compiled program. A BASIC compiler, for example, will produce object code that will run from the DOS prompt without the need for running the BASIC interpreter. Some languages, like Microsoft Quick BASIC, incorporate both interpreter and compiler in the same package.

When PCs were young, getting the best performance required using a low-level language. High-level languages typically include error routines and other overhead that bloats the size of programs and slows their performance. Assembly language enabled programmers to minimize the number of instructions they needed and to ensure that they were used as efficiently as possible.

Optimizing compilers do the same thing but better. By adding an extra step (or more) to the program compiling process, the optimizing compiler checks to ensure that program instructions are arranged in the most efficient order possible to take advantage of all the capabilities of a RISC microprocessor. In effect, the optimizing compiler does the work that would otherwise require the concentration of an assembly language programmer.

In the end, however, the result of using any language is the same. No matter how high the level of the programming language, no matter what you see on your computer screen, no matter what you type to make your machine do its daily work, everything the microprocessor does is reduced to a pattern of digital pulses to which it reacts in knee-jerk fashion. Not exactly smart on the level of an Albert Einstein or even the trouble-making kid next door, the microprocessor is nvertheless fast, efficient, and useful. It is the foundation of every PC.

Chapter 4
Numeric Coprocessors

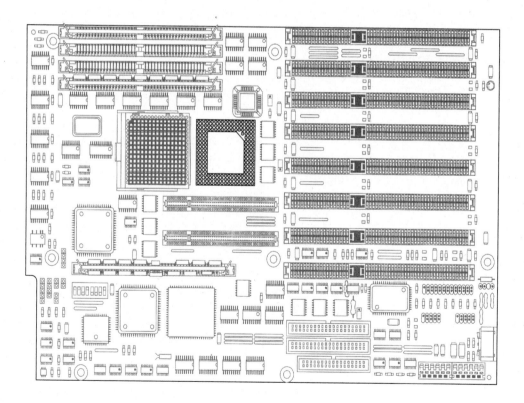

Most microprocessors are generalists designed to carry out a variety of logical operations. Adding a specialist chip called a numeric coprocessor can speed the complex mathematic operations carried out in a PC nearly a hundredfold. Each of Intel's early microprocessors had its own matching numeric coprocessor, but the latest generations of chips have integrated the coprocessor function into their silicon, making the stand-alone coprocessor obsolete.

Although the first microprocessors were designed for pocket calculators, neither they nor their immediate successors were designed to solve the most complex mathematical problems with the highest speed. By their very nature, these microprocessors were designed to handle a multitude of functions, of which complex math operations were of peripheral interest. After all, all mathematical operations can be created by judiciously manipulating simple addition—math by repeating addition ad nauseum; subtraction by looking at things backward and inverting the addition; division by inverting the multiplication, looking a long way back; and so on. Even the most complex math operations such as determining trigonometric functions or square roots can be carried out by variations on the addition theme. After all, you can build a mile-high building out of Legos if you have the mind to.

Maybe not. The problem would be time—stacking a billion or so blocks would take more waking moments than the Fates deal us. Similarly, for the microprocessor, multiplying by a million using addition alone means a million or so steps. And even at microprocessor rates, carrying out each step can take substantial time—not enough that you'll go gray—but you may feel like you are.

To accelerate numeric operations, most microprocessors incorporate more than simple addition operations in their command repertories. In the Intel family of microprocessors, no chips include *all* possible math operations. There are just too many that are used too rarely to make the added design work and complex silicon work worthwhile. As a result, general purpose Intel microprocessors can be unbearably slow at complex mathematical operations.

The *coprocessor* is a special integrated circuit that works cooperatively with your microprocessor to speed up its operation. The most familiar of coprocessors are those designed to accelerate the same high-order math operations that were left out of the command set of the general purpose microprocessor. Other coprocessors are optimized to handle other specific functions—for example, making images on your display screen. Because the coprocessor is designed for a specific purpose, it can handle its particular functions many times faster than the ordinary general purpose microprocessor. In effect, the coprocessor relieves the microprocessor from needing to handle the hard stuff.

The coming generation of RISC chips also slights on the number of instructions that they understand. Most, however, include their own floating-point units equal to the best external coprocessors. As a result, most RISC chips handle math functions substantially faster than CISC chips even without external math coprocessors. Consequently, most RISC-based systems don't need—and make no provisions for—add-on math coprocessor chips.

Even if you have a PC based on an Intel-style CISC microprocessor, the blessings brought by math coprocessors vary with the work you do. A math coprocessor can dramatically accelerate calculations—but only certain calculations. While the coprocessor chip can crunch numbers like a junkyard hydraulic ram, most of what you use your PC for, including number-intensive bookkeeping, may not benefit from a math coprocessor at all. In fact, Intel has estimated that only about 1 percent of the work performed by a typical PC involves floating-point operations.

If that's not confusing enough, the math coprocessor marketplace is quickly becoming crowded and is dying at the same time. Although once your choice of coprocessors was limited to exactly one chip that would work with your PC, today you have a choice of many from a range of vendors that at times (depending on lawsuit status) includes Cyrix Corporation, Integrated Information Technology, Intel Corporation, ULSI, and Weitek Corporation. All now offer or have offered chips that plug into one of the coprocessor sockets that are standard in nearly all PCs today.

However, Intel Corporation developed a new strategy to get rid of its competition in the lucrative coprocessor market by making the future need for coprocessors unpredictable, even entirely eliminating the need for the chips at all. First, Intel followed the RISC lead and made the coprocessor effectively obsolete by including all of its functions in the 486DX and Pentium microprocessors. But after eliminating the need for coprocessors with the 486DX, Intel brought back the coprocessor with the budget-chip 486SX and its matching 487SX math coprocessor. Then Intel again destroyed the need for a coprocessor by effectively replacing the 487SX with its OverDrive line of upgrade chips.

For PCs that can use them—which essentially limits the market to a historic one, machines with older chips from 8088 to 486SX—a modest investment in a coprocessor chip can bring immense performance improvements, or maybe not. The results you get depend on who you believe and the software that you run. For example, the benchmark tests written by the math coprocessor makers point to performance improvements of up to 100-fold by plugging in a coprocessor. On most applications, however, the benefits of a math coprocessor are about as elusive as catching a glimpse of Comet Kahoutek. Most programs that you are apt to run won't gain any extra speed at all. Even the number-crunching that most businesspeople use their PCs for—spreadsheet-based accounting—benefits little if at all from using a math coprocessor. Only computationally-intense chores like statistics, engineering, and graphics stand much to gain, and the margin of improvement a math coprocessor brings them hardly rises to the 100-fold claims of the chip manufacturers.

That's not to say that math coprocessors are over-rated or worthless. If you have a job and a PC that can take advantage of one, there's no more cost-effective power-boost you can give your system. Today, the bottom line for coprocessors is that most people don't need them, but they don't hurt anything (except if you have to pay extra for the additional silicon) and are essentially unavoidable at the high end of the market. If you don't have a coprocessor in your PC today, you will eventually, one way or another—by adding one to what you have, by buying a system based on a chip with an integral coprocessor, or by moving to RISC where the microprocessor is its own coprocessor.

Fundamentals

The concept of a coprocessor is straightforward. A coprocessor is simply something that works in cooperation with your PC's microprocessor. The goal is performance won by greater efficiency through specialization and division of labor—the electronic equivalent of a miniature Industrial Revolution. To divide the labor, the coprocessor takes charge of some particular task normally relegated to the general purpose microprocessor, relieving the main chip of some of its load. At the same time, the coprocessor is a specialist, designed to handle one particular task—and one task only—with the greatest possible efficiency. In sacrificing the need to be all things to all software, the specialist coprocessor can be trimmed down to the bare essentials required to perform its task most efficiently.

At heart, a coprocessor is a microprocessor, but unlike a general purpose microprocessor it is dedicated to its specific function as a special purpose device. Because its repertory is somewhat limited, it can concentrate on being best in its field.

As microprocessors, coprocessors work just like all other microprocessors. They simply run programs that consist of a series of instructions. Unlike the main microprocessor in a PC, however, the coprocessor may not directly control the bulk of the machine. Instead, its lifeline is through the main microprocessor, which may send the coprocessor the program instructions it requires and then carry away the results.

In normal operation, the microprocessor handles all the functions of running the computer. When, however, it encounters a task that's best handled by the coprocessor, it passes the data and instructions over and patiently awaits the answers.

Coprocessors do not share the same instruction set with the microprocessors that they complement. They have their own, special command sets. Consequently, programs must be specially written to take advantage of coprocessors. They must use the special coprocessor instructions if they want the coprocessor to do anything. Programs that are not written using the coprocessor will not benefit by its availability.

The rule is worth repeating: By itself, a coprocessor does not improve the performance of your computer. You need to run software that has been specially written to include coprocessor instructions to take advantage of the speed and power of the coprocessor. Programs that do use the coprocessor can often run many times faster, a speed on the same order of magnitude as moving from a PC to an AT or PS/2.

The coprocessor won't automatically kick in when a tough problem crops up. Moreover, not only must an application be written to use a numeric coprocessor, but also it must match a particular coprocessor. If an application does not have coprocessor instructions that match those recognized by the coprocessor, the numeric coprocessor won't do anything.

The only way to ensure that the coprocessor will be active during the execution of a specific program is to check for an explicit statement from the program's publisher to that effect. There's no easy way to tell whether the coprocessor is working other than comparing performance with and without having the chip installed.

Coprocessors have been designed for a variety of tasks, but the best known are those discussed in this chapter—the math coprocessor, which is also termed *numeric coprocessor,* or the *floating-point unit* (or *FPU*). As the name implies, these chips specialize in manipulating numbers. In particular, they are designed to handle all the complex functions that gave you nightmares while you were daydreaming in high school: long division, trigonometric functions, roots, and logarithms. These operations yield floating-point numbers, the type that math coprocessors are most adept at handling.

Floating-point describes a way of *expressing* values, not a mathematically defined type of number like integer, rational, or real number. The essence of a floating-point number is that its decimal point "floats" between a pre-defined number of significant digits rather than being fixed in place the way dollar values always have two decimal places.

Mathematically speaking, a floating-point number has three parts: a *sign,* which indicates whether the number is greater or less than zero; a *significant*—sometimes called a *mantissa*—which comprises all the digits that are mathematically meaningful; and an *exponent,* which determines the order of magnitude of the significant, essentially the location to which the decimal point floats. Think of a floating-point number as being like those represented by scientific notation. But where scientists are apt to deal in base ten—the exponents in scientific notation are powers of ten—math coprocessors think of floating-point numbers digitally in base two, all ones and zeros in powers of two.

In carrying out complex mathematic operations on floating-point numbers, the math coprocessor works much in the same way as a general purpose microprocessor. Using digital logic, it processes patterns of bits containing information (the floating-point numbers) under the control of other bit patterns making up instructions. These operations are carried out in registers, special internal memory areas inside the coprocessor.

To make a computation, the math coprocessor first loads one of the numbers that it is to work upon into one of its registers, then loads the second number into another register. Next it reads the program instruction that tells the chip what particular operation it should carry out on the two numbers. The instruction starts another miniature computer program running inside the coprocessor chip, and that program causes the circuitry of the coprocessor to actually calculate the desired answer. The entire set of programs inside the math coprocessor that respond to the various instructions that the chip understands is called its *microcode.*

Once a result has been calculated, getting the answer out of the coprocessor requires the execution of another instruction. Alternately, the next instruction can make the coprocessor carry out another operation on the results of the first.

In that general purpose microprocessors operate exactly the same way—load values, read instructions, and execute microcode—the math coprocessor can only earn a speed advantage in handling floating-point numbers by carrying out commands faster. The basic commands understood by the general purpose microprocessor are, in fact, handled with great efficiency. Instead of streamlining these common operations, most (but not all) numeric coprocessors concentrate on complex operations that would otherwise require a long series of steps. By combining all the steps into one operation that can quickly be computed, the coprocessor beats the general purpose microprocessor at the numbers game. For example, a general purpose microprocessor can compute an irrational root, but it may have to execute a loop of simple instructions hundreds of times to come up with the answer, performing hundreds of iterations of integer math. The coprocessor solves the same problem with a single instruction.

Certainly a microprocessor can be designed so that it could carry out all of the complex instructions handled by a math coprocessor. The Intel 486 microprocessor comes close to doing exactly that, appearing like a coprocessor to your programs, although having a distinct internal structure comprising a general purpose processor and special purpose floating-point unit. The coprocessor exists as a separate element for reasons tied to the history of the standardization of floating-point calculations and the technology of integrated circuits.

Addressing

To work properly with the main microprocessor in a PC, a coprocessor must share data. Somehow the microprocessor must be able to pass floating-point problems along to the coprocessor, and the coprocessor must be able to route the answers right back. Certainly the potential range for communication method is wide—from Pony Express to telepathy—but practicality (not to mention functionality) leave but two main choices: linking to the main microprocessor through a direct connection of input and output ports through which they send and receive data and instructions, and exchanging data and instructions with the main microprocessor by passing bytes through memory. The first type of coprocessor design is generally called *I/O- mapped*; the second type, *memory-mapped*. Because of fundamental differences in the way the two coprocessor designs operate, program code must be written to use one or the other technology. Most coprocessors work through one method or the other, although one coprocessor (the Cyrix EMC87) has two operating modes, one I/O-mapped, one memory-mapped.

I/O-Mapped Coprocessors

In the I/O mapped design, both the microprocessor and the coprocessor are connected to the data lines that carry information—program instructions as well as the data that they work on—inside your PC. Normally, the main microprocessor carries out all of the instructions in most computer programs. Certain instructions are recognized by the math coprocessor as its own, however, and it can carry them out directly.

In a way, the I/O-mapped math coprocessor operates as a leech, a parasite that cannot live without the microprocessor to which it clings. Only the microprocessor has circuitry to control your PC's address lines to find information. Consequently, proper operation of the coprocessor requires careful coordination of its work with that of the main microprocessor. The effort of the two chips is kept together through a direct hardware link up—wires connecting the two chips— that is electrically controlled through input/output ports. These ports are internal to the two chips and, unlike the I/O ports used by your PC's peripherals, cannot be accessed directly by you.

Both the main microprocessor and the coprocessor have their own registers (in which all calculations take place) and internal control circuitry. As a result, the two chips can operate somewhat independently and simultaneously. That is, while your math coprocessor is wrestling with a particularly difficult problem, the microprocessor can do something else.

In theory, this design could add a degree of parallel processing to your PC. In reality, it often does not. Most programs send the math chip scurrying off in search of an answer and leave the microprocessor to wait until the results are found. Only a few programs take advantage of this parallel-processing capability.

Memory-Mapped Coprocessors

To communicate with your programs and microprocessor, memory-mapped coprocessors use memory addresses as mailboxes. A small range of addresses (typically a 4K page) in far away paragraphs of your system's RAM—well above the 16 megabytes that most 386-based computers can use for physical RAM but within the four-gigabyte addressing range of the microprocessor— is cordoned off for such communications. The microprocessor pushes instructions for the coprocessor to one group of addresses and data to be worked on to other addresses. The coprocessor responds with its results in the same manner. No actual RAM chips are installed at these locations. Rather, the memory for holding the commands and data is part of the coprocessor's circuitry.

One obvious requirement of the memory-mapped design is that the coprocessor chip must have access range to the address lines used by the microprocessor. Because I/O-mapped coprocessors have no need for this address information, address lines are not available at coprocessor sockets designed for I/O-mapped chips. Memory-mapped coprocessors thus require larger sockets with more pins to accommodate all the address lines to which they need access. These special sockets for memory-mapped coprocessors are termed *EMC sockets* because they use an Extended Math Coprocessor interface.

Because of the additional address-decoding logic they require, memory-mapped coprocessors are inherently more complex than I/O-mapped chips. They are more difficult to design and make and generally more expensive than equivalent (if there is such a thing) I/O-mapped chips.

In theory, a memory-mapped coprocessor can be faster than an I/O-mapped chip because the exchange of commands and data through memory is quicker than through the I/O route. While I/O-mapped chips must move instructions and data in separate operations over several clock cycles, memory-mapped chips can acquire all the data and instruction they need in a single operation. Because address lines and data lines can be used simultaneously to move data and instructions between microprocessor and coprocessor, the memory-mapped coprocessor effectively has a 64-bit link with a 32-bit microprocessor (much as multiplexed data transfers give 32-bit Micro Channel machines a 64-bit data path).

In addition, once the information has been loaded into its memory range, the memory-mapped coprocessor is on its own. The I/O-mapped coprocessor requires more hand-holding. The main microprocessor first must read the instruction for the coprocessor, then poke the data into the proper port to get it to the coprocessor.

The big disadvantage of the memory-mapped coprocessor is that the interface has not been standardized. Each memory-mapped coprocessor has its own commands and uses its own distinct address range. In order to take advantage of the coprocessor, programs must know these secrets so that each memory-mapped math coprocessor requires its own version of a particular application. Few programs actually have such built-in support.

Intel Architecture

All coprocessors made by Intel Corporation and those from other manufacturers aimed to be compatible—that is, the chips designed to work with Intel's microprocessors from the 8088 up to the 486SX—share a number of common characteristics. All use the I/O-mapped design. More importantly, in conformance with the IEEE floating specification, all work with 80-bit registers, leaving the 8-, 16-, 32-, and 64-bit registers of Intel's microprocessors far behind.

Eighty bits seems somewhat arbitrary in a computer world that's based on powers of two and a steady doubling of register size from 8 to 16 to 32 to 64 bits. But 80-bit registers are exactly the right size to accommodate 64 bits of significance with 15 bits left over to hold an exponent value and an extra bit for the sign of the number held in the register.

The registers in Intel coprocessors (and the coprocessor circuits of the latest microprocessors) are not limited to this single data format, however. They can calculate on 32-, 64-, or 80- bit floating-point numbers, 32- or 64-bit integers, and 18-digit Binary Coded Decimal (BCD) numbers as well. (Binary Coded Decimal numbers simply use a specific four-bit digital code to represent each of the decimal digits between zero and nine.) Figure 4.1 shows the formats of the different number types supported under the IEEE specification.

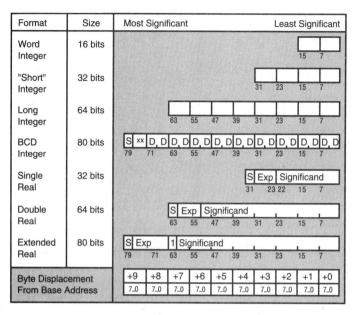

Figure 4.1. Number types supported under the IEEE specification.

Each Intel chip has eight of these 80-bit registers in which to perform its calculations. Instructions in your programs tell the math chip what format of numbers to work on and how. The only real difference is the form in which the math chip delivers its results to the microprocessor when it's done. All calculations are carried out using the full 80-bits of the chip's registers, unlike Intel microprocessors, which can independently manipulate their registers in byte-wide pieces.

The eight 80-bit registers in an Intel coprocessor also differ from those in a microprocessor in the way they are addressed. Commands for individual microprocessor registers are directly routed to the appropriate register as if sent by a switchboard. Coprocessor registers are arranged in a stack, sort of an elevator system. Values are pushed onto the stack, and with each new number the old one goes down one level. Stack machines are generally regarded as lean and mean computers. Their design is austere and streamlined, which helps them run more quickly.

Numeric History

In the mid-1970s there were no math coprocessors as they are known today. Nor were there any microprocessors. The only computers were mainframes and minicomputers. All of them were floating-point operations. Oddly enough, however, all the different computers in the world came up with different answers when challenged by complex calculations. Not that they added two and two and deduced random numbers. Rather, when they calculated irrational numbers and rounded the values to something that could be stored and expressed in something less intractable than an infinite series of digits, the last few decimal places varied depending on what make and model of computer did the thinking.

The core of the problem was, of course, that irrational numbers can only be approximated by the finite set of digits in our numerical system. Every computer and software-designer PC had his own preferred means of dealing with the challenge of irrationality—rounding up or down at one or another decimal place in whatever numeric base was handiest—binary, octal, decimal, or whatever.

Of course, scientists weren't really thrilled to have the results of their calculations vary with the hardware on which they were computed. Before they became as irrational as their numbers, the Institute of Electrical and Electronic Engineers (the IEEE) formed an industry committee to develop standards for floating-point calculations.

At the same time scientists and engineers were trying to approach numbers more rationally, Intel was taking a more irrational approach to the design of its microprocessors. It already had created the successful 8080 and 8085 chips and was working on successors. As part of the development of its next generation of chips, the company decided to create a hardware implementation of the IEEE floating-point standard to handle the irrationalities. The new microprocessor would become the 8086, the immediate predecessor of the 8088 that served as the foundation of the IBM PC.

The decision had little to do with making PC programs run faster. At the time, only a few hobbyists were dabbling with desktop machines. But Intel foresaw advanced floating-point capabilities as being useful in robotic and numeric control applications, considered one of the brightest markets for microprocessors back then.

From a marketing viewpoint, a microprocessor with elaborate floating-point capabilities seemed a good bet, but integrated circuit technology pushed the odds in the other direction. When the 8086 microprocessor was being developed in the years before its introduction in 1978, creating an integrated circuit was a much more exotic process than it is today. The technology was still primitive, and the size and number of components that could be grown and etched onto a wafer of silicon limited the complexity of possible (or at least affordable) integrated circuits. At the time, microprocessors were the most complex circuits ever designed.

The larger the chip, the more likely it was (and is) to contain some defect that would make it unusable. On the other hand, technology constrained how small the details of the chip design could be. If layouts were too small, they were more likely to suffer manufacturing defects, again making the chip unusable. For example, the smallest possible details in the 8086 microprocessor measured five to ten microns across. (Today some chips are made with details one-tenth that width.)

Together these two limits conspired to put an effective lid on the complexity of a given circuit at a given level of technical development. The 8086 by itself pressed hard against those limits.

Making the chip even more complex was out of the question even for the potentially lucrative market of digitally controlled electronic milling machines, and probably unnecessary. Other chips made do without the need for dedicated floating-point units. There were no coprocessors for the 8080 and Z80 chips that were popular in the rudimentary desktop computers available at the time. Even the 4004, designed to be the heart of the handheld calculator, lacked advanced floating-point capabilities. Most computer applications back then just didn't need a floating-point processor that followed the evolving IEEE standard.

The 8087

As a result of these very practical—if not rational—issues, Intel chose not to include advanced math functions in the silicon of the 8086 chip. Instead, the eminently useful and marketable math functions were relegated to a separate element, which eventually was produced as a commercial product in 1980—the 8087 math coprocessor.

The two-year lag between the introduction of the 8086 and its companion coprocessor arose from technical rather than marketing issues. The 8087 was just hard to design. According to Intel, when the 8087 was introduced, it was the most complex large-scale integrated circuit ever commercially manufactured.

Despite its complexity, the 8087 was not self-sufficient. It could only function in conjunction with an 8086 in a tightly bound symbiotic relationship. To simplify the too complex circuitry of the 8087, the chip's engineers took advantage of the interfacing and control circuitry built into the 8086. The main microprocessor reads and writes all program instructions from memory. When it encounters a numeric coprocessor instruction, it simply passes it along to the 8087. The 8086 also tells the 8087 what data it needs to act upon, but the 8087 has its own bus connections to reach out and get what it needs. When the 8087 comes up with an answer, it passes the results back to the 8086. The microprocessor then can fit results back into the program.

The twin-chip approach to floating-point coprocessing has one big advantage—the 8087 can be paired with other microprocessors without the need to redesign the silicon. Intel wisely crafted the 8087 to complement the entire family of 8086-derived microprocessors. These include the 8088 used in PCs and XTs as well as the 80186 and 80188.

The 8087 fits into a 40-pin DIP socket that provides the chip with the same addressing and data handling capabilities of the chips it was built to match. While it can accept data from a 16-bit bus, it also works without modification with the eight-bit bus of the 8088, automatically adapting itself as necessary. The 8087 ordinarily shares the same clock frequency with its microprocessor cohort and operates at the same speed.

Three versions of the 8087 (differing by speed rating) have been made. The original chip, the plain *8087*, was designed to operate at system clock speeds up to five megahertz; the *8087-2* operates at speeds up to eight megahertz; and the *8087-1* operates at up to ten megahertz.

Other than the rated speed, there is little difference between these chips. They understand the same commands and run the same software. The faster chips just produce results faster *in a faster computer.* Although a higher speed 8087 works at a clock rate slower than its rating, there is no advantage to doing so. The speed of the system clock determines how fast the chip calculates. The rating of the chip only determines how fast a system the chip can work in.

All IBM PCs, XTs, 8086-based PS/2s, and nearly all compatible computers have sockets designed to accommodate the 8087. The IBM PC and XT line need nothing more exotic than the ordinary 8087. PS/2s and higher speed (so-called Turbo XT) compatibles generally require the 8087-2.

The 80287

In the original design of the 8087, Intel had the foresight to divide the chip's circuitry into two functional elements: a *bus interface unit* and the actual *floating-point unit.* The former links the chip to the rest of the system in which it is installed (the microprocessor in particular) and the latter performs the heavy-duty calculations. As a result, the math side of the 8087 could easily be adapted to match other microprocessors and environments by modifying only the bus interface. After all, that was the whole point of the IEEE floating-point standard. The form, function, and answers derived by the 8087 are defined by the standard, so they don't vary with the microprocessor or the computer built around it.

Intel took advantage of the split design of the 8087 to develop its next floating-point processor effort, the *80287.* As introduced in 1985, the original 80287 took advantage of the floating-point section of the 8087 and coupled it with new interface logic to match the Intel's 80286 microprocessor chip. In the translation, however, some modifications were made to the floating-point unit to reflect changes in the nascent IEEE standard.

As with the 8087, the bus control logic of the 80287 is designed to link to an 80826 and rely on the microprocessor host for system support. The 8087 itself won't work with the 80286 because of the wider address bus used by the newer microprocessor. In fact, the 80287 mates more tightly with the 80286 than its predecessor did with its microprocessor. The 80287 doesn't even have access to the address lines of the computer in which it is installed. All of its memory-related operations must be handled by the main 80286 microprocessor.

This addressless design allows the 80287 to deal with both the real and protected modes of the 80286 processor and enables the 80287 to address the full 16 megabyte range of that microprocessor. The 8087 operates only in real mode.

As with the 8087, the 80287 is packaged in a 40-pin DIP socket, but it obviously is not pin-for-pin compatible with the 8087 (see fig. 4.2). Moreover, the 80287 is designed to operate asynchronously while the 8087 normally is locked to the same clock that drives its host microprocessor. As a result, the 80287 does not necessarily operate at the same speed as its host microprocessor. The two chips—microprocessor and coprocessor—know how to adjust their operations, waiting as necessary, to match their data transfer cycles.

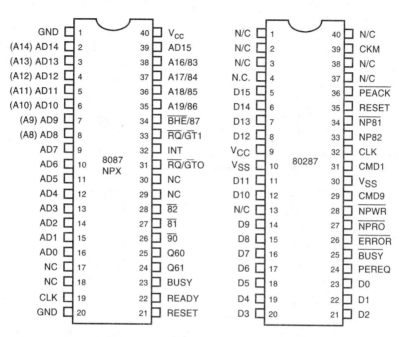

Figure 4.2. A comparison of the pin-out of the 8087 and 80287.

Ordinarily, the 80287 is connected with the same oscillator that runs the rest of an 80286-based PC. An internal divider, however, slows down the clock frequency entering the 80287 to one-third its original speed before it reaches the floating-point circuitry. An 80287, therefore, operates at one-third the clock speed that is presented to it. In most 80286-based systems, the clock that runs the microprocessor is divided in half before being connected to the 80286. Typically, the original double-speed clock is connected to the 80287 so that the coprocessor effectively operates at two-thirds the microprocessor speed. For example, in an eight megahertz IBM AT the 80287 coprocessor runs at 5.33Mhz.

Because the 80287 operates asynchronously, there's no need for its clock to be a multiple or submultiple of the microprocessor clock. In fact, some PCs give their 80287s their own dedicated clocks, allowing the engineers designing these systems to operate the coprocessors at whatever speed they want. By using a dedicated clock, they can boost the data throughput of their 80287s substantially (providing, of course, the chips can handle the racy speeds the engineers design in).

The 80287 is also compatible with the 80386 microprocessor. The 80287, however, is not capable of operating at the same speeds as the 80386 and requires special interface designs to match it to the data bus used by the 80386. Moreover, because the 80287 is essentially a 16-bit chip, all communications between it and a host 80386 must be handled in 16-bit words, a potential (but not substantial) performance roadblock.

At various times Intel has offered 80287 chips with four different speed ratings, none of which are obsolete. All four have been replaced by two new coprocessors, the 287XL and 287XLT, which are based on a new floating-point unit design first implemented in the second generation of 387 coprocessors. Both of these chips are designed to operate at speeds up to 12.5MHz. The 287XL plugs into any socket designed to accommodate an ordinary 287 chip no matter the speed. The 287XLT is specifically designed for low-power applications and is not socket-compatible with other 287s. It fits a PLCC (Plastic Leadless Chip Carrier) socket, while the XL is compatible with the 40-pin DIP sockets used by earlier 80287 implementations.

The obsolete 80287 chips can be distinguished by their speed rating designations. The plain *80287* or *80287-3* operates at up to five megahertz; the *80287-6* runs at up to six megahertz; the *80287-8* runs at up to eight megahertz; and the *80287-10* goes all the way to ten megahertz. The four chips can be used interchangeably as long as the clock rate supplied to them is within their operating range. There is no advantage to using a chip rated faster than the clock when a slower 80287 will work—and the prices for quicker chips tend toward the stratosphere.

Note that no Intel 80287 is rated to operate faster than the 12.5MHz 286XL and XLT. Other companies, however, offer higher speed clones of the 80287 capable of speeds up to 20MHz (providing the computer host can supply the necessary clock signal to its coprocessor socket). These chips are identified by their manufacturers' part numbers, which contain the designation "287" and end with the speed rating "-20."

The Intel bus control logic design of the 80287 that makes the coprocessor rely on its microprocessor host for addressing information means that the 80287 is not limited by the 16-megabyte memory-handling capabilities of the 80286. The versatile design allows the 80287 to operate with 386 microprocessors, and for two years it was the official Intel coprocessor for the 386.

But the 80286 had shortcomings in the 386 environment. The 80286 was designed with a 16-bit interface, while the 386 was capable of 32-bit operations. The 386 host had to translate wide data down to narrow size to slide it into the 80287. Moreover, the 80287 had been left behind by the still-evolving IEEE floating-point standard. In fact, only after the 80287 was in production was the IEEE floating-point standard finally put into its final form, now known as *ANSI/IEEE 754-1985*. In some subtle ways, the 80287 and the finalized standard were at variance. Consequently, the 80287 is not the ideal math coprocessor, particularly for 386-based PCs. Nevertheless, a slow 80287 is faster on floating-point operations than a 386 by itself, so even a lowly 80287 can be a worthy addition to a PC that can accommodate one.

The 387

When Intel began to design a coprocessor to match the 386, the old 8087 design was beginning to look long in the tooth. Not only had the venerable floating-point unit not kept up with the mutating IEEE proto-standard, it had not kept up with modern semiconductor design technology. Consequently, Intel decided to revamp the entire chip—bus-control logic and floating-point unit—when developing a matching coprocessor addition for the 386 microprocessor.

Intel put a design team to work on the 387 in Israel in parallel with its U.S.-based 386 design effort. The math coprocessor proved a bigger challenge than was anticipated, however, and the 387 lagged behind the introduction of the 386 by about two years. Meanwhile, the venerable 80287 served as the arithmetic assistant to the 386.

When the new floating-point unit design was introduced, it not only implemented final IEEE standards but also proved faster than the old 8087/80287 floating-point unit by a factor of about five. After its introduction in 1987 as part of the 387 math coprocessor, the new floating-point unit became the foundation of all later Intel math coprocessors. It also serves as the foundation of the 387SX and the newest revisions of the 80287, the 287XL and 287XLT coprocessors. Much of its design is also carried over into the 486 microprocessor's floating-point section.

The 387 has a similar degree of backward compatibility with the 80287 as the 80287 does with the 8087. The primary differences appear in error handling, mostly because of changes in the IEEE standard. These differences are easily managed by properly written software. On some problems the 387 or 387SX may, in fact, deliver slightly different answers than would an 80287—not to the extent of adding two and two and getting twenty-two but deriving transcendental functions that may differ in the far right decimal place. Not that either microprocessor is wrong; the 387 and 387SX just conform better to the current IEEE standard.

Another change Intel made in updating the floating-point units of the 387 was endowing the chip with a greater range of transcendental functions, including sine, cosine, tangent, arctangent, and logarithmic functions. As a result, while the 387 and 387SX should be able to run all programs written for the 80287, the reverse is not necessarily true. Programs that take advantage of all the power of the 387 or 387SX may not run on the lesser chip. In general, however, code meant for the 8087 and 80287 will run on either the 387 or 387SX.

Although it can operate asynchronously, a 387 generally operates at the same speed as the 386 it is installed with. Available versions have tracked the speed of the 386 as that microprocessor has become available in faster versions, all the way up to 33 megahertz.

The 387 even looks like an 386, only smaller. Its square 68-pin Pin Grid Array (PGA) case has the same slate-like appearance as the microprocessor (see fig. 4.3). The speed rating of the chip is given in megahertz following the part number. A 387-20, therefore, is rated to operate at 20 megahertz.

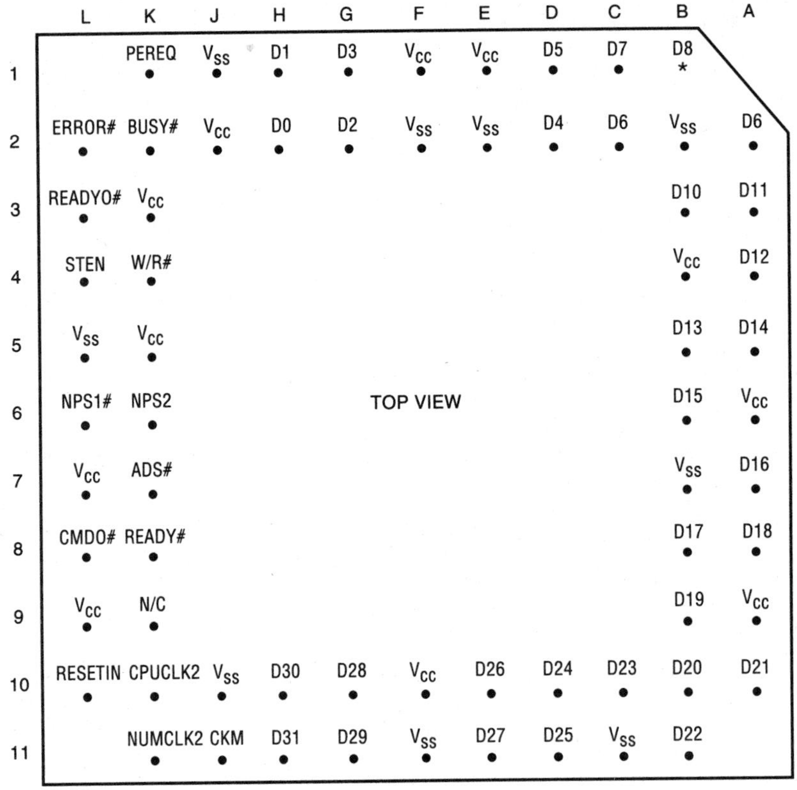

	L	K	J	H	G	F	E	D	C	B	A
1		PEREQ	V_{SS}	D1	D3	V_{CC}	V_{CC}	D5	D7	D8 ★	
2	ERROR#	BUSY#	V_{CC}	D0	D2	V_{SS}	V_{SS}	D4	D6	V_{SS}	D6
3	READYO#	V_{CC}								D10	D11
4	STEN	W/R#								V_{CC}	D12
5	V_{SS}	V_{CC}								D13	D14
6	NPS1#	NPS2				TOP VIEW				D15	V_{CC}
7	V_{CC}	ADS#								V_{SS}	D16
8	CMDO#	READY#								D17	D18
9	V_{CC}	N/C								D19	V_{CC}
10	RESETIN	CPUCLK2	V_{SS}	D30	D28	V_{CC}	D26	D24	D23	D20	D21
11		NUMCLK2	CKM	D31	D29	V_{SS}	D27	D25	V_{SS}	D22	

Figure 4.3. 387DX NPX pin configuration.

The 387 design has not been static. When it became necessary to boost the 387 to 33 MHz, further design improvements proved essential. Intel switched from N-channel Metal Oxide Semiconductor (NMOS) technology to Complementary Metal Oxide Semiconductor (CMOS) and used new manufacturing processes that allowed details as fine as one micron to be etched in the chip's silicon. (Older 387s were limited to 1.5 micron details.) These improvements, along with some tinkering in the floating-point unit itself, yielded a performance improvement of about 20 percent. The same basic design is used for 50MHz chips.

On October 1, 1990, Intel upgraded its 16, 20, and 25MHz versions of the 387 chip to the same new technology used by the 33MHz and faster versions, giving each an extra 20 percent performance. The new chips are socket-compatible with the old and are essentially identical in appearance. The only way you can distinguish old technology 387s from new technology chips is by the numeric code under the part number. Old 387s always begin this line of ten numbers with the letter "S." New technology chips lack the "S."

The 387SX, a math coprocessor complement for the 386SX microprocessor, was introduced in January 1990 with this technology as well. Essentially, the 387SX is the same chip as the 387DX but was redesigned with a modified bus-interface unit to work with the 16-bit bus of the 386SX instead of a full 32-bit data bus. Intel offers versions of the 387SX to match all of its 386SX microprocessors, including speed ratings of 16, 20, and 25MHz.

487SX

The design of the original 486 microprocessor entirely eliminated the need for an external floating-point coprocessor. Intel simply put floating-point circuitry inside the main microprocessor (using the latest, fastest 387 design). Not only does the internal coprocessor design save a package (and eliminate the vagaries of one set of connections), but it also streamlines the communications between the main processor and coprocessor. With no external circuits to traverse, chip engineers can design an optimum transfer path operating at whatever width and speed yields the best match. Advances in chip design and fabrication technology made the more complex design possible with acceptable yields.

But not all computer chores require the power of a floating-point coprocessor. Although advancing technology allowed the incorporation of coprocessor circuitry along with the main microprocessor on the same slab of silicon, the combination was still more expensive to make than the general-purpose processor alone. Eliminating the coprocessor circuitry would yield the manufacturer a less expensive 486. In effect, the 486 without a coprocessor would be a fast 386—a chip with the benefit of the more efficient processing of the 486 but without the costly baggage of an unnecessary (for some applications) coprocessor. The 487SX was born from this idea.

Conceptually, the 487SX is a second chance. If you bought a PC based on a 486SX and later discovered that you needed coprocessor power to get the most performance from your applications, the 487SX gave you the necessary math speed. The 486SX also allowed you to buy a less-expensive 486SX and upgrade it to full 486DX power, spreading the capital cost out. Of course, Intel might have had more mundane reasons for introducing the 486SX—for example, it provided an outlet for 486DX chips with defective coprocessor units.

Whatever the reason for the existence of the 486SX-487SX pair, it labored under a handicap. One of the chief advantages of the 486DX was that it put microprocessor and coprocessor in a single package. The 486SX-487SX pairing split that design apart.

To sidestep that shortcoming, Intel developed a novel solution—the 487SX—a coprocessor that is basically a 486DX in a slightly different package. The 487SX has an extra pin (see fig. 4.4). Otherwise, all 487SX chips come in Pin Grid Array packages at speeds to match each of the 486SX microprocessors in the Intel line-up. Plugging in a 487SX automatically switches off the 486SX in a PC and substitutes the circuitry of the 487SX for all system operations. The extra pin on the 487SX handles this function—it also prevents you from substituting a 486DX for a 487SX and vice versa. Although the 486SX chip is switched off when you install a 487SX, the 487SX design requires that you leave the 486SX in your PC. This expedient brings a benefit— for Intel, at least. You can't pry out your old 486SX and drop it into another PC, potentially eliminating another microprocessor sale for Intel. Intel, however, admits that in some systems you can unplug the 486SX and drop a 487SX *in its place*. They neither recommend this procedure nor guarantee that it will work in all systems.

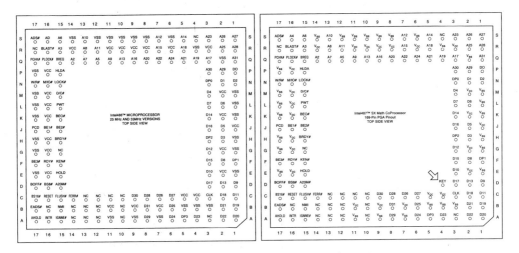

Figure 4.4. A comparison of the pin-out of the 486DX and 486SX.

Be that as it may, the 487SX has been rendered obsolete by Intel's OverDrive chips. For about the same price as the simple coprocessor function of the 487SX, an OverDrive chip brings clock-doubling *and* floating-point functions. The OverDrive is a better buy.

Strategically, the OverDrive line also gives the coprocessor competition a bigger challenge. No longer is cloning a coprocessor sufficient—the entire processor-coprocessor package must be duplicated. That's a big hurdle for the competitors to leap.

Considering the OverDrive and the poor publicity garnered by the "crippled" 486SX chip, the 487SX likely marks the end of Intel's dedicated coprocessor line. Certainly the company will manufacture coprocessors for older microprocessors as long as the market demands them (and keeps their manufacture profitable), but new floating-point units probably aren't in Intel's plans.

Pentium

The integral math coprocessor in the Pentium family of Intel microprocessors marks yet another new generation. The floating-point unit inside is totally redesigned and streamlined. The end result is the best coprocessor yet for the Intel family, able to offer up to five times the performance of the older 387-style design. In fact, the chief performance boost that the Pentium offers over the 486 family on many applications is this improvement in math speed.

The coprocessor circuitry of the Pentium remains backwardly compatible with the 387 generation of chips and complies fully with the IEEE floating-point standard. The redesign merely reflects the lessons learned in years of designing coprocessor circuitry. The new design outperforms all add-on coprocessors for the Intel family (including Weitek chips). Additional chips are simply irrelevant to the Pentium.

Third-Party Coprocessor Designs

The perfect product, according to apocryphal authorities, is one that costs a nickel to make, sells for a dollar, and is addictive. Coprocessors aren't quite addictive (although anything that improves the performance of your PC comes close), but otherwise fits the mold. Coprocessors, which at one time had list prices upwards of $1000, cost but a few dollars to make. They represented one of the most lucrative areas of the semiconductor business. Understandably, most chip-makers found crafting a successful coprocessor as alluring as a supposed sure-thing would be to an inveterate gambler.

Although Intel licensed other chip-makers to produce its microprocessor and coprocessor designs for the 80286 and 80287 families, the company has staunchly refused to license the 386 and 387. With the low cost of their production and high market prices, those chips proved immensely profitable for Intel—so profitable that a number of envious entrepreneurs invested in designing their own compatible products. Among these were Chips and Technology, Cyrix Corporation, Integrated Information Technology, and ULSI.

All of these coprocessors were designed through reverse engineering using "clean-room" techniques. That is, the designers don't pry into the exact layout of the original products but instead seek to duplicate the prototype working back from its functions. Each of the resultant clones differs significantly from the Intel design. In fact, most compatible coprocessor manufacturers claim their products are superior to the original because of more efficient designs, aided by the big benefit of hindsight.

While the clean-room technique sidesteps many copyright issues—the clone chips don't actually copy any part of the Intel design—they can run afoul of other legal protections instituted by Intel. For example, Intel Corporation holds many patents on chip fabrication, which it can choose to license or not. Withholding such a license can effectively block a company from making any chips, let alone clone coprocessors. Intel has asserted this protection to block some coprocessor manufacturers (successful, at least temporarily, against ULSI). It has also initiated suits against the other compatible coprocessor vendors, but has not prevented the sale of other clone chips. In true American tradition, the other vendors have responded with their own suits against Intel. As a result, clone coprocessors are shrouded with legal uncertainties.

Leave the complex legal maneuvering for the lawyers to worry about. If you buy a compatible coprocessor, you won't have to worry about the complexities of the law—leave the bickering to the corporations. No one will knock on your door and confiscate an unauthorized coprocessor. Rather, you should investigate all of your available options and take advantage of the one that suits you, your PC, and your budget best. You have several choices.

Chips and Technologies SuperMathDX

Chipset maker Chips and Technologies broadened its product line first by releasing Intel-compatible microprocessors in 1991, then a line of 387-compatible coprocessors in 1992. The embodiment of the latter is the company's SuperMathDX line.

Although outwardly a 387, the SuperMathDX chip uses an entirely different internal design. According to Chips and Technologies, the SuperMathDX chips can carry out some operations as much as six times faster than their Intel equivalents. Of course, this gain reflects only floating-point performance, and gain on typical applications is much smaller.

Socket-compatible with Intel's own 387-series of coprocessors, the SuperMathDX line uses the same 68-pin PGA package as the Intel chips. Compared to the Intel 387DX, however, the SuperMathDX line goes a bit further at the high end—Chips and Technologies coprocessors are available at speeds up to 40MHz.

Unique to the SuperMathDX series among today's coprocessors is on-chip power management circuitry, similar to that in laptop computer microprocessors, which reduces the power needs of the SuperMathDX chips. Typically, the chip needs about half a watt (100 milliamps at 5 volts) during operation.

The SuperMathDX series conforms to the IEEE 754-1985 floating-point specification. According to Chips and Technologies, the entire series of chips is 100 percent compatible with Intel's 387 coprocessor line-up.

Cyrix 83D87

Cyrix Corporation was founded in 1988 to design and market advanced solid-state components. After the company was formed, it decided to develop Intel-compatible math coprocessors as its first product because of the ready market in an area that was without significant competition. The first of Cyrix's FasMath series of coprocessors was introduced in October 1989 as the 83D87, a pin-compatible replacement for the Intel 387. A lower-cost version for 386SX computers, the 83S87 was introduced in March, 1990.

The Cyrix products are designed to be completely compatible with the Intel 387 family of coprocessors, although the Cyrix chips are engineered with an entirely different logic design based on the documented and undocumented functions of the Intel products. One important difference is that the Cyrix chips rely more on hard-wired logic than microcode. Because of this design alternative, Cyrix chips often can achieve substantially greater speed than Intel's chips on floating-point operations.

Hard-wired logic is exactly what it sounds like. The bit-patterns that make up commands directly trigger state-changes in the solid-state circuitry of the chip. Each pattern—each logical instruction—must be specifically designed into the hardware of the coprocessor.

In microcode designs, instructions sent to the microprocessor cause the chip to run through several steps that make up the miniature internal program. The internal program tells the more general purpose logic of the chip to carry out the function required of it.

The microcode design is the more structured approach. It gives the designer greater flexibility and can help get products to the market faster. It also allows complex instruction sets to be handled by general purpose circuits. But microcode can slow down the thinking process of the chip. Executing the microcode imposes another layer of overhead on every calculation.

On pure floating-point operations, the Cyrix chips can think nearly twice as fast as the official Intel 387 equivalents. The actual performance you get on commercial application software shows a more modest difference, however. Because of all the other operating overhead, you should expect to see only about a 10 percent difference between the Cyrix and Intel products.

Cyrix offers the 83D87 rated at any of four speeds: 20, 25, 33, and 40MHz. Designed for low power operation, it averages only about 35 milliwatts when running at 20MHz, in part because it switches into an automatic idle mode when not executing floating-point instructions.

Cyrix 83S87

For PCs equipped with 386SX microprocessors, Cyrix offers its own version of the 387SX, which it calls the *83S87*. Although externally identical to the Intel chip (and thus, it may be substituted for the 387SX in virtually any PC that calls for it), Cyrix claims several improvements over the Intel product. Using essentially the same core logic as the 83D87, the 83S87 can better the Intel chip by a factor of three on some operations. It also consumes less power, only about 5 milliamps when idling and about 40 when running at 16MHz.

Cyrix 87DLC and 87SLC

Functionally equivalent to Intel's 387-series of floating-point processors, the Cyrix 87-series consists of OEM products designed for manufacturers to install when they need a low-power (but powerful) math coprocessor. The *87SLC* takes the place of an Intel 387SX, and the *87DLC* replaces the 387DX. The chips are not pin-compatible, however, but packaged as small (14 millimeters square) surface-mount components in 80-pin quad flat packages. To achieve power economy, these Cyrix chips use a fully static CMOS design that operates at 3.3 volts.

Cyrix CX487

Although the Cyrix *CX487* was designed to complement 486SX-style processors as does Intel's 487SX, the philosophy behind the Cyrix chip differs substantially from Intel's. Where Intel provides what amounts to a second microprocessor along with the coprocessor circuitry, the CX487 is simply an add-on floating-point unit. Meant to be integrated on the system board when the board is manufactured, the CX487 fits into an 80-pin quad flat pack. Cyrix offers both 3.3 and 5 volt versions.

Cyrix EMC87

Hoping to legitimize itself as more than merely the maker of clone chips, Cyrix has attempted to vault past the inherent limitations of I/O-mapped coprocessors by marketing its own memory-mapped design, the EMC87. Although based on the same processor architecture as the 387, with eight 80-bit registers, and though it has essentially the same command set, the EMC87 has completely revamped bus control logic. Cyrix claims a fivefold performance improvement over the Intel part. Again, however, most of the difference disappears when running actual applications because of other system overhead.

Unlike other memory-mapped coprocessors, however, Cyrix has built in complete Intel 387 compatibility in the EMC87. The Cyrix chip can operate either as I/O mapped or memory-mapped, depending on the instructions given to it in your applications. With I/O mapped instructions, it operates almost exactly like an Intel 387. With memory-mapped instructions, it rushes ahead in its native mode.

Of course, getting that memory-mapped speed requires software particularly written for the EMC87. Most existing applications have only Intel 387-style I/O-mapped instructions. Moreover, the EMC87 is incompatible with code written for other memory-mapped coprocessors including the family of chips built by Weitek Corporation. Weitek and Cyrix memory-mapped chips use entirely different architectures for their floating-point units.

Because the EMC87 is memory-mapped, it requires access to all the address lines used in 386 computers. It therefore has a full complement of 121 pins and fits into the EMC socket normally reserved for a Weitek coprocessor (see fig. 4.5).

Understanding the need for the availability of software to create a demand for the chip, Cyrix offers a code converter which adapts assembly language code from I/O-mapped to memory-mapped instructions for the EMC87. This code-converter only works with assembly language files, including those produced by higher-level language compilers, such as Pascal or C. While these free code-converters may be interesting for software developers, they are of no value to you as an end user. They cannot convert commercial applications to make them compatible with the EMC87.

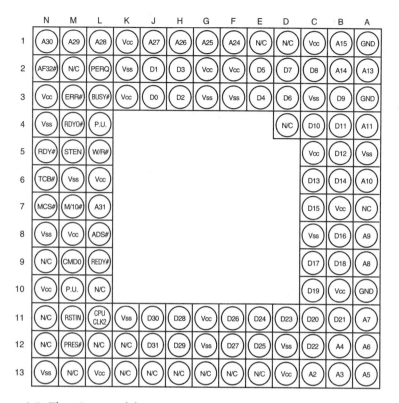

Figure 4.5. The pin-out of the Cyrix EMC87 coprocessor.

Until (and if) software publishers opt to take advantage of the EMC87, the chip will remain more a curiosity than an added enhancement. To help foster a user base, Cyrix priced the EMC87 identically with its 83D87. In that the two chips offer the same compatibility with Intel I/O-mapped instructions, the only reason to choose the 83D87 is the lack of socket accommodations in your PC for the physically larger EMC87.

IIT 3C87

At heart, Integrated Information Technology is a coprocessor company, producing both floating-point and video chips. Founded in 1988 by two engineers who left Intel to work for Weitek (one was actually a co-founder of Weitek), the company now offers chips compatible with Intel's 80287 and 387 using full CMOS designs based on 1.2 micron technology.

The IIT coprocessor design differs from the Intel original in that the IIT 3C87 has 32 80-bit registers instead of a mere eight. These registers are divided into four banks and are designed to facilitate 4 × 4 matrix math, which can accelerate drawing performance in graphics applications.

Using just one of those four banks simulates an Intel-architecture coprocessor. Using all four requires specially written programs that use the IIT 4x4 matrix instruction.

IIT claims that the 3C87 can calculate 50 percent faster than an Intel 387 in its math functions. As with the Cyrix chips, however, actual program throughput is much more modest because of system overhead.

Unlike the Cyrix chips, the IIT coprocessor doesn't exactly duplicate the operation of the Intel 387. The exception handling of the Intel and IIT chips differs, much as it does between the 80287 and 387. Some chip-makers have exploited that difference by writing special programs that show anomalous results when run on the IIT chips. With a bit of P. T. Barnum in their salesmanship, they claim that such results prove the 3C87 is inaccurate. According to IIT, however, such odd answers only crop up when you purposely try to exacerbate the exception handling differences by dividing by a near-zero number, such as 1027. On normal application software, no anomalous results should appear.

IIT acknowledges that an early iteration of its 3C87 chip did have an internal bug that resulted in errors in using its arctangent operation when running AutoCAD under Unix (and only with that application and operating system). This bug was corrected in June 1990, and the company reports that no other problems have been reported in the 100,000 chips it has shipped.

ULSI 83C87

No longer a coprocessing contender—at least temporarily—the MathCo 83C87 from ULSI was removed from the market by legal action taken by Intel Corporation. Intel claimed that ULSI violated certain of Intel's chip patents in the manufacture of the 83C87, and the court agreed, enjoining ULSI from selling its chip products in early 1992.

ULSI stands for Ultra Larges Scale Integration, the company's specialty—developing tiny products full of lots of circuitry. The MathCo 83C87 was a reverse-engineered clone of the Intel 387. According to ULSI, the products of the MathCo 83C87 line were entirely socket-compatible with the various Intel chips that they mimic.

The ULSI products used CMOS technology and a streamlined design, claiming to be more efficient than the Intel products. Each calculation performed by the MathCo 83C87 required fewer clock cycles than did the same operation on an Intel chip. For example, while an Intel chip requires 18 clock cycles to carry out a simple "add" instruction, the ULSI chip needed only three. Division, which takes an Intel chip about 80 cycles, was handled by the ULSI chips in 40. Of course these quicker calculations mean nothing if you cannot buy the chips, and the cloudy legal issues make the future of the ULSI coprocessors doubtful.

Weitek 1167

While other companies have concentrated on cloning Intel's own coprocessors, Weitek Corporation, based in Sunnyvale, California, has gone its own direction, building memory-mapped coprocessors to its own standards. Founded by former Intel employees, Weitek has a better relationship with the world's favorite microprocessor maker than the manufacturers of other clone chips. The company was formed in 1981 and by 1985 was producing floating-point coprocessors for a variety of workstations including those based on Motorola 68020 and Sun SPARC microprocessors. Around that time, Intel contracted with Weitek to develop a coprocessor for the 386 microprocessor. According to Weitek, the in-house Intel 387 program was behind schedule and Weitek developed its product in parallel with the 387 team.

Unlike the 387, however, Weitek's effort was developed from multi-platform design. The initial Weitek product for the Intel environment split the one-package coprocessor into its constituent parts, using the same floating-point chips but different bus interface chips from coprocessors created for other microprocessor architectures. The first Weitek chip, the WTL1167, was consequently not a single chip but a multiple chip assembly on a small L-shaped printed circuit board. Three Weitek proprietary VLSI modules—the 1163, 1164, and 1165—were combined to create the coprocessor.

Although odd-looking and expensive, the WTL1167 has one great strength—it delivers even higher performance than the 387 on many numeric operations, in particular, CAD. Moreover, it works on all numeric operations, not just transcendental functions. According to Weitek Corporation, the WTL1167 could deliver from three to four times the performance of a 387 in machines designed to handle it. Again, such promises are meaningless because no one runs applications that exercise the coprocessor exclusively.

The Weitek WTL1167 and its successors accelerate your PC's floating-point performance purely through inherent processor efficiency, not by using an exotic command set. In fact, the Weitek chips lack both the rich command repertory and wider register width of the Intel chips. All Weitek coprocessors use 32-bit registers optimized to handle addition, subtraction, multiplication, division, negation, absolute value, comparison testing, data movement, and format conversion functions. Transcendental functions—the 387 specialty—are available through a subroutine library.

As with Intel coprocessors, the WTL1167 and other Weitek chips rely on special instructions passed to them by their host microprocessors, although those instructions are entirely different from those used by Intel's chips. The Weitek coprocessor instructions cause the host microprocessor to address certain areas of memory, well outside the range used by DOS or OS/2 programs. The addressing action itself (the activation of certain patterns of these special address lines) tells the Weitek processor what operation to carry out.

The WTL1167 plugs into a special 121-pin socket with a pin-out that is a superset of that used by the 387 (see fig. 4.6). Thus, either a 387 or WTL1167 often can be slipped into computers that use this socket.

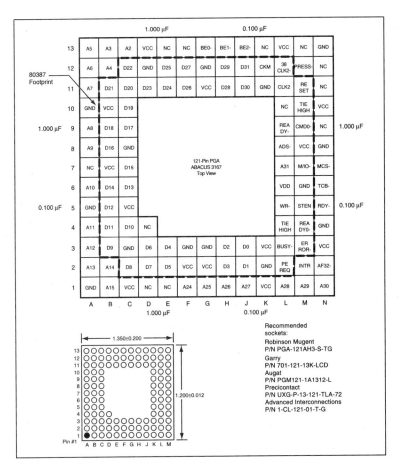

Figure 4.6. The pin-out of the Weitek 1167 coprocessor.

A socket on the WTL1167 board provides a home for the expatriated 387, allowing you to put both chips in one system to reap the benefits of both. Even when you put both chips into your PC, however, the two coprocessors do not interact or work with one another. Instead, each one runs only the code designed specifically for it.

Weitek 3167

A three-chip design is inherently more expensive to build and less reliable than a single chip. Consequently, Weitek distilled the entire three-chip WTL1167 into a single chip, the Abacus 3167, which was introduced in April 1988. With the exception of packaging, however, the 1167 and 3167 are essentially equivalent. They run the same applications and deliver the same performance.

Weitek 4167

In November 1989, Weitek announced the 4167, a math coprocessor based on the 3167 but designed to enhance the Intel 486 microprocessor. According to Weitek, the 4167 can process floating-point math three to five times faster than a 486 alone, giving a 486-based PC the same math power as a RISC-based minicomputer (see fig. 4.7).

Pin A1 identifier	1	2	3	4	5	6	7	8	9	10	11	12	13	14	15
A	X	X	VCC	GND	GND	VCC	GND	GND	VCC	GND	GND	VCC	GND	DPI	D7
B	D22	D23	D21	D19	GND	D17	DP2	GND	D14	D12	GND	D10	D8	VCC	GND
C	DP3	GND	VCC	D20	VCC	D18	D16	VCC	D15	D13	VCC	D11	D9	D6	D5
D	D24	D25	D26										VCC	GND	GND
E	D27	D28	D29										D4	D3	VCC
F	D30	GND	VCC										D2	D1	GND
G	D31	VCC	VCC										VCC	GND	GND
H	GND	GND	VCC										D0	DP0	VCC
J	RESET	PCHK-	CLK										NC	NC	GND
K	BOFF-	NC	VCC										VCC	GND	GND
L	INTR	RDY IN-	GND										NC	NC	NC
M	RDY OUT-	GND	VCC										VCC	GND	NC
N	W/R-	TCR-	MCS-	A28	VCC	A26	A14	VCC	A11	A8	VCC	A5	A2	BE1-	PRES-
P	NC	M/IO-	A30	A27	GND	A25	A13	GND	A10	A7	GND	A4	BE2-	BE0-	NC
R	ADS-	A31	A29	NC	GND	A15	A12	GND	A9	A6	GND	A3	NC	NC	GND

Center: 15X15 142-PIN PGA TOP VIEW

Figure 4.7. The pin-out of the Weitek 4167 coprocessor.

The Abacus 4167 maintains full backward compatibility (Weitek calls it "full upward object-code-compatible") with the Abacus 3167 and runs all the same applications that execute on the 3167. The Abacus 4167, however, is not hardware compatible with the 3167. The 4167 offers sixteen 32-bit registers for adventurous programmers to play with and requires a 142-pin socket.

Coprocessor Applications

On the surface, coprocessors are a compelling concept. They show substantial performance improvements on floating-point mathematical operations, their precise design goal. If your work comprised nothing but floating-point operations, you could expect a coprocessor chip to work miracles. You'd gain more speed by adding a coprocessor than from upping the speed of your system by the next increment or two.

Unfortunately no computer program—with the exception of benchmarks, tests, and demonstrations developed by coprocessor makers—consists of nothing but floating-point operations. Even most number-intensive applications make scant use of floating-point operations. Even on heavy-duty calculations, most applications only devote a fraction of their code to the actual math. They also need to devote time to processing display information, disk operations, and other house-keeping functions that are not aided by coprocessor operation. Consequently, only a fraction of the work done through any commercial application relies on the power of a coprocessor.

Some programs have less overhead than others and thus accelerate more with the addition of a coprocessor. But all applications are sensitive to the tasks you call on them to carry out. For example, a spreadsheet used as a database will gain little from a coprocessor. Put the same program to work on financial projections, however, and the coprocessor will shift into high gear. Consequently, the value of a coprocessor varies not only with the application that you run but what you do with the application.

To gain any performance improvement from a coprocessor, you must have a need for transcendental functions. Typical accounting calculations have no such requirement (unless, perhaps, you're planning for the hereafter). Engineering and scientific chores are those most likely to require transcendentals. Financial calculations that involve compound interest and the like will also take some advantage of a coprocessor.

Computer-Aided Design programs all benefit from the addition of a math coprocessor, but the advantage gained varies with the operation carried out. Loading images and screen regenerations can be handled in about half the time when a coprocessor is available. Hidden-line removal benefits only a little more than 10 percent.

No matter the application, normal data entry performance won't change at all with the addition of a math coprocessor. Nor will the speed of standard DOS operations.

Whether you need a coprocessor becomes a personal choice. If you have an application that demands floating-point work, you would be foolish not to purchase one if you want to get the most out of your existing PC. Even with a "mere" 50 percent performance improvement on spreadsheet recalculations, there's no more cost-effective speed boost you can give to your PC. But if you really need math performance, the ultimate choice is to move to a new system—either one based on the Pentium family of chips with its superb integral coprocessor, or a PC with a RISC chip that needs no extra tutoring in math.

Chapter 5
Memory

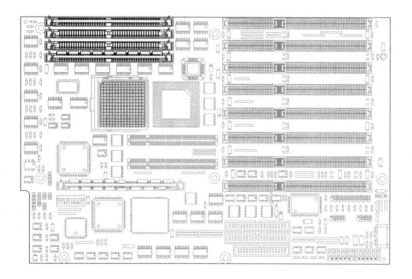

Memory is mandatory to make a microprocessor work. It's where all the bytes must be that your PC's microprocessor needs to operate. Memory holds both the raw data that needs to be processed and the results of the processing. Memory can even be a channel of communication between the microprocessor and its peripherals. Memory comes in many types, described and delimited by function and technology. Each has its role in the proper function of your PC.

The difference between genius and mere intelligence is storage. The quick-witted react fast, but the true genius can call upon memories, experiences, and knowledge to find real answers—the difference between pressing a button fast and having the insight to know which button to press.

PCs are no different. Without memory, a PC is nothing more than a switchboard. All of its reactions would have to be hard-wired in. The machine could not read through programs or retain data. It would be stuck in a persistent vegetative state, kept alive by electricity but able to react only autonomously.

A fast microprocessor is meaningless without a place instantly at hand to store programs and data for current and future use. Its internal registers can hold only a handful of bytes (and they can be slippery critters, as you know if you've tried to grab only one), hardly enough for a program that accomplishes anything truly useful. Memory puts hundreds, thousands, even millions of bytes at the microprocessor's disposal, enough to hold huge lists of program instructions or broad blocks of data. Without memory, a microprocessor is worthless even as a doorstop (most are too thin); with memory, the same chip is the herald of the information revolution.

That memory can take a variety of forms. A binary storage system, the kind used by today's PCs, can be built from marbles, marzipan, or metal-oxide semiconductors. Not all forms of memory work with equal effectiveness (as you'll soon see), but the concept is the same with all forms of memory—preserving bits of information in recognizable and usable form. Some forms of memory are just easier for an electronic microprocessor to recognize and manipulate.

The primary characteristic required by computer memory is that electricity be able to alter it. After all, today's computers think with electricity. They are made from electronic integrated circuits. Little wonder that the most practical memory for computers is also made from integrated circuits. But the memory that's available in IC form comes in a variety of ways, differing, for example, in function, accessibility, technology, capacity, and speed.

Primary and Secondary Storage

Function distinguishes what is generally termed *computer memory* from the kind of data storage kept by disks and tapes. Both normal memory and disk storage preserve information that the computer needs, but for different purposes. Normal computer memory systems function as *primary storage.* That is, they store the information in a form that is immediately accessible by the computer or microprocessor. Anything that is kept in primary storage is immediately accessible, ready to be used. This form of memory is sometimes also called *on-line* storage because it is always connected to the computer—for example, directly accessible through the address lines of a microprocessor. Because any specific part of this memory, any random byte, can be instantly found and retrieved, it often is termed *random access memory* or *RAM*.

Primary storage is, in effect, the short term memory of the computer. It's easy to get at but tends to be limited in capacity—at least compared to other kinds of storage.

Disk and tape storage, regarded as a computer's *secondary storage* system, operates as the machine's long-term memory. Not only does disk and tape memory maintain information that must be kept for a long time, but also it holds the bulk of the information that the computer deals with. Secondary storage may be tens, hundreds, or thousands of times larger than primary storage. This data is held off-line and is not directly accessible by the computer. To be used, the data must be transferred from secondary storage into primary storage. In other words, the most important aspect of primary storage is access *speed*; the most important aspect of secondary storage is *capacity*. Secondary storage often is termed *mass storage* because of its voluminous capacity: it stores a huge mass of data.

Bits and Bytes

In digital computer systems, memory operates on a very simple concept. In principal, all that computer memory needs to do is preserve a single *bit* of information so that it can later be recalled. *Bit*, an abbreviation for *binary digit*, is the smallest possible piece of information. A bit doesn't hold much intelligence—it only indicates whether something is or isn't—on or off, up or down, something (one) or nothing (zero). It's like the legal system: everything is in black and white, and there are no shades of gray (at least when the gavel comes down).

When enough bits are taken collectively, they can code meaningful information. A pattern of bits can encode more complex information. In their most elementary form, for example, five bits could store the number 5. Making the position of each bit in the code significant increases the amount of information a pattern with a given number of bits can identify. (The increase follows the exponential increase of powers of two—for n bits, 22 unique patterns can be identified.) By storing many bit patterns in duplicative memory units, any amount of information can be retained.

People don't remember the same way computers do. For us human beings, remembering a complex symbol can be as easy as storing a single bit. While two choices may be enough for a machine, we prefer a multitude of selections. Our selection of symbols is as broad as the imagination. Fortunately for typewriter makers, however, we've reserved just a few characters as the symbol set for our language—26 uppercase letters, a matching number of lowercase letters, 10 numerals, and enough punctuation marks to keep grammar teachers preoccupied for entire careers. Representing these characters in binary form makes computers wonderfully useful, so computer engineers tried to develop the most efficient bit patterns for storing the diversity of symbols we finicky humans prefer. If you add all those letters, numbers, and punctuation marks, you'll find that the lowest power of two that could code them all is 128 (or 27). Computer engineers went one better—by using an 8-bit code yielding a capacity of 256 symbols, they found that all the odd diacritical marks of foreign languages and similar nonsense (at least to English speakers) could be represented by the same code. The usefulness of this 8-bit code has made 8 bits the standard unit of computer storage, the ubiquitous byte.

Half a byte—a four-bit storage unit—is called a *nibble* because, at least in the beginning of the personal computer revolution, engineers had senses of humor. Four bits can encode 16 symbols—enough for 10 numerals and six operators (addition, subtraction, multiplication, division, exponents, and square roots), making the unit useful for numbers-only devices such as handheld calculators.

The generalized term for a package of bits is the digital *word*, which can comprise any number of bits that a computer might use as a group. The term *word* has developed a more specific meaning in the field of PCs, however, because Intel defines a word as 2 bytes of data, 16 bits. According to Intel, a *double-word* comprises 2 words, 32 bits; a *quad-word* is 4 words, 8 bytes, or 64 bits.

To remember a single bit—whether alone or as part of a nibble, byte, word, or double-word—computer memory needs only to preserve a single state—whether something is true or false, positive or negative, a binary one or zero. Almost anything can suffice to remember a single state—whether a marble is in one pile or another, whether a dab of marzipan is eaten or molding on the shelf, whether an electrical charge is present or absent. The only need is that the memory unit has two possible states and that it will maintain itself in one of those states after it is put there. If a memory element changes on its own, randomly, it would be useless because it does not preserve the information that it's supposed to keep.

While possibilities of what can be used for remembering a single state are nearly endless, how the bits are to be used makes some forms of memory more practical than others. The two states must be readily changeable and readily recognizable by whatever mechanism is to use them. A string tied around your finger will help you remember a bit state but would be inconvenient to store information for a machine, for example. Whatever the machine, it would need a mechanical hand to tie the knot and some means of detecting its presence on your finger—a video camera, precision radar set, or even a gas chromatography system.

Random Access Memory

In digital computers, it is helpful to store a state electrically so that the machine doesn't need eyes or hands to check for the string, marble, or marzipan. Possible candidates for electrical state-saving systems include those that depend on whether an electrical charge is present or whether a current will flow. Both of these techniques are used in computer memories for primary storage systems.

The analog of electricity, magnetism, also can be readily manipulated by electrical circuits and computers. In fact, a form of magnetic memory called *core* was the chief form of primary storage for the first generation of mainframe computers. Some old-timers still call primary storage *core memory* because of this history. Today, however, magnetic storage is mostly reserved for mass storage because magnetism is one step removed from electricity. Storage devices have to convert electricity to magnetism to store bits and magnetic fields to electrical pulses to read them. The conversion process takes time, energy, and effort—all of which pay off for long-term storage, at which magnetism excels, but are unnecessary for the many uses inside the computer.

Using electrical circuits endows primary storage with the one thing it needs most—speed. Only part of its swiftness is attributable to electricity, however. More important is the way in which the bits of storage are arranged. Bits are plugged into *memory cells* that are arranged like the pigeon holes used for sorting mail—and for the same reason. Using this arrangement, any letter or bit of memory can be instantly retrieved when it is needed. The microprocessor does not have to read through a huge string of data to find what it needs. Instead it can zero-in on any storage unit at random. Consequently, this kind of memory is termed *random access memory*, more commonly known by its acronym, *RAM*.

Dynamic Memory

The most common memory inside today's personal computers brings RAM to life using minute electrical charges to remember memory states. Charges are stored in small *capacitors*. The archetypical capacitor has two metal plates separated by a small distance that's filled with an electrical insulator. A positive charge can be applied to one plate and, because opposite charges attract, it draws a negative charge to the other nearby plate. The insulator separating the plates prevents the charges from mingling and neutralizing each other.

The capacitor can function as memory because a computer can control whether the charge is applied to or removed from one of the capacitor plates. The charge on the plates can thus store a single state and a single bit of digital information.

In a perfect world, the charges on the two plates of a capacitor would forever hold themselves in place. One of the imperfections in the real world results in no insulator being perfect. There's always some possibility that a charge will sneak through any material; although better insulators lower the likelihood, they cannot eliminate it entirely. Think of a perfect capacitor as being like a glass of water, holding whatever you put inside it. A real-world capacitor inevitably has a tiny leak through which the water (or electrical charge) drains out. The leaky nature of capacitors is made worse by the circuitry that charges and discharges the capacitor because it, too, allows some of the charge to leak off.

This system seems to violate the primary principal of memory—it will not reliably retain information for very long. Fortunately, this capacitor-based system can remember long enough to be useful—a few milliseconds—before the disappearing charges make the memory unreliable. Those few milliseconds are sufficient that practical circuits can be designed to periodically recharge the capacitor and *refresh* the memory. Refreshing memory is akin to pouring extra water into a glass from which it is leaking out. Of course, you have to be quick to pour the water while there's a little left so you know which glass needs to be refilled and which is supposed to be empty.

Because of the changing nature of this form of capacitor-based memory and its need to be actively maintained by refreshing, it is termed *dynamic* memory. Integrated circuits that provide this kind of memory are termed *dynamic RAM* or *DRAM* chips.

In personal computer memories, special semiconductor circuits that act like capacitors are used instead of actual capacitors with metal plates. A large number of these circuits are combined to make a dynamic memory integrated circuit chip. As with true capacitors, however, dynamic memory of this type must be periodically refreshed.

Static Memory

While dynamic memory tries to trap evanescent electricity and hold it in place, *static* memory allows the current flow to continue on its way. Instead, it alters the path taken by the power, using one of two possible courses of travel to mark the state being remembered. Static memory operates as a switch that potentially allows or halts the flow of electricity.

A simple mechanical switch will, in fact, suffice as a form of static memory. It, alas, has the handicap that it must be manually toggled from one position to another by a human or robotic hand.

A switch that can be controlled by electricity is called a *relay*, and this technology was one of the first used for computer memories. The typical relay circuit provided a *latch*. Applying a voltage to the relay energizes it, causing it to snap from not permitting electricity to flow to it. Part of the electrical flow could be used to keep the relay energized which would, in turn, maintain the electrical flow. Like a door latch, this kind of relay circuit stays locked until some force or signal causes it to change, opening the door or the circuit.

Transistors, which can behave as switches, also can be wired to act as latches. In electronics, a circuit that acts as a latch is sometimes called a *flip-flop* because its state (which stores a bit of data) switches like a political candidate who flip-flops between the supporting and opposing views on sensitive topics. A large number of these transistor flip-flop circuits, when miniaturized and properly arranged, together make a static memory chip. *Static RAM* often is shortened to *SRAM* by computer professionals. Note that the principal operational difference between static and dynamic memory is that static RAM does not need to be periodically refreshed.

Read-Only Memory

Note that both the relay and the transistor latch must have a constant source of electricity to maintain their latched states. If the current supplying them falters, the latch relaxes and the circuit forgets. Even static memory requires a constant source of electricity to keep it operating. Similarly, if dynamic memory is not constantly refreshed, it too forgets. When the electricity is removed from either type of memory circuit, the information that it held simply evaporates, leaving nothing behind. Consequently, these electrically dependent memory systems are called *volatile.* A constant supply of electricity is necessary for them to maintain their integrity. Lose the electricity, and the memory loses its contents.

Not all memory must be endowed with the capability to be changed. Just as there are many memories that you would like to retain—your first love, the names of all the constellations in the zodiac, the answers to the chemistry exam—a computer is better off when it can remember some particularly important things without regard to the vagaries of the power line. Perhaps the most important of these more permanent rememberings is the program code that tells a microprocessor that it's actually part of a computer and how it should carry out its duties.

In the old-fashioned world of relays, you could permanently set memory in one position or another by carefully applying a hammer. With enough assurance and impact, you could guarantee that the system would never forget. In the world of solid-state, the principal is the same but the programming instrument is somewhat different. All you need are switches that don't switch—or, more accurately, that switch once and jam. This permanent kind of memory is so valuable in computers that a whole family of devices called *read-only memory* or *ROM* chips has been developed to implement it. These devices are called read-only because the computer that they are installed in cannot store new code in them. Only what is already there can be read from memory.

In contrast, the other kind of memory, to which the microprocessor can write as well as read, is logically termed *read-write memory.* That term is, however, rarely used. Instead, read-write memory goes by the name RAM even though ROM also allows random access to its contents.

Mask ROM

If ROM chips cannot be written by the computer, the information inside must come from somewhere. In one kind of chip, the *mask* ROM, the information is built into the memory chip at the time it is fabricated. The mask is a master pattern that's used to draw the various circuit elements on the chip during fabrication. When the circuit elements of the chip are grown on the silicon substrate, the pattern includes the information that will be read in the final device. Nothing, other than a hammer blow or its equivalent in destruction, can alter what is contained in this sort of memory.

Mask ROMs are not common in personal computers because they require that their programming be carried out when the chips are manufactured; changes are not easy to make and the quantities that must be made to make things affordable are daunting.

PROM

One alternative is the *programmable read-only memory* chip or *PROM*. This style of circuit consists of an array of elements that work like fuses. Too much current flowing through a fuse causes the fuse element to overheat, melt, and interrupt the current flow, protecting equipment and wiring from overloads. The PROM uses fuses as memory elements. Normally, the fuses in a PROM conduct electricity just like the fuses that protect your home electrical disaster. Like ordinary fuses, the fuses in a PROM can be blown to stop the electrical flow. All it takes is a strong enough electrical current, supplied by a special machine called a *PROM programmer* or PROM burner.

PROM chips are manufactured and delivered with all of their fuses intact. The PROM then is customized for its given application using a PROM programmer to blow the fuses one by one according to the needs of the software to be coded inside the chip. This process is usually termed *burning* the PROM.

As with most conflagrations, the effects of burning a PROM are permanent. The chip cannot be changed to update or revise the program inside. PROMs are definitely not something for people who cannot make up their minds—or for a fast changing industry.

EPROM

Happily, technology has brought an alternative, the *erasable programmable read-only memory* chip or *EPROM*. Sort of self-healing semiconductors, the data inside an EPROM can be erased and the chip reused for other data or programs.

EPROM chips are easy to spot because they have a clear window in the center of the top of their packages. Invariably, this window is covered with a label of some kind, and with good reason. The chip is erased by shining high-intensity ultraviolet light through the window. If stray light should leak through the window, the chip could inadvertently be erased. (Normal room light will not erase the chip because it contains very little ultraviolet. Bright sunshine does, however, and can erase EPROMs.) Because of their versatility, permanent memory, and easy reprogrammability, EPROMs are ubiquitous inside personal computers.

EEPROM

A related chip is called *electrically erasable programmable read-only memory* or *EEPROM* (usually pronounced double-E PROM). Instead of requiring a strong source of ultraviolet light, EEPROMs need only a higher than normal voltage (and current) to erase their contents. This electrical erasability brings an important benefit—EEPROMs can be erased and reprogrammed without popping them out of their sockets. EEPROM gives electrical devices such as computers and their peripherals a means of storing data without the need for a constant supply of electricity.

EEPROM has one chief shortcoming—it can be erased only a finite number of times. Although most EEPROM chips will withstand tens or hundreds of thousands of erase-and-reprogram cycles, that's not good enough for general storage in a PC that might be changed thousands of times each second you use your machine. This problem is exacerbated by the manner in which EEPROM chips are erased—unlike ordinary RAM chips in which you can alter any bit whenever you like, erasing an EEPROM means eliminating its entire contents and reprogramming every bit all over again. Change any one bit in an EEPROM, and the life of every bit of storage is shortened.

Flash RAM

A new twist to EEPROM is *flash RAM*. Instead of requiring special, higher voltages to be erased, flash RAM can be erased and reprogrammed using the normal voltages inside a PC. For system designers, that makes flash RAM easy to use. Unfortunately, flash RAM is handicapped by the same limitation as EEPROM—its life is finite (although longer than ordinary EEPROM) and (in most but not all cases) it must be erased and reprogrammed as a block.

On the other hand, the convenience of using flash RAM has led many developers to create disk emulators from it. For the most effective operation and longest life, however, these emulators require special operating systems (or modified versions of familiar operating systems) that minimize the number of erase-and-reprogramming cycles.

Memory Operation

No matter the type of memory—RAM or ROM, dynamic or static, erasable or flash—it all works the same. Essentially, memory is an elaborate set of pigeon holes like the post office workers use to sort local mail. A memory location called an *address* is assigned to each piece of information to be stored. Each address corresponds to one pigeon hole, unambiguously identifying the location of each unit of storage. The address is a label, and it is not the storage location itself (which is actually one of those tiny electronic capacitors, latches, or fuses).

Because the address is most often in binary code, the number of bits available in the code determines how many such unambiguous addresses can be accessed directly in a memory system. As noted before, an 8-bit address code permits 256 distinct memory locations ($2^8 = 256$). A 16-bit address code can unambiguously define 16,256 locations ($2^{16} = 16,256$). The available address codes generally correspond to the number of address lines of the microprocessor in the computer, although strictly speaking they need not.

The amount of data stored at each memory location depends on the basic storage unit, which varies with the design of the computer system. Generally, each location contains the same number of bits that the computer processes at one time—so an 8-bit computer (like the original PC) stores 1 byte at each address and a 32-bit machine keeps a full double-word at each address.

The smallest individually addressable unit of today's 32-bit Intel microprocessors—the 386, 486, and Pentium—is actually four double-words, and 16 bytes: a unit Intel calls a *line* of memory. Smaller memory units cannot be individually retrieved because the four least significant address lines are absent from these microprocessors. Because the chips prefer to deal with data one line at a time, greater precision in addressing is unnecessary.

Most PCs that follow the IBM standard actually use more bits for each storage unit than these examples describe. IBM adds one extra bit called a *parity check bit* to every byte of storage. The parity check bit enables the computer to verify the integrity of the data stored in memory. When a byte is written into memory, the value stored in the parity check bit is set to a logical 1 or 0 in such a way that the total of all 9 bits storing the byte is always odd. Every time memory is read, the PC totals up the 9 bits of each byte, verifying that the total remains odd. If the system detects an even total, it immediately knows that something has happened to cause 1 bit of the byte to change, making the stored data invalid.

Because IBM's engineers believe that having bad data is worse than losing information through a system crash—wrong data can result in erroneous paychecks, undecipherable inventory reports, and bridges collapsing, while a crash immediately notifies you that something is wrong—most PCs are designed to shut down when incorrect parity is discovered. If your system finds a wrong parity total in its motherboard memory, it automatically blasts the ominous message `Parity Check 1` onto your monitor screen and freezes its operations. A wrong total on expansion-board memory elicits a `Parity Check 2` error with the same fatal failing.

Parity checking can locate only an error of 1 bit in a byte. More elaborate error-detection schemes can detect larger errors. Better still, when properly implemented, these schemes can fix single-bit errors without crashing your system. Called *error correction code,* or ECC, this scheme in its most efficient form requires three extra bits per byte of storage. The additional bits enable your system not only to determine the occurrence of a memory error but to locate any single bit that changed so that the error can be reversed.

IBM uses ECC on its larger computers and some high-end PCs designed to be used as network file servers. Memories in PCs were small and reliable enough that IBM's engineers did not think the additional expense of ECC bits were justified. As total system capacities stretch beyond 16M, however, ECC may become a standard part of the memory systems of some PCs.

A growing number of low-budget PCs skimp on memory by omitting the extra bits needed for parity checking. This simple expedient saves a little more than 10 percent of the cost of memory. It also enables a PC to keep running even if a bit in memory goes bad. Because a bad bit in a program crashes the system just as a parity error does, this might not seem like a bad idea. But a bad bit in program data could have far-reaching implications. Although you might not notice a single pixel of the wrong color on your monitor screen, one number changed while bidding on an important contract (say to build a bridge across Lake Erie) could lead to unfortunate consequences—say under- or overbidding by an order of magnitude.

One school of thought holds that today's RAM chips are so reliable that parity-checking is unnecessary. Another school holds that a single error can be so costly that the extra cost of parity-checking is insignificant. Whether you need parity-checking in your PC depends on what school you went to.

Memory chips do not connect directly to the microprocessor's address lines. Instead, special circuits in the *memory controller* translate the binary data sent to the memory address register into the form necessary to identify the memory location requested and retrieve the data there. The memory controller can be as simple as address decoding logic circuitry or an elaborate application-specific integrated circuit that combines several memory-enhancing functions.

To read memory, the microprocessor activates the address lines corresponding to the address code of the wanted memory unit during one clock cycle. This action acts as a request to the memory controller to find the needed data. During the next clock cycle, the memory controller puts the bits of code contained in the desired storage unit on the microprocessor's data bus. This operation takes two cycles because the memory controller cannot be sure that the address code is valid until the end of a clock cycle. Likewise, the microprocessor cannot be sure the data is valid until the end of the next clock cycle. Consequently, all memory operations take at least two clock cycles.

Writing to memory works similarly—the microprocessor first sends off the address to write to, the memory controller finds the proper pigeon hole, and then the microprocessor sends out the data to be written. Again, the minimum time requires is two cycles of the microprocessor clock.

Reading or writing can take substantially longer than two cycles, however, because microprocessor technology has pushed into performance territory far beyond the capabilities of today's affordable DRAM chips. Slower system memory can make the system microprocessor—and the rest of the PC—stop while it catches up, extending the memory read/write time by one or more clock cycles.

Memory Speed

Memory speed deficiencies first appeared when IBM introduced the first AT computers with 80286 microprocessors. Ordinary memory chips could not keep pace with the speed of such a fast (by the standards of 1984, remember) microprocessor. The 80286 could request bytes in such short order that memory was unable to respond. Consequently, *wait states* were added when the microprocessor requested information for memory.

A wait state is exactly what it sounds like; the microprocessor suspends whatever it's doing for one or more clock cycles to give the memory circuits a chance to catch up. The number of wait states required in a system depends on the speed of the microprocessor in relation to the speed of memory.

Microprocessor speeds are usually expressed as a frequency in megahertz—millions of cycles per second—while memory chips are rated by time in nanoseconds—billionths of a second. The two measurements are reciprocal. At a speed of 1 MHz, one clock cycle is 1000 nanoseconds long; 8 MHz equals 125 nanoseconds; 16 MHz, 62.5 nanoseconds; 20 MHz, 50 nanoseconds; 25 MHz, 40 nanoseconds; 33 MHz, 33 nanoseconds; and so on.

Dynamic memory chips are speed-rated; usually with a number emblazoned on the chip following its model designation. This number reflects the *access time* of the chip given in nanoseconds with the rightmost zero left off to make the expression a little more compact. A chip that has a -12 labeled on it, therefore, has an access time of 120 nanoseconds.

If this were the number of merit for chip speed, most of today's computers would have no problem. At 25 MHz, for example, one clock cycle is 40 nanoseconds and the microprocessors require at least two cycles between memory operations—a total of 80 nanoseconds. Chips rated at 70 nanoseconds are readily available and relatively inexpensive. In general, you will do no harm installing quicker chips than a computer calls for—for example, putting 70-nanosecond chips into a system that calls for 80-nanosecond parts. The only detriment is that faster chips will likely cost you more—you will be paying for speed that you don't need. Slower chips may not work or, more likely, work sporadically, leaving you vulnerable to parity-check errors at unexpected times.

The access time is not the only—or the most important—figure to describe a memory chip, however. More relevant is the *cycle time*, which does measure how quickly two back-to-back accesses can be made to the chip. The cycle time is generally about two to three times the access time of the chip. Even a 70-nanosecond DRAM chip, therefore, is not capable of reliably serving a 25 MHz PC.

Static RAM chips have no need to be refreshed. Not only do their cycle times equal their access times, but they can operate faster. Static chips are readily available with ratings of 25 or 35 nanoseconds while the fastest common DRAM chips are rated at 60 or 70 nanoseconds. Unfortunately, because static chips are much more expensive than DRAM, they rarely are used for the primary storage of PCs.

To cope with the speed limitations of affordable DRAM memory chips, PC makers use a number of designs for their memory systems. The most straightforward of these is simply to use the fastest possible chips, but even today's quickest DRAM chips lag far behind a 50 MHz or 66 MHz microprocessor. Another quick fix is to impose as many wait states as necessary—with not-so-quick results. A single wait state extends a normal memory cycle from two to three clock ticks—that's a big performance hit. With one wait state, a PC operates at only two-thirds its potential speed. Two wait states cut performance in half.

Page-Mode RAM

A better way around the problem of speed mismatch is to look to technology. Special RAM chips that combine features of both dynamic and static memory can cut the effects of wait states down to size. Two hybrid technologies have been used by PCs: *page-mode RAM* and *static-column RAM*.

Page-mode RAM chips allow part—but not all—of their storage to be read without wait states. These chips divide up their total address range into smaller sections called *pages*. Each individual page can be accessed repeatedly without the imposition of wait states. Back-to-back accesses to different pages require wait states, but no more than standard DRAM rated at the same speed.

Static column RAM chips split their memory into rows and columns. Back-to-back accesses within a column can be made without wait states. Memory accesses crossing the boundaries between memory columns require the addition of wait states.

Technically, page-mode and static-column RAM are distinct chip technologies. In the static-column RAM arrangement, memory is logically laid out as a two-dimensional array and sequential memory bits are organized in adjacent rows within a single column. Page-mode RAM chips break the total chip capacity into a number of pages, usually containing two kilobits.

Despite this physical difference, in most practical applications the two technologies yield exactly the same results: repeated accesses within a given range occur without wait states. Because most of the time programs require sequential bytes (the next instruction in a sequence or the adjacent character of data), this wait-state cutting technique is particularly effective. Wait state reductions of 60 percent or more are readily achieved.

The performance of static-column or page-mode memory systems depends on the page or column size that's used. The larger the page, the more likely the next bit of memory will be inside it and the better the chances of reading it without wait states. The performance improvement can be dramatic. Most programs execute within the limits of a 2K page most of the time, so overall system performance is boosted to near what it would be if system RAM was entirely static.

Interleaved Memory

Another clever technique, called *interleaved memory*, is like page-mode RAM in that it picks up speed on sequential memory accesses, but it does not suffer the limitation of small page sizes. Interleaved memory works by dividing the total RAM of a system into two or more banks. Sequential bits are held in alternate banks, so the microprocessor goes back and forth between banks when it reads sequential bytes. While one bank is being read, the other is cycling, so the microprocessor does not have to wait. Of course, if the microprocessor must read logically noncontiguous bits, whether or not it encounters wait states is governed by the laws of probability.

In a typical interleaved memory system, system RAM is divided into two banks, so the probability of encountering a wait state is about 50 percent. A four-way interleave can reduce wait states by 75 percent.

Because interleaved memory does not require special memory chips, it is perhaps the most affordable method of speeding up system operation. Memory interleaving also can be combined with page-mode memory chips to further enhance system performance. Of course, you need an even number of memory banks to achieve a two-way interleave. With today's 32-bit microprocessors, the smallest single bank is typically 4M. Such systems often require 8M for a simple two-way interleave, or 16M for a four-way interleave.

Memory Caching

With today's highest-performance microprocessors, the most popular memory-matching technique is memory caching. A memory cache interposes a block of fast memory—typically high-speed static RAM—between the microprocessor and the bulk of primary storage. A special circuit called a *cache controller* attempts to keep the cache filled with the data or instructions that the microprocessor is most likely to need next. If the information the microprocessor requests next is held within the static RAM of the cache, it can be retrieved without wait states. This fastest possible operation is called a *cache hit*. If the needed data is not in the cache memory, it is retrieved from ordinary RAM at ordinary RAM speed. The result is called a *cache miss*.

Not all memory caches are created equal. Memory caches differ in size, logical arrangement, location, and operation.

A major factor that determines how successful the cache will be is how much information it contains. The larger the cache, the more data that is in it, and the more likely any needed byte will be there when your system calls for it. Obviously, the best cache is one that's as large as and duplicates the entirety of system memory. Of course, a cache that big is also absurd. You could use the cache as primary memory and forget the rest. The smallest cache would be a byte, also an absurd situation because it guarantees that the next read is not in the cache. Practical caches range from a 1K (as used internally by some Cyrix microprocessors) to several megabytes. With today's multitasking operating systems, a cache size of about 256K is most favored.

The disadvantage of a larger cache is cost. Faster SRAM chips inevitably cost more, pushing up the overall cost of the system. Some manufacturers give you an option—scaleable caches. These caches enable you to start small and add more SRAM as you can afford it. If you expect to find the end of a rainbow sometime after buying your new 486, such a system deserves consideration.

The logical configuration of a cache involves how the memory in the cache is arranged and how it is addressed—how the microprocessor determines whether needed information is available inside the cache. You have three major choices: direct-mapped, full associative, and set-associative.

The *direct-mapped cache* divides the fast memory of the cache into small units, call lines (corresponding to the lines of storage used by Intel 32-bit microprocessors, which allow addressing in 16-byte multiples, blocks of 128 bits), each of which is identified by an *index bit*. Main memory is divided into blocks the size of the cache, and the lines in the cache correspond to the locations within such a memory block. Each line can be drawn from a different memory block, but only from the location corresponding to the location in the cache. Which block the line is drawn from is identified by a *tag*. For the cache controller—the electronics that ride herd on the cache—determining whether a given byte is stored in a direct-mapped cache is easy—just check the tag for a given index value.

The problem with the direct-mapped cache is that if a program regularly moves between addresses with the same indexes in different blocks of memory, the cache needs to be continually refreshed—which means cache misses. While such operation is uncommon in single-tasking systems, it can occur often during multitasking and slow down the direct-mapped cache.

The opposite design approach is the *full-associative cache*. In this design, each line of the cache can correspond to (or be associated with) any part of main memory. Lines of bytes from diverse locations throughout main memory can be piled cheek-by-jowl in the cache. The major shortcoming of the full-associative approach is that the cache controller must check the addresses of every line in the cache to determine whether a memory request from the microprocessor is a hit or miss. The more lines to check, the more time it takes. A lot of checking can make cache memory respond more slowly than main memory.

A compromise between direct-mapped and full associative caches is the *set-associative cache*, which essentially divides up the total cache memory into several smaller direct-mapped areas. The cache is described as the number of ways into which it is divided. A four-way set-associative cache, therefore, resembles four smaller direct-mapped caches. This arrangement overcomes the problem of moving between blocks with the same indexes. Consequently, the set-associative cache has more performance potential than a direct-mapped cache. Unfortunately, it is also more complex, making the technology more expensive to implement. Moreover, the more "ways" there are to a cache, the longer the cache controller must search to determine whether needed information is in the cache. This penalty ultimately slows down the cache, mitigating the advantage of splitting it into sets. Most PC makers find a four-way set-associative cache to be the optimum compromise between performance and complexity. Figure 5.1 illustrates the difference between direct-mapped, full-associative, and set-associative memory caches.

Caches can be internal or external to the microprocessor they serve. An *internal cache* is often also termed a *primary cache* and is built into the microprocessor's circuitry like the 8K cache of the 486 series of microprocessors. An external or *secondary cache* uses an external cache controller and memory chips.

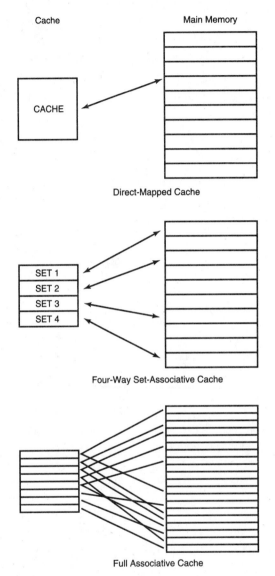

FIGURE 5.1. Direct-mapped, full-associative, and set-associative memory caches.

The primary cache holds more speed-up potential than a secondary cache because of its direct connection with the internal circuitry of the microprocessor. In 486 microprocessors, for example, the data path between the internal cache and the rest of the microprocessor is one 16-byte line wide. A transfer between the cache and microprocessor still requires two cycles, but in those two cycles all 16 bytes can be transferred. Because the 486 microprocessor has only 32 data lines, those same 128 bits normally require four times longer—eight cycles—to transfer.

Some secondary caches are implemented with 128-bit buses and take advantage of a streamlined addressing mode of the 486 called *burst mode* that allows four sequential data transfers without intervening address cycles. In other words, to move the cache data into the microprocessor takes five cycles (one address and four data transfers) instead of eight (four alternating address/10 data cycles). The internal cache still has a 2-to-5 performance advantage over this advanced addressing mode.

The shortcoming of the primary cache is capacity. The 8K internal cache of the 486 microprocessor occupies about one-third of the silicon used by the chip, for example. Making the cache any larger would add prohibitively to the expense of making the microprocessor.

When a cache is used for storing any kind of information, be it instructions or data bytes, it is termed a combined cache or an I+D (instructions plus data) cache. Sometimes primary caches are divided functionally into separate *instruction caches* and *data caches*. The instruction cache solely stores microprocessor instructions and the data cache holds only data. This segregation can yield improvements in overall performance and is used effectively by Intel's Pentium, some Motorola microprocessors, and most RISC chips. The Intel 486 series of microprocessors uses a single, combined cache for data and instructions. Older Intel chips have no integral memory caches.

Caches also differ in the way they treat writing to memory. Most caches make no attempt to speed up write operations. Instead they push write commands through the cache immediately, writing to cache and main memory (with normal wait-state delays) at the same time. This *write-through cache* design is the safe approach because it guarantees that main memory and cache are constantly in agreement. Most Intel microprocessors through the current versions of the Pentium use write-through technology.

The faster alternative is the *write-back cache*, which allows the microprocessor to write changes to cache memory, which the cache controller eventually writes back to main memory as time allows. The problem with the write-back cache is that there are times when main memory and the cache have different contents assigned to the same memory locations—for example, when a hard disk is read and information is transferred into memory through a control system (the DMA system) that does not involve the microprocessor. The cache controller must constantly check the changes made in main memory and ensure that the contents of the cache properly track such alteration. This "snooping" capability makes the design of a controller more complex—and, therefore, expensive. For the utmost in performance, however, the write-back cache is the optimum design.

One preferred solution is to delegate all responsibilities for supervising the cache to dedicated circuits designed for that purpose. In the PC environment, a number of cache controller chips are available. Some chipsets also incorporate memory caching into their circuitry (see Chapter 9).

Video Memory

Memory access problems are particularly prone to appear in video systems. Memory is used in display systems as a *frame buffer,* where the on-screen image is stored in digital form with one unit of memory (be it a bit, byte, or several bytes) assigned to each element of the picture. The entire contents of the frame buffer are read from 44 to 75 times a second as the stored image is displayed on the monitor screen. All the while, your PC may be attempting to write new picture information into the buffer to appear on-screen.

With normal DRAM chips, these read and write operations cannot occur simultaneously. One has to wait for another. The waiting negatively affects video performance, your system's speed, and your patience.

The wait can be avoided with special memory chips that have a novel design twist—two paths for accessing each storage location. With two access paths, this memory acts like a warehouse with two doors—your processor can push bytes into the warehouse through one door while the video system pulls them out through another. Strictly speaking, this memory can take two forms: true *dual-ported memory* allows simultaneous reading and writing, and *video memory* chips (often called *VRAM* for video random access memory) give one access port full read-and-write random access while the other port only allows sequential reading (which corresponds to the needs of scanning a video image).

Memory Location

One memory speed issue arises not from semiconductor technology but from system design. Where memory is located and how it is connected to the system microprocessor can have a dramatic effect on memory performance.

Memory usually is connected to the microprocessor's local bus—that means it runs at the microprocessor's clock speed and connects through a bus as wide as the microprocessor's data bus. Many motherboards lack sufficient space for memory expansion and consequently relegate expansion memory to daughterboards. These daughterboards can link to the motherboard either with a proprietary connection that operates at full microprocessor speed and bus width, or through a standard expansion bus like ISA, EISA, or Micro Channel.

The first kind of memory boards, which often are termed *proprietary memory boards*, generally impose no performance penalty on expansion memory. The latter boards can impose severe penalties in all systems more powerful than 8 MHz AT compatibles.

Higher speed machines (those with microprocessors operating in excess of 8 MHz) suffer severely when memory is added through expansion slots. The slots typically operate at 8 MHz or so, notwithstanding the higher speed of the microprocessor. Accessing this add-in memory thus requires the system to slow down to the 8 MHz rate. A 66-MHz machine would be effectively slowed to one-eighth the speed when accessing expansion board memory.

The memory in classic AT bus slots imposes an additional slowdown on 386DX, 486, and Pentium microprocessors because of the maximum 16-bit width of the bus. Because the memory bus would be only half or less the width of the microprocessor data bus, transferring data from memory to microprocessor automatically takes twice as long as it would with the full-width connection used by the motherboard and proprietary memory board RAM. The Pentium's 64-bit data bus mades the problem even more severe.

The simple rule is to keep memory out of normal expansion slots in any PC faster than an ancient 8-MHz AT if you want full performance. In some cases, however, sliding a few megabytes into an expansion slot makes eminent sense, such as when you have no other expansion, when a specialized application doesn't require the utmost in memory speed, or when you already have a memory expansion board.

Some PCs have limited motherboard-expansion capabilities, and slotted memory may be the only kind that you can add. An all-too-common scenario is the system board that uses a proprietary memory expansion board, and you cannot acquire the needed proprietary board because the manufacturer is unreachable, out of business, or never bothered to make the boards in the first place.

If you just need a RAM disk to speed up program compiles or database sorts, expansion board memory may suffice. Although the RAM drive would not be as fast as one created using motherboard memory, it would nevertheless far outrace any mechanical disk drive.

If you already have a populated memory expansion board, there's no reason to put it to pasture if your PC accepts it. As long as you configure the memory on the board to be addressed above the top of all system board memory, it will be the last to be used by your applications. Only when a program needs every last byte will it reach into slow-down territory. Certainly, performance will suffer at that point, but you will be able to run software you wouldn't otherwise be able to.

Moreover, if you're using an environment like Windows that takes advantage of virtual memory techniques, the slow slotted memory will still outperform the virtual memory that is emulated by a mechanical disk drive. Although such slotted memory is not an ideal solution, it can be acceptable, affordable, and workable.

Logical Memory Organization

Although it may be made from the same kind of chips, not all memory in a PC works in the same way. Some programs are restricted to using only a fraction of the available capacity; some memory is off-limits to all programs.

Memory handling is, of course, determined by the microprocessor used to build a computer. Through the years, however, the Intel microprocessors used in PCs have dramatically improved their memory capabilities. In less than seven years, the microprocessor-mediated memory limitation was pushed upward by a factor of 4,000, far beyond the needs of any program written or even conceived of—at least today.

But neither PCs nor applications have kept up with the memory capabilities of microprocessors. Part of the reason for this divergence has to do with some arbitrary design decisions made by IBM when creating the original PC. But the true underlying explanation is your own expectations. You expect new PCs to be compatible with the old, run the same programs, and use most of the same expansion hardware. To achieve that expected degree of compatibility, the defects and limitations of the original PC's memory system have been carried forward for ensuing generations to enjoy. A patchwork of improvements adds new capabilities without sacrificing (much of) this backward compatibility, but they further confuse the PC's past memories.

The result is that PCs are stuck with a hierarchy of memory types, each with different capabilities and compatibilities, some useful to some applications, some useless to all but a few. Rather than improving with age, every advance adds more to the memory mix up.

Conventional Memory

Once upon a time, there was only one kind of memory to worry about: the kind of memory that your programs could use. There was only one operating system anyone was concerned about: DOS. Under its strictures, only 640K was available to your programs. For years all programs abided by this 640K DOS memory limit. Since those early days, however, programs and operating systems have changed—as have your memory concerns. While strictly speaking, DOS (starting with Version 5.0) is no longer confined to using just 640K of RAM, many familiar applications remain bound by the original DOS constraints.

The DOS memory limit cannot be credited to the crafters of the operating system, but rather was thrust upon them by the design of the original PC. The PC's limit was, in turn, caused by a combination of pragmatic engineering and microprocessor limits.

To be used by a microprocessor, memory must be addressable. The 8088 microprocessor around which the PC was built imposed a memory addressing limit of 1M. As noted in Chapter 3, this 1M is termed *real mode memory*.

Out of this basic 1M addressing range, IBM's engineers reserve certain sections for special system functions. In the initial design of the PC, just over half of its memory was reserved. The top half of the 8088 address range, 512K, was given over to providing an addressing range for the system's BIOS code and direct microprocessor access to the memory used by the video system. The first few kilobytes were reserved for specific hardware and operation system functions, to provide space for remembering information about the system and the location of certain sections of code that are executed when specific software interrupts are made.

The purposes assigned to each address range of memory can be charted to give a visual representation of memory usage. The result is a chart called a *memory map*. Figure 5.2 shows a memory map of the original IBM PC.

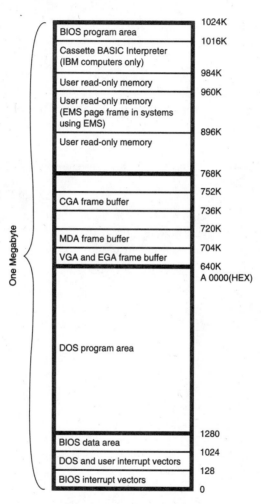

FIGURE 5.2. Memory map of the original PC and compatible computers.

Even though 512K seemed generous in the days when 64K was the most memory other popular computers could use, the wastefulness of the original limit soon became apparent. Less than one year after the original PC was introduced, IBM engineers rethought their memory division and decided that an extra 128K could safely be reassigned to program access. That change left 384K at the upper end of the address range for use by video memory and BIOS routines.

This division persists, leaving us with the lower 640K addressing range assigned to the DOS memory area, also termed *conventional memory*. This range corresponds to the maximum contiguous memory area within the addressing range of the 8088 microprocessor and represents the extent of addresses that normal DOS programs can access. The design of DOS constrains programs to using memory that is logically contiguous. DOS permits programs to address any memory within an upper and lower bound (which it defines based on available memory and its assignment to utility functions). If there were a hole in DOS memory, for example, a range of addresses that did not correspond to memory chips, a program might inadvertently try to use the nonexistent range with detrimental results. The program (and your system) would crash. Until the advent of modern memory management hardware and software, this need for logical memory contiguity meant that DOS applications could only use 640K of RAM, no matter how much memory was installed in your PC.

The upper limit to the DOS memory area is set by IBM's assignment of VGA memory, which begins immediately after the DOS 640K. The memory assigned to the original monochrome display system starts 64K higher. Some memory expansion boards and memory managers take advantage of the placement of monochrome display memory by giving DOS access to the 64K range used by VGA. With a propitious hardware/software combination, DOS and the applications that run under it can thus have access to a 704K range of RAM.

The lower limit to the DOS addressing range does not start at the first memory address because IBM has reserved some of this area for storing information needed by DOS and your programs. Included among the bytes at the bottom of the addressing range are *interrupt vectors*, pointers that tell the microprocessor the addresses used by each interrupt it needs to service. Also kept in these bottom bytes is the *keyboard buffer*—16 bytes of storage that hold the code of the last 16 characters you pressed on the keyboard. This temporary storage enables the computer to accept your typing while it is temporarily busy on other tasks. It then can go back and process your characters when it's not as busy. The angry beeping your PC makes sometimes when you hold down one key for too long is the machine's way of complaining that the keyboard buffer is full and that it has no place to put the latest characters, which it steadfastly refuses to accept until it can free up some buffer space. In addition, various system *flags*, indicators of internal system conditions that can be equated to the code of semaphore flags, are stored in this low memory range.

The hardware design of the PC restricts not just DOS but all operating systems to using only 640K of real mode memory. Consequently, the bottom 640K of memory often is described with the more general term *base memory*. It is the standard foundation on which all IBM-compatible systems must be built.

Extended Memory

Memory beyond the megabyte addressable by the 8088, which can be accessed through the protected mode of the 80286 and 80386 microprocessors, is generally termed *extended memory*. Up to 15M of extended memory can be added to a 286-based computer; nearly four gigabytes to a 386 or 486.

The usefulness of extended memory to DOS applications varies with the microprocessor installed in a PC. Only protected-mode applications can use extended memory in 286 machines. But with 386 and later microprocessors, Virtual 8086 mode allows software to split extended memory into 1M or smaller ranges that each act like base memory of an individual PC.

To be useful to DOS and its applications, using extended memory for Virtual 8086 mode requires some kind of memory management software. DOS versions before 5.0 required an add-on memory manager such as Qualitas 386Max or Quarterdeck Office Systems Q-EMM. Current versions of Windows have built-in memory management. Extra memory management is irrelevant to OS/2 because it is a protected mode operating system designed to use extended memory.

Note, however, no matter how much memory you have installed in your PC and no matter what memory management scheme you use, your DOS applications will be limited to addressing no more than 1M and more typically only 640K. That's because the memory addressing limits of DOS applications are built into the applications themselves. Although you can often use extended memory to run several standard DOS applications under Windows or OS/2, each program is still internally constrained by the old DOS 640K addressing limit.

A few powerful DOS programs are exceptions to this rule. They can stretch into extended memory using *DOS extenders*, software toolkits comprising precoded memory-management routines that become embedded in the application. When a program is written using a DOS extender, it gets its own built-in memory manager. (You never see the DOS extender; you only can appreciate its results.)

DOS extenders work by loading a program through DOS in real mode, and then switching program control to protected mode. The DOS extender then provides all services normally given by DOS (because DOS can operate only in real mode). When an application in protected mode needs to step back for a function normally provided by DOS in real mode, the extender translates virtual protected-mode addresses into physical addresses, copies necessary data from extended memory into conventional memory, and switches back to real mode to carry out the function. When the real-mode function completes, the extender reverses the process and switches back to protected mode.

Most applications that use DOS extenders typically have *386* in their names—for example Paradox 386 or AutoCAD 386—because they are designed to run on 386 and later microprocessors. Most of these programs, however, are disappearing from the marketplace because the *386* name makes them seem obsolete in a world now dominated by 486 microprocessors. Moreover, programs specifically written to use OS/2 or Windows have access to extended memory without the need for a built-in DOS extender. (Of course, programs written for OS/2 or Windows are not DOS applications but OS/2 or Windows applications.)

The larger expanses of extended memory add greater potential for program problems. With multiple megabytes out there for the taking, you can be tempted to run several extended DOS programs or operating systems that each have a built-in memory manager at the same time. Because DOS does not control how programs interact in extended memory, two programs in extended memory could potentially run into conflicts if both try to use the same block of RAM.

To prevent such conflicts, software writers have developed several methods for allocating extended memory among programs. The most primitive way is for a program that uses extended memory to reserve the blocks of extended memory it needs. Each extended memory program steals its own chunk of memory and that's that. The big problem is that programs only make this allocation when they load so it cannot change with the program's needs. Should an application need multiple megabytes for only one little-used task, it would have to reserve all those megabytes when it starts, depriving all other programs of access to that memory.

Three standards have developed for extended memory managers to allow extended memory programs to work together: Extended Memory Specification, Virtual Control Program Interface, and DOS Protected Mode Interface.

Extended Memory Specification

Extended Memory Specification (XMS) was developed by AST Research, Intel Corporation, Lotus Development, and Microsoft Corporation to take advantage of several extended memory capabilities. First appearing in 1987, XMS functions with all microprocessors that address extended memory (286 or better) and allows real-mode (DOS) applications to use that extended memory as well as a special block of real-mode memory normally out of DOS's reach. XMS is normally added to your system by loading an Extended Memory Manager driver in your PC's CONFIG.SYS file. The most familiar extended memory manager is HIMEM.SYS, which accompanies more recent versions of DOS and Windows.

Virtual Control Program Interface

Virtual Control Program Interface (VCPI) was developed by Phar Lap Software (the publisher of a popular DOS extender) and Quarterdeck Office Systems (creator of Q-EMM/386, an extended memory manager), and also first appeared in 1987. VCPI was developed specifically for the 386 microprocessor as a means of making Virtual 8086-mode programs cooperate and communicate using a software interrupt— specifically 67(Hex). Each VCPI application includes its own 386 control program. The first VCPI program loaded into your system takes the responsibility for linking control of that interrupt with each subsequent VCPI program loaded, so the first program acts as a memory manager for all the others.

DOS Protected Mode Interface

DOS protected mode interface is the most recent extended memory management system that first appeared commercially along with (and built into) Windows 3.0. Version 1.0 of the standard was formally released in November 1990, and applies to all microprocessors with extended memory capabilities. Although initially conceived by Microsoft as a proprietary standard that included all the functions of a DOS extender as well as a memory manager, the extent of the formal standard was scaled back to avoid conflicts with DOS extenders and administration of the standard was given to an independent industry organization (the DPMI committee).

Expanded Memory

In April 1985—just months after the AT was introduced with its multiple megabytes of extended memory range—a major software publisher, Lotus Development Corporation, and a hardware maker, Intel Corporation, formulated their own method for overcoming the 640K limit of older DOS computers based on the 8088 microprocessor. A few months later, they were joined by Microsoft Corporation, and the development was termed the Lotus-Intel-Microsoft Expanded Memory Specification (for its originators), LIM memory, EMS, or simply expanded memory. The initial version was pioneered by Lotus and Intel, and they numbered it as EMS Version 3.0 to indicate its compatibility with then-current DOS 3.0. There was no EMS 1.0 and no EMS 2.0. When Microsoft joined the initial twosome, the spec was slightly revised and denominated as Version 3.2. This version remained unchanged for about two years until it was revised to Version 4.0.

The new memory system differed from base memory and extended memory because it was not within the normal address range of its host microprocessor. Instead, it relied on hardware circuitry to switch banks of memory within the normal address range of the 8088 microprocessor where the chip can read and write to it. This technique, called *bank-switching*, was neither novel nor unusual; it was applied to CP/M computers based on the Z80 microprocessor to break through their inherent 64K addressing limit, for example. Only the cooperative effort at standardization by oftentimes competing corporations was surprising.

The original EMS specification dealt with its expanded memory in banks of 16K. It mapped out a 64K range in the non-DOS memory area above the bytes used for display memory to switch these banks, up to four at a time, into the address range of the 8088. Up to 8M of 16K banks of expanded memory could be installed in a system.

The Expanded Memory Specification included the definition of several function calls (pre-defined software routines) contained in special EMS software called the Expanded Memory Manager that were to be used by programs to manipulate the expanded memory. Because the memory areas beyond the DOS 640K range had been assigned various purposes by IBM, when the bank-switching area is assigned an arbitrary location, it could potentially conflict with the operation of other system expansion. Consequently, the specification allows several address locations for the bank- switching area within the range 784K to 960K.

Because programs had to be specially written to include the function calls provided by the EMS drivers, expanded memory does not allow ordinary software to stretch beyond the DOS limit. Moreover, the original Expanded Memory Specification put a burdensome limit on the uses of this additional memory—it could be used only for data storage. Program code could not execute in the EMS area. Adding EMS memory to your system also required special expansion boards with the required bank-switching hardware built into them. You couldn't just buy a handful of no-name memory boards and expect to put all their bytes to work.

The introduction of the AT and its potential of 16M of addressability overshadowed EMS until the hard reality of the inaccessibility of extended memory hit home. Only after three years did an extended memory operating system (OS/2 Version 1) become available, giving expanded memory a three-year headstart in applications software development.

In fact, one of the most important uses of extended memory before the advent of truly useful extended memory programs like DOS 5.0, Windows 3.0, and OS/2 2.0 was emulating expanded memory. Special programs called *expanded memory managers* or *LIMulators* could make any kind of memory—from base to extended to disk memory—EMS compatible.

These software-only EMS products could be divided into two classes: those that took advantage of the paged virtual memory mapping capabilities built into the 80386 microprocessor (as well as 286 machines with the memory mapping hardware such as Micro Channel PS/2s and AT-compatible machines built from the right chipsets) and those that copy 16K banks of memory from extended into base memory. The 386-style programs have a performance edge in that they can switch nearly instantly instead of requiring the host PC to go through the extra work of copying memory blocks. However, when you need EMS and the only way of getting it is with a copying-style LIMulator, the slower performance is but a small penalty.

Enhanced Expanded Memory Specification

Shortly after the introduction of EMS, a competing system was proposed by another cooperative association of otherwise competing computer products companies: AST Research, Quadram, and Ashton-Tate. Called the *Enhanced Expanded Memory Specification* or *EEMS*, it was an elaboration of the EMS idea—a superset of EMS—that allowed program execution and multitasking in the expanded memory area. Its design enhancements included the capability to switch banks of up to 64K as well as use part of the DOS 640K area for switching banks into. EEMS, too, required a special driver, special hardware, and software written to take advantage of its refinements—all different from those created for EMS.

EMS Version 4.0

In August 1987, the two systems (EMS and EEMS) were brought together with the adoption of EMS Version 4.0. Because both EMS and EEMS are subsets of Version 4.0, software written for either system can run under it. Beyond the previous standards, Version 4.0 supports up to 32M of bank-switched memory, all of which can support program execution and multitasking, and provides more than double the number of function calls to aid programmers in creating products to take advantage of this memory. While EMS 4.0 is compatible with previous hardware designs, it requires new memory management software to bring it to life. Although applications must be specially written to use its advanced function calls, those written for previous EMS or EEMS standards will operate within the limits of the specification for which they were designed.

According to its creators, the purpose of EMS 4.0 is to extend the life of 8088- and 8086-based computers—which, back in 1987, might still have had some limited prospects. Although the specification can be useful as an alternative to a protected mode operating system to give programs access to greater memory, EMS 4.0 is not an operating system in itself. It merely affords facilities to software and operating system developers and requires an EMM program to be used effectively as a multitasking environment. With newer PCs and operating systems, any version of EMS is simply unnecessary.

High DOS Memory

Memory-management software, including that in the latest versions of DOS, creates several other kinds of specialized memory in receptive computers to optimize the storage available to programs in the real mode addressing range. These include high DOS memory or upper memory blocks and the high memory area.

Note that these memory definitions apply only to DOS. Advanced operating systems make the full extent of protected mode available to their programs so that they don't have to rely on these memory tricks.

The reserved memory addresses beyond the nominal top of DOS memory and the upper limit of real mode memory—that is, the area between physical addresses 640K and 1,024K—provide more space than is usually necessary for all the functions in a PC. Typically, tens or hundreds of thousands of memory addresses in this area are unused even in fully expanded PCs. Because these unused addresses appear in the real mode addressing range, they can be used by DOS. This entire range of 384K is called *high DOS memory.*

By themselves, the vacant addresses in high DOS memory are meaningless because no memory is assigned to them. However, PCs that support memory mapping—machines equipped with 386 or better microprocessors as well as 286 computers with the proper support circuitry—can remap extended memory into this address range. Although this remapped memory is not useful to DOS applications (because it is not contiguous), it can be used for executing self-contained chunks of code such as driver software or terminate-and-stay-resident utilities.

Many memory-management programs (including DOS 5.0 and later) take advantage of the combination of these otherwise unused addresses and memory mapping to create what Microsoft calls *upper memory blocks*. Using special program loaders (such as DOS's LOADHIGH), driver and TSR software can be located in upper memory blocks rather than the normal DOS 640K to leave more DOS memory for your applications. The trick to taking advantage of upper memory blocks is finding the best fit between drivers and TSRs and the memory blocks. Each driver or program must fit entirely within the confines of a single contiguous memory block.

To make high DOS memory work in your PC, you must have suitable hardware (a 386, 486, Pentium, or a 286 with a chipset that supports memory mapping), a memory manager, and the special loader—and have physical memory available to remap. If your system has only 640K of memory, you cannot remap anything into the high DOS range.

High Memory Area

Microprocessors with extended memory capabilities have an interesting quirk—they can address more than 1M of memory in real mode. When a program running on an 8088 or 8086 microprocessor tries to access memory addresses higher than 1M, the addresses "wrap" around and start back at zero. However, with a 286 or more recent microprocessor, if the 21st address line (which 8088s and their kind lack) is activated, the first segment's worth of accesses in excess of one megabyte will reach into extended memory. This address line (A20) can be activated during real mode using a program instruction. As a result, one segment in additional memory is accessible by 286 and better microprocessors in real mode.

This extra memory, a total of 64K minus 16 bytes, is called the *High Memory Area*. Because it is not contiguous with the DOS 640K, it cannot be used as extra memory by ordinary DOS applications. However, it can be used like upper memory blocks for driver or TSR software. Unlike upper memory blocks, however, only one driver or utility, no matter what its size (at least as long as it fits—that means it must be less than 65,520 bytes) can be loaded into the high memory area. DOS versions 5.0 and newer are written to allow you to move the system kernel (about 40K or so of program code that's the operating system's essential core) into the high memory area, which it will do automatically in systems in which the high memory area is accessible. This relocation frees up 40K of the normal DOS 640K for use by your DOS applications.

Figure 5.3 shows a memory map of a modern PC that uses a memory manager to establish a complete range of memory types.

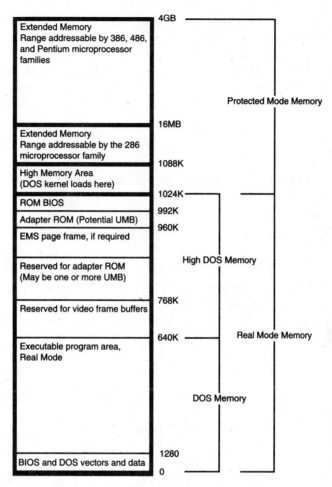

FIGURE 5.3. PC memory map using a memory manager.

Shadow Memory

The latest 32-bit and 64-bit computers provide a means to access memory through 8-, 16-, 32-, or 64-bit data buses. It's often most convenient to use a 16-bit data path for ROM BIOS memory (so only two expensive EPROM chips are needed instead of the four required by a 32-bit path or eight by a 64-bit path). Many expansion cards, which may have on-board BIOS extensions, connect to their computer hosts through 8-bit data buses. As a result, these memory areas cannot be accessed nearly as fast as the host system's 32-bit RAM. This problem is compounded because BIOS routines, particularly those used by the display adapter, are among the most often used code in the computer (at least when running DOS).

To break through this speed barrier, many designers of 80386 computers use *shadow memory*. They copy the ROM routines into fast 32-bit or 64-bit RAM and use the page virtual memory mapping capabilities of the 80386 and newer microprocessors to switch the RAM into the address range used by the ROM. Execution of BIOS routines then can be speeded up by a factor of four or more—more because greater wait states often are imposed when accessing slower ROM memory. Of course, the shadow memory is volatile and must be loaded with the BIOS routines every time the computer is booted up.

Shadowing has some detrimental effects on its host PC. Any ROM memory that is shadowed must be duplicated in RAM, and the bytes used for the duplication will be stolen away from the total RAM in your system. This memory is reallocated for its purpose by your PC's BIOS and is invisible to the rest of your system—including your applications. Consequently, the total RAM installed in your PC often exceeds the amount reported by your system's POST (power-on self test).

The ROM that is moved must go somewhere. Almost any address space can be assigned to it because once it is relocated, it should not need to be called upon again. When shadowing first appeared in machines made by Compaq Computer Corporation, the company's engineers assigned the range just above the 16M for the relocation because these systems were designed to address no more than 16M of RAM. Letting the shadow fall up there prevented programs from bumping into it. Most computer and motherboard makers copied the Compaq prototype and chose this address space for ROM relocation.

This address choice posed no problems as long as PCs and their applications needed only a few megabytes. Today, however, 16M is where many people want to start with memory. However, PCs that plant relocated ROM at the 16M border cannot go higher. Their memory must be contiguous and the relocated ROM puts a big hole in the address range that prevents any RAM at higher addresses from being used. In other words, in some PCs adding more physical RAM beyond 16M will not yield any more useful RAM.

This problem has an easy solution—switch off ROM shadowing. Most modern PCs make shadowing an option that can be switched on or off during their advanced setup procedure. Switching off shadowing prevents the relocated ROM from interfering with normal RAM addressing. In modern PCs, there's little penalty for switching shadowing off, anyway. The most important effect of shadowing is to accelerate video BIOS routines. However, most advanced applications and operating systems (like Windows and OS/2) avoid the video BIOS and instead write directly to display memory. These operations are *not* aided by shadowing, so they operate at the same speed whether shadowing is on or off. In other words, if most of your work is in Windows, ROM shadowing doesn't have any effect, so you might as well switch it off.

The other problem with shadowing is that not all the ROM in a PC comes as standard equipment. Many peripherals—for example, video boards, disk controllers, and network adapters—add their own ROM to your PC's native endowment. Most PCs make an effort at shadowing this ROM memory, too. Sometimes, however, the code in these add-in ROMs is not designed to be relocated, and trying to shadow it can crash your system even before it boots up. To avoid such problems, most PC makers give you the option of shadowing ROM in blocks, letting you switch shadowing on and off for each individual block. Switching on shadowing for a given address range should be approached carefully, particularly when you are uncertain whether the code in that address range is amenable to shadowing.

Memory Constraints

All else being equal, more memory is better. Unfortunately, the last time all else was equal was before chaos split into darkness and light. You may want an unlimited amount of memory in your PC, but some higher authority may mitigate against it—simple physics for one. The Pauli exclusion principle made practical: You can't stuff your system with more RAM than will fit into its case.

Long before you reach any such physical limit, however, you'll face a more steadfast barrier. (After all, you always can buy a bigger case for your PC.) Many aspects of the design of real-world PCs limit the amount of memory that the system actually can use. Important factors include the addressing limits of microprocessors, the design limits of systems, and the requirement that program memory be contiguous.

Microprocessor Addressing

Every Intel microprocessor has explicit memory-handling limits dictated by its design. Specifically, the amount of memory that a particular microprocessor can address is constrained by the number of address lines assigned to that microprocessor and internal design features. Ordinarily, a microprocessor can directly address no more memory than its address lines will permit. Although modern microprocessors make this constraint pretty much irrelevant, for older chips these limits are very real.

A microprocessor needs some way of uniquely identifying each memory location it can access. The address lines permit this by assigning a memory location to each different pattern that can be coded by the chip's address lines. The number of available patterns then determines how much memory can be addressed. These patterns are, of course, simply a digital code.

The on/off patterns of the 20 address lines of the 8088 and 8086 microprocessors can uniquely define 2^{20} addresses, the 1M-addressing limit of DOS, a total of 1,048,576 bytes. Because 286 microprocessors have 24 addressing lines, they can directly access up to 2^{24} bytes of RAM— that's 16 M or 16,777,216 bytes. Other chips, such as the 386SL, suffer similar limits (32M in the case of the 386SL). No PC with a 286 microprocessor can directly address more than 16M of RAM; a 386SL, 32M.

With the introduction of chips with a full 32 address lines—such as the 386CS, 486, and Pentium—direct memory addressing has become practically unlimited. These microprocessors can directly access 4 gigabytes of memory—that's 4,294,967,296 bytes. You're unlikely to need more than that amount of addressability soon, particularly considering that most programs still are written with the DOS constraints in mind. If you could find RAM at $25 per megabyte, reaching the limit of the Pentium would cost you $102,400 for memory alone. Adding it would make itself an interesting upgrade, one that would keep you plugging in SIMMs for the better part of a day—if you could find a PC with enough sockets to fill.

System Capacity

Not all computers can take advantage of all the memory that their microprocessors could address. Many 386-based PCs that use the class AT bus for expansion generally permit the direct addressing of only 16M, for example. The reason for this memory-addressing shortfall is that the AT bus was designed with only 24 addressing lines rather than the full 32 of the microprocessor. Newer classic-bus computers break through this limit by the expedient of forcing you to keep all memory in proprietary expansion. Once no longer constrained by the bus, memory capacity could be expanded to the limits of the PC's microprocessor, but hardly any ISA machines give you that option. A nagging few of them still maintain the 16M bus limit even on motherboard memory because designing and building PCs with such limits is easier and cheaper. Some other systems restrict you to 32M or so because of constraints built into their support chips.

The second-generation PC expansion buses, EISA and Micro Channel, extend their address buses to a full 32 bits (although you are well advised not to use these buses for memory expansion). Today's local bus implementations (both VL Bus and PCI) have exactly the same 32-bit constraint. Addressability is not an issue with them.

Other aspects of computer design also may limit internal addressing to levels below those allowed by the system's microprocessor. Most of the first generation of 386-based EISA computers allowed up to 32M of RAM to be installed—more than AT-bus machines but far within the four gigabyte constrains imposed by their microprocessors. Many machines now available have pushed the limit to 64M. Some of the latest machines have no inherent limit except for the number of memory sockets they provide. The only way to be certain about the addressing limit of a given PC is to check its specification sheet.

Some special architectures allow microprocessors to address more memory than the amount for which they were designed. The most popular of the techniques is the *bank-switching* method used by EMS. Note, however, that the expanded memory standard restricts bank-switched memory to far less capacity than today's top microprocessors can address directly. Consequently, bank-switching as a means to add extra RAM to PCs has fallen into disfavor.

Although desktop systems that lack a full 16M capacity on the system board allow you to stuff in that much RAM in expansion slots, most laptop and notebook PCs lack true AT-style expansion slots, substituting proprietary connectors for modems and memory. Consequently, nearly all notebook PCs leave you stuck with a memory limit ordained by the manufacturer. While the

PCMCIA 2.0 standard allows for full 32-bit addressing, other design factors limit the expandability of notebook machines with slots for PC cards.

Contiguity Problems

Nearly all applications and operating systems assume that your system's memory is *contiguous*—there are no gaps in the entire range from beginning to end. One reason is that most programs contain instructions called *relative jumps*—the instruction tells the program to leap from one point in memory to another. The distance to jump is defined as the number of bytes separating the old point of execution from the new rather than indicating exact memory addresses. A relative jump tells a program to look for its next instruction a given number of bytes from its last instruction. Relative jumps make programs flexible because they allow the software to load into memory without any reference to an absolute address. Programs can slip into RAM anywhere without a problem. This flexibility enables the same program to run in systems with different memory capacities, even with different resident software loaded.

If a hole appears in memory—if the RAM addresses are not all contiguous—there's always a chance that a relative jump will drop program execution in the middle of nowhere, where there is no waiting instruction, and likely no memory at all. Not knowing that to do, the program stops or does something unexpected, which means that it usually crashes your system (see fig. 5.4).

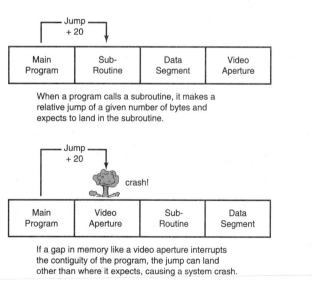

FIGURE 5.4. Jumping to data causes crashes.

Ordinarily, this need for contiguity is no problem because most PCs require their memory to be contiguous and will not let you install it otherwise. However, you may face contiguity problems in some special cases: when using ROM shadowing and memory apertures.

ROM shadowing, the popular PC speed-up technique, can have detrimental effect on memory expansion. The extended memory holding the remapped ROM code has to come from somewhere. Most machines simply steal 256K or so of extended memory from the very top of the available addresses. But an annoying number of older PCs assume that you will never want to put more than 16MB in your PC, so they fix the address range used for shadowing right at the 16MB border. If you stuff such a PC with more than 16MB of RAM, shadowing will still steal what it needs from that fixed address at the 16MB limit, which puts a gaping chasm in the machine's address range. Operating systems and programs butt against the hole and can go no farther no matter how much more memory you install in your system.

Thankfully this limit is easy to sidestep—switch off shadowing using your PC's advanced setup procedure. Memory will likely benefit your system more than sha-dowing.

Memory apertures are address ranges used by PC peripherals for memory-mapped input/output operation and control. Your PC sends data and control signals to the memory-mapped device by writing to a given range of memory addresses. The device picks up the data there and does its thing, whatever that may be. A Weitek math coprocessor is one example of a memory-mapped device. Fortunately (actually, by plan), the Weitek chip uses an address range in the gigabyte range, far from where you would want to install any RAM.

Another device that's like to demand a dedicated memory address range—and one that's more likely to pop into your PC soon—is a direct memory aperture video board. Until IBM intro-duced its XGA system in 1991, most display adapters followed the VGA standard for memory use. Their frame buffers were bank-switched from a 64K frame within the real-mode address range. But bank-switching complicates the programming of graphic software and slows down video speed. IBM's XGA added a *direct memory aperture* addressing mode, which reserved a range in extended memory for directly addressing the XGA frame buffer.

Although other manufacturers have been slow to adopt the XGA standard, many have embraced the direct memory aperture concept. Many graphics adapters now use direct memory apertures to address their frame buffers in their higher resolution modes.

Because display adapters include their own video memory, these memory apertures don't steal any of the RAM you install in your PC. Moreover, because the frame buffer memory is not used by your programs for execution, it need not be contiguous with the rest of RAM. In theory, there should be no problem.

With advanced expansion buses that can address a full 4GB, there almost never is a problem with a memory aperture. So many addresses are available, there's no chance of conflict. But with old ISA, the memory aperture can severely restrict your RAM expansion. Because you are forced to install display adapters in an expansion slot and because ISA is limited to 16M, the memory aperture used by a display adapter in an ISA system must appear somewhere below the 16M border. And it does—Wham! The aperture blasts a huge hole in your RAM address range somewhere below the 16M border. Memory above the aperture but below 16M cannot be reached by most operating systems because it becomes noncontiguous because of the aperture's hole. The aperture itself steals a megabyte or two, so you're left with a PC that can give your programs no more than about 14M no matter how much RAM you install.

In many PCs, the situation is even worse. You might be limited to only 8M of total RAM no matter how much you install in the system. Most PCs have eight 9-bit SIMM sockets and let you install SIMMs of just about any capacity. But the aperture makes SIMMs larger than 1M useless. Installing a single bank of 4M SIMMs puts overall capacity at 16M and guarantees a conflict with a memory aperture that's limited to that range by ISA. The most memory you can install in such systems is two banks of four 1M SIMMs—that's just 8M.

This aperture limit usually does not occur with Micro Channel, EISA, VL Bus, or PCI because all four of those buses permit 32-bit addressing and do not force the aperture below the 16M border. As long as the maker of the video board enables you to move the board's aperture above the address range used by your system's DRAM, you should face no problem.

Memory Packaging

An actual memory chip is a sliver of silicon smaller than a fingernail and so delicate that exposure to ordinary air will cause it to self-destruct. To make it easier to handle, memory chips (like all semiconductors) are hermetically sealed in a larger case that protects the silicon and provides a convenient means of handling the chip and attaching it to circuit assemblies. This case is called the chip's *packaging*.

Almost universally, memory chips are individually packaged as integrated circuits that commonly are called discrete chips. Early PCs were designed to accept these discrete chips in their memory sockets, normally nine chips per memory bank. With the advent of 32-bit microprocessors, memory needs have become so large that discrete chips are inconvenient or impractical for memory. One bank typically would include 36 chips, and multiple banks would quickly consume more board space than is available in most PCs.

The modern alternative are the memory modules, which simply put several discrete chips on a single small plug-in circuit board. Memory modules are more compact than discrete chips for two reasons. Chips are soldered to memory modules, eliminating space-wasting sockets and allowing the chips to be installed closer together (because no individual access is required). Moreover, because the discrete chips that are installed in the memory module never need to be individually manipulated except by machine, they can use more compact surface-mount packages. A single memory module just a few inches long thus can accommodate a full bank of memory.

If the instruction materials accompanying your computer did not specify the type of memory that it uses, you can tell just by taking a quick look. Discrete memory chips are nearly always located in a rectangular array on the system board, typically in multiple rows (usually four) of nine chips each, although some machines may use 18-chip rows or more than four rows. Some of the rows may be vacant sockets, allowing for the memory expansion that you want.

The give-away in identifying a computer that uses discrete memory chips is that all the chips in this chip array are identical—all usually will have the same identifying numbers on their cases. It is possible, however, for black-sheep chips to appear because different chip manufacturers use different part numbers. Moreover, some computers may use different chip types in different rows of memory. Nevertheless, an array of multiple, similar chips is a good indicator of discrete memory.

You can tell if your computer is equipped with memory modules of some type by looking for several tiny circuit boards sticking up from your system board, usually at a right angle. A few computer designers spread out the memory modules, perhaps placing them between expansion slots. Usually, however, they're all located together in a patch about four inches square.

Discrete Chips

The evolution of the RAM chip has closely followed the development of the personal computer. The success of the small computer fueled demand for memory chips. At the same time, the capacity of memory chips increased and, except for a temporary rise in the late 1980s due to a worldwide shortage, their price has tumbled.

At the time the first PC was introduced, the standard RAM chip could store 16 kilobits of information—that is 16,384 bits or 2048 bytes. These, the smallest capacity memory chips used by any PC-compatible computer, are now difficult to find (and consequently expensive) because they were quickly outmoded. Only a few tens of thousands of PCs used them, and the useful lives of most of those machines have ended.

By the time the XT was introduced less than one year later, chips with larger capacities—64 kilobits—proved to be more cost-effective. Although able to store four times more data, 64-kilobit chips cost less than four times the price of 16-kilobit chips. The PC system board was revised to accommodate the better memory buy, and the XT was designed to accept these chips. In a few years, 64-kilobit chips became so popular that their price fell below that of 16-kilobit chips.

By 1984, the best value in memory had become the next step larger, the 256-kilobit chip, and RAM chips of this size were chosen for later model 286-based computers (although the original AT used its own novel—or weird—memory solution: two 64-kilobits soldered together to make a 128-kilobit stack).

As the first 386-based PCs came on the market, the standard memory chip capacity had increased to 1 megabit. Today, 4-megabit chips are being marketed and 16-megabit chips are appearing.

Most chip manufacturers aim at a factor of four when increasing in the capacity of their products, so the next generations of RAM chips will likely be 64-kilobit and 256-megabit capacity. The first 256-megabit chips are expected to become available by 1998. With the trend toward using more convenient memory modules, however, you're unlikely to deal with discrete chips of these capacities—or even 4-megabit chips.

Mixing discrete chips of different capacities in one PC can be chancy. Some PCs accept different capacities of chip but require that all chips installed in the system have the same capacity. The machine might be able to use 64-kilobit, 256-kilobit, or 1-megabit chips, but will not accept combinations of different chip capacities. Other systems may accept mixtures of chip sizes provided that all the chips in a given bank have the same capacity. (You will have to check your PC manual or that of its motherboard to determine the rule your system follows.) The reasoning underlying this general rule is that if one chip in a bank had a smaller capacity than the others, then some address would not have sufficient bits to pack a complete unit of storage. Errors would be inevitable. This rule is violated only in one case—when using 4-bit chips—but this situation imposes even stricter requirements.

Discrete chip packages differ in ways besides capacity. They also can have different physical configurations—the plastic packages may be different shapes and the pins that fit their sockets (or are soldered to circuit boards) vary in their arrangement. The most common memory chips remain those that use the *dual in-line pin* (or DIP) package, a small slab of plastic with two parallel rows of chips that emerge from either side of the package and then bend down at right angles to it. In general, the pins are spaced 1/10 inch apart and the two parallel rows are separated from each other by 4/10 inch. The *single in-line pin* (or SIP) package turns the DIP on edge and drops all pins straight down from one edge with 1/10 inch spacing between the pins. The *zig-zag in-line pin* (or ZIP) package resembles the SIP but has two rows of pins 1/10 inch apart and alternating at 1/10 inch intervals. In effect, the pins in the two rows are offset from one another by half the spacing between the pins to create a zig-zag pattern. ZIP chips allow more connections for the same size chip as compared to SIPs.

Memory chips also are available in surface-mount packages, tiny (typically half-inch) square blocks of epoxy designed to be soldered in place. These chips cannot be used for expanding system board memory because they will not fit into any standard socket. Figure 5.5 shows a sample chip package.

Discrete chips also differ in how their capacity is accessed. The typical computer memory chip stores information in a series of addresses, typically about 256,000, one bit wide. The same capacity can be split four ways so that each address stores four bits. In that way, a 256-kilobit memory chip would store four bits at each of about 64,000 addresses. This style of chip, growing in popularity in display adapters and a few computer systems, is called a 4 x 64-kilobit chip, distinguishing it from the 1 x 256-kilobit conventional chip—although both can be legitimately be called 256-kilobit chips. Similarly, 1-megabit parts are available either as 1 x 1024-kilobit chips or as 4 x 256-kilobit chips

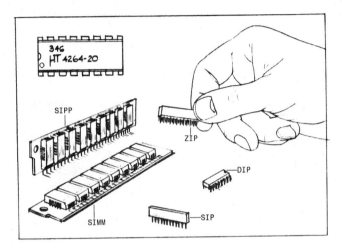

FIGURE 5.5. Discrete memory chip packages.

The chief advantage of wider chips is that fewer are needed per memory bank, so when a system designer wants to skimp on the memory he packs in a system, he may use wider chips. You only need two 4-bit chips for byte-wide memory, for example, while you would need eight single-bit chips for the same memory width. In PCs, 4-bit chips allow a building bank of memory from three chips (you need one additional chip for parity checking), so the minimum 32-bit bank needed to power a 386 or 486 PC requires only 12 chips instead of 36, conserving motherboard space. This type of memory arrangement—with each byte consisting of one 1-bit chip and two 4-bit chips—is the only exception to the rule that you cannot mix chip capacities in a single memory bank. But in this case you need to have chips of the correct capacity—and be sure to get the right capacity in the right place.

When you order memory, you must be certain to get chips with the proper width. 1-bit and 4-bit chips are not compatible even when they have the same total capacity.

The only certain way of identifying memory chips is through the manufacturer's designation stenciled on the top of the chip case. However, most computers use a style of memory chip that's so ubiquitous that it is nearly generic—bit-wide, dynamic RAM chips in DIP packages. Odds are that if your computer uses discrete memory chips, it uses this variety. If so, your only concern is the capacity of the individual chips—64 kilobit, 256 kilobit, 1 megabit, or 4 megabit.

To confound you, every manufacturer uses its own nomenclature for this garden variety kind of memory chip. Table 5.1 lists the part numbers used by many major manufacturers for different chips.

TABLE 5.1. Memory Chip Part Numbers

64 Kilobit Dynamic Ram Chips
(listed as 150 nanosecond, change suffix for other speeds)

Fujitsu	MBM8264-15
Intel	P2164B-15
Mitsubishi	M5K4164P-15
Motorola	MCM4164BP-15
Oki	MSM3764-15
Panasonic	MN4164P-15
Samsung	KM416A-15
Texas Instruments	TMS4164-15nl

256 Kilobit Dynamic Ram Chips
(listed as 150 nanosecond, change suffix for other speeds)

Fujitsu	MB81256P-15
Hitachi	HM50256P-15
Intel	P21256-15
Mitsubishi	M5m4256P-15
Motorola	MCM6256AP-15
NEC	UPD41256C-15
Oki	M41256-15
Samsung	KM41256-15
Texas Instruments	TMS4256-15
Toshiba	TMM41256P-15

1-Megabit Dynamic Ram Chips
(1-bit wide organization, fast page mode)

Fujitsu	MB81C1000P/PJ/PSz
Hitachi	HM511000AP/AJP/AZP
Micron	MT4C1024PD/DJA/ZB
Mitsubishi	M5M41000AP/AJ/AL
NEC	uPD421000C/LA/V
Oki	MSM511000RS/JS/ZS

continues

TABLE 5.1. Continued

1-Megabit Dynamic Ram Chips

Siemens	HYB511000
Texas Instruments	TMS4C1024N/DJ
Toshiba	TC411000BP/BJ/BZ/BFT
Vitelic	V53C100

(1-bit wide organization, nibble mode)

Fujitsu	MB81C1001P/PJ/PSZ
Hitachi	HM511001AP/AJP/AZP
Micron	MT4C1025PD/DJA/ZB
Mitsubishi	M5m41001AP/AJ/AL
NEC	uPD421001C/LA/V
Oki	MSM511001RS/JS/ZS
Texas Instruments	TMS4C1025N/DJ
Toshiba	TC411001BP/BJ/BZ/BFT

1-Megabit Dynamic Ram Chips

(1-bit wide organization, static column)

Fujitsu	MB81C1002P/PJ/PSZ
Hitachi	HM511002AP/AJP/AZP
Micron	MT4C1026PD/DJA/ZB
Mitsubishi	M5M41002AP/AJ/AL
NEC	uPD421020C/LA/V
Oki	MSM511002RS/JS/ZS
Siemens	HYB511002
Texas Instruments	TMS4C1026n/DJ
Toshiba	TC411002BP/BJ/BZ/BFT
Vitelic	V53C102

(4-bit wide organization, fast page mode)

Fujitsu	MB81C4256P/PJ/PSZ
Hitachi	HM514256AP/AJP/AZP
Micron	MT4C4256PD/DJA/ZB

1-Megabit Dynamic Ram Chips

Mitsubishi	M5M44256BP/BJ/BL/BVP/BRV
NEC	uPD424256C/LA/V
Oki	MSM514256RS/JS/ZS
Texas Instruments	TMS44C256N/DJ
Toshiba	TC514256BP/BJ/BZ/BFT
Vitelic	V53C104

1-Megabit Dynamic Ram Chips

(4-bit wide organization, staic column)

Fujitsu	MB81C4258P/PJ/PSZ
Hitachi	HM514258AP/AJP/AZP
Micron	MT4C4258PD/DJA/ZB
Mitsubishi	M5M44248BP/BJ/BL/BVP/BRV
NEC	uPD424258C/LA/V
Oki	MSM514258RS/JS/ZS
Toshiba	TC514258RS/BJ/BZ/BFT
Vitelic	V53C106

(4-bit wide organization, fast page write per bit)

Hitachi	HM514266AP/AJP/AZP
Mitsubishi	M5M44266BP/BJ/BL/BVP/BRV
NEC	uPD424266C/LA/V
Toshiba	TC514266BP/BJ/BX/BFT
Vitelic	V53C105

4-Megabit Dynamic Ram Chips

(1-bit wide organization, fast page mode)

Fujitsu	MB814100
Hitachi	HM514100AJ/AS/Az
Micron	MT4C1004
Mitsubishi	M5m44100J/L
Mosaic	MDM14000
Motorola	MCM514100
NEC	MPD424100

continues

TABLE 5.1. Continued

4-Megabit Dynamic Ram Chips

Oki	MSM51400RS/JS/ZS
Panasonic	MN41C4000SJ/L
Samsung	KM41C4000
Siemens	HYB514100
Texas Instruments	TMS44100
Vitelic	V53C400
(1-bit wide organization, nibble mode)	
Hitachi	HM514101AJ/AS/AZ
Mitsubishi	M5M44101J/L
NEC	MPD424101
Oki	MSM51401RS/JS/ZS
Samsung	KM41C4001
(1-bit wide organization, static column)	
Hitachi	HM514102AJ/AS/AZ
Mitsubishi	M5M44102J/L
NEC	MPD424102
Oki	MSM51402RS/JS/ZS
Panasonic	MN41C4002J/L
Samsung	KM41C40012
(4-bit wide organization, fast page mode)	
Fujitsu	MB81440
Hitachi	HM51440AJ/AS/AZ
Micron	MT4C4001
Mitsubishi	M5M44400J/L
Mosaic	MDM41000
Motorola	MCM514400
NEC	MPD424400
Oki	MSM514400RS/JS/ZS
Panasonic	MN41C41000SJ/L
Samsung	KM44C1000
Siemens	HYB514400

4-Megabit Dynamic Ram Chips

Texas Instruments	TMS44400
Toshiba	TC514400AP/AJ/ASJ/AZ
Vitelic	V53C404
(4-bit wide organization, static column)	
Hitachi	HM514402AJ/AS/AZ

5 Megabit Dynamic Ram Chips

Mitsubishi	M5Mj44402J/L
NEC	MPD424402
Oki	MSM514402RS/JS/ZS
Toshiba	TC514402AP/AJ/ASJ/AZ
(4-bit wide organization, static column)	
Hitachi	HM51440aJ/AS/AZ
Mitsubishi	M5m44410J/L
NEC	MPD424410
Panasonic	MN41C41002SJ/L
Toshiba	TC514410AP/AJ/ASJ/AZ

The major exceptions to the generic memory rule are the few 80386-based machines that use more exotic chips to achieve greater performance than DRAM can deliver—static-column or page-mode chips. To determine the memory technology your computer uses, compare the legends on its memory chips to Table 5.1. If you find a match, you're probably safe in expanding your system's memory with that chip or its equivalent.

As with coprocessors or any other chips you might install inside your computer, memory chips must be aligned properly in their sockets. Pin number 1 of the chip must fit into the corresponding pin 1 hole of the socket.

All chips have some means of identifying pin 1 or the end of the chip at which pin 1 is located. Usually the pin one end of the chip is notched. Occasionally, a small circular depression—an indented dot—is located directly adjacent to pin 1. The end of the chip that is so marked is oriented to match the notch in the chip socket. Sometimes pin 1 of the socket also is identified with a silk-screened legend on the circuit board. Occasionally, all the pins in a socket will be denoted with numbers molded into the plastic of the socket.

An improperly oriented chip probably will fail immediately when you power-up your computer. In fact, the backward chip may short out and prevent your computer from booting at all. To avoid such disasters, double-check the orientation of every chip before you switch on your computer after adding any chips.

Sliding chips into sockets is not foolproof. The legs of ICs have a nasty tendency to go exactly where you don't want them. Sometimes they fold outward and slide down outside the socket instead of making a connection. Sometimes they bend underneath the chip and don't make a connection. If a chip leg misses its place, you will encounter memory errors when you boot up your computer, although the bent pin is unlikely to cause other damage to your system. Avoid such problems by carefully investigating each leg of every chip you install. Make certain that it fits properly into the hold provided in its socket.

If you discover that a leg that is misplaced, simply pry the chip out of its socket, straighten the pin as best you can (don't flex the leg too much because they easily break off), and reinsert the chip.

You will want to be careful when installing memory chips in your PC. Although it takes electricity to power a computer, the same force can be the worst enemy of your memory. A shuffle across a wool rug can charge you up to 20,000 volts, just rarin' to zap a memory chip designed to operate on five. While taking all the recommended precautions may be overkill—you don't have to ground yourself to a cold water pipe—there's no sense in taking chances. Grounding can be simply a matter of touching the case of your PC, or even touching the plastic tube or foam your memory chips come in to your computer before you begin. The key move is to make yourself, your computer, and the memory chips at the same potential, which simply means linking them together before you actually touch the legs of the memory chip.

A few companies recommend that you leave the power cord plugged into your computer to ground it while you're making the installation. You will be safer to ignore that advice and unplug *all* cables from your computer before you begin. That way, you cannot accidentally try to install memory chips while the computer is running—an exercise guaranteed to be fatal to the memory chips.

Memory Modules

Memory modules are the large economy size RAM in a bigger package to better suit the dietary needs of today's PCs. Besides the more convenient package that enables you to deftly install a number of chips in one operation, the memory module also better matches the way your PC uses memory. Unlike most chips, which are addressed at the bit level, memory modules usually operate in bytes. Where chip capacities are measured in kilobits and megabits, memory modules are measured in megabytes.

The construction of a memory module is straightforward; it's simply a second level of integration above the basic memory chip. Several chips are brought together on a small glass-epoxy circuit board with their leads soldered down to the circuit traces and the entire assembly terminated in an external connector suitable for plugging into a socket or soldering to another circuit board. This basic arrangement splits into two primary variations based on connector type.

Single in-line memory modules, more commonly known as *SIMMs*, use edge connectors. Like expansion boards, the connector is just a circuit board trace brought out to the edge of the module and, typically, plated with gold to prevent corrosion and to guarantee better contact. As with expansion boards, a SIMM is designed solely to plug into matching edge-connector sockets. The design allows the SIMM to be repeatedly added or removed without tools or damage.

Single in-line pin package modules, often shortened to *SIPPs*, use pin connectors. Like SIPP chip packages, the connections of a SIPP module are brought out as wire-like pins that hang down from the basic board in a single collinear row. The leads on a SIPP are designed for soldering in place, although sometimes they are installed in special sockets much like SIPP chips. A SIPP socket often is nothing more than line of holes reinforced by contact cups in the circuit board to which the SIPP mates. Figure 5.6 shows SIMM and SIPP packages.

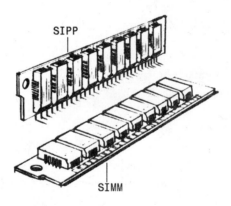

FIGURE 5.6. SIMM and SIPP packages.

Functionally, SIMMs and SIPPs can carry the same memory chips, technologies, and capacities. However, their differing mounting schemes make them mutually incompatible. When you want to add more memory to your PC or replace a defective module, you will have to specify whether it uses SIMMs or SIPPs.

Beyond packaging, you will find a number of differences in memory modules. As with memory chips, these include access, capacity, and technology.

Although most memory modules have their storage arranged in bytes, they do not necessarily have an 8-bit bus width. Most PC memory modules are designed to the same standard as discrete chip memory systems—that means parity checking. Consequently, the most popular PC memory modules have 9-bit access—eight data bits and one extra for the parity check. The connections to a 9-bit SIMM are spread among 30 pins (see fig. 5.7).

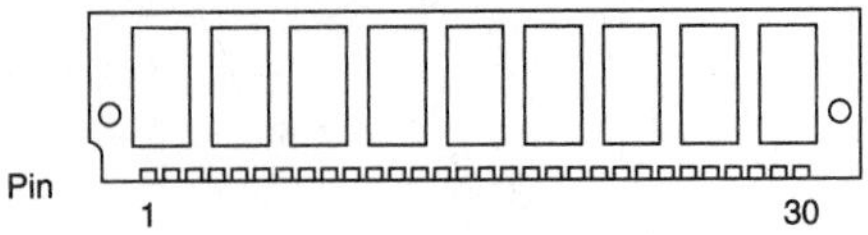

Pin   1   30

Pin connections

1	VCC	7	A2	13	DQ3	19	A10	25	DQ7
2	$\overline{CAS}$	8	A3	14	A6	20	DQ5	26	Q8
3	DQ0	9	VSS	15	A7	21	$\overline{WE}$	27	$\overline{RAS}$
4	A0	10	DQ2	16	DQ4	22	VSS	28	CAS8
5	A1	11	A4	17	A8	23	DQ6	29	D8
6	DQ1	12	A5	18	A9	24	NC	30	VCC

FIGURE 5.7. 9-bit (30-pin) SIMM pin-out.

Some computer systems (notably many Apple Macintoshes and some low-end ISA machines) and some specialized applications (such a printer and video memory) use 8-bit modules that lack parity checking. These are for people who like to live dangerously, saving slightly on the cost of memory while risking errors in their data. Manufacturers like them because they do save dollars on the price of memory for every PC—and they don't have to live with the consequences. But you do.

Note that although 8-bit and 9-bit SIMMs have the same number of pins (30), their pin-outs are different and you cannot substitute one for the other (see fig. 5.8).

You'll find one more interesting difference in SIMMs—3-chip versus 9-chip models. The 3-chip variety is like a 3-chip memory bank. It links two nibble-wide chips for data storage and a bit-wide chip for parity. 9-chip SIMMs put each bit of every byte of storage in a separate chip. Functionally these two types of SIMMs should be interchangeable, and in most PCs they are. Alas, a few PCs are more particular and prefer one type of SIMM to the other (for example, a handful of systems simply won't work with 3-chip SIMMs). Moreover, to avoid difficulties you should never mix 3- and 9-chip SIMMs in the same memory bank.

As with discrete chips, the minimum memory you can add to a microprocessor will be a bank that matches the microprocessor's bus width. If you have a 32-bit microprocessor such as a 386DX or 486, you will need four 9-bit memory modules per bank. Memory expansion also will have to be made in four-module increments.

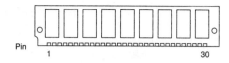

Pin

1   30

Pin connections

1	VCC	7	A2	13	DQ3	19	A10	25	DQ7
2	$\overline{\text{CAS}}$	8	A3	14	A6	20	DQ5	26	—
3	DQ0	9	VSS	15	A7	21	$\overline{\text{WE}}$	27	$\overline{\text{RAS}}$
4	A0	10	DQ2	16	DQ4	22	VSS	28	—
5	A1	11	A4	17	A8	23	DQ6	29	—
6	DQ1	12	A5	18	A9	24	NC	30	VCC

FIGURE 5.8. 8-bit SIMM pin-out.

Some memory modules are designed for individual 32-bit addressing. One module delivers full 32-bit bus width so you can expand a 386 or 486 system that uses such modules one module at a time. (These wider modules have become very popular with Pentium PCs because you only need two for a 64-bit memory bank—rather than eight byte-wide SIMMs.) Because these SIMMs provide a 32-bit bus complete with 4 bits of parity checking, they also are termed *36-bit SIMM*s. They also are sometimes referred to as *72-pin SIMM*s because their connectors have 72 connections. Because these wide-bus SIMMs were initially used in IBM's PS/2 series of computers, they are often termed "IBM-style" SIMMs.

These wide-bus SIMMs are versatile enough that the same 36-bit SIMMs can be used in 16-bit as well as 32-bit PS/2s (see fig. 5.9).

In addition, the IBM standard for these SIMMs includes coding pins that allow your PC to determine the speed rating of every one that you install (see fig. 5.10). Many PCs use this feature to adjust their memory timing and number of wait states to automatically optimize memory performance.

Possible memory module capacities are as wide as the imagination of the person soldering them together, though a number of standard sizes have arisen. The smallest commonly available modules store 256K. The most popular capacities among 9-bit SIMMs are 1M and 4M. Larger sizes such as 8M and 16M SIMMs haven't yet caught on among 9-bit SIMMs because the smallest bank potentially made from them—32M—is bigger than most people currently want.

IBM-style 36-bit SIMMs are available in capacities including 1M, 2M, 4M, 8M, 16M, and 64M. Because only one such SIMM is required as standard system memory or as an expansion increment (two in a 64-bit Pentium system), the larger sizes are both useful and popular. Table 5.2 lists model numbers, capacities, and technologies of popular memory modules.

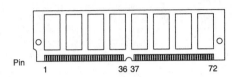

Pin   1   36 37   72

Pin connections

1	VSS	13	A1	25	DQ24	37	DQ17	49	DQ9	61	DQ14
2	DQ0	14	A2	26	DQ7	38	DQ35	50	DQ27	62	DQ33
3	DQ18	15	A3	27	DQ25	39	VSS	51	DQ10	63	DQ15
4	DQ1	16	A4	28	A7	40	$\overline{CAS0}$	52	DQ28	64	DQ34
5	DQ19	17	A5	29	NC	41	$\overline{CAS2}$	53	DQ11	65	DQ16
6	DQ2	18	A6	30	VCC	42	$\overline{CAS3}$	54	DQ29	66	NC
7	DQ20	19	A10	31	A8	43	$\overline{CAS1}$	55	DQ12	67	PD0
8	DQ3	20	DQ4	32	A9	44	$\overline{RAS0}$	56	DQ30	68	PD1
9	DQ21	21	DQ22	33	NC	45	NC	57	DQ13	69	PD2
10	VCC	22	DQ5	34	$\overline{RAS2}$	46	NC	58	DQ31	70	PD3
11	NC	23	DQ23	35	DQ26	47	$\overline{WE}$	59	VCC	71	NC
12	A0	24	DQ6	36	DQ8	48	NC	60	DQ32	72	VSS

FIGURE 5.9. 36-bit SIMM pin-out.

Speed in nanoseconds	Code pin	Pin 67	Pin 68	Pin 69	Pin 70
60		+5V	0	0	0
70		+5V	0	+5V	0
80		+5V	0	0	+5V

Note: +5V indicates nominal supply voltage; 0 indicates no connection on the SIMM hence no voltage.

Source: Kingston Technology Corporation

FIGURE 5.10. Speed code for 36-bit SIMMs.

TABLE 5.2. SIMM Part Numbers

256 Kilobyte SIMMs

8-bit

Hitachi	HB561008
Micron	MT8C8256
Mitsubishi	MH25608
NEC	MC157
Oki	MSC2328
TI	TM4256GU8
Toshiba	THM82500

9-bit

Fujitsu	MB85240
Hitachi	HB561003
Micron	MT8C9256
Mitsubishi	MH25609
NEC	MC41256A9
NMB	MM256K0J9
Oki	MSC2331
Texas Instrumentas	TM42566U9
Toshiba	THM92500

8-bit width

Fujitsu	MB85230
Hitachi	HB56A18
Micron	MT8C8024
Mitsubishi	MH1M08A0J
Motorola	MCM81000
NEC	MC42100A8
NMB	MM1M100J8
Oki	MSC2313
Texas Instruments	TM024GAD8
Toshiba	THM81000

continues

TABLE 5.2. Continued

9-bit width

Fjuitsu	MB85235
Hitachi	HB56A19
Micron	MT8C9024
Mitsubishi	MH1M09A0J
Motorola	MCM91000
NEC	MC421000A9
NMB	MM1M100J0
Oki	MSC2312
Texas Instruments	TM024EAD9
Toshiba	THM91000
Oki	MSC2327
Toshiba	THM322500

36-bit width

Fujitsu	MB85236
Hitachi	MB56D25636
Micron	MT9D36256
Mitsubishi	MH25636AJ
Motorola	MCM36256
NEC	MC424256A36
Oki	MSC2320
Toshiba	THM362500

2M SIMMs

36-bit width

Hitachi	HB56D51236
Micron	MT8C36512
Mitsubishi	MH51236AJ
NEC	MC424512A36
Oki	MSC2321
Toshiba	THM365120

4M SIMMs

    8-bit width

Hitachi	HB56A48
Mitsubishi	MH4M08
Motorola	MCM84000
Oki	MSC2341
Toshiba	THM84000

9-bit width

Fujitsu	MB85285
Hitachi	HB56A49
Hyundai	HYM594000
Mitsubishi	MH4M09A0J
Micron	MT9D49
Motorola	MCM9L4000
Oki	MSC2340
Texas Instruments	tMS4100EBD9
Toshiba	THM94000

32-bit width

Hitachi	HB56D132
Toshiba	THM321000
Hitachi	HB56D136
Mitsubishi	MH1M36
Oki	MSC2350
Toshiba	THM361020

Memory modules follow the same mixing rules as chips: all the modules in a given bank of memory must have the same capacity. In a 32-bit computer, for example, the four modules that comprise one bank must have the same capacity. The seeming exceptions to this rule are machines that use IBM-style 36-bit SIMMs, which generally can be mixed without regard to capacity (although some memory boards may be more particular—check your manual). The important difference is that one IBM-style SIMM typically makes up an entire bank, so the rule really is not violated.

Because memory modules are made from discrete chips, they use the same underlying technologies. SIMMs made using static, dynamic, video, and page-mode RAM technologies are available. As with discrete chips, different module technologies are not interchangeable, so you need to specify the correct type when ordering memory for your PC.

One way to identify memory modules is by part number. The manufacturer's part number given to a memory module often is stenciled on the side of the board opposite that carrying the individual memory chips. If the number is not there—or anywhere else, as is often the case—you can identify the memory module from the nomenclature on its chip components. A module made from nine 256-kilobit chips rated at 80 nanoseconds, for example, is a 256-*kilobyte*, 80-nanosecond memory module.

For a better look when attempting to identify memory modules, you may want to pop the module from its socket. Just be careful because memory modules are made from discrete chips and consequently have the same sensitivity to static electricity. If you take the proper precautions, however, the removal process for SIPPs is easy—just pull each one out, applying even pressure to the two ends of the SIPP.

SIMMs are more difficult. Normally SIMMs are latched into place by plastic fingers at either end of the slot in their connectors. Look closely and you will see that the plastic of the socket has two latching fingers at each end. You must carefully pry these fingers away from the SIMM before you can put it out. You then can lean the SIMM over a bit and pull it out. When you reinsert the SIMM, you must press it firmly in place until the fingers lock it down again and little round tabs appear in the latching holes in the SIMM near the fingers.

When installing SIMMs or SIPPs, remember that their orientation is important. In general, all SIMMs and SIPPs in a PC will face in the same direction. With SIMMs in modern, slanted sockets, that generally means the chips on the SIMM circuit board will be on the top of the SIMM once you lean it down into the socket. Most SIMM sockets have keying tabs on them to prevent your putting a SIMM in backward. If you try to insert a SIMM and discover that it refuses to fit, you probably have it in the wrong orientation or improperly seated.

Memory Errors

Memory chips (and memory modules) sadly seem to be the most likely solid-state part of your computer to fail. They can fail in one of two ways: with *soft errors* or *hard errors*.

Soft Errors

For memory chips, a soft error is a transient change. One bit in a chip may suddenly, randomly change state. Typically, one of the slightly radioactive atoms in the epoxy case of the chip will spontaneously decay and shoot out an alpha or beta particle into the chip. (There are a number of radioactive atoms in just about everything—they don't amount to very much but they are there.) If the particle hits a memory cell in the chip, the particle can cause cells to change state, blasting the memory bit it contains.

This error can be detected thanks to the parity-check bit assigned to each byte of memory. As soon as the error is detected (in general, when the address containing the error is accessed), your machine shuts down with a parity error. However, the chip itself has suffered no damage from the particle blast, and as soon as you reboot your computer, the error will be gone. Because such radioactive decay is rare and unpredictable, your machine is likely to resume processing and not have an error again for a long time.

There's nothing you can do to prevent soft errors, and there's nothing to do after they occur. The best you can hope for is to understand them.

Hard Errors

When some part of a memory chip actually fails, the result is a hard error. A jolt of static electricity can wipe out one or more memory cells, for example. As a result, the initial symptom is the same as that of a soft error—a parity failure followed by computer shut down. The difference is that the hard error recurs. Your machine may not pass its memory test when you try to reboot it, or you may encounter repeated, random errors when a memory cell hovers between life and death.

Hard errors require attention. The chip in which the error originates should be replaced.

Finding a Bad Bank

Machines that follow the IBM standard facilitate finding memory errors by putting diagnostic messages on-screen during the Power On Self Test procedure that your system goes through every time you turn it on. Sometimes these diagnostic error codes will appear after a parity error.

Unfortunately, the memory failure messages—and almost all other diagnostic messages provided by computers—are designed for service technicians rather than normal human beings. The messages appear in a numeric code that must be translated to zero-in on the defective chip. Appendix C gives guidance in finding errors in some popular discrete-chip PCs.

When PCs had dozens of memory chips in every bank, finding the one chip that went bad was a challenge. Trial-and-error chip swapping was out of the question unless you had time on your hands and a chip puller in them. You had to rely on diagnostics to locate the bad chip. Ultimately, this meant consulting a look-up table or deciphering a complex formula to find the bad chip from the obscure numerical message.

With modern SIMM-based PCs, however, the math of the chip-finding formula often takes longer than swapping a few modules. Most PCs have only four to eight memory modules, so you usually can locate the bad module in a few minutes simply by swapping modules. If you want the most efficient means of locating a bad module, you can use a formula similar to the one for calculating the Tower of Hanoi puzzle. You could shift a couple modules around and look for changes in the diagnostic error message, but the limited access in most PCs makes you remove the outermost modules to get to the inner ones. You ultimately end up pulling out most of the modules anyway. If you ever do encounter a hard error in one of your system's SIMMs, you probably will find repair easier if you just exchange one module from inside your PC for a known good module (the replacement) and work your way through a memory bank.

Chapter 6
The Expansion Bus

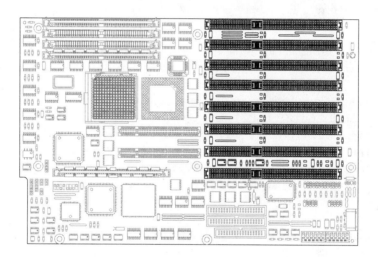

Your PC's expansion bus allows your system to grow. It provides a high-speed connection for internal peripherals that enhance the power of your PC. Standardized buses have spawned an entire industry dedicated to making interchangeable PC expansion boards. Where once a single standard sufficed, PC expansion has become specialized with expansion buses optimized for multiuser computers, high-performance video systems, and notebook machines.

PCs earn their versatility with expansion slots. You can make your PC into anything you want it to be with an appropriate selection of plug-in boards—within reason, of course. Adding the slicing and dicing power of a Ginsu knife or the warm affection of Pygmalion-style dreams requires more elaborate accessorizing, but expansion boards can make a modest PC into a multimedia extravaganza, an infallible data collection clerk, a high-speed information retrieval system, or an expensive desktop paperweight.

An *expansion slot* is just a space for the board. The real power for pushing the capabilities of your system comes from the connections provided by the slot—the *expansion bus*. The expansion bus is the electrical connector sitting at the bottom of the slot. The expansion bus is your PC's electrical umbilical cord, a direct connection with the PC's logical circulatory system that allows whatever expansion brainchild you have to link to your system.

The purpose of the expansion bus is straightforward: it enables you to plug things into the machine and, hopefully, enhance the PC's operation. The buses themselves, however, are not quite so simple. Buses are much more than simple electrical connections like you make when plugging in a lamp. Through the bus circuits, your PC transfers not only electricity but also information. Like all the data your PC must deal with, that information is defined by a special coding in the sequence and pattern of digital bits. The bus connection must flawlessly transfer that data. To prevent mistakes, every bus design also includes extra signals to control the flow of that information; adjust its rate to accommodate the speed limits of your PC and its expansion accessories; and adjust the digital pattern itself to match design variations. Different buses each take their own approach to the signals required for control and translation, and these design variations govern how your computer can grow. As a result, the standard that your PC's bus follows is a primary determinant of what enhancement products work with it—whether they are compatible. The design of the expansion bus also sets certain limits on how the system performs and what its ultimate capabilities can be.

For nearly the first decade of the personal computer industry's existence, PCs were defined by the expansion bus they used. Mainstream machines almost universally adhered to the standard set by IBM's early PC and AT computers. After all, when the first PC came on the market, its bus gave the world a single standard where none seemingly existed before. Manufacturers of expansion boards have a set of dimensions and layout of electrical signals to guide them in crafting their products. (The timing of those signals, however, was never explicitly defined by IBM.) The AT extended this original design to match the performance capabilities of more modern peripherals while retaining almost complete compatibility with the original.

The real virtue of the PC and AT bus designs was not technical, however, but simply that they had IBM's backing. That alone was the most compelling reason to use it. At the time, the IBM name meant business computer; IBM was the major computer maker in the world. IBM set standards and the world followed—blindly, perhaps. Compared to other expansion buses used up to that time, however, the PC bus was nothing remarkable. In fact, the design is remarkable mostly because of its simplicity. Most of its underlying design decisions were arbitrary and associated with expedience and lower costs. Still, everything needed was there, and the bus was entirely workable. When the IBM PC became a runaway success, board makers had to adopt the PC bus to sell their products. The standard was born.

As computers grew in power and shrank in size, however, the shortcomings of the original design became readily apparent. The original bus offered limited performance and even wasted the power of the PC's microprocessor. Adding expansion devices to it was cumbersome, confusing, and too often tinged with mysticism. It was too big for small computers and too small for big computers.

About six years after the PC bus appeared on the scene, a second generation of buses followed—revolutionary designs that added convenience and speed while sacrificing simplicity and cost. The two second-generation contenders, IBM's *Micro Channel Architecture* and the consortium-designed rival *Enhanced Industry Standard Architecture*, spent their critical early years battling one another instead of fighting their ways into users' hearts. They stumbled because they required rewriting software to take advantage of their special capabilities.

The industry now has stepped into the third generation of expansion bus designs with three new standards. Rather than being direct competitors, however, each is a specialist. The Personal Computer Memory Card International Association created a standard for credit card-size expansion boards designed for notebook computers and other compact, low-power systems. Intel Corporation crafted a high-performance expansion bus that breaks free of the constraints imposed by any specific microprocessor family and will likely be the most important expansion standard among third-generation PCs. The Video Electronics Standards Association developed a bridge design that adds extra performance to existing first- and second-generation expansion buses while minimizing redesign needs and costs. Each bus has its own role in the future of PCs.

Bus Basics

Although the concept of an expansion bus is simple—extend and link the signals of your system—practical expansion buses are not. Each bus represents a complex system of design choices—some made by necessity; many picked pragmatically. Not all buses share the same capabilities because they may be designed for different purposes and systems. Even the expansion buses crafted for PCs vary in the facilities they provide.

The range of bus resources is wide. Among these are all the data and address lines from the microprocessor. In addition, special signals are required to synchronize the thoughts of the add-in circuitry with those of the host computer. Newer bus designs also include means of delegating system control to add-in products and tricks for squeezing extra speed from data transfers. The most important of the bus functions supplied by some personal computer expansion buses are discussed in the following sections.

Data Sharing

The most important function of any expansion bus, indeed the defining characteristic of a bus, is the capability to share information between the computer host and the expansion accessories. The bus must provide the connections needed for moving data between the add-in circuits and the microprocessor and the rest of the computer.

Although the information can be transferred either by serial or parallel means, PCs use parallel data buses that allow the transfer of information one or more bytes at a time. Ideally, the expansion bus should provide a data path that matches that of the microprocessor. That way, an entire digital word or one of the double-words used by today's 32-bit chips could ride across the bus in a single exchange. When the bus is narrower than a device that sends or receives the signals, the data must be repackaged for transmission—a double-word might have to be broken into two words or four bytes to fit a 16- or 8-bit bus. Circuitry to handle this packaging complicates both motherboards and expansion boards, and, of course, a narrower bus slows transfers because moving a double-word may take two or four exchanges of data.

The fundamental factor in describing an expansion bus is thus the number of data lines it provides. More is always better, although adding more beyond the number of data connections on the host microprocessor adds undue complexity.

Addressing

As long as a program knows what to do with data, a bus can transfer information without reference to memory addresses. Having address information available, however, increases the flexiblity of the bus. For example, making addressing available on the bus enables you to add normal system memory on expansion boards. Addressing allows memory-mapped information transfers and random access to information, and allows data bytes to be routed to the exact location at which they will be used or stored. Imagine the delight of the dead letter office of the Post Office and the ever-increasing stack of stationery accumulating there if everyone decided that appending addresses to envelopes was superfluous. Similarly, expansion boards must be able to address origins and destinations for data. The easiest method of doing this is to provide address lines on the expansion bus that correspond to the address lines of the microprocessor.

As with microprocessor address lines, those of the bus determine the maximum memory range addressable by the bus. Usually, a computer bus provides the full range of address lines used by a PC's host microprocessor. Some buses shortchange on the number of address lines. When the addresses not included are at the top of the range (the most significant bits of each address), this strategy puts some addresses off-limits to expansion boards. For example, the old expansion buses designed for 286 microprocessors duplicated the chip's 24 address lines to allow access to 16 megabytes of memory. When a 386DX or better microprocessor is connected to one of these old buses, its upper address range is out of reach—which effectively wastes 4,278,190,080 potential memory locations.

On the other hand, because 386DX and better microprocessors grab data in 32-bit double-words, they have no need to find individual bytes. When they do want to retreive a single byte, they just grab a whole double-word at once and sort out what they need internally. Consequently, 32-bit expansion buses designed to accommodate these chips commonly delete the two least significant address bits. Although they have only 30 address lines, they can access the full four gigabyte range used by 32-bit microprocessors. Although omitting two address lines limits how precisely memory can be identified, that degree of precision is unnecessary with a 32-bit data bus. The bus simply does not need to be more specific.

Power

Although all electrical devices need some source of electricity to operate, no immutable law requires an expansion bus to provide that power. For example, when you plug a printer into your PC, you also usually plug the printer into a wall outlet. Similarly, expansion boards could have their own sources of needed electricity. Providing this power on the expansion bus makes the lives of engineers much easier. They don't have to worry about the design requirements, meta-physics, or costs of adding power sources like solar panels, magnetohydrodynamic generators, or cold fusion reactors to their products.

By today's conventions, most digital logic circuits require five volts of direct current to operate, so most expansion buses are designed to provide a copious flow at that potential. A few devices have more extensive requirements—for example, a negative five-volt supply or twelve volts (positive and negative) for special functions—so that most PC buses also make those voltages available. However, older buses make no provision for the 3.3 volt logic used by low-power microprocessors and their associated circuitry. That omission doesn't make old buses totally incompatible with new logic because on-board voltage regulators can drop the off-board supply down to the correct level. New designs have built-in provision for the new, lower-voltage circuit designs.

All complete electrical circuits require two wires, one to send the power out from its source and a return line. For example, every battery has a positive and negative terminal, both of which must be connected to make electricity flow. In a personal computer, the return circuit for all power connections is system *ground*, and all voltages on the expansion buses are referenced to ground. The positive five volt power conductor measures five volts *higher* than ground potential. The negative five volt power conductor measures five volts *lower* than ground. Consequently, the difference between the plus five and minus five volt conductors on a personal computer expansion bus is *ten* volts.

All the circuits inside a personal computer—both logic signals and power—share a common return line, the system ground. Although ground signals may appear in several places on a bus connector, all are the same and are electrically linked.

Timing

Expansion cards are like children: they can be totally independent, like the kids who go their own way and only choose to drop a card to the parents at the odd moments that financial need arises, or they can be completely committed, like kids who live at home and keep their lives in lockstep with father and mother and their bank balance. Many tightly coupled expansion boards are designed to operate in lockstep with the circuitry of their computer hosts. Such a bus is synchronized to the clock of its host and is described as a *synchronous* expansion bus. To keep the circuitry on the expansion board synchronized with the rest of the system, the host provides a *system clock* signal on the expansion bus.

The purest example of a synchronous expansion bus is found in the original IBM PC. The clock that controls the PC bus operates at exactly the same speed as the clock that operates the microprocessor. In fact, it is exactly the same clock, controlled by the same vibrating quartz crystal.

Although this design was satisfactory for the PC because of the modest speed potential of the 8088 microprocessor, more recent microprocessors are designed to operate at substantially higher clock speeds. Their backwardly compatible expansion slots, however, tempt people to plug in boards made any time in the history of the PC. That means an ancient old slow expansion board could easily find its way into a new slot. The result is about the same as hitching an old buggy to a jet airliner—something's going to crash.

System designers worked around this problem by adding a new synchronizing signal, the *bus clock*, to provide a reference frequency to expansion boards that may or may not be the same speed as the clock that runs the microprocessor. These systems can still maintain synchronous operation by operating at a submultiple (or even fraction) of the microprocessor's clock—for example, an 8.25 MHz bus clock in a system running at 33 MHz.

More advanced expansion buses are designed with even greater speed flexibility. By incorporating special circuitry to negotiate data transfers, holding back data until the host system is at the right instant in its clock cycle to receive it, expansion boards can run any speed the system designer wants. These *asynchronous* expansion buses still have bus clock signals, but the bus clock frequency need have no mathematical relationship to the system clock. Although asynchronous designs also increase the complexity of bus control logic, modern technology has shrunk all the required components onto a single ASIC (Application-Specific Integrated Circuit), making asynchronous buses both practical and affordable. Microprocessor-independent expansion buses generally operate asynchronously to allow full flexibility in the choice host microprocessor.

Flow Control

Even when the operation of an expansion board is synchronized with its host PC, the board might not be able to keep up with the speed needs of the computer. For example, a serial board might be able to accept data at 1,000 characters per second while the computer is generating information a thousand times faster. If the PC pushes out all the data it makes as fast as it can, the serial board would soon be swamped with information. Bailing itself out would mean throwing away the data it was supposed to send. To avoid such data losses when a speed disparity arises between an expansion board and its host, most expansion buses include *flow control* signals. In the simplest form, the board sends a special "not ready" signal across the bus, warning the host to wait until the board catches up. Switching off the "not ready" signals the host to dump more data on the board.

The original expansion bus design follows the microprocessor pattern for making data transfers (after all, the original PC bus was simply a direct extension of the microprocessor). Each transfer requires at least two clock cycles even without flow-control slowdowns. First, the microprocessor uses one clock cycle to signal what memory location is being addressed. Moving the data requires a second clock cycle. As a result, actual data throughput is less than half what the bus clock speed implies. This two-cycle-per-transfer mode holds one great advantage. Because each data transfer includes an individual address, it allows full random access. Any transfer can be made to or from any valid memory location. On the other hand, the one-move-in-two-cycles speed is inefficient.

When random access is not required, modern buses can switch into higher speed modes. Most microprocessors—and buses derived from them—now offer a *burst mode* during which several data transfers occur after a single address cycle. For example, the 486 microprocessor supports its own burst mode in which a single address cycle is followed by four data cycles. Moving one line of data—four 32-bit double-words (16 bytes), the basic unit with which the 486 prefers to work—thus requires five clock cycles rather than eight, a performance improvement of over 60 percent.

Some advanced expansion buses go farther by extending burst-like transfers to longer blocks of data and work independently from the design of the host microprocessor. In what is now called *Streaming Data Mode*, a single address cycle can be followed by as many data cycles as can be pushed across the bus before some other system function (such as memory refreshing) requires access. When moving large blocks of bytes, streaming data mode can nearly double bus through-put. Its primary drawback is its capability to shift only contiguous, sequential data. It sacrifices random access for speed.

Both expansion boards and the host computer must be designed to handle burst and streaming data modes. They also require special handshaking signals to request and accept such block transfers.

System Control

In a modern PC, peripherals often do more than shift information around. Many PCs need to communicate with the host microprocessor—for example, to break into a running program when they have "hot" data that needs to be processed. The peripheral needs to be able to send interrupt signals to the microprocessor to gain its attention. All PC expansion buses have provisions for one or more interrupt signals for this purpose. Most PC buses also make provisions for giving expansion boards control over the Direct Memory Access (DMA) controllers in the computer host. Some buses even include control lines for resetting or shutting down the host system entirely.

Bus-Mastering and Arbitration

In the early days of PCs, the entire operation of the expansion bus was controlled by the microprocessor in the host computer. The bus was connected directly to the microprocessor; in fact, the bus was little more than an extension of the connections on the chip itself. A bus connected directly to the microprocessor data and address lines is termed a *local bus* because it is meant to service only the components in the close vicinity of the microprocessor. However, another technology has usurped the "local bus" term, and in common parlance a local bus computer is generally one that has both a local bus-style expansion interface as well as other bus technologies.

Using this direct-connection design, every byte transferred across the bus is moved by the microprocessor. Using the data moving instructions, the microprocessor pushes bytes to addresses indicating memory located on expansion boards. For example, when the microprocessor wants to put a byte from one of its registers into memory, on one bus cycle it sends out the address to which it wants to send the data. The memory system then prepares that address to receive the data. On the next cycle, the microprocessor puts the bit values of the data on the bus, and the memory subsystem collects the bits and stores them in DRAM chips. The speed of this simple bus-transfer operation is governed by the bus speed, which is directly linked to the microprocessor speed. Most bus operations are not so simple, however. The microprocessor must go through gyrations of machine language instructions for every byte it transfers. With these more complex transfers, the actual speed of the microprocessor dominates all other factors in determining bus performance. This load is dropped on the microprocessor whether or not it is the source or target of the bus transfers and even when the chip should have no need to get involved at all—for example, when bytes must move from hard disk to video memory to place a stored image on the monitor screen.

The microprocessor need not be burdened with controlling the expansion bus, however. Just as an executive delegates all his work to underlings, a computer's microprocessor can delegate the control of the bus to special circuitry dedicated to the task. A *Direct Memory Access* or *DMA* controller does exactly that. But even with a DMA chip controlling the actual movement of data, the microprocessor often still must set up and oversee the DMA transfers, tying up the chip throughout the bus transfer.

Newer buses break the direct microprocessor connection by vesting the authority to control bus transfers in special logic circuits to make an *arbitrated expansion bus*. In the arbitrated bus design, the microprocessor abdicates its all-powerful position and takes a place as an equal to the expansion boards in the system. Although the microprocessor still controls the bus transfers that it originates or receives, it need not become involved in transfers between other devices in the system.

A device that takes control of the expansion bus to mediate its own transfers is a *bus master*. The device that receives the data from the bus master is termed the *bus slave* or *target*. The centralized circuitry in this design really does nothing more than determine which device takes control of the bus, a process called *bus arbitration*. Figure 6.1 illustrates the difference in the logical arrangement of the classic PC bus and an arbitrated expansion bus.

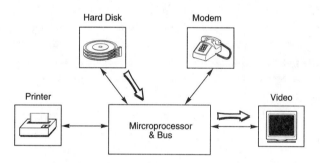

a. Non-arbitrated bus (PC/AT bus, true local bus)

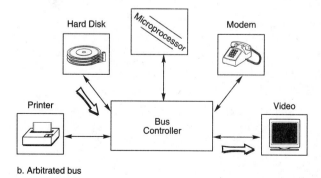

b. Arbitrated bus

FIGURE 6.1. Differences between PC bus and arbitrated bus.

Slot-Specific Signals

Buses are so named because their signals are "bused" together—that is, directly connected to one another with wiring, traditionally called *bus wires* in the electrical industry. In other words, pin one in every connector on the bus is linked to pin one in every other connector on the bus, and the signal that appears on any given pin number appears in all slots on exactly the same pin number. This design makes every slot equal and enables you to slide any expansion board into every slot.

This straightforward, straight-through design has a significant drawback: communicating to an expansion board individually is difficult. Typically, some elaborate protocol is needed. The host must send a signal that switches off all but the desired card by using some form of identification system.

A number of newer PC expansion buses include *slot-specific signals* that connect individually and uniquely to each slot. The host computer can use this signal to switch on or off features on individual cards or even entire cards.

Most systems use only a single slot-specific signal on a dedicated pin (the same pin in each slot, but a different slot-specific signal on the pin in each slot). This slot-specific signaling is used chiefly during testing and setup. Each board can be individually activated for testing, and the board (or separately controllable parts) can be switched off if defective. Slot-specific signals also are used to poll expansion boards individually about their resource usage so that port and memory conflicts can be managed automatically by the host system. This *automatic configuration* simplifies system setup by eliminating the need to adjust DIP switches or jumpers on individual expansion boards.

Multiple-Bus Computers

No law dictates that computers have only one expansion bus. In fact, a single bus imposes a great hardship—the speed and design restrictions of the original PC. When memory and expansion peripherals are connected to the same bus, all have to slow to the operating speed of the most laggardly device in the system. Because memory beyond that built into the computer's motherboard must be connected to the microprocessor's bus, a one-bus computer must submit its memory to the same speed restrictions imposed on the expansion bus by the slowest of slow boards. In other words, a 50 MHz PC slows to 8.25 MHz every time it accesses memory—which means most of the time.

To get the most speed out of a machine, you want the microprocessor and memory to race along as fast as possible. But you can't just jazz up the whole system because you'll outrun the cards you plug into the expansion bus. The answer, of course, is a divorcing of memory and input/output functions.

Just as the microprocessor and the expansion bus need not run at the same speeds, there's no real need (other than design ease) to throttle memory down to I/O speed. You can split the expansion bus in two at the bus controller level, providing parallel data paths to memory and the input/output expansion bus. Memory can run at whatever ridiculous speed you can buy chips to operate. The expansion bus can be kept down to eight megahertz or so, so that off-the-shelf expansion components run reliably.

In early 1987, Compaq Computer Corporation cleverly sidestepped this problem with the introduction of its first Deskpro 386, which operated at 16 MHz. The first *dual-bus PC*, the Deskpro was the first machine to provide a separate bus for its memory, operating at microprocessor speed, and for input/output operations, operating at the lower speeds that expansion boards can tolerate. All modern PCs now use this dual-bus design or an even more complex derivative.

For two critical PC functions—high resolution graphics and mass storage—two buses aren't enough. The amount of information that needs to be moved to mass storage or a video system by a high-speed microprocessor far exceeds the capacity of the traditional expansion bus. But the control needs of mass storage and graphics complicate—and slow down—the memory bus. Consequently, as early as 1991 designers began incorporating a third bus inside their systems—a high-speed bus especially designed for the needs of hard disks and video systems, in addition to the memory bus and traditional expansion bus compatible with conventional expansion boards. Because the new high-speed bus was often operated at microprocessor speed much like the original PC local bus design, this third bus is often called a *local bus*. Local-bus PCs are actually three-bus computers that have this local bus in addition to the other two conventional expansion buses.

Connector Layout

Without undue headaches, engineers can design electronic circuits to operate at any reasonable speed—into the range of gigahertz. When it comes to expansion buses, however, they are teased by several quirks of technology. Some quirks are purely electronic issues that cause high-speed buses to operate erratically and therefore interact detrimentally with other electronic circuits by generating interference. In addition, engineers must please people as well as the electrons in their circuits. Often, people are unwilling to accept their best design efforts—witness the lukewarm reception of some advanced expansion buses.

Expansion buses pose more engineering problems than other circuits because they require the balancing of several conflicting needs. The expansion bus must operate as fast as possible to achieve the highest possible transfer rate. The expansion bus also must provide a number of connectors for attaching peripherals, and these connectors must be spread apart to allow a reasonable thickness for each peripheral. In other words, the bus must stretch over several inches.

As speeds go up, so does the radiation potential of the signal; as circuit lengths increase, so does the radiation potential of the signal they carry. One way to minimize radiation is to keep speed low; another is to keep the bus short. Neither choice is entirely satisfactory if you want fast expansion that accommodates several peripherals. With the proper layout of bus signals—for example, interleaving of signals and grounds—the interaction between circuits can be kept to a minimum. However, older expansion buses are plagued by radiation problems that limit their maximum speed because old buses needed to maintain compatibility with the first PC expansion bus, laid out with little regard to radiation and high-frequency operation. At the time, no one ever thought buses would need to be faster—and no FCC rules governed computer radiation.

Slot Limits

High frequencies, radiation, and other electrical effects also conspire to limit the number of expansion slots that can be attached in a given bus system. These limits become especially apparent with local bus systems that operate at high clock speeds. All current local bus standards limit to three the number of high-speed devices that can be connected to a single bus.

Note that the limit is measured in devices and not slots. Many local bus systems use a local bus connection for their motherboard-based display systems. These circuits count as one local bus device, so PCs with local bus video on the motherboard can offer at most two local bus expansion slots.

The three-device limit results from speed considerations. The larger the bus, the higher the capacitance between its circuits (because they have a longer distance over which to interact). Every connector adds more capacitance. As speed increases, circuit capacitance increasingly degrades its signals. The only way to overcome the capacitive losses is to start with more signals. To keep local bus signals at reasonable levels and yet maintain high speeds, the standards enforce the three-device limit.

Local bus advocates are quick to point out that the three-device limit offers no practical disadvantage. Most PCs only need the high-performance edge offered by local bus technology for three devices—the video system, the mass storage system, and a network connection. A high-speed SCSI (Small Computer Systems Interface) host adapter allows the single local bus slot allocated to mass storage to link to multiple hard disks, disk arrays, and other devices. If you need more high-speed expansion than is afforded by a three-slot local bus system, you probably need more computer than an ordinary PC.

Working around the slot-limit problem is possible. A single computer can accommodate multiple expansion buses connected together. Each of these sub-buses then uses its own bus-control circuitry. In effect, this design is equivalent to multiple PCs intimately linked together.

Compatibility

For an expansion bus to be at all useful, it must be compatible with expansion boards. With which boards a bus achieves compatibility and how this compatibility is achieved have a strong effect on the usefulness and success of a given expansion bus standard.

For most people, the most important level of compatibility is that with conventional PC-style expansion boards—those used by systems as far back as 1981's IBM PC and 1984's AT. Systems compatible with these two standards offer major benefits. Old-board compatibility means that any old expansion boards that you've already bought and paid for still can be useful, if just as spares. Moreover, there's safety—and economy—in numbers. You'll find a wider variety of expansion boards adhering to the old PC standard than fit any other bus. If you're looking for some obscure function, it most likely is available as an old-bus board. Competition and simple design (not to mention low quality standards in some cases) have driven the prices of these boards down to trivial levels.

Two levels of old-board compatibility are available. *Slot-level* compatibility ensures that old boards plug into the same slot as boards that follow whatever standard is used in the host computer. In other words, with slot-level compatibility, you can slide any old board into any slot and expect it to work. *System-level* compatibility means that you can find at least one slot in the computer system that enables you to plug in your favorite ancient expansion board. Other slots in the system accommodate the new bus standards.

Most people don't require slot-level compatibility because taking advantage of your investment in old ISA boards does not require access to every slot. One reason for advancing to a new bus design is to gain the performance of new boards. You'll only want to retain the old boards that have no higher speed equivalents because of some speed limit other than the bus, such as an industry standard. For example, no modem is going to stress the capabilities of an expansion bus because even the quickest modems with weird modulation schemes and data compression can move data faster than about 38,400 bits per second. All you need is a PC with system level compatibility that has a number of old-style slots large enough to accommodate your old boards. You can slide the old boards into one or more slots inside the system that are dedicated to backward compatibility. Use the other slots to take advantage of the speed of the new local bus standards.

Bus History

Pinpointing the origins of computer bus technology depends on the definition you choose. Early mainframe computers were massive entities, made from many racks of equipment, and connected by snarls of cables. Through the expedience of plugging and unplugging subassemblies, the additional capabilities could be added to the computer. You could consider those cables as rudimentary buses, but in the context of today's machines, the wires were more like the circuit board traces connecting one integrated circuit to another. After all, one of today's ICs performs many more functions than a whole rack of tube-based computer gear. Nor did the cables of the first mainframe computers enable you to add off-the-shelf components because each early mainframe was a unique machine.

Buses before the PC

As mainframe computers matured, however, they developed into assemblies of identical parts connected in a bus-like structure. But what's usually considered the first computer bus appeared in the first downsizing of computers from the traditional mainframe to the new minicomputer, essentially invented by Digital Equipment Corporation. The first products DEC offered were plug-in boards that held building block circuits that could be used in the design or testing of computers. As the DEC modules became more complex, they evolved into complex boards that could be combined to make a minicomputer. When DEC started selling minicomputers, they were based on this bus-oriented design. But the bus was proprietary, as were the bus designs of the products of competing minicomputer companies that came to the market.

When computers first moved down to the next step, the initial designs were single-board machines. They were the work of experimenters, not commercial products, and expansion was as simple as grafting a new circuit onto a breadboard or strapping in another module with a ribbon cable—much as the original mainframe assemblies were linked together. After all, experimenters had little motivation to add expansion buses when they had nothing to expand with.

The machine most people regard as the first personal computer, Altair, was originally put together as a single-board system by its creator, Ed Roberts. The machine was publicized in that form in the January, 1975, issue of *Popular Electronics* magazine. But when the prototype disappeared in shipping, Roberts turned his setback into an opportunity—he redesigned the Altair to use a bus-oriented design. In the process, he laid the groundwork for the first personal computer expansion bus. Originally called the Altair bus after the name of the machine that introduced it to the world, its adoption by other manufacturers lead to a more neutral name, *S-100*, which first appeared in late 1976. Later, a standard based on the S-100 design was officially agreed upon by the Institute of Electrical and Electronic Engineers as IEEE 696. In this form, the bus is still used in obscure corners of the computer industry.

Roberts' original design choices set the pattern for today's most popular expansion buses. First, he chose edge connectors popular in electronic equipment at the time because they could be cheaply etched into circuit boards when the other interconnecting traces were formed. The off-the-shelf connectors had two rows of 50 contacts each spaced at 0.1-inch increments. The 100 contact total became the basis for the later S-100 name. Roberts' original Altair design only used 86 contacts, allowing future expansion to take over the remaining 14. This forethought allowed the Altair bus, originally created for 8-bit microprocessors, to be readily adapted to 16-bit technology.

Although S-100 was popular, it suffered several flaws that prevented it from becoming the dominant standard when the popularity of personal computers took off. It was designed originally for true bus-oriented computers—the bus itself was passive, nothing more than a parallel set of wires. It had no official operating speed because that would be set by the boards attached to it (though most machines using S-100 operated at about 2.5 MHz). Later computer designs were more like single-board systems with grafted-on expansion buses, which allowed much of the support circuitry to be held in common on the motherboard. The S-100 design required substantial duplication of circuitry. For example, S-100 boards had to devote space and cost to power-hungry voltage regulation circuitry on every expansion board.

By the late '70s, other manufacturers had developed their own expansion buses more suited to the needs of microcomputers. None was truly dominant. Designers of other early computers, such as the Apple II, simplified their expansion buses and lowered the cost and complication of expansion.

But the Apple design added more complications because each slot was not equal; slots were individually addressed.

PC Bus

All PC expansion buses trace their roots to the bus built into IBM's original PC, introduced with the PC on August 1, 1981. The design of this prototype bus owed nothing to any great brain trust, research and development, or design innovation. It was nothing more than an extension of the connections of the 8088 microprocessor, buffered so that the signals would be strong enough to power external circuits; demultiplexed so that the signals that shared pins on the chip would have their own connections on the bus; and arranged on an industry-standard connector in a way that easily matched available componentry.

The PC bus had all the virtues of the S-100 and other expansion buses popular at the time. It allowed the versatility of adding different options to the system (ports, memory, display adapters). Moreover, the bus approach was necessary in the first PC because all the circuitry to make a PC would not fit on the motherboard that used the technology that existed at the time. The expansion bus gave engineers a chance to add more features and make substitutions as technology progressed.

Little attention was paid to the technical aspects of bus design because IBM never expected sales of the PC to exceed 100,000. Although technically on par with the Apple II and S-100 buses, today the layout of the original PC bus appears almost haphazard, having little regard for signal integrity or radio frequency emissions. Then again, at the low operating speed of the bus and with the lack of FCC regulation, none of those concerns was critical.

The starting point for the original PC bus was the local bus of the 8088 microprocessor. The addressing and width of the data path of the PC bus was exactly matched to the 8088 microprocessor, and the bus operated at the 8088's speed under the microprocessor's direct control. But to make this nearly pure local bus useful, IBM mixed in a few additional signals, among them five control lines to signal hardware interrupts. The control of input/output ports was achieved by a control line that toggled the address bus between memory and the I/O ports. However, IBM chose only to decode the ten least significant bits of I/O port addresses in the circuitry of its first expansion boards. As a result, only 1,024 of the 65,536 possible I/O ports were usable by these early expansion boards.

A few electrical characteristics needed to be changed to allow system expansion and isolate the microprocessor from more nefarious expansion board designs. All the connections to the chip were not assigned separate pins on the chip package. A few were combined together—multiplexed—to give the 8088 more legroom. These connections must be demultiplexed before they can be used by the computer's other circuits. These demultiplexed connections were then extended to the PC bus. In addition, the 8088 chip itself was not designed to supply enough power to run the numerous devices that might be plugged into an expansion slot. Consequently, the microprocessor connections were repowered—run through a digital amplifier called a *buffer* that boosts the current available for running accessories.

The PC bus design put the microprocessor in direct contact and direct control of everything on the expansion bus. Because of its local connection, the operating frequency of the PC bus exactly matched the microprocessor in PCs. That means it operated at the same speed and bus width— 4.77 MHz and one byte wide. Because every bus cycle required two ticks of the system clock (on the first tick, an address was put on the bus; on the second, the data was actually moved), the maximum speed at which information could be transferred across the bus was 2.38 M/sec. But even that speed was restricted to short periods between other system functions, such as refreshing memory. Nevertheless, the PC bus operated as fast as anything could in the PC. Not only was there no speed penalty for plugging into the bus, using the bus also was the only way to attach memory beyond the first 64K (or 256K in later models) into a system.

Industry Standard Architecture

By 1984, the rudimentary design of the PC bus had already fallen behind the times. As IBM's engineers worked on a revolutionary new product (for then) based on a fast 286 microprocessor designed to run at 8 MHz (though initially limited to 6 MHz), they confronted a bus unsuited for the performance level of the new machine. Because the 286 used a full 16-bit data bus, IBM decided to add more data signals (as well as address and control signals) to the PC bus to match the capabilities of the new and more powerful chip. The bus speed of the AT also was matched to the microprocessor, so again no performance penalty was incurred in connecting a peripheral—even expansion memory—to the bus.

Not only was the PC bus limited in its memory handling and the width of its data path to the capabilities of a microprocessor on the road to oblivion (the 8088), but also many of the available system services were in too short supply for growth of the PC beyond a desktop platform for simple, single-minded jobs. Most systems, for example, ran out of hardware interrupts long before they ran out of expansion slots or clever ideas, and expansion boards needing interrupts for control. At the same time, engineers were faced by the profusion of PC bus-based expansion products, many of these made by IBM, which would be rendered incompatible if the bus were radically changed. A complete redesign required creating an entirely new line of expansion products for IBM and the compatibles industry, probably creating an outcry loud enough to weaken the IBM standard.

As a result of balancing these conflicting needs, the new AT bus was born a hybrid. It retained compatibility with most earlier PC expansion products, while adding functionality needed to push forward into full 16-bit technology. In addition, the AT bus contained a few new ideas (at least for PC-compatible computers) that hinted at—and perhaps even foretold—the Micro Channel. Inherent in the AT bus, but almost entirely unused, are provisions for cohabiting microprocessors inside the system, able to take control and share resources.

The big physical difference between the PC/XT bus and the AT bus was the addition of a second connector to carry more data and address lines—four more address lines and eight data—for a total of 16 data lines and 24 address lines, enough to handle 16 megabytes, the physical addressing limit of the 80286 chip. To make up for some of the shortcomings of the PC, which limited its expandability, the new AT bus also included several new interrupt and DMA control lines. In addition, IBM added a few novel connections—one in particular helps make expansion boards compatible across the 8- and 16-bit lines of the IBM PC; it signals to the host that the card in the socket uses the PC or AT bus.

Maintaining physical compatibility with the older PC bus was accomplished with the simple but masterful stroke of adding the required new bus connections on a supplementary connector rather than redesigning the already entrenched 62-pin connector. Expansion cards that required only an 8-bit interface and needed no access to protected mode memory locations or the advanced system services of the AT, could be designed to be compatible with the full line of 8- and 16-bit IBM-standard computers. Cards needing the speed or power of the AT could get it through the supplemental connector. The design even allowed cards to use either 8- or 16-bit expansion, depending on the host in which they were installed.

Because of its initial speed and data-path match with the 286 microprocessor, the original AT bus substantially out-performed the PC bus—the 16-bit data path combined with the 8 MHz clock (in its most popular form) yielded a potential peak transfer rate of 8 M/sec. Its 24 address lines put 16M of memory within reach. However, the number of useful I/O ports was still limited to 1,024 because of compatibility concerns with PC bus expansion boards.

The AT bus design incorporated one major structural difference over the original PC bus, however. Where the PC had a single oscillator to control all its timing signals including bus and microprocessor, the AT used several separate oscillators. The microprocessor speed, time-of-day clock, system timer, and bus speed were separated and could be altered independently. As a result, separate clocks could be used for the microprocessor and the expansion bus (as well as the system timers). This change enabled expansion boards to operate at a lower speed from that of the microprocessor. Because of this change, the ultra-compatible AT bus could be used with higher performance PCs as they became available. Although expansion boards might not work at the 25 MHz or 33 MHz clock speed of 386 and new microprocessors, the bus could be held back to its 8 MHz rate (or a slightly higher sub-multiple of the microprocessor clock frequency) to ensure backward compatibility with old expansion boards. At first, the lower speed of the bus presented no problem because nothing anyone wanted to plug into the bus needed to transfer data faster than 8 M/sec. For example, the fastest devices of the time—state-of-the-art ESDI drives—pushed data around at a 1.25 M/sec rate, well within the peak 8 M/sec limit of ISA. Eventually, however, the speed needs of peripherals (and memory) left the AT bus design far behind.

The AT bus suffered another shortcoming. Although IBM documented the function of every pin on the AT bus, IBM never published a rigorous set of timing specifications for the signals on the bus. As a result, every manufacturer of AT expansion boards had to guess at timing and hope that their products would work in all systems. Although this empirical approach usually did not interfere with operation at 8 MHz, compatibility problems arose when some PC makers pushed the AT bus beyond this speed. The timing specifications of the AT bus were not officially defined until 1987 when a committee of the IEEE (Institute of Electrical and Electronic Engineers) formally approved a bus standard that became known as *Industry Standard Architecture* or simply *ISA*. It also goes under several other names: ISA, *classic bus*, and its original name, *AT bus*.

The problem with holding the speed of the ISA bus at 8 MHz for backward expansion board compatibility first became apparent when people wanted to add extra memory to their higher speed PCs. When the microprocessor clock speed exceeded the bus speed, the microprocessor had to slow down (by adding wait states) whenever it accessed memory connected through the expansion bus. System performance consequently suffered—sometimes severely.

System designers at Compaq solved the problem by devoting a special, second bus to memory in the company's 1987 Deskpro 386. All current ISA-based PCs follow this design—a separate bus for high-speed memory and another for I/O expansion.

Since the time the IEEE set the ISA specification, its bus signals have remained essentially unchanged. The introduction of the *Plug and Play ISA* specification on May 28, 1993, a joint development by Intel and Microsoft, alters the way expansion boards work in conjunction with the bus.

Plug and Play ISA is designed to give ISA systems the same if not better self-configuration capabilities enjoyed by more recent expansion bus designs. In fully compliant systems, you can plug in any combination of expansion boards and never worry about such things as DIP switch settings, jumper positions, interrupts, DMA channels, ports, or ROM ranges. Each Plug and Play ISA card can tell the computer host exactly what resource it requires. If the resource requests of two or more cards conflict, the Plug and Play system automatically straightens things out.

Instead of altering the bus, Plug and Play ISA substitutes an elaborate software-based isolation protocol. Effectively, it keeps an expansion board switched off until it can be uniquely addressed, so that one card can be queried at a time. The host system then can determine the resources the board needs, check to make sure that no other board requires the same resources, and reserve those resources for the target board.

Although Plug and Play ISA does not require them, it can make use of slot-specific address-enable signals. The use of such signals—which now are not part of the ISA specification—can eliminate the complex software-query system used for isolating cards. Although software-based Plug and Play configuration is possible with current systems, using the streamlined hardware-based scheme requires new motherboards.

Micro Channel Architecture

When bus shortcomings became apparent in 1987, the world thought IBM was introducing its solution in the guise of Micro Channel Architecture (MCA). Unfortunately, IBM's engineers saw the PC bus problem differently from the rest of the world.

What PC owners were looking for was performance to match the then-powerful 386 microprocessor. With speeds that started at 16 MHz, four gigabytes of memory, and a 32-bit data path, the 386 far outstripped the 8 MHz, 16 megabyte, 16-bit AT bus. Whetted with the perceived need for at least a factor of four increase in performance and need to address 256 times more bytes of RAM, a bus that brought no real addressing increase and an clock speed increase of 25 percent would be quickly assayed a disappointment. Once salted with features that most of the world did not understand and few existing products could use—and a total incompatibility with everything past—the failure of the new introduction might have seemed certain. Actually, Micro Channel sold millions and influenced all buses that have come since. Despite its initial handicaps and publicity that would give nightmares to an advertising account representative specializing in product tampering and airline disaster cases, Micro Channel made its mark because *technically* it was the most creative and best-designed PC bus yet introduced. Unfortunately, it was a product designed for technical quality rather than for the PC market.

Long before the introduction of Micro Channel, IBM saw the PC as a platform to link up with its mainframe computers, using the bus as a means to add peripherals. Moreover, because the IBM engineers were familiar with mainframe computers, they believed that all computers should be adept at handling multiple tasks at the same time. After all, that's what the mainframes do. At the same time, IBM was interested in reserving power to mainframe computers (where most of its profits lay) and did not want to implant too much capability in PCs too soon.

Early in the PC revolution, IBM added the capability to give add-in devices control of PCs—first giving its XT a special slot for the purpose and then giving the AT the capability to let any slot give over control to an external master. The shortcoming of these designs was that only one device could take control; multiple add-in masters could not be accommodated safely. Consequently even before the AT and its improved expansion bus were introduced, IBM began working on a total redesign of personal computer expansion in 1983.

Micro Channel brought many mainframe computer design ideas to PC bus expansion and absolved many of the original sins of the PC bus. Micro Channel's architects completely redesigned the bus with high-speed operation in mind, relocating and redefining signals. Unlike the PC and AT buses, the Micro Channel put a ground or power supply conductor within three pins of every signal to shield against radio frequency interference.

Most importantly, Micro Channel took bus control from the system microprocessor and gave it a circuit IBM called the *Central Arbitration Point.* Transfers across the bus were managed by devices called *bus masters,* of which the microprocessor was but one. Other bus masters could operate from individual expansion slots. Multiple bus masters were permitted, and the bus provided a dynamic hierarchical method of assigning priorities and bus access to each master.

Far from stripping the microprocessor of power, however, this design lightened its overhead so that the microprocessor had more time for microprocessing. Although the Micro Channel design did little to improve performance of the bus, it gave the overall system more potential. The nominal bus clock was upped to 10 MHz, and the data path expanded to 32-bits, providing a peak data rate of 20 M/sec. IBM designed Micro Channel to be microprocessor-independent and operate asynchronously, so that the speed could be varied. Using what IBM called *Matched Memory Cycles,* some 32-bit memory boards operated at 16 MHz (peak data rate, 32 M/sec).

The new bus architecture required devices to negotiate for every access to the bus, for every transfer made. To cut this overhead, IBM added what it called a *Burst Mode* that permitted a single device to maintain control of the bus without renegotiation for up to about 12 milliseconds. Even with this Burst Mode, all Micro Channel transfers each still required two clock cycles—one for addressing; one for data transfer.

The original Micro Channel was a full 32-bit design with 32-bit addressing that allowed up to 4 gigabytes (G) of memory on the bus, but initial IBM products only allowed 16M to be accessed by a computer's DMA controller. That limitation tied down Micro Channel with effective memory-handling capabilities no better than the AT bus because most products assume that DMA reaches all memory addresses. On the other hand, all Micro Channel expansion boards were required to decode all 65,536 I/O ports addressable by Intel microprocessors.

Although Micro Channel did not change the number of available interrupts, it allowed the existing interrupts to be shared. To facilitate sharing and improve reliability, interrupts were maintained by level-sensitive signals instead of being edge-triggered.

To prevent any attempt at using old bus cards in Micro Channel machines, IBM specified a new miniaturized connector for expansion board. This incompatibility and the initial high royalty IBM demanded to use proprietary aspects of Micro Channel technology dampened enthusiasm for the new bus. Whereas most industry insiders viewed these measures as IBM trying to regain control of the PC market by promoting a proprietary standard, IBM actually documented Micro Channel more fully than it ever documented the AT bus.

Technically, Micro Channel rated as a masterstroke, essentially embodying the best of mainframe technology distilled down to PC size. But in a fit of corporate hubris, IBM tied use of MCA's proprietary technologies to hefty licensing fees. The rest of the PC industry, accustomed to taking advantage of IBM-developed technology for free, balked. Moreover, IBM cursed Micro Channel with marketing so inept it might have besmirched the reputation of Florence Nightingale, and failed to satisfactorily explain why backward compatibility with PC and AT expansion boards was such an ill-considered concept. IBM's rationale was that the truly bad engineering behind the old bus and boards would hold back performance of new MCA systems. Advanced features, such as level-sensitive interrupts, would not tolerate old boards that used edge-triggered interrupts. Starting with a brand new standard opened the opportunity for doing things right, entirely re-engineering the bus for optimum high-speed operation and reliability. Most people, however, believed the Micro Channel design was more a means for IBM to steal back the industry by making the products of other manufacturers obsolete.

Enhanced ISA

In 1988, to frustrate the perceived attempt by IBM at hegemony over the PC industry, a consortium of nine companies (termed by industry wags as the "Gang of Nine") made up of AST Research, Compaq Computer Corp., Epson, Hewlett-Packard, NEC, Olivetti, Tandy, Wyse, and Zenith Data Systems developed *Extended Industry Standard Architecture*, more commonly known as *EISA*. Compaq led the effort, but passed control and management of the standard to an independent organization, BCPR Services, which now officiates the standard.

The basic design of EISA amounts to the features of Micro Channel implemented in technologies free from IBM's control. Although the exciting new bus standard certainly incorporates some original and clever thoughts, EISA really amounts to the greatest hits of computer buses—the best ideas drawn from other bus designs and the whole computer industry.

This description is not meant to be derogatory any more than it is accidental that EISA is so derivative. From its very beginnings, EISA was outrightly designed not as an original concept but as an enhancement to the familiar AT bus. The reality of EISA goes far beyond merely specifying how to add 16 new data lines to the classic AT bus. By borrowing the best ideas from other bus designs—features such as bus mastering, automated setup, and interrupt sharing—then mixing in its own new data transfer modes, EISA has become a powerful and useful expansion design.

Of course, one contrary viewpoint is to label EISA the computer equivalent of a camel—rather than a horse—drawn by committee, a standard so executed by the Gang of Nine. The goal, announced September 13, 1988, was to design a 32-bit successor to Industry Standard Architecture—one that remained compatible with it instead of replacing it.

To improve performance, EISA relied on four advanced transfer modes that trim the number of clock cycles needed to move each byte. The most efficient mode compresses a transfer cycle into a single clock tick, putting the address cycle on the rising edge and data cycle on the falling edge of a single clock pulse. With its 32-bit bus width, a nominal 8.33 MHz clock speed carried over for compatibility with ISA, and its advanced transfer modes, EISA can reach a peak transfer rate of 33 M/sec.

At more than 50 percent faster, EISA was designed to make Micro Channel look second-rate. IBM's response was to add new modes to Micro Channel to allow higher throughput and increase data integrity. The revised Micro Channel specification optionally includes a Streaming Data Mode, which doubles burst speed. A block transfer begins by putting a starting address on the address bus. Thereafter, the entire block moves at a one transfer-per-clock-cycle rate.

Because the address bus is not used during these data streams, IBM allowed for it to serve as an auxiliary data channel, effectively broadening the data bus to 64-bits during bursts and again doubling the transfer rate. Together, these new modes quadrupled the Micro Channel transfer rate to 80 M/sec.

Another new Micro Channel option allowed doubling the bus clock rate to 20 MHz while accommodating 10 MHz boards. This option pushes the bus to a potential peak transfer rate of 160 M/sec. Note, however, that all these advanced features are optional, and no existing PC uses the complete package.

Faced with technology outrunning their bus, the EISA consortium has gone back to work and is now developing an EISA-2 specification. Coupling EISA existing advanced transfer modes with the streaming data and multiplexed transfer con-cepts borrowed from Micro Channel, EISA-2 promises a potential transfer rate of 132 MB/sec.

Proprietary Local Buses

Both Micro Channel and EISA suffer several handicaps that have prevented major market penetration. Price and availability are the biggest problems—both PCs and expansion boards using either advanced bus demand high premiums. The range of products has always been smaller than ISA. Both advanced buses were designed to use "switch-free" software setup, which should be an advantage, but the cure has until recently been worse than the disease (at least for some people)—the substitution of a complex, often confusing software setup procedure. Complicating system setup further, most peripherals require special software drivers to take advantage of the high-speed transfer modes of Micro Channel or EISA.

Worse, until recently neither Micro Channel nor EISA improved perceived system performance. The added expense of a new bus did nothing to make PCs seem faster. By 1991, high-perfor-mance PCs were suffering bus throughput problems, although most people were not aware of them. All on-screen graphics were forced through the standard input/output bus. Even motherboards with built-in video circuitry electrically used the I/O bus as a link. The handicap was substantial—high-performance microprocessors could move screen data at speeds approaching 132 M/sec, but the old ISA bus could only push bytes at a 8 M/sec rate—but it became apparent only with the rise in acceptance of high resolution video and graphical operating environments.

With early PCs, video throughput was not a problem because most applications were *character-mapped.* A full screen of information was simply an 80 × 25 array of characters stored in memory as two bytes per character. (One byte in modified ASCII code; the other an attribute byte that specified color or emphasis.) An entire screen of text data comprises only 4K bytes, which takes an insignificant time to transfer even across the original PC bus (the actual transfer time would be less than 1/500th second on a 4.77 MHz bus one byte wide).

With graphics, the transfer needs increase dramatically. A screen of standard VGA 16-color graphics—today's least common denominator—consists of about 150K. Move up to a True Color (24-bit) image at 1,024 × 768 resolution, and one screen of data increases to about 2.3M. If a system had no other overhead, that one screen would take one full second to transfer across the PC bus. In reality, such a transfer takes much, much longer when mediated by the system microprocessor, which also must allocate its time for memory refreshing, subtle background processes (servicing the timer interrupt, for example), and calculating the image data bound for the screen.

The only real improvement in video performance between 1981 and 1991 was when Compaq pushed video onto the 16-bit ISA connection with the introduction of its Deskpro 386 in 1987, doubling the old 8-bit transfer rate. Although IBM demonstrated the use of bus-mastering to speed video updates with its XGA system introduced in late 1990, XGA never found wide application. Moreover, as with Micro Channel and EISA, XGA also requires software to be specifically written to take advantage of its bus-mastering feature. The vast majority of applications cannot cash in on XGA speed, and the weak acceptance of XGA gives programmers little incentive to create XGA code.

The bus breakthrough that has most affected video has been a return to the native, the same local bus technology used by the first PCs. By adding a third bus that operates at or near the speed of today's high performance microprocessors with a full 32-bit (or even 64-bit) bus width, local bus holds the potential for increasing the transfer of display data by up to eight times. Better still, that acceleration requires no software changes. Best of all, you can see the difference readily.

The appearance of improvement made by local bus video systems is the greatest marketing strength of the entire local bus concept. With local bus, your PC seems to be operating faster. In fact, on tasks constrained by display speed—Computer-Aided Design and Windows applications, for example—local bus makes the overall operation of a PC faster. Moreover, this local bus technology can improve the performance of any bus-connected peripheral that demands high data throughput. The first machines to demonstrate the local bus concept—NEC's PowerMate desktop PCs, introduced in 1991—used this concept solely to increase display performance. The motherboard-mounted display systems of these machines were connected to a new, third bus almost directly to the microprocessor to augment its Compaq-style separate memory bus and conventional ISA expansion bus. Given the name that stuck—*local bus*—by NEC, the nearly direct-to-microprocessor link allowed the PowerMate to move pixel data at (or near) the native speed of the microprocessor instead of at the lower rate imposed by the expansion bus bottleneck.

The major drawback to the NEC design was that the local bus connection was embedded in the motherboard circuitry with no possibility of external connections. To improve the display system in an older PowerMate (for example, for higher resolution) meant foregoing its local bus performance.

To try to keep up, many PC makers copied the NEC design. To make their systems upgradable, some put their local buses on proprietary expansion connectors. Unfortunately, the profusion of proprietary standards hindered wide industry support. They suffered the disadvantage of any proprietary design—your options are limited to what the manufacturer provides. Even when local bus slots are present, you are still limited by proprietary bus designs to the few expansion boards offered by the PC's manufacturer.

Although OPTi, the maker of PC chipsets, proposed an open local bus standard based on its products, the proprietary design never found wide adoption. Early in 1992, OPTi developed its local bus as an adjunct to its DXBB PC/AT chipset (which consists of the company's 82C496 system/data controller, 82C206 integrated peripheral controller, and optionally 82C497 cache controller). As part of the data provided on this chipset, the company included a suggested local bus connector design based on an EISA connector (access keys in the OPTi connector prevent standard EISA boards from plugging into an OPTi slot). The company has made no effort to ensure conformance with this design, and some manufacturers have opted for different connectors (for example, Hauppauge Computer Works uses a Micro Channel connector with OPTi-derived signals).

VESA Local Bus

OPTi never achieved wide industry acceptance because it was overshadowed by the more widely supported local bus standards, also first promoted in 1992. One standard was hammered out by the Video Electronics Standards Association (VESA) and called *VESA Local Bus* or *VL Bus*; the other was developed at Intel Corporation and termed *Peripheral Component Interconnect* or *PCI*.

The VESA Local Bus standard—VL Bus—was formally announced August 28, 1992. Industry acceptance was instant. In fact, because preliminary specifications had been circulating for months, compatible products were announced immediately. Figure 6.2 shows a VESA VL bus.

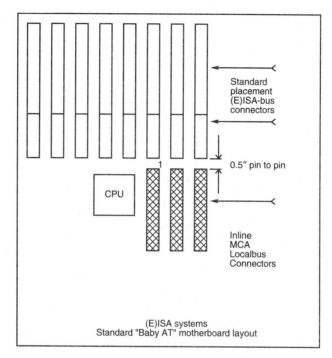

FIGURE 6.2. A VESA VL bus showing in-line ISA connectors. (Drawing from the VESA specification.)

VL Bus gave the PC industry what it wanted most—a standardized connector and protocol for a local bus expansion system for PCs. Inherent in that standard is the potential for interchangeable display adapters (and other expansion boards) that allow for a free and open market for new peripherals. Although originally targeted at advanced video systems, the resulting specification was made broad enough to be equally adept at handling other peripherals that require high-bandwidth transfers as mass storage and network interfaces.

Reflecting the introduction of the 64-bit Pentium in 1993, VESA developed a second generation VL Bus standard (Version 2.0). Besides broadening the bus and clarifying details, the revised specification redefines the maximum number of VL Bus slots permitted in a single circuit.

Peripheral Component Interface

In July 1992, Intel Corporation introduced Peripheral Component Interconnect. Long awaited as a local bus specification, the initial announcement proved to be both more and less than the industry hoped for. The first PCI specification fully documented Intel's conception of what local bus should be—and it wasn't a local bus. Instead, Intel defined mandatory design rules, including hardware guidelines to help ensure proper circuit operation of motherboards at high speeds with a minimum of design complication. It showed how to link together PC circuits—including the expansion bus—for high-speed operation. But the initial PCI announcement fell short exactly where the industry wanted the most guidance: the pin-out of an expansion bus connector that allows the design of interchangeable expansion boards. PCI turned out not to be a local bus at all, but a high-speed interconnection system a step removed from the microprocessor—but one that runs more closely to microprocessor speed than does a traditional expansion bus. A conceptual drawing of one possible PCI bus arrangement is shown in Figure 6.3.

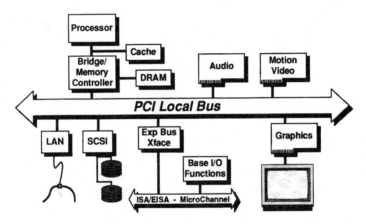

FIGURE 6.3. A PCI bus, showing PCI attachments. (Drawing courtesy of PCI SIG.)

Although in its initial form, PCI was not incompatible with VL Bus, Intel positioned its design more as a VL Bus alternative by introducing PCI Release 2.0 in May, 1993. The new specification extended the original document in two primary ways. It broadened the data path to 64 bits to match the new Pentium chip, and it gave a complete description of expansion connectors for both 32-bit and 64-bit implementations of a PCI expansion bus. The design is unlike and incompatible with VL Bus. Foremost, PCI 2.0 was designed to be microprocessor-independent rather than limited to Intel's own chips. Instead of linking almost directly to the microprocessor, the PCI 2.0 specification provided a compatibility layer, making it what some industry insiders call a *mezzanine bus*. Whereas VL Bus was designed to augment more traditional expansion buses in a PC (the specification defines ISA, MCA, and EISA design alternatives), PCI tolerates older buses but can also replace them. In fact, machines that combine PCI with a traditional bus may serve as a foundation to move from ISA to PCI as the primary personal computer expansion standard.

PCMCIA

All the above bus standards presuppose one thing: that they will be used in a desktop box that has room and power available for expansion. But this underlying assumption runs directly contrary to one of the strongest currents in the PC mainstream—machine miniaturization that has led to notebook, subnotebook, and palmtop computers. After all, an individual expansion board for one of these desktop standards likely stretches out longer than the largest dimension of most notebook machines. And a single board might draw more power than an entire notebook computer.

The world of movable computers had its own demands for expansion that were becoming apparent in 1987, by which time memory manufacturers were packing expansion RAM for notebook computers in slide-in, credit card-size boards. In fact, memory cards of charge card dimension can trace their heritage back to the ROM cards used to store laser printer fonts as early as 1984.

Although such memory cards were becoming popular in 1987, no single standard existed. The industry leader at that time was Mitsubishi, whose memory cards used a proprietary 60-pin package. Fujitsu Microelectronics had a similar, competing line of memory cards and *smart cards* (Fujitsu's term for any small card with integrated circuits on it), but these were based on a 68-pin connector design.

John Reimer, upon being appointed marketing manager for microcomputer products at Fujitsu in 1987, quickly determined that he had inherited what amounted to a product looking for a purpose. It seemed to Reimer that card memory had the potential to serve as a data exchange medium that lacked the environmental vulnerability of floppy disks (such as LBLdust, temperature, shock, and impact).

While exploring marketing opportunities for his memory cards, Reimer discovered that the Poqet Computer Company was itself investigating the use of memory cards as an alternative to disk drives for a new product that was ultimately to become the first true subnotebook PC. (Fujitsu had invested in the Poqet startup and has since acquired the company.) But Poqet was so concerned about the lack of standards among the various memory cards that it hesitated to select a memory card product because of uncertainty about which designs would succeed.

Sensible as was Poqet's desire to standardize memory cards throughout the industry, Reimer found that realizing the desire was a practical impossibility. No single standards organization was set up to rule on all the required aspects of such a design: physical card size, number and function of the connector pins, data file formats, and software interface. And to run the different facets of a card design through the whole gamut of separate standards sanctioning organizations might take longer than the useful life of the product.

While promoting the idea that the personal computer industry should itself develop a memory card standard, Reimer discovered that Lotus Development was contemplating putting its software on ROM cards. Lotus had been among the first to embrace putting software on the larger cartridges of the ill-fated PCjr. But Lotus, too, balked at the prospect of a profusion of incompatible card designs, and offered its support when Reimer proposed to bring together parties interested in memory card standardization. Reimer found enough initial support among other major suppliers of software, semiconductors, and personal computers, to convene a meeting of representatives from about 25 manufacturers that took place at the Fairmont Hotel in San Jose in June 1988.

That first informal meeting pointed out the possibilities—including the potential for an antitrust suit. So with $10,000 contributed by Fujitsu, Reimer hired lawyers to draft guidelines that would avert legal tangles and organized the group that became the *Personal Computer Memory Card Industry Association,* or *PCMCIA.* At that early point, however, the role and future of the organization were uncertain. Early on, Reimer entertained the possibility that PCMCIA would craft a standard and quietly fade away, mission accomplished. But the organization gained its own momentum at its monthly meetings, and the standard expanded in scope from a PC enhancement to a universal digital data exchange mechanism.

PC Card, Release 1.0, the first generation of the PCMCIA standard, was introduced in September 1990. It contemplated only the use of solid-state memory on the card as a means of data storage. But the PC Card intrigued both the makers of subnotebook computers and peripheral developers, who believed that the standard could be expanded to incorporate I/O devices as well as memory.

As a result, the PC Card standard was updated in September 1991 to comprise a more generalized interface that would accommodate both storage and input/output devices. Additionally, the new Release 2.0 standard allowed the use of thicker cards, permitting the incorporation of a wider variety of semiconductor circuits. It also allowed programs stored on PC Cards to be executed in the card memory instead of requiring the code to be downloaded into standard RAM.

In keeping with good practice, backward compatibility was maintained: Cards designed under PCMCIA Release 1.0 plug into and work in Release 2.0 machines. Because Release 2.0 adds a wealth of features that older hardware may not understand, however, all the functions of a new card may not work in an older system. Because normal thickness cards of both generations are physically the same, new cards will fit slots in old systems. No combination of card and system will result in damage at either end of the connection.

Backward compatibility at that early stage was, of course, practically a non issue. The only device limited solely to PCMCIA Release 1.0 form factor slots was the Poqet subnotebook. Although the Hewlett-Packard 95LX conforms to Release 1.0 electrically, its socket accommodates the thicker cards permitted by Release 2.0.

The completed PCMCIA 2.0 is far more than a simple set of physical specifications for card dimensions and a bus pin-out. The standard also describes file formats and data structures, a method through which a card can convey its configuration and capabilities to a host, a device-independent means of accessing card hardware and software links independent of operating systems; it currently remains the only standard for the expansion of notebook and smaller PCs.

Bus Design and Operation

Just as a highway system is more than pavement, a bus is more than a set of wires or copper traces on a printed circuit board. Roads are governed by an elaborate set of rules, followed by the majority of drivers, that ensure the smooth and trouble-free flow of traffic—even making allowances for the few scofflaws who flout the regulations and dare to travel even one mile-per-hour over the posted limits. Computer expansion buses similarly are governed by rules that dictate which signals flow when and where. These rules determine how fast and successful information passes across the bus, what resources are available to expansion boards, and whether the overall computer works.

Although all computer buses are designed to achieve the same purpose—the capability to expand the power of your PC—the variation in rules that govern buses controls how well this goal is achieved. The general goal in the evolution of bus designs has been to push as much information as possible across the copper traces in as little time as possible. At the same time, designers opted to increase the flexibility of their bus designs so that more and different expansion devices can be connected, to lighten the load on the host system so that more of its power can be put to work, and to reduce your involvement in setting up the devices connected to the bus. To reach these worthy goals, computer makers have set up truly elaborate rules for bus operation. Understanding them gives you insight in how the expansion bus of your PC operates, what you can expect from it, and why you may prefer one design over another.

What follows is a discussion of all the expansion buses used in today's PCs, from the oldest designs that stick around like dinosaur bones buried in the earth to the latest standards that your next PC is likely to support.

Industry Standard Architecture

If any one characteristic has defined a PC, it is Industry Standard Architecture. For many manufacturers, ISA is The One True Bus. If you want to add something to your PC, odds are it is available in ISA. It is the *sine qua non* of the personal computer. When poets need to note some unimaginably large number, they can add the installed base of ISA boards to classics like the grains of sand on the beach, the stars in the universe, and celebrity spouses. Greek philosophers probably would have ranked ISA as one of the grand ultimates—along with Truth, Beauty, Justice, and the five-cent cigar. You get the idea. ISA is the ultimate blessing for the PC, yet still something that's not quite perfect. But it's what we have—what we're stuck with—and we'll make do, even if we have to delude ourselves.

Like the rest of our universe, ISA did not spring fully armed from the head of Zeus, but underwent a prolonged and painful birth. Its development parallels that of the entire PC industry. From pragmatic beginnings in the first PC, it grew to double its size, went through a troubled and troubling adolescence, and finally matured into the accepted standard known today. To know it isn't exactly to love it, but knowing it gives you valuable insight into why PCs are the way they are.

Eight-Bit Subset

Historically and operationally, the classic PC bus is the best place to start examining how all the bus signals work together. It's both the oldest design you'll still find in PCs and the most primitive. Just as humans can trace the salt water in their cells back to the primordial ooze from which our ancestors first crawled, the classic eight-bit bus marks where PC buses began. Its original constituents still echo through the latest bus incarnations.

Board Dimensions. When IBM originally designed the PC, the engineers had to balance size constraints. Expansion boards had to be large enough to hold a reasonable amount of circuitry so that they fit all the functions they needed using only the discrete logic available to them. But the boards were constrained by the need to keep the overall size of the PC within bounds. After all, if they made the machine itself too large there might be no difference between it and a mainframe.

The chosen design reflects that and other compromises. The boards are long and thin to fit the short, deep case of the PC. The expansion connector itself is relegated near one end of the board, giving the boards an "L" shape. This all-at-one-end arrangement facilitated motherboard design (more contiguous space for circuitry) and allowed the engineers to put the bus interface circuitry at one end of the board and the circuits for the bus functions at the other end.

The original design called for boards extending the full length of the PC case and 3 inches high, not including the expansion connector dipping off the bottom. All five slots in the original PC accommodated full-length boards. When the XT was introduced, the value of expansion had proven itself—and the number of slots in the PC proved too few. To up the XT quota to eight, the slots were more tightly spaced (0.8 inches versus a full inch apart in the PC), and two slots were squeezed in behind the drive bays. These slots accommodated only short boards, those measuring no more than seven inches long. But IBM promulgated no standards, so short boards might be any length that fit the confines behind the drive bays.

The expansion connector for each slot, located on the system board, had two rows of 31 pins each with center-to-center pin spacing of 0.1 inch. The mating contacts on each expansion board were simply etched in place when the board traces were etched. Most but not all boards had these board edge-connector contacts gold-plated for reliability. Figure 6.4 shows the dimensions of a full-size 8-bit expansion board.

Basic Signals. Of the 62 pins used by the PC/XT bus, three are grounds; five are lines to supply the various voltages needed around the computer (two 5 volt direct current as well as one each -5, 12, and -12 volts); twenty are address lines; eight are data lines; ten are devoted to interrupts; and several are special purpose connections to bring it all to life. Table 6.1 shows how these signals are arrayed.

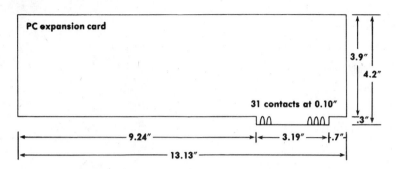

FIGURE 6.4. Dimensions of a full-size 8-bit expansion board.

TABLE 6.1. Pin-Out of Standard 8-Bit PC Bus

Used by PC, XT, Portable Personal Computer, most compatibles

Pin	Signal	Pin	Signal
B1	Ground	A1	Input/Output Channel Check
B2	Reset Driver	A2	Data 7
B3	+5 VDC	A3	Data 6
B4	Interrupt Request 2	A4	Data 5
B5	-VDC	A5	Data 4
B6	DMA Request 2	A6	Data 3
B7	-12 VDC	A7	Data 2
B8	Card Selected	A8	Data 1 (XT Only)
B9	+12 VDC	A9	Data 0
B10	Ground	A10	Input/Output Channel Ready
B11	Memory Write	A11	Address Enable
B12	Memory Read	A12	Address 19
B13	Input/Output Write	A13	Address 18
B14	Input/Ouput Read	A14	Address 17
B15	DMA Acknowledge 3	A15	Address 16
B16	DMA Request 3	A16	Address 15
B17	DMA Acknowledge 1	A17	Address 14
B18	DMA Request 1	A18	Address 13
B19	DMA Acknowledge 0	A19	Address 12

continues

TABLE 6.1. Continued

Used by PC, XT, Portable Personal Computer, most compatibles

Pin	Signal	Pin	Signal
B20	Clock	A20	Address 11
B21	Interrupt Request 7	A21	Address 10
B22	Interrupt Request 6	A22	Address 9
B23	Interrupt Request 5	A23	Address 8
B24	Interrupt Request 4	A24	Address 7
B25	Interrupt Request 3	A25	Address 6
B26	DMA Acknowledge 2	A26	Address 5
B27	Terminal Count	A27	Address 4
B28	Address Latch	A28	Address 3 Enable
B29	+5 VDC	A29	Address 2
B30	Oscillator	A30	Address 1
B31	Ground	A31	Address 0

Although the list of bus functions is complicated by a wealth of specialized terminology that makes it look as forbidding as the list of ingredients on a candy bar, everything is completely straightforward.

The *Oscillator* line supplies a signal derived directly from the crystal oscillator that runs all the clocks and timers inside the computer. Operating at 14.31818 megahertz, in the PC bus design, this oscillator is the single frequency standard of the entire computer.

The odd frequency on which PCs were based was actually derived from a very practical consideration. It's exactly three times the speed at which the microprocessor operates and four times the frequency that televisions (and inexpensive computer monitors) use to lock their color signals to. This one oscillator can serve multiple purposes through simple frequency dividers, running both the microprocessor and display system.

The *Clock* line on the bus is one of those signals derived from the Oscillator. It's the one electrically divided by four—to 4.77 megahertz—and supplied to the microprocessor and other system circuitry to time and synchronize all logical operations.

The *I/O Channel Check* line provides the microprocessor with an integrity check of the memory and devices connected to the PC bus. If the signal on this line is interrupted, it indicates to the microprocessor that a parity check error has occurred. Grounding this line effectively crashes the system.

Supplying a pulse to the *Reset Driver* line of the PC bus instructs the whole system to reset or initialize itself. A signal is generated on this line whenever the system is turned on or power is interrupted.

The *Data Lines* carry digital information in parallel form throughout the computer. These same lines are used to move information to and from both memory and input/output devices. Eight data lines are used in the PC, identified with numbers from zero to seven, with zero indicating the line carrying the least significant bit of each digital word of information.

The *Address Lines* are used for specifying locations in memory to and from which bytes of information are moved. The twenty total lines are identified with numbers 0 through 19, again with line zero being the least significant.

Bus Control. To read or write memory, the microprocessor sends the memory address that it wants to use down the address lines and then pulses a special line called the *Address Latch Enable* to indicate to devices connected to the bus that it sent a valid address and that the devices should remember it (by "latching"—electronically locking their circuits to that address). Finally, the microprocessor sends a signal down the *Memory Read Command,* which tells the memory controller to put the data at the indicated address on the data lines. Alternatively, the microprocessor can send a signal down the *Memory Write Command* line, which indicates that the microprocessor has put a byte of information on the data lines and that the memory controller should store that information at the indicated addresses.

The same data lines are used for moving bytes to input/output devices through other special purpose lines on the bus. The *I/O Read Command* line tells a device to move information from an input port onto the data lines so that the microprocessor can read it into its registers. The *I/O Write Command* line instructs an input/output device to take the information on the data lines, put there by the microprocessor, and move it to its output port.

Because the microprocessor can generate or demand data quicker than an input/output device or even memory might be able to handle it, the PC bus also includes a provision for making the microprocessor wait while the other part of the system catches up. By removing the ready signal from the *I/O Channel Ready* line, the memory controller or input/output device tells the microprocessor to pause for one or more clock cycles.

If the microprocessor does not find a ready on this line at the beginning of a clock cycle when it tries to use the bus, it waits until the start of the next clock cycle before trying again—and continues to wait as long as the ready signal is not present. IBM specifications do not allow these delays to extend for longer than ten clock cycles.

DMA Control. Information can be moved from one place in a PC to another much faster under DMA control than through the use of the microprocessor. To make those moves, however, the DMA controller must take command of both the address and data lines. In addition, devices connected to the bus must be able to signal to the DMA controller to make these moves, and the controller needs to be able to signal back to the system when it's done. Several bus lines are used for these functions.

The *Address Enable* line is used to tell the DMA controller that the microprocessor has disconnected itself from the bus to let the DMA controller take command. After this signal is asserted, the DMA controller has charge of the address and data lines, in addition to the memory and input/output read and write control lines.

At the end of a DMA memory move, a pulse is sent down the *Terminal Count* line, which is called this because the pulse represents the termination (end) of a count of the number of bytes moved in the DMA transfer. (The number of bytes to be moved must be declared before the transfer begins so that they can be appropriately counted.)

Devices indicate to the DMA controller that they want to make DMA transfers by sending signals down one of the three *DMA Request* lines. Each line is assigned a priority level that corresponds to its numerical designation, with one having the highest priority and three having the lowest.

To indicate that a request has been received by the DMA controller as well as to provide the rest of the system with an acknowledgment of the DMA request, four *DMA Acknowledge* lines are provided. Three lines are used to confirm the DMA requests across the bus itself, designated by numbers corresponding to the request acknowledged. The fourth line, designated zero, acknowledges memory refreshing (which also deprives other devices access to the PC bus).

Finally, the PC bus provides for five *Interrupt Request* lines, which are used for hardware signals from various devices to the microprocessor to capture its attention and temporarily divert it to a different process. The Interrupt Request lines are designated with numbers two through seven, in order of decreasing priority.

Interrupts zero and one are not available on the bus, but are used internally by the PC in its system board circuitry. Interrupt zero is controlled by the system timer and generates a periodic interrupt at a rate of 18.2 per second, and one is devoted to servicing the keyboard, generating an interrupt with each keypress. In addition, a special interrupt called the *Non-Maskable Interrupt,* or *NMI* because it cannot be masked or switched off in the normal operation of the system through software, is used to signal the microprocessor about parity errors.

Note that the NMI can be switched off through the *NMI Mask Registers,* available at I/O port 0A0(hex) in the PC and XT. (Similar functions are available in other IBM computers but at different ports.) By loading 00(hex) into this register, the NMI can be masked off and the computer does *not* shut down on parity errors. Loading 80(hex) to this register turns the NMI back on. Table 6.2 shows an example of how to do this using the DOS program Debug.

TABLE 6.2. Turning NMI Off Using DEBUG

To turn NMI off and prevent system halting with parity errors:

```
DEBUG                 ; Load the Debug program
-rax                  ; Read the AX register
```

To turn NMI off and prevent system halting with parity errors:

AX 0000	; System responds with current AX value
;0a	; Load the register with the port number, 0A(hex)
-o 00	; Output 00(hex) to the port in AX
-q	; Quit Debug to return to DOS

To turn NMI on and halt system upon detection of parity errors:

DEBUG	; Load the Debug program
-rax	; Read the AX register
AX 0000	; System responds with current AX value
;0a	; Load the register with the port number, 0A(hex)
-o 80	; Output 80(hex) to the port in AX
-q	; Quit Debug to return to DOS

Note:

Port 0A(Hex) applies to PC-class machines. AT-class computers control NMI through port 070(Hex). Substitute this port number when using this routine on AT-style computers.

XT Slot Eight. Normally, in a PC with an eight-bit expansion bus, all the connectors on a bus have exactly the same signals available at the same positions. IBM made an exception for its XT. In the IBM XT, system units slot eight—the short slot nearest the power supply—differs electrically from all other eight-bit IBM PC-bus slots. One connection, noted as reserved in the original PC bus, is devoted to the slot-specific function that IBM called *card selected.* Because of this special signal, slot eight is regarded separately by the host computer in now rare computers that follow the XT prototype. In ordinary operation, system board drivers pay no attention to slot eight. Only when the card selected line is activated does the system board respond and link up to the circuitry on the card. The card itself controls its isolation. This feature is designed to be taken advantage of by special purpose adapters, for instance the multiboard emulation facility of the 3270 PC.

If you have an old PC that follows this XT standard, you'll find that should you slide an expansion board that makes no special provision for slot eight into the slot, it won't work properly. In the early days of PCs, products that would not function in slot eight had warnings to that effect in their instructions. Many vendors of short PC-bus expansion cards (the only ones that fit into slot eight) included a jumper or DIP switch on their boards to allow them to adapt to this special expansion slot. If you have a vintage computer that follows the XT slot-eight standard and run into a problem with a specific board in the special slot, the solution is simple—

move the board. Better still, get a new PC to replace your fossil. Modern PCs don't add this extra layer of complication to their ISA expansion buses.

Sixteen-Bit Extension

To push the already aging 8-bit PC bus into the 16-bit world of the AT, IBM grafted on a second connector. The auxiliary edge connector, with the same pin-spacing (0.1 inch center-to-center) but fewer pins (38 versus 62), was added in front of the old connector to give good backward compatibility. Because the 8-bit connector retained its normal position, 8-bit boards would readily slide into 16-bit slots by simply ignoring the extra connector. At the same time, 16-bit boards would fit into most 8-bit slots with their auxiliary connectors hanging free and unused. Bus signals (or lack of them) indicated to both board and computer that the auxiliary connector was unused.

Board Dimensions. Despite the connector arrangement, backward compatibility was not complete. Eight-bit boards with *skirts*—extended depth along the bottom of the card to allow extra circuitry—do not fit 16-bit slots. Moreover, in some cases 16-bit boards do not fit 8-bit (nor even some 16-bit) systems. The greater headroom of the AT case allowed for taller expansion boards. (PC and AT cases were the same depth, so the length of 16-bit expansion boards was unchanged from the 8-bit design.) Expansion boards could extend almost as tall as the case to accommodate more circuitry. The largest possible AT expansion board measured 4.75 by 13.5 inches (see fig. 6.5). Because not all compatible full 16-bit PCs copied the tall AT case, however, many manufacturers restricted the height of their 16-bit expansion product to the same height as old 8-bit boards.

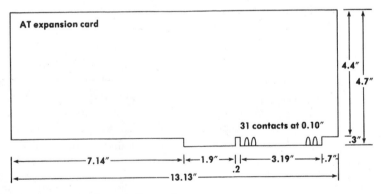

FIGURE 6.5. AT expansion board dimensions.

The 16-Bit Data Bus. Table 6.3 shows the complete pinout of the 16-bit AT bus. The obvious addition required when moving from 8 to 16 data bits is eight additional data lines. These eight new lines, designated Data 8 through 15, complete the sequence started with the first eight, increasing in significance with their designations.

TABLE 6.3. Pin-Out of the Standard 16-Bit AT (ISA) Expansion Bus

Pin	Signal	Pin	Signal
B1	Ground	A1	Input/Output Channel Check
B2	Reset Driver	A2	Data 7
B3	+5 VDC	A3	Data 6
B4	Interrupt Request 9	A4	Data 5
B5	-VDC	A5	Data 4
B6	DMA Request 2	A6	Data 3
B7	-12 VDC	A7	Data 2
B8	Zero Wait State	A8	Data 1
B9	+12 VDC	A9	Data 0
B10	Ground	A10	Input/Output Channel Ready
B11	Real Memory Write	A11	Address Enable
B12	Real Memory Read	A12	Address 19
B13	Input/Output Write	A13	Address 18
B14	Input/Ouput Read	A14	Address 17
B15	DMA Acknowledge 3	A15	Address 16
B16	DMA Request 3	A16	Address 15
B17	DMA Acknowledge 1	A17	Address 14
B18	DMA Request 1	A18	Address 13
B19	Refresh	A19	Address 12
B20	Clock	A20	Address 11
B21	Interrupt Request 7	A21	Address 10
B22	Interrupt Request 6	A22	Address 9
B23	Interrupt Request 5	A23	Address 8
B24	Interrupt Request 4	A24	Address 7
B25	Interrupt Request 3	A25	Address 6
B26	DMA Acknowledge 2	A26	Address 5
B27	Terminal Count	A27	Address 4
B28	Address Latch Enable	A28	Address 3
B29	+5 VDC	A29	Address 2
B30	Oscillator	A30	Address 1

continues

TABLE 6.3. Continued

Pin	Signal	Pin	Signal
B31	Ground	A31	Address 0
D1	Memory 16-bit Chip Select	C1	System Bus High Enable
D2	I/O 16-bit Chip Select	C2	Unlatched Address 23
D3	Interrupt Request 10	C3	Unlatched Address 22
D4	Interrupt Request 11	C4	Unlatched Address 21
D5	Interrupt Request 12	C5	Unlatched Address 20
D6	Interrupt Request 15	C6	Unlatched Address 19
D7	Interrupt Request 14	C7	Unlatched Address 18
D8	DMA Acknowledge 0	C8	Unlatched Address 17
D9	DMA Request 0	C9	Memory Read
D10	DMA Acknowledge 5	C10	Memory Write
D11	DMA Request 5	C11	Data 8
D12	DMA Acknowledge	C12	Data 9
D13	DMA Request 6	C13	Data 10
D14	DMA Acknowledge 7	C14	Data 11
D15	DMA Request 7	C15	Data 12
D16	+5 VDC	C16	Data 13
D17	Master	C17	Data 14
D18	Ground	C18	Data 15

Because both 8- and 16-bit devices may be present in one computer, some provision must be made to indicate how may bits are actually to be used for each memory and input/output operation. IBM uses several signals to facilitate such matters. One of these is called *System Bus High Enable*, and it must be active for 16-bit data transfers to take place. In addition, expansion cards indicate to the host system that the data transfer taking place is a 16-bit operation with the *Memory 16-bit Chip Select* and *I/O 16-bit Chip Select* signals, depending on whether the transfer is from or to memory or an input/output device.

Besides slowing down memory access with the *I/O Channel Ready* signal, the AT bus also provides for a speedup signal. The *Zero Wait State* signal indicates that the current bus cycle can be completed without wait states.

The 24-Bit Address Bus. To accommodate the full 16 megabyte physical address range of the 80286 microprocessor used in the AT, IBM expanded the number of memory address lines to 24. Instead of adding just four new lines, however, IBM added eight.

The new address lines differ from the old in that they do not latch—that is, their value is not held by the system board throughout the memory cycle. Instead, they are asserted only until the memory read or write command is given, at which point their value becomes undefined. The expansion board is charged with the responsibility for remembering the address for any longer period that it needs. This technique can allow faster operation on the bus.

The *Memory Read* and *Memory Write* functions of the AT bus are shifted to the supplementary connector, whereas the bus connections at the positions used by the Memory Read and Memory Write functions of the original (eight-bit) PC bus are devoted only to operation on real mode memory.

Memory transfers within the one megabyte real addressing range require that both the new and old memory read or write lines be activated. When a read or write request is made to the area above the one megabyte limit of real memory, however, only the supplementary connector Memory Read or Write lines are activated. An eight-bit card, therefore, never receives a command (nor is able to issue one) that it cannot act upon.

Added System Services. To make up for the shortages of interrupts and DMA channels that often occur in PCs and XTs when multiple serial ports, hard disks, tape systems, and other peripherals are installed, IBM virtually doubled the number of each. Two sets of DMA controllers are available—one that yields four 8-bit channels, one with four 16-bit channels of which one is reserved for use only on the system board. The operation and priorities assigned to DMA channels follow the pattern set with the PC. DMA channel 0 has the highest priority; DMA channel 7 the lowest.

The number of interrupts also was nearly doubled in the AT, from 8 to a total of 15. Not all these appear on the expansion bus, however. Five interrupts are reserved to the system board: interrupts 0, 1, 2, 8, and 13. In addition, the AT makes provisions for interrupt sharing so that one interrupt can be used for several functions.

Bus Sharing. As with the XT's slot eight, IBM made a token effort toward adding more power on the PC bus. In the AT, however, IBM gave specific support to running more than one microprocessor on the bus, and this support was not restricted to a single slot.

The bus sharing of ISA works like a DMA cycle. The expansion card that contains the visiting microprocessor first activates a DMA request and receives back an acknowledgment. After receiving the acknowledgment, the visiting microprocessor activates the *Master* line on the bus, which gives the chip complete control of all address, data, and control lines of the bus. For a short period, it is the master, in charge of the computer.

The short period is delimited by memory refreshing, which requires host system access to RAM. If the visiting microprocessor tries to steal more than 15 microseconds at a time from the bus, the host may lose its memory and mind because the chip gets *total* control, and the host cannot even refresh its own memory.

To prevent unwanted interruptions during memory refresh cycles, the AT bus also provides for a *Refresh* signal, which serves as a warning as to what is going on.

Plug and Play ISA

The ISA standard leaves issues of system setup to you. You have to ensure that every expansion board plugged into the system gets the interrupt service, memory address range, port addresses, and DMA access that it requires. You also must ensure that the needs of each board conflict with none of the others in the system. Before you slide each expansion board into your system, you have to check jumpers or DIP switch settings to ensure that they do not conflict with setting anything else in your system, or should you be blessed with a board that includes its own software setup procedure, you get to wade through a program written by someone intent on creating a cipher the CIA cannot understand. When the inevitable conflict arises, you are left with the limitless joy of a computer or peripheral that absolutely refuses to work, and will not say why. You, as the manager of the PC are to blame, and your punishment is to devote a substantial fraction of your life to penance—that is, surrounding yourself with manuals, notepads, and a hexadecimal calculator to sort things out.

Plug and Play ISA gives all that brainwork to the electronic entity closest to the problem, your PC itself. Using the features specified by the standard, individual expansion boards can tell the system their needs and what substitutions they accept, and your system then can make the necessary arrangements.

Plug and Play works without modification to the ISA bus, although it allows for advanced systems to streamline their configuration process by adding a single slot-specific signal to each bus connector. The main modification required by Plug and Play ISA is the addition of special registers to each expansion board and the capability for each card to deselect itself, essentially disconnecting from the bus so that the card does not respond to commands and signals meant for other boards.

Isolation Sequence. The key to setting up individual boards in a Plug and Play ISA system is the capability to isolate each board from the other boards. The Plug and Play ISA specification standardizes the isolation sequence used.

When you switch on your system or give it a cold boot, all the Plug and Play ISA cards inside it come up in their *Wait for Key* state. In this condition, the expansion boards refuse to respond to any signal on the ISA bus until they receive their initiation key. When a board receives the initiation key code, it switches to its *Sleep* state. The card (and all the other cards in the PC) then wait again for a *Wake[Card Select Number]* command. Upon receiving this command, all cards in the system shift to their *Isolation state*, which allows them to listen to bus signals.

The host computer then executes a series of 72 reads of consecutive read-only registers that store a board identification number. Every Plug and Play ISA expansion board (not merely every model) is assigned a number during manufacture that should be unique in every PC. After the number of a card is uniquely identified, all the other boards in the system are forced back into Sleep state, and a unique number is written to the Card Select Number register on the board. Writing this number back to the card causes the designated card to enter its *Config* state. The board now can be configured independently from any other board in the system (all the others will be in the Sleep state), or the system can switch the selected card back to its Sleep state by sending a `Wake[0]` command to it. However, the uniquely assigned CSN number can be used any time thereafter to isolate and individually command the selected board.

When a board has a Card Select Number assigned, it drops out of the isolation sequence. The system continues to step through the process until each board has been assigned a unique Card Select Number.

Assigning Resources. Plug and Play ISA allows for any board to ask for up to four non contiguous ranges of memory base addresses; up to eight non contiguous base addresses for input/output ports; up to two separate interrupt levels; and up to two DMA channels. The system can query a board as to its needs only when the board is in its Config state. Only one board can be in Config state at a time; this state is selected either during the isolation sequence or by sending a Wake command using the board's unique Card Select Number (which must be assigned earlier during the isolation sequence).

Micro Channel Architecture

As long as the system is managing one resource or operating with one bus master, the ISA system works well. But computers often are called upon to manage a number of tasks and devices simultaneously. When the going gets tough, the ISA system has a tough time going. IBM was aware of the need for more flexibility and power in the expansion bus even before the AT and its 16-bit bus was introduced. The Card Selected signal in XT slot eight was only an indication of the direction IBM was going.

With the introduction of its PS/2 line of computers, IBM unveiled its solution—a stunning *tour de force* that represented a total break with the classic bus design that incorporates a multitude of the best ideas used in mainframe computers, including bus-mastering with full prioritized arbitration. In addition, the new design provided an IBM-sanctioned 32-bit expansion bus to an industry without a 32-bit expansion standard.

Although Micro Channel no longer rates as a mainstream PC product—today most new Micro Channel products are file servers, minicomputer systems, and upgrade parts for the aging base of PS/2 computers—its influence has been pervasive. Every PC bus designed since the introduction of Micro Channel owes a large debt to it.

Physical Characteristics

Actually, Micro Channel Architecture refers to more than just the layout of an expansion bus, it also redefined physical aspects of expansion boards, how system boards operate, some construction practices, how systems are set up, and how software interacts with the bus.

The physical embodiment of Micro Channel Architecture includes the definition of the size and physical arrangement of the bus connectors used, the electrical signals coursing through those connectors, and the logical function of those signals. The bus allows for many variations: a 16-bit implementation, a 32-bit implementation, an optional extension to allow the exchange of video signals, and another optional extension that permits the bus speed to be increased from 10 to 16 MHz to provide higher speed memory transfer for 16 MHz computers. Some additional signals also were grafted on in the first major Micro Channel revision in 1990.

Table 6.4 shows the complete pin-out of the Micro Channel Architecture bus, 16-bit implementation.

TABLE 6.4. Micro Channel Architecture Bus Pin-Out, 16-Bit Implementation

Pin	Function	Pin	Function
A1	Card setup	B1	Audio ground
A2	Memory address enable 24	B2	Audio
A3	Ground	B3	Ground
A4	Address line 11	B4	14.3 MHz oscillator
A5	Address line 10	B5	Ground
A6	Address line 9	B6	Address line 23
A7	+5VDC	B7	Address line 22
A8	Address line 8	B8	Address line 21
A9	Address line 7	B9	Ground
A10	Address line 6	B10	Address line 20
A11	+5VDC	B11	Address line 19
A12	Address line 5	B12	Address line 18
A13	Address line 4	B13	Ground
A14	Address line 3	B14	Address line 17
A15	+5VDC	B15	Address line 16
A16	Address line 2	B16	Address line 15
A17	Address line 1	B17	Ground
A18	Address line 0	B18	Address line 14

Pin	Function	Pin	Function
A19	+12VDC	B19	Address line 13
A20	Address decode latch	B20	Address line 12
A21	Preempt	B21	Ground
A22	Burst	B22	Interrupt request 9
A23	–12VDC	B23	Interrupt request 3
A24	Arbitration line 0	B24	Interrupt request 4
A25	Arbitration line 1	B25	Ground
A26	Arbitration line 2	B26	Interrupt request 5
A27	–12VDC	B27	Interrupt request 6
A28	Arbitration line 3	B28	Interrupt request 7
A29	Arbitration/-Grant	B29	Ground
A30	Terminal count	B30	Data parity enable
A31	+5VDC	B31	Data parity 0
A32	Status 0	B32	Channel check
A33	Status 1	B33	Ground
A34	Memory/-Input Output	B34	Command
A35	+12VDC	B35	Channel ready return
A36	Card Channel Ready	B36	Card selected feedback
A37	Data line 0	B37	Ground
A38	Data line 2	B38	Data line 1
A39	+5VDC	B39	Data line 3
A40	Data line 5	B40	Data line 4
A41	Data line 6	B41	Ground
A42	Data line 7	B42	Channel Reset
A43	Ground	B43	Streaming data strobe
A44	Data size 16 return	B44	Streaming data request 0
A45	Refresh	B45	Ground
A46	KEY	B46	KEY
A47	KEY	B47	KEY
A48	+5VDC	B48	Data line 8
A49	Data line 10	B49	Data line 9

continues

TABLE 6.4. Continued

Pin	Function	Pin	Function
A50	Data line 11	B50	Ground
A51	Data line 13	B51	Data line 13
A52	+12VDC	B52	Data line 14
A53	Data parity 1	B53	Data line 15
A54	System byte high enable	B54	Ground
A55	Card data size 16	B55	Interrupt request 10
A56	+5VDC	B56	Interrupt request 11
A57	Interrupt request 14	B57	Interrupt request 12
A58	Interrupt request 15	B58	Ground

Auxiliary Video Extension

Pin	Function	Pin	Function
AV10	Vertical sync	BV10	ESYNC
AV9	Horizontal sync	BV9	Ground
AV8	Blanking	BV8	P5
AV7	Ground	BV7	P4
AV6	P6	BV6	P3
AV5	EDCLK	BV5	Ground
AV4	DCLK	BV4	P2
AV3	Ground	BV3	P1
AV2	P7	BV2	P0
AV1	EVIDEO	BV1	Ground
KEY	KEY		

Note:

Both the Matched-memory and Video extensions extend the Micro Channel connector above pin one, away from the 32-bit extension. A key separates the Video extension from the rest of the bus connector; the Matched-memory extension merely extends the connector.

Some of the changes from the familiar PC bus seem so obvious to be almost trivial. It uses physically different—smaller—connectors from those used by the aging PC bus. This fact alone makes hardware meant for the PC bus incompatible with the Micro Channel.

The new connector choice seemed almost devious. In effect, IBM rendered all third-party peripherals obsolete in one bold stroke. The company honored itself with an instant head start against all other vendors in the design of enhancements for the more profitable top end of the PS/2 line.

If you didn't have a few million dollars tied up in PC expansion inventory and product designs, you might see a bright side to the adoption of miniaturization connectors. For one, these connectors make it easier to engineer expansion boards based on *surface mount components*, miniaturized microchips that pack more functions into less space than ever before. Because the pin spacing on the new Micro Channel connectors—increments of 0.050 inch—corresponds to that of surface mount circuit components, the job of the layout artists (or drafting machine) is easier. On the negative side, they aren't amenable to garage-based engineering because soldering these connectors to circuit boards demands special equipment.

IBM complemented the smaller connectors and smaller surface mount components by reducing the size of expansion boards, from the 4.75 x 13.5 of AT boards to 3.5 x 11.5 inches (see fig. 6.6). Surface mount components also help in this size reduction because they require less power and thus produce less heat, allowing more miniaturization. For people who just use computers and don't have to worry about designing and building them, the smaller connectors, surface mount components, and expansion cards are good news. Less of your desk needs to be overrun by rampaging computer equipment.

Smaller boards help manufacturers cut costs, at least after the price for developing new designs is paid. They require less in the way of the glass-epoxy base materials from which the boards are built. That's only a small advantage, however, because the cost of components, development, and labor far outweigh the price of the glass-epoxy that makes up the board substrate.

On the interference front, the Micro Channel marks a quantum improvement over the PC bus design. The radically altered arrangement of signals on the Micro Channel puts an electrical ground on every fourth pin. The many grounds and their proximity to the high frequency digital signals on the bus help reduce interference more than is possible in PCs or ATs. This, in turn, makes achieving FCC certification less of a headache, giving designers one less thing to sit up nights worrying about.

The better arrangement of signals in the Micro Channel also aids in increasing the maximum speed at which expansion boards can operate because it increases the bandwidth of the bus. That means higher frequencies and higher data rates are possible. Unfortunately, IBM only provided for a modest clock speed increase when Micro Channel was first introduced (to 10 MHz). The 1990 revision, which allowed for double speed—20 MHz operation—showed that the bus redesign confers substantial upward potential. In fact, some independent tests show that the Micro Channel bus can be safely operated at speeds up to 80 MHz.

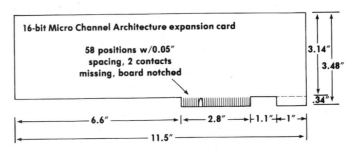

FIGURE 6.6. Micro channel board dimensions.

Signal Enhancements

Electrically, the Micro Channel provides for either a 16-bit or 32-bit data bus and full 24-bit addressing. Initially, 32-bit memory addressing was possible with DMA support limited to the first 16MB, but current designs allow full 32-bit addressing of up to 4,096 megabytes of physical RAM.

The Micro Channel uses special signals to indicate the bus width of each card inserted into a connector. *Card Data Size 16* is generated by devices connected to the bus to tell expansion cards that 16-bit information is available to them. The card signals back on *Data Size 16 Return* that it can handle 16-bit data. Similarly, the signals *Card Data Size 32* and *Data Size 32 Return* indicate and confirm 32-bit operations in 80386-equipped PS/2s such as the Models 70 and 80.

Byte Enable Bits 0 through 3 are used to identify the type of data transfer carried across the bus. They permit Micro Channel components to move information 8, 16, 24, or 32 bits at a time without ambiguity. This aids Micro Channel adapters in using any bus width that's an even multiple of a byte so that 8-, 16-, and 32-bit expansion accessories can be mixed in the same computer.

Memory Address Enable 24, when not turned on, indicates that the microprocessor or other device on the bus is using the extended 32-bit addressing range of the 80386 microprocessor instead of the 24-bit range of the 80286.

Instead of using separate lines for memory and input/output operations as does the PC bus, the Micro Channel uses a combination of three signals—*Memory/Input-Output*, *Status Bit One*, and *Status Bit Two* to define the type of bus cycle to be made.

Like the I/O Channel Check line of the PC bus, the *Channel Check* line of the Micro Channel is used to indicate serious errors conditions, such as parity check errors.

Other extensions made to both the 16- and 32-bit Micro Channel designs allow for integrating a single-channel analog audio signal of medium fidelity—for example, synthesized voice or music—with the IBM bus structure. This *Audio* signal is the only analog signal that's a standard part of based Micro Channel connectors. The audio signal itself is optional and allows expansion cards on the channel to exchange and independently process audio signals.

Although originally this audio extension far outreached the sound capabilities of then-marketed PCs, it pales in comparison to today's CD-based audio systems. Micro Channel's audio quality was designed to be not even as good as FM radio—and noisy even then—with a frequency range up to about ten kilohertz. (Technically, the response is 50 Hz to 10 KHz +/— 3 dB.) The Micro Channel specification allows an analog noise level of up to 50 millivolts, against a maximum analog signal of 2,500 millivolts, an inauspicious signal-to-noise ratio of about 32 dB.

The video extension to the Micro Channel—a small auxiliary connector, generally only on one slot in each PS/2—allows expansion cards to access the Video Graphics Array circuitry built into some motherboards. Non-Micro Channel machines require a separate VGA or VESA feature connector on the motherboard and a separate additional cable to link motherboard and expansion board. The Micro Channel video extension enables you to plug a video coprocessor card into your system and have it connect to your monitor without an additional cable.

The video extension uses several important signals. Present here are horizontal and vertical synchronizing signals, and a special control line called *ESYNC* or *Enable Sync.* This line determines whether the synchronizing signals used in the video system are original on the planar board or from an adapter plugged into the Micro Channel. ESYNC normally is held to logical high; bringing it low enables the system to use the synchronizing signals from the Micro Channel adapter.

Video data is transferred across the Micro Channel video extension in digital form using eight *Video Data Lines.* The data here is used to drive the VGA Digital-to-Analog converter on the system board.

Two clock signals and a special *blanking* signal also are provided. The last signal switches off the output VGA Digital-to-Analog converter to blank the screen. When this signal is high, the screen remains lit; a low signal darkens the screen.

To allow more effective system management, some new signals have been defined on the Micro Channel bus (besides those used by the new hardware arbitration feature). For example, *Card Selected Feedback* provides an indication from an expansion card to the host that the card is at the address it is supposed to be. It's primary use is during setup and diagnostics to help the system decipher what options are installed in it.

The *Channel Ready* line differs substantially from the I/O Channel Ready line of the PC bus. In the Micro Channel, it is used by devices connected to the bus to signal that they need more time to complete an operation, not to exceed 3.5 microseconds. Each connector has its own independent, slot-specific signal that is not bused together with those from other connectors. All the signals from every connector are combined logically at the bus controller circuit on the motherboard. Only if all the Channel Ready signals indicate that no additional time is needed, another special signal—*Channel Ready Return*—is created to make monitoring the condition of the bus easier.

Each connector in the Micro Channel also has its own *Card Setup* line, which is used during setup and error-recovery procedures. Activating this signal allows the configuration data space on the expansion board in the connector to be read.

Matched Memory Cycles

In addition to the wider 32-bit bus and the faster allowable clock speed of the Micro Channel, 32-bit versions of the system allow for a new data transfer mode. Called *Matched Memory,* this mode endows the Micro Channel with the potential of further quickening the pulse of data transfers between the planar board and expansion cards. The new signals take the form of another extension to the 32-bit bus that indicates to the 80386 that the data moving between devices can synchronize at a higher rate. When memory or a 16- or 32-bit internal peripheral is capable of operating at this higher speed, it can use the Matched Memory provisions of the Micro Channel to speed each information transfer by 25 percent, from 250 nanoseconds per cycle to 187.

The Matched Memory extension to the Micro Channel adds eight possible connections—three are reserved for future use and two are grounds. The *Matched Memory Cycle* signal is activated by the host microprocessor to indicate that it can handle matched memory transfers. The *Matched Memory Cycle Request* line is driven active by a device on the bus to indicate that it wants transfers to be made in the faster Matched Memory mode, either as 16- or 32-bit data. A third signal, *Matched Memory Command,* indicates that a Matched Memory cycle is active.

Bus Arbitration

The Micro Channel's biggest break with traditional PC design, and its most copied aspect, is its *hardware-mediated* bus arbitration scheme. This feature allows multiple microprocessors and ancillary devices to share the bus in an organized manner inside a single PC. The arbitration system allows not only multitasking but also parallel processing.

The key words are *hardware-mediated.* The AT allows bus sharing, but requires special software to control the system. All prioritizing is accomplished through programming, and little support was given to the programmer. With Micro Channel, all the hard work is handled by the hardware with a minimum of software support. Only a few bus cycles are required to pass along control of the bus. A software scheme would likely require dozens of program instructions (and even more clock cycles).

The original Micro Channel implementation of hardware bus arbitration allows up to eight microprocessors and eight other devices such as DMA controllers all to share the single data bus of a Micro Channel PC. Unfortunately, for the system to work properly, it requires all expansion cards—even cards that do not exploit bus arbitration to take control—to implement its circuitry.

This alone mandates incompatibility with old ISA expansion boards. As long as the cards were being redesigned, IBM's engineers must have figured, adding the rest of the Micro Channel features could just come along for the ride.

As forbidding as bus mastering and arbitration under Micro Channel standard sounds, its operation is actually easy to conceptualize. It's just a system of several signals that serve as semaphores to let each device sharing the bus know when its turn to control the data bus has come up. The system allows up to 16 different devices inside a single PC to share the bus, with each assigned its own level of priority.

To provide a familiar analogy to the Micro Channel, IBM used the metaphor of a superhighway in its initial explanations. Like the interstate, the Micro Channel provides, according to IBM, multiple lanes going in every direction at the highest possible safe speed. Because it has more lanes, it can handle more traffic, speeding the flow of data around inside the system.

It's a good metaphor, and could be better only if it actually described how the Micro Channel works. At best, however, it's misleading. The Micro Channel provides only two parallel paths for high speed traffic running next to its (up to) 32 bits of data—one for its auxiliary audio signal, and one for video information.

Rather than a superhighway, the Micro Channel works like the humble traffic cop, breaking up gridlock with a mixture of nerve, willpower, and guts. Just as the officer, armed with naught but his white gloves, keeps hacks and hitchhikers out of harm's way and keeps traffic flowing, the Micro Channel's hardware bus arbitration gives each processor sharing the bus its own turn, ensuring that nothing bogs down. Data processing flows along in as orderly and efficient a manner as possible.

Micro Channel bus arbitration accomplishes this task by specifying the hierarchy of signals that each device must use to gain access to the data bus. The arbitration scheme also provides a means of resolving conflicting claims when two or more devices demand their right to ride the bus. Hardware arbitration prevents the confusion of two devices from trying to appropriate control of the Micro Channel at the same time.

To implement this arbitration strategy, the Micro Channel uses several new lines to the old PC bus. Four of these, called *Arbitration Bus Priority Levels 0 through 3*, carry signals that code the level of priority assigned to each device that wants to take control of the Micro Channel, allowing for its 16 levels of priority.

In addition, two additional levels of priority are used by the devices on the system board host PCs and do not appear on the Micro Channel. These special levels are used to assign the absolute top priority to memory refreshing (which preserves data integrity) and the non-maskable interrupt (the familiar parity check error signal).

Bus arbitration involves three additional signals. One called *Pre-empt* is used by expansion cards to indicate that they require access to the Micro Channel. *Arbitrate/Grant* is sent out from the

Micro Channel *Central Arbitration Control Point* (which manages use of the bus) to start a haggling process for bus access. A final signal, *Burst,* allows Micro Channel devices to retain control while they transfer multiple blocks of related data so that the devices do not have to go through arbitration until the entire transfer is complete. It's a Do Not Disturb sign for block data transfers.

The arbitration process begins when one or more devices want to take control of the Micro Channel and send the message to the Central Arbitration Point (or CAP). When a pause appears on the data bus, the CAP signals all devices connected to the Micro Channel that they should start bidding for control.

Each Micro Channel device that wants bus access then sends out its assigned priority level on the four *Arbitration Bus Priority Level* lines. Each Micro Channel expansion card checks the these signals and ceases its efforts if it finds that a higher priority level is being asserted. Conflicting claims of the same priority level should never appear because the Micro Channel design does not allow two devices to be assigned the same priority.

These priority levels are assigned during the configuration process of each Micro Channel board and are stored on disk in the *Adapter Description Files*—disk files associated with each Micro Channel device during the Programmable Option Select process.

Sequential Transfer Modes

Although the modest clock speed increase of the original Micro Channel specification did little to improve the flow of randomly accessed data across the bus, IBM's engineers added a new transfer mode that speeds the movement of sequential data. Because many applications often require the movement of large sequential blocks of data, this new mode can boost overall system throughput.

The key to accelerating sequential transfers is Micro Channel's *burst mode.* Instead of relying on the two-step microprocessor data-moving process, the Micro Channel lets bursts of data blocks be transferred to and from input and output devices at rates of nearly 19 million characters or bytes per second (that's nearly 152 million bits per second) *without* the intervention of the microprocessor. To prevent congestion in the microprocessor, the Micro Channel also defines eight additional high-speed block-oriented paths between the input/output bus and memory.

Burst mode also requires some overhead, but much less than with PC- and AT-style block transfers. In burst mode, the system first is set up for moving the data by specifying the destination of the first byte to be transferred. Then the block of data is moved one byte right after another. Rather than a local or express bus trip, burst mode works like a chartered tour. It's a direct point-to-point operation that keeps together a group of sightseers.

Instead of using software signals to indicate that a transfer is taking place or has ended, the Micro Channel uses hardware—a special connection in the expansion bus. Operation of the burst mode is controlled by Micro Channel circuitry without the intervention of the microprocessor, so burst mode transfers can take place while the microprocessor is engaged in other activities (such as processing data that previously moved across the bus).

When IBM needed to quote higher throughput figures to make Micro Channel sound more competitive with EISA, it did so by adding a special, faster data transfer protocol—essentially an improved burst mode—called *streaming data mode.*

Designed to speed the movement of data between bus masters and slaves, streaming data mode is an optional Micro Channel implementation—meaning that not all computers or peripherals have to be made to be able to use it. Systems and devices designed to use it benefit from data transfers up to eight times faster. Systems that cannot accommodate it do not encounter compatibility problems, however. They simply use normal transfer methods if instructed to use the faster mode. In other words, under the Micro Channel specification systems and peripherals operate at the highest speed they can, but do not suffer compatibility problems if they cannot handle the fastest transfers. Because few expansion boards, little software, and no Micro Channel computers made before 1990 support the streaming data mode, its capabilities are mostly of academic (and advertising) interest.

Nevertheless, the speed increase can be substantial. With no change in a system's timings or its signal definitions, streaming data mode can accelerate transfers by two to four times the initial or default data transfer rate of the system in which it operates.

To add even more speed, the 1990 Micro Channel revision allows for a data multiplexing technique that yields an effective doubling of the data bus width—from 32 bits to 64 bits—for streaming data transfers. Altering system timing can double the transfer rate again. Ultimately, the existing streaming data protocol allows up to a sixteenfold increase in the speed of data transfers across the bus. Because multiplexed data transfers rely on streaming data mode, only the few elite systems that support streaming data can take advantage of multiplexing. These features have, however, been grafted onto EISA to improve its throughput potential.

Interrupt Sharing

The Micro Channel also changed how many of the familiar signals carried over from the traditional PC bus work. For example, interrupts, which are edge-triggered on the PC bus, were made level-sensitive on the Micro Channel. Systems based on the technology of the old PC sense any interrupts only at the instant when the interrupt request changes state. In the Micro Channel design, the interrupt signal remains active during the interrupt.

While either edge-triggering or level-sensing works for interrupt signals, the latter design confers several benefits in computers in which interrupts are shared. The computer knows an interrupt is active just by examining a level-sensitive interrupt line. It must remember that an edge-triggered line has been set. As a result, level-sensing simplifies the design of the logic-sharing circuitry on expansion boards. It reduces the sensitivity of the interrupt controller to noise and transients, and it allows for a mixture of sharing and non-sharing hardware on the same interrupt level.

Except for the change from edge-triggering to level-sensing, the interrupts of the Micro Channel bus are essentially unchanged—the same interrupts are devoted to the same purposes as ISA. They perform the same function. A device asserts an *Interrupt Request* line associated with a specific interrupt. The line is directly linked to the interrupt controller, which prioritizes the interrupts (by number) and relays the need to the microprocessor.

Software Interface

By itself, Micro Channel's bus mastering is a powerful and useless concept. Without some way for the computer to control the new feature through its software and operating system, the new hardware design can hardly be exploited to full potential. What's needed is some means to link the new hardware with the personal system's programs.

Subsystem Control Block Architecture serves that function. An architecture like Micro Channel Architecture, Subsystem Control Block Architecture is a software structure, a set of rules, and a philosophy. Its basic purpose is to define how operating systems can control one or more bus masters connected to the Micro Channel expansion bus. To do this, it provides a means for applications to take control over hardware resources. It specifies data structures (that is, the syntax of commands) and the method through which they are exchanged between parts of the computer system.

The responsibilities of Subsystem Control Block Architecture range from the mundane to the exotic. For example, part of the architecture provides error and status reporting protocols so that all programs can depend on a standard interface to monitor the operation of the entire system. At the other end of the control continuum, it allows the dynamic assignment of system facilities among multiple masters.

One innovation introduced by Subsystem Command Block Architecture is *Command Chaining*, a powerful concept through which multiple bus masters can decide—according to prescribed algorithms—which of several potential control paths to follow. The path selection capability of Command Chaining allows for the several bus master operations to be coordinated and pre-defined as *macro* operations. Unlike a simple series of commands, however, the chain of command can be interactive, allowing the bus master subsystems the latitude to respond to changing conditions while they are operating.

In some ways, Subsystem Control Block Architecture is a way to avoid the mass proliferation of system interrupts. It provides a means of control independent of them and helps avoid the overhead of interrupt operation. Subsystem Control Block Architecture owes its heritage to mainframe computer design (as does much of the Micro Channel), and it anticipates the further migration of mainframe operating system principles into the personal systems.

Subsystem Control Block Architecture provides the primary means for controlling complex hardware configurations that have multiple intelligent subsystems. The use of Subsystem Control Block Architecture extends the capabilities of the Micro Channel to support distributed multiprocessing—multiple microprocessors in a single system chassis serving a number of diverse users. Because today's major applications and operating systems do not support Subsystem Control Block Architecture, the technology probably will not reach the mainstream. In high-end systems where the use of Micro Channel survives, however, this technology provides a means for managing and controlling the Micro Channel bus.

Software Setup

Micro Channel also broke with the past with its *Programmable Option Select* or *POS* feature, designed to make installation and expansion of system enhancements much easier and less confusing than in earlier PCs. POS did away with all DIP switches, jumpers, and headers that made configuring a system only a slightly less arcane ritual than an exorcism. It served as an inspiration for both EISA and the new Plug-and-Play PC systems.

Using low-power, battery-backed-up CMOS memory much like the AT uses for storing its disk drive types and memory endowment, each Micro Channel PC is designed to remember its own hardware configuration. That includes which board is supposed to be in each of its expansion slots and how that board is supposed to function in relation to the rest of the system.

Each different expansion board designed for the Micro Channel is assigned a unique identifying number coded into its firmware. When the system boots up, it compares the options it finds installed with a list it keeps in CMOS setup memory to detect changes to ensure the integrity of the setup. Identifying numbers serve to link each Micro Channel board data files holding information on using and installing the option. The setup files are incorporated into the software setup procedure on the system *Reference Disk* automatically, so you see one seamless (but sometimes unseemly) installation procedure. That way one simple and familiar installation procedure can take care of any expansion board, no matter its origins.

Standards and Coordination

Although fallen from favor in the PC mainstream, Micro Channel remains very much alive. An independent organization, the Micro Channel Developers Association, promotes the technology and links together engineers and companies working with it:

Micro Channel Developers Association
22280 N. Bechelli Lane, Suite B
Redding, California 96002
(916) 222-2262

Enhanced Industry Standard Architecture

Committees often are accused of creating camels when horses are intended, but the committee that crafted the first 32-bit enhancement to ISA had to work the other direction. They had to train the camel to race more like a horse to bring the original ISA kludge in line with current personal computer technical standards. Those standards were high—set by Micro Channel.

The EISA committee was both motivated and constrained by conflicting design goals. They strove to create a 32-bit expansion standard for PCs that incorporated as many of the innovations of Micro Channel as possible without infringing on IBM's intellectual property rights in Micro Channel's technologies (so no licensing fees would be due). While pushing up performance, they wanted to maintain backward compatibility with the huge installed base of ISA expansion boards.

In the end, the EISA committee didn't make a horse. In the final assessment, it appears they more likely added another hump to the ISA camel. By necessity, their lofty goals were amended. The touted backward compatibility was incomplete: ISA boards work in EISA but not vice versa, and adding an ISA board to an EISA system disables part of the EISA system's capabilities (for example, the capability to share an interrupt). Moreover, EISA was unable to escape the need to license technology from IBM. After all, IBM owns basic patents on technologies required to build any PC, whether or not Micro Channel ideas are included.

Despite the diminished expectations, however, the resulting EISA specification has become the basis of many high-performance computers. EISA works effectively. Although it, like Micro Channel, has failed to be a major force in the PC mainstream, the reasons relate to applications and cost rather than technical capability (again, like Micro Channel). Although EISA shows some promise for the next generation of PCs, it will likely be eclipsed by newer designs like PCI.

Physical Characteristics

At the heart of the EISA specification was its highly promoted backward compatibility with ISA. Under EISA, all existing PC expansion boards are plug-compatible (at least to some extent) with newer, high-performance EISA computers, although the opposite is not true and some exceptions do exist. To achieve this required some big compromises—for example, retaining the 8 MHz bus speed limit. In addition, EISA demanded an entirely new kind of connector and unprecedented cooperation in a competitive industry.

The physical specifications between the old and new standards are remarkably similar. EISA expansion boards are the same size and shape as AT boards, with the standard setting the maximum (at 13.4 inches long and 4.5 inches high, from the top of the board to its bottom edge of the board), with smaller boards such as so-called *short cards*, still accepted. But EISA makes some specific changes aimed at ensuring future products are even more inter-compatible than PC boards are today.

A seemingly minor change holds the potential for making a big difference. All measurements for EISA boards are specified from a common origin—that is, you measure all dimensions from a common starting point. For EISA, that point is the center of the expansion connector rather than an edge of the card. As a result, tolerances are smallest and the fit of boards is best where it counts most, at the expansion connector. EISA boards should fit better than their predecessors.

Another EISA change may have greater implications for existing PC expansion boards. While EISA accepts all physical configurations of current expansion boards, it prohibits from future products the addition of skirts—except for a *mini-skirt* located between the expansion connector and card-retaining bracket.

The centerpiece of the EISA specification is its expansion connector, the design of which ensures backward compatibility with PC-bus cards while allowing full 32-bit expandability of EISA peripherals. It adds 90 new connections (55 new signals) without increasing the size of the connector itself and accepts both EISA and classic-bus boards indiscriminately.

The clever, two-tier design of the this connector actually represents a revision on the original EISA concept. The EISA connector originally announced in 1988 relied on what was in effect two parallel connectors—one that provided the compatible link-up with existing expansion boards and a second connector, offset from the expansion board, for 32-bit data transfers and addressing. The parallel-connector design was criticized for various deficiencies including its need for inordinately high insertion force (the effort required to plug a board into a slot). Such effort was believed to be required to squeeze a board into this connector that it nearly precluded the use of cost-saving automatic insertion machinery in the building of new computers.

Because the new EISA connector is physically the same size as a traditional expansion connector, it requires about the same insertion force—35 pounds—versus the 100-plus estimated for the proposed parallel connector. This connector should cause no problems for automatic insertion machinery.

The new connector achieves its combination of compatibility and full 32-bit expandability by branching out vertically instead of horizontally. In the new EISA connector, the contacts for enhanced functions are built into a second, lower level. Existing PC expansion boards can be inserted only about halfway into EISA slots to engage only the PC bus contacts. Five keys— plastic stops molded into the EISA connector—prevent older boards from going farther in. EISA boards have cut-outs that fit into the keys and allow the boards to be fully inserted into the connector. This keying prevents old-bus cards from shorting out the EISA connections, which holds the potential of damaging the EISA computer. When the card is fully inserted, both the upper and lower sets of contacts engage pads on the EISA board.

Because of its need for this deeper insertion, the edge connector on an EISA board is consequently a bit longer (about 0.2 inch) than that of a classic bus board (see fig 6.7).

Nothing stops EISA boards from fitting into ordinary 16-bit AT expansion slots, however. In fact, because of the odd arrangement of contacts on EISA boards, inadvertently inserting an EISA board into a old AT connector can potentially send signals into the wrong circuits—not enough fireworks to give Mr. Scott apoplexy, but sufficient to render the host system dysfunctional. Consequently, EISA boards should never be inserted into non-EISA computers even though they physically can fit the slots.

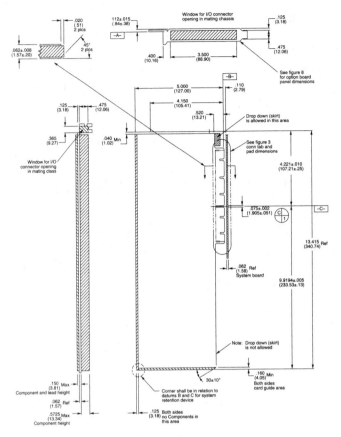

FIGURE 6.7. EISA expansion board dimensions.

EISA also strives to maintain compatibility with the power demands of old-bus expansion boards. Under the EISA specification, a generous availability of power is assumed for each expansion slot, freeing peripheral designers from the need to use special low-power components. Over 45 watts at four different voltages are available to each EISA expansion slot.

Of course, such availability takes an optimistic view of the total reserves of the system power supply. Filling the eight slots envisioned in a complete EISA system with hungry expansion boards would require over 325 watts. Even without considering the needs of mass storage devices and the system board itself, a fully-expanded EISA computer would require a huge power supply. Then again, nothing about the EISA design implies expansion boards require any more power than old-bus cards, so traditional power levels likely are adequate. Figure 6.8 shows the pin-out of the EISA bus.

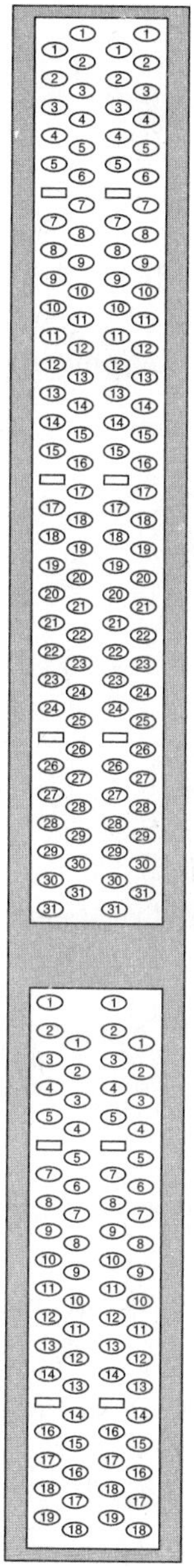

Row F

1	Gnd
2	+5V
3	+5V
4	XXXXXX
5	XXXXXX
Access key	
7	XXXXXX
8	XXXXXX
9	+12V
10	M–10
11	Lock*
12	Reserved
13	Gnd
14	Reserved
15	BE*<3>
Access key	
17	BE*<2>
18	BE*<0>
19	Gnd
20	+5V
21	LA*<29>
22	Gnd
23	LA*<26>
24	LA*<24>
Access key	
26	LA<16>
27	LA<14>
28	+5V
29	+5V
30	Gnd
31	LA*<10>

Row B

1	Gnd
2	RESDRV
3	+5V
4	IRQ<9>
5	-5V
6	DRQ<2>
7	-12V
8	NOWS*
9	+12V
10	Gnd
11	SMWTC*
12	SMRDC*
13	IOWC*
14	IORC*
15	DAK*<3>
16	DRQ<3>
17	DAK*<1>
18	DRQ<1>
19	Refresh*
20	BCLK
21	IRQ<7>
22	IRQ<6>
23	IRQ<5>
24	IRQ<4>
25	IRQ<3>
26	DAK*<2>
27	B
28	Dale
29	+5V
30	OSC
31	Gnd

Row E

1	CMD*
2	Start*
3	EXRDY
4	EX32*
5	Gnd
Access key	
7	EX16
8	SLBurst*
9	MSBurst*
10	W–R
11	Gnd
12	Reserved
13	Reserved
14	Reserved
15	Gnd
Access key	
17	BE*<1>
18	LA*<31>
19	Gnd
20	LA*<30>
21	LA*<28>
22	LA*<27>
23	LA*<25>
24	Gnd
Access key	
26	LA<15>
27	LA<13>
28	LA<12>
29	LA<11>
30	Gnd
31	LA*<9>

Row A

1	IOCHK*
2	D<7>
3	D<6>
4	D<5>
5	D<4>
6	D<3>
7	D<2>
8	D<1>
9	D<0>
10	CHRDY
11	AENx
12	SA<19>
13	SA<18>
14	SA<17>
15	SA<16>
16	SA<15>
17	SA<14>
18	SA<13>
19	SA<12>
20	SA<11>
21	SA<10>
22	SA<9>
23	SA<8>
24	SA<7>
25	SA<6>
26	SA<5>
27	SA<4>
28	SA<3>
29	SA<2>
30	SA<1>
31	SA<0>

Row H

1	LA<8>
2	LA<8>
3	LA<5>
4	+5V
5	LA<2>
Access key	
7	D<16>
8	D<18>
9	Gnd
10	D<21>
11	D<23>
12	D<24>
13	Gnd
14	D<27>
Access key	
16	D<29>
17	+5V
18	+5V
19	MAKx*

Row D

1	M16*
2	IO16*
3	IRQ<10>
4	IRQ<11>
5	IRQ<12>
6	IRQ<13>
7	IRQ<14>
8	DAK*<0>
9	DRQ<0>
10	DAK*<5>
11	DRQ<5>
12	DAK*<6>
13	DRQ<6>
14	DAK*<7>
15	DRQ<7>
16	+5V
17	Master 16*
18	Gnd

Row G

1	LA<7>
2	Gnd
3	LA<4>
4	LA<3>
5	Gnd
Access key	
7	D<17>
8	D<19>
9	D<20>
10	D<22>
11	Gnd
12	D<25>
13	D<26>
14	D<28>
Access key	
16	Gnd
17	D<30>
18	D<31>
19	MREQx*

Row C

1	SBHE*
2	LA<23>
3	LA<22>
4	LA<21>
5	LA<20>
6	LA<19>
7	LA<18>
8	LA<17>
9	MRDC*
10	MWTC*
11	D<8>
12	D<9>
13	D<10>
14	D<11>
15	D<12>
16	D<13>
17	D<14>
18	D<15>

Rows A, B, C, and D are upper (ISA) contacts
Rows E, F, G, and H are lower (EISA) contacts

FIGURE 6.8. EISA pin-out.

32-Bit Extension

The original impetus behind the search for a new bus standard was the 16-bit classic AT bus' incapability to deal with the 32-bit needs of the newer Intel microprocessors (specifically, the 386DX and 486). The first step in wringing full performance from these chips is to move data around in the largest blocks they can manipulate in a single operation, specifically 32-bit double-words. Widening the *data path* to 32-bits in itself can double the speed of data transfers in an AT-style computer, all else being equal (which it definitely is not in the case of EISA). To gain this instant advantage over the classic bus, EISA adds 16 new data lines, shown as D17, through D31 on Figure 6.8, the pin-out of the EISA connector.

The classic AT bus imposes another limit on higher powered microprocessors. Its 24 *address lines* enforce a maximum size of 16 megabytes on directly-addressable memory (as opposed to bank-switched memory, like that available under the EMS standard). To accommodate the complete addressing capabilities of the 32-bit Intel microprocessors—four gigabytes—EISA also broadens the address bus to a full 32-bits. The new address lines are labeled with the prefix LA in the pin-out.

Note that EISA's endowment is more generous than a mere eight additional address lines. The standard also adds new lines for indicating some of the lower-order address bits, to some extent duplicating the function of the classic bus but with an important change. The EISA lower-order address lines (LA2 through LA16) are *latching*, that is, they provide stable signals through the address cycle instead of just at its beginning. Note that the EISA address extensions (the upper eight bits) to the classic bus also latch. Unlike Micro Channel, EISA permitted full DMA reach to all four gigabytes of memory addresses from its inception.

Sometimes all 32-bits of the data bus are not needed in a data transfer. For example, a program may need only to move a byte from one memory location to another. EISA provides four new signals to indicate which bytes of the double-word of data on the bus are significant—the *Byte Enable* signals BE0 through BE4.

To maintain compatibility with as many classic bus expansion boards as possible, EISA is designed to accommodate devices that have either 8-, 16-, or 32-bit interfaces. This diversity requires some method of preventing a device from trying to dump 32-bits of data to another that has only a 16-bit interface (in which case half the data would be lost).

EISA provides to signals to indicate what size data transfers a device can handle. To indicate that it has access to the full 32-bits of the EISA bus, a device sends the *EX32* signal. Similarly, the *EX16* signal indicates that a device supports only 16-bit transfers. If neither signal is present, the system must assume that the particular device can handle only eight bits of data at a time. (These signals supplement those on the classic bus that indicate 8- or 16-bit transfer width.)

EISA doesn't stop with bus-width signaling. The standard also provides for the automatic translation of the width of bus signals, for instance breaking down the 32-bit signal of an EISA card into four sequential eight-bit signals that can be digested by old classic bus expansion boards. A special integrated circuit, the EISA Bus Controller, moves data into the appropriate byte-lanes and translates the control signals on the bus accordingly.

Advanced Transfer Modes

EISA goes well beyond simply providing extra signals to add new data and addressing capacity to the classic bus. Other EISA enhancements also require new signals to be assigned to bus connections. These signals include support for *burst-mode* data transfers (*MBURST* and *SLBURTS*), new timing signals to help manage fast data transfers (*START* and *CMD*), even a signal to slow down the bus with wait states (*EXRDY*).

Under EISA, all the other signals on the classic bus retain their former definitions and functions to maintain backward compatibility with older expansion boards. The big challenge faced by the EISA engineers was to fit all these signals on a connector that would still allow the use of old expansion boards.

Compatibility also is among the most formidable problems in squeezing more raw speed—more megahertz—from the AT bus. Simply upping the clock speed that synchronizes data transfers across the bus is out of the question because any speed increase can cause conniptions for existing expansion boards. Many classic bus boards cannot operate at bus speeds much higher than the eight megahertz used in the AT or ten megahertz used by some compatibles.

To help ensure compatibility, EISA does not increase the raw speed of the clock driving the expansion bus. The specification calls for a bus clock (*BCLK*) oscillating at a fixed rate between 6 and 8.33 megahertz, the latter figure being one-quarter the 33 MHz clock speed of today's faster microprocessors.

The bus speed is a submultiple of the system clock frequency because the EISA is nominally a *synchronous bus*—it operates in lock-step with the host microprocessor—but not necessarily. Bus masters can take over control and alter some aspects of system timing to achieve higher data throughputs.

Such altered timings are necessary because the bus speed limit is more severe than the megahertz would imply. The actual data transfer rate of ISA is limited by its two-cycle per transfer limitation with the bus going through an elaborate hierarchy of commands for every byte that's transferred. Although EISA allows this data transfer method, it also adds two faster schemes of its own: *compressed transfers* and burst mode. Compressed transfers are 50 percent faster in that data can be moved every one and a half bus cycles. Burst mode moves data every cycle, resulting in an effective transfer rate of 33 megabytes per second (8.33 MHz. bus speed and 32-bit data path).

The key to EISA's compressed cycle operation is a special timing signal (*CMD*), which serves as a supplement to the bus clock. During compressed transfers, the CMD signal operates at twice the speed of the bus clock, and the data transfer is required to take place during its duration.

In burst mode, the addresses for data transfer are asserted at the beginning (for writing data) or the end (for reading data) of every clock cycle. The data is actually put on the bus one-half or one and a half cycles later, locked to CMD.

The EISA burst data mode has advantages as well as limitations. EISA burst mode can move noncontiguous data because an address is given with each transfer. However, EISA allows only the least significant ten address bits to change during a burst cycle, effectively limiting a burst data to addresses within a block of 1,024 double-words in memory. In addition, EISA does not permit reads and writes to be mixed in a single burst because of the differences in the timing of these signals.

Don't confuse the fast 33 megabyte per second maximum data transfer rate with the even faster 33 megahertz operation of some once-regarded-as-fast PCs. Although both the EISA bus and the system memory of these computers is 32 bits wide, the maximum EISA bus clock speed remains 8.33 MHz, effectively one-quarter the speed of system board memory. In other words, in EISA computers slotted memory is still slower than system board memory, just as it is in classic bus machines. High performance (which, for practical purposes, means all) EISA computers still are built with proprietary memory expansion slots that operate at the full speed of the system (not the bus) clock.

DMA Modes

If any part of the old AT needed improvement, it was the Direct Memory Access system. While DMA controllers have the potential for speeding system operation, PCs and ATs failed to deliver on this promise. DMA transfers on these systems can be painfully slow—so slow that DMA was abandoned for hard disk transfers in the AT.

On an AT, for example, DMA transfers ordinarily take place at the agonizing rate of one megabyte per second. Although a speed of two megabytes per second is theoretically possible using the three 16-bit DMA channels in the AT, DOS is limited to eight bit transfers and, thus, the lower rate.

New DMA timings and techniques show some of the most creative aspects of the EISA design. Besides AT-compatible DMA transfers, EISA adds three new types—Types A, B, and C (the last also known as *Burst DMA*)—and all three can make 8-, 16-, or 32-bit transfers. In addition, multiple transfers also can be chained to send the same bytes to different locations. Under EISA, a maximum DMA data transfer rate of 33 megabytes per second is available with 32-bit transfers in burst mode.

The default DMA timing is the slowest mode, AT-compatible 8-bit transfers. The EISA specification envisions the other modes being brought to life with software drivers. With the proper drivers, most classic bus expansion board can take advantage of Type A transfers; a few also can take advantage of double-speed Type B transfers. EISA boards are required to use Type C or 32-bit transfers of any type.

Each type of DMA brings an improvement in data transfer rate. For a given width of data path, Type A transfers are about 30 percent faster than AT-style DMA. Type B transfers double the AT speed. Type C transfers are more than four times faster than AT transfers.

For the most part, these speed increases are made simply by specifying different data transfer protocols that involve fewer bus cycles in each DMA move. In the AT environment, each DMA move (8- or 16-bit) requires eight bus cycles, during most of these cycles, nothing is really happening. Type A transfers merely trim two of the wasted bus cycles from each DMA move. Type B transfers are more extreme, cutting the number of cycles per DMA move to four. Because newer expansion boards can operate at higher rates, many classic bus expansion cards can operate at these speeds.

Under the EISA specification, Type C DMA transfers compress all the necessary signal manipulations into a single bus cycle, with specific signal transitions occurring at the leading and trailing edges of the bus clock. Only EISA expansion cards are capable of this transfer method, and even they have their limitations. Only the ten lowest-order bits of the address bus are allowed change within the confines of this tight timing, with the result that Burst Mode DMA transfers on EISA are limited to addresses within a single 1,024-byte page.

Besides creating new, high-speed transfer modes, the EISA specification also expands the reach of DMA. Because of addressing limitations, classic bus systems could provide DMA transfers only through the lowest 16 megabytes of memory addresses. EISA allows DMA transfers anywhere within a four gigabyte range of physical memory.

The rate at which data can move during a DMA transfer depends on how many bits are moved at a time. All seven EISA DMA channels support up to 32-bits; the channels differ only in priority. The higher-numbered channels (5, 6, and 7) are serviced more often when an EISA system is heavily loaded.

Bus Mastering

The most significant borrowing that EISA makes from Micro Channel is bus mastering. In EISA systems, both the operation and nomenclature differ from the IBM design—not just for the sake of originality but also because IBM's designs are protected by patents and other intellectual property rights. In an EISA system, the arbitration control element is called the *Integrated System Peripheral* chip (and, strangely, not the EISA Bus Controller). The *ISP* acts just like the Micro Channel Central Arbitration Point and determines which system function gets control of the expansion bus.

Every arbitration system has rules. Mom, confronted with caring for a crowd of kids from the neighborhood may, for example, let the kid who screams the loudest go first in line just to get some peace and quiet. EISA has a much more pragmatic, more deterministic set of rules for priority. Control rotates through three classes: memory refreshing, DMA transfers, and a combination of the microprocessor and bus masters. In every control cycle, each element receives control in turn. If, however, several DMA channels request bus control, only one gets it per control cycle. In effect, control is like a menu in an old-fashioned Chinese restaurant—in each arbitration cycle, the system selects one from column A, memory refreshing; one from column B, DMA; and one from column C, the bus masters/microprocessor.

Which of the six EISA DMA channels gets control rotates through the circle of those needing it until DMA channels all are served. Actually, this rotation is a pair of cycles, wheels within wheels. Three high-priority DMA channels (corresponding to the 16-bit channels in an AT system but allowed any transfer width under the EISA specification) going through one rotation and three lower priority channels in another rotation. One low-priority channel gets control for each complete cycle of three high-priority channels.

The microprocessor and bus masters form another wheel-within-wheel arrangement. Each time the microprocessor/bus master column is selected, either the microprocessor *or* a bus master gets control, whichever was *not* selected on the last cycle. In other words, the microprocessor is served half the time; the bus masters the other half. Another cycle selects which of the various bus masters gets served when the bus master selection pops up.

Consequently, memory refreshing is assigned the highest priority in an EISA system. Every arbitration cycle includes memory refresh—as it should be because without memory refreshing, the system would crash. DMA transfers are next highest in that one active DMA channel would get attention every cycle. The microprocessor has the next highest level of priority, getting control at least every other cycle. At best, any given bus master can match only the priority level of the microprocessor. If several are active, each gets control only after a delay of many arbitration cycles.

Considering the complexity of this arbitration hierarchy, the hardware that brings it to life is actually simple. Only two slot-specific signals are necessary for each expansion board. The controlling logic is all contained inside the ISP chip, so the designers of expansion boards need not worry about complex decision-making circuitry.

When a bus master board wants to request bus access, the board only needs to assert its *Memory Request* (abbreviated *MREQx*, where x is the slot number, in EISA nomenclature) line. The ISP informs the bus master that it can take control of the bus by asserting the *Memory Acknowledge* (or *MAKx*) signal associated with the slot in which the bus master is located.

The EISA standard also allows a form of bus master to be built solely using the AT bus. Such cards use the DMA signals to control the bus, the DMA Request (DRQ) line indicating a need to use the bus. Permission is sent back to the board on the associated DMA Acknowledge line (DAK).

Because these classic bus masters don't have access to all the EISA timing signals, they hold the potential for overstaying their welcome, getting so involved in a transfer, they do not yield control to the one function that absolutely must have it—memory refresh. Consequently, the EISA design requires these boards to have built-in timing circuits to limit the duration of their bus access.

Interrupt Sharing

Speed and data connections are not the only things in short supply in classic bus systems. System interrupts amount to a paltry few after even a modest number of expansion boards are plugged in. Nearly every device connected to the input/output channel—from hard disks to serial ports to video controllers—demands at least one interrupt for optimum performance.

Seven additional interrupts were added to the AT system design when the eight of the original PC proved too few. EISA could have done likewise and dosed new systems with new interrupt channels, but that strategy becomes overly complex and expensive as the number of interrupts increases.

The more moderate solution is to share interrupts between peripherals. With sharing, the 15 existing interrupts could potentially serve needs of an EISA system no matter how much it might be expanded.

Maintaining classic bus compatibility and implementing interrupt sharing is a technological nightmare, however. The principal reason for this problem is the edge-triggered interrupts used by the AT bus. Level-sensitive interrupts are, of course, inherently less susceptible to noise and confusion, but using level-triggered interrupts in the PC environment is problematic. Getting level-sensitive interrupts to work with software that uses edge-triggered interrupts is one difficulty. Maintaining compatibility with existing edge-triggered boards is another, particularly considering that the two kinds of interrupts won't work together on a given interrupt control line. To maintain full backward compatibility, however, EISA must be able to mix the two types of interrupts without causing additional problems.

The EISA approach is to make each interrupt individually programmable between edge-triggered and level-sensitive operation. Old boards can use the edge-triggered interrupts they prefer, one board per interrupt. New EISA expansion boards can share the other interrupts programmed to be level-sensitive.

The one remaining obstacle with this system is that level-sensitive interrupts require a different kind of hardware than does the edge-triggered variety. Because of this difference, plugging a board designed to use an edge-triggered interrupt effectively blocks the use of that interrupt by level-sensitive boards.

This difference in technology also holds the potential for damaging the hardware involved in the conflict. Thankfully, the EISA design minimizes this danger by specifying the inclusion of a current-limiting resistor in the interrupt lines of level-sensitive EISA boards. Nevertheless, EISA supports interrupt sharing only on EISA boards. Existing classic bus expansion cards cannot share interrupts with each other or EISA cards.

Software Setup

At minimum, setting up all the technical wizardry that EISA's engineers have conjured into a system might seem to require a magic wand—with addressing and interrupt considerations, not to mention four DMA types, the data transfer modes, and the rest of the EISA variables. Even without the innovations, setting up an expansion board meant for the classic bus generally is an exercise in frustration that requires the careful matching of DIP switch and jumper settings with the needs of the board and the available interrupts and memory in the host system. Make one mistake—which is almost assured owing to the deplorable state of most documentation—and the host system probably cannot even boot, let alone diagnose the problem. Fortunately, EISA incorporates several strategies to alleviate these setup problems.

The EISA design automatically prevents conflicts in the assignment of some system resources. In addition, it incorporates a software-mediated setup procedure that finds, flags, and even corrects conflicts to the extent of automatically configuring the system. If that's not enough versatility, EISA also allows old-fashioned switch and jumper configuring of boards as well.

One inspired aspect of EISA automatically eliminates the conflict of input/output port assignments. In classic-bus computers, expansion boards can choose from any ports in the range 100(Hex) to 3FF(Hex) for their needs. You have the job of assigning ports from a range within the range that the board-maker selected to use. You also have the responsibility of detecting and resolving conflicting port assignments.

In contrast, the EISA design assigns a unique range of ports to each expansion slot. Boards are still confined to a limited range of three-digit hexadecimal addresses, but each expansion slot adds an extra digit to distinguish the ports used by its associated board from those in the other slots. This scheme makes it physically impossible for two boards to try to use the same I/O port addresses.

Each board also can be individually addressed to ferret out information stored in common locations. Besides the slot-specific signals for managing bus arbitration (*MREQx* and *MAKx*), each EISA slot incorporates one additional slot-specific signal that redefines a signal assignment on the classic bus, now called *AENx*. It enables each expansion board to respond independently of the others so that each board can be individually addressed and controlled. By selectively activating the AENx bus line for each slot, the host EISA system can query individual boards, isolate them, or simply identify them.

The nomenclature of these slot-specific signals alone limits EISA to its avowed maximum of 15 expansion slots per system (the *x* in the signal names is replaced by the hexadecimal designation of the slot), although the specification states that systems with more than eight slots are unlikely.

Each make and model of EISA expansion board is assigned a unique *EISA Product Identifier,* which is stored on the board at input/output port addresses 0xC80(Hex) to 0xC83(Hex). The first two bytes store, in compressed form, a three-letter abbreviation identifying the board manufacturer (the characters "ISA" reserved to indicate generic classic-bus boards). The next byte encodes a two-digit product number, and the final byte encodes a two-digit revision number. The manufacturer's abbreviation is assigned by BCPR Services, the organization that distributes the EISA specification. Manufacturers create their own product and revision numbers. System boards are assigned identification numbers using a similar scheme.

Supplementing this slot- and card-identification arrangement is an *automated setup system*. Through a standardized setup program, you can allocate the resources of your EISA system or let the system set itself up.

This system brings together several diverse elements. Setup information is maintained in a hardware extension to the CMOS configuration memory used by AT-class computers. Additional battery-backed-up CMOS memory is assigned to remembering the essential parameters of the board installed in each expansion slot.

To load this information into memory, each EISA system manufacturer provides a setup program, either on disk or in ROM. This program integrates with each product that requires setup through Configuration Files, disk-based database records holding setup information in a standardized format set by the EISA specification. The setup program reads the disk-based data to customize itself for the setup needs of each specific product installed in the computer host.

The product identification numbers are used as a key. Stored in CMOS memory, they are used to look up Configuration Files each time the system is switched on. This system centralizes the non-volatile memory needed for memorizing the setup of each board, eliminating the expense of incorporating such memory into each expansion product.

Even the interface of the setup program has been standardized across EISA machines so that if you can set up one, you know how to configure them all. If you don't, mastering the procedure is easy—you only need to pull down menus to choose the options you want.

Specifications and Coordination

Although the original Gang of Nine EISA committee was brought together by Compaq, management of the standard was given over to a separate entity called BCPRS Services, Inc., which now publishes the EISA specification and coordinates the efforts of EISA developers.

EISA Specification
BCPR Services, Inc.
1400 L Street Northwest
Washington, D.C. 20005

VESA Local Bus

Despite the technical prowess incorporated into Micro Channel and EISA, the better bus yielded little apparent improvement in system performance. The primary reasons were twofold. Taking advantage of their higher performance meant rewriting software, which no one wanted to do because the effort was costly and not justified by the modest user base each bus had won. Moreover, back in 1987, few expansion boards actually chafed at the limits of good old ISA. In other words, the better buses yielded no benefits but added extra cost.

When high-resolution graphics finally made the limitations of ISA obvious, integral local bus systems yielded an excellent solution: they raised video throughput visibly without adding perceptibly to the cost of PCs. The penalty was a lack of upgradability. If you wanted to add a higher-resolution display system, you were stuck sliding it into an expansion slot and losing the benefit of local bus. The obvious answer was to give the local bus its own slot—an idea so good that nearly everyone tried his hand at designing the connection. But these slots were proprietary, meaning upgrades were limited to those offered (often at outrageous prices) by the original maker of the PC.

The rapid proliferation of PCs with proprietary local bus display systems in late 1991 and early 1992 inspired the Video Electronics Standards Association to develop a unified design for local bus expansion for PCs that has come to be known as VESA Local Bus or VL Bus. Although originally targeted at advanced video systems, the resulting specification was made broad enough to be equally adept at handling other peripherals that required high-bandwidth transfers, such as mass storage and network interfaces.

Perhaps the most important aspect of the VL Bus design is that it specifies the pin-out of a connector for local bus circuits. When the design was introduced, no other industry-accepted standard for a local bus existed. The availability of such a standard permits the design of inter-changeable display adapters (and other expansion boards) that allow for a free and open market for new peripherals.

Architectural Overview

Reflecting its origins in the PC industry, VL Bus was designed around the needs of Intel microprocessors, specifically the 486. It virtually duplicates the signal needs of that chip with the exception that a few signals are more broadly defined to allow compatibility with older 386 microprocessors. Other microprocessor families can be accommodated only using *bridge logic*, circuits that translate signals and protocols.

The most important innovation inherent in VL Bus—and the reason anyone cares about it —is the high operating speed. Although the VL Bus specification sets no upper limit or required speed, technical considerations put the maximum at 66 MHz. The best combination of features and performance come with 33 MHz operation. Coupled with its full 32-bit design (with the capability to handle 16-bit operations), the 33 MHz speed gave the original VL Bus a claimed peak throughput of 132 sec.

In truth, VL Bus is quick but not that quick. The fastest at which VL Bus can transfer data is its burst mode, which follows the Intel's definition of the term for the 486 chip: A *burst* is a single address cycle followed by four data cycles—five clock cycles for the transfer of four double-words (each of which is four bytes or 32-bits). At a 33 MHz bus speed, that's 105 sec not counting other overhead. For other (non-burst) transfers, VL Bus requires the same two-clock cycles (address, then data) for each transfer as do other buses, yielding a peak throughput of 66 sec.

Even that figure is generous. At operating speeds above 33 MHz, at least one wait state is added to each read and write operation; at 33 MHz and below no wait state is required for write operations (but one may be inserted); and one is required for reads. One wait state reduces non-burst throughput by 50 percent—that is, the 66 M/sec peak transfer rate effectively becomes 44 M/sec. Burst speed is nearly halved (nine cycles for four 32-bit transfers or 58 M/sec.) Moreover, individual VL Bus devices may add still more wait states by sending signals to the bus controller indicating they are not ready for the next cycle.

Architecturally, VL Bus approaches a true local bus in design and in simplest form provides little more than a set of unbuffered address, data, and control signals directly connected to the host microprocessor. PC makers can add buffering to extend the reach of the bus (that is, more slots), but then sacrifice speed. More connectors means more capacitance, which enforces a lower speed limit.

The original VL Bus specification recommended designers use no more than three local bus devices in any system operating at speeds of 33 MHz or lower. The recommended limit did not distinguish between slot-mounted devices and those integrated into the system board. Consequently, a PC with local bus video built into its motherboard would likely be constrained to a maximum of two VL Bus connectors. Higher speeds limit the count further: at 40 MHz, only two devices (one of which could be a slot) were recommended. At 50 MHz, only one VL Bus integrated into the system board was recommended.

The small count of bus connectors was not seen as a handicap because few devices can truly benefit from local bus speed. Most PCs need only the three high-speed connections recommended for 33 MHz operation—one each for video, mass storage, and network host adapters.

Manufacturers who want to add more than three VL Bus slots can, simply by building multiple VL Bus subsystems into a single PC. Each subsystem can add three slots (assuming a 33 MHz design), and no limit exists on the number of subsystems that can be installed in a PC.

Physical Characteristics

The VESA design aims at adding to, rather than replacing, a conventional expansion bus, although a PC could be built with nothing but a VL Bus. VESA imagined that all PC makers would want to use the VL Bus regardless of their allegiance to an earlier bus standard. Consequently, VESA designed three separate physical standards for VL Bus boards: one for ISA; one for Micro Channel; and one for EISA.

In each case the VL Bus connector fits in the same slot as a traditional (ISA, EISA, or Micro Channel) bus connector, collinear with it. VL Bus expansion cards are permitted (but not obligated) to include two connectors—one for the VL Bus and one for the traditional bus (see fig. 6.9). The latter option allows a VL Bus peripheral to take advantage of the resources of the other expansion bus—interrupts, DMA control, and so on—which are not provided by VL Bus. The VL Bus itself includes only one hardware interrupt control line (IRQ9).

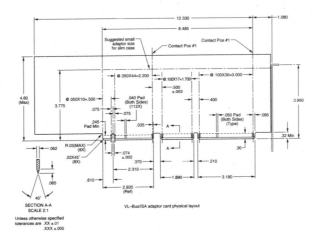

FIGURE 6.9. VL bus/ISA adapter card physical layout.

The physical embodiment of VL Bus is a standard 16-bit Micro Channel-style connector with 0.05 inch spacing of its 112 contacts in two rows of 56. Obviously, this connector cannot handle all the signals on 168 pins of a 486 microprocessor. Consequently, the signals of the 486 that are redundant or not relevant to an expansion bus are not carried through to the VL Bus. Table 6.5 shows the pin-out of the standard VL Bus connector.

TABLE 6.5. VL-Bus Slot Pinout

B Side			A Side	
64 bit	*32 bit*	*Pin #*	*32 bit*	*64 bit*
	DAT00	01	DAT01	
	DAT02	02	DAT03	
	DAT04	03	GND	
	DAT06	04	DAT05	
	DAT08	05	DAT07	
	GND	06	DAT09	
	DAT10	07	DAT11	
	DAT12	08	DAT13	
	VCC	09	DAT15	
	DAT14	10	GND	
	DAT16	11	DAT17	
	DAT18	12	VCC	
	DAT20	13	DAT19	
	GND	14	DAT21	
	DAT22	15	DAT23	
	DAT24	16	DAT25	

64 bit	32 bit	Pin #	32 bit	64 bit
B Side			*A Side*	
64 bit	*32 bit*	*Pin #*	*32 bit*	*64 bit*
	DAT26	17	GND	
	DAT28	18	DAT27	
	DAT30	19	DAT29	
DAT63	ADR31	21	ADR30	DAT62
	GND	22	ADR28	DAT60
DAT61	ADR29	23	ADR26	DAT58
DAT59	ADR27	24	GND	
DAT57	ADR25	25	ADR24	DAT56
DAT55	ADR23	26	ADR22	DAT54
DAT53	ADR21	27	VCC	
DAT51	ADR19	28	ADR20	DAT52
	GND	29	ADR18	DAT50
DAT49	ADR17	30	ADR16	DAT48
DAT47	ADR15	31	ADR14	DAT46
	VCC	32	ADR12	DAT44
DAT45	ADR13	33	ADR10	DAT42
DAT43	ADR11	34	ADR08	DAT40
DAT41	ADR09	35	GND	
DAT39	ADR07	36	ADR06	DAT38
DAT37	ADR05	37	ADR04	DAT36
	GND	38	WBACK#	
DAT35	ADR03	39	BE0#	BE4#
DAT34	ADR02	40	VCC	
LBS64#	NC	41	BE1#	BE5#
	RESET#	42	BE2#	BE6#
	D/C#	43	GND	
DAT33	M/10#	44	BE3#	BE7#
DAT32	W/R#	45	ADS#	
		KEY		
		KEY		
	RDYRTN#	48	LRDY#	

continues

TABLE 6.5. Continued

B Side			A Side	
64 bit	32 bit	Pin #	32 bit	64 bit
	GND	49	LDEV<X>#	
	IRQ9	50	LREQ<X>#	
	BRDY#	51	GND	
	BLAST#	52	LGNT<X>#	
	ID0	53	VCC	
	ID1	54	ID2	
	GND	55	ID3	
	LCLK	56	ID4	ACK64#
	VCC	57	NC	
	LBS16#	58	LEADS#	

In addition to the 486-derived signals, the VL Bus specification adds several signals of its own. So that devices attached to the original VL Bus can determine the microprocessor architecture of the system to which they are attached, the bus provides static status signals on four pins. Two pins reveal the type of microprocessor in the host. Of four possible definitions, two were reserved for future designations; the other two indicate 386 or 486 chips. Another pin indicates whether the host PC can accept high-speed writes—that is, PCs without wait states. The fourth pin indicates whether the host PC operates lower (or equal to) or higher than 33 MHz.

VL Bus allows for bus-mastering operation following the capability built into the 486, but uses slightly different signaling. When a bus master wants to take control of the bus, it sends out a special signal to the host system. It then can only take command upon receiving a confirmation signal from the system host. Unlike Micro Channel or EISA, the VL Bus specification does not set the priorities of bus mastering devices. Arbitrating competing requests to use the bus is left to the motherboard and the proclivities of its designer.

As with microprocessors, the VL Bus includes signals to indicate whether addresses on the bus refer to memory or input/output ports and whether a read or write operation should be carried out and also can distinguish data from program instructions that use another signal—a distinction irrelevant to the 486, but useful to the Pentium (which uses separate internal caches for code and data).

Although a PC could be built with only these few VL Bus slots, the VESA design is aimed at adding to rather than replacing a conventional expansion bus.

Automatic configuration is not part of the VL Bus specification. Board makers can design products that are setup traditionally—with jumpers and DIP switches—or devise their own software setup systems. In either case, VL Bus is invisible to software. No drivers need be used for your PC and peripherals to take advantage of the higher speed transfers possible with the VL Bus design. Used in conjunction with ISA, VL Bus provides higher performance than EISA or Micro Channel with none of the compatibility worries.

Signal Enhancements

In addition to the 486-derived signals—principally 32 data lines and 30 address lines (enough to address four gigabytes; in the 486 the two least-significant lines of 32-bit addressing are not brought out because the 486 chip addresses memory in four bytes at a time)—the VL Bus specification adds several signals of its own.

So that devices attached to the original VL Bus can determine the microprocessor architecture of the system to which they are attached, the bus provides static status signals on four pins. Two (ID0 and ID1, bus pins B53 and B54) reveal the type of microprocessor in the host. Of four possible definitions, two are reserved for future designations; the other two indicate 386 or 486 chips. Another pin (ID2 at A54), when high, indicates the host PC can accept high-speed writes—those without wait states. The fourth pin (ID3 at A55), when high, indicates the host PC operates lower than (or equal to) 33 MHz.

VL Bus allows for bus-mastering operation patterned after that built into the 486, but the VL Bus system uses slightly different signaling. When a bus master wants to take control of the bus, it sends out a special slot-specific signal (LREQ(X)# on pin A50) to the host system. It then can only take command upon receiving a confirmation signal (LGNT(X)# on pin A52) from the system host. Unlike Micro Channel or EISA, the VL Bus specification does not set the priorities of bus mastering devices. Arbitrating competing requests to use the bus is left to the motherboard and the proclivities of its designer. VL Bus supports up to three bus masters per subsystem. A board in a VL Bus slot that also connects with a more traditional expansion bus can be designed to function as a master on either or both buses and even can transfer data between the two buses.

As with microprocessors, the VL Bus includes signals to indicate whether addresses on the bus refer to memory or input/output ports (MI/O# on pin B44) and whether a read or write operation (W/R# on pin B45) should be carried out. It can also distinguish data from program instructions that use another signal (D/C# on pin B43), a distinction irrelevant to the 486 but useful to the Pentium (which uses separate internal caches for code and data).

Automatic configuration is not part of the VL Bus specification. Board makers can design products that are setup traditionally—with jumpers and DIP switches—or devise their own software setup systems. In either case, VL Bus is invisible to software. No drivers need be used for your PC and its peripherals to take advantage of the higher speed transfers possible with the VL Bus design. That makes configuration of VL Bus products exactly the same as ISA—set the switches—although the standard does not preclude manufacturers from using separate installation software to alter on-board EEPROM memory for configuration.

The combination of high speed and easy installation made VL Bus an instant winner. Used in conjunction with ISA, VL Bus provides higher performance than EISA or Micro Channel with none of the compatibility worries.

Revision 2.0

Reflecting the introduction of the 64-bit Pentium in 1993, VESA is working on a second generation VL Bus standard (Version 2.0), in preliminary form at this writing. The revised specification redefines the maximum number of VL Bus slots permitted in a single circuit. VESA recommendations allow for up to three slots at 40 MHz and two slots at 50 MHz if low capacitance is maintained in the design. Again PCs can sidestep these limits by using multiple VL Bus subsystems.

The new 2.0 specification will add bits as well as slots and defines a 64-bit interface based on a 32-bit Micro Channel connector. The wider bus and higher clock push theoretical throughput up to 400 M/sec, subject to the same real world adjustments as the 132 M/sec claim of the VL Bus original. The 2.0 update also includes support for write-back caching (using the formerly reserved signal, WBACK# on pin A38). A new, fifth status signal (ID4 at pin A56) helps identify 486-based systems that support burst protocols.

The VL Bus 2.0 specification requires backward compatibility. Boards designed to the new standard will work in old VL Bus PCs and vice versa. In fact, 64-bit boards operate in 32-bit systems at 32-bit cards. Ratification of the standard is expected later this year.

Standards and Coordination

As the adoption of VL Bus 2.0 indicates, the VESA committee regularly reviews the standards it governs and updates them as necessary. You can reach VESA at the following address:

Video Electronics Standards Association
2150 North First Street, Suite 440
San Jose, California 95131-2020
(408) 435-0333

Peripheral Component Interconnect

The bus of tomorrow is today perhaps the best way to characterize Intel's Peripheral Component Interconnect. Of all the expansion systems currently in use in desktop PCs, PCI holds the best promise of replacing ancient ISA once and for all. Three characteristics back this promise. PCI is fast, an excellent match for the current generation of microprocessors. In addition, PCI is microprocessor-independent, so if the world of PCs does move away from the Intel microprocessor standard, PCI will still give machines expansion reach no matter what chip is inside. Finally, PCI has solid backing and no real competition. Unlike VL Bus, PCI is designed to replace rather than supplement conventional expansion buses and is supported (and was developed) by the largest microprocessor maker and standalone semiconductor firm in the world, arguably one of two companies powerful enough to steal the mantle from IBM as computer-industry standard setter. (The other? Microsoft, of course.)

Although PCI got off to a rocky start when the initial chipsets for empowering it proved flawed, computer makers have almost universally announced support. The first PCI machines will bridge the standards, offering both ISA and PCI expansion. As the new standard gains momentum, however, there may be less and less reason to ever look back. Finally, the PC may be able to break free from the chains imposed by the pragmatic design of the first PC.

Architectural Overview

The original explicit purpose of the PCI design was to make the lives of those who engineer chipsets and motherboards easier. It wasn't so much an expansion bus as an interconnection system, hence its pompous name—*peripheral component* is just a pompous way of saying *chip*, and *interconnect* means simply *link*. And that is what PCI is meant to be—a fast and easy chip link.

Even when PCI was without pretensions of being a bus standard, its streamlined linking capabilities held promise for revolutionizing PC designs. Where each new Intel microprocessor family required the makers of chipsets and motherboards to completely redesign their products with every new generation of microprocessor, PCI promised a common standard, one independent of the microprocessor generation or family. As originally envisioned, PCI would allow designers to link together entire universes of processors, coprocessors, and support chips without *glue logic*—the pesky profusion of chip needed to match the signals between different integrated circuits—with a connection the speed of which was unfettered by frequency (and clock) limits. All PC chips that follow the PCI standard can be connected together on a circuit board without the need for glue logic. In itself, this standard could lower PC prices by making designs more economical while increasing reliability by minimizing the number of circuit components.

As a chip link, PCI was designed to operate at the full clock speed of Intel's top-of-the-line microprocessors—33 MHz and beyond. That high speed makes the layout of circuit traces on the motherboard critical. Consequently, the original PCI specification gave guidelines for the physical configuration of the chips to be connected on the motherboard. Intel believed that PCI devices should physically be arranged as close together as possible so that chip connections to the high-speed parallel circuit traces (an on-board bus that Intel called the *PCI Speedway*) are spaced about one inch apart. The chips straddle the speedway, on alternating sides of the speedway, so that those located on a given side appear at two-inch increments. This staggered design minimizes the length of the bus and the capacitive effects that limit its operating frequency. Figure 6.10 illustrates the PCI Speedway.

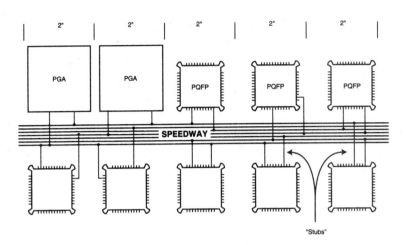

FIGURE 6.10. The PCI Speedway.

The published design was entirely open because Intel intended PCI to become the single industry standard to which chipmakers would design their products. Such an open standard would foster third-party manufacturers creating a wide variety of chips with specialized functions that could easily attach to PCI—not just video but also SCSI controllers, LAN adapters, and audio and video products for multimedia systems.

PCI was initially released into a world that clamored for a local bus standard just before the VL Bus standard was officially ratified. The original PCI was a local bus, but one that stuck to the motherboard. Although the signals needed for an external expansion bus were noted in the specifications, the one thing the expansion industry clamored for was absent: a pin-out for an expansion connector. On the surface, motherboard-oriented PCI appeared to be compatible with VL Bus. That compatibility, however, was not to stay in Intel's long-range plans.

When Intel upgraded the PCI specifications to match the Pentium processor, they also tightly plugged the one hole in the original design. By specifying not only a connector pin-out but also an entire expansion board architecture, Intel's engineers pushed PCI into the forefront of expansion design.

As with VL Bus, the revised PCI was designed to work inside PCs based on more traditional buses, such as ISA, Micro Channel, or EISA. Unlike VL Bus, however, the new PCI was self-contained and need not affiliate with another bus. The PCI bus standard envisioned PCI boards connecting only to the PCI bus and getting all the signals they need from the PCI connector. The new standard defined physical compatibility so that the same board can be adapted easily to fit the form factor of a ISA/EISA or Micro Channel system.

A key tenant of the PCI design is processor independence; that is, its circuits and signals are not tied to the requirements of a specific microprocessor or family.

This independence alone removes PCI from being a true local bus. Although the standard was developed by Intel, the PCI design is not limited to Intel microprocessors. In fact, some computers based on DEC's Alpha chip are expected to use PCI.

Although PCI can deliver performance on par with the host microprocessor's local bus, it is one step removed from the microprocessor. This intermediary position has given PCI the title *mezzanine bus.*

That said, the speed of operation of the PCI bus is dependent on the host microprocessor's clock. PCI components are normally synchronized with the host microprocessor. The standard foresees operation in a frequency range from 20 to 33 MHz, although PCI itself is designed for operation down to 0 Hz, a dead stop.

To accommodate devices that cannot operate at the full speed of the PCI bus, the design incorporates three flow control signals that indicate when a given peripheral or board is ready to send or receive data. One of these signals halts the current transaction. Consequently, PCI transactions can take place at a rate far lower than the bus speed implies.

Physical Characteristics

Just as the basic underpinnings of PCI differ from other expansion buses, so does its physical embodiment. When installed on a motherboard, the PCI connector is offset from the plane of an ordinary expansion board in a given slot. If a PCI slot and traditional expansion slot share the same physical space, the PCI connector is laterally offset from (or next to) the other bus connector. Although it is possible for a given expansion board to have both a PCI and traditional bus connector, the offset connector design of PCI enables you to have your choice in a single slot— the new bus or the old one (see fig. 6.11).

The PCI design provides for expansion connectors extending the bus off the motherboard, but limits such expansion to a maximum three connectors (none are required by the standard). As with VL Bus, this limit is imposed by the high operating frequency of the PCI bus. More connectors would increase bus capacitance and make full speed operation less reliable.

To attain reliable operation at high speeds without the need for terminations (as required by the SCSI bus), Intel chose a reflected rather than direct signaling system for PCI. To activate a bus signal, a device raises (or lowers) the signal on the bus only to half its required activation level. As with any bus, the high-frequency signals meant for the slots propagate down the bus lines and are reflected back by the unterminated ends of the conductors. The reflected signal combines with the original signal, doubling its value up to the required activation voltage.

The basic PCI interface requires only 47 discrete connections for slave boards (or devices), with two more on bus-mastering boards. To accommodate multiple power supply and ground signals and blanked off spaces to key the connectors for proper insertion, the physical 32-bit PCI bus connector actually includes 124 pins. Every active signal on the PCI bus is adjacent to (either next to or on the opposite side of the board from) a power supply or ground signal to minimize extraneous radiation (see Table 6.6).

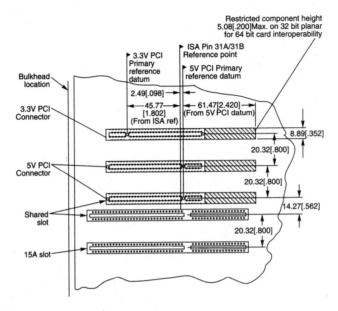

FIGURE 6.11. PCI connector layout.

TABLE 6.6. PCI Connector Pinout

	5V System Environment		3.3V System Environment		
Pin	Side B	Side A	Side B	Side A	Comments
1	-12V	TRST#	-12V	TRST#	32-bit connector start
2	TCK	+12V	TCK	+12V	
3	Ground	TMS	Ground	TMS	
4	TDO	TDI	TDO	TDI	
5	+5V	+5V	+5V	+5V	
6	+5V	INTA#	+5V	INTA#	
7	INTB#	INTC#	INTB#	INTC#	
8	INTD#	+5V	INTD#	+5V	
9	PRSNT2#	Reserved	PRSNT1#	Reserved	
10	Reserved	+5V (I/O)	Reserved	+3.3V (I/O)	

Pin	5V System Environment		3.3V System Environment		Comments
	Side B	Side A	Side B	Side A	
11	PRSNT2#	Reserved	PRSNT2#	Reserved	
12	Ground	Ground	Connector Key		3.3 volt key
13	Ground	Ground	Connector Key		3.3 volt key
14	Reserved	Reserved	Reserved	Reserved	
15	Ground	RST#	Ground	RST#	
16	CLK	+5V (I/O)	CLK	+3.3V (I/O)	
17	Ground	GNT#	Ground	GNT#	
18	REQ#	Ground	REQ#	Ground	
19	+5V (I/O)	Reserved	+3.3V (I/O)	Reserved	
20	AD[31]	AD[30]	AD[31]	AD[30]	
21	AD[29]	+3.3V	AD[29]	+3.3V	
22	Ground	AD[28]	Ground	AD[28]	
23	AD[27]	AD[26]	AD[27]	AD[26]	
24	AD[25]	Ground	AD[25]	Ground	
25	+3.3V	AD[24]	+3.3V	AD[24]	
26	C/BE[3]#	IDSEL	C/BE[3]#	IDSEL	
27	AD[23]	+3.3V	AD[23]	+3.3V	
28	Ground	AD[22]	Ground	AD[22]	
29	AD[21]	AD[20]	AD[21]	AD[20]	
30	AD[19]	Ground	AD[19]	Ground	
31	+3.3V	AD[18]	+3.3V	AD[18]	
32	AD[17]	AD[16]	AD[17]	AD[16]	
33	C/BE[2]#	+3.3V	C/BE[2]#	+3.3V	
34	Ground	FRAME#	Ground	FRAME#	
35	IRDY#	Ground	IRDY#	Ground	
36	+3.3V	TRDY#	+3.3V	TRDY#	
37	DEVSEL#	Ground	DEVSEL#	Ground	
38	Ground	STOP#	Ground	STOP#	
39	LOCK#	+3.3V	LOCK#	+3.3V	

continues

TABLE 6.6. Continued

Pin	5V System Environment		3.3V System Environment		Comments
	Side B	Side A	Side B	Side A	
40	PERR#	SDONE	PERR#	SDONE	
41	+3.3V	SBO#	+3.3V	SBO#	
42	SERR#	Ground	SERR#	Ground	
43	+3.3V	PAR	+3.3V	PAR	
44	C/BE[1]#	AD[15]	C/BE[1]#	AD[15]	
45	AD[14]	+3.3V	AD[14]	+3.3V	
46	Ground	AD[13]	Ground	AD[13]	
47	AD[12]	AD[11]	AD[12]	AD[11]	
48	AD[10]	Ground	AD[10]	Ground	
49	Ground	AD[09]	Ground	AD[09]	
50	Connector Key		Ground	Ground	5 volt key
51	Connector Key		Ground	Ground	5 volt key
52	AD[08]	C/BE[0]#	AD[08]	C/BE[0]#	
53	AD[07]	+3.3V	AD[07]	+3.3V	
54	+3.3V	AD[06]	+3.3V	AD[06]	
55	AD[05]	AD[04]	AD[05]	AD[04]	
56	AD[03]	Ground	AD[03]	Ground	
57	Ground	AD[02]	Ground	AD[02]	
58	AD[01]	AD[00]	AD[01]	AD[00]	
59	+5V (I/O)	+5V (I/O)	+3.3V (I/O)	+3.3V (I/O)	
60	ACK64#	REQ64#	ACK64#	REQ64#	
61	+5V	+5V	+5V	+5v	
62	+5V	+5V	+5V	+5V	32 bit connector end
	Connector Key		Connector Key		
	Connector Key		Connector Key		

The 64-bit implementation of PCI uses a 188-pin connector (see Table 6.7). As with VL Bus, PCI connectors are patterned after connectors used by Micro Channel, with 0.050-inch spacing between pins.

TABLE 6.7. PCI Connector Pin-Out

Pin	Side B	Side A	Side B	Side A	Comments
	Connector Key		Connector Key		
	Connector Key		Connector Key		
63	Reserved	Ground	Reserved	Ground	64-bit connector start
64	Ground	C/BE[7]#	Ground	C/BE[7]#	
65	C/BE[6]#	C/BE[5]#	C/BE[6]#	C/BE[5]#	
66	C/BE[4]#	+5V (I/O)	C/BE[4]#	+3.3V (I/O)	
67	Ground	PAR64	Ground	PAR64	
68	AD[63]	AD[62]	AD[63]	AD[62]	
69	AD[61]	Ground	AD[61]	Ground	
70	+5V (I/O)	AD[60]	+3.3V (I/O)	AD[60]	
71	AD[59]	AD[58]	AD[59]	AD[58]	
72	AD[57]	Ground	AD[57]	Ground	
73	Ground	AD[56]	Ground	AD[56]	
74	AD[55]	AD[54]	AD[55]	AD[54]	
75	AD[53]	+5V (I/O)	AD[53]	+3.3V (I/O)	
76	Ground	AD[52]	Ground	AD[52]	
77	AD[51]	AD[50]	AD[51]	AD[50]	
78	AD[49]	Ground	AD[49]	Ground	
79	+5V (I/O)	AD[48]	+3.3V (I/O)	AD[48]	
80	AD[47]	AD[46]	AD[47]	AD[46]	
81	AD[45]	Ground	AD[45]	Ground	
82	Ground	AD[44]	Ground	AD[44]	
83	AD[43]	AD[42]	AD[43]	AD[42]	
Pin	Side B	Side A	Side B	Side A	
84	AD[41]	+5V (I/O)	AD[41]	+3.3V (I/O)	
85	Ground	AD[40]	Ground	AD[40]	
86	AD[39]	AD[38]	AD[39]	AD[38]	
87	AD[37]	Ground	AD[37]	Ground	
88	+5V (I/O)	AD[36]	+3.3V (I/O)	AD[36]	
89	AD[35]	AD[34]	AD[35]	AD[34]	
90	AD[33]	Ground	AD[33]	Ground	

continues

TABLE 6.7. Continued

Pin	Side B	Side A	Side B	Side A	Comments
91	Ground	AD[32]	Ground	AD[32]	
92	Reserved	Reserved	Reserved	Reserved	
93	Reserved	Ground	Reserved	Ground	
94	Ground	Reserved	Ground	Reserved	64-bit connecter

Data Transfer Cycles

Although the number of connections sounds high, Intel actually had to resort to a powerful trick to keep the number of bus pins manageable. The address and data signals on the PCI bus are time multiplexed on the same 32 pins. That is, the address and data signals share the same bus connections (AD00 through AD31). On the one clock cycle, the combined address/data lines carry the address values and set up the location to move information to or from. On the next cycle, the same lines switch to carrying the actual data.

This address/data cycling of the bus does not slow the bus. Even in non-multiplexed designs, the address lines are used on one bus cycle and then the data lines are used on the next. Moreover, PCI has its own burst mode that eliminates the need for alteration between address and data cycles. PCI also can operate in its own burst mode. During burst mode transfers, a single address cycle can be followed by multiple data cycles that access sequential memory locations.

PCI achieves its multiplexing using a special bus signal called *Cycle Frame* (FRAME#). The appearance of the Cycle Frame signal identifies the beginning of a transfer cycle and indicates the address/data bus holds a valid address. The Cycle Frame signal is then held active for the duration of the data transfer.

Use of this signal allows PCI to offer a burst mode that does not suffer the 4-cycle, 16-byte limit of the burst mode of VL Bus and today's 486 microprocessors. During burst mode transfers, a single address cycle can be followed by multiple data cycles that access sequential memory locations, limited only by the needs of other devices to use the bus and other system functions (such as memory refresh). The burst can continue as long as the Cycle Frame signal remains active. With each clock cycle that Cycle Frame is high, new data is placed on the bus. If Cycle Frame is active only for one data cycle, an ordinary transfer takes place. When it stays active across multiple data cycles, a burst occurs. In effect, the PCI burst mode is equivalent to the streaming data modes of Micro Channel and EISA.

This burst mode underlies the claimed 132 M/sec throughput claimed for the 32-bit PCI design. (With the 64-bit extension, PCI claims a peak transfer rate of 264M/sec.) Of course, PCI attains that rate only *during* the burst. The initial address cycle steals away a bit of time and lowers the data rate (the penalty for which declines with the increasing length of the burst). System overhead, however, holds down the ultimate throughput.

Even though PCI anticipates all devices following the standard will use its full 32-bit bus width, the standard allows for transfers of smaller widths. Four Byte Enable signals (C/BE0# through C/BE3#) are used to indicate which of four byte-wide blocks of PCI's 32-bit signals contain valid data. In 64-bit systems, another four signals (C/BE4# through C/BE7#) indicate the additional active byte lanes.

To accommodate devices that cannot operate at the full speed of the PCI bus, the design incorporates three flow control signals: Initiator Ready (IRDY# at pin B35), Target Ready (TRDY# at pin A36), and Stop (STOP# at pin A38). Target Ready is activated to indicate that a bus device is ready to supply data during a read cycle or accept it during a write cycle. When Initiator Ready is activated, it signals that a bus master is ready to complete an on-going transaction. A Stop signal is sent from a target device to a master to stop the current transaction.

Data Integrity Signals

To ensure the integrity of information traversing the bus, the PCI specification makes mandatory the parity-checking of both the address and data cycles. One bit (signal PAR) is used to confirm parity across 32 address/data lines and the four associated Byte Enable signals. A second parity signal is used in 64-bit implementations. The parity signal lags the data it verifies by one cycle, and its state is set so that the sum of it, the address/data values, and the Byte Enable values is a logical high (1).

If a parity error is detected during a data transfer, the bus controller asserts the Parity Error signal (PERR#). The action taken on error detection—for example, re-sending data—depends on how the system is configured. Another signal, System Error (SERR#) handles address parity and other errors.

Parity-checking of the data bus becomes particularly important as bus-width and speed grow. Every increase in bus complexity also raises the chance of errors creeping in. Parity-checking prevents such problems from affecting the information transferred across the bus.

Bus Mastering and Arbitration

The basic PCI design supports arbitrated bus mastering like other advanced expansion buses, but PCI has its own bus command language (a four-bit code) and supports secondary cache memory.

Bus mastering on PCI works like that of VL Bus. A bus master board sends a signal to its host to request control of the bus and starts to transfer when it receives a confirmation. Unlike Micro Channel and EISA, in which the arbitration control signals are bused together, each PCI board gets its own slot-specific signals to request bus control and receive confirmation that control was granted. This approach allows great flexibility in assigning the priorities, even the arbitration protocol, of the complete computer system. The designer of a PCI-based computer can adapt the arbitration procedure to suit his needs rather than having to adapt to the ideas of the obscure engineers who conceived the original bus specification.

Bus mastering across the PCI bus is achieved with two special signals, Request (REQ#) and Grant (GNT#). A master asserts its Request signal when it wants to take control of the bus. In return, the *central resource* (Intel's name for the circuitry shared by all bus devices on the motherboard, including the bus control logic) sends a Grant to the master to give permission to take control. Each PCI device gets its own dedicated Request and Grant signal.

As a self-contained expansion bus, PCI naturally provides for hardware interrupts. PCI includes four level-sensitive interrupts (INTA# through INTD# at pins A6, B7, A7, and B8) that enable interrupt sharing. The specification does not define what the interrupts are or how they are to be shared. Even the relationship between the four signals is left to the designer (for example, each can indicate its own interrupt, or all can combine to define up to 16 separate interrupts as binary values). Typically, these details are implemented in a device driver for the PCI board. The interrupt lines are not synchronized to the other bus signals and therefore may be activated at any time during a bus cycle.

Low-Voltage Evolution

The PCI specification also anticipates an eventual switchover from standard five volt logic to power-saving 3.3-volt operation. To accommodate the development of low-voltage "green" PCs, PCI specifies two connector types and three different connector regimes—a 5-volt connector for today's prevailing circuit designs; a 3.3-volt connector for low-power designs; and the capability to combine both connectors on a single expansion board for a smooth transition between designs. A key on 5-volt sockets (blocking pins 50 and 51) prevents the insertion of 3.3-volt boards. (Five-volt boards have a slot corresponding to the key.) A key on 3.3-volt sockets (at pins 12 and 13) restricts the insertion to correspondingly slotted 3.3-volt boards. Boards capable of discriminating the two voltage regimes have slots in both places (see fig. 6.12).

The signals on the PCI bus are odd, based on reflected rather than direct voltages. To activate a bus signal, a device raises (or lowers) the signal on the bus only to half its required voltage level. The signal then propagates down the bus and is reflected back because the bus operates unterminated. The reflected signal combines with the original signal, doubling its value, up to the required activation voltage.

Automated Setup

As with Micro Channel and EISA, PCI contemplates system configuration without the need to set jumpers or DIP switches. Under the PCI specification, expansion boards include registers that store configuration information that can be tapped to set up systems automatically. PCI requires 256 registers. This configuration space is tightly defined by the PCI specification to ensure compatibility. A special signal, *Initialization Device Select (IDSEL)*, dedicated to each slot is used to activate the configuration read and write operations.

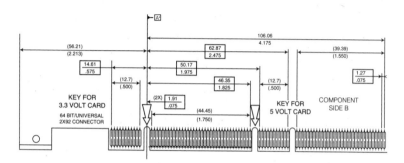

FIGURE 6.12. PCI voltage encoding.

Standards and Coordination

The PCI standard is managed and maintained by the PCI Special Interest Group. The latest revision of the specification is available from the following address:

PCI Special Interest Group
M/S HF3-15A
5200 N. E. Elam Young Parkway
Hillsboro, Oregon 97124-6497
(503) 696-2000

PC Card

While the desktop remains a battlefield for bus designers, notebook computer makers have selected a single standard to rally around: *PC Card,* promulgated by the Personal Computer Memory Card Industry Association. As desktop systems have become smaller and greener, PC Card has quietly slipped into a few. Soon it may become an accepted desktop expansion standard as well.

Such dramatic predictions reflect the virtues and versatility of the underlying standard, and the features of the PC Card design read like a wish list for the expansion standard of the future. PC Cards are compatible with all the old buses you've grown to know and hate—ISA, Micro Channel, EISA, and so on. Because they are operating system and device independent, you can plug the same PC Card peripheral into a PC, Mac, Newton, or whatever the next generation holds in store. Moreover, PC Card is designed not to be limited to PCs, but also can be used in any digital electronic device—from calculators to hair curlers or CAD workstations to auto-everything cameras. Someday you may even find a PC Card lurking in your toaster oven or your music synthesizer.

The PC Card system is self-configuring, so you do not have to deal with DIP switches, fiddle with jumpers, or search for a Reference Diskette. PC Card differs from other bus standards in that it allows for external expansion—you don't have to open up your PC to add a PC Card. The design is so robust that you can insert or remove a PC Card with the power on without worrying that you will damage it, your PC, or data stored on the card. The PC Card standard is even ready for tomorrow's battery-saving low-voltage computer designs.

Although initially intended simply to add programs to miniature computers that lack disk drives, in the last year or so PC Cards have grown to embrace a full repertoire of expansion functions. Besides memory and firmware, high-speed modems and hard disks have been encapsulated into PC Cards. In coming months, you can expect to find nearly anything that fits on a PC expansion board downsized to squeeze into a PC Card.

Unfortunately, the universal scope of the PC Card standard has interfered with its growth. PC Card requires layers of software to ensure its compatibility across device architectures, even to prevent one card from working inside (or destroying) a hostile machine. Sorting out the software side of PC Card has proven problematic, to the extent that mortals may have difficulty making some cards work in systems where by right and design they should. The software also can steal memory space from applications, making the universally agreeable standard disagreeable to put to work.

Eventually, the software will get sorted out, and the PC industry will adapt to the needs and peculiarities of PC Cards. When this happens, PC Card will be posed to become a major force in both portable and desktop computers, perhaps even outstripping the potentials of PCI.

Architectural Overview

At first glance, PCMCIA 2.0 looks a bit archaic as an expansion bus. It provides only a 16-bit interface; it lacks such advanced features as bus mastering; and it offers only a single interrupt request (IRQ) line. However, because the versatile design of PCMCIA is fundamentally different from the design of ordinary expansion buses, such shortcomings are temporary. (PCMCIA is working on support for bus-mastering adapters, for example.)

PCMCIA's expansion system is not a simple extension to the bus circuitry of a computer. Rather, it is a system that includes everything—from a computer and host-independent socket for the PC Cards to program calls that link software into the PCMCIA system. Figure 6.13 shows an overview of the PCMCIA expansion system.

A hardware device supporting the PCMCIA standard can have from 1 to 255 PCMCIA adapters; that is, circuits that match the signals of PC Cards to the host. Up to 16 separate PC Card sockets can be connected to each adapter, much as you can connect two hard disks to an IDE controller or seven devices to a SCSI host adapter. Consequently, PCMCIA 2.0 allows for the possibility of plugging up to 4,080 PC Cards into one system.

The memory and I/O registers of each PC Card are individually mapped into the address range of the host device. Therefore the addresses on the card need not be identical with those of the host. The host accesses the PC Card resources through one or more windows, which are memory or register ranges that can be directly addressed by the host. The entire memory on a PC Card can be mapped into a single large window (for simple memory expansion, for example), or it can be paged (like EMS memory) through one or more windows. The PC Card determines the access method through configuration information it stores in its memory.

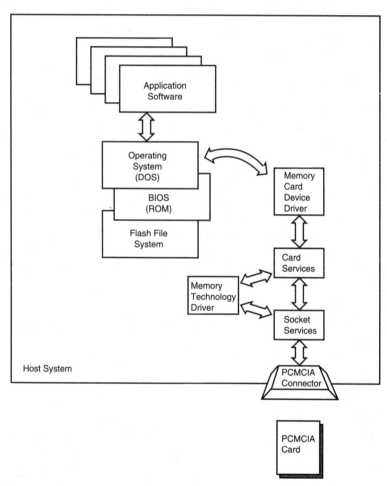

FIGURE 6.13. Overview of the PCMCIA expansion system.

Physical Characteristics

The centerpiece of PCMCIA 2.0 is the PC Card itself. Measuring 54 by 85 millimeters (2.126 by 3.37 inches) and 3.3mm (just over ⅛ inch) thick, the PC Card physically follows the form factor of earlier memory cards (including the IC Card) standardized by JEIDA (the Japan Electronic Industry Design Association). The first release of the PCMCIA specification paired this single-size card with a Fujitsu-style 68-pin connector. Under the current PCMCIA 2.0 specification, this form factor is designated as the Type I PC Card.

The thinness of the Type I card proved an unacceptable limitation. Even without allowing for the PC Card packaging, some solid-state devices are thicker than 3.3mm. Most important among these "fat" devices are the EPROMs, used for nonvolatile storage. (Most PCs use EPROMs to store their system BIOS, for example.) Unlike ordinary, thin ROMS, EPROMs can be reprogrammed, but this operation requires a transparent window to admit the ultraviolet radiation used to erase the programming of the chip. The windowed packaging makes most EPROMs 3.3 mm or thicker.

Fujitsu faced this problem when developing the firmware to be encoded on memory cards and developed a somewhat thicker card that could be plugged into the same sockets as standard memory cards. Modem and other peripheral makers found the Fujitsu fat card more suited to their purposes. To accommodate them, PCMCIA 2.0 standardized an alternative, Type II PC Card. Essentially based on the old Fujitsu developmental EPROM form factor, Type II PC Cards are 5.0 millimeters thick, but otherwise conform to the same dimensions as Type I cards. Figures 6.14, 6.15, and 6.16 show standard card dimensions.

The PCMCIA 2.0 standard puts the extra thickness in a planar bulge, called the *substrate area*, in the middle of the card. This thicker area measures 48mm wide and 75mm long. Three millimeters along each side of the Type II PC Card are kept to the thinness of the Type I standard so that the same card guides can be used for either card type. Similarly, the front 10mm of a Type II card maintain the 3.3mm thickness of the Type I standard so that the same connector can be used for either card type. Naturally, the actual card slot for a Type II PC Card must be wide enough to accommodate the maximum thickness of the card.

In September 1992, PCMCIA approved a third, Type III form factor for PC Cards. These still-thicker cards expand the bulge of Type II from 5mm to 10.5mm and are designed to accommodate miniaturized hard disks and similar mechanical components. As with Type II cards, Type III PC Cards remain thin at the edges to fit standard card guides and standard connectors.

Under Release 2.0, both Type I and Type II cards can be implemented in extended form—their depth can be increased by an additional 50mm (to 135mm) to hold additional componentry. Such extended cards project about two inches more from standard PCMCIA slots.

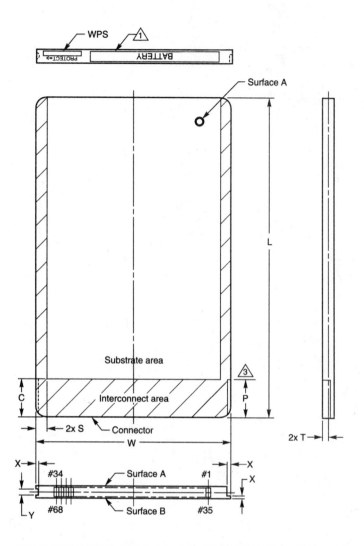

C Min	L±0.008	P Min △	S Min	T △	W±0.004	X±0.002	Y±0.002
.294	3.370	.394	.118	.065	2.126	.039	.063
(10.0)	(85.60)	(10.0)	(3.0)	(1.65)	(54.0)	(1.00)	(1.60)

△1 Recommended battery location. The battery holder should be designed so that the positive side of the battery is up.

2. The PC card shall be opaque (non-see thru)

△3 Polarization key length

△4 Interconnect area tolerance = ±.002
subtrate area tolerance = ±.004

5. Millimeters are in parenthesis ( ).

FIGURE 6.14. PCMCIA package card dimensions.

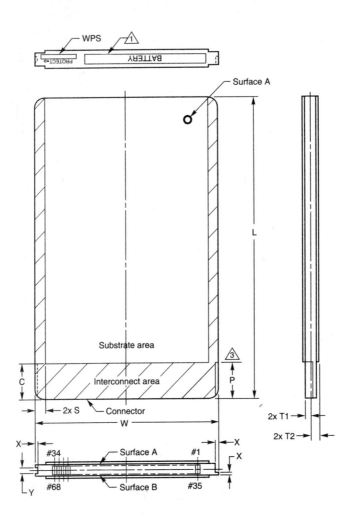

C Min	L±0.008	P Min /2\	S Min	T1±0.002	T2 MAX	W±0.004	X±0.002	Y±0.002
.394	3.370	.394	.118	.065	.098	2.126	.039	.063
(10.0)	(85.60)	(10.0)	(3.0)	(1.65)	(2.50)	(54.0)	(1.00)	(1.60)

/1\ Recommended battery location. The battery holder should be designed so that the positive side of the battery is up.

2. The PC card shall be opaque (non-see thru)

/3\ Polarization key length

4. Millimeters are in parenthesis ( ).

FIGURE 6.15. More PCMCIA package card dimensions

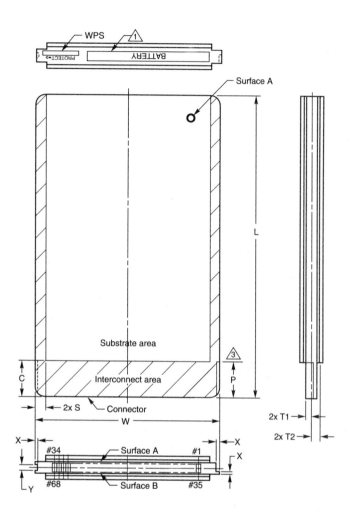

C Min	L±0.008	P Min /3\	S Min	T1±0.002	T2 MAX	W±0.004	X±0.002	Y±0.002
.394	3.370	.394	.118	.065	.196	2.126	.039	.063
(10.0)	(85.60)	(10.0)	(3.0)	(1.65)	(5.0)	(54.0)	(1.00)	(1.60)

/1\ Recommended battery location. The battery holder should be designed so that the positive side of the battery is up.

2. The PC card shall be opaque (non-see thru)

/3\ Polarization key length

4. Millimeters are in parenthesis ( ).

FIGURE 6.16. More PCMCIA package card dimensions.

To ensure that all cards easily and securely mate with their connectors, the PC Card standard requires that card guides be at least 40mm long and that the PC Card connector must engage and guide the connector pins for 10mm before the connector bottoms out.

The layout of a PC Card is essentially symmetrical, meaning that it could inadvertently be inserted upside down. The PC Card design allows for such cases of brain fade by eliminating the risk of damage. Although the cards do not work while inverted, neither they nor the computers into which they are plugged suffer damage.

Because the size and placement of labels on the cards is part of the standard, when you are familiar with the layout of one PC Card, you know the proper orientation of all the cards. Moreover, other physical aspects of the cards—the position of the write-protect switch (if any) and battery (if needed)—are standardized as well. The PCMCIA standard also recommends that the batteries in all cards be oriented in the same direction (positive terminal up).

In addition to the physical measures that facilitate getting the cards into their sockets, two pins—one on each side of the connector—allow the PC host to determine whether the card is properly seated. If the signal (ground) from one pin is present and the other is not, the system knows that the card is skewed or otherwise improperly inserted in the connector.

The one part of the PC Card not yet standardized is the rear edge, where connections are made to communications products such as modems. PCMCIA is currently working on this area and hopes to develop specifications for the connectors and their placement.

Bus Connection

All types of PC Cards use the same 68-pin connector, whose contacts are arranged in two parallel rows of 34 pins. The lines are spaced at 1.27mm (0.050 inch) intervals between rows and between adjacent pins in the same row. Male pins on the card engage a single molded socket on the host.

To ensure proper powering up of the card, the pins are arranged so that the power and ground connections are longer (3.6mm) than the signal leads (3.2mm). Because of their greater length, therefore, power leads engage first so that potentially damaging signals are not applied to unpowered circuits. The two pins (36 and 67) that signal that the card is inserted all the way are shorter (2.6mm) than the signal leads.

Signals and Operation

The standard PCMCIA 2.0 connector itself allows for two PC Card variations: *memory-only* (which essentially conforms to the Release 1.0 standard) and *I/O cards*. Table 6.8 lists the pin assignments. All but ten pins of the standard 68 share common functions between the two card styles (these are designated in the table with asterisks). Four memory card signals are defined differently for I/O cards (pins 16, 33, 62, and 63); three memory card signals are modified for

I/O functions (pins 18, 52, and 61); and three pins reserved on memory cards are used by I/O cards (pins 44, 45, and 60).

TABLE 6.8. PCMCIA PC Card Pin 1 to Pin 68 Assignments

Memory Only Card Interface
(Always Available at Card Insertion)

Pin	Signal	I/O	Function	+/−
1	GND		Ground	
2	D3	I/O	Data bit 3	
3	D4	I/O	Data bit 4	
4	D5	I/O	Data bit 5	
5	D6	I/O	Data bit 6	
6	D7	I/O	Data bit 7	
7	CE1	I	Card enable	−
8	A10	I	Address bit 10	
9	OE	I	Output enable	−
10	A11	I	Address bit 11	
11	A9	I	Address bit 9	
12	A8	I	Address bit 8	
13	A13	I	Address bit 13	
14	A14	I	Address bit 14	
15	WE/PGM	I	Write enable	
16	RDY/BSY	O	Ready/busy	+/−
17	Vcc			
18	Vpp1		Programming Supply Voltage 1	
19	A16	I	Address bit 16	
20	A15	I	Address bit 15	
21	A12	I	Address bit 12	
22	A7	I	Address bit 7	
23	A6	I	Address bit 6	
24	A5	I	Address bit 5	
25	A4	I	Address bit 4	

continues

TABLE 6.8. PCMCIA PC Card Pin 1 to Pin 68 Assignments

Memory Only Card Interface
(Always Available at Card Insertion)

Pin	Signal	I/O	Function	+/-
26	A3	I	Address bit 3	
27	A2	I	Address bit 2	
28	A1	I	Address bit 1	
29	A0	I	Address bit 0	
30	D0	I/O	Data bit 0	
31	D1	I/O	Data bit 1	
32	D2	I/O	Data bit 2	
33	WP	O	Write protect	+
34	GND		Ground	
35	GND		Ground	
36	CD1	O	Card detect	–
37	D11	I/O	Data bit 11	
38	D12	I/O	Data bit 12	
39	D13	I/O	Data bit 13	
40	D14	I/O	Data bit 14	
41	D15	I/O	Data bit 15	
42	CE2	I	Card enable	–
43	RFSH	I	Refresh	
44	RFU		Reserved	
45	RFU		Reserved	
46	A17	I	Address bit 17	
47	A18	I	Address bit 18	
48	A19	I	Address bit 19	
49	A20	I	Address bit 20	
50	A21	I	Address bit 21	
51	Vcc			
52	Vpp2		Programming Supply Voltage 2	
53	A22	I	Address bit 22	
54	A23	I	Address bit 23	

Memory Only Card Interface
(Always Available at Card Insertion)

Pin	Signal	I/O	Function	+/–
55	A24	I	Address bit 24	
56	A25	I	Address bit 25	
57	RFU		Reserved	
58	RESET	I	Card Reset	+
59	WAIT	O	Extend bus cycle	–
60	RFU		Reserved	
61	REG	I	Register select	–
62	BVD2	O	Battery voltage detect 2	
63	BVD1	O	Battery voltage detect 1	
64	D8	I/O	Data bit 8	
65	D9	I/O	Data bit 9	
66	D10	I/O	Data bit 10	
67	CD2	O	Card detect	–
68	GND		Ground	

I/O and Memory Card Interface:
(Available Only After Card and Socket Are Configured)

Pin	Signal	I/O	Function	+/–
1	GND		Ground	
2	D3	I/O	Data bit 3	
3	D4	I/O	Data bit 4	
4	D5	I/O	Data bit 5	
5	D6	I/O	Data bit 6	
6	D7	I/O	Data bit 7	
7	CE1	I	Card enable	–
8	A10	I	Address bit 10	
9	OE	I	Output enable	–
10	A11	I	Address bit 11	
11	A9	I	Address bit 9	

continues

TABLE 6.8. Continued

I/O and Memory Card Interface:
(Available Only After Card and Socket Are Configured)

Pin	Signal	I/O	Function	+/–
12	A8	I	Address bit 8	
13	A13	I	Address bit 13	
14	A14	I	Address bit 14	
15	WE/PGM	I	Write enable	–
16	IREQ	O	Interrupt Request	–
17	Vcc			
18	Vpp1		Programming and Peripheral Supply	
19	A16	I	Address bit 16	
20	A15	I	Address bit 15	
21	A12	I	Address bit 12	
22	A7	I	Address bit 7	
23	A6	I	Address bit 6	
24	A5	I	Address bit 5	
25	A4	I	Address bit 4	
26	A3	I	Address bit 3	
27	A2	I	Address bit 2	
28	A1	I	Address bit 1	
29	A0	I	Address bit 0	
30	D0	I/O	Data bit 0	
31	D1	I/O	Data bit 1	
32	D2	I/O	Data bit 2	
33	IOIS16	O	IO Port is 16 bit	–
34	GND		Ground	
35	GND		Ground	
36	CD1	O	Card detect	–
37	D11	I/O	Data bit 11	
38	D12	I/O	Data bit 12	
39	D13	I/O	Data bit 13	

I/O and Memory Card Interface:
(Available Only After Card and Socket Are Configured)

Pin	Signal	I/O	Function	+/–
40	D14	I/O	Data bit 14	
41	D15	I/O	Data bit 15	
42	CE2	I	Card enable	–
43	RFSH	I	Refresh	
44	IORD	I	IO Read	–
45	IOWR	I	IO Write	–
46	A17	I	Address bit 17	
47	A18	I	Address bit 18	
48	A19	I	Address bit 19	
49	A20	I	Address bit 20	
50	A21	I	Address bit 21	
51	Vcc			
52	Vpp2		Programming and Peripheral Supply 2	
53	A22	I	Address bit 22	
54	A23	I	Address bit 23	
55	A24	I	Address bit 24	
56	A25	I	Address bit 25	
57	RFU		Reserved	
58	RESET	I	Card Reset	+
59	WAIT	O	Extend bus cycle	–
60	INPACK	O	Input Port Acknowledge	–
61	REG	I	Register select & IO Enable	–
62	SPKR	O	Audio Digital Waveform	–
63	STSCHG	O	Card Statuses Changed	–
64	D8	I/O	Data bit 8	

continues

TABLE 6.8. Continued

I/O and Memory Card Interface:
(Available Only After Card and Socket Are Configured)

Pin	Signal	I/O	Function	+/−
65	D9	I/O	Data bit 9	
66	D10	I/O	Data bit 10	
67	CD2	O	Card detect	−
68	GND		Ground	

When a PC Card is plugged into a slot, the host computer's PCMCIA adapter circuitry initially assumes that it is a memory card. The card defines itself as an I/O card through its on-board CIS data, which the host computer reads upon initializing the PC Card.

The PCMCIA 2.0 standard allows for card implementations that use either 8- or 16-bit data buses. In memory operations, two Card Enable signals (pins 7 and 42) set the bus width; pin 7 enables even-numbered address bytes; and 42 enables odd bytes. All bytes can be read by an 8-bit system by activating pin 7 but not 42 and toggling the lowest address line (A0, pin 29) to step to the next byte.

Although the current PCMCIA standard allows for only 16 data lines, the specification is flexible enough to allow for multiplexed 32-bit operation in custom designs. Properly implemented, such a card would work with a standard 16-bit interface in devices that comply with Release 2.0, but it could gain full 32-bit power in machines matched to a proprietary enhancement of the standard. PCMCIA is discussing a 32-bit extension to the PC Card design, but as yet no timetable has been set for developing it.

Twenty-six address lines are used, allowing the direct addressing of up to 64M of data. The memory areas on each card are independent. That is, each PC Card can define its own 64M address range as its Common Memory. Not all this memory range is directly addressable by some hosts: 8088-based systems are limited by their microprocessors to 1M of directly addressed memory, for example. The entire 64M range can be addressed by such systems through a PCMCIA window, however.

In addition to Common Memory, each card has a second 64M address space devoted to the Attribute Memory that holds the card's setup information. The entire range need not have physical memory associated with it. In fact, most PC Cards probably will devote only a few kilobytes of the available addressing range to CIS storage.

Activating the Register Select signal (pin 61) shifts the 26 address lines normally used to address Common Memory to specifying locations in Attribute Memory instead. The address space assigned to Attribute Memory need not correspond to a block of memory separate from Common Memory. To avoid the need for two distinct memory systems, a PC Card can be designed so that activating the Register Select signal simply points to a block of Common Memory devoted to storing setup information. All PC Cards limit access to Attribute Memory to an 8-bit link using the eight least-significant data lines.

To open or close access to data read from a PC Card, the host computer activates a signal on the card's Output Enable line (pin 9). A Ready/Busy line (pin 16) on memory cards allows the card to signal when it is busy processing and cannot accept a data transfer operation. The same pin is used on I/O cards to make interrupt requests to the host system. During setup, however, an I/O card can redefine pin 16 back to its Ready/Busy function. Under Release 2.0, memory or I/O PC Cards also can delay the completion of an operation in progress—in effect, slowing the host to accommodate the time needs of the card—by activating an Extend Bus Cycle signal on pin 59.

The Write Protect pin (pin 33) relays the status of the write-protect switch on memory cards to the computer host. On I/O cards, this pin indicates that a given I/O port has a 16-bit width.

Pins 62 and 63 on memory cards output two battery status signals. Pin 63 indicates the status of the battery: When activated, the battery is in good condition; when not activated, it indicates that the battery needs to be replaced. Pin 62 refines this to indicate that the battery level is sufficient to maintain card memory without errors; if this signal is not activated, it indicates that the integrity of on-card memory already may be compromised by low battery power.

Memory cards that use EPROM memory often require higher than normal voltages to reprogram their chips. Pins 18 and 52 on the PCMCIA interface provide these voltages when needed.

The same 26 lines used for addressing Common and Attribute Memory serve as port selection addresses on I/O cards. Two pins, I/O read (44) and I/O write (45) signal that the address pins are used for identifying ports and whether the operation is a read or a write.

Unlike memory addresses, however, the I/O facilities available to all PC Cards in a system share "only" one 67,108,864-byte (64M) range of port addresses. Considering that the AT bus allows only 64K of I/O ports, of which some systems recognize a mere 16K, the shared port address space represents no real limitation. Even assigning 16K ports to each of the 4,080 possible PC Cards in a system leaves a few port addresses unused. Whether ports are 8- or 16-bit is indicated by the signal on pin 33.

I/O PC Cards each have a single interrupt request signal. The signal is mapped to one of the PC interrupt lines by the computer host. The PC Card generates a generic interrupt, and it is the host computer's responsibility to route the interrupt to the appropriate channel.

The PCMCIA specification requires all PC Cards to be able to generate edge-triggered (PC and AT-style) interrupts and level-sensitive interrupts (as used by Micro Channel and EISA in some modes). Every card conforms to the host's requirements.

An audio output line also is available from I/O PC Cards. This connection is not intended for high-quality sound, however, for it allows only binary digital (on/off) signals. The audio lines of all PC Cards in a system are linked together by an XOR (exclusive OR) logic gate, fed to a single common loudspeaker.

PC Card, Release 2.0, adds a single Reset signal to all cards at pin 58. When the host computer activates this signal, the card returns to preinitialization settings, with I/O cards returning to their power-on memory card emulation.

PCMCIA 2.0 contemplates the use of PC Cards that operate at either the standard TTL 5-volt level or at a power-saving reduced voltage level of 3.3. The current standard requires that cards initialize operating at 5 volts then shift to lower voltage operation under the direction of the card's configuration information. PCMCIA is currently working on extending the standard to embrace PC Cards that operate solely at 3.3 volts.

Software Interface

To link the PC Card to an Intel-architecture PC host, PCMCIA has defined a software interface called Socket Services. By using a set of function calls under interrupt 1A (which Socket Services shares with the CMOS time-of-day clock), software can access PC Card features without specific knowledge of the underlying hardware. In other words, Socket Services make access to the PC Card hardware independent, much like the BIOS of a PC. In fact, Socket Services are designed so that they can be built into the PC BIOS. Socket Services also can be implemented in the form of a device driver, however, so that PCMCIA functionality can be added to existing PCs.

Using Socket Services, the host establishes the windows used by the PC Card for access. Memory or registers then can be directly addressed by the host. Alternatively, individual or multiple bytes can be read or written through Socket Services function calls.

In September 1992, PCMCIA approved a Card Services standard that defines a program interface for accessing PC Cards. This standard establishes a set of program calls that link to those Socket Services independent of the host operating system. Like the Socket Services associated with interrupt 1A, Card Services can be implemented either as a driver or built in as part of an operating system. (Protected-mode operating systems such as OS/2 and Windows NT require the latter implementation.)

For an advanced system such as PCMCIA 2.0 to work effectively, each PC Card must be able to identify itself and its characteristics to the computer host. Specifically, it must be able to tell the computer how much storage it contains; the device type (solid-state memory, disk, I/O devices, or other peripherals); the format of the data; the speed capabilities of the card; and any of a multitude of other variables about how the card operates.

Automated Setup

Asking you to enter all the required data every time you install a PC Card would be both inconvenient and dangerous. Considerable typing would be required, and a single errant keystroke could forever erase the data from the card. Therefore, PCMCIA developed a self-contained system through which the basic card setup information can be passed to the host regardless of the data structure of the on-card storage or of the operating system of the host.

Called the *Card Identification Structure (CIS)* or *metaformat* of the card, the PCMCIA configuration system works through a succession of compatibility layers to establish the necessary link between the PC Card and its host. As with the hardware interface, each layer of CIS is increasingly device-specific.

Only the first layer, the *Basic Compatibility Layer,* is mandatory under PCMCIA 2.0. This layer indicates how the card's storage is organized. Only two kinds of information are relevant here: the data structures used by the layer itself; and standard and physical device information such as the number of heads, cylinders, and sectors of a physical or emulated disk.

The next layer up is the *Data Recording Format Layer,* which specifies how the stored data is organized at the block level. Four data formats are supported under Release 2.0: unchecked blocks, blocks with checksum error correction, blocks with cyclic redundancy error checking, and unblocked data that does not correspond to disk organization (for example, random access to the data, such as is permitted for memory).

The third CIS layer, the *Data Organization Layer,* specifies how information is logically organized on the card; it specifies the operating system format to which the data conforms. PCMCIA recognizes four possibilities: DOS, Microsoft's Flash File system for Flash RAM, PCMCIA's own execute-in-place (or XIP) ROM image, and application-specific organization. Microsoft's FlaSh file system is an operating system specifically designed for the constraints of Flash memory. It minimizes rewriting specific memory areas to extend the limited life of the medium and to allow for speedy updates of required block writes.

Execute-in-place or XIP is PCMCIA's own specification that allows program code in read-only memory to execute without being first loaded into main system (read/write) memory. Application-specific organization allows card developers to create data organizations unique to their products so as to implement special features.

The fourth CIS layer is assigned to system-specific standards that comply with particular operating environments. For example, the XIP standard defines how programs encoded on ROM cards are to be read and executed.

The setup information for all these layers is stored in a reserved area on the PC Card called *Attribute Memory.* This area is isolated from the card's ordinary storage, which under PCMCIA 2.0 is called *Common Memory.* The CIS information is structured as a linked chain of data blocks called *tuples,* each of which can be up to 128 bytes long. To give all systems a common starting point to search for CIS data, the first tuple of the metaformat is located at the first address in Attribute Memory. This ensures that the data is within the addressing range of even primitive microprocessors that can address only one megabyte of RAM. Because the CIS system must work in any PC or other host, the card assumes that memory can be accessed only in byte widths.

The first 2 bytes of each tuple, as well as the format of many predefined tuples, are strictly defined. The first byte encodes the function of the tuple and the parameters it describes. The second byte links to the next tuple in the chain (if any); it specifies the number of data bytes in the tuple, which, of course, indicates where the next tuple begins. The PCMCIA 2.0 specifications define the options available for many common tuples as shown in Table 6.9. PC Card manufacturers are free to add their own tuples to store data for setting up cards that contain proprietary features.

TABLE 6.9. Common PCMCIA Tuples

Code	Name	Description
0	CISTPL_NULL	Null tuple; ignore
1	CISTPL_DEVICE	The device-information tuple (Common Memory)
2-7	CISTPL_CHECKSUM	(Reserved for future, upward-compatible versions of the device-information tuple)
8-0Fh	CISTPL_LONGLINK_A	(Reserved for future, incompatible version of the device-information tuple)
10h	CISTPL_LONGLINK_C	The checksum-control tuple
11h	CISTPL_LINKTARGET	The long-link-control tuple
12h	CISTPL_NO_LINK	The long-link-control tuple (to Common Memory)
13h	CISTPL_VERS_1	The link-target-control-tuple
14h	CISTPL-ALTSTR	The no-link-control tuple
15h	CISTPL_DEVICE_A	The Level-1 version/product-information tuple
16h	CISTPL_JEDEC_C	The alternate-language-string tuple
17h	CISTPL_JEDEC_A	Attribute Memory device information
18h	CISTPL_CFIG	JEDEC programming information for Common Memory
19h	CISTPL_ENTRY	JEDEC programming information for Attribute Memory
1Ah	CISTPL_DEVICE_OC	The configurable-card tuple
1Bh	CISTPL_DEVICE_OA	The configuration-entry tuple
1Ch	CISTPL_VERS_2	Other operating conditions device information for Common Memory
1Dh	CISTPL_FORMAT	Other operating conditions device information for Attribute Memory
1Eh-3Fh	CISTPL-GEOMETRY	(Reserved for future standardization)
40h	CISTPL_BYTEORDER	The Level-2 version tuple
41h	CISTPL_DATE	The format tuple

As the storage and expansion needs of PCs and other electronic devices continue to evolve, the PCMCIA PC Card standard will likely follow in lockstep. Undoubtedly, it is the PC expansion system of the future—and the first truly universal data interchange system.

Standards and Coordination

One key to the PC Card's success is that the it is not a proprietary standard foisted on the industry by a single company or small coterie. The design is the product of a group called the Personal Computer Memory Card International Association (PCMCIA), which has more than 220 members involved in all aspects of the computer and electronics industry. The PCMCIA standard is completely open, and all specifications are available to anyone requesting them from the organization. (The charge for the latest specification release was not set at the time of this writing, but it is estimated to be between $200 to $300.)

Rather than operate completely independently, PCMCIA cooperates with other standard-setting organizations. For example, by working jointly with the Japan Electronic Industry Development Association (JEIDA) in December 1989, PCMCIA was able to ensure that the standards it developed would be truly international in scope. Today each organization sends a delegation to the meetings of the other.

Besides the efforts at extending PCMCIA to future technologies such as 32-bit data paths and bus mastering, PCMCIA is also developing standards for incorporating specific device types into the system. Already the group has fully described the needs for XIP, which allows programs to execute from their storage locations on PC Cards instead of needing to be loaded as if from disk into normal system RAM. PCMCIA has also developed standards for linking AT Attachment-style IDE hard disks into PC Card sockets.

To obtain more information about PCMCIA products and standards, contact the following address:

Personal Computer Memory Card International Association
1030 East Duane Avenue, Suite G
Sunnyvale, California 94086
(408) 720-0107
fax: (408) 720-9416

Chapter 7

The Basic Input/Output System

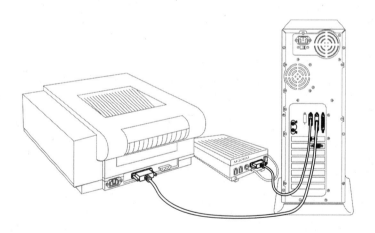

Every PC gets its personality from a set of built-in software routines called the Basic Input/Output System or BIOS. Although only a fraction of the size of a typical application program—often less than 32K of code—the BIOS controls many of the most important functions of the PC—how it interprets keystrokes, how it puts characters on the screen, how it communicates through its ports.

The BIOS tests the computer every time you turn it on. It can even allocate your system's resources for you automatically. The BIOS also determines the compatibility of the computer and its flexibility in use. Although all BIOSs have the same function, they all are different.

Just as the Minotaur—a man-beast, half-breed—ruled the unfathomable Labyrinth, the inner mysteries and maze of your PC are governed by an odd mating of hardware and software called the *Basic Input/Output System* or *BIOS*. More than just a bullheaded guard, however, the BIOS also serves as a demigod that links the material hardware world of your PC and its circuits to the transcendent realm of software ideas and instructions.

The BIOS is not just a link between hard and soft worlds, it *is* both hardware and software. Like software, the BIOS is a set of instructions to the computer's microprocessor. Like hardware, however, these special instructions do not need to be evanescent. Instead, in many PCs, they are entirely coded into the hard, worldly silicon of PROM chips. Because of the twilight state of this kind of BIOS, existing in the netherworld between hardware and software, it and other PROM-based programs often are termed *firmware*.

Today, many PCs and operating systems enhance the basic BIOS firmware with additional instructions loaded from disk-like ordinary software. This software-based code performs the same role as the traditional BIOS firmware, however, linking your PC's hardware to the software programs that you run.

The BIOS code of most PCs has more than one function. Typically, it comprises routines that test the computer, data that give the machine its personality, special program routines that allow software to take control of the PC's hardware so that it can more smoothly mesh with the electronics of the system, and even a complete system (in some PCs) for determining which expansion boards and peripherals you have installed and ensuring that they do not conflict in their requests for input/output ports and memory assignments. In a few PCs—mostly IBM's older machines—the BIOS also includes a rudimentary programming language that allows you to use the machine without any other software (or even a disk drive to load it).

The personality comes from the firmware code. This code determines how the computer performs the basic functions needed to make a working computer—how quickly and smoothly they are completed. The BIOS firmware can be elaborate and exotic, storing even the look of graphics screens (in the case of the code in Apple Computer's Macintosh). PC BIOSs are more rudimentary. The display code, for example, includes only the most basic instructions for putting individual dots, characters, or lines of text on the screen. More advanced functions are left to software, such as operating systems or application programs.

In many PCs, the BIOS firmware also governs how system board components interact, the chipset features that are used, and even how much of the microprocessor's time is devoted to keeping memory working. The setup procedures in most new PCs also are held in the BIOS.

The BIOS starts to work as soon as you switch your system on. When all modern Intel microprocessors start to work, they immediately set themselves up in *real mode* and look at a special memory location that is exactly 16 bytes short of the top of the one-megabyte real mode addressing range, absolute address 0FFFF0(Hex). This location holds a special program instruction, a *jump* that points to another address where the BIOS code actually begins.

In most PCs, the first thing the BIOS tells the microprocessor to do is to run through all the known components of the system—the microprocessor, memory, keyboard, and so on—and to test whether they are operating properly. After the system is sure of its own integrity, it checks to see whether you have installed any expansion boards that hold additional BIOS code. If you have, the microprocessor checks the code and carries out any instructions that it finds. A modern PC may even check to see if any new expansion boards are plugged in without being set up properly. The BIOS code might then configure the expansion board so that it functions properly in your PC.

When the microprocessor runs out of add-in peripherals, it begins the actual *boot-up* process, which engineers call the *Initial Program Load* or IPL. The BIOS code tells the microprocessor to jump to a section of code that tells the chip how to read the first sector of your floppy or hard disk. Program code then takes over from the BIOS and tells the microprocessor how to load the operating system from the disk to start the computer running.

After the operating system has taken control of the microprocessor, the BIOS does not rest. Its firmware also includes several sets of routines that programs can call to carry out everyday functions—typing characters on the screen or to a printer, reading keystrokes, timing events. Because of this basic library, programmers can create their grand designs without worrying about the tiny details.

Hardware/Software

The BIOS earns its name from its function as the software-to-hardware interface of your machine. It is a control *system* that operates at the lowest possible level—the most *basic*—at which the *input* and *output* of your computer are designed to link to programs. In effect, it is like a remote control for a television set. The BIOS allows your software to press buttons at a distance from the hardware, just as you control the channel of your TV from your easy chair—and without prying open the set and ratcheting its tuning circuits. In operation, the BIOS is a universal remote control. It lets you push the same buttons, no matter what model or brand of television at which you point it.

The purpose of this one-step-removed BIOS design is to allow PC hardware to be revised and updated without the need to change software correspondingly. It helps guarantee the backward compatibility of PCs. The extra BIOS step is needed, because all computers have many hardware elements that are located at specific addresses in memory or within the range of certain input/output ports. Other computer components may have registers of their own, used in their control, that also are addressed at specific locations. Because of the number of separate components inside any computer, the potential number of possible variations in the location of these features is limitless. Software that attempts to control any of this hardware must properly reach out to these registers. As long as all computers are crafted exactly the same, with the same ports used for exactly the same hardware with exactly the same registers, no problems should occur. But if a computer designer wants to change the hardware to a technology that delivers better performance or greater reliability, he may be stymied by the old addresses. Software may expect to reach the old design at one set of ports while the new, improved design may be memory-mapped and not use ports at all. The old software would not know how to reach the new hardware, and the new design simply would not work.

The BIOS gives the software a link. The software reaches into the BIOS for the hardware function it wants. Then the BIOS dips down into the hardware. If the design of a computer system is changed radically, only the BIOS needs to be changed to reflect the new way of getting at the features of the PC. The changed BIOS still works the same way as the software, so all older programs run exactly as they did before the change. In effect, the new system design requires a new route to get to an old destination—a detour. The new BIOS is an update road map that shows only the detour.

With the first PC, IBM put its reliance on BIOS technology and reserved the right to alter the hardware at will. The company made no guarantee that any of the ports or registers of the PC would be the same in any later computer. In the well-ordered world envisioned by IBM, programs would never need to directly address hardware. Instead, they would call up a software routine in the BIOS which would have the addressing part of the instruction permanently set in its code. Later computers with different hardware arrangements would use BIOS routines that worked like the old ones and were indistinguishable from the old ones when used by application software. The addresses inside the routines would be changed, however, to match the updated hardware. The same software could work, then, with a wide variety of hardware designs, giving the designer and manufacturer the flexibility to upgrade the entirety of system hardware, if necessary.

Software Interrupts

The BIOS design IBM created for its PCs does its linking through a system of *software interrupts*. To gain access to the underlying hardware, a program sends out an interrupt, a special instruction to the microprocessor. The software interrupt causes the microprocessor to stop what it is doing and start a new routine. It does this by suspending the execution of the code on which it is working, saving its place, and looking in a table held in memory that lists *interrupt vectors*. Each interrupt vector is a pointer that tells the microprocessor where the code associated with the interrupt is located. The microprocessor reads the value of the vector, and starts executing the code located at the value stored in the vector.

The table of interrupt vectors begins at the very start of the microprocessor's memory, address 00000(Hex). Each vector comprises four bytes, and all vectors are stored in increasing order. The default values for each vector are loaded into RAM from the ROM containing the BIOS when your computer boots up. Programs can alter these vectors to change the meaning of software interrupts. Typically, *terminate-and-stay-resident programs* (*TSRs*—pop-up programs like SideKick and background programs like Pro-Key) make such modifications for their own purposes.

Parameter Passing

Because fewer interrupts are available for the many things one would want to do with the BIOS, different functions are available for many of the interrupts. These separate functions are identified by *parameter passing.* Information is handed over to the BIOS routine as a parameter, a value held in one or more of the registers at the time the software interrupt is issued. The BIOS routine may also achieve some result and pass it back to the program that called it. Table 7.1 summarizes the principal BIOS interrupts.

TABLE 7.1. BIOS Interrupt Vectors

Absolute Address (Hex)	Interrupt Value	Function	Corresponding Hardware Interrupt
0000:0000	00H	Divide by Zero Interrupt Header	
0000:0004	01H	Single Step Interrupt Handler	
0000:0008	02H	Non-Maskable Interrupt	
0000:000C	03H	Breakpoint	
0000:0010	04H	Arithmetic Overflow Handler	
0000:0014	05H	Print Screen	
0000:0018	06H	Reserved	
0000:001C	07H	Reserved	
0000:0020	08H	Timer Interrupt (18.21590/sec)	

continues

TABLE 7.1. Continued

Absolute Address (Hex)	Interrupt Value	Function	Corresponding Hardware Interrupt
0000:0024	09H	Keyboard Service	
0000:0028	0AH	VGA Retrace (AT Slave)	IRQ2
0000:002C	0BH	Serial Port 2	IRQ3
0000:0030	0CH	Serial Port 1	IRQ4
0000:0034	0DH	Hard Disk	IRQ5
0000:0038	0EH	Floppy disk	IRQ6
0000:003C	0FH	Parallel Port	IRQ7
0000:0040	10H	Video Services	
0000:0044	11H	Equipment Check	
0000:0048	12H	Memory Size Check	
0000:004C	13H	Floppy and Hard Disk I/O	
0000:0050	14H	RS-232 Service	
0000:0054	15H	System Services	
0000:0058	16H	Keyboard	
0000:005C	17H	Printer I/O	
0000:0060	18H	Basic ROM Entry point (startup)	
0000:0064	19H	Initial Program Load (IPL) Bootstrap Loader	
0000:0068	1AH	Time of Day	
0000:006C	1BH	Keyboard Break	
0000:0070	1CH	User Timer	
0000:0074	1DH	Monitor ROM Pointer	
0000:0078	1EH	Disk Control Table Pointer	
0000:007C	1FH	Character Generator Pattern Table Pointer	
0000:0080	20H	DOS Terminate Program	

Absolute Address (Hex)	Interrupt Value	Function	Corresponding Hardware Interrupt
0000:0084	21H	DOS Function Calls	
0000:0088	22H	DOS Terminate Address	
0000:008C	23H	DOS Ctrl-break Exit Address	
0000:0090	24H	DOS Fatal Error Exit Address	
0000:0094	25H	DOS Absolute Disk Read	
0000:0098	26H	DOS Absolute Disk Write	
0000:009C	27H	DOS Terminate and Stay Resident	
0000:00A0	28H	DOS Idle Loop	
0000:00A4	29H	DOS Console Device Raw Output Handler	
0000:00A8	2AH	DOS Network Communications	
0000:00AC	2BH-2DH	Reserved	
0000:00B8	2EH	DOS Execute Command	
0000:00BC	2FH	DOS Print Spool Control	
0000:00C0	30H-31H	DOS Internal Use	
0000:00C8	32H	Reserved	
0000:00CC	33H	Mouse Driver Calls	
0000:00D0	34H-3EH	Reserved	
0000:00FC	3FH	LINK (internal use)	
0000:0100	40H	Floppy and Hard Disk Handler	
0000:0104	41H	Pointer to Hard Disk Parameters	
0000:0108	42H	EGA Video Vector Screen BIOS Entry	
0000:010C	43H	EGA Initialization Parameters	

continues

TABLE 7.1. Continued

Absolute Address (Hex)	Interrupt Value	Function	Corresponding Hardware Interrupt
0000:0100	44H	EGA Graphics Character Patterns	
0000:0114	45H	Reserved	
0000:0118	46H	Pointer to Second Fixed Disk Parameters	
0000:011C	47H	Reserved	
0000:0120	48H	PCjr Cordless Keyboard	
0000:0124	49H	PCjr Non-Keyboard Scan Code Table	
0000:0128	4AH	Alarm Routine	
0000:012C	4BH-4FH	Reserved	
0000:0140	50H	Periodic Alarm from Timer	
0000:0144	51H-59H	Reserved	
0000:0168	5AH	Cluster Adapter BIOS-entry Address	
0000:016C	5BH	Cluster Boot	
0000:0170	5CH	NETBIOS Entry Point	
0000:0174	5DH-5FH	Reserved	
0000:0180	60H-66H	User program interrupts	
0000:019C	67H	Expanded Memory Manager Routines	
0000:01A0	68H-6BH	Unused	
0000:01B0	6CH	System Resume Vector	
0000:01B4	6DH-6FH	Unused	
0000:01C0	70H	Real Time Clock	IRQ8
0000:01C4	71H	LAN Adapter (IRQ2 replacement)	IRQ9
0000:01C8	72H	Reserved	IRQ10
0000:01CC	73H	Reserved	IRQ11

Absolute Address (Hex)	Interrupt Value	Function	Corresponding Hardware Interrupt
0000:01D0	74H	Mouse	IRQ12
0000:01D4	75H	80287 NMI Error	IRQ13
0000:01D8	76H	Hard disk controller	IRQ14
0000:01DC	77H	Reserved	IRQ15
0000:01E0	78H-7FH	Unused	
0000:0200	80H-85H	BASIC	
0000:0218	86H	NetBIOS	
0000:021C	87H-F0H	BASIC	
0000:03C4	F1H-FFH	Reserved for Program Interrupts	

Entry Points

The various code routines in each BIOS start and end at addresses assigned to the BIOS function in the PC memory map. The address at which each routine starts is called that routine's *entry point*. The entry point of a BIOS function is completely different from the interrupt that calls that function. When the BIOS in your PC sets itself up—either before or during the actual boot-up—it loads the addresses of the entry points into a table in memory that becomes the interrupt vectors. In theory, an entry point can be at any location for any BIOS function—it needs only to be loaded into the slot in the BIOS interrupt vector table to be properly recognized. Unfortunately, some program writers decided to call BIOS routines by their entry points instead of using interrupts, because the direct approach is faster. Consequently, a few applications require that some entry points be at specific physical BIOS addresses. If the entry point of a BIOS differs from that which the program expects, the result is likely to be a system crash.

IBM has maintained the same entry points with all of its BIOSs, and many compatible BIOSs use exactly the same addresses. A few do not, however. In general, the BIOSs with varying entry points have been written as programming modules that can be combined in various ways to suit the needs of a PC designer. What these modular BIOSs add in flexibility, they lose in compatibility.

Unlike programs that write directly to system hardware, however, programs that require specific BIOS entry points are rare. With the popularity of compatible computers and modular BIOSs, they are sure to become more rare. Modern software, nevertheless, is getting away from a dependency on complete compatibility down to the level of specific entry points. In fact, many programs avoid the BIOS entirely.

The chief beneficiaries of the BIOS are individual programmers who need to create code quickly. In many cases, using BIOS routines can simplify the writing of a program. Certain system operations always are available and can be accessed easily through software. They are reasonably well-documented and well-understood, removing many of the programmer's concerns.

Penalties

The problem with BIOS routines—and the primary reason software avoids using them—is that the steps added by the routines can slow many computer functions. BIOS performance problems are most evident in the video display. All IBM BIOS routines, for example, are designed for putting information on the video display one character at a time using dozens of microprocessor instructions to place each one. Text can be blasted onto the screen much faster by directly manipulating the hardware.

Using BIOS routines, software first has to load particular registers with the character to display its attribute (color or underlining or the like), perhaps even its location on the screen. Then, the program issues a software interrupt to give the BIOS control to do its job. The BIOS then runs through a dozen or more assembly language instructions to move the character onto the screen.

Taking direct control—avoiding the BIOS—means writing directly to the display memory on the video card. A program can write directly to the screen simply by loading the appropriate address and moving the needed byte value to that address in one assembly language step. The dozens of steps saved in writing each character add up to real performance gains, the difference between watching changes slowly scroll down the screen and instant updates.

Another limitation imposed by handling all system operations through the BIOS is that the computer cannot do anything that the BIOS does not know about. Consider, for instance, floppy disk drives. When operated in their standard modes, the BIOS routines function well and allow you to read, write, and format floppy disks using the standard IBM disk formats. At the same time, however, they impose limits on what the drives can do. Controlled through the BIOS, drives act only like products that have been blessed by IBM. But floppy disk drives are more versatile than the BIOS suggests. They can read and write the disk formats used by other computer systems and others that can be used for copy-protecting diskettes. Taking advantage of a disk drive's abilities beyond the powers officially sanctioned by IBM means sidestepping the BIOS.

Bypassing the BIOS with programs that directly address the system hardware is not difficult, even if at heart such a concept is forbidden by the original IBM dream. In fact, so many software writers have taken their liberties with direct hardware control that many of the hardware features of personal computers are more standardized than the BIOS. Most prominent among these is the location of display memory. Writing directly to display memory has been so common that IBM has even thrown in the towel and stated that it plans to use its best efforts to preserve the status quo in the addresses used by display memory. Serial ports, too, have developed beyond BIOS control. Every program that uses a serial port at speeds higher than 9600 bits per second (19,200 on some machines) must sidestep the BIOS's serial communication routines.

The PC hardware standard, moreover, may just be a tighter standard than that set by the BIOS. Most compatibles do an exact job of mimicking all the hardware of a PC. The BIOS's that they use, however, are certain to be somewhat different because of the demands of copyright laws. Hardware actually is more standardized (in many respects) than is the BIOS firmware. Even IBM admitted, in effect, some of the shortcomings of the BIOS-only restriction in conceding that the hardware memory locations used by the video display are supported for as long as possible.

Testing and Initialization

Every time your PC switches on, the BIOS immediately takes command. Its first duty is to run through a series of diagnostic routines—system checks—called the *Power-On Self Test* routine or POST that insures every part of your PC's hardware is functioning properly before you trust your time and data to it. One by one, the POST routine checks the circuits of your system board and memory, the keyboard, your disks, and each expansion board. After the BIOS makes sure that the system is operating properly, it initializes the electronics so that they are ready for the first program to load.

The BIOS tests are relatively simple. The BIOS sends data to a port or register then looks to see the results. If it receives expected results, the BIOS assumes all is well. If it finds a problem, however, it reports the failure as well as it can. If the display system is working, it posts a code number on your monitor screen. (The limited amount of memory available prevents the BIOS from storing an elaborate—that is, understandable—message for all the hundreds of possible error conditions.) If your PC is so ill that the display system will not even work, the BIOS sends out a coded series of beeps through your system's loudspeaker.

Although the exact codes used by a BIOS vary with the supplier of the BIOS, certain codes have earned a more general definition. Table 7.2 lists the numbers assigned to specific problem areas. Table 7.3 shows the beep codes used by many BIOSs.

The digits of a three-digit code, the first two digits of a four-digit code, or the first three digits of a five-digit error code isolate the subsystem harboring the failure; the final two digits localize the error. These numbers give you an indication of where a test failure or error has occurred in your PC.

TABLE 7.2. Common Error Codes

0100-Series:	***System Board Errors***
0101	Interrupt failure
0102	ROM checksum error (PC, XT), Timer (AT)
0103	ROM checksum error (PC, XT), Timer interrupt (AT)
0104	Interrupt controller (PC, XT), Protected mode (AT)
0105	Timer (PC, XT)
0106	System board circuitry
0107	System board circuitry or an adapter card
0108	System board circuitry
0109	DMA test
0121	Unexpected hardware interrupt
0151	Real-time clock (or CMOS RAM)
0152	System board circuitry
0161	CMOS power failure
0162	CMOS checksum error
0163	Clock date error
0164	Memory size (POST finds value different from CMOS)
0165	Adapter added/removed (PS/2)
0199	Device list not correct
0200-Series:	***Memory***
0300-Series:	***Keyboard***
0301	Stuck key/improper response
0302	Keyboard test error
0302	Keyboard locked
0303	Keyboard interface error (on system board)
0304	Non-specific keyboard error
0365	Keyboard failure
0366	Keyboard cable failure
0400-Series:	***Monochrome Display***
0401	Memory or sync test failure
0432	Parallel port text failure

0500-Series:	***Color Graphics Adapter***
0501	Memory or sync test failure
0556	Light pen failure
0564	Screen paging error
0600-Series:	***Floppy Disk System***
0601	Drive or adapter test failure
0602	Drive failure
0603	Wrong drive capacity
0606	Disk verify function error
0607	Write-protected diskette
0608	Bad command
0610	Disk initialization error
0611	Timeout error
0612	Bad controller chip
0613	DMA failure
0614	DMA boundary error
0621	Seek error
0622	CRC error
0623	Record not found
0624	Bad address mark
0625	Controller seek failure
0626	Data compare error
0627	Change line error
0628	Disk removed
0700-Series:	***Floating-Point Unit***
0900-Series:	***LPT1***
1000-Series:	***LPT2***
1100-Series:	***COM1***
1200-Series:	***COM2***
1300-Series:	***Game Control Adapter***
1301	Adapter failure
1302	Joystick failure

continues

TABLE 7.2. Continued

1400-Series:	*Printer*
1500-Series:	*Synchronous Data Line Control (SDLC) Communications Adap*
1600-Series:	*Display Station Emulation Adapter (DSEA)*
1700-Series:	*Hard Disk System*
1701	Drive not ready; Disk or adapter test failure
1702	Time out; Disk or adapter error
1703	Drive error
1704	Adapter or drive error
1705	Record not found
1706	Write fault
1707	Track 0 error
1708	Head select error
1709	Bad error correction code
1710	Read buffer overrun
1711	Bad address mark
1712	Nonspecific error
1713	Data compare error
1714	Drive not ready
1730	Adapter error
1731	Adapter error
1732	Adapter error
1780	Drive C: boot failure
1781	Drive D: failure
1782	Controller boot failure
1790	Drive C: error
1791	Drive D: error
1800-Series:	*PC or XT Expansion Chassis*
2000-Series:	*First Bisynchronous Communications (BSC) Adapter*
2100 Series:	*Second Bisynchronous Communications (BSC) Adapter*
2200-Series:	*Cluster Adapter*
2400-Series:	*Enhanced Graphics Adapter*
2401	Adapter test failure
2456	Light pen failure

2500-Series:	*Second Enhanced Graphics Adapter*
2600-Series:	*PC/370-M Adapter Adapter*
2700-Series:	*PC/3277 Emulation Adapter*
2800-Series:	*3278/79 Emulator Adapter*
2900-Series:	*Printer*
3000-Series:	*Network Adapter*
3001	Adapter ROM test failure
3002	Adapter RAM test failure
3006	Interrupt conflict
3100-Series:	*Second Network Adapter*
3300-Series:	*Compact Printer*
3600-Series:	*IEEE-488 (GPIB) Adapter*
3800-Series:	*Data Aquisition Adapter*
3900-Series:	*Professional Graphics Controller Adapter*
4400-Series:	*5278 Display Attatchment Unit and 5279 Display*
4500-Series:	*IEEE-488 (GPIB) Adapter*
4600-Series:	*Artic Interface Adapter*
4800-Series:	*Internal Modem*
4900-Series:	*Second*
5600-Series:	*Financial Communication System*
7000-Series:	*Phoenix Bios Chipset*
7000	CMOS failure
7001	Shadow memory
7002	CMOS configuration error
7100-Series:	*Voice Communication Adapter*
7300-Series:	*3.5-Inch Floppy Disk Drive*
7301	Drive or adapter test failure
7307	Write-protected diskette
7308	Bad command
7310	Track zero error
7311	Timeout
7312	Bad controller or DMA
7315	Bad index
7316	Speed error
7321	Bad seek

continues

TABLE 7.2. Continued

7100-Series:	*Voice Communication Adapter*
7300-Series:	*3.5-Inch Floppy Disk Drive*
7322	Bad CRC
7323	Record not found
7324	Bad address mark
7325	Controller seek error
7400-Series:	*8514/A Display Adapter*
7401	Test failure
7426	Monitor failure
7600-Series:	*Page Printer*
8400-Series:	*Speech Adapter*
8500-Series:	*2MB Memory Adapter*
8600-Series:	*Pointing Device*
8900-Series:	*MIDI Adapter*
10000-Series:	*Multiprotocol Communications Adapter*
10100-Series:	*Modem and Communications Adapter*
10400-Series:	*ESDI Disk Controller*
10450	Write/read test error
10451	Read verify test error
10452	Seek test error
10453	Device type mismatch
10454	Controller buffer failure
10455	Controller failure
10461	Format error
10463	Write/read sector error
10464	Drive map unreadable
10465	ECC error
10466	ECC error
10467	Soft seek error
10468	Hard seek error
10469	Soft seek error
10470	Controller diagnostic error
10499	Controller failure

10700-Series:	***5.25-Inch External Floppy Disk Drive***
11200-Series:	***SCSI Adapter***
12900-Series:	***Processor Platform***
12901	Processor error
12902	Cache error
14900-Series:	***Plasma Display and Adapter***
16500-Series:	***Streaming Tape Drive***
16520	Drive error
16540	Controller error
16600-Series:	***First Token-Ring Network Adapter***
16700-Series:	***Second Token-Ring Network Adapter***
19400-Series:	***Adapter Memory Module***
2100-Series:	***SCSI Hard Disk or Host Adapter***
21500-Series:	***CD-ROM System***

TABLE 7.3. BIOS Beep Codes

1	POWER-ON SELF-TEST PASSED
1-<PAUSE>-1-<PAUSE>-3	CMOS WRITE/READ FAILURE
1-<PAUSE>-1-<PAUSE>-4	ROM BIOS CHECKSUM ERROR
1-<PAUSE>-2-<PAUSE>-1	PROGRAMMABLE INTERVAL TIMER FAILURE
1-<PAUSE>-2-<PAUSE>-2	DMA INITIALIZATION FAILURE
1-<PAUSE>-2-<PAUSE>-3	DMA PAGE REGISTER WRITE/ READ FAILURE
1-<PAUSE>-3-<PAUSE>-1	RAM REFRESH VERIFICATION FAILURE
1-<PAUSE>-3-<PAUSE>-3	FIRST 64K RAM CHIP OR DATA LINE FAILURE MULTI-B
1-<PAUSE>-3-<PAUSE>-4	FIRST 64K ODD/EVE LOGIC FAILURE
1-<PAUSE>-4-<PAUSE>-1	ADDRESS LINE FAILURE 64K OF RAM
1-<PAUSE>-4-<PAUSE>-2	PARITY FAILURE FIRST 64K OF RAM

continues

TABLE 7.3. Continued

2-<PAUSE>-1-<PAUSE>-1	BIT 0 FIRST 64K RAM FAILURE
2-<PAUSE>-1-<PAUSE>-2	BIT 1
2-<PAUSE>-1-<PAUSE>-3	BIT 2
2-<PAUSE>-1-<PAUSE>-4	BIT 3
2-<PAUSE>-2-<PAUSE>-1	BIT 4
2-<PAUSE>-2-<PAUSE>-3	BIT 6
2-<PAUSE>-2-<PAUSE>-4	BIT 7
2-<PAUSE>-3-<PAUSE>-1	BIT 8
2-<PAUSE>-3-<PAUSE>-2	BIT 9
2-<PAUSE>-3-<PAUSE>-3	BIT 10
2-<PAUSE>-3-<PAUSE>-4	BIT 11
2-<PAUSE>-4-<PAUSE>-1	BIT 12
2-<PAUSE>-4-<PAUSE>-2	BIT 13
2-<PAUSE>-4-<PAUSE>-3	BIT 14
2-<PAUSE>-4-<PAUSE>-4	BIT 15 FIRST 64K RAM FAILURE
3-<PAUSE>-1-<PAUSE>-1	SLAVE DMA REGISTER FAILURE
3-<PAUSE>-1-<PAUSE>-2	MASTER DMA REGISTER FAILURE
3-<PAUSE>-1-<PAUSE>-3	MASTER INTERRUPT MASK REGISTER FAILURE
3-<PAUSE>-1-<PAUSE>-4	SLAVE INTERRUPT MASK REGISTER FAILURE
3-<PAUSE>-2-<PAUSE>-4	KEYBOARD CONTROLLER TEST FAILURE
3-<PAUSE>-3-<PAUSE>-4	SCREEN INITIALIZATION FAILURE
3-<PAUSE>-4-<PAUSE>-1	SCREEN RETRACE TEST FAILURE
4-<PAUSE>-2-<PAUSE>-1	TIMER TICK FAILURE
4-<PAUSE>-2-<PAUSE>-2	SHUTDOWN TEST FAILURE
4-<PAUSE>-2-<PAUSE>-3	GATE A20 FAILURE
4-<PAUSE>-2-<PAUSE>-4	UNEXPECTED INTERRUPT IN PROTECTED MODE
4-<PAUSE>-3-<PAUSE>-1	RAM TEXT ADDRESS FAILURE
4-<PAUSE>-3-<PAUSE>-3	INTERVAL TIMER CHANNEL 2 FAILURE
4-<PAUSE>-3-<PAUSE>-4	TIME OF DAY CLOCK FAILURE
4-<PAUSE>-4-<PAUSE>-3	MATH COPROCESSOR FAILURE

Most systems follow the previous scheme, however some systems with the AMI BIOS may use an alternate beep code system as follows:

AMI BIOS:

1	DRAM refresh failure
2	Parity Circuit failure
3	Base 64K RAM failure
4	System Timer failure
5	Processor failure
6	Keyboard Controller Gate A20 error
7	Virtual Mode Exception error
8	Display Memory R/W Test failure
9	ROM-BIOS Checksum failure

After the actual testing is complete, it begins to execute initialization routines that configure the various options inside your PC. Exactly what happens next depends on the design of the BIOS. A conventional BIOS merely looks for add-in BIOS routines, initializes devices using the routines already in the BIOS, and starts the disk boot-up. A new *Plug and Play* system runs through a more structured initialization process that amounts to completely setting up system resources each time the computer boots.

Every PC assumes that many of its peripherals are loaded with specific data values when it starts up. That is, all the default operating values are loaded by the BIOS so your timer knows what to time and the speaker knows the frequency at which to beep. The serial ports are set to their default speed.

By design, the BIOS knows how to search beyond the confines of the system board. It knows how to locate the extra instructions and data that get added in with some expansion boards. Where some computers require you replace the BIOS PROMs with new chips to add new features, IBM designed its BIOS to be *extendible*. That is, the full extent of the BIOS is not forever cast in the silicon of the firmware. The extendible BIOS is capable of accepting additional code as its own into one integrated whole. Rather than *replacing* the BIOS PROM, this extendibility means that you can add more PROM chips containing their own BIOS routines to your PC. The BIOS incorporates the new routines into itself.

All BIOSs that follow the IBM design (which means all compatible BIOSs) are extendible with one exception—those inside the very earliest PCs that allowed only 64K of memory to be installed on their systems boards. Few of these machines are around any more, and most of them have been updated with replacement BIOSs. The Ancient History Appendix documents how to identify one of these venerable machines, determine whether its BIOS is extendible, and upgrade it if it is not.

The key to making the IBM BIOS extendible is itself an extra firmware routine that enables the BIOS to look for add-in code. During the initialization process, the BIOS code reads through the address range that IBM set aside for firmware, looking for code stored on add-in boards. If it finds a valid section of code, it adds those instructions to the BIOS repertory. New interrupt routines may be added, for instance, or the function of existing routines may be changed.

The routine to extend the BIOS works as follows: Following the actual testing portion of the Power On Self Test, after basic system board functions have been initialized (for example, the interrupt vectors have been loaded into RAM), the resident BIOS code instructs the computer to check through its ROM memory for the occurrence of the special *preamble bytes* that mark the beginning of add-in BIOS routines. The original IBM BIOS searches for these preamble bytes in the absolute address range 0C8000(Hex) to 0F4000(Hex); newer BIOSs check the range from 0C0000(Hex) to 0EFFFF(Hex). Either of these subsets of the full, reserved, high memory range—that is, 0A0000(Hex) to 0FFFFF(Hex)—exclude the areas used by video memory and the BIOS itself to prevent confusing data with preamble bytes.

If the BIOS finds the special preamble bytes, it verifies that the subsequent section of code is a legitimate BIOS extension by performing a form of cyclical redundancy check on the specified number of 512 byte blocks. The values of each byte in the block are totaled using Modulo 0100(Hex) addition—the effect is the same as dividing the sum of all the bytes by 4096. A remainder of zero indicates that the extension BIOS contains valid code.

The preamble bytes take a specific form. Two bytes indicate the beginning of an extension code section—055(Hex) followed by 0AA(Hex). Immediately following the two byte preamble bytes is a third byte that quantifies the length of the additional BIOS. The number represents the number of a block 512 bytes long needed to hold the extra code. Plug and Play peripherals have a more structured header that follows the preamble bytes.

After a valid section of code is identified, system control (BIOS program execution) jumps to the fourth byte in the extension BIOS and performs any functions specified there in machine language. Typically, these instructions tell the BIOS how to install the extra code. Finally, when the instructions in the extension BIOS are completed, control returns to the resident BIOS. The system then continues to search for additional blocks of extension BIOS. When it finally completes its search by reaching the absolute address 0F4000(Hex), it starts the process of booting up your computer from disk.

The ROM chips containing this extra BIOS code do not have to be present on the system board. The memory locations used also are accessible on the expansion bus. This feature allows new ROM chips that add to the BIOS to be part of expansion boards that can be slid into the computer. The code necessary to control the expansion accessory loads automatically whenever the system boots up.

Multiple sections of this add-on code fit into any computer, limited only by the address range available. One complication is that no two sections of code can occupy the same memory area. As a result, the makers of conventional ISA expansion boards typically incorporate jumpers, DIP switches, or EEPROM memory on their products to allow you to reassign the addresses used by their BIOS extensions and avoid conflicts. Plug and Play designs have made this conflict resolution automatic during the setup process.

Data Storage

As with any computer program, the BIOS code uses data for its operations and produces data as its result. The BIOS stores some of this data to be used as a reference by your programs. The BIOS acquires some of this information as it sets up the system. By storing it all in one place, it eliminates the need for every program to waste its time looking up common features. Other data is encoded as part of the BIOS itself so that programs can determine what kind of computer— and what kind of BIOS—with which they have to work.

BIOS Data Area

During the initialization process, the BIOS searches through the system for specific features. It checks the number and kinds of ports installed, the type of display adapter (monochrome or color), and other options. Included among the data that it stores are *equipment flags*, the base addresses of input/output adapters, keyboard characters, and operating modes. The BIOS then stores this information in specific memory locations so that your programs can check to see which features are available or being used. For example, the BIOS looks for serial ports at specific addresses (see Chapter 19, "Modems"). As it finds them, the BIOS records the base address that each serial port uses.

All of this self-descriptive information about your system is stored in a special part of RAM called the *BIOS data area*. Located just above the interrupt vectors, the BIOS data area comprises 256 bytes of memory, starting at absolute memory location 000400(Hex) and running to 0004FF(Hex). Table 7.4 lists the definition of some of the more important (and interesting) bytes in the BIOS data area.

TABLE 7.4. BIOS Data Area Assignments

Absolute Address	Function
0000:0400	COM1 base address
0000:0402	COM2 base address
0000:0404	COM3 base address
0000:0406	COM4 base address
0000:0408	LPT1 base address

continues

TABLE 7.4. Continued

Absolute Address	Function
0000:040A	LPT2 base address
0000:040C	LPT3 base address
0000:040E	Reserved
0000:0410	Equipment flag
0000:0412	Initialization flag
0000:0413	Memory size in kilobytes
0000:0415	Reserved
0000:0416	Reserved
0000:0417	Keyboard monitor flag
0000:0419	Alternate keypad entry
0000:041A	Keyboard buffer head pointer
0000:041C	Keyboard buffer tail pointer
0000:041E	Keyboard buffer (32 bytes)
0000:043E	Drive recalibration status
0000:043F	Motor status
0000:0440	Motor control time-out counter
0000:0441	Diskette status return code
0000:0442	Diskette drive controller status (7 bytes)
0000:0449	Video mode
0000:044A	Number of columns on monitor screen
0000:044C	Length of video regen buffer in bytes
0000:044E	Starting address of video regen buffer
0000:0450	Cursor position (8 bytes, one for each of 8 pages)
0000:0460	Cursor mode (starting and ending line of cursor)
0000:0462	Active page
0000:0463	Base address of 6845 video controller

Absolute Address	Function
0000:0465	Video mode setting
0000:0466	Video palette setting
0000:0467	Pointer to reset code (warm boot; 2 bytes)
0000:046B	Interrupt flag
0000:046C	Timer counter
0000:0470	Timer overflow (24 hour rollover flag)
0000:0471	Break key status
0000:0472	Reset flag (2 bytes)
0000:0474	Hard disk status
0000:0475	Number of hard disk drives
0000:0476	Fixed disk drive control byte for XT
0000:0477	Fixed disk drive controller port for XT
0000:0478	LPT1 time-out value
0000:0479	LPT2 time-out value
0000:047A	LPT3 time-out value
0000:047C	COM1 time-out value
0000:047D	COM2 time-out value
0000:047E	COM3 time-out value
0000:047F	COM4 time-out value
0000:0480	Pointer to start of keyboard buffer (2 bytes)
0000:0482	Pointer to end of keyboard buffer (2 bytes)
0000:0484	
0000:0485	
0000:0487	System information byte
0000:0488	System information byte
0000:0489	System flags
0000:048A	VGA Display Combination Code table index
0000:048B	Floppy disk control
0000:048C	Hard disk status register

continues

TABLE 7.4. Continued

Absolute Address	Function
0000:048D	Hard disk error register
0000:048E	Hard disk interrupt control flag
0000:048F	Combination hard/floppy disk card
0000:0490	Floppy drive 0 media state
0000:0491	Floppy drive 1 media state
0000:0492	Floppy drive 2 media state
0000:0493	Floppy drive 3 media state
0000:0494	Drive 0 track (cylinder) currently seeked
0000:0495	Drive 1 track (cylinder) currently seeked
0000:0496	Keyboard mode and type flags
0000:0497	Keyboard LED flags
0000:0498	Offset address to user wait complete flag
0000:049A	Segment to user wait complete flag
0000:049C	User wait count (2 bytes—microseconds)
0000:04A0	Wait active flag
0000:04A1	LAN Adapter DMA channel flags
0000:04A2	LAN Adapter 0 status
0000:04A3	LAN Adapter 1 status
0000:04A4	Hard disk interrupt vector (4 bytes)
0000:04A8	BIOS video save table (4 bytes)
0000:04AC	Reserved (8 bytes)
0000:04B4	Keyboard NMI control flags
0000:04B5	Keybarod break pending flags (2 bytes)
0000:04B9	Port 60 queue
0000:04BA	Scan code of last key typed
0000:04BB	Pointer to beginning of NMI buffer
0000:04BC	Pointer to end of NMI buffer
0000:04BD	MNI scan code buffer (16 bytes)

Absolute Address	*Function*
0000:04CE	Day counte
0000:04D0	Reserved (32 bytes)
0000:04F0	Application program area (16 bytes)

Date

Nearly every BIOS identifies itself with a copyright message and (usually) a version number so that you can determine who made it. (More specifically, the copyright message protects the writers of the BIOS from other people copying their work.) This identification information may appear anywhere within the BIOS code range.

In addition, IBM reserved a special place for the BIOS to list its latest revision date so that you can identify how recently its code was updated. This BIOS date is not only interesting, it is a useful diagnostic. As PCs have expanded their abilities, BIOSs have been revised to enable new operations. Sometimes older BIOSs will not work with new peripherals. The most important recent example occurred with early AMI BIOSs which did not work properly with AT interface hard disk drives. After April, 1990, the problems were corrected. Many PCs remain equipped with the old code, however. Checking the BIOS date tells you if your system uses a BIOS predating the revision. AMI BIOSs dated 4-09-90 and later incorporate the fix.

Most BIOS chips have their date and revision number printed on labels affixed over their EPROM windows along with a copyright message. You can determine the BIOS date of your PC, however, without opening your PC or even knowing what an EPROM chip looks like. You can examine the revision date embedded in the BIOS code using the DEBUG program supplied with DOS or the Microsoft Diagnostics program accompanying Windows 3.1. Any of a number of commercial system exploration utilities also let you check your PC's BIOS date.

DEBUG is the one universal means of determining system resources. Nearly every PC will have DEBUG available, so it makes a dependable and fast means of snooping your BIOS. To check the BIOS date of your PC (or other computer—this procedure works on nearly all models), simply run the DEBUG program.

At the hyphen prompt, type the following instruction:

```
D F000:FFF0
```

A mysterious-looking line of numbers and letters should appear on your screen. This line is divided horizontally into three parts. At left is the label of a memory location at which the display of 16 bytes begins—in this case, 0FFFF0(Hex). The central block of characters shows you the individual contents of each of those 16 bytes of memory. The right block gives the

ASCII representation of those values (if the value is a printable character). You should be able to read the date of the BIOS directly as it appears in the right column.

Run the Debug program that comes with most versions of DOS. You'll need to have the program DEBUG.COM in the currently logged disk and directory or accessible through the path command. Then type

```
DEBUG
```

Once the Debug program loads, you'll see a hyphen prompt on the screen. Type the following command in response to the prompt:

```
D F00:FFF0
```

Debug will respond with a display like that shown below; the BIOS date appears in the right column:

```
F000:FFF0 EA AC 86 00 F0 20 30 39-2F 32 33 2F 38 37 FC 45 ..... 09/23/87.E
```

To Exit Debug, at the hyphen prompt type the Quit command, simply the letter Q, as shown below:

```
-Q
```

Debug will then return you to the DOS prompt.

System Identification Bytes

Also part of the IBM ROM but not strictly part of the BIOS are IBM's *System Identification Bytes*. These two bytes of code can be read by programs so that the program knows what kind of computer or system board on which it is attempting to run.

Originally, IBM assigned one byte to this purpose. Starting with the XT Model 286, however, IBM added a second byte to permit more specific identification. In IBM nomenclature, these are called the *Model Byte* and the *Submodel Byte*.

The Model Byte is located at absolute memory address 0FFFFE(hex) and the Submodel byte follows it. Table 7.5 lists the model and submodel byte values for various IBM computers. Compatible computers generally use the byte value of the system to which they are the closest match.

TABLE 7.5. Model and Submodel Byte Values

Model Byte	Submodel Byte	Revision	BIOS Date	Computer Model
F8	00	00	30-Mar-87	PS/2 Model 80 (Type 1)
F8	00	01	30-Mar-87	PS/2 model 80
F8	00	02	19-Jun-89	PS/2 Model 80

Model Byte	Submodel Byte	Revision	BIOS Date	Computer Model
F8	01	00	7-Oct-87	PS/2 Model 80 (Type 2)
F8	04	02	11-Apr-88	PS/2 Model 70 (Type 2)
F8	04	03	17-Mar-89	PS/2 Model 70
F8	04	04	15-Dec-89	PS/2 Model 70
F8	09	02	11-Apr-88	PS/2 Model 70 (Type 1)
F8	09	03	17-Mar-89	PS/2 Model 70
F8	09	04	15-Dec-89	PS/2 Model 70
F8	11	00	1-Oct-90	PS/2 Model 90 (Type 1)
F8	13	00	1-Oct-90	PS/2 Model 90 (Type 2)
F8	14	00	1-Oct-90	PS/2 Model 95 (Type 1)
F8	16	00	1-Oct-90	PS/2 Model 95 (Type 2)
F8	19	05	15-Mar-91	PS/2 Model 35SX/40SX
F8	19	06	4-Apr-91	PS/2 Model 35SX/40SX
F8	19	07	4-Jun-91	PS/2 Model 35SX/40SX
F8	23	00	4-Jun-91	PS/2 Model L40SX
F8	26	00	10-May-91	PS/2 Model 57SX
F8	80	01	21-Nov-89	PS/2 Model 80
F8	80	02	15-Feb-90	PS/2 Model 80
F8	0B	00	1-Dec-89	PS/2 Model 70
F8	0B	02	1-Dec-89	PS/2 Model 70
F8	0C	00	2-Nov-88	PS/2 Model 55SX
F8	0C	01	2-Nov-88	PS/2 Model 55SX
F8	0D	00	8-Jun-88	PS/2 Model 70 (Type 3)
F8	0D	01	20-Feb-88	PS/2 Model 70
F8	1B	00	1-Dec-89	PS/2 Model 70 (Type 4)
F8	1C	00	8-Feb-90	PS/2 Model 65SX
F8	1E	00	8-Feb-90	PS/2 Model 55LS
F8	2C	01	24-Apr-91	PS/2 Model 95 (Type 3)
F8	2D	01	24-apr-91	PS/2 Model 90 (Type 3)
F8	2E	01	24-Apr-91	PS/2 Model 95 (Type 3)
F8	2F	01	24-Apr-91	PS/2 Model 90 (Type 3)

continues

TABLE 7.5. Continued

Model Byte	Submodel Byte	Revision	BIOS Date	Computer Model
F9	00	00	13-Sep-85	PC Convertible
FA	00	00	2-Sep-86	PS/2 Model 30
FA	00	04	31-Jan-89	PS/2 Model 30
FA	01	00	26-Jun-87	PS/2 Model 25
FA	01	01	2-Nov-88	PS/2 Model 25
FB	00	01	10-Jan-86	XT
FB	00	01	10-Jan-86	XT
FB	00	02	9-May-86	XT
FC	04	00	13-Feb-87	PS/2 Model 50 (Type 1)
FC	04	01	13-Feb-87	PS/2 Model 50
FC	04	02	2-Nov-89	PS/2 Model 50 (Type 1)
FC	04	03	28-Jan-88	PS/2 Model 50 (Type 2)
FC	04	04	12-May-88	PS/2 Model 50
FC	05	00	13-Feb-87	PS/2 Model 60
FC	09	00	25-Aug-88	PS/2 Model 30 286
FC	09	01	30-Nov-88	PS/2 Model 30 286
FC	09	02	30-May-89	PS/2 Model 30 286
FC	09	03	30-May-89	PS/2 Model 30 286
FC	00	00	10-Jan-84	AT
FC	00	01	10-Jun-85	AT
FC	01	00	15-Nov-85	AT
FC	02	00	21-Apr-86	XT Model 286
FD	00	00	1-Jun-83	PCjr
FE	00	00	8-Nov-82	XT
FF	00	00	24-Apr-81	PC
FF	00	01	19-Oct-81	PC
FF	00	02	27-Oct-82	PC

ROM BASIC

Although not truly part of the BIOS, the same ROM that holds the BIOS in most IBM personal computers also stores another set of code routines comprising a rudimentary BASIC language interpreter. Called *Cassette BASIC* (sometimes, ROM BASIC) because it enabled the very first PCs to operate from cassette tapes without the need for floppy disk drives or an operating system, this feature is truly an artifact of a by-gone error. The language doesn't let you do much—you can type in simple programs or load them from cassette tape, but you can only save them to cassette. Cassette BASIC has no provisions for dealing with disk drives of any type.

The defining purpose of the Cassette BASIC language was to enable the original IBM PC to do something—anything!—without the need for a floppy disk drive. When you booted an IBM personal computer that lacked a system disk in any of its boot drives (hard or floppy), the machine started executing the Cassette BASIC language.

With Cassette BASIC in its BIOS, a PC isn't a vegetable when it lacks a boot disk. It has just enough intelligence to frustrate you.

At the time the IBM PC was introduced, floppy disks were by no means a standard. Many small computers got along fine using only cassette recorders for mass storage. Cassette BASIC enabled the PC to boot up and load a program from tape (as well as run simple BASIC programs).

A more advanced version of the BASIC language was included with PC DOS. This BASIC code was designed to augment the Cassette BASIC already in an IBM computer's ROM, however. Since the code was already in the machine, it was not necessary to duplicate it on the DOS disk. Loading BASIC or BASICA from disk simply adds new routines that augment Cassette BASIC.

Cassette BASIC has its charming points—seeing its prompt makes a diskless system friendlier than one that sticks out its fat electronic tongue with a message like "Non-system disk or disk error." It also can give you quick answers to math questions or run simple programs—though you will not want to try complex programs without having a disk for loading or saving. Most people never need or use the BASIC language, and a truncated cassette form is even less useful. No compatible computer maker has seen the need to pack Cassette BASIC into its ROM chips, consequently. These systems will not work with IBM's BASICA that was included with early versions of IBM's PC DOS.

Because modern versions of BASIC (for example Quick BASIC) have no attachment to Cassette BASIC, the ROM-based language is irrelevant. In fact, some advanced memory management programs map the code used by Cassette BASIC in many IBM machines out of existence to recover the address range it uses—0F0000(Hex) to 0F8000(Hex)—so that they can load high-utility programs and drivers into that range.

System Configuration

In order to properly test a computer, the BIOS needs to know exactly what it is testing—what peripherals are installed, how much memory it must look through, and whether you have installed a coprocessor. In order to boot a computer, the BIOS needs to know exactly what kind of disk is connected to it. In order for you to see what is going on when your system boots up, the BIOS needs to know what kind of display system you have.

In some cases, the BIOS code itself can be written to search out and find the vital information it needs to get your system going. Such a search is not always accurate. Nor is it easy to write the proper search method into a few kilobytes of BIOS code. Even if the proper program could be written and packed into ROM, you probably do not want to sit around and wait—and wait— while the BIOS probes into every nook and cranny to see if something is there.

To let the BIOS (and the rest of the PC) know what options are installed in a given system, all PCs record vital setup information that can be referenced quickly. The storage system for this data—that is, *system setup memory*—has one requirement: It must be non-volatile. Other than that, the storage format and method are flexible because the BIOS isolates them from the rest of your software. The BIOS looks up this system data and transfers it to the BIOS data area for reference by your programs.

This flexibility has given designers freedom to use a number of storage technologies for this setup information. Among the most popular have been physical memory (switches), non-volatile electronic memory, and magnetic (disk) memory. Since the AT was introduced about a decade ago, however, the basic form of this setup memory used by most PCs has been the same: a few bytes of CMOS memory kept fresh—continuously operating—by battery power.

CMOS

When the world and PCs were young, all the differences between PCs could be coded by one or two banks of DIP switches. But as the options began to pile up, the switch proved to be more of a problem than a panacea. A reasonable number of switches couldn't allow for the number of options possible in a modern PC. Another problem with switches is that they are prone to mechanical problems—both of their own making and otherwise. Switch contacts naturally go bad, and they can be helped along the path of their own destruction by people who attempt to adjust them with pencils (the graphite that scrapes off the point is conductive and can short out the switches). People often set switches wrong and wonder what is awry.

IBM developed a better scheme for the AT. Vital system parameters would be stored in a special, small block of battery-backed CMOS memory, a total of 64 bytes, in the form of a special chip, a Motorola MC146818, which also held a *real-time clock*. The lower 14 of those bytes are used by the real-time clock to hold the current time and an alarm time, leaving 40 for storage of setup information. Locations were assigned for storing information about floppy and hard disk, the presence of a coprocessor, the amount of installed memory, and the type of display system (monochrome or color). Table 7.6 summarizes these updated assignments. A battery keeps this memory fresh and the real-time clock running. (See Chapter 9, "The Power Supply.")

TABLE 7.6. CMOS Byte Assignments

Byte	Assignment	Purpose
00	Seconds	Real-time Clock
01	Second Alarm	Real-time Clock
02	Minutes	Real-time Clock
03	Minute Alarm	Real-time Clock
04	Hours	Real-time Clock
05	Hours Alarm	Real-time Clock
06	Day of the Week	Real-time Clock
07	Date of the Month	Real-time Clock
08	Month	Real-time Clock
09	Year	Real-time Clock
10	Status Register A	Real-time Clock
11	Status Register B	Real-time Clock
12	Status Register C	Real-time Clock
13	Status Register D	Real-time Clock
0A	Status Register A	
0B	Status Register B	
0C	Status Register C	
0D	Status Register D	
0F	Shutdown Status	
10	Diskette Drive Type	
11	Reserved	
12	Hard Disk Type	
13	Reserved	
14	Equipment Type	
15	Low Base Memory	
16	High Base Memory	
17	Low Expansion Memory	

continues

TABLE 7.6. Continued

Byte	Assignment	Purpose
18	High Expansion Memory	
19	Reserved	
1A	Reserved	
1B	Reserved	
1C	Reserved	
1D	Reserved	
1E	Reserved	
20	Reserved	
21	Reserved	
22	Reserved	
23	Reserved	
24	Reserved	
25	Reserved	
26	Reserved	
27	Reserved	
28	Reserved	
29	Reserved	
2A	Reserved	
2B	Reserved	
2C	Reserved	
2D	CMOS Checksum	
2E	CMOS Checksum	
30	Low Expansion Memory	
31	High Expansion Memory	
32	Date Century	
33	Information Flags	
34	Reserved	
35	Reserved	
36	Reserved	
37	Reserved	

Byte	Assignment	Purpose
38	Reserved	
39	Reserved	
3A	Reserved	
3B	Reserved	
3C	Reserved	
3D	Reserved	
3E	Reserved	
3F	Reserved	

Unlike normal system memory, this *CMOS setup memory* was I/O mapped. That is, its contents were accessed through two input/output ports. Port 070(Hex) indicates the memory byte you want to access, and port 071(Hex) provides the pathway to the indicated byte. Reading or writing a byte of CMOS setup memory requires two steps. First, you write to port 070(hex) with the byte location in the CMOS range you want to read or write. Reading port 071(hex) tells you the value stored at the location you have chosen. Writing to port 071(Hex) changes the byte value at the appointed location.

The contents of most of the storage locations in this CMOS setup memory are monitored by storing a checksum in bytes 02E and 02F(Hex). If the checksum does not agree with the modular total of the monitored bytes, your system reports a CMOS memory error. The diagnostic status byte—00E(Hex)—indicates the gross nature of the error and additionally reports whether battery power has failed. If all systems are go, this byte has a zero value; any bit set indicates a specific error (with two bits reserved).

Newer PCs have elaborated on this CMOS storage scheme, adding more bytes to hold the status of other system features. In function and operation, however, all follow the pattern set by the AT.

Setup

The AT setup memory system has one weakness. In order for your system to boot, it needs to know which kind of disk is installed in it—information encoded in CMOS. But in order to load the CMOS, the computer first must boot so that you can set it up. Somehow, you have to be able to load all the setup information into the CMOS memory.

In its original system, IBM supplied a setup program on floppy disk. It queried you for the proper values and recorded your answers into the CMOS. To get the program running, however, the system had to assume you had a floppy disk and try to boot from it.

This scheme works, providing your PC has a general idea of what kind of floppy disk is installed inside it. With the profusion of floppy disk types, however, certainty about disk type disappears faster than popcorn at a movie premiere. The floppy-based setup system often has another drawback—the floppy disk itself. Misplace your setup floppy, and you cannot alter your basic system resources.

To eliminate these problems, most BIOS manufacturers now include a setup program in their BIOS code. Pressing the right combination of keys (sometimes only within a special time window during the POST procedure) brings up a setup menu through which you can type in setup values. Some BIOSs also include *advanced setup* procedures that allow you to alter vital system operating parameters that are controlled by the motherboard chipset. Typically, advanced setup is a second menu (or series of menus) accessed through the initial setup menu.

The range of features controlled by advanced setup varies with both the BIOS and the chipset inside your PC. Altering the options can have a dramatic effect on the performance of your PC. In most cases, tinkering often can lead to having a machine that will not work. Performance becomes zero. Worse, the machine will not operate at all—it may not even run through its POST procedure—which means you cannot alter whatever weird settings you've put into CMOS. To protect you from yourself, most motherboard makers give you an out: a jumper that resets the CMOS to its factory settings so your PC can boot up and give you another try at setup. PCs lacking this feature can usually be reset to their defaults by disconnecting the CMOS battery and waiting for the setup system to entirely discharge (which may take 15 minutes or more). After you've given the system long enough to discharge, reattach the battery before attempting to turn on your PC.

Some of the options available with different chipsets and BIOSs include:

Parity Check

Some systems permit you to switch off memory parity checking, disabling error detection. Taking this option prevents your system from halting when memory parity errors are detected. You are well-advised to leave parity checking enabled except when attempting to find elusive memory problems. Because this option is meaningful only for PCs that have parity-checked memory, it offers you no savings as would a system that used 8-bit SIMMs instead of parity-checked 9-bit SIMMs. Your system is likely to halt when a parity-error occurs in program code, but the crash is less controlled than an error-warning message. Files may be destroyed. If the error occurs within data, you may never know when your information is inaccurate.

Cache

Some systems require that you set the size of secondary (external) memory cache you have installed. You'll want to change this setting only if you install additional SRAM chips to increase the size of your PC's memory cache.

Some BIOSs allow you to switch on or off the cache. Some allow the individual control of the internal (that is, primary) cache inside your microprocessor and the external (secondary) cache. The only time you should switch off your system's caches is when you want to pin down software problems or diagnose hardware errors.

Wait States

This setting controls the number of wait states injected during memory accesses. Typically, you have a choice of 0, 1, 2, and possibly 3 wait states. Some systems allow the separate setting of read and write wait states. Choosing fewer wait states makes your PC faster, but choosing too few to accommodate the speed of your system's memory leads to memory errors. Set this value too low and your PC may not boot at all. If you are a die-hard tinkerer and want to explore the potentials of this setting, adjust it downward one step at a time. Then run your PC for a while to check its reliability. Toying with this may also familiarize you with the location of the CMOS reset jumper.

Bus Clock

Many ISA systems allow you to adjust the clock speed of their expansion buses so you can eke the most performance from your old expansion boards. Some systems give you a choice of clock speeds in megahertz; others express the speed in terms of the microprocessor clock (for example, CLOCKIN/4 implies one-quarter the microprocessor clock speed, 8.25 MHz with a 33 MHz system). Higher speeds (lower divisors) can deliver more performance, but rates above about 12 MHz may sacrifice reliability.

ROM Shadowing

Manufacturers may provide any of a number of options to enable or disable the shadowing of ROM code in fast RAM memory. Some merely allow the simple enable/disable choice. Others allow you to control ROM elements separately. One variety of BIOS lets you individually enable/disable system ROM and expansion ROM. System ROM means the BIOS code on your motherboard; expansion ROM is the code on expansion boards, which typically includes your video card and hard disk host adapter. Another variety of BIOS gives the choice of system, video, and adapter. A fourth BIOS type lets you choose whether to shadow ROM memory by address range, letting you select enabling or disabling by 16K, 32K, or 64K blocks.

Experimenting with shadowing can also lead to a system that does not boot. It is best to enable one block or shadowing feature at a time, and then run your system to observe the result.

Boot Sequence or Boot Device

Some BIOSs allow you to select the order in which your system tries to boot from disk, either floppy (A:) first or hard disk (C:) first. Some enable or disable the ability to boot from floppy at all. Choosing the boot from hard disk makes your system boot faster and allows you to lodge a floppy disk in the drive without pernicious error messages every time you turn on your PC. If you encounter a hard disk failure, however, you must use setup to change the boot procedure to load your operating system from floppy.

Concurrent Refresh

Most early PCs must devote 10% or more of their active time to refreshing memory. Newer systems are able to refresh memory concurrently—that is, while they are performing normal tasks. Concurrent refreshing ekes more performance from your system, so it is the preferred operating mode.

Page Interleave

Some systems with two or four identical banks of RAM chips or memory modules can operate in an interleaved fashion, that is, alternating banks in back-to-back memory requests. Statistically, interleaving can cut wait-states by nearly half. Although the effect is less pronounced in modern cached systems, enabling page interleave (when supported with sufficient memory) can improve performance.

Page Mode

Page-mode memory chips and modules also can trim wait states. Page mode SIMMs can make repeated accesses to one memory page without wait states. If you equip your system with page mode memory and enable this option, you should get better performance.

Programmable Option Select

Because of the innovations in the PS/2 design, IBM had to revise many aspects of its BIOS to handle added functions when it introduced its new system design. An additional section of code also was added to help with multitasking software. The result was that BIOS firmware was more tightly integrated with the rest of the system than ever before. The BIOS was part of a complete system that included new system board hardware and special software for aiding in setup. The additions help the computer better adjust itself for the options and accessories that you install inside it. In the first few years of supporting PCs, IBM discovered the vast majority of system problems arose from mis-set DIP switches on expansion boards or the interaction between mis-configured expansion boards. To eliminate these problems, IBM added a software-based configuration scheme called *Programmable Option Select* or *POS* to its Micro Channel computers.

POS removed the need for jumpers and DIP switches entirely. All configuration was handled through software—not just the rudimentary setup data of the AT, but all system resource (memory, DMA, I/O port, and interrupt assignment) usage. This system configuration information was stored in additional CMOS memory that linked to special disk files. The new PS/2 BIOS was designed to automatically load the stored resource allocation information from memory into each expansion board every time the system is booted up. The BIOS also included procedures to insure the integrity of this setup information.

The Programmable Option Select process was keyed to adapter identification numbers, unique designations assigned to each model of Micro Channel adapter. These identification numbers were coded as four digits and stored as two bytes of data. Every Micro Channel expansion board must have such a number. Although IBM initially took no part in the assignment, it grudgingly began acting as a clearinghouse and now attempts to prevent conflicts. Assignment of numbers to products now is coordinated by the Micro Channel Developers Association. The makers of some early Micro Channel accessories, however, invented their own numbers, creating the possibility of conflicts. Some also copied the numbers used by IBM for similar adapters, perhaps to add legitimacy or an aura of compatibility to their products. Neither strategy was recommended or necessary because a dearth of identifying numbers never has existed, and none is expected. The two byte approach makes 65,536 numbers possible, a total unlikely to be exhausted before a new expansion standard makes Micro Channel irrelevant.

POS has two parts—an initial configuration performed when you install an expansion board in a system, and a setup process that runs each time the system boots up. The configuration process runs from disk and gives you a menu- driven procedure for assigning each expansion board the memory ranges, interrupts, I/O ports, and DMA channels it uses. The process has been standardized so that each expansion board maker needs only supply a floppy disk with data files relevant to its products, and the configuration software automatically incorporates the information into its menu system.

The configuration process begins when you boot from the *Reference Diskette* that accompanied your Micro Channel system and select the option to configure your system. (Some newer systems put the configuration code on the hard disk.) The configuration procedure then begins its work by individually selecting each expansion slot and querying it for the presence of an adapter. If no adapter resides in the slot, no response will be forthcoming, and the slot is ignored. If an adapter is present, the POS procedure queries it for its adapter identification number.

The configuration procedure uses this number as a key to find an *Adapter Description File* on the Reference Disk. This special file contains the setup information for configuring the associated adapter.

An Adapter Configuration File can be recognized by its filename extension .ADF. The four numbers in the filename are the same as the identifying number assigned to the associated adapter. Before a Micro Channel expansion board can be properly configured, its associated .ADF file must be transferred to your working copy of your Reference Diskette. The configuration procedure provides an option for carrying out this copying process as the menu selection, "Copy an option diskette."

If an adapter description file is found for the expansion board, the values in the file are read and integrated into the configuration menu. Then the next slot is queried, and so on, until all the boards in all slots have been queried and their configuration options loaded.

The POS process permits both manual and automatic resource allocation. In manual mode, you select which resources each board uses from the options each board allows using a menu-driven interface. In automatic mode, the configuration software makes the allocation and automatically resolves resource conflicts.

This conflict-resolution process evolved over a few years. Originally, the configuration process went through the list of installed peripherals only once when it attempted an automatic setup. If it encountered a problem, it made no attempt to go back and reassign the resources given to a board that it had already configured. More recent versions of the POS configuration program cycle through all peripherals until all conflicts are resolved or until it runs out of options. The configuration procedure then saves each expansion board's identification number as well as the manually or automatically selected resource options to the system's extended CMOS memory.

To update your configuration procedure to the newer, reiterative mode, you usually only need to install a new peripheral. IBM provided most manufacturers with updated configuration programs, which they distributed with their data files. Most new Micro Channel expansion boards, consequently, come with a code that updates your system's configuration routines, automatically giving you the benefits of the updated configuration procedure.

The boot-up side of the Programmable Option Select process starts with the BIOS individually querying each expansion slot for the identification number assigned to the board inside it. This number is compared to the value stored in CMOS memory assigned to that slot so that the system can insures its own integrity. That is, your computer knows when you add, move, or remove an expansion board. If the numbers match, the BIOS downloads the option values to the expansion board. If the numbers do not match, the BIOS alerts you to the error, giving you the option to continue or pull out your Reference Diskette and reconfigure your system.

The centralized CMOS storage removes the need for each Micro Channel expansion board to incorporate non-volatile memory. Only one battery is needed to maintain the setup data for the entire system.

Besides adapter description files, some Micro Channel option diskettes also include *diagnostic code modules* and *Power-On Self-Test Error Message Files*, which are identified by their filenames.

These filenames also are keyed to the identifying number of the option, which normally are transferred to the working copy of your Reference Diskette when you copy adapter description files.

EISA Configuration

The engineers who designed EISA followed the configuration and setup pattern set by Micro Channel. Configuration is handled through a disk-based software procedure, and the BIOS is enhanced to properly set up each expansion board at boot time. The one notable change is that conflicting I/O port assignments automatically are eliminated by assigning each EISA expansion slot its own range of 511 I/O port addresses to use (see Chapter 6, "The Expansion Bus").

Instead of adapter identification numbers, each EISA board is assigned its own, unique *EISA Product Identifier.* Through a standardized *automated setup system,* you can manually or automatically allocate the various system resources. As with the Programmable Option Select procedure, the EISA system stores configuration in extended CMOS setup memory, and maintains a record of which board is in which slot using the EISA Product Identifier numbers. The EISA BIOS uses these numbers to verify that your system has been properly configured (that is, no expansion boards have been changed) and to load setup data into each expansion board every time the system boots up.

Plug and Play

One of the gravest shortcomings of the PCs based on the ISA expansion bus has been their lack of the automatic configuration procedures offered by Micro Channel and EISA. The Plug and Play initiative is designed to change that, to make the configuration of ISA (and other) PCs fully automatic—no switches, no jumpers, no headaches. The straightforward goal belies an arduous journey. Making Plug and Play work requires will require changes in every PC's BIOS, expansion bus, expansion boards, and the operating system. The universal adoption of Plug and Play will involve a lengthy transition as compliant products course into the market and older equipment retires.

Origins

The first stab at a Plug and Play specification appeared last year when the original Intel-Microsoft specification for ISA was released on May 28, 1993. That effort inspired other companies to join in, and related standards are being developed to extend Plug and Play to other troubling configuration processes, particularly SCSI expansion. Compaq Computer Corporation and Phoenix Technologies joined Intel to develop a BIOS specification for Plug and Play, first released November 1, 1993. The first Plug and Play PCs were scheduled to arrive in mid-1994, and, by the end of that year, it will have been integrated into at least one operating system (Windows 95).

By design, Plug and Play products will automatically ease the transition. All will work with non-Plug and Play equipment by sacrificing some of their inherent Plug and Play abilities. In other words, a new Plug and Play PC will accommodate old expansion boards and give you true Plug and Play operation with compliant peripherals. But a PC without Plug and Play can't ever take full advantage of the technology. In other words, you'll want to be sure the next system you buy has complete Plug and Play support—or some means of adding it in, such as its BIOS in flash memory. Otherwise, your frustration may be exceeded only by your regrets.

Plug and Play works by shifting the responsibility for remembering and assigning setup options from you to your computer system. After all, your PC likely has a better memory than you do, and it doesn't mind running through a check up procedure, however many times as is needed.

The basic Plug and Play procedure is a three-step process that lends itself to automation: First, your system checks what resources each expansion device needs. Next it coordinates the assignments to avoid conflicts. Finally, it tells your system and software which choices it has made.

Implementing this procedure is complicated, however, by the shortcomings of the decade-old ISA design. For example, the ISA bus provides no way of singling out an individual expansion board to determine exactly what resources it might require. Boards can be used individually only after they are configured and your software is notified which resources they use.

ISA expansion boards, too, lack the facilities required for automatic configuration. They require some means to allow their resource needs to be set automatically. Instead of jumpers and switches, they must have software latches. And they must understand a common command set for making their adjustments.

In addition, an automatic configuration procedure itself needs its own control system. That is, it needs a program to step through the configuration procedure. And it requires some method for communicating the addresses and assignment it makes to your software so that your applications can reach your PC's peripherals.

These shortcomings show that building an automatic configuration system will involve changes in nearly every aspect of a PC. To individually address expansion boards, the ISA expansion bus needs revision. To permit automatic configuration, ISA expansion board design must change. The setup procedure needs to be built into your PC's test procedure, which requires changes to the system BIOSs. And linking with software is best implemented by redesigning the overall operating system.

These are not changes to be taken lightly. They require the cooperation of the entire PC industry. Plug and Play has, for the first time, brought together that industry, chiefly because the benefits of cooperation are so great, both for you (no headaches) and them (dramatically lower support costs).

Backward Compatibility

The anemic acceptance shown previously attempts at incorporating automatic configuration—Micro Channel and EISA—have shown how unwilling the vast installed user base of ISA is to give up its familiar bus for any breakthrough, however compelling. Consequently, the Plug and Play players designed the system to allow a gradual phase-in. Although a completely hassle-free system will require your PC to be equipped with a new BIOS and nothing but Plug and Play expansion boards, setup headaches will nevertheless fade away as you add new operating systems and expansion boards to your current PC.

With existing PCs that lack explicit Plug and Play support in their BIOSs, the automatic configuration system will divide the task of sorting through resource conflicts between you and the operating system. Although the Plug and Play operating system will manage Plug and Play expansion boards, you'll still have to configure your conventional expansion boards. Even updating your PC to one with a Plug and Play BIOS won't help resolving conflicts between conventional expansion boards because the hardware-mediated resource allocation on conventional boards can't be changed by software alone. Once you've eliminated non-Plug and Play products from your system, however, your setup headaches will disappear.

Expansion Board Changes

The Plug and Play configuration process calls upon specific hardware features of Plug and Play expansion boards. Most importantly, each Plug and Play board is able to inactivate itself so that it does not respond to the normal control signals inside your PC. The board disconnects itself from all system resources so that when it is inactive, it cannot possibly cause conflicts.

In addition, each Plug and Play board has several new on-board registers that are reached through a standardized set of three I/O port addresses so that the BIOSs or operating system can control the configuration of the board. These ports are designated Address, Write Data, and Read Data.

The *Address Port* functions as a pointer that expands the number of control registers directly accessible to your system without stealing more system resources. Loading a register number in the Address Port makes that register available for reading or writing through the Write and Read Data ports.

The Plug and Play specification explicitly defines eight card control registers and reserves two large ranges, one of 24 registers for future elaboration of the standard, and a second 16-port range that board makers can assign to their own purposes. In addition, the Plug and Play specification allows cards to be configured as multiple logical devices, and it assigns ports for their control. The Address port allows the Write Data port to select which of the logical devices is active and the resources used by each.

Plug and Play expansion boards act in one of two ways, depending on whether they are needed for booting the system. Boards that are required for boot-up—that is, display adapters and disk controllers—start up active. That is, they come on-line exactly like conventional expansion boards using the resources assigned them as power-on defaults. They will grab the resources that they need, participate in the normal power-on self-test procedure, and let you operate your PC normally. They may also cause the same old resource allocation problems, as will any conventional expansion boards that don't support Plug and Play. The other Plug and Play devices (those not needed in booting your PC) automatically inactivate themselves when your system comes on, waiting to be told what configuration to use by your operating system.

Plug and Play boards not required during boot up normally start up inactive. They do nothing until specifically activated, typically by the Plug and Play operating system.

Every Plug and Play board has specific circuitry for managing its configuration. This circuitry operates independently from the normal functions of the board. Unlike the functional circuits on the board that can be disconnected from the bus interface, the Plug and Play circuits always monitor the signals on the bus. However, the Plug and Play circuitry operates in one of four states—Wait for Key, Isolation, Configuration, and Sleep—without regard to whether the functional circuitry is active or inactive.

Boot Sequence

All Plug and Play boards, whether active or inactive, boot up in their *Wait for Key* state. In this condition, the boards refuse to respond to any signal on the ISA bus until they receive an explicit command called an *Initiation Key*. The Initiation Key is actually a precisely defined 32-step interaction between the host Plug and Play system and circuitry on each set (one at a time), and the host sends a data byte to the board. Each Plug and Play board compares its internal values to those received from the host. All 32 comparisons must be correct for the Initiation Key to be successful. Upon properly receiving the Initiation Key, Plug and Play expansion boards shift into Sleep mode.

A circuit on the board called a *Linear Feedback Shift Register* generates a new pattern at each step (by shifting its bits one at a time) and the host sends a data byte to the board. Each Plug and Play board compares its internal values to those received from the host. All 32 comparisons must be correct for the Initiation Key to be successful. Upon properly receiving the Initiation Key, Plug and Play expansion boards shift into Sleep mode.

Because an ordinary PC BIOS does not know how to carry out the Initiation Key process, it cannot remove Plug and Play boards from the Wait for Key state. The configuration circuitry of the Plug and Play boards does not activate (if at all) until the Plug and Play operating system loads.

In a fully Plug and Play PC, the BIOSs automatically sends out the Initiation Key. It can then take control of individual boards, interrogate each Plug and Play device about the system resources it requires, and resolve conflicts between boot-up devices. The BIOS ordinarily does not, however, make resource assignments or activate the boards not involved in boot-up. Instead, it leaves that decision-making to the operating system.

In order to configure each expansion board, the Plug and Play BIOSs or operating system must be able to individually communicate with each board to independently instruct each what to do. Ordinarily that's difficult in the ISA system because all signals are broadcast in common to all expansion boards. The Plug and Play creators envisioned that ISA bus being modified to include slot-specific signals to unambiguously identify each expansion board. Knowing that such changes would take years to creep onto desktops, however, they also developed a board-identification system compatible with the existing ISA bus that allows individual addressing except when multiple identical boards are installed in a single PC. In this Plug and Play system, a *Card Select Number* (CSN) identifies each board. Each board is dynamically assigned its CSN by the Plug and Play BIOS (if your PC has one) or the Plug and Play operating system.

The CSN is actually a convenience that works as a handle, much like the file handles used by DOS. The ROM on each Plug and Play board model includes a serial identifier, an eight-byte code coupled with a one-byte checksum. Two bytes store a three-letter manufacturer identification in compressed ASCII code (five bits per character). Two more store the model number of the board, and four more bytes code a board-specific serial number.

In contrast, the CSN is an individual byte value that is more convenient to store and manipulate. Moreover, CSN numbers allow you to install multiple copies of a given board model in one PC without conflict—provided your PC has a means of individually addressing each expansion slot.

All Plug and Play boards boot up with a CSN of zero (0). To assign a unique CSN to a Plug and Play board, the Plug and Play BIOSs or operating system must isolate individual boards from the bus. It does this by first arousing all boards from the Sleep state into their Isolation state by broadcasting a Wake command that specifies the default CSN of zero to the Write Data ports of all boards.

In the *Isolation* state, each board interacts with your PC (and the Plug and Play BIOSs or operating system) in a precisely defined manner called the Isolation Sequence. The Plug and Play BIOSs or operating system uses the serial identifier to uniquely locate each board. The system merely compares the bit patterns of the serial identifiers, ignoring their information content.

The *Isolation Sequence* involves simultaneously scanning all serial identifiers one bit at a time in the Lineral Feedback Shift Register. The host system sends out 72 consecutive one-bit read operations (one operation for each of the 64 bits in the code plus its 8-bit checksum). At every step, each Plug and Play board compares one bit in its LFSR to that of the other boards by observing bus signals.

When the board has a high bit (digital 1) in its LFSR, it asserts a data signal across the bus; boards with low bits (digital 0) at that position in their serial identifiers do not. When a board with a low bit detects the signal from one or more boards with high bits in a given position in their ID codes, it drops out of the isolation sequence by slipping back into its Sleep state. This bit-comparison process continues until, at the end of 72 evaluations, only one board has not dropped off to sleep.

Once a single board is thus uniquely identified, the operating system then assigns that board its unique CSN number. The board then stores the CSN for future reference in a special CSN register and it, too, goes into its Sleep state. Then the Plug and Play BIOSs or operating system initiates another Isolation Sequence to assign the next CSN, and so on until all boards have been assigned their CSNs. Only the boards with a CSN of zero participate in later Isolation Sequences because only they respond to the Wake command that starts the sequence.

After all Plug and Play boards have been isolated and assigned CSNs, the BIOSs or operating system then checks the resource needs of each one. To do this, the BIOSs or operating system individually switches each board into its Configuration mode to read its resource needs from the data stored on the board.

A board with a valid CSN switches into Configuration mode when it detects a Wake command specifying its CSN. Only one board is permitted in Configuration mode at a time, so other boards automatically switch to Sleep mode when they detect the Wake command meant for another board.

In PCs with a Plug and Play BIOS, the BIOS checks each board by reading registers through its Read Data port to compile a list of resource requirements, and then finishes the boot-up process. The Plug and Play operating system takes over at that point. In PCs without Plug and Play BIOSs, the operating system merely jumps from the isolation to the configuration process.

After a given expansion board has been configured, the operating system can activate it by writing to the appropriate register on the board. A single expansion board may have several functions, each called a virtual device, which the operating system can separately activate.

After the configuration process is completed (or at any other necessary time) the operating system can switch the designated expansion board out of its Sleep state and back to its Configuration state to activate it, deactivate it, or change its configuration. It controls each board individually using the Wake command and specifying an CSN. This process allows the operating system to dynamically modify the resource usage of any board in the system as applications require.

BIOS Structure

Besides introducing several new steps to the standard BIOS-mediated POST procedure, Plug and Play adds a new structure to add-in BIOS code. It allows a given expansion board to include code targeted to specific operating systems so that a given expansion board can take on different personalities depending upon the operating system that's in control.

The Plug and Play BIOS swings into action mimicking the BIOS convention originated by IBM backing in 1981 by scanning through the memory address range used for BIOS code to look for add-in code held on expansion boards. As with the standard ISA POST procedure, the Plug and Play BIOS looks for a special add-in ROM signature—the two-byte 055(Hex), 0AA(Hex) code—which indicates a block of add-in BIOS code follows.

The Plug and Play system adds more information to this signature[em]a pointer that immediately follows it to indicate the location of an *Expansion Header* in the BIOS code or a chain of several headers. Each header is identified by a special four-byte preamble—024(Hex), 050(Hex), 06E(Hex), 050(Hex)—that corresponds to the ASCII characters $PnP. Each header can be keyed to an individual operating system using additional codes. Unlike conventional expansion boards, the operating system and not the PC's own BIOS reads through this add-in code on Plug and Play boards because the boards are inactive and effectively de-coupled from the bus during a normal BIOS scan.

Using the CSNs given by the BIOS (or the operating system itself), the operating system can identify each Plug and Play board, read through its BIOS area, and find each header. Information encoded in each expansion header includes the type of devices on the board and the location of program code to boot the PC (if a device on the board can boot the computer). A *Device Indicator* byte in the header indicates whether the ROM on the board initializes as a device driver, may be shadowed, can be cached, or operates as a boot, display, or input device. A *Device Type Code* helps the system BIOS determine which devices should be used for booting the system if none is overtly specified. It identifies exactly what kind of peripheral is connected through the expansion slot. The serial identifier is also included in the header.

The Plug and Play specification allows each board maker a generous apportionment of the available memory and port addresses. Each board can have up to four non-contiguous ranges of memory base addresses for BIOS code and up to eight non-contiguous base addresses for input/output ports. In addition, a board can use from zero to two separate interrupt levels and up to two DMA channels. Each manufacturer determines the number of resources that a given board can use. Which it uses, however, is a matter left to the board maker.

Resource requirements need not be configurable. A board with minimal Plug and Play support merely tells what resources it wants and stodgily sticks there. Most Plug and Play products will, however, allow for several options in their resource requirements. Even when irresolvable conflicts arise between boards, the Plug and Play system can keep a PC operating by inactivating one of the conflicting boards.

The Plug and Play scheme allows the ROM on each expansion board to hold interface and driver code for multiple operating systems, each coded by its own expansion header. An operating system can identify the code that applies specifically to it by reading the headers.

IBM Advanced BIOS

All BIOSs provide basically the same support and features as the original IBM BIOS. Because this prototypical BIOS was written for 8088-based computers, it was designed solely with real mode in mind. It offered no support for protected mode. It did not even acknowledge that protected mode existed.

With the introduction of the Micro Channel PS/2, IBM revised its standard BIOS with the addition of new, protected-mode routines designed to facilitate the use of OS/2 and other advanced applications. Instead of integrating them into the existing BIOS, IBM chose to make the new routines a separate entity so that the PS/2 BIOS consists of two sections that take up nearly 128K of Read-Only Memory. The first is called the *Compatibility BIOS* or *CBIOS*. It addresses only the first megabyte of system memory and is used by PC DOS. It is fully compatible with the previous IBM BIOS, hence its designation. The second section of BIOS code was the *Advanced BIOS* or *ABIOS*. It was able to address all the memory within the 16-megabyte range of the 80286 microprocessor in its protected mode and was specifically designed to provide support for multitasking systems.

Most manufacturers of BIOSs for compatible PCs choose simply to ignore the ABIOS. Today, most PCs rely on supplemental software code, rather than BIOS firmware extensions, to handle protected mode and extended memory.

The ABIOS was radically different from the old BIOS in both the way it was written and the way in which it operated. Instead of using software interrupts and parameter passing for accessing hardware devices, the ABIOS is based on a *call system* that is meant to integrate with programming language subroutines. To make use of an ABIOS routine, a program just transfers control to a subroutine, which sends control back to the program after the routine has been completed.

Unlike the CBIOS, the ABIOS uses *re-entrant* code. This feature allows it to issue a second call while waiting for the results of the first call. A program may request that the ABIOS read a cluster of data from the system's floppy disk drive, for example. The disk might not be ready to transfer data, however. The ABIOS routine would let you know that the disk was not ready, but would continue to keep trying to read the disk. Because the ABIOS routine is re-entrant, the underlying program can issue a second call, such as to another disk drive, while the first is executing, without confusing the system. This re-entrant feature permits the ABIOS of Micro Channel PS/2s to operate in a true multitasking mode. Most new compatible BIOS now use re-entrant code.

One reason few BIOS makers or PC vendors have chosen to clone the ABIOS is because many of its features were designed to simplify the mode-switching of the 286 microprocessor. Most BIOS makers now care little about microprocessors older than the 386. The one operating system designed to truly benefit from the ABIOS—OS/2—has itself been thoroughly rewritten for greater compatibility without the need for the ABIOS at all. In fact, OS/2 loads its own software-based ABIOS code as it boots up. Having ABIOS code in ROM is irrelevant today.

Compatibility

After the IBM BIOS made its debut, it became the most copied set of software routines in the world. The PC BIOS laid out all the entry points used by subsequent IBM BIOS and most compatible BIOSs as well. It also defined the functions that could—and must—be expected in any BIOS. And it established the way that the BIOS works. The AT BIOS that is now mandatory in every PC added a few enhancements without disturbing the underlying PC design. The IBM PC and AT BIOSs are therefore the point of departure for understanding how a BIOS works.

The goal of the compatible computer manufacturer is to match the BIOS used by his machine to that inside the IBM AT. Even today's latest and most powerful machines must be able to duplicate everything the old AT did. That minimum level of functionality is what all programs expect from a PC.

No matter how good it may be, the match cannot be perfect. The code used by IBM is protected by copyrights which forbid others from legally duplicating it. Instead, compatible makers are charged with writing their own BIOS routines without copying IBM's.

Because the copyright laws forbid any copying of someone else's work, compatible BIOSs are written "clean." That is, the programmers are kept from ever viewing the source code or having any knowledge of the routines it contains. Instead, they work from a list of instructions and the functions that the BIOS carries out when given each specific instruction. In other words, they look at the BIOS they want to copy as a black box that takes an input and gives an output. The programmers then deduce the instructions for the inside of the box that will give the desired results.

Working in this way is time-consuming and expensive. Few computer companies have the resources to do it all themselves. The vast majority of compatible PC manufacturers buy the necessary BIOS firmware from specialist firms such as American Megatrends, Inc., Award Software, Phoenix Technologies, Ltd. or Mr. BIOS. This expedience gives them a BIOS that is known to work without worries about violating copyright protection.

Bought in bulk (that is, to be installed in a full production run of PCs) the rights to use a compatible BIOS can be quite inexpensive—only a few dollars per copy. Buying an individual BIOS for a machine is more expensive because you do not get the benefit of a manufacturer's mass-order bargaining power. You must buy the PROM chip that holds the code, while computer-makers often buy the code on disk or tape, making the copies they need (and have paid for) themselves. Consequently, buying a single copy of a BIOS can cost you $20 to $50 depending on what you buy and from whom.

Because each BIOS vendor must develop its own product separately, the exact code used by each BIOS version is different. As a result, BIOSs vary in their compatibility with the IBM XT standard. Some BIOSs strive to match the IBM entry points, for example, and some do not.

In the early days of compatible computers, programmers simply wrote solely for the IBM PC and considered the difficulties encountered by so-called "compatible" computers to be problems that the hardware maker could solve. In those golden years, IBM computers represented the majority of the PCs in use. Today, with IBM only one of a multitude of PC manufacturers, the situation has changed. Software writers have to be sure that their products work on the un-washed masses of PCs. They have to make allowances for all the compatible BIOSs. That fact means that they must stick closer to IBM's original intentions—that software must match at the BIOS interrupt level rather than at the entry points. BIOS compatibility today is essentially a non-issue—at least at the software level.

Another compatibility issue with BIOSs exists, however, and arises if you ever want to replace the BIOS in your PC. You must insure that any replacement BIOS is compatible with the computer in which you want it to work. The job is not one to be taken lightly. By design, every BIOS is created to match specific hardware. That is part of its job—uniting different hardware designs so that they work interchangeably with all software. Every BIOS is customized for the PC it controls, consequently. Computer motherboard manufacturers modify BIOSs to suit their own purposes. That modification means no generic BIOS works in any PC. If you want to change or upgrade your PC's BIOS for any reason, you need to get one that matches the exact model of computer that you own.

Performance Effects

A BIOS either works or does not work, generally speaking. Your system runs the applications you want, or it crashes dismally whenever you press the Enter key. If there is any possible quality difference between BIOSs, it is in performance. The BIOS in a PC can affect the system's performance in two ways—the efficiency of the BIOS code itself and the control it affords over system resources. A better BIOS could, therefore, give a PC a performance edge—at least on functions that take advantage of the BIOS.

Because BIOS routines look like black boxes to programs with their specific contents essentially unknown (and not cared about), the assembly language instructions of each BIOS routine can vary considerably among different BIOSs. Some routines may have more instructions for a given function than do others. Those routines with the fewest instructions to carry out a given function are the most efficient. A program needs to execute fewer steps using fewer clock cycles every time it calls BIOS routines. As a result, the system runs faster.

Of course, this difference only appears when a program takes advantage of BIOS routines. Because most high-performance programs and operating systems sidestep the BIOS to take direct hardware control, a better BIOS will not make much of an overall improvement on the quickest programs. For most people and software, the difference is nothing to worry about.

Another performance issue arises because of the technology used for storing BIOS code—PROM. Most PROM chips do not respond as quickly as today's fast RAM chips, so that calling a BIOS routine from PROM may add wait states and slow down the system's microprocessor. Most PCs today configure their BIOS with a 16-bit bus width, even in 32-bit PCs. As a result, just loading the BIOS code into the microprocessor takes twice as long as it would from RAM that operates with the full bus width. To minimize such problems, most PCs today support *ROM shadowing*. That is, they copy the BIOS code from slow PROM into fast RAM and remap all the addresses so programs see the standard BIOS routines in RAM at their normally expected addresses. This ROM shadowing can effectively double the speed of execution of BIOS code. As with a more efficient BIOS, however, ROM shadowing makes a difference only to programs that actually use the BIOS routines.

A more important performance difference depends on how a BIOS initiates its host computer. Some BIOSs do a better job than others in optimizing the relationship between the microprocessor's local bus and the input/output channel. With most modern chipsets, the relationship between the two is completely programmable. Most chipsets allow many performance-enhancing features—such as memory interleaving—to be switched on or off and others—such as cache operation—to be optimized. A simple BIOS can bring a PC to life without ever trying to take optimum advantage of these features, shortchanging on the performance potential built into the PC. A better BIOS automatically checks for the best operation of all available features. Through advanced setup procedures, it may also give you manual control of these vital system parameters so you can second-guess its settings.

Unfortunately, you have no way of knowing how well a BIOS works simply by looking at a PC. The only way to judge is to run your applications on the system and see what it does—and how fast it does them. Although you will only rarely be able to narrow down performance difference to BIOS effects (rarely, you can find two PCs with the same system board but different BIOSs), at least you are able to determine if a given system responds quickly enough to keep you happy.

Chapter 8
Support Circuitry

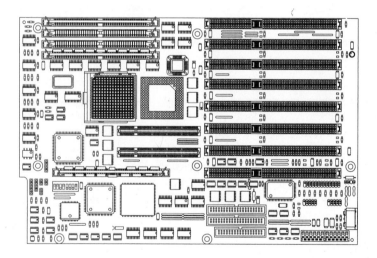

Support circuits are the glue that holds a PC together, providing the signals that the microprocessor needs to operate as well as those that link the PC and its peripherals. Over the years of development, the form and nature of those support circuits has changed, but their function has remained consistent, part of the definition of an IBM-compatible PC.

Just as you can't build a house without nails, you can't put together a computer without support chips. A wealth of circuits are needed to hold together all the functions of a PC, to coordinate its operation, and to control the signals inside it. After all, you need more than a microprocessor to make a computer—otherwise a microprocessor *would* be a computer. While some systems come close to being little more than microprocessors and some microprocessors come close to being complete computers, today most personal computers require a number of support functions to make their microprocessors useful—and make the microprocessors work. Support chips provide a PC's microprocessor with the signals it needs to operate as well as generating the signals the rest of your PC requires to operate. Some support chips merely link motherboard components together.

Those with a penchant for details can take glee in pointing out that it *is* possible to build a house without nails, what with space-age adhesives, drywall screws, and even peg-and-tenon construction. They're right. The art of PC construction has advanced so that where dozens of support chips once were needed, two or three suffice for most systems. In fact, all the essential support can now be packaged in a single chip, sometimes inside the same package as the system microprocessor—no nails, no glue, just one prefabricated assembly.

Despite the physical lack of support chips in some of today's systems, the functions performed by these vital circuits remain as vital as they were for the first PCs. Every computer needs the same essential elements to work: a clock or oscillator to generate the signals that lock the circuits together; a memory controller to ensure that each byte goes to the proper place and stays there; bus-control logic to command the flow of data in and out of the chip and the rest of the system; direct memory access control to assist in moving data; and interrupt control to meet the needs of interactive computing. Only the form of these circuit elements has changed to protect the profits—they are more compact in combination, and more affordable, too.

Chipsets

In early PCs, support circuits were constructed from a variety of discrete circuits—small, general-purpose integrated circuits such as logic gates—and a few functional blocks that each had a specific function, although not one limited to a specific model or design of computer. These garden-variety circuits were combined together to build all the necessary computer functions into the first PC.

As PCs became increasingly popular, enterprising semiconductor firms combined many of the related computer functions together into a single package. Eliminating the discrete packages and all their interconnections helped make PCs more reliable. Moreover, because a multitude of circuits could be grown together at the same time, this integrated approach made the PC support circuitry less expensive. At first, only related functions were grouped together. As semiconductor firms became more experienced and fabrication technology permitted smaller design rules and denser packaging, however, all the diverse support functions inside a PC were integrated into a few VLSI components individually termed *Application-Specific Integrated Circuits* or *ASICs*, collectively called a *chipset*.

The chipset changed the face of the PC industry. With discrete support circuitry, designing a PC motherboard was a true engineering challenge because it required a deep understanding of the electronic function of all the elements of a PC. Using a chipset, a PC engineer need only be concerned with the signals going in and out of a few components. The chipset might be a magical black box for all the designer cares. In fact, in many cases the only skill required to design a PC from a chipset is the ability to navigate from a roadmap. Most chipset manufacturers provide circuit designs for motherboards to aid in the evaluation of their products. Many motherboard manufacturers (all too many, perhaps) simply take the chipset maker's evaluation design and turn it into a commercial product.

Today, even chipsets are disappearing. A single chip is sufficient to hold all the support circuitry of an entire PC. Moreover, chipmakers have already taken the final step—integration of the support circuitry with the microprocessor. The premiere example today is Intel's 486SL. This is a full-fledged 486DX microprocessor designed for low power and total system control—a whole computer inside.

Although a single-chip design has its benefits, particularly in space-critical applications such as notebook and handheld PCs, it is not always the best approach. A multi-chip design allows hardware engineers more freedom to customize and optimize their products—which means a greater ability to tune in more speed. The semiconductor costs of one-chip and three-chip implementations are not significantly different, and the extra chips impose little penalty on desktop-size motherboards.

Timing Circuits

Although anarchy has much to recommend it, anarchy is an anathema to computer circuits. Today's data processing designs depend on organization and controlled cooperation—timing is critical. The meaning of each pulse passing through a PC is dependent on time relationships. Signals must be passed between circuits at just the right moment for the entire system to work properly.

This time is critical in PCs because their circuits are designed using a technology known as *clocked logic*. All the logic elements in the computer operate synchronously. They carry out their designated operations one step at a time, and each circuit makes one step at the same time as all the rest of the circuits in the computer. This synchronous operation helps the machine keep track of every bit that it processes, ensuring that nothing slips between the cracks.

Clocks and Oscillators

The system *clock* is the conductor who beats the time that all the circuits follow, sending out special timing pulses at precisely controlled intervals. The clock, however, must get its cues from somewhere, either its own internal sense of timing or some kind of metronome.

An electronic circuit that accurately and continuously beats time is termed an *oscillator*. Most oscillators work on a simple feedback principle. Like the microphone that picks up its own sounds from public address speakers too near or turned up too high, the oscillator, too, listens to what it says. As with the acoustic feedback squeal that the public address system complains with, the oscillator, too, generates its own howl. Because the feedback circuit is much shorter, however, the signal need not travel as far and its frequency is higher, perhaps by several thousand fold.

The oscillator takes its output as its input, then amplifies the signal, sends it to its output where it goes back to the input again in an endless—and out of control—loop. By taming the oscillator by adding impediments to the feedback loop, by adding special electronic components between the oscillator's output and its input, the feedback and its frequency can be brought under control.

In nearly all PCs, a carefully crafted *crystal* of quartz is used as this frequency control element. Quartz is one of many *piezoelectric* compounds. Piezoelectric materials have an interesting property—if you bend a piezoelectric crystal, it generates a tiny voltage. Or if you apply a voltage to it in the right way, the piezoelectric material bends.

Quartz crystals do exactly that. But beyond this simple stimulus/response relationship, quartz crystals offer another important property. By stringently controlling the size and shape of a quartz crystal, it can be made to *resonate* at a specific frequency. The frequency of this resonance is extremely stable and very reliable—so much so that it can help an electric watch keep time to within seconds a month. Although PCs don't need the absolute precision of a quartz watch to operate their logic circuits properly, the fundamental stability of the quartz oscillator guarantees that the PC operate at a clock frequency within the design limits always available to it.

The very first IBM Personal Computer was designed around a single such oscillator built from a crystal that resonated at 14.31818 megahertz (MHz). The odd frequency was chosen for a particular reason—it's exactly four times the subcarrier frequency used in color television signals (3.58 MHz.). The engineers who created the original PC thought compatibility with televisions would be an important design element of the PC. They were anticipating multimedia but looking for a cheap way of putting PC images on-screen. When the PC was released, no inexpensive color computer monitors were available (or necessary for almost non-existent color graphic software).

The actual oscillator in these early machines was made from a special integrated circuit, type 8284A, and the 14.31818 MHz crystal. One output at the crystal's fundamental frequency was routed directly to the expansion bus. Another oscillator output was divided down by a discrete auxiliary chip to create the 1.19 MHz frequency that was used as a timebase for the PC's timer/counter circuit. The same chip also divided the fundamental crystal frequency by three to produce a frequency of 4.77 MHz (the actual clock signal used by the microprocessor in the PC), determining the operating speed of the system microprocessor. This same clock signal also synchronized all the logic operations inside the PC and related eight-bit bus computers.

Because the 14.31818 crystal determines the speed that a PC or related computer operates, you may think that you could speed up such a system and improve its overall performance simply by replacing the crystal with one that operates at a higher frequency. Although this strategy actually increases the operating speed of a PC, it is not a good idea for several reasons.

One problem is easily solved. Although the standard 8088 microprocessor in the PC is rated at only five megahertz and may not operate properly at higher speeds, you can swap it out for one that can handle a faster clock—an 8088-2 or NEC V-20, for example. But you need to upgrade other parts of the system to higher speed, too. A bigger obstacle is the one-oscillator design of the PC. Because all timings throughout the whole PC system are locked to that one oscillator, odd things happen when you alter its frequency. The system clock won't keep very good time, perennially kept in a high-speed time warp. Software that depends on system timings may crash. Expansion boards may not work at the altered bus speed. Even your floppy disks may operate erratically with some software.

The goal in the oscillator/clock design of the PC seems to have been frugality rather than flexibility, versatility, or usability. In those early systems, one master frequency was cut, chopped, minced, and diced into whatever else was needed inside the computer. But as with trying to make a cut-rate system speed up, altering the frequency of any part of a computer with the PC oscillator design is likely to throw off all the other frequency-critical components. Consequently, when IBM rethought the basic concept of a personal computer and came up with its Advanced Technology approach, the oscillator was completely redesigned.

The more enlightened AT design broke the system clock free from the bondage of the timer and its oscillator. Instead of just one crystal and oscillator, the AT and every subsequent computer based upon its design (which means nearly all PCs) uses three. One is used to derive the system clock for synchronizing the bus, microprocessor, and related circuits. Another operates at 14.31818 MHz and provides input to a timer/counter chip and a 14.31818 bus signal for compatibility with the PC. The third oscillator controls the CMOS time-of-day clock that runs on battery power even when the computer is switched off.

The oscillator of the original AT was much the same as that of the PC, to the extent of being based on the same 8284A timer chip and 14.31818 MHz crystal. Its output was routed directly to the bus. Another output was divided down to 1.19 MHz to feed the timer/counter circuit to maintain backward compatibility with the first PCs.

In the original AT, a special circuit was dedicated to generating the system clock signal, a type *82284 System Clock Generator* chip. The operating frequency of the microprocessor was governed by the crystal associated with this chip. The 82284 divides the crystal frequency in half to produce the clock that controls the speed of the microprocessor, bus, and associated circuitry. The original AT operated with a 6 megahertz clock derived from a 12 megahertz crystal; later ATs ran at 8 megahertz, derived from a 16 megahertz crystal.

Replacing the crystal used by the 82284 oscillator alters the speed of the microprocessor. This change likely can also affect the operating speed of the expansion bus. In the original AT design, the bus clock frequency was locked to the microprocessor clock. The bus and the microprocessor ran in lockstep. As designers pushed microprocessor speeds higher, however, bus devices could not keep up. Consequently, most modern PCs using the ISA expansion bus put a frequency divider between the microprocessor clock and the expansion bus.

Because the expansion bus clock is directly derived from the microprocessor clock, the two clocks are locked together, providing synchronous operation of the bus. However, the bus speed can be kept at a frequency low enough to be tolerated by most expansion boards. Most ISA systems strive to run the bus at the submultiple of the microprocessor clock that comes closest to the eight megahertz that most expansion boards are designed to accommodate. The EISA bus design dictates a nominal 8 megahertz bus speed as well.

IBM took the oscillator designs of its PS/2 series in new directions but went to great lengths to maintain compatibility with previous systems. Even the first PS/2s merged much of the support circuitry on their motherboards into ASICs, with the system's oscillators and clocks among these newly integrated functions.

For example, the initial ISA PS/2s, the Models 25 and 30, put their timer, oscillator, and clock functions into two VLSI chips that IBM called the *System Support Gate Array* and the *I/O Support Gate Array.* The former circuit generates the system clock, starting with the output of a 48 MHz external oscillator. The System Support Gate Array divides this frequency down by a factor of six to achieve the eight megahertz that serves as the system clock. It also controls the refreshing of system memory, a function that in previous systems required the use of a channel of the system timer. In addition to these functions, the System Support Gate Array also controls which functions and devices (microprocessor, coprocessor, DMA controller, and so on) have command of the system bus.

The I/O Support Gate Array controls the serial and parallel port, the floppy and hard disk controllers, the video system, and the real-time clock but does not contain the full circuitry for these functions. It also generates the 1.19 MHz signal used by the system timer.

The direction of current PC clock and oscillator designs is exemplified by Chips and Technologies 82C836 (also called SCATsx). It's a one-chip VLSI device that incorporates most of the motherboard logic needed to construct an AT-style computer using a 386SX microprocessor. The 82C836 accepts a single, crystal-controlled oscillator signal (typically 32, 40, or 50 MHz) and provides isolated output clock signals for the system microprocessor, the expansion bus, and the DMA system. It also provides a 14.31818 MHz I/O clock derived from a separate crystal or oscillator. The 82C836 produces a microprocessor clock that's either exactly equal to or at one-half, one-quarter, or one-eighth of the oscillator signal provided at its input. The bus clock can be set at either one-quarter, one-fifth, or one-sixth the input frequency. The DMA clock can be set at bus speed or one-half the bus speed. Using a chipset like the 82C836, the PC designer need only provide a single oscillator frequency, and all the necessary clock signals are automatically derived for him without further work or worry. Nevertheless, the designer is still allowed the flexibility of choosing among several bus and DMA speeds to match his particular system requirements.

Timers

The signals developed by the clocks and oscillators inside a PC are designed for internal consumption only. That is, they are used for housekeeping functions—locking together the operation of various circuit components. System timers serve more diverse functions. Unlike clocks and oscillators, which are fixed in frequency and purpose by hardware design, the PC's timers are programmable, so their output frequencies can be altered to suit the needs of special applications.

The timer signals in the original PC were generated from the system clock using a *8253 timer/counter* integrated circuit chip. Actually three 16-bit timers in one, the 8253 derives several important signals from the system clock. One of its outputs controls the time-of-day clock inside the PC, another controls the memory refresh circuitry of the computer, and the third is used to generate the tones made by the PC's speaker.

The 8253 timer/counter operates by counting the clock pulses it receives by reducing the value it holds in an internal register by one with each pulse it receives. In the PC series of computers, the signal that the 8253 timer/counter actually counts is a submultiple of the system clock, divided by four, to about 1.19 MHz.

The 8253 can be set up (through I/O ports in the PC) to work in any of six different modes, two of which can only be used on the speaker channel. In the most straightforward way, Mode 2, it operates as a frequency divider or rate generator. You load its register with a number, and it counts to that number. When it reaches that number, it outputs a pulse and starts all over again. Load the 8253 register with 2, and it sends out a pulse at half the frequency of the input. Load it with one thousand, and the output becomes 1/1000th the input. In this mode, the chip can generate an interrupt at any of a wide range of user-defined intervals. Because the highest value you can load into its 16-bit register is 2^{16} or 65,536, the longest single interval it can count is about .055 second—that is, the 1.19 MHz input signal divided by 65,536.

The six modes of the PCs 8253 timer/counter and their functions and programming are given in Table 8.1.

TABLE 8.1. Operating Modes of 8253 Timer/Counter Chip

Mode	Operation
0—Interrupt on Terminal Count	Timer is loaded with a value and counts down from that value to zero, one counter per clock pulse.
1—Hardware Retriggable One-Shot	A trigger pulse causes timer output to go low; when the counter reaches zero, the output goes high and stays high until reset. The process repeats every time triggered. Pulse length set by writing a control word and initial count to chip before first cycle.
2—Rate Generator	Timer divides incoming frequency by the value of the initial count loaded into it.
3—Square Wave	Produces a series of square waves with a period (measured in clock pulses) equal to the value loaded into the timer.
4—Software Retriggerable Strobe	Timer counts down the number of clock cycles loaded into it; then pulses its output. Software starts the next cycle.
5—Hardware Retriggerable Strobe	Timer counts down the number of clock cycles loaded into it; then pulses its ouput. Hardware-generated pulse initiates the next cycle.

The time-of-day signal in the original PC used the 8253 timer/counter to count out its longest possible increment, generating pulses at a rate of 18.2 per second. The pulses cause the time-of-day interrupt, which the PC counts to keep track of the time. These interrupts can also be used by programs that need to regularly investigate what the computer is doing; for instance, checking the hour to see whether it's time to dial up a distant computer. Note that reprogramming this channel of a PC has interesting effects on the time-of-day reported by the system, generally making the hours whiz by.

The speaker section of the 8253 works the same way, only it generates a waveform that is used to power the speaker and make sounds. Programs can modify any of its settings to change the sound of the speaker. Programs can also modify the channel that drives the memory controller, which may likely crash your computer.

The timer/counter of the AT is similar to that of earlier IBM computers except that it is based on a chip. In the AT, it provided three outputs—one to generate the 18.2 per second pulse that drives the time-of-day signal and interrupt; the second to provide a trigger for memory refresh cycles, fixed in the case of the AT to produce a signal with a period of 15 milliseconds; and a third to drive the speaker. Controls for these operate in the same way as those for the related PC functions and are found at the same I/O ports.

In its PS/2 series, IBM maintained the timer as a separate circuit, an 8253, just as in IBM's previous PCs and XTs. The timer is accessed and controlled through the same ports with the same commands. The newer IBM design differed, however, in the assignment of its three outputs. One still generates the 18.2 per second pulses to serve as the system timer, and another controls the speaker. The other channel, used for DMA operations in PC and XTs, is only used for diagnostics in the Models 25 and 30. Its output is unconnected. Its former function is handled by the System Support Gate Array.

In Micro Channel PS/2 models, the oscillator and timing functions are integrated into VLSI chips, but the function of the circuits remains compatible with the timers in previous computer models. However, some system timer functions were revised to help forestall disasters. As with the Models 25 and 30, the system timer has been freed of its DMA duty, that chore being handled by a gate array. The timer channel and I/O port address nominally assigned to that function—041(Hex)—are undefined in Micro Channel PS/2s. A third timer channel is instead assigned a "watchdog" function, overseeing the Micro Channel expansion bus.

This timer channel monitors the 18.2 times per second time-of-day interrupt. It counts the number of these interrupts that do not arrive on schedule. Should the total number of missed interrupts reach a critical value, it reports an error to the system. If a program goes awry and interferes with proper operation of the system interrupts, the watchdog reports an error, allowing corrective action to be taken.

In a single-user, single-tasking system, the watchdog is of dubious value. When the interrupts go away, both the executing program and the machine have effectively crashed. In a multitasking system, however, the watchdog gives the system a chance to save properly executing applications from the effects of one that crashes.

The watchdog can be defeated or its timing values adjusted through the I/O ports that control the timer (see fig. 8.1).

Modern PCs based on commercial chipsets duplicate the functions of the AT's 8254-2 timer chip in their own silicon. The time-of-day and speaker timers in these machines are programmable exactly as they are in the AT. Many systems use a third timer channel in the traditional manner to determine the intervals at which to refresh system memory. A few aim to prevent unintended disasters by relegating the memory refresh function to other circuits beyond the reach of your programs. As long as you don't plan to tinker with timers (that is, you don't do any hardware-level programming yourself) there's no reason to prefer one design over the other.

Register I/O Port address	Function
040 (Hex)	Timer 0 count
041 (Hex)	Timer 1 count
042 (Hex)	Timer 2 count
043 (Hex)	8253 Control register

Bit 0 - 0 = Binary counter 16-bits
      1 = Binary-coded decimal (BCD) counter (four decades)

Bits 1 to 3 -- Mode select in binary form

Bit 3	Bit 2	Bit 1	Mode
0	0	0	0
0	0	1	1
X	1	0	2
X	1	1	3
1	0	0	4
1	0	1	5

Bits 4 to 5 -- Read/load

Bit 5	Bit 4	Function
0	0	Counter latching operation
0	1	Read/load least significant byte only
1	0	Read/load most significant byte only
1	1	Read/load least significant byte first, then the most significant byte

Bits 6 to 7 -- Select counter

Bit 7	Bit 6	Function
0	0	Select counter 0
0	1	Select counter 1
1	0	Select counter 2
1	1	Illegal instruction

FIGURE 8.1. Registers and control of 8253 timer.

Real-Time Clock

Perhaps the most annoying characteristic of the first PCs was their bad habit of asking the time and date every time you switched them on. The inevitable response was to press down twice on the Enter key to load in the defaults. Obediently, the system would assume the day to be 1 January 1980 and the time midnight, and all your files would be time-stamped as if you had spent the wee hours of New Year's Day slaving away.

The AT and all more recent computers have avoided the problem by including a *real-time clock* among their support circuits. IBM set the pattern by using a specific clock circuit, the MC146818 chip, which also holds the CMOS memory that stores system setup information. Based on low-power CMOS circuitry, the MC146818 is designed to run constantly whether your PC is switched on or off. A battery of some kind in your system supplies power when the PC is unplugged or otherwise turned off.

The MC146818 measures time by counting pulses of a crystal oscillator operating nominally at 32.768 kilohertz, so it can be as accurate as a quartz watch. (The MC146818 can be programmed to accept other oscillator frequencies as well.) Many compatible PCs tell time as imaginatively as a four-year old child, however, because their manufacturers never think to adjust them properly. Most put a trimmer (an adjustable capacitor) in series with their quartz crystal, allowing the manufacturer—or anyone with a screwdriver—to alter the resonate frequency of the oscillator. Giving the trimmer a tweak can bring the real-time clock closer to reality—or further into the twilight zone. (You can find the trimmer by looking for the short cylinder with a slotted shaft in the center near the clock crystal, which is usually the only one in a PC with a kilohertz rather than megahertz rating.)

The real-time clock has a built-in alarm function. The MC146818 can be programmed to generate an interrupt when the hour, minute, and second of the time set for the alarm arrives. The alarm is set by loading the appropriate time values into the registers of the MC146818.

Many chipsets emulate the MC146818 in their internal circuitry. In addition, special real-time clock modules (which also mimic the MC146818) with integral batteries are also available.

Reading the clock inside the MC146818 (or the chipsets that emulate the MC146818) requires the same two-step process as reading or writing setup information. The clock is addressed through the same two I/O ports as setup memory: one port—070(Hex)—to set the location to read or write, and a second port—071(Hex)—to read or write the value. The assignment of clock data to byte locations is listed in Chapter 7, "The Basic Input/Output System" in Table 7.6.

Interrupt Controllers

Intel microprocessors understand two kinds of interrupts—software and hardware. A software interrupt is simply a special instruction in a program that's controlling the microprocessor. Instead of adding, subtracting, or whatever, the software interrupt causes program execution to temporarily shift to another section of code in memory.

A hardware interrupt causes the same effect but is controlled by special signals outside of the normal data stream. The only problem is that the microprocessors recognize far fewer interrupts than would be useful—only two interrupt signal lines are provided. One of these is a special case, the Non-Maskable Interrupt. The other line is shared by all system interrupts.

IBM's personal computer architecture nevertheless allows for several levels of interrupt, which are prioritized—a more important interrupt takes priority over one of lesser importance.

To organize the hardware interrupts of the PC series of computers, IBM selected the *8259 Interrupt Controller*. This chip handles eight interrupt signals, numbered zero through seven, assigning each one a decreasing priority as the numeric designation increases. Table 8.2 lists the interrupt assignments of the PC, XT, Portable PC, and PCjr computers.

TABLE 8.2. PC and XT Interrupt Assignments

Interrupt Number	Function
NMI	"Memory Parity Errors, Coprocessor"
IRQ0	Timer Output 0
IRQ1	Keyboard (Buffer Full)
IRQ2	"EGA Display; Network, 3278/79 Adapter"
IRQ3	Serial Port 2; Serial Port 4; SDLC Communications; BSC Communications; Cluster Adapter; Network (alternate); 3278/79 (alternate)
IRQ4	Serial Port 1; Serial Port 3; SDLC Communications; BSC Communications; Voice Communications Adapter
IRQ5	Hard Disk Controller
IRQ6	Floppy Disk Controller
IRQ7	Parallel Port 1; Cluster Adapter (alternate)

Source: IBM Corporation

Eight hardware interrupts—of which but six were available on the expansion bus—quickly proved inadequate for complex systems, so IBM nearly doubled that number in the AT. The arrangement, assignment, and interplay of these interrupts were altered substantially from the PC design.

The near-doubling of interrupts was accomplished by adding a second interrupt controller chip (another 8259A) to the system architecture by cascading it to the first. Therefore, the new chip is connected to another which, in turn, connects to the microprocessor. The chip closest to the microprocessor operates essentially as the single interrupt controller in a PC or XT. However, its interrupt two input is no longer connected to the PC bus. Instead, it receives the output of the second 8259A chip.

The interrupt channel on the bus that formerly led to the interrupt two input is now connected to interrupt nine on the second chip. This interrupt works the same with its new connection—the signal only needs to traverse two controllers instead of one before the interrupt swings into action. Despite its new number, AT interrupt nine functions just like PC interrupt two, with the same priority activated by the same control line.

Although each 8259A controller still handles individual interrupts on a priority level corresponding to the reverse of the numerical designation of their inputs, the cascaded arrangement of the two controllers results in an unusual priority system. Top priority is given to interrupts zero and one on the first chip. Because the second chip is cascaded to interrupt two on the new chip, the new, higher numbered interrupts that go through this connection get the next highest priority.

In fact, interrupt nine (which, remember, is actually the interrupt zero input of the second 8259A controller) gets top priority of all interrupts available on the expansion bus. The rest of the interrupts connected to the second controller receive the next priority levels in ascending order up to interrupt 15. Finally, the remaining interrupts on the first chip follow in priority, from interrupt three up to interrupt seven. AT interrupt assignments are shown in Table 8.3.

TABLE 8.3. AT Interrupt Assignments

Interrupt Number	*Function*
IRQ0	Timer Output 0
IRQ1	Keyboard (Buffer Full)
IRQ2	Cascade from IRQ9
IRQ3	Serial Port 2; Serial Port 4; SDLC Communications; BSC Communications; Cluster Adapter; Network (alternate); 3278/79 (alternate)
IRQ4	Serial Port 1; Serial Port 3; SDLC Communications; BSC Communications; Voice Communications Adapter
IRQ5	Parallel Port 2
IRQ6	Floppy Disk Controller
IRQ7	Parallel Port 1; Cluster Adapter (alternate)
IRQ8	Real-time Clock
IRQ9	Software redirected to INT 0A(Hex); Video; Network; 3278/79 Adapter
IRQ10	Reserved
IRQ11	Reserved
IRQ12	Reserved
IRQ13	Coprocessor
IRQ14	Hard Disk Controller
IRQ15	Reserved

Source: IBM Corporation

Just in case the 15 available interrupts (16 counting the special non-maskable interrupt) still don't stretch far enough, the AT bus makes provisions for *interrupt sharing*. IBM does not, however, implement interrupt sharing. That's left up to the designers of add-in componentry. It involves designing device hardware to allow interrupt sharing and writing not only the code for the software routines that get carried out as a result of the interrupt but program code to sort through the shared possibilities, arbitrate conflicting interrupt calls, and put everything back together again at the end of the interrupt. Best done in assembly language, it's not stuff that timid programmers play with.

Micro Channel Architecture brought the next revision in the interrupt structure of personal computers by switching to level-sensitive interrupts to make interrupt sharing more reliable. Although the level-sensitive interrupts work differently from and are incompatible with the edge-triggered interrupts used in previous IBM personal computers, the circuitry that controls them is familiar indeed. Micro Channel PS/2s use two *8259A* interrupt controllers—exactly the same chips as other IBM personal computers—arranged exactly as are those in an ordinary AT. That is, the second 8259A is cascaded to the interrupt two channel of the first. Interrupt priorities are the same in both the AT and Micro Channel designs.

The 8259A chip is capable of either edge-triggered or level-sensitive operation. In Micro Channel computers, the chips are initialized in level-sensitive mode. Circuits external to the 8259A chips prevent their being set up in edge-triggered mode.

In EISA machines, the same interrupts are supported as in ISA computers. EISA interrupts, however, can operate as either edge-triggered or level-sensitive, depending on whether servicing an ISA board (which would use edge-triggered signaling) or EISA board (which would use level-sensitive interrupts). Interrupt sharing is possible but only between EISA boards.

VL Bus links to the interrupt circuitry of the more conventional bus with which it works. Its single interrupt ties to interrupt channel nine of the primary bus.

PCI changes the interrupt structure entirely. Only four interrupt lines are available, and their function is left up to the designer of each individual expansion board. The PCI specification puts no limits on how these interrupt signals are used (the software driver that services the board determines that) but specifies level-sensitive interrupts so that the four signals can be reliably shared. The interrupt control circuitry is built into the bus control logic of the PCI chipset.

With the exception of PCI machines, the chipsets used by modern PCs, including most EISA machines, incorporate the interrupt controller function that mimics the AT interrupt structure, cascading two levels of interrupts. Some, however, reorganize the interrupt structure to eliminate the two-tier approach. In general, this change causes no problems. A few peripherals and programs depend on finding the exact AT interrupt structure and can demonstrate incompatibilities with these altered designs. The problems often can be avoided by reassigning interrupts so that the troublesome devices or software access interrupts that strictly follow the AT standard. In other words, if a device has difficulty when using interrupt two or nine in a PC, the problem often can be remedied by assigning it another interrupt.

Direct Memory Access

The best way to speed up system performance is to relieve the host microprocessor of all its housekeeping chores. Among the more time consuming is moving blocks of memory around inside the computer; for instance, shifting bytes from a hard disk (where they are stored) through its controller into main memory (where the microprocessor can use it). The memory moving chores can be handled by a special device called a *Direct Memory Access* or *DMA* controller.

This specialized chip only needs to know the base location of where bytes are to be moved from, the address to where they should go, and the number of bytes to move. After it has received that information from the microprocessor, the DMA controller takes command and does all the dirty work itself. The DMA controller used in all IBM computers is completely programmable and operated through a series of I/O registers.

DMA operations can be used to move data between I/O devices and memory. In theory, DMA operations could also expedite the transfer of data between memory locations, but this mode of operation is not supported by the basic IBM system design.

IBM first chose the 8237A-5 DMA controller for the PC and used the same chip in all later personal computers up to Micro Channel PS/2 models. The -5 in the designation is the speed rating of the chip (five megahertz) which closely matches the one and only clock in the PC and XT, 4.77 MHz. Each transfer of a byte under DMA control requires five cycles of the system clock, a total of 1,050 nanoseconds.

The 8237A-5 affords these computers four separate DMA channels, which can be used independently for memory moves. The PC design reserves one of these channels for refreshing system memory. The other three channels are available on the I/O bus. The PC and XT DMA can address only one megabyte, the maximum memory of those systems and the addressing limit of the eight-bit PC expansion bus.

In most IBM software, only one DMA channel is used at a time. Only on rare occasions, such as backing up a hard disk to floppy, are two channels needed. In such cases, it is convenient to pull data from the hard disk and immediately write it to the backup device. Many floppy disk-based backup systems do, in fact, use two DMA channels simultaneously for this purpose.

Normally, such operations should cause no problems. However, in 10-15 percent of the original PCs, such operations do not work properly because of defective 8237A chips. The chip errors don't normally show up (and didn't in the testing of the chips) because only one channel is typically used at a time.

The only sure cure for this problem is to replace the chip should its symptoms be noted. As this replacement is not easy—the ailing chip is soldered in place—and because the error is likely only to occur with a few backup programs, the procedure usually is not worthwhile. The better (and more affordable) strategy is to live with the bad chip, which won't otherwise misbehave, and avoid the software that causes the problem. This problem does not occur with other computers because the design of the 8237A chip has been revised to eliminate it.

The AT and most more recent PCs based on the AT model use the same DMA chip as the PC and XT, the 8237A-5, but augment it with a second chip. As with the AT interrupt controller, one channel of one of the DMA controller chips is used to cascade the second chip. With four channels per chip and one used for cascading, the net yield to the system is seven DMA channels. Each of these channels can address the full 16 megabyte range of the 80286 microprocessor, the addressing limit of the AT expansion bus.

Four of these DMA channels are eight bits wide and operate identically to those of the PC and XT. The other three channels on the second chip are a full 16-bits wide.

In the AT, each of the DMA controllers operates at one-half the microprocessor speed to stay within its speed rating. Therefore, in a six megahertz AT, the 8237A-5 operates at three megahertz. In an eight megahertz AT, the 8237A-5 operates at four megahertz. Because each DMA cycle requires five clocks, each takes 1,666 nanoseconds in a six-megahertz machine or 1,250 nanoseconds in an eight-megahertz machine. Note that even in an eight-megahertz AT in eight-bit mode, DMA transfers actually occur more slowly in the AT than in the PC. In 16-bit mode, however, AT DMA transfers are faster because the wider bus width permits more data to move through the controller.

DMA transfers in AT systems are faster than those in PCs but still not that fast. In fact, IBM determined the speed to be inadequate for hard disk access. Consequently, AT-style systems avoid DMA control for hard disk access and instead use programmed I/O; that is, the microprocessor itself manages hard disk transfers. Of course, this eliminates problems of simultaneously using two DMA channels when backing up the hard disk.

In IBM's Micro Channel Architecture, the DMA controller is incorporated into one of the very large-scale integration circuits on the system board. The design is functionally compatible with that of the AT and can mimic the operation of a pair of 8237A chips. However, the Micro Channel machines make an additional DMA channel available and offer an additional extended command set for control.

In a Micro Channel machine, DMA timing is essentially independent of the system clock. In general, each DMA cycle requires 600 nanoseconds from system board memory or 500 from an expansion board on the Micro Channel. Another few hundred nanoseconds of overhead is required to set up the entire transfer (which may consist of up to 64K cycles). Transfers can be either 8 or 16 bits at a time. Overall, Micro Channel DMA transfers are more than twice as fast as those of the AT, giving the newer computers a substantial performance advantage.

The initial Micro Channel design limited DMA addressing to 24 address lines, capping the reach of DMA to 16 megabytes of RAM. Starting with the PS/2 Models 90 and 95, Micro Channel DMA was given full 32-bit addressing.

EISA makes DMA more complex because of the three high-speed modes (Types A, B, and C) that are available in addition to ordinary AT DMA to accelerate data transfers (see Chapter 6, "The Expansion Bus"). EISA systems also support full 32-bit DMA addressing.

PCI doesn't allow conventional DMA control—no DMA signals are allocated—but accomplishes the same end through its bus arbitration. A bus master can act like a DMA controller and make transfers across the bus independently of the host microprocessor.

Modern PCs that require DMA controllers typically integrate the circuitry with the rest of the system support inside the chipset. They mimic a pair of cascaded 8237A DMA controllers, but most extend their addressing capabilities to the full four-gigabyte range supported by modern microprocessors.

Other Support Functions

One additional support chip is necessary in every PC, a *keyboard decoder*. This special purpose chip, an Intel 8042 in most PCs, an equivalent chip, or part of a chipset that emulates an 8042, links the keyboard to the motherboard. The primary function of the keyboard decoder is to translate the serial data that the keyboard sends out into the parallel form that can be used by your PC. As it receives each character from the keyboard, the keyboard decoder generates an interrupt to make your PC aware that you have typed a character. The keyboard decoder also verifies that the character was correctly received (by performing a parity check) and translates the scan code of each character. The keyboard decoder automatically requests the keyboard to retransmit characters that arrive with parity errors.

Each character in the serial data stream sent to the keyboard decoder comprises 11 bits—a start bit, eight bits of data, a parity bit, and a stop bit. The bits are synchronized to a clock signal originating inside the keyboards. In AT and more recent keyboards, the keyboard decoder also can send data to the keyboard to program its internal microprocessor. (Keyboards and scan codes are discussed more completely in Chapter 11, "Input Devices.")

Chipsets often include a variety of other functions to make the PC designer's life easier. These can include everything from controls for indicator lights for the front panel to floppy disk controllers. Exactly which functions are built into the chipset depends on the magnanimity of the chipset maker. Although adding more functions makes the chipset more complex and costly, a more feature-packed chipset also can give its maker a marketing advantage. Most modern chipset makers offer full-featured products that include floppy disk control circuitry, input/output ports (parallel, serial, mouse, keyboard, and game ports), and a connector for an embedded controller (IDE) hard disk. Some chipset manufacturers incorporate video (VGA) circuitry into their products as well.

If you are buying rather than designing a PC, you may find no particular advantage in the extreme integration of today's single-chip PCs. Although a single-chip solution is, in theory, more reliable than a three-chip PC, the difference may be between whether the machine ultimately fails when your great-great-grandchildren are playing with the system or when their children are reveling in the primitive glory of playing with an ancient PC. Probably the only important support circuit issue to ponder when purchasing a new PC is whether port, video, and floppy disk control circuitry on the motherboard can be defeated to eliminate I/O and interrupt conflicts with other expansion products. (IDE ports don't need defeatability because an unused IDE port acts as an expansion connector with nothing plugged in.) Other support chip issues represent only different paths to the same destination.

If a system doesn't have the right combination of support circuitry, it simply won't work like a PC. And if it has the right support circuitry, all you need is exactly what you should expect—a trouble-free PC that runs your favorite programs.

Chapter 9
The Power Supply

PCs require a continuous supply of carefully conditioned low-voltage direct current at several potentials. The power supply provides the necessary electricity, but does not protect against problems associated with utility-supplied power. Surge suppressors and backup power systems help to ensure that your PC gets the proper electrical diet.

All practical computers made today operate electronically. Moving electrons—electricity—are the media of their thoughts. Electrical pulses course from one circuit to another, switched off or on in an instant by logic chips. Circuits combine the electrical pulses together to make logical decisions and send out other pulses to control peripherals. The computer's signals stay electrical until electrons colliding with phosphors in the monitor tube push out photons toward your eyes or generate the fields that snap your printer into action.

Of course, your computer needs a source for the electricity that runs it. The power does not arise spontaneously in its circuits, but must be derived from an outside source. Conveniently, nearly every home in America is equipped with its own electrical supply that the computer can tap into. Such is the wonder of civilization.

But the delicate solid-state semiconductor circuits of today's computers cannot directly use the electricity supplied by your favorite utility company. Commercial power is an electrical brute, designed to have the strength and stamina to withstand the miles of travel between generator and your home. Your PC's circuits need a steady, carefully controlled trickle of power. Raw utility power would fry and melt computer circuits in a quick flash of miniature lightning.

For economic reasons, commercial electrical power is transmitted between you and the utility company as *alternating current,* the familiar *AC* found everywhere. AC is preferred by power companies because it is easy to generate and adapts readily between voltages (even to very high voltages that make long distance transmission efficient). It's called *alternating* because it reverses polarity—swapping positive for negative—dozens of times a second (arbitrarily 60 Hz in America; 50 Hz in Europe).

The changing or oscillating nature of AC enables transformers to increase or decrease voltage (the measure of driving force of electricity) because transformers only react to electrical changes. Electrical power travels better at higher voltages because waste (as heat generated by the electrical current flowing through the resistance of the long distance transmission wires) is inversely proportional to voltage. Transformers permit the high voltages used in transmitting commercial power—sometimes hundreds of thousands of volts—to be reduced to a safe level (nominally 117 volts) before it is led into your home.

As wonderful as AC is to power companies, it's an anathema to computer circuits. These circuits form their pulses by switching the flow of electricity tapped from a constant supply. Although computers can be designed that use AC, the constant voltage reversal would complicate the design so that juggling knives while blindfolded and riding a roller coaster would seem tame in comparison. Computers (and most electronic gear) use *direct current* or *DC* instead. Direct current is the kind of power that comes directly from a primary source—a battery—a single voltage that stays at a constant level (at least constant as long as the battery has the reserves to produce it). Moreover, even the relatively low voltage that powers your lights and vacuum cleaner would be fatal to semiconductor circuits. Tiny distances separate the elements inside solid state circuits, and high voltages can flash across those distances like lightning, burning and destroying the silicon along the way.

The intermediary that translates AC from your electrical outlets into the DC that your computer's circuits need is called the *power supply*. As it operates, the power supply of your PC attempts to make the direct current supplied to your computer as pure as possible, as close to the ideal DC power produced by batteries. The chief goal is *regulation*, maintaining the voltage as close as possible to the ideal desired by the circuits inside your PC.

Notebook and subnotebook computers have it easy. They work with battery power, which is generated inside the battery cells in exactly the right form for computer circuits—low voltage DC. However, even notebook computers require built-in voltage regulation because even pure battery power varies in voltage depending on the state of charge or discharge of the battery. In addition, laptop and notebook computers also must charge their batteries somehow, and their charges must make exactly the same electrical transformations as a desktop computer's power supply.

Power Supply Technologies

In electronic gear, two kinds of power supplies are commonly used: *linear* and *switching*. The former is old technology, dating from the days when the first radios were freed from their need for storage batteries in the 1920s. The latter rates as high technology, requiring the speed and efficiency of solid-state electronic circuitry to achieve the dominant position they hold today in the computer power market. These two power supply technologies are distinguished by the means used to achieve their voltage regulation.

Linear Power Supplies

The design first used for making regulated DC from utility-supplied AC was the *linear power supply*. At one time, they were the only kind of power supply used for any electronic equipment. When another technology became available, they were given the linear label because they then used standard linear (analog) semiconductor circuits, although a linear power supply need not have any semiconductors in it at all.

In a linear power supply, the raw electricity from the power line is first sent through a *transformer* that reduces its voltage to a value slightly higher than that required by the computer's circuits. Next, one or several *rectifiers*, usually semiconductor diodes, convert the now low-voltage AC to DC by permitting the flow of electricity in only one direction, blocking the reversals. Finally, this DC is sent through the *linear voltage regulator*, which adjusts the voltage created by the power supply to the level required by your computer's circuits.

Most linear voltage regulators work simply by absorbing the excess voltage made by the transformer, turning it into heat. A *shunt regulator* simply shorts out excess power to drive the voltage down. A *series regulator* puts an impediment—a resistance—in the flow of electricity, blocking excess voltage. In either case, the regulator requires an input voltage higher than the voltage it supplies to your computer's circuits. This excess power is converted to heat (that is, it is wasted). The linear power supply achieves its regulation simply by varying the waste.

Switching Power Supplies

The design alternative is the *switching power supply*. Although more complex, switching power supplies are more efficient and often less expensive than their linear kin. While designs vary, the typical switching power supply first converts the incoming 60 Hertz utility power to a much higher frequency of pulses (in the range of 20,000 Hz, above the range of normal human hearing) by switching it on and off using an electrical component called a *triac*.

At the same time the switching regulator increases the frequency of the commercial power, it regulates the commercial power using a digital technique called *pulse-width modulation*. That is, the duration of each power pulse is varied in response to the needs of the computer circuitry being supplied. The width of the pulses is controlled by the electronic switch; shorter pulses result in a lower output voltage. Finally, the switched pulses are reduced in voltage down to the level required by the computer circuits by a transformer and turned into pure direct current by rectification and filtering.

Switching power supplies earn their efficiency and lower cost in two ways. Switching regulation is more efficient because less power is turned into heat. Instead of dissipating energy with a shunt or series regulator, the switching regulator switches all current flow off, albeit briefly. In addition, high frequencies require smaller, less expensive transformers and filtering circuits. For these two very practical reasons, nearly all of today's personal computers use switching power supplies.

PC Power Needs

Modern computer logic circuits operate by switching voltages with the two different logic states (true or false, one or zero, for example) coded as two voltage levels—*high* and *low*. Every family of logic circuits has its own voltage standards. Most PCs today are built around the requirements of *Transistor-Transistor Logic* or *TTL*. In a TTL design, "high" refers to voltages above about 3.2 volts, and "low" means voltages lower than about 1.8 volts. The middle ground is undefined logically, an electrical guard band that prevents ambiguity between the two meaningful states. Besides the signals, TTL logic circuits also require a constant supply voltage that they use to power their thinking—it provides the electrical forces that throws their switches. TTL circuits nominally operate from a five volt supply. The power supplies used by all full-size IBM personal computers and PS/2s are designed to produce this unvarying five volts in great abundance—commonly 20 or more amperes.

PCs often require other voltages as well. The motors of most disk drives (hard and floppy) typically require 12 volts to make their spin. Other specialized circuits in PCs sometimes require bipolar electrical supplies. A serial port, for example, signals logic states by varying voltages between positive and negative in relation to ground. Consequently the mirror image voltages, -5 and -12 volts, must be available inside every PC, at least if it hopes to use any possible expansion boards.

In notebook computers, most of which have no room for generic expansion boards, all of these voltages are often unnecessary. For example, many new hard disks designed for notebook computers use five volt motors, eliminating the need for the 12 volt supply.

In addition, the latest generation of notebook computer microprocessors and support circuits are designed to operate with a 3.3 volt supply. These lower voltage circuits cut power consumption because—all else being equal—the higher the voltage, the greater the current flow, and the larger the power usage. Dropping the circuit operating voltage from 5 to 3.3 volts cuts the consumption of computer power by about half (the power usage of a circuit is proportional to the square of the current consumed).

Voltages and Ratings

The power supplies that you are most likely to tangle with are those inside desktop PCs, and these must produce all four common voltages to satisfy the needs of all potential combinations of circuits. In practical desktop PC power supplies, each of these four voltages (+5, -5, +12, and -12) is delivered in different quantities (amperages) because of the demands associated with each. The typical PC has much logic circuitry so it needs copious quantities of 5 volt power (20 to 25 amperes); it has two or three disk drives, so it needs quite a bit less 12 volt power (perhaps four or five amperes); and it has a few, almost trivial components requiring negative voltages (fractions of an ampere).

Most power supplies are rated and advertised by the sum of all the power they can make available, as measured in watts. The power rating of any power supply can be calculated by individually multiplying the current rating of each of the four voltages it supplies and summing the results. (Power in watts is equal to the product of voltage times current in amperes.) The power supplies in IBM computers range from 63.5 watts to 325; compatibles cover a similar range. Most modern full-size computers have power supplies of 200-220 watts.

Note that this power rating does not correspond to the wattage that the power supply draws from a wall outlet. All electronic circuits—and power supplies in particular—suffer from inefficiencies, linear designs more so than switching. Consequently, a power supply requires a wattage in excess to that it provides to your computer's circuits—at least when it is producing its full output. PC power supplies, however, rarely operate at their rated output. As a result, efficient switching power supplies typically draw less power than their nominal rating in normal use. For example, a PC with a 220 watt power supply with a typical dosage of memory (say four megabytes) and one hard disk drive likely draws less than 100 watts while it is operating.

When selecting a power supply for your PC, the rating you require depends on the boards and peripherals with which you want to fill your computer. A system board may require 15-25 watts; a floppy disk drive, 3-20 (depending on its vintage); a hard disk, 5-50 (also depending on its vintage); a memory or multifunction expansion board, 5-10. Table 9.1 lists the typical power demands of items you're likely to plug into your PC. Sum things up, and you see that 200 watts, even 150 watts, is more than adequate for any single-user system equipped with state-of-the-art components.

TABLE 9.1. Typical Device Power Demands

Device Class	Device Type	Power	Example
Floppy disk 5.25 inch	Full-height	12.6 watts drive	IBM PC diskette drive
Floppy disk drive	Half-height, 5.25 inch	12.6 watts	QumeTrak 142
Floppy disk drive	One-inch high, 3.5 inch	1.4 watts	Teac FD-235J
Graphics board	Two-board old technology	16.2 watts	IBM 8514/A
Graphics board	High performance, full length	13.75 watts	Matrox MGA
Graphics board	Accelerated half-card	6.5 watts	ATI VGA Wonder, Graphics Ultra+
Hard disk	Full-height, 5.25 inch	59 watts	IBM 10MB XT hard disk
Hard disk	Half-height, 5.25 inch	25 watts	[estimated]
Hard disk	One-inch high, 3.5 inch	6.5 watts	Quantum ProDrive LPS120S
Hard disk	2.5 inch	2.2 watts	Quantum Go Drive 120AT
Hard disk	Full-height, 3.5 inch	12 watts	Quantum ProDrive 210S
Modem	Internal, half-card	1.2 watts	Boca V.32bis
Network adapter	Ethernet, half-card	7..9 watts	Artisoft AE-2/T

Device Class	Device Type	Power	Example
System board	286, AT-size	25 watts	[estimated]
System board	386, XT-size	12 watts	Monolithic Systems MSC386 XT/AT
System board	486 or Pentium, AT-sized	25 watts	[estimated]

Source: Manufacturers' data sheets for selected representative products

Supply Voltage

Most power supplies are designed to operate from a certain line voltage and frequency. In the United States, utility power is supplied at a nominal 115 volts and 60 Hertz. In other nations, the supply voltage and frequency may be different. In Europe, for instance, a 230 volt, 50 Hertz standard prevails.

Most switching power supplies can operate at either frequency, so that shouldn't be a worry when traveling. (Before you travel, however, check the ratings on your power supply to be sure.) Linear power supplies are more sensitive. Because their transformers have less reactance at lower frequencies, 60 Hz transformers draw more current than their designers intend when operating on 50 Hz power. Consequently, they are liable to overheat and fail, perhaps catastrophically.

The switching power supplies in most PCs are also switchable. That is, they have a small switch on the rear panel that selects their operating voltage. Make sure that the switch is in the proper position for the available power before you turn on your computer (see fig. 9.1).

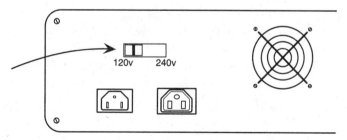

FIGURE 9.1. Power supply voltage selector.

When traveling in a foreign land, always use this power supply switch to adjust for different voltages. Do not use inexpensive voltage converters. Often these devices are nothing more than rectifiers that clip half the incoming waveform. Although that strategy may work for light bulbs, it can be disastrous to electronic circuitry. Using such a device can destroy your computer. It's not a recommended procedure.

IBM computers introduced since the XT Model 286 and a few compatibles have auto-adjusting, autoranging, or *universal power supplies* that automatically adjust themselves to the prevailing voltage and frequency. If you have a computer with such a power supply, all you need to do is plug the computer in, and it should work properly. Note that some of these universal power supplies accommodate any supply voltage in a wide range; others are limited to two narrow ranges, bracketing the two major voltage standards. Because you are unlikely to encounter a province with a 169.35 volt standard, these dual-range supplies are universal enough for world-wide use.

The Power-Good Signal

Besides the voltages and currents the computer needs to operate, IBM power supplies also provide another signal called *Power-Good.* Its purpose is to tell the computer that all is well with the power supply and the computer can operate normally. If the Power-Good signal is not present, the computer shuts down. The Power-Good signal prevents the computer from attempting to operate on odd-ball voltages (for example, those caused by a brown-out) and damaging itself. A bad connection or failure of the power-good output of the power supply also causes your PC to stop working just as effectively as a complete power supply failure.

Portable Computer Power

As with any PC, electricity is the lifeblood of notebook machines. With these machines, how-ever, emphasis shifts from power production to consumption. To achieve freedom from the need for plugging in, these totable PCs pack their own portable power—batteries. Although they are free from concerns about lightning strikes and utility bill shortfalls, they face a far less merciful taskmaster—gravity. The amount of power they have available is determined by their batteries and weight constrains battery size to a reasonable value (the reasonableness of which varies inversely with the length of the airport concourse and the time spent traveling). Compared to the almost unlimited electrical supply available at your nearby wall outlet, the power provided by a pound of batteries is minuscule, indeed, with total available energy measuring in the vicinity of five watt-hours.

The power supply in a notebook computer is consequently more concerned with minimizing waste rather than regulating. After all, battery power is close to ideal to begin with—smooth, unchanging DC at a low potential (voltage) that can be tailored to match computer circuitry with the proper battery selection. Regulation needs are minimum: a protection circuit to prevent too much voltage from sneaking in and destroying the computer and a low-voltage detection circuit to warn before the voltage output of the battery supply drops too low to reliably run the machine. Power-wasting shunt or series regulators are unnecessary because battery voltage is entirely predictable—it simply grows weaker as the charge is drained away.

Rather than regulation, management is the principal power issue in a portable PC. Circuitry inside the system monitors which resources are being used and, more importantly, which are not. Anything not being used gets shut off—for example, the backlight on the display screen, the spin of the hard disk, even the microprocessor in some systems.

With but a few exceptions, notebook computers also rely on a battery charger of some kind so that you can use rechargeable batteries for power. In essence and operation, the battery charger is little more than a repackaged power supply. Line voltage AC goes in, and low voltage DC (usually) comes out. The output voltage is close to that of the system's battery output, always a bit higher. (A slightly higher voltage is required so that the batteries are charged to their full capacity.)

Most of the time, the battery charger/power supply is a self-contained unit external to the notebook PC. Although they typically contain more than just a transformer, most people call these external power supplies *transformers* or *power bricks*. The name was apt when all external battery chargers used linear designs with heavy transformers, giving the device the size and heft approaching that of an actual clay brick. Modern external power supplies use switching designs, however, and can be surprisingly compact and light.

Manufacturers favor the external power supply design because it moves unnecessary weight out of the machine itself and eliminates high voltages from anywhere inside the computer. The design also gives you something else to carry and leave behind as well as a connection that can fail at an inopportune time.

The brick typically only reduces line voltage to an acceptable level and rectifies it to DC. All the power management functions are contained inside the PC.

No standard exists for the external battery chargers/power supplies of notebook computers. Every manufacturer—and often every model of PC from a given manufacturer—uses its own design. They differ as to output voltage, current, and polarity. You can substitute a generic replacement only if the replacement matches the voltage used by your PC and generates at least as much current. Polarity matching gives you two choices—right and wrong—and the wrong choice is apt to destroy many of the semiconductors inside the system. In other words, make certain of power polarity when plugging in a generic replacement power supply. (With most PCs, the issue of polarity reduces to a practical matter of whether the center or outer conductor of the almost-universal coaxial power plug is the positive terminal.) Also available are cigarette lighter adapters that enable you to plug many models of notebook computers into the standard cigarette lighter jack found in most automobiles. Again, you must match these to the exact make and model of the PC you plan to use, being particularly careful of the polarity of the voltage.

Most external power supplies are designed to operate from a single voltage (a few are universal, but don't count on it). That means you are restricted to plugging in and charging your portable PC to one hemisphere (or thereabouts) or the other. Moving from 117 volt to 230 volt electrical systems requires a second, expensive external charger. Experienced travelers often pack voltage converters to take care of electrical differences. Two kinds of converters are available: one that works with notebook PC chargers, and one that will likely destroy the charger and the computer as well.

Rectifying Power Converters

The simplest, smallest, lightest, and cheapest converter is nothing more than a diode (rectifier) that blocks half the AC wave from getting through, effectively cutting the voltage in half—sort of. The result is an odd-ball half-wave electrical supply apt to wreak both havoc and disaster with critical electronic circuits, such as your PC and its power supply. Although these converters work well with electric razors and hair dryers, never plug your PC into one.

Transformers

The other kind of converter is a simple transformer. Like all transformers, these converters are heavy (making them a joy to pack into an overnight bag). They are also relatively expensive. They are safe for powering your PC because they deliver normal AC at their outputs. Of course, they require that you carry two power adapter bricks with your notebook computer—its power supply and the converter—that together probably weigh more than the machine itself. In the long run—and the long concourse—you are better off buying a second battery charger/power supply for your PC.

Batteries

Think back to elementary school, and you probably remember torturing half a lemon with a strip of copper and one of zinc in another world-relevant experiment meant to introduce you to the mysteries of electricity. Certainly those memories come in handy if you are stuck on a desert island with a radio, dead batteries, a case of lemons, and strips of zinc and copper, but they probably seem as meaningless in connection with your PC as DOS 1.1. Think again. That juicy experiment should have served as an introduction to battery technology (and recalling the memories of it makes a good introduction to this section).

Battery Technologies

The lemon demonstrates the one way that chemical energy can be put to work, directly producing electricity. The two strips of metal act as *electrodes*. One gives off electrons through the chemical process of oxidation, and the other takes up electrons through chemical reduction. In other words, electrons move from one electrode, the *anode*, to another called the *cathode*. The acid in the lemon serves as an *electrolyte*, the medium through which the electrons are exchanged in the form of ions. Together the three elements make an electricity-generating device called a Galvanic *cell*, named after eighteenth-century chemist Luigi Galvani. Several such cells connected together comprise a *battery*.

Connect a wire from cathode to anode, and the electrons have a way to dash back and even up their concentration. That mad race is the flow of electricity. Add something in the middle—say a PC—and that electricity performs work on its way back home.

All batteries work by the same principle. Two dissimilar materials (strictly speaking, they must differ in oxidation potential, commonly abbreviated as E^0 value) serving as anode and cathode are linked by a third material that serves as the electrolyte. The choice of materials is wide and allows for a diversity of battery technologies. It also influences the storage density (the amount of energy that can be stored in a given size or weight of battery) and nominal voltage output.

Primary and Secondary Cells

Batteries can be divided into two types: *primary* and *secondary* or *storage*. In primary batteries, the creation of electricity is irreversible; one or both of the electrodes is altered and cannot be brought back to its original state except by some complex process (like re-smelting the metal). Secondary or storage batteries are rechargeable; the chemical reaction is reversible by the application of electricity. The electrons can be coaxed back whence they came. After the battery is discharged, the chemical changes inside can be reversed by pumping electricity into the battery again. The chemicals revert back to their original, charged state and can be discharged to provide electricity once again.

In theory, any chemical reaction is reversible. Clocks can run backwards, too. And pigs can fly, given a tall enough cliff. The problem is that when a battery discharges, the chemical reaction affects the electrodes more in some places than others; recharging does not necessarily reconstitute the places that were depleted. Rechargeable batteries work because the chemical changes inside them alter their electrodes without removing material. For example, an electrode may become plated with an oxide, which can be removed during recharging.

Primary and secondary (storage) batteries see widely different applications, even in PCs. Nearly every modern PC has a primary battery hidden somewhere inside, letting out a tiny electrical trickle that keeps the time-of-day clock running while the PC is not. This same battery also maintains a few bytes or kilobytes of CMOS memory to store system configuration information. Storage batteries are used to power just about every notebook computer in existence. (A few systems use storage batteries for their clocks and configuration memory.)

The most common batteries in the world are primary cells based on zinc and carbon electrodes. In these zinc/carbon batteries—formally called a *Leclanche dry cell* but better known as the flashlight battery—zinc (the case of the battery) serves as the anode; a graphite rod in the center acts as the cathode; and the electrolyte is a complex mixture of chemicals (manganese dioxide, zinc chloride, and ammonium chloride). *Alkaline batteries* change the chemical mix to increase storage density and shelf life. Other materials are used for special-purpose batteries, but with the exception of lithium these have not found wide application in PCs.

Ordinarily, alkaline batteries cannot be recharged, but Rayovac Corporation has developed a series of standard-sized alkaline cells called *Renewal batteries* that accept 25 to 100 recharges. To achieve their reusability, these cells combine novel fabrication techniques and a special microprocessor-controlled charger. The charger pulses power into discharged cells and measures the effect of each pulse. Renewal batteries cannot be charged with conventional battery chargers; in fact, they may explode if you try.

The most common storage batteries in the world are the *lead-acid batteries* used to start automobiles. These have electrodes made from lead (anode) and lead oxide (cathode) soaked in a sulfuric acid electrolyte. Not only are these batteries heavy—they are filled with lead, after all—but they contain a corrosive liquid that can spill anywhere. Some lead-acid batteries are sealed to avoid leakage.

Gelled-electrolyte lead-acid batteries, often called simply *gel cells,* reduce this problem. In these batteries, the electrolyte is converted to a colloidal form like gelatin, so it is less apt to leak out. Unlike most lead-acid batteries, however, gel cells are degraded by the application of continuous low-current charging after they have been completely charged. (Most lead-acid batteries are kept at full capacity by such "trickle" charging methods.) Consequently, gel cells require special chargers that automatically turn off after the cells have been fully charged.

Nickel-Cadmium Cells

In consumer electronic equipment, the most popular storage batteries are *nickel-cadmium cells,* often called *nicads.* These batteries use electrodes made from nickel and cadmium, as the name implies. Their most endearing characteristic is the capability to withstand in the range of 500 full charge/discharge cycles. They are also relatively lightweight, have a good energy storage density (although about half that of alkaline cells), and tolerate trickle charging. On the downside, cadmium is toxic.

The output voltage of most chemical cells declines as the cell discharges because the reactions within the cell increase its internal resistance. Nicads have a very low internal resistance—meaning they can create high currents—which changes little as the cell discharges. Consequently, the nicad cell produces a nearly constant voltage until it becomes almost completely discharged, at which point its output voltage falls precipitously. This constant voltage is an advantage to the circuit designer because fewer allowances need to be made for voltage variations. However, the constant voltage also makes determining the state of a nicad's charge nearly impossible. As a result, most battery-powered computers deduce the battery power they have remaining from the time they have been operating rather than by actually checking the battery state.

Nicads are known for another drawback: memory. When some nicads are partly discharged, left in that condition, and then later recharged, they may lose capacity. The cure for the memory problem is *deep discharge*—discharging the battery to its minimum working level and then charging the battery again. Deep discharge does not mean totally discharging the battery, however. Draining nearly any storage battery absolutely dry will damage it and shorten its life. If you discharge a nicad battery so that it produces less than about one volt (its nominal output is 1.2 volts), it may suffer such damage. Notebook computers are designed to switch off before their batteries are drained too far, and deep discharge utilities do not push any farther so you need not worry in using them. But don't try to deeply discharge your system's batteries by shorting them out—you risk damaging the battery and even starting a fire.

According to battery makers, newer nicads are free from memory effects. In any case, to get the longest life from nicads the best strategy is to operate them between extremes—operate the battery through its complete cycle. Charge the battery fully; run it until it is normally discharged; then fully charge it again.

Nickel-Metal Hydride Cells

A relative newcomer in battery technologies is the nickel-metal hydride cell (abbreviated NiMH). These cells have all the good characteristics of nicads, but lack the cadmium—substituting heavy metals that may also have toxic effects. Their chief strength is the capability to store up to 50 percent more power in a given cell. In addition, they do not appreciably suffer from memory effects.

Both nicads and nickel-metal hydride cells suffer from *self-discharge*. Even sitting around unused, these cells tend to lose their charge at a high rate in the vicinity of 30 percent per month.

Most PC batteries and battery chargers are designed to be plugged in continuously without any detrimental effects on the battery. In fact, the best strategy is to leave your PC plugged in even after it is fully charged, detaching it from its charger only when you need to take the machine on the road. The trickle charge will not hurt it (in fact, the battery charging circuitry may switch off once the battery is charged), and you will always be ready to roam.

Clock Batteries

Nearly every PC since the AT was introduced in 1984 has had a time-of-day clock built into its system board circuitry. To keep proper track of the hours, days, and eons, this clock needs to run continuously even when the computer itself is switched off or unplugged. The source for the needed power is a small battery.

Different manufacturers have taken various approaches to supplying this power. IBM led the way by using *lithium primary batteries* in a plastic holder accessible at the rear of the system unit.

With the first PS/2 computers, the battery moved inside, but still relied on lithium technology. Some more recent machines use Dallas integrated clock modules (Dallas being the name of the manufacturer). These, too, have built-in lithium cells.

Lithium cells have several notable aspects. They offer a high-energy density, packing much power for their size. Moreover, they have a very long shelf life. Whereas conventional zinc/carbon dry cells lose potency after a year or so even when no power is being drawn from them, lithium cells keep most of their power for a decade. These qualities make lithium cells suited to providing clock power because today's solid-state clocks draw a minuscule amount of power—so small that when battery and circuit are properly matched, battery life nearly equals shelf life.

The downside of these lithium cells is that they are expensive and often difficult to find. Another shortcoming is that the metals used in them result in an output voltage of three volts per cell. A one-cell lithium battery produces too little voltage to operate standard digital circuits; a two-cell lithium battery produces too much.

Of course, engineers can always regulate away the excess voltage, and that is typically done. Poor regulator design, however, wastes more power than is used, robbing the battery of its life. Some PCs suffer from this design problem and consequently give frightfully short battery life.

One advantage of the Dallas clock module is that its circuitry is matched with its built-in battery to optimize its life, which is nominally ten years. The disadvantage of the module is that most are soldered to system boards—meaning that in ten years you are guaranteed to need a visit to the repair shop to have the module replaced.

Many IBM-compatible computer makers avoid the expense and rarity of lithium batteries by adding battery holders for four (or so) type AA cells. Because zinc/carbon and alkaline cells produce 1.5 volts each, a four pack puts out the same six volts as a dual-cell lithium battery and can suffer the same problems in improperly designed PCs—only more so because the cells have shorter lives. A three-pack of AA cells produces 4.5 volts, which is adequate for most clock circuits and need not be hampered by regulation. Special alkaline PC battery modules are available that combine three ordinary cells into one package with the proper connector to match most system boards. The pin connectors used on system boards designed to accommodate such batteries follow a de facto standard, as shown in Figure 9.2.

Notebook Power

Portable computers put contradictory requirements on their batteries; they must produce as much power for as long as possible, yet be as small and light as possible. Filling those needs simultaneously is impossible, so notebook computer batteries are always a compromise.

All three of the most popular storage batteries—lead-acid, nicad, and nickel-hydride—are used in notebook and subnotebook computers. From your perspective as an end user, however, the technology doesn't matter as long as the result is a PC that you can carry without stretching your arms too long and use without getting caught short too often. Odds are, however, you will see nickel-hydride batteries increasing in popularity in notebook computers because of their greater storage density and less hazardous nature.

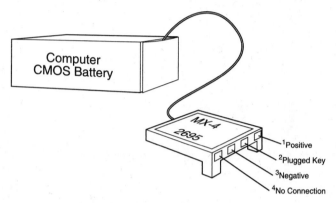

FIGURE 9.2. Battery Power Connector.

Notebook computer makers traditionally design the packaging for the batteries of their machines. These custom designs enable them to better integrate the battery with the rest of the notebook package. It also makes you dependent on the computer manufacturer for replacement batteries. (Most packs have standard-size cells inside. You can crack the battery pack open and replace the cells, but the effort is rarely worth the reward.)

This situation is changing. One battery manufacturer (Duracell) has proposed standard sizes for rechargeable batteries for notebook computers (see figs. 9.3, 9.4, and 9.5).

Rather than battery type or packaging, care is most important with computer batteries. If you take proper care of your PC's batteries, they will deliver power longer—both more time per charge and more time before replacement.

Battery Safety

The maximum current any battery can produce is limited by its internal resistance. Zinc/carbon batteries have a relatively high resistance and produce small currents, on the order of a few hundred milliamperes. Lead-acid, nickel-cadmium, and nickel-hydride batteries have very low internal resistances and can produce prodigious currents. If you short the terminals of one of these batteries, whatever produces the short circuit—wires, a strip of metal, a coin in your pocket—becomes hot because of resistive heating. For example, you can melt a wrench by placing it across the terminals of a fully charged automotive battery. Or you can start a fire with something inadvertently shorting the terminals of the spare nickel-cadmium battery for your notebook or subnotebook computer. Be careful and never allow anything to touch these battery terminals except the contacts of your notebook PC.

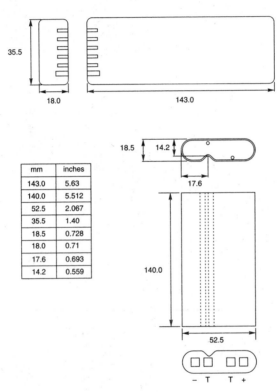

mm	inches
143.0	5.63
140.0	5.512
52.5	2.067
35.5	1.40
18.5	0.728
18.0	0.71
17.6	0.693
14.2	0.559

FIGURE 9.3. Duracell standard notebook PC battery.

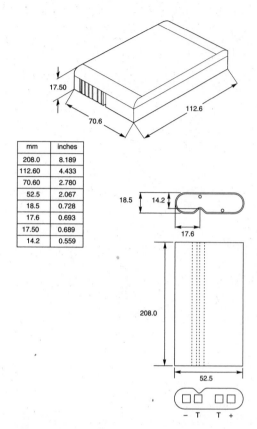

mm	inches
208.0	8.189
112.60	4.433
70.60	2.780
52.5	2.067
18.5	0.728
17.6	0.693
17.50	0.689
14.2	0.559

FIGURE 9.4. Duracell standard notebook PC battery.

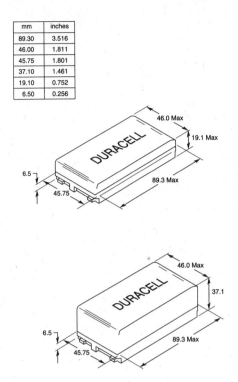

mm	inches
89.30	3.516
46.00	1.811
45.75	1.801
37.10	1.461
19.10	0.752
6.50	0.256

FIGURE 9.5. Duracell standard notebook PC battery.

When a battery is charged, a process called *electrolysis* takes place inside. If you remember your high school science experiments, electrolysis is what you did to break ordinary water into hydrogen and oxygen using electricity. Hydrogen is an explosive gas; oxygen is an oxidizer. Both are produced when charging batteries. Normally these gases are absorbed by the battery before they can do anything (such as explode), but too great a charging current (as results from applying too high a voltage) can cause them to build up. Trying to charge a primary battery produces the same gas build-up. As a result, the battery can explode from too great an internal pressure, or from combustion of the gases. Even if the battery does not catastrophically fail, its life will be greatly reduced. In other words, use only the charger provided with a portable PC battery and never try to hurry things along.

Nearly all batteries contain harmful chemicals of some kind. Even zinc-carbon batteries contain manganese, which is regarded as hazardous. All batteries present some kind of environmental hazard, so be sure to properly dispose of them. Some manufacturers are beginning to provide a means of recycling batteries. Encourage them by taking advantage of their offers.

Desktop PC Power Supplies

Most PCs package their power supplies as a subassembly that's complete in itself and simply screws into the chassis and plugs into the system board and other devices that require its electricity. The power supply itself is ensconced in a metal box perforated with holes that let heat leak out and prevent your fingers from poking in.

In fact, the safety provided by the self-contained and fully-armored PC power supply is one of the prime advantages of the original IBM design. All the life-threatening voltages—in particular, line voltage—are contained inside the box of the power supply. Only low, non-threatening voltages are accessible—that is, touchable—on your PC's system board and expansion boards. You can grab a board inside your PC even when the system is turned on and not worry about electrocution (although you may burn yourself on a particularly intemperate semiconductor or jab an ill-cut circuit lead through a finger).

Grabbing a board out of a slot of an operating computer, however, is not safe for the computer's circuits. Pulling a board out is apt to bridge together some pins on its slot connector, if but for an instant. As a result, the board (and your PC's motherboard) may find unexpected voltages attacking, possibly destroying, its circuits. These surprises are most likely in EISA systems because of their novel expansion connectors. In other words, never plug in or remove an expansion board from a PC that has its power switched on. Although you may often be successful, the penalty for even one failure should be enough to deter your impatience.

In most PCs, the power supply serves a secondary function. The fan that cools the power supply circuits also provides the airflow that cools the rest of the system. This fan also supplies most of the noise that PCs generate while they are running. In general, the power supply fan operates as an exhaust fan—it blows outward. Air is sucked through the other openings in the power supply from the space inside your system. This gives dust in the air taken into your PC a chance to settle anywhere on your system board before getting blown out through the power supply.

Power Supply Selection

Two standards have emerged for the physical size of the PC power supply package—one that fits into the chassis of the original PC and XT, and another that fits the full-size AT chassis. AT-size power supplies are taller and wider than PC/XT models, measuring 5-7/8 x 8-3/8 x 5-7/8 inches (HWD) with a notch taken out of the inboard bottom corner to allow extra space inside the computer chassis for the system board. PC/XT-size power supplies measure about 4-3/4 x 8-3/8 x 5-1/2 inches.

Although it is obvious that the AT power supply cannot fit into the smaller XT-size chassis, you may be surprised to discover that the smaller XT power supply also cannot fit properly into an AT chassis. The placement of screws and other functional parts is different enough that the little box cannot fit correctly in the big box.

Other system design variations may frustrate your power supply replacement efforts. The more effort that a PC maker uses in designing its own identifiable system, the farther that system varies from the accepted standards. Larger manufacturers—AST, Compaq, Dell, IBM, NEC, and others—typically use a ground-up design philosophy that requires power supplies be matched to a custom designed case. This means that they forego either of the two standard power supply packages for something that suits their purposes better. As a result, a power supply failure in one of these systems is a more expensive disaster than in systems from smaller manufacturers who use standard-size parts. A proprietary power supply may cost $400 or more, whereas a standard power supply retails for $50 or less.

Beyond mere size, power supplies come in two classes—the generic and the glamorous. Generic power supplies make no claims except that they deliver the volts and amps you need. They likely originate in some part of the Far East that you can't pronounce and even less imagine. They are the cheap ones with prices often below $50—and they work, at least for a while. In fact, many are likely to be the same units that nestle themselves in your favorite compatible computers.

The glamorous watt-makers promise some grand advantage over their generic siblings. More watts, less noise, more wind, and so on. The glamorous demands a premium price and may earn a premium guarantee. Whether you need one depends on your sensibilities and motivations. Most PCs are adequately served by the low-end power supplies. If your PC operates without problems on a 100-degree day, you probably don't need better cooling, although a quieter fan gives anyone's ears a break. In other words, peace and quiet can overrule purely budgetary sense, but the decision is entirely personal.

Power Supply Mounting

Standard-size power supplies also are standard in their mounting. In all cases, the big chrome power supply box is held in place by four screws in the back panel of the computer. The front is secured by two fingers stamped from the computer chassis so that the power supply does not stress the rear panel of the PC.

After you remove the top of your computer's case and locate the power supply, you see that four of the screws in the rear panel roughly coincide with the four corners of the backside of the power supply. When you face the rear of the computer, the four screws are on the left half of the rear panel, arranged roughly in a rectangle (see fig. 9.6). Remove these screws, and the power supply will be loose inside the chassis but not entirely free.

Before you attempt to lift the power supply out, remove the power supply connectors from each disk drive and the two connectors from the system board. Finally, slide the power supply box about one inch forward in the chassis until it bumps lightly against the rear of the disk drive bay or disk drives. The power supply should then lift out of the chassis without further ado.

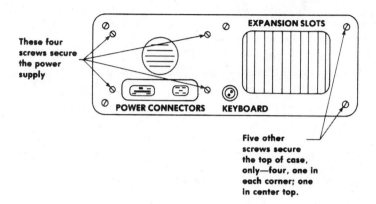

FIGURE 9.6. Power supply rear panel screws.

Installing a new or replacement power supply is equally easy. First, properly orient the supply so that the power switch protrudes through the notch cut in the top of the chassis. Then lower the power supply straight down into the chassis into the empty space left by the old power supply.

Before attempting to screw the new power supply into place, push it toward the front of the chassis and gently into the drive bays. Then, while pressing it down, push the power supply back toward the rear panel of the chassis. This front-then-back slide should slip the two steel fingers on the computer chassis through the slots at the bottom of the power supply to hold it in place. You may also want to attach the power supply connectors before you screw the power supply down.

Finally, screw the power supply into place. Start all four screws, but give them no more than two full turns before you have all four started. This enables you to move the power supply slightly to line up all four holes. If you tighten one screw first, you may find that the rest of the holes in the power supply do not line up with those in the chassis. When all four screws have been started, drive them all home.

Power Connections

All IBM-standard PC, XT, and AT power supplies have two kinds of connectors dangling from them. Two of them go to the system board; the rest are designed to mate with tape and disk drives.

Mass Storage Power

The tape and disk drive connectors supply five and twelve volts respectively to operate those devices. The connectors come in two sizes and both are polarized so that you can install them properly. The original drive power connector was roughly rectangular in cross-section, but had two of its corners chamfered so that it fit in its matching jack on the drive in only one orientation. The newer, miniaturized power connectors used by many 3.5-inch drives has a polarizing ridge that enables you to insert it only in the proper orientation. If either kind of drive connector doesn't seem to fit, don't force it! Instead, rotate it 180 degrees and try again. Likely it will slide into place (see fig. 9.7).

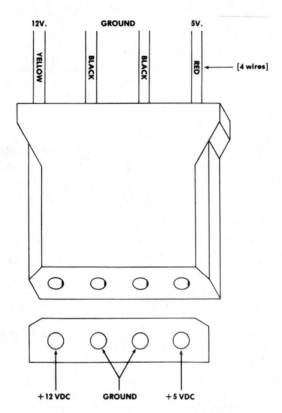

FIGURE 9.7. Mass storage device power connector.

PCs and some compatible computers are decisively frugal with their power connectors, supplying only two outlets. Powering more than two drives requires a Y-adapter that splits the power lines two ways. Figure 9.8 shows a Y-adapter cable that increases the available drive power connectors by one. Although you can make such a cable if you have the right connectors, it is easier and often cheaper to buy one from a drive vendor ready-made. An even better idea is to replace the meager PC power supply with one that can supply more current because the factory standard supply really doesn't have the capacity for operating multiple mass storage devices other than their standard two-floppy endowment.

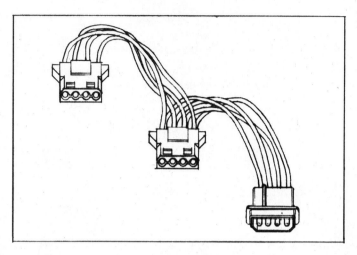

FIGURE 9.8. A sample Y-cable.

System Board Power

The two system board power connectors on standard power supplies are not identical. Each has its own repertory of voltages. On most PC power supplies these connectors are labeled *P8* and *P9*. The lower number attaches to the mating connector on the PC system board, typically the one nearer the rear of the chassis.

Not all system boards match the two Burndy connectors standard on most power supplies. PS/2s often (but, again, not always) combine the two connectors into one. Other system board manufacturers sometimes use slightly different Molex connectors. Unfortunately, Burndy and Molex connectors are not entirely compatible.

One difference between the two connector types is that the pins of a Burndy are rectangular. Molex system board connectors use smaller, square pins. Only with great effort can you mate dissimilar connectors together. Check the style of pins required by your system board before you order a power supply. The only way to be sure about the style of the connector is to disconnect one of them (with your PC switched off, of course) to examine the shape of its pins.

The Burndy connectors used by most power supplies are supposed to be keyed so that you cannot put one in the wrong place. Unfortunately, many replacement power supplies are shipped without the proper keying.

If you examine the power connectors meant to attach to the system board, you see that one side of the connector has one or more small tabs sticking out. If just one is longer than the rest, the connector is keyed. If all are the same length, the connector has not been keyed. You can key it by cutting off all but the one right tab using a pair of diagonal cutters (see fig. 9.9).

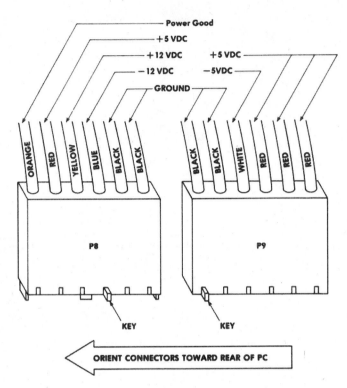

FIGURE 9.9. Keying of system board power connectors.

Another way to make sure that the system board connectors are in their proper positions is by the color codes of the wires. Proper installation puts black wires in the middle—that is, the black wires on the connectors adjoin one another.

Power Protection

Normal line voltage is often far from the 115 volt alternating current you pay for. It can be a rather inhospitable mixture of aberrations like spikes and surges mixed with noise, dips, and interruptions. None of these oddities is desirable, and some can be powerful enough to cause errors to your data or damage to your computer. Although you cannot avoid them, you can protect your PC against their ill effects.

Power Line Irregularities

Power line problems can be broadly classed into three basic categories: overvoltage, undervoltage, and noise. Each problem has its own distinct causes and requires a particular kind of protection.

Overvoltage

The deadliest power line pollution is *overvoltage*—lightning-like high-potential spikes that sneak into your PC and actually melt down its silicon circuitry. Often the damage is invisible—except for the very visible lack of image on your monitor. Other times, you can actually see charred remains inside your computer as a result of the overvoltage.

As its name implies, an overvoltage gushes more voltage into your PC than the equipment can handle. In general—and in the long run—your utility supplies power that's very close to the ideal, usually within about 10 percent of its rated value. If it always stayed within that range, the internal voltage regulation circuitry of your PC could take its fluctuations in stride.

Short duration overvoltages larger than that may occur too quickly for your utility's equipment to compensate, however. Moreover, many overvoltages are generated nearby, possibly within your home or office, and your utility has no control over them. Brief peaks as high as 25,000 volts have been measured on normal lines, usually due to nearby lightning strikes. Lightning doesn't have to hit a power line to induce a voltage spike that can damage your PC. When it does hit a wire, however, everything connected to that circuit is likely to take on the characteristics of a flash bulb.

Overvoltages are usually divided into two classes by duration. Short-lived overvoltages are called *spikes* or *transients* and last from a nanosecond (billionth of a second) to a microsecond (one millionth of a second). Longer duration overvoltages are usually termed *surges* and can stretch into milliseconds.

Sometimes power companies do make errors and send too much voltage down the line, causing your lights to glow brighter and your PC to teeter closer to disaster. The occurrences are simply termed overvoltages.

Most AC-power PCs are designed to withstand moderate overvoltages without damage. Most machines tolerate brief surges in the range of 800 to 2,000 volts. On the other hand, power cords and normal home and office electrical wiring breaks (by arcing over between the wiring conductors) at potentials between about 4,000 and 6,000 volts. In other words, electrical wiring limits the maximum surge potential your PC is likely to face to no more than about 6,000 volts. Higher voltage surges simply can't reach your PC.

Besides intensity and energy, surges also differ in their *mode*. Modern electrical wiring involves three conductors: *hot, neutral,* and *ground.* Hot is the wire that carries the power; neutral provides a return path; and ground provides protection. The ground lead is ostensibly connected directly to the earth.

A surge can occur between any pairing of conductors: hot and neutral, hot and ground, or neutral and ground. The first pairing is termed *normal mode*. It reflects a voltage difference between the power conductors used by your PC. When a surge arises from a voltage difference between hot or neutral and ground, it is called *common mode*.

Surges caused by utility switching and natural phenomena—for the most part lightning—occur in the normal mode. They have to. The *National Electrical Code* requires that the neutral lead and the ground lead be bonded together at the service entrance (where utility power enters a building) as well as at the utility line transformer typically hanging from a telephone pole near your home or office. At that point, neutral and ground must have the same potential. Any external common mode surge becomes normal mode.

Common mode surges can, however, originate within a building because long runs of wire stretch between most outlets and the service entrance, and the resistance of the wire allows the potential on the neutral wire to drift from that of ground. Although opinions differ, recent European studies suggest that common mode surges are the most dangerous to your equipment. (European wiring practice is more likely to result in common mode surges because the bonding of neutral and ground is made only at the transformer.)

Undervoltage

An *undervoltage* occurs when your equipment gets less voltage than it expects. Undervoltages can range from *sags*, which are dips of but a few volts, to complete outages or *blackouts*. Durations vary from nearly instantaneous to hours—or days, if you haven't paid your light bill recently.

Very short dips, sags, and even blackouts are not a problem. As long as they are less than a few dozen milliseconds—about the blink of an eye—your computer should purr along as if nothing happened. The only exceptions are a few old computers that have power supplies with very sensitive Power Good signals. A short blackout may switch off the Power Good signal, shutting down your computer even though enough electricity is available. (See Appendix A, "Ancient History.")

Most PCs are designed to withstand prolonged voltage dips of about 20 percent without shutting down. Deeper dips or blackouts lasting for more than those few milliseconds result in shut down. Your PC is forced to cold start, booting up afresh. Any work you have not saved before the undervoltage is lost.

Noise

Noise is a nagging problem in the power supplies of most electronic devices. It comprises all the spurious signals that wires pick up as they run through electromagnetic fields. In many cases, these signals can sneak through the filtering circuitry of the power supply and interfere with the signals inside the electrical device.

For example, the power cord of a tape recorder might act like an antenna and pick up a strong radio signal. The broadcast could then sneak through the circuitry of the recorder and mix with the music it is supposed to be playing. As a result, you might hear a CB radio maven croaking over your Mozart.

In computers, these spurious signals could confuse the digital thought coursing through the circuitry of the machine. As a practical matter, they don't. High-quality computers are designed to minimize the leakage of their signals from inside their cases into the outside world to minimize your computer's interfering with your radio and television. The same protection against signals getting out works extremely well against other signals getting in. Personal computers are thus well-protected against line noise. You probably won't need a noise filter to protect your computer.

Then again, noise filtering doesn't hurt. Most power-protection devices have noise filtering built into them because it's cheap, and it can be an extra selling point (particularly to people who believe they need it). Think of it as a bonus. You can take advantage of its added protection—but don't go out of your way to get it.

Overvoltage Protection

Surges are dangerous to your PC because the energy they contain can rush through semiconductor circuits faster than the circuits can dissipate it—the silicon junctions of your PC's integrated circuits fry in microseconds. Spikes and surge protectors are designed to prevent most short-duration, high-intensity overvoltages from reaching your PC. They absorb excess voltages before they can travel down the power line and into your computer's power supply. Surge suppressors are typically connected between the various conductors of the wiring leading to your PC. They work by conducting electricity only when the voltage across their leads exceeds a certain level, that is they conduct and short out the excess voltage in spikes and surges before it can pop into your PC. The voltage at which the varistor starts conducting and clipping spikes and surges is termed its *clamping voltage.*

The most important characteristics of overvoltage protection devices are how fast they work and how much energy they can dissipate. Generally, a faster *response time* or *clamping speed* is better. Response times can be as short as picoseconds—trillionths of a second. The larger the energy handling capacity of a protection device, the better. Energy handling capacities are measured in watt-seconds or joules. Devices claiming the capability to handle millions of watts are not unusual.

Four kinds of devices are most often used to protect against surges: Metal Oxide Varistors (MOVs), gas tubes, avalanche diodes, and reactive circuits. Each has its own strengths and weaknesses. Typically, commercial surge protectors use several technologies in combination.

Metal Oxide Varistors

The most popular surge protection devices are based on *Metal Oxide Varistors* or *MOVs*, disc-shaped electronic components typically made from a layer of zinc oxide particles held between two electrodes. The granular zinc oxide offers a high resistance to the flow of electricity until the voltage reaches a breakover point. The electrical current then forms a low-resistance path between the zinc oxide particles that shorts out the electrical flow.

MOVs are the most popular surge protection component because they are inexpensive to manufacture and easy to tailor to a particular application. Their energy-handling capability can be increased simply by enlarging the device (typical MOVs are about an inch in diameter; high power MOVs may be twice that).

The downside to MOVs is that they degrade. Surges tend to form preferred paths between the zinc oxide particles, reducing the resistance to electrical flow. Eventually, the MOV shorts out, blowing a fuse or (more likely) overheating the MOV until it destroys itself. The MOV can end its life in flames or with no external change at all—except that it no longer offers surge protection.

Gas Tubes

Gas tubes are self-descriptive: tubes filled with special gases with low dielectric potential designed to arc-over at predictable low voltages. The internal arc short circuits the surge. Gas tubes can conduct a great deal of power—thousands of kilowatts—and react quickly, typically in about a nanosecond.

On the negative side, a gas tube does not start conducting (and suppressing a surge) until the voltage applied to it reaches two to four times the tube's rating. The tube itself does not dissipate the energy of the surge; it just shorts it out, allowing your wiring to absorb the energy. Moreover, the discharge voltage of a gas tube can be affected by ambient lighting (hence most manufacturers shield them from light).

Worst of all, when a gas tube starts conducting, it doesn't like to stop. Typically, a gas tube requires a reversal of current flow to quench its internal arc, which means that the power going to your PC could be shorted for up to 8.33 milliseconds. Sometimes gas tubes continue to conduct for several AC current cycles, perhaps long enough for your PC power supply to shut down. (Many PC power supplies switch off when power interruptions exceed about 18 milliseconds.)

Avalanche Diodes

Avalanche diodes are semiconductor circuits similar to zener diodes that offer a high resistance to electrical flow until the voltage applied to them reaches a breakover potential. At that point, they switch on and act as conductors to short out the applied current. Avalanche diodes operate more quickly than other protection devices, but have limited energy capacity, typically from 600 to 1,500 watts.

Reactive Circuits

While MOVs, gas tubes, and avalanche diodes share the same operating principle—shorting out the surge before it gets to your PC—the *reactive surge suppressor* is different. The typical reactive surge suppressor uses a large inductance to resist the sharp voltage rise of a surge and spread it out over a longer time. Adding a capacitor tunes the reactance so that it can convert the surge into a semblance of a normal AC waveform. Other noise on the power line is also automatically absorbed.

Unfortunately, this form of reactive network has severe drawbacks. It doesn't eliminate the surge—only spreads out its energy. The size of the inductor determines the spread, and a large inductor is required for effective results. In addition, the device only works on normal mode surges. The reactance also can cause a common mode surge in the wiring leading to the device by raising the neutral line above ground potential.

Most commercial surge suppressors combine several of these technologies along with noise reduction circuitry, and better surge suppressors arrange them in multiple stages, isolated by inductors, to prolong life and improve response time. Heavy-duty components such as gas tubes or large MOVs form the first stage and absorb the brunt of the surge. A second stage with tighter control (more MOVs or avalanche diodes) knocks the surge voltage down farther.

Thanks to the laws of thermodynamics, the excess energy in a surge cannot just disappear; it can only change form. With most surge suppression technologies (all except reactive devices), the overvoltage is converted into heat dissipated by the wiring between the device and the origin of the surge as well as inside the surge suppressor itself. The power in a large surge can destroy a surge suppressor so that it yields up its life to protect your PC.

Because they degrade cumulatively with every surge they absorb, MOVs are particularly prone to failure as they age. Eventually, an MOV will fail, sometimes in its own lightning-like burst. Although unlikely this failure will electrically damage the circuits of your computer, it can cause a fire—which can damage not just your PC, but your home, office, or self. Some manufacturers (for example, IBM) forego putting MOVs in their power supplies to preclude the potential for fire, which they see as less desirable than a PC failure.

An MOV-based surge suppressor also can fail more subtly—it just stops sucking up surges. Unbeknownst to you, your PC can be left unprotected. Many commercial surge suppressors have indicators designed to reveal the failure of an internal MOV.

In any case, a good strategy is to replace MOV-based surge suppressors periodically to ensure that they do their job and to lessen the likelihood of their failure. How often to replace them depends on how dirty an electrical diet you feed them. Every few years is generally a sufficient replacement interval.

Three devices help your computer deal with undervoltages. *Voltage regulators* keep varying voltages within the range that runs your PC, but offer no protection against steep sags or blackouts. The *standby power system* and *uninterruptible power system* (or *UPS*) fight against blackouts.

Voltage regulators are the same devices your utility uses to try to keep the voltage it supplies at a constant level. These giant regulators consist of large transformers with a number of *taps* or *windings*—outputs set at different voltage levels. Motors connected to the regulators move switches that select the taps that supply the voltage most nearly approximating normal line voltage. These mechanical regulators are gargantuan devices. Even the smallest of them is probably big enough to handle an entire office. In addition, they are inherently slow on the electrical time scale, and they may allow voltage dips long enough for data to be lost.

Solid-state voltage regulators use semiconductors to compensate for line voltage variations. They work much like the power supply inside your computer, but can compensate over a wider range.

The *saturable reactor* regulator applies a DC control current to an extra control coil on the transformer, enough to "saturate" the transformer core. When saturation is achieved, no additional power can pass through the transformer. Regulating the DC control current adjusts the output of the transformer. These devices are inherently inefficient because they must throw away power throughout their entire regulating range.

Ferroresonant transformer regulators are "tuned" into saturation much the same as a radio is tuned—using a capacitor in conjunction with an extra winding. This tuning makes the transformer naturally resist any change in the voltage or frequency of its output. In effect, it becomes a big box of electrical inertia that not only regulates, but also suppresses voltage spikes and reduces line noise.

The measure of quality of a voltage regulator is its *regulation*, which specifies how close to the desired voltage the regulator maintains its output. Regulation is usually expressed as the output variation for a given change in input. The *input range* of a regulator indicates how wide a voltage variation the regulator can compensate for. This range should exceed whatever variations in voltage you expect to occur at your electrical outlets.

Blackout Protection

Both standby and uninterruptible power systems provide blackout protection in the same manner. They are built around powerful batteries that store substantial current. An *inverter* converts the direct current from the batteries into alternating current that can be used by your computer. A battery charger built into the system keeps the reserve power supply fully charged at all times.

Because they are so similar, the term UPS is often improperly used to describe both standby and uninterruptible power systems. They differ in one fundamental characteristic: the electricity provided by a standby power system is briefly interrupted in the period during which the device switches from utility power to its own internal reserves. An uninterruptible power system, as its name indicates, avoids any interruption to the electricity supplied to the device it protects. If your PC is sensitive to very short interruptions in its supply of electricity, this difference is critical.

Standby Power Systems

As the name implies, the standby power system constantly stands by, waiting for the power to fail so that it can leap into action. Under normal conditions—that is, when utility power is available—its battery charger draws only a slight current to keep its source of emergency energy topped off. The AC power line from which the standby supply feeds is directly connected to its output, and thence to the computer. The batteries are out of the loop.

When the power fails, the standby supply switches into action—*switch* being the key word. The current-carrying wires inside the standby power supply that lead to the computer are physically switched from the utility line to the current coming from the battery-powered inverter.

The switching process requires a small but measurable amount of time. First, the failure of the electrical supply must be sensed. Even the fastest electronic voltage sensors take a finite time to detect a power failure. Even after a power failure is detected, another slight pause occurs before the computer receives its fresh supply of electricity while the switching action itself takes place. Most standby power systems switch quickly enough that the computer never notices the lapse. A few particularly unfavorable combinations of standby power systems and computers, however, may result in the computer shutting down during the switch.

Most standby power systems available today switch within one-half of one cycle of the AC current they are supplied—that's less than ten milliseconds, quick enough to keep nearly all PCs running as if no interruption occurred. Although the standby power system design does not protect again spikes and surges, most SPSes have other protection devices installed in their circuitry to ensure that your PC gets clean power.

Uninterruptible Power Systems

Traditionally, an uninterruptible power system supplied uninterrupted power because its output did not need to switch from line power to battery. Rather, its battery was constantly and continuously connected to the output of the system through its inverter. This kind of UPS always supplied power from the batteries to the computer. The computer was thus completely isolated from the vagaries of the AC electrical line. New UPS designs are more like standby systems, but use clever engineering to bridge over even the briefest switching lulls. They, too, deliver a truly uninterrupted stream of power, but can be manufactured for a fraction of the cost of the traditional design.

In an older UPS, the batteries are kept from discharging from the constant current drain of powering your computer by a large built-in charger. When the power fails, the charger stops charging, but the battery—without making the switch—keeps the electricity flowing to the connected computer. In effect, this kind of UPS is the computer's own generating station only inches away from the machine it serves, keeping it safe from the polluting effects of lightning and load transients. Dips and surges can never reach the computer. Instead, the computer gets a genuinely smooth, constant electrical supply exactly like the one for which it was designed.

Newer UPSes connect both the input power and the output of their inverters together through a special transformer, which is then connected to your PC or other equipment to be protected. Although utility power is available, this kind of UPS supplies it through the transformer to your PC. When the utility power fails, the inverter kicks in, typically within half a cycle. The inductance of the transformer, however, acts as a storage system and supplies the missing half-cycle of electricity during the switchover period.

The traditional style of UPS provides an extreme measure of surge and spike protection (as well as eliminating sags) because no direct connection bridges the power line and the protected equipment—spikes and their kin have no pathway to sneak in. Although the transformer in the new style of UPS absorbs many power line irregularities, overall it does not afford the same degree of protection. Consequently, these newer devices usually have other protection devices (such as MOVs) built in.

Backup Power System Specifications

The most important specification to investigate before purchasing any backup power device is its *capacity* as measured in volt-amperes (VA) or watts. This number should always be greater than the rating of the equipment to which the backup device is to be connected.

In alternating current (AC) systems, watts do not necessarily equal the product of volts and amperes (as they should by the definition that applies in DC systems) because the voltage and current can be out of phase with one another. That is, when the voltage is at a maximum, the current in the circuit can be at an intermediary value. So the peak values of voltage and amperage may occur at different times.

Power requires both voltage and current simultaneously. Consequently, the product of voltage and current (amperage) in an AC circuit is often higher than the actual power in the circuit. The ratio between these two values is called the *power factor* of the system.

What all this means to you is that volt-amperes and watts are not the same thing. Most backup power systems are rated in VA because it is a higher figure thanks to the power factor. You must make sure that the total VA used by your computer equipment is less than the VA available from the backup power system. Alternatively, you must make sure that the wattage used by your equipment is less than the wattage available from the backup power system. Don't indiscriminately mix the VA and watts in making comparisons.

To convert a VA rating to a watt rating, multiply the VA by the power factor of the backup power supply. To go the other way—watts to VA—divide the wattage rating of the backup power system by its power factor. (You can do the same thing with the equipment you want to plug into the power supply, but you may have a difficult time discovering the power factor of each piece of equipment. For PCs, a safe value to assume is 2/3.)

Standby and uninterruptible power systems also are rated as to how long they can supply battery power. This equates to the total energy (the product of power and time) that they store. Such time ratings vary with the VA the backup device must supply—because of finite battery reserves, it can supply greater currents only for shorter periods. Most manufacturers rate their backup systems for a given number of minutes of operation with a load of a particular size instead of in more scientific fashion using units of energy. For example, a backup system may be rated to run a 250 volt-ampere load for 20 minutes.

If you want an idea of the maximum possible time a given backup supply can carry your system, check the ratings of the batteries it uses. Most batteries are rated in ampere-hours, which describes how much current they can deliver for how long. To convert that rating to a genuine energy rating, multiply it by the nominal battery voltage. For example, a 12 volt, 6 amp-hour battery could, in theory, produce 72 watt-hours of electricity. That figure is theoretical rather than realistic because the circuitry that converts the battery DC to AC wastes some of the power and because ratings are only nominal for new batteries. However, the numbers you derive give you a limit. If you have only 72 watt-hours of battery, you can't expect the system to run your 250 VA PC for an hour. At most, you could expect 17 minutes; realistically, you might expect 12 to 15.

You probably will not need much time from a backup power system, however. In most cases, five minutes or less of backup time is sufficient because the point of a backup supply is not to keep a system running forever. Instead, the backup power system is designed to give you a chance to shut down your computer without losing your work. Shutting down shouldn't take more than a minute or two.

Different backup power systems also vary as to their output *waveform*. The perfect waveform is one that matches that the utility company makes—*sine wave* (or sinusoidal) power in which the voltage and current smoothly alternates between polarities 120 times a second (a frequency of 60 Hz). Although the most desirable kind of power, smooth sine waves are difficult to generate. Electronic circuits such as those in a backup power system more easily create *square waves*, which abruptly switch between polarities. The compromise between the two—called *modified square waves* or *modified sine waves* (depending on who's doing the talking)—approximates the power factor of sine waves by modifying the duty cycle of square waves or stepping between two or more voltage levels in each power cycle. Figure 9.10 shows the shapes of these different wave forms.

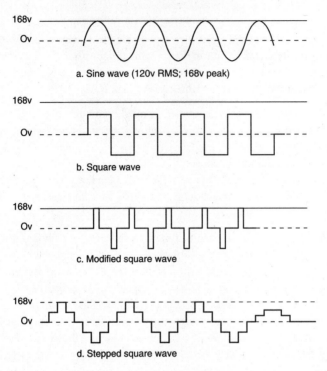

FIGURE 9.10. Power supply wave forms.

Considerable debate surrounds the issue of whether sine or square waves are better for your equipment. In truth, however, most waveform arguments are irrelevant for PC backup power systems. Although a backup power system should produce square waves most efficiently, commercial products show little correspondence between efficiency and output waveform. On the other hand, square waves are richer in harmonics that can leak into sensitive circuits as noise. But the filters in all PC power supplies effectively eliminate power line-related noise.

Perhaps the biggest shortcoming attributed to square waves is that they can cause transformers to overheat. All PC power supplies, however, use high-speed switching technology, which breaks the incoming waveform into a series of sharp pulses regardless of whether it is made from sine or square waves. Most monitors also use switching power supplies. Only linear power supplies, now rare in electronic equipment, may be prone to overheating from square waves. Moreover, standby power systems, the inverters of which are designed to operate your equipment for less than 30 minutes, do not provide local power long enough to create a severe overheating problem.

Chapter 10
Cases

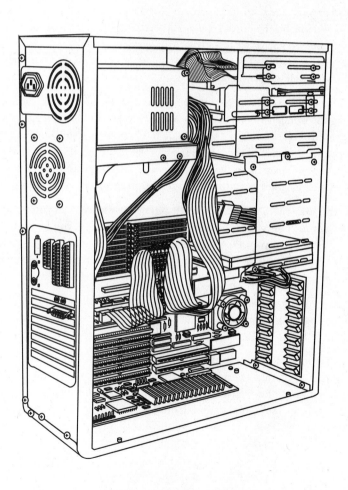

What holds your whole PC together is its case, but a case is more than a mere box. The case provides secure mountings for circuit boards and mass storage devices. It protects delicate circuitry from all the evils of the outside world—both mechanical and electrical—and it protects the world and you from what's inside the PC—both interference and dangerous voltages. Cases come in various sizes, shapes, and effectiveness at their protective tasks to match your PC and the way you plan to use it.

The case is the physical embodiment of your PC. In fact, the case *is* the body of your PC. It's a housing, vessel, and shield that provides the delicate electronics of the computer a secure environment in which to work. It protects against physical dangers—forces that may act against its circuit boards, bending, stressing, even breaking them with deleterious results to their operation. It also prevents electrical short circuits that may be caused by the in-fall of the foreign objects that typically inhabit the office—paper clips, staples, letter openers, beer cans, and bridgework. The case also guards against invisible dangers, principally strong electrical fields that could induce noise that would interfere with the data handling of your system, potentially inducing errors that would crash your system.

The protective shield of the case works both ways. It also keeps what's inside your PC inside your PC. Among the wonders of the workings of a computer, two in particular pose problems for the outside world. The electrical voltages inside the PC can be a shocking discovery if you accidentally encounter them. And the high-frequency electrical signals that course through the computer's circuits can radiate like radio broadcasts and interfere with the reception of other transmissions—which includes everything from television to aircraft navigational beacons.

Your PC's case also has a more mundane role. Its physical presence gives you a place to put the things that you want to connect to your computer. Drive bays allow you to put mass storage devices within ready reach of your PC's logic circuits while affording the case's protection to your peripherals. In addition, your PC's case gives your expansion boards a secure mounting and provides them the same mechanical and electrical shelter as the rest of the system.

The case can play a more mundane role, too. It also can serve as the world's most expensive monitor stand, raising your screen to an appropriate viewing, elevated high above the clutter and confusion of your desktop.

Compounding the function of your computer's case is the need to be selective. Some of what's inside your PC needs to get out—heat, for instance. And some of what's outside needs to get in—such as signals from the keyboard and power from your electrical outlets. In addition, the computer case must form a solid foundation upon which your system can be built. It must give disk drives a firm base and hold electrical assemblies out of harm's way. Overall, the simple case may not be as simple as you think.

Mechanical Matters

The obvious function of the case is mechanical—you can see it and touch it as a distinct object. And it steals part of your desktop, floor, or lap when you put it to work. It has a definite size—always too small when you want to add one more thing but too large when you need to find a place to put it (and particularly when that place happens to be inside your carry-on luggage). The case also has a shape, which allows you the best access to all those computer accouterments, like the slot into which you shove your backup tapes. But shape and color also are part of your PC's style, which can set one system apart from the boring sameness of its computer kin.

In computers, form dictates function as much (if not more) than it does for any other type of office equipment. Computers have the shape they have so that they can hold what you want to put inside them—primarily all those expansion options that give your machine power and ability. It needs to be large enough to accommodate the expansion boards you want to plug in as well as provide adequate space for all the floppy and hard disks, optical, and tape drives your PC and life would not be complete without.

The sizes of both boards and drives are pre-ordained—set long ago and forever invariant. The case must be designed around the needs of each. But creating a case is more than a matter of allocating box-like space for options. The case also needs to provide a place for such mandatory system components as power supplies and loudspeakers. In addition, everything must be arranged to allow air to freely flow around everything to bring your PC's circuitry and peripherals a breath of cooling fresh air.

Not all computer manufacturers, however, give that much thought to the cases into which they pack their products. Many (if not most) simply select a case from some other manufacturer that specializes in molding plastic and bending steel. Thanks to a mixture of the forethought of the case-maker and dumb luck, these amalgamations work out and everyone is happy—the case-maker who made the original sale, the computer-maker who gets a cheap box to slide his equally cheap electrical works into, and you get a deal on the system that you buy.

Nevertheless, you still have options open to you when you select a PC or buy a case into which to put your own computer creation. To make the right decision—and to ensure that your computer as a whole suits your needs and continues to do so for a long life—you need to know your options and all of their ramifications.

XT Size

The place to begin a discussion of cases is with the first case design, the metal package that surrounded the original IBM PC and its younger cousin, the XT. These set the pattern for all machines to come. Although dimensions may vary, the majority of desktop computers still abide by some variation of the PC/XT layout. Moreover, even after nearly a decade and a half, the package is still current. You can buy ready-built computers in this exact size case or find empty shells widely available on the parts market. It has become an industry standard called *XT size*, after IBM's most popular product in this package. The last IBM product to use this exact case design was the Model XT 286.

Although superficially identical, the cases of IBM's PC and XT computers were different, reflecting their difference in expansion slot spacing and number (one-inch spacing of five slots for the PC; 0.8-inch spacing and eight slots for the XT). Squeezing in the extra slots drew its own penalty. Because the space used by the slots overlapped that of the drive bays, two slots could not extend the full length of the case. These *short slots* would accept expansion boards no longer than seven inches. Despite this shortfall in slot length, all of the cases of current PCs and those sold in the replacement market follow the XT pattern.

The success of the XT design is a case of success breeding success. Not that IBM's designers had any extraordinary insights and somehow managed to create the "one true computer case." The original design was more pragmatic with its fundamental design dictated by function and fit. Space at the front for two disk drives of the then-current "miniature" format (full-height 5.25-inch drives), a power supply tucked behind the drives, and a system board lining the rest of the case to the left—its size determined by the amount of circuitry required to build a computer. The height of the case was set by the needs of the full-height drives and the expansion board format.

Mix in the competing need to keep things compact, and the result was functional, if not inspired. The *footprint* of the XT case (the amount of desk space it needed) measured 21 inches wide by 17 inches deep. Its height, to allow for expansion boards and three-eighths inch underneath (just enough so you could lose a pencil—maybe the designers did have *some* kind of inspiration!), measured 5.5 inches (see fig. 10.1).

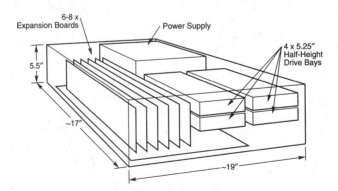

FIGURE 10.1. PC/XT size case.

Fabrication was designed to be easy—and cheap—as suited a machine of unknown destiny. The bottom of the case formed the computer's *chassis*, the frame or foundation to which all the important mechanical components of the system are bolted. The top was simpler still—a flat piece of steel with the sides rolled down to a bottom lip. With this design, the chassis provided a full steel bottom, front, and back. The steel lid provided sides top, left, and right giving the PC built into the case steely protection and interference prevention on all sides. A molded plastic front panel added a decorative touch.

The chassis and lid mated at the rear panel, which quickly proved to be the weakest part of the design. Originally, IBM provided only three screws to hold the top to the bottom and electrically connect the full-surround of shielding. This was one of the biggest weaknesses of the original desk. When IBM made a true commitment to the PC design and upgraded the original machine to hold an astounding 256K of RAM on its system board (up from 64K), it added two screws, for a total of five, to ensure better mechanical and electrical integrity. Other vendors may use a differing number of screws, but the fastening system remains one of the most predictable in the business.

The other weak aspect of the original PC/XT case design was its provision for mounting disk drives. Full-height floppy disk drives slid into either of two bays formed from a steel tray. Drives were held in place on only one side because the side-by-side installation of two drives made the space (and screw holes) between the drives inaccessible. Consequently, drives were insecure in their mountings—so insecure IBM had to add a screw through the bottom of the case to keep the hard disk of the XT in place. Moreover, the bay made no provision for half-height devices— an understandable situation considering that no half-height drives were readily available when the machines were introduced. Later IBM machines did provide for half-height drive mounting. Most other case vendors do likewise: all that's needed is punching a second set of drive-mounting slots in the sides of the drive bay.

AT Size

The XT case has another drawback: size. The power of PCs grew faster than could be accommodated within the confines of the XT case. Even today, a fully expanded PC may demand more space than the XT case can accommodate. The need for room to roam arises particularly with each new generation of microprocessor—when a new design is introduced support circuits usually haven't had enough development time to be reduced to a single ASIC. The motherboard needs a lot of real estate for circuit layout, more than can be crammed into the XT footprint even after liberally coating the motherboard with grease and persuading it to fit by gently bending, folding, stapling, and mutilating.

IBM faced this problem when it introduced its first "advanced" personal computer, the AT. A new, more commodious case relieved the size restrictions on motherboards and has since remained a primary standard for case design in the PC industry. The foundation of the AT design was basically a continuation—a chassis with a matching lid, both fabricated from steel, and a decorative plastic front panel (and an easily removable decorative plastic panel to fit over the rear of the machine).

To accommodate the larger system board required by the AT's then-advanced design, the system unit was broadened by two inches (to 23 by 17 inches), and its height was increased by nearly an inch, allowing both taller expansion boards and accommodations for a stack of three half-height devices in the mass storage bays. A taller power supply with greater reserves was also fitted. To accommodate the large system board, however, the base of the power supply had to be cut away.

As with the PC, two side-by-side mass storage bays were installed, but IBM reserved the inboard (left) bay for hard disk drives that required no access to their front panels for media changes. Because the large system board required space for its circuits under the drive bay, this inboard bay had to end more than an inch above the bottom of the case, restricting it to a single full-height device while the outboard (right) bays provided space for three half-height drives, two of which had front panel access (see fig. 10.2).

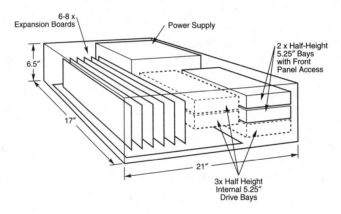

FIGURE 10.2. AT-size case.

Drive mounting was the real innovation of the AT case. Mass storage devices are secured on both sides by sturdy mounting rails that slide into channels on either side of the drive bay. The two-sided mounting prevents the drive in the bay from bouncing or rattling around during shipment as they would in one-sided PC mounting.

The new design made drive removal and installation relatively easy—providing you had hands small enough or skin tough enough so that you didn't bloody your knuckles reaching behind the drive to connect or disconnect its various cables. The mounting rails were secured by two brackets that screwed into the front panel of the chassis.

True AT size cases use exactly this mounting scheme with rails that match those used by IBM down to a fraction of an inch. Other manufacturers developed individual variations on the IBM theme, either to distinguish themselves or to make manufacturing easier.

One additional AT case innovation was motivated by security concerns. A PC and its data are vulnerable to anyone who can switch on a machine and probe its mass storage. Or the entire mass storage system can disappear by simply popping open the case with a screwdriver. Replace the lid, and the damage won't be obvious until someone boots the machine, possibly days later.

To help prevent such problems, IBM added access control to its AT cases, a strategy that most computer and case-makers now follow. The AT case set the pattern. A *keylock* using a cylindrical key (the high-security type similar to the ones you find on pay phones and Coke machines) both physically latched the lid on the case and electrically disabled the keyboard. Twist the key off, and you keep your fingers out of the box and prevent their doing damage by dancing on the keyboard.

The keylock complemented a small *control panel* that incorporated a power-on indicator, which helped diagnose monitor problems. (Nothing on your screen? Is the little green light on the computer lit?) In addition, a disk activity indicator—a small red LED light—let you know when your hard disk was accessing data (just in case you couldn't feel your desk shake).

IBM never developed the AT case beyond this arrangement, but various compatible computer makers refined the details. Most AT-compatible computers have added front panel access to all of the drive positions in the case. The internal bays of most machines also have been subdivided to accommodate either a pair of half-height drives or a single full-height device. Some PC makers have even elaborated on the control panel with indicators to entertain you and incidentally help in diagnosing system problems. All retain the generous space available for a large motherboard.

Mini-AT Size

A few inches may not seem like much, but the change between XT and AT cases represents a huge increase in apparent mass. While an XT resided on a desktop, an AT dominated it. But the larger size of the AT brought its own benefits, primarily the ability to use larger expansion boards that could pack more circuitry and features into an expansion slot.

Some compatible manufacturers hit upon the great compromise—an XT-size footprint in an AT-height case. The result was the *mini-AT*. A better description might be "tall-XT" cases because all their horizontal dimensions and accommodations (including system board size) match the XT standard; they equal the AT only in expansion slot area and drive-bay height.

The advantage of this design is simply the smaller space it requires on your desk—compared to the ordinary AT—coupled with the capability to accommodate any expansion board. Although not as popular as they once were, tall AT-size expansion boards still appear on the market, often as the basis for some of the most desirable, high-performance products. The downside of the mini-AT case is its inevitable compromises—slicing off those inches eliminates some space in the expansion board area so one or two slots may be pared off or truncated into short slots. Also, the access inside is tighter (see fig. 10.3).

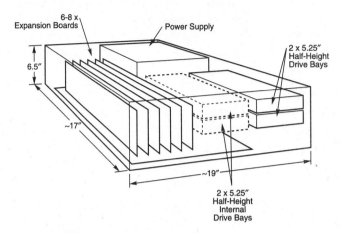

FIGURE 10.3. Mini-AT case.

The mini-AT case is one of the most popular available. Although its overall space savings is actually modest compared to a full AT-size box, it is aesthetically pleasing. And it affords designers all sorts of possibilities for squeezing in small drive bays. For XT-size and smaller motherboards, it is probably the best overall compromise.

Small-Footprint PCs

With today's advanced chipsets and integrated microprocessors such as Intel's 486SL, motherboards measuring only a few square inches are possible and even the XT and mini-AT cases loom like caverns in accommodating one of them. True miniaturization demands a case of smaller dimensions. The generic term for such boxes is the *small-footprint PC*. In general, the term describes a case trimmed smaller than the XT horizontal dimensions yet still able to accommodate those taller AT-size expansion boards.

Achieving that smaller size requires a big trade-off: accommodations. The principal loss is in expansion slots. To shave down the height of these tiny cases while conserving the capability of handling tall AT-size expansion boards, small footprint machines move their options on edge. Instead of boards sliding into slots vertically, these tiny PCs align them horizontally. Typically their system boards remain horizontal in the case and have a single ISA expansion slot. A special expansion board rises vertically with additional ISA slot connectors on one side to allow you to slide in several ordinary expansion boards (typically three) parallel to the system board.

Drive accommodations suffer, too. Although the exact assortment of drive possibilities varies with system design, most small footprint machines roughly halve the number of bay possibilities in larger designs. Instead of two side-by-side stacks of two drives, some machines have a single stack. Others put two half-height bays side by side. More modern machines squeeze in at least one 3.5-inch or smaller internal drive bay (see fig. 10.4).

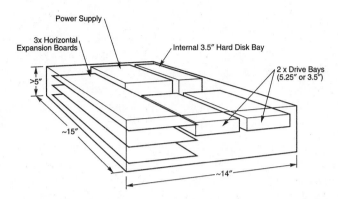

FIGURE 10.4. Small footprint case.

With the capacities possible inside today's 3.5-inch hard disk drives (500MB and beyond), the overall storage capabilities of these machines is not a major concern. The chief shortcoming is in variety of drive options. Two bays means one floppy disk drive and one something else—your choice: second floppy, tape backup, removable cartridge hard disk, CD-ROM, whatever. Although you can add other peripherals externally, you pay more for self-contained products and add to your office mess with a clutter of wires.

Another problem besides the obvious space and expansion limitations of the small-footprint design is that horizontal mounting of expansion boards also has a shortcoming. The horizontal boards impede the normal convective air flow that would otherwise cool the components on the board. Moreover, the lower boards can serve as stoves, heating the boards installed atop them.

As fewer expansion boards are installed into PCs (because of more functions being integrated on the system board) and large scale integration trims the power consumption and heat generated by circuits, this problem decreases in magnitude. Moreover, the demonstration Green PCs that forego traditional bus expansion for low-power PCs entirely eliminates the problem. Nevertheless, if you want to squeeze conventional expansion into a small case, you need to put the most component-laden of your expansion boards in the top slot so the other boards can keep their cool.

IBM embraced the downsizing philosophy with the introduction of its initial PS/2 machines, essentially trying to eliminate the 5.25-inch form factor. With the introduction of the Models 57 and 90, for example, the need for drive accommodations for CD-ROM had become mandatory and IBM allowed for larger bays. If you have visions of expanding your PC into the realm of multimedia, today or a year from now, you'll need to think about the space requirements of your drives.

Tower-Style Cases

At the other end of the packaging continuum from the small-footprint PC is the machine designed to be as large as logic allows—the *tower-style* system. Designed to stand upright on the floor, they are free from the need of minimizing the desk space they require. Instead, they concentrate on expandability, allowing as many expansion boards as standard system board designs permit and a wealth of drive bays.

Standing on edge is enough to qualify a PC as a tower. The internal accommodations vary as much as the aesthetic tastes. Most—but not all—larger machines can happily house an AT-size motherboard. Most—but not all—can accommodate at least five 5.25-inch half-height devices. You can't tell by looking at the outside of the case what fits inside. The accommodations need to be enumerated. Figure 10.5 shows a typical tower-style configuration.

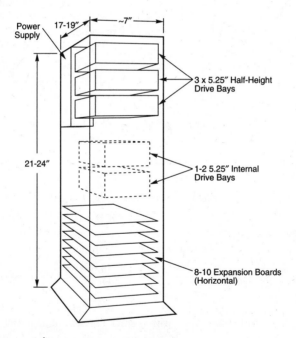

FIGURE 10.5. Tower style case.

The AT first brought legitimacy to installing personal computers on edge, using an after-thought mounting scheme—a cocoon to enclose a conventional AT machine on its end. The first mainstream PCs designed from the start for floor-mounting were IBM's tower-style PS/2s, the venerable Models 60 and 80. Compatible computers took to towers to take advantage of their more commodious drive accommodations. With some models having space for eight or more drives, freestanding tower-style PCs have become the choice for multi-gigabyte network servers.

Vertically mounting computer components causes no problems. Electronic circuits don't know which way is up. However, some hard disks (in particular, massive older models that require a full-height 5.25-inch drive bay) may complain about installation on edge. In some cases, drives that have been low-level formatted in horizontal orientation show an inordinate number of errors when operated vertically. The weight of a sturdy, old head mechanism can be enough to skew the head away from the center of the disk tracks with the result that errors reading the disk can become appallingly frequent. The simple solution is to low-level format the disk in the same vertical orientation in which it will be used.

Another flaw in some tower-style cases is cooling. Most towers align expansion boards horizontally, stacking them one atop another much like small-footprint PCs. Unless care is taken in providing cooling air flow, power-hungry boards low in the stack can cook those boards higher up. IBM anticipated such problems with its tower-style PS/2s by incorporating a plastic channel to direct air current across the expansion boards in those systems. Better tower-style PCs incorporate supplemental cooling fans.

Choose a PC with a tower-style case for its greater physical capacity for internal peripherals and its flexibility of installation wherever there are a few vacant feet of floorspace. You also need to be critical about the provisions for physically mounting mass storage devices. Some towers provide only flimsy mounting means or require you to work through a Chinese puzzle of interlocking parts to install a drive. You need a system that provides a simple, secure mounting scheme for drives, typically something akin to the AT rail system.

Aberrations

Originality has never been the strong suit of the case designs for IBM-compatible computers. In general, that's good because compatible manufacturers have relied on tried and true designs. Along the way, however, some odd and impractical—if stylish—designs have emerged.

Mini-tower PCs fit the same oxymoronic classification as "jumbo shrimp," "military intelligence," or "user-friendly operating system" by taking a design created for maximum capacity and altering it for compact quarters. On the positive side, mini-towers minimize the materials that would go into making a PC case, and they suffer no shortcomings beyond those of a true tower-style case. They require as much floor space, however, as a full-height tower without the added capacity for mass storage devices. In other words, style overpowers function.

Short cases were offered by some manufacturers to make machines less demanding of your desktop. The design strategy was simple: slice a few inches of depth off the case to make it more compact. Some of the air between the drive bay and disk bays could be squeezed out.

The problem with this design should be obvious. The depth of the standard XT and AT cases was set by the length of expansion boards. Trimming the case makes the chassis too short for full length boards. For example, a number of machines offered by Tandy through its Radio Shack stores would only accommodate boards eleven inches or shorter. The implication is obvious: many common expansion products won't work in these systems.

Flip-top cases seem like a good idea—they mimic the standard XT configuration but instead of using a lid that slides forward, they substitute a cover that lifts hatch-style. Although this design at first appears compelling—you can get easy access to what is inside your computer simply by lifting the lid as if you were opening the hood of your car—but in the long run it may not be as desirable as you think. You still must pull whatever's atop the machine off to get inside. Worse yet, you may need to pull the plug on some of the peripherals that you have plugged into the expansion slots because the pivoting back end of the lid shears down upon them. You must pull the plugs or you can't access your expansion boards. The flip-top adds nothing but bother.

Notebook Packaging

Back in the days before microminiaturization, anything instantly became portable the moment you attached a handle. The first generation of portable televisions, for example, was eminently portable—at least for anyone accustomed to carrying a carboy under each arm. The first generation of PCs had similar pretenses of portability, challenging your wherewithal with a weighty bottle of gas and photons, and a small but hardly lightweight picture tube. The typical weight of a first-generation portable PC was about 40 pounds—about the limit of what the market (or any reasonable human being) would bear.

These portables were essentially nothing more than a repackaging that combined a conventional PC with an integral monitor. Some—for example, IBM's ill-starred PC Portable—used motherboards straight from desktop systems (the PC Portable was just an XT in schleppable clothing). Drive bays were moved and slots sacrificed for a package that appealed to the visual senses, no matter the insult to your musculature.

Replacing the bottle with a flat-panel display gave designers a quick way to cut half the weight and repackage systems into *lunchbox* PCs. The name referred to the slab-sided design with a handle on top reminiscent of what every kid not party to the school lunch program toted to class—but with some weighing in at 20 to 25 pounds, these packages were enough to provide Paul Bunyan with his midday meal. The largest of these did allow the use of conventional motherboards with space for several conventional expansion slots. Overall, however, the design was one that only a mother could love, at least if she advocated an aggressive weight-training program.

The ultimate in computer compression is the *notebook* PC, machines shrunk as small as possible while allowing your hands a grip on their keyboards (and eyes a good look at the screen) and as thin as componentry allows. Making machines this small means everything has got to give—you can find compromises in nearly every system component.

The fewest of these compromises appears in mass storage. The need for tiny, flyweight drives for both notebook computers and machines of even smaller dimensions has been the principal driving force behind the miniaturization of floppy and hard disks. Drive manufacturers have been amazingly successful at reducing physical size while increasing capacity and improving performance and reliability. Moreover, many notebook system manuacturers are now relegating the hard disk drive to removable status, opting to install drives in PCMCIA Type 3 slots so that your dealer can easily configure a system or you can readily upgrade your own.

Today the biggest compromises made for the sake of compact size appear in the user interfaces. Making a portable computer portable means making it a burden that a human being can bear, even one that will be willingly borne. And the portable must be something that can be packed rather than needing to be tethered with mooring ropes. Unfortunately some aspects of the user interface can't be compressed without losing usability—it's unlikely that human hands will be downsized to match the demand for smaller, lighter PCs so the optimum size required for a keyboard won't shrink. But the temptation remains for the manufacturer to trim away what's viewed as excess—a bit around the edges from the function keys or eliminating some keys altogether in favor of key-combinations only contortionists can master.

A number of subnotebook machines have been developed with keyboards reduced to 80 percent of the standard size. These include the Gateway HandBook series and the Zeos Contenda. Most people adapt to slightly cramped keyboards and continue to touch-type without difficulty. Smaller than that, however, and touch-typing becomes challenging. In other words, handheld PCs are not for extensive data entry.

Besides length and width, notebook computer makers also have trimmed the depth of their keyboards, reducing the height of keytops—not a noticeable change—as well as key travel. The latter can have a dramatic effect on typing feel and usability. Although the feel and travel of a keyboard is mostly user preference, odds favor greater dissatisfaction with the shrunken, truncated keyboards in miniaturized computers compared to full-size machines.

Displays, too, are a matter of compromise. Bulky picture-tube displays are out, replaced with flat screens of size limited by the dimensions of the rest of the notebook package.

Although old notebook systems have explored a number of variations on the screen-mounting theme, today's most common case is the *clamshell*. Like the homestead of a good old geoduck, the clamshell case is hinged to open at its rear margin. The top holds the screen. When folded down, it protects the keyboard; when opened, it looms behind the keyboard at an adjustable angle. In general, the hinge is the weakest part of this design.

To make their systems more ergonomic, some notebook manufacturers try to follow the desktop paradigm by cutting the keyboard, screen, or both free from the main body of the computer. The appeal of these designs is adjustability: you can work the way you want with your hands as close or far from the screen as feels most comfortable. When used in an office, this design works well. When mobile—for example, in a coach seat on a commuter plane bounding between less civilized realms in the Midwest— the extra pieces to tangle with (and lose) can be less a blessing than a curse. The worst compromise is the keyboard. Making a machine portable demands that the weight of every part be minimized. But lightweight keyboards coupled with cables that are too short and too springing can be frustrating to use—the keys, then the entire keyboard, slipping away from under your fingers.

Although a few notebook systems allow the use of ISA expansion boards, the match is less than optimal. Expansion boards designed for desktop use are not built with the idea of conserving power, so a single board may draw as many watts as the rest of a notebook computer, cutting battery life commensurately. Consequently, most notebook PCs and nearly all notebook machines forswear conventional expansion boards in favor of proprietary expansion products or the credit-card size expansion modules that follow the PCMCIA standard.

Access is one major worry with notebook cases. If you plan to expand the memory of your system, you need a notebook that lets you plug in memory modules or memory cards without totally disassembling the PC. The easiest machines to deal with have slots hidden behind access panels that allow you to slide in a memory card as easily as a floppy disk. Others may have access hatches that accommodate the addition of memory modules. The only shortcoming of either of these expansion methods is the amount of additional memory such machines support—generally one to eight megabytes—enough for current applications, perhaps, but insufficient for the massive applications programmers stay up nights creating. Many notebook computers, especially the lower cost models wearing the house brands of mail-order companies, require that you remove the keyboard to access memory module sockets—a tricky job that demands more skill and patience than you may want to devote to such a task. A few even require unbolting the screen for accessing expansion sockets. If you plan on expanding a notebook or notebook system in the future, check both the permitted memory expansion capacity and the method for adding more RAM.

The key design feature of any notebook or subnotebook computer is portability. You need a machine that's packaged to be as compact and light as possible—commensurate with the ergonomic features that you can tolerate. Older notebooks had built-in handles; newer machines have foregone that luxury. With PCs now weighing in under five pounds and sometimes measuring smaller than a stack of legal pads, that lack has become tolerable—you can either wrap your palm around the machine or tuck it into a carrying case.

At one time the toughest notebook computers had cases crafted from metal, often tough but light magnesium, but nearly all machines today are encased in high-impact plastic. In general, they are tough enough for everyday abuse but won't tolerate a tumble from desktop to floor any more than would a clock, a camera, or other precision device. Inside you find foil or metal-enclosed subassemblies, but these are added to keep radiation within limits rather than minimize the effects of sudden deceleration after free fall. In other words, notebook and subnotebook computers are made to be tough, but abuse can be as fatal to them as any other business tool.

Motherboard Mounting

A motherboard must somehow be mounted in its cabinet, and PC manufacturers have devised a number of ways of holding motherboards down. This simple-sounding job is more complex than you may think. The motherboard cannot simply be screwed down flat. The projecting cut ends of pin-in-hole components make the bottom uneven, and torquing the board into place is apt to stress it, even crack hidden circuit traces. Moreover, most PC cases are metal and laying the motherboard flat against the bottom panel is apt to result in a severe short circuit. Consequently, the motherboard must not only be held secure, but it must be spaced a fraction of an inch (typically in the range 3/8 to 1/2) above the bottom of the case.

IBM originally solved the motherboard-mounting problem ingeniously in its first PC. The motherboards in these machines—and those of the entire IBM line until the introduction of the PS/2—use a combination of screws and specialized spacers that make manufacture (and board replacement) fast and easy. The design is actually amazingly frugal, using just two (sometimes three) screws.

The balance of the mounting holes in the IBM's motherboards are devoted to nylon fasteners which insulate the boards from the metal chassis while holding them in place. These fasteners have two wings that pop through the hole in the motherboard and snap out to lock themselves in place. The bottom of these fasteners slides into a special channel in the bottom of the PC case.

Mechanically, the two or three screws hold the IBM motherboards in place and the nylon fasteners are designed to space the board vertically and fit special channels in the metal work of the case, allowing the boards to slide into place.

In the IBM design, removing the screws allows you to slide the motherboard to the left, freeing the nylon fasteners from their channel. Installing a motherboard requires only setting the board down so that the fasteners engage their mounting channel, then sliding the board to the right until the vacant screw holes line up with the mounting holes in the chassis. Because the number of screws is minimized, so is the labor required to assemble a PC—an important matter when you plan to make hundreds of thousands of machines.

In the PS/2 series, IBM simplified motherboard mounting by molding the required spacers into the plastic shell of the computers. Nevertheless, most machines still minimize the number of screws used for motherboard mounting.

Other personal computer makers developed their own means of mounting motherboards inside their machines.

Some of these manufacturers save the cost of welding the fastener mounting channels in place by drilling a few holes in the bottom of the case and supplying you with a number of threaded metal or plastic spacers (usually nothing more than small nylon tubes) and screws. These spacers are meant to hold the system board the same height from the bottom of the chassis as would the IBM-style fasteners. Other makers have developed their own variations of the PS/2 scheme or entirely original mechanical configurations.

When installing a replacement motherboard in a case using screws and spacers, you have two choices. Either screw the spacers into the case, put the motherboard atop them, then screw the motherboard to the spacers. Or you could screw the motherboard to the spacers then try to get the spacers to fit the holes in the bottom of the case. Neither method is very satisfactory because you're faced with getting 10 or so holes and screws to line up which, owing to the general lack of precision exercised by cut-rate manufacturers in making these cases, they never do. The best thing to do is compromise. Attach the spacers loosely to the motherboard, then try to get the screws at the bottom of the spacers to line up with the holes in the case. You should be able to wiggle them into the holes.

Sometimes when you want to upgrade or repair a PC by replacing its motherboard, you find that the holes in the case and motherboard are at variance. In such circumstances, the best strategy is to modify your case by drilling holes in it to match the motherboard, then use screws and spacers for mounting. Never modify the motherboard by drilling holes in it. You can damage circuit board traces, some of which are invisible and buried within layers of the motherboard.

Drive Mounting

Not only must devices fit into the chassis of a personal computer, they must securely attach in some way. Other components, too, require some means of attachment to the chassis so that your PC doesn't turn into a basketful of parts as soon as you touch it.

The most important of the components that somehow must fit and be affixed to the chassis is the power supply. For the most part, installing power supplies presents few problems. Most power supplies are standardized boxes that simply screw in place. Four screws suffice. (Power supply installation is covered in Chapter 9.)

Note, however, that all power supplies do not fit into all cases for both size and configuration reasons. Most power supplies follow the IBM style and put a big red on/off switch on an extension bracket to the right of the box. The cases of most systems—in particular, those that explicitly follow the old XT and AT standards—are notched at its right rear to allow access to these switches. A few cases, however, are designed to use power supplies with rear panel power switches. Usually the company that sells one variety of case offers power supplies that match (and vice versa). But if you're just replacing the case or the power supply, you need to be careful.

Don't forget that power supplies for XT- and AT-size cases are different sizes themselves, and one does not fit in a case meant for the other. It's an obvious problem but one that can be eliminated if it's anticipated.

Mass storage devices present their own case-matching considerations. When you buy a complete computer system, you don't need to worry about interfaces, controllers, and the like. The manufacturer has done all the work and properly matched everything for optimum operation (you hope). Adding a new mass storage device to enhance your PC or replacing one that has failed provides you with several interesting challenges. Not only must the prospective product be matched electrically to your system, but also it must physically match your PC's case. After all, any device meant to be installed inside your system must, at minimum, physically fit in place.

Form Factors

Disk drives come in a variety of heights and widths. The basic unit of measurement of the size of a drive is the *form factor*. A form factor is simply the volume of a standard drive that handles a particular medium. Several form factors regularly find their way into discussions of personal computers ranging in size from eight inches to 1.3 inches, most of which allow for one or more device heights.

A full-size drive, one which defines the form factor and occupies all of its volume, is usually a first generation machine. Its exact dimensions, chosen for whatever particular reason, seemed fitting, perhaps allowing for the mood of the mechanical engineer on the day he was drafting the blueprints. If the drive is a reasonable size and proves particularly successful—successful enough that other manufacturers eagerly want to cash in, too—others follow suit and copy the dimension of the product, making it a standard. Dimensions of the various standard accepted form factors are shown in figures 10.6 and 10.7.

Device Heights

The second generation of any variety of hardware inevitably results in some sort of size reduction. Cost cutting, greater precision, experience in manufacturing, and the inevitable need to put more in less space gang up to shrink things down. The result of the downsizing process is a variety of fractional size devices, particularly in the 5-1/4 inch and 3-1/2 inch form factors. At 5-1/4 inches, devices are measured in sub-increments of the original full-height package. Devices that are two-thirds height, half-height, one-third, or quarter-height have all been manufactured at one time or another.

At the 3-1/2 inch form factor, sizes are more pragmatic, measured as the actual height in inches. The original 3-1/2 inch drives may be considered full-height and typically measure about 1.6 inches high. The next most widely used size was an even inch in height (five-eighths height, for the fractious folk who prefer fractions). Sub-inch heights have been used for some devices, some as small as 0.6 inches.

However, before 3-1/2 inch drives had a chance to slim down to two dimensions, smaller form factors came into play—2.5, 1.8, and 1.3 inches. The 2.5-inch devices were designed primarily for notebook computers. Smaller drives fit palmtop computers, even on credit-card size expansion boards. The 1.8-inch size has won particular favor for fitting into Type 3 PC Cards that follow the most recent PCMCIA standard.

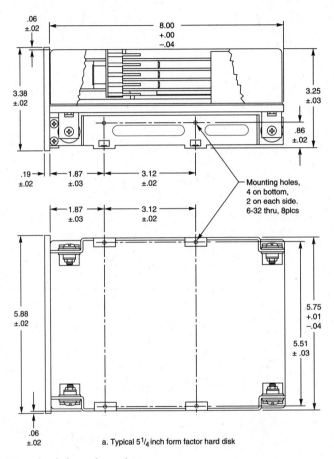

FIGURE 10.6. Standard drive form factors.

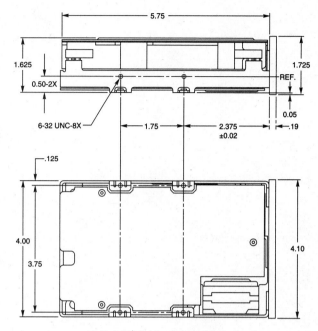

b. Typical 3½ inch form factor hard disk

FIGURE 10.7. Standard drive form factors.

Note that all of these applications for sub-3.5 inch drives are the type in which the system (or at least its case or other packaging) is designed around the drive. In other words, only the PC manufacturer needs to fret about the exact dimensions of the drive and what fits where (see fig. 10.8, 10.9, and 10.10).

To bring order to the chaos of drive sizes with each manufacturer determining what fits best for its own purposes, several drive makers formed a consortium to standardize drives. Called the Small Form Factor Committee (SFF), the organization does not officially sanction standards, but rather creates specifications that are then submitted for approval to other standard-setting organizations (such as the IEEE and ANSI). Because SFF became active only in 1992, it initially began work on drives with form factors smaller than 3.5 inches (as fits its name). However, the committee is also working on defining firm specifications for larger drives. The form factors smaller than 3.5 inches shown in figures 10.8 to 10.10 are those that have received SFF sanction.

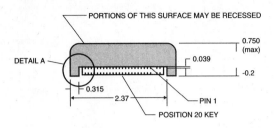

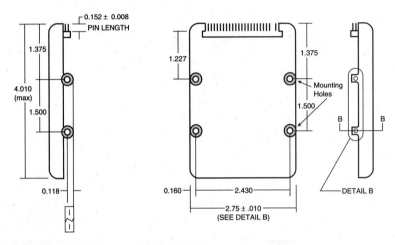

FIGURE 10.8. Small form factor disk drives.

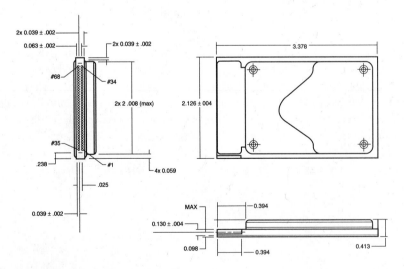

FIGURE 10.9. Small form factor disk drives.

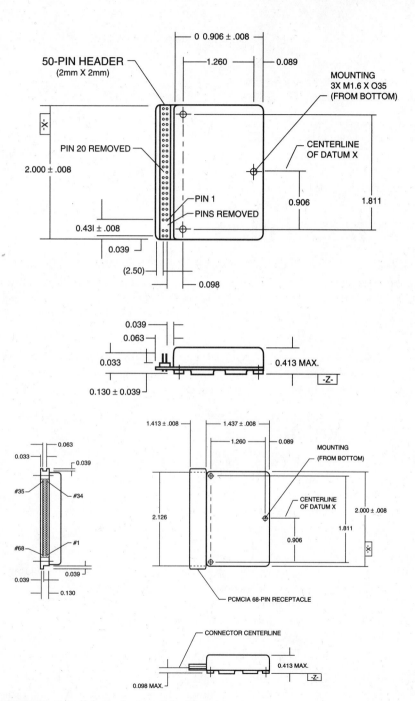

FIGURE 10.10. Small form factor disk drives.

The specifications developed by the SFF committee are published by

ENDL Publications
14426 Black Walnut Court
Saratoga, California 95070

The one important rule regarding small drives is that a device can always be adapted to fit a drive bay designed for a larger form factor. For example, kits to adapt 3.5-inch drives for 5-1/4 inch bays are readily available—often included with the drive itself. You can always install a smaller drive in place of a larger one with a suitable adapter (or even by making mounting holes in your chassis yourself). Going the other way is more difficult.

Drive Installation

Internal installation of any mass storage device in a drive bay is actually quite simple. Most disk and tape drives are replete with multiple tapped holes on each side and bottom that accept screws to hold the drive in place. Add the right screws and a few twists and you can install a device in a few minutes. Anyone who knows the right end of a screwdriver to grab is qualified to physically install or remove a device from a drive bay.

But matters—and drive bays—are not quite so simple. You need to get access to the drive bay itself as well as the holes through which you must twist the screws. Some systems make playing hide-and-seek with the invisible man less of a challenge.

Direct Mounting

The logical way to attach a disk drive to a computer is to screw it in. Disk drives provide tapped holes on three sides to accommodate your efforts as well as the most vexing drive placement schemes concocted by misanthropic engineers. All you need to do is find where the case maker provided space for the drive, figure out how to get the drive in place, and screw everything together. Some schemes make external drives the most desirable alternative.

The most straightforward direct-mounting scheme is that used by the original PC, XT, and compatible computers patterned after them. Bays are accommodated in a mounting tray, the sides of which are bent upward with holes provided to match the two tapped mounting holes on each side of the standard full-height 5-1/4 inch mass storage device. These screws are visible on the right side of drives in the right drive bay and the left side of drives in the left bay. Gaining access to the latter typically requires a short screwdriver, a great deal of dexterity, and a tolerance for blood loss—or removing all or most of the expansion cards inside the computer.

The only challenge is lining up the holes tapped into the side of a device with the holes or slots in the sides of the drive bay. Slots impose an additional layer of merriment. You must align the front of the device with the front panel of the computer. You also need to use screws with large heads (*binder head* screws are best if you can acquire them from your hardware store) that won't slip through the slots.

As noted earlier, two screws on one side of a device provides less than adequate mounting security, particularly in inexpensive cases made from sheet-metal so thin you may expect it to be recycled soup cans. Slide a tape-cartridge drive into one of these bays and you can probably fold the entire bay half an inch over every time you shove in a tape. IBM added an extra screw for its XT hard disk drives for the sake of mechanical integrity, and you would be well advised to do the same. You need to mark the place on the bay that lines up with one of the screw holes in the bottom of the device you want to install and drill a matching hole in the bottom of the mounting tray. You then need to drill a matching hole in the bottom of the case large enough for the entire screw (and screwdriver) to be pushed up to the bottom of the mounting tray.

Another difficulty you may face is installing half-height devices in very early machines (such as IBM's PC and XT) that were designed before half-height devices became popular. Although you can install a single half-height drive in each slot simply by using these mounting holes and filling the empty space above the drive with blank half-height panel, packing a pair of drives in one bay is more challenging. Try to install two half-height drives in a single full-height bay and you could be screwing in the air. The solution is to create a pair of half-height *adapter plates*. Basically just thin pieces of steel with a number of slots or holes in them, adapter plates allow you to assemble two half-height drives into a single unit that installs into a full-height drive bay (see fig. 10.11).

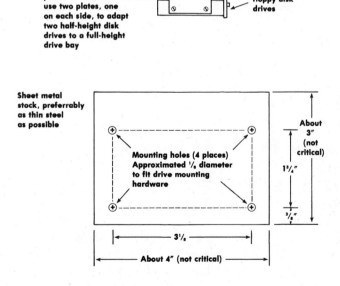

FIGURE 10.11. Half-height drive adapter plate.

Installing drives with these adapters is more difficult than you may think. You can't just connect two drives with them and slide the whole assembly into the drive bay—the screw heads (and maybe plates themselves) make the drive package too wide to slide through the front panel opening in the chassis.

The first step to a double-half-height installation is to connect the two drives together on the side opposite that which attaches the mounting tray. Once one plate is installed, you should be able to slide the drive stack into the computer as a single piece.

Once the two-drive stack is in its proper place but while you can still maneuver the drives in and out of the bay, install all the cables to both drives. Once everything is plugged in, slip the other mounting plate between the drives and the side of the drive bay. Secure this mounting plate and the drive by screwing through the two holes in the bay, through the mounting plate, and into the screw holes in the bottom drive. Finally, finish your work by screwing the top drive into place.

Systems that have proper holes for mounting half-height drives into full-height slots also benefit from using an adapter plate. Installing a single adapter on the side of the drive stack opposite the attachment screws adds stability.

A number of small-footprint PCs use special internal bays for 3.5-inch hard disks. In most cases, you need to remove the bay itself—which is little more than a bent sheet-metal cage—before you can install the drive. After removing the bay from the chassis, you then can screw the drive directly to the bay. Then reinstall the entire drive-and-bay assembly.

Most makers of modern miniaturized hard disks warn that you should use the shortest possible screws for direct mounting of the drive. When you tighten long screws, they may press against the side of the drive's case or its electronics, physically distorting the drive itself. Because the drive is a precision instrument, even the slightest distortion can be fatal. Some drives require screws as short as one-quarter inch.

Rail Mounting

The improved drive mounting scheme developed for the AT and compatible systems following its case design imposes an additional step on device installation: *mounting rails.* The sides of the drive bay are fabricated into channels. Rails installed on each side of each drive slide into these channels, securing the drive on both sides.

Rail-mounting solves and adds problems to drive installation. On the positive side, they make a truly secure mounting system that can withstand even moderate earthquakes. A tight fit between the channel and rail ensures that the drive is kept in place vertically. A stop at the back of the channel and a mounting bracket at the front prevent fore-and-aft rattling. On the negative side, however, the process of installing the rails themselves allows you to make several missteps that you won't discover until too late, giving you the pleasure of screwing rails on and off your drive several times.

The rail-mounting scheme has proven so satisfactory that IBM has used it with little change for more than a decade (compared to the three years it used direct mounting). Many other manufacturers have adopted the same or a similar mounting system. You may find many AT-compatible cases that simply duplicate the IBM mounting scheme in all of its dimensions. Others—particularly the larger manufacturers (such as Compaq)—have opted for their own rail designs.

IBM preserved the AT-rail system in its PS/2 systems that accept 5-1/4 inch devices but adapted the containment system to make the installation of drives free from the need for tools after rails have been attached to each device. Instead of a fully enclosed bay, the PS/2 line uses a cage with channels for drive rails on either side.

The first challenge in installing rails on a device is coming up with the rails themselves. True AT-style rails are easy to find. Many device vendors package AT-style rails with their products or pre-install AT-style rails before sending the device to you. The rails in compatible computers are so varied that finding the exact size you need means contacting the computer maker or an authorized dealer who stocks a complete array of parts. Many makers of AT-style computers now alleviate this problem by filling all drive bays in their systems with rails, whether or not a drive is installed in each bay. Figure 10.12 shows the dimensions of the standard AT drive mounting rail and the similar rail used by Compaq.

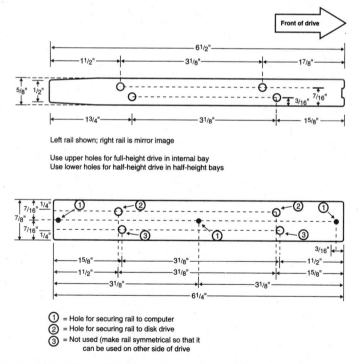

FIGURE 10.12. IBM AT and Compaq drive mounting rails.

Even with AT-style rails, you face a choice. All sorts of rails are available. Official IBM rails are different for the right and left side of the drive and have only two installation holes. Aftermarket rails may have four or eight holes or slots and may be entirely symmetrical, even squared off at both ends. These rails are meant to be interchangeable between the right and left sides of the device you want to install. Although that's a laudable design consideration, the multiplicity of holes also imposes on you the challenge of finding which pair of the eight puts the device at the proper height in the bay and the proper distance from the front panel.

With true, unsymmetrical IBM rails, proper orientation points the tapered end of the rail toward the rear of the drive. The screws to hold the rails in place then go into the lower pair of the two sets of mounting holes on the drive. With non-IBM AT-style rails, the general rule is to use the lower holes on the rail (when its tapered end is pointed toward the rear of the drive) to mate with the lower holes in the side of the device. Some odd rails may have holes in different positions, however. If you install rails on a new drive, make sure that the drive lines up in the proper vertical position before you secure its mounting brackets and try to reinstall the lid of the case.

Once you've installed rails on a device, slide it into the bay in which you plan to use. Push the device to the back of the bay to ensure that the device fits at the proper height and depth to match with the computer's fascia panel. Once you're satisfied that the device fits properly, pull it part way out and make all the electrical connections to it. Then push the drive back to its final resting place. Then with AT-style cases, screw in the front panel brackets to hold the rails and device in place. With some compatibles, the bracket is part of the rail itself. These mate directly against the front panel of the computer.

In computers that follow the AT pattern, most of the brackets are L-shaped. However, one (which fits between the left and right bays) is U-shaped. With either style of bracket, the arm or arms of the bracket that project backward press against the drive mounting rail and hold it at the end of its travel in its channel.

In IBM's tool-free PS/2 line, rail-mounted drives are secured by vertical pressure against their rails instead of end brackets. A turn of a screw provides the needed force. Big, blue daisy-like knobs of plastic turn the screws, designed to be spun without tools by firm pressure from the palm of your hand.

Installing a single drive in one of these systems simply requires lowering the drive decked out in its mounting rails through the open center of the cage. The top of the channel is cut away in the middle so that you can properly push the drive down. When you do, the drive should be oriented so that the connectors at its rear will end up nearest the center of the chassis once the drive is positioned. Once you've lowered the drive into the cage, simply push it to the end of its travel (either toward the front or back of the chassis, your choice) and tighten down the blue daisies.

Two drive systems require a more complicated installation because one drive blocks access to the central open area of the chassis. The drive to be located at the rear of the chassis should be inserted first, as for a single drive installation. The second drive can then slide into the cage through the opening in the front of the chassis. You need to snap out the front panel bezel to gain access. The front-mounted drive is tightened into place as for the rear unit.

Sled Mounting

In the PS/2 series of computers, IBM refined its device mounting schemes so that all devices could be installed or removed from their computer hosts without the use of tools. Devices conforming to the 3-1/2 inch form factor install on special plastic mounting sleds while 5-1/4 inch drives in most systems retain the AT rail system.

IBM-style drive sleds are one-piece plastic castings that screw into the bottom of 3-1/2 inch devices. The sled slides into guide rails cast into the drive bay and snaps into place using a plastic latch that's part of the sled. The IBM design holds the potential for making the sled an integral part of the device chassis, but such designs have not been accepted by drive makers. Figure 10.13 shows a device sled.

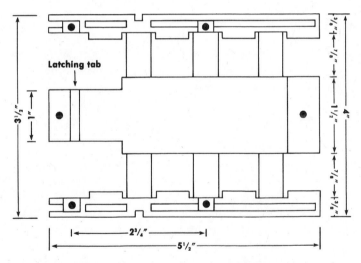

FIGURE 10.13. PS/2 3.5-inch hard disk mounting sled (dimensions approximate).

To access the drive bay to install or remove one of these sleds, you need to remove the front fascia panel from your PS/2. These are secured by plastic snaps molded into the fascia. Just pry the front panel free at the seam running around it about half an inch behind its face. You should be able to pull it off using your fingers.

A "floating" connector (one with some freedom of movement) at the rear of the bay automatically mates with an edge connector on the drive. Besides carrying the signals, this connector also supplies power to the drive, eliminating the need for a separate power connector.

Once the drive is pushed fully into its bay, a latch at the bottom of the drive snaps down, locking the drive securely in place. To remove the drive, this latch must be released. To do so, simply lift up on the tab that's centered under the drive. Firmly pull the drive forward while lifting the tab to release the latch. After some initial effort required to pull the drive from the connector at the back of the bay, the drive pulls easily and smoothly from the bay.

Tray Mounting

Other manufacturers were as quick to adopt IBM's drive sleds as they were the Micro Channel expansion bus. You may find few compatible machines using sleds. However, some computer makers use a variation on the theme—the *drive tray*. One example is the Advanced Logic Research tower-style case. In these systems, drives mount through their bottom screw-holes to trays, much as drives mount to IBM sleds. The trays, however, then screw into the side of the tower. The cover-plate on the other side of the case is slotted to support the other side of each tray.

Cooling

A case can be confining. It can keep just about everything from escaping, including the heat electronic circuits produce as a by-product performing their normal functions. Some of the electricity in any circuit (except one made from superconductors) is turned into heat by the unavoidable electrical resistance of the circuit. Heat is also generated whenever an element of a computer circuit changes state. In fact, nearly all of the electricity consumed by a computer eventually turns into heat.

Inside the protective but confining case of the computer, that heat builds up thus driving up the temperature. Heat is the worst enemy of semiconductor circuits; it can shorten their lives considerably or even cause their catastrophic failure. Some means of escape must be provided for the excess heat. In truth, the heat build-up in most PCs may not be immediately fatal to semiconductor circuits. For example, most microprocessors shut down (or simply generate errors that shut down your PC) before any permanent damage occurs to them or the rest of the components inside your PC. However, heat can cause circuits to age prematurely and can trim the lives of circuit components.

The design of the case of a PC affects how well the machine deals with its heat build-up. A case that's effective in keeping its internal electronics cool can prolong the life of the system.

Passive Convection

The obvious way to make a PC run cooler is to punch holes in its case to let the heat out—but to keep the holes small enough so that other things such as mice and milkshakes can't get in. In due time, *passive convection*—less dense hot air rising with denser cool air flowing in to take its place—lets the excess thermal energy drift out of the case.

Any impediment to the free flow of air slows the passive cooling effect. In general, the more holes in the case, the merrier the PC will be. Remove the lid, and the heat can waft away along with temperature worries.

Unfortunately, your PC's case should be closed. Keeping a lid on it does more than just restrict cooling—it is also the only effective way to deal with interference. It also keeps your PC quieter, prevents foreign objects and liquids from plummeting in, and gives your monitor a lift.

Moreover, passive cooling is often not enough. Only low-power designs (such as notebook and Green PCs) generate little enough heat that convection can be entirely successful. Other systems generate more heat than naturally goes away on its own.

Active Cooling

The alternative to passive cooling is, hardly unexpectedly, *active cooling*, which uses a force of some kind to move the heat away from the circuits. The force of choice in most PCs is a *fan*.

Usually tucked inside the power supply, the computer's fan forces air to circulate inside both the power supply and the computer. It sucks cool air in to circulate and blows the heated air out.

The cooling systems of early PCs, however, were particularly ill-conceived for active cooling. The fans were designed mostly to cool off the heat-generating circuitry inside the power supply itself and only incidentally cool the inside of the computer. Moreover, the chance design of the system resulted in most of the cool air getting sucked in through the floppy disk drive slots. Along with the air, in come all the dust and grime floating around in the environment, polluting whatever media you have sitting in the drive. At least enough air coursed through the machine to cool off the small amount of circuitry that the meager power supply of the PC could provide.

The XT added more electricity from the power supply but no better ventilation. And that brought its own problem. The airflow around expansion cards and the rest of the computer was insufficient (actually too ill-placed) to keep the temperature throughout the machine down to an acceptable level. As a correction to later models of the XT, IBM eliminated a series of ventilation holes at the bottom of the front of the chassis. The absence of these holes actually improves the air circulation through the system unit and keeps things cooler (see Appendix D, "Ancient History").

Unfortunately, most computer manufacturers rely on cooling that has not advanced beyond the XT system. At most, they graft a *heatsink* onto the system microprocessor to provide a greater area to radiate heat. But most still rely on the fan in the power supply to move the cooling air through the system.

Advanced Cooling

Some systems have more carefully thought-out cooling systems. IBM's tower-style PS/2s are exemplary, channeling the flow of cooling air to the places it is most needed. A few manufacturers add extra fans to supplement the air flow generated by the power supply fan.

In most systems, however, the cooling system can be improved. Booster fans that clamp on the rear panel of the computer and power supplies with beefed-up fans are available. These do, in fact, increase air circulation through the system unit, potentially lowering the internal temperature and prolonging the lives of components. Note that there is no reliable data on whether this additional cooling increases the life of the components inside your PC. Unless you stuff every conceivable accessory into your machine, however, you're unlikely to need such a device except for the added measure of peace of mind it provides.

On the other hand, blocking the airpath of the cooling system of any PC can be fatal, allowing too much heat to build up inside the chassis. Never locate a PC in cramped quarters that lacks air circulation (like a desk drawer or a shelf on which it just fits). Never block the cooling slots or holes of a computer case.

Fan Failure

The fan inside a PC power supply is a necessity, not a luxury. If it fails to operate, your computer won't falter—at least not at first. But temperatures build up inside. The machine—the power supply in particular—may even fail catastrophically from overheating.

The symptoms of fan failure are subtle but hard to miss. You hear the difference in the noise your system makes. You may even be able to smell components warming past their safe operating temperature.

Should you detect either symptom, hold you hand near where the air usually emerges from your computer. (On PCs and ATs, that's near the big round opening that the fan peers through.) If you feel no breeze, you can be certain your fan is no longer doing its job.

A fan failure constitutes an emergency. If it happens to your system, immediately save your work and shut the machine off. Although you can safely use it for short periods, the better strategy is to replace the fan or power supply as soon as you possibly can.

Limiting Radiation

Besides heat, all electrical circuits radiate something else—electromagnetic fields. The flow of electrical energy sets up an electromagnetic field that radiates away. Radio and television stations push kilowatts of energy through their antennae so that this energy (accompanied by programming in the form of modulation) radiates over the countryside, eventually to be hauled in by a radio or television set for your enjoyment or disgruntlement.

The electrical circuits inside all computers work the same way but on a smaller scale. The circuit board traces act as antennae and radiate electromagnetic energy whenever the computer is turned on. When the thinking gets intense, so does the radiation.

You can't see, hear, feel, taste, or smell this radiation, just as you can't detect the emissions from a radio station (at least not without a radio), so you would think there would be no reason for concern about the radiation from your PC. But even invisible signals can be dangerous, and their very invisibility makes them more worrisome—you may never know if they are there or not. The case of your PC is your primary (often only) line of defense against radiation from its electronic circuitry.

The problems of radiation are twofold: the radiation interfering with other, more desirable signals in the air; and the radiation affecting your health.

Radio Frequency Interference

The signals radiated by a PC typically fall in the microwatt range, perhaps a billion times weaker than those emitted by a broadcasting station. You would think that the broadcast signals would easily overwhelm the inadvertent emissions from your PC. But the strength of signals falls off dramatically with distance from the source. They follow the inverse-square law; therefore a signal from a source a thousand times farther away would be a million times weaker. Radio and television stations are typically miles away, so the emissions from a PC can easily overwhelm nearby broadcast signals, turning transmissions into gibberish.

The radiation from the computer circuitry occurs at a wide variety of frequencies, including not only the range occupied by your favorite radio and television stations but also aviation navigation systems, emergency radio services, and even the eavesdropping equipment some initialed government agency may have buried in your walls. Unchecked, these untamed radiations from within your computer can compete with broadcast signals not only for the ears of your radio but that of your neighbors. These radio-like signals emitted by the computer generate what is termed *radio frequency interference* or *RFI*, so called because they interfere with other signals in the radio spectrum.

The government agency charged with the chore of managing interference—the Federal Communications Commission—has set strict standards on the radio waves that personal computers can emit. These standards are fully covered in Appendix A, "Regulations." At their hearts, however, the FCC standards enforce a good neighbor policy. They require that the RFI from PCs be so weak that it won't bother your neighbors, although it may garble radio signals in your own home or office.

The FCC sets two standards: Class A and Class B. Computer equipment must be verified to meet the *FCC Class A* standard to be legally sold for business use. PCs must be certified to conform with the more stringent *FCC Class B* standard to be sold for home use.

Equipment makers, rather than users, must pass FCC muster. You are responsible, however, for ensuring that your equipment does not interfere with your neighbors. If your PC does interfere, legally you have the responsiblity for eliminating the problem. While you can sneak Class A equipment into your home, you have good reasons not to. The job of interference elimination is easier with Class B certified equipment because it starts off radiating lower signal levels, so Class B machines give you a head start. Moreover, meeting the Class B standards requires better overall construction, which helps assure that you get a better case and a better PC.

Health Concerns

Some radiation emitted by PCs is of such low frequencies that it falls below the range used by any radio station. These Very Low Frequency and Extremely Low Frequency signals (often called VLF and ELF) are thought by some people to cause a variety of health problems (see Appendix A, "Regulations").

Your PC's case is the first line of defense against these signals. A metal case blocks low frequency magnetic fields, which some epidemiological studies have hinted might be dangerous, and shields against the emission of electrical fields. Plastic cases are less effective. By themselves they offer no electrical or magnetic shielding. But plain plastic cases would also flunk the FCC tests. Most manufacturers coat plastic cases with a conductive paint to contain interference. However, these coatings are largely ineffective against magnetic fields. Most modern systems now use metal cases or internal metal shielding inside plastic cases to minimize radiation.

No matter the construction of your PC, you can minimize your exposure to radiation from its case by ensuring that it is properly and securely assembled. Minimizing interference means screwing in the retaining brackets of all the expansion boards inside your PC and keeping the lid tightly screwed into the chassis. Keeping a tight PC not only helps keep you safe, it keeps your system safe and intact as well.

Chapter 11
Input Devices

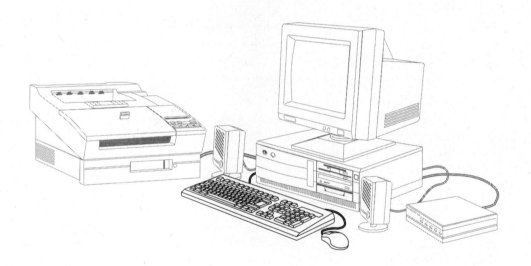

Input devices are the means by which you move information into your PC—the primary means by which you interact with your personal computer. The various available devices span an entire range of technologies, from the tactile to the vocal. Although they work in different ways, all accomplish the same task: they enable you to communicate with your computer.

Even when computers are held at lowest esteem—"garbage in, garbage out"—they still have an essential need. They must have some way of getting data in, if only just to let it out in the same miserable form. To be at their best and carry out your commands, the need is still the same. If the computer doesn't have raw material to work upon, it simply cannot do any work. If you can't tell it what to do, the computer can't do anything.

The one needed element is the input device, a channel through which you can pass data and commands to your PC. Absent a silico-cerebral mind link, that connection inevitably involves some kind of mechanical device. Commands, data, and ideas need to be reduced to physical form to exit your mind and enter your PC. The input device converts the mechanical into the electronic form that your PC can understand.

The basic electro-mechanical interface is the switch. A computer can detect the state of a switch by sensing the electrical flow through it (the switch is on if electricity flows; off it does not). Thus with a single switch, you can communicate with your PC exactly one bit at a time—a daunting task if you want to create a multi-megabyte database.

You can speed the communications by employing several switches—a whole bank of them. In fact, early computers were programmed exactly that way—as are computers today. However, instead of using old-fashioned toggle switches, today's computers use pushbuttons. Each button is assigned a code to send to the computer—a letter of the alphabet or other symbol. The entire bank of switches is called a keyboard. The keyboard remains the primary input device used by today's PCs.

Keyboards have shortcomings. The primary one is that they are relatively inefficient at relaying spatial information to your computer; they send symbols. A number of applications, however, depends on knowing where rather than what—moving a cursor, for example. The computer knows what you want to move (the cursor); it just needs the spatial information about where to put it. A whole menagerie of input devices has arisen to improve keyboards—mice, trackballs, pens, and digitizing tablets.

As computers moved into the graphic realm with the aid of pointing devices, they also developed the need to acquire huge blocks of graphic data from external sources, a means of converting a physical (optical) image into electronic form. The scanner fills this need.

Keyboards

The primary input device for most computer systems is the keyboard, and until voice recognition systems are perfected to the point that they can recognize continuous speech, the dominance of the keyboard is not likely to change. Even then the keyboard will probably remain unapproachable for speed and accuracy for years to come. The keyboard also is more suited to data entry in open offices, airplanes, and anywhere your privacy is not ensured.

As long as you are stuck with it, you may as well understand how it works. The keyboard concept—a letter for every pushbutton—is almost ancient, dating back to the days of the first typewriter. The basic layout and function has changed little since the last half of the 19th century. Even PC keyboards seem to have changed little. Look at one, and they seem the same since 1987. But while the keycaps have held their positions, the technology underneath them has changed over the years.

Technologies

No matter how their keys are arranged, all keyboards have the same function: detecting the keys pressed down by your fingers and relaying that information to your computer. Even though two keyboards may look identical, they may differ considerably in the manner in which they detect the motion of your fingers. The technology used for this process—how the keyboard works electrically—can affect the sturdiness and longevity of the keyboard. Although all keyboards operate in effect as switches by altering the flow of electricity in some way, the way those changes are detected evolved into an elaborate mechanism.

Nearly every technology for detecting the change in flow of electricity has been adopted to keyboards at one time or another. The engineer's goal has been to find a sensing mechanism that combines accuracy—detecting only the desired keystroke and ignoring errant electrical signals—with long life (you don't want a keyboard that works for six words), along with the right "feel," the personal touch. In past years, keyboard designers found promise in complex and exotic technologies like Hall-effect switches, special semiconductors that react to magnetic field changes. The lure was the wonder of magnetism—nothing needs to touch to make the detection. A lack of contact promised a freedom from wear, a keyboard with endless life.

In the long run, however, the quest for the immortal keyboard proved misguided. Keyboards rated for tens of millions of keypresses met premature ends with a splash from a cup of coffee. The two most common designs in PCs are the capacitive and hard contact keyboards.

Capacitive

When the PC was introduced, it inherited the keyboard technology used by its predecessors—terminals and workstations. At the time, the basic switch had severe shortcomings for heavy-duty office use: it didn't last long when confronted with long-term use and environmental hazards. Even oxidation—an effect of ordinary air—caused them to become unreliable. Consequently, IBM adapted a proven design that sequestered the switches from the air. Instead of relying on the contacts of a switch to change the flow of electricity, IBM opted to detect a change in capacitance.

Capacitance is essentially a stored charge of static electricity. Capacitors store electricity as opposite static charges in one or more pairs of conductive plates separated by a non-conductive material. The opposite charges create an attractive field between one another, and the insulating gap prevents the charges from coming together and canceling out one another. The closer the two charged plates are, the stronger the field and the more energy can be stored. Moving the plates in relation to one another changes their capacity for storing charge, which in turn can generate a flow of electricity to fill up the increased capacity or drain off the excess charge as the capacity decreases.

These minute electrical flows are detected by the circuitry of a capacitive keyboard. The small, somewhat gradual changes of capacity are amplified and altered so that they resemble the quick flick of a switch.

Capacitive keyboards are generally built around an etched circuit board. Two large areas of tin and nickel plated copper form pads under each switch station (in keyboard terminology, each key is called a station). The pads of each pair are neither physically nor electrically connected to one another. They act as the plates of a capacitor.

In the IBM capacitive keyboard design, pressing any key on the keyboard forces a circle of metalized-plastic down, separating a pair of pads that lies just below the key plunger. Although the plastic backing of the circle prevents making a connection that allows electricity to flow between the pads, the initial proximity of the pads results in a capacity charge. Separating them causes a decrease in this capacitance—a change on the order of 20 to 24 picofarads decreasing to 2 to 6 picofarads. The reduction of capacitance causes the necessary small but detectable current flow in the circuitry leading to the pads.

Some compatible capacitive keyboards do the opposite of the IBM design. Pressing a key pushes capacitive pads together and increases the capacitance. This backward process has the same effect, however. It alters the flow of current in a way that can be detected by the keyboard.

Capacitive keyboard designs work well. Most have rated lives of over 10 million keypresses at each station. If they have a shortcoming it is that their sensing is indirect. It's like hooking up an intercom to listen in on a distant door bell. It works, but a direct approach—moving the door bell itself—would be more efficient with less complication and fewer things to go wrong.

Contact

The direct approach in keyboards is using switches to alter the flow of electricity. The switches in the keyboard do exactly what all switches are supposed to do—open and close an electrical circuit to stop or start the flow of electricity. Using switches requires simpler (although not trivial) circuitry to detect each keystroke, although most switch-based PC keyboards still incorporate a microprocessor to assign scan codes and serialize the data for transmission to the system unit.

Design simplicity and corresponding low cost have made switch-based keyboards today's top choice for PCs. These keyboards either use novel technology to solve the major problem of switches—a short life—or just ignore it. Cost has become the dominant factor in the design and manufacture of keyboards. In the trade-off between price and life, the switch-based design is the winner.

Three switch-based keyboard designs are used in PCs: mechanical switches, rubber domes, and membrane switches.

Mechanical switches use the traditional switch mechanism, precious metal contacts forced together. The switch under each keyboard station can be an independent unit that can be individually replaced, or the entire keyboard can be fabricated as one assembly. Although the former may lend itself to easier repair, the minimum labor charge for computer repair often is higher than the cost of a replacement keyboard.

The contact in a mechanical switch keyboard can do double-duty, chaperoning the electrical flow and positioning the keycaps. Keyboard contact can operate as springs to push the keycap back up after it has been pressed. Although this design is compelling because it minimizes the parts needed to make a keyboard, it is not suited to PC-quality keyboards. The return force is difficult to control and the contact material may suffer from fatigue and break. Consequently, most mechanical switch keyboards incorporate springs to push the keycaps back into place as well as other parts to give the keyboard the right feel and sound.

Rubber dome keyboards combine the contact and positioning mechanisms into a single piece. A puckered sheet of elastomer—a stretchy, rubber-like synthetic—is molded to put a dimple or dome under each keycap with the dome bulging upward. Pressing on the key pushes the dome down. Inside the dome is a tab of carbon or other conductive material that serves as one of the keyboard contacts. When the dome goes down, the tab presses against another contact and completes the circuit. Release the key and the elastomer dome pops back to its original position, pushing the keycap back with it.

The rubber dome keyboard design was first used by IBM for the PCjr. Although the original product was maligned for having small keys (derisively termed "Chicklets"), the underlying mechanism has proven itself and is now widely used in full-size keyboards. One-piece construction makes rubber-dome keyboards inexpensive. Moreover, proper design yields a keyboard with excellent feel—individual domes can be tailored to enable you to sense exactly when the switch makes contact. A poor design, however, makes each keypress feel rubbery and uncertain.

Membrane keyboards are similar to rubber domes except that they use thin plastic sheets—the membrane—printed with conductive traces rather than elastomer sheets. The contacts are inside dimples in the plastic sheets. Pressing down on a key pinches the dimples together, closing the switch contact. The membrane design often is used for keypads to control calculators and printers because of its low cost and trouble-free life. The materials making contact can be sealed inside the plastic, impervious to harsh environments. By itself, the membrane design makes a poor computer keyboard because its contacts require only slight travel to actuate. However, an auxiliary key mechanism can tailor the feel (and key travel) of a membrane keyboard and make typing on it indistinguishable from working with a keyboard based on another technology.

Touch

Today the principal dividing line between keyboards is not technology but touch—what typing actually feels like. A keyboard must be responsive to the touch of your fingers—when you press down, the keys actually have to go down. More than that, however, you must feel like you are typing. You need tactile feedback, sensing through your fingers when you have activated a key.

The most primitive form of tactile feedback is the hard stop—the key bottoms out and stops moving at the point of actuation. No matter how hard you press, the key is unyielding, and that is the problem. To ensure yourself that you are actuating the key, you end up pressing harder than necessary. The extra force tires you out more quickly.

One alternative is to make the key actuate before the end of key travel. Because the key is still moving when you realize that it registered your keystroke, you can release your finger pressure before the key bottoms out. You don't need to expend as much effort, and your fingers don't get as tired.

The linear travel or linear touch keyboard requires that you simply press harder to push a key down. In other words, the relationship between the displacement of the key and the pressure you must apply is linear throughout the travel of the key. The chief shortcoming of the linear touch keyboard is that your fingers have no sure way of knowing when they have pressed down far enough. Audible feedback, a click indicating that the key has been actuated can help, as does the appearance on-screen of the character you typed. Both slow you down, however, because you are calling more of your mind into play to register a simple keystroke. If your fingers could sense the actuation of the keys themselves, your fingers could know when to stop reflexively.

Some keyboards provide this kind of tactile feedback by requiring you to increase pressure on the keyboard keys until they actuate and then dramatically lowering the force you need to press down farther until you reach the limit of travel. Your fingers detect the change in effort as an over-center feel. Keyboards that provide this positive over-center feel are generally considered to be the best for quick touch-typing.

A spring mechanism, carefully tailored to abruptly yield upon actuation of each key, gives the classic IBM keyboard its tactile feel and delivers the infamous click of every keypress. The spring mechanism also returns the key to the top of its travel at the end of each keystroke. So called soft-touch keyboards often use foam as a spring mechanism and to cushion the end of each keystroke. Soft-touch keyboards give a more linear feel but are preferred by some people for exactly the same reason others dislike them—their lack of snap and quiet operation.

Another influence on the feel of a keyboard is the force required to actuate a key. Some keyboards require you to press harder than others. In general, however, most keyboards require between 1.9 and 2.4 ounces of pressure to actuate a key. Stiff keyboards can require as much as three ounces.

Keyboards also differ in how far you must press down a key to actuate it. Full-travel keyboards require your fingers to move down between 0.14 and 0.18 of an inch to actuate a key. Studies show that the full-travel design helps typists achieve high speeds and lower error rates. In laptop and notebook computers where every fraction of an inch counts, however, keyboards sometimes are designed with less than full travel. A short-travel keyboard actuates with less than about 0.10 inch of key travel. Whether you can live with—or even prefer—a short-travel keyboard is a personal issue.

Electrical Function

In the macroscopic world in which we live, switches operate positively without hesitation or doubt. Switch on a light, and it comes on like, well, a light. In the realm of microelectronics, however, switches are not so certain in their first steps toward changing state. As a switch makes contact, it hesitates, letting tiny currents flow and then halting them; then letting more flow. These initial jitters are called switch bounce, and it results from many causes. The contact materials of most switches are far from perfect. They may become coated with oxidation or other impurities, and they often don't mesh together perfectly. The contacts touch, bounce, cut through the crud, and finally mate firmly together. In the process, many tiny pulses of electricity can slip through. These pulses aren't enough to affect a light bulb, but can be more than sufficient to confuse a semiconductor circuit.

For use in computer circuits, switches require special electronics to remove the jitters, to debounce their contacts. Such debouncing circuits monitor the switch contacts and change the hesitating initial stabs at changing state into a sharp, certain switch. Unfortunately, each switch contact requires its own debouncer. This is not much of a concern with a single switch, but can be a nightmare for the designer who must debounce the 101 switches in a typical keyboard.

Instead of individual debouncing, computer keyboards use a different process for eliminating the hesitation from keyboard switches. The keyboard electronics do not detect when each switch changes, but check periodically to see if a switch has changed. When the electronics note a change in the state of a switch corresponding to the press of a key, they generate an indication of the switching that is sent along to your PC.

This process has its own shortcomings. The go-and-look method of detection adds a brief wait to signaling each keypress. Moreover, each key must be individually checked. But the high speed of today's computer circuits makes this system entirely workable. The process is reduced to a routine—the keyboard electronics scan each key at rates approaching a million times every second, looking for a change in the state of any key. In general, a microprocessor (an 8048-series device in the most popular keyboards) scans the keyboard for current changes every few microseconds, and the minute current flow caused by a keystroke can be detected. Because a slight chance exists that random noise—the stuff that must be debounced away—could cause a current pulse similar to that generated by a keystroke, keyboards may require that the increased current flow be detected during two or more consecutive scans of the keyboard.

Scan Codes

When a keystroke is detected, the microprocessor built into the keyboard then generates a scan code indicating which key was struck. The scan code is then converted to serial data and relayed to the microprocessor in the computer's system unit.

Each press of a key generates two different scan codes—one when the key is pushed down, and another when it pops back up. The two-code technique allows your computer system unit to tell when a key is pressed and held down—for example, when you hold down the Alt key while pressing a function key.

Each key generates a unique scan code. Even if the same legend appears on two keys, such as the duplicate number keys in the alphanumeric and numeric-and-cursor keypads, the individual keys generate the same codes. The code for a given key is the same whether the Caps Lock or other shift key is in effect. Table 11.1 shows the scan codes sent by the keys of the different IBM keyboards.

TABLE 11.1. Scan Codes on U.S. Keyboards

Alphanumeric Key Area (all keyboards)

Key	Make Code	Break Code
A	1E	9E
B	30	B0
C	2E	AE
D	20	A0
E	12	92
F	21	A1
G	22	A2
H	23	A3
I	17	97
J	24	A4
K	25	A5
L	26	A6

Key	Make Code	Break Code
M	32	B2
N	31	B1
O	18	98
P	19	99
Q	10	90
R	13	93
S	1F	9F
T	14	94
U	16	96
V	2F	AF
W	11	91
X	2D	AD
Y	15	95
Z	2C	AC
0 or)	0B	8B
1 or !	02	82
2 or @	03	83
3 or #	04	84
4 or $	05	85
5 or %	06	86
6 or ©	07	87
7 or &	08	88
8 or *	09	89
9 or (	0A	8A
° or ™	29	A9
- or _	0C	8C
= or +	0D	8D
[or {	1A	9A
] or }	1B	9B
¶ or ®	2B	AB

continues

TABLE 11.1. Continued

Alphanumeric Key Area (all keyboards)

Key	Make Code	Break Code
; or :	27	A7
' or "	28	A8
, or <	33	B3
/ or ?	35	B5
Left Shift	2A	AA
Left Ctrl	1D	9D
Left Alt	38	B8
Right Shift	36	B6
Right Alt	E0 38	E0 B8
Right Ctrl	E0 1D	E0 9D
Caps Lock	3A	BA
Backspace	0E	8E
Tab	0F	8F
Space bar	39	B9
Enter	1C	9C

Numeric/Cursor Keypad

Key	Make Code	Break Code
Scroll Lock	46	C6
Num Lock	45	C5
*	37	B7
-	4A	CA
+	4E	CE
Enter	E0 1C	E0 9C
1 or End	4F	CF
2	50	D0
3 or Pg Dn	51	D1
4	4B	CB
5	4C	CC
6	4D	CD
7 or Home	47	C7

Key	Make Code	Break Code
8	48	C8
9 or PgUp	49	C9
0 or Ins	52	D2
Num Lock	E0 35	E0 B5

Note:

When the keyboard is in a shifted state, the make code of the Num Lock key changes to AA, and the break code changes to E0 B5 2A.

Function Keys (F11 and F12 on Advanced and Compact Keyboards only)

Key	Make Code	Break Code
Esc	01	81
F1	3B	BB
F2	3C	BC
F3	3D	BD
F4	3E	BE
F5	3F	BF
F6	40	C0
F7	41	C1
F8	42	C2
F9	43	C3
F10	44	C4
F11	57	D7
F12	58	D8

Dedicated Cursor Area and Related Keys (Advanced and Compact Keyboards)

Key	Make Code	Break Code
↑	E0 48	E0 C8
↓	E0 50	E0 D0
←	E0 4B	E0 CB

continues

TABLE 11.1. Continued

Dedicated Cursor Area and Related Keys (Advanced and Compact Keyboards)

Key	Make Code	Break Code
→	E0 4D	E0 CD
Insert	E0 52	E0 D2
Home	E0 47	E0 C7
Page Up	E0 49	E0 C9
Key	Make Code	Break Code
Delete	E0 53	E0 D3
End	E0 4F	E0 CF

Note:

The keys send out different scan codes when the keyboard is in a shifted or Num Lock condition, effectively cancelling the effect of the locked shift. When the key is shifted, its scan code is preceded by E0 AA, mimicking the effect of pressing Shift before the key and temporarily nullifying the shift. The break code is followed by E0 2A, restoring the keyboard back to its shifted condition. Similarly, when the keyboard is in Num Lock state, the make codes of these keys are preceded by E0 2A, and the break codes are followed by E0 AA.

Page Down	E0 51	E0 D1
Scroll Lock	46	C6
Pause	E1 1D E1 9D C5	[None—Make only]
Print Screen	E0 2A E0 37	E0 B7 E0 AA

Note:

When the keyboard is in a shifted state or the Ctrl key is held down when the Print Screen key is pressed, it sends out a make code of E0 37 and a break code of E0 B7. When the Alt key is held down, the make code of Print Screen becomes 54, and the break code becomes D4. The Pause key also acts differently in the shifted or Ctrl state, sending out the make code E0 46 E0 C6.

Your computer receives these scan codes at a special I/O port. When a scan code is received by your computer, the keyboard controller chip issues an interrupt to notify the microprocessor that a scan code is available to be read. When that happens, your computer sorts through the scan codes and determines which keys are pressed and in which combination. The program code for doing this is part of your system's BIOS. The computer remembers the condition of the locking shift keys by changing special memory locations, called *status bytes*, to reflect each change made in their condition.

Normally, you do not have to deal with scan codes. The computer makes the translation to numbers and letters automatically and invisibly. The converted information is used in generating the information that appears on your monitor screen, to the applications you run, and even the programs you write. Sometimes, however, when you write your own programs, it is useful to detect every key change. You may, for example, want to cause something to happen when a certain key combination is pressed. Your program only needs to read the keyboard input port and compare what it finds there to a scan code chart.

Compatibility

The scan codes produced by all PC-compatible keyboards are the same, but not all keyboards are the same. When IBM developed its Personal Computer AT, the inner function of the keyboard was reconsidered, and IBM elected to make the keyboard programmable. Old keyboards—those shipped with the 8088-based PC and XT models—were one-way devices, sending scan codes to their host computers in a constant monologue. Today's keyboards accept commands from the computer and even have their own language.

Although you will never have to deal with the keyboard language (it's for programmers and hardware designers), it does make the pre- and post-AT keyboard designs incompatible. An AT keyboard does not work with PC and XT system units, nor does an XT keyboard work with today's computers.

IBM eliminated worries about keyboard compatibility in its own product line by changing its keyboard connectors in 1987 (but too late—for three years the company manufactured AT computers with the same keyboard connector as used by XT systems). Other keyboard makers compensated by putting switches on their products to select their compatibility. A few keyboards automatically detect the type of circuitry in your computer and adjust themselves accordingly.

Some keyboards, however, are not adjustable. Because XT-style systems and keyboards have been left far behind, many keyboard makers now feel safe in ignoring backward compatibility with them. Unless you have an ancient system that pre-dates the 1984 AT keyboard design change, you should not have to worry about the compatibility of your keyboard.

Connections

The scan-code system simplifies the connection scheme used by PC keyboards. Scan codes are sent from the keyboard to the computer serially so that only one wire conductor is needed to convey the keyboard data information. A second conductor is required to serve as a return path for the data signal, and as a ground, it serves as a common return for all other circuits in the keyboard cable. To synchronize the logic in the keyboard with that in the computer, a separate wire is used for a keyboard clock signal. A fourth and final wire is used to supply the keyboard with the five-volt direct current power that it needs to operate. These four conductors are all that is necessary to link keyboard to computer.

Most PCs follow the keyboard wiring system IBM designed for its original series of personal computers, based on a standard five-pin DIN connector. Pin one of the connector is assigned the keyboard clock signal; two, the keyboard data signal; four, the ground; five, the five-volt electrical supply. One of the connections provided by the keyboard plug—pin three—is assigned to carry a signal to reset the keyboard, but it is normally not used and need not be connected in normal keyboard cabling. Figure 11.1 shows the pin-out of a standard PC keyboard connector.

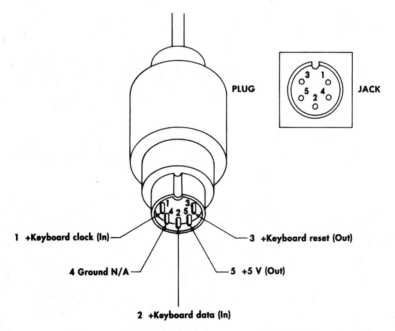

PLUG

JACK

1 +Keyboard clock (In)

3 +Keyboard reset (Out)

4 Ground N/A

5 +5 V (Out)

2 +Keyboard data (In)

FIGURE 11.1. IBM PC, XT, AT keyboard connectors, 5-pin DIN connector.

IBM adopted a new wiring scheme for its PS/2 series of machines that few other manufacturers have deigned to follow—Compaq being the only significant advocate of the new design. The PS/2 wiring system is based on a six-pin miniature DIN connector. Again, only four pins are significant to keyboard use: pin one is assigned keyboard data; pin three, ground; pin four, five volts; and pin five, keyboard clock. Pins two and six are reserved, and the shield is attached as a chassis ground. The pin-out connector is shown in Figure 11.2.

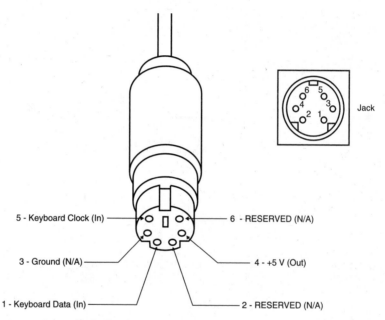

FIGURE 11.2. Systen end of a keyboard connector pin-out.

With the PS/2 series, IBM also designed its keyboard to accept different keyboard cables by making the cable detachable from the keyboard. This detachable design makes the cable easy to service (by replacing it) and a single keyboard adaptable to between five-pin and six-pin cabling standards. The keyboard-to-cable connection uses a modular (AMP) jack on the rear of the keyboard with a matching plug on the cable. It has the following assignments: A, reserved; B, keyboard data; C, ground; D, keyboard clock; E, five volts; F, reserved. When looking at the gold contacts of the connector, the contacts are labeled in reverse alphabetical order from left to right (see fig. 11.3).

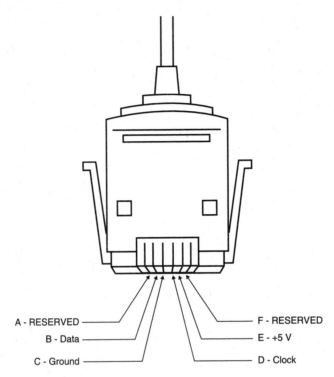

FIGURE 11.3. Keyboard end of a keyboard connector pin-out.

Key Layouts

Rather than technology, the appeal of a particular keyboard is governed by a more mundane matter—the key layout. At one time the proper layout of the function keys and other ancillary keys was debated as fervently as religious beliefs. The issue now has been resolved by the simple practicality that almost all systems now come equipped with keyboards arranged in the manner of IBM's 101-key Enhanced Keyboard of 1987.

Achieving this keyboard standard was not easy. IBM offered at least eight different keyboards with its personal computers. Four really were not mainstream products: two designs were meant only for the PCjr, one fit the Portable PC, and one was designed particularly for the 3270 PC. Three of the others marked a progression of adjustments in key layout and convenience features. The last design provides a smaller, more convenient alternative for crowded desks.

83-Key

IBM's first design accompanied its first personal computers and offered 83 keys, as shown in Figure 11.4. Most of the arrangement followed the typewriter standard—a big set of alphabetical keys in the middle of the keyboard. In addition, IBM put two vertical rows of function keys at the left of the main alphanumeric keypad, and forced cursor controls to share the same keypad with a calculator-style array of numbers for direct data entry. The Enter key was small and ambiguously identified with a bent arrow legend, and no indicators were provided for the three locking shift keys (Caps Lock, Num Lock, and Scroll Lock). This design remained standard through the introduction of the AT in 1984.

FIGURE 11.4. Layout of the original IBM PC and XT keyboards.

The complaints about the original design concerned mainly the layout of peripheral keys. The left-hand function keys did not correspond to the bottom-of-the-screen listings of function key assignments used by most programs. The lack of indicators lead to many mistypings of numbers for cursor movements and capital letters for lowercase. Spreadsheets needed both a numeric keypad and cursor control keys, and the Enter key was too small.

84-Key

After years of complaints in the press, IBM took heed and introduced a new keyboard layout with the AT. This new layout had an additional key—Sys Req, designed primarily for use with multiuser applications. Enter was made bigger, Selectric-size, and indicators were provided for the locking shift keys (see fig. 11.5).

FIGURE 11.5. Original IBM AT keyboard layout.

101-Key

With the introduction of the upgraded AT, IBM also unleashed another new keyboard, termed the Advanced Keyboard by IBM but also commonly called the Enhanced Keyboard. Although electrically similar to the original AT product—to the extent that they can be plugged in interchangeably and it remains incompatible with PCs and XTs—the layout was altered again.

The advance the Enhanced Keyboard made was a greater endowment of keys—to a total of 101 in the standard United States model; international models gain one more (see fig. 11.6).

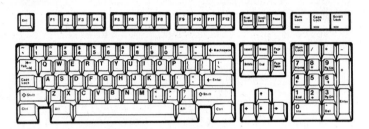

FIGURE 11.6. IBM Advanced Keyboard layout.

The key additions were several. A new, dedicated cursor control pad was provided separate from the combined numeric and cursor pad, and several other control keys were duplicated in another small pad. Two new function keys (F11 and F12) were added, and all 12 were moved to a top row, above and slightly separated from the alphanumeric area. Duplicate Ctrl and Alt keys were provided at either side of the space bar, and Caps Lock was moved to the former location of the Ctrl key.

One supposed blessing provided by the Advanced design—the top row function keys—was something demanded by computer writers since the introduction of the PC. Finally, the function keys corresponded to the positions of on-screen key labels, and the complainers learned that the left twin rows of function keys were much more convenient to use, particularly when needed in combination with Alt or Ctrl. What once could be done with one hand now required two.

Moreover, the relocated function keys proved to be more cumbersome to use. The smaller Enter key of the new design was more apt to be missed in fast typing. The new keyboard was designed more for hunt-and-peck key bangers than proficient typists—probably the exact people who complained most loudly about the earlier designs. In fact, probably the same people who complained that the letters are not arranged in alphabetic order.

The PS/2 line universally uses the IBM Advanced Keyboard or a special reduced-size keyboard designed primarily for the tiny Model 25. The layout of the latter is shown in figure 11.7.

Compatible Keyboards

Compatible computer makers have tried to keep pace with IBM and have adapted their keyboards to the prevailing standard. Thus they followed suit in adopting the Advanced design, its drawbacks notwithstanding. Some manufacturers compounded the confusion created by IBM's troika of key layouts by adding their own subtle refinements, a complete elaboration of which would probably require a book of its own. Anything out of the normal alphanumeric contingent is a candidate for roving around the keyboard.

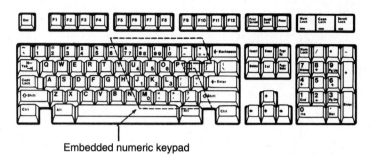

Embedded numeric keypad

FIGURE 11.7. IBM Compact keyboard layout.

Several also include extra key caps to enable you to swap the position of the left-hand Ctrl and Caps Lock keys so that Ctrl falls in its more familiar position. The electrical relocation is handled either through another keyboard switch or through software that you must run on the host computer. Although these features cannot be added to an existing keyboard, they are worth looking at when buying a replacement.

QWERTY

The one unvarying aspect of keyboards also seems the oddest—the unalphabetical arrangement of the alphabet keys. Anyone new to typing will be amazed and perplexed at the seemingly nonsensical arrangement of letters on the keys of the typical computer keyboard. Even the name given to this esoteric layout has the ring of some kind of black magic or odd cabala—QWERTY. Simply a list of the first six characters on the top row of the nominal arrangement, the absurdity harks back to the keyboard of the first practical typewriter.

A legend surrounds the QWERTY arrangements. The typewriter was invented in 1867 by Christopher Sholes, and his first keyboard had its letter keys arranged alphabetically. Within a year of his invention, however, Sholes discovered what he viewed as a superior arrangement, QWERTY.

According to the common myth, Sholes created QWERTY because typists pounded on keys faster than the simple mechanisms of the first typewriters could handle. The keys jammed. The odd QWERTY arrangement slowed down the typists and prevented the jams.

Sholes left no record of how he came upon the QWERTY arrangement, but it certainly was not to slow down speedy typists. High typing rates imply modern-day touch typing, 10 fingers flying across the keyboard. This style of typing did not arise until about 10 years after Sholes had settled on the QWERTY arrangement. Typewriter development was indeed slow—the Shift key wasn't added to the basic design to permit lowercase characters until 1878!

Other hypotheses about the QWERTY placement also lead to dead-ends. For example, breaking a strict alphabetic order to separate the keys and prevent the type bars (the levers that swing up to strike letters on paper) from jamming doesn't make sense because the arrangement of the type bars has no direct relationship to the arrangement of keys.

There is no doubt that the standard arrangement is not the only possible ordering of the alphabet—in fact, there are 26 (or 26 factorial, exactly 403,291,461,126,605,635,584,000,000) different possible arrangements of letters alone, not to mention the further complications of using rows of different lengths and non-alphabetic keys. QWERTY is not the only possible layout, and it's probably not the best. Nor is it the worst. But it is the standard that millions of people have spent years mastering.

Dvorak-Dealey Keyboard

The most familiar challenger to QWERTY, one that crawls in a distant second in popularity and use, is the Dvorak-Dealey letter arrangement, named for its developers, August Dvorak and William L. Dealey. The name is often shortened to Dvorak.

The Dvorak-Dealey design incorporates several ideas that should lead to faster typing. A basic goal is to foster the alternation of hands in typing. After you strike one letter with a key under a finger of your left hand, the next key you'll want to press likely is under a right-hand finger. This hand alteration is a faster typing strategy. To make hand alternation more likely, the Dvorak-Dealey arrangement places all vowels in the home row under the lefthand's fingertips and the consonants used most often in the right hand's home row. Note that the Dvorak-Dealey arrangement was developed for speed and does nothing to make the keyboard more alphabetic or easier to learn to use (see fig. 11.8).

FIGURE 11.8. The Dvorak-Dealey key layout (as implemented in the PC-compatible Key Tronic KB 5150D).

The first publication of the Dvorak-Dealey keyboard was in the 1936 book *Typewriting Behavior*, authored by the developers of the new letter arrangement. To back up the philosophic and theoretical advantages attributed to the Dvorak-Dealey arrangement, tests were conducted in the 1930s on mechanical typewriters, amounting to typing races between the QWERTY and Dvorak-Dealey key arrangements. Dvorak and Dealey ran the tests, and—not surprisingly—they came out the winner by factors as large as 30 percent.

Dvorak believed in both his keyboard and his test results and wrote papers promoting his ideas. Alas, the more he wrote, the greater his claims became. Articles like "There Is a Better Typewriter Keyboard" in the December, 1943 issue of *National Business Education Quarterly* has been called by some experts "full of factual errors." Tests run by the United States Navy and the General Accounting Office reported much more modest results for Dvorak.

Notwithstanding the exaggerated claims, the Dvorak layout does offer some potential advantages in typing speed, at least after you become skilled in its use. The penalty for its increased typing throughput is increased difficulty in typing when confronted with a QWERTY keyboard.

The design of the PC makes converting to Dvorak relatively easy. Whereas typewriters have to be redesigned for the new key arrangement, you can just plug a new keyboard into your PC. Commercial Dvorak keyboards often are available by special order.

In fact, if you don't mind your keytop legend bearing no likeness to the characters that actually appear on your screen (and in your files), you can simply reprogram your PC to think that it has a Dvorak keyboard by intercepting the signals sent by the keyboard to your computer and converting them on the fly.

Mice

For many people, the keyboard is the most formidable and forbidding aspect of a PC. The keys may as well be teeth ready to chomp down on their fingers as soon as they try to type. Typing isn't something that comes naturally to most people. Learning to type takes months or years of practice—practice that's about as welcome as a piano lesson on a sunny afternoon when the rest of the neighborhood kids are playing outside.

One idea aimed at making the computer more accessible is the mouse. The idea was developed by Douglas C. Engelbart during his tenure at the Stanford Research Institute between 1957 and 1977 and first found fame as the pointing device coupled with a graphical/menu-driven on-screen user interface developed at the Palo Alto Research Laboratory of Xerox Corporation. The underlying concept is to allow a computer user to indicate what function he wants his computer to carry out by selecting from a list of commands presented as a menu. The user points at the menu selection by physically moving the pointing device, which causes a corresponding on-screen movement of the cursor. One or more buttons atop the device enables the user to indicate that he wants to select a menu item.

The device is small enough to fit under the palm of a hand with the button under a fingertip. The cord connecting the device to its computer host trailing like a tail and the need to make the device scurry around the desktop to carry out its function, quickly earned it the name mouse. The whole process of moving the mouse and its on-screen representation is termed dragging the mouse.

Apple Computer, understanding the need to make computers more accessible by making them easier to use, incorporated the best of the Palo Alto ideas into its Macintosh, including the mouse. IBM, more performance than ease-of-entry oriented, only made the mouse a built-in feature of its personal computers with the introduction of the Micro Channel PS/2 line. Each machine incorporates a special mouse port in its motherboard circuitry.

Mice can be distinguished by four chief differences: the technology they use; the number of buttons they have; the manner in which they connect with their computer hosts; and the protocol or language they use to encode the information they send to your PC.

Mechanical Mice

The first mouse was a mechanical design based on a small ball that protruded through its bottom and rotated as the mouse was pushed along a surface. Switches inside the mouse detected the movement and relayed the direction of the ball's rotation to the host computer.

Although the ball is free to rotate in any direction, only four directions are detected, corresponding to two axes of a two-dimensional coordinate system. The movement in each of the four directions is quantified (in hundredths of an inch) and sent to the host as a discrete signal for each discrete increment of movement.

The mechanical mouse works on just about any surface. In general, the rotating ball has a coarse texture and is made from a rubbery compound that even grips on smooth surfaces. In fact, you can even turn a mechanical mouse upside down and spin the ball with your finger (although you'll then have difficulty fingering the pushbuttons!).

On the other hand, the mechanical mouse requires that you move it across a surface of some kind, and all too many desks do not have enough free space to give the mouse a good run. (Of course, if all else fails, you can run a mechanical mouse across your pants leg or skirt, but you're likely to get some odd looks.) In addition, mechanical parts can break. A mechanical mouse tends to pick up dirt and lint that can impede its proper operation. Regularly clean your mechanical mouse even if you think your desktop is spotless.

Optical Mice

The alternative technology to the mechanical mouse is the optical mouse. Instead of a rotating ball, the optical mouse uses a light beam to detect movement across a specially patterned mouse pad. No moving parts means that the optical mouse has less to get dirty or break.

The typical optical mouse uses two pairs of LEDs and photodetectors on its bottom, one pair oriented at right angles to the other. Its matching mouse pad is coated with an overlapped pattern of blue and yellow grids. Each pair of LEDs and photodetectors detects motion in either direction across one axis of the grid. A felt-like covering on the bottom of the mouse makes it easy to slide across the plastic-coated mouse pad.

The big disadvantage of the optical mouse is that it requires that you use its special mouse pad. The pad itself can get dirty and become damaged. The plastic coating can stick to your bare forearm on a humid day and lift off in sheets. In a normal, air-conditioned office environment, however, it should prove long-lasting and trouble-free.

Buttons

In its purest form, the mouse has exactly one pushbutton. Movement of the mouse determines the position of the on-screen cursor, but a selection is made only when that button is pressed, preventing any menu selections that the mouse is inadvertently dragged across from being chosen.

One button is the least confusing arrangement and the minimum necessary to carry out mouse functions. Operating the computer is reduced to nothing more than pressing the button. Carefully tailored menu selections allow the single button to suffice in controlling all computer functions. The Apple Macintosh uses this kind of mouse with one button.

Two buttons allow more flexibility, however. For example, one can be given a "Do" function, and a second, an "Undo" function. In a drawing program, one might "lower" the pen analog that traces lines across the screen while the other button "lifts" the pen.

Of course, three buttons would be even better. The programmer would have yet more flexibility. Maybe four buttons would—but as the number of mouse buttons rises, the mouse becomes increasingly like a keyboard. It becomes a more formidable device with a more rigorous learning curve. A profusion of mouse buttons is counterproductive.

Three buttons is the practical limit because three positions are available for index, middle, and ring fingers while the thumb and pinkie grab the sides of the mouse. Most applications use two or fewer buttons, and the most popular mice are the two-button variety. There's nothing wrong with three-button mice—they can do everything two-button mice can and more—but most applications don't require the extra button.

Interfaces

To communicate its codes to your computer, the mouse must be connected in some way. Mice connect with PCs through any of three ways: a serial port, a built-in dedicated mouse port, or a special adapter that plugs into an expansion slot. Mice that use these methods are called (respectively) serial mice, proprietary mice, and bus mice.

Serial Mice

Most mice adapt to a port that is generally available—the standard serial port. Serial mice simply plug in and deliver their movement codes to the serial port. Driver software for operating the mouse gives the mouse priority by generating an interrupt whenever a new mouse movement code appears at the port. The driver then passes along the mouse code to the software in control.

In general, mice make no onerous demands on the serial port. They operate at a low communication rate, 1,200 bits per second, and adapt to any available port. However, because every mouse movement generates a serial-port interrupt, if your system has more than two serial ports, you have to be careful which port you assign your mouse. Because serial ports 1 and 4 (that is, the ports that DOS calls COM1 and COM4) share interrupt four and serial ports 2 and 3 (COM2 and COM3) share interrupt three, a mouse can conflict with another device connected to the other port sharing its interrupt. It's always best to plug your mouse into the port that does not have to share its interrupt (for example, COM1 if your PC has three serial ports) to avoid surprises—the kind that can crash your PC.

Bus Mice

Another way to avoid serial port conflicts is to avoid serial ports. Sometimes this strategy is forced upon you—your PC has only two ports and you have a modem and plotter connected and want to plug in a mouse. The alternative is attaching the mouse to a dedicated mouse adapter that plugs into your computer's expansion bus. These so-called bus mice work identically to serial mice except that they use their own dedicated ports.

In most cases, these special mouse ports conform to the RS-232 standard and act just like serial ports except that they cannot be directly accessed by DOS because the operating system doesn't know to what I/O addresses the ports are assigned. Otherwise, a bus mouse is just like any other mouse. It can use optical or mechanical technology and have any number of buttons.

If you have a spare serial port, you probably will want a serial mouse because you pay extra for the bus mouse's adapter card. If you are short on serial ports, however, you likely will want a bus mouse.

Proprietary Mice

Some PCs, such as the IBM PS/2 series and some Compaq computers, have built-in mouse ports. These make mouse matters elementary. You simply plug the mouse into the mouse port without worrying about interrupt conflicts or tying up a serial port. At heart, these proprietary mouse ports are just bus mouse connections built into your PC. (Some compatible machines just slide a bus adapter into an expansion slot. IBM builds the circuitry onto the motherboard.)

From a performance standpoint, the style of mouse you choose makes little difference. All three kinds of mouse interfaces use the equivalent of a serial connection. The principal factors in choosing one over the other are the resources of your PC.

Obviously, you need a serial port if you want to attach a serial mouse that plugs into such a port. If you have a spare serial port, a serial mouse is the least expensive way of adding a pointing device to your PC.

Most people, however, have designs on all their serial ports and consequently do not want to tie them up with a mouse cable. The bus mouse provides a way out. The bus mouse host adapter does not steal a COM port from DOS nor does it share one of the serial port interrupts, the sharing of which often causes problems with modem communications. The only problems associated with using a bus mouse are finding a spare slot into which to slide the host adapter and the extra cash to pay for the additional hardware. A bus mouse and a serial mouse work effectively the same way. Which you choose makes no difference to your software.

If your system has a built-in mouse port, you may be stuck needing a proprietary mouse. Although your source of supply may be more limited (and the mice consequently more costly), a proprietary mouse is the easiest of all to install.

Protocols

Mice convert the motions they detect into a digital code that can be processed or analyzed by your PC. The only loose end is what code the mouse uses. A standard mouse code would help software writers craft their products to better take advantage of mice. A standard mouse code would be so useful, in fact, that the industry has come up with four distinct standards, called mouse protocols. These standards were developed by four of the major forces in the mouse industry, and each bears its originator's name. These include: Microsoft, Mouse Systems Corporation (for a period known as MSC Corporation), Logitech, and IBM Corporation. The first three were designed for individual mouse products created by the respective companies. The IBM protocol was introduced with the PS/2 series of computers, which came equipped with a built-in jack that accepted a mouse.

In truth, you don't need to know the details of any of these protocols. You only need to know that they exist, and that they are different. Match the protocol used by your mouse to your applications.

Today, the Microsoft mouse protocol is the most prevalent. Many applications are written to directly accept code from Microsoft-compatible mice. For example, Windows 3.1 makes direct contact with any mouse compatible with the Microsoft mouse protocol. You can use other mice with these applications, but setting things up is a bit more difficult because other mice require the use of software drivers to convert their protocols into a form that the applications understand.

Note that PS/2 mouse ports are more hardware-specific and require mice that use the IBM protocol. A growing number of applications are being written to directly accept this protocol as well.

Most mice sold today can emulate the Microsoft mouse protocol. Those that have this emulation built into their hardware can be directly substituted for a Microsoft mouse. Others require the use of drivers to make the match.

The important issue is to check your applications for what mouse protocols they will accept. You then can use any mouse that can match those protocols. Figures 11.9 through 11.11 list the codes used by many popular mice.

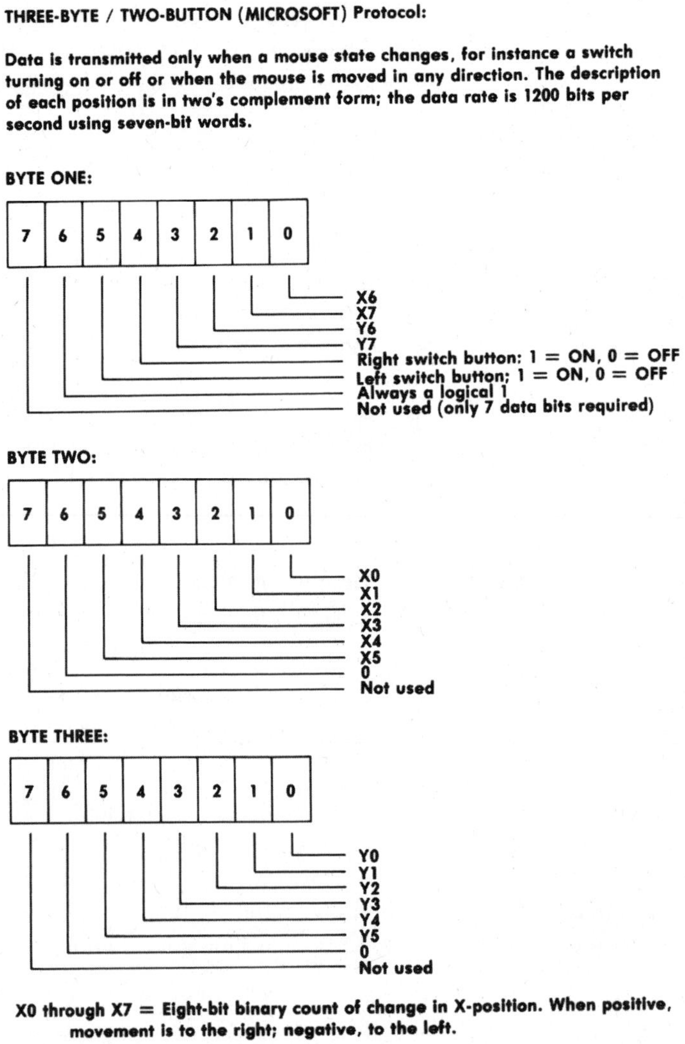

THREE-BYTE / TWO-BUTTON (MICROSOFT) Protocol:

Data is transmitted only when a mouse state changes, for instance a switch turning on or off or when the mouse is moved in any direction. The description of each position is in two's complement form; the data rate is 1200 bits per second using seven-bit words.

BYTE ONE:

| 7 | 6 | 5 | 4 | 3 | 2 | 1 | 0 |

- X6
- X7
- Y6
- Y7
- Right switch button: 1 = ON, 0 = OFF
- Left switch button; 1 = ON, 0 = OFF
- Always a logical 1
- Not used (only 7 data bits required)

BYTE TWO:

| 7 | 6 | 5 | 4 | 3 | 2 | 1 | 0 |

- X0
- X1
- X2
- X3
- X4
- X5
- 0
- Not used

BYTE THREE:

| 7 | 6 | 5 | 4 | 3 | 2 | 1 | 0 |

- Y0
- Y1
- Y2
- Y3
- Y4
- Y5
- 0
- Not used

X0 through X7 = Eight-bit binary count of change in X-position. When positive, movement is to the right; negative, to the left.

FIGURE 11.9. Mouse control codes (courtesy of MSC Technologies, Inc.).

BYTE ONE:

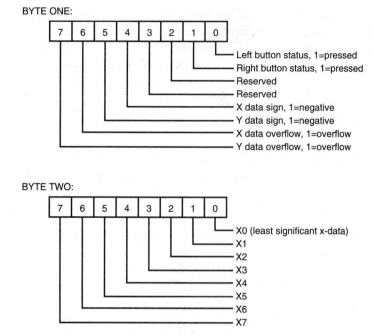

Left button status, 1=pressed
Right button status, 1=pressed
Reserved
Reserved
X data sign, 1=negative
Y data sign, 1=negative
X data overflow, 1=overflow
Y data overflow, 1=overflow

BYTE TWO:

X0 (least significant x-data)
X1
X2
X3
X4
X5
X6
X7

BYTE THREE:

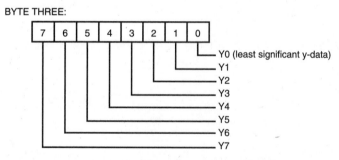

Y0 (least significant y-data)
Y1
Y2
Y3
Y4
Y5
Y6
Y7

FIGURE 11.10. Mouse control codes (courtesy of MSC Technologies, Inc.).

Resolution

Mice are sometimes rated by their resolution—the number of Counts Per Inch or CPI that they can detect. When a mouse is moved, it sends a signal indicating each increment of motion it makes as a single count. The number of these increments in an inch of movement equals the mouse's CPI rating.

The higher the CPI, the finer the detail in the movement the mouse can detect. Unless the mouse driver compensates, higher resolution has an odd effect. More resolution translates into faster movement of the mouse pointer on-screen because the screen pointer is controlled by the number of counts received from the mouse, not the actual distance the mouse is moved. Consequently, a higher resolution mouse is a faster mouse, not a more precise mouse.

The true limit on how precisely you can position your mouse cursor is your own hand. If you want to be more accurate with your mouse, you can compensate for your human limitations by opting for less resolution from your mouse. Because you have to move your mouse physically farther for each on-screen change, a lower mouse resolution helps you put the cursor where you want it.

Trackballs

Just like the namesake in the Rodentia, the computer mouse needs room to roam and ends up almost anywhere. A mouse does not stay put because moving around is in its nature—and that's how you use it.

The problem is that many folks do not have room for a roaming rodent. Their desks are just too cluttered or they are traveling with a laptop and neglected to carry a desk along with them into the coach-class cabin. More insidious issues also involve mice. Pushing a plastic rodent requires clumsy, wasteful, and tiring whole-arm movements. Mice are inefficient and exhausting.

The leading mouse alternative, the trackball, eliminates these problems. Essentially a mouse turned upside down, the trackball is much like it sounds—an often big ball that, when rotated, causes the screen pointer (mouse cursor) to track its movements. The trackball spins in place and requires no more desk space than its base, a few square inches. Portable trackballs are designed to clip onto laptop and notebook computers, extending the width of the machine by no more than a few inches.

Y0 through Y7 = Eight-bit binary count of change in Y-position. When positive, movement is downward; negative indicates upward.

FIVE-BYTE / THREE-BUTTON (MOUSE SYSTEMS) Protocol:

Five bytes are used as a data block. The beginning of the data block is indicated by a sync byte the first five bits of which are always 10000 (binary). The remaining three bits code the state of the three mouse pushbuttons. The next four bytes encode the change in the mouse's position since the last data block. The second and third bytes encode the change in the X- and Y-positions of the mouse since the last data block; the fourth and fifth byte encode the change in X- and Y-positions since the readings given in the second and third bytes. In effect, each data block encodes two changes of mouse position as two's complement, 8-bit binary numbers.

X7 and Y7 define the direction of mouse travel. When X7 is 0, it indicates motion to the right; Y7 at 0 indicates motion upward or in the direction of the mouse cord.

Codes are transmitted as eight-bit words at 1200 bits per second with no parity.

BYTE ONE:

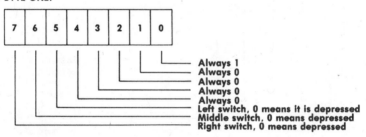

BYTE TWO:

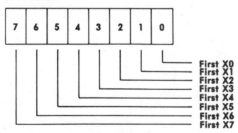

FIGURE 11.11. Mouse control codes (courtesy of MSC Technologies, Inc.).

BYTE THREE:

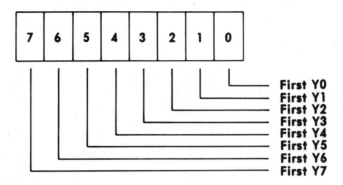

BYTE FOUR:

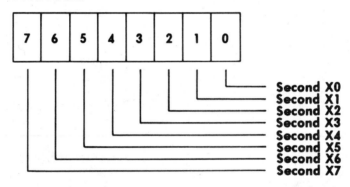

BYTE FIVE:

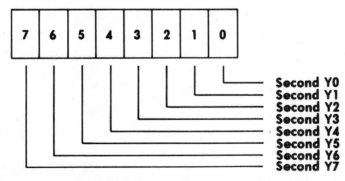

FIGURE 11.11, cont. Mouse control codes (courtesy of MSC Technologies, Inc.).

Switches

As with mice, trackballs also require switches so that you can indicate when the cursor is pointing to what you want. Most trackballs have two or three pushbuttons that duplicate the selection functions of mouse buttons. Although some trackballs boast four buttons, the foursome typically functions as two duplicate pairs—mirror images—so that one trackball can serve either a right or left hand.

No standard exists for switch placement on trackballs because no consensus exists on how you are supposed to operate a trackball. Some are designed so that you spin the ball with your fingers. Others prefer that your thumb do the job. Which is better depends on whom you believe and how you prefer to work.

A company which makes trackballs that operate with the fingers maintains that your fingers are more agile than your thumb, so they are more precise at spinning the ball. A competing company that makes a trackball designed for thumb control says that the thumb has more muscle control than the fingers. Some makers wisely don't take sides and make trackballs that can be used equally adeptly by the thumb or the fingers.

Ball Size

Another trackball design choice is the size of the ball itself and how it is retained inside the mechanism. Various products range in dimensions from the size of a shooter marble to those equaling cue balls. Bigger once was thought to be better, but the trackballs built into laptop and notebook computers are making smaller sizes popular. (In fact, the most compelling reason that big trackballs are big is that a ready supply of balls is available on the pool table.)

Because no definitive study has shown the superiority of any particular size for a trackball, the best advice is to select one that feels best to you—or the one that comes already attached to your PC.

As with the balls in mechanical mice, trackballs naturally attract dirt. Although the trackball doesn't pick up dirt from rolling around, dust does fall upon the ball and the oils from your fingers collect there, too. A readily removable ball can be quickly and easily cleaned. This sort of serviceability is absent from many trackball designs—something to consider if you plan to use your trackball for a long time.

Handedness

Most mice are symmetrical. Although two- and three-button mice define different functions for their left- and right-side buttons, most enable you to flip the functions of the buttons to suit right or left hand operation if what button falls under a given finger is important to you.

Trackballs, however, are sometimes asymmetrical. In itself, that can be good. An asymmetrical trackball can better fit the hand that it is designed for, either right or left. But this handedness among trackballs poses a problem when you make your purchase; you need to determine whether you want a right- or left-handed trackball. Which you need does not necessarily correspond to the way you write. Some left-handed people prefer right-handed trackballs (and some righties like lefties). Consequently, a right-handed trackball isn't always the best choice for a right-handed person. Before you buy a one-handed trackball, make sure that you know which hand you will favor in using it. If you switch hands when you tire from using one hand for spinning your trackball all day long, you may not want a product with definite handedness at all.

Protocols

To communicate with your programs, trackballs must send positioning information back to your PC exactly as mice must. Because mice came first and have established workable protocols, trackball makers simply adopted the various mouse standards as their own. Consequently, most trackballs mimic the Microsoft mouse and use exactly the same protocol. Other trackballs are designed to plug directly into IBM's PS/2s as mouse substitutes, so they use IBM's mouse protocol.

As with mice, the protocol used by a trackball must match that supported by your PC and its software. Other than that issue of compatibility, you don't need to worry about trackball protocols.

Resolution

As with mice, trackballs are sometimes rated in resolution, the number of counts per inch of movement (CPI). As with mouse resolution, these numbers don't necessarily indicate precision. A higher number of counts per inch actually makes a trackball less precise to use. A trackball with a high number of counts per inch moves your on-screen pointer a greater distance for every degree of spin you give the ball. As a result, the high CPI trackball makes the on-screen cursor move faster but with less control. A low number of counts per inch means that you must spin the ball farther to move the cursor, giving you greater precision in your control.

Most trackball manufacturers now give you several choices for the effective resolution of their products so that you can tailor its actions and reactions to match the way you work. In addition, most trackball makers offer ballistic operation in which the translation of ball movement to on-screen cursor change varies with the speed of the ball's spin. This yields fast positioning without loss of precision. The only problem is getting used to such non-linear control in which the speed at which you spin the trackball has as much (sometimes more) effect as how far you spin it.

Unlike most other peripherals, no one trackball is objectively better than the rest. Operating any of them is an acquired talent like brain surgery, piano-playing, or hair-combing. Any judgment must be subjective, and which is better suited to a particular user depends most on personal preference and familiarity.

Non-Ball Trackballs

In the endless quest for the ultimate pointing device for laptop and notebook computers, designers have developed a number of intriguing ideas that either have not caught on or have not yet had time to catch on. Two of the most promising are the Isopoint device and the pointing stick.

Invented by Craig Culver, the Isopoint device acts like a trackball that uses a rolling bar instead of a ball. Designed to be located just below the space bar of your keyboard, the Isopoint is perfectly placed for you to operate with one of your thumbs. To move your on-screen cursor vertically, you roll the Isopoint bar as if it were a one-dimensional trackball. To move left or right, you push the spring-loaded roller, and the force you apply determines the speed at which the cursor races along. To click as you would a mouse, press down on the roller. Auxiliary switches on either side of the roller can be added to replicate the function of the extra buttons on two- and three-button mice.

The technology behind the Isobar isn't revolutionary—it just uses switches and encoders like a mouse or trackball. The genius is the shape and location. Easy to grope and find, it fits right under your thumb without taking up too much room. Unlike the trackballs added to laptop computers, you don't need to take your fingers from the home row to use the Isopoint device. The disadvantage of the product is, as with any other revolutionary idea, it's different.

The pointing stick (called Trackball II in IBM notebooks) was developed by Ted Selker and Joseph D. Rutledge of IBM's Thomas J. Watson Research Center and first used in IBM notebook computers. In principle, the pointing stick is a miniature joystick that's stuck between the "G" and "H" keys of a conventional keyboard. The pointing stick protrudes just two millimeters above the normal typing surface. Its position enables you to maneuver it with either index finger while the rest of your fingers remain in the home row. Because in normal touch-typing your fingers should never cross the G-H boundary, it does not interfere with normal typing. The selection function of mouse buttons is passed over to bar keys at the lower edge of the keyboard, adjacent to the space bar.

Unlike joysticks, the pointing stick itself does not move. Instead, it reacts to pressure. IBM believes the key to the success of the pointing stick is the algorithm it uses to determine the speed to move your on-screen cursor. In general, the more force you apply to the pointing stick, the faster the cursor moves—up to a maximum speed that corresponds to your ability to follow the cursor motion (as determined by human-factor experiments in the Watson lab).

Light Pens

Sometimes what you want to do with your computer is so obvious you could just point at the screen. If only you could move things around by pointing at them you would have instant, easy control.

A light pen enables you to do exactly that. Shaped like a pen but trailing a cord, the light pen allows your computer to register positions on-screen by pointing at them. The trick is inside the pen. At the tip is a photodetector that can detect changes in brightness. The picture tube in a computer monitor is lit by a scanning electron beam that lights tiny patches on-screen by scanning them back-and-forth and top-to-bottom. As each patch of the screen is struck by the beam, it briefly glows. The beam repeats its scan of the tube face so fast—50 to 70 times a second—that it appears continuously lit to you but not to the sharp eye of the light pen.

The light pen registers the instant the patch on-screen lights up, then signals to your computer at that instant. Your computer can determine exactly where the pen is because it knows where the scanning electron beam is all the time. From the light pen, the computer can tell where you are pointing on-screen.

You can use the light pen for anything that requires pointing. For example with a painting program, you can draw on your monitor screen with a light pen as if it were filled with ink and the screen were paper. The light pen is used in graphic editing so that artists need only point to the screen or circle design elements they want to change or move.

The light pen is a wonderful idea but one that is inefficient and has low resolution, limited to the sharpness that your monitor can display. It also makes your arm tired when you stretch it toward the screen all day long. Consequently, light pens have fallen from favor. A light-pen interface was once part of IBM's graphics adapters (CGA and EGA), but today's VGA boards have no provisions for connecting a light pen. The light pen interface is not included on the IBM Monochrome Display Adapter because most light pens do not work with the IBM monochrome display. The lingering glow of the IBM green screens does not give the sharp on-off transition the light pen needs to detect its position on-screen. On the graphics adapters supporting light pens, the connector is simply a header on the card itself that requires you to route a cable from inside the computer outside to the light pen.

By itself, the light pen does little that's useful. It simply provides a signal at an input/output port. Your software must determine what to do with the signal. To make a light pen useful, you need a special software driver or an application specifically written to use a light pen.

Today's pen-based computers do not use light pens. Instead they use electromagnetic sensing, the same technology as digitizing tablets.

Digitizers

If a trackball is a mouse turned upside down, the digitizer is a mouse turned inside out. A digitizer puts the pointing element in your hand and surrounds it with its sensing mechanism. More than mere mechanics, however, the digitizer turns the concept of the mouse inside out. Whereas the mouse cares about only where it is moving from, the digitizer is locked to its surroundings. For the mouse, everything is relative; for the digitizer, all is absolute.

From appearance alone, you may miss these differences. A digitizer uses a pointing device that moves around on a dedicated pad. The pointing device itself may resemble a mouse with cross-hairs or an overweight fountain pen. They seem to work the same—move the pointing device, and a cursor on-screen travels in sync. Work with both for a while, however, and the big difference quickly becomes apparent. Lift the mouse and move it, and the on-screen cursor still starts from where you left it. Move the digitizer and plunk it down, and the cursor on-screen immediately leaps to the new location.

That is the difference between relative and absolute. The mouse is a relative positioning device. It builds each move on the preceding move. It has no memory and does not keep track of where it is. The digitizer is locked to its surroundings, and its absolute position determines where the cursor appears on-screen.

If you are tracing a drawing or sketching without looking at the screen, the difference can be dramatic. The digitizer follows your work. The mouse forces you to concentrate on the screen. Each has its own advantages, and either can surpass the capabilities of the keyboard when it comes to working with graphics.

The difference between absolute and relative positioning holds only for the native mode of digitizers, however. Most of today's digitizing tablets include mouse drivers that allow them to emulate one or another mouse (Microsoft's mouse is the most popular emulation). Equipped with such an emulation, the digitizing tablet becomes more versatile than the mouse because it can deliver both absolute and relative positioning information, depending on what the application software requires.

Pointers

The part of a digitizer you hold in your hand goes by various names. Two entirely different styles are popular.

The kind that resembles the mouse is most often called a cursor, although some manufacturers call it a puck or sometimes tracer. The style that resembles a pen with a pituitary problem is called—not surprisingly—a *pen* (some manufacturers prefer to use the more scientific-sounding term *stylus*).

The shape and feel of a cursor or pen is the most subjective aspect of using a digitizing tablet. In general, a pen feels like using an bloated ballpoint, not unlike the typical technical pen. For the most part, the cursor is simply a hunk of plastic you can conveniently hold that provides a vehicle for pushbutton switches. While no cursor is as hand-pleasing as a Microsoft or KeyTronic mouse, they range from an ok grip to a cramp and a gripe about style over function.

The number of buttons you need on a cursor depends mostly on how many of your favorite applications it supports; pattern is a matter of preference. The endowments of most cursors range from 2 to 16 buttons. Two buttons give you the same point-and-click capability as a mouse. A 16-button cursor means that you may rarely need to go back to your keyboard to elicit functions, but you will probably still need to squint at the cursor or scratch your head to remember which button does what.

Pens differ in the number of buttons they offer, too. In general, all pens give at least one switch that's activated by pressing down on the point, the tip-switch. A second button (and sometimes a third) on the side of the pen near the tip may also be available. How useful additional buttons are depends on the software you use. Each button simply sends out a different code, which your software must interpret.

Many digitizer pens have internal ink supplies so that you can draw on paper as you transmit data back to your PC. Sometimes a manufacturer distinguishes its digitizer pens from a digitizer stylus in that the latter doesn't contain an ink supply. With few exceptions, pens can be equipped with dummy inkless cartridges to make them into styli.

A new kind of pen, the pressure pen, is rapidly becoming popular. Instead of merely indicating on or off, the pressure pen sends out a digital value corresponding to the effort applied to the pen tip. This force can then be used by an application to indicate the width, weight, or color of a line drawn in that application, a feature particularly useful in freehand sketching. Pressure pens vary in the range of forces they can detect and the number of pressure levels they can digitize, typically from 64 to 256.

From a usefulness and versatility standpoint, the most important distinguishing characteristic between different pens and cursors is cordlessness. Most pointing devices must be tethered to the tablet by a cable used in communicating position information to the tablet electronics. Some of the most recent tablet designs are now cordless.

Cordlessness can be a great convenience. Not only is there no cable to tangle, snarl, and resist your drawing efforts but cordless operation also enables you to instantly switch between using a pen and a cursor. Moreover, a cordless pen can be as elegant to draw with as a Waterman fountain pen.

Of course, cordlessness can be a problem, too. A cordless pen can easily be misplaced or pocketed. Whereas a disappearing ballpoint pen is a small worry, a $250 digitizer pen can lead to grand larceny. A cord may not prevent a thief from liberating the pointing device, but it can slow down most ne'er-do-wells and even help refresh your own memory.

Technology

A variety of technologies underlie today's digitizers. All can be fine-tuned to deliver essentially the same resolution (most digitizers can resolve down to about one-hundredth of an inch) with the same response speed.

Electromagnetic

The most widely used technology relies on electromagnetic sensing. Hidden under the top surface of the tablet is a wire grid. The electronics of the tablet set up an electromagnetic field that sweeps across the grid. The cursor or pen acts as an antenna, receiving a signal from the grid. By carefully calculating the timing of the signal's reception in relation to the sweep of the grid signal, the digitizer electronics can calculate the location of the pointing device. The electronics translate the position into coordinates that are then relayed to your PC so that your application can determine the location of the pointing device.

Resistive

Resistive decoding technology does away with the wire grid used in more conventional electro-magnetic tablets and substitutes a thin-film coating of a conductive material. The resistive decoding system works by creating a voltage gradient across this film. This voltage capacitively induces another detectable voltage inside the cursor or pen. The voltage is pulsed from each of the four sides of the digitizing area in succession, and from the ratio of analog voltages developed from each pulse inside the pointing device, the system detects the location of the pointing device. (Because the system works with ratios, absolute values of the signal are unimportant and variables like the distance the pointing device is above the resistive surface automatically disap-pear.) The analog ratios are converted to digital form and are then processed by a patented error-correction circuit to compensate for non-linearities in the system.

By choosing the proper material for the resistive film, such as transparent indium-tin oxide, the tablet of a resistive digitizer can be made clear. If you want to trace drawings, a clear tablet has an important advantage: you can shine a light through it and the drawing you want to trace.

Magneto-Strictive

Sometimes called give-and-receive resonance, magneto-strictive digitizers rely on the energy briefly stored in resonant circuits. The electromagnetic field in the tablet itself excites an LC circuit in the pen (a tuned circuit combining an inductive coil and a capacitor). The inductive coil does double-duty and also serves to electrically couple the pointing device with the tablet. When the LC circuit discharges, the resulting signal flowing through the coil is picked up by a matrix of flat-wound coils in the tablet. The relative strength of the signal in the tablet coils helps determine the location of the pointing device.

Pressing a button on the pointing device alters the tuning of its LC network, and the resulting change in phase angle can be detected by the tablet. Because the LC circuit in the pointing device is entirely passive, no batteries or other power source (besides the current induced from the tablet) is necessary for its operation.

Note that the coils in the pointing device do not need to be connected to the tablet to produce this phase angle change. Consequently, this technology readily lends itself to cordless pointing devices.

Acoustic

Some digitizers rely on a form of sonar, measuring the timing of acoustic signals sent out by pointing devices. One commercial product uses pointing devices with piezo-electric elements or spark gaps, which emit sharp clicks (much as do bats) when triggered by a 600 volt pulse from the control unit. A pair of separated microphones—bat-like ears—in the control unit listens for the noise, filtering out all sounds except those in the range 65-75 kilohertz, which masks most ambient noise. From the speed of sound, the distance from pointing device to microphone is easily calculated, and through triangulation the X-Y coordinates of the pointing device's position can be determined. Although the noise emitted by the devices is broadband, its level is kept low enough that the sound is inaudible unless you hold a pen or cursor up to your ear.

Resolution and Accuracy

The position detection accuracy of digitizers is rated in by resolution and accuracy. Although related, the terms indicate different qualities.

The resolution of a digitizer indicates the finest movement the device can measure. Accuracy indicates how close to reality the coordinates reported by the digitizer really are. Most digitizers claim a resolution of 1,000 points (or lines) per inch. Most are accurate, however, only to about one-hundredth of an inch (that is, 100 points per inch). Even that degree of accuracy far exceeds your human ability to position the cross-hairs of a cursor or move a pen.

Speed

Digitizers differ in the number of individual points they can distinguish and transmit back to your PC within one second. If you are drawing freehand, speed may be the most important digitization issue to you. A tablet must be fast enough to follow the quickest motions of your hand. A slow tablet may not be able to keep up with fast freehand drawing. If you are merely sampling individual points from a blueprint, however, even a slow tablet will suffice.

The actual speed of a digitizer is limited by the circuitry inside the digitizer and the communications rate of the connection between tablet and host. Most use serial connections with data rates of 9,600 bits per second or faster.

Size

Unlike much else in the world, bigger is often better with digitizers. Bigger digitizers enable you to work with bigger drawings and to work more precisely because they offer more digitizable points. On the other hand, bigger also means bulkier and more expensive.

Technically, you'll find no difference between tablets of different sizes. They use the same operating principles and offer the same resolution and accuracy.

Size does not necessarily translate into working area, however. The useful space on a tablet varies with several outside factors. Both the application you run and the digitizing tablet driver you use with it control how much of the work-surface is put to work. For example, AutoCAD provides the TABLET CFG command that enables you to shrink the tablet space actually devoted to screen manipulation and define portions of the tablet as menu areas.

Standards

The most important consideration with any digitizing tablet is the software with which it can be used. Support for digitizers may be built into applications, or the digitizer may include emulation software to match a given tablet to the standard used by some other pointing device. For example, most digitizers include software drivers allowing them to emulate a Microsoft mouse.

Many applications already have built-in support for digitizing tablets. With these programs, it's important that the tablet you choose works like one that your favorite applications know. Most tablets can emulate one or another of the more popular data formats used by digitizing tablets. The most popular emulations include those of Calcomp and Summagraphic digitizers. Make sure that the tablet you choose emulates something your software supports.

Touch Screens

Pointing is so natural (if impolite) that other technologies have been developed to exploit this human ability to data processing control. The most natural pointing device is, of course, the index finger. Giving the computer some means of detecting what a finger is aiming at would turn the humble appendage into a true digital interface.

The touch screen is designed for exactly that purpose. This technology can detect the presence and location of a finger on or near the display screen of the computer. At least two methods of finger-detection have been employed. One form relies on actual contact with the surface of the screen to capacitively detect the presence of the finger. Another, used by Hewlett-Packard's Touch-Screen system uses a special frame around the screen. This frame is lined on two perpendicular sides with LEDs emitting invisible light, and on the two sides opposite photodetectors. A finger approaching the screen breaks the constant light beam and allows the computer to determine its location.

Although a very natural interface, touch screen technology suffers its own logistical problems. As with light pens, reaching to the screen to perform normal daily work is a great way to build biceps and triceps and otherwise tire yourself out. You're also apt to cover your screen with oily smudges and—if you share your computer with others less kempt than yourself—unknown contaminants and organisms.

The biggest problem with touch screens is the very practical matter of accuracy. Whereas light pens can zero in on any given pixel, the touch screen is much patchier in its pointing capabilities. The screen is divided into a checkerboard pattern with resolution of about 16 x 16. Whereas the touch screen can be used for making menu choices, it is hardly adequate for drawing or graphic editing on-screen.

Touch screens have been effectively used to interface computers with a general public not versed in the intricacies of computing, enabling them to point at the function they want to carry out. However, for skilled computer users, the touch screen is an exotic aberration.

Scanners

A mouse or other pointing device enables you to easily put an original drawing into your PC. But when you have an existing drawing or photograph that you want to convert into electronic form, the time it takes to manipulate a pointing device makes the effort seem pointless—particularly when there's a more expedient alternative. The best way to capture images into your PC is by using a scanner.

The scanner can convert anything you have on paper—or, for that matter, anything reasonably flat—into computer-compatible electronic form. Dot-by-dot, a scanner can reproduce photos, line drawings—even collages—in detail sharper than your laser printer can duplicate. Better yet, equip your PC with optical character-recognition software, and the images your scanner captures of typed or printed text can be converted into ASCII files for your word processor, database, or publishing system. Just as the PC opened a new world information management to you, a scanner opens a new world of images and data to your PC.

The essence of any scanner is elementary. The scanner uses an array of light sensors to detect differences in the brightness of reflections off an image or object. In most cases, the scanner has a linear array of these sensors, typically charge-coupled devices (CCDs), squeezed together hundreds per inch in a narrow strip that stretches across the full width of the largest image that can be scanned. The width of each scanning element determines the finest resolution the scanner can detect within a single line. The narrower each scanning element and the closer they are all packed together, the higher the resolution and the finer the detail that can be captured.

This line-up of sensors registers a single, thin line of the image at a time. Circuitry inside the scanner reads each sensing element one by one in order and creates a string of serial data representing the brightness of each point in each individual scan line. Once the scanner has collected and arranged the data from each dot on the line, it advances the sensing element to read the next line.

Types

How the view of the scanning sensor moves to the next line is the fundamental design difference between scanners. Somehow the long line of sensing elements must shift their attention with extreme precision over the entire surface of the image to be captured. Nearly all scanners require a mechanical sweep of the sensors across the image. To make this sweep, two primary strategies have emerged in scanner technology. One requires the image sensor to move across a fixed original; the other moves the original in front of a fixed scanner.

Drum scanners exemplify the latter technology. They work like printing presses in reverse. You feed into the scanner a piece of paper that bears the image you want to capture, and the paper wraps around a rotating drum that spins the image past a sensor string that's fixed in place inside the machine.

Two designs take the opposite tack and move the sensor instead of the image. A *flatbed scanner* use an automatic mechanism to move the sensor. It earns its name from the flat glass surface upon which you must place the item to be scanned, face down. The scanning sensors are mounted on a bar that moves under the glass, automatically sweeping across the image. The glass surface allows the sensors to see up to the image. *Hand scanners* make you the motive force that propels the sensor over the image. You hold the T-shape hand scanner in the palm of your hand and drag it across the image you want to scan. The string of sensors peers through a plastic window in the bottom of the hand scanner.

Flatbed and drum scanners are designed with precision mechanisms that step the sensors or image a small increment at a time, each increment representing a single scan line. The movement of the mechanism, which is carefully controlled by the electronics of the scanner, determines the width of each line (and thus the resolution of the scanner in that direction).

Hand scanners must cope with the vagaries of the sweep of your all-too-human hand. If you move your hand at a speed other than that at which the scanner expects, lines will be scanned as too wide or too narrow, resulting in image distortion. At best, the aspect ratio may be off; at worse, the scanned image will look as wavy at the Atlantic under the influence of an errant typhoon. To avoid such disasters, the hand scanner uses a feedback mechanism that tracks the position of the image. Most have a roller that presses down against the image you're scanning to sense how fast you drag the scanner along. The rate at which the roller spins gives the scanner's electronics the feedback it needs about scanning speed. From this information, the software that controls the hand scanner can give each scanned dot its proper place.

Each of these three technologies has its advantages and disadvantages. Some scanner designs are suited to some applications more than others.

The least expensive is the hand scanner because it requires no precision (and expensive) scanning mechanism. The hand scanner also is compact and easy to carry. You could plug one into your notebook PC (with an appropriate interface adapter) and carry the complete system to the neighborhood library to scan from books in its collection. Hand scanners can also be quick because you can make quick sweeps of small images instead of waiting for the lumbering mechanism of another scanner type to cover a whole sheet. Hand scanners may also adapt to some non-flat surfaces and three-dimensional objects. For example, most will easily cope with the pages of an open atlas or gothic novel—although few can do a good job on a globe or watermelon.

On the downside, the small size of the hand scanner means a single pass of the scanner will cover an image no more than about four inches wide. Although that's enough for a column of text and most scanners offer a means of pasting together parallel scans of larger drawings and photos, the narrow strips of scan make dealing with large images inconvenient. On the other hand (and in the other direction), because a hand scanner is not limited by a scanning mechanism, it can allow you to make absurdly long scans, typically limited only by the scanning software you use.

Note that hand scanning is like typing—a learned skill. To use a hand scanner effectively, you'll have to practice until you learn to move the scanner smoothly and at the proper speed, which means very slowly at high resolutions.

Drum scanners are moderate in price and compact in size because their mechanisms are relatively simple. However, that mechanism imposes a stiff penalty—only thin, flexible images can be scanned. In general, that means normal paper. Books (at least while intact) and solid objects are off limits. Only certain sizes of paper may be accepted. While this may be no disadvantage in a character-recognition application, it may be frustrating when you want to pull an image off a large sheet without resorting to scissors or a photocopier first.

Flat-bad scanners are like copying machines in that anything that you can lay flat on their glass faces can be scanned—books, magazines, sections of poster, even posteriors and other parts of your anatomy if you get imaginative, bored, or drunk. Of course, the scanned image can be no larger than the scanner bed. The big drawback of the flatbed scanner is price. Their precision mechanisms makes the technology the most expensive among popular scanners.

Slide scanners are not a special technology but rather a special implementation of flat-bed scanner technology. A slide scanner is optimized for the higher-resolution needs of scanning small photographic transparencies or negatives, but it relies on a modified flat-bed scanner mechanism. It needs only more precision in its control because of the smaller side of the scanned area.

Color

Scanners perceive reality either in color or black-and-white. The former type of scanners are quite naturally called *color scanners*. The latter are generally termed *gray-scale scanners* because they convert all colors into shades of gray.

Color scanners are clearly the best. They can do anything a gray-scale scanner can do but with full spectral fidelity. Moreover, most can stoop to making quick scans in monochrome. You can even convert captured color images to grayscale at any later date when your needs require it.

Most color scanners register from 256 to 16.7 million different hues. While that may be more than you or your software wants to manage, their palettes can easily be scaled back, either through hardware controls or through software. Some scanner programs even optimize the scanner output so that those hundreds of thousands of colors can be accurately represented by a sampling as small as 256.

Older color flatbed scanners impose a speed penalty because they need a separate pass of their image sensors for each primary hue. Most newer color flatbed scanners use single-pass designs. Instead of changing the color that's scanned at the end of a full image, they quickly alternate colors on each line by quickly flashing different colors of light. A three-pass scanner may need five minutes to assay a full-sheet image. A single-pass scanner may do a sheet in a minute.

Just as color scanners have different spectral ranges, gray-scale scanners differ in the number of shades they can detect. At the bottom are the plain black and white machines that recognize no intermediary tones. From there, the gray-scale range increases at powers of two. A few years ago, a scanner with a range of 16 grays was top of the line. Today most gray-scale scanners have a range of 256 levels, which matches eight-bit encoding (one byte per pixel) and matches most monitor display capabilities.

Most gray-scale scanners can also be set to recognize fewer gray tones, usually the selection is between 2 (black and white), 16, 64, and 256 grays. The more grays you select, the larger the resulting image file will be and the more realistic the image will appear. A limited gray range is useful for text recognition and for capturing line drawings, but you'll want a wide ranges of grays to capture photographs.

Color can be an issue even with monochrome scanners. Most scanners provide their own sources of illumination for scanning images. (This eliminates one variable from the scanning process and makes for more uniform and repeatable scans.) Although the color of illumination might seem immaterial for a monochrome scanner, it might not necessarily be so. Illumination color becomes important when you want to scan from color originals.

For example, some hand scanners use red light-emitting diodes (LEDs) for illumination. LEDs have long, trouble-free lives. But when colored objects are illuminated in their red light, the brightness reflected from the image does not correspond to the brightness the human eye would perceive in white light. Green illumination gives a better approximation of the human eye's perception of tones. Colored images captured by a scanner that uses red illumination may seem tonally incorrect. Flesh tones, in particular, scan too lightly. For line drawing and text-recognition applications, however, red can sometimes be better. Red pencil or ink marks on an image won't reproduce, so you can sketch or comment in red and not have it show in your scans.

Resolution

Scanners differ in the resolution at which they can capture images. All scanners have a maximum mechanical limit on their resolution that is equal to the smallest step that their sensor can be advanced, typically about 300 dots per inch, but often higher. Special-purpose slide scanners achieve resolutions as high as 6000 dots per inch.

Beyond the mechanical resolution of a given scanner, the control software accompanying the scanner often pushes the claimed resolution even higher. To achieve the higher resolution figures, the control software *interpolates* dots. That is, the software computes additional dots in between those that are actually scanned. Although interpolating higher resolution adds no more information to a scan—which means it cannot add to the detail that you've scanned—it can make the scan look more pleasing. The greater number of dots reduces the jaggedness or stair stepping in the scan and makes lines look smoother.

The new dots created by interpolation add to the size of the resulting scanned file, possibly making a large file cumbersome indeed. Because interpolation adds no new information, it need not be done at the time of scanning. You can store a file made at the mechanical resolution limit of your scanner, and then later increase its apparent resolution through interpolation without wasting disk space storing imaginary dots.

As with colors and shades of gray, a scanner can easily be programmed to produce resolution lower than its maximum. Lower resolution is useful to minimize file size, to match your output device, or simply to make the scanned image fit on a single screen for convenient viewing. Many scanners shift their resolution in distinct increments—75, 150, and 300 dpi, for example—while others make resolution continuously variable.

Optical Character Recognition

Scanners don't care what you point them at. They will capture anything with adequate contrast: drawing or text. However, text captured by a scanner will be in bit-image form, which makes it useless to word processors that use ASCII code. You can translate text into graphic form and into ASCII codes in two ways—by typing everything into your word processor or by *Optical Character Recognition* (OCR). Add character-recognition software to your scanner, and you can quickly convert almost anything you can read on your screen into word processor, database, or spreadsheet files. Once in the realm of mainframe computers and special hardware costing tens of thousands of dollars, OCR is now within the reach of most PCs and budgets.

Early OCR software used a technique called *matrix-matching*. The computer would compare small parts of each bit-image it scanned to bit-patterns it had stored in a library to find what character was the most similar to the bit pattern scanned. For example, a letter "A" would be recognized as a pointed tower 40 bits high with a 20 bit wide crossbar.

Matrix-matching suffers a severe handicap—it must be tuned to the particular typeface and type size you scan. For example, an italic *A* has a completely different pattern signature from a roman A, even within the same size and type family. Consequently, either a matrix-matching OCR system must have an enormous library of bit patterns (requiring a time-consuming search for each match), or the system must be limited to matching a few type styles and fonts. Even then, you will probably have to tell the character-recognition system which typeface you want to read so that it can select the correct pattern library. Worse, most matrix matching systems depended on regular spacing between characters to determine the size and shape of the character matrix, so these systems worked only with monospaced printing such as that generated by a typewriter.

Most of today's OCR systems use *feature-matching*. Feature-matching systems don't just look and compare, but they also analyze each bit pattern that's scanned. When it sees the letter A, it derives the essential features of the character from the pattern of bits—an upslope, a peak, and a downslope with a horizontal bar across. In that every letter A has the same characteristic features—if they didn't your eyes couldn't recognize each one as an A—the feature-matching system doesn't need an elaborate library of bit patterns to match nearly any font and type size. In fact, feature-matching recognition software doesn't need to know the size or font of the characters it is to recognize beforehand. Even typeset text with variable character spacing is no problem. Feature-matching software can thus race through a scan very quickly while making few errors.

Electrical Interfacing

At least four different interface designs are used by scanners—SCSI (the Small Computer System Interface), GPIB (General-Purpose Interface Bus), proprietary, and standard serial.

The least desirable of these is the last. Standard serial ports are simply too slow to handle the data generated by a scanner. Most desktop scanners are moving to the SCSI interface for its high speed. Hand scanners generally use proprietary connections because the tiny devices have neither the room nor the need for standardized interface circuitry. GPIB was originally developed by Hewlett-Packard Company (hence, its original moniker, the Hewlett-Packard Interface Bus) for interconnecting its test and measurement equipment. It provides a medium- to high-speed connection (fitting neatly between serial and SCSI).

Application Interfacing

As with other input devices, scanners have their own control and signaling systems that must link to your software to be used effectively (or at all). Early scanners used their own proprietary application interfaces to relay commands and data. Consequently, each scanner required its own software or drivers.

Today that situation has changed. Most scanners now follow the *Twain* standard. First released in early 1992, Twain was developed by an industry consortium called the Working Group for Twain, which included Aldus Corporation, Caere Corporation, Eastman Kodak Company, Hewlett-Packard, and Logitech.

During its development, the proto-standard was originally called Direct Connect. Later it became the Connecting Link for Applications and Source Peripherals (CLASP). The now-official Twain name is not an acronym but, according to the Working Group, a descriptive label that expresses how the standard unites applications and input devices—making the twain meet.

Twain links programs and scanner hardware, giving software writers a standard set of function calls by which to control the features of any scanner. One set of Twain drivers will handle any compatible scanning device. The Twain connection has two ends: your scanner and your software; to take advantage of it requires that both ends be Twain-compatible.

Twain defines its hardware interface as its *Source*. The Source is hardware or firmware in a scanner that controls the information that flows from the scanner into Twain. The scanner maker designs the Source to match its particular hardware and interface. Your software links to the Twain Source through a *Source Manager*, which is essentially a set of program calls. In the Windows environment, the Source Manager is a DLL (Dynamically Linked Library), although it can also take the form of a software driver.

This architecture allows your software to make calls using a standardized set of commands. The calls go to the source manager, which links them to the source. The source then interprets the commands and forwards them to your scanner. Similarly, your scanner passes along data to the source. Your application can pick up that data by making the appropriate calls to the source manager.

Twain gives the scanner manufacturer a common software interface. For you, that means you don't have to worry about compatibility—Twain takes care of everything. All you need do is assure that your scanner is Twain-compatible.

Chapter 12
The Display System

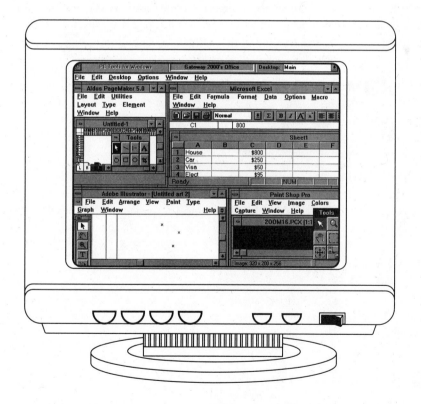

Your PC's Display System allows you to see exactly what your PC is doing as it works. Because it gives you instant visual feedback, the display system makes your PC interactive. The display system also affects the speed of your PC and your pleasure (or pain) in using your machine. PCs use a number of different technologies in creating their displays, and the choice determines what you see, how sharply you see it, and how quickly.

Seeing is believing. If you couldn't see the results of your calculations or language manipulations, the personal computer would be worthless as a tool. You need some way of viewing the output of the computer system to know what it has done and why you're wasting your time feeding it data. Today's choice for seeing things that come from your computer is the video display, sort of like a television that substitutes a cable to your CPU for an antenna.

Nearly every PC today comes already equipped with a standardized video system called VGA, named after IBM's pioneering Video Graphics Array that was introduced in 1987 along with the PS/2 series of computers. Although the minimum expected in a new PC, the VGA system is actually able to create better images than any television set. And that's just for starters. The best display systems put more than six times as much detail on your screen.

Display Fundamentals

PC displays were not always this good—and they are not always as good as they can be. While some programs stretch your display system to its limits, others reach back to the uncertain first days of computers—a time before monitors, even before monitor technology was developed.

Computers like Harvard Mark I existed even before there was television, at least commercial television as we know it. These first data processors shared the same output device that was used by their predecessor, the mechanical adding machine—printed output. Before video, computers directly operated printers of some kind to show their results to an almost disbelieving world.

Teletype Output

The printer of choice was the teletype machine, long used to convey words and numbers across continents. These early computers fed characters to the teletype printer as if they had begun at some different keyboard—one character at a time in a long series.

Video Terminals

Although the teletype has reached a status somewhere between endangered species and museum piece, the method of data transmission and display that it used still does service to today's high-tech toys. Instead of hammering away at paper, however, these machines send their character strings at the electronic equivalent of the teletype, the computer terminal. These terminals are often called *Video Data Terminals* (sometimes Video Display Terminals) or *VDTs* because they rely on video-displays to make their presentations to you. They are terminal because they reside at the end of the communications line, in front of your eyes.

A terminal at its most rudimentary is the classic dumb terminal, which merely displays each character exactly as it is received, on a phosphor-coated screen instead of paper. The refinements are few—instead of rattling off the edge of the paper, a too-long electronic line more likely will "wrap" or scroll down to the line below. The terminal never runs out of paper—it has a fresh supply of blank screen below that rolls upward as necessary to receive each additional line. Alas, the output it generates is even more tenuous than the flimsiest tissue and disappears at the top of the screen, probably never to be seen again.

A smart terminal, on the other hand, has innate intelligence—that is, it has some of the data processing abilities of a computer. It recognizes special commands for formatting its display and may even be able to do some computer-like functions on its own. Often, however, the smartest of terminals is relegated to working like an ordinary dumb terminal.

A few other characteristics also distinguish the operation of a mechanical teletype. The paper it prints upon moves in only one direction. Neither the paper nor the output of the teletype ever goes backward. Like a stock ticker, the teletype merely churns out an unending string of text. The teletype cannot type over something it did before, and it cannot jump ahead without patiently rolling its paper forward as if it has printed so many blank lines.

In the electronic form of the computer terminal, the teletype method of text-handling means that when one character changes on the screen, a whole new screen full of text must be generated and sent to the terminal. The system cannot backup to change the one character, so it must rush headlong forward, reworking the whole display along the way.

Mammoth primeval computers and rattling teletypes might seem to have little in common with the quiet and well-behaved PC sitting on your desk. The simplest of programs, however, still retain this most primitive way of communicating with your video screen. They generate characters and send them one by one to the video display, only instead of traveling across the globe, the text merely shuffles from one place in memory to another inside the machine. These programs in effect operate as if the video system of your computer were the screen of a terminal that mimics an age-old teletype.

Many computers are limited to this form of video imagery, which, understandably, is often called a Teletype display. For most PCs, teletype displays are a vestige of their ancestry that's used only by rudimentary programs—and sophisticated software on which the programmers have shirked responsibility for making things look better. Teletype-type output is, however, the highest level of support provided by the system BIOS in most PCs.

The basic PC BIOS gives several layers of teletype output. In the most primitive, a program must load one character at a time into a microprocessor register, issue a video interrupt—010(Hex)—and wait while the microprocessor checks where to put the character (a several step process in itself), pushes the character into the appropriate place in memory, and finally returns back to the program to process the next character. The most advanced teletype mode lets a program put an entire line of text on the screen through a similar, equally cumbersome process.

Because of this software overhead, the actual speed of teletype displays depends on the available microprocessor power. The faster the processor, the quicker the software runs, and the snappier the on-screen display.

In basic teletype mode, characters are written on the screen from left to right, from screen top to bottom, merely scrolling after each line is full or ended with a carriage return. More advanced display technologies are able to write anywhere on the monitor screen using formatting instructions much as smart terminals do. For example, commands in the PC BIOS let your programs locate each character anywhere on the screen.

Character Mapping

For years the most common means of displaying text on a PC screen was the character-mapped display. Using this technology, a special range of addresses called *screen memory* or *display memory* is reserved for storing the characters that will appear on the screen, and programs write text on the screen by pushing bytes into the proper places in that memory. Just as a street on a road map corresponds to the location of a real street, each byte of display memory corresponds to a character position on the screen.

In the most common of the character-mapped display systems used by PCs, the screen is divided into a matrix (essentially a set of pigeon holes with each hole corresponding to one position on the screen) that measures 80 characters wide and 25 high. To display a character on the screen, a program loads the corresponding code into the matrix cell. To put the image on the screen, the display system reads the entire matrix, translates into a serial data stream that scans across the monitor screen, and moves the data to the video output. From there, the signal is the monitor's problem.

Speed in making changes is one virtue of the character-mapped display system. Programs can push characters into any screen location in any order that they please—top, bottom, left, or right, even lobbing one letter atop another, overwriting the transitory existence of each. Screen updates occur quickly because the system has direct access to the screen and need not go through the multiple steps the BIOS requires. Moreover, only the character (or characters) needing to be changed have to be pushed into place. Once a character has been pushed into the display memory matrix, it stays there until changed by the program that put it there—or any other software that reaches into that area of memory.

For your programs, writing characters to the screen is simply a matter of writing directly to screen memory. Consequently this display technique is often called *direct writing*. It is the fastest way to put information on a PC screen.

The ability of the PC BIOS to position characters on the screen uses a two-step form of character mapping: one BIOS command lets a program specify the location to start writing anywhere on the screen, and a second command can then write a character in that position. As with teletype displays, however, BIOS-mediated character mapping suffers the speed penalty of software overhead. Where direct-writing takes only a few commands to display each character, BIOS-mediated character-mapping takes dozens.

For character-mapping to work, your applications need to know the exact location of each screen memory address. For all applications to work on all PCs, the addresses used by each system must be the same—or there needs to be some means of determining what addresses are used. In the original PC, IBM's engineers reserved two blocks of addresses (one for color text, one for monochrome) in High DOS Memory for holding characters for screen memory, but it refused to make them an official standard. In their vision, only the BIOS was supposed to be used to put characters into video memory. Software writers, however, found that the only way to get acceptable speed from their software was to use this character-mapped mode. The industry's reliance on these addresses made them into unofficial standards with which no manufacturer bothers to tamper.

In basic text modes, your PC uses one set of screen memory addresses when it is operating in color and the other set when in monochrome. To determine which mode your system is currently using, the IBM BIOS provides a special flag—called the *video mode flag*, although originally termed the video equipment flag by IBM—located at absolute memory location 0463(hex). When this flag is set to 0D4(hex), your system is running in color and the chain of addresses starting at 0B8000(hex) is used for screen text memory. In monochrome, the flag is set to 0B4(hex) to indicate the use of addresses starting at 0B0000(hex). For compatibility reasons, all newer IBM video systems are also capable of operating through these same addresses even though they may store additional video information elsewhere.

The storage of graphics information of early display adapters used these same addresses. More modern display adapters use a separate range for graphics information, the 64K memory block starting at absolute address 0A0000(Hex). A few display systems move display memory to the protected mode area. Beyond the video mode flag, the BIOS provides no character-mapped display support.

Character Boxes

In text modes, the display memory addresses hold codes that have nothing to do with the shapes appearing on the monitor screen except as a point of reference. The actual patterns of each character that appears on the screen are stored in a special ROM chip called the *character ROM* that's part of the video circuitry of the computer. The byte that defines the character is used by the video circuitry to look up the character pattern that matches it. The bit-pattern from the character ROM is scanned and sent to the screen to produce the final image.

Modern display adapters allow you to download your own fonts (typefaces) into on-board RAM that's reserved from the same block that would serve as the character map. These downloaded fonts can be used as if they were located in ROM with the same ease of manipulation as ROM-based fonts. Downloaded fonts appear just the same whether pushed on the screen through the teletype or direct-access technique.

Each on-screen character is made from an array of dots, much like the text output of a teletype or dot-matrix printer. The several video standards used by IBM and other manufacturers build individual characters out of different size dot arrays. The framework in which the dots of an individual character are laid out, called the *character box*, is a matrix like a crossword puzzle. The character box is measured by the number of dots comprising its width and its height. For instance, a standard Video Graphics Array (VGA) text screen uses a 9 x 16 character box. Each character takes up a space on the screen measuring nine dots wide and sixteen dots high. Other display systems use character boxes of different sizes. The standard Monochrome Display Adapter character box measures 9 x 14; the standard Color Graphics Adapter character box, 8 x 8; the Enhanced Graphics Adapter character box, 8 x 14.

Individual characters do not necessarily take up the entire area that a character box affords. For instance, text characters on most monochrome displays keep one row of dots above and one below those used by each character to provide visible separation between two adjacent lines of text on the screen.

Video Attributes

The character-mapped displays of most PC video systems do not store each letter adjacent to the next. Instead, each on-screen character position corresponds to every other byte of memory; the intervening bytes are assigned as attribute bytes. Even numbered bytes store character information; odd bytes, attributes.

The attribute byte determines the highlighting or color of the displayed character that's stored in the preceding memory byte. Monochrome and color attributes use different codes. Monochrome characters are allowed the following attributes: normal, highlighted (brighter on-screen characters), underlined, and reverse-video characters (dark on light instead of the normal light on dark). The different attributes can be combined. Note, however, that highlighted reverse-video characters make the character background brighter instead of highlighting the character shape itself. Monochrome display attributes are shown in Figure 12.1.

Color systems store two individual character hues in the attribute byte. The first half of the byte (the most significant bits of the digital code of the byte) code the color of the character itself. The latter half of the attribute (the least significant bits) code the background color. Because four bits are available for storing each of these colors, this system can encode 16 foreground and 16 background colors for each character (with black and white considered two of these colors). In normal operation, however, one bit of the background color code indicates a special character attribute: blinking. This attribute allows any color combination to blink, but it also cuts the number of hues available for backgrounds in half (to eight colors—all intensified color choices eliminated). When your software needs to be able to display 16 background colors, a status bit allows the character-flashing feature to be defeated. Color display attributes are shown in Figure 12.2.

	Bit 7	6	5	4	3	2	1	0
Non-blinking characters	0	x	x	x	x	x	x	x
Blinking characters	1	x	x	x	x	x	x	x
Non-display	x	0	0	0	x	0	0	0
Underline	x	0	0	0	x	0	0	1
White-on-black	x	0	0	0	x	1	1	1
Reverse video	x	1	1	1	x	0	0	0
Normal intensity	x	x	x	x	0	x	x	x
High intensity (bright)	x	x	x	x	1	x	x	x

Even byte: ASCII character value — bits 7 6 5 4 3 2 1 0
Odd byte: Display attribute — bits 7 6 5 4 3 2 1 0

Key: x = don't care
0 = binary 0
1 = binary 1

FIGURE 12.1. Monochrome text display attributes.

Because each character on the screen requires two bytes of storage, a full 80-character column by 25-character row of text (a total of 2000 characters) requires 4000 bytes of storage. In the basic PC monochrome video system, 16 kilobytes are allotted to store character information. The basic (and basically obsolete) color system reserved 64 kilobytes for this purpose.

Video Pages

The additional memory does not go to waste, however. It can be used to store more than one screen of text at a time, with each separate screen called a *video page*. Either basic video system is designed to quickly switch between these video pages so that on-screen images can be changed almost instantly. Switching quickly allows a limited degree of animation.

The basic PC color system also has a special mode in which it displays text in 40 columns across the screen, an accommodation to people trying to use televisions instead of computer monitors as displays. Televisions are not as sharp as computer monitors, so fine, 80-column characters blur together on their screens. Half as many columns requires half as much storage, which in turns allows twice as many pages of video text.

Through the years, improving video standards has refined the quality of the display systems and increased the amount of memory devoted to video. In character-based displays, this additional memory has been put to work by allowing an increased number of video pages, by offering new character-based video modes that put more rows of text on the screen, or both.

Some video systems offer text modes that permit up to 60 rows of text and 132 columns of characters on a single screen. These increases in the number of on-screen characters often are not complemented by increases in resolution, however. To squeeze all those letters and numbers on the screen, these systems shrink the character box down to eyestrain-size dimensions. For example, a display with 60 rows by 132 columns may squash each individual character into a 5 x 7 dot box. You can see more characters, but each one is tinier and harder to read. To gain an overview you lose detail.

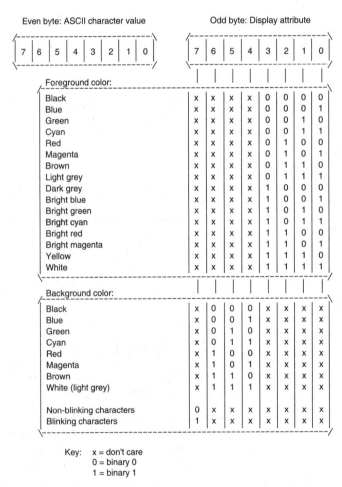

FIGURE 12.2. Color text display attributes.

Block Graphics

Teletypes, able only to smash numbers and letters on paper, never excelled at printing graphics. By proper selection of characters, standing far from printouts, and squinting, you could imagine you saw pictures in some printouts (a triangle of text might vaguely resemble a Christmas tree, for example). But these text-based images could hardly be confused with photographs unless your vision was quite bad, your standards quite low, or your camera very peculiar.

When PCs operate like teletypes, their graphic output faces the same limitations as printouts—characters can only approximate real-world images. To try to improve matters, the designers of the original PC took advantage of the extra potential of storing characters as byte values. Because one byte can encode 256 different characters, and the alphabet and other symbols total far short of that number, IBM's designers assigned special characters to some of the higher-numbered bytes in its character set. Beyond dingbats and foreign language symbols, a few of the extra characters were reserved for drawing graphic images from discrete shapes and patterned blocks that partly or entirely fill in the character matrix.

Graphic images can be made by strategically locating these character blocks on the screen so that they form larger shapes. Other extra characters comprise a number of single and double lines as well as corners and intersections of them to draw borders around text areas. The characters are building blocks of the graphics images, and consequently this form of graphics is termed *block graphics*. Table 12.1 shows the block graphic characters used in most PCs.

To a PC display system, block graphics are considered text and are handled exactly like ordinary text characters. All of the text attributes are available to every character of block graphics, including all of the available text colors, highlighting, and inverse video characteristics.

Moreover, because block graphic displays are built in text mode, they can be pushed into video memory and onto the screen just as quickly as any other text—which is fast indeed. Block graphics are, in fact, the fastest graphics available on the PC.

On the other hand, block graphics offer the worst quality of the graphic display systems that PCs can use. The images made with block graphics are jagged and lumpy—in a word, blocky. Intricate shapes and fine details are impossible to create using large character blocks. Block graphic images are chunky, clunky, and otherwise aesthetically unappealing for most applications.

Then again, block graphics comprise the only graphics available on all PCs no matter their vintage, no matter whether color- or monochrome-equipped. They are the minimum graphic standard and the least common graphic denominator among IBM display systems.

Table 12.1. Block graphic characters.

ASCII	Character	ASCII	Character
169	⌐	170	¬
176	░	177	▒
178	▓	179	│
180	┤	181	╡
182	╢	183	╖
184	╕	185	╣
186	║	187	╗
188	╝	189	╜
190	╛	191	┐
192	└	193	┴
194	┬	195	├
196	─	197	┼
198	╞	199	╟
200	╚	201	╔
202	╩	203	╦
204	╠	205	═
206	╬	207	╧
208	╨	209	╤
210	╥	211	╙
212	╘	213	╒
214	╓	215	╫
216	╪	217	┘
218	┌	219	█
220	▄	221	▌
222	▐	223	▀

Bit-Mapped Graphics

One way to improve the poor quality of block graphics would be to make the blocks smaller. Smaller blocks would build an image with finer grain that could show more detail. The smaller the blocks, the better the image. Unfortunately, physical aspects of the display system impose a distinct and unbreakable limit on how small each block can be—the size of the individual dots that make up the image on the video screen. The sharpest and highest quality image that could be shown by any display system would individually control every dot on the screen.

These dots are often called *pixels*, a contraction of the descriptive term picture element. Like atomic elements, pixels are the smallest building blocks from which known reality can be readily constructed.

The terms dot and pixel are often used as synonyms, but their strict definitions are somewhat different. When a system operates at its limits, putting as many dots on the screen as it is physically capable of handling, the number of dots and the number of pixels are the same. Often, however, systems operate with somewhat less sharpness than they are capable, with the result that one pixel may be made from several on-screen dots.

The most straightforward way of handling the information to be displayed on such a screen is to assign some part of memory to each pixel, just as two bytes are given over to each character of a character-mapped display. In the PC scheme of things, because the data controlling each pixel is stored as one or more memory bits, this kind of display system is often called *bit-mapped graphics*. Alternately, because each pixel or point on the video screen can be separately addressed through memory, this method of controlling the video display is often called *All Points Addressable graphics* or an *APA display*.

In the bit-mapped graphics system, display memory stores an exact electronic representation of the on-screen image. It's actually a time-slice of what you see—the software running on your PC is constantly sending new data into display memory to update the screen image. The memory temporarily stores or buffers the changes until it is read out as a complete image frame dozens of times per second. Because of this function, graphic display memory is often called the *frame buffer*.

As with character-mapped memory, programmers have their choice of methods to write bit-mapped graphics to your monitor screen. The PC BIOS provides basic support that allows any bit on the screen to be altered by programs. Using the BIOS to alter individual pixels is, however, a slow and painstaking process. Most applications write directly to the frame buffer to achieve satisfactory performance.

Bit-mapped graphics hold the potential for being much sharper than block graphics. More pixels means more detail. The number of dots on a screen and the ultimate number of pixels are many times the number of characters that are displayed on that same screen, from 64 to 126 times greater. However, bit-mapped graphics impose its own, interrelated penalties—memory usage and speed.

The amount of memory required by a graphic display system depends on two factors: the sharpness of the display image and the number of colors (or grey levels) that are to be displayed. Each increase in sharpness and number of colors means that your PC is putting more detail (more information) on its screen and storing more information in its display buffer. As a result, it must move around more information (more bytes) and that means more work. And the harder your PC works, the longer it takes to complete its job.

Resolution

The number that quantifies the possible sharpness of a video image is called *resolution*. It indicates how many individual pixels an image contains that your display system will spread across the width and height of the screen. Because your PC generates the image as an electrical signal completely independent from your computer monitor (it would make the same image even if your monitor wasn't connected to the computer at all) physical properties of the monitor (such as its physical dimensions) play no part in resolution measurements. In other words, the number of pixels in an image does not vary with the size of the screen that it is displayed upon. Resolution is expressed without reference to units of linear measurement—resolution is described in pixels or dots rather than dots per inch. For example, a standard VGA display has a resolution of 640 pixels horizontally by 480 pixels vertically in its native graphics mode. (A peculiarity of the VGA system makes its text and graphics resolutions different. VGA text has a resolution of 720 x 400 pixels.)

Dots-per-inch is a measure of actual on-screen sharpness, and it depends both on resolution and the size of the resulting image. At the same resolution a larger screen has less sharpness than a smaller screen—all else being equal. For example, a VGA image that measures 15 inches diagonally will have 640 pixels across one of its 12-inch long horizontal lines. On a perfect monitor, its sharpness would be 53 dots per inch. On a perfect 10-inch screen, the sharpness would measure 80 dots per inch.

The higher the resolution of an image, the more pixels it will contain. The more pixels, the more memory needed to store them.

Graphic Attributes

How much memory required for a given resolution depends on a second factor in addition to the number of pixels—the number of bits assigned to each pixel. At minimum, each pixel requires a single bit of storage. That bit can be used to code either of two conditions—whether the pixel is illuminated on the screen or invisibly dark. In the simplest bit-image graphic system, one bit of memory would then be used to map the condition of each pixel in the video display.

What's lacking from this primitive mapping system are contrast and color. All bits are treated the same and their associated pixels look about the same, either on or off. The result is a single-hued picture with no variation or shading, essentially the same sort of an image as a line drawing. While that may be sufficient for some purposes—for instance, the display of a chart or graph that mimics the monochrome look of ink-on-paper—color and contrast can add impact.

The way to add color to bit-mapped images is much the same as adding color to character-based displays, adding attribute information. Additional memory is devoted to storing the attribute of each bit. The bit-mapped system works somewhat differently from the character-based mode, however. All of the memory devoted to a bit is used to describe it. Not a byte needs to be devoted to identifying a character or pattern for each picture element because each one is essentially a featureless dot.

Color Planes

A single bit per pixel results in what graphics folk call a *two-color system* because it puts every-thing in black and white—each pixel is either on or off. Putting more color in the image requires encoding more information—more bits and more memory. Adding a second bit per pixel doubles the number of possible displayable colors. (*Shades*—degrees of darkness or light—are considered different colors in the terminology of computer graphics.) Every additional bit assigned to each pixel likewise doubles the number of possible colors. Hence with n bits, 2n colors are possible.

In computer graphics, the number of bits that are assigned to coding color information is sometimes described as the number of color planes. This term relates to the organization of display memory. The memory map of the graphic image can be visualized much like a Mercator projection of the world with latitude and longitude lines corresponding to the different positions of the bits corresponding to pixels in the image. Additional bits per each pixel add a third dimension, much like layers of maps stacked atop one another, a series of flat planes containing the color information.

Because the more colors used in an image the better the apparent image-quality and the more lifelike its appearance, the temptation is to increase the bit-depth of each pixel as high as possible. But the more colors or color planes, the more storage is needed for encoding each pixel. Moreover, much to the dismay of purveyors of video memory, the human eye is limited in its ability to resolve individual colors—most people can distinguish only a few million distinct colors. Color monitors are even more limited in the number of colors that they can display. Most monitors top out at about 262,144 colors, corresponding to the capabilities of an 18-bit display system. Once these limits are reached and enough memory is assigned each pixel, further improvements do not improve appearances.

The practical limit on color is a bit-depth of 24 bits, which allows a system to store and theoreti-cally display any of 16,777,216 hues. Display systems with this bit-depth are termed *24-bit color* or *true color* systems because they can store sufficient information to encode more colors than anyone could possibly see—they hold a truly accurate representation of any color.

Although some of the capabilities of true color display systems are superfluous because they exceed human abilities to distinguish colors, true color is a convenient system for designers because it assigns one byte of storage for each of the three additive primary colors (red, green, and blue) to each pixel. This three-byte-per-pixel memory requirement imposes severe processing overhead on high-resolution systems. It can also strain storage systems.

Some newer display systems have a 32-bit color mode. Instead of allocating the additional byte of storage to color information, however, most of these 32-bit systems put the extra bits to work as an alpha channel. The bits in the alpha channel hold control rather than color information. In effect, the alpha channel provides a storage place for special effects information. The bits in the alpha channel normally are not tallied in counting color planes.

The math for finding the amount of memory required to display a color graphics screen is straightforward. Simply multiply the number of pixels on the screen—that is, the resolution—by the bit-depth of each pixel, then divide by eight to translate bits into bytes. For example, a VGA graphics screen comprises 307,200 pixels (that's simply 640 pixels times 480 pixels). With a bit depth of four (allowing 16 colors on the screen), the minimum memory required is 1,228,800 bits. Divided by eight bits per byte, that equates 153,600 bytes of storage. The next-highest standard increment of memory is 256K, so you'd need at least 256K of RAM to store a 16-color VGA image.

Color planes are related to memory banks but are not exactly the same thing. For instance, to map more memory into the limited address space reserved for video under the IBM standard, some IBM video adapters use bank-switching techniques to move video memory bytes in and out of the address range of the host microprocessor. In some video modes, these banks correspond exactly to the color planes used by the video adapter. In other modes, several planes of video information may be stored in each bank by using bits in each byte of screen memory to indicate individual colors.

Color Coding

The best and the worst display systems assign the same number of bits to each of the three primary colors—a bit or an entire byte. For intermediary color depths, however, the base-two digital nature of the PC and the three-fold nature of color vision come into direct collision. For example, if you want to assign a single byte to store the colors of each pixel, how can you evenly allocate eight bits among three colors? With two bytes per pixel, how do you divide 16 by 3 evenly?

You don't. But you don't have to. You don't even have to code colors as a mix of red, green, and blue.

Because the human eye is most sensitive to green and its shadings (probably because primitive humans lived in an environment lush with chlorophyll green plants), some color-coding systems split their bit assignments evenly and assign the odd bit to green. For example, when IBM's engineers designed a 16-bit color system, they assigned five bits to red and blue and gave six to green.

Some image storage systems encode colors by an entirely different manner. One of the most common (used by the Kodak PhotoCD system) is to encode colors by brightness (technically called *luminence* and abbreviated as Y) and two color (or chromaticity) values (abbreviated C1 and C2) that essentially correspond to coordinates on a map of colors. Print-oriented workers prefer to think and store colors corresponding to the ink colors used in printing, cyan, magenta, and yellow, which are often abbreviated CMY (or sometimes, CMYK—the K stands for black, which is used in four-color process printing to add depth to the colors).

These coding methods are useful to particular output devices—CMYK colors for storing images that eventually will be printed and published; luminance and chrominance coding for images that will eventually be used in broadcast-style (as opposed to computer) video systems. To be displayed by normal computer monitors, they must be translated from their native format to the RGB signals used by PC monitors.

Color Mapping

Another method of encoding colors in memory that requires translation has found greater use in PCs. A technique called *color mapping* stores only code numbers, each of which could refer to almost any color. Each pixel is assigned a place to hold one code number in display memory. The display system matches the stored numeric values to a *Color Look-Up Table* or *CLUT* that tells which color corresponds to each number, then that color is sent along to the monitor. Because of the nature of colors in the real world, color mapping can lead to substantial economies in display memory.

When the values stored in screen memory directly indicate what color appears on the screen, as it does in the above example, the colors are said to be *direct mapped.*

Direct mapping allows any pixel to be any color, but most images are made from far fewer colors. After all, there are only 307,200 pixels on the VGA screen, so you can't possibly display them all at once. If you're judicious about your color pruning and the colors you display, you can make amazingly realistic images using a few bytes of storage by limiting the number of colors you put on the screen (which limits the storage you need). The problem is, of course, the optimum color selection for one image isn't the same as another. A polar bear in a snowstorm is predominantly white; a black bear in a cave on a starless night would be predominantly black; and a still frame from a blockbuster movie would likely be mostly red.

The colors assigned to storage can be made to adapt to the image using the Color Look-Up Table. In effect, the CLUT serves as a spectral map. A limited amount of storage makes up the guideposts or pointers which indicate which particular color in an wide overall selection called a palette belongs to a particular pixel. The number of guideposts determines how many different colors can be on the screen at the same time. The number of colors in the palette is constrained by the size of the pointer. Each pixel on the screen needs only enough storage to indicate which pointer to use. For example, a VGA system using a single byte of storage for each pixel could access a color look-up table with 256 pointers—that is, 2^8—allowing 256 different colors on the screen at a time. Each pointer has 18 bits of storage, allowing access to a palette of 262,144 different hues.

Color Look-Up Tables conserve both memory and speed. The march of technology makes these issues increasingly irrelevant, however. As memory and microprocessor power become cheaper, CLUTs will become rarer, at least in new display standards. With progress currently stuck on VGA, however, CLUTs will be around for a long while.

Raster and Vector Graphics

This form of video display system, which organizes the screen into a series of lines that's continually scanned dozens of times a second, is termed a *raster display*. Although it's workable and is the basis of all PC displays—as well as today's television and video systems—it's not the only way to put a computer image on a monitor. A completely different technique does not regularly scan the screen at all. Instead, it precisely controls the circuitry operating the horizontal and vertical deflection yokes. It doesn't trace scan lines but instead draws figures the same way you would as a series of strokes of a paintbrush. To keep the screen lit, it constantly retraces the figures.

Because the signals controlling the monitor drive the electron beam in the CRT as a series of vectors, this image-making technique is termed *vector graphics*. Alternately, this kind of display system is sometimes called a *stroker* because of the kinship to drawing brushstrokes. Although not used on PCs, the term pops up occasionally in the descriptions of expensive computerized workstations.

Video Controllers

Images are loaded into screen memory by your PC's microprocessor or by dedicated video circuitry (which may itself include a full-fledged microprocessor). In simple display systems, your PC's microprocessor does all the work with either direct commands from your software to move bytes to specific memory locations or through program calls to your PC's BIOS, which then handles the detail work (and commands the microprocessor to load values into particular screen memory locations). In more complex display systems, the microprocessor sends codes to the video processor which either directly moves the data into screen memory or generates the image, then moves it into memory. In any case, the final destination for screen-bound data is in the screen memory of your PC.

Getting those bytes from memory to monitor is a much more complex matter. The image must be transformed from its comparatively static position in screen memory to a signal controlling a fast moving electron beam inside the picture tube of your monitor. The conversion is not as direct as you might think. The resemblance between the memory map and the on-screen image is only metaphoric. The bytes of video information are scattered among eight or more memory chips and must somehow get organized and find their way to the monitor. In addition, the monitor itself must be brought under the control of the computer.

These are the jobs of the video controller, generally a special VLSI chip designed specifically for the task of turning memory bytes into video. The first PC color and monochrome adapters relied on an off-the-shelf chip, the 6845, to handle their displays. Today, however, most manufacturers have switched to custom- designed and -manufactured chips.

The primary job of the video controller in desktop PCs that use picture tubes is to serialize the data in display memory. The picture tubes are technically termed *Cathode Ray Tubes* or *CRT*s because they shoot electron beams from a cathode (an electron emitter) to light the phosphors of the screen—to serialize the data in display memory. The information that's so nicely laid out in two logical dimensions (horizontal and vertical) in the memory map must be converted to a long, serial train of pulses in a single dimension—time.

The principle underlying the conversion is elegant in its simplicity. Addresses in the memory map are just read off in sequential order, one row at a time. However, to make sure the one-dimensional video information is not misinterpreted by your monitor, the video controller must mix a host of synchronizing and control signals with the stream of data.

When display systems not based on CRTs are used—for instance, the flat-panel *Liquid Crystal Display* or *LCD* of most laptop computers—data for the display might not be serialized but nevertheless must be manipulated into a format that can be handled by the display. The flat panel display is addressed in two dimensions (exactly like display memory), but the data often has to be channeled through a narrow electrical path. The video controller circuitry must convert the screen memory data into transferable form and reconstruct it once it gets to the display panel.

Retrace

CRT-based systems have particular signal requirements. To make the image you see, the electron beam in the CRT traces a nearly horizontal line across the face of the screen, then in an instant, flies back to the side of the screen from which it started but lower by the width of the line it already traced out. This quick zipping back is termed *horizontal retrace*, and, although quick, it cannot take place instantly because of the inertia inherent in electrical circuits. Consequently, the smooth flow of bytes must be interrupted briefly at the end of each displayed line (else the video information would vanish in the retrace). The video controller must take each retrace into account as it serializes the image.

In addition, another variety of retrace must occur when the electron beam reaches the bottom of the screen when it's finished painting a screen-filling image: *vertical retrace*. The beam must travel as quickly as possible back up to its starting place, and the video controller must halt the flow of data while it does so.

Blanking

During retrace, if the electron beam from the gun in the tube were on, it would paint a bright line diagonally across the screen as the beam returned to its proper position. To prevent the appearance of this distracting line, the beam is forcibly switched off not only during retrace but also during a short interval on either side to give the beam time to stabilize. The interval in which the beam is forced off and cannot be turned on by any degree of programming is called *blanking* because the electron beam can draw nothing but a blank on the screen.

Most computer monitors don't fill their entire screens with data. They center (or try to) the image within darkened borders to minimize the image distortions that sneak in near the edges of the screen. To produce these darkened, protected areas, the electron beam is held at the level that produces a black image for a short while before and after the data of each image line is displayed. These short intervals are termed the *front porch* and *back porch* of the signal. If you examined the signal, you'd see that it dips down for blanking and pops up to an intermediate height (called *black level*) to create the porches between blanking and data. Use your imagination and the black-level signals look like shelves—or porches.

Vertical Interval

The period during which the screen is blanked during the vertical retrace is called, appropriately, the *vertical interval*. Its physical manifestation is the wide, black horizontal bar that's visible between image frames when your television screen or computer monitor picture rolls and requires adjustment of the vertical hold control. Figure 12.3 shows what the waveform of a typical line of video data looks like.

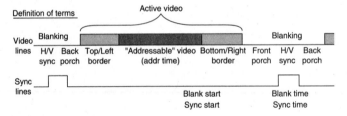

FIGURE 12.3. Video waveform.

Synchronizing Signals

The electron beam in the monitor is swept across the screen by a combination of magnetic fields. One field moves the beam horizontally, and another vertically. Circuitry in the monitor supplies a steadily increasing voltage to two sets of deflection coils to control the sweep of the beam. These coils are electromagnets, and the increasing voltage causes the field strength of the coils to increase and deflect the beam farther. At the end of the sweep of a line, the field that controls the horizontal sweep of the electron beam is abruptly switched off, returning the beam to the starting side of the screen. Likewise, when the beam reaches the bottom of the screen, the field in control of the vertical sweep switches off. The result is that the electron beam follows a tightly packed zig-zag path from the top of the screen to the bottom. Although LCD screens don't need to worry about retrace (or even scanning across the screen), in order to be compatible with the video signals already used by PCs, they must make allowances for retrace and blanking.

The primary difference between the two sweeps is that several hundred horizontal sweeps take place for each vertical one. The rate at which the horizontal sweeps take place is called the *horizontal frequency* or the *line rate* of the display system. The rate at which the vertical sweeps take place is called the *vertical frequency* or *frame rate* of the system because one complete image frame is created every time the beam sweeps fully down the screen.

The electronics that generate the sweep frequencies used by a monitor are inside the monitor itself. The signals themselves, however, must be synchronized with the data stream coming from the computer so that characters appear at their proper positions on the screen. Lose sync, and the ordinarily orderly screen display takes on the countenance of the Tower of Pisa—or the present day appearance of the Colossus at Rhodes.

To keep things organized, the video controller sends out special synchronizing signals, one kind (*horizontal sync*) before each line is sent to the display, and another (*vertical sync*) before each frame. The monitor detects these synchronizing signals and knows to reset its sweep to the beginning of a line or frame.

Digital and Analog Display Systems

Two kinds of signals are used by different display systems to move video information from your PC to your monitor. The older display standards, MDA, CGA, and EGA, all use digital signals, often termed *TTL* (for *transistor-transistor logic*, the family of electronic components used in their circuitry). The VGA and later standards use *analog* signals. The difference between the two is how they encode color information—and the number of colors each system can encode.

Digital signals are like the thoughts of your PC—each signal has one of two states. Information is conveyed by the pattern of several signals. Digital monitor signals use a parallel code that's been specifically tailored to monitors. Under the Color Graphics Adapter system, IBM's first PC color display standard, the digital video code comprises four signals, three (one for each of the additive primary colors) that determine whether a specific electron gun assigned one of those colors is on or off. The fourth signal increases the intensity of all four signals simultaneously. This digital signal code is often called *RGBI* for the names of the four signals—red, green, blue, and intensity. RGBI signals can encode 16 colors because a four-bit system has 16 possible values. The more refined (but still primitive by today's standards) *Enhanced Graphics Adapter* system uses a six-bit code—three signals for the primary colors and an intensity signal assigned to each. The resulting six-bit code allows the transmission of 64 different colors. The MDA system uses only a single video signal but one that can have three states, corresponding to black, moderate intensity, and high intensity images.

Analog signals can assume practically any value, and so can encode a virtually unlimited number of colors—as many as the phosphors in the monitor are capable of displaying. The signals are called analog because their electrical strength equates to (is analogous to) the brightness of the electron beam inside the CRT and the image on the tube face. Because analog signals are more versatile, nearly all newer video standards (VGA and up) now use them.

Digital-to-Analog Converters

Internally your PC uses nothing but digital signals in its digital circuits. To translate those digital codes into the analog signals used by today's monitors, display adapters use special integrated circuits called *Digital-to-Analog Converters*. Often abbreviated as DAC, the same chips also masquerade under the name RAMDAC, which is short for Random Access Memory Digital-to-Analog Converter.

DACs are classified by the number of digital bits in the digital code they translate. For example, an eight-bit DAC converts the levels encoded in eight-bit digital patterns into 256 analog levels. In color systems, each primary color or channel requires a separate DAC, a total of three. Total up the number of bits of each DAC, and you'll get the number of bit-planes of color which a system can display, its palette. The number of simultaneous on-screen colors is limited by the amount of display memory. With adequate storage, three eight-bit DACs yield a 24-bit True Color system.

In most display systems, all DACs are created equal. Today, all three necessary DAC channels are integrated into a single chip that may in turn be integrated with the video controller. Some older boards, however, may use separate DACs for each color channel.

For a couple of years, two specialized DACs tantalized the PC industry with a promise of better, more realistic quality without increasing the memory needs of standard VGA adapters.

The *Color-Edge Graphic* system developed by Edsun Laboratories (now part of Analog Devices) tinkered with the VGA's Color Look-Up Table codes and reserved the uppermost 32 of them to indicate blending ratios of the colors of adjacent pixels rather than individual colors. The result was smooth transitions between colors at their borders or edges. Colors (more than a million blends are possible) could gradually blend together—with a minimum loss of sharpness. The CEG system never caught on partly because it lagged behind the market demands for the higher speeds needed for higher resolutions and because it required programs to know the chip's special codes for color mixing. Few applications were written to take advantage of it.

HiColor RAMDACs from Sierra Semiconductor pushed the color capabilities of display adapters from 256 simultaneous on-screen colors to 32,768 or 65,536 using the simple expedient of allocating more bits for image storage—instead of the eight-bit maximum of VGA, it allows up to 16 bits to store codes. The first HiColor chips and their more recent updates (SC11481/SC11486/SC11488) followed the standard set by TruVision's TARGA board with five bits assigned to each primary color. Other HiColor chips (SC11485/SC11487/SC11489) also allowed the use of the 16-bit system of XGA. With the advent of integrated three-channel, eight-bit DACs in most products, however, these products have spent their 15 minutes of fame.

Bus Links

The video system in your PC must somehow link up with the rest of its circuitry. In most display systems, the connection is intimate; your PC's microprocessor must be able to directly intervene, injecting data right into screen memory. That means that the screen memory must be within the addressing range of the microprocessor. While some high performance video systems (typically those with their own video processors) put their memories outside the reach of your PC's regular microprocessor, these systems cannot display the signals of standard display systems, MDA to VGA to XGA.

Either of two electrical connections can provide the logical link between screen memory and your PC's microprocessor. The link can be made at the I/O bus, which essentially equates to your PC's expansion bus, or directly to the microprocessor at its local bus. The functional difference between these two connections is speed. In most modern PCs, the microprocessor's local bus operates several times faster than the I/O bus. On the face of it, that singular advantage should give the local bus connection a big edge in performance. On actual applications, local bus is somewhat faster but nowhere near its theoretical potential.

I/O Bus

The I/O bus connection is almost traditional. The first PCs put their video circuits on expansion boards installed in ordinary expansion slots. The choice of location was pragmatic—the required circuitry would not fit on the motherboard, so it had to go into the slots. Slot-mounted memory also gives versatility to video designers and PC owners alike. One video adapter design fits all PCs, opening a wide market to vendors. PC owners in turn got access to a huge selection of products. Moreover, upgrading the quality of display systems was easy—simply slide out one board and slip in a new one.

With the advent of the AT and its 16-bit ISA expansion bus, the advantage of using a wider bus connection became obvious. Display adapter boards with 16-bit interfaces proved themselves substantially faster than boards with eight-bit connectors. With twice the bus width, 16-bit adapters could acquire display data quicker, delivering almost the expected doubling of performance.

Around 1987, some PC manufacturers, including industry leaders Compaq and IBM, rethought the reason for plugging video into expansion slots. The increased scale of integration left room on the motherboard that might be used by display circuitry. Moreover, where once several standards vied for acceptance as the one true video standard, VGA had assumed the role. Video was no longer a luxury, and the VGA standard made one video system the choice for nearly all PCs. As a result, these companies moved their display adapter circuitry onto the motherboard.

While this redesign changed the physical location of display adapter circuitry, it changed nothing about its logical connection. The video circuits still linked into the PC as if it were on the expansion bus, giving the microprocessor access to video memory through the old standard addresses. Electrically, the motherboard-based video circuits remained connected to the I/O bus, notwithstanding the proximity of the high-speed microprocessor.

The I/O bus connection gives the system designer important advantages even when video circuits are installed on the motherboard. Generally available video control circuitry is limited in its speed potential. Many of the chips simply cannot operate at the high speeds of today's microprocessors. The I/O bus is geared down to a rate tolerated by most video controllers by the bus control circuits on the motherboard. The video circuits also need access to system memory addresses, which requires tapping into address signals. The I/O bus provides the necessary address signals so nothing more needs to be added to the PC to graft video onto the motherboard.

The I/O bus connection means that ordinary motherboard video circuitry operates exactly as if it were installed in an expansion slot. Some motherboard video systems, such as those in early IBM PS/2s, use eight-bit I/O bus connections on the motherboard, holding back performance behind that which was available from expansion bus video boards. In fact, the only advantages of motherboard video connected through the I/O bus is lower cost and the saving of one expansion slot because you need no separate display adapter.

The I/O bus connection proved satisfactory for video for such a long time (from 1981 to 1991) because the video needs of older applications were minimal. For example, with early PCs it was not a problem because most applications were character-mapped. A full screen of information was simply an 80 by 25 array of characters stored in memory as two bytes per character (one byte in modified ASCII code, the other an attribute byte that specified color or emphasis). Because an entire screen of text data comprised only 4K bytes, it took an insignificant time to transfer even across the original PC bus (the actual transfer time would be less than 1/500th second on a 4.77 MHz bus one byte wide).

With the increasing emphasis on graphics applications in recent years, video transfer needs have increased dramatically. A screen of standard VGA 16-color graphics (today's least common denominator) consists of 163,200 bytes of data. Move up to a True Color (24-bit) image at 1024 by 768 resolution, and one screen of data increases to about 2.3 megabytes. If a system had no other overhead, that one screen would take a full second to transfer across the PC bus. In reality, such a transfer takes much, much longer when mediated by the system microprocessor, which must also allocate its time for memory refreshing, subtle background processes (servicing the timer interrupt, for example), and calculating the image data bound for the screen. Clearly, the several seconds per screen update required by I/O bus connections in this instance is unacceptable performance.

Local bus video systems take advantage of a more direct connection to the microprocessor using the address circuits available nearer the microprocessor that operate at microprocessor speed. These signals are available thanks to new chipsets specifically designed to give access to them. The video circuits themselves have to respond faster to keep up with the higher speeds—or they have to inject wait states to prevent operation outside their ratings. The local bus connection to the video circuitry can be made on the motherboard itself or it can be extended to another expansion bus such as VL Bus. When using a standard local bus design like VL Bus, the video system may still reside on the motherboard or it may fit on an expansion board linked through a local bus expansion connector. As with the conventional I/O-bus video connection, the physical location of the local bus video circuitry does not affect its operation or speed.

Because *local bus* video requires a special connection to the microprocessor in a PC, it cannot be added to existing machines the way you make other display system upgrades. Taking advantage of local bus requires a big investment—you need to either buy a new PC equipped with local bus or upgrade your existing computer with a motherboard that offers it.

The term local bus itself describes a technology and not an implementation. Before the PC industry adopted the VL Bus and PCI standards, a number of PC makers developed systems built around proprietary local bus designs. To achieve compatibility with today's applications, they mimicked ordinary VGA connections by using the same addresses for memory and the registers of their video controllers. As long as the PC designers maintained the same degree of compatibility achieved by VGA expansion boards, the details of the motherboard local bus connection were irrelevant to you as a mere PC user. The board would act exactly like an ordinary VGA system only it would react faster. The local bus standard used on one of these motherboards was about as important to you as the kind of cardboard from which a milk carton was made. As long as it worked and didn't spawn anything dangerous, it served its purpose without worry. These designs did have a big drawback, however. Upgrading one of these proprietary, integrated local bus systems canceled the local bus performance advantage. Any new display adapter slid into an ordinary expansion slot that followed a conventional (that is, slow) bus standard.

The VL Bus and PCI standards discussed in Chapter 6, "The Expansion Bus," eliminated that drawback. These local bus designs allow transfers between your system and the frame buffer at substantially faster rates than through the traditional I/O bus. They are particularly efficient at moving full-screen bit-images, the greatest throughput challenge faced by any display system. While useful, another new technology minimizes the need to move blocks of data to the display system—the graphic accelerator.

Graphics Acceleration

The chief strength of any local bus implementation is the ability to quickly move data to display memory from other places in your PC. The recent trends in display circuitry designs, however, have focused on minimizing the need to move large blocks of video data from one place to another. By constructing and manipulating the on-screen image with processor power that's directly connected display memory (rather than using a microprocessor that has to reach through a bus into display memory), massive transfers of video data can be minimized. Because less data moves across the bus, there's less of a handicap from bus overhead no matter whether the I/O bus or a local bus is used as the transfer channel.

Two technologies are built around the concept of moving the processing power closer to display memory. *Graphic accelerators* use VLSI chips specially designed for carrying out important, commonly used graphic operations such as drawing lines, filling areas, or creating Windows dialog boxes. Graphic coprocessors are full-fledged microprocessors that are designed primarily for carrying out graphic operations. As with a true microprocessor, a graphic coprocessor can be fully programmed—for example, to carry out the operations of a graphic accelerator. But a *graphic coprocessor* can do more, almost anything within the imagination of its programmer. While the functions and operations of a graphic accelerator are set by its hardware design (consequently graphic accelerators are sometimes called *fixed-function chips*), the graphic coprocessor can change its personality with a change of its software.

In contrast, a traditional display system has no processing power of its own, instead relying on the intelligence of the host computer's microprocessor. Because this older design has no inherent intelligence to control the display memory that buffers each frame of the image, it is often termed a *dumb frame-buffer* design.

Both graphic accelerators and graphic coprocessors add intelligence to your PC's display system to help break the bus bottleneck while lightening the load on your PC's microprocessor. Instead of the microprocessor needing to execute the instructions to create on-screen images, the graphics chips take over the chore. Where the microprocessor must move all screen-bound data into display memory through either the I/O bus or local bus, the graphics chips are directly connected to screen memory and don't require bus transfers. Instead of shipping data across the I/O bus, your PC's microprocessor sends only the software's drawing commands to the graphics chips, pushing a few bytes instead of thousands of them across the bus. The load on the bus is so light it makes little difference whether the graphics chips connect to your system through the I/O bus or local bus.

Only one kind of image data doesn't benefit from this graphics speed-up—those pesky stored bit-images. If you have a bit-image saved on hard disk that you want to put on the screen (for example, a photograph that you scanned in) the disk-based data must be transferred without modification directly to display memory.

The graphics chips bring another performance advantage. Just as numeric coprocessors can help your PC crunch through transcendental functions faster, these special purpose graphics chips can accelerate the performance of your system in drawing images on your monitor. The instruction set of a general purpose microprocessor is designed for versatility. The creators of the chip have no idea what some designer will do with their product, so they add in the ability to do nearly anything, sacrificing overall efficiency at any particular task. The makers of the graphic processor know exactly what their creation will be used for—graphics—so they can optimize the chip's command set for graphics functions.

Graphic accelerators and coprocessors often go hand-in-hand with higher resolution display systems. While dumb frame buffers work for any resolution level (as long as your PC's microprocessor can access the addresses used by display memory), the prodigious amounts of data at high resolutions require the extra speed of the graphic chips for adequate performance. Graphic chips can deal with huge amounts of graphics information (hundreds of thousands of pixels) in a fraction of the time it would take your computer's native microprocessor to ponder them.

A graphics accelerator or coprocessor often makes a greater difference in the video performance of a PC than would moving to the next most powerful microprocessor. For example, adding a graphic accelerator to a 33 MHz 486 PC boosts the speed at which it paints the screen beyond the level achievable by a 50 MHz machine using a dumb frame buffer. The actual performance improvement varies with the application software you use—programs that merely transfer bit-images won't benefit from an accelerator or coprocessor while those that draw on the screen (such as CAD) race ahead several times faster.

Overlay Boards

Multimedia systems often suffer from another slowdown: image processing time. The image produced by a multimedia system often combines picture information from several sources. Typically, you'll have a Windows display combined with a video image. Although combining this image data is no problem for a PC, it can be time consuming—so time consuming as to make real-time video displays impossible. Hardware designers have found a better way to combine video with other PC graphic information. As you might expect, they do it in hardware. They use special hardware to add together the different image signals.

The one design problem these engineers faced was how to tell the hardware where to locate the video image. After all, they couldn't overwrite the entire screen (if they did, there would be no reason to combine images), nor could they write on the screen at random, because they would risk obscuring important information.

To supply the needed location information, these design engineers turned to an old television technology called *chroma keying*. This process works by substituting one image for a key part of another image. Typically the key would be identified by its color or chroma, and the color of choice was a sky blue. This color is preferred because it's optically the opposite of average Caucasian flesh tones, so it is least apt to make parts of people disappear on the screen.

Multimedia display systems work similarly. They instruct Windows (or whatever software you use) to mark the area in which the video is to be displayed by painting it a particular color. Then the display hardware *overlays* the video image on that color. Your graphic software doesn't need to deal with the changing video information; it just passes along the video image from the hardware on which it originated to your display adapter. Because they overlay one image onto another, display adapters that perform this function are usually called *overlay boards*.

High-Level Commands

The secret weapon of any high-speed graphics system is the high-level graphic command. Ordinary programs tell the system microprocessor how to build or manipulate an image using its normal command set. The microprocessor can only accomplish the functions for which it was designed using the system facilities at its disposal. Even with the addition of a graphic chip, the microprocessor continues to execute all of these ordinary instructions, never asking the auxiliary chip to take over part of the action.

To bring the graphic chip into play, the microprocessor must send it instructions about what to do—those high-level graphic commands. The commands don't appear out of thin air. They must be part of the software you run on your system. Your PC's microprocessor detects the instructions and relays them to the graphic chip, which then carries them out.

The range of commands is large. Each graphic acceleration product has it own repertory. Several among them are basic and are invariably implemented. These include:

➤ Bit block transfers, instructions that tell the graphic chip to move data from one place to another in display memory. Instead of moving each byte of screen data through memory, the microprocessor only needs to tell the graphic chip what block to move (the source of the data) and where to put it (the destination). The graphic chip then carries out the entire data transfer operation on its own.

Often shortened to BitBlt, bit block transfers are most commonly used for scrolling the image up the screen. You can easily see the effect the command makes in video performance. When you scroll a bit image up the screen using a graphic chip, the top part of the image often snaps into its new position, leaving a black band at the bottom of the screen that slowly fills with the remainder of the image. The initial quick move of the top of the image is made entirely in display memory using BitBlts. The rest of the image must be brought into display memory through the I/O bus or local bus, resulting in delays.

➤ Drawing commands tell the graphic chip how to construct part of an image on the screen—drawing a line, rectangle, or arc, or filling a closed figure with a solid color or pattern. Often called *graphic primitives*, these commands break the image into its constituent parts that can be coded digitally to build a shape on the screen.

Before your PC's microprocessor puts a line on the screen, it first has to compute where each bit of the line will appear. It must compute the coordinates of each pixel to appear on the screen, then transfer the change into display memory across the bus. With a graphic chip, the microprocessor only needs to indicate the starting and ending points of a line to the chip. The graphic chip then computes the pixels and puts the appropriate values in display memory.

➤ Sprites are small images that move around the screen as a unit, much like an on-screen mouse pointer. General purpose microprocessors have no provisions for handling sprites, so they must compute each bit of the sprite image anew every time the sprite moves across the screen. Many graphic chips have built in abilities to handle sprites. They store the bit-pattern of the sprite in memory and only need instructions telling where to locate the sprite on the screen. Instead of redrawing the sprite, the graphic chip need only change the coordinates assigned its on-screen image, essentially only remapping its location.

➤ Windowing is one of the most common features of today's multitasking systems. Each task is given an area of the screen dedicated to its own operations and images. Keeping straight all the windows used by every task is a challenge for a general-purpose microprocessor. Graphic acceleration chips, however, are usually designed to manage windows using simple commands. Once an on-screen window is defined, it can be manipulated as a single block rather than moving individual bytes around. The windowing operations can be strictly software manipulations or the graphic chip may include special hardware provisions for streamlining the control of the windows.

In a conventional windowing system, software controls the display of each window. The layout of the screen is calculated, and the proper values for each pixel are plugged into the appropriate locations in the memory map. The image is generated by reading each memory location in sequence and using the information it contains to control the intensity of the electron beam in the display as it sweeps down the screen. Every memory location is scanned sequentially in a rigid order.

➤ Hardware windowing works by slicing up the memory map. Although each dot on the screen has one or more bits of memory assigned to it, the map no longer needs to be an exact representation of the screen. The video chip no longer scans each memory location in exact sequential order as the video beam traces down the screen. Instead, the memory scanned to control the beam is indicated by pointers, which guide the scan between different memory areas. Each memory area pointed to represents an on-screen window.

Each window can be individually manipulated. The memory used by a window can even be mapped into the address range of the system microprocessor while the rest of the screen is handled separately. As a consequence, most of the calculating normally required to change a window is eliminated. Screen updates speed up substantially.

➤ Hardware panning takes advantage of the display memory that's not needed as a frame buffer. For example, the extra 100K of the 256K on a VGA board needs only about 160K for a full image. The extra memory can hold an image that's bigger than that displayed on the monitor screen—the monitor image essentially becomes a window into display memory. Instead of stretching out for 640 by 480 pixels, for example, the extra display memory might allow the filling of an 800 by 600 matrix of which only the center 640 by 480 matrix is displayed. To pan the on-screen image one way or another on the screen, the display circuits only need to change the address of the area routed through the output of the board (see fig. 12.4). Changing addresses is much faster than moving blocks of bytes with BitBlt instructions, so hardware panning takes place very quickly—as long as the entirety of the image to be displayed is held in memory.

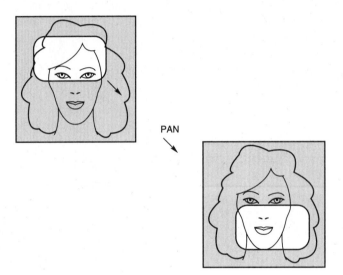

FIGURE 12.4. Hardware panning.

Graphic Environments

If there is any weakness in improving display performance with graphic accelerators and graphic processors, it is the need for these special high level commands. Unless a program includes the requisite instructions, the graphic chips will never swing into action. Any investment in this extra-cost hardware would be wasted.

Consequently, programs must be specially written to take advantage of your system's graphic hardware. In itself that need might not seem troublesome—until you consider that more than a dozen graphic chips are in use and each has its own individual command set. To recognize and use all the available chips, a program would have to pack itself with instructions for each of the chips with which it might potentially be used. With the proliferation of different chips, the necessary code would grow inside programs like a digital cancer, swelling programs with tumors of code that will eventually doom performance.

Software drivers help programmers sidestep the need for overloading their programs with graphic code. The program itself is written to the most common subset of high-level graphic commands available from most graphic chips. The programmer uses his own, proprietary command for each of those functions. He then creates a separate program called a *software driver* that translates his commands into those used by a specific graphic chip or board build from a specific chip. When the microprocessor in the PC encounters one of the program's graphic instructions, the software driver tell the microprocessor the proper instruction to send to the graphic chip which then carries out the operation.

While this design makes your life easier, it fosters nightmares for most programmers—if they can even get enough sleep to have a nightmare. This strategy requires the programmer of even the simplest graphic program to be familiar with all available graphic hardware. He needs to be both a software and hardware wizard in a world where expertise in one or the other field is rare enough already.

The computer industry has circumvented this problem in two ways—leaving the writing of software drivers to the makers of display adapters (which simply shifts the requirement of double expertise from the software company to the hardware company) and the graphic operating environment. This latter approach is simply another step like that which brought you the software driver—adding yet one more layer of software. The graphic operating environment serves as a software bridge between your applications and advanced video systems that allows a single driver to be used for all applications that run under the environment. The first PC graphic environments were simply programs that added on to a basic text-oriented operating system. Today, the graphic environment is an integral part of operating systems like OS/2, Windows NT, and Windows 4.0. The Apple Macintosh goes a step deeper and makes the graphic environment part of the system BIOS.

The environment works by giving the programmer a set of software routines called *hooks* that the programmer can use to elicit certain images on the video display. The operating environment translates the hook commands into its own common language which is translated by the graphic environments driver software into a form understood by the graphic accelerator, coprocessor, or other video innovation. Application writers need only concern themselves with the operating environment hooks. The operating environment designers, on the other hand, match their products to as many of the competing non-standard video systems as they can—or let the hardware companies do the work.

Application Program Interfaces

The entire set of program hooks is called the *application program interface* or *API*. IBM nomenclature omits the redundant word program, so these hooks are sometimes called simply the *application interface* or *AI*. Whatever the name, these command compendia make the intermediate translation step that allows software and hardware to come together. The application program interface is the official means of controlling the display system (or linking with display software) that's documented by the maker of the device. The connection can take work through any of a variety of links—from direct control of hardware registers to a top layer of software that interacts with specific drivers.

For example, the application program interface created for the 8514/A display system comprised a set of commands to make the display board execute bit-block transfers, draw lines, fill areas, generate patterns, and mix colors. It also includes text commands for proportionally spaced fonts and alphanumeric operations based on the those of the IBM 3270 terminal. Commands to the 8514/A application program interface took the form of BIOS function calls, except that they are entered through CALL instructions rather than software interrupts.

For the programmer, the application program interface is an instruction manual that tells him how to work with the various features built into a display system. You, as a PC user, never need to deal with the application program interface. Your only concern is that a specific display system you choose is compatible with the application program interface of your software. For example, if you have a program that requires an XGA display system, you want to be sure your hardware supports the XGA application program interface—which means you want true XGA compatibility.

Sometimes programmers sidestep the official application program interface to take control of a display device at a lower, more intimate level. For example, many applications (and even the Windows 3.1 operating environment) skirt around the 8514/A application interface and send commands directly to the display board's hardware registers to improve the performance of the system.

Graphic Development Systems

If you strip the graphic operating environment of its user interface, you'll end up with a set of software hooks that help applications match to hardware. Several such products, termed *graphic development systems*, are available to application developers to help them write the programs that use the operating environments. These are wonderful products because you don't have to worry about them. The programmer uses the software tools supplied by the development system to make his job of writing flashy code easier and to broaden the market for his product across a wide range of hardware. You, as the user of the application, don't have to fret about complications other than loading the appropriate driver when you start your system.

Graphic Accelerator Chips

As with the microprocessors, graphic accelerators come in wide varieties with different levels of performance and features. In fact, the number of different graphic accelerators available to display board builders appears limited only by the number of different chip makers. After just a few years of development, the chips have jumped into their second generation with overall performance several times improved over their forefathers.

The first significant fixed-function graphic accelerators were made by S3 Corporation (the company prefers to think of its name as S-cubed, but their name is generally pronounced S-three (the name is derived from Solid State Systems). The company's 86C911 chip set the pace for the first generation of accelerators. Stripped to its essentials, the chip was a hardware implementation of the features most relevant to Windows applications, drawn from the instruction set of the IBM Extended Graphics Array (XGA) coprocessor. Designed to match the ISA bus, the S3 86C911 used 16-bit architecture all around—internally and linking it to its 1MB maximum of VRAM. Although it could handle resolutions up to 1280 to 1024, its color abilities were limited by its RAMDAC connection.

Other manufacturers followed with their own 16-bit chips; most jumped directly into the second generation with 32-bit chips. Now video chipmakers are using 64-bit and wider technology, both for internal processing and for accessing the frame buffer. Over a dozen companies now offer graphic accelerator chips. Table 12.2 lists these manufacturers and compares their products.

TABLE 12.2. Graphic Accelerators

Manufacturer	Part Number	Channel Width to System	Bus Support
ATI Technologies	Mach 32	32	ISA, EISA, MCA, VL, PCI
ATI Technologies	Mach 64	32	ISA, EISA, VL, PCI
ATI Technologies	Mach 8	16	ISA, MCA
Avance Logic	ALG2101	16, 32	ISA, EISA, VL, PCI
Avance Logic	ALG2201	16, 32	ISA, EISA, VL, PCI
Avance Logic	ALG2228	16, 32	ISA, EISA, VL, PCI
Avance Logic	ALG2301	16, 32	ISA, EISA, VL, PCI
Cirrus Logic	CL-GD5428	16	ISA, EISA, MCA, VL
Cirrus Logic	CL-GD5429	16	ISA, EISA, MCA, VL
Cirrus Logic	CL-GD5430	16, 32	VL, PCI
Cirrus Logic	CL-GD5434	16, 32	VL, PC
Cirrus Logic	CL-GD5452/GD5453	16, 32	ISA, VL, PCI
Matrox Electronic System	MGA 64-Bit	32	ISA, MCA, VL, PCI
NCR Microelectronics	77C32BLT	32	VL
NCR Microelectronics	77C832	32	PCI
Oak Technology	OTI-64107	32	ISA, VL, PCI
S-MOS Systems	Pixel 3D	32	PCI
S-MOS Systems	SPC 8110FOA	32	VL, PCI
S3, Inc	Vision 864	32	ISA, VL, PCI
S3, Inc	Vision 964	32	ISA, VL, PCI
Trident Microsystems	TVGA8900D	16	ISA
Trident Microsystems	TVGA9000C	16	ISA
Trident Microsystems	TVGA9000i	16	ISA
Trident Microsystems	TVGI9400CXi	32	VL
Trident Microsystems	TVGI9420DGi	32	VL, PCI
Tseng Labs	ET4000	16	ISA, EISA, MCA, VL
Tseng Labs	ET4000/W32	8, 16, 32	ISA, EISA, MCA, VL
Tseng Labs	W32i	16, 32	ISA, EISA, MCA, VL
Tseng Labs	W32p	16, 32	VL, PCI
Weitek	Power 9000	32	VL, PCI

Channel Width to Memory (Bits)	Internal Register Width (Bits)	Frame Buffer Memory Type	Frame Buffer Sizes Supported	Integral DAC
32	32	VRAM or DRAM	512K, 1MB, 2MB, 4MB	NO
16, 32 ,64	64	VRAM or DRAM	512K, 1MB, 2MB, 4MB, 8MB	NO
16, 32	16	VRAM	512K, 1MB	NO
32	32	DRAM	512K, 1MB, 2MB	NO
32	32	DRAM	512K, 1MB, 2MB	NO
32	32	DRAM	512K, 1MB, 2MB	NO
32	32	DRAM	512K, 1MB, 2MB	NO
32	16	DRAM	512K, 1MB, 2MB	YES
16, 32	32	DRAM	512K, 1MB, 2MB	YES, 8-bit
16, 32	32	DRAM	512K, 1MB, 2MB	YES, 8-bit
16, 32, 64	32	DRAM	1MB, 2MB, 4MB	YES, 8-bit
32, 64	32	VRAM	1MB, 2MB, 3MB, 4MB	YES, 8-bit
64	64	VRAM	2MB, 3MB, 4MB, 4.5MB,18.5MB	NO
32	32	DRAM	1MB, 2MB, 3MB, 4MB	NO
32	32	DRAM	1MB, 2MB, 3MB, 4MB	NO
64	64	DRAM	1MB, 2MB, 3MB, 4MB, 8MB	NO
64	32	VRAM	2MB, 4MB, 6MB, 8MB	NO
32	16	DRAM	1MB	YES, 6-bit
64	64	DRAM	1MB, 2MB, 4MB, 8MB	NO
64	64	VRAM	1MB, 2MB, 4MB, 8MB	NO
32	16	DRAM	256K, 512K, 1MB	NO
16	16	DRAM	256K, 512K	NO
16	16	DRAM	256K, 512K	YES, 8-bit
32	32	DRAM	512K, 1MB, 2MB	YES, 8-bit
32	32	DRAM	512K, 1MB, 2MB	YES, 8-bit
8, 16, 32	8	DRAM	256K, 512K, 1MB	NO
8, 16, 32	8	DRAM	256K, 512K, 1MB, 2MB, 4MB	NO
16, 32, 64	8	DRAM	512K, 1MB, 2MB	NO
64	8	DRAM	512K, 1MB, 2MB	NO
64	64	VRAM	1MB, 2MB, 4MB	NO

➤*continues*

TABLE 12.2. continued

Manufacturer	Part Number	Integral VGA	Speed Ratings Available (in Megahertz)
ATI Technologies	Mach 32	YES	80, 135
ATI Technologies	Mach 64	YES	135
ATI Technologies	Mach 8	NO	80
Avance Logic	ALG2101	YES	80, 90
Avance Logic	ALG2201	YES	80, 90
Avance Logic	ALG2228	YES	80, 90
Avance Logic	ALG2301	YES	80, 90
Cirrus Logic	CL-GD5428	YES	80
Cirrus Logic	CL-GD5429	YES	86
Cirrus Logic	CL-GD5430	YES	80, 86
Cirrus Logic	CL-GD5434	YES	80, 110
Cirrus Logic	CL-GD5452/GD5453	YES	80, 90, 100, 110, 135
Matrox Electronic System	MGA 64-Bit	YES	80, 90, 100, 110, 135, 170, 200
NCR Microelectronics	77C32BLT	YES	110, 120, 135
NCR Microelectronics	77C832	YES	110, 120, 135
Oak Technology	OTI-64107	YES	110
S-MOS Systems	Pixel 3D	YES	N/S
S-MOS Systems	SPC 8110FOA	YES	65
S3, Inc	Vision 864	YES	80, 90, 100, 110, 135, up to 200
S3, Inc	Vision 964	YES	80, 90, 100, 110, 135, up to 200
Trident Microsystems	TVGA8900D	YES	80
Trident Microsystems	TVGA9000C	YES	
Trident Microsystems	TVGA9000i	YES	80
Trident Microsystems	TVGI9400CXi	YES	80
Trident Microsystems	TVGI9420DGi	YES	80
Tseng Labs	ET4000	YES	80
Tseng Labs	ET4000/W32	YES	80
Tseng Labs	W32i	YES	80, 90
Tseng Labs	W32p	YES	135
Weitek	Power 9000	YES	250

Resolution and Bit Depths Supported

1600 by 1200	1280 by 1024	1024 by 768	800 by 600	640 by 480
	4, 8	4, 8, 16	4, 8, 16, 24	4, 8, 16 ,24
4, 8, 16, 24	4, 8, 16, 24	4, 8, 16, 24	4, 8, 16, 24	4, 8, 16, 24
	4, 8	4, 8	4, 8	4, 8
	4, 8	4, 8, 16	4, 8, 16, 24	4, 8, 16, 24
	4, 8	4, 8, 16	4, 8, 16, 24	4, 8, 16, 24
	4, 8	4, 8, 16	4, 8, 16, 24	4, 8, 16, 24
	4, 8	4, 8, 16	4, 8, 16, 24	4, 8, 16, 24
	4, 8	4, 8, 16	4, 8, 16	4, 8, 16, 24
	4, 8	4, 8, 16	4, 8, 16	4, 8, 16, 24
	4, 8	4, 8, 16	4, 8, 16	4, 8, 16, 24
	4, 8, 16	4, 8, 16, 24	4, 8, 16, 24	4, 8, 16, 24
	4, 8, 16, 24	4, 8, 16, 24, 32	4, 8, 16, 24, 32	4, 8, 16, 24, 32
	4, 8, 16, 24	4, 8, 16, 24	4, 8, 16, 24	4, 8, 16, 24
4, 8	4, 8	4, 8, 16, 24	4, 8, 16, 24	4, 8, 16, 24
4, 8	4, 8	4, 8, 16, 24	4, 8, 16, 24	4, 8, 16, 24
4	4, 8	4, 8, 16, 24	4, 8, 16, 24	4, 8, 16, 24
4, 8, 16, 24	4, 8, 16, 24	4, 8, 16, 24	4, 8, 16, 24	
			4, 8	4, 8
	4, 8, 16, 24	4, 8, 16, 24	4, 8, 16, 24	4, 8, 16, 24
	4, 8, 16, 24	4, 8, 16, 24	4, 8, 16, 24	4, 8, 16, 24
		4, 8	4, 8, 16	4, 8, 16, 24
		4	4, 8	4, 8
		4	4, 8	4,
	4, 8	4, 8	4, 8, 16	4, 8, 16, 24
	4, 8	4, 8	4, 8, 16	4, 8, 16, 24
	4	4, 8	4, 8, 16	4, 8, 16, 24
	4, 8	4, 8	4, 8, 16	4, 8, 16, 24
	4, 8	4, 8, 16	4, 8, 16	4, 8, 16, 24
	4, 8	4, 8, 16	4, 8, 16, 24	4, 8, 16, 24
8, 16	8, 16, 24	8, 16, 24	16, 24	8, 16, 24

Source: Manufacturer-supplied data.

The performance and output quality of a graphic accelerator depends on a number of design variables. Among the most important of these are the following:

➤ Register Width: Graphic accelerators work like microprocessors dedicated to their singular purpose, and internally they are built much the same. The same design choice that determines microprocessor power also affects the performance of graphic accelerator chips. The internal register width of a graphic accelerator determines how many bits the chip works with at a time. As with microprocessors, the wider the registers, the more data that can be manipulated in a single operation.

The first generation of graphic accelerators were 16-bit chips. Second-generation chips moved to 32-bit architecture, while a few jumped all the way to 64-bit designs.

Because each graphic accelerator has its own language or command set, you should have no concern about wasted width, as you would with 16-bit DOS running on 32-bit microprocessors. Each chip runs at its full potential.

➤ Bus type and width: Bus bandwidth is extremely important to graphic accelerators because they are the element inside your PC with the most voracious appetite for information.

The first generation of graphic accelerators had 16-bit interfaces because they were designed before local bus technology appeared on the scene. They only needed to match to ISA, and 16 bits sufficed. The advent of local buses forced the new generation of chips onto the scene to take advantage of the higher possible bus throughput. Most current-generation graphic accelerators have full 32-bit interfaces to match the leading local buses.

Besides needing a link to the system bus, graphic accelerators also couple with their own frame buffers. The width of this connection need not match that of the bus interface. For better performance, many graphic accelerators use wider connections to their video memory. Some chips have a 64-bit memory connection. Chips with 128-bit memory buses are in development.

➤ Memory handling: The maximum amount of memory in the frame buffer sets upper limits on the color and resolution support of a graphic accelerator, although other design choices may further constrain these capabilities. The more memory, the higher the resolution and the greater the depth of color the accelerator can manage.

You can easily compute the frame buffer memory required by any graphic accelerator for a given resolution level and color depth. The minimum memory is the product of the horizontal resolution, vertical resolution, and color depth in bytes. For example, at the 1280 by 1024 resolution level with True Color capabilities (24-bit color—3-byte color depth), the required memory for the frame buffer is 1280 x 1024 x 3 or 3,932,160 bytes.

➤ Memory type: Graphics accelerators can be designed to use standard dynamic memory (DRAM), dual-ported video memory (VRAM), or either type. VRAM memory delivers better performance because it can handle its two basic operations (writing and reading, corresponding to image updates and writing to the screen) simultaneously. VRAM is, however, substantially more expensive than DRAM and, in the quantities used with modern display adapters, the cost difference can be substantial. Only boards aimed at squeezing out the last bit of video performance are likely to use VRAM.

➤ Resolution support: Every graphic accelerator supports three basic resolutions: standard VGA 640 by 480 pixel graphics, SuperVGA 800 by 600 pixels, and 1024 by 768 pixels. Beyond the basic trio, designers often push higher, depending on other constraints. Besides the standard increments upward (1280 by 1024 and 1600 by 1200 pixels) some makers throw in intermediate values so that you can coax monitors to their maximum sharpness.

➤ Color depth support: Many of today's graphics accelerators are all-in-one video solutions, so they contain DACs as well as control circuitry. These built-in DACs obey the same rules as standalone chips. Foremost in importance is the color-depth the chips can produce. Some graphic accelerators rely on standard VGA-style DAC and are limited to 18-bit VGA-style color (six bits of each primary color) and can only discriminate between 262,144 colors. Most newer graphic accelerators with built-in DACs have full 24-bit (or 32-bit) color support, enabling them to display the 16.7 million hues of True Color.

➤ Speed rating: The higher the resolution a graphic accelerator produces, the more pixels it must put on the screen. At a given frame rate, more pixels means each one must be produced faster—it gets a smaller share of each frame. Consequently higher resolution accelerator chips must be able to operate at higher speeds. For 1024 by 768 resolution with a 75 Hz frame rate, 80 MHz is sufficient; for 1280 by 1024, 100 MHz is sufficient (110 MHz is better); for 1600 by 1200 resolution, 150 MHz is needed, although 135 MHz is sufficient should screen updating be limited to lower frame rates.

➤ VGA support: Every video board boots up in an IBM-compatible mode. In modern PCs, that means VGA. So every video board must have VGA support of some kind. Many graphic accelerator makers have integrated all the needed VGA functions into their chips. Other rely on external chips for VGA text and images.

Functionally, your software won't notice a difference between the location of the VGA support circuitry. You may, however. Because the design of VGA circuits varies with different chipsets, their performance varies, too. Some graphic accelerators have indifferent VGA performance. As a result, DOS screens and low resolution graphics may be slow while high resolution graphics perform superbly. Of course, accelerators with external VGA support can suffer the same indignity if their designers don't choose top VGA chips.

From a practical standpoint, VGA support may be irrelevant to you if you jump immediately from the DOS prompt to Windows or run OS/2. If, however, you often work in text mode or rely on standard VGA graphics, you should concern yourself with the performance of a given graphic accelerator both in its native high-resolution modes and in VGA.

A graphic accelerator does not automatically guarantee a performance improvement on all graphic applications. Software not designed to work with the application interface of the graphic accelerator won't gain any of the benefits of the acceleration. Often, the opposite is the case. A standard DOS program may operate more slowly through a graphic system designed to accelerate Windows performance. As with other PC hardware, your choice of a graphic accelerator depends on the applications that you want to run.

Graphic Coprocessors

Fixed-function graphic accelerator technology evolved from the general purpose graphic coprocessor, which in turn developed from the general purpose microprocessor. Each step of this evolution involved greater specialization—manufacturers carving a market niche by optimizing their products for a specific application. New niches open when an application develops into a sufficiently large market to support development costs.

The workstation market triggered the graphic coprocessor. Microprocessor makers altered their general purpose designs into products that were particularly adept at manipulating video images. Because the workstation market was multi-faceted with each different hardware platform running different software, the graphic coprocessor had to be as flexible as possible—programmable just like their microprocessor forefathers.

These coprocessors joined the PC revolution in applications which demanded high performance graphics. But the mass acceptance of Windows made nearly every PC graphics-intensive. The coprocessor was left behind as chipmakers targeted the specific features needed by Windows and trimmed off the excess—programmability.

Of the variety of graphics coprocessor chips, some never successfully made it into the PC mainstream. For example, both the Hitachi HD63484 and Intel 82786 found application in specialized graphic controllers but few PC products. The most successful graphic coprocessors in the PC market (and the only ones you'll likely encounter before the technology is as forgotten as wig-powdering) were the Texas Instruments TMS34010 and its improved update TMS34020.

At heart both chips were essentially TI's microprocessors optimized for handling graphics. They show how TI could have been a formidable microprocessor maker, were its products DOS compatible. For example, the TMS34010 was a chip with awesome potential. It has the equivalent of 31 registers 32 bits wide. That's twice as many 32-bit registers as the 68000 microprocessor used in the Macintosh and nearly four times as many as used in Intel's 80386 microprocessor, which the TI chip beat to the market. The architecture of the TMS34020 was much the same, but its implementation was improved so that the chip could yield double the performance of its predecessor.

In graphics, a large number of registers is particularly valuable because they permit the many parameters often used in graphics manipulation to stay inside the processor instead of being shifted continually between the chip and memory. The pointless swapping of information out of the processor and into memory and back again is called *thrashing* and is deadly to performance. Because of its microprocessor base and its many registers, the TMS34010 and TMS34020 could handle pixel calculation tasks better than any other single programmable chip.

The TMS coprocessor family also had the best industry support, mostly thanks to the TI-designed application interface *TIGA* (which stands for the Texas Instruments Graphic Architecture). TIGA gave software writers a single standard to follow. On the other hand, in the TIGA system the frame buffer is usually not addressable by the microprocessor in your PC.

Consequently, most of these boards required a separate display system when running without benefit of the TIGA environment, for example, for normal DOS applications. TIGA boards had to co-reside with another display adapter or have standard display-adapter circuitry built-in in addition to the TIGA circuitry. (Such "built-in" circuits were often optional, such as a daughtercard that attached to the main display board to add DOS capabilities.)

The natural mode of operation for these boards was through a monitor separate from that used for DOS applications. In such two-monitor systems, one monitor showed a DOS display (such as the commands you give a CAD program) while the other display showed what the TIGA board was doing (such as the wireframe being created by the CAD program). While the DOS display ran in a standard mode such as VGA, the TIGA display presented a high resolution image.

For the people who couldn't afford a second monitor or didn't want one cluttering their desks, most TIGA adapters allowed one-monitor operation, either with on-board VGA circuitry or by allowing the output of a standard video board to loop through the TIGA board (the two boards are connected together, and the output of the standard board appears at the connector on the TIGA board).

Because the TI chips were true microprocessors, they required memory to carry out their functions. Consequently, TIGA boards have two kinds of memory: display memory for the frame buffer and instruction memory for the chip's operations. As with other graphic systems, the amount of display memory partly determines the maximum resolution of the board and the number of color planes that can be stored.

More instruction memory could be used to improve the performance of the overall display system. For example, it can be used to temporarily store the results of graphics commands to draw images so that images can be quickly regenerated without the need for carrying out all the math over again. Some computer-aided design applications call this feature *display list memory*.

When introduced, the TMS-series chips delivered the best graphic performance available. Today's fixed-function graphic accelerators carry out Windows tasks faster and cost less. Although programmability has its powers, getting the most from your PC and budget are not among them in graphics today.

Chapter 13
Display Adapters

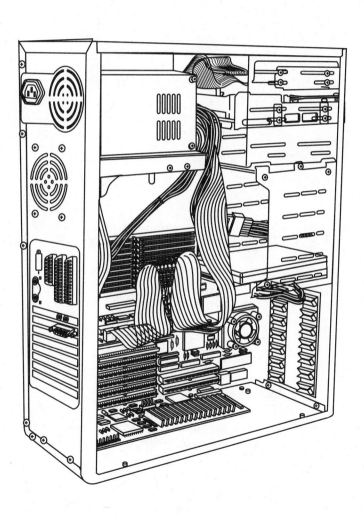

The hardware that changes your pulsing digital PC's thoughts into the signals that can be displayed by a monitor is called the *display adapter*. Over the years, the display adapter has itself adapted to the demands of PC users, gaining color and graphics abilities as well as increasing its resolution and range of hues. A number of standards—and standard setters—have evolved, each improving the quality of what you see on your monitor screen. Although display adapters themselves may disappear from PCs, they will leave a legacy in the standards they set.

Making light of electronic signals requires no extraordinary skill or complex circuitry. All it takes is a lightbulb and a press of a finger on a willing wall switch. Beyond that, however, things get more difficult. Imagine mastering more than 300,000 lightbulbs, each with a dimmer rather than a switch, and perfectly adjusting each half a hundred times a second.

Of course that's exactly the kind of chore you bought your computer for. Not just any computer will do, though. It needs special circuitry to take control of that light show. Not only must it be able to switch on and off the lights, dimming them when appropriate, but it also has to remember how each is supposed to be set. And it has to imagine, visualize, and draw the patterns that the lights will reveal. In a modern PC, all of these functions are adeptly handled by a display adapter, circuitry that adapts computer signals to those that control your monitor. In most machines, the display adapter is a special expansion board that serves primarily to make graphic images, hence the display adapter is often called a graphics board.

No matter its name, the function of display circuitry is the same—control. But there is one more essential element. Just any control won't do. Give a room full of monkeys control of your 300,000 light dimmers (you'll need a mighty large room or a special breed of small, social simians), and the resulting patterns might be interesting—and might make sense at about the same time your apes have completed duplicating the works of Shakespeare.

As important to the control of your light show is the communication it supplies—the ability to translate the sense of your computer's thoughts into an image that makes sense to you. Key to this ability is standardization—rules that let your computer and its display adapter know the correct way to control the image on your monitor. Computer makers build their display circuits to conform to certain industry standards, and programmers write their magnum opuses to match.

Since the introduction of the PC, display adapters and display standards have evolved hand-in-hand. Programmers have followed close behind, often prodding to push things ahead even faster. Over the years, several standards have emerged, unleashing their momentum as great waves, splashing across the industry, ebbing away, and leaving puddles of advocates slowly evaporating in the heat of the latest innovations. If you're not careful, you can step into one of those lingering puddles. You'll not just wet your feet but muddy your vision.

Today one standard ranks as truly universal, the one now built into every PC, the one that nearly every program supports, the least common denominator among displays, programs, and possibilities. It's called VGA, and if you've bought a computer in the last half decade, odds are 99 out of 100 that you've got it inside. With a modern PC, however, VGA is but a point of departure. Nearly every PC acknowledges VGA as the minimum among its potentials. Most go well beyond its minimal offerings to double or more on-screen resolution. Yet a lingering percent (or so) of machines cheap out by opting for older standards or specialize with esoteric display systems optimized for particular applications (such as huge monochrome screens or broadcast video outputs). Although these other display systems and standards have their places, the cheap ones can be as annoying as the mud on your shoes after you inadvertently step in a puddle or worse (say, behind a bull).

Display standards have originated in one of two ways—either a lone manufacturer creates a product that the rest of the industry studiously copies or the industry bands together to hammer out (or cobble together) a standard that all agree to follow. When display adapter makers took their first, uncertain steps, they imitated the market leader—IBM—and slavishly copied its products and standards. Nowadays, however, no company has a monopoly on good ideas, and no company is the undisputed leader in technology or the marketplace. The setting of display standards has shifted to an industry-wide endeavor. As a result, you have a wider choice of resolutions and color support than ever before, with few compatibility worries—at least if you know and understand the standards.

In the beginning, display standards weren't an issue. There was only one—one model of IBM Personal Computer, one kind of display adapter, and one kind of monitor you could plug into it. As with Model T's, you had exactly one choice of color (green rather than Henry Ford's enforced black) but you still had no options or alternatives.

Although beauty lies in the beholder's eye, the first PC's screen was something only a zealot (or a secretary under duress) could love—ghostly green text that lingered on as the screen scrolled, crude block graphics, the kinds of stuff you thought you outgrew when you graduated from crayons to pencils. The most positive thing you could say for the IBM's original display, called MDA, was that you never had any trouble making up your mind about what you wanted. Nor did you have to worry about compatibility—or such trivialities as art, color, aesthetics, or creativity. Only later did IBM add color in its CGA system, which required an entirely different and incompatible display system. A second standard was born. When IBM tried to integrate color and monochrome systems, the result was yet a third standard—EGA—with varying degrees of compatibilities with the two that came before.

VGA represented a thorough rethinking of display technology. It has proven to be such an enduring standard because it provides sharpness on small monitor screens that matches your ability to see detail and a complete integration of color and monochrome display systems. Although it suffered a few shortcomings, such as too few colors for realistic images, the technology allowed engineers to easily add enhancements to accommodate such innovations.

Somewhere along the way, IBM fell victim to corporate hubris and lost its standard-setting capability. Its next step up, 8514/A, was slow to win favor because of IBM's reluctance to provide full details of its operation and because the rest of the PC industry viewed its interlaced displays as a shortcoming. By the time IBM improved the 8514/A standard into XGA, it had lost its ability to define industry trends and standards.

In its stead, VESA has become the mediator of PC display industry standards. VESA developed today's standards for resolutions beyond VGA—including refined versions of both 8514/A and XGA. VESA, the Video Electronics Standards Association, was first conceived in 1987 by an engineer at NEC Technologies, the company that offered the best-selling multi-scanning monitor, the original MultiSync. Jim Schwabe of NEC claims to have coined the VESA name while standing in his kitchen amid dishes packed for moving from California to Chicago. Within the first three years of its existence, VESA came to embrace literally every maker of display adapters, most monitor manufacturers, and even large computer companies like IBM and Compaq.

The more relevant inspiration for VESA was the lack of a standard for display system resolutions beyond VGA. Every display adapter maker followed its own whims as to the specific timing of signals and means for controlling the display circuitry. Because of timing variances, once you switched your display system beyond VGA, the image might shift anywhere on the monitor screen. You'd have to reach up and twiddle the knobs to see everything—and hope the monitor had enough adjustment range. Although the problem originated in the display adapter, monitor makers bore the brunt of the blame because that's where the problem showed up. By standardizing timing, VESA was able to make image-making more predictable. At the same time, VESA also developed a standard for a software interface for resolutions beyond VGA.

VESA quickly grew into the display industry forum. All current standards beyond VGA widely recognized by the PC industry have been developed by VESA. Although the traditional display adapter is disappearing as standard equipment in modern PCs, replaced by motherboard circuitry, the display standards governed by VESA will remain an intrinsic part of every PC on the market.

VGA

The minimum display system in any modern PC follows the standard set by the VGA circuitry that IBM introduced in 1987 as an integral part of its Micro Channel PS/2s. VGA was, in fact, the only part of the PS/2 that was completely adopted by the PC industry.

The VGA name is derived from the name IBM gave to a VLSI chip. This chip, the Video Graphics Array, integrated all the functions of the video controllers used in previous IBM designs so that it was entirely backwardly compatible with older software. The Video Graphics Array used gate array technology (which means a lot of logic circuits dedicated to their function instead of being programmable like a microprocessor). Because it generated video signals, the Video Gate Array name was a natural.

For IBM, VGA appeared like the end of the line for standard PC display systems. The company has made no basic improvements or changes to the VGA design. To this day it remains the standard display system in the vast majority of IBM's personal computers. Only after four years did the company deign to add something better as standard equipment—and only then to the machines at the very top of the IBM line.

Actually, there's little to criticize in VGA as standard equipment. Although higher resolutions always look better, a dramatic step up from VGA would be invisible on the small monitors that are attached to most PCs. The detail would simply be too fine to see at normal working distances. VGA resolution is about all that's necessary for normal screen sizes, normal eyes, and normal viewing distances—and yesterday's software.

Graphic operating environments (and particularly those with multitasking abilities—as in OS/2—or multitasking pretensions—as in Windows) have placed greater demands on display systems. When you put several windows on the screen, you need more than a tidbit each to know what's going on, so you naturally want to squeeze as much on one screen as possible. Higher resolution lets you put more information in front of your eyes. Moreover, larger screens are becoming both available and popular, so more on-screen detail becomes both visible and desirable.

Even when VGA was first getting off the ground and into everyone's heart and eyes, many companies tried to push beyond its 640 by 480 graphic resolution. The motivation was to offer something more in their products. After all, adding higher resolution modes required no extra memory—designers could skimp colors at high resolution (four colors instead of sixteen) without sacrificing big numbers in advertising copy. Chipset makers added extra high resolution modes to their products, and display adapter makers followed suit.

Because of its designed-in backward compatibility, the VGA system carries a lot of baggage, most of it odd-shaped and tattered. Ordinary VGA systems operate at any of four resolutions depending on the video mode your software requests. Its signals switch between three images heights and two refresh (vertical synchronizing) rates as it changes resolution.

Text Modes

The default operating mode of the VGA system is a character-mapped carry-over from the very first PC display system. This allows your PC to boot up with text messages on your screen so that you can read diagnostic messages and enjoy the copyright messages of the various BIOS add-ins you've installed. This text is arrayed in 80 columns across your screen, 25 rows high. Each character is formed in a 9 by 16 dot box, so the screen displays a total of 720 pixels horizontally and 400 vertically.

Depending on your PC and monitor, the VGA system defaults to either color or monochrome operation. In color mode, the VGA system locates its character buffer at base address 0B8000(Hex) and allows you or your software to choose any of 16 foreground colors and 8 background colors for each text character. You can also make individual characters blink. (Some software exchanges the ability to make individual characters blink with an extra eight background colors.) In monochrome mode, the character buffer is located at base address 0B0000(Hex). In monochrome text mode, you can select character attributes instead of colors. The available attributes include character intensity (bright or dim), underlining, reverse video, and blinking.

The VGA system provides an automatic means to detect whether you have a monochrome or color monitor attached to your PC using a special signal in the monitor cable, discussed below. Not all PC and monitor makers choose to implement this feature. You can, however, switch between monochrome and color operation using the DOS MODE command.

The distinction between color and monochrome text modes is important because software that writes directly to video memory may not be able to find the screen if your system is in the wrong mode. For example, if you've installed a program to operate in monochrome mode and your VGA system is operating in color mode, the program will write to the wrong address range. The characters will miss the character buffer and disappear—and you'll be stuck staring at a screen that's nearly completely blank. All you're likely to see is a lonely cursor. Running the mode command to switch to the proper mode (color or monochrome) before starting the offending program will solve the problem. Better still, reinstall the program so that it operates in the mode that properly matches the one your VGA system normally uses.

In color modes, monochrome monitors won't produce colors on the screen. They will, however, translate colors into shades of grey. To approximate the way that the colors would appear to your eye in monochrome, the VGA system interprets them into 16 levels of grey with 8 matching background grey levels (or 16, depending on whether the individual character blinking feature is enabled).

For compatibility with older software, the VGA system can also operate in a 40-column text mode. In this mode, characters are still formed in a 9 by 16 dot box, but the screen is traced with 360 by 400 pixel resolution to produce double-width characters. The memory used for this mode always starts at base address 0B8000(Hex).

The basic VGA system includes three fonts, its native 9 x 16 characters and two for backward compatibility with lower resolution standards, an 8 x 8 font and a 9 x 14 font. In addition, it allows the downloading of up to eight more fonts, each with 256 characters. By sacrificing eight of the possible character foreground colors, the VGA system allows the use of up to 512 different characters on the screen at a time. The necessary 512-character font (up to four may be used) are simply downloaded in the positions used by two of the smaller fonts.

A familiar part of every text mode screen is the flashing cursor that identifies where the next character to be typed will appear on your monitor screen. The VGA chip in your PC generates the cursor. Although you can change the on-screen size of the cursor by sending commands to registers on the VGA chip, you cannot alter the rate at which the cursor flashes. The blink rate is forever fixed by the VGA chip. The size of the cursor is varied by altering two registers. You load the cursor start register (bits 0 to 4) with binary value of the row in the character matrix which you want to be the top line of the cursor, and you load the cursor end register (bits 0 to 4) with the last line of the cursor. By altering these values, you can make the cursor a block that fills an entire character position, a single scan line, or anything in between. Normally, the cursor is a two-scan line underline. You can turn the cursor completely off by altering bit 5 of the cursor start register.

To send values to the cursor start register, you must load the CRT Controller Address register (which is part of the VGA chip)—which is located at 03B5(Hex) during monochrome operation, 03D5(Hex) during color—to a value of 0A(Hex). You reach the cursor end register by setting the CRT Controller Address register to 0B(Hex).

Graphics Modes

The native graphics mode of the VGA system operates with a resolution of 640 pixels horizontally and 480 pixels vertically. This resolution is the highest supported by standard VGA systems. Because most monitor screens have an aspect-ratio of 4:3, each pixel occupies a perfectly square area on the screen. Other display standards (indeed, other VGA display modes) produce elongated pixels that complicate the math needed to draw shapes on the screen.

At its highest resolution, the most basic VGA systems operate with either of two color-depths, one or four bits, allowing for either 2 or 16 simultaneous on-screen colors. These color depths are constrained by the 256K of memory used by bottom-line VGA boards. The 307,200 pixels require at least 153,600 bytes of frame buffer for 16 color operation.

To accommodate older software, the VGA system has compatibility modes that are addressed as 320 by 200 pixels, 640 by 200 pixels, and 640 by 350 pixels. The first of these allows for up to 256 simultaneous on-screen colors; the others, 16 colors. The latter limit results not from inherent constraints of the VGA system but rather by carrying through the capabilities of earlier display systems. Most modern video boards with VGA abilities have more than 256K of memory, but this excess memory is not supported under the VGA standard.

To broaden its apparent range of colors and to generate more life-like images, the VGA standard takes advantage of a color look-up table to map hues. Each of the 256 entries in the color look-up table encodes one of 262,144 hues.

The hue limit results from the color generation system of the VGA electronics. The VGA system produces analog signals to drive its monitors, and these analog signals are derived from three six-bit digital-to-analog converters (DAC). In the prototype IBM VGA circuitry, all three DAC channels were integrated into a single chip, an Inmos 6171S. Each six-bit DAC channel encodes 64 intensities of a primary color (red, blue, or green). Combined together, 64 times 64 times 64 (that is 64^3, or 2^{18}) distinct combinations of color levels are possible, the 262,144 hue potential.

The actual color look-up table in the original VGA circuitry was part of the Inmos DAC chip, which provided 256 registers, each capable of storing the necessary 18-bit color code.

Monochrome Integration

Color and monochrome graphics are integrated together in the VGA system, so you can interchangeably plug a color or monochrome monitor into any VGA video system. Although that seems like no great feat (you'd expect to pull your car into the garage no matter what color it's painted), this compatibility has not always been the case. Early PC video standards drew a hard line between monochrome and color. Plug one in where the other is expected, and you would get an image resembling a sleet storm slashed onto the screen by a two-year-old. Worse, the mismatch connection could lead to monitor melt-down. The VGA system eliminated all such hardware incompatibilities.

Software is another matter. Translating Technicolor into grey flannel can be tricky business. Although translating the relative brightness of colors into shades of grey seems straightforward, the aesthetics can be daunting. The human eye is color-fickle: it prefers some colors to others, being most sensitive to green, least to blue. Direct translations of brightness don't take such human prejudices into account. Moreover, color and monochrome imagery differ in how they affect your human sensitivities and make impact. A monitor screen that's striking in color may become a yawn in monochrome. In fact, the image could completely disappear in the translation.

Most of these matters are beyond the concern of hardware designers, but they still have to make a system that works well for everyone. To help software writers compensate for the individual needs of color and monochrome display systems, the hardware engineers provide a means by which your PC and its software can determine whether you've plugged a monochrome or color monitor into your VGA system. The secret is a special extra signal added to the VGA interface. This extra signal is simply feedback from the display that tells the VGA circuitry what kind of monitor you've plugged in. VGA monitors are designed to send out the proper signal—at least they are supposed to be.

Two pins in the VGA connector allow the detection of display type. Monochrome monitors assign Pin 12 the function of video ground and provide no pin or connection on Pin 11. Color displays are wired in the opposite manner: the connector from the monitor has no Pin 12 and uses Pin 11 as a video ground. This digital ground function is also duplicated on Pin 10, so monitors lacking either sensing pin will still properly receive all image signals.

As a default, the VGA circuitry sends out only the signal assigned to the color green when it detects a monochrome monitor. Of course, the color repertory of the VGA system is compromised by this operation, but the VGA compensates by translating the colors into up to 64 shades of grey, a result of the green signal being capable of handling 26 discrete intensities, limited by the 6-bit green channel of the DAC. Proper monochrome monitors don't have connections for the red or blue signals, so they naturally get only the green signal. Many PCs simply operate as they would for color monitors, even when a monochrome display is attached, and let the hardware take care of the differences. Critical software can, however, detect the presence of a monochrome monitor and adjust its display palette (or even image making) to optimize the contrast that appears on the screen.

Memory

The VGA system faces a small problem in addressing its full 256K memory capacity: not enough address space was reserved for such a large frame buffer in the original PC specification. The available address ranges are simply too small. To fit the frame buffer within the confines of the available addresses, the VGA uses the time-honored trick of bank-switching. The full expanse of the system's display memory is usually split four ways into 64K banks, although a two-way 128K-bank split is also possible. A register called the Map Mask Register, which is part of the VGA chip, controls which banks the system microprocessor addresses through a 64K range of high memory addresses. The VGA specification puts the Map Mask Register at I/O port 03C5(Hex). Several registers actually share this port address to economize on port usage. The VGA Sequencer Register at port address 03C4(Hex) controls the function of the port used by the Map Mask Register. When the Sequencer Register is set to the value 02(Hex), port 03C5(Hex) gives access to the Map Mask Register.

The Map Mask Register has four control bits. In the VGA's native 16-color mode, each bit nominally controls a bit plane and switches the intensity red, green, and blue signals (listed from most significant bit to least) on or off. Unlike most bank switching systems, the VGA system allows multiple banks to be switched on simultaneously. This scheme allows an on-screen hue that's mixed from more than one color to be loaded in a single cycle. For example, if your system could only activate the VGA banks individually, writing a bright white dot would take four separate operations—writing a bit of one color, switching banks, then writing another color, and so on. By activating all four banks simultaneously, writing the white bit takes only one switch and write operation.

Addressing within each bank is linear in the native 16-color VGA graphic mode. That is, the memory arrangement puts on-screen pixels and lines into memory in the same order that they appear on the screen. The bit data in a byte from most significant to least significant bit corresponds to an on-screen sequence of eight pixels in a line from left to right.

In 256-color mode, each byte of memory defines the color of a single pixel. The bank-control logic of the VGA system divides the 256K of memory for on-screen pixels into four 64K blocks. These banks essentially duplicate one another but provide a convenient way of scanning color plane data into the DAC. Because there are eight color signals per pixel, and the VGA system is designed to scan four color planes at a time, the 256-color pages are scanned twice to make the transfer.

In text modes, the memory banks are similarly interleaved: odd bytes of display memory in the first bank; even bytes in the second bank. In normal text mode operation, this corresponds to putting the character values in the first bank and attribute data in the second bank. The various pages of character memory start at each 2K paragraph address boundary. For example, the first page will be based at 0B8000(Hex), the second page at 0B8800(Hex), and so on.

The VGA system normally locates its frame buffer in the 64K memory segment beginning at absolute address 0A0000(Hex). To maintain compatibility with older video standards, however, the VGA system can relocate the base address of its video memory. A VGA board uses the same physical memory no matter the base address at which it is used.

The mechanics of this relocation are relatively straightforward. A register in the VGA control circuitry acts as the switch. The Memory Map Register controls the base address of the VGA's video memory and the page size of each bank. Accessing the Memory Map Register is a two-step process. First the Graphic Address Register at microprocessor I/O port must be set with a value of 06(Hex) to enable writing to the Memory Map Register through the VGA's Miscellaneous Register at microprocessor port address 03C2(hex), an address shared with a number of other functions. Bits 2 and 3 in the Memory Map Register control bank address and size.

Setting Bit 3 of the Memory Map Register to zero locates the base address of the frame buffer at 0A0000(Hex). Bit 2 then controls bank size. Set to zero, it specifies two 128K banks; set to one it indicates four 64K banks.

When Bit 3 of the Memory Map Register is set to one, bank size is set at 32K and Bit 2 controls the base address used by the two permitted banks. With Bit 2 set to zero, the buffer base address is 0B0000(Hex); when set to one, the buffer base address is 0B8000(Hex).

Monitor Requirements

The VGA system requires monitors capable of synchronizing in a fixed horizontal sweep frequency of 31.5 kHz. The monitor must also be able to accommodate two frame rates, 60 and 70 Hz. The VGA system shifts between these frame rates depending on the mode in which it operates. Text and lower resolution graphic modes (all those except 640 by 480 pixels) use the 70 Hz rate. High resolution VGA graphics slip back to the 60 Hz rate to maintain operating frequencies within acceptable limits—the slower frame rate allows squeezing more lines on the screen without significantly altering system timing.

The VGA system creates displays that may be built from one of three possible numbers of horizontal display lines—either 350 (for backward compatibility with old digital monochrome display adapters and 640 by 350-line graphic images), 400 lines (for its native text modes), and 480 lines (for native graphics modes). In addition, the VGA system generates 400 lines in its video modes measuring 200 pixels high. To make this conversion, the VGA system uses double-scanning. That is, each pixel in the image is sent to the monitor twice, once in each of two sequential scan lines. This technique does not increase the resolution of the image. It merely trims the number of different image line counts and makes building a VGA system easier.

The tripart VGA line count creates a tough enough problem. All else being equal, a display made out of fewer lines will fill less of the monitor screen. The image will be shorter because the width of monitor display lines is reasonably constant; the height of the image depends only on the number of lines piled up. Practically speaking, a 350-line display would be less than three-quarters the height of a 480-line image. In other words, some pictures would be scrunched up like electronic roadkill; others would bulge out like a dieter's rebound.

The VGA system compensates for this height difference by requiring the monitor to alter its vertical gain in accordance with the number of lines it is displaying. Raising the vertical gain effectively makes each line wider, which can compensate for a lower line count. On many monitors you can make this adjustment yourself by twisting the control labeled vertical gain or height.

Twiddling dials may give you a feeling of mastery over your machine, but after a while you'll know that the chore actually makes the machine the master. Nothing is more bothersome than having to readjust your system every time it changes video modes. Consequently, the designers of the VGA incorporated a method by which the monitors could automatically adjust for different image line counts.

The obvious way to determine the correct vertical gain setting would be to count the number of lines in every frame. Given sufficient intelligence, monitors have no problem counting lines. Most of today's monitors have built-in microprocessors, so the task is trivial. The chips can handle transcendental equations, so counting is no big deal. But when the VGA system was created, monitors had less intelligence than your average flatworm. To make things easier on numerically challenged monitors, the VGA designers developed a system to tell the monitor how many lines were in the image. The VGA circuitry simply sends a code to the monitor to indicate how many vertical lines it is sending in each frame. Instead of adding a new signal to the array of those the VGA system sends out, the engineers took advantage of two signals that were already available. By altering the polarities of the vertical and horizontal synchronizing signals, the engineers were able to send the monitor an indication of each of four distinct VGA modes.

Only three of the possible codes are used by the VGA system. The code specifies 480 line operation when both sync signals are negative-going. For 400-line mode, vertical sync is negative-going and horizontal is positive-going. For 350-line mode, the code is vertical sync positive-going and horizontal sync negative-going.

VGA Connectors

Because the signals generated by the VGA are so different from those of previous IBM display systems, IBM finally elected to use a different, incompatible connector so the wrong monitor wouldn't be plugged in with disastrous results. Although only nine connections are actually needed by the VGA system (11 if you give each of the three video signals its own ground return as IBM specifies), the new connector is equipped with 15 pins. It's roughly the same size and shape as a nine-pin D-shell connector, but before IBM's adoption of it, this so-called high-density 15-pin connector was not generally available. Table 13.1 shows the signal assignments to this connector.

TABLE 13.1. Video Graphics Array Pin-Out

15-pin high-density D-shell connector

Pin	Function
1	Red
2	Green
3	Blue
4	RESERVED
5	Digital Ground
6	Red Return
7	Green Return
8	Blue Return
9	Plug
10	Digital Ground
11	RESERVED
12	RESERVED
13	Horizontal Sync
14	Vertical Sync
15	RESERVED

Many early multiscanning monitors were able to handle VGA signals but were equipped with nine-pin connectors that harkened back to earlier monitor standards. To plug one of these displays into an IBM-standard VGA connection, you'll need an adapter cable (see fig.13.1).

Compatibility

One of the initial design thrusts of the VGA system was to maintain complete compatibility with the software that was available when the standard was introduced. As the standard became popular and new manufacturers entered the field, compatibility concerns shifted to achieving a perfect match with the original design. Today neither compatibility issue is much of a concern because all widely available chipsets match the standard perfectly.

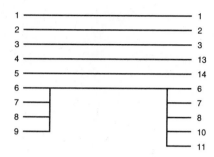

FIGURE 13.1. DB-9 to DB-15 adapter wiring.

In earlier times, two levels of compatibility determined what software would work with a given VGA adapter. BIOS compatibility indicated that a particular board reacted identically to the original that it is copied from when it receives a software command to its on-board firmware. The video BIOS did the dirty work, poking the appropriate values into the registers on the display adapter. The video BIOS isolated your software from the idiosyncrasies of early VGA hardware.

The VGA design made the BIOS the cure-all for compatibility issues. But a large number of programs soon took advantage of all the features available in VGA hardware by directly manipulating registers. For programs written at this level to function properly, all the registers of a video board must work exactly like those of the prototype that they are copying. When perfect, this register-level compatibility assures that all programs written for one video board will work on the so-called compatible board.

VGA Auxiliary Video Connector

For third-party manufacturers making VGA boards for PC-bus computers, true hardware compatibility with the VGA standard goes beyond the register level. It also requires one additional item, duplication of the video extension to the IBM Micro Channel expansion bus that's called the VGA auxiliary video connector. On many VGA-compatible boards, this connector is termed the VGA Feature Connector. This special connection permits add-on accessories to share signals and control with VGA circuitry. Add-ons can even overpower the VGA and switch it off, claiming the video output as their own.

This edge connector is usually included on most VGA-compatible display adapters. If you plan on adding auxiliary high-resolution display systems (such as an 8514/A-compatible board) to your PC, you'll need this connector. In fact, display adapters lacking this connector cannot truly be called VGA hardware compatible.

A derivative of this design is called the VESA Feature Connector. The VESA connector includes the same signals as the VGA Feature Connector but uses a pin connector instead of the VGA's edge connector (see fig. 13.2). Consequently, products expecting a VGA Feature Connector cannot plug into a VESA Feature Connector (and vice versa). Each of the two standards requires its own particular connecting cable. If you need to plug an auxiliary video board into your PC's VGA board, you'll want to check which type of expansion connector it uses.

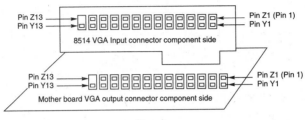

Figure 1

Pins are assigned from a top view on the component side of the respective PWB's

VESA Standard VS890803

Mother Board Header

Pin Z1	Ground	Pin Y1	Pixel data 0
Pin Z2	Ground	Pin Y2	Pixel data 1
Pin Z3	Ground	Pin Y3	Pixel data 2
Pin Z4	Future (Note 1)	Pin Y4	Pixel data 3
Pin Z5	Future (Note 2)	Pin Y5	Pixel data 4
Pin Z6	Future (Note 3)	Pin Y6	Pixel data 5
Pin Z7	N/C (Not used)	Pin Y7	Pixel data 6
Pin Z8	Ground	Pin Y8	Pixel data 7
Pin Z9	Ground	Pin Y9	Pixel clock
Pin Z10	Ground	Pin Y10	Blanking
Pin Z11	Ground	Pin Y11	Horizontal sync
Pin Z12	N/C (Not used)	Pin Y12	Vertical sync
Pin Z13	No Pin (Key)	Pin Y13	Ground

Table 2

Notes: (1) Low enable external pixel data input to the motherboard DAC.

(2) Low enable external sync and blanking inputs to the motherboard DAC.

(3) Low enable external pixel clock input to the motherboard DAC.

FIGURE 13.2. VGA/VESA feature connectors.

Both the VGA and VESA feature connectors are limited to the signals used by the VGA system itself. They are not useful beyond a 640 by 480-pixel resolution in 256 colors. But higher resolution systems sometimes require interconnections, too. To satisfy the need for a high-performance channel for linking graphics and video systems, VESA designed a new, high-performance connection called the VESA Advanced Feature Connector. Although it has limited backward compatibility with the standard VESA Feature Connector, the new VAFC transcends the limitations of VGA. It passes video data at a rate up to 150 megabytes per second. The connector provides a 16-bit or 32-bit data channel that operates at a maximum clock speed of

37.5 MHz and supports resolutions up to 1024 by 768. In its fullest 32-bit implementation, the VAFC uses an 80-pin high-density connector with 0.1 by 0.05-inch pin spacing. Its pinout is shown in Table 13.2.

TABLE 13.2. VESA VAFC Standard 1.0

Name	Pin #	Pin #	Name
RSRV0	1	41	GND
RSRV1	2	42	GND
GENCLK	3	43	GND
OFFSET0	4	44	GND
OFFSET1	5	45	GND
FSTAT	6	46	GND
VRDY	7	47	GND
GRDY	8	48	GND
BLANK*	9	49	GND
VSYNC	10	50	GND
HSYNC	11	51	GND
EGEN*	12	52	GND
VCLK	13	53	GND
RSRV2	14	54	GND
DCLK	15	55	GND
EVIDEO*	16	56	GND
P0	17	57	P1
GND	18	58	P2
P3	19	59	GND
P4	20	60	P5
GND	21	61	P6
P7	22	62	GND
P8	23	63	P9
GND	24	64	P10
P11	25	65	GND
P12	26	66	P13
GND	27	67	P14

continues

TABLE 13.2. Continued

Name	Pin #	Pin #	Name
P15	28	68	GND
P16	29	69	P17
GND	30	70	P18
P19	31	71	GND
P20	32	72	P21
GND	33	73	P22
P23	34	74	GND
P24	35	75	P25
GND	36	76	P26
P27	37	77	GND
P28	38	78	P29
GND	39	79	P30

A typical application uses the VAFC to link a video system that captures images with a television camera to a computer graphic system for special effects. Equipment on either side of the connector can use signals from either side of it to create composite images.

Memory Controller Gate Array

A few early IBM PS/2 models cut corners with a degraded subset of the VGA display system called the Memory Controller Gate Array. The compromise was to link to VGA hardware but slice away three-quarters of the memory demand of VGA along with much of its functionality. Top resolution and color modes both fall short of the VGA standard. As with VGA, this system was named after IBM's term for the chip that first (and last) implemented it, the Memory Controller Gate Array or MCGA.

The MCGA system allows for two text modes, one with 40-column characters and one with 80-column characters. The MCGA system, however, eliminated the circuitry required to put 720 pixels across each line. Consequently, its text resolution was limited to 640 x 400 pixels, with each text character drawn in an 8 x 16 dot box. Although the MCGA system allows for the full VGA palette of 256K because it uses the same DAC chip as VGA, the maximum number of simultaneous colors was limited to 16. Because its designers envisioned the system working only with color monitors, the MCGA system doesn't provide the monochrome modes that VGA does and locates its character buffer only at 0B8000(Hex).

For graphics, the MCGA system produces four distinct modes. Three operate at lower resolutions, 320 x 200 pixels and 640 x 200 pixels, double-scanned like VGA images to produce 400 on-screen lines that are compatible with VGA monitors. As with VGA, this double-scanning does not increase the sharpness of the image. At the lowest of these resolutions, MCGA can paint screen pixels with any four colors drawn from the full 256K color VGA palette or it can take advantage of VGA's 256-color mode. In the higher of these resolutions, two colors are possible, foreground and background, also drawn from the full 256K VGA palette.

The top MCGA graphics mode mimics the native mode of the VGA system with full 640 by 480 pixel resolution. However, with only 64K bytes available, your choice of colors is severely restricted. Only a single color plane fits the available memory, so the only possibilities are foreground and background. The color mapping abilities of the VGA system allow your software to choose these two screen colors from the full 256K VGA palette.

The MCGA system lacks full VGA BIOS compatibility, but its register structure is quite similar to the VGA system so that it can support its VGA graphics modes. On the hardware side, the MCGA system uses VGA-style displays and VGA connectors. Systems originally equipped with MCGA are upgradable to VGA by installing a VGA expansion board and deactivating the motherboard circuitry. There's little reason to bother with such upgrades. Systems equipped with MCGA are obsolete; none used the 386-class microprocessor that today's applications require.

VESA

Beyond VGA resolution there is at once one standard and no standard. Almost universally, higher resolution boards—no matter the number of pixels that they display—follow the standard set by The Video Electronics Standards Association. But VESA's standard is a non-standard. It doesn't tell manufacturers how to build a display adapter, as IBM's VGA spec does. Instead, it tells your software how to find out exactly what the display adapter does. The VESA specifications are more keys than hard and fast rules.

Moreover, the VESA display adapter specs have many facets. The organization has set standards for both sides of the video adapter—in addition to how your programs connect to your display adapter, they also lay out the rules for connecting your monitor. The VESA specifications for higher resolutions have stepped through three minor revisions, and a major revision is on the horizon. The VESA BIOS extensions version 1.0 (Oct. 1,1989) had standardized higher resolution control. Version 1.1 (June 2, 1990) clarified the more rough points. Version 1.2 (Oct. 22, 1991) added new fields to Function 01 (Hex) and Return Mode Info. Finally, version 2.0 (Nov. 12, 1993) added direct memory aperature (flat-frame buffer) support, bit-to-wait for vertical refresh (some functions), support for dual-and multiple-display controllers, protected-mode support, and support for relocating BIOS code.

VESA uses the term Super VGA for all modes and resolutions beyond the basic 640 by 480 graphics mode of VGA. Today these include standards at resolution levels of 800 by 600, 1024 by 768, 1280 by 1024, and 1600 by 1200 pixels.

VESA BIOS Extension

One problem faced when advancing beyond the basic VGA specification is the software connection. Because no single organization provided guidance for Super VGA as IBM had for lower resolutions, every display adapter manufacturer ventured off in his own direction. By using software drivers, even the most esoteric display hardware could link to your applications. But there was a major problem. Designing display drivers for all major applications and operating environments was a big challenge to programmers—and a costly demand for display adapter makers. In fact, only the largest manufacturers could afford the development costs for a full array of application drivers for their products.

The VESA solution to this problem was to develop the VESA BIOS Extension, an add-on BIOS extension for PCs that encapsulated vital data about Super VGA display systems. The VESA BIOS Extension gave programs (in particular, software drivers) vital information about the display system. As with any BIOS code, the VESA BIOS Extension provides an intermediary link between software and hardware. By keeping the BIOS interface the same, the underlying hardware can be changed without affecting the connection with programs.

The basic VESA BIOS interface takes advantage of the standard IBM video function calls that are activated with software interrupt 010(Hex). The VESA BIOS Extension adds one additional function call, 04F(Hex), which is otherwise unused. By loading different parameters when making this function call, software can elicit a number of functions from the VESA BIOS Extension.

Compared to the standard video support built into the basic PC BIOS, that provided by the VESA extension is modest. The additional code holds no new text or individual bit-handling routines. Instead the extension simply provides information that your video drivers and applications need to be able to use the higher resolutions of a Super VGA display adapter. Rather than a secret recipe, the VESA BIOS Extension is the key that unlocks the secret. The video driver software uses the key to put display bits into the proper pixel positions.

One of the most important functions of the VESA BIOS Extension is to report which modes a particular display adapter understands and displays from among the range supported by the VESA standard. These cover all the major resolution levels and color depths currently used by display adapters.

VESA developed its very first mode to extend ordinary VGA systems to 800 by 600 pixel resolution. By the time the association had begun its work, individual manufacturers had already developed their own modes. VESA chose to number its own mode 06A(Hex) and used it as a phantom mode—when this VESA mode was elicited, the display adapter actually switched to one of its own native modes that supported the 800 by 600 pixel resolution level.

Originally, IBM provided eight bits for tracking video modes. To prevent confusion between proprietary video modes and VESA standards, VESA extended the range to 15 bit values. All modes agreed upon after the original 800 by 600 pixel standard were given 15-bit mode numbers, and the original 06A(Hex) mode was given an alternate number, 101(Hex). Table 13.3 lists the VESA video modes.

TABLE 13.3. Video Mode Numbers

Mode Number	Text or Graphic	Originator	Graphic Resolution Horizontal	Vertical	Colors	Text Resolution Columns	Rows
0	Text	IBM				40	25
1	Text	IBM				40	25
2	Text	IBM				80	25
3	Text	IBM				80	25
4	Graphic	IBM	320	200	4		
5	Graphic	IBM	320	200	4		
6	Graphic	IBM	640	200	2		
7	Text	IBM				80	25
8	Graphic	IBM	160	200	16		
9	Graphic	IBM	320	200	16		
A	Graphic	IBM	640	200	4		
B	Graphic	Proprietary	704	519	16		
D	Graphic	IBM	320	200	16		
E	Graphic	IBM	640	200	16		
F	Graphic	IBM	640	350	2		
10	Graphic	IBM	640	350	16		
11	Graphic	IBM	640	480	2		
12	Graphic	IBM	640	480	16		
13	Graphic	IBM	320	200	256		
25	Graphic	Proprietary	640	480	16		
26	Graphic	Proprietary	640	480	16		
50	Graphic	Proprietary	640	480	16		
53	Graphic	Proprietary	800	560	16		
58	Graphic	Proprietary	800	600	16		
59	Graphic	Proprietary	720	512	16		

continues

TABLE 13.3. Continued

Mode Number	Text or Graphic	Originator	Graphic Resolution Horizontal	Vertical	Colors	Text Resolution Columns	Rows
6A	Graphic	VESA	800	600	16		
70	Graphic	Proprietary	800	600	16		
71	Graphic	Proprietary	800	600	16		
71	Graphic	Proprietary	800	600	16		
73	Graphic	Proprietary	640	480	16		
77	Graphic	Proprietary	752	410	16		
79	Graphic	Proprietary	800	600	16		
100	Graphic	VESA	640	400	256		
101	Graphic	VESA	640	480	256		
102	Graphic	VESA	800	600	16		
103	Graphic	VESA	800	600	256		
104	Graphic	VESA	1024	768	16		
105	Graphic	VESA	1024	768	256		
106	Graphic	VESA	1280	1024	16		
107	Graphic	VESA	1280	1024	256		
108	Text	VESA				80	60
109	Text	VESA				132	25
10A	Text	VESA				132	43
10B	Text	VESA				132	50
10C	Text	VESA				132	60
10D	Graphic	VESA	320	200	32K		
10E	Graphic	VESA	320	200	64K		
10F	Graphic	VESA	320	200	16M		
110	Graphic	VESA	640	480	32K		
111	Graphic	VESA	640	480	64K		
112	Graphic	VESA	640	480	16M		
113	Graphic	VESA	800	600	32K		
114	Graphic	VESA	800	600	64K		

Mode Number	Text or Graphic	Originator	Graphic Resolution Horizontal	Vertical	Colors	Text Resolution Columns Rows
115	Graphic	VESA	800	600	16M	
116	Graphic	VESA	1024	768	32K	
117	Graphic	VESA	1024	768	64K	
118	Graphic	VESA	1024	768	16M	
119	Graphic	VESA	1280	1024	32K	
11A	Graphic	VESA	1280	1024	64K	
11B	Graphic	VESA	1280	1024	16M	
11C	Graphic	VESA	1600	1200	32K	
11D	Graphic	VESA	1600	1200	64K	
11E	Graphic	VESA	1600	1200	16M	

For software using the VESA BIOS Extensions, finding the available modes is only a start. Your software uses the information reported back by the VESA BIOS extension to determine whether it can operate at the resolution and color level you want. Once the software is certain it can operate in the proper mode, it must then find out how. By sending another function code to the VESA BIOS Extension, your software can determine the location and control system for the memory banks used by the frame buffer for a given video mode.

Under the current VESA specification, a Super VGA board can provide for one or two apertures into display memory, which the spec calls (without much originality) windows. The size and number of windows is left to the designer of the display system. The VESA BIOS Extension merely reports to inquiring software where they are, how large, and how to control shifting them. It also indicates the memory map, that is, the correspondence of pixel information to display memory. A software driver can then take advantage of this information and write directly to the memory on the VESA-compatible display adapter.

Under version 2.0 of the VESA BIOS Extension (which, at the time of this writing, remains a proposal rather than a completed specification), the standard itself is extended to include multimedia facilities including control of audio and MIDI control systems. Each of these uses its own function call to send the appropriate information to inquiring software.

VESA Monitor Standards

At the other end of the display adapter, VESA supplies a full list of monitor timing specifications. Although these are commonly represented as a table of horizontal and vertical synchronizing frequencies used at various resolution levels, the VESA standards go deeper. They also indicate the exact relationship between the synchronizing signals and the on-screen display, specifying the delay between blanking and on-screen information. The net result is that the specifications completely describe the shape of the display waveform at each resolution level. The wave shape directly translates to the on-screen position of the active image. In other words, if a display adapter follows the VESA specification, it will put its image at the same place exactly as every other display adapter that follows the VESA spec—no more images jumping around the screen.

The initial increment up from VGA was 800 by 600 pixel resolution. True to its committee origins, VESA endowed this resolution with several options. Initially the specifications describe two guidelines and a single standard. These guidelines allowed for Super VGA systems operating at 56 and 60 Hz to earn the VESA imprimatur—and let manufacturers with monitor designs pre-dating the original standard sell their products as VESA compliant. The 56 Hz guideline accommodated older monitors designed with a bandwidth aimed only as high as handling the 35.5 KHz horizontal frequency IBM set for its 8514/A system. The 60 Hz guideline compromised between electronics cost and refresh rate. The official VESA standard at the 800 by 600 pixel resolution level requires an eye-pleasing 72 Hz refresh rate.

8514/A

In 1987, IBM's view of higher than VGA resolutions was that they were required only by special applications. The vast majority of PC users didn't require anything better than graphics made from an array of 640 by 480 pixels. For those who aspired higher, the company offered an expensive (initially about $1000) special-purpose display adapter with fixed-function acceleration circuitry, the 8514/A, so named because it was the Adapter to match the company's model 8514 monitor, also designed for the 1024 by 768-pixel resolution level.

Besides its high price, the 8514/A graphics board had three additional strikes against it: IBM made the product available only for Micro Channel computers. The outputs of the adapter provided an interlaced video signal, which even then was viewed as substandard by most of the PC industry—particularly monitor makers, most of whose products lacked the long-persistence phosphors needed to eliminate the image flicker interlacing inevitably caused. Finally, because IBM did not disclose the circuitry that made the 8514/A work (unlike what it had done with other display systems), the resulting system proved difficult to clone. Few manufacturers even bothered.

Like a troublesome coyote in a cartoon thriller, however, 8514/A refused to die, no matter what sort of disasters it set itself up for. But unlike any celluloid villain, the 8514/A standard has redeemed itself, mostly by sidestepping the issues that made the PC video industry avoid it. The problems with 8514/A have been resolved in a remarkable way—troublesome parts of the standard have been deemed never to have been part of the standard in the first place. And where IBM refused to tread, VESA has stepped in. These expedients have revived 8514/A. Moreover, because VESA had laid the entire architecture of 8514/A out plainly, it transcends other VESA standards. Where normal VESA-compatible products still require individual software drivers to work at the 1024 by 768-pixel resolution level, the necessary video handling routines can be incorporated into software. Support for the 8514/A standard is built into Windows, OS/2, and a wide variety of applications.

The most troubling aspect of the 8514/A standard was one of implementation. To keep the 8514 monitor that matched the board affordable, IBM skimped on its bandwidth. To keep its horizontal frequency under control while attempting to minimize flicker, IBM made the monitor interlace images in its 1024 by 768-pixel mode. Despite the use of long persistence phosphors and a relatively high refresh rate (for an interlaced system—a frame rate of 44 Hz and field rate of 88 Hz), users complained of flicker.

Nevertheless, the 8514/A standard survived for about three years as IBM's high-resolution PC display system. Just as clone-makers were developing their own compatible products, IBM summarily abandoned 8514/A in favor of its new XGA system. The application interface of the 8514/A standard lives on, however, as part of the XGA system.

After nearly three years of development, independent chip makers finally cloned the hardware aspects of the 8514/A display adapter. Western Digital was first to produce a truly register-compatible 8514/A controller chip, which several manufacturers used to build boards which could be plugged into the ISA bus. (Several board-makers had earlier released products compatible with the 8514/A adapter interface but not fully register compatible.) Most of these hardware-compatible boards improved on the basic standard by recognizing that the need for hardware compatibility extended only back to the system from the display adapter itself. The most maligned aspect of the standard (its interlaced monitor signals) could be avoided because software never touched this side of the adapter.

Most non-IBM 8514/A adapters include provisions for selecting monitor frequencies while maintaining the 1024 by 768 resolution of the standard. Besides the IBM interlaced frequencies, most provided for 60Hz and 70Hz (or higher) non-interleaved operation. The interleaved mode allows the use of dual-frequency monitors such as IBM's original 8514 and its successor 8515. The non-interleaved modes require multi-scanning monitors with the capability of operating at high refresh rates—48KHz with 60Hz refresh, 56KHz with 70Hz refresh.

Resolution

The most important characteristic of the 8514/A standard was its resolution, 1024 by 768 pixels, which put about 2.5 times as much data on the screen as VGA. It uses the same DAC as the VGA system, allowing it the same potential range of 262,144 hues, although memory limits the number which can be simultaneously displayed as a substantially lower value.

Memory

One-half megabyte of memory was made the standard equipment of the 8514/A, more than enough for a 1024 x 768 pixel image four bits deep. This memory is arranged into four bit-planes, each comprising a megabit of storage, allowing 16 simultaneous on-screen colors.

That arrangement leaves 128K of memory to spare, 256 kilobits in each of the bit-planes. The memory used for the on-screen display takes up the lowest portion of that storage. The rest is put to work as auxiliary memory for the data needed to carry out such functions as area-filling and holding loadable character sets. Although this additional memory can be addressed directly by the host microprocessor just like the rest of the memory of the 8514/A, this ability is not supported by IBM. That means writing to it may destroy information that the 8514/A has stored there for another purpose.

In its VGA-compatible mode, the 8514/A divides up its half-megabyte into eight 1024 x 512 bit planes arranged in two independent banks four bit-planes deep. The hardware design of the 8514/A does not allow combining these planes into one eight-bit plane.

IBM offered a half-megabyte expansion option for the 8514/A as a daughter card. This additional memory was designed to increase the color capability of the display adapter, moving its spectrum to eight bit-planes and 256 simultaneous on-screen colors. In addition, with the extra memory both VGA-mode maps of the 8514/A also gain eight-bit depth and a full range of 256 simultaneous colors.

Dual Screen Operation

The 8514/A system operates independently of the VGA circuitry built into its computer host. Operations that change the memory of one will not necessarily change that of the other. When the 8514/A is in its VGA mode, the two VGA systems duplicate one another. However, some operations (such as loading a palette or changing modes) may affect the 8514/A screen differently, revealing incorrect colors or a skewed greyscale. When the 8514/A is in its native mode, the two screens can be used independently. Typically, you will put text displays on the VGA screen while the 8514/A makes drawings.

Connections

The 8514/A display adapter shares the same high-density 15-pin D-shell connector with the VGA standard. Pin assignments are somewhat different. In addition to the separate signal leads provided for each color and its return, and horizontal and vertical sync, three additional leads replace the one devoted to identifying the display attached to the adapter (see table 13.4).

TABLE 13.4. 8514/A Pin-Out

Pin	Function
1	Red video
2	Green video
3	Blue video
4	Monitor ID bit 2
5	Ground
6	Red return
7	Green return
8	Blue return
9	Key (no connection)
10	Sync return
11	Monitor ID bit 0
12	Monitor ID bit 1
13	Horizontal sync
14	Vertical sync
15	Not used (reserved)

The monitor identification signals provide feedback to the 8514/A board so that it knows what kind of display it is working with. These signals prevent the 8514/A from sending a high-resolution/interlaced image to a fixed-frequency VGA display that might be plugged into its connector. This feedback scheme assures that the display and adapter function properly together and avoids the problems that might be encountered plugging a monochrome display into a CGA adapter. Table 13.5 shows how the polarities of the synchronizing signals code different display types.

TABLE 13.5. VGA and 8514/A Sync Code

Mode #	Mode Function	Lines on-screen	Horiz. sync polarity	Vert. sync polarity
1	EGA	350	Positive	Negative
2	VGA text or CGA compatibility	400	Negative	Positive
3	VGA graphics	480	Negative	Negative
4	8514/A	768	Positive	Positive

XGA

Other manufacturers were slow to adopt the 8514/A standards, and their hesitation was amply rewarded in 1990 with IBM's introduction of its Extended Graphics Array video system, commonly termed XGA. Just as a few manufacturers had released display adapters that matched both the 8514/A adapter interface and its hardware registers, IBM made that standard obsolete. Its XGA was backwardly compatible with only the 8514/A adapter interface. The 8514/A registers that had proved so troublesome to clone were ignored by the new standard.

From another perspective, XGA is IBM's replacement for its 8514/A display adapter. In some ways, you won't even see a difference—the current incarnation of XGA is designed to use the same monitor (IBM's 8515, a 15-inch color display that replaced the original 8514), operating at the same frequencies (35.5 KHz horizontal, 44 Hz interlaced vertical). XGA also incorporates the 8514/A Adapter Interface to allow backward compatibility with 8514/A software. Both XGA and 8514/A are made to fit only Micro Channel computers.

But XGA makes several improvements on the 8514/A. For one, it does not mandate monitor interlacing, which finally puts IBM in league with the makers of 8514/A-compatible display adapters. Aftermarket vendors have supported both interlaced and non-interlaced displays at frame rates up to 70 Hz when following the 8514/A standard. XGA permits IBM to follow the same strategy.

Unlike those compatible boards, however, XGA is not hardware-compatible with 8514/A and won't run software that takes direct register control of the 8514/A board. IBM sees XGA as a standard in its own right, one that only tips its hat at 8514/A then continues further on into the world of graphics coprocessing.

Wanting to prevent the recurrence of the yawn that greeted 8514/A, IBM made XGA an open standard by fully disclosing its features and operation. Anyone with a few electronic parts and idle millions (to cover development costs) can clone it in relatively short order—say a year or so.

The world greeted XGA with a yawn anyway because the first XGA system that IBM produced matched 8514/A in its greatest perceived flaw, its use of an interlaced monitor. However, the XGA system did have its strong points—enough that most Windows accelerators incorporate most of its functions. Nor was interlacing required by the system; as with third-party 8514/A adapters, the XGA system was designed to work with either interlaced or non-interlaced monitors. To free XGA from its status as a proprietary standard, VESA setup a committee (of which IBM is a member) to develop XGA into an independent industry standard, a status it had not yet reached in mid-1992.

The XGA board itself incorporates its own coprocessor, an IBM proprietary design, which is optimized for Windows and OS/2 Presentation Manager displays. Some of the functions it carries out include BitBlts, (Bit-block transfers), similar pixel-block transfers, line drawing, area filling, logical and arithmetic mixing, map masking, scissoring, and x-y axis addressing. (In contrast, the fixed-function 8514/A was primarily aimed for operation with Computer-Aided Design software.)

Of course, the IBM XGA coprocessor is not a mandatory part of the design of XGA boards. Manufacturers who work with the TMS34010-series of coprocessors believe that that chip can be adapted to XGA operation with appropriate software or firmware.

Modes

XGA has two operating modes, one in which it emulates a VGA board, the other its own Extended Graphics Mode. In VGA mode, it is hardware compatible with a conventional VGA adapter and includes all VGA features. When operating in the latter mode, it generates either 640 by 480 or 1024 by 768 pixel resolution, selected by your software. XGA also supports its own 132-column text modes with 200, 350, or 400 scan lines using characters that each measure eight pixels wide.

The VGA circuitry of the XGA adapter cannot coexist with another VGA adapter in the same PC. IBM allows for the VGA portion of its XGA adapter to be switched off for such installations. Up to eight XGA systems can be installed in a single PC.

The XGA system requires a contiguous eight-kilobyte block of memory addresses for its BIOS extension, and this block must be somewhere within the address range C0000(Hex) to DFFFF(Hex) in the High DOS memory area. The upper one kilobyte of this block is reserved for the XGA's control registers, which are used to send commands to the XGA coprocessor.

Color

To achieve full backward compatibility, XGA allows use of the color storage scheme of the VGA system. As with VGA, XGA incorporates modes that allow up to 256 simultaneous on-screen colors selected from a palette of 262,144.

Memory determines the maximum number of colors that can be displayed on the screen at a time: the low-end board with 512K of video memory allows 256 colors at the lower resolution, 16 at the higher resolution. With its current maximum of one-megabyte of VRAM, XGA allows 65,536 colors at lower resolution, 256 at high.

Because XGA uses the same DAC as VGA and 8514/A boards, it is limited to the same 262,144-color palette as the older boards are. XGA, however, also incorporates a direct addressing mode which sidesteps the palette register and gives direct access to 256 on-screen colors.

In addition, XGA adds its own 16-bit direct-color storage format. The 16-bits are allocated between primary colors with five for red and blue and six for green. This allows 65,536 simultaneous on-screen colors. Although that range may seem limited compared to the real-world spectrum, it doubles the capability of the TruVision TARGA system of 15-bit color, five bits each for red, green, and blue. In that the TARGA system has been found adequate for most video displays, XGA should be even better.

The XGA coprocessor is limited to the palette-mapped colors and cannot manipulate 16-bit direct color values. Consequently, direct color mode requires that the XGA board be used as a dumb frame buffer. However, the coprocessor can work on XGA memory at the same time as your PC's microprocessor uses the memory for direct color effects.

Memory

XGA also incorporates an innovative means for software to address screen memory. Actually, three different addressing schemes are supported, called memory apertures, and their accessibility and use depend on the type of microprocessor in your system and the bus width of the slot into which the XGA adapter is plugged.

The most basic of these is the 64K aperture, which can correspond to standard VGA addressing at the first 64K segment in the base of High DOS memory (addresses starting at A0000(Hex)). Alternately, this aperture can be relocated to the B0000(Hex) range. Its value is set by an on-board register. Unlike VGA, however, this aperture provides addressing to all of the memory of the XGA system (up to four megabytes) by paging. This aperture allows 8088 and 8086 micro-processors to use XGA memory in their limited real-mode addressing range.

A one megabyte aperture allows XGA memory to be controlled through a one-megabyte window, which can be located on any one-megabyte boundary within the first 16MB of extended memory. Again, this aperture is paged to allow access to all four megabytes of XGA memory. This aperture is designed to allow the 286 and 386SX microprocessors convenient access to XGA memory. It is also the widest aperture available when the XGA board is plugged into a 16-bit expansion slot.

Finally, the XGA's memory can be addressed through a four megabyte aperture located in extended memory above the first 16MB, giving a 386DX or 486 microprocessor that uses an expansion bus (or other connection to the video frame buffer) with addressing beyond the 16MB permitted by ISA direct (rather than paged) access to the maximum RAM of the XGA board.

Hardware Sprite

XGA also adds a wealth of new features and modes to PC displays. One of these is a hardware-controlled sprite, a 64-by-64 pixel graphic image that overlays the main on-screen image without disturbing the contents of the main video memory. The sprite is moved around the screen using simple positioning commands without requiring the entire screen to be rewritten. That makes it particularly suited for moving screen elements such as a fast mouse cursor.

Bus Mastering

The XGA board is designed for bus mastering operation, allowing its coprocessor to take direct memory control, not just of its own on-board VRAM but also the entire system RAM in your PC. The XGA coprocessor is designed to carry out graphics calculations on data held in your PC's main memory, then speedily transfer the resulting image into the VRAM screen memory as a bus master.

Control of the XGA board is achieved through a number of memory-mapped registers that fit along with 7K of BIOS extension code into the High DOS area of your PC (memory addressed above the old DOS 640K limit). To send a command to the XGA, your software only needs to write specific bytes to certain of these memory addresses.

Pre-VGA Standards

There have been a few sidetrips along the path of display system development. For instance, before the wide acceptance of the VGA standard, the monochrome graphics system developed by Hercules Computer Technology was the primary choice for bit-image graphics on monitor screens. (Some low-cost PCs are still sold with Hercules-compatible display adapters.) Some software still holds its allegiance to the older IBM video standards set by now-obsolete display adapters. Nearly all of these not-quite-abandoned standards are still displayable on the latest equipment (thanks to the blessing of backward compatibility deliberately engineered into IBM's display products). Even the first, rudimentary display system still hangs around as the lowest cost way to see on screen what your PC's doing.

Consequently, that's where any discussion of the display adapters used by PCs needs to mention the first video board IBM plugged into its first PCs—the Monochrome Display Adapter. A technological fossil perhaps, but as enduring as its mineral-based analog. Although technology may have passed it by, the Monochrome Display Adapter remains part of many PCs, including a bewildering number of new machines.

Monochrome Display Adapter

The first display standard for PCs was introduced in 1981 along with IBM's original Personal Computer. That machine came equipped with a display system that would not have looked out of place in a 1950's Nike base with myopic infantrymen peering intently at radar sweeps that revealed the Bomb winging over the North Pole. The monitor was cryptic green, each character fading slowly with every scroll of the screen, but it was sharp—and it was all you could get.

The signals were generated by what IBM called the Monochrome Display and Parallel Printer Adapter, but everyone quickly shortened the title to Monochrome Display Adapter or, better still, MDA. In truth, the green screen was not unlike the picture tubes of computer terminals of the time, and the MDA functioned almost exactly like one. It was a character-mapped display system with no provision for graphics other than the IBM extended character set for block graphics.

MDA Dot Box

For legibility on par with terminals used with its larger computer systems, IBM set the character box for the MDA at 9 x 14 pixels with a typical character using a 7 x 9 matrix in the box. The extra dots spaced individual lines apart for greater readability, something that's most appreciated when it's not available. To put this character box on the screen in the default arrangement used by most VDTs, 80 columns and 25 rows, requires 720 pixels horizontally and 350 vertically, a total of 252,000 dots on every screen.

MDA Frame Rate

IBM compromised on how to display all those dots. At a high frame rate, displaying that amount of information would require a wider bandwidth monitor than was available (at least inexpensively) when the PC was introduced. IBM instead slowed down the frame rate to 50 Hz and compensated for whatever flicker might develop by using long persistence phosphors in its standard monochrome display.

The lower frame rate gave the horizontal sweep of the scanning electron beam extra time to cover each line of the image. However, even with the lower frame rate, the dot density of the IBM monochrome standard demanded a higher horizontal frequency than was used by popular video monitors (and television sets), 18.1 kHz versus 15,525 kHz.

The MDA Signal Standard

The signals generated by the MDA are digital—nominally five volts to indicate a logical high, zero for a low—that conforms to the level used by standard Transistor-Transistor Logic or TTL. IBM calls the MDA signals direct drive because they need not undergo any digital-to-analog conversion but are instead directly connected to the drive circuits of the attached monitor.

Because of this signal standard, monitors that connect with MDA boards are often called TTL monochrome displays or just digital monochrome monitors. These names are important because only special TTL or MDA monitors will work with MDA boards. More common composite monochrome monitors are incompatible, as are monochrome VGA monitors. Fortunately, both of these types of monitors use different connectors than the MDA system, so you cannot plug them into an MDA board even inadvertently.

The MDA system uses four signals: a drive signal for the electron gun, an intensity bit (which causes highlighted dots and characters to glow more brightly), and horizontal and vertical synchronizing signals. These signals are assigned pins on a female nine-pin D-shell connector on the retaining bracket of the MDA. The pin-out of this connector is shown in Figure 13.3.

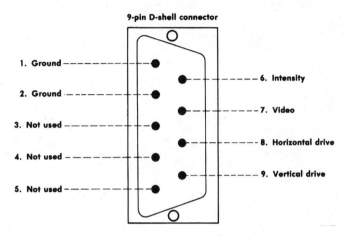

FIGURE 13.3. MDA pin-out.

6845 Video Controller

The MDA set the pattern for all display adapters to come. It was built around a 6845 video controller, which all video systems use or emulate. The 6845 chip was linked to four kilobytes of dual-ported static RAM for holding a single-page character-map.

The 6845 is a completely programmable device that's controlled through a series of registers. Programs can load values into the various registers of the 6845 and change the characteristics of the video signal it (and the display adapter built around it) produces (see Table 13.6).

TABLE 13.6. 6845 Video Controller Registers

Register	Description	Prog. Unit	Read/Write
R0	Horizontal total	Character	Write Only
R1	Horizontal displayed	Character	Write Only
R2	Horizontal sync position	Character	Write Only
R3	Horizontal sync width	Character	Write Only

continues

TABLE 13.6. Continued

Register	Description	Prog. Unit	Read/Write
R4	Vertical total	Row	Write Only
R5	Vertical total adjust	Scan line	Write Only
R6	Vertical displayed	Row	Write Only
R7	Vertical sync position	Row	Write Only
R8	Interlace mode	None	Write Only
R9	Maximum scan line address	Scan line	Write Only
R10	Cursor start	Scan line	Write Only
R11	Cursor end	Scan line	Write Only
R12	Start address (High)	None	Write Only
R13	Start address (Low)	None	Read/Write
R14	Cursor (High)	None	Read/Write
R15	Cursor (Low)	None	Read/Write
R16	Light pen (High)	None	Read Only
R17	Light pen (Low)	None	Read Only

One of the functions of the 6845 is generating the MDA's hardware cursor. The MDA design saddled the industry with a hardware cursor with a flash rate fixed in hardware.

Hercules Graphics

Because it is only a character-based system in a world that has moved on to graphic operating environments, ordinary MDA boards are rarely encountered. MDA technology still persists in the lowest priced PCs and display systems in display boards that follow the standard set by the Hercules Graphics Card or HGC, which was developed by Hercules Computer Technology, Inc., headed by Kevin Jenkins.

The Hercules Graphics Card grafted a bit-image graphic system onto the MDA foundation. It used the same 6845 controller as MDA but took advantage of additional modes and incorporated 64K of RAM functionally arranged in two contiguous 32K banks with base addresses of 0B0000(Hex) and 0B8000(Hex).

In text mode, the Hercules Graphics Card operates as a superset of MDA. Characters were formed in the same 9 x 14 pixel dot-box on a screen with a full-screen resolution of 720 x 350 pixels, a horizontal sync frequency of 18.1 kilohertz, and a 50 Hertz frame rate. All attributes of the IBM MDA—underline, blink, high-intensity, and inverse video—are supported by the

HGC. The HGC even included a parallel printer port with a based address of 03BC(Hex), same as the MDA. The extra memory of the Hercules card can be used as additional text pages, a total of 16.

In its graphics mode, the Hercules card generated a 720 by 348 bit-mapped image with two brightness levels: black and white. Two graphics pages (each about 30.5K) fit into the 64K video memory on the board. In graphics mode eight contiguous on-screen pixels are controlled by each memory byte, 90 bytes to each 720 pixel line. The most significant bit of each byte corresponds to the leftmost on-screen pixel stored in the byte. Screen lines are interleaved in the frame buffer, however, so that contiguous lines in memory display four lines apart on the screen.

The frame buffer of the Hercules Graphics Board is too large to fit into the 32K address range reserved for monochrome memory at absolute address 0B0000(Hex) and overlaps the 32K range allowed for the Color Graphics Adapter (CGA) at 0B8000(Hex). To prevent compatibility problems, Hercules boards boot up with only half of their memory in the monochrome address range active. A configuration register located at I/O port 03BF(Hex) activates the second bank. Poking zero into the second bit (Bit 1) of the register at this port disables the second bank of memory. Poking a one enables the second bank.

The first bit of this register switches the Hercules Graphics Card between text and graphics mode. Poking a one into the first bit of the register at I/O port 03BF(Hex) enables graphics mode; a zero puts the board in text mode and disables graphics mode.

The Hercules Graphics Card is completely compatible with MDA hardware and its text-mode software, but does not comply with any other graphic standard. Applications must be specially written with support for the HGC.

The design of the Hercules Graphics Card proved easy to copy. Nearly all inexpensive monochrome video boards now follow the standard set by it.

Color Graphics Adapter

The first bit-mapped display adapter that IBM developed for the PC was the Color Graphics Adapter or CGA. Introduced as an alternative to the MDA in 1982, its first images dazzled a world accustomed to plain green computer screens. Compared to today's display systems, however, its spectrum was rather stark—CGA boasted the ability to show 16 bright, pure colors (a total which misleadingly includes black, dark grey, light grey, and white). To put those colors to work other than making multi-hued text, the CGA board also featured a host of graphics modes with several different levels of resolution ranging from marginal to awful.

As the name implies, the CGA system was designed to put graphics on a color screen. It also featured text modes, however, and could work with monochrome displays as well—but not the IBM Personal Computer Display that was designed for the MDA board. The CGA display adapter could work with both monochrome and color composite monitors, and it even featured an output for a modulator for use with a television set. (You cannot plug a television directly into the CGA board unless, of course, the television features a monitor-style composite video input.) In addition, the CGA board also made provisions for connecting a light pen.

The CGA was designed to be a multi-mode display adapter. It could use both the character-mapped and bit-mapped display techniques, and allowed several options under each. To store its images, the CGA board was equipped with a whopping 16 kilobytes of memory which functioned as a dumb frame buffer, directly accessible by your system's microprocessor.

CGA is effectively obsolete. Display adapters matching the standard are available only as close-outs and bargain-basement imported clone boards that cost as little as $10. Matching monitors are almost impossible to find except used or as close-outs. CGA lives on, however, in every other display system created by IBM. The color text modes of the latest display adapters mimic the CGA addressing scheme. Nearly all modern display adapters also offer graphics modes that are backwardly compatible with software written to use CGA displays. The CGA standard will probably live on for generations of products to come, if only as a software artifact.

CGA Character Modes

The enduring text mode of the CGA system is designed much like that of the MDA system. Text mode is the boot-up default and is character-mapped in the CGA system. The chief differences between the CGA text mode and the MDA system are the base addresses used for memory and the character attributes that are supported.

CGA hardware also distinguished the two early IBM standards. While MDA was designed to work with a proprietary monitor with nonstandard horizontal and vertical frequencies to produce a sharper image, the CGA system opted for more standard frequencies. It was designed around the horizontal and vertical scan rates of composite video displays, which endowed the CGA system with compatibility with the greatest range of monitors available at the time—but with a sacrifice in on-screen quality.

To fit its operation under the confines of the composite video standard (which uses a 15,525 Hz horizontal rate and 60 Hz vertical rate), the CGA system divides the display into a pixel array numbering 640 horizontally and 200 vertically. To put the same 2000 text characters on the screen in the same 80 x 25 arrangement used by the MDA allows only a dot box measuring 8 x 8 pixels. Visually and arithmetically, that means worse quality than the output of a nine-wire dot-matrix printer running in its lowest-quality draft mode.

The 16 kilobytes of memory on the CGA is sufficient to handle four pages of text. Normally, only a single page, the first one, is used in text mode. The others are, however, accessible by you and programs through both the BIOS and directly through the mode register on the CGA.

CGA Character Quality

In the CGA system, each character is allocated a 7 x 7 matrix with one dot reserved for descenders and one for letter spacing. Obviously, a descending character will occupy the full height of the dot box and thus bump into an ascending character on the line below with no separation. The fewer dots mean that on-screen text will otherwise look more crude and less pleasing than that made by the MDA.

Forty-Column Text

Even those rudimentary characters are more than can be imaged sharply on a standard color television set. On most televisions, lines of text 80 characters wide appear blurry if not indecipherable because of the resolution limits of both the signals inside the set and the picture tube. To allow adequate text renderings on color televisions, IBM added a special low-resolution text mode that cuts the number of columns of text from 80 to 40. The number of rows, 25, is left the same as for other displays because it is not a problem for televisions.

Characters in 40-column text mode are made within the same 8 x 8 dot box used in 80-column mode, and they suffer the same quality limitations. They look rough but they may be more legible than 80-column characters because they are wider.

Although 40-column mode was rarely used in serious computing even in the dark ages of PCs, many programs (including many DOS utilities) make allowance for it by generating lines of text no wider than 40 characters each. That's why some of their displays look so odd most of the time. The 40-column mode is the least common denominator of all IBM text display systems. To assure that utilities would work even on the cheapest PCs, programmers wrote their utilities in this 40-column mode.

Text Colors

In any text mode, the CGA system of attributes allows up to the full 16 color palette to be displayed on the screen at once. Any character of text can be any one of the 16 colors allowed. This same attribute system is maintained today by the VGA system in its text mode.

Under the CGA attribute system, the background of the character (the dots in the 8 x 8 box that are not part of the character shape) can be separately set to one of those same 16 colors, with one limitation. In the default operating mode of the system, only eight background colors are possible because the bit in the attribute byte which controls the brightness or intensity of the background color is assigned a different task. It controls the blinking of the character.

A register on the CGA board alters the definition of this attribute bit. By loading values into this register, you or a program can toggle its function between blinking and high-intensity background colors. Note, however, that this register affects all text on the screen. You cannot have both blinking characters and a high-intensity background on the screen at the same time.

The CGA forces programmers to directly manipulate this register. More advanced IBM display adapters add an extra BIOS routine that handles this function.

Border Color

Another register on the CGA controls the border color. The screen border is the screen area outside of the active data area in which text appears. The default colors of the CGA display (white text on a black background) hide the matching black border circling the screen. Change the background color of the text and the border appears, with an obnoxious sharp demarcation between it and the edge of the perimeter characters in the text display.

Setting the CGA register for a border color, which can be any of the 16 colors displayable by the CGA system, makes for a more pleasant on-screen image. This register is called the color select register and is available at the I/O port 03D9(Hex). The lower four bits of this register control the border color.

Flicker and Snow

One of the most notable (and to many people, the most obnoxious) characteristics of the CGA and many other display systems is its tendency to flash the text display off and on when the display scrolls in high resolution text mode. Called *flicker*, it is a direct result not of the display adapter but of the sorry, slow processing speed of some PCs in which the graphics adapters are installed interacting with impatient programs.

Scrolling an image up the screen requires that every byte used by the display must be moved because every character on the screen (and its associated attribute) must change position. The IBM display system is designed so that information is written to the screen only during the brief period called vertical retrace, when the scanning electron beam travels back from the bottom of the screen at the end of one frame to the top for the beginning of the next. During vertical retrace, the electron beam is blanked, switched off, so no matter what is sent to it, nothing gets on the screen.

If the CGA or other display memory is changed at some other time—that is, when the beam is not blanked—the display system may scan through video memory while it is being changed, with the result that all sorts of odd pulses may be picked up and sent to the screen. On the screen, you see this effect as a flurry of bright dots that look like a flash of animated cartoon unconsciousness. The formal name of the quick flashes of odd images is *video noise*, more popularly called *snow*, because the randomly placed dots look somewhat like a snowstorm (if you have enough imagination).

The CGA card provides a status bit which indicates when vertical retrace is occurring. This is a "Coast is clear" signal that programs or the BIOS can query to see when it is okay to write to the screen. The vertical retrace period provides enough time for only a few lines to be updated, however. So to avoid snow, the scrolling must take place slowly, in chunks, during several retrace periods, or snow may occur. IBM sidestepped this issue by turning off the electron beam for the whole time that the screen is being updated during a scroll. Instead of momentarily going black during the invisible vertical retrace, the screen turns black for a substantial—and readily visible—fraction of a second. That whole-screen blanking causes the flicker.

With a CGA adapter, the trade-off is flicker for snow. Other video adapters use faster memory that can be entirely updated within a single retrace period or different types of memory which can be updated while being read to eliminate both problems. Even with these faster boards, however, waiting for video retrace can slow down screen response. Some application software gives you the choice of abiding by the rules and updating the screen using IBM's snow-elimination procedure or blasting bytes to video memory without guarantee they will slip in place without snow. With fast PCs and display adapters, this latter mode will yield higher speed without visible on-screen effects.

Graphics Modes

The CGA standard allows for graphics at three different levels of resolution named low, medium, and high—labels appropriate when the system was introduced. Today, even the CGA's highest resolution is low compared with most display systems.

With each CGA graphics resolution level, the number of on-screen dots is traded off against the number of displayable colors. The 16K of available memory creates serious limitations.

Low Resolution

The lowest resolution graphics mode of the CGA (which is not supported by IBM) breaks the screen into a display of 160 lines, each 200 dots wide. Because this display requires 32,000 pixels, only half a byte is available for storing attributes, allowing four color planes, enough for 16 colors. All of the 16 colors possible with the CGA system can be put on a single screen in low resolution mode, but displays are so chunky that this mode is little-used.

Medium Resolution

As a compromise between color and sharpness, IBM created medium resolution mode. Based on displays of 320 lines, each 200 dots wide, the medium resolution standard allows for two color planes that permit up to four simultaneous colors to be displayed.

The four colors cannot be chosen at random, however. IBM allows four possible palettes to chose from: red, green, brown, and black ; white, magenta, cyan, and black (or a selected background color); and the previous two but in high intensity colors. The palette to be used is selected using a special Bit five selects between the red/green palette (set at 0) and magenta/cyan palette (set at 1). Bit 4 selects the intensity—0 for dim, 1 for intensified. Bits 0 through 3 select the background color. The default values, set by the BIOS, are for the intensified magenta/cyan palette with a black background.

High Resolution

The highest resolution mode of the CGA assigns one bit to each pixel on the screen, allowing for individual control of an array of pixels 640 horizontally by 200 vertically. Because no additional memory is available on the CGA for storing attribute information, all pixels must be the same color and intensity. You can, however, choose what color you want them to be with the color select register.

CGA Memory Arrangement

In graphics mode, the CGA uses an unusual storage arrangement. It stores even-numbered scan lines, starting with zero, one after the other, starting at absolute memory location 0B8000(Hex). The odd-numbered scan lines are stored in sequence starting at an address 2000(Hex) higher. The unusual arrangement was chosen for entirely practical hardware-design reasons.

When multiple bits are assigned to an individual pixel, they are stored as sequential bits in a given byte of storage, four pixels per byte in medium resolution mode (see fig. 13.4). The strange arrangement should not bother you because all graphic software and language automatically takes it into account.

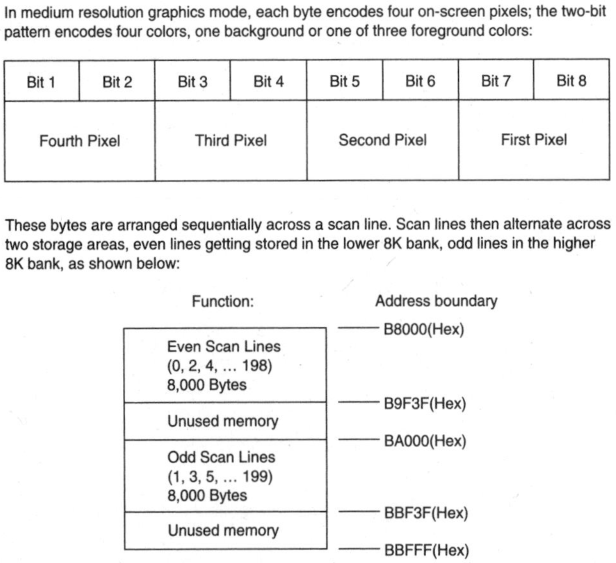

In medium resolution graphics mode, each byte encodes four on-screen pixels; the two-bit pattern encodes four colors, one background or one of three foreground colors:

Bit 1	Bit 2	Bit 3	Bit 4	Bit 5	Bit 6	Bit 7	Bit 8
Fourth Pixel		Third Pixel		Second Pixel		First Pixel	

These bytes are arranged sequentially across a scan line. Scan lines then alternate across two storage areas, even lines getting stored in the lower 8K bank, odd lines in the higher 8K bank, as shown below:

Function:	Address boundary
	—— B8000(Hex)
Even Scan Lines (0, 2, 4, ... 198) 8,000 Bytes	
	—— B9F3F(Hex)
Unused memory	
	—— BA000(Hex)
Odd Scan Lines (1, 3, 5, ... 199) 8,000 Bytes	
	—— BBF3F(Hex)
Unused memory	
	—— BBFFF(Hex)

FIGURE 13.4. CGA medium resolution graphics data storage arrangement.

Outputs

You can connect your video display to the CGA through one of three different connectors. The one that you choose depends on the kind of display you want to connect.

The preferred display is an IBM 5151 Personal Computer Color Display that uses TTL digital inputs through a nine-pin D-shell connector. Separate on-and-off digital signals are provided for each of three color guns (red, green, and blue), an intensity bit (which brightens all three guns simultaneously), horizontal sync, vertical sync, and ground. The pinout is shown in Figure 13.5.

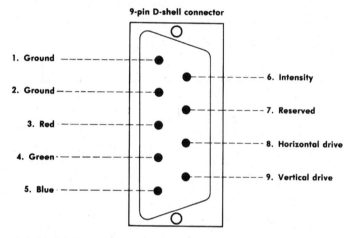

9-pin D-shell connector

1. Ground
2. Ground
3. Red
4. Green
5. Blue
6. Intensity
7. Reserved
8. Horizontal drive
9. Vertical drive

FIGURE 13.5. CGA RGB interface pin-out.

All of these signals are positive-going—that is, a digital high turns on the appropriate gun or indicates a synchronizing pulse—with the exception of vertical sync. When this style of connection was first becoming popular, this arrangement caused untold problems for developers because horizontal sync is normally negative-going. IBM's signal thus appears upside down.

The composite output of the CGA is provided both on an RCA-style pin jack on the retaining bracket of the card and as part of a header on the surface of the board. The signals provided at the RCA jack are compatible with both color and monochrome displays that follow the NTSC standard.

The composite output provided on the card itself is meant to operate a modulator. Other pins of this single-row header supply the voltage needed to operate the modulator (see fig. 13.6).

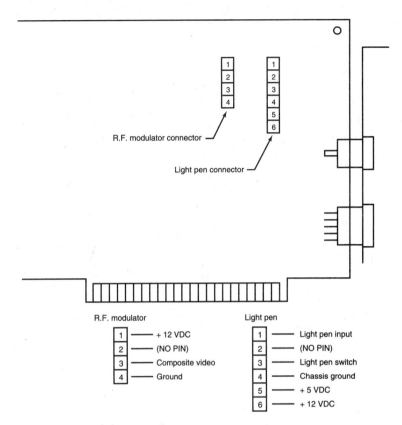

FIGURE 13.6. CGA modulator output pin-out.

Black-and-White Mode

When a monochrome composite monitor is connected to the CGA, the screen will sometimes shift to an eye-straining jumble of vertical lines and shadings instead of solid color. Text can be almost impossible to read. This odd display is caused by the color subcarrier that's part of the composite video signal. It limits the bandwidth of the video signal and interferes with monochrome information, creating the odd patterns on the screen.

You can clear up the problem by switching to black-and-white mode, which turns off the color subcarrier. Although you can control this by loading values into a CGA register, the MODE command supplied with DOS does the job more easily. Just type

```
MODE BW
```

to switch off the color subcarrier.

Double-Scanned CGA

In these days of VGA resolution, which promises more than twice the on-screen sharpness of CGA, you might think that the PC's first graphic display standard would have been left far behind by new hardware. In fact, new PCs capable only of CGA graphic response continue to be introduced. Nearly all of these systems are monochrome, and most deliver higher resolution than the nominal 640 by 200 pixels of ordinary CGA. Universally, these graphic systems are found in laptop and notebook computers using Liquid Crystal Displays (LCDs).

These display systems achieve higher resolution than CGA graphics by using double-scanning of the CGA image. That is, instead of displaying 640 by 200 pixels on the screen, the display system shows 640 by 400 pixels. This double-scanning technique allows for sharper images without sacrificing the ability to use the CGA standard. Most importantly, double-scanned CGA allows the use of a less expansive LCD panel than a higher-quality VGA system would. Few lines on the screen means fewer pixels in the panel, which means lower manufacturing costs.

If double-scanned CGA were simply double-scanned, it would look as bad as any CGA screen. In text mode, however, double-scanned systems use a different character generator than ordinary CGA systems. Instead of duplicating pixels to stretch the character matrix, the double-scanned systems actually generate individual characters from an 8 by 16 matrix. In other words, the double-scanned text characters are double-sharp, almost as high in quality as those produced by today's standard top-quality display adapters.

Where double-scanned CGA comes up short is graphics. These systems maintain ordinary CGA addressing, so their double-scanning produces no increase in graphic sharpness. Each pixel in an on-screen image is simply doubled in the vertical dimension. The result is bigger pixels than would be produced by a 640 by 400-pixel display system, corresponding to bigger grains in a photographic image. The bottom line is that ordinary double-scanned CGA graphics are not any sharper than plain old ordinary CGA graphics. In other words, the advantage of double-scanning is thus limited to sharper text and graphic compatibility but not higher quality in graphics.

Sometimes, however, you can improve the quality of double-scanned CGA graphics. Some non-standard display systems—for instance, that used by the AT&T model 6300 PC-compatible computer—make 640 by 400 images in their native mode. Some software drivers for these AT&T display systems will drive double-scanned CGA systems, yielding full 400-line quality in graphics mode. If you have a double-scanned display system, it's always worth a try to set up your graphics applications for AT&T display systems to see the effects. If the AT&T drivers work, your reward will be graphics that are twice as sharp. If the drivers don't work, your only loss will be the few minutes spent on experimentation.

Enhanced Graphics Adapter

By 1984 the shortcomings of the CGA system had become obvious—if just from the skyrocketing white cane sales to the people who were using it regularly. The hard-to-read text displays and coarse graphics probably generated more eyestrain than anything since the insurance industry invented two-point type.

IBM's answer was a system based on a new video adapter called the Enhanced Graphics Adapter or EGA. The enhancements wrought by the new system were severalfold. It increased on-screen resolution. It brought the possibility of graphics to monochrome screens such as the venerable green IBM Personal Computer Display. And it added new BIOS routines that augmented and extended the existing ROM-based video support built into the PC and XT.

EGA was designed to be backwardly compatible with CGA, so programs written for the older display system would work with the new board. EGA's sharper images, however, required higher-frequency signals—and that meant an entirely new style of monitor.

In the long run, EGA proved to be an interim step—better but not quite good enough. After a three year heyday, it was relegated to the background and backward compatibility. It survives as a few display modes in the VGA system. Support for EGA products (and the products themselves) is disappearing because today higher resolution technologies are simply cheaper.

EGA Resolution

The important improvement that EGA brought to the PC world was the sharper images it put on IBM's matching monitor, its Enhanced Graphics Display. EGA pushed resolution up to 640 x 350 pixels, forming characters in dot boxes measuring 8 x 14. Although the EGA dot box was a dot narrower than that used by the MDA, each character was made from the same 7 x 9 matrix. More importantly, EGA provided enough extra space between lines on the screen so that descenders and ascending characters on adjacent rows did not touch. Color text was finally as readable as monochrome.

The EGA system also extended its 640 x 350 resolution to graphics. All previous IBM-supported graphics modes were also included in the capabilities of the VGA so that it was entirely downwardly compatible with CGA graphics.

EGA Frequencies

To fit EGA's extra dots into a video signal, IBM had to extend the horizontal scanning frequency used by the system. Instead of the television-compatible 15.575 kilohertz horizontal scan rate of CGA, EGA substituted 23.1 kilohertz. To minimize image flicker, however, the EGA design maintains the 60 Hz frame rate of CGA.

EGA Colors

Even more notable was the increase in color capability brought by the EGA standard. By altering the adapter-to-display interface, the possible palette in the EGA system was increased to 64 different hues (again, counting black and various shades of grey as separate colors). In addition, the greater memory capabilities of the EGA standard meant that the wider rainbow was possible at higher resolution levels. At its maximum resolution and maximum memory endowment, the EGA could spread 16 different shades from its 64 color palette on a 640 x 350 screen at one time.

EGA Monochrome Graphics

The EGA was also designed to eliminate the two-standard system that reigned in the IBM universe. The EGA adapter was equally adept at handling color and monochrome displays. By setting DIP switches that were cleverly arranged to be accessible through a cut-out in the card retaining bracket without popping the top off your PC, the EGA could be adapted to any standard IBM display. (Note, however, that this clearly does not include composite monitors—the EGA does not have composite output. Then again, IBM never made a composite display for its personal computers.)

More importantly, the support of monochrome displays extended to graphics. The EGA provided IBM's first monochrome graphics standard. Note, however, that IBM went its own direction and did not accommodate the graphics standard used by the Hercules Graphics Card. Instead, it substituted its own standard, one compatible with EGA color graphics so that no extra effort was required to write programs compatible with both EGA monochrome and color graphics. Adopting the Hercules standard would have required programmers to develop separate code for color and monochrome graphics on the EGA.

EGA Memory

By the time the EGA was introduced, many applications had been written that moved bytes directly to video memory rather than endure the sluggishness of using IBM's primitive BIOS routines. Changing the memory arrangement used by the EGA would have made the adapter incompatible with those existing applications.

The EGA designers faced another problem. More colors and resolution automatically requires more memory. That would not be a problem except that only a finite range of addresses were reserved out of the 8088 microprocessor's range for holding video information.

The IBM solution was to make the EGA a bank-switched memory card, a heritage that carried over into VGA and most Super VGA boards. In standard (minimal) configuration, the EGA was equipped with 64 kilobytes of RAM, split into four 16K banks. To the host system, the adapter looked like a CGA board as long as the advanced EGA modes and their bank-switching was not brought into play.

64K was not sufficient for the wide palette, high resolution modes of the EGA, so IBM provided expansion up to 256K through a memory expansion daughter card. Expansion EGA memory was allotted equally among the banks on the card, so the maximum configuration gave four banks of 64K each.

The memory of the EGA board can be switched to either the base address of the CGA or MDA to achieve compatibility with programs that write directly to video memory. In EGA modes, however, the base address of the board's memory is shifted downward to 0A0000(Hex). As a result, the entire 64K to 256K of video memory is no longer constantly addressable by the host PC's microprocessor, and writing directly to screen memory takes somewhat more ingenuity on the part of programmers. The alternative, however, was untenable—devoting a full 256K of address range to the frame buffer, which would leave almost no High DOS memory for other purposes (such as EMS—coincidentally another bank-switching system). This address-stretching solution set the pattern for all other display systems until the introduction of XGA.

EGA Interface

The EGA retained the digital signal format used by the MDA and CGA before it. To accommodate its additional color capabilities, the CGA wiring scheme was altered slightly by redefining one connection and adding two new ones. Each color gun was given two signals, essentially the individual drive signals as used on the CGA and individual intensity signals. Instead of all three guns being controlled by a single intensity signal, each gun could be brightened by itself. The two-bit digital code given to each gun allowed it four intensities—off, bright, and two intermediary levels. The combination of four levels per gun times three guns allows up to 64 hues to be displayed from the various combinations.

For compatibility with all IBM monitors, the EGA used the same connector as previous video boards, a nine-pin, female D-shell connector. The definitions of its signal pins were controlled by the setup DIP switches depending on the type of monitor that was to be connected to the board. Both the monochrome and CGA-compatible color schemes corresponded exactly with the MDA and CGA standards to allow complete compatibility. For EGA displays, the CGA intensity pin was used for the intensity signal of the green gun. Additional intensity signals were added for the red and blue guns. See Figure 13.7 for the pinout.

EGA Monitor Compatibility

Because the EGA adapter cannot determine which variety of display that it is connected to, you must be certain to properly match its setup to your display or risk damage to your monitor. Supplying the wrong synchronizing signals to a monochrome IBM Personal Computer Display for more than a short period can permanently damage the monitor. The symptom of an improper mating of display adapter and monitor is a blank or unreadable screen, typically crossed by a number of thin horizontal lines, and a high-pitched squeal from inside the monitor.

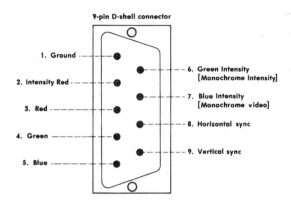

FIGURE 13.7. EGA pin-out.

Should you encounter these symptoms when connecting a display system, turn off your PC immediately and double-check the compatibility of your monitor and the display adapter.

At the other end of the EGA connection, matters are just as critical with IBM color and monochrome displays introduced before the EGA. Fortunately, the IBM Enhanced Color Display can determine whether it is connected to an EGA or CGA display and adjust itself to accommodate the correct synchronizing frequency. Rather than determine the frequency of the signal, however, the EGA display examines the polarity of the horizontal synchronizing signal. If the horizontal sync is positive, the monitor operates with a 15,575 Hertz sync frequency. If the horizontal sync is negative-going, the display switches to a 23.1 kilohertz sync frequency.

EGA Compatibility with Other Display Adapters

In the IBM scheme of things, you are allowed to connect one monochrome, one color, or one of each sort of display to a system, but you can never connect more than one of each. You could, for instance, add both a CGA and MDA to your computer, but you could never use two CGAs at once. That's because both CGAs would try to locate their memories at the same addresses. Monochrome and color systems use different memory addresses, however.

The EGA follows this philosophy. If you set up an EGA to operate a color display, then it will happily co-reside with an MDA board. If you set up your EGA as a monochrome adapter, then you can also add a CGA to your system. You cannot, however, add two EGAs—even if one is set up as monochrome and one as color—because their BIOS codes and memory assignments would conflict. While a jumper on the EGA board allows you to alter its base address, the alternate address is not supported by the IBM EGA BIOS code.

Addressing the EGA

In its compatibility modes, the EGA looks to your system as if it were an MDA or CGA, depending on how you have it set up. It even sets the equipment flags appropriately to match the location assigned to its memory so that your programs might never know that they are working with an EGA. You can write simple assembly (or higher level) language procedures that directly address video memory, and they will work properly with the EGA, provided that you operate within its compatibility modes.

In the EGA's advanced graphics modes, however, you're in for surprises because you can address only one of its four pages unless you toggle the page register. Fortunately, the EGA BIOS and most application software takes care of that automatically.

Chapter 14
Monitors

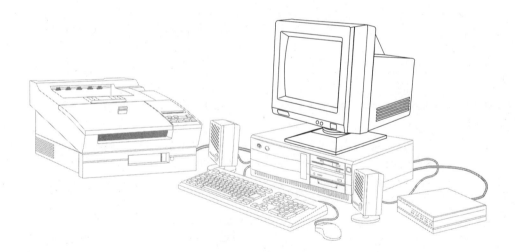

A display is the keyhole you peer through to spy on what your PC is doing. You can't do your work without a display, and you can't work well without a good one. The final quality of what you see—the detail, sharpness, and color—all depends on the display you use. No longer a function only of TV-like monitors, today's computer displays increasingly rely on new technologies to achieve flat screens and high resolutions.

You cannot see data. The information that your computer processes is nothing but ideas, and ideas are intangible no matter whether in your mind or your computer's. Whereas you can visualize your own ideas, you cannot peer directly into the pulsing digital thought patterns of your computer. You probably have no right to think that you could—if you can't read another person's thoughts, you should hardly expect to read the distinctly non-human circuit surges of your PC.

Although most people—at least those not trained in stage magic—cannot read thoughts *per se*, they can get a good idea of what's going on in another person's mind by carefully observing his external appearances. Eye movements, facial expressions, gestures, and sometimes even speech can give you a general idea about what that other person is thinking, although you will never be privy to his true thoughts. So it is with computers. You'll never be able to see electrons tripping through logical gates, but you can get a general idea of what's going on behind the screens by looking into the countenance of your computer—its display. What the display shows you is a manifestation of the results of the computer's thinking.

The display is your computer's line of communication to you, much as the keyboard enables you to communicate with it. Like even the best of friends, the display doesn't tell you everything; but it does give you a clear picture, one from which you can draw your own conclusions about what the computer is doing.

Because the display has no direct connection to the computer's thoughts, the same thoughts— the same programs—can generate entirely different on-screen images while working exactly the same way inside your computer. Just as you can't tell a book's contents from its cover, you cannot judge the quality of a computer from its display.

What you can see is important, however, because it influences how well you can work with your computer. A poor display can lead to eyestrain and headaches, making your computer literally a pain to work with. A top quality display means clearly defined characters, sharp graphics, and a system that's a pleasure to work with.

Monitors Versus Displays

Although the terms are often used interchangeably, a display and a monitor are distinctly different. A display is the image-producing device itself, the screen that you see. The monitor is a complete box that adds support circuitry to the display. This circuitry converts the signals set by the computer (or some other device, such as a videocassette recorder) into the proper form for the display to use. Although most monitors operate under principles like those of the television set, displays can be made from a variety of technology including liquid crystals and the photon glow of some noble gases.

Because of their similar technological foundations, monitors to a great extent resemble the humble old television set. Just as a monitor is a display enhanced with extra circuitry, the television is a monitor with even more signal conversion electronics. The television incorporates into its design a tuner or demodulator that converts signals broadcast by television stations or a cable television company into about the same form as those signals used by monitors. Beyond the tuner, the television and monitor work in much the same way. Indeed, some old-fashioned computer monitors work as televisions as long as they are supplied the proper signals.

New monitors have developed far beyond their television roots, however. They have greater sharpness and purity of color. To achieve these ends, they operate at higher frequencies than television stations can broadcast.

Computer displays and monitors use a variety of technologies to create visible images. A basic bifurcation divides the displays of desktop computers and those of laptop machines. Most desktop computers use systems based on the same cathode ray tube technology akin to that used in the typical television set. Laptop and notebook computers chiefly use liquid crystal displays. Occasionally, a desktop or portable system is equipped with a gas-plasma display, but these are unusual and costly.

Cathode Ray Tubes

The oldest electronic image-generating system still in use is the cathode ray tube. The name is purely descriptive. The device is based on a special form of vacuum tube—a glass bottle that is partially evacuated and filled with an inert gas at very low pressure. The cathode—another name for a negatively charged electrode—of the tube shoots a beam or ray of electrons toward a positively charged electrode, the anode. (Electrons, having a negative charge, are naturally attracted to positive potentials.) Because it works like a Howitzer for electrons, the cathode of a CRT is often called an electron gun.

Phosphors

At the end of the electrons' short flight, from the gun in the neck of the tube to the inside of its wide, flat face, lies a layer of a phosphors compound with a wonderful property—it glows when struck by an electron beam. To move the beam across the breadth of the tube face (so that the beam doesn't light just a tiny dot in the center of the screen), a group of powerful electromagnets arranged around the tube called the yoke bend the electron beam in the course of its flight. The magnetic field set up by the yoke is carefully controlled and causes the beam to sweep each individual display line down the face of the tube.

The image you see in a CRT is the glow of the electrically-stimulated phosphor compounds, simply termed phosphors in the industry. Not all the phosphorous compounds used in CRTs are the same. Different compounds and mixtures glow various colors and for various lengths of time after being struck by the electron beam.

A number of different phosphors are used by PC-compatible monitors. Table 14.1 lists some of these phosphors and their characteristics.

TABLE 14.1. Phospors and Their Characteristics

Type	Steady-state Color	Decay Color	Decay Time(ms)*	Uses or Comments
P1	Yellow-Green	Yellow-Green	15	Oscilloscopes, radar
P4	White	White	.1	Display, television
P7	White	Yellow-Green	unavail.	Oscilloscopes, radar
P11	Blue	Blue	.1	Photography
P12	Orange	Orange	unavail.	Radar
P16	Violet	Violet	unavail.	Ultraviolet
P19	Orange	Orange	500	Radar
P22R	Red	Red	.7	Projection
P22G	Yellow-Green	Yellow-Green	.06	Projection
P22B	Blue	Blue	.06	Projection
P26	Orange	Orange	.2	Radar, medical
P28	Yellow-Green	Yellow-Green	.05	Radar, medical
P31	Yellow-Green	Yellow-Green	.07	Oscilloscope, display
P38	Orange	Orange	1000	Radar
P39	Yellow-Green	Yellow-Green	.07	Radar, display
P40	White	Yellow-Green	.045	Med. persist. display
P42	Yellow-Green	Yellow-Green	.1	Display
P43	Yellow-Green	Yellow-Green	1.5	Display
P45	White	White	1.5	Photography
P46	Yellow-Green	Yellow-Green	.16	Flying spot scanners

Type	Steady-state Color	Decay Color	Decay Time(ms)*	Uses or Comments
P55	Blue	Blue	.05	Projection
P56	Red	Red	2.25	Projection
P101	Yellow-Green	Yellow-Green	.125	Display
P103	White	White	.084	P4 w/bluish background
P104	White	White	.085	High efficiency P4
P105	White	Yellow-Green	100+	Long persistence P7
P106	Orange	Orange	.3	Display
P108	Yellow-Green	Yellow-Green	125	P39 w/bluish background
P109	Yellow-Green	Yellow-Green	.08	High efficiency P31
P110	Yellow-Green	Yellow-Green	.08	P31 w/ bluish background
P111	Red/green	Red/Green	unavail.	Voltage penetration
P112	Yellow-Green	Yellow-Green	unavil.	Ir lightpen doped P39
P115	White	White	.08	More yellow P4
P118	White	White	.09	Display
P120	Yellow-Green	Yellow-Green	.075	P42 w/bluish Background
P122	Yellow-Green	Yellow-Green	.075	Display
P123	Infrared	N/A	unavail.	Infrared
P124	Yellow-Green	Yellow-Green	.130	Yellow part of P4
P127	Green	Yellow-Green	unavail.	P11+P39 for light pens
P128	Yellow-Green	Yellow-Green	.06	Ir lightpen doped P31
P131	Yellow-Green	Yellow-Green	unavail.	Ir lightpen doped P39
P133	Red to green	Red to green	varies	current-sensitive
P134	Orange	Orange	50	European phosphor
P136	White	White	.085	Enhanced contrast P4
P137	Yello-Green	Yellow-Green	.125	High efficiency P101
P138	Yellow-Green	Yellow-Green	.07	Enhanced contrast P31

continues

TABLE 14.1. Continued

Type	Steady-state Color	Decay Color	Decay Time(ms)*	Uses or Comments
P139	Yellow-Green	Yellow-Green	70	Enhanced contrast P39
P141	Yellow-Green	Yellow-Green	.1	Enhanced contrast P42
P143	White	Yellow-Green	.05	Enhanced contrast P40
P144	Orange	Orange	.05	Enhanced contrast P134
P146	Yellow-Green	Yellow-Green	.08	Enhanced contrast P109
P148	Yellow-Green	Yellow-Green	unavail.	Lightpen applications
P150	Yellow-Green	Yellow-Green	.075	Data displays
P154	Yellow-Green	Yellow-Green	.075	Displays
P155	Yellow-Green	Yellow-Green	unavail.	Lightpen applications
P156	Yellow-Green	Yellow-Green	.07	Lightpen applications
P158	Yellow	Yellow	140	Medium persistence
P159	Yellow-Green	Yellow-Green	unavail.	Enhanced contrast P148
P160	Yellow-Green	Yellow-Green	.07	Data displays
P161	Yellow-Green	Yellow-Green	.07	Data displays
P162	Yellow-Green	Yellow-Green	.1	Data displays
P163	White	White	2	Photography
P164	White	Yellow-Green	.1	Displays
P166	Orange	Orange	unavail.	Ir lightpens
P167	White	White	.075	Display
P168	Yellow-Green	Yellow-Green	.075	Projection
P169	Yellowish	Yellowish	1.5	Display
P170	Orange	Orange	unavail.	Enhanced contrast P108
P171	White	Yellow-Green	.2	Display
P172	Green	Green	unavail.	Lightpen displays
P173	Infrared	N/A	unavail.	Lightpen

Type	Steady-state Color	Decay Color	Decay Time(ms)*	Uses or Comments
P175	Red	Red	.6	Display
P176	Yellow-Green	Yellow-Green	.2	Photography
P177	Green	Green	.1	Data displays
P178	Yelow-Green	Yellow-Green	.1	Displays
P179	White	White	1	Displays
P180	Yellow-Orange	Yellow-Orange	.075	Displays
P181	Yellow-Green	Yellow-Green	unavail.	Color shutter displays
P182	Orange	Orange	50	Displays
P183	Orange	Orange	unavail.	Lightpen displays
P184	White	White	.075	Displays
P185	Orange	Orange	30	Enhanced contrast P134
P186	Yellow-Green	Yellow-Green	25	Displays
P187	Yellow-Green	Yellow-Green	unavail.	Lightpen P39
P188	White	White	.05	White displays
P189	White	White	unavail.	White displays
P190	Orange	Orange	.1	Displays
P191	White	White	.12	White displays
P192	White	White	.2	White displays
P193	Whtie	White	.08	White displays
P194	Orange	Orange	17	Displays
P195	White	White	.125	Inverse displays

Approximate time in milliseconds for display to decay to 10 percent of its emission level.

The type of phosphor determines the color of the image on the screen. Several varieties of amber, green, whitish phosphors are commonly used in monochrome displays. Color CRT displays use three different phosphors painted in fine patterns across the inner surface of the tube. The patterns are made from dots or stripes of the three additive primary colors—red, green, and blue—arrayed next to one another. A group of three dots is called a color triad or color triplet.

One triad of dots makes up a picture element, often abbreviated as pixel (although some manufacturers prefer to shorten picture element to pel).

The makers of color monitors individually can choose each of the three colors used in forming the color triads on the screen. Most monitor makers have adopted the same phosphor family (P22), so the basic color capabilities of most multi-hued monitors are the same.

The color monitor screen can be illuminated in any of its three primary colors by individually hitting the phosphor dots associated with that color with the electron beam. Other colors can be made by illuminating combinations of the primary colors. By varying the intensity of each primary color, an infinite spectrum can be generated.

Monochrome displays have their CRTs evenly coated with a single, homogenous phosphor so that wherever the electron beam strikes, the tube glows in the same color. The color of the phosphors determines the overall color that the screen glows.

Three colors remain popular for monochrome computer displays—amber, green, and white. Which is best is a matter of both preference and prejudice. Various studies support the superiority of each of these colors:

> **Green.** Green screens got a head start as PC displays because they were IBM's choice for most of its terminals and the first PC display. It is a good selection for use where ambient light levels are low; part of its heritage is from the days of oscilloscope and radar screens (most of which remain stubbornly green). Over the last few years, however, green has fallen from favor as the screen of choice.

> **Amber.** In the 1980s, amber-colored screens rose in popularity because they are, according to some studies, easier on the eyes and more readable when the surrounding environmental light level is bright. Yellow against black yields one of the best perceived contrast combinations, making the displays somewhat easier on your eyes. Amber also got a push as being a *de facto* European monitor standard.

> **White.** Once white screens were something to be avoided, if just from their association with black-and-white televisions. A chief reason was that most early monochrome displays used a composite interface and gave low on-screen quality.

> Apple's Macintosh and desktop publishing forced the world to re-evaluate white. White is the color of paper that executives have been shuffling through offices over the ages. White and black also happens to be among the most readable of all color combinations. IBM added impetus to the conversion of the entire world to white with the introduction of the VGA and its white-screen monochrome display.

> If you look closely, you might see fine specs of colors, such as a bright yellow dappled into so-called "white" phosphors. Manufacturers mix together several different phosphors to fine tune the color of the monochrome display—to make it a cool, blue television "white" or a warm, yellowish paper "white."

No good dividing line exists between ordinary white and paper-white displays. In theory, paper-white means the color of the typical bond paper you type on, a slightly warmer white than the blue-tinged glow of most "white" monitors. But "paper-whiteness" varies with who is giving the name.

➤ **Background color.** Often ignored yet just as important to screen readability as the phosphor colors is the background color of the display tube. Monochrome screen backgrounds run the full range from light grey to nearly black. Darker screens give more contrast between the foreground text and the tube background, making the display more readable, particularly in high ambient light conditions.

➤ **Matrix color.** The background area on a color screen—that is, the space in between the phosphor dots—is called the matrix, and it is not illuminated by the electron beam. The color of the matrix determines what the screen looks like when the power is off—pale grey, dark green-grey, or nearly black. Darker and black matrices give an impression of higher contrast to the displayed images. Lighter grey matrices make for purer white. The distinctions are subtle, however, and unless you put two tubes side-by-side, you're unlikely to judge the difference.

Color Temperature

If your work involves critical color matching, the color temperature of your monitor can be an important issue. White light is not white, of course, but a mixture of all colors. Alas, all whites are not the same. Some are richer in blue, some in yellow. The different colors of white are described in their color temperature, the number of kelvins (degrees Celsius above absolute zero) that a perfect luminescent body would need to be to emit that color.

Like the incandescence of a hot iron horseshoe in the blacksmith's forge, as its temperature gets higher the hue of a glowing object shifts from red to orange to yellow and on to blue-white. Color temperature simply assigns an absolute temperature rating to these colors.

For example, ordinary lightbulbs range from 2,700 to 3,400 kelvins. Most fluorescent lights have non-continuous color spectra rich in certain hues (notably green) while lacking others that makes assigning a true color temperature impossible. Other fluorescent lamps are designed to approximate daylight with color temperatures of about 5,000 kelvins.

The problem with color matching arises because pigments and paper only reflect light, so their actual color depends on the temperature of the light illuminating them. Your monitor screen emits light, so its color is independent of illumination—it has its own color temperature that may be (and is likely) from that lighting the rest of your work. Monitors are designed to glow with the approximate color temperature of daylight rather than incandescent or fluorescent light.

Alas, not everyone has the same definition of daylight. Noonday sun, for instance, ranges from 5,500 to 6,000 kelvins. Overcast days may achieve a color temperature of 10,000 kelvins because the scattered blue glow of the sky (higher color temperature) dominates the yellowish radiation from the sun. The colors and blend of the phosphors used to make the picture tube screen and the relative strengths of the electron beams illuminating those phosphors determine the color temperature of a monitor. Some engineers believe the perfect day is a soggy, overcast afternoon suited only to ducks and Englishmen and opt to run their monitors with a color temperatures as high as 10,000 kelvins. Others, however, live in a Kodachrome world where the color temperature is the same 5,300 kelvins as a spring day with tulips in the park.

Persistence

CRT phosphors also differ in persistence, which describes how long the phosphor glows after being struck by the electron beam. Most monitors use medium persistence phosphors.

Persistence becomes obvious when it is long. Images take on a ghostly appearance, lingering for a few seconds and slowly fading away. Although the effect may be bothersome, particularly in a darkened room, it's meant to offset the effect of another headache-producer: flicker.

Exactly what it sounds, flicker is the quick flashing of the screen image caused by the image decaying before it gets re-scanned by the electron beam. The persistence of vision (a quality of the human visual system) makes rapidly flashing light sources appear continuously lit. Fluorescent lights, for example, seem to glow uninterruptedly even though they switch on and off 120 times a second (twice the nominal frequency of utility-supplied electricity).

The lingering glow of long persistence phosphors bridges over the periods between passes of electron beams when they stretch out too long for human eyes to blend them together. Long persistence phosphors are thus often used in display systems scanned more slowly than usual, such as interlaced monitors (see below). The IBM Monochrome display, perhaps the most notorious user of long-persistence green phosphors, is scanned 50 times a second instead of the more normal (and eye-pleasing) 60 or higher.

Long-persistence phosphors need not be green, however. Long-persistence color systems also are available for use in applications where flicker is bothersome. Most often, long-persistence color phosphors are used in interlaced systems that are scanned more slowly than non-interlaced displays.

Long-persistence phosphors also frustrate light pens, which depend on detecting the exact instant a dot of phosphor lights up. Because of the lingering glow, most light pens perceive several dots to be lit simultaneously. The pen cannot zero in on a particular dot position on the screen.

Electron Guns

Monochrome CRTs have a single electron gun that continuously sweeps across the screen. Most color tubes have three guns, although some color televisions and monitors boast "one-gun" tubes. The gun count depends on the definition of a gun. Like all color CRTs, the one-gun tubes have three distinct electron-emitting cathodes that can be individually controlled. The three cathodes are fabricated into a single assembly that allows them to be controlled as if they were generating only a single beam.

In a three-gun tube, the trio of guns is arranged in a triangle. One-gun tubes arrange their cathodes in a straight line, often earning the epithet in-line guns. In theory in-line guns should be easier to set up, but as a practical matter excellent performance can be derived from either arrangement.

The three guns in a color CRT emit their electrons simultaneously, and the three resulting beams are steered together by the yoke. Individual adjustments are provided for each of the three beams, however, to ensure that each beam falls exactly on the same triplet of color dots on the screen as the others. Because these controls help the three beams converge on the same triad, they are called convergence controls. The process of adjusting them is usually termed alignment.

Convergence

The three electron beams inside any color monitor must converge on exactly the right point on the screen to illuminate a single triad of phosphor dots. If a monitor is not adjusted properly—or if it is not designed or made properly—the three beams cannot converge properly to one point. Poor convergence results in images with rainbow-like shadows and a loss of sharpness and detail. Individual text characters no longer appear sharply defined but become two- or three-color blurs. Monochrome monitors are inherently free from such convergence problems because they have but one electron beam.

Convergence problems are a symptom rather than a cause of monitor deficiencies. Convergence problems arise not only from the design of the display, but also from the construction and setup of each individual monitor. It can vary widely from one display to the next and may be aggravated by damage during shipping.

The result of convergence problems is most noticeable at the screen periphery because that's where the electron beams are the most difficult to control. When bad, convergence problems can be the primary limit on the sharpness of a given display, having a greater negative effect than wide dot-pitch or low bandwidth (discussed below).

Many monitor makers claim that their convergence is a given fraction of a millimeter at a particular place on the screen. If a figure is given for more than one screen location, the center of the screen invariably has a lower figure—tighter, better convergence—than a corner of the screen.

The number given is how far one color may spread from another at that location. Lower numbers are better. Typical monitors may claim convergence of about 0.5 (one-half) millimeter at one of the corners of the screen. That figure often rises 50 percent higher than the dot-pitch of the tube, making the convergence the limit on sharpness for that particular monitor.

Misconvergence problems often can be corrected by adjustment of the monitor. Many monitors have internal convergence controls. A few, high-resolution (and high-cost) monitors even have external convergence adjustments. But adjusting monitor convergence is a job for the specialist—and that means getting a monitor converged can be expensive, as is any computer service call.

Many monitor makers now claim that their products are converged for life. Although this strategy should eliminate the need to adjust them (which should only be done by a skilled technician with the correct test equipment), it also makes it mandatory to test your display before you buy it. You don't want a display that's been badly converged for life.

Shadow Masks

Just pointing the electron beams at the right dots is not enough because part of the beam can spill over and hit the other dots in the triplet. The result of this spillover is a loss of color purity—bright hues become muddied. To prevent this effect and make images as sharp and colorful as possible, all color CRTs used in computer displays and televisions alike have a shadow mask—a metal sheet with fine perforations in it, located inside the display tube and a small distance behind the phosphor coating of the screen.

The shadow mask and the phosphor dot coating on the CRT screen are critically arranged so that the electron beam can only hit phosphor dots of one color. The other two colors of dots are in the "shadow" of the mask and cannot be seen by the electron beam.

The spacing of the holes in the shadow mask to a great degree determines the quality of the displayed image. For the geometry of the system to work, the phosphor dots on the CRT screen must be spaced at the same distance as the holes in the mask. Because the hole spacing determines the dot spacing, it is often termed the dot-pitch of the CRT.

The dot-pitch of a CRT is simply a measurement of the distance between dots of the same color. It is an absolute measurement, independent of the size of the tube or the size of the displayed image.

The shadow mask affects the brightness of a monitor's image in two ways. The size of the holes in the mask limits the size of the electron beam getting through to the phosphors. Off-axis from the guns—that is, toward the corners of the screen—the round holes appear oval to the gun and less of the beam can get through. As a result, the corners of a shadow mask screen are often dimmer than the center, although the brightness difference may not be distinguishable.

The mask also limits how high the electron beam intensity can be in a given CRT. A stronger beam—which makes a brighter image—holds more energy. When the beam strikes the mask, part of that energy is absorbed by the mask and becomes heat, which raises the temperature of the mask. In turn, this temperature rise makes the mask expand unpredictably, distorting it minutely and blurring the image. To minimize this heat-induced blur, monitor makers are moving to making shadow masks from materials that have a low coefficient of thermal expansion. That is, they change size as little as possible with temperature. The alloy Invar is favored for shadow masks because of its capability to maintain a nearly constant size as it warms.

Aperture Grilles

With all the problems associated with shadow masks, you might expect someone to come up with a better idea. Sony Corporation did exactly that, inventing the Trinitron picture tube.

The Trinitron uses an aperture grille—slots between a vertical array of wires—instead of a mask. The phosphors are painted on the inner face of the tube as interleaved stripes of the three additive primary colors. The grille blocks the electron beam from the wrong stripes just as a shadow-mask blocks it from the wrong dots. The distance between two sequential stripes of the same color is governed by the spacing between the slots between the wires—the slot-pitch of the tube. Because the electron beam fans out as it travels away from the electron gun and stripes are farther from the gun than the mask is, the stripes are spaced a bit farther apart than the slot-pitch. Their spacing is termed screen-pitch. For example, a 0.25 millimeter slot-pitch Trinitron might have a screen-pitch of 0.26 millimeter.

The wires of the aperture grille are quite thick, about two-thirds the width of the slot-pitch. For example, in a Trinitron with a 0.25 slot-pitch, the grille wires measure about 0.18 millimeters in diameter because each electron beam is supposed to illuminate only one-third of the screen. The wires shadow the other two-thirds from the beam to maintain the purity of the color.

The aperture grille wires are held taut, but they can vibrate. Consequently, Trinitron monitors have one or two thin tensioning wires running horizontally across the screen. Although quite fine, these wires cast a shadow on the screen that is most apparent on light-colored screen backgrounds. Some people find the tensioning wire shadows objectionable, so you should look closely at a Trinitron before buying.

Trinitrons hold a theoretical brightness advantage over shadow-mask tubes. Because the slots allow more electrons to pass through to the screen than do the tiny holes of a shadow mask, a Trinitron can (in theory) create a brighter image. This added brightness is not borne out in practice. However, Trinitrons do excel in keeping their screens uniformly bright. The aperture grille wires of a Trinitron block the beam only in one dimension, and so don't impinge as much on the electron beam at the screen edges.

Thanks to basic patents, Sony had exclusive rights to the Trinitron design. However, those patents began expiring in 1991, and other manufactures were quick to begin working with the technology. Other patents, however, cover manufacturing and other aspects of building successful Trinitrons. Consequently, an expected flood of Trinitron clones never appeared. In fact, the only new alternative to the Trinitron was introduced by Mitsubishi in 1993. Called Diamondtron by its manufacturer, the new design is based on aperture grille technology, but uses a refined electron gun. Whereas the Trinitron combines three guns into a single focusing mechanism, the Diamondtron gives each gun its own control. According to Mitsubishi, this refinement allows more precise beam control and a more accurate and higher resolution image.

Required Dot-Pitch

No matter whether a monitor uses a shadow-mask with a dot-pitch or an aperture grille with a slot-pitch, the spacing of image triads on the screen is an important constituent in monitor quality. A monitor simply cannot put dots any closer together than the holes in a mask or grille allow. It's easy to compute the pitch necessary for a resolution level in a computer system. Just divide the screen size by the number of dots required to be displayed.

For example, a VGA text display comprises 80 columns of characters each nine dots wide, for a total of 720 dots across the screen. The typical twelve-inch (diagonal) monitor screen is roughly 9.5 inches or 240 millimeters across. Hence, to properly display a VGA text image, the dot pitch must be smaller than .333 (or 240/720) millimeter, assuming the full width of the screen is used for display. Often a monitor's image is somewhat smaller than full screen width and such displays require even finer dot-pitch. The larger the display, the coarser the dot-pitch can be for a given level of resolution.

Screen Curvature

Most CRTs have a distinctive shape. At one end, a narrow neck contains the electron gun or guns. Around the neck fits the deflection yoke, an external assembly that generates the magnetic fields that bend the electron beams to sweep across the inner surface of the wide face of the tube. The tube emerges from the yoke as a funnel-like flaring, which enlarges to the rectangular face of the screen itself. This face often (but becoming much less common) is a spherically curving surface.

The spherical curve of the face makes sense for a couple of reasons. It makes the distance traveled by the electron beam more consistent at various points on the screen, edge to center to edge. A truly flat screen would require the beam to travel farther at the edges than at the center and would require the beam to strike the face of the screen obliquely, resulting in image distortion. Although this distortion can be compensated for electrically, the curving screen helps things along.

In addition, the CRT is partly evacuated, so normal atmospheric pressure is constantly trying to crush the tube. The spherical surface helps distribute this potentially destructive force more evenly, making the tube stronger.

Screen curvature has a negative side effect. Straight lines on the screen appear straight only from one observation point. Move your head closer, farther away, or to one side, and the supposedly straight lines of your graphics images will bow this way and that.

Technology has made the reasons underlying spherical curved screens less than compelling. The geometry of in-line guns simplifies tube construction and alignment sufficiently that cylindrically curved screens are feasible. They have fewer curvilinear problems because they warp only one axis of the image. Trinitrons characteristically have faces with cylindrical curves. Most shadow-mask tubes have spherical faces.

In the last few years, the technical obstacles to making genuinely flat screens have been surmounted. A number of manufacturers now offer flat-screen monochrome displays, which are relatively simple because compensation for the odd geometry is required by only one electron beam.

The first color flat screen was Zenith's flat tension-mask system. The tension-mask solves the construction problems inherent in a flat screen color system by essentially stretching the shadow mask. Its flat face and black matrix make for very impressive images, only the case of the monitor itself is bulky and ugly to look at; and an internal fan made the first model as much a pain for the ears as the screen was a pleasure for the eyes. Since then, such monitors have become less power hungry, but they remain more costly than more conventional designs.

Today's so-called flat-square tubes are neither flat nor square. They are, however, flatter and squarer than the picture tubes of days gone by so they suffer less curvilinear distortion.

Resolution Versus Addressability

The resolution of a video system refers to the fineness of detail that it can display. It is a direct consequence of the number of individual dots that make up the screen image and thus is a function of both the screen size and the dot-pitch.

Because the size and number of dots limit the image quality, the apparent sharpness of screen images can be described by the number of dots that can be displayed horizontally and vertically across the screen. For example, the resolution required by the Video Graphics Array system in its standard graphics mode is 640 dots horizontally by 480 vertically. The XGA display system produces an image 1,024 by 768 dots in its highest resolution mode.

Sometimes, however, the resolution available on the screen and that made by a computer's display adapter are not the same. For example, a video mode designed for the resolution capabilities of a color television set hardly taps the quality available from a computer monitor. On the other hard, the computer-generated graphics may be designed for a display system that's sharper than the one being used. You might, for instance, try to use a television in lieu of a more expensive monitor. The sharpness you actually see would then be less than what the resolution of the video system would have you believe.

Actual resolution is a physical quality of the video display system—the monitor—that's actually being used. It sets the ultimate upper limit on the display quality. In color systems, the chief limit on resolution is purely physical—the convergence of the system and the dot-pitch of the tube. In monochrome systems, which have no quality-limiting shadow masks, the resolution is limited by the bandwidth of the monitor, the highest frequency signal with which it can deal. (Finer details pack more information into the signals sent from computer system to monitor. The more information in a given time, the higher the frequency of the signal.)

A few manufacturers persist in using the misleading term addressability to describe the quality of their monitors. Addressability is essentially a bandwidth measurement for color monitors. It indicates how many different dots on the screen the monitor can point its electron guns at. It ignores, however, the physical limit imposed by the shadow mask. In other words, addressability describes the highest quality signals the monitor can handle, but the full quality of those signals are not necessarily visible to you on-screen.

Anti-Glare Treatment

Most mirrors are made from glass, and glass tries to mimic the mirror whenever it can. Because of the difference between the index of refraction of air and that of glass, glass is naturally reflective. If you make mirrors, that's great. If you make monitors—or worse yet, use them—the reflectivity of glass can be a big headache. A reflection of a room light or window from the glass face of the CRT can easily be brighter than the glow of phosphors inside. As a result, the text or graphics on the display tends to "wash out" or be obscured by the brightness.

The greater the curvature of a monitor screen, the more apt it is to have a problem with reflections because more of the environment gets reflected by the screen. A spherical monitor face acts like one of those huge convex mirrors strategically hung to give a panoramic view of shoplifters or cars sneaking around an obscured hairpin turn. The flatter the face of the monitor, the less of a worry reflections are. With an absolutely flat face, a slight turn of the monitor's face can eliminate all glare and reflections.

You can't change the curve of your monitor's face. However, help is available. Anti-glare treatments can reduce or eliminate reflections from the face of most CRTs. Several glare-reduction technologies are available, and each varies somewhat in its effectiveness.

Mesh

The lowest tech and least expensive anti-glare treatment is a simple fabric mesh, usually nylon. The mesh can either be placed directly atop the face of the screen or in a removable frame that fits about half an inch in front of the screen. Each hole in the mesh acts like a short tube, allowing you to see straight in at the tube, but cutting off light from the sides of the tube. Your straight-on vision gets through unimpeded, while glare that angles in doesn't make it to the screen.

As simple as this technique is, it works amazingly well. The least expensive after-market anti-glare system uses mesh suspiciously similar to pantyhose stretched across a frame. Unfortunately this mesh has an unwanted side effect. Besides blocking the glare, it also blocks some of the light from the screen and makes the image appear darker. You may have to turn the brightness control up to compensate, which may make the image bloom and lose sharpness.

Mechanical

Glare can be reduced by mechanical means—not a machine that automatically intercepts glare before it reaches the screen, but mechanical preparation of the screen surface. By lightly grinding the glass on the front of the CRT, the face of the screen can be made to scatter rather than reflect light. Each rough spot on the screen that results from the mechanical grinding process reflects light randomly, sending it every which direction. A smooth screen reflects a patch of light all together, like a mirror, reflecting any bright light source into your eyes. Because the light scattered by the ground glass is dispersed, less of it reaches your eyes and the glare is not as bright. However, because the coarse screen surface disperses the light coming from inside the tube as well as that reflected from the tube face, it also lessens the sharpness of the image. The mechanical treatment makes text appear slightly fuzzier and out-of-focus, which to some manufacturers is a worse problem than glare.

Coating

Glare can be reduced by applying coatings to the face of the CRT. Two different kinds of coatings can be used. One forms a rough film on the face of the CRT. This rough surface acts in the same way as a ground-glass screen would, scattering light.

The screen also can be coated with a special compound like magnesium fluoride. By precisely controlling the thickness of this coating, the reflectivity of the surface of the screen can be reduced. The fluoride coating is made to be a quarter the wavelength of light (usually of light at the middle of the spectrum). Light going through the fluoride and reflecting from the screen thus emerges from the coating out of phase with the light striking the fluoride surface, visually canceling out the glare. Camera lenses are coated to achieve exactly the same purpose, the elimination of reflections. A proper coating can minimize glare without affecting image sharpness or brightness.

Polarization

Light can be polarized, that is, its photons can be restricted to a single plane of oscillation. A polarizing filter allows light of only one polarization to pass. Two polarizing filters in a row can be arranged to allow light of only one plane of polarization to pass (by making the planes of polarization of the filters parallel), or the two filters can stop light entirely when their planes of polarization are perpendicular.

The first filter lets only one kind of light pass; the second filter lets only another kind of light pass. Because none of the second kind of light reaches the second filter, no light gets by.

When light is reflected from a surface, its polarization is shifted by 90 degrees. This physical principle makes polarizing filters excellent reducers of glare.

A sheet of polarizing material is merely placed a short space in front of a display screen. Light from a potential source of glare goes through the screen and is polarized. When it strikes the display and is reflected, its polarization is shifted 90 degrees. When it again reaches the filter, it is out of phase with the filter and cannot get through. Light from the display, however, only needs to go through the filter once. Although this glow is polarized, there is no second screen to impede its flow to your eyes.

Every anti-glare treatment has its disadvantage. Mesh makes an otherwise sharp screen look fuzzy because smooth characters are broken up by the cell structure of the mesh. Mechanical treatments are expensive and tend to make the screen appear to be slightly "fuzzy" or out of focus. The same is true of coatings that rely on the dispersion principle. Optical coatings, Polaroid filters, and even mesh suffer from their own reflections. The anti-glare material itself may add its own bit of glare. In addition, all anti-glare treatments—polarizing filters in particular—tend to make displays dimmer. The polarizing filter actually reduces the brightness of a display to one-quarter its untreated value.

Even with their shortcomings, however, anti-glare treatments are amazingly effective. They can ease eyestrain and eliminate the headaches that come with extended computer use.

Overscan and Underscan

Most computer displays are rated as to their screen size. As with television sets, the measurement of the cathode ray tube (CRT or picture tube) in a computer monitor is made diagonally across its face. The active display area of a 12-inch monitor thus may measure somewhat less than nine by seven inches.

Two monitors with the same size screens may have entirely different on-screen image sizes. Composite monitors are often afflicted by overscan; they attempt to generate images larger than their screen size, and the edges and corners of the active display area may be cut off. (The overscan is often designed in so that as the components inside the monitor age and become weaker, the picture shrinks down to normal size—likely over a period of years.) Underscan is the opposite condition—the image is smaller than nominal screen size.

Overscan may be perfectly normal—designed into a particular display— and does not necessarily indicate any underlying problems. Image geometry is easier to control nearer the center of the screen than it is at the edges. Pulling in the reins on the image can ensure that straight lines actually are displayed straight. Excessive overscan can be intimidating and counterproductive. If overscan is excessive, you are actually getting a smaller display than you are paying for. When comparing monitors, take into account the actual image size displayed rather than screen size.

Aspect Ratio

The relationship between the width and height of a monitor screen is termed its aspect ratio. Today the shape of the screen of nearly every monitor is standardized as is that of the underlying CRT that makes the image. The screen is 1.33 times wider than it is high, resulting in the same 4:3 aspect ratio used in television and motion pictures before the wide-screen phenomenon took over.

The image on-screen need not have the same aspect ratio of the tube, however. The electronics of monitors separate the circuitry that generates the horizontal and vertical scanning signals and results in their independent control. As a result, the relationship between the two can be adjusted, and that adjustment results in an alteration of the aspect ratio of the actual displayed image. For example, by increasing the amplification of the horizontal signal, the width of the image is stretched, raising the aspect ratio.

Normally, you should expect that the relative gains of the horizontal and vertical signals will be adjusted so that your display shows the correct aspect ratio on its screen. A problem develops when a display tries to accommodate signals based on different standards. This mismatch is particularly troublesome with VGA displays because the VGA standard allows images made with three distinct line counts—350, 400, and 480.

All else being equal, an image made from 350 lines is less than three-quarters the height of a 480-line image. A graphic generated in an EGA-compatible mode shown on a VGA display would thereby look quite squashed. A circle drawn on the screen would look like an ellipse; an orange would more resemble a watermelon.

Image Sizing

Monitors that match the VGA standard compensate for such obtuse images with the sync-polarity detection scheme. The relative polarities of the horizontal and vertical sync signals instruct the monitor in which mode and line count the image is being set. The monitor then compensates by adjusting its vertical gain to obtain the correct aspect ratio no matter the number of lines in the image.

Not all monitors take advantage of this sync signaling system. Shifting display modes with such a monitor can lead to graphics displays that look crushed. Others use a technique called autosizing that allows the monitor to maintain a consistent image size no matter what video signal your display adapter is sending it without regard to VGA sync coding. Monitor makers can achieve autosizing in several ways. True autosizing works regardless of the signal going to the monitor and scales the image to match the number of display lines. Mode-sensitive autosizing works by determining the display mode used for an image from the frequency of the signal. It then switches the size to a pre-set standard to match the number of lines in the signal. Monitors often combine VGA sync-sensing with mode-sensitive autosizing.

Image Controls

A few (far from a majority) monitors make coping with underscan, overscan, and odd aspect ratios simply a matter of twisting controls. These displays feature horizontal and vertical size (or gain) controls that enable you to adjust the size and shape of the image to suit your own tastes. With these controls—providing they have adequate range—you can make the active image touch the top, bottom, and sides of the screen bezel or you can shrink the bright area of your display to a tiny (but geometrically perfect) patch in the center of your screen.

Size and position controls give you command of how much screen the image on your monitor fills. With full-range controls, you can expand the image to fill the screen from corner to corner or reduce it to a smaller size that minimizes the inevitable geometric distortion that occurs near the edges of the tube. A full complement of controls includes one each of the following: horizontal position (sometimes termed phase), vertical position, horizontal size (sometimes called width), and vertical size (or height).

A wide control range is better than a narrow one. Some monitors skimp on one or more controls and limit you in how large you can make the on-screen image. Worse, sometimes a monitor maker doesn't include a control at all. For example, some monitors have no horizontal size controls. As a result you cannot adjust both the size and aspect ratio of the image.

The optimum position for these controls is on the front panel where you can both adjust them and view the image at the same time. Controls on the rear panel require you to have gorilla-like arms to reach around the monitor to make adjustments while checking their effect.

Image controls come in two types, analog and digital. Analog controls are the familiar old knobs like you find on vintage television sets. Twist one way and the image gets bigger; twist the other and it shrinks. Analog controls have one virtue—just by looking at the knob you know where they are set, whether at one or the other extreme of their travel. The control itself is a simple memory system; it stays put until you move it again. Analog controls, however, become dirty and wear out with age, and they usually enable you to set but one value per knob—one value that must cover all the monitor's operating modes.

Digital controls give you pushbutton control over image parameters. Press one button, and the image gets larger or moves to the left. Another compensates in the opposite direction. Usually digital controls are linked with a microprocessor, memory, and mode-sensing circuitry so that you can pre-set different image heights and widths for every video standard your monitor can display.

Digital controls don't get noisy with age and are more reliable and repeatable, but you never know when you are approaching the limit of their travel. Most have two-speed operation—hold them in momentarily and they make minute changes; keep holding down the button and they shift gears to make gross changes. Of course, if you don't anticipate the shift, you'll overshoot the setting you want and spend a few extra moments zeroing in on the exact setting.

Size and position controls are irrelevant to LCD and similar alternate display technologies. LCD panels are connected more directly to display memory so that memory locations correspond nearly exactly to every screen position. There's no need to move the image around or change its shape because it's forever fixed where it belongs.

Most CRT-based displays also carry over several controls from their television progenitors. Nearly every computer monitor has a brightness control, which adjusts the level of the scanning electron beam; this in turn makes the on-screen image glow brighter or dimmer. The contrast control adjusts the linearity of the relationship between the incoming signal and the on-screen image brightness. In other words, it controls the brightness relationship that results from different signal levels—how much brighter high-intensity is. In a few displays, both the brightness and contrast function are combined into a single "picture" control. Although a godsend to those who might get confused by having to twiddle two knobs, the combined control also limits your flexibility in adjusting the image to best suit your liking.

Other controls ubiquitous to televisions usually are absent from better computer monitors because they are irrelevant. Vertical hold, color (saturation), and hue controls only have relevance to composite video signals, so they are likely only to be found on composite-interfaced displays. The vertical hold control tunes the monitor to best decipher the vertical synchronizing signal from the ambiguities composite video signal. The separate sync signals used by other display standards automatically removes any ambiguity. Color and hue only adjust the relationship of the color subcarrier to the rest of the composite video signal and have no relevance at all to non-composite systems.

Flat Panel Display Systems

CRTs are impractical for portable computers, as anyone who has toted a forty-pound first-generation portable computer knows. The glass in the tube itself weighs more than most of today's portable machines, and running a CRT steals more power than most laptop or notebook machines budget for all their circuitry and peripherals.

LED

In lieu of the tube, laptop designers have tried just about every available alternate display technology. These include the panels packed with light-emitting diodes—the power-on indicators of the 1980s—that glow at you as red as the devil's eyes. But LEDs consume extraordinary amounts of power. Consider that a normal, full-size LED can draw 10 to 100 milliwatts at full brilliance and that you need 100,000 or so individual elements in a display screen; you get an idea of the magnitude of the problem. Certainly the individual display elements of an LED screen would be smaller than a power-on indicator and consume less power, but the small LED displays created in the early days of portable PCs consumed many times the power required by today's technologies. LEDs also suffer the problem that they tend to wash out in bright light and are relatively expensive to fabricate in large arrays.

Gas-Plasma

One alternative is the gas-plasma screen, which uses high voltage to ionize a gas and cause it to emit light. Most gas plasma screens have the characteristic orange-red glow of neon because that's the gas they use inside. Gas-plasma displays are relatively easy to make in the moderately large sizes perfect for laptop computer screens and yield sharpness unrivaled by competing technologies. However, gas-plasma screens also need a great deal of power—several times the requirements of LCD technology—at high voltages, which must be synthesized from low-voltage battery power. Consequently, gas-plasma displays are used primarily in AC-power portables. When used in laptops, the battery life of a gas-plasma-equipped machine is quite brief, on the order of an hour.

LCD

The winner in the display technology competition was the Liquid Crystal Display, the infamous LCD. Unlike LED and gas-plasma displays, which glow on their own emitting photons of visible light, LCDs don't waste energy by shining. Instead, they merely block light otherwise available. To make patterns visible, they either selectively block reflected light (reflective LCDs) or the light generated by a secondary source either behind the LCD panel (backlit LCDs) or adjacent to it (edgelit LCDs). The backlight source is typically an electroluminescent (EL) panel, although some laptops use Cold-Cathode Fluorescent (CCF) for brighter, whiter displays with the penalty of higher cost, greater thickness, and increased complexity.

Nematic Twists

A number of different terms describe the technologies used in the LCD panels themselves, terms like supertwist, double supertwist, and triple supertwist. In effect, the twist of the crystals controls the contrast of the screen, so triple supertwist screens are have more contrast than ordinary supertwist.

The history of laptop and notebook computer displays has been lead by innovations in LCD technology. Invented by RCA in the 1960s (General Electric still receives royalties on RCA's basic patents), LCDs came into their own with laptop computers because of their low power requirements, light weight, and ruggedness.

An LCD display is actually a sandwich made from two plastic sheets with a very special liquid made from rod-shaped or nematic molecules. One important property of the nematic molecules of liquid crystals is that they can be aligned by grooves in the plastic to bend the polarity of light that passes through them. More importantly, the amount of bend the molecules of the liquid crystal gives to the light can be altered by applying an electrical current through them.

Ordinary light has no particular orientation, so liquid crystals don't visibly alter it. But polarized light aligns all the oscillations of its photons in a single direction. A polarizing filter creates polarized light by allowing light of a particular polarity (or axis of oscillation) to pass through. Polarization is key to the function of LCDs.

To make an LCD, light is first passed through one polarizing filter to polarize it. A second polarizing filter, set to pass light at right angles to the polarity of the first, is put on the other side of the liquid crystal. Normally, this second polarizing filter stops all light from passing. However, the liquid crystal bends the polarity of light emerging from the first filter so that it lines up with the second filter. Pass a current through the liquid crystal and the amount of bending changes, which alters in turn the amount of light passing through the second polarizer.

To make an LCD display, you need only to selectively apply current to small areas of the liquid crystal. The areas to which you apply current are dark; those that you don't are light. A light behind the LCD makes the changes more visible.

Over the past few years, engineers have made several changes to this basic LCD design to improve its contrast and color. The basic LCD design outlined above is technically termed twisted nematic technology or TN. The liquid molecules of the TN display in their resting state always bend light by 90 degrees, exactly counteracting the relationship between the two polarizing panels that make up the display.

By increasing the bending of light by the nematic molecules, the contrast between light and dark can be increased. An LCD design that bends light by 180 to 270 degrees is termed a supertwist nematic or simply supertwist display. One side effect of the added twist is that the appearance of color artifacts results in the yellowish green and bright blue hues of many familiar LCD displays.

This tinge of color can be canceled simply by mounting two supertwist liquid crystals back-to-back so that one bends the light the opposite direction of the other. This design is logically termed a double supertwist nematic or simply double supertwist display. This LCD design is currently popular among laptop PCs with black-and-white VGA-quality displays. It does have a drawback, however. Because two layers of LCD are between you and the light source, double supertwist panels appear darker or require brighter backlights for adequate visibility.

Triple supertwist nematic displays instead compensate for colorshifts in the supertwist design by layering both sides of the liquid crystal with thin polymer films. Because the films absorb less light than the twin panels of double supertwist screens, less backlight—and less backlight power—is required for the same screen brightness.

Active Versus Passive

LCDs also come in two styles based on how the current that aligns their nematic molecules is applied. Most LCD panels have a grid of horizontal and vertical conductors, and each pixel is located at the intersection of these conductors. The pixel is darkened simply by sending current through the conductors to the liquid crystal. This kind of display is called a passive matrix.

The alternate design, the active matrix, is more commonly referred to as Thin Film Transistor (TFT) technology. This style of LCD puts a transistor at every pixel. The transistor acts as a relay. A small current is sent to it through the horizontal and vertical grid, and in response the transistor switches on a much higher current to activate the LCD pixel.

The advantage of the active matrix design is that a smaller current needs to traverse the grid, so the pixel can be switched on and off faster. Whereas passive LCD screens may update only about half a dozen times per second, TFT designs can operate at ordinary monitor speeds—ten times faster. That increased speed equates to faster response—for example, your mouse won't disappear as you move it across the screen.

The disadvantage of the TFT design is that it requires the fabrication of one transistor for each screen pixel. Putting those transistors there requires combining the LCD and semiconductor manufacturing processes. That's sort of like getting bricklayers and carpenters to work together.

To achieve the quality of active matrix displays without paying the price, engineers have upped the scan on passive panels. Double-scanned passive work exactly like the name says: they scan their screens twice in the period that a normal screen is scanned only once. As a result, they eke out extra brightness, contrast, and speed. They do not, however, reach the quality level set by active matrix screens.

Color adds other complications to LCD design and manufacture—and considerable expense, on the order of an extra $2,500 for a laptop equipped with color LCD. A number of technologies have been tried for color LCD screens, both additive (which put red, green, and blue-colored pixels side-by-side so that their output can visually combine) and subtractive (which layer cyan, yellow, and magenta-absorbing screens to produce colors). The most striking results have been achieved by coupling TFT technology with color to achieve bright, fast, and expensive displays. Although the best units look wonderful—often better than color CRTs—today their price puts them in the interesting-but-impractical class.

Resolution

On-screen resolution is an important issue with LCD screens; it determines how sharp text characters and graphics will appear. Today, three resolution standards are dominant: CGA (640 by 200); double-scanned CGA (640 by 400); and VGA (640 by 480).

Most people prefer the last because it's exactly equivalent to today's most popular desktop displays so it can use the same software and drivers.

CGA resolution is visibly inferior, producing blocky, hard-to-read characters and remains used only in the least expensive laptops.

Double-scanned CGA offers a good compromise between cost and resolution. It's actually as sharp as text-mode CGA. Graphics pose a problem as double-scanned CGA mode is not supported by a wide base of software. Under Windows, however, many double-scanned CGA systems are compatible with Toshiba and AT&T 640 by 400 pixel drivers.

VGA poses particular problems for LCD displays because it's really three standards under a single name, operating with modes that put 350, 400, or 480 lines on the screen. Most VGA display panels have 480 rows of dots to accommodate these lines.

A problem develops with VGA images made with lower line counts. Many laptop LCD screens display only the active lines and leave the rest of the screen blank. For example, 80 lines are left blank when 400-line mode is displayed on a 480-line LCD. The result is a black band at both the top and bottom of the screen.

This banding is particularly obnoxious because VGA text normally displays in 400-line mode. A number of manufacturers have improved on this situation by shifting VGA text into 640×480 mode using larger, more legible characters to fill the screen. If you have a choice, you'll probably want your next laptop to operate this way.

Monitor Electronics

The image you see on screen is only part of the story of a complete display system. The video signals from your PC must be amplified and processed by the electronics inside the monitor to achieve the right strength and timing relationships to put the proper image in view.

The basic electronic components inside a monitor are its video amplifiers. As the name implies, these circuits simply increase the strength (amplify) of the approximately one-volt signals they receive from your PC to the thousands of volts needed to drive the electron beam from cathode to phosphor. Monochrome monitors have a single video amplifier; color monitors, three (one for each primary color).

In an analog color monitor, these three amplifiers must be exactly matched and absolutely linear. That is, the input and output of each amplifier must be precisely proportional, and it must be the same as the other two amplifiers. The relationship between these amplifiers is called color tracking. If it varies, the color of the image on the screen won't be what your software had in mind.

The effects of such poor color tracking are all bad. You lose precision in your color control. This is especially important for desktop publishing and presentation applications. With poor color tracking, the screen can no longer hope to be an exact preview of what eventually appears on paper or film. You may even lose a good fraction of the colors displayable by your video system.

What happens is that differences between the amplifiers cause one of the three primary colors to be emphasized at times and de-emphasized at others, casting a subtle shade on the on-screen image. This shading effect is most pronounced in grey displays—the dominate color(s) tinge the grey.

Although you don't have to worry about color tracking in a monochrome display, the quality of the amplifier nevertheless determines the range of greys that can be displayed. Aberrations in the amplifier cause the monitor to lose some of its grey scale range.

The relationship between the input and output signals of video amplifiers is usually not linear. That is, a small change in the input signal may make a greater than corresponding change in the output. In other words, the monitor may exaggerate the color or grey scale range of the input signal—contrast increases. The relationship between input and output is referred to as the gamma of the amplifier. A gamma of one would result in an exact correspondence of the input and output signals. However, monitors with unity gammas tend to have washed out, pastel images. Most people prefer higher gammas, in the range 1.5 to 1.8, because of the greater contrast of their images.

If you want a monitor that works both with today's VGA, Super VGA, and sharper display systems as well as old graphics adapters like CGA and EGA, you need a monitor with TTL capability. Most modern computer monitors have only analog inputs, which cannot properly display the digital (TTL) signals used by these older standards. You also have to check the color support of such monitors. To be compatible with the CGA standard, a monitor must be capable of handling a 16-color digital input, sometimes called RGBI for the four (red, green, blue, and intensity) signals from which it is made. EGA compatibility requires 64-color capability.

Synchronizing Frequency Range

Today's variety of signal standards makes it almost mandatory that your monitor be able to synchronize to a wide range of synchronizing frequencies. You have two frequencies to worry about. Vertical frequency, sometimes called the refresh rate or frame rate, determines how often the complete screen is updated. The horizontal synchronizing frequency (or horizontal scan rate) indicates the rate at which the individual scan lines that make up the image are drawn.

These frequency ranges are important to you because they determine with which video standards the monitor can work. The CGA system requires a horizontal frequency of 15.75 KHz; MDA, 18 KHz; EGA, 22 KHz; and VGA, 31.5 KHz. At Super VGA resolution, horizontal frequencies depend on the refresh rate used. At a 56 Hz refresh rate, 35 KHz is adequate; but at the VESA 72 Hz spec, 48 KHz is required.

The lowest frame rate normally required is the 50 Hz used by MDA signals. VGA and most other video standards use refresh rates between 60 and 70 Hz. Table 14.2 lists the frequency requirements of all recognized PC video standards.

TABLE 14.2. Frequencies Required by Various Monitor Standards

Standard	Resolution in pixels	Vert. Sync (frame rate)	Horz. Sync (line rate)	Sync Position Vert.
MDA	720 × 350	50 Hz	18.3 KHz	Pos.
CGA	640 × 200	60 Hz	15.75 KHz	Pos.
EGA	640 × 350	60 Hz	21.5 KHz	Pos.
MDGA	640 × 480	60 or 70 Hz	31.5 KHz	Neg.
VGA (original)	640 × 480	60 or 70 Hz	31.5 KHz	Neg.
Macintosh	640 × 480	67 Hz.	35.0 KHz	N/A
XGA-2	640 × 480	75 Hz	39.38 KHz	Neg.
VESA	640 × 480	75 Hz	37.5 KHz	Neg.
Apple Portrait	640 × 870	76.5 Hz	70.19 KHz	N/A
VESA guideline	800 × 600	56 Hz	35.5 KHz	Either
VESA guideline	800 × 600	60 Hz	37.9 KHz	Pos.
VESA standard	800 × 600	72 Hz	48.1 KHz	Pos.
VESA standard	800 × 600	75 Hz	46.875 KHz	Pos.
RasterOps & Supermac	1024 × 768	75.1 Hz	60.24 KHz	N/A
VESA guideline	1024 × 768	60 Hz	48.3 KHz	Neg.
VESA standard	1024 × 768	70.1 Hz	56.5 KHz	Neg.
VESA standard	1024 × 768	75 Hz	60 KHz	Pos.
8514/A	1024 × 768	44 Hz*	35.5 KHz	Pos.
XGA	1024 × 768	44 Hz*	35.5 KHz	Pos.
XGA-2	1024 × 768	75.8 Hz	61.1 KHz	Pos.
Apple 2-page	1152 × 870	75 Hz	68.68 KHz	N/A
VESA standard	1280 × 1024	75 Hz	80 KHz	Pos.

* Because 8514/A and XGA, the current XGA standards, operate in interlace mode, they require monitors that can synchronize to their field rate, which is twice the frame rate, 88 Hz.

Interlaced systems like the 8514/A and the first implementations of XGA used a trick developed for television to help put more information on-screen using a limited bandwidth signal. Instead of scanning the image from top to bottom, one line after another, each frame of the image is broken in half into two fields. One field consists of the odd-numbered lines of the image; the other the even-numbered lines. The electron beam sweeps across and down, illuminating every other line and then starts from the top again and finishes with the ones it missed on the first pass.

This technique achieves an apparent doubling of the frame rate. Instead of sweeping down the screen 30 times a second (the case of a normal television picture), the top-to-bottom sweep occurs 60 times a second. Whereas a 30 frame per second rate would noticeably flicker, the ersatz 60 frame per second rate does not—at least not to most people under most circumstances. Some folks' eyes are not fooled, however, so interlaced images have earned a reputation of being flickery.

Interlacing is used on computer display signals to keep the necessary bandwidth down. A lower frame rate lowers the required bandwidth of the transmission channel. Of all the prevailing standards, only the original high-resolution operating mode of the 8514/A display adapter and the first generation of XGA use interlacing. Their frame rate, 44 Hz, would cause distinct flicker. Interlacing drives the field rate up to 88 Hz. Note that you need a monitor that can lock to the vertical frequency of the higher field rate rather than the frame rate of an interlaced monitor.

Bandwidth

Perhaps the most common specification usually listed for any sort of monitor is bandwidth, which is usually rated in megahertz. Common monitor bandwidths stretch across a wide range—figures from 12 to 100 MHz sometimes encountered.

In theory, the higher the bandwidth, the higher the resolution and sharper the image displayed. In the case of color displays, the dot-pitch of the display tube is the biggest limit on performance.

In a monochrome system, however, bandwidth is a determinant of overall sharpness. The PC display standards do not demand extremely wide bandwidths. Extremely large bandwidths are often superfluous.

The bandwidth necessary in a monitor is easy to compute. A system ordinarily requires a bandwidth wide enough to address each individual screen dot plus an extra margin to allow for retrace times. (Retrace times are those periods in which the electron beam moves but does not display, for instance at the end of each frame when the beam must move from the bottom of the screen at the end of the last line of one frame back up to the top of the screen for the first line of the next frame.)

A TTL monochrome display operating under the MDA standard shows 252,000 (or 720 × 350) pixels 50 times per second—12.6 million pixels per second. A composite display shows 128,000 (or 640 × 200) pixels 60 times per second—7.68 million pixels per second. A VGA display, 288,000 (or 720 × 400 in text mode) shows pixels 70 times per second—20.16 million pixels per second.

Allowing a wide margin of about 25 percent for retrace times, it can thus be seen that for most PC applications, a bandwidth of 16 megahertz is acceptable for TTL monitors, and 10 megahertz of bandwidth is sufficient for sharp composite video displays, figures well within the claims of most commercial products. For VGA, 25 megahertz is the necessary minimum. Table 14.3 summarizes the bandwidth required by the various IBM display standards.

TABLE 14.3. Dot-Clocks (Bandwidths) of IBM Video Standards

Video Standard	Dot-Clock
MDA	16.3 MHz
CGA	14.3 MHz
EGA	16.3 MHz
PGC	25 MHz
VGA (350- or 480-line mode)	25 MHz
VGA (400-line mode)	28 MHz
8514/A	44.9 MHz

Because in real-world applications the worst-case display puts an illuminated pixel next to a dark one, the actual (as opposed to theoretical) bandwidth required by a display system is half the dot-clock plus system overhead.

Monitor Types

The world of PC monitors is marked by a profusion of confusion. To make sure that you get the right type of display, you must describe it with specificity. Saying color or monochrome is not enough. You must also indicate the signal standard to which the monitor must abide. The standard is dictated by the video adapter used by the monitor; but some monitors work with different adapters, and many adapters are flexible in regard to your monitor choice. However, certain terms are used to describe and distinguish particular monitor types.

Monochrome

Monochrome means exactly what its root words say—mono means one and chrome indicates color. Monochrome monitors show their images in one color, be it green, amber, white, puce, or alizarin crimson. Monochrome does not describe what sort of display adapter the monitor plugs into. Among the monitors available, you have three choices that give you long odds at finding the right combination by chance. A fourth, the multiscanning monochrome display, accepts almost any monochrome signal.

TTL Monochrome

The original display type offered by IBM—the one that plugs into the Monochrome Display Adapter—is distinctly different from any monitor standard made for any other purpose. It uses digital input signals and separate lines for both its horizontal and vertical synchronizing signals.

Its digital signals match the level used by integrated circuits of the Transistor-Transistor Logic (TTL) family. These chips operate with tightly defined voltage ranges indicating a logical one or zero. (Five volts is nominally considered a digital one, although that's the input voltage level of TTL chips. The maximum level TTL signals ever reach is about 4.3 volts.) Because of their use of TTL signals, such monitors are often called TTL monochrome displays. They can only be plugged into MDA or compatible display adapters (including the Hercules Graphics Board).

TTL monochromes are the least expensive monitors (and the oldest monitor technology) still sold with computer systems today. When manufacturers want to skimp somewhere, they may substitute a TTL monochrome display system for a monochrome VGA system. Avoid such systems if you can because fewer applications support Hercules graphics than support VGA. Consequently, you should consider such a monitor if you only want text displays, and a few dollars are very important to you.

Composite Monochrome

A monitor bearing no description other than merely "monochrome" is most likely a composite monochrome monitor. This type of monitor offers the lowest resolution of any monochrome system available for PCs, the same level as a CGA color display but without the redeeming virtue of color. Because the composite monochrome monitor uses the same signal as home and professional video systems, it is as ubiquitous as it is hard on the eyes. Designed for the mass market, the composite monochrome monitor is likely to be the least expensive available. It can only be plugged into a CGA or compatible display adapter. The built-in display of the unlamented IBM Portable Personal Computer is actually a composite monochrome monitor. About the only real use of a monochrome composite display today is in multimedia systems to preview video images.

VGA Monochrome

As with TTL monochrome monitors, VGA monochrome monitors follow a unique frequency standard. Because the Monochrome VGA display quickly won acceptance, it spawned a number of compatibles. These all are incompatible with other video standards but plug into any VGA-style output.

A VGA monochrome monitor works with any VGA display adapter without change. It displays VGA graphics without a hitch—but also without color, of course.

Multiscanning Monochrome

Unlike the other three monochrome display types, which are designed to operate at certain fixed frequencies, the multiscanning monochrome display adapts to the signals sent to it within a wide range of frequencies. Usually, this kind of monitor can handle any standard monochrome signal, from composite to VGA. It offers no advantage over the fixed-frequency displays except an impunity from errors. You can shift it between monochrome-equipped computer systems no matter what standards they follow.

Multiscanning monochrome monitors are rare today. They appear on the market occasionally, and typically disappear when demand turns out to be as great as for CP/M-based computers.

Color Monitors

Five types of color displays are generally available for connecting to PCs and PS/2s. Among these are composite color, RGB (or CGA), Enhanced RGB (or EGA), VGA, and mulitscanning monitors.

Composite Color

Generic video monitors—the kind you're likely to connect to your VCR or video camera—use the standard NTSC composite video signal. This signal standard has long been used with PCs—starting with the CGA adapter and the PCjr's built-in display system. Composite signals have never really gone away. They are still used where computer-generated graphics are destined for television and video productions. They also link into some multimedia systems. The 3.58 megahertz color subcarrier specified by the NTSC standard limits their color sharpness, however, so the best you can expect should you want to use a composite color display for general use is readable 40-column text. In other words, composite color is a special purpose product, nothing you want to connect for average, everyday computing.

RGB

The original color display for the IBM PC—the Personal Computer Color Display, IBM model 5151—used three discrete digital signals for each of the three primary colors. From these signals, the display type earned the nickname RGB from the list of additive primary colors: Red, Green, and Blue. To be completely accurate, of course, this style of monitor should be termed RGBI, with the final "I" standing for intensity, per the CGA standard.

Except for the interface signal, the RGB monitor works like a composite color monitor, using the same frequencies, but substituting digital signals for analog. Because there's no need for the NTSC color subcarrier, bandwidth is not limited by the interface, and RGB monitors appear much sharper than composite monitors, even though they display the same number of lines. RGB monitors work with the CGA, EGA (in its degraded CGA mode), and compatible display adapters as well as the PCjr. Because of the low resolution of CGA systems, CGA monitors are about as dead and forgotten as the PCjr.

Enhanced RGB

Moving up to EGA quality requires a better display, one able to handle the 22.1 KHz horizontal synchronizing frequency of the EGA standard. In addition, its interface is somewhat different. While still digital, it must accommodate intensity signals for each of the three primary colors. The EGA signals require a matching EGA connection on the display.

As with CGA, EGA is essentially obsolete. No new systems are sold with it anymore. Rather than getting a new monitor to work with your existing EGA card when your old monitor fails, you'll probably save time and headaches by upgrading to VGA.

VGA Displays

VGA displays were introduced by necessity with the PS/2s. They use analog inputs and a 31 KHz horizontal synchronizing frequency to match with the VGA standard. VGA is now the minimum you should demand in a computer monitor.

Multiscanning Color Displays

Color multiscanning displays were introduced even before the monochrome models. At the time, at least two competing IBM color standards were in use while only one monochrome standard was popular. Among the first color multiscanning systems was NEC's Multisync, a monitor so successful that any monitor in this entire class is often erroneously referred to as being a "multisync."

Multiscanning displays do not lock their horizontal and vertical synchronizing frequencies to any particular standard. Instead, they try to match the sync pulses sent to them by your computer system. By automatically adjusting themselves to the available signal, color multiscanning displays can work with just about any video standard.

The range of frequencies they can latch on to is limited, however. For example, a manufacturer might specify that a display can handle horizontal sync frequencies from 48 to 60 Hz. Such a display could not cope with the 70 Hz signals used under the VGA standard.

Most multiscanning displays are designed to handle signals even beyond the VGA standard. EGA Plus cards were initially created to capitalize on this potential. After IBM introduced its 8514/A display adapter, many manufacturers extended the range of their system to make them compatible with that standard. Now most multiscanning monitors accommodate signals affording resolutions of 1,024 by 768 pixels and higher.

Inputs and Connectors

Monitors can be grouped by the display standard they support, mostly based upon the display adapter card they are designed to plug into. One basic guide that helps you narrow down the compatibility of a display just by inspecting its rear panel is the input connector used by the monitor. After all, if you cannot plug a monitor into your computer, odds are it is not much good to you.

Three styles of connectors are shared by different PC video standards. By name, these three connectors are the RCA-style pin jack, the nine-pin D-shell, and the 15-pin "high-density" D-shell. In addition, some high-resolution monitors use three or more BNC connectors for their input signals.

Three is just enough fewer than the number of major PC video standards (four) that you can get into serious trouble with. Plugging the wrong kind of monitor into a display adapter connector that it seemingly fits can result in fatal damage to your monitor. Obviously, you'll want to know which is acceptable, and what is fatal.

Pin Jacks

The bull's eye jack used on stereo and video equipment is used by most manufacturers for the composite video connections in PC display systems, although a wealth of monitors and television sets made by innumerable manufacturers also use this connector. This connector does give you many choices for alternate displays—that is, if you don't mind marginal quality.

Composite monitors (those dealing with the composite video and NTSC color only) rank among the most widely available and least expensive in both color and monochrome. Even better quality television sets have such jacks available.

Although you can use any composite video display with a CGA or compatible color card, the signal itself limits the possible image quality to okay for monochrome, acceptable for 40-column color, and unintelligible for 80-column color. Nevertheless, a composite video display—already a multipurpose device—becomes even more versatile with a computer input.

Daisy-Chaining

A side benefit of pin plug/composite video displays is that most have both input and output jacks. These paired jacks enable you to daisy-chain multiple monitors to a single video output. For example, you can attach six composite video monitors to the output of your computer for presentations in classroom or boardroom.

In many cases, the jacks just loop through the display (that is, they connect together). The display merely bridges the input video signal and alters it in no other manner. You can connect a nearly unlimited number of monitors to these loop-through connections with no image degradation. Some monitors, however, buffer their outputs with a built-in video amplifier. Depending on the quality of the amplifier, daisy-chaining several of these monitors can result in noticeable image degradation.

One way to tell the difference is by plugging the output of the display into the output of your computer. Most amplifiers don't work backwards, so if the display has a buffering amplifier nothing appears on-screen. If you do get an image comparable to the one you get when plugging into the input jack, the signal just loops through the display.

Analog Voltage Level

The specifications of composite monitors sometimes include a number describing the voltage level of the input signal. This voltage level can be important when selecting a composite display because all such monitors are essentially analog devices.

In analog monitors, the voltage level corresponds to the brightness the electron beam displays on-screen. A nominal one volt peak-to-peak input signal is the standard in both the video and computer industries and should be expected from any composite monitor. The VGA system requires a slightly different level—0.7 volts.

Termination

For proper performance, a composite video signal line must be terminated by an impedance of 75 ohms. This termination ensures that the signal is at the proper level and that aberrations do not creep in because of an improperly-matched line. Most composite input monitors (particularly those with separate inputs and outputs) feature a termination switch that connects a 75 ohm resistor across the video line when turned on. Only one termination resistor should be switched on in any daisy-chain, and it should always be the last monitor in the chain.

If you watch a monitor when you switch the termination resistor on, you'll notice that the screen gets dimmer. That's because the resistor absorbs about half the video signal. Because composite video signals are analog, they are sensitive to voltage level. The termination cuts the voltage in half and consequently dims the screen by the same amount. Note that the dim image is the proper one. Although bright might seem better, it's not. It may overload the circuits of the monitor or otherwise cause erratic operation.

Composite monitors with a single video input jack and no video output usually have a termination resistor permanently installed. Although you might try to connect two or more such monitors to a single CGA composite output (with a wye cable or adapter), doing so is unwise. With each additional monitor, the image gets dimmer (the signal must be split among the various monitors) and the CGA adapter is required to send out increasing current. The latter could cause the CGA to fail.

Nine-Pin D-Shell Connectors

Three different PC video standards share the nine-pin D-shell connector: monochrome, standard RGB, and enhanced RGB. To confuse things further, many monitor makers also use the same connector for VGA and proprietary display systems.

Because of the huge potential for confusion, you must follow one important rule—Know what kind of display adapter you are about to plug into. Making the wrong choice can be fatal to your display, particularly if you try to plug an IBM Monochrome Display into a CGA adapter. The mismatch of synchronizing frequencies leads to the internal components of the display overheating and failing.

A mismatch is easy to spot—you simply can't make sense of the image on the screen. You may see a Venetian-blind pattern of lines; the screen may flash; or it may look like the vertical hold failed in a dramatic way. Should you observe any of these patterns or hear a high-pitched squeal from your display and see nothing on-screen, immediately turn off your display. Hunt for the problem while the life of your monitor is not ticking away.

Fifteen-Pin High-Density D-Shell Connectors

The only monitors you are likely to find 15-pin high-density D-shell connectors in are those that are VGA-compatible, whether dedicated to that purpose or multiscanning.

So far, PC display standards have done a good job of ensuring that problems like the nine-pin mismatch do not occur with these connectors. Although both monochrome and color displays use the same connectors, the VGA circuit can sense which is connected and handle either one properly.

IBM's 8514 and 8515 displays as well as 8514/A and XGA display adapters also use the same connector even though they at times use different signals. Again, however, IBM has incorporated coding in the signals to ensure that problems do not arise. The 8514/A and XGA adapters can sense the type of display connected to it, and do not send out conflicting signals. The 8514 and 8515 monitors operate happily with VGA signals, so problems do not occur if they are plugged into an ordinary VGA output.

BNC Connectors

True high resolution systems use a separate coaxial cable for every signal they receive. Typically, they use BNC connectors to attach these to the monitor. They have one very good reason. Connectors differ in their frequency handling capabilities, and capacitance in the standard

15-pin high-density D-shell connector can limit bandwidth, particularly as signal frequencies climb into range above 30 MHz. BNC connectors are design for frequencies into the gigahertz range, so they impose few limits on ordinary video signals.

Monitors can use either three, four, or five BNC connectors for their inputs. A three-connector system integrates both horizontal and vertical synchronizing signals with the green signal. The resulting mix is called sync-on-green. Others use three connectors for red, green, and blue signals and a fourth for horizontal and vertical sync combined together. This scheme is called composite sync. Five connector systems use three color signals: one for horizontal sync, and one for vertical sync. These are called separate sync systems.

Audio Inputs

Although the number of monitors (particularly those with composite inputs) with audio and video capabilities had been declining, they have enjoyed a resurgence over the last year. IBM, Apple, and many clone monitors are adding audio (both input and output). This can be useful in at least two cases—to take advantage of the new voice synthesis and voice digitization options now becoming available for PC systems, and to amplify the three-voice audio output of the PCjr. Most monitor audio amplifiers, even those with modest specifications (limited audio frequency bandwidth and output powers less than a watt), can handle either job adequately.

Only recently has music making become a passion among PC makers, and even the most favored systems still relegate audio to plug-in accessories. Although you can add accessories to transform the musical mission of your PC, you'll also want to add better quality audio circuitry than you'll get with any PC. A patch cord to connect the add-on accessories to your stereo system will do just fine.

Chapter 15
Audio

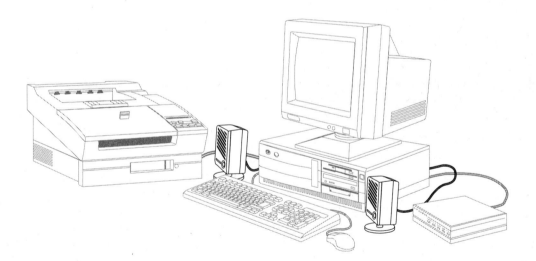

The noise-making spectrum of PCs ranges from the beeps and squeaks of the tiny internal speaker to an aural rush equal in quality to today's best stereo CDs. PCs can generate, manipulate, record, and play back sounds of all sorts and even control other noise-makers such as music synthesizers. Today's high-quality sound capability distinguishes multimedia PCs from ordinary, visual-bound systems.

Of the five senses, most people only experience personal computers with four: touch, smell, sound, and sight. Not that computers are tasteless—although a growing body of software doesn't even aspire that high—but most people don't normally drag their tongues across the cases of their computers. Touch is inherent in typing and pushing around a mouse or digitizer cursor. Smell is more limited still—what you appreciate in opening the box holding your new PC or what warns you when the fan in the power supply stops, internal temperatures rise, and roasting resistors and near inflammatory components begin to melt.

Most interactions with PCs involve sight: what you see on the monitor screen and, if you're not a touch typist, a peek down at the keyboard. High-resolution graphics make sight perhaps the most important part of any PC—or at least the most expensive.

To really experience your PC, however, you need an added sensual dimension—sound. In fact, sound distinguishes the ordinary PC from today's true multimedia machine. Most PCs are mainly limited to visual interaction. A multimedia PC extends the computer's capabilities of interacting with the world to include sound. It can generate sounds on its own, acting like a music synthesizer or noise generator, and it can control external devices that do the same thing through a MIDI interface. It can record or sample sounds on any standard computer medium (the hard disk being today's preferred choice) with sonic accuracy every bit as good (even better) than commercial stereo CDs. All the sounds it makes and stores can be edited and manipulated: tones can be stretched; voices shifted; noises combined; music mixed. It can play back all the sounds it makes and records with the same fidelity, pushing the limits of even the best stereo systems.

Unfortunately, the native endowment of most PCs is naught but a squeaker of a loudspeaker that makes soprano Mickey Mouse sound like the Mormon Tabernacle Choir in comparison. The designers of the first PCs simply thought sound unnecessary. After all, the noise that calculating machines made was to be avoided. All they thought important were warning signals, so that's all the PC got. Images fared little better: little did text screen hint at today's graphic potential of the PC.

The audible omission of the PC's designers can be corrected by adding a sound board. A basic requirement of a multimedia PC, the sound board gives your PC the capability to synthesize and capture a variety of sounds, play them back, and control external devices.

Physics of Sound

Sound is a physical phenomenon, best understood as the rapid change in air pressure. When a physical object moves, it forces air to move also. After all, air and the object cannot take up the same place at the same time. Air is pushed away from the place the object moves to and rushes into the empty place where the object was. Of course, the moving air has to come from somewhere. Ideally, the air pushed out of the way would retreat to the vacuum left behind when the object moved. Unfortunately the air, much like any physical entity, cannot instantly transport itself from one place to another. The speed at which the air moves depends on its density; the higher the pressure, the greater the force pushing the air around. Indeed, moving the object creates an area of high pressure in front of it—where the air wants to get out of the way—and low pressure behind. Air is dumb—or in today's politically correct language, knowledge challenged. The high pressure doesn't know that an exactly matching area of low pressure exists behind the object, so the high pressure pushes out in all directions. As it does, it spreads out and the pressure decreases.

Simply moving an object creates a puff of air. Sound arises when the object moves rapidly, vibrating. As it moves one way, it creates the high pressure puff that travels off. It moves back, and a corresponding low pressure pulse pops up and follows the high pressure. As the object vibrates, a steady train of these high-and-low pressure fronts moves steadily away from it.

The basic principles of sound should be obvious from this rudimentary picture. Sound requires a medium for transmission. The speed of sound depends not on the moving object but on the density of the air (or other medium). The higher the density, the faster the sound moves. The intensity of the sound pressure declines with distance as more and more air interacts with the compression-decompression cycles. Unconstrained, this decline would follow the infamous inverse-square law because as the sound travels in one dimension, it must spread over two. By confining or directing the air channel, however, you can alter the rate of this decay.

Human beings have a mechanism called the ear that detects pressure changes or sound waves. The ear is essentially a mechanical device that's tuned to react to pressure changes that occur over a range that's commonly listed as between 20 and 20,000 times per second. (Everyone's hearing is different, and the upper limit that an individual can perceive declines with age. Women tend to have wider hearing ranges than men.)

The job of the audio circuitry in your PC is to set the air in motion, making sounds that you can hear to alert you, to entertain you, and to amaze you.

Motherboard Circuitry

From the standpoint of a computer, sound is foreign stuff. Indeed, it's something that happens to stuff—air—while the computer deals with the non-stuff of logical thoughts. Video images are much more akin to computer electronics—at least the photons that you see are electromagnetic.

Sound is purely mechanical, and that makes the computer's job of dealing with it tough. To make sound audible, it somehow needs to do something mechanical. It needs a transducer, a device that transmits energy from one system to another—from the electrical PC to the kinetic world of sound.

Computers are not alone in their need to convert electrical signals into mechanical sound. Nearly every sound-producing home entertainment device (with the exception of ancient hand-cranked phonographs) has the same need, as do telephones, voice pagers, even amplified bullhorns. The technology has been around since Alexander Graham Bell first sent sound through wires in 1876. The most common audio transducer, the dynamic loudspeaker was invented in 1921 by Kellogg Rice. In the loudspeaker, a current drives a voice-coil (a solenoid or coil of wire that gives the speaker its voice) attached to a diaphragm or speaker cone that vibrates—pushing out then back in repeatedly—to move the air.

Every PC has a speaker of some kind in it. The most common kind is minimal: a tiny little object about 2.5 inches in diameter. Although that size is sufficient to make noise, it falls short on quality, range, and loudness. These shortcomings are again a matter of physics.

A number of factors influence what the output of a loudspeaker sounds like. Two of the most important are the size of the loudspeaker and how it is packaged.

The loudness of a sound depends on the volume of moving air; louder means more air in motion. To move more air, the diaphragm of the loudspeaker needs either to make larger excursions or be larger itself. Practical considerations like holding the loudspeaker together limit excursion length, so larger speakers are normally louder.

Physics also requires that more air move at lower frequencies to achieve the same pressure changes or loudness, so larger speakers do a better job generating low frequency sounds. But the packaging of the speaker also influences its low frequency reproduction. At low frequencies, the pressure waves created by a loudspeaker can travel a substantial distance in the time it takes the speaker cone to move in and out. In fact, when frequencies are low enough, the air has time to travel from the high pressure area in front of the speaker to the low pressure area behind an outward-moving speaker cone. The moving air cancels out the air pressure changes and the sound. At low frequencies—typically those below about 150 Hz—a loudspeaker in free air has little sound output.

This low-frequency cancellation can be reduced or eliminated by blocking the air flow from the front to the back of the speaker. Putting the loudspeaker in an enclosure or speaker baffle accomplishes exactly that. Although speaker baffles have their own problems—they absorb sound energy and have resonances that alter the quality of the loudspeaker's sound—in general they improve sound quality.

The internal loudspeakers in PCs are not baffled, so they have two strikes against them when it comes to accurate sound generation at low frequencies. (Although the speaker in a PC is enclosed in the case of the PC, the speaker is actually suspended in free air inside the case.) To get realistic sound reproduction, a PC consequently requires an external baffled loudspeaker—preferably two for modern stereophonic sound.

All it takes is a current to drive the loudspeaker to make sound. Unfortunately, engineers try to design normal computer circuits to minimize the use of current. After all, the greater the current, the greater the heat and power consumption. Many PCs added a special line-driver integrated circuit to provide enough power to run the internal loudspeaker, although some modern systems incorporate this circuitry into the basic motherboard chipset.

Because baffled loudspeakers are less efficient than free-air loudspeakers (in general, they trade-off efficiency to achieve the capability to reproduce a wider range of frequencies), the barely sufficient power of a PC's internal speaker driver is woefully inadequate for external baffled loudspeakers. To achieve the necessary power for external speakers, the level of the audio signal inside the PC must be increased by an amplifier. Add-in sound boards typically include modest amplifiers for powering external loudspeakers.

The standard PC design also adds a low-pass filter and a current limiting resistor between the driver and the loudspeaker. The low-pass filter eliminates frequencies higher-than-normal hearing range (and some in the upper ranges that you probably can readily hear). PCs often use higher frequencies to make audible sounds, and the low pass filter prevents these artifacts from leaking into the speaker.

A resistor (typically about 33 ohms) in series with the loudspeaker prevents the internal loudspeaker of a PC from drawing too much current and overloading the driver circuit. A resistor also lowers the loudness of the speaker because it absorbs some power as part of the current-limiting process. Although some circuit-tinkerers bypass this resistor to make their PCs louder, doing so risks damage to the driver circuit.

The quality of the standard PC sound system is marginal at best not just because of the tiny, unbaffled loudspeaker. In fact, the abysmal loudspeaker in most PCs is well matched to the rudimentary sound-generation capabilities designed into the basic circuitry of the PC. The original PC's design made no attempt to generate appealing sounds. Instead of having some dedicated sound synthesizing circuitry, the PC's designers relied on the oscillators already available in the digital logic of the motherboard.

In a PC, the digital computer signal is routed directly through the driver to the loudspeaker. Specifically, the driver is directly connected to one of the channels of the 8253 or 8254-2 timer/counter integrated circuit chip (or its equivalent integrated into the system's chipset). The timebase set for the oscillator determines the frequency of the speaker's output. In addition, the input to the driver combines two other signals to add a degree of richness to its output.

This digital signal limits the dynamics of the signal. Sounds are normally distinguished by their loudness. The digital signal delivered to the PC's loudspeaker is at a constant level—the standard digital signal level—so the sound level produced by the speaker does not vary. All the sounds produced by the PC's motherboard have the same level. Some noises generated by the PC sound louder than others primarily because they are more obnoxious. They are made from the exact combination of frequencies to nag at the aesthetic parts of your brain. That's about all they were designed to do. Listen long enough and you'll agree that the PC's designers succeeded beyond their wildest dreams at creating obnoxious sound.

Sound Boards

The only way to get better sound from a PC is to add a completely new sound system, one designed from the ground up to create sound that's pleasing rather than irritating. The necessary addition to your PC is the sound board—a circuit board with the required audio circuitry—that plugs into your PC's expansion slots.

To cope with the needs of multimedia software and the demands of human hearing and expectation, sound boards carry out several audio-related functions. They convert stored sounds from digital to analog form so that you can hear them; record sounds for later playback; create sounds of their own with built-in synthesizers; mix the results together; and amplify the final audio product so that you can actually hear it.

The important differences between sound boards are twofold: the quality of what they deliver to your speakers and the compatibility with your software. Of the two, the latter is most important because if your software can't coax a whimper from your sound board, you won't hear anything no matter how well the circuitry on the board might be able to do its job. After you have the basic compatibility that your software needs, however, your ears will prefer the board with the better quality. A bad sound board shrieks and crackles worse than a radio in a thunderstorm; a good one can rival the best audiophile stereo system.

Sound boards have three primary jobs: creating sounds from instructions sent to them by your programs; playing back sounds created by some other source; and controlling other sound-making devices. Creating sounds is called synthesis, and when done well it's as far from the simple oscillator of a PC as a metal toy drum is from a symphony orchestra. The sounds played back range from the contents of ordinary audio CDs to reproducing those sounds that you've captured onto your hard disk, perhaps sampled by the sound board itself. Control of other sound-making devices requires a special electrical connection. In multimedia systems, sound boards take control through the Musical Instrument Device Interface or MIDI. Through a more conventional interface, your sound-control software also can control the operation of a CD-ROM player. The CD-ROM interface is often part of a sound board, although it need not be.

Synthesis

Making a sound electronically is easy. After all, any AC signal with a frequency in the range of human hearing makes a noise when connected to a loudspeaker. Even before the age of electronics, Hermann Helmholtz discovered that any musical tone is made from vibrations in the air that correspond to a periodic (but complex) waveform. Making an electronic signal sound like something recognizable is not so simple, however. You need exactly the right waveform.

The basic frequency-generating circuit, the oscillator, produces a very pure tone, so pure that it sounds completely unrealistic—electronic. Natural sounds are not a single frequency but collections of many, related and unrelated, at different strengths.

A tone from a musical instrument, for example, comprises a single characteristic frequency (corresponding to the note played) called the fundamental and a collection of other frequencies, each a multiple of the fundamental, called overtones by scientists or partials by musicians. The relationship of the loudness of the overtones to one another gives the sound of the instrument its distinctive identity, its timbre, and makes a note played on a violin sound different from the same note played on a flute. Timbre is a product of the many resonances of the musical instrument, which tend to reinforce some overtones and diminish others.

Noises differ from musical tones because they comprise many, unrelated frequencies. White noise, for example, is a random collection of all frequencies.

The one happy result of all sounds being combinations of frequencies (a principle discovered in relation to periodic waves by Jean Baptiste Joseph Fourier in the late 18th century) is that creating any sound requires only putting together frequencies in the right combination. So synthesizing sounds should be easy—all you need to know is the right combination. At that, synthesis becomes a little daunting. Trial-and-error experimentation at finding the right combinations is daunting at best because the number of frequencies and the possible strengths of each frequency are both infinite, so you end up dealing with numbers that strain most pocket calculators—like infinity times infinity. Add in the fact that natural sounds vary from one instant to the next, meaning that each instant represents a different frequency combination giving you yet another infinity to deal with, and sound synthesis suddenly seems to slip to the far side of impossible.

In truth, the numbers are much more manageable than the dire situation outlined in the preceding paragraph. For example, musical sounds involve only a few frequencies—the fundamental and overtones within the range of human hearing (both in frequency range and strength). But synthesizing sounds from scratch remains a challenge.

Electronic designers have devised several strategies that synthesize sound with varying degrees of success. Two techniques are popular in today's synthesizers, Frequency Modulation and Wave Table Synthesis.

Compatibility is most important when you call upon a sound board to create sounds from program instructions. If a given sound board is not completely compatible with your software, it cannot produce the sounds that the programmer originally intended.

Subtractive Synthesis

The first true music synthesizers (as opposed to electronic instruments, which seek to replicate rather than synthesize sounds) used analog technology. The first of these machines were created in the late 1950s and were based on the principle of subtractive synthesis. These early synthesizers generated tones with special oscillators called waveform generators that made tones already rich in harmonics. Instead of the pure tones of sine waves, they generated square waves, sawtooth waves, and odd intermediary shapes. In itself, each of these oscillators generated a complex wave rich in harmonics that had its own distinctive sound. These initial waveforms were then mixed together and shaped using filters that emphasized some ranges of frequencies and attenuated others. Sometimes one tone was used to modulate another to create waveforms so strange they sounded like they originated in foreign universes.

Analog synthesis was born in an age of experimentation when the farthest reaches of new music was being explored. Analog synthesizers made no attempt to sound like conventional instruments—after all, conventional instruments could already do that and the outposts of the avant garde had traipsed far beyond the fringes of conventional music. The goal of analog synthesis was to create new sounds—sounds not found in nature; sounds never before heard; sounds like the digestive system of some giant dyspeptic dinosaur. Analog synthesizers sounded unmistakably electronic.

As the depths of new music were being plumbed, digital technology appeared as an alternative to analog designs. The first digital synthesizers sought merely to duplicate the function of the analog units using an alternate technology that provided greater control. In fact, digital synthesis provided so much control over sounds that it became possible not just to create new sounds, but also to create (or at least approximate) any sound. The goal of synthesis also shifted to mimicking conventional instruments—that is, expensive, hand-crafted instruments—with cheap, sound-nearly-alike digital substitutes. With one mass-produced electronic box—the digital synthesizer—a musician could put an entire orchestra at his fingertips.

Additive Synthesis

Recreating the sounds of actual instruments required entirely different technologies than had been used in new-sound synthesizers. The opposite of a subtractive synthesizer is an additive synthesizer. Instead of starting with complex waves and filtering away the unwanted parts, the additive synthesizer builds sounds in the most logical way—by adding together all the frequencies that make up a musical sound. Whereas this chore was difficult if not impossible with analog circuitry, the precision of digital electronics made true additive synthesis a reality. The digital additive synthesizer mathematically created the pattern that mixing tones would create. The resulting digital signal would then be converted into an analog signal (using a digital-to-analog converter) that would drive a loudspeaker or recording system.

The additive synthesizer faced one large problem in trying to create life-like sounds: the mix of frequencies for each note of an instrument is different. In fact, the mix of frequencies changes from the initial attack when a note begins (for instance, when a string is struck by a piano hammer) to its final decay. To produce sounds approaching reality, the synthesizer required a complete description of every note it would create at various times in its generation. As a result, a true additive-type digital synthesizer is a complex—and expensive—device.

Practical sound synthesis for PC peripherals is based on much more modest technologies than purely additive synthesis. Two primary alternatives have become commercially popular in the synthesizers incorporated into PC sound boards. These are FM synthesis and wave table synthesis.

FM Synthesis

While working at Stanford Artificial Intelligence Laboratories in 1973, John M. Chowning made an interesting discovery. Two pure sine wave tones could be combined together to make interesting sounds using frequency modulation. Although the principle corresponded to no natural phenomenon, it could be used to create sounds with close-to-natural attacks and decays.

The resulting FM synthesis works by starting with one frequency or tone called a carrier and altering it with a second frequency called a modulator. When the modulator is a low frequency of a few Hertz, the carrier frequency rises and falls much like a siren. When the carrier and modulator are close in frequency, however, the result is a complex wave. Varying the strength of the modulator changes the mix of frequencies in the resulting waveform, altering its timbre. (Changing the strength of the carrier merely makes the sound louder or softer.) By changing the relationship between the carrier and modulator, the timbre changes in a natural-sounding way.

A basic FM synthesis system needs only two oscillators producing sine waves to work. However, a synthesizer with a wider combination of carriers and modulators can create an even more complex variety of waveforms and sounds. Each of the sine waves produced by an FM synthesizer is called an operator. Popular synthesizers have four to six operators.

The greatest strength of FM synthesis is that it is inexpensive to implement; all it takes is a chip. On the other hand, FM synthesis cannot quite duplicate real world sounds. The sounds created through FM synthesis are recognizable—both as what they are supposed to represent and as synthesized sounds.

Wave Table Synthesis

An alternate technique used for creating sounds is wave table synthesis. Also known as sampling, wave table synthesis starts not with pure tones but with representative waveforms for particular sounds. The representations are in the form of the sound's exact waveform, and all the waveforms that a product can produce are stored in an electronic table, hence the name of the technology. The waveforms for a given instrument or sound are only templates that the synthesizer manipulates to produce music or what is supposed to pass as music. For example, the wave table may include a brief burst of the tone of a flute playing one particular note. The synthesizer can then alter the frequency of that note to play an entire scale and alter its duration to generate the proper rhythm.

Although wave table synthesis produces more life-like sounds than FM synthesis, they are not entirely realistic because it does not replicate the complete transformation of musical sounds from attack to decay nor the subtle variation of timbre with the pitch produced by a synthesized instrument. Some wave table synthesizers have specific patterns for the attack, sustain, and decay of notes, but mathematically derive the transitions between them. These come closer to reality, but still fall short of perfection. In general, wave table synthesized notes all have the same frequency mix and consequently have a subtle but unreal sameness to them.

Standards

Technologies like FM and wave table synthesis don't do anything until they are put to work in an implementation. They require an architecture and method of control to work. In other words, you need to build a synthesizer around the technology.

If you want to put the synthesizer under the control of your PC, it needs to link to your hardware and software. If the synthesizer is to be used by a variety of applications, it must follow a recognized control standard. Among sound board synthesizers, two widely popular standards are Ad Lib and Sound Blaster.

In fact, the standards define the product of the synthesis rather than the type of synthesis—that is, the noises created and how they are controlled.

Ad Lib. One of the first sound boards to gain popularity was made by a company no longer in the sound-board business called Ad Lib. Because it had the widest user base early when noisy games were becoming popular, many game programmers wrote their products to take advantage of the specific hardware features of the Ad Lib board. The capability to mimic the Ad Lib hardware became the minimal standard for sound creation compatibility.

Sound Blaster. Another company, Creative Labs, entered the sound board business and built upon the Ad Lib base. Its Sound Blaster product quickly gained industry acceptance as a superset of the Ad Lib standard; it did everything the Ad Lib board did and more. The Sound Blaster found a huge market and raised the standard for sound synthesis among game products. Because programmers directly manipulated the hardware registers of the sound Blaster to make the sounds they wanted, to run most games and produce the proper sounds you need a sound board that is hardware compatible with the Sound Blaster. Several iterations of Sound Blaster hardware were produced; the minimal level of compatibility to expect today is with Sound Blaster version 1.5.

The Sound Blaster relies on a particular integrated circuit to produce its array of synthesized sounds, the Yamaha YM3812. This chip has a single output channel, so it can produce only monophonic sound even when it is installed on a sound board that's otherwise called stereo. Some sound boards use two of these chips to produce stereo. The YM3812 has a fixed repertoire of eleven voices, six of which are instrumental and five for rhythm.

A newer FM synthesis chip has become popular on better sound boards, the Yamaha YMF262 or OPL3. Not only does the OPL3 have more voices (20), but it also uses more sophisticated algorithms for synthesis. It also can produce a full stereo output.

Digitization and Sampling

Reality cannot yet be synthesized. Even the best synthesis systems only approach the sound of real-world musical instruments and not-so-musical noises. The best—or most real—sound quality produced by a sound board is thus not synthesized but recorded. As with Compact Discs, sound boards use the high-tech, high-quality, high-fidelity, digital sound recording system.

Digital recording of sound turns music into numbers. That is, a sound board examines audio waveforms thousands of times every second and assigns a numerical value to the strength of the sound every time it looks; it then records the numbers. To reproduce the music or noise, the sound board works backward. It takes the recorded numbers and regenerates the corresponding signal strength at intervals exactly corresponding to those at which it examined the original signal. The result is a near-exact duplication of the original audio.

The digital recording process involves several arbitrary variables. The two most important are the rate at which the original audio signal is examined—called the sampling rate—and the numeric code assigned to each value sampled. The code is digital and is defined as a given number of bits, the resolution of the system. The quality of sound reproduction is determined primarily by the values chosen for these variables.

The sampling rate limits the frequency response of a digital recording system. The highest frequency that can be recorded and reproduced digitally is half the sampling frequency. This top frequency is often called the Nyquist frequency. Higher frequencies become ambiguous and can be confused with lower frequency values producing distortion. To prevent problems, frequencies higher than half the sampling frequency must be eliminated—filtered out—before they are digitally sampled. Because no audio filter is perfect, most digital audio systems have cut-off frequencies somewhat lower than the Nyquist frequency. The Compact Disc digital audio system is designed to record sounds with frequencies up to about 15KHz, and it uses a sampling rate of about 44KHz.

The number of bits in a digital code determines the number of discrete values it can record. For example, an eight-bit digital code can represent 256 distinct objects, be they numbers or sound levels. A recording system that uses an eight-bit code can thus record 256 distinct values or steps in sound levels. Unfortunately, music and sounds vary smoothly rather than in discrete steps. The difference between the digital steps and the smooth audio value is distortion. This distortion also adds to the noise in the sound recording system. Minimizing distortion and noise means using more steps. High-quality sound systems—that is, CD-quality sound—require a minimum of a 16-bit code.

Sampling rate and resolution determine the amount of data produced during the digitization process, which in turn determines the amount that must be recorded. In addition, full stereo recording doubles the data needed because two separate information channels are required. The 44.1KHz sampling frequency and 16-bit digital code of stereo CD audio result in the need to process and record about 150,000 bits of data every second, about nine megabytes per minute.

For full CD compatibility, most newer sound boards have the capability to digitize at the CD level. To save disk space and processing time, however, most give you the option of using less resource-intensive values. Moreover, many older sound boards were not powerful enough for full CD-quality. Consequently, you will find sound boards that support intermediary sampling frequencies and bit densities. Many older sound boards also limit themselves to monophonic operation. The MPC specification only requires eight-bit digitization support. Most sound boards support 22 and 11 KHz sampling; some offer other intermediate values such as 8, 16, or 32KHz.

If you are making original recordings of sounds and music, you will want to use as high a rate as is consistent with your PC's resources. If you want to play back sounds recorded on another PC (or pre-recorded), choose a sound board that supports the original recording format. Don't expect to get the quality of a recording studio from a sound board even though it may boast full CD-level digitization. In operation, the electronic noise rattling around inside your PC leaks into the sound board and its signals, degrading your recordings with an electronic background cacophony.

The digital signal processing circuitry inside most CD players is typically more sophisticated than that on sound boards. You get better sound quality out of your stereo system than from a sound board. In fact, most sound boards have analog inputs that enable you to send the audio output of a CD-ROM player converted from digital to analog form through your PC sound system. Most sound boards enable you to digitize or sample this signal, record it in digital form or mix it with other sounds, and reproduce it through the speakers connected to your PC. Because the signals sent along to your sound board in analog form require no further digital processing, playing them puts no load on your PC.

Control

Another way you and your PC can make beautiful music is by controlling external electronic musical instruments. Instead of generating sounds itself, your PC becomes a sequencer, a solid-state surrogate conductor capable of leading a big band or orchestra of electronic instruments in the cacophony of your own creation. A sequencer is nothing more than a memory and messaging system with editing capabilities. The memory required by the sequencer is supplied by your PC's hard disk. The editing is the software for your music making.

MIDI

The principle messaging system used for electronic instruments is the MIDI interface. MIDI is the standard connection for plugging electronic instruments and accessories together. In essence, MIDI is both hardware (a special kind of serial port) and software (a protocol for transferring commands through the port). Amazingly, it's one of the few sound board standards actually standardized enough to work with just about everything that says MIDI-compatible. MIDI enables synthesizers, sequencers, home computers, rhythm machines, and so on to be interconnected through a standard interface.

Although MIDI is used for linking electronic music-making instruments, the MIDI connection itself carries no music. The MIDI wire is only for control signals. Like a remote control for your television, it turns things on and off but doesn't carry the sound (or picture) at all.

Hardware

The MIDI interface hardware itself is electronically and logically simple. It's just another kind of serial port designed to provide a moderate-speed port to pass commands to musical interfaces. Each device connected has both transmitting and receiving circuits, although some may have only one or the other. A MIDI transmitter packages signals into the standard MIDI format and sends them on their way. A MIDI receiver listens for commands on the MIDI bus and executes those meant for it.

Every MIDI port has at its heart a UART chip that converts parallel computer data into serial form. MIDI transmitters link to the MIDI bus using a line driver, which increases the strength of the UART signal so that it can drive a five milliamp current loop. The driver also buffers the UART from problems with the connection. The transmitter signal is designed to power exactly one MIDI receiver.

Each MIDI receiver links to the bus through an optoisolator, a device that uses an incoming electrical signal to power a light-emitting diode (LED). A photocell senses changes in brightness in the LED and creates a corresponding electrical signal. The intermediary light (optical) beam isolates the incoming electrical signal from those inside the MIDI device, preventing all sorts of nasties like electrical shocks (which can harm you) and ground loops (which can harm the integrity of the MIDI signal).

The physical embodiment of a MIDI transmitter is the Out connector on a MIDI device. The In connector links to a MIDI receiver. A Thru connector, when present, is a second MIDI transmitter directly connected to the receiver using the In connector.

The MIDI connectors themselves are standard full-size five-pin DIN jacks (such as Switchcraft 57 GB5F). Only three connections are used: pin 2 is ground; pin 4 is the positive-going side of the differential signal; pin 5 is the negative-going side. Pins 1 and 3 are not used and are unconnected. Unlike with serial ports, there's no need to cross over conductors in going from one MIDI port to another; all three connections are the same at both ends of the cable.

MIDI cables have matching male 5-pin DIN plugs on either end. They use shielded twisted-pair wire and can be up to 50 feet long (15 meters). The shield of the cable connects to pin 2 at both ends of the cable.

The UARTs in the MIDI system provide an asynchronous serial connection that operates at a fixed speed of 31,250 bits per second. Because every byte transferred is framed with a start bit and stop bit, it allows information to be exchanged at 3,125 bytes per second. Each data frame measures 320 microseconds long. The actual MIDI electrical signals are inverted; that is, a logical 0 on the MIDI bus is indicated by switching the current on.

MIDI interfaces mate with your PC exactly as do any other ports. They communicate with your system by exchanging bytes through an input/output port. Most MIDI port adapters prefer to use the input/output port address of 330(Hex), because much MIDI software expects to find MIDI there and often refuses to recognize MIDI at other locations. Alternatively, many sound boards use 220(Hex), which often is the better choice because many SCSI host adapters also prefer the 330(Hex) base address for communications. In any case, make sure that your MIDI software is aware of the port address you choose for your MIDI adapter.

The wiring of even the most complex MIDI system can be as easy as stringing Christmas tree lights or plugging in stereo components. All MIDI devices are daisy-chained together. That is, you connect the MIDI Out of one device to MIDI In on the next. Signals then travel from the first transmitter through all the devices down to the last receiver. Ordinarily, the first transmitter is your keyboard or sequencer; the rest of the devices in the chain are synthesizers or electronic instruments.

Thru connectors make your MIDI project more thought-provoking. Because the signals at the Thru connector on a device duplicate those at the In connector rather than the Out connector, the information the device sends out does not appear on the Thru connector. Ordinarily, this situation presents no problems because most downstream MIDI devices are musical instruments that act only as receivers. If you have a keyboard connected to a sequencer, however, any device plugged into the sequencer's Thru connector listens to and hears the keyboard, not the sequencer. To hear both, you need to use the sequencer's Out connector.

Protocol

The most complex part of the MIDI system is its communications protocol, the signals sent over the wiring. MIDI devices communicate with one another through the MIDI connection by sending messages, which are nothing more than sequences of bytes. Each message begins with a status byte that identifies the type of message being sent; for example, to switch on or off a musical note. The status byte is usually followed by Data Bytes in groups of one or two (depending on the command), which hold the information about what to do; for example, which note to switch on. Status Bytes are unambiguously identified by always having their most significant bit as a logical one. Data Bytes always have zero as their most significant bit.

Each MIDI system has 16 channels that can be individually addressed. The sounds generated by the synthesizers or instruments in the MIDI system are called voices. What a voice sounds like depends on the synthesizer generating it. A voice controls a program on the synthesizer, and the program is a property of the synthesizer. The same MIDI messages may elicit different sounds from different synthesizers. Because you may expect some consistency between synthesizers, electronic instrument makers defined 128 programs, assigning a numeric value and descriptive name to each. The result is called General MIDI. Table 15.1 summarizes the assignments of the General MIDI standard.

TABLE 15.1. General MIDI Instrument Program Map

Prog# (1-8)	Instrument Piano	Prog# (9-16)	Instrument Chrom Percussion
1	Acoustic Grand	9	Celesta
2	Bright Acoustic	10	Glockenspiel
3	Electric Grand	11	Music Box
4	Honky-Tonk	12	Vibraphone
5	Electric Piano 1	13	Marimba
6	Electric Piano 2	14	Xylophone
7	Harpsichord	15	Tubular Bells
8	Clav	16	Dulcimer
(17-24)	*Organ*	*(25-32)*	*Guitar*
17	Drawbar Organ	25	Acoustic Guitar (nylon)
18	Percussive Organ	26	Acoustic Guitar (steel)
19	Rock Organ	27	Electric Guitar (jazz)
20	Church Organ	28	Electric Guitar (clean)
21	Reed Organ	29	Electric Guitar (muted)
22	Accordian	30	Overdriven Guitar
23	Harmonica	31	Distortion Guitar
24	Tango Accordian	32	Guitar Harmonics

continues

TABLE 15.1. Continued

(33-40)	Bass	(41-48)	Strings
33	Acoustic Bass	41	Violin
34	Electric Bass (finger)	42	Viola
35	Electric Bass (pick)	43	Cello
36	Fretless Bass	44	Contrabass
37	Slap Bass 1	45	Tremolo Strings
38	Slap Bass 2	46	Pizzicato Strings
39	Synth Bass 1	47	Orchestral Strings
40	Synth Bass 2	48	Timpani
(49-56)	Ensemble	(57-64)	Brass
49	String Ensemble 1	57	Trumpet
50	String Ensemble 2	58	Trombone
51	SynthStrings 1	59	Tuba
52	SynthStrings 2	60	Muted Trumpet
53	Choir Aahs	61	French Horn
54	Voice Oohs	62	Brass Section
55	Synth Voice	63	SynthBrass 1
56	Orchestra Hit	64	SynthBrass 2
(65-72)	Reed	(73-80)	Pipe
65	Soprano Sax	73	Piccolo
66	Alto Sax	74	Flute
67	Tenor Sax	75	Recorder
68	Baritone Sax	76	Pan Flute
69	Oboe	77	Blown Bottle
70	English Horn	78	Skakuhachi
71	Bassoon	79	Whistle
72	Clarinet	80	Ocarina
(81-88)	Synth Lead	(89-96)	Synth Pad
81	Lead 1 (square)	89	Pad 1 (new age)
82	Lead 2 (sawtooth)	90	Pad 2 (warm)

(81-88)	*Synth Lead*	(89-96)	*Synth Pad*
83	Lead 3 (calliope)	91	Pad 3 (polysynth)
84	Lead 4 (chiff)	92	Pad 4 (choir)
85	Lead 5 (charang)	93	Pad 5 (bowed)
86	Lead 6 (voice)	94	Pad 6 (metallic)
87	Lead 7 (fifths)	95	Pad 7 (halo)
88	Lead 8 (bass+lead)	96	Pad 8 (sweep)

(97-104)	*Synth Effects*	(105-112)	*Ethnic*
97	FX 1 (rain)	105	Sitar
98	FX 2 (soundtrack)	106	Banjo
99	FX 3 (crystal)	107	Shamisen
100	FX 4 (atmosphere)	108	Koto
101	FX 5 (brightness)	109	Kalimba
102	FX 6 (goblins)	110	Bagpipe
103	FX 7 (echoes)	111	Fiddle
104	FX 8 (sci-fi)	112	Shanai

(113-120)	*Percussive*	(121-128)	*Sound Effects*
113	Tinkle Bell	121	Guitar Fret Noise
114	Agogo	122	Breath Noise
115	Steel Drums	123	Seashore
116	Woodblock	124	Bird Tweet
117	Taiko Drum	125	Telephone Ring
118	Melodic Ton	126	Helicopter
119	Synth Drum	127	Applause
120	Reverse Cymbal	128	Gunshot

To be controlled, voices (and thus the assigned programs) are assigned to channels, although the correspondence need not be one-to-one. For example, all voices can share one channel or one voice can be controlled by all channels. Which voice responds to which channel is controlled by sending messages through the system to set up each receiver.

The least significant nibble (that is, the last four bits) of the status byte of the message defines the channel to which it is addressed. The most significant nibble (the first four bits) of the status byte defines the function controlled by the channel message. The various channel messages are defined in Table 15.2.

TABLE 15.2. MIDI Channel Mode Messages

Status	Data	Data	Function
BX	00	7A	Local control off
BX	7F	7A	Local control on
BX	00	7B	All notes off
BX	00	7C	Omni Mode off
BX	00	7D	Omni Mode on
BX	00	7E	*Mono Mode on; Poly Mode off
BX	00	7F	Poly Mode on; Mono Mode off

*The Mono Mode on command requires a mandatory third data byte which specifies the number of channels in which voice messages are to be sent in the range 1 to 16. The receiver assigns channels to voices starting with the Basic Channel sequentially up through the number given in this third byte. However, if the third data byte is zero, the receiver will assign all of its voices, one per channel, from the Basic Channel through 16.

A MIDI system divides its channels into two types, Voice Channels and Basic Channels. A Voice Channel controls an individual voice. A Basic Channel sets up the mode of each MIDI receiver for receiving voice and control messages. Typically, a MIDI receiver is assigned one Basic Channel as a default; later the device can be reconfigured. For example, an eight-voice synthesizer could be reconfigured to respond as two four-voice synthesizers, each with its own Basic Channel. The MIDI sequencer or keyboard could then send separate messages to each four-voice synthesizer as if it were a physically separate instrument.

Messages sent to individual channels in the MIDI system are termed channel messages. Messages sent through the voice channel are termed voice messages because they control a voice; those sent through the basic channel are mode messages because they control the mode of the device listening to the channel. Mode messages determine how a device responds to voice messages. Although voice messages may also be sent through the basic channel, mode messages can use only the basic channel.

MIDI allows four modes to govern how the receiver routes the channel messages to individual voices. These modes are distinguished by three characteristics that act as flags: Omni, Mono, and Poly.

Omni controls whether the channels are treated individually or as a single-minded group. When Omni is on, the channels are grouped together. In effect, the messages come in from all directions—control is omnidirectional. The MIDI voices respond as if all the control signals get funneled together. When Omni is off, voices listen solely to the one channel to which they are assigned. Each channel and voice is individually linked, separate from the others.

Mono is short for monophonic. If Omni is on, Mono combines together all channel messages and sends them to a single designated voice. When Omni is off, Mono allows the assigning of channels to individual voices. That is, each voice has individual control through a separate channel.

Poly is short for polyphonic and routes the messages on one channel to all the voices in the MIDI receiver. When Omni and Poly are on, all messages combine together and go to all voices. When Omni is off but Poly is on, one channel controls all voices. In other words, when Poly is on, all voices play the same notes. Note that Poly and Mono are mutually exclusive. When Poly is on, Mono is off. Table 15.3 summarizes MIDI receiver modes.

TABLE 15.3. MIDI Receiver Modes

Mode number	*Omni status*	*Poly/Mono*	*Function*
1	On	Poly	Voice messages received from all Voice channels assigned to voices polyphonically.
2	On	Mono	Voice messages received from all Voice Channels control only one voice, monophonically.
3	Off	Poly	Voice messages received in Voice channel N are assigned only to voices polyphonically.
4	Off	Mono	Voice messages received in Voice channels N thru N+M-1 are assigned monophonically to voices 1 thru M, respectively. The number of voices M is specified by the third byte of the Mono Mode Message.

When Poly is on, MIDI transmitters send all voices through a designated channel. When Poly is off, Omni determines whether one or multiple voices are controlled. When on, voice messages for one voice are sent through the designed channel. When Omni is off, a number of channels carry voice messages for a like number of individually controlled voices. Table 15.4 summarizes MIDI transmitter modes.

TABLE 15.4. MIDI Transmitter Modes

Mode number	*Omni status*	*Poly/Mono*	*Function*
1	On	Poly	All voice messages transmitted in Channel N.
2	On	Mono	Voice messages for one voice sent in Channel N.

continues

TABLE 15.4. Continued

Mode number	Omni status	Poly/Mono	Function
3	Off	Poly	Voice messages for all voices sent in Channel N.
4	Off	Mono	Voice messages for voices 1 thru M transmitted in Voice Channels N thru N+M-1, respectively. (Single voice per channel.)

MIDI devices, whether receivers or transmitters, can operate only under one mode at a time. In most cases, both the transmitter and receiver operate in the same mode. If a receiver cannot operate in a mode that a transmitter requests from it, however, it may switch to an alternate mode (in most cases, this will be Omni on, Poly on); or it ignores the mode message. When powered up, all MIDI instruments default the Omni on, Poly on mode.

Mode messages affect only voice channels and not the definition of the basic channel. Consequently, a receiver recognizes only those mode messages sent over its assigned Basic Channel even if it is in a mode with Omni on. A mode command (with the exception of those turning local control on or off) automatically turns all notes off.

Besides voice and mode messages, each receiver in the MIDI system listens to system messages. Because these are universal messages, the status byte of each one does not define an individual channel. Three types of system messages are defined: common messages are meant to be heard by all receivers in the MIDI system; exclusive messages are sent to all receivers but are keyed by a manufacturer's code so that only devices keyed to that code respond; and real-time messages are used to synchronize the various devices in the MIDI system.

Exclusive and real-time messages are exceptions to the rule that all messages have a status byte followed by multiples of one or two data bytes. The status byte of an exclusive message can be followed by any number of data bytes. Its length is defined by a special End of Exclusive Flag Byte—that is a value of 0F8(hex) or 11110111(binary)—or any other status byte. A real-time message consists only of a status byte. Manufacturers of MIDI equipment assign an ID code through which an exclusive message accesses the equipment. The MIDI standard requests that manufacturers publish the ID codes they use so that programmers can address and control it with exclusive messages. The manufacturer also controls the format of the Data Bytes that follow their ID.

Real-time messages can be (and often are) sent at any time, even during other messages. The action called for by a real-time message is immediately executed; then normal function of the system continues. For example, the entire MIDI system is synchronized with the real-time clock message (0F8(hex)/byte value) sent from the transmitter at a rate of 24 clocks to the quarter note (a crotchet). Some MIDI transmitters periodically send out Active Sensing messages—byte value 0FE(Hex)—to indicate that the transmitter is still connected to the system and operating.

The Song Position Pointer tracks the number of MIDI beats that have elapsed since the beginning of a song. One MIDI beat equals six MIDI clocks, one-quarter of a quarter note—a semiquaver. To move to any position in a song (with a resolution of one beat), a Song Position Pointer status byte can be sent followed by two data bytes indicating the pointer value.

MIDI works by simply sending out strings of bytes. Each device recognizes the beginning of a command by detecting a status byte with its most significant bit set high. With voice and mode messages, the status byte simply alerts the MIDI receiver to the nature of the data bytes that follow. Each device knows how many data bytes are assigned to each command controlled by a status byte, and waits until it has received all the data in a complete command before acting on the command. If the complete command is followed by more data bytes, it interprets the information as the beginning of another command. It awaits the correct number of data bytes to complete this next command and then carries it out. This feature—one status byte serving as the preamble for multiple commands—is called Running Status in the MIDI scheme of things. Running Status ends as soon as another status byte is received, with one exception. If the interrupting message is a real-time message, the Running Status resumes after the real-time message is complete. If a subsequent status byte interrupts a message before it is complete (for example, between the first and second data bytes of a message requiring two data bytes), the interrupted message is ignored. The MIDI device won't do anything until it receives a full and complete message (which may be the interrupting message).

Badly formatted or erroneous MIDI commands are generally ignored. If a given MIDI receiver does not have a feature that a command asks for, it ignores the status and data bytes of that command. If a MIDI transmitter inadvertently sends out a status byte not defined by the MIDI specification, the status byte and all following data bytes are ignored until a valid status byte is sent.

Because of the MIDI coding system's nature, data bytes can have a value only from 0 to 127. Higher values would require the most significant bit of the data byte to be set high, which would cause MIDI devices to recognize it as a status byte. Most MIDI values consequently fall in the range of 0 to 127. For example, MIDI recognizes 128 intensities and 128 musical notes.

MIDI encodes musical notes as discrete numeric values in steps generally corresponding to the twelve-tone scale used in most Western music, but it need not. For example, electronic percussion instruments may recognize note values for different non-chromatic drum sounds. In the MIDI scheme of things, middle C is assigned a value of 60. Each semitone lower is one number lower; each semitone higher is one number higher. The MIDI coding scheme thus covers a range 40 notes wider than the 88 keys of most pianos, 21 notes below and 19 above. Table 15.5 lists MIDI values and the corresponding chromatic notes.

TABLE 15.5. MIDI Note Values

MIDI Value	Note	Frequency (Hz)	MIDI Value	Note	Frequency (Hz)
1	C#/D-flat	17.32	31	G	98.00
2	D	18.35	32	G#/A-flat	103.83
3	D#/E-flat	19.45	33	A	110.00
4	E	20.60	34	A#/B-flat	116.54
5	F	21.83	35	B	123.47
6	F#/G-flat	23.12	36	C	130.81
7	G	24.50	37	C#/D-flat	138.59
8	G#/A-flat	25.96	38	D	146.83
9	A	27.50	39	D#/E-flat	155.56
10	A#/B-flat	29.14	40	E	164.81
11	B	30.87	41	F	174.61
12	C	32.70	42	F#/G-flat	185.00
13	C#/D-flat	34.65	43	G	196.00
14	D	36.71	44	G#/A-flat	207.65
15	D#/E-flat	38.89	45	A	220.00
16	E	41.20	46	A#/B-flat	233.08
17	F	43.65	47	B	246.94
18	F#/G-flat	46.25	48	C	261.63
19	G	49.00	49	C#/D-flat	277.18
20	G#/A-flat	51.91	50	D	293.66
21	A	55.00	51	D#/E-flat	311.13
22	A#/B-flat	58.27	52	E	329.63
23	B	61.87	53	F	349.23
24	C	65.41	54	F#/G-flat	369.99
25	C#/D-flat	69.30	55	G	391.99
26	D	73.42	56	G#/A-flat	415.30
27	D#/E-flat	77.78	57	A	440.00
28	E	82.41	58	A#/B-flat	466.16
29	F	87.31	59	B	493.88
30	F#/G-flat	92.50	60	Middle C	523.25

MIDI Value	Note	Frequency (Hz)	MIDI Value	Note	Frequency (Hz)
61	C#/D-flat	554.37	92	G#/A-flat	3322.43
62	D	587.33	93	A	3520.00
63	D#/E-flat	622.25	94	A#/B-flat	3729.31
64	E	659.25	95	B	3951.07
65	F	698.46	96	C	4186.01
66	F#/G-flat	739.99	97	C#/D-flat	4434.92
67	G	783.99	98	D	4698.63
68	G#/A-flat	830.61	99	D#/E-flat	4978.03
69	A	880.00	100	E	5274.04
70	A#/B-flat	932.33	101	F	5587.65
71	B	987.77	102	F#/G-flat	5919.91
72	C	1046.50	103	G	6271.92
73	C#/D-flat	1108.73	104	G#/A-flat	6644.87
74	D	1174.66	105	A	7040.00
75	D#/E-flat	1244.51	106	A#/B-flat	7458.62
76	E	1318.51	107	B	7902.13
77	F	1396.91	108	C	8372.02
78	F#/G-flat	1479.97	109	C#/D-flat	8869.84
79	G	1567.98	110	D	9397.27
80	G#/A-flat	1661.22	111	D#/E-flat	9956.06
81	A	1760.00	112	E	10548.08
82	A#/B-flat	1864.65	113	F	11175.30
83	B	1975.53	114	F#/G-flat	11839.81
84	C	2093.00	115	G	12543.84
85	C#/D-flat	2217.46	116	G#/A-flat	13289.74
86	D	2349.31	117	A	14080.00
87	D#/E-flat	2489.01	118	A#/B-flat	14917.24
88	E	2637.01	119	B	15804.26
89	F	2793.82	120	C	16744.03
90	F#/G-flat	2959.95	121	C#/D-flat	17739.68
91	G	3135.95	122	D	18794.54

continues

TABLE 15.5. Continued

MIDI Value	Note	Frequency (Hz)	MIDI Value	Note	Frequency (Hz)
123	D#/E-flat	19912.12	126	F#/G-flat	23679.62
124	E	21096.15	127	G	25087.69
125	F	22350.59	128	G#/A-flat	26579.47

*Note: Frequency values assume modern Western Tuning, A=440 Hz.

After a MIDI system has been set up by assigning modes and programs, tunes can be played by sending out voice messages. A Note On status byte plays a single note of the voice on the channel indicated in the byte. The pitch of the note is defined by the first data byte, and its velocity (corresponding to how hard the key on the keyboard is pressed—at least on velocity-sensing keyboards) is defined by the second data byte. The note continues as defined by the program until a Note Off (either a specific Note Off or a general All Notes Off) message is sent, although in the meantime the program may cause the note to decay to inaudibility. The individual Note Off message also allows the control of a release velocity, a feature rare but available on some synthesizers.

MIDI provides for further control. Messages also control after touch, a feature of some keyboards that enables you to change the sound of a note by pressing harder on a key after you've first depressed it to sound the note. MIDI provides for two kinds of after touch: general—using Status Byte 0D(Hex)—that applies to all notes currently being played in the channel; and specific—using Status Byte 0Ax(Hex)—that applies only to an individual key.

Another Status Byte allows MIDI to send the state of dials or switches on the keyboard called controllers. One important controller, the shift wheel, has its own Status Byte—0Ex(Hex)—assigned to its control. Another Status Byte—0Bx(Hex)—relays data about up to 122 other controllers.

CD-ROM Connections

Sound boards also include connections to control CD-ROM players and link them into a single multimedia system. The sound board passes commands through this connection to the CD-ROM player to access specific tracks and activate functions and receive data back from the CD-ROM drive.

The CD-ROM connections are standard (or near-standard) system-level interfaces. Most CD-ROM players use SCSI connections, and many sound boards provide a suitable interface to match these drives. Creative Labs' Sound Blaster board uses a proprietary interface modeled after the AT Attachment disk interface for attaching Panasonic CD-ROM players that use a matching interface. Both are useful, and you may want to avoid them.

The reason to avoid the proprietary connection is because it's proprietary. Although the Creative Labs interface is similar to the AT Attachment design, Creative Labs does not guarantee that other ATA devices work with the connection or that the Panasonic drives designed for it work with other ATA boards. Although this proprietary connection is effective, it prevents you from plugging in a better CD-ROM player—one with faster access or a higher transfer rate.

The SCSI connection on sound boards is best avoided if you want to attach more than one SCSI device to your PC. Sound board SCSI connections lack the high performance attributes of dedicated SCSI host adapters. If you try to plug in a hard disk or other peripheral to your sound board in addition to your CD-ROM player, you'll be disappointed. You'll probably have difficulty getting it to work. If you do get it to work, the performance you get from a sound board SCSI port will be on the shy side of satisfactory, shortchanging the high-speed potentials of today's hard disks.

You can install two SCSI host adapters in one PC, so you can use the SCSI port on your sound board for a CD-ROM player and a separate, high-performance host adapter for your hard disk. Alternatively, with the correct driver software, you can connect your CD-ROM player to the high performance host adapter used by your hard disk. The drive allows program commands to get to the CD-ROM player without needing to go through the sound board.

Output Connections

Most sound boards have integral audio amplifiers designed for powering external speakers. Because of constraints imposed by your PC, however, these amplifiers are rudimentary. Typically, they produce little output power—usually between 100 milliwatts and one watt. Worse, many cut off low frequencies below 100 Hertz, the very frequencies that have the most impact on the sound effects often played through sound boards. Although you can connect an auxiliary amplifier and speaker system to your sound board to overcome the power shortage, you usually cannot overcome the low frequency cut-off.

Most sound board outputs are high level, meant for direct connection with loudspeakers. Using high-power buffer circuits, they can drive low impedance loads presented by loudspeakers, typically four to sixteen ohms. Although these connections are designed for loudspeakers, they match the high-level audio inputs of most preamplifiers and receivers well enough that you can usually connect them directly with a patch cord.

Do not worry about blasting a full watt into the input of your receiver. The input circuits of your receiver or preamplifier are sensitive to the voltage level rather than the power in the signal. Because amplifier inputs typically have a high input impedance—at least 2,000 ohms and possibly as high as 100,000 ohms—little of the current in the sound board output can flow through the amplifier input circuit. The voltage levels match well enough that the signals are compatible, although you may have to adjust the volume control on high-powered sound boards to prevent overloading your receiver's inputs with too much voltage.

A sound board with a one-watt output into a four ohm load produces a two volt output. A 100-milliwatt sound board produces a 0.62 volt output, again assuming a four ohm impedance. Most high-level receiver and preamplifier auxiliary inputs operate with a voltage level of 0.1 to 1 volt. Do not, however, plug the speaker output signals of your sound board into microphone inputs. The voltage levels in the sound board signal will likely overload most microphone inputs.

If you choose to make a direct connection to a receiver or other external amplifier, turn down the volume or loudness control on both your sound board and receiver to a minimal level before you begin. Play some sound through your sound board and slowly increase the volume control on your receiver to the position you use for your normal listening level. Finally, increase the level of your sound board until it reaches a pleasing listening level through your receiver.

If you don't want to use your stereo system but still want more power than most sound boards deliver, you can use powered speakers, available in several styles. An increasing number of speaker systems designed specifically for multimedia are becoming available. Some are individual satellite speakers you can place anywhere, whereas others come pre-installed in a cabinet that matches your PC and fits on top of your system unit between it and your monitor. Ordinary powered speakers that you might plug into your Walkman-like portable stereo also will work, although you may need an adapter cable to match the jack on your sound board to the plugs on the speakers. These amplified speakers are normally designed to accept speaker-style outputs, so you can plug them directly into the outputs of your sound board without worry.

Digital Signal Processors

In the next few years, PC-based audio systems will likely change as dramatically as have video systems. Just as graphics resolution and speed have jumped up from a cartoon-colored caricature of reality to Technicolor artistry thanks to high-powered video systems, the sound-related circuitry in the PC is developing quality that pushes the limits of human perception and flexibility unmatched in the aural world.

The nucleus of this change is the Digital Signal Processor, the audio equivalent of the graphic coprocessor. A DSP endows sound circuits with programmability so that traditional signal processing such as filtering (to diminish or augment certain frequencies), synthesis, or even digital-to-analog conversion is controlled by software, changeable as easily as putting a syntax error into a BASIC program.

In function, the basic DSP starts a wire that conducts audio signals unchanged and then by software command transforms the signals any way you want. In fact, the journey through the DSP is not a straight path. Incoming analog signals get transformed into digital code that the DSP works on mathematically, making its signal transformations under the control of algorithms specified by a program; then the signals are converted back into analog form. If this digital manipulation sounds familiar, it should. A DSP need be nothing more than a microprocessor optimized for processing audio signals. (DSP designs also can manipulate video signals—after all, video and audio are both analog signals that differ only in frequency—but today's PCs put DSPs to work only in audio applications.)

Just as graphic coprocessors are designed to work with image data, the DSP is optimized to work with sound and sound-like signals. The challenges of this sound work, however, are entirely different from those confronted by ordinary microprocessors. The DSP need not be as powerful as the main chip in your PC, but it must be faster. Think of the wire that the DSP emulates; signals go in and come out without slowing down. There's no delay between input and output. The DSP must carry out its functions in real time. If it had to pause to carry out its computations, the result would be a hole in the sound generated. You could hear such pauses as pops or distortion—not exactly what you would expect from adding audio processing power.

At the same time, the DSP doesn't need 32-bit heft. Sixteen bits are sufficient to encode sound without a trace of audible distortion (at least to most ears). There's no point to piling in more bits. Most DSPs are 16-bit designs (with some 32-bit registers to handle the results of multiplying 16-bit numbers).

That multiplication is the chief difference between the processing demands on a DSP and a general-purpose microprocessor. Most audio filtering and other sound manipulations require multiplying signals by trigonometric functions. The DSP needs math capabilities on par with a floating-point processor. Most RISC processors also excel at math, so many DSPs have RISC processors at their core. In fact, some engineers believe in putting ordinary RISC chips to work as DSPs, although application-specific DSPs can be substantially less expensive.

These DSP chips can be distinguished from RISC processors by special-purpose internal circuits that facilitate their use inside PCs. For example, the most popular DSPs used in PCs, the Texas Instruments TMS320M500 and TMS320M520, incorporate interface circuits to link to the ISA bus, telephone lines, microphones, and speakers. This design lets the DSP do everything audio that your PC needs. It can be a synthesizer, modem, or heart of a speech-recognition system.

Because the programs rather than hardware define the precise function of a DSP, a DSP-based modem can switch between communications standards as easily as downloading a configuration file. You can upgrade a DSP-based modem to match any new communication standard without touching the hardware at all. Similarly, a DSP board can duplicate the function of the audio circuitry on any sound board—additive, FM, and wave-table synthesis are but simple chores for the DSP.

What's the catch? Why doesn't every sound board, modem, and PC have a DSP inside? Part of the reason is newness: DSP technology is young and many designers lack experience using them. After all, building with DSPs requires a different mindset from creating with conventional audio hardware. It's a job more for programmers than chip jockeys. Moreover, no single standard dominates the DSP industry. Whereas PCs are dominated by Intel microprocessors, no single DSP owns the majority of the market. In fact, no single design dominates. Several chip makers manufacture DSPs to their own specifications, each with its own internal architecture.

The first applications in which DSPs appeared are hardware devices that hide the DSP from your PC's circuitry. The product designer—not your PC—controls what the DSP does. Usually, the DSP performs a specific function, such as controlling a modem. The true versatility of the DSP will not be realized until your PC can take full control and send programs directly to it.

Standing in the way is the lack of a common standard. Each DSP design runs only the software written specifically for it. No common language exists among DSPs—at least not yet. DSP makers have, however, created their own proprietary standards—each hoping their design becomes accepted as the one true specification by the PC industry.

These standards take several different forms. For example, the standard may be an operating system to control DSP functions; an architecture based on a layered structure of software and hardware; or simply a command set. Currently, four such standards have a major presence in the industry: Windows DSP Architecture, MWave, VCOS, and Signal Computing Architecture.

MWave

Originally a joint effort between Texas Instruments and IBM, MWave linked TI's coprocessor expertise with IBM's strength in software and system architecture design. The core of the design was TI's series of 16-bit DSPs coupled with an IBM-designed software kernel. The software runs on a host PC to give it control of the DSP functions.

The original goal of the MWave effort was to make it an open standard that could win industry support. IBM went so far as to develop a board that implemented the MWave specification and could function as a sound board and a modem in a PC, giving the rest of the industry a working model to copy. Early on, MWave showed promise if just because the TI DSPs had the largest share of the overall market. In 1993, however, Texas Instruments withdrew its support from MWave, leaving IBM the solitary MWave standard bearer.

Signal Computing Architecture

Analog Devices manufactures DSPs and quite naturally designed a control system to link them to computers. Called Signal Computing Architecture, the Analog Devices design is based on a layered model that functionally divides the overall DSP system. Four of the layers involve the host computer. The top layer is the user interface, how you work with the system. One step down is the application software you run on your PC to control the DSP. Next comes the API (application program interface), the set of program hooks that translate program instructions into the language understood by the DSP. The final host layer is the operating system of the computer, which provides the environment for running software, controlling how the program interacts with your PC.

The other three layers concern the DSP and its software. The fifth layer is the algorithm layer, which develops the mathematical form of the commands requested by the host. The sixth layer is the DSP's own operating system, and the seventh layer is the language layer, which is the actual code that runs on the DSP.

The layered approach makes the links more important than the underlying design. A hardware designer can change the internal structure of a DSP, and as long as the chip properly links with the language layer the rest of the system does not notice the difference. Similarly, programmers need only concern themselves with the upper layers, letting the lower layers and hardware take care of itself.

VCOS

To control its own line of digital signal processors, AT&T developed its own operating system called VCOS. The operating system runs on the DSP and is controlled by function calls from the host computer's software. Developers write the proper calls into their C language or Windows programs, and AT&T offers its own set of algorithms as a multimedia module library.

VCOS allows the DSP and its host to share memory. This sharing lets either processor take a hand in signal manipulation. In addition, sharing memory can cut the overall cost of adding a complete DSP system to a PC—memory costs can be a significant part of a DSP board. To prevent memory access problems (a DSP needs fast access to operate in real time), a DSP running VCOS internally caches blocks of memory instead of randomly accessing bytes. Unlike normal PC memory caching, however, the data in the cache is controlled by the programmer writing VCOS code, giving the application developer complete control over the speed of signal processing.

The current version of VCOS (1.1, announced in August 1993) gives designers power far in excess of that yielded by a single DSP. The operating system can spread multimedia tasks over several DSPs to further improve performance, balancing the load between chips and applications.

Windows DSP Architecture

Late in 1993, a new dominant force entered the DSP standards arena—PC software giant Microsoft Corporation. Rather than develop its own DSP interface, however, Microsoft joined with Spectron Microsystems to create an interface to allow Windows applications to control DSPs for communications and multimedia applications. The result of this marriage was Windows Digital Signal Processor software architecture, a hybrid of PC-based software and an operating system for DSPs. In concept, Windows DSP architecture gives developers a hardware-independent application interface that can be used to operate any DSP for audio or video processing.

The foundation for Windows DSP architecture was the SPOX DSP operating system, which Spectron developed earlier. Originally designed as a 32-bit operating system, SPOX was revised just before the Microsoft affiliation into a product better suited to 16-bit DSP applications.

The underlying SPOX design is a three-part entity that includes a software kernel that runs on the DSP to control hardware functions; a set of communications links between the DSP and the host computer; and a set of high-level math functions for defining the actual signal processing. Microsoft added in links to the Windows environment.

Even before joining with Microsoft, Spectron was working on SPOX development kits for Texas Instruments, Analog Devices, and Motorola DSPs, so the resulting collaborative product gives programmers access to the major DSP families. Because Windows is the dominant multimedia environment, Windows DSP Architecture will likely be the force that pushes DSPs into PCs.

Chapter 16
Parallel Ports

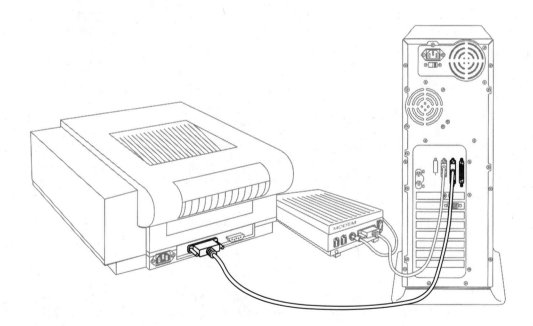

Parallel ports are well-defined, convenient, and quick—probably the most trouble-free connection you can make with your PC. Once the exclusive province of printers, with the advent of the Enhanced Parallel Port, they promise to be the universal interface—the duct tape of PC ports. An increasing number of peripherals are taking advantage of the fast, sure, parallel connection. But all parallel ports are not the same, nor are all parallel connections. A port that works for a printer may fail dismally when you attempt to transfer files across it. It is all a matter of design.

When it comes to connecting peripherals to your PC, the parallel port appears to be the answer to your prayers. You plug in a cable, and everything works. No switches to worry about, no mode commands, no breaking out the break-out box to sort through signals with names that sound suspiciously similar to demons from Middle Earth. The parallel port is as close to Plug and Play as anything that comes in the realm of the PC.

But the parallel port is no simple thing, and no single standard suffices for every one of them. Through the years, three parallel port standards have developed. All look the same. They all use the same connectors. And all send signals to things that you plug in. In fact, you might become aware of the differences only when you start to scratch your head and wonder why your friends can unload files from their notebook computers 10 times faster than you can.

Standard equipment on even the first PCs, the parallel port is almost synonymous with "printer port." The name is self-descriptive. The port is parallel because it conducts its signals through eight separate wires—one for each bit of a byte of data—that are enclosed together in a single cable. The signal wires literally run in parallel from your PC to their destination.

In theory, having eight wires means that you can move data eight times as fast through a parallel connection than through a single wire. In practice, the advantage is much greater. Where today's standard serial ports top out at 115,200 bits per second, an Enhanced Parallel Port spits out bits more than 100 times faster. In other words, there is more to a parallel port than just wires.

Despite the three different types of parallel port, a parallel connection remains the easiest, most foolproof way of connecting a printer or other compatible peripherals to your PC. Just plug it in, and the odds are that whatever it is works flawlessly—or that flaws in its operation have nothing to do with the interconnection.

Well, that is almost true. The devil is in the details. Some printers (thankfully a minuscule and dwindling number) react negatively to the conventions of the original parallel port—negatively enough that they might forever cease to function. Some peripherals and software try to take advantage of the speed and versatility of the updated parallel port designs and find that they are making demands that some ports cannot fill.

Although at heart all parallel ports are based on the same concepts, creative thinking has grafted more power into the parallel package. The first parallel printer ports, today termed *Standard Parallel Ports*, operated at speeds high for their day but modest today—between 50 and 150 kilobytes per second. True to their design goal, they pushed information in one direction only, from PC to printer. The second generation of ports, the *PS/2 Parallel Port*, made parallel technology a two-way street, allowing the interface to mate a variety of devices that expect communications to be give-and-take. The latest innovation in port design, the *Enhanced Parallel Port*, gives the venerable design added impetus, upping the potential parallel transfer rate to 2000 kilobytes per second. That puts the parallel port in a league with some expansion buses— It is nearly the same as a slot in an eight-bit PC and close to the limit of ISA.

Technology

The parallel port reflects a hardware engineer's concept of the way in which communication should work. A signal that is in one place is connected to the distant location at which it is wanted by running a wire from point to point. For every signal, another wire is added. Eight data signals take eight wires. In addition, all the control functions—for example, the signaling back and forth between PC and printer to prevent buffer overflow—get their own separate wires.

Such a design saves on the complex circuitry needed to bundle signals together to travel down one or two conductors. The whole connection, in fact, works like a marionette—the PC operates the printer or remote device by electronically tugging on the appropriate strings. It is difficult to imagine a simpler, more straightforward system.

No conversion circuitry impedes the flow of information. The eight conductors serve as an expressway for information, moving bytes at the same speed at which a single bit can traverse the connection.

What the design engineer saves in time and port circuitry is made up for in the cost of cables. Instead of the two wires used by telephones and serial computer circuits, a parallel port requires at least eight wires (one for each data bit) plus more for a ground and control signals. The standard parallel port design demands a full 25 separate connections. Enhanced Parallel Ports require special, double-shielded cables. In either case, the result is a big, fat cable that is hard to bend when, for example, you want to back your PC against a wall to give yourself more desk space. Connectors need to grow larger to accommodate all the wires and signals, too. And more wires mean that more time needs to be spent soldering or crimping the cable and connector together.

You should note that one trade-off with the parallel interface is that the expense of extra port circuitry is balanced by the cost of a fatter cable. From the perspective of a company that manufactures computers and leaves the acquisition of printer cables to the purchaser, you can see why the parallel design makes sense.

Cable cost is not the only downside of a parallel link. The parallel nature of the parallel port also is its undoing from an electrical standpoint. Data and control signals must travel together in a tight group down that big, thick cable. By itself, that is no problem. Parallel ports do, in fact, work well. The multiple signal paths, however, tend to react with each other as they travel down the parallel cable that connects the port on your computer to the one on your printer. Signals from one lead tend to leak into others, a problem called *crosstalk*. (In telephone systems, the same tendency causes conversations in one circuit to cross over into others.)

The longer the cable or the higher the speed of the signal, the greater the leakage. Most manufacturers, consequently, recommend that standard PC-style parallel connections be kept under 10 feet in length to prevent problems. Enhanced Parallel Ports must be kept even shorter, no more than about six feet (two meters). Computers and printers vary in their sensitivity to parallel port crosstalk, however. Some systems work with lengthy parallel connections, up to 50 feet long; others balk with anything over 10 feet. Enhanced Parallel Ports are much more finicky. The only way to tell how long a cable your system can handle is to experiment.

Logical Interface

All parallel ports, no matter the speed or technology, must somehow interface with your PC and its operating system. They need to be connected to the logic circuitry in your PC and, from there, linked to your software.

The logical interface used by all parallel ports is the same. It was conceived during the development of the first IBM Personal Computer and remains essentially unchanged over the years since. Standard parts of this design include the input/output ports used to send data from programs to parallel ports, the names that DOS (and other operating systems) use to identify ports, and the inherent limits on the number of parallel ports that can be installed in a single PC.

Port Assignments

Each parallel port in a PC logically connects with the rest of the system through three input/ output ports. One of the ports is used for transferring data to the parallel connection. Your PC's microprocessor typically retrieves the information to be printed from memory and transfers it to the I/O port used by the parallel adapter. This data is buffered and sent to the parallel connector. The other two I/O ports are used for manipulating control signals and monitoring the signals sent back by the printer indicating its operating status.

The basic PC design allows for up to three parallel ports to be installed, each with its own triad of input/output ports. Three ranges of three I/O port addresses are reserved for parallel ports, at base addresses of 03BC(Hex), 0378(Hex), and 0278(Hex). In any system, each of these I/O address triplets must be uniquely assigned to a single parallel port. Two parallel ports cannot share the same base address.

The first of these, 03BC(Hex), originally was reserved for the parallel port that was installed on the IBM Monochrome Display Adapter card. Because the MDA card cannot be used with PS/2s, which have their own built-in display adapters, this same set of addresses was assigned to the standard equipment parallel port in each PS/2. Most compatible computers with system board video systems also use this address for their on-board parallel ports. The other two starting addresses typically are available for additional parallel ports.

Compatible systems lacking motherboard-mounted video often avoid using the 03BC(Hex) ports because there still is a small chance you might want to install an MDA video adapter in such a machine. Instead, these systems usually provide for a base address of 0378(Hex) and some provision for reassigning the address used by the port, typically jumpers or DIP switches.

Device Names

You never need to use the I/O base addresses in the daily operation of your PC. If you need to reference a parallel port, you can instead use its DOS designation. The names LPT1, LPT2, and LPT3 are reserved for the three parallel ports the systems support. (Think of LPT as an abbreviation for Line PrinTer.) The device name PRN is equivalent to LPT1.

These logical names do not necessarily match with a given set of I/O port addresses, however. At boot-up, the BIOS code of your PC searches for parallel ports at each of the three supported base addresses. The search always is performed in the order listed—03BC(Hex), then 0378(Hex), then 0278 (Hex). The first parallel port that is found in the system is assigned the name LPT1; the second, LPT2; the third, LPT3. If you have a monochrome display adapter or a PS/2 with built-in parallel port, that port always is LPT1. The values of the port available in your PC are stored in the BIOS data area starting at absolute memory location 0000:0408, with one 16-bit word reserved for storing each based address value.

As a consequence of this allocation scheme, you are assured of having an LPT1 (and PRN) device in your system no matter which I/O ports are assigned to your parallel ports—providing that you have at least one parallel port! If, however, you have two ports assigned to the same base I/O addresses, your system assigns both ports the same name, and neither is likely to work.

Interrupts

Two hardware interrupts are used by parallel ports in handling their communications. Normally interrupt 07(Hex) is assigned to the first parallel port, and interrupt 05(Hex) is assigned to the second.

Port Limit

Because parallel ports come embedded in many products, it is common to find the number of parallel ports in your PC mysteriously higher than you think it should be. You can easily run into port conflicts even when you have not intentionally added extra ports. You might even exceed the official IBM parallel port maximum of three without knowing it. Or, you might make two ports think they are the same one, with confusing and crashing consequences. Before you add a parallel port to your system, it is a good idea to check the number and base addresses of the ports already installed. You can check either through DEBUG or using a commercial feature reporting program.

Standard Parallel Ports

In designing the now-standard parallel port that first appeared inside its original PC, IBM elected to follow the pattern of control signals set by one once-prominent printer manufacturer, Centronics. The connection was not formalized at the time IBM borrowed the design—Centronics had just developed a set of control signals that well served the control of computer printers. Other printer companies also were adopting the Centronics design when IBM appropriated it.

Connections

IBM, however, chose to go in its own direction for parallel port connectors. Where a true Centronics printer port uses a 36-conductor Amphenol connector, IBM selected a 25-pin D-shell connector. Since then, printer makers have stuck with the 36-pin design, and IBM and nearly every other computer maker has maintained the 25-pin standard. Consequently, you need a special adapter cable to plug your printer into your PC in almost every case. Fortunately, the ubiquity of PCs has made the odd adapter cable a standard accessory. Table 16.1 shows the connections for this adapter.

TABLE 16.1. IBM to Centronic Parallel Printer Pin Mapping

Connect these	To these	Connect these	To these
25-pin connector	36-pin connector	25-pin connector	36-pin connector
1	1	16	31
2	2	17	36
3	3	18	19-30,33
4	4	19	19-30,33
5	5	20	19-30,33
6	6	21	19-30,33
7	7	22	19-30,33
8	8	23	19-30,33

Connect these	To these	Connect these	To these
25-pin connector	36-pin connector	25-pin connector	36-pin connector
9	9	24	19-30,33
10	10	25	19-30,33
11	11		
12	12		
13	13		
14	14		
15	32		

Of the 25 contacts on a parallel port connector, a full 19 are required transferring 8 bits of data. Table 16.2 shows where each connection is assigned on the standard IBM parallel port connector. The function of each of these is as follows:

Table 16.2. Standard Parallel Port Cable Pin Assignments

25-pin connector	Function	25-pin connector	Function
1	Strobe	16	Initialize printer
2	Data bit 0	17	Select input
3	Data bit 1	18	Ground
4	Data bit 2	19	Ground
5	Data bit 3	20	Ground
6	Data bit 4	21	Ground
7	Data bit 5	22	Ground
8	Data bit 6	23	Ground
9	Data bit 7	24	Ground
10	Acknowledge	25	Ground
11	Busy		
12	Paper end (out of paper)		
13	Select		
14	Auto Feed		
15	Error		

Data Lines

The information that is to be sent to the printer to become hard copy first is loaded onto eight data lines, located on pins 2 through 9 of the parallel connector, one for each bit of a byte of ASCII code. As with the other signals on the standard parallel port connector, those on the data lines are compatible with standard TTL voltages—nominally a "high" or five volts indicating a digital one; a "low" or zero volts indicating a logical zero.

Strobe Line

Just loading bits onto the data lines is not sufficient to indicate to the printer that it should print a character. The data bits are constantly changing, and the system provides no insurance that all eight are going to simultaneously pop to the right value—and even if it did, the printer would have no way of knowing that it should (or should not) print the same character twice or more. Some way is required to signal that the computer is finished loading bits onto the data lines and that a character can be printed. The Strobe line on pin one serves exactly that purpose.

The strobe signal in the standard parallel scheme is a negative-going pulse. When data bits are not read, it is high. When a byte of data is to be transmitted, it goes low.

The timing of the data signals and the strobe signal is critical. All data lines must be at their proper value before the strobe signal is triggered so that the printer circuits have adequate time to assume the proper values. About one-half microsecond is required. The strobe signal should last for a full microsecond (long enough for the printer to realize that it is present!), and the data signals should persist slightly (another half microsecond) after the completion of the strobe. The overlap helps protect against errors.

Busy Line

This data-strobe-and-data process allocates a minimum of two microseconds per character. At that rate, the parallel interface could dump 500,000 characters per second into some poor, defenseless printer. The printer needs a way to fight back, to tell the computer that it is busy blasting a character onto the paper. The busy signal on pin 11, sent from printer to computer, accomplishes this task. It is a hold-your-horses signal. As soon as the printer receives the strobe and starts the process of printing a character (be it only to shove the data into an internal buffer), it trips the busy signal, sending it high.

The busy signal stays high as long as it takes the printer to prepare to receive the next byte of data. This busy condition can persist momentarily as the byte is loaded into a buffer, or for an extended period during which the printer would be unable to accept another character for printing. For instance, the buffer may fill up, the ribbon could jam, or the printer might not have fully initialized after being turned on.

Acknowledge Line

While the busy line is a negative signal—it commands "Don't send data"—another parallel port line is used for positive flow control. The acknowledge line carries a signal from the printer to your computer on pin 10 that indicates the previous character has been properly received and dashed to paper, and that the printer is ready for the next character. As with the strobe signal, acknowledge normally is a logical high that shifts low to indicate that the printer is ready for the next character. This negative-going pulse typically lasts about eight microseconds.

Printer Feedback

The parallel interface does more than just move data. Dedicated lines in the parallel circuit are used by the printer to signal various aspects of its condition to the host computer. The signals tell the computer that the printer is ready, willing, and able to do its job. They endow the computer with a modicum of remote sensing abilities.

Select

The select line on pin 13 indicates that the printer is "selected," which means that it is in its online condition, ready to receive information. The select line acts exactly like the online light on the front panel of the printer. But instead of being visible to your eyes, it is registered by and through the parallel port.

The select line goes high when the printer is online. If the select line is not high, the parallel port does not transmit data.

Paper Empty

The most common problem encountered during a print job is running out of paper. When that happens, your printer could just run the busy signal high—which effectively stops your computer from pouring data into it. In fact, most printers do exactly that. But they do more—to give you some idea of what is happening, in case you cannot see the printer or do not realize your paper pile has been depleted.

To indicate to your computer the exact nature of its problem, your printer pulls the paper-empty line on pin 12 high. Again, it operates just like the paper-out light on the printer but supplies its signal in a form that your computer can understand.

Fault

One further signal is used as a catch-all for other printer problems—fault, on pin 15. This signal indicates to your computer that something is wrong without indicating the exact problem—not enough wires are in a cable to indicate all possible printer problems. Fault could indicate, for example, that the lid to the printhead chamber is open; the printhead has jammed; the printhead does not index (for instance, the drive belt broke); or whatever other error conditions your printer can detect on its own.

The fault signal is negative-going. It normally is held high. When an error occurs, it goes low.

Many printers do not use a single-barreled defense. When something goes wrong, all the flags are raised. Busy, select, and fault all go to their warning states.

Computer Control

In the IBM parallel port scheme, three additional signals are used to control various aspects of the printer through hard-wired port connections. These signals initialize the printer and switch it to an online condition (when the printer allows such a remote-controlled change), and line feeding begins.

Initialize Printer

The computer and printer are two separate organisms that can grow and change independently. You can send commands to the printer to change its operation, set new fonts, change character pitch, and so on. On its own, your computer does nothing to keep track of the commands it sends to your printer—the printer could turn into a monster that would dump the next 47 pages of your monthly report as an amorphous blob in graphics mode, and your computer would not know the difference.

The printer always starts at the same point, however, with fonts, pitches, and modes all sent in a predetermined way. You can reset the printer to this condition by turning it off and then on, initializing all of its important operating parameters. The *initialize printer* or *input prime signal* on pin 16 is an alternate means of accomplishing the same end. It is like a reset button for the printer. Drive this line low from its normal high condition, and the printer initializes itself, running through its own boot-up operation.

Select Input

Some printers are designed to be switched on- and offline by their computer hosts. The signal used for commanding the switch is called *select input* and is located on pin 17. When this signal is low, printers accept data; when high, they do not. Many printers allow you to defeat this control by operating a DIP switch that causes the machine to always hold this line low.

Auto Feed XT

The lowly carriage return can be a confusing thing. Some printers assume that a carriage return should automatically advance paper to the beginning of the next line; others think a carriage return merely swerves the printhead back to the beginning of the line currently being printed. Most printers give you a choice—a DIP switch determines how the printer reacts to carriage returns.

The auto feed XT signal on pin 14 gives your computer the choice. By holding this signal low, the printer is commanded to automatically feed one line when it detects a carriage return. Make it high, and a line feed character is required to roll the paper up to the next line.

Control

The various signals in the parallel cable are controlled through a set of three input/output ports in your PC. Each standard parallel port has its own set of I/O ports, the first of which is located at the base address assigned during hardware setup, and the others as the next two ports in sequence. If the first standard parallel port in your PC has a base address of 0378(hex), this parallel port also uses I/O ports 0379(Hex) and 037A(Hex).

The I/O port at the base address of the parallel port serves as the data latch. This register operates as the point of exchange for data from your PC. The eight bits of this port are connected to the data lines of the parallel port so that the most significant bit of the register and the port correspond. To set a value to send to your printer, your PC's microprocessor outputs the appropriate value to this register. The values are maintained (latched) until your microprocessor writes to the port again.

The next I/O port, at offset one from the base address of the parallel port, is the printer status register. The various bits in this register carry messages from the printer back to your PC. The five most significant bits of this register correspond to five lines in the parallel cable: bit 7 controls the Busy signal; bit 6, Acknowledge; bit 5, Paper Empty; bit 4, Select; and bit 3, Error. The three least significant bits (bits 2, 1, and 0) are unused by a standard parallel port.

The third I/O port, at offset two from the base address of the parallel port, is the printer control register. This register relays commands from your PC's microprocessor to the printer. Only the five least significant bits of this register are used. Four of these directly control corresponding parallel port lines. Bit 3 controls the Select line; bit 2, the Initialize line; bit 1, the Auto Feed XT line; and bit 0, the Strobe line.

Bit 4 of the printer control register enables the printer to send an interrupt to your PC's microprocessor. When this bit is set high, the Acknowledge signal from the printer triggers the interrupt. When the printer has received a character, processed it, and is ready for another, it changes the Acknowledge signal from high to low. When bit 4 is set, and after your microprocessor detects this change (by reading the printer status register), it executes the hardware interrupt assigned to the port—which typically leads to sending another character to the printer.

In normal operation, your PC's microprocessor micro-manages the details of sending data through a standard parallel port. It goes through an elaborate series of commands to carry out this simple function. First, it checks the printer status, then loads the values into the data latch, then triggers the strobe line, and checks status again. This series of commands typically is carried out through a BIOS routine entered through interrupt 017(Hex), the printer interrupt, although programs can take direct control of the I/O ports assigned the standard parallel port.

Performance

This multi-step process is one of the principal speed limits on parallel port performance. Processing overhead at both ends of the connection slows the orderly parallel flow substantially. The computer, for instance, must receive the Acknowledge signal, then run through a BIOS routine to understand it, then load the next character into the parallel port, and finally send the strobe signal out the port. Even if the printer is equipped with its own buffer, it must go through an equivalent electronic ritual each time a character is received. Faster computers and faster printers result in quicker transfers.

The maximum operating speed of the standard parallel port connection is determined by a number of factors. The cable itself sets the ultimate limit on the frequencies of the signals that can be used. As long as it is less than about 10 feet long, however, the effects of the cable on the data throughput of a standard parallel port are minimal. Instead, the performance of a parallel port is mostly controlled by the values arbitrarily chosen for pulsing of the strobe and Acknowledge lines used for normal parallel port flow control. When system timing is set to yield the minimal lengths of these signals, a complete character transmission cycle requires about 10 microseconds—a speed sufficient to move 100,000 bytes in a second—that is, 800,000 bits per second. Newer systems can squeeze a bit more speed out of the standard parallel port (about 50 percent) by trimming some of these cycle times.

Bi-Directional Parallel Ports

Because standard parallel ports originally were conceived to serve solely as printer outputs, the flow of data was designed to be in one direction only—from PC to printer. Only a few of the parallel port control signals needed to go the other way. All early PCs, consequently, were equipped with unidirectional parallel ports. That is, they could send but not receive data.

This one-way nature was a result of the intrinsic electrical design of the port. The standard parallel port was not designed to be able to supply a significant level of current. Grounding one of the data lines of the port, as might happen when sending data to it, could be destructive to the circuitry of the port. By disallowing any equipment from altering the port outputs (in effect, discouraging sending information to the port), the standard parallel port design effectively precludes using a port for data acquisition or reception.

PS/2 Design

IBM evidently rethought this design after the first PCs were produced and began to make parallel ports that were capable of bi-directional operation. The standard parallel port of the AT allows for bi-directional data flow. IBM did not officially support bi-directional operation, however, until it introduced the PS/2 line.

This bi-directional support does not otherwise alter the signal definitions or connector pin assignments or other aspects of the design of standard parallel ports. PS/2 parallel ports are backwardly compatible with standard parallel ports.

The parallel port support built into the very early models of IBM personal computers does, in fact, permit reading of the various data lines. As long as care is taken to keep from grounding the data lines (for instance, controlling them through resistors to keep currents low), it is possible to use even the earliest PC parallel ports bi-directionally. Because the PS/2 design allows the system to source 2.6 milliamps, resistors of 2.2 kilohms are sufficient. Standard parallel ports can sink (absorb) up to 24 milliamps.

The whole issue of unidirectional and bi-directional ports would be academic, except that the former is easier and cheaper to build. While all reputable computer makers install bi-directional ports in their products, the makers of inexpensive parallel adapters or multifunction boards are apt to skimp on the circuitry. They may equip their parallel ports with unidirectional buffers.

If you wanted only to print, you need not worry whether a port is unidirectional or bi-directional. Today, however, you can plug a variety of devices into a parallel port. Some of these include SCSI adapters, network adapters, and data interchange systems. All of these products are designed to take advantage of the high speed of a parallel connection, but none works with one of these unidirectional ports on a cheap parallel adapter.

Bus Mastering

Along with the acknowledgment of bi-directional operation, PS/2s added a speed-enhancing capability—bus-mastering—to parallel ports. In systems with parallel ports bus mastering, data transfers to the parallel port can be made by the DMA controller without microprocessor intervention, trimming the overhead associated with parallel transfers. With a quick DMA system, data throughput can approach the limits imposed by standard parallel port hardware. The first systems with built-in bus-mastering PS/2 parallel ports were the IBM PS/2 Models 90 and 95.

More important than the data throughput to the parallel port, however, is the release of the microprocessor from the drudgery of parallel control. By shifting responsibilities to the DMA system, the microprocessor gains back much of its bandwidth. As a result, overall system performance improves, particularly in a multiuser or multitasking environment. Bus mastering generally is unavailable in systems using ISA designs and has not won favor for parallel transfers in other architectures that do support mastering. The high processing speed of modern microprocessors and comparatively low throughput of standard parallel ports make the bus mastering of them an unnecessary complication. The speed and simplified transfer protocol of Enhanced Parallel Ports give bus mastering a definite throughput edge, particularly when coupled with local bus technology. The bus mastering of parallel ports may eventually prove popular.

Enhanced Parallel Ports

In days of printers that clacked out a few dozen characters every minute, the standard parallel port offered more than sufficient performance. When bi-directionality made the PS/2 parallel port a feasible channel for connecting computers, the speed limit still seemed unimportant. The one product originally designed for PS/2 parallel ports—IBM's Data Migration Facility, a combination of a cable and software—foresaw only one-time use as a means of moving files from PCs with 5.25-inch floppy disk drives to new PS/2s with incompatible 3.5-inch floppies.

As with many products introduced by IBM, the idea behind the Data Migration Facility was intriguing, but the implementation left a lot to be desired—little things like a comfortable interface and performance. It was enough, however, to inspire other designers to develop data transfer programs that took advantage of the speed advantage that the PS/2 parallel port held over ordinary PC serial ports.

Although standard parallel port speed was sufficient for most people (at least, at the time), some folks found it limiting. Specifically, engineers at Xircom Incorporated discovered that the low speed of the standard parallel port put the external network adapters they developed in 1989 at a severe disadvantage compared to slot-mounted host adapters. Engineers at Zenith Data Systems struggled with the parallel port speed limit in looking for a way to get information in and out of notebook computer systems without adding mass and complexity to their products. As a result Zenith and Xircom banded together with Intel (a company that supports just about any new technology that sells more PCs and, with them, microprocessors) to form the Enhanced Parallel Port Partnership.

On August 10, 1991, the EPP Partnership released the initial description of an Enhanced Parallel Port. After a few revisions, the standard reached its present form (Release 1.7) in March, 1992, in which it was submitted to the IEEE as a prospective industry standard. The design was first implemented in Zenith's MasterPort SLe notebook computer and Intel's 386SL microprocessor chipset.

The Enhanced Parallel Port earns its speed in two ways: a streamlined, logical interface and explicit definition of electrical parameters. The former lets your PC move data into the port faster. The latter ensures that the data gets where it is going.

Logical Interface

In the initial Intel EPP chip design (integrated into the 386SL chipset), the Enhanced Parallel Port was created as a superset of the standard and PS/2 parallel ports. Altering a register can switch the function of the port from standard parallel, to bi-directional, to enhanced. This design allows the Enhanced Parallel Port to be backwardly compatible with the preceding designs. In fact, when a PC with the Intel chip initially boots up, the Enhanced Parallel Port defaults to operating as a standard serial port.

In the Intel chipset, software can control the operating mode of the parallel port through the fast parallel port control register. Setting the most significant bit (bit 7) of this register high switches on enhanced operation; when low (the default), the port operates in standard mode. Bit 6 of this register controls whether the port is bi-directional (bit 6 set high) or unidirectional (bit 6 low).

Just as standard parallel ports use three input/output ports for control and moving data, the Enhanced Parallel Port uses eight. Those used by the Enhanced Parallel Port start with the same base address options as standard ports and take up five additional ports in sequence.

The first new port (offset three from the base port address) is the *EPP address port.* It is used for device/register selection operations in future refinements of the Enhanced Parallel Port specifications. This I/O port is used to pass along address values to select among multiple devices that may be connected to the same parallel connector, much as data would be sent through the data latch in a standard parallel port.

The upper four ports (starting at offset four from the base port) serve as the EPP data buffer through which information is transferred to the Enhanced Parallel Port data lines, much like the standard parallel port data latch. To increase port performance, the EPP design allows the host computer to write to all four ports simultaneously, writing a single 32-bit double-word in a single clock cycle. The Enhanced Parallel Port circuitry then takes care of reorganizing the data into four bytes, which the port loads onto the data lines in the proper order. The EPP specification also allows for byte-wide and word-wide (16- bit) writes to the EPP data buffer ports.

Unlike standard parallel ports, the Enhanced Parallel Port requires no other signals from the host computer to carry out a data transfer. The data strobe signal on the bus is automatically generated when the host writes data to the data buffer port. Similarly, reading data from the port automatically triggers the data strobe signal to indicate the system is ready to receive more data. The host, consequently, can push data through the port as fast as it can cycle—providing, of course, that the device at the other end of the connection can accept bytes that quickly.

Connections

The Enhanced Parallel Port uses the same 25-pin, D-shell connectors as standard parallel ports. In its SPP mode, all signal definitions are essentially the same as a standard parallel port.

When its enhanced functions are enabled, however, only the eight data lines and five signals actually are used. These five signals change definition with the switch to Enhanced Parallel Port operation.

Write

The signal on pin one, Write, tells devices connected to the Enhanced Parallel Port that data is being passed along on the data lines of the connection. This signal, designated WRITE#, goes low when active. It takes over the pin used by the standard parallel port Strobe signal.

Data Strobe

The signal on pin 14, Data Strobe, indicates that the signals on the eight data lines contain valid data and can be read. In normal operation, the PC or other device sending data across the Enhanced Parallel Port first activates its data lines, then, after the correct signal values have become established, activates the Data Strobe signal. Using this two-step process prevents signals in transition from being misinterpreted. This signal is designated as DATASTB# and goes low when it is active. It takes over the pin used by the standard parallel port Autofeed signal.

Address Strobe

The signal on pin 17, Address Strobe, performs a function similar to the data strobe signal in ensuring the integrity of values on the data lines. The presence of the address strobe, however, indicates that the values on the data lines represent an address, which can be used to select a register or device connected to the bus. Designated ADDRSTB#, this signal goes low when active. It takes over the pin used by the standard parallel port Select Input signal.

Wait

The signal on pin 11, Wait, is used to confirm that a data transfer was successful. Normally, this signal is active. It gets switched off to acknowledge that the preceding transfer is complete and that the receiving device is ready for another transfer. Designated WAIT#, this signal is active when low; switching high acknowledges the receipt of data.

Interrupt

The Interrupt signal, on pin 10, is used by devices connected to the Enhanced Parallel Port to request an interrupt from the host computer. Designated INTR, this signal normally is low and is switched high to request an interrupt. It takes over the pin used by the standard parallel port Acknowledge signal.

The Enhanced Parallel Port specification allows the four other pins used in standard parallel port operation to be used for application-specific purposes when in high-speed EPP mode. These four pins are 12 (Paper End), 13 (Select), 15 (Error), and 16 (Initialize). Table 16.3 shows the pin-out of an Enhanced Parallel Port in its native high-speed mode.

Cable

The high data speeds made possible by the logical design of the Enhanced Parallel Port far exceed the limits imposed by the loose wiring specifications of the standard parallel port. The EPP specifications, consequently, precisely detail a special cable for high-speed operation.

Unlike standard parallel wiring, the data lines in the EPP cable are double-shielded. The eight wires for conducting the data signals and a drain wire (corresponding to the ground on pin 18) are wrapped in a shield of aluminum foil and mylar which is then encircled by the remaining 16 wires grouped in pairs of signal and matching ground. Figure 16.1 shows the conductor arrangement of an EPP card. Under the EPP specification, this cable should be two meters long.

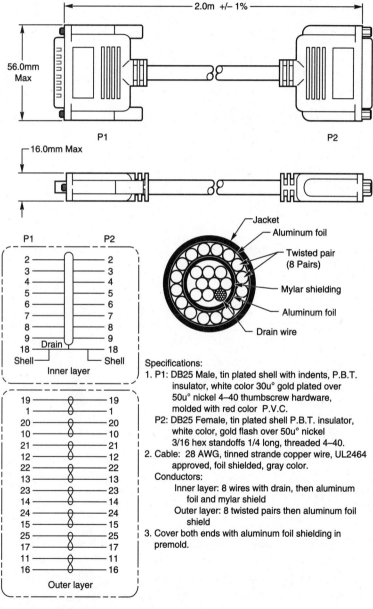

FIGURE 16.1. Enhanced parallel port cable.

TABLE 16.3. Enhanced Parallel Port Cable Pin Assignments

25-pin connector	Function	25-pin connector	Function
1	Write #	16	Initialize printer (paired with pin 11)
2	Address/Data bit 0	17	Address strobe #
3	Address/Data bit 1	18	Ground (Data)
4	Address/Data bit 2	19	Ground (paired with pin 1)
5	Address/Data bit 3	20	Ground (paired with pin 10)
6	Address/Data bit 4	21	Ground (paired with pin 12)
7	Address/Data bit 5	22	Ground (paired with pin 13)
8	Address/Data bit 6	23	Ground (paired with pin 14)
9	Address/Data bit 7	24	Ground (paired with pin 15)
10	Interrupt #	25	Ground (paired with pin 17)
11	Wait # (paired with pin 16)		
12	Paper end (Out of paper) #		
13	Select #		
14	Data strobe #		
15	Error #		

Performance

Under the EPP specification, the timing of signals in the initial implementation of the design allows for data transfer rates of about two megabytes per second with a cycle time of about 500 nanoseconds. By tightening the constraints and requiring the data to become valid quicker (within 100 nanoseconds), future implementations can increase the parallel transfer rate to eight megabytes per second. Although this rate is beyond the capability of parallel ports connected through the ISA bus, it is readily achievable by high-performance PCs using local bus designs. It puts parallel port performance on par with other PC interfaces (the AT interface and SCSI) and creates a multitude of possibilities for devices connected through Enhanced Parallel Ports.

Extended Capabilities Ports

Although the Enhanced Parallel Port provides means for making high-speed data transfers to peripherals, the specifications don't tell designers exactly how each transfer should be carried out every step of the way from program to printed page.

Hewlett-Packard combined efforts with Microsoft to create the *Extended Capabilities Port* (ECP), an extension that takes up where the EPP leaves off. Version 1.0 of the ECP specification for ISA-based computers was first published in November 1992, and numerous refinements have been made since then. ECP adds two modes to the EPP design: a fast two-way communication mode between a PC and its peripherals, and another two-way mode with performance further enhanced by simple integral data compression.

As with EPP, the ECP design is aimed at compatibility. An ECP port functions as a standard parallel port when dealing with old-fashioned devices like printers. With advanced devices, however, the ECP port can adeptly transfer data at the same high speeds as EPP but with additional versatility.

ECP includes a complete protocol for exchanging data across a parallel connection. Every ECP (as opposed to a standard parallel port) transfer is negotiated. The host computer can query a given device connected to the ECP system to determine its capabilities. Peripherals that support ECP signal that they can accept high-speed transmissions and the format of the data they are capable of receiving—for example, compressed or uncompressed. The ECP system includes full handshaking and error detection so that you and your system know when transfers are unsuccessful.

Data Compression

To boost effective throughput, ECP takes advantage of a simple form of data compression called *Run Length Encoding* (RLE). The RLE algorithm works at the byte level to reduce the transmission of a long sequence of the same byte to a two-byte code that indicates the repeated byte and the number of times that byte is repeated in the data stream. The ECP algorithm works over repeated byte strings up to 128 bytes long. Its two-byte coding thus allows a maximum compression ratio of 64 to 1.

Because repeated identical bytes occur often in raster images, RLE coding is particularly effective in sending bit-image graphics from a PC to a printer. Normal text usually does not contain sequences of identical characters more than two letters long, so RLE encoding helps little in text transmission speed. Then again, printing straight text rarely strains the capabilities of even an ordinary parallel port.

Channel Addressing

ECP is designed to link multiple devices to a single port. In order that signals can be routed to a particular device without other peripherals reacting to them, the ECP standard includes its own addressing scheme. To route a packet or stream of data to a particular peripheral, the host computer sends out a *channel address command* down the parallel port bus. The command tells all devices except the one identified by the command to ignore all data that is sent until the next channel address command or the end of the data stream. If no channel address is specified for a given transfer, the address defaults to zero and the information is broadcast across the parallel connection. The ECP standard allows for 128 different channel addresses.

Control and Configuration

The Extended Capabilities Port is controlled through a set of registers located at the same base addresses as are assigned to ordinary parallel ports. In addition to the data, status, and control registers of ordinary parallel ports, however, the ECP also uses an additional set of registers offset at port addresses 0400(Hex) higher than the base registers. The function of all ECP ports varies with the mode of operation of the ECP. By writing to the Extended Control Register (located at the I/O port located at the base address plus 0402(Hex)), the host computer can switch from standard parallel to PS/2 parallel port, EPP, or ECP modes. The host computer determines how the ECP operates.

In its default mode, the ECP behaves exactly like a standard parallel port. Writing bytes to the data register (located at the port's base address) sends the information down the data lines of the parallel bus. Bytes to be sent out the port then are written to the ECP buffer register, which may have an 8-, 16-, or 32-bit interface. Other registers monitor and control other aspects of the data transfer. Table 16.4 lists the registers used by the ECP and the modes in which they function.

TABLE 16.4. Extended Capabilities Port Register Definitions.

Name	Address	Mode	Function
Data	Base	PC, PS/2	Data register
ecpAFifo	Base	ECP	ECP FIFO (Address) buffer
DSR	Base+1	All	Status register
DCR	Base+2	All	Control register
cFifo	Base+400	EPP	Enhanced Parallel Port FIFO (data) buffer
ecpDFifo	Base+400	ECP	ECP FIFO (data) buffer
tFifo	Base+400	Test	Test FIFO

Name	Address	Mode	Function
cnfgA	Base+400	Configuration	Configuration register A
cnfgB	Base+401	Configuration	Configuration register B
ecr	Base+402	All	Extended control register

The ECP specification also redefines the signals and connections of the standard parallel port when it is operating in its ECP mode. Table 16.5 lists the ECP signal descriptions.

TABLE 16.5. Extended Capabilities Port Pin-Out

Host Pin	Slave Pin	Name	Function
1	1	nStrobe	Registers address or data into slave
2	2	Data 7	Data bit
3	3	Data 6	Data bit
4	4	Data 5	Data bit
5	5	Data 4	Data bit
6	6	Data 3	Data bit
7	7	Data 2	Data bit
8	8	Data 1	Data bit
9	9	Data 0	Data bit
10	10	nAck	Indicates valid data when asserted
11	11	Busy	Indicates peripheral can receive data when not asserted
12	12	PError	Acknowledges change in direction of transfer
13	13	Select	Indicates printer is on line
14	14	nAutoFd	Requests byte of data when asserted

continues

TABLE 16.5. Continued

Host Pin	Slave Pin	Name	Function
15	32	nFault	Generates interrupt when asserted
16	31	nInit	Sets transfer direction (asserted=reversed)
17	36	nSelectIn	Never asserted in ECP mode
18	33	Ground	Aux-Out
19	19	Ground	Return for strobe
20	21	Ground	Return for data 1
21	23	Ground	Return for data 3
22	25	Ground	Return for data 5
23	27	Ground	Return for data 7
24	29	Ground	Return for busy
25	30	Ground	Return logic ground
NC	15	Unused	
NC	16	Unused	
NC	17	Unused	
NC	20	Ground	Grounded on connector
NC	22	Ground	Grounded on connector
NC	24	Ground	Grounded on connector
NC	26	Ground	Grounded on connector
NC	28	Ground	Grounded on connector
NC	34	Unused	
NC	35	Unused	

Chapter 17
Printers and Plotters

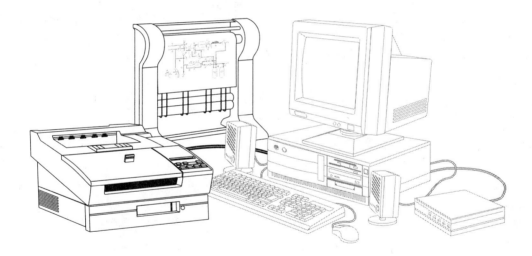

Of all the external peripherals people attach to their PCs, the most popular is undoubtedly the printer. Little wonder, considering that the printer is the primary means of converting your computer's intangible thoughts into the hard copy of the material world. Printers use a variety of technologies to put your PC's thoughts on paper, and each has its own advantages and disadvantages.

The term "printer" is perhaps the broadest in the language of data processing, uniting technologies as diverse as hammers, squirt guns, and flashlights. The range of performance is wider than with any other peripheral. Various printers operate at speeds from lethargic to lightning-like, from slower than an arthritic typist with one hand tied behind his back to faster than Speedy Gonzales having just munched tacos laced with amphetamines. They are packaged as everything from one-pound totables to truss-stressing monsters and look like anything from Neolithic bricks to Batman's nightmares. Some printers place ink dots on paper with text quality that rivals that of a professional publisher, and some chart out graphics with speed and sharpness that puts a plotter to shame. Some make a two-year-old's handiwork look elegant.

The classification of printers runs a similar, wide range. You can distinguish machines by their quality, speed, technology, purpose, weight, color, or any other of their innumerable (and properly pragmatic) design elements.

A definitive discourse on all aspects of printer technology would be a never-ending tale because the field is constantly changing. New technologies often arise, and old ones are revived and refined. Innovations are incorporated into old machines. And, seemingly obsolete ideas recur.

Printer Mechanics

Obviously, the term "computer printer" is a general one that refers not to one kind of machine but to several. Even in looking at the mechanical aspects of the typical printer's job of smudging paper with ink, you discover that many ways exist to put a computer's output on paper, just as more than one method exists for getting your house cat to part with its pelt.

Impact Printers

One of the most evident demarcations between printer technologies is whether anything mechanical actually impacts the paper on which you want to print. Impact printers beat your paper to death. Non-impact printers cuddle and squeeze it—perhaps even electrocute it—but never slam it hard. They can use any of a diverse array of technologies, from laser beams to miniature toaster heating-elements that fry pigment to paper, to bubbles of ink blown into place. The sole characteristic that can be assumed for any non-impact printer is that nothing forcibly smashes into the paper during the image-making process.

Typewriter Origins

Some of the most popular—and, not incidentally, least expensive—printers rely on impact technology. They are direct descendants of the original office typewriter and are perhaps best understood by examining their aged forefather.

Although an old-fashioned typewriter is a mechanical complexity (as anyone knows who has tried putting one back together after taking it apart), its operating principle is quite simple. Strip away all the cams, levers, and keys, and you find that the essence of the typewriter is its hammers.

Each hammer strikes against an inked ribbon, which is then pressed against a sheet of paper. The impact of the hammer against the ribbon shakes and squeezes ink onto the paper. Absorbed into the paper fibers, the ink leaves a visible mark or image in the shape of the part of the hammer that struck at the ribbon, typically a letter of the alphabet.

One way or another, all impact printers rely on this basic typewriter principle. Like Christopher Sholes first platen-pecker, all impact printers smash a hammer of some kind against a ribbon to squeeze ink from the ribbon onto paper, making their mark by force. In fact, if any difference exists between an impact printer and a typewriter at all, it is that the typewriter directly links your fingers to the mechanism that does the printing. A printer, on the other hand, inserts your personal computer between your mind and the printed word.

In the earliest days of personal computers—before typewriter makers were sure that PCs would catch on and create a personal printer market—a number of companies adapted typewriters to computer output chores. The Bytewriter was typical of the result—a slow, plodding computer printer with full typewriter keyboard. It could do double-duty as fast as your fingers could fly, but it was no match for the computer's output.

One device, short-lived on the marketplace, even claimed that you could turn your typewriter into a printer simply by setting a box on the keyboard. The box was filled with dozens of solenoids and enough other mechanical parts to make the Space Shuttle look simple. The solenoids worked as electronically controlled "fingers," pressing down each key on command from the host computer. Interesting as it sounds, they tread the thin line between the absurd and surreal. More than a little doubt exists as to whether these machines, widely advertised in 1981, were ever actually sold.

Today, the most popular low-cost printers are impact dot-matrix printers, most often clipped to simply the name "dot-matrix." Although they use a different character-forming method than the classic typewriter, they rely on the same hammer-and-ribbon impact printing principle.

Impact Advantages

As with typewriters, all impact printers have a number of desirable qualities. Owing to their heritage of more than a century of engineering refinement, they represent a mature technology. Their designs and functions are relatively straightforward and familiar.

Most impact printers can spread their output across any medium that ink has an affinity for, including any paper you might have lying around your home, from onion skin to thin cardstock. While both impact and non-impact technologies have been developed to the point that either can produce high-quality or high-speed output, impact technology takes the lead when you share one of the most common business needs, making multi-part forms. Impact printers can hammer an impression not just through a ribbon, but through several sheets of paper as well. Slide a carbon between the sheets or, better yet, treat the paper for non-carbon duplicates, and you get multiple, guaranteed-identical copies with a single pass through the mechanism. For a number of business applications—for example, the generation of charge receipts—exact carbon copies are a necessity, and impact printing is an absolute requirement.

Impact Noise

Impact printers reveal their typewriter heritage in another way. The hammer bashing against the ribbon and paper makes noise, a sharp staccato rattle that is high in amplitude and rich in high-frequency components, penetrating and bothersome as a dental drive or angry horde of giant, hungry mosquitoes. Typically, the impact printer rattles and prattles louder than most normal conversational tones, and it is more obnoxious than an argument. The higher the speed of the impact printer, the higher the pitch of the noise and the more penetrating it becomes.

Some printer makers have toned down their boisterous scribes admirably—some printers as fast as 780 characters per second are as quiet as 55 dB, about the level of a quiet PC fan. But you still want to leave the room when an inexpensive impact printer (the best-selling of all printers) grinds through its assignment.

Non-Impact Printers

The obvious opposite to impact technology is non-impact printing. A number of other ways of putting images on paper without the typewriter-like hammer impact have been developed through the application of new technologies and a good deal of imagination. The five leading, non-impact technologies are the inkjet, thermal, laser, wax-transfer, and dye-diffusion.

Image-Forming Methods

The terms "impact" and "non-impact" describe the kind of devilry involved in getting any marks at all to appear on paper. But the method of making those marks is independent of what they are and how they are shaped. While differing printing technologies have some effect on the quality of the image and what the printer is used for, other considerations are just as important in regard to image quality. Among the most important is the character-forming method used by the printer.

Fully Formed Character Printers

The original typewriter and all such machines made through the 1970s were based on the same character-forming principle as the original creation of Johannes Gutenberg. After laboriously carving individual letters out of wood, daubing them with sticky black ink, and smashing paper against the gooey mess, Gutenberg brought printing to the West by inventing the concept of movable type. Every letter he printed was printed fully formed from a complete, although reversed, image of itself. The character was fully formed in advance of printing. Every part of it, from the boldest stroke to the tiniest serif, was printed in one swipe of the press. Old-fashioned typewriters adapted Gutenberg's individual-character type to an impact mechanism.

In the early days of personal computing, a number of machines used this typewriter technology and were grouped together under the term fully formed character printers. Other names for this basic technology were letter-quality printers, daisy-wheel printers, and a variation called the thimble printer.

Nearly all of the fully formed character printers that are likely to be connected to a personal computer use the impact principle to get their ink on paper. Rather than having a separate hammer for each letter, however, the characters are arranged on a single, separate element that is inserted between a single hammer and the ribbon. The hammer, powered by a solenoid that is controlled by the electronics of the printer and your computer, impacts against the element. The element then squeezes the ink off the ribbon and on to the paper. To allow the full range of alphanumeric characters to be printed using this single-hammer technique, the printing element swerves, shakes, or rotates each individual character that is to be formed in front of the hammer as it is needed.

Most often, the characters are arranged near the tips of the spokes of a wheel. These machines are called "daisy-wheel" because the hubs resemble flower petals. Hold the daisy horizontally and bend those petals upward, and the printing element becomes the thimble (or what you might call a "tulip-wheel").

Fully formed character technology produces good-quality output, in line with better typewriters. The chief limitation, in fact, is not the printing technology but the ribbon that is used. Some daisy-wheel printers equipped with a mylar film ribbon can give results almost on-par with the work of a phototypesetter.

While daisy-wheel printers still are available, they are *passé*, from the PC perspective. Gutenberg-era technology finally is showing its age. The movable-type design limits them solely to text printing and crude graphics. Fully formed character printers also limit you to a few typefaces. You can print only the typefaces—and font sizes—available on the image-forming daisy-wheels or thimbles. These machines also are slow—budget-priced machines hammer out text at a lazy 12 to 20 characters per second, and even the most expensive machines struggle to reach 90 characters per second. Other technologies (in particular, laser printers) now equal or exceed the quality of fully formed character printers, run far ahead in speed, and impose little or no price penalty.

Bit-Image Printers

The way to break free from the binding of Gutenberg is to go him one further. Gutenberg broke the page into tiny, separate elements—individual letters. The next step would be to follow suit with the letters themselves—break them into dots. The result is the bit-image printer.

Where fully formed character printers remember the shape of each letter mechanically, the bit-image printer stores each shape electronically. It forms each character on-the-fly based on the bit arrangements stored in memory.

The raw material for characters on paper is much the same as it is on the video screen—dots. A number of dots can be arranged to resemble any character that you want to print. To make things easier for the printer (and its designer), printers that form their characters from dots usually array those dots in a rectilinear matrix like a crossword puzzle grid. Because most bit-image printers form their characters from dots placed within a matrix, they are usually termed dot-matrix printers. Most people, however, restrict the use of the dot-matrix term to impact dot-matrix machines.

Bit-Image Technologies

All popular, non-impact printers and the surviving impact technology use bit-image technology. The reason is versatility. A bit-image printer can generate both text and graphics at virtually any level of quality. The dot patterns that make up individual characters are computer-controlled and can be changed and varied by your computer (or the computer-like control electronics built into the printer) without your needing to make any mechanical adjustments to the machine. A daisy-wheel, fully formed character printer may allow you to shift from Roman to Italic typeface or from Pica to Elite type size simply by swapping printing elements (the daisy-wheels themselves), but matrix printers make the switch even easier and the repertory wider. Just send a computerized instruction to the printer, and you can change the typeface in mid-line, double the height of each character, squeeze type to half its width, or shift to proportionally spaced script. The same dots can be formed into a chart, graph, drawing, or simulation of a half-tone photograph. Using bit-image techniques, one printer can put virtually any image on paper.

The quality and speed of the output of bit-image printers vary with the technology used. At the low end, dot-matrix printing can look simply awful. At the high end, better laser printers can generate book-quality output. Speeds vary from less than a page a minute to dozens of pages in the same period. The following paragraphs describe how each of the most important bit-image printer technologies works.

Impact Dot-Matrix Printers

The prototypical, bit-image printer is that impact dot-matrix machine. It uses a printhead that shuttles back and forth across the width of the paper. A number of thin printwires act as the hammers that squeeze ink from ribbon to paper.

In most dot-matrix printers, a seemingly complex, but efficient mechanism controls each of the printwires. The printwire normally is held away from the ribbon and paper, and against the force of a spring, by a strong permanent magnet. The magnet is wrapped with a coil of wire that forms an electromagnet, wound so that its polarity is the opposite of that of the permanent magnet. To fire the print wire against the ribbon and paper, this electromagnet is energized (under computer control, of course), and its field neutralizes that of the permanent magnet. Without the force of the permanent magnet holding the print wire back, the spring forcefully jabs the print wire out against ribbon, squeezing ink onto the paper. After the printwire makes its dot, the electromagnet is de-energized, and the permanent magnet pulls the printwire back to its idle position, ready to fire again.

The two-magnets-and-spring approach is designed with one primary purpose—to hold the printwire away from the paper (and out of harm's way) when no power is supplied to the printer and the printhead. The complexity is justified by the protection it affords the delicate printwires.

The printhead of a dot-matrix printer is made from a number of these print wire mechanisms. Most first-generation personal computer printers and many current machines use nine wires arrayed in a vertical column. To produce high quality, an increasing number of newer, impact dot-matrix printers use even more wires, typically 18 or 24. These often are arranged in parallel rows with the printwires vertically staggered, although some machines use different arrangements.

To print a line of characters, the printhead moves horizontally across the paper, and each wire fires as necessary to form the individual characters, its impact precisely timed so that it falls on exactly the right position in the matrix. The wires fire on the fly—the printhead never pauses until it reaches the other side of the paper.

A major factor in determining the printing speed of a dot-matrix machine is the time required between successive strikes of each print wire. Physical laws of motion limit the acceleration each print wire can achieve in ramming toward the paper and back. Thus, the time needed to retract and re-actuate each printwire puts a physical limit on how rapidly the printhead can travel across the paper. It cannot sweep past the next dot position before each of the print wires inside it is ready to fire. If the printhead travels too fast, dot positioning (and character shapes) would become rather haphazard.

To speed up operation, some impact dot-matrix machines print bidirectionally, rattling out one row from left to right then the next row right to left. This mode of operation saves the time that would ordinarily be wasted when the carriage returns to the left side of the page to start the next line. Of course, the printer must have sufficient memory to store a full line of text so that it can be read out backwards.

Inkjets

If the term "inkjet" conjures up images of the Nautilus and giant squid or a B-52 spraying out blue fluid instead of a fluffy white contrail, your mind is on the right track. Inkjet printers are electronic squids that squirt out ink like miniature jet engines fueled in full color. While this technology sounds unlikely— a printer that sprays droplets of ink onto paper—it works well enough to deliver image sharpness on par with most other output technologies.

In essence, the inkjet printer is a dot-matrix printer with the hammer impact removed. Instead of a hammer pounding ink onto paper, the inkjet flings it into place from tiny nozzles, each one corresponding to a print wire of the impact dot-matrix printer. The motive force can be an electromagnet or, as is more likely today, a *piezo-electric crystal* (a thin crystal that bends when electricity is applied across it). A sharp, digital pulse of electricity causes the crystal to twitch and force ink through the nozzle into its flight to paper.

One secret to the success of the inkjet is that it has no ribbon to blur the image. On-paper quality can equal that of more expensive laser printers. The laser-less technology of the inkjet machines equates to lower costs—and lower prices—budget inkjets rival low-end dot-matrix printers in affordable price.

But inkjets are slower at producing high quality than laser printers because they rely on a printhead that mechanically scans across each sheet instead of lightning-fast optics. Inkjets also require periodic maintenance because they use liquid ink. If not properly cared for, the ink can dry in the nozzles and clog everything up.

To avoid such problems, better inkjets have built-in routines that clean the nozzles with each use. Most nozzles now are self-sealing, so that when they are not used, air cannot get to the ink. Some manufacturers even combine the inkjet and ink supply into one easily changeable module. If, however, you pack an inkjet away without properly cleaning it first, it is not likely to work when you resurrect it months later.

Because inkjets are non-impact printers, they are much quieter than ordinary dot-matrix engines. About the only sound you hear from them is the carriage coursing back and forth. On the other hand, inkjets require special paper with controlled absorbency for best results—that means you are likely to pay more per page. If you try to get by using cheap paper that is too porous, the inks wick away into a blur. If the paper is too glossy, the wet ink can smudge.

The liquid ink of inkjet printers can be a virtue when it comes to color. The inks remain fluid enough even after they have been sprayed on paper to blend together. This gives color inkjet printers the ability to actually mix their primary colors together to create intermediary tones. The range of color quality from ink-jet printers is wide. The best yield some of the brightest, most saturated colors available from any technology. The vast majority, however, cannot quite produce a true-color palette.

As important as the underlying print mechanism is the choice of ink. After all, a color printer cannot make colors that are not in its inks. Ink-jet ink tends to blur (which reduces both sharpness and color contrast) because it dries at least partly by absorption into paper. Most ink-jet printers work with almost any paper stock, but produce the best results—sharpest, most colorful—with specially coated papers that have controlled ink absorption. On non-absorbent media (for example, projection acetates), the ink must dry solely by evaporation, and the output is subject to smudging until the drying process completes.

To avoid the complications of ink absorption by paper, printer makers developed a new inkjet technology called the solid-inkjet or phase-change printer. Classic inkjets spray volatile inks based on solvents, but phase-change printers melt wax that is dyed the appropriate color, fling it at paper, and let it harden there without getting absorbed. As with other inkjets, phase-change printers spray tiny dots of ink. When the hot dots hit the paper, they quickly cool, changing phase from liquid to solid (hence the name of the technology). Because the paper becomes little more than a carrier, phase-change printers are almost completely insensitive to the paper you feed through them. The solid ink is resistant to smudging even on non-absorbent media.

The original phase-change printer, Howtek Pixelmaster, stopped there, leaving little lumps of plastic-based inks on the paper—or clogging the printhead. Tektronix improved on this original by adding a cold fuser, a steel roller that then squashes the ink dots flat, or nearly so, as the printing medium rolls out of the printer. To make the fuser work, they also reformulated the inks from plastic compounds to a fatty wax base, something akin to a Crayola. Because they do not get absorbed into the paper, phase-change inks have greater saturation than traditional inkjet inks. Heat alone can remove clogs from a phase change printhead.

Thermal

A printer that works on the same principle as a wood-burning set might seem better for a Boy Scout than an on-the-go executive, but today's easiest-to-tote printers do exactly that—the equivalent of charring an image on paper. Thermal printers use the same electrical heating of the word-burner, a resistance that heats up with the flow of current. In the case of the thermal printer, however, the resistance element is tiny and heats and cools quickly, in a fraction of a second. As with inkjets, the thermal printhead is the equivalent of that of a dot-matrix printer, except that it heats rather than hits.

Thermal printers do not, however, actually char the paper on which they print. Getting paper that hot would be dangerous, precariously close to combustion (although it might let the printer do double-duty as a cigarette lighter). Instead, thermal printers use special, thermally sensitive paper that turns from white to near-black at a moderate temperature.

Thermal technology is ideal for portable printers because few moving parts are involved—only the printhead moves, nothing inside it. No springs and wires means no jamming. The tiny, resistive elements require little power to heat, actually less than is needed to fire a wire in an impact printer. Thermal printers can be lightweight, quiet, and reliable. They can even run on batteries.

The special paper they require is one drawback. Not only is it costly (because it is, after all, special paper) but it feels funny and is prone to discolor if it is inadvertently heated to too high a temperature. The paper cannot tell the difference between a hot printhead and a cozy corner in the sun.

Gradually, thermal printers are becoming special application machines. Inkjets have many of the same virtues and more reasonable paper; therefore low-cost inkjets are invading the territory of the thermal machines.

Thermal Transfer

Engineers have made thermal technology more independent of the paper or printing medium by moving the image-forming substance from the paper to a carrier or ribbon. Instead of changing a characteristic of the paper, these machines transfer pigment or dyes from the carrier to the paper. The heat from the printhead melts the binder holding the ink to the carrier, allowing the ink to transfer to the paper. On the cool paper, the binder again binds the ink in place. In that the binder is often a wax, these machines are often called thermal-wax transfer printers.

These machines produce the richest, purest, most even and saturated color of any color print technology. Because the thermal elements have no moving parts, they can be made almost arbitrarily small to yield high resolutions. Current thermal-wax print engines achieve resolutions similar to those of laser printers. However, due to exigencies of printhead designs, the top resolution of these printers extends only in one dimension (vertical). Top thermal-wax printers achieve 300 dots per inch horizontally and 600 dots per inch vertically.

Compared to other technologies, however, thermal-wax engines are slow and wasteful. They are slow because the thermal printing elements must have a chance to cool off before advancing the 1/300th of an inch to the next line on the paper. And they are wasteful because they use wide ink transfer sheets, pure colors supported in a wax-based medium clinging to a plastic film base—sort of like a mylar typewriter ribbon with a gland condition. Each of the primary colors to be printed on each page requires a swath of inked transfer sheet as large as the sheet of paper to be printed—that is nearly four feet of transfer sheet for one page. Consequently, printing a full-color page can be expensive, typically measured in dollars rather than cents per page.

Because thermal-wax printers are not a mass market item and each manufacturer uses its own designs for both mechanism and supplies, you usually are restricted to one source for inksheets— the printer manufacturer. While that helps ensure quality (printer makers pride themselves on the color and saturation of their inks), it also keeps prices higher than they might be in a more directly competitive environment.

For color work, some thermal-wax printers give you the choice of three- or four-pass transfer sheets and printing. A three-pass transfer sheet holds the three primary colors of ink—red, yellow, and blue—while a four color sheet adds black. Although black can be made by overlaying the three primary colors, a separate black ink gives richer, deeper tones. It also imposes a higher cost and extends printing time by one-third.

From these three primary colors, thermal-wax printers claim to be able to make anywhere from seven to nearly seventeen million colors. That prestidigitation requires a mixture of transparent inks, dithering, and ingenuity. Because the inks used by thermal wax printers are transparent, they can be laid one atop another to create simple secondary colors. They do not, however, actually mix.

Expanding the thermal-wax palette further requires pointillistic mixing, laying different color dots next to each other and relying on them to visually blend together in a distant blur. Instead of each dot of ink constituting a picture element, a group of several dots effectively forms a super pixel of an intermediate color.

The penalty for this wider palette is a loss of resolution. For example, a super pixel measuring five by five dots would trim the resolution of a thermal-wax printer to 60 dots per inch. Image quality looks like a color halftone—a magazine reproduction—rather than a real photograph. Although the quality is shy of perfection, it is certainly good enough for proofs of what is going to a film recorder or the service bureau to be made into color separations.

A variation of the thermal wax design combines the sharpness available from the technology with a versatility and cost more in-line with ordinary dot-matrix printers. Instead of using a page-wide printhead and equally wide transfer sheets, some thermal wax machines use a line-high printhead and a thin transfer sheet that resembles a mylar typewriter ribbon. These machines print one, sharp line of text or graphics at a time, usually in one color—black. They are quiet as inkjets but produce sharper, darker images.

Dye-Diffusion

For true photo-quality output from a printer, today's stellar technology is the thermal dye-diffusion process, sometimes called thermal *dye-sublimation*. Using a mechanism similar to that of the thermal-wax process, dye-diffusion printers are designed to use penetrating dyes rather than inks. Instead of a dot merely being present or absent, as in the case of a thermal-wax printer, diffusion allows the depth of the color of each dot to vary. The diffusion of the dyes can be carefully controlled by the printhead. Because each of the three primary colors can have a huge number of intensities (most makers claim 256), the palette of the dye-diffusion printer is essentially unlimited.

What is limited is the size of the printed area in some printers. The output of most dye-diffusion printers looks like photographs in size, as well as color. Another limit is cost. The newer, more exotic technology pushes dye-diffusion machines into the pricing stratosphere. Although one manufacturer promises thermal and dye-diffusion quality near $1000, most machines cost in excess of $5000.

Laser Printers

The one revolution that changed the faces of both offices and forests around the world was the photocopier. Trees plummet by the millions to provide fodder for the duplicate, triplicate, megaplicate. Today's non-impact, bit-image laser printer owes its life to this technology.

At heart, the principle is simple. Some materials react to light in strange ways. Selenium and some complex organic compounds modify their electrical conductivity under the influence of light. Copiers and laser printers capitalize on this by focusing an optical image on a photo conductive drum that has been given a static electrical charge. The charge drains away from the conductive areas that have been struck by light but persist in the dark areas. Pigment called toner is then spread across the drum, and it sticks to the charged areas. A roller squeezes paper against the drum to transfer the pigment, which is fixed in place by heating or "fusing" it.

The trick to the laser printer is that the laser beam is made, as if by magic, to scan across the drum (magic because most printers use rotating mirrors to make the scan). By turning the drum, it automatically advances to the next line as the scanning is done. The laser beam is modulated, rapidly switched on for light areas, off for dark areas, one minuscule dot at a time to form a bit-image. Similar optical printers use LCD-shutter technology, which puts an electronic shutter (or an array of them) between a constant light source (which need not be a laser) and the drum to modulate the beam. LED printers modulate ordinary Light-Emitting Diodes as their optical source.

As exotic as these different technologies sound, these imaging parts of the laser printer are of small concern in buying such a machine. Nearly all laser and laser-like printers produce similar results—you need an eye loupe to tell the difference—with today's incarnation of the technology producing resolution of 300 to 600 dots per inch. You find that the biggest differences between lasers and related LCD shutter printers are found in their paper-handling and data-handling.

As far as color is concerned, today's affordable laser printer gives you the Model T choice—any color you want as long as it is black. The printers themselves are designed for monochrome operation and can yield other colors with toners of different hues (few of which are available).

Bit-Image Quality

The quality of the characters printed by the bit-image printer is determined by three chief factors—the number of dots in the matrix, the addressability of the printer, and the size of the dots. The denser the matrix (the more dots in a given area), the better the characters look. Higher addressability allows the printer to place dots on paper with greater precision. Smaller dots allow finer details to be rendered.

The minimal matrix of any printer measures 5 x 7 (horizontal by vertical) dots and is just sufficient to render all the upper-and lowercase letters of the alphabet unambiguously—but not aesthetically. The dots are big and they look disjointed. Worse, the minimal matrix is too small to let descending characters ("g," "j," "p," "q," and "y") droop below the general line of type and instead makes them look cramped and scrunched up. Rarely do you encounter this minimal level of quality today except in the cheapest, close-out printers.

The minimum matrix used by most commercial dot-matrix printers measures 9 x 9 dots, a readable arrangement but still somewhat inelegant in a world accustomed to printed text. Newer 18- and 24-pin impact dot-matrix printers can form characters with 12 x 24 to 24 x 24 matrices.

Other bit-image technologies go even further. Laser printers pack tiny dots very densely, 300 or 600 per inch. At a 10-per-inch character pitch, a single letter is formed from a 30 x 50 or 60 x 100 matrix. The latest generation of inkjet and impact dot-matrix printers also approaches that quality level. Newer lasers can double or quadruple that matrix quality. For comparison, commercial type-setting equipment achieves character matrices of about 240 x 400 for 12-point (that is, 10-pitch) type.

As with computer displays, the resolution and addressability of dot-matrix printers often are confused. When resolution is mentioned, most of the time addressability is intended, particularly on dot-matrix printer specification sheets. A printer may be able to address any position on the paper with an accuracy of, say, 1/120th inch. If a printwire is larger than 1/120th inch in diameter, however, the machine never is able to render detail as small as 1/120th inch.

The big dots made by the wide printwires blurs out the detail. Better quality impact dot-matrix printers have more printwires, and they are smaller. Also, the ribbon that is inserted between the wires and paper blurs each dot hammered out by an impact dot-matrix printer. Mechanical limits also constrain the on-paper resolution of impact machines.

Impact dot-matrix printers use a variety of tricks to improve their often marginal print quality. Often, even bidirectional printers slow down to single-direction operation when quality counts. To increase dot density, they retrace each line two or more times, shifting the paper half the width of a dot vertically, between passes, filling in the space between dots. Unidirectional operation helps insure accurate placement of each dot in each pass.

With non-impact bit-image printers, resolution and addressability usually are the same, although some use techniques to improve apparent resolution without altering the number of dots they put in a given area.

Laser Resolution Issues

The best resolution available in moderate cost PC printers comes from laser machines. The minimum resolution offered by these machines is 300 dots per inch, and newer machines are pushing the expected standard to 600 dots per inch (some go to 1200 dpi). Several factors control the resolution that slides out of a laser printer.

In most lasers, the resolution level is fixed primarily by the electronics inside the printer. The most important part of the control circuitry is the *Raster Image Processor,* also known as the RIP. The job of the RIP is to translate the string of characters or other printing commands into the bit-image that the printer transfers to paper. In effect, the RIP works like a video board, interpreting drawing commands (a single letter in a print stream is actually a drawing command to print that letter), computing the position of each dot on the page, and pushing the appropriate value into the printer's memory. The memory of the printer is arranged in a raster just like the raster of a video screen, and one memory cell—a single bit in the typical black-and-white laser printer—corresponds to each dot position on paper.

Most dot-matrix printers accept dot-addressable graphics on the fly. That is, the printer obediently rattles data bytes to paper as soon as the bytes are received or, at most, after a full line has been accepted. They operate one line at a time, as line printers.

Lasers cannot work so quickly. They work a page at a time, (earning them the epithet *page printers*) digesting an entire sheet of graphics before committing a dot to paper. The laser mechanism is tuned to run at exactly one speed, and it must receive data at the proper rate to properly form its image. In addition, many lasers recognize higher level graphics commands to draw lines and figures across the entire on-paper image area. To properly form these images, the laser needs to get the big picture of its work.

For these and other reasons, lasers require prodigious amounts of memory to buffer full-page, bit-mapped images in their highest resolution modes. The size of the memory in the laser printer, consequently, limits the resolution of graphics that can be printed. Enough memory must be present to store a whole page at the resolution level to be printed. If not enough memory is available, only a portion of a page can be imaged or the full page must be imaged at a lower resolution. An 8 x 10.5 -inch image (about a full page on an 8.5 x 11-inch sheet) at 300 dpi requires 945,000 bytes—essentially one megabyte of printer memory. The 512K that is packed in some printers as standard equipment allows only 150 dpi across a full 8.5 by 11-inch sheet. Even more memory is needed if you want to use the printer's memory for functions other than storing a raster—for instance, holding downloadable fonts.

(Most lasers operate in a character-mapped mode when rendering alphanumerics, so memory usage is not as great. The printer can store a full-page image in ASCII or a similar code, one byte per letter, and generate the dots of each character as the page is scanned through the printer.)

The RIP itself may by design limit a laser printer to a given resolution. In many lasers, however, the RIP can be replaced by an add-in processor using the video input of the printer. The video input earns its name because its signal is applied directly to the light source in the laser in raster scanned form (like a television image), bypassing most of the printer's electronics. The add-in processor can modulate the laser at higher rates to create higher resolutions.

Hewlett-Packard's LaserJet III series of printers introduced another way to improve sharpness that the company called *Resolution Enhancement Technology*. This technique works by altering the size of toner dots at the edges of characters and diagonal lines to reduce the jagged steps inherent in any matrix bit-image printing technique. With Resolution Enhancement, the actual on-paper resolution remains at 300 dpi, but the optimized dot size makes the printing appear sharper.

Moving from 300 dpi to 600 dpi and 1200 dpi means more than changing the RIP and adding memory, however. The higher resolutions also demand improved toner formulations because, at high resolutions, the size of toner particles limits sharpness much as the size of printwires limits impact dot-matrix resolution. With higher resolution laser printers, it becomes increasingly important to get the right toner, particularly if you have toner cartridges refilled. The wrong toner limits resolution just as a fuzzy ribbon limits the quality of impact printer output.

Graphics Printing Techniques

Bit-image printers compatible with the IBM character set give you two methods for printing graphics, *block graphics* and *all-points-addressable graphics.* The principle differences between the two are quality and compatibility. Block graphics are ugly, but any software that can generate them operates any printer that can print them. Bit-image graphics are sharper, but require that your software know exactly how to control your printer.

Block Graphics

Think of block graphics as an extra set of characters built into a printer that permits you to draw pictures out of building blocks of simple shapes—like squares, rectangles, triangles, horizontal and vertical lines, and so on. Each of these shapes is electronically coded and recognized by the printer as if it were a letter of the alphabet, and the printer merely lays down line after line of these block characters to make a picture, like filling in each square on a piece of graph paper with different shapes. The pictures look a little chunky because the building blocks are big, just a little under 1/8th inch across in most printer's default text modes.

All-Points-Addressable Graphics

The native mode of most bit-image printers allows you to decide where to place individual dots on the printed sheet using a technique called *all-points-addressable graphics* or APA graphics. With a knowledge of the appropriate printer instructions, you or your software can draw graphs in great detail or even make pictures resembling the halftone photographs printed in newspapers. The software built into the printer allows every printable dot position to be controlled—specified as printed (black) or not (white). An entire image can be built up like a television picture, scanning lines several dots wide (as wide as the number of wires in the printhead) down the paper.

This graphics printing technique takes other names, too. Because each individual printed dot can be assigned a particular location or "address" on the paper, this feature is often called dot-addressable graphics. Sometimes, that title is simplified into dot graphics. Occasionally, it appears as bit-image graphics, because each dot is effectively the image of one bit of data.

The problem with all-points-addressable graphics is that your software must know the codes for telling your printer where to put each dot. Although a number of standards has arisen in the printer industry, some manufacturers have elected to go in their own directions and use their own codes. Most, however, follow the codes set by the industry leaders. For example, most nine-pin and 24-pin impact dot-matrix printers use the same codes as Epson or IBM printers. Most laser printers use the same codes as Hewlett-Packard LaserJet printers.

Printer Control

To make what you see on paper resemble what you preview on your monitor screen, your printer requires guidance from your computer and your software to tell it exactly how to make a printout look. The computer must send the printer a series of instructions, either to control the most intimate operation of the dumb printer or to coax special features from the brainy machine.

The instructions from the computer must be embedded in the character stream because that is the only data connection between the printer and its host. These embedded instructions can take on any of several forms.

Control Characters

Some of the most necessary instructions are the most common, for instance to backspace, tab, or even underline characters. In fact, these instructions are so commonplace that they were incorporated into the ASCII character set and assigned specific values. To backspace, for instance, your computer just sends your printer a byte with the ASCII value 08, the backspace character. Upon receiving this character, the printer backspaces instead of making a mark on the paper. The entire group of these special ASCII values are termed control characters.

Escape Sequences

The number of ASCII characters available for printer commands are few, and the number of functions that the printer can carry out are many. To sneak additional instructions through the data channel, most printers use special strings of characters called escape sequences.

An escape sequence is a series of ASCII characters that begins with a special code symbol assigned the ASCII value of 27. This special character is often called escape by programmers, and is abbreviated ESC.

In most commands, the escape character by itself does nothing. It serves only as an attention-getter. It warns the printer that the ASCII character or characters that follow should be interpreted as commands rather than printed out.

ANSI Escape Sequences

The American National Standards Institute has defined a standard set of escape sequences for controlling printers. A partial listing of these ANSI escape sequences is given in Table 17.1.

TABLE 17.1. ANSI Control Characters

ASCII value	Control value	Mnemonic	Function
0	^@	NUL	Used as a fill character
1	^A	SOH	Start of heading (indicator)
2	^B	STX	Start of text (indicator)
3	^C	ETX	End of text (indicator)
4	^D	EOT	End of transmission; disconnect character
5	^E	ENQ	Enquiry; request answerback message
6	^F	ACK	Acknowledge
7	^G	BEL	Sounds audible bell tone
8	^H	BS	Backspace
9	^I	HT	Horizontal tab
10	^J	LF	Line feed
11	^K	VT	Vertical tab
12	^L	FF	Form feed
13	^M	CR	Carriage return
14	^N	SO	Shift out; changes character set
15	^O	SI	Shift in; changes character set
16	^P	DLE	Data link escape
17	^Q	DC1	Data control 1, also known as XON
18	^R	DC2	Data control 2
19	^S	DC3	Data control 3, also known as XOFF
20	^T	DC4	Data control 4
21	^U	NAK	Negative acknowledge
22	^V	SYN	Synchronous idle
23	^W	ETB	End of transmission block (indicator)
24	^X	CAN	Cancel; immediately ends any control or escape sequence

continues

TABLE 17.1. Continued

ASCII value	Control value	Mnemonic	Function
25	^Y	EM	End of medium (indicator)
26	^Z	SUB	Substitute (also, end-of-file marker)
27	^[	ESC	Escape; introduces escape sequence
28	^\	FS	File separator (indicator)
29	^]	GS	Group separator (indicator)
30	^^	RS	Record separator (indicator)
31	^_	US	Unit separator (indicator)
32		SP	Space character
127		DEL	No operation
128		Reserved	Reset parser with no action (Esc)
129		Reserved	Reset parser with no action (Esc A)
130		Reserved	Reset parser with no action (Esc B)
131		Reserved	Reset parser with no action (Esc C)
132		IND	Index; increment active line (move paper up)
133		NEL	Next line; advance to first character of next line
134		SSA	Start of selected area (indicator)
135		ESA	End of selected area (indicator)
136		HTS	Set horizontal tab (at active column)
137		HTJ	Horizontal tab with justification
138		VTS	Set vertical tab stop (at current line)
139		PLD	Partial line down
140		PLU	Partial line up
141		RI	Reverse index (move paper down, backwards, one line)
142		SS2	Single shift 2
143		SS3	Single shift 3
144		DCS	Device control string
145		PU1	Private use 1
146		PU2	Private use 2
147		STS	Set terminal state
148		CCH	Cancel character

ASCII value	Control value	Mnemonic	Function
149		MW	Message writing
150		SPA	Start of protected area (indicator)
151		EPA	End of protected area (indicator)
152		Reserved	Function same as Esc X
153		Reserved	Function same as Esc Y
154		Reserved	Function same as Esc Z
155		CSI	Control sequence introducer
156		ST	String terminator
157		OSC	Operating system command (indicator)
158		PM	Privacy message
159		APC	Application program command

Some of the preceding also are implemented as standard escape sequences for use in seven-bit environments:

Esc D	Index
Esc E	Vertical line
Esc H	Set horizontal tab
Esc Z	Set vertical tab
Esc K	Partial line down
Esc L	Partial line up
Esc M	Reverse index
Esc N	Single shift 2
Esc O	Single shift 3
Esc P	Device control string
Esc [	Control sequence introducer
Esc \	String terminator
Esc]	Operating system command
Esc ^	Private message
Esc _	Application program command

Characters shown as implemented by Digital Equipment Corporation.

De Facto Command Standards

As is so often the case with personal computer products, the standard escape sequences are not that standard. The ANSI list is chiefly designed to handle the printing of text using fully formed character printers. Many printers have advanced graphics and other functions that transcend the ANSI design. Nearly every printer manufacturer, consequently, has broadened, adapted, or ignored the standard to suit the special needs of its own printer.

Whatever standards do exist among printers are de facto, after the fact, earning their status as standards simply because lots of people follow them. Usually the codes and commands used by a large manufacturer with a top-selling product are followed by smaller companies making compatible products.

Daisy-Wheel Commands

Initially, the market for fully formed character printers was dominated by two companies, the Diablo division of Xerox and Qume, owned by the ITT conglomerate at the time the PC was introduced. (The company has changed hands several times since then.) The commands used by the printers manufactured by those two companies have emerged as compatibility standards among letter-quality printers. Even some laser printers boast either Diablo- or Qume-compatibility so that they can take over for old technology machines and work with aged word processors. The two command sets are very similar, differing only in a few instructions. A condensed listing of the two command sets is given in Table 17.2.

TABLE 17.2. Diablo and Qume Control Codes and Escape Sequences

Control Codes

ASCII value	Control value	Mnemonic	Function
1	^A	SOH	Perform user test continuously
2	^B	STX	Perform user test once
5	^E	ENQ	Halt continuous user test
7	^G	BEL	Sounds audible bell tone
8	^H	BS	*Backspace
9	^I	HT	*Horizontal tab
10	^J	LF	*Line feed
11	^K	VT	*Vertical tab
12	^L	FF	*Form feed
13	^M	CR	*Carriage return
27		Esc	Return to normal mode

ASCII value	Control value	Mnemonic	Function
31		US	Program mode carriage motion
127		DEL	*No Operation

Escape Sequences

Escape Sequence	Function
Esc BS	*Backspace 1/120 inch
Esc LF	*Negative (backwards) line feed
Esc SO	Shift to primary mode
Esc SI	Return to normal mode
Esc RS n	*Define vertical spacing increment as n-1
Esc US n	*Set horizontal space increment to n-1
Esc VT n	*Absolute vertical tab to line n-1
Esc HT	*Absolute tab to column n-1
Esc SP	Print special character position 004
Esc SUB I	Initialize printer
Esc SUB SO	Terminal self-test
Esc CR P	Initialize printer
Esc 0	*Set right margin
Esc 1	*Set horizontal tab stop
Esc 2	*Clear all horizontal tab stops
Esc 3	*Graphic on 1/60 inch
Esc 4	*Graphics off
Esc 5	*Forward print
Esc 6	*Backward print
Esc 8	*Clear horizontal tab stop
Esc 9	*Set left margin
Esc .	Auto line feed on
Esc ,	Auto line feed off
Esc <	Auto bi-directional printing on
Esc >	Auto bi-directional printing off
Esc +	Set top margin

continues

TABLE 17.2. Continued

Escape Sequence	Function
Esc –	Set bottom margin
Esc @T	Enter user test mode
Esc #	Enter secondary mode
Esc $	*WPS (proportional spaced printwheel) on
Esc %	*WPS (proportional spaced printwheel) off
Esc (n	Set tabs at n (n can be a list)
Esc)n	Clear tabs at n (n can be a list)
Esc /	Print special character position 002
Esc C n m	Absolute horizontal tab to column n
Esc D	*Negative half-line feed
Esc E n m	Define horizontal space increments
Esc F n m	Set form length
Esc G	*Graphics on 1/120 inch
Esc H n m 1	Relative horizontal motion
Esc I	Underline on
Esc J	Underline off
Esc K n	Bold overprint on
Esc L n n	Define vertical spacing increment
Esc M n	Bold overprint off
Esc N	No carriage movement on next character
Esc O	Right margin control on
Esc P n	Absolute vertical tab to line n
Esc Q	Shadow print on
Esc R	Shadow print off
Esc S	No print on
Esc T	No print off
Esc U	*Half-line feed
Esc W	Auto carriage return/line feed on
Esc V n m 1	Relative vertical paper motion
Esc X	Force execution
Esc Y	Right margin control off
Esc Z	Auto carriage return/line feed off

Escape Sequence	Function
Esc e	Sheet feeder page eject
Esc i	Sheet feeder insert page from tray one
Esc x	Force execution

Qume Sprint 11 commands shown; *indicates commands shared by Diablo 630

Epson and IBM Nine-Wire Commands

The closest to de facto standards that exists in dot-matrix printers are the code and commands used by IBM and Epson. These are closely related if simply because the first IBM Graphics Printer was based on the Epson MX-80. The chief differences between the two were their character sets. IBM used the upper half of the 256 ASCII values for a variety of special symbols, the IBM extended character set, but Epson used those values for italics. The commands used by these two printers have become a de facto standard for nine-wire dot-matrix printers. A condensed table of these commands is given in Table 17.3.

TABLE 17.3. Epson Control Characters and Escape Sequences

Control Codes

ASCII value	Control value	Mnemonic	Function
7	^G	BEL	Sounds audible bell tone
8	^H	BS	Backspace
9	^I	HT	Horizontal tab
10	^J	LF	Line feed
11	^K	VT	Vertical tab
12	^L	FF	Form feed
13	^M	CR	Carriage return
14	^N	SO	[2]Turns enlarged print mode on
15	^O	SI	[2]Turns condensed print mode on
17	^P	DC1	[2]Select printer
18	^R	DC2	Turns condensed print mode off
19	^S	DC3	[2]Deselect printer
20	^T	DC4	Turns enlarged print mode off
24	^X	CAN	Cancel line
127	DEL		No operation

continues

TABLE 17.3. Continued

Escape Sequences

Escape Sequence	Function
Esc SO	[2]Turns enlarged print mode on
Esc SI	[2]Turns condensed print mode on
Esc EM	[2]Cut sheet feeder control
Esc SP	[2]Selects character space
Esc !	[2]Selects mode combinations
Esc #	[2]MSB mode cancel
Esc $	[2]Set absolute horizontal tab
Esc %	[2]Selects active character set
Esc :	[2]Copies ROM to user RAM
Esc &	[2]Defines user characters
Esc /	[2]Set vertical tab
Esc \	[2]Move printhead
Esc <	Turn unidirectional (left-to-right only) printing on
Esc >	[2]MSB set (MSB=0)
Esc =	[2]MSB reset (MSB=1)
Esc @	[2]Initialize printer
Esc -n	Underline mode
	n=1 or 49, turns underline mode on
	n=0 or 48, turns underline mode off
Esc *n	[2]Select bit-image mode (data follows n)
	n=0, normal density
	n=1, dual density
	n=2, double-speed dual density
	n=3, quadruple density
	n=4, CRT graphics
	n=6, CRT graphics II
Esc ^	Nine-pin graphics mode
Esc 0	Set line spacing at 1/8 inch

Escape Sequence	Function
Esc 1	Set line spacing at 7/72 inch
Esc 2	Set line spacing at 1/6 inch
Esc 3 n	Set line spacing at n/216 inch (n between 0 and 255)
Esc 4	[2]Turns alternate character (italics) set on
Esc 5	[2]Turns alternate character (italics) set off
Esc 6	[1]Select character set 1
	[2]Deactivate high-order control codes
Esc 7	[1]Select character set 2
	[2]Restores high-order control codes
Esc 8	Turns paper-end detector off
Esc 9	Turns paper-end detector on
Esc A n	Set line spacing at n/72 inch (n between 0 and 85
Esc B	[2]Set vertical tab stop
Esc C n	Sets form length to n inches (n between 1 and 22)
Esc D	Set horizontal tab stop
Esc E	Turns emphasized mode on
Esc F	Turns emphasized mode off
Esc G	Turns double-strike mode on
Esc H	Turns double-strike mode off
Esc I	[2]Control code select
Esc J n	Tentative n/216-inch line spacing
Esc K	Normal-density bit-image data follows
Esc L	Dual-density bit-image data follows
Esc M	Elite-sized characters on
Esc N n	Set number of lines to skip-over perforation
	n=number of lines to skip between 1 and 127
Esc O	Turn skip-over perforation off
Esc P	[2]Elite mode off/Pica-sized characters on
Esc Q n	[2]Sets the right margin at column n
Esc R	[1]Returns to default tabs

continues

TABLE 17.3. Continued

Escape Sequence	Function
Esc R n	[2]Selects international character set
	n=0, USA
	n=1, France
	n=2, Germany
	n=3, England
	n=4, Denmark I
	n=5, Sweden
	n=6, Italy
	n=7, Spain
	n=8, Japan
	n=9, Norway
	n=10, Denmark II
Esc S n	Superscript/subscript on mode
	n=0 or 48, superscript mode on
	n=1 or 49, subscript mode on
Esc T	Turns superscript/subscript off
Esc U n	Unidirectional/bidirectional printing
	n=0 or 48, turn bidirectional printing on
	n=1 or 49, turn unidirectional printing on
Esc W n	Enlarged (double-width) print mode
	n=1 or 49, enlarged print mode on
	n=0 or 48, enlarged print mode off
Esc X	[1]Sets margins
Esc Y	Double-speed, dual-density bit image data follows
Esc Z	Quadruple-density bit-image data follows
Esc a	[2]Justification
Esc b	Set vertical tab
Esc e n	Set tab unit
	n=0 or 48, sets horizontal tab unit
	n=1 or 49, sets vertical tab unit

Escape Sequence	Function
Esc f n	Set skip position setting
	n=0 or 48, sets horizontal skip position
	n=0 or 49, sets vertical skip position
Esc g	[2]Select 15 width
Esc i	[2]Immediate print (typewriter mode)
Esc j	[2]Immediate temporary reverse paper feed
Esc k	[2]Select family of type styles
Esc l n	Sets the left margin at column n
Esc m n	Special character generator selection
	n=0, control codes accepted
	n=4, graphics characters accepted
Esc p n	Proportional printing
	n=0 or 48, turn proportional printing off
	n=1 or 49, turn proportional printing on
Esc s	Half-speed printing
	n=0 or 48, turn half-speed printing off
	n=1 or 49, turn half-speed printing on
Esc z	Select letter quality or draft

Includes codes used by many printers.

[1]IBM command only

[2]Epson command only

Epson 24-Wire Commands

When dot-matrix technology advanced from nine-wire printers to 24-wire designs, graphics commands needed to be augmented to take additional print modes into account. Again, the commands for Epson's 24-wire series of printers have become as close to a standard as exists in the personal computer industry.

The generalized command form is as follows:

```
Esc*m c1 c2 [graphics data]
```

Where m is the code number from table 17.4 and c1 and c2 specify the number of columns to use for graphics.

TABLE 17.4. 24-Pin Graphics Mode Codes

Mode	Pins	Code	Density Dots/inch
Single-density	8	0	60
Double-density	8	1	120
High-double density	8	2	120
Quadruple density	8	3	240
CRT I	8	4	80
CRT II	8	6	90
Single-density	24	32	60
Double-density	24	33	120
CRT III	24	38	90
Triple-density	24	39	180
Hex-density	24	40	360

The values of c_1 and c_2 specify the number of column dots to use for the graphics display. Because one byte can code only 256 values, a second byte is used to encompass the total number of dot-columns possible. The c_1 value is least significant. To determine the proper values, divide the desired number of graphic columns by 256. The quotient is the value of c_2; the remainder is c_1.

Each 24-pin column of data in a line is encoded with three separate bytes: the first byte codes the top eight wires; the second codes the middle eight; the last codes the bottom eight. The least significant bit in each byte codes the bottom dot of the octet associated with that byte; the most significant bit codes the top dot of the octet. A value of one indicates that a dot will appear on paper.

Postscript

Laser printers are more than mere printers. Most have the brains of a complete computer. Many are smarter than the computers that they are plugged into. The instructions that they understand reflect this intelligence. Rather than mere commands, the software controls for laser printers are more like programming languages.

Among people working extensively with graphics, the most popular printer control method is Adobe System's Postscript page description language. Originally developed in 1985, Postscript comprises a group of commands and codes that describe graphic elements and indicate where they are to appear on the printed page. Your computer sends high-level Postscript commands to your laser printer, and the printer executes the commands to draw the image itself. In effect, the data processing load is shifted to the printer, which, in theory, has been optimized for implementing such graphics commands. Nevertheless, it can take several minutes for the printer to compute a full page image after all the Postscript commands have been transferred to it. (Older Postscript printers might take half an hour or more to work out a full page of graphics.)

The advantage of Postscript is its versatility. It uses outline fonts, which can be scaled to any practical size. PostScript is device- and resolution- independent, which means that the same code that controls your 300 dpi printer runs a 2500 dpi typesetter—and produces the highest possible quality image at the available resolution level. You can print a rough draft on your LaserJet from a Postscript file and, after you have checked it over, send the same file to a typesetter to have a photo-ready page made.

In June 1990, Adobe Systems announced a new version of Postscript, Level 2, which incorporated several enhancements. The most obvious are speed and color. Postscript Level 2 can dash through documents four to five times quicker thanks to getting the font-rendering technology used in Adobe Type Manager. In addition, Postscript incorporates a new generalized class of objects called "resources" that can be pre-compiled, named, and cached and downloaded to the memory (or disk) inside a Postscript device. Nearly anything that is printed can be classed as a resource—artwork, patterns, forms—handled in this streamlined manner. Postscript Level 2 also manages its memory use much better, no longer requiring that programs pre-allocate memory for downloaded fonts and bit-mapped graphics. It also incorporates new file management capabilities to handle disk-based storage inside PostScript devices. In addition, Postscript Level 2 has built-in compression/decompression abilities so that bit-mapped images (and other massive objects) can be transmitted more quickly in compressed form and then expanded inside the printer or other device.

Color first was grafted onto Postscript in 1988, but Postscript Level 2 takes color to heart. Where each Postscript device had its own proprietary color-handling methods, with Postscript Level 2, color is device-independent. To improve color quality, the new version also allows color halftone screening at any angle, which helps eliminate more patterns and make sharper renderings.

Level 2 also enhances font handling. Old Postscript limited fonts to 256 characters each. Level 2 allows for composite fonts that allow an essentially unlimited number of characters. Larger fonts are particularly useful for languages that do not use the Roman alphabet (such as Japanese) or those that have a wealth of diacritical marks.

Level 2 also incorporates Display PostScript, an extension that is designed to translate Postscript code into screen images. Device-independent support for many of the more generalized printer features is also available so that paper trays, paper sizes, paper feeding, and even stapling can be controlled through Postscript.

Of course, ordinary Postscript printers cannot take advantage of these new features, but Level 2 machines are generally (though not completely) backwardly compatible with older code. In most cases, a Postscript Level 2 printer handles ordinary Postscript commands without a problem, but realizing the full features of Level 2 requires new Postscript 2 software drivers.

PCL

Hewlett-Packard's Printer Control Language, most often abbreviated with its initials, PCL, was first developed as a means to control a rudimentary (by current standards) inkjet printer. As HP has introduced increasingly sophisticated laser printers, the language has been expanded and adapted. It now is on its fifth major revision, called PCL5.

PCL functions like an elaborate printer command set, with long strings of characters initiating the various Laserjet functions. It is not a true page description language.

Versions of PCL before the current one have amounted to little more than a system of control codes for eliciting various printer functions, including font selection. PCL5 goes further by including more line-drawing commands and the capability to handle scalable (outline) fonts.

PCL5 was formally introduced with the announcement of the LaserJet III on February 26, 1990 and followed four earlier versions of the PCL language. Although PCL is normally associated with LaserJet printers, the initial two versions of PCL predated the introduction of the first laser printer by any manufacturer. The first printer to use the original version of PCL was the HP ThinkJet, an inkjet engine. PCL3, the third version—was the language that controlled HP's first laser printer, the original LaserJet.

Printers compatible with the PCL3 standard can use only cartridge fonts in their text modes. Full pages graphics must be generated by their computer hosts and transferred bit-by-bit to the printer.

The next major revision to PCL was a response to the needs of early desktop publishing and similar applications that demanded more than just a few cartridge-based fonts. This revision was PCL4, which added the capability to have multiple fonts on the same page and to use down-loaded fonts. These were bit-mapped fonts, however, and you could print only one orientation on a given page. You also could do some rudimentary box drawing and filling of boxes.

Besides scalable fonts, PCL5 adds vector graphics; sophisticated page formatting capability; and the ability to handle portrait and landscape orientations on the same page, print white-on-black, and turn fonts into some pattern or shade. In addition, PCL5 incorporates a pared-down version of the HP-GL, Hewlett-Packard's Graphics Language that has become an industry-standard means of commanding plotters.

PCL5 can yield on-paper images that are effectively identical to those made on PostScript printers, but there are substantial differences between PCL 5 and PostScript. PostScript is essentially device-independent. The PostScript code sent out of a PC is the same no matter whether it is meant to control a relatively inexpensive desktop laser or an expensive typesetting machine.

As a printer language, PCL5 is device-dependent. It currently works only with 300 dpi laser printers, so its code cannot be used to drive typesetters. But PCL5 is less expensive than PostScript because it requires no license to use.

PCL5 would be a curiosity if it were only to be used in Hewlett-Packard printers, as it has been for the first year of its existence. But that situation is changing and making PCL5 into the latest de facto standard for controlling laser printers.

A number of companies have developed controllers for laser printers that understand PCL5. These controllers are bought by printer manufacturers to build their products. Now that printer makers have easy access to these high-performance controllers, the market is likely to be compatible with PCL5-compatible printers. That means you can get PostScript quality at a lower price, more than enough reason to look for PCL5 compatibility in your next laser printer.

Fonts

All laser printers (and their kin, LED and LCD shutter printers) are simply glorified dot-matrix printers. Individual characters are formed from dots just like a castle can be built from a child's building blocks. Every character position is divided into a matrix like a giant tic-tac-toe playing field, and the shape of individual characters is determined by which positions in the field are light and dark.

Fonts differ in how the information for coding these light and dark patterns is stored. Generally, fonts are stored using one of two technologies, termed bit-mapped and outline.

Bit-mapped fonts encode each character as the pattern of dots that form the matrix, recording the position and color of each individual dot. Because larger character sizes require more dots, they require different pattern codes than smaller characters. In fact, every size of character, weight of character (bold, condensed, light, and so on), even each character slant (Roman versus Italic), requires its own code. In other words, a single type family may require dozens of different, bit-mapped fonts.

Outline fonts encode individual characters as mathematical descriptions, essentially the stroke you would have to make to draw the character. These strokes define the outline of the character, hence the name for the technology. Your computer or printer then serves as a raster image processor that executes the mathematical instructions to draw each character in memory to make the necessary bit pattern for printing. With most typefaces, one mathematical description makes any size of character—the size of each individual stroke in the character is merely scaled to reflect the size of the final character (consequently outline fonts are often termed scalable fonts). One code, then, serves any character size, although different weights and slants require somewhat different codes. A single type family can be coded with relatively few font descriptions—normal, bold, Roman, and Italic combinations.

Simply scaling fonts produces generally acceptable results. To make the clearest, most readable text, however, small characters typically are shaped somewhat differently than large characters. For example, the serifs on each letter may need to be proportionally larger for smaller characters, or else they would disappear. Bit-mapped fonts automatically compensate for these effects because each size font can be separately designed. In outline fonts, the equations describing each stroke can include hints on what needs to be changed for best legibility at particular sizes. Outline fonts that include this supplementary information are termed *hinted* and produce clearer characters, particularly in large, headline and tiny, contract-style sizes.

PostScript Level 2 takes outline fonts a level further. With its Multiple Master fonts, some typefaces of the same family can be encoded as a single font. That is, one font definition can cover italic, Roman, and bold characters (as well as all sizes) of a given typeface.

The complex equations used for storing an outline font typically require more storage (more bytes on disk or in memory) than bit-mapped fonts, but storing an entire family of outline fonts requires substantially less space than a family of bit-mapped fonts (because one outline font serves all sizes). For normal business printing, which generally involves fewer than a dozen fonts (including size variations), this difference is not significant. For graphic artists, publishers, and anyone who likes to experiment with type and printing, however, outline fonts bring greater versatility.

On the other hand, bit-mapped fonts print faster. Outline fonts have to go through an additional step—raster image processing—computations which add to printing time. Bit-mapped fonts are directly retrieved from memory without any additional footwork.

Storage and Retrieval

The information describing font characters has to be stored somewhere. Considering that many megabytes may be involved, the location of font storage can have important implications on how you use your PC and printer.

Like every dot-matrix printer, the laser printer has a few fonts built in. Ubiquitous among lasers is the familiar, old 10-pitch Courier, the default typeface held over from typewriter days. The bit patterns for this typeface are forever encoded into the ROMs of nearly every machine. It can—and usually is—pulled up at an instant's notice simply by giving a command to print a character. Probably the most endearing characteristic of Courier (at least to software and printer designers) is that it is monospaced—every character from "i" to "m" is exactly the same width, making page layout easy to control.

A few other faces may be resident in the ROM of printers. The number depends on many factors—generally if the manufacturer is large, as few faces as possible are packed in ROM; smaller manufacturers include more to give their products a competitive edge.

Font Cartridges

Additional fonts can be added in several ways. The easiest to manage is the font cartridge. The dot patterns for forming alternate character fonts are stored in ROM chips held inside each cartridge. The cartridge itself merely provides a housing for the chip and a connector that fits a mate in the printer. By sliding in a cartridge, you add the extra ROM in the cartridge to that in the printer. Many impact and laser bit-image printers have been designed to use font cartridges.

Note that each manufacturers' cartridges are different and incompatible (sometimes the cartridges of two models of printers made by the same manufacturer are incompatible), although several laser printer makers are making their machines compatible with Hewlett-Packard laser printer cartridges.

The disadvantage of the font cartridge technique—besides the cost of the fonts themselves—is the limited number of cartridge slots available. A single cartridge may hold six to twelve fonts. With bit-image fonts in particular, such a small capacity can be confining. To sidestep this issue, several enterprising developers have packed dozens of fonts into a single cartridge.

Downloadable Character Sets

Most laser printers also allow you to download fonts. That is, you can transfer character descriptions from your PC's memory to the RAM inside your laser printer, where the individual characters can be called up as needed just as if they were in ROM. These are called downloadable character sets or soft fonts because they are transferred as software. Typically, you buy soft fonts just like software, on floppy disk, that you can copy to your PC's hard disk. You can store as many soft fonts as your hard disk can hold for use in your laser printer.

Soft fonts have many disadvantages, each with its own work-around. For example, soft fonts can be inconvenient. Somehow, you must transfer them from your PC to your printer, typically every time you want to use them can avoid this problem with font manager software. Each soft font you load into your printer steals a chunk of your printer's RAM. The memory limit of your laser printer constrains the number of soft fonts you can load at any given time, although the prodigious amount of memory allowed by newer prints ameliorates the problem somewhat (but not, of course, the cost of additional printer memory).

Some software can generate the bit patterns of fonts it needs by itself, the equivalent of having soft fonts built into the program. It then transmits the resulting bit-patterns to your printer (instead of sending a stream of characters that the printer renders into bit-patterns). Windows sometimes uses this font generation method, depending on the fonts and printer you choose. In fact, TrueType uses this strategy to simplify printing with Windows; it eliminates most of the need to download fonts to your printer. On the other hand, this technique imposes a hefty penalty—bit-patterns take more memory than characters, requiring more memory inside your laser printer, more than a megabyte to print a full page at highest resolution. Worse, the greater amount of data requires longer to transmit to the printer, increasing print time.

With older printers following the Hewlett-Packard LaserJet printing standard, all but the simplest graphics required this kind of bit-image transmission, as did printing anything but cartridge fonts and soft fonts. Page description languages allow the transmission of an entire page—text and graphics—in fast, coded form. Consequently, the trend in better laser printers is to use page description languages.

The best-known of these are the previously mentioned PostScript and PostScript Level 2. Both versions of PostScript take advantage of outline fonts. In fact, 35 outline fonts are built into most PostScript printers (some budget machines have as few as 17 as standard equipment).

PCL versions 3 and 4 can only use bit-mapped fonts (including those in cartridge and soft-font form). PCL5 printers understand and use outline fonts.

The bottom line is that you need a PostScript, PostScript-compatible, or PCL5-compatible printer to take advantage of most downloadable fonts.

Font Formats

All outline fonts are not the same, however. Several standards have arisen, and you must match the fonts you add to the standard used by your hardware and software. Your principal choices are Intellifont, Type 1 (PostScript), Speedo, and TrueType.

The native font format of the LaserJet III series of printers (and PCL5) is called Intellifont. Developed jointly by Agfa Compugraphic and Hewlett-Packard, it is notably fast in rasterizing and may just have the most widespread use, considering the popularity of LaserJet printers. Although you do not have to worry about font formats with cartridge fonts—if the cartridge fits, it should work—the cartridges you plug into your LaserJet or compatible printer use Intellifont characters. Downloadable outline fonts for LaserJet III and compatible printers use Intellifont format.

PostScript printers use Type 1 fonts, the format that probably offers more font variety than any other. You can use Type 1 fonts with Windows using Adobe Type Manager. Support for Type 1 fonts is built into OS/2 Versions 1.3 and later.

Many programs use Bitstream fonts, which have their own format called Speedo. In general, this software works by generating the characters in your PC and transferring them in bit-image form to your printer. Speedo fonts are used by Lotus 1-2-3 and Freelance (in their DOS versions). You also can use Bitstream's Speedo fonts with Windows using Bitstream's FaceLift for Windows.

Microsoft Windows 3.1 has its own format, called TrueType, that also is used by Apple's System 7 operating system for the Macintosh. Thirteen TrueType fonts come with Windows 3.1, and you can easily install more using the Windows Control Panel. TrueType is compatible with printers that use other font formats. For example, with LaserJets, for each font you want to use, TrueType generates a bit-map LaserJet font from one of its outline fonts, then downloads the font to your printer. That way, it only needs to send characters rather than bit-maps to your printer. For PostScript printers, TrueType similarly converts its fonts to PostScript outlines or bit-maps (depending on the font) and sends those to your printer.

Windows gives you font flexibility. All outline fonts packages are equipped with programs that allow them to be installed in Windows. Font managers are available for other major font formats (Adobe Type Manager, FaceLift for Windows, Intellifont for Windows).

Color Printing

A growing number of applications demand color output, and the printer industry has responded with a number of different technologies to suit individual color applications, from low cost to photo-like quality.

A number of impact dot-matrix printers allow you to add color to both the alphabets and graphics they put on paper. A few have two color ribbons (like old-fashioned typewriters) and special software instructions to control shifting between them.

Most color printers now use ribbons soaked with three or four colors of ink and can achieve seven colors on paper by combining color pairs. For example, laying a layer of blue over a layer of yellow results in an approximation of green. To switch colors that they print, they merely shift the ribbon up or down. The extra mechanism required is simple and inexpensive, costing as little as $50 extra. (Of course, the color ribbon costs more and does not last as long as its monochrome equivalent.) A few machines use multiple ribbons, each one a different color, to achieve the same effect.

Non-impact matrix printers excel at color. Inkjets are well suited to the task because their liquid inks can actually blend together on the paper before they dry. Color inkjet printers are, however, substantially more complex and expensive than their monochrome equivalents because each primary color requires its own separate ink reservoir and nozzle. Most thermal-wax matrix printers are designed particularly for color output. They achieve on-paper color mixing by using transparent inks that allow one color to show through another. The two hues blend together optically.

The only problem with color printers is that they need special software to bring their rainbows to life. Without the right software, you have to understand computer programming to take advantage of multi-color capabilities. Today, most impact color printers follow the standard set by the Epson JX-80, which adds one escape code to its normal command set for changing ribbon color. Thermal-wax and phase-change printers normally use PostScript, and PostScript 2 gives them a common color language.

Page description languages can actually slow down graphic printing—particularly color printing—when you deal extensively with bit-images. To print a bit-image with a page description language, your PC must first translate the bit-image into commands used by the page description language. Then the printer must convert the commands into the image raste before it can print out the image. This double conversion wastes time. Printers that sidestep the page description language by using their own specialized drivers typically send only the bits of the image through the printer interface. The printer can then quickly rasterize the image bits. The downside of the special driver technique is that each application (or operating environment) requires its own driver software—which usually means that such printers work only with Windows and a handful of the most popular applications.

Paper Handling

If shuffling the printhead back and forth were a printer's sole goal in life, all your printouts would be long, thin documents exactly one line long. The printer must advance the paper line by line just as a typewriter does when you slam the carriage back. The various schemes developed to help printer and operator deal with this chore—the way the printout paper is handled and the kind of paper that can be handled—must be carefully considered to match a printer to your needs.

Friction Feed

The old-fashioned typewriter moved paper through its mechanism by squeezing it between the large rubber roller, called a platen, and smaller rollers. The paper also is held around the platen above the area where the hammers strike it by a bail arm, which usually pivots out of the way when you load paper. The friction between the platen, smaller rollers, and bail arm keeps the paper from slipping as it is rolled past the printhead, so this paper feeding system is often called friction feed.

In most cases, friction feed implies that loading paper is a manual operation—you must pull out the bail arm, insert each individual sheet, line it up to be certain that it is square (so that the printhead does not type diagonally across the paper), lock it and the bail arm down, and finally signal to the machine that all is well. Easier said than done, of course—and more tedious, too, if you decide to print a computerized version of the Encyclopedia Britannica. Worse yet, you have to stand-by and give the machine your undivided attention, constantly shuffling in a fresh new sheet of paper every time the printer finishes one.

On the positive side, however, most friction feed mechanisms will handle any kind of paper you can fit through the mechanism, from your own engraved stationery to pre-printed forms, from W-2's to 1040's, envelopes, and index cards.

Automatic Sheet Feeder

Anything you can do, someone can design a machine to do, too. Whether the machine can be made affordably is another matter. Feeding paper through a friction-fed printer is no exception. A device, quite logically termed the automatic sheet feeder (although occasionally called bin-feed) can relieve your tedium and tantrums by loading most standard size forms and plain papers into your printer without your intervention or attention. Unfortunately, sheet feeders have been among the most complex accessories you can add to your computer system, many of them being much akin to the inventions of Rube Goldberg. Price rises with complexity, and sheet feeders tend also to be expensive, quite capable of ripping a multiple hundred dollar hole in your pocket. Most sheet feeders are designed for single-layer paper, which means two separate printings of separate sheets—no carbons. Your printing project can run into double and triple time when you need more than one copy.

Roll Feed

The alternative to adding a complex paper-handling mechanism to a printer is to redesign the paper. One way to reduce the number of times you must slide a sheet of paper into the friction-feed mechanism is to make the paper longer. In fact, you could use one, long continuous sheet. Some systems do exactly that, wrapping the long sheet around a roll (like toilet paper). The printer just pulls the paper through as it needs it. By rigidly mounting a roll-holder at the back of the printer, the paper can be kept in reasonable alignment and skew can be eliminated.

The shortcoming of this system is, of course, that you end up with one long sheet. You have to tear it to pieces or carefully cut it up when you want traditional 8-1/2 by 11 output.

Pin-Feed and Tractor-Feed

Although roll-fed paper could be perforated at eleven-inch intervals so that you could easily and neatly tear it apart, another problem arises. Most friction mechanisms are not perfect. The paper can slip so that, gradually, the page breaks in the image and page breaks at the perforations no longer correspond. In effect, the paper and the image can get out of sync.

By locking perforations in the edge of the paper inside sprockets that prevent slipping, the image and paper breaks can be kept coordinated. Two different paper-feeding systems use sprocketed paper to avoid slippage. *Pin-feed* uses drive sprockets which are permanently affixed to the edges of the platen roller. The pin feed mechanism, consequently, can handle only one width of paper, the width separating the sprockets at the edges of the platen. *Tractor-feed* uses adjustable sprockets that can be moved closer together or farther apart to handle nearly any width paper that fits through the printer.

As the names imply, a uni-directional tractor only pulls (or pushes) the paper through in a single direction (hopefully forward). The bi-directional tractor allows both forward and backward paper motion, which often is helpful for graphics, special text functions (printing exponents, for instance) and lining up the top of the paper with the top of the printhead.

Push and Pull Tractors

The original tractor mechanism for printers was a two-step affair. One set of sprockets fed paper into the printer, and another set pulled it out. For the intended purpose of tractor feeding, however, the two sets of sprockets are one more than necessary. All it takes is one set to lock the printer's image in-sync with the paper.

A single set of sprockets can be located in one of two positions, either before or after paper wraps around the platen in front of the printhead. Some printers allow you to use a single set of tractors in either position. In others, the tractors are fixed in one location or the other.

Push tractors are placed in the path of the paper before it enters the printer. They push the paper through the machine, in effect. The platen roller helps to ease paper through the printer while the push tractor provides the principal force and keeps the paper tracking properly. This form of feeding holds a couple of advantages. You can rip the last sheet of a printout off without having to feed an extra sheet through the printer or rethread it. The tractor also acts bidirectionally with relative ease, pulling the paper backwards as well as pushing it forward.

Pull tractors are located in the path of the paper after it emerges from the printmaking mechanism. The pull tractor pulls paper across the platen. The paper is held flat against the platen by its friction, and the resistance of pulling it up through the mechanism. The pull tractor is simpler and offers less potential hazards than push designs.

Although most pull tractors operate only unidirectionally, they work well in high speed use on printers with flat, metal (instead of round rubber) platens. Because of their high-speed operation, typically several pages per minute, the machines naturally tend to be used for large print jobs during which the waste of a single sheet is not a major drawback.

Sheet Feeders

By necessity, every laser printer has to have the complex cut-sheet mechanism that is so often an expensive option with other printer designs. The laser printer must be able to slip a single sheet from a stack, waft it through the complex image forming mechanism, and deliver it back to you. That today's laser printers work as well as they do is a tribute to the mechanical ingenuity of their engineers. But significant differences exist in the philosophy and convenience of the paper handling of different laser printers.

One is capacity. Some laser printers are made only for light, personal use and have modestly sized paper bins that hold about 50 sheets. That means that every 10 to 15 minutes, you must attend to the needs of the printer, loading and removing the wads of paper that course through it. If you have a big print job, that means baby-sitting the printer—not an exciting way to spend the day.

When lasers disgorge their output, it can fall into the output tray one of two ways—face up or face down. Although it might be nice to see what horrors you have spread on paper immediately, rather than saving up for a heart attack, face down is the better choice. When sheets pile on top of one another, face down means that you do not need to sort through the stack to put everything in proper order.

Duplex printers take the final step—printing on both sides of each sheet of paper. If you print a lot of reports, the cost savings in cutting your paper consumption in half may more than pay for a more expensive duplex printer.

Paper Control

Friction and tractor-fed printers differ to a great degree in how precisely they can move paper through their mechanisms. Some are designed to allow exacting tolerances and move each sheet in increments of the tiniest fractions of an inch (as small as 1/216th inch). A few still cling to their typewriter heritage and restrict you to shifting paper to one line (or half-line) at a time.

The trend has been to more precise control because it allows more format versatility in printing text—for instance, you can change line spacings from six lines per inch for manuscripts to eight per inch for business letters or add a few extra inch-fractions to each line to stretch ten pages into twelve pages when you have a tough essay assignment—and more accuracy in printing graphics.

Printers also vary in the control they afford in the other direction, the horizontal movement of the printhead across the paper. A few primitive machines still stick with the mechanical cog of the typewriter. Most modern machines, however, let you vary the character pitch in text mode and the spacing of dots and speed of printing in graphics modes. This versatility is necessary for the rendering of proportionally-spaced text and for printing multiple graphic densities.

Smart and Dumb Printers

A printer is not just a brute-force paper-pounder. It must have brains, too. Even the cheapest impact dot-matrix printer has to be smart enough to know the one exact instant it must trigger each of its printwires to ram one dot of the image on exactly the right spot on the paper. Lasers must match each character in their font cartridges with the proper on-paper position and possibly flick their light beams seven million or more times for each sheet that rolls through. Daisy-wheel machines time their hammer blows to the exact instance the right character on its spinning wheel is lined up properly. Behind the scenes, all printers must sort embedded commands from printed characters to carry out advanced operations, such as printing bold characters or changing fonts.

Printers vary substantially in their native intelligence. While many printers operate as little more than slaves, taking orders and carrying them out, many printers have much greater abilities. Some can go so far as to format the data as they print it.

The old-line printer, typified by the classic all-mechanical teletype, was so dumb that it did not even know when it came to the edge of the paper. It would gladly perforate its platen with the text of an entire novel if the data it was sent was not broken into short lines with the appropriate carriage return and line feed characters mixed in with the text. Many of today's printers have brains almost equally as primitive and rely on the computer and its software to tell them exactly what to do. Some computer programs, like word processors designed to be used with specific printers, may include special printer drivers software that adds in all sorts of extra ASCII code symbols to the data stream. Every fractional-inch movement of the printhead between proportionally-spaced characters, every character to be pecked, every roll of the platen, is specifically indicated by the computer program and sent to the printer.

On the other hand, smart printers can take over these same text-processing functions on their own. They can accept a nearly completely unformatted string of text, break it into proportionally spaced lines, and leave the proper margins at the top and bottom of the page. To handle these and other chores, even inexpensive printers nowadays have their own built-in microprocessors. The internal microbrain helps the printer position the proper petal of the daisy-wheel in front of the print hammer or calculate when to fire the wire of a dot-matrix printhead.

Horizontal and Vertical Tabbing

One place the intelligence of a printer can be put to use is in optimizing printhead motion, making every movement of the printhead the most efficient possible. The internal microprocessor in a printer can look ahead in the memory, see what is coming up next and optimize the positioning of the printhead or print wheel by finding the shortest difference between consecutive lines. The goal is to move between printhead positions as quickly as possible. Often called logic seeking printers, these machines use a number of techniques to optimize printhead movement. Using horizontal tabbing, they can breeze over oceans of blank space in each line without dwelling on each individual space and deciding what not to print. With vertical tabbing, they can be equally adept at skipping blank lines on the page. Both techniques, combined with bidirectional printing, allow a printer so blessed to type normal documents faster than machines with the same characters-per-second speed rating that lack these features.

Consumables

Consumables are those things that your printer uses up, wears out, or burns through as it does its work. Paper is the primary consumable, and the need for it is obvious with any printer. Other consumables are less obvious, sometimes even devious in the way they can eat into your budget.

You probably think you are familiar with the cost of these consumables. A couple months after the old dot-matrix ribbon starts printing too faintly to read, you finally get around to ordering a new $5 ribbon to hold you through for the rest of the decade. But if you buy one of today's top-quality printers—laser, thermal-wax, and dye-diffusion—you may be in for a surprise. When the toner or transfer sheet runs out, the replacement may cost as much as did your old dot-matrix printer.

The reason that laser printer consumables cost so much is that a bit of the machine is used up with every page that rolls out. The organic photoconductor drum on which images are made gradually wears out. (A new drum material, silicon, is supposed to last for the life of the printer, but few printer models currently use silicon drums.) Toner is spread across each page. The charging corona or other parts may also need to be periodically replaced. Although thermal-wax printers do not waste their mechanisms, they do slurp up ink—up to four pages full of ink for every page of paper that spools through.

These consumables costs can add up. With laser printers, consumables—not including paper—cost between two and five cents a page. With thermal-wax printers, costs can range as high as five dollars a page.

Over the life of a printer, the cost of consumables can quickly exceed what you paid for the printer. More importantly, consumables costs differ with various printer models. Over the life of the typical printer, the difference in consumables cost can far overwhelm a difference in purchase price.

Because thermal-wax printers cost substantially more than laser printers, the difference in consumables costs between them do not reflect so dramatically against the purchase prices, but you still can save a dollar or more per page by opting for a machine with inexpensive consumables.

Some printers appear wasteful in their need for consumables. Hewlett-Packard's LaserJets, for example, are designed with one-piece cartridges that contain both the drum and toner. The whole assembly is replaced as a single unit when the toner runs out. Other laser printers are designed so that the toner, drum, and sometimes the fuser, can be replaced individually.

The makers of the latter style of printer contend that the drum lasts for many times more copies than a single shot of toner, so dumping the drum before its time is wasteful. On the other hand, the all-in-one cartridge folks contend that they design their drums to last only as long as the toner.

Surprisingly, from a cost standpoint, the choice of technology does not appear to make a difference. (From an ecology standpoint, however, the individual replacement scheme still makes more sense.)

Cartridge Refilling

One way to tiptoe around the high cost of laser printer consumables is to get toner cartridges refilled. Most manufacturers do not recommend this—because they have no control over the quality of the toner, they can't guarantee that someone else's replacement works right in their machines. Besides, they miss the profits in selling toner.

Quality really can be an issue, however. The Resolution Enhancement technology of the HP's LaserJet III and IV-series, for example, requires toner with a particle size much smaller than that of toner used by other printers. You cannot tell the difference in toner just by looking at it—but you can when blotchy grey pages pour out of the printer. When you get cartridges refilled, you must be sure to get the proper toner quality.

Another consideration: With all-in-one cartridges, just refilling the cartridge with toner will not affect the drum or charger in the cartridge. Although these are engineered for extra life, the extra might not stretch twofold. Order a refilled cartridge, and you could get fresh toner packed with a worn-out drum.

On the other hand, some people report excellent results with refilled toner cartridges. Whether you are going to be happy with refills depends on your personal standards, as well as the quality of the refill work.

Paper

When comparing the costs of using different printer technologies, do not forget to make allowances for machines that require special paper. In most cases, approved media for such printers is available only from the machine's manufacturer. You must pay the price the manufacturer asks which, because of the controlled distribution and special formulation, is sure to be substantially higher than buying bond paper at the office supply warehouse.

Certainly, you can load any kind of paper that fits into a printer. With some printers, particularly thermal machines, you do not get any image output if you use the wrong medium. With most printers, however, the penalty is a substandard image. Inkjet images, for instance, are blurrier with less saturated colors because of the ink absorption by the paper. Other effects may be more subtle. With laser printers, feeding might be erratic, leading to more jams, and blacks might become spotty or grey with the wrong paper. Some laser printers make particular requirements for the humidity content of the paper for proper printer operation.

If you want to use a non-approved paper with your printer, the best bet is to try and see the results you get.

Printer Sharing

Two printers are not necessarily better than one—they are just more expensive. In a number of business situations, you can save the cost of a second printer by sharing the one with two or more PCs and their users. This strategy works because no one prints all the time—if he did, he would have no time left to create anything worth printing. Because normal office work leaves your printer with idle time, you can put it to work for someone else.

You have your choice of several printer-sharing strategies, including those that use nothing but software and those that are hardware-based.

The least expensive—in terms of out-of-pocket cost—is a simple A/B switch box. As the name implies, this device consists of a box of some kind that protects a multi-pole switch. The switch allows you to reroute all 25 connections of a printer cable from one PC to another. For example, in position A, your computer might be connected to the printer; in position B, a coworker's PC would be connected. It is the equivalent of moving the printer cable with the convenience of a switch.

True sharing systems give you the greater convenience of automatic operation. Of the various techniques, software printer sharing is generally the least costly. Most *zero-slot local area networks* have provisions for sharing printers. A zero-slot LAN allows you to connect several PCs together as a network using their serial ports. The only expenses involved in sharing printers this way are the software itself and some (relatively cheap) cable to connect the systems together.

But a non-monetary cost exists, too—the performance hit the printer server suffers. The PC connected to the printer is forced to spend some of its time spooling the print job and controlling the printer, which can steal a good deal of performance. No worker in your office is likely to want to use that PC for his daily work—unless his work mostly involves checking the output quality of the office coffee maker.

Hardware printer-sharing eliminates that problem by substituting a dedicated box for spooling operations. Each PC is connected to the sharing box which, in turn, connects directly to the printer. The disadvantage of this system is simply the expense of the added hardware.

Not all printer sharing boxes are alike. They differ in the amount of memory they make available and in their arbitration systems. The memory is used to buffer print jobs so that when one PC is printing, others can continue to send printing instructions as if they are running the printer, too. No time is lost by programs waiting for printer access. More memory is generally better, although you might not need a lot if you standardize your office on Windows or UNIX or some other software environment with a built-in software print spooler. With today's graphic printing job, you want at least a megabyte in any hardware printer sharing device.

Arbitration systems determine which PC has priority when two or more try to print at once. The best sharing systems allow you to assign a priority to every PC based upon its need and the corporate pecking order. You should expect to get control software to let you manage the entire printing system to accompany the more versatile sharing devices.

Sharing devices also differ as to the number and kind of ports that they make available. You need a port for every PC you want to connect. You want parallel ports for easy connections, but serial ports if PCs are located some distance (generally over 10-25 feet) from the sharing device.

Some printer sharing devices plug into the I/O slots of printers. Although these devices limit the number of available ports because of size constraints, they also minimize costs because no additional case or power supply is required. A few printers are designed to be shared, having multiple or network inputs built-in.

When printers are expensive—as better-quality machines like lasers and thermal-wax printers—sharing the asset is much more economical than buying a separate printer for everyone and smarter than making someone suffer with a cheap printer while the quality machine lies idle most of the day.

Plotters

In a world in which technologies change as quickly as a chameleon climbing paisley wallpaper, plotters remain as resolute and steadfast as the Great Stoneface or your brother-in-law's bad habits. In less than a decade, microprocessors have raced ahead twenty times faster, printers have gone from hammers to lasers, hard disks have grown from five to five hundred megabytes, and plotters...

For example, let's say you step into a time warp, slip back 10 years, and the only proof of your travels you carry is one of today's state-of-the-art desktop plotters. One look at it, and not a soul from a decade ago would believe you are a time traveler. Plotters today look the same as yesterday— they work the same, and they deliver nearly the same results.

But the story of the plotter involves more than that. Subtle changes have been made electronically and philosophically. More importantly, however, today's desktop plotters are just as useful as they ever were, notwithstanding a broadside of new competition from every quarter.

Today's desktop plotters offer the highest resolution of almost any hard copy device you can plug into your PC, typically addressable to one-thousandth of an inch. With such high accuracy, they can sketch smooth curves and skew lines without a trace of jagginess. They are quick enough to serve as your only graphic output device or, in major installations, they are cheap enough to attach to workstations to take the load off a larger plotter when only drafts are required.

The subtle changes that have been made to desktop plotters over the last few years have made them more accessible, more usable, and generally more compatible with you and your software. While plotters work the same way they always have—they simply control the movement of an ink pen across one or another drafting medium—they have become smarter—and so have their makers.

Most plotters today are microprocessor-based. The smartest process the instructions they receive to move their pens as economically as possible, optimizing pen travel and pen selection to waste the least time. Manufacturers have wised up and adopted one standard language for controlling their products.

Most available plotters are designed to recognize the commands of Hewlett-Packard's HP-GL plotter language. Manufacturers now document all the details of setting up their equipment to operate with PCs and the most popular software. You no longer need to stay up nights experimenting to find the right cable connections and set-up parameters.

Plotter Designs

Plotter technology itself is unchanged, divided into two families, (1) the flatbeds or X-Y plotters and (2) roller-beds or drum plotters. The difference is simply a matter of what moves. The flatbed plotter is the magic moving hand in action. The plotting medium is held fast against the flat plotting surface (the "bed" of the "flatbed" name), and the mechanism moves the pen across the paper in two dimensions (the "X" and "Y" of the alternate name), just as you would draw a picture by hand.

The roller-bed plotter restricts its pen to travel in one dimension—laterally across the width of the drafting medium—and lends new impetus to the paper. That is, to draw lines perpendicular to the movement of the pen, the paper slides underneath the pen. The "roller" in the bed is a cylinder or drum underneath the paper which provides the motive force.

Neither technology is an all-around winner. When accuracy counts, the flatbed design is the low-cost winner. Building an accurate flatbed is inherently less expensive because control over only one mechanism—that which moves the pen—is required. Roller-beds require two discrete and fundamentally different systems, one for the pen, one for the paper, in order to be precisely coordinated. This added complexity can translate into higher costs. But when price overrules resolution, roller-bed plotters can sacrifice milli-inches of precision for affordability.

On the other hand, roller-bed plotters have an inherent speed advantage. Paper is simply less massive than overreaching mechanical arms and pen carriages, and Newton's Second Law (for those needing a refresh in freshman physics: F=ma, force equals mass times acceleration) says that it is less work to speed up a lighter object. Little wonder the fastest plotters tend to be roller-bed machines.

Flatbed plotters have one advantage: they let you use virtually any size of drafting medium up to their physical limits. Most drum or roller-bed plotters constrain your choice of widths of drafting medium because they grip it only at its edges and, for design reasons, the paper-grippers are a fixed distance apart. Narrower widths of drafting media just cannot be properly gripped. However, one manufacturer, Hitachi, offers a roller-bed plotter that used a full-width drum that can grasp any width paper down to postcard size.

With a flatbed plotter, however, you do not face minimum size limits. After all, flatbeds are just drafting tables with automated arms attached. Anything that the table holds can be drawn upon—with the proper software instructions, of course.

Plotters range in size from those that fit on top of your desk to machines that ink sheets bigger than wallpaper. The most common machines handle drafting media up to the ANSI *B-size*, that is, with metes and bounds measuring 11 by 17 inches.

As with drafting tables, flatbed plotters require some means of securing paper to the drawing surface. Ordinary drafting tape will suffice but is hardly an elegant solution. Plotter makers have adopted several strategies to eliminate the pesky stickiness of tape. Some plotters use the magic of static electricity to hold the drafting medium down, a sticking strategy that works for all but a few media. Alternately, one manufacturer uses magnets instead of electricity to hold down drafting copy, a tactic that should work with any medium except thin sheets of iron.

Output Quality

The most important difference between cheap and expensive plotters is precision. A better plotter has a smaller resolution or step size.

Step size is limited by a number of factors. The ultimate limit is the plotter's mechanical resolution, the finest movements the hardware can ever make, owing to the inevitable coarseness of the stepper motors that move their pens. In most, but not all cases, step size is further constrained by addressability. The smallest increments in which HP-GL can move a plotter pen is 0.001 (one-thousandths) inch. The least expensive plotters often have mechanical resolutions more coarse than the addressing limits of HP-GL. In these cases, the mechanism itself limits quality.

The smaller the step size, the smoother the curves a plotter can draw. Each step shows as a right-angle bump in a diagonal or curved line. At the 0.001-inch limit of HP-GL, steps are less than a third the size of a laser-printer dot—very fine indeed, essentially invisible. With less expensive plotters, however, each step may be plainly visible, resulting in a self-describing condition called the jaggies.

Color

Desktop plotters also differ in the number of pens from which they can select automatically. Although a rough correspondence exists between color capabilities and the number of pens that a plotter can handle, you can make multi-colored plots even with a one-pen engine. Most plotters allow you to pause their work and exchange pens, giving you manual control over the hues of their output. In other words, a four-pen plotter is not necessarily limited to four colors; it can ink drawings in as many tints as are available in compatible pens. More pens is a matter of convenience only.

A larger number of pens, however, enables you to run your plotter on auto-pilot. Start the plot and you can empty the coffee pot and socialize the morning away. You do not need to stand over the machine and anticipate when to make the change.

Besides sheer numbers, plotters offer you a choice of pen types that you can load. Which to use depends on the type of output you want to create—paper and film plots require different kinds of ink, perhaps different pen types. Some manufacturers offer refillable pens. These offer you the higher quality (thinner, more consistent lines) of a drafting pen without the hefty expense of making you buy a new one when the ink runs out.

If you have a choice of pens, you should choose the most popular to have the widest possible selection. The closest to a standard among plotter pens is the design used by Hewlett-Packard machines and followed by several manufacturers. As with anything else, proprietary pen designs limit your options—and may require you to pay a higher price.

Interfacing

With plotters, compatibility is a major issue. Traditionally, plotter-makers have viewed their products as professional tools, which means that they were designed to give smug engineers their comeuppance. At minimum, you needed to have a special cable manufactured for your particular installation.

Most of that frustration lies in the past, however. The typical plotter today includes a Centronics-style parallel port that makes it as easy to connect as a dot-matrix printer.

Several machines still depend on RS-232 serial connections. Others make it an option. If you choose to use a serial link, you probably want to buy the plotter maker's own serial cable that has been designed to match the needs of the particular plotter. The $50 or so you spend staves off the Thorazine and straight-jackets to which sorting out a serial link usually lead.

Unless you already have other peripherals that use it, you probably do not want to tangle with the cost, intricacies, and special software drivers required to use the IEEE-488 (also known as GPIB, the General Purpose Interface Bus, or HP-IB, the Hewlett-Packard Interface Bus) connection that some plotters make available.

Control Languages

Most plotter manufacturers now have adopted Hewlett-Packard Graphic Language (HP-GL) to control their machines, making that language the standard in this country. (Although HP-GL is used internationally, GP-GL is more prevalent in some markets.) Another alternative is Digital Microprocessor Plotter Language (DMPL), developed by Houston Instrument, which has several built-in functions that are not present in HP-GL, such as built-in fonts, the ability to do closed area fill with a single command, and built-in smoothing algorithms. Other plotters have their own native languages, which often work faster than HP-GL with programs that support them. But plotters that understand HP-GL work with just about any program with a plotter output.

Performance

As with printers, most plotters have built-in RAM to buffer plotting instructions. The buffer memory helps free up your computer when you plot. A large buffer allows the plotter to absorb most or all of the instructions sent out of your PC and process them while your computer does something else. Some plotters take further advantage of their buffers by looking ahead at plotting instructions and calculating how to minimize pen movement or pen changes, drawing all black lines before switching to the red pen, for example. Such optimization can substantially trim the time required for making plots. The buffer can also allow you to make multiple copies of a plot without tying up your PC. Speed differences between plotters can be dramatic: some machines plot in half the time of others.

The output quality among plotters tends toward uniformity except in the lowest cost machines. Text renderings, however, depend on a plotter's interpretation of HP-GL and the characteristics of any internal character sets.

Plotter Alternatives

Putting pen to paper in these days when words, music, and money flash electronically through wires at the speed of light seems about as anachronistic as stoking the furnace or paying cash. Other technologies are quicker, more colorful, and cheaper. Yet plotters persist for several reasons.

When it comes to fast graphic output, the laser printer is without peer. A typical full graphic page might pour out in less than a minute while a plotter struggles five or ten minutes on the same chore. But most lasers—and all affordable machines—are limited to a single color and media no larger than ANSI A size (8-1/2 by 11 inches). Plotters deftly draw in any color in which you can find a pen to match and create nearly limitless combinations of colors (as long as you are willing to manually change pens at the appropriate times). On the other hand, even the most compact of these desktop plotters handle sheets up to B size. And they are almost indifferent to the medium you give them to plot upon—just match the proper pens, and they happily ink paper, vellum, mylar, or whatever you lay on their beds.

The comparison to color inkjet printers is nearly the same. Inexpensive inkjets do not handle large sheets. Those that accept B-size paper likely cost more than a comparable plotter. But inkjets can stretch their color spectra through dithering and mixing inks on paper. They can even add a more natural look by shading from one hue to another, although not under direct manual control.

Plotters beat nearly all printers when it comes to accuracy: most move in steps of about one-thousandth of an inch, more than three times finer than the 300 dots per inch delivered by the typical laser engines. This extreme resolution is put to good use drawing curves from which every trace of jagginess has been expunged.

But lasers lead when it comes to fine detail. Although the plotter can draw almost absolutely smooth diagonals, thanks to their high resolution, the finest details they can create are limited to the widths of the lines drawn by their pens. Typically, the finest pen available for plotting inks a line three-tenths of a millimeter wide, about twelve times the width of the plotter's resolution or step size and about four times wider than the thinnest laser line.

On the other hand, plotters can draw in solid colors rather than the spotty digital dots fused to paper by the lasers or sprayed by the inkjets (not to mention the pointillism of impact dot-matrix engines). Plotter colors are pure and consistently-toned.

Direct-speed comparisons between printers and plotters are impossible because they use different imaging techniques. Printers are raster-based devices; plotters draw vectors. As a result, which is faster depends on what you want to draw.

Plotters might possibly finish simple drawings first, but lag when images become more complex than a few lines. Dot-addressed printers (as opposed to those that use a language like PostScript), on the other hand, devote about as much time to the simplest or most complex drawings. They have to scan an entire sheet, no matter how many lines are to be drawn. (Postscript printers take somewhat longer for more complex drawings because transfer and processing times must be added.)

Bottom line: Plotters are moderately priced, colorful, accurate, and slow. Affordable laser printers are faster but lack color capabilities and the 1/1000th inch resolution of plotters. Color lasers are quick, costly, and not quite as sharp. Color inkjets provide multiple hues, moderate speed, and costs comparable to plotters, but lack the capability to create smooth, detailed drawings. For many applications, plotters still deliver the right combination.

Chapter 18
Serial Ports

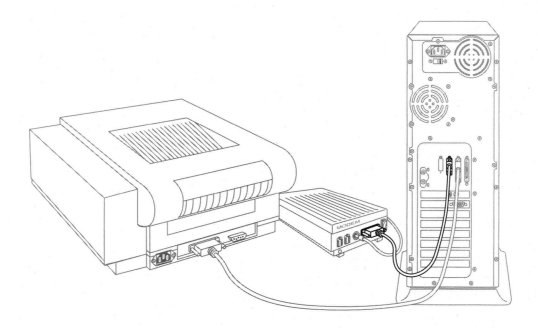

The serial port is the least common denominator of computer communications. Even the most primitive PCs and peripherals sport a serial connection. But serial communications is a many-splendored—and many terrored—thing. Where once most products followed a single industry standard, new variations have blossomed and a revolutionary serial connection is in the offing.

The typical PC has the personality of the local mile-a-minute gossip—the neighbor with so much to say and so little time to say it that you expect the chatterbox's head to explode from overfilling with the backlog of words. The backlog can build quickly—your PC likely can process data at a rate of tens of millions of bytes per second, yet the only truly universal two-way access it has to the outside world is the serial port that hobbles along trying to exchange a few thousands of bytes per second. The demand for communications—bulletin boards, E-mail services, and the Internet—grows prodigiously year by year while the standard serial port has locked itself in slow gear. Despite America going on-line, the laggardly serial port remains the one universal communication channel.

The serial port in your PC wears a number of different names. IBM, in the spirit of bureaucracy, sanctions an excess of syllables, naming the connection an asynchronous data communications port. Time-pressed PC users clip that to async port or comm port. Officialdom bequeaths its own term. The variety of serial links accepted by the PC industry operates under a standard called RS-232C (one that was hammered out by an industry trade group, the Electronics Industry Association or EIA), so many folks call the common serial port by its numerical specification, an RS-232 port.

No matter the name, all PC serial ports are the same, at least functionally. Each takes the 8, 16, or 32 parallel bits your computer exchanges across its data bus and turns them sideways—from a broadside of digital blips into a pulse chain that can walk the plank, single-file. This form of communication earns its name *serial* because the individual bits of information are transferred in a long series.

The change marks a significant difference in coding. The bits of parallel data are coded by their positions; the designation of the bus line they travel confers value. The most significant bit travels down the line designated for the most significant signal. With a serial port, the significance is awarded by timing. The position of a bit in a pulse string gives it its value. The later in the string, the more important the bit.

In a perfect world, a single circuit—nothing more than two wires, a signal line, and a ground—would be all that was necessary to move this serial signal from one place to another without further ado. Of course, a perfect world also would have fairies and other benevolent spirits to help usher the data along and protect it from all the evil imps and energies lurking about trying to debase and disgrace the singular purity of serial transfer.

The world is, alas, not perfect, and the world of computers even less so. Many misfortunes can befall the vulnerable serial data bit as it crawls through its connection. One of the bits of a full byte of data may go astray, leaving a piece of data with a smaller value on arrival as it had at departure—a problem akin to shipping alcohol by a courier service operated by dipsomaniacs.

With the vacancy in the data stream, all the other bits will slip up a place and assume new values. Or the opposite case—in the spirit of electronic camaraderie, an otherwise well-meaning signal might adopt a stray bit like a child takes on a kitten, only later to discover that this breeds a progeny of errors that ripple through the communications stream, pushing all the bits backward. In either case, the prognosis is not good. With this elementary form of serial communications, if one mistaken bit goes either way, every byte that follows will be in error.

Establishing reliable serial communications means overcoming these bit-error problems and many others as well. Thanks to some digital ingenuity, however, serial communications work and work well—well enough for you and your PC to depend on them.

Serial Transmission Methods

Two chief serial transmission methods are used to avoid the disaster of serial bit errors. In synchronous communication, the sending and receiving systems are synchronized using some kind of auxiliary signal so that both ends of a connection are always in step, synchronous and asynchronous communications.

Synchronous Communications

In a synchronous communications system, a clock precisely times the period separating each data bit. The clock synchronizes the timing of the sending and receiving units. A missing bit or extra bit can be detected quickly because it or its absence will show up at an unexpected position (actually, time) in the stream of bits. It's like having all the shuttle aircraft at an airport scheduled to arrive exactly on the hour. Any airplane that hits the tarmac at another time can reasonably be expected not to be a shuttle (assuming that the shuttle service has a good reputation for on-time arrivals—possible only in the perfect world of examples, of course). Just by checking the clock, you can determine shuttles from other aircraft—or, in computer communications, a real data bit from interloping noise. This time-synchronized form of serial transfer called synchronous communication is a technique used primarily in mainframe systems.

This synchronized system fails whenever the sending and receiving systems lose their mutual signal lock, however. The data stream then becomes little more than noise.

Asynchronous Communications

The alternative is to add place-markers to the bit stream to help track each data bit. One marker could indicate the position assigned to a bit, for example. A bit occurring without its marker could be assumed errant. Of course, such a simple scheme would be grievously wasteful, requiring two digital signals (the marker and the data bit) for every bit of information transferred.

More workable is a compromise system. Instead of indicating each bit, the marker could indicate the beginning of a short stream of bits. The position of each bit in the stream could be defined by timing the bit at regular intervals. Although this method is similar to synchronous transfer, the sending and receiving systems don't have to be locked together except for the brief interval between markers. The arrival of a marker tells the receiving system to start looking for bits and run a short-term timer. The problem of the sending and receiving timers getting out of sync is eliminated by restarting the clock with each marker. By keeping the period between markers short, there's not enough time for either timer to wander too far astray.

This timed short-term system is commonly termed asynchronous communication because the sending and receiving systems need not be precisely synchronized to one another. The marker bits provide the temporary lock needed to distinguish a short stream of data bits that follow. Most PC serial communications use this scheme.

In most asynchronous systems, the data is broken up into small pieces, each roughly—though not exactly—corresponding to one byte. Each of these chunks is called a word; and may consist of five to eight data bits. The most widely used word lengths are seven and eight bits; the former because it accommodates all upper- and lowercase text characters in ASCII code, the latter because each word corresponds exactly to one data byte.

As serial data, the bits of a word are sent one at a time down the communication channel. As a matter of convention, the least significant bit of the word is sent out first. The rest of the bits follow in order of their increasing significance.

Added to these data bits is a very special double-length pulse called a start bit, and it indicates the beginning of a data word; a stop bit indicates the end of the word. Between the last bit of the word and the first stop bit, a parity bit is often inserted as a data integrity check. Together the data bits, the start bit, the parity bit, and the stop bits make up one data frame (see fig 18.1).

Parity Bits

Five kinds of parity bits can be used in serial communication, two of which actually offer a means of detecting bit-level transmission errors. This error detection works by counting the number of bits in the data word and determining whether the result is even or odd. In odd parity, the parity bit is set on (made a logical one) when the number of bits in the word is odd. Even parity switches on the parity bit when the bit total of the word is even.

In mark parity the parity bit is always on, regardless of the bit total of the word. Space parity always leaves the parity bit off. No parity means that the frame doesn't even provide space for a parity bit. Although you lose a bit of data integrity (which can be provided by other means), you will have more efficient communications by squeezing more information in a given number of transmitted bits.

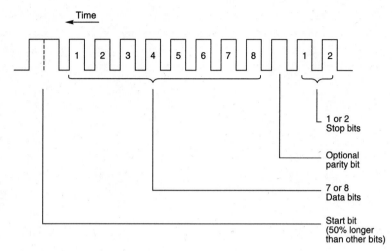

Figure 18.1. Serial data frame.

Signal Polarity

All of the bits of an RS-232 standard serial signal are sent down the communication line as negative-going pulses superimposed on a normal positive voltage that's maintained on the data line. The presence of a bit in a serial word will interrupt a continuous positive voltage with a brief negative pulse. Compared to normal logical systems, RS-232 standard data looks upside down. There's no particularly good reason for the inversion except that it's the way things have always been done and, when it comes to communications, things work best when everybody sticks to the same standard.

Bit Rates

Another important characteristic of every serial signal is the rate at which the bits in the serial data train are nominally sent. The standard form of this measurement is amazingly simple—the number of bits per second that are sent—with the standard unit being one bit per second or bps.

For somewhat arbitrary reasons, bit rates are enumerated in a rather odd increment. The usual minimum speed is 300 bps, although slower submultiples of 50, 100, and 150 bps are available. Faster standard speeds merely double the preceding rate, so the sequence runs 600, 1200, 2400, 4800, 9600, to 19,200, the fastest speed supported by many computer BIOSs.

These slow, BIOS rates are mandatory because software control of the serial port imposes such a load on some system microprocessors that slower chips cannot deal with the fastest transmission rates. Because the highest rates cannot be supported by all software, IBM chose not to sanction higher rates in its older computers. Other computer makers follow IBM's lead.

PCs equipped with Micro Channel, EISA, VL Bus, and PCI computers potentially have a means of avoiding the serial bottleneck by eliminating microprocessor overhead. In these machines, serial ports can take advantage of bus-mastering DMA control. Using this expedient, IBM increased the officially sanctioned speed of the serial ports in some systems to 38,400 bps.

Even this speed is too limiting for modern modems and other communication products. One avenue around the bottleneck is to avoid BIOS control and to directly manipulate PC hardware. This technique can push serial port speeds up to 115,200 bits per second before other limits take over. Another strategy is to use an enhanced serial port, which adds intelligence to the port itself to give high communications rates without compromising on control. In the future, a radically different serial connection (which is now a working proposal of the IEEE and designated P1394) promises serial transmission speeds as high as 100 million bits per second, potentially even higher.

Most PC communications today, however, are stuck with the classic serial port, with all its limitations. Getting the most from it requires a bit of knowledge about how it works.

Serial Hardware

The circuit at the heart of the serial ports of most PCs is a special chip with the express purpose of transforming parallel bus signals into a train of serial pulses. Called a Universal Asynchronous Receiver/Transmitter or UART, this chip accepts eight data lines as a parallel input and provides a fully structured serial output. From the name, you can tell that the UART is designed to work both ways—sending and receiving. One chip can thus convert serial signals on a communication line into the parallel kind that your PC wants as well as making serial from parallel. Every serial port has a UART at its heart, as do products with embedded serial ports such as internal modems.

8250

The term UART describes both the function and family of integrated circuits. The exact chip goes under a numerical designation assigned by its manufacturer. Three types of UART are used in the various computers that follow the PC standard. The oldest, slowest, and minimal chip was that used by the original PC and XT, installed on IBM's Asynchronous Communications Adapter card. Designated the 8250, this chip was adapted by most makers of compatible communications and multifunction boards so that they could precisely mimic the IBM product. The same chip was (and sometimes is) used as part of many lower-speed internal modems.

Besides providing the basic parallel-to-serial-and-back conversion, the 8250 UART also controls the flow of information and speed at which the exchange takes place. It sets the data rate of the serial signal by dividing down a 1.8432 MHz oscillator clock supplied by your PC. A divisor loaded into one of the chip's registers sets the UART's data rate. Similarly, other registers control the word length, parity, and number of stop bits set. Other registers enable your PC to monitor the chip and the progress of the communications it manages.

Wonderful as it sounds, the 8250 represents old technology. Even back in the dark ages when the original IBM PC was introduced, the chip was not highly regarded. The problem of the 8250 is that it is slow and cannot keep up with even the modest speed of AT-class computers. The chip has a one-byte internal buffer, which means that your PC must read every byte that's sent to the chip before the next byte arrives. If your PC doesn't get the byte fast enough, a subsequent byte may overwrite it. The result is called an overrun error.

On the other hand, the 8250 chip is cheap. When a manufacturer sells a board with two serial ports for $12, you can bet it's not going to squander $10 each for two UARTs for the board when an elderly 8250 retails for change. After all, they have to put something on the board because the basic design of the 8250 has become a mandatory part of every PC. This happened because programmers had taken direct control of the registers in the chip (rather than writing their software to access it through the BIOS, which was the prime culprit in limiting serial port speed). As a result, to maintain software compatibility, all later serial ports have had to duplicate the register function of the 8250 in order to remain backwardly compatible.

16450

In quest of better performance, hardware designers in 1984 turned to the register-compatible successor of the 8250, the 16450 UART. This chip can accommodate higher operating speeds than the 8250 and has become one of the mainstays of most serial ports. But at high communication rates and multitasking software, it still can produce overrun errors.

The 16450 retains the one-byte buffer of the 8250. While a 486 microprocessor can usually service the chip fast enough to retrieve characters before the overrun (at 115,200 bits per second, it must be able to fetch a character about every 90 microseconds), multitasking systems often delay access of the chip. If the microprocessor is involved in one task when the UART is controlled by another, a second character can bump into the UART buffer before the microprocessor can shift between applications. As a result, one or more new characters overwrite the old character while the microprocessor has its mind on other matters. Overrun occurs.

16550A

By 1987, the problems with the 16450 became obvious, and the chip of choice shifted to the higher performance 16550. The early versions of this chip proved buggy, and its design was revised to the 16550A, which is best known by the full designation 16550AFN (the final characters refer to the package and temperature rating). The 16550 UART boosts the speed potential of a PC serial port by more than an order of magnitude. The trick was beefing up the single-character buffer of the 8250 and 16450 to a 16-byte first-in first-out (FIFO) buffer. With that addition, the 16550 can receive characters for 1440 microseconds before overrun errors occur. That's long enough for most multitasking systems to switch tasks and grab the byte before they get overwritten.

The buffer in the 16550 does not automatically swing into action. The chip starts up in a backward-compatible mode that mimics the earlier UART models with single byte buffers. The chip must be expressly programmed through its register to enable the buffer.

A new write-only register controls the buffer in the 16550. Called the FIFO Control Register, in PCs this register is addressed at the third byte from the base address of the COM port. To enable the FIFO buffer, you must set the least significant bit of the FCR high.

The 16550 has a built-in timer that triggers an interrupt to your PC should no new characters pop into the buffer after a period equal to about the time required to receive four characters. This prevents characters from getting lost in the 16550 during a break in communications.

Because the 16550 is functionally compatible with the 16450, you can replace the older chip with the newest one in a few minutes; the sole requisite is that the UART in your PC or serial card be socketed rather than soldered. The upgrade is not costly, and UARTs are available at retail from companies that sell individual electronic components. Be sure to get the latest 16550A version when you order.

Although the 16550 is not pin-for-pin compatible with earlier UARTs, it is close enough that older UARTs can be upgraded. Only 2 of the 40 pins of the 16550 have definitions different from those of the earlier UARTs, and in most serial ports these redefined pins are not significant. Specifically, the changes occur in pin 24 and 29. If these connections are used on a particular serial board, the connections usually can be safely removed without affecting the operation of the port. The easiest way is to simply bend these pins on the UART so they do not fit into the socket.

Chipsets

The UART chip itself is disappearing, however. Its functions are being taken over by application-specific integrated circuits (ASICs). The chipsets that most PCs are built from today typically include the circuitry of one or two UARTs. In modern one- and three-chip PCs, the UART function is hidden on the same slab of silicon along with the rest of the logic functions of the PC. In addition, some manufacturers have begun packaging several communications functions in a single package for using in multifunction boards. The Western Digital 16C552, for example, combines the electrical equivalent of two 16550 UARTs and a parallel port into one chip. Even with these more advanced chips, the internal designs of embedded UARTs keep mimicking the stand-alone versions to assure complete system compatibility.

Enhanced Serial Ports

For high-speed communications, the 16-byte buffer of the 16550A UART can be inadequate. To overcome this problem, Hayes Microcomputer Products (the modem people) created in 1990 an enhanced serial port adapter that mates a 16550A (actually a pair of them to yield two ports per expansion board) but augments the chip with transmit-and-receive FIFO buffers of 1,024 bytes and a special coprocessor to control communications. The coprocessor is an Intel 8031, an 8-bit chip similar to the Intel 8042 used in PC keyboards. The ESP defines the basic functions of the 8031 with 8 kilobytes of ROM. To carry on its operations, the 8031 has access to 8 kilobytes of RAM, half of which is used by the buffers (1 kilobyte for each of two transmit-and-receive buffers). This memory is local to the 8031 and is not within the address space of the host PC.

The ESP operates in two distinct modes: compatibility mode to provide full backward compatibility with standard serial ports and an enhanced mode that takes advantage of the larger buffer.

As a default in the compatibility mode, the ESP operates with a single-byte buffer that appears to software as identical to a 16450 UART. Even in this mode, however, the ESP allows limited additional buffering to be activated to improve throughput. With an appropriate command, the ESP will activate a 16550-style 16-byte buffer and can be programmed to counteract all attempts to disable this buffer. Your software never knows the buffer is operating and cannot override it. If, however, your application software tries to activate the FIFO buffer as if the ESP were a 16550A, the ESP pretends that it is nothing more than a 16550A chip. To minimize the overhead on your system, the ESP also can manage hardware handshaking in its compatibility mode.

When the ESP operates in its enhanced mode, the on-board coprocessor takes control of the 1,024-byte buffer. The coprocessor also manages the port's handshaking and can even take control of DMA transfers with the host system. Enhanced mode is not invisible like compatibility mode, however. You must install a software driver so that your applications can recognize the enhanced-mode features. An application must have a special driver to take advantage of any enhanced-mode features.

You control the ESP through registers using a command set defined by Hayes and called the Enhanced Serial Interface specification. Commands reach the ESP through a set of seven input/output ports that control twelve 8-bit registers (for the two ports on a single ESP board). You can assign any base address to the ESP's I/O ports that does not conflict with other peripherals. Of course, you must configure the ESP software driver with the same base address.

The ESP registers include the following:

1. Register Ready, which indicates which of the other registers need to be read. The eight bits of this register correspond to the readable registers of the port, and a high bit in any position indicates that the corresponding register holds unread data. Bits in this register get cleared automatically when your software reads the designated register.

2. Service ID identifies the reason that the ESP sends an interrupt to your PC. The Service ID register indicates the nature of the interrupt and the port needing service. Possible interrupt conditions include that the receive buffer needs to be read, the transmit buffer is nearing empty, a DMA transfer has concluded, or a transmission error has occurred. This register is the first one read when your PC services a communications interrupt.

3. Received Data is the port through which your PC picks up incoming data from the ESP. Each port on a two-port ESP board has its own 8-bit Received Data register.

4. Transmit Data is the port through which your PC sends data to the ESP to be transmitted down the serial line. Each of the two ports on an ESP board has its own Transmit Data register. However, following the pattern of the original 8250 UART, the Receive Data and Transmit Data registers share the same address. The function of the register at the address is determined by whether your software reads or writes to the shared address.

5. Command is a pair of two registers shared by the two ports on a single two-port ESP board. Command 1 sends the actual commands (opcodes) to both ports; Command 2 sends the data for those commands (operands).

6. Status is a pair of two registers shared by both ports on a single ESP card that relays responses to ESP commands sent to the Command register. As with Receive Data and Transmit Data, the Command and Status ports share the same address space. The function at the designated address depends on whether your send carries out a read or write operation.

7. DMA Transmit provides a channel from the DMA controller in your PC to the ESP.

8. DMA Receive provides a path to your PC's DMA controller for data the ESP receives. Again, the DMA Transmit and DMA Receive ports share the same address space. These ports are mostly a convenience. In most cases, a fast microprocessor will outperform the system DMA controller.

9. The Hayes Enhanced Serial Interface defines 30 commands and intimately describes the 12 registers used by the ESP. The specification is available from the Hayes Developer Support Department at

Hayes Microcomputer Products, Inc.
P. O. Box 105203
Atlanta, Georgia 30348
(404) 840-9200

After you install a serial port in your PC, it acts as a simple extension to the computer's circuitry. Your PC just moves data from memory or a microprocessor register into the UART, which makes the necessary conversion from parallel to serial data. The output of the UART is then channeled through a serial line driver integrated circuit which converts the 5-volt logic used by the computer to the bipolar, higher voltage (15) system specified by the RS-232 standard.

I/O Addressing

To access the registers of the UART, your PC's microprocessor must send commands through system input/output ports. The data sent and received by the modem is also transferred to your PC through another I/O port. In fact, standard PC architecture assigns a block of eight I/O ports to each UART (and thus each asynchronous communication adapter—serial port—in your PC), although only seven are actually used.

Under DOS, four ranges of ports can be used by each asynchronous communication adapter. Each range encompasses eight contiguous ports, with the ranges starting at I/O port addresses 3F8(Hex), 2F8(Hex), 3E8(Hex), and 2E8(Hex). OS/2 also communicates with asynchronous adapters through ranges of eight I/O ports but except for the first two uses different port ranges than does DOS. The OS/2 and other operating systems that are capable of full 16-bit addressing assign different addresses to the higher ports. The series of these addresses starts at 03F8(Hex) and progresses through 02F8(Hex), 3220(Hex), 3228(Hex), 4220(Hex), 4228(Hex), 5220(Hex), and 5228(Hex).

These addresses are hidden from most software and from you at the DOS prompt by the BIOS and your operating system, which together assign other names to each asynchronous communication adapter. When your PC boots up, the BIOS hunts through the addresses available for serial ports and transfers the base addresses of the serial ports it finds to the BIOS data area at absolute memory address 0000:0400(Hex). It searches for ports in a specific order—the order in which the I/O port base addresses are listed in this section. DOS assigns the names COM1 through COM4, in that order, to the ports it finds listed in the BIOS data area. OS/2 calls its serial ports SERIAL 1 through SERIAL 8 and has the appropriate addresses built in.

Windows 3.1 uses another means for locating the registers assigned to serial ports COM3 and COM4. You must explicitly declare the base addresses used by these ports in your SYSTEM.INI file found in your PC's WINDOWS directory. Under the [386Enh] section of the file, you'll find listings for the COM3Base and COM4Base. The values listed should correlate with the values used by your ports. Windows 3.1 automatically assumes the standard base addresses of COM3 at 3E8(Hex) and COM4 at 2E8(Hex). If you have additional serial ports, you'll have to specify their base addresses to Windows here, too.

Register Function

The register at the base address assigned to each serial port is used for data communications. Bytes are moved to and from the UART using the microprocessor's OUT and IN instructions. The next six addresses are used by other serial port registers, in this order: the Interrupt Enable Register, the Interrupt Identification Register, the Line Control Register, the Modem Control Register, the Line Status Register, and the Modem Status Register. Another register, called the

Divisor Latch, shares the base address used by the Transmit and Receive registers and the next higher register used by the interrupt enable register. It is accessed by toggling a setting in the Line Control Register.

This latch stores the divisor that determines the operating speed of the serial port. Whatever value is loaded into the latch is multiplied by 16. The resulting product is used to divide down the clock signal supplied to the UART chip to determine the bit rate. Because of the factor of 16 multiplication, the highest speed the serial port can operate at is limited to 1/16 the supplied clock (which is 1.8432 MHz). Setting the latch value to its minimum, one, results in a bit rate of 115,200.

Registers not only store the values used by the UART chip but also are used to report back to your system how the serial conversation is progressing. For example, the line status register indicates whether a character that has been loaded to be transmitted has actually been sent. It also indicates when a new character has been received.

Although you can change the values stored in these registers manually using Debug or your own programs, for the most part you'll never tangle with these registers. They do, however, provide flexibility to the programmer.

Instead of being set with DIP switches or jumpers, the direct addressability of these registers allows all the vital operating parameters to be set through software. By loading the proper values into the line control register, for example, you alter the word length, parity, and number of stop bits used in each serial word.

Flow Control

Besides data transmissions, the UART also creates and reacts to other signals which control its operation and how the serial conversation it engages in is managed. Control is afforded through several registers that are accessed by your computer through I/O ports. To change the speed at which the serial port communicates, for example, you merely need to load a register with the proper number. The conversation control is handled by voltages that appear or are received on the serial port connectors on the rear panel of your personal computer.

One of these other UART functions is to arrange for the control of the flow of data across the serial line. Every serial interchange is a true conversation with two sides. When one side speaks, the other has to listen. Just as with polite conversation, if the listener isn't paying attention, nothing will get communicated. And if the speaker rambles along too fast, the listener can be overwhelmed and miss most of what's said. Serial communications among computers is fraught with the same problems. Without properly gauging their delivery, they may shovel out data and have it disappear into the ether unused. Even when the connection is good, the receiving equipment may be otherwise engaged and not able to give its attention to the serial information being delivered to it. Or the serial data may arrive at such a high speed that it exceeds the capacity of the receiving system to do anything with it on the fly—even saving the information for later inspection. Consequently, some means is needed for the receiving system to signal the sending system to hold on and wait until it is ready to acquire data. Several techniques for controlling the flow of serial data have evolved, all generally classed as methods of handshaking, agreeing to the terms of the transmission method.

The easiest solution is to use a special wire as a signal line that the receiving system can use to indicate that it is actually ready to receive. Because this method uses extra hardware—the flow control wire—it is termed hardware handshaking. This is the default flow control method used by the serial ports of today's IBM-compatible personal computers.

Some communications channels do not allow the use of an extra signal wire. The telephone connection used by modems (the prototypical serial communications device) only provides the two wires necessary for carrying data. With no hardware signaling means available, some alternate method of flow control is needed. The logical way of managing such communications is to give the listener special characters that it can use as semaphores to signal the speaker to slow down or stop. Another character then can be used to indicate when it's all right to speed up again. This form of flow control is termed software handshaking because, well, it's not hardware. Moreover, the flow-control indicators have the same tentative existence as the ideas embodied in software code.

With software used as most handshaking methods, the receiving system uses two distinct characters to tell the sending system when it is ready to receive a data transmission and when it can temporarily no longer accept more data. Two character pairs are commonly used in software handshaking. ETX/ACK uses the control code represented by the ASCII hexadecimal character 03(hex)—also called ETX (End TeXt) or Control-C—to indicate that it requires a pause in data transmission, and the ASCII character 06(hex)—ACK (ACKnowledge) or Control-F—to indicate that it's okay to resume. More common among PC products today is XON/XOFF handshaking, which uses the ASCII characters 13(hex)—also called DC1, XOFF, or Control-S—and 11(hex)—or DC3, XON, or Control-Q—to ask for pauses or resumptions of data flow.

Although most PC peripherals that use a serial connection offer the option of software handshaking without special driver software, they will not work properly with an IBM-compatible PC. The computer doesn't even listen for the flow control characters, so it will never act on them. The result is data overflow and characters lost from the transmission. If you use a serial printer and the handshaking does not work, for example, characters, words, or whole paragraphs may mysteriously disappear from your printouts.

Software flow control is, however, built into many application programs for controlling peripherals such as printers or for relaying through modems (which cannot pass along hardware-handshaking signals) to remote data sources. Many multiuser or multitasking operating systems (for example, OS/2) also come with special drivers that allow you to use the software handshaking through your system's serial ports without special applications.

Interrupts

The UART interacts with the microprocessor in your PC. It has to in order to transfer information so that the microprocessor can process the data to display or store it. To achieve the highest speed, the UART must be able to pass along data as quickly as it is received. Every time it uses flow control to stop the in-rush of information, transmission speed slows. Consequently, the UART has to pass along the data it gets as soon as possible—immediately if not sooner. It needs to get the microprocessor's attention right away. The UART can get the immediate attention it demands by sending a hardware interrupt to the microprocessor.

Most serial ports require that you assign them an interrupt for them to work properly. (Serial communications will work without interrupt control, but they will be severely speed constrained.) Ideally, each serial port should be assigned its own interrupt to avoid conflicts. However, the PC has few hardware interrupts available and IBM attempted to limit the number assignable to serial ports. Two interrupts are commonly used: IRQ3 and IRQ4. The COM1 serial port normally should be given hardware Interrupt Request (IRQ) 4. Serial port COM2 normally uses IRQ3. Although there's no standard for the higher DOS ports, most manufacturers used IRQ4 for COM3 (shared with COM1), and IRQ3 for COM4 (shared with COM2).

This primitive interrupt-sharing system has its drawbacks. Two or more serial devices can operate at the same time and send interrupts to your microprocessor. If two devices using the same interrupt vie for the microprocessor's attention, the chip may lose track of which port needs immediate service. As a result, commands can get confused and data lost. When assigning serial ports, it's important to avoid assigning the same interrupt to two serial devices that operate at the same time.

Mice are constantly active, always ready to issue commands to your PC. Consequently a mouse should never share an interrupt with another device if you can avoid such an assignment. If you attach a serial mouse to COM1 (which uses IRQ4), do not attach a modem to COM3 (which also uses IRQ4), for example.

Of course, the application (actually environment) with which you're most likely to use a mouse is Microsoft Windows, and Microsoft's designers were well aware of the problems of mice, interrupts, and serial ports when they wrote Windows 3.1. To help you sidestep interrupt conflicts, Windows allows you to designate any interrupt that you wish for serial port three and four. You make the necessary declaration in your PC's SYSTEM.INI file, which is ordinarily found in your WINDOWS subdirectory. Under the heading [386Enh], you'll find entries for COM3Int and COM4Int. Just edit the file so that these entries specify the interrupts that you want to use. Of course, these values apply only to your use of those serial ports when you use Windows. If you have serial ports beyond four, you'll have to specify their interrupts similarly. The Windows settings won't be understood by ordinary DOS programs (unless, of course, you use the standard interrupt settings or are able to configure your DOS applications to match the interrupts used by your serial ports).

Connectors

The external manifestation of a serial port is the connector it provides for you to plug in serial devices. You can identify serial ports on an IBM-compatible computer by the type of connectors you find. Two kinds of connectors are typically used. IBM PCs, XTs, and PS/2s all use male 25-pin D-shell connectors for their serial ports. ATs use male 9-pin D-shell connectors. The smaller connectors of the AT were mandated by the tight confines of the card retaining bracket of the combined serial/parallel port board used in those systems. Not all 25 pins in a serial connector are actively used in the IBM scheme, allowing the use of the shorter connectors, while the parallel port uses all of its pin allotment. Obviously, the serial port was the likely candidate for this size reduction.

Parallel ports, which also use 25-pin D-shell connectors, can be distinguished because they are female (that is, the connectors show holes instead of pins). Old-style MDA/CGA/EGA video connectors, which use 9-pin D-shell connectors like those of AT serial ports, also use female connectors.

In that most serial cables are equipped with 25-pin connectors at either end, an adapter is usually required to convert the AT's 9-pin connection to 25. Commercial adapters are generally available, or you can make your own. Figure 18.2 shows the proper wiring of an IBM 9-to-25 pin serial converter.

25-pin connector	9-pin connector
2	3
3	2
4	7
5	8
6	6
7	5
8	1
20	4
22	9

Figure 18.2. Wiring for a 9- to 25-Pin Serial Port Adapter

Serial Device Types

Understanding how serial ports are supposed to work requires taking a giant step backward to the dark ages when huge lizards roamed the earth and personal computers were not to be found anywhere. Originally, RS-232 ports were designed to connect data terminals with modems to connect the terminals to a giant mainframe computer in some far-off city. The connection scheme was based on a typical division of labor that was near-ubiquitous in a world that had only semi-miniaturized electronics. The terminal reduced keystrokes to digital pulses and converted other pulses to characters on-screen. The modem transformed the digital signals from the terminal into analog signals that could be transmitted over telephone lines. The serial port linked them together.

In the RS-232 system, certain tightly-defined names were assigned to the devices at either end of the connection. The terminal earned the epithet Data Terminal Equipment or DTE. The modem was called Data Communication Equipment or DCE. The difference between the two is more than just the names. Communication between the two is mediated by a very elaborate hierarchy of query signals and responses. The two behave differently and are wired differently.

Regardless of whether it's a DTE or DCE, the serial port on a device must function as a two-way street. Information is allowed to flow in both directions so that both ends of the connection must be able to operate as both sending and receiving devices. Every connection has two ends. One end may be the terminal and modem just considered. Those devices may talk to a computer, another terminal, or a printer, always using another modem. No matter which end of the connection it is attached to, as long as the modem is DCE and the terminal/computer/printer is DTE, everything will work fine.

Because of the complication of both ends sending and receiving data, often simultaneously, a single communication circuit is not sufficient to implement a true RS-232 connection. Thus, to prevent serial devices from becoming confused by hearing—and reacting to—their own transmissions, the standard serial connection uses separate wires for sending and receiving. (Modems avoid the need for separate wires by using two different signals on the same wire link.)

This use of separate wires for sending and receiving signals leads to a problem. The wire one system uses for sending must be the wire the other system uses for receiving, and vice versa. If both devices sent down the same wire, no one would be listening, and no communications would take place.

By convention, the connector pins numbered 2 and 3 are used for the two communication signals. Ordinarily, DTE devices use pin 2 to send and pin 3 to receive, and DCE devices use pin 3 to send and pin 2 to receive. The 9-pin equipped AT is an exception, however. Although considered DTE, it uses pin 3 on its DB-9 connector to send and pin 2 to receive. The normal 9-to-25 pin adapter supplied by IBM converts the AT to a standard 25-pin DTE-style connection.

The one important point about the sending and receiving pins of serial ports is that when a normal straight-through cable is used, one in which the pins at one end are directly connected to the pins with the same number at the other end, DTE devices must always be connected to DCE devices, and DCE devices will work only when connected to DTE devices.

Operation

The RS-232 specification assigns particular functions to the wires in a serial cable. Beside the two conductors used for data, several other connections are required for hardware handshaking and to make everything work properly. The various connections and their names on standard 25-pin (DTE) and 9-pin IBM serial connectors are shown in table 18.1.

TABLE 18.1. IBM Serial Port Pin-Outs

25-Pin Connector

Pin	Function	Mnemonic
2	Transmit data	TXD
3	Receive data	RXD
4	Request to send	RTS
5	Clear to send	CTS
6	Data set ready	RTS
7	Signal ground	GND
8	Carrier detect	CD
20	Data terminal ready	DTR
22	Ring indicator	RI

Current Loop Connections (Only on IBM Async Adapter, Now Obsolete)

Pin	Function
9	Transmit current loop return
11	Transmit current loop data
18	Receive current loop data
25	Receive current loop return

9-Pin (AT-Style) Connector

Pin	Function	Mnemonic
1	Carrier detect	CD
2	Receive data	RXD
3	Transmit data	TXD
4	Data terminal ready	DTR
5	Signal ground	GND
6	Data set ready	DSR
7	Request to send	RTS
8	Clear to send	CTS
9	Ring indicator	RI

The most important of all these assignments is number 7, signal ground. This wire provides the necessary return path for both the data signals and the handshaking signals. This wire must be present in all serial cables.

Signal ground is separate and completely different from pin 1, chassis ground. The pin in the serial connector corresponding to this wire is connected directly to the metal chassis or case of the equipment much as the third prong of a three-wire AC cable is. In fact, this connection provides the same safety function as the electrical ground. It ensures that the outside metal parts of the two serial devices are at the same electrical potential. It prevents you from getting a shock by touching the two devices at the same time. It carries whatever electricity might flow between the two units instead of letting your body do it (and potentially electrocuting you).

Proper Grounding

This connection is not always necessary, however, and not always desirable. It's not necessary when both devices in a serial link-up are already grounded together through their AC cables. It may not be desirable when the two serial devices are separated by a great distance and derive their power from different sources. Electrical ground potentials vary (because of differing resistances that are present in every ground return path), and it is entirely possible that grounded AC cables could put the two devices at widely different potentials. The chassis ground circuit might then carry substantial current as a ground loop. If the current in the loop is great enough, it can cause electrical interference. A small chance exists that it might be large enough to melt the chassis ground conductor and start a fire.

The best strategy is to follow these rules: If both serial devices in a connection are grounded through their AC cords, you do not need the chassis ground wire. If only one is grounded through its AC wire, the best bet is to ground the other device through its AC wire, too. Otherwise, you should use the chassis ground connection in your serial port.

Signal Functions

Trying to engage in serial communication would be fruitless if one or the other device at an end of the connection were turned off. Without a second device to listen, information from one device would pour down the serial line and vanish into the ether, wasted. Consequently, the RS-232 specification includes two wires dedicated to revealing whether a device is attached to each end of the connection and turned on.

The signal on pin 20 is called data terminal ready or simply DTR. It is a positive voltage sent from the DTE device to indicate that the device is plugged in, powered up, and ready to begin communication.

The complementary signal appears on pin 6. Called data set ready or DSR, a positive voltage on this line indicates that the DCE is turned on and ready to do its job.

In a normal RS-232 serial connection, both of these signals must be present before anything else happens. The DTE sends the DTR signal to the DCE, and the DCE sends the DSR signal to the DTE. Both devices then know that the other device is ready.

Normal modem hardware handshaking is implemented on two entirely different conductors. The DCE puts a positive voltage on the connection on pin 5, which is called clear to send or CTS, to indicate whether it is all right to send data to the DCE. In effect, it signals to the DTE that the coast is clear. At the other end of the connection, the DTE puts a positive voltage on pin 4, called request to send or RTS, to indicate to the DCE that it wants to receive information, too.

The important rule to remember is that unless both CTS and RTS have positive voltages on them, no data will flow in either direction. If no positive voltage is on the CTS wire, the DTE will not send data to the DCE. If no positive voltage is on RTS, then the DCE will not send data to the DTE.

The DCE issues one further signal that can affect the flow of data. Called carrier detect or sometimes data carrier detect, abbreviated CD or DCD, a positive voltage on this conductor indicates that the DCE modem has a carrier signal from the modem at the other end of the connection. If no carrier is detected, then the serial signal may likely be nothing but the garbage of line noise. The CD signals helps the DTE know when to be on its guard. In some cases, when CD is not positive, the DTE will refuse to accept data.

The signal on pin 22 is called ring indicator or RI and is used by a DCE modem to signal to the DTE terminal to which it is attached that it has detected ringing voltage on the telephone line. In other words, a positive voltage on RI alerts the terminal that someone is calling the modem. In most serial communications systems, this can be regarded as an optional signal because its absence usually will not prevent the flow of serial data.

A normal serial communication session follows a very particular protocol. Before anything else can happen, the hardware at both ends of the connection must be turned on and ready to go. The DTE, your computer, will assert its DTR signal and the DCE, your modem, will assert its DSR. When a telephone call awakens the modem from its lethargy, it will send an RI to the computer, which may trigger a message on-screen. Once the modem negotiates the connection with the other modem at the distant end of the call, the local modem will send a CD signal to your computer. If they were not already on during the wait before the call, your computer will assert its RTS and the modem will assert its CTS.

Type something at the computer keyboard to send to the modem or send some data from a file, and if the modem can send the bytes out fast enough to keep up, it will drop its CTS signal to tell your PC to hold off for a while. When it again makes CTS positive, your computer will resume sending data to it.

If data rolls in from the modem and your computer needs to take care of something more important—such as saving part of the transmission to disk—it will drop its RTS signal, and the modem will stop dumping data to it. When your computer finishes with its disk chores, it will assert RTS again, and data will again flow from the modem.

DTE-to-DTE Communications

As long as you want to connect a computer serial port that functions as DTE to a modem that functions as DCE, this serial connection scheme will likely work flawlessly the first time you try it. Simply sling a cable with enough conductors to handle all the vital signals between the computer and modem and, Voila! Serial communications without a hitch. Try it, and you're likely to wonder why so many people complain about the capricious nature of serial connections.

The problem is that you may want to connect something besides a modem to a serial port. Other common serial devices include printers, plotters, mice, digitizing pads, even video display terminals. Many of these devices are not set up to be DCE but are themselves DTE, patterned after the first computer printers that did double duty as terminals.

Connect two DTE devices together with an ordinary serial cable and the result will be that you have two serial devices tied together with a cable. You will not have a communications system at all. The two DTE units will not even listen to one another because each one will listen on the line that the other is listening on and talk on the line that the other talks on—if they even get that far. Lacking proper voltages on their DSR pins, they will not even try to talk.

All IBM-compatible computers (except the very special case of ATs with 9-pin serial connectors) are DTE. Modems and most mice are DCE and can be directly connected to IBM-style 25-pin serial ports. Serial printers operate as DTE, however, and present problems, as do many plotters and other peripherals.

The simple solution to the problem of connecting a serial printer to a PC is to only use parallel printers with PCs. But that's not always feasible—the serial connection gives a printer greater reach. Moreover, the serial connection may be the only one available to you.

If you need to connect another DTE device such as a printer to your PC's serial port, you will have to reverse pins 2 and 3 somewhere between the two ports. Special cables called cross-over cables do exactly that. In addition, most cross-over cables also swap the DTR and DSR leads as well as the RTS and CTS leads. In this way, the two DTE devices talk and listen to each other. The DTR signals from each device tell the other that it is ready, and the RTS signals act as flow control. A typical cross-over cable is shown in Figure 18.3.

In the best of all possible worlds, such a cross-over cable between two DTE devices would work just as well as an ordinary straight-through cable between DTE and DCE. The real world is different.

The first problem is that the CD line has no corresponding match. The DTE device sends out nothing similar to a CD signal. Without the CD signal, the DTE device may be inhibited from ever sending out data.

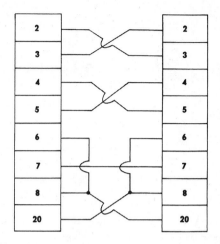

Figure 18.3. A generalized cross-over cable.

The simple thing to do is to create a CD from something that's already at hand. Both CD and CTS have to be present for the DTE to send data out. They could be tied together, and the DTE would never know the difference. When CTS is asserted, the DTE would see CD at the same time and would know it was safe to transmit.

A variation on this theme makes the system easier to wire and more reliable. Because a DTE device must be turned on if it's going to produce any signal—let alone the DTR and RTS, which are flipped into DSR and CTS to let the other DTE that's party to the connection to know it can send—the RTS can serve both functions. Thus one signal, RTS, through a cross-over cable, can control three at the other end—DSR, CTS, and CD. These wires can actually be bridged together within the connector attached to a serial cable. In a great many cases, this cable will allow two DTE devices to communicate with one another.

This specialized cross-over cable does not work in all circumstances because not all DTE devices are wired the same. Some printers, for example, are designed with the intention of connecting them to the serial outputs of computers that function as DTE. They consequently use a special flow control pin on their serial connectors that is different from DTR but works in the same way. Perhaps the most common of these, used by Digital Equipment Corporation and NEC on some of their printers, devotes pin 19 to flow control. While DTR from the computer is used to control the other device, pulling its DSR, CTS, and CD high, pin 19 on these printers does the same thing. A cross-over cable that works with many such serial printers is shown in figure 18.4.

A few serial ports enable you to avoid the confusion of crossed wires and rerouted signals by making the port identity—DTE or DCE—selectable. By flipping switches or moving jumpers, you can reassign the pin definitions of these products and make them work with many serial devices using nothing more than a straight-through cable.

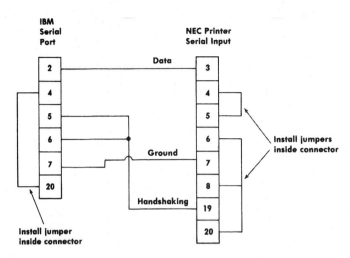

Figure 18.4. Cross-over cable for NEC and similar printers.

These indecisive ports are not a panacea, however. The serial printers that posed problems for cross-over cables by defining themselves as DTE and using pin 19 for flow control thwart the elegance of this strategy. A properly configured DCE will not provide working flow control when connected to such a DTE port through a straight-through serial cable.

One way to avoid the hassle of finding the right combination of hardware handshaking connections would appear to be letting software do it—avoiding hardware handshaking and instead using the XON-XOFF software flow control available with most serial devices. Although a good idea, even this expedient can cause hours of headscratching when nothing works as it should—or nothing works at all.

When trying to use software handshaking, nothing happening is a common occurrence. Without the proper software driver, your PC or PS/2 has no idea that you want to use software handshaking. It just sits around waiting for a DSR and a CTS to come rolling in toward it from the connected serial device.

Moreover, switching to software flow control does nothing to change the sending and receiving connections of DTE and DCE. If you plan on connecting a DTE computer to a DTE printer, for example, you still need a cross-over cable even if you use software handshaking.

Null Modems

Software handshaking does free you from many of the other concerns about serial connections, however. By using local voltages, you can fool a serial port into believing that it's getting what it wants from the distant end of the cable. You can substitute the positive voltage that the PC itself provides as the DTR signal to make it believe that it has received the full complement of DSR, CTS, and CD signals by wiring the four pins together inside your serial connector, for example.

A cable or adapter that provides this tomfoolery (usually in both directions, to both ports that it is connected to) is sometimes called a null modem. This term has, however, lost much of its specificity. Ask for a null modem cable and you're just as likely to receive a simple cross-over cable, a cable with all of the handshaking circuits wired together, or a combination of the two that flips the data pair (pins 2 and 3) and connects the handshaking lines. Figure 18.5 shows the wiring of a true null modem.

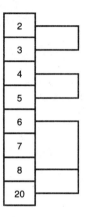

Figure 18.5. The wiring of a true null modem.

The only way to be sure that such a cable is wired properly is to make it yourself. If even that's not a guarantee that it will work (or if, indeed, your skills are such that it may be a guarantee that it will not work), thoroughly scrutinize a cable-wiring diagram or cable description before making your purchase.

Three-Wire Connections

If the DTE device that you want to connect to your PC is a plotter or printer, you don't always have to worry about all the serial port signals. With hardware handshaking, the only thing that the printer has to say to your PC is when to stop and start. A single wire can handle that. One wire also suffices for one-way data flow. A single ground will serve both the handshaking and data signals, allowing you to hook up your serial device with as few as three wires—one for data on TXD, one for a signal ground, and one for a handshaking line.

The reasons for making such a slimmed-down cable are several. Because there are fewer connections to make, there are fewer things to go wrong. And, when you're trying to get a system to work and you must resort to the brute force method of trial and error, the three-wires technique can greatly simplify your experimentation. Figure 18.6 shows two possible three-wire cables for such connections: straight-through and crossover.

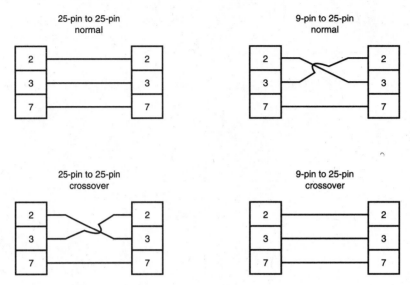

Figure 18.6. Three-wire serial cables.

P1394

Compared to the performance you've come to expect from your PC, serial ports are slow at best. They are constrained not only by the pragmatic aspects of their design—UART chips and the clocks that control them—but also by the medium through which the signals travel. Single-ended signals and cables of dubious quality are the communications equivalent of unleashing a go-kart with a lawnmower engine on an Autobahn that's unfettered by speed limits. The chances your data will get where it's going unscathed are slim and, even if successful, the trip will be slow. As long as the medium remains the same, improvements in serial signal speed will be chancy if possible at all.

The best way to accelerate the serial trip is to redefine the medium and method. The IEEE embarked on exactly that goal and is working on a proposal called P1394 to be the serial port of the future. The goal of the effort is to give computer and peripheral makers a low-cost but high-speed interface for linking devices and systems. Rather than replacing the RS-232 port alone, proponents see P1394 as a substitute for all the odd and varied ports on the back of your PC. P1394 has the potential for replacing not only your serial port but the parallel port, SCSI port, even the video connector.

The key to the power of P1394 is speed. The initial design of P1394 sets up a 100 megabit per second data transfer protocol. In addition, the standard defines two higher-speed data rates for future upgrades, 200 and 400 megabits per second.

From a manufacturer's standpoint, size and cost are as important as speed. P1394 has the potential of reducing the cost of external connections to PCs both in terms of money spent and panel usage. Both of these savings originate in the design of the P1394 connector. P1394 envisions a single 6-wire plastic connector replacing most if not all of the standard port connectors on a PC.

The connector itself will cost manufacturers a few cents while the connectors alone for an RS-232 port can cost several dollars (and that can be a significant portion of the price of a peripheral or even PC). Moreover, a standard serial connector —25-pin D-shell connector—by itself is much too large for today's miniaturized systems. It cannot fit a PCMCIA card by any stretch of the imagination or plastic work.

Those savings have a price. Far from simply needing a UART, P1394 is a complex communications system with its own transfer protocol. It will require complex circuits to work. But throughout the history of PCs, the cost of standard silicon circuits has plummeted while the cost of connectors has continued to climb. Just as the electrically more complex AT interface replaced older interfaces for hard disks, P1394 stands to step in place of the serial port.

The future imagined by P1394 advocates is much like the early Macintosh computers that depended on a single SCSI port for all system expansion. P1394 beats old SCSI both in connector simplicity and cost. But it also joins SCSI—P1394 is one of the hardware channels incorporated into the proposed SCSI-3 standard.

As with existing SCSI systems, P1394 enables you to connect multiple devices and uses an addressing system so the signals sent through a common channel are recognized only by the proper target device. The linked devices can independently communicate among themselves without the intervention of your PC. But P1394 gives you greater wiring flexibility than the current SCSI standards. To link multiple peripherals, you can daisy-chain them or split the cable into branches. In effect, the P1394 connection behaves like a small (but fast) network.

P1394 is a true architecture that is built from several layers, each of which defines one aspect of the serial connection. These layers include a bus-management layer, a transaction layer, a link layer, and a physical layer.

Bus Management Layer

This part of the P1394 standard defines the basic control functions as well as the control and status registers required by connected devices to operate their ports. This layer handles channel assignments, arbitration, mastering, and errors.

Transaction Layer

The protocol that governs transactions across the P1394 connection is called the transaction layer. This layer mediates the read and write operations. To match modern PCs, the transaction layer is optimized to work with 32-bit double words, although the standard also allows block operations of variable length. This layer's operation was derived from the IEEE 1212 parallel data-transfer standard.

Link Layer

The logical control on the data across the P1394 wire is the link layer, making the transfer for the transaction layer. Communications are half-duplex transfers, but the link layer provides a confirmation of the reception of data. Double-word transfers are favored, but the link layer also permits exchanges in variable-length blocks.

Physical Layer

The actual physical connections made by P1394 are governed by the physical layer. This part of the standard includes both a protocol and the medium itself. The physical protocol sublayer controls access to the connection with full arbitration. The physical medium sublayer comprises the cable and connectors.

In initial form, the physical part of P1394 will be copper wires. The standard cable is a complex weaving of six conductors. Data will travel down two shielded twisted pairs. Two wires will carry power at 8 to 40 volts with sufficient current to power a number of peripherals. Another shield will cover the entire collection of conductors. A small, 6-pin connector will link PCs and peripherals to this cable. Figure 18.7 shows this connector.

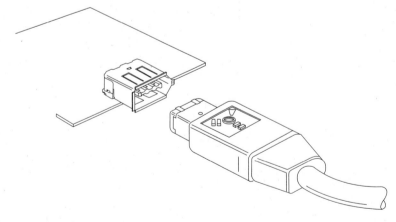

Figure 18.7. P1394 Connector.

The P1394 wiring standard allows for up to 32 hops of 4.5 meters (about 15 feet) each. As with current communications ports, the standard allows you to connect and disconnect peripherals without switching off power to them. You can daisy-chain P1394 devices or branch the cable between them. When you make changes, the network of connected devices reconfigures itself to reflect the alterations.

Chapter 19
Modems

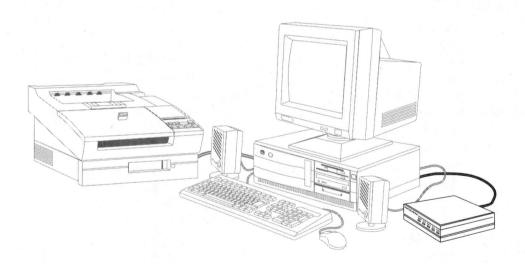

The greatest power and strength in using a computer comes not from sitting at a solitary keyboard but by connecting with other machines and exchanging files, programs, images, and information across telephone lines. But because today's telephone lines are analog and computers are digital, you need a modem to match them. Modem speeds and variety (including fax modems) are greater than ever before.

For some unknown reason, you need a modem to match your PC to a telephone line; the need for the extra device seems so absurd because both computer and telephone use the same things for making and moving messages: electrical signals. Were not the giant corporations specializing in computers and telephones not such avowed rivals, you might suspect that they were in cahoots to foist such a contrived accessory on the computer marketplace.

Step back and look at what a modem does, however, and you will gain new respect for the device. In many ways, the modern modem is a miracle worker. The best of today's modems can squeeze more than a dozen data bits through a cable where only one should fit. A fax modem can even cram a full-page image through a thin 22-gauge telephone wire in about 15 seconds. Even the least expensive generic modem operates like a specialized time machine that can bridge the century-wide chasm between state-of-the-art computer and old-fashioned telephone technologies.

Modems are a necessary bridge between digital and analog signals. The modern modem usually does much more than connect. Most modems are boxes chock-full of convenience features that can make using them fast, simple, and automatic. The best of today's modems not only make and monitor the connection but even improve it. They dial the phone for you, remembering the number you want, and they will try again and again. A modem will listen in until it's sure of good contact, and only then lets you transmit across the telephone line. Some modems even have built-in circuits to detect and correct the inevitable errors that creep into your electrical conversations.

Modems are a necessary evil in the modern world of telecommunications because the telephone system was designed even before electronics were invented, and solid-state digital circuitry was almost 100 years off. The first words out of Dr. Bell's speaking telegraph were analog electrical signals, the same juice that flows through the receiver of your own telephone. Although strictly speaking, digital communications are older—the conventional telegraph predates the telephone by nearly 30 years (Samuel F. B. Morse wondered what God had wrought in 1844)—current digital technology is only a recent phenomenon.

The telephone system was designed only to handle analog signals because that's all that speaking into a microphone creates. Over the years, the telephone system has evolved into an elaborate international network capable of handling millions of these analog signals simultaneously and switching them from one telephone set to another anywhere in the world. Although telephone companies are increasingly using digital signals to move trunk-line communications between switching centers, the input and output ends of the circuit still end in conventional analog-based telephones, at least for the time being. In the future, you will undoubtedly connect to an all-digital telephone system (ISDN, discussed later, is just a first step), but for today, you're still stuck with analog connections and modems.

Modem Operating Principles

A modem is a signal converter that mediates the communications between a computer and the telephone network. In function, a modern PC modem has five elements.

PC Interface

For a modem to work with your PC, the modem needs a means to connect to your PC's logic circuits. All modems use a standard or enhanced serial port. In the case of an internal PC modem, the serial port is embedded in the circuitry of the modem, and the expansion bus of the PC itself becomes the interface. Besides giving a hardware connection, this interface converts the parallel data of your PC into serial form suitable for transmission down a telephone line. Modern modems operate so fast that the choice of serial port circuitry (particularly the UART) becomes critical to achieving the best possible performance.

Any modem, whether installed as a box outside your PC or inside in an expansion slot, will steal one serial port (COM1, COM2, COM3, or COM4) from your PC. With an external modem, the loss is obvious because you fill the port's jack with the plug of a cable running off to your modem. With an internal modem, the loss is less obvious. You may not even detect it until something doesn't work because both your modem and your mouse (or some other peripheral) try to use the same port at the same time.

The serial ports built into internal modems are just like any other serial ports. You must assign them an input/output address and an interrupt. Most modems let you make these selections either by hardware (with jumpers or switches) or during software setup. Any modern modem or communications program will let you use any of the four standard PC serial ports. Older hardware and software products may not, so it is important to check each for flexibility and compatibility when acquiring a modem. In other words, if your PC's two serial ports already are plugged with a mouse and a hand scanner, then you will want both a modem and communications package that let you use COM3 or COM4. You still can use a modem (or software package) that doesn't support COM3 and COM4, but you will have to rearrange the other serial devices plugged into your PC.

Data Preparation

Modern modem communications require that the data you want to send be properly prepared for transmission. This pretransmission preparation helps your modem deliver the highest possible data throughput while preventing errors from creeping in.

Most modem standards change the code used by the serial stream of data from the PC interface into code that's more efficient—for example, stripping out data framing information for quicker synchronous transfers. The incoming code stream may also be analyzed and compressed to strip out redundant information. The modem may also add error-detection or correction codes to the data stream.

At the receiving end, the modem must debrief the data stream and undo the compression and coding of the transmitting modem. A micro controller inside the modem performs these functions based on the communications standard you choose to use. If you select a modem by the communications standards it uses, you don't have to worry about the details of what this micro controller does.

Modulator

The heart of the modem is the circuitry called a *modulator* that converts the direct current pulses of the serial digital code from the micro controller into an analog signal containing the same information but compatible with the worldwide telephone network. The very name modem is derived from this term and the reciprocal circuit (the demodulator) that's used in reception. Modem is a foreshortening of the words MOdulator/DEModulator. The conversion process from digital to analog is termed *modulation*.

Modulation, and hence modems, is necessary because analog telephone connections do not allow digital, direct-current signals to pass. The modulation process creates analog signals that contain all the digital information of the computer original but which can be transmitted through the voice-only channels of the telephone system.

The modulation process begins with a constant signal called the *carrier*, which carries or bears the load of the digital (modulating) information. In most systems, the carrier is a steady-state signal of constant amplitude (strength), frequency, and coherent phase. The signal that's electrically mixed with the carrier to modify some aspect of it is given the same name as the process: modulation. Changes in the modulation result in a change in the carrier-and-modulation mix. The change in the modulation makes a corresponding change in the carrier but not necessarily a change in the same aspect of the carrier. In FM or frequency modulation, for example, a change in the strength of the modulation is reflected as a change in the frequency of the carrier.

Modulation brings several benefits—more than enough to justify the complication of combining signals. Because electronic circuits can be tuned to accept the frequency of one carrier wave and reject others, multiple modulated signals can be sent through a single communications medium. This principle underlies all radio communication and broadcasting. In addition, modulation allows digital, direct-current-based information to be transmitted through a medium, like the telephone system, that otherwise could not carry direct current signals.

In demodulation, the carrier is stripped away and the encoded information is returned to its original form. Although logically it is just the complement of modulation, demodulation usually involves entirely different circuits and operating principles, which adds to the complexity of the modem.

User Interface

The fourth element in the modem is what you see and feel. Most modems give you some way of monitoring what they do either audibly with a speaker or visually through a light display. These features don't affect the speed of the modem or how it works but can make one modem easier to use than another. Indicator lights are particularly helpful when you want to troubleshoot communication problems.

Line Interface

Finally, the modem needs circuitry to connect with the telephone system. This line-interface circuitry (in telephone terminology, a data-access arrangement) boosts the strength of the modem's internal logic-level signals to a level matching that of normal telephone service. At the same time, the line-interface circuitry protects your modem and computer from dangerous anomalies on the telephone line (a nearby lightning strike, for example), and it protects the telephone company from odd things that may originate from your computer and modem (a pulse from your PC in its death throes, for example).

From your perspective, the line interface of the modem is the telephone jack on its back panel. Some modems have two jacks so that you can loop through a standard telephone. By convention, the jack marked "Line" connects with your telephone line; the jack marked "Phone" connects to your telephone.

Over the years, this basic five-part modem design has changed little. But the circuits themselves, the signal-processing techniques that they use, and the standards they follow have all evolved to the point that modern modems can move data as fast as the theoretical limits of telephone transmission lines allow.

Short-Haul Modems

Some devices that are called modems don't follow this five-part design and aren't really modems at all. Inexpensive short-haul modems advertised for stretching the link between your PC and serial printer actually involve minimal circuitry, typically nothing more than digital buffers. Definitely not enough to modulate and demodulate signals. There's so little circuitry, in fact, that it is often entirely hidden inside the shell of a simple cable connector.

All that the short-haul modem does is convert the digital output of a computer to another digital form that can better withstand the rigors of a thousand feet of wire. Don't confuse short-haul modems with the real thing. A short-haul modem will not communicate over a dial-up telephone system and isn't even legal to plug into your telephone wiring.

Leased-Line Modems

Another distinction between modems is between *dial-up modems* and *leased-line modems*. The dial-up modem is what you think of when you hear the word modem. The dial-up modem connects with a standard telephone line just as an ordinary telephone set would. The dial-up modem links to the telephone system and can dial a line to make a connection just like a telephone would. You tie up your telephone line and pay for the service only when the dial-up modem is connected (or is making a connection) to a distant modem. When you have no more data to send or receive, the dial-up modem hangs up so that you don't get charged for telephone time you don't need.

In contrast, the leased-line modem is always connected to a dedicated telephone line leased from the telephone company (hence the name). The leased-line modem stays in constant contact, and you pay for a continuous telephone connection.

The leased-line modem has its own advantages. You never have to worry about a busy signal or a connection not getting through (although you can be disconnected because of line trouble). Moreover, the telephone company leases lines of various quality levels, some that are much better than ordinary dial-up circuits. Better phone lines mean greater data capacity, so leased-line modems often are faster than the dial-up variety. Finally, the constant connection means that you're always in touch. You get instant response. Remote terminals, such as those on computerized airline reservation systems, typically use leased-line modems for this reason.

Channel Limits

Like a great artist, the modem is constrained to work within the limits of its medium, the telephone channel. These limits are imposed by the characteristics of analog communications and the communications medium used—primarily the unshielded twisted-pair wire that runs between your business or home and the telephone company's central office. Just as an artist must overcome the limitation of his medium, turning its weaknesses into strengths, the modem must struggle within the confines of the telephone line and turn the ancient technology to its advantage.

Signal Bandwidth

The primary limit on any communications channel is its *bandwidth*, and bandwidth is the chief constraint on modem speed. Bandwidth merely specifies a range of frequencies from the lowest to the highest that the channel can carry or a range of frequencies present in the signal. It is one way of describing the maximum amount of information that the channel can carry.

An unmodulated carrier wave has a nominal operating frequency. In radio broadcasting, for example, it's the number you dial in when you tune in your favorite station. Without modulation, a pure carrier wave uses only that one frequency and has essentially zero bandwidth. It also carries the least possible amount of information—simply that it's there. It's the equivalent of one, unchanging digital bit.

The modulation that's added to the carrier contains information that varies at some rate. Traditional analog signal sources (music or voice signals, for example) contain a near-random mix of frequencies between 20 Hz and 20,000 Hz. Although digital signals start off as direct current, which also has no bandwidth, every change in digital state adds a frequency component. The faster the states change (the more information that's squeezed down the digital channel, as measured in its bit rate), the more bandwidth the signal occupies. The on-and-off rate of the digital signal is its frequency, and modulating the carrier with the rate adds to the frequency range demanded by the carrier-and-modulation combination. In other words, mixing in modulation increases the bandwidth needed by the carrier; the more information that's added, the more bandwidth that's needed.

Sidebands

In the simplest modulation systems, a modulated carrier requires twice the bandwidth of the modulation signal. Although this doubling sounds anomalous, it's the direct result of the combining of the signals. The carrier and modulation mix and result in modulation products corresponding to the frequency of the modulation both added to the carrier together with the frequency of the modulation and subtracted from the carrier. The added result often is called the *upper sideband*, and the subtracted result is correspondingly called the *lower sideband*.

Because these upper and lower modulation products are essentially redundant (they contain exactly the same information), one or the other can be eliminated without loss of information to reduce the bandwidth of the modulated carrier to that of the modulation. (This form of bandwidth savings, termed single sideband modulation, is commonly used in broadcasting to squeeze more signals into the limited radio spectrum.)

Even with sideband squeezing, the fundamental fact remains that any modulated signal requires a finite range of frequencies to hold its information. The limits of this frequency range define the bandwidth required by the modulated signal.

Channel Bandwidth

The bandwidth of a communications channel defines the frequency limits of the signals that they can carry. This channel bandwidth may be physically limited by the medium used by the channel or artificially limited by communications standards. The bandwidths of radio transmissions, for example, are limited artificially, by law, to allow more different modulated carriers to share the air waves while preventing interference between them.

In wire-based communications channels, bandwidth often is limited by the wires themselves. Certain physical characteristics of wires cause degradations in their high frequency transmission capabilities. The capacitance between conductors in a cable pair, for example, increasingly degrades signals as their frequencies rise, finally reaching a point at which a high frequency signal might not be able to traverse more than a few centimeters of wire. Amplifiers or repeaters, which boost signals so that they can travel longer distances, often cannot handle very low or very high frequencies, imposing more limits.

Most telephone channels also have an artificial bandwidth limitation imposed by the telephone company. To get the greatest financial potential from the capacity of their transmissions cables, microwave systems, and satellites, telephone carriers normally limit the bandwidth of telephone signals. One reason bandwidth is limited is so that many separate telephone conversations can be stacked on top of one another through multiplexing techniques, which allow a single pair of wires to carry hundreds of simultaneous conversations.

Although the effects of bandwidth limitation are obvious (it's why your phone doesn't sound as good as your stereo), the telephone company multiplexing equipment works so well that you are generally unaware of all the manipulations made to the voice signals as they are squeezed through wires.

Bandwidth Limitations

One of the consequences of telephone company signal manipulations is a severe limitation in the bandwidth of an ordinary telephone channel. Instead of the full frequency range of a good quality stereo system (from 20 Hz to 20,000 Hz), a telephone channel will allow only frequencies between 300 Hz and 3000 Hz to freely pass. This very narrow bandwidth works well for telephones because frequencies below 300 Hz contain most of the power of the human voice but little of its intelligibility. Frequencies above 3000 Hz increase the crispness of the sound but don't add appreciably to intelligibility.

Although intelligibility is the primary concern with voice communications (most of the time), data transfer is oriented principally to bandwidth. The comparatively narrow bandwidth of the standard telephone channel limits the bandwidth of the modulated signal it can carry, which in turn limits the amount of digital information that can be squeezed down the phone line by a modem.

Try some simple math and you will see the harsh constraints faced by your modem's signals. A telephone channel typically has a useful bandwidth of about 2700 Hz (from 300 Hz to 3000 Hz). At most, a carrier wave at exactly the center of the telephone channel, 1650 Hz, burdened by two sidebands, could carry data that varies at a rate no greater than 1650 Hz. Such a signal would fill the entire bandwidth of the telephone channel without allowing for a safety margin.

Shannon's Limit

Fortunately for your modem, it can use modulation technologies that are much more efficient than this simple example. But the modem still faces an ultimate limit on the amount of data that it can squeeze through an analog telephone line. This ultimate limit combines the effects of the bandwidth of the channel and the noise level in the channel. The greater the noise, the more likely that it will be confused with the information that has to compete with it. This theoretical maximum data rate for a communication channel is called *Shannon's limit.*

With two-way *dial-up* telephone connections under ideal conditions, the limit for conventional modem technologies reaches about 19,200 bits per second. New modem designs are pushing the limit higher, however, to about 30,000 bits per second.

Most of these technologies rely on the power of digital signal processors to take advantage of novel technologies, such as line probing, multidimensional trellis coding, signal shaping, and protocol spoofing.

Line probing lets a pair of modems determine the optimal transfer method for a given telephone connection. The two modems send a sequence of signals back and forth to probe the limits of the connection and ascertain the higher modulation rate, best carrier frequency, and coding technique that gives the highest throughput.

Multidimensional trellis coding is a way of making modem signals more resistant to errors caused by noise in the telephone connection by carefully selecting the modulation values assigned to the transmitted code.

Signal shaping improves signal-to-noise performance of the modem connection by altering the power of the signal in certain circumstances. Signal points that occur frequently are transmitted at a higher power, and less frequent points are transmitted at a reduced power.

Protocol spoofing removes the redundant parts of data-transfer protocols so that less data needs to be transferred. In effect, it compresses the protocol to speed transmissions much as data compression speeds data transfer. At the receiving end, the protocol is fully reconstructed before being passed along for further processing.

Asynchronous Operation

At lower speeds most modems are designed to operate asynchronously: the timing of one modem's signals doesn't matter as long as it is within wide limits. More important is the actual bit pattern that is sent. That pattern is self-defining. Each character frame holds enough data not only to identify the information that it contains but also to define its own beginning and end.

Normally, the time at which a pulse occurs in relation to the ticking of a computer's system clock determines the meaning of a bit in a digital signal, and the pulses must be synchronized to the clock for proper operation. In asynchronous transmissions, however, the digital pulses are not locked to the system clock of either computer. Instead, the meaning of each bit of a digital word is defined by its position in reference to the clearly (and unambiguously) defined start bit. In an asynchronous string, the start bit is followed by seven or eight data bits, an optional parity bit for error detection, and one or two stop bits that define the ends of the frame. (See Chapter 18, "Serial Ports.") Because the timing is set within each word in isolation, each word of the asynchronous signal can be independent of any time relations beyond its self-defined bounds.

Synchronous Operation

When speed's the thing (as it almost always is with PCs), asynchronous communications rank as wasteful. All those start and stop bits eat up time that could be devoted to squeezing in more data bits. Consequently, high-speed modem transmission standards and protocols as well as most leased-line modems do away with most extra overhead bits of asynchronous communication by using synchronous transmission. In this method of transmitting data across phone lines, the two ends of the channel share a common time base, and the communicating modems operate continuously at substantially the same frequency and are continually maintained in the correct phase relationship by circuits that monitor the connection and adjust for the circuit conditions.

In synchronous transmissions, the timing of each bit independently is vital, but framing bits (start and stop bits) are unnecessary, which makes this form of communication transmitted faster by two or three bits per byte.

Duplex

Communication is supposed to be a two-way street. Information is supposed to flow in both directions. You should learn something from everyone you talk to, and everyone should learn from you. Even if you disregard the potential for success of such two-way communication, one effect is undeniable: it cuts the usable bandwidth of a data communication channel in one direction in half because the data going the other way requires its own share of the bandwidth.

With modems, such a two-way exchange of information is called *duplex communications*. Often it is redundantly called full duplex. A full-duplex modem is able to simultaneously handle two signals, usually (but not necessarily) going in opposite directions, so it can send and receive information at the same time. Duplex modems use two carriers to simultaneously transmit and receive data; each carrier has half the bandwidth available to it and its modulation.

Half Duplex

The alternative to duplex communications is *half duplex*. In half-duplex transmission, only one signal is used. To carry on a two-way conversation, a modem must alternately send and receive signals. Half-duplex transmission allows more of the channel bandwidth to be put to use but slows data communications because often a modem must switch between sending and receiving modes after every block of data crawls through the channel.

Switching Modems

To push more signal through a telephone line, some modems attempt to mimic full-duplex operation while actually running in half-duplex mode. *Switching modems* are half-duplex modems that reverse the direction of the signal at each end of the line in response to the need to send data. This kind of operation can masquerade as full duplex most of the time communications go only in one direction. You enter commands into a remote access system, and only after the commands are received does the remote system respond with the information that you seek. Although one end is sending, the other end is more than likely to be completely idle.

On the positive side, switching modems are able to achieve a doubling of the data rate without adding any complexity to their modulation. But the switching process is time-consuming and inevitably involves a delay because the modems must let each other know that they are switching. Because transmission delays across long-distance lines are often a substantial fraction of a second (most connections take at least one trip up to a satellite and back down, a 50,000 mile journey that takes about a quarter of a second even at the speed of light) the process of switching can eat huge holes into transmission time.

Most software-modem protocols require a confirmation for each block of data sent, meaning the modem must switch twice for each block. The smaller the block, the more often the switch must occur. Just one trip to a satellite would limit a switching modem with an infinitely fast data rate using the 128-byte blocks of some early modem protocols to 1,024 bits per second at the two-switches-per-second rate.

Asymmetrical Modems

Because of this weakness of switching modems, *asymmetrical modems* cut the waiting by maintaining a semblance of two-way duplex communications while optimizing speed in one direction only. These modems shoehorn in a low-speed (typically 300 bps) channel in addition to a high-speed channel. As with switching modems, asymmetrical modems can flip-flop the direction of the high speed communications. They rely on algorithms to determine which way is the best way. Typically, the high speed channel is used for transferring blocks of data, and the confirmations trickle back on the lower speed channel. Some fax modem standards use this scheme.

Interactive two-way communications have the same problem with asymmetrical modems as file-transmission protocols have with switching modems. When the direction of communication changes often, speed plummets. Consequently, most modern modem development has been full duplex. The latest modem standards all specify full-duplex operation.

Echoplex

The term duplex often is mistakenly used by some communications programs for PCs to describe echoplex operation. In *echoplex mode*, a modem sends a character down the phone line, and the distant modem returns the same character, echoing it. The echoed character then is displayed on the originating terminal as confirmation that the character was sent correctly. Without echoplex, the host computer usually writes the transmitted character directly to its monitor screen. Although a duplex modem generates echoplex signals most easily, the two terms are not interchangeable.

Guard Bands

Duplex does more than cut in half the bandwidth available to each channel. Separating the two channels is a *guard band*, a width of unused frequencies that isolates the active channels and prevents confusion between their separate carriers. The safety margin is, in effect, also a guard between the carriers and the varying limit of the bandwidth.

Once you add in the needs of duplex communication and the guard bands, the practical bandwidth limit for modem communications over real telephone channels that have an innate 2700 Hz bandwidth works out to about 2400 Hz. That leaves 1200 Hz for each of the two duplex channels. Getting the most information through that limited bandwidth is a challenge to the inventiveness of modem designers and modem standards in picking the best possible modulation method.

Modulation Technologies

Just as AM and FM radio stations use different modulation methods to achieve the same end, modem designers can select from several modulation technologies to encode digital data in a form compatible with analog transmission systems. The different forms of modulation are distinguished by the characteristics of the carrier wave that are changed in response to changes in data to encode information. The three primary characteristics of a carrier wave that designers may choose to vary for modulation are its amplitude, its frequency, and its phase.

Amplitude Modulation

The *amplitude* is the strength of the signal or the loudness of a tone carried through a transmission medium, such as the telephone wire. Varying the strength of the carrier in response to modulation to transmit information is called *amplitude modulation*. The carrier tone gets louder or softer in response to the modulating signal.

One way that digital information could be coded with amplitude modulation is as two discrete strengths of the signal corresponding to the two digital states. In fact, the most rudimentary form of amplitude modulation uses the two limits of carrier strength, full power and zero power, for its code. This type of amplification is called carrier wave or CW transmission (see fig. 19.1).

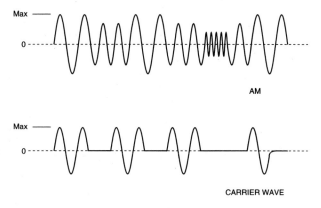

Amplitude modulation encodes information as the signal strength (height of carrier waveform). Carrier wave is a special case of AM where the signal varies from zero to full strength.

FIGURE 19.1. Amplitude and carrier wave modulation.

Pure amplitude modulation has one big weakness. The loudness of a telephone signal is the characteristic most likely to vary during transmission. As the signal travels, the resistance and impedance of the telephone wire tends to reduce the signal's strength; the telephone company's amplifiers attempt to keep the signal at a constant level. Moreover, noise on the telephone line mimics amplitude modulation and might be confused with data. Consequently, pure amplitude modulation is not used by modems.

Phase Modulation

Another carrier state that can be altered to encode information is its phase. An unmodulated carrier is a constant train of identical waves that follow one after another precisely in step. The peaks and troughs of the train of waves flow by at constant intervals. If one wave were delayed for exactly one wavelength, it would fit exactly on top of the next one.

By delaying one of the waves without altering its amplitude or frequency, a detectable state change called a *phase shift* is created. The onset of one wave is shifted in time compared to the waves that preceded it. Information can be coded as phase modulation by assigning one amount of phase shift from the constant carrier to a digital 1 and another phase shift to a digital 0.

One particular type of phase modulation called *quadrature modulation* alters the phase of the signal in increments of 90 degrees. The modulated carrier will differ from the unmodulated carrier wave by a phase angle of 0, 90, 180, or 270 degrees. Although this form of modulation is useful in modem communications, it is most often used with other modulation techniques (see fig. 19.2).

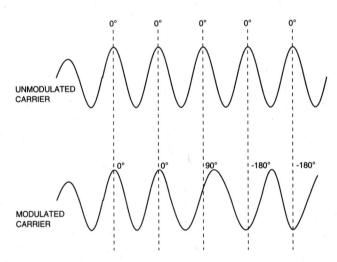

FIGURE 19.2. Quadrature modulation.

Frequency Modulation

The other alternative-modulation technique alters the frequency of the carrier in response to the modulation. A higher amplitude of modulation, for example, might cause the carrier to shift upward in frequency. If you listened to the pitch of the carrier wave, it would vary or warble when it was modulated. This technique, called *frequency modulation*, is commonly used in radio broadcasting by FM stations (see fig. 19.3).

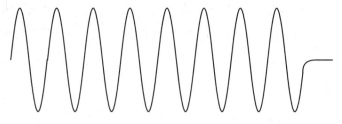

UNMODULATED CARRIER

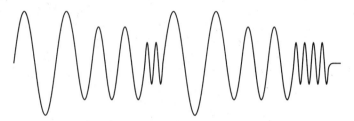

MODULATED CARRIER

FIGURE 19.3. Frequency modulation.

Frequency Shift Keying

In the most rudimentary digital form of frequency modulation, a digital 1 would cause the carrier wave to change from one frequency to another. One frequency would signify a digital 1 and another discrete frequency would signify a digital 0. This form of modulation is called *frequency shift keying* or *FSK* because information is encoded in (think of it being "keyed to") the shifting of frequency.

The "keying" part of the name is actually left over from the days of the telegraph when this form of modulation was used for transmitting Morse code. The frequency shift came with the banging of the telegraph key. Frequency shift keying is used in the most rudimentary of popular modems, the once-ubiquitous 300 bits-per-second modem that operated under the Bell 103 standard.

Baud Rates

In frequency shift keying modems, one bit of data causes one corresponding change of frequency in the carrier wave. Every change of frequency or state carries exactly one bit of information. The unit of measurement used to describe the number of state changes taking place in the carrier wave in one second is the *baud*. The term baud was named after J.M.E. Baudot, a French telegraphy expert. His full name (Baudot) is used to describe a 5-bit digital code used in Teletype systems.

In the particular case of the FSK modulation, one change of state per second (one baud) conveys exactly 1 bit of information per second, and 1 baud is equal to a transfer of digital information at a 1 bit-per-second rate. Depending on the number of states used in the communication system, however, a single transition (1 baud) can convey less than or more than 1 bit of information. Several different frequencies of tones (several different changes in carrier frequency) might be used to code information, for example. The changing from one frequency to another would take place at 1 baud, yet because of the different possible changes that could be made, more than 1 bit of information could be coded by that transition. Hence, strictly speaking, 1 baud is not the same as 1 bit per second, although the terms often are incorrectly used interchangeably.

This 300 bits-per-second rate using the simple FSK technique requires a bandwidth of 600 Hz. The two 300-baud carriers, which require a 1200 Hz bandwidth (two times 600 Hz) and a wide guard band fit comfortably within the 2700 Hz limit.

Under the Bell 103 standard, which is used by most 300 bits-per-second modems, the two carrier frequencies are 1200 Hz and 2200 Hz. Space modulation (logical zeros) shifts the carrier down by 150 Hz, and mark modulation pushes the carrier frequency up by an equal amount.

Because the FSK modulation technique is relatively simple, 300-baud modems are generally inexpensive. Because these modems don't push out to the limits of the available bandwidth, they are generally reliable even with marginal connections.

Using the same simple modulation technique and exploiting more of the 2700 Hz bandwidth of the typical telephone line, modem speeds can be doubled to 600 baud. Beyond that rate, however, lies the immovable bandwidth roadblock.

Group Coding

A data-communications rate of 300 or even 600 bits per second is slow, slower than most folks can read text flowing across the screen. If long distance communications were limited to a 600 bits-per-second rate, the only people who would be happy would be the shareholders of the various telephone companies. Information could, at best, crawl slowly across the continent.

By combining several modulation techniques, modern modems can achieve much higher data rates despite the constraints of ordinary dial-up telephone lines. Instead of merely manipulating the carrier one way, the modems may modify two (or more) aspects of the constant wave. In this way, every baud carries multiple bits of information.

These more complex forms of modulation don't add extra bandwidth to the communications channel; remember, that's a function of the medium, which the modem cannot change. Instead, these forms take advantage of the possibility of coding digital data as changes between a variety of states of the carrier wave. The carrier wave, for example, can be phase-modulated with quadrature modulation so that it assumes one of four states for every baud.

Although you might expect these four states to quadruple modem speed, the relationship is not quite that direct. To convert states into digital information, modems use a technique called *group coding* in which one state encodes a specific pattern of bits. The modem needs a repertoire of unique states wide enough to identify every pattern possible with a given number of bits. Two digital bits can assume any one of four distinct patterns: 00, 01, 10, and 11. So, to encode those two bits into a single baud, a modem needs four different states to uniquely identify each bit pattern. The ultimate speed of a modem on an ideal connection would thus be determined by the number of states that are available for coding.

Group coding is the key to advanced modulation techniques. Instead of dealing with data one bit at a time, bits of digital code are processed as groups. Each group of data bits is encoded as one particular state of the carrier.

As the example illustrates, however, the relationship between states and bits is not linear. As the number of bits in the code increases by a given figure (and thus the potential speed of the modulation technique rises by the same figure), the number of states required increases to the corresponding power of two, the inverse logarithm of the number of available states (tones, voltage, or phases). A 2 bit-for-baud rate requires four separate carrier states for encoding; a 4 bit-for-baud rate needs 16 separate carrier states; and an 8 bit-for-baud system requires 256 states.

Most 1200 bits-per-second modems operate at 600 baud with four different carrier states made possible by quadrature modulation. Modems that operate at data rates of 2400 bps use a modulation method that's even more complex than quadrature modulation and yields 16 discrete states while still operating at 600 baud. Each state encodes one of the 16 different patterns of four digital bits. One baud on the telephone line carries the information of 4 bits going into the modem.

Trellis Modulation

More complex modulation systems combine two or more modulation methods to cram more bits into every baud. A modem can use combinations of several different frequencies and amplitudes to create distinct states. The group code values can be assigned to each state in a two-dimensional system that arrays one modulation method on one axis and a second modulation method on another. You then can assign a group code value to each discrete coordinate position. The result is a matrix that, viewed graphically as the intersection of coordinate lines, with enough imagination looks like a trellis. Consequently, this kind of multiple modulation is called *trellis modulation*.

You could assign group code values at random to positions in the coordinate space of the trellis. Carefully choose the values, however, and you can optimize the performance of the system. International modem standards set the correspondence between modulation and code values at each operating speed (see fig. 19.4).

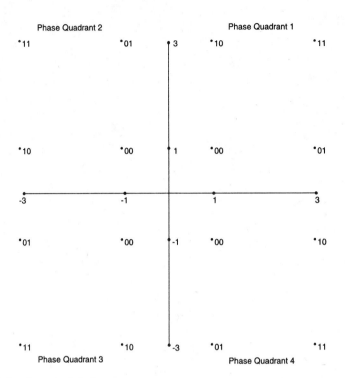

FIGURE 19.4. Lattice modulation.

According to the free lunch principle, this system of seemingly getting something for nothing using complex modulation must have a drawback. With high speed modems, the problem is that the quality of the telephone line becomes increasingly critical as the data rate is increased. Moreover, as modem speeds get faster, each phone line blip (baud) carries more information, and a single error can have devastating effects.

Line Compensation

Although a long distance telephone connection may sound unchanging to your ear, its electrical characteristics vary by the moment. Everything from a wire swaying in the Wichita wind to the phone company's automatic rerouting of the call through Bangkok when the direct circuits fill up can change the amplitude, frequency, and phase response of the circuit. The modem then faces two challenges: not to interpret such changes as data and to maintain the quality of the line to a high enough standard to support its use for high-speed transmission.

Under modern communications standards, modems compensate for variations in telephone lines by equalizing the telephone line. Two modems exchange tones at different frequencies and observe how signal strength and phase shift with frequency changes. The modems then change their signals to behave in the exact opposite way to cancel out the variations in the phone line. The modems compensate for deficiencies in the phone line to make signals behave the way they would have in absence of the problems. If the modems observe that high frequencies are too weak on the phone line, for example, the modems will compensate by boosting high frequencies before sending them.

Modern modems also use echo cancellation to eliminate the return of their own signals from the distant end of the telephone line. To achieve this goal, a modem sends out a tone and listens for its return. Once it determines how long the delay is before the return signal occurs and how strong the return is, the modem can compensate by generating the opposite signal and mixing it into the incoming data stream.

Fallback

Most modems use at most two carriers for duplex communications. These carriers are usually modulated to fill the available bandwidth. Sometimes, however, the quality of the telephone line is not sufficient to allow reliable communications over the full bandwidth expected by the modem even with line compensation. In such cases, most high-speed modems incorporate fallback capabilities. When the top speed does not work, the modems attempt to communicate at lower speeds that are less critical of telephone-line quality. A pair of modems might first try 9600 bps and be unsuccessful. They next might try 4800, then 2400, and so on until reliable communications are established.

Most modems fall back and stick with the slower speed that proves itself reliable. Some modems, however, constantly check the condition of the telephone connection to sense for any deterioration or improvement. If the line improves, these modems can shift back to a higher speed.

Multiple-Carrier Modems

Although most modems rely on a relatively complex form of modulation on one or two carriers to achieve high speed, one clever idea now relegated to a historical footnote by the latest modem standards is the *multiple-carrier modem*. This type of modem used relatively simple modulation on several simultaneous carrier signals. One of the chief advantages of this system comes into play when the quality of the telephone connection deteriorates. Instead of dropping down to the next incremental communications rate, generally cutting data speed in half, the multiple-carrier modems just stop using the carriers in the doubtful regions of the bandwidth. The communication rate may fall off just a small percentage in the adjustment. (Of course, it could dip by as much as a normal fallback modem as well.)

Data Compression

Although there's no way of increasing the number of bits that can cross a telephone line beyond the capacity of the channel, the information-handling capability of the modem circuit can be increased by making each bit more meaningful. Many of the bits that are sent through the telecommunication channel are meaningless or redundant—they convey no additional information. By eliminating those worthless bits, the information content of the data stream is more intense, and each bit is more meaningful. The process of paring the bits is called *data compression*.

The effectiveness of compression varies with the type of data that's being transmitted. One of the most prevalent data-compression schemes encodes repetitive data. Eight recurrences of the same byte value might be coded as two bytes, one signifying the value and the other the number of repetitions. This form of compression is most effective on graphics, which often have many blocks of repeating text. Other compression methods may strip out start, stop, and parity bits.

At one time, many modem manufacturers had their own methods of compressing data so that you needed two matched modems to take advantage of the potential throughput increases. Today, however, most modems follow international compression standards so that any two modems using the same standards can communicate with one another at compressed-data speeds.

These advanced modems perform the data compression on the fly in their own circuitry as you transmit your data. Alternately, you can precompress your data before sending it to your modem. Sort of like dehydrating soup, precompression (also known as file compression) removes the unnecessary or redundant parts of a file, yet allows the vital contents to be easily stored and reconstituted when needed. This process gives you two advantages: the files you send and receive require less storage space because they are compressed, and your serial port operates at a lower speed for a given data throughput.

Note that after a file is compressed, it usually cannot be compressed further. So modems that use on-the-fly compression standards cannot increase the throughput of precompressed files. In fact, using one on-the-fly modem data compression system (MNP5) actually can increase the transmission time for compressed files as compared to not using modem data compression.

Error-Checking and Error-Correction

Because all high-speed modems operate closer to the limits of the telephone channel, they are naturally more prone to data errors. To better cope with such problems, nearly all high-speed modems have their own built-in error-checking methods (which detect only transmission errors) and error-correction (which detects data errors and corrects the mistakes before they get passed along to your PC). These error-checking and error-correction systems work like communications protocols, grouping bytes into blocks and sending cyclical redundancy checking information.

These systems differ from the protocols used by communications software in that they are implemented in the hardware instead of your computer's software. That means that they don't load down your computer when it's straining at the limits of its serial ports.

It also can mean that software communications protocols are redundant and a waste of time. As mentioned before in the case of switching modems, using a software-based communications protocol can be counterproductive with many high-speed modems, slowing the transfer rate to a crawl. Most makers of modems using built-in error-checking advise against using such software protocols.

All modem error-detection and error-correction systems require that both ends of the connection use the same error-handling protocol. In order that modems can talk to one another, a number of standards have been developed. Today, the most popular standards are MNP4 and V.42. You also may see the abbreviations LAPB and LAPM describing error-handling methods.

LAPB stands for link access procedure, balanced, an error-correction protocol designed for X.25 packet-switched services like Telebit and Tymnet. Some high-speed modem makers adapted this standard to their dial-up modem products before the V.42 standard (described later) was agreed on. The Hayes Smartmodem 9600 from Hayes Microcomputer Products includes LAPB error-control capabilities, for example.

LAPM is an acronym for link access procedure for modems and is the error correction protocol used by the CCITT V.42 standard which is described later in the chapter.

Modem Standards

Neither men nor modems are islands. Above all, they must communicate and share their ideas with others. One modem would do the world no good. It would just send data out into the vast analog unknown, never to be seen (or heard) again.

But having two modems isn't automatically enough. Like people, modems must speak the same language for the utterances of one to be understood by the other. Modulation is part of the modem language. In addition, modems must be able to understand the error-correction features and data-compression routines used by one another. Unlike most human beings, who speak any of a million languages and dialects, each somewhat ill-defined, modems are much more precise in the languages they use. They have their own equivalent of the French Academy: standards organizations.

In the United States, the first standards were set long ago by the most powerful force in the telecommunications industry, which was the telephone company—more specifically, the American Telephone and Telegraph Company and the Bell System, which promoted various Bell standards, the most famous being Bell 103 and Bell 212A. After the Bell System was split into AT&T and the seven regional operating companies (RBOCs, also known as the Baby Bells), other long-distance carriers broke into the telephone monopoly. In addition, other nations have become interested in telecommunications.

As a result of these developments, the onus and capability to set standards moved to an international standards organization that's part of the United Nations, the International Telecommunications Union (ITU) Telecommunications Standards Sector, which was formerly the Comité Consultatif International Télégraphique et Telephonique (in English, that's International Telegraph and Telephone Consultative Committee). The initials of the latter, CCITT, grace nearly all of the high-speed standards used by modems today, such as V.22bis, V.32, V.32bis, V.42, and V.42bis.

Along the way, a modem and software maker, Microcom, developed a series of modem standards prefixed with the letters MNP, such as MNP4 and MNP5. The letters stand for Microcom Networking Protocol. Some modems boast having MNP modes, but these are falling from favor as the ITU (CCITT) standards take over.

Standards are important when buying a modem because they are your best assurance that a given modem can connect successfully with any other modem in the world. In addition, the standards you choose will determine how fast your modem can transfer data and how reliably it will work. The kind of communications you want to carry out will determine what kind of modem you need. If you're just going to send files electronically between offices, you can buy two nonstandard modems and get more speed for your investment. But if you want to communicate with the rest of the world, you will want to get a modem that meets the international standards. The following sections discuss the most popular standards for modems that are connected to PCs.

Bell Standards

Bell 103 comes first in any list of modem standards because it was the first widely adopted standard, and it remains the standard of last resort, the one that will work when all else fails. It allows data transmissions at a very low speed. Bell 103 uses very simple FSK modulation, so it is the only standard in which the baud rate (the rate at which signals change) is equal to the data rate.

Bell 212A is the next logical step in a standards discussion because it was the next modem standard to find wide application in the United States. It achieves a data transfer rate of 1200 bits per second by adding quadrature modulation to a frequency modulated 600-baud signal. Consequently, a Bell 212A modem operates at 600 baud and transfers information at 1200 bits per second. Although Bell 212A was, at one time, the most widely used communication standard in America, many foreign countries prohibited the use of Bell 212A, preferring instead the similar international standard, V.22.

MNP Standards

Microcom Networking Protocol is an entire hierarchy of standards, starting with MNP Class 1, an out-of-date error-correction protocol, to MNP Class 10, Adverse Channel Enhancements, which is designed to eke the most data transfer performance from poor connections. MNP does not stand alone but works with modems that may conform to other standards. The MNP standards specify technologies rather than speeds. MNP Classes 2 through 4 deal with error control and are in the public domain. Classes 5 through 10 are licensed by Microcom and deal with a number of modem operating parameters.

MNP Class 1 uses an asynchronous byte-oriented half-duplex method of exchanging data designed to make a minimum demand on the processor in the PC managing the modem. It was originally designed to enable error-free communications with first generation PCs that had little speed and less storage. Using MNP Class 1 steals about 30 percent of the throughput of a modem, so a 2400 bits-per-second modem using MNP Class 1 achieves an actual throughput of about 1690 bps.

MNP Class 2 takes advantage of full-duplex data exchange. As with MNP Class 1, it is designed for asynchronous operation at the byte level. MNP Class 2 achieves somewhat higher efficiency and takes only about a 16 percent toll on throughput.

MNP Class 3 improves on MNP2 by working synchronously instead of asynchronously. Consequently, no start and stop bits are required for each byte, trimming the data transfer overhead by 25 percent or more. Although MNP3 modems exchange data between themselves synchronously, they connect to PCs using asynchronous data links, which means that they plug right into RS232 serial ports.

MNP Class 4 is basically an error-correcting protocol but also yields a bit of data compression. It incorporates two innovations. *Adaptive packet assembly* allows the modem to package data in blocks or packets that are sent and error-checked as a unit. The protocol is adaptive because it varies the size of each packet according to the quality of the connection. *Data phase optimization* eliminates repetitive control bits from the data traveling across the connection to streamline transmissions. Together these techniques can increase the throughput of a modem by 120 percent at a given bit rate. In other words, using MNP4, a 1200 bits-per-second modem could achieve a 1450 bits-per-second throughput. Many modems have MNP4 capabilities.

MNP Class 5 is purely a data-compression protocol that squeezes some kinds of data into a form that takes less time to transmit. MNP5 can compress some data by a factor up to two, effectively doubling the speed of data transmissions. On some forms of data, such as files that have been compressed already, however, MNP5 may actually increase the time required for transmission.

MNP Class 6 is designed to help modems get the most out of telephone connections independent of data compression. Using a technique called universal link negotiation, modems can start communicating at a low speed, and then, after evaluating the capabilities of the telephone line and each modem, switch to a higher speed. MNP6 also includes statistical duplexing, which allows a half-duplex modem to simulate full-duplex operation.

MNP Class 7 is a more efficient data compression algorithm (Huffman encoding) than MNP5, which permits increases in data throughput by a factor as high as three with some data.

MNP Class 9 (there is no MNP Class 8) is designed to reduce the transmission overhead required by certain common modem operations. The acknowledgment of each data packet is streamlined by combining the acknowledgment with the next data packet instead of sending a separate confirmation byte. In addition, MNP9 minimizes the amount of information that must be retransmitted when an error is detected by indicating where the error occurred. Although some other error-correction schemes require all information transmitted after an error to be re-sent, an MNP9 modem needs only the data that was in error to be sent again.

MNP Class 10 is a set of adverse channel enhancements that help modems work better when faced with poor telephone connections. Modems with MNP10 will make multiple attempts to set up a transmission link, adjust the size of data packets they transmit according to what works best over the connection, and adjust the speed at which they operate to the highest rate that can be maintained reliably. One use envisioned for this standard is cellular modem communications (the car phone).

CCITT/ITU Standards

V.22 is the CCITT equivalent of the Bell 212A standard. It delivers a transfer rate of 1200 bits per second at 600 baud. It actually uses the same form of modulation as Bell 212A, but it is not compatible with the Bell standard because it uses a different protocol to set up the connection. In other words, although Bell 212A and V.22 modems speak the same language, they are unwilling to start a conversation with one another. Some modems support both standards and allow you to switch between them.

V.22bis was the first true world standard, adopted into general use in both the United States and Europe. It allows a transfer rate of 2400 bits per second at 600 baud using a technique called trellis modulation that mixes two simple kinds of modulation: quadrature and amplitude modulation. Each baud has 16 states, enough to code any pattern of four bits. Each state is distinguished both by its phase relationship to the unaltered carrier and its amplitude (or strength) in relation to the carrier. There are four distinct phases and four distinct amplitudes under V.22bis, which, when multiplied together, yield the 16 available states.

V.32 is an international high-speed standard that permits data-transfer rates of 4800 and 9600 bits per second. At its lower speed, it uses quadrature amplitude modulation similar to Bell 212A but at the higher baud rate of 2400 baud. At 9600 bits per second, it uses trellis modulation similar to V.22bis but at 2400 baud and with a greater range of phases and amplitudes.

Note that, while most Group III fax machines and modems operate at 9600 bits per second, a fax modem with 9600 bps capability is not necessarily compatible with the V.32 standard. Don't expect a fax modem to communicate with V.32 products.

V.32bis extends the V.32 standard to 14,400 bits per second while allowing fallback to intermediary speeds of 7200 and 12,000 bits per second in addition to the 4800 and 9600 bits-per-second speeds of V.32. (Note that all these speeds are multiples of a basic 2400-baud rate.) The additional operating speeds that V.32bis has and V.32 does not are generated by using different ranges of phases and amplitudes in the modulation.

At 14,400 bits per second, there are 128 potentially different phase/amplitude states for each baud under V.32bis, enough to encode seven data bits in each baud. Figure 19.1 shows a plot of codes and their corresponding phase/amplitude relationships at 14,400 bps. Other data rates (including V.32) use similar relationships for their data coding. Because there are so many phase and amplitude differences squeezed together, a small change in the characteristics of a telephone line might mimic such a change and cause transmission errors. Consequently, some way of detecting and eliminating such errors becomes increasingly important as transmission speed goes up.

V.34 is the official designation of the high-speed standard once known as V.fast. Under the V.34 standard, as adopted in June 1994, modems can operate at data rates as high as 28,800 bits per second without compression over ordinary dial-up telephone lines. The V.34 standard also will allow lower transmission rates at 24,000 and 19,200 bits per second and include backward compatibility with V.32 and V.32 bis.

The V.34 standard calls for modems to adapt to telephone-line conditions to eke out the greatest usable amount of bandwidth. Where V.32 modems operate at a fixed bandwidth of 2400 Hz, with a perfect connection V.fast modems will be able to push their operating bandwidth to 3429 Hz. V.34 modems will use line-probing techniques to try each connection, and then apply advanced equalization to the line. To squeeze in as much signal as possible, V.34 modems use multidimensional trellis coding and signal shaping.

V.34 was immediately preceded by two nonstandards, V.32 terbo and V.FC (or V.Fast Class), that were supported by various modem industry groups and chip manufacturers, but which were not formally sanctioned by the ITU. Because technology provided the power to allow higher speeds before the ITU could reach a consensus on a standard, these quasi-standards were widely available until V.34 products became available.

V.32 terbo appeared in June 1993, when AT&T Microelectronics introduced modem chips that operated at 19,200 bits per second using an extension of the V.32 modulation scheme. The terbo in the name is a poor play on words. *Bis* in modem standards stands for second; similarly ter means third (as in tertiary). *Terbo* means nothing but conjures up the sound of respectability (ter for the third iteration of V.32) and speed (turbo as in a high-performance automobile with a turbocharger). The technology was designed for picture phone technologies. V.32 terbo is backwardly compatible with V.32bis standards and will connect with older modems at the highest speed at which both can operate. With compression such as MNP5 or V.42 bis, V.32 terbo modems can operate at effective data rates as high as 115,200 bits per second.

V.FC modems represent the interpretation of some modem makers and a chip maker (Rockwell International) of a preliminary version of the V.34 standard. These V.FC modems deliver true 28,800 bits per second speed using V.34 technology, but they don't use the same handshaking to set up communications as V.34. (The V.FC products predate the final V.34 agreements.)

V.42 is a world wide error-correction standard that is designed to help make V.32, V.32bis, and other modem communications more reliable. V.42 incorporates MNP4 as an "alternative" protocol. That is, V.42 modems can communicate with MNP4 modems but a connection between the two will not use the more sophisticated V.42 error-correction protocol. At the beginning of each call, as the connection is being negotiated between modems, a V.42 modem will determine whether MNP4 or full V.42 error correction can be used by the other modem. V.42 is preferred, and MNP4 is the second choice. In other words, a V.42 first will try to set up a V.42 session; failing that, it will try MNP4; and failing that, it will set up a communications session without error correction.

V.42bis is a data-compression protocol endorsed by the CCITT. Different from and incompatible with MNP5 and MNP7, V.42bis is also more efficient. On some forms of data, it can yield compression factors up to four, potentially quadrupling the speed of modem transmissions. (With PCs, the effective maximum communication rate may be slower because of limitations on serial ports, typically 38,400 bits per second.) Note that a V.42bis-only modem cannot communicate with an MNP5-only modem. Unlike MNP5, a V.42 modem never increases the transmission time of "incompressible" data. Worst-case operation is the same speed as would be achieved without compression.

Digital Services

The V.34 standard may be the modem's last stand. Eventually today's modem standards will be replaced by the next step in PC-to-PC communications, all digital dial-up telecommunications. After all, nearly all traffic between telephone exchanges throughout the world is digital. The only archaic analog step is the stretch between the exchange and your home or office (called POTS by those in the know, which stands for Plain Old Telephone Service). Although the last 10 years have seen improvements in the speed of moving digital data through this ancient link (dial-up modems have moved from transfer rates of the paltry 300 bits per second of Bell 103A to a 115,200 bps under V.34), it has no future.

Certainly you still will talk on the telephone for ages to come (if your other family members give you a chance, of course) but the nature of the connection may finally change. Eventually, digital technology will take over your local telephone connection. In fact, in many parts of America and the rest of the world, you already can order a special digital line from your local telephone company and access all-digital switched systems. You get the equivalent of a telephone line, one that allows you to choose any conversation mate who's connected to the telephone network (with the capability of handling your digital data, of course) as easily as dialing a telephone.

At least three such services currently or will soon be available in many locations. All are known by their initials: SDS 56, ISDN, and SMDS. Eventually you will probably plug your PC into one of them or one of their successors.

SDS 56

Already available from some telephone-operating companies in some exchanges, *Switched Data Services 56* (sometimes shortened to Switched-56) gives you a single digital channel capable of a 56 kilobit-per-second data rate. Its signals are carried through conventional copper twisted-pair wiring (the same old stuff that carries your telephone conversations). To link to your PC, you need special head-end equipment—the equivalent of a modem—for your PC. This equipment is priced in the range of better V.32 modems. Of course, because the signal stays digital, there's no need for modulation or demodulation. The signal stays error-free through its entire trip.

In some locales, SDS 56 is no more expensive than an ordinary business telephone line. Installation costs, however, can be substantially higher and some telephone companies may add extra monthly maintenance charges in addition to the normal dial-up costs.

To take advantage of SDS 56, you also need to communicate with someone who has SDS 56 services. Currently, SDS 56 is not an internationally agreed upon standard, so your access to the service and its subscribers will be less universal than a telephone-based modem link. The chief advantages of linking through SDS 56 are higher speed, greater reliability, and data integrity.

ISDN

The initials stand for *Integrated Services Digital Network*, although waggish types will tell you it means "I Still Don't Know" or "It Still Does Nothing." The latter seems most apt because ISDN has been discussed for years with little to show for all the verbiage. But ISDN is an internationally supported standard, one that promises eventually to replace your standard analog telephone connection.

The first real movement toward getting ISDN rolling occurred in November 1992 when AT&T, MCI, and Sprint embraced a standard they called ISDN-1. Under the new standard, ISDN now has a consistent interface to connect end-user equipment, local telephone companies, and trunk carriers. This common interface now makes coast-to-coast ISDN transmission possible.

Today, two versions of ISDN are generally available. The simplest is the Basic Rate Interface (BRI), which takes advantage of the copper twisted-pair wiring that's already in place linking homes and offices to telephone exchanges. Instead of a single analog signal, an ISDN line carries three digital channels: two B (for Bearer) channels that can carry any kind of data (digitally-encoded voice, fax, text, and numbers) at 64,000 bps, and a D (or Delta) channel, operating at 16,000 bps, that can carry control signals and serve as a third data channel. The three channels can be independently routed to different destinations through the ISDN system.

A single BRI wire enables you to transfer uncompressed data bidirectionally at the 64,000 bps rate, exactly like a duplex modem today but with higher speed and error-free transmission thanks to its all-digital nature. Even during such high-speed dual-direction connections, the D channel still would be available for other functions.

The more elaborate form of ISDN service is called the Primary Rate Interface. This service delivers 23 B channels (each operating at 64,000 bits per second) and one D channel (at 16,000 bits per second). As with normal telephone service, use of ISDN is billed by time in use, not the amount of data transmitted or received.

The strength of BRI service is that it makes do with today's ordinary twisted-pair telephone wiring. Neither you nor the various telephone companies need to invest the billions of dollars required to rewire the nation for digital service. Instead, only the central office switches that route calls between telephones (which today are mostly plug-in printed circuit boards) need to be upgraded.

Of course, this quick fix sounds easier than it is. The principal barriers aren't technological, however, but economic. The changeover is costly and, because telephone switching equipment has long depreciation periods, does not always make business sense for the telephone company.

Once you have access to ISDN, you will not be able to plug your PC directly into your telephone line, however. You still will need a device to interface your PC to the ISDN line. You will need to match your equipment to the line and prevent one from damaging the other using a device called an ISDN Adapter. Such adapters may have analog ports that will allow you to connect your existing telephones into the ISDN network. ISDN Adapters are becoming available for use in the limited areas that already have ISDN.

SMDS

If you need to move more data fast, the alternative is *Switched Multimegabit Data Service*. Still in its infancy, SMDS isn't backed by any universal standard but is instead easing itself onto the market. One implementation provides some government offices with dial-up links supporting 1.45 megabits-per-second data transfers. Other systems with 1.2 to 30 megabits-per-second rates have been proposed.

Modem Control

Besides its basic purpose of converting digital data into modulated audio signals, the modem often is called upon to handle other chores of convenience. You probably want your modem to automatically dial or answer your phone or just tell you whether the line is busy or ringing when you dial. These features of the modem must be able to be controlled by your computer, and the modem must be able to signal your computer about what it does and what it finds out.

Dual Modes

Most modems operate alternately in one of two modes. In *command mode*, the modem receives and carries out instructions sent by your computer. In *communications mode*, it operates as transparently as a modem can, merely converting data.

Changing modes is mostly a matter of sending control characters to the modem. The characters can be received and processed only in command mode. In communication mode, the characters would be passed along down the telephone line.

Shifting from command mode to communications mode is easy; the modem is already handling commands, so adding one more to its repertoire is no big deal. Shifting back from communications mode to command mode is more problematic. In communications mode, the modem is supposed to be relaying all the data it receives down the telephone line. The most widely used method for initiating the switch from communications to command mode involves a guard period, a brief interval during which no data is sent. Then, a set of characters unlikely to be found in a normal communications string is sent, followed by a final guard period. This mode-switching method is patented by Hayes Microcomputer Products and must be licensed by all modems that use it. Most modems use guard periods of one second and three plus signs as the command character sequence.

Hayes Command Set

Today, most modems use a standardized set of instructions called the Hayes command set, named after the Hayes company which developed it for its modems. For the most part, the Hayes command set comprises several dozen modem instructions that begin with a two-character sequence, *AT*, called *attention characters*. The letters must be in uppercase. Other characters specifying the command follow the attention character. Because the AT is part of nearly every command, the Hayes command set also is termed the AT command set. A modem that understands the Hayes command set (or the AT command set) is said to be Hayes-compatible. The AT command set itself is not patented (although it is not useful without incorporating the patented mode-switching method). Table 19.1 lists the basic Hayes command set.

TABLE 19.1. Hayes Extended Command Set

Command	Function
AT	Attention (used to start all commands)
ATIn	Request product code and ROM checksum
	0=modem sends its 3-digit product code
	1=request numeric checksum of firmware ROM
	2=request OK or ERROR state of ROM checksum

continues

TABLE 19.1. Continued

Command	Function
Command	*Function*
A/	Repeat last command (No AT or Return)
A	Answer without waiting for ring
Bn	Bell mode—set 1200 bps protocol compatibility: 0=CCITT v.22/v.22bis 1=Bell 212A
Cn	Carrier state: 0=off 1=on
Dn	Dial telephone number n
	Special dialing commands
	P Pulse Dialing
	R Reverse mode (use answer frequencies when originating a call)
	S Dial stored number
	T Tone dialing
	W Wait (for second dial or access tone)
	@ Wait for quiet answer
	, Pause (a delay in dialing sequence)
	! Flash (on hook for 1/2 second)
	; Return to command mode after dialing
En	Echo modem commands; 0=no 1=yes
Fn	Full- or half-duplex operation; 0=half 1=full
Hn	Hook; 0=on hook (hang up) 1=off hook
Ln	Loudness or speaker volume; 0=low 1=low 2=medium 3=high

Command	Function
Mn	Mode of speaker operation; 0=off 1=on 2=always on 3=disable speaker when modem receives a carrier signal while modem is dialing
On	On-line state 0=modem returns to the on-line state 1=modem returns on-line and retries equalizer (2400 bps mode only)
Qn	Quiet command for result codes; 0=commands are sent 1=commands are not sent
Sn=x	S-register commands n=S-register number x=value to set register to
Sn?	Display value of S-register n
Vn	Verbose mode for result codes 0=use digits 1=use words
Xn	Enable extended result code and mode setting 0=basic (9300 bps) 1=extended (no dial tone or busy signal detection) 2=extended (detects dial tone or busy signal detection) 3=extended (no dial tone detect but detects busies) 4=extended (detects both dial tones and busies)
Yn	Long space disconnect 0=disabled 1=enabled; disconnects after receiving 1.6 sec break
Z	Fetch configuration profile from non-volatile memory
&Cn	Data Carrier Detect handling 0=modem keeps DCD (RS-232 pin 8) always on 1=DCD tracks data carrier detected by modem

continues

TABLE 19.1. Continued

Command	Function
&Dn	Data Terminal Ready handling 0=modem ignores DTR line (RS-232 pin 20) 1=modem assumes asynch command state when DTR goes off 2=DTR off switches modem off hook, out of answer mode and back to command state 3=DTR switching off initialized modem
&F	Fetch factory configuration profile from ROM
&Gn	Guard tone selection 0=no guard tones 1=550 Hz guard tones 2=1800
&Jn	Telephone jack selection 0=RJ-11/RJ-41S/RJ-45S 1=RJ-12/RJ-13
&Ln	Leased-line or dialup line selection 0=dialup operation 1=leased-line
&Mn	Asynchronous/Synchronous mode selection 0=asynchronous 1=synchronous mode 1—async dialing, then switch to synchronous operation 2=synchronous mode 2—stored number dialing 3=synchronous mode 3—manual editing
&Pn	Pulse dial make/break pulse length selection 0=39% make, 61% break (US and Canada standard)
&Rn	Request to Send/Clear to send handling (sync mode only); 0=CTS (RS-232 pin 5) tracks RTS (pin 4) 1=modem ignores RTS and turns CTS on when ready to receive synchronous data
&Sn	Data Set Ready handling 0=modem forces DSR on whenever modem is turned on 1=DSR (RS-232 pin 6) operates according to EIA specifications

Command	*Function*
&Tn	Test mode
	0=terminate any test in progress when last command on a line
	1=initiates local analog loopback test
	3=initiate local digital loopback
	4=conditions modem to perform remote digital loopback when requested by another modem
	5=prohibits remote digital loopback
	6=initiates remote digital loopback with another modem
	7=initiates remote digital loopback with self-test
	8=initiates remote digital loopback with self-test
&W	Write active configuration profile to memory
&Xn	Select synchronous transmit clock source (sync mode only)
	0=modem generates timing and sends through pin 15
	1=modem's host computer generates timing and sends it to modem on pin 24, which modem routes to pin 15
	2=modem derives timing from incoming signal and supplies it to pin 15
&Zn	Store telephone number
	n=string of digits compatible with Dial command

Most AT commands follow the attention characters with one letter that specifies the family of the command and another character that indicates the nature of the command. H is standard for Hook, for example. H0 means put the phone "on the hook" or hang up. H1 indicates that the modem should take the phone off the hook, that is, make a connection to the line.

Several commands and their modifiers can be combined on a single line after an initial attention command. To command a Hayes or Hayes-compatible modem to dial information on a tone-dialing line, for example, the proper sequence of commands would read: ATDT155511212. The AT is the attention signal, D is the Dial command, the T tells the modem to use tones for dialing, and the 155511212 is the number of the telephone company information service.

All AT commands must be followed by a carriage return. The modem waits for the carriage return as a signal that the computer has sent the complete command and that the modem should start processing it.

Extended Modem Command Sets

At the time the Hayes command set was developed, modems had relatively few special features. As modems became more sophisticated, they became more laden with capabilities and features. The original Hayes command set had to be extended to handle all the possibilities. Note that many Hayes-compatible modems recognize only the original command set. All of their features may not work with software that expects the extended Hayes set.

Because the 26 letters of the alphabet proved too few to handle all these extended commands, modem makers developed new commands with special preamble characters. Hayes first extended beyond the alphabet using an ampersand (&) followed by a letter. Other manufacturers have used percent signs (%) and backslashes (\) as preamble characters.

Because modem makers have added unique features to many of their products, they have often defined their own unique extended modem commands. Each manufacturer, and often each modem, recognizes a different set of commands. Although modem makers have attempted to avoid assigning the commands used by another manufacturer for a different purpose, many extended modem commands have multiple definitions. Only the most basic commands can be assumed universal. Others are product-specific, and you need to check your modem's manual to be sure what command does what.

Table 19.2 lists extended modem commands and designates which of these have universal or near-universal application.

TABLE 19.2. Extended modem commands

Command	Function	Source	
A	Force answer mode	Hayes	*
A/	Re-execute last command	Hayes	*
A>	Repeat mode; redials up to 10 times for connection	USR	
AT	Attention command; must precede all other commands (except A/, A>, and +++)	Hayes	*
B0	ITU (CCITT) Handshaking	Hayes	*
B1	Bell handshaking	Hayes	*
B15	Initiate calls using V.21 at 300 cps	PP	
B16	Initiate calls using Bell 103 at 300 cps	PP	

Command	Function	Source	
B41	Initiate calls using V.32 at 4800 bps	PP	
	Initiate calls using V.32 at 9600 bps	PP	
C0	Carrier (transmitter) off	Hayes	*
C1	Carrier (transmitter) on	Hayes	*
D	Dial command	Hayes	*
Dn	Dial number stored as n	Hayes	
DL	Dial last number dialed	USR	
DSn	Dial number stored in modem's memory at location n	USR	
E0	Echo characters typed at /sent by PC	Hayes	*
E1	Do not echo characters typed at/sent by PC	Hayes	*
F0	Select auto-detect mode (same as N1)	Boca	
F0	On-line echo on (half duplex)	Hayes	
F1	Select V.21 or Bell 103	Boca	
F1	On-line echo off (full duplex)	Hayes	
F3	Select V.23; 75 bps send, 1200 bps receive	Boca	
F4	Select V.22; 1200 bps	Boca	
F5	Select V.22bis; 2400 bps	Boca	
F6	Select V.32/V.32bis; 4800 bps	Boca	
F7	Select V.32bis; 7200 bps	Boca	
F8	Select V.32/V.32bis; 9600 bps	Boca	
F9	Select V.32bis; 12,000 bps	Boca	
F10	Select V.32bis; 14,400 bps	Boca	
H0	Hang up line	Hayes	*
H1	Take line off-hook	Hayes	*
I0	Returns 3-digit product code	Boca	
I1	Returns ROM checksum	Boca	
I2	Validate ROM checksum	Boca	

continues

TABLE 19.2. Continued

Command	Function	Source	
I2	Display results from RAM test	USR	
I3	Returns firmware revision code	Boca	
I3	Display duration of last call	USR	
I4	Returns modem identifier string	Boca	
I4	Display current modem settings	USR	
I5	Returns country code	Boca	
I5	Display non-volatile RAM settings	USR	
I6	Returns data pump mode and revision code	Boca	
I6	Display dial diagnostics of last call	USR	
I7	Display product configuration information	USR	
I8	Reserved	USR	
I9	Reserved	USR	
I10	Display dial security account status information	USR	
I11	Reserved	USR	
K0	Display current call duration when on-line; last call duration when off-line	USR USR	
K1	Return actual time at ATI3	USR	
L0	Lowest speaker volume	Hayes	*
L1	Low speaker volume	Hayes	*
L2	Medium speaker volume	Hayes	*
L3	Highest speaker volume	Hayes	*
M0	Speaker always off	Hayes	*
M1	Speaker on until carrier detected	Hayes	*
M2	Speaker always on	Hayes	*
M3	Speaker on only during answering	Boca	
M3	Speaker switches on after last number is dialed, switches off after carrier is established (suppresses dialing)	Hayes	

Command	Function	Source	
N0	Disable auto-mode detection; S37 determines speed	Boca	
N1	Enable auto-mode detection (same as F0)	Boca	
O0	Enter data (on-line) mode	Hayes	*
O1	Enter data (on-line) mode and retrain modem	Hayes	*
P	In dialing string, switch to pulse dialing	Hayes	*
Q0	Result codes sent to PC	Hayes	*
Q1	Quiet mode: result codes not sent to PC	Hayes	*
Q2	Result codes not sent to PC in answer mode	USR	
R	In dialing string, reverse frequencies to force dialing using answer frequencies	Hayes	*
S	In dialing string, dial stored number	Hayes	*
Sn	Establishes S-register n as the default	Boca	
Sn=v	Sets S-register n to value v	Hayes	*
Sn?	Returns value of S-register n	Hayes	*
T	In dialing string, switch to DTMF dialing	Hayes	*
V0	Send terse (numeric) responses	Hayes	*
V1	Send verbose (plain language) responses	Hayes	*
W	In dialing string, wait for second dial tone	Hayes	*
W0	Reports only connect speed	Boca	
W1	Reports line speed, error correction protocol, and computer-to-modem speed	Boca	
W2	Reports only modem connection speed	Boca	
X0	Sends OK, CONNECT, RING, NO CARRIER, ERROR and NO ANSWER	Boca	
X0	Sends OK, CONNECT, RING, NO CARRIER, and ERROR	USR	
X1	Sends CONNECT speed in addition to X0	Boca	

continues

TABLE 19.2. Continued

Command	Function	Source	
X1	Adds CONNECT (SPEED) to X0	USR	
X2	Send NO DIALTONE in addition to X1	Boca, USR	
X3	Sends BUSY in addition to X2	Boca	
X3	Adds BUSY and NO ANSWER to X2; deletes NO DIALTONE	USR	
X4	Sends all responses	Boca	
X4	Adds NO DIALTONE to X3	USR	
X5	Adds RINGING and VOICE to X3	USR	
X6	Adds RINGING and VOICE to X4	USR	
X7	As X6 but drops VOICE	USR	
Y0	Disables long-space disconnect	Hayes	*
Y1	Enables long-space disconnect	Hayes	*
Z	Restore factory default settings	Hayes	*
Z0	Reset to defined profile 0	Boca	
Z1	Reset to profile 1	Boca	
&A0	ARQ result codes disabled	USR	
&A1	ARQ result codes enabled	USR	
&A2	Additional VFC, HST, or V3 modulation indicator	USR	
&A3	Additional error correction indicator (LAPM, HST, MNP, SYNC, or NONE) and data compression type (V.42bis or MNP5)	USR	
&B0	Serial port rate set variable	USR	
&B1	Serial port rate fixed	USR	
&B2	Serial port rate fixed for ARQ calls, variable for non-ARQ calls	USR	
&C0	Forces DCD on	Hayes	*
&C1	DCD follows remote carrier	Hayes	*
&D0	Modem ignores DTR line	Hayes	
&D0	DTR always on	USR	

Command	*Function*	*Source*	
&D1	Modem assumes command state when DTR switches	Hayes	
&D2	DTR switches modem off hook, out of answer mode, and back to command state	Hayes	
&D3	DTR switches off, initializes modem	Hayes	
&F	Loads pre-set factory parameters	Hayes	
&Fn	Load factory present configuration n	USR	
&G0	Disables guard tone	Hayes	*
&G1	Disables guard tone	Boca	
&G1	Enables 550Hz (European) guard tone	Hayes	
&G2	Enables 1800Hz (U.K.) guard tone	Hayes	*
&H0	PC-to-modem flow control disabled	USR	
&H1	PC-to-modem hardware flow control (CTS)	USR	
&H2	PC-to-modem software flow control (XON/XOFF)	USR	
&H3	PC-to-modem hardware and software flow control	USR	
&I0	Modem-to-PC software flow control (XON/XOFF) disabled	USR	
&I1	Modem passes type flow control to remote system	USR	
&I2	Modem acts on software flow control, does not forward to remote system	USR	
&I3	Software flow control using ENQ/ACK in host mode	USR	
&I4	Software flow control using ENQ/ACK in terminal mode	USR	
&I5	Software flow control over modem link without error control	USR	
&J0	Select RJ-11/ RJ-41S/ RJ-45S jack	Hayes only	
&J1	Select RJ-12/ RJ-13 jack	Hayes only	
&K0	Disables flow control	Boca, PP	
&K0	Disables data compression	USR	

continues

TABLE 19.2. Continued

Command	Function	Source
&K1	Enable RTS/CTS hardware flow control	PP
&K1	Auto enable data compression (compression on only when serial port rate is variable)	USR
&K2	Enable XON/XOFF software local flow control	PP
&K2	Data compression enabled	USR
&K3	Enables RTS/CTS flow control	Boca,PP
&K3	Selective data compression (MNP5 disabled)	USR
&K4	Enables XON/XOFF software local flow control	Boca,PP
&K5	Transparent XON/XOFF: Commands acknowledged but not acted upon	PP
&K6	Enable XON/XOFF with pass-through	PP
&K7	Enable RTS/CTS local with XON/XOFF pass-through	PP
&L0	Dial-up operation	Hayes only
&L1	Leased-line operation	Hayes only
&M0	Selects asynchronous mode	Hayes
&M1	Synchronous mode 1; asynchronous dialing then switches to synchronous operation	Hayes only
&M1	On-line synchronous mode without V.25bis	USR
&M2	Synchronous mode 2; stored number dialing	Hayes only
&M3	Synchronous mode 3; manual dialing	Hayes only
&M4	Normal/ARQ Mode; if ARQ connection unsuccessful reverts to &M0	USR
&M5	Enter ARQ synchronous mode; disconnect if unsuccessful	USR
&M6	Enter V.25bis synchronous mode	USR

Command	Function	Source
&M7	Enter V.25bis synchronous mode with HDLC protocol	USR
&N0	Connection rate variable, negotiated by modems	USR
&N1	Connection rate set at 300bps (if remote modem supports)	USR
&N2	Connection rate set at 1200bps (if remote modem supports)	USR
&N3	Connection rate set at 2400bps (if remote modem supports)	USR
&N4	Connection rate set at 4800bps (if remote modem supports)	USR
&N5	Connection rate set at 7200bps (if remote modem supports)	USR
&N6	Connection rate set at 9600bps (if remote modem supports)	USR
&N7	Connection rate set at 12,000bps (if remote modem supports)	USR
&N8	Connection rate set at 14,400bps (if remote modem supports)	USR
&N9	Connection rate set at 16,800bps (if remote modem supports)	USR
&N10	Connection rate set at 19,200bps (if remote modem supports)	USR
&N11	Connection rate set at 21,600bps (if remote modem supports)	USR
&N12	Connection rate set at 24,000bps (if remote modem supports)	USR
&N13	Connection rate set at 26,400bps (if remote modem supports)	USR
&N14	Connection rate set at 28,800bps (if remote modem supports)	USR
&P	Pulse dialing make/break ratio of 39:61	PP

continues

TABLE 19.2. Continued

Command	Function	Source	
&P0	Make/break dial ratio of 39:61 at 10 pps	Hayes	*
&P1	Make/break dial ratio of 33:67 at 10 pps	Hayes	*
&P2	Make/break dial ratio of 39:61 at 20 pps	Boca	
&P3	Make/break dial ratio of 33:67 at 20 pps	Boca	
&Q0	Selects direct asynchronous mode	Boca	
&Q5	Modem negotiates error-correction	Boca	
&Q6	Selects autosynchronous mode with speed buffering	Boca, PP	
&Q8	Select MNP operation	PP	
&Q9	Conditional data compression	PP	
&R0	CTS tracks RTS in sync mode	Hayes	
&R0	RTS/CTS delay with received data	USR	
&R1	Modem ignores RTS and turns CTS on when receiving synchronous data	Hayes	
&R1	Modem ignores RTS	USR	
&R2	Hardware flow control of received data	USR	
&S0	Forces DSR continuously on	Hayes	*
&S1	DSR active after carrier detect; off after carrier loss	Hayes	*
&S2	On loss of carrier, modem sends pulsed DSR with CTS following CD	USR	
&S3	As &S2 but without CTS following CD	USR	
&S4	Modem sends PC a DSR at same time as CD	USR	
&T0	End test in progress	Boca, Hayes	
&T1	Starts local analog loopback test	Boca, Hayes	
&T3	Starts local digital loopback test	Boca, Hayes	
&T4	Responds to remote modem request for digital loopback	Boca, Hayes	

Command	Function	Source
&T5	Ignores remote modem request for digital loopback	Boca, Hayes
&T6	Request remote digital loopback without self-test	Boca, Hayes
&T7	Same as &T6 but with self-test	Boca, Hayes
&T8	Starts local analog loopback with self-test	Boca, Hayes
&U	Enable trellis code modulation	PP
&U0	Enable trellis code modulation	PP
&U1	Disable trellis code modulation	PP
&V	Displays current and stored profiles and stored numbers	Boca, PP
&W	Write current profile to memory	Hayes only
&W0	Sets profile 0 as current configuration	Boca
&W1	Sets profile 1 as current configuration	Boca
&X0	Set synchronous clock source to modem internal clock	Hayes only
&X1	Set synchronous clock to PC source provided on pin 24	Hayes only
&X2	Set synchronous clock to incoming modem signal	Hayes only
&Y0	Modem uses profile 0	Boca
&Y0	Break handling: break is destructive but not sent from modem	USR
&Y1	Modem uses profile 1	Boca
&Y1	Break handling: break is destructive and expedited	USR
&Y2	Break handling: break is nondestructive and expedited	USR
&Y3	Break handling: break is nondestructive and not expedited (send in sequence with received data)	USR

continues

TABLE 19.2. Continued

Command	Function	Source
&Zn	Store telephone number n	Hayes only
&Zn=x	Stores telephone number x at memory location n	Boca, USR
&Zn?	Display telephone number stored at memory location n	USR
&ZCs	Write string s to non-volatile memory	USR
%An	Create and configure security account n	USR
%B0	Configure modem serial port rate to 110 bps	USR
%B1	Configure modem serial port rate to 300 bps	USR
%B2	Configure modem serial port rate to 600 bps	USR
%B3	Configure modem serial port rate to 1200 bps	USR
%B4	Configure modem serial port rate to 2400 bps	USR
%B5	Configure modem serial port rate to 4800 bps	USR
%B6	Configure modem serial port rate to 9600 bps	USR
%B7	Configure modem serial port rate to 19,200 bps	USR
%B8	Configure modem serial port rate to 38,400 bps	USR
%B9	Configure modem serial port rate to 57,600 bps	USR
%B10	Configure modem serial port rate to 115,200 bps	USR
%C0	Disable data compression	Boca
%C0	Defer configuration changes until current call ends	USR
%C1	Enable MNP5 compression	Boca

Command	Function	Source
%C1	Cancel configuration changes made during remote access	USR
%C2	Enable V.42bis compression	Boca
%C2	Force immediate configuration changes	USR
%C3	Enables both MNP5 and V.42bis	Boca
%E=1	Erase local access password	USR
%E=2	Erase autopass password	USR
%E=3	Erase passwords in accounts 0-9	USR
%E=4	Erase phone numbers in accounts 0-9	USR
%E=5	Disable account, dialback, and new number fields in accounts 0-9	USR
%E0	Disables line-quality monitoring and auto-retraining	Boca
%E1	Enables monitoring and retraining	Boca
%E2	Enables monitoring and fallback/ fall forward	Boca
%E3	Enables monitoring, retraining, and fast disconnect	Boca
%F0	Set data format to no parity, 8 data bits	USR
%F1	Set data format to mark parity, 7 data bits	USR
%F2	Set data format to odd parity, 7 data bits	USR
%F3	Set data format to even parity, 7 data bits	USR
%L	Reports received signal level in -dBm	Boca
%L=	Assign an account password at the local access password	USR
%P0=	Disable password security	USR
%P1=	Disable password security	USR
%P0=s	Specify password string s for viewing privileges only	USR

continues

TABLE 19.2. Continued

Command	Function	Source
%P1=s	Specify password string s for view and configuration privileges	USR
%Pn?	Display password n	
%Q	Reports line signal quality	Boca
%S=n	Obtain access to security accounts without disabling security	USR
%T	Enables off-hook modem to detect tone frequencies of dialing modems	USR
%V=PWn	Assign password in account n as autopass password	USR
\A0	64-character maximum MNP block size	Boca
\A1	128-character maximum MNP block size	Boca
\A2	192-character maximum MNP block size	Boca
\A3	256-character maximum MNP block size	Boca
\Bn	When error-correction not active, sends break to remote modem for n tenth second	Boca
\G0	Disables XON/XOFF flow control with remote modem	Boca
\G1	Enables XON/XOFF flow control with remote modem	Boca
\Kn	Defines break type	Boca
\L0	Uses stream mode for MNP connection	Boca
\L1	Uses interactive block mode for MNP connection	Boca
\N0	Normal data link with speed buffering	Boca
\N1	Selects serial interface	Boca
\N2	Selects error-correction mode	Boca
\N3	Selects auto-reliable (error-correction) mode	Boca
\N4	LAPM error correction only	Boca
\N5	MNP5 error correction only	Boca
$H	Help command; display help summary	PP

Command	Function	Source	
, (comma)	In dialing string, pause for two seconds	Hayes	*
; (semicolon)	In dialing string, return to command mode after dialing	Hayes	*
" (quote)	Dial letters literally	USR	
! (exclamation)	In dialing string, flash hook switch	Hayes	*
@ (a sign)	In dialing string, wait for second dial tone	USR	
/ (slash)	Pause for 125 milliseconds	USR	
+++	Return to command mode (must have one second of silence before and after)	Hayes	*

Note: Only those commands with an asterisk in the last column can be assumed universal. Multiple occurrences of a command indicate different functions assigned by different manufacturers.

S-Registers

Most modem commands are designed to work interactively to change the function of the modem or to make the modem perform a defined action. As communications have become more varied and challenging, modems have become more complex and flexible. Many modem features are entirely programmable, designed to be changed to suit the needs of the connection you want to make.

This increased flexibility requires a more elaborate control system, one that reaches far beyond a simple command set. Modems require a means of control to adjust their settings and a means to store those settings.

Hayes developed a control system with exactly those features. This second-layer system uses a series of registers as both a channel to communicate with the modem and a portal into the modem's memory. In the Hayes-designed system, you access these registers using the S command. Consequently, they are called *S-registers*.

Early Hayes modems had provisions for 28 of these registers, although the functions of some were not initially defined. Each register was named with an S-number, from S0 through S27. As modems became more complex, even this bountiful endowment proved insufficient, and later modems made by Hayes and other manufacturers added more S-registers until today some products use register names as high as S100.

As with AT commands, each manufacturer has added to the repertory of S-registers to suit the needs of its own products. Most modem makers have attempted to assign unique designations to the registers exclusive to their products. That is, they have tried to avoid using register names used by other manufacturers for different purposes. While such efforts are to be applauded, they have led to a profusion of incompatible registers and functions. In fact, some manufacturers even define many of the basic 28 Hayes S-registers in their own ways.

In general, only the lower 13 Hayes S-registers (that is, S0 through S12) and part of S16 are anywhere near universal among modems. Any S-registers above this minimal endowment must be considered manufacturer-unique.

S-registers are of two types. One accepts an integer value to define a parameter—for example, the length of a tone or delay in increments of a fraction of a second. To set these registers, you only need to write the appropriate integer value to the register. Out-of-range values generally will result in your modem responding with an error message while leaving the previous register contents intact. Other S-registers are bit-mapped. That is, the state of a bit (or bit pattern) determines whether a given modem feature is on or off. Each bit (or pattern) in the register operates independently. To set these registers, you must first determine the value of each of the eight bits stored in the register and encode these values together as an eight-bit binary number. Bit 0 of the bit-map is the least significant bit of the resulting number, and bit 7 the most significant. Next, convert the binary number to decimal, and write the decimal value to the S-register.

Table 19.3 lists the basic, near-universal, S-registers. Table 19.4 illustrates the chaos beyond these basic registers, listing the conflicting functions a number of manufacturers have assigned to the other S-registers.

TABLE 19.3. Commonly used S-register functions (based on original Hayes S-register set)

Register	Range	Units	Default	Description	Scope of Application
S0	0-255	rings	0	answer on ring #	Near universal
S1	0-255	rings	0	count number of rings	Near universal
S2	0-127	ASCII	43	escape code	Near universal
S3	0-127	ASCII	13	character used as return	Near universal
S4	0-127	ASCII	10	character used as line feed	Near universal

Register	Range	Units	Default	Description	Scope of Application
S5	0-32,127	ASCII	8	character used as backspace	Near universal
S6	2-255	sec.	2	time to wait for dial tone	Near universal
S7	1-255	sec.	30	time to wait for carrier	Near universal
S8	0-255	sec.	2	length of comma pause	Near universal
S9	1-255	0.1"	6	response time, carrier detect	Near universal
S10	1-255	0.1"	7	delay before hang up	Near universal
S11	50-255	0.001"	95	DTMF duration	Definition varies
S12	20-255	0.02"	50	escape code dead time	Widely used, not universal
S14	bit-mapped	modem options	AA(Hex)		Definition varies
	Bit 0	reserved			
	Bit 1	command echo			
				0=no echo	
				1=echo	
	Bit 2	result codes			
				0=enabled	
				1=disabled	
	Bit 3	verbose mode			
				0=short form result codes	
				1=verbose result codes	

continues

TABLE 19.3. Continued

Register	Range	Units	Default	Description	Scope of Application
	Bit 4	dumb mode			
				0=modem acts smart	
				1=modem acts dumb	
	Bit 5	dial method			
				0=tone	
				1=pulse	
	Bit 6	reserved			
	Bit 7	originate/ answer mode			
				0=answer	
				1=originate	
S16	bit-mapped		0	modem test options	Widely used, not universal
	bit 0	local analog loopback			
				0=disabled	
				1=enabled	
	bit 1	reserved			
	bit 2	local digital loopback			
				0=disabled	
				1=enabled	

Register	Range	Units	Default	Description	Scope of Application
	bit 3	status bit			
				0=loopback off	
				1=loopback in progress	
	bit 4	initiate remote digital loopback			
				0=disabled	
				1=enabled	
	bit 5	initiate remote digital loopback with test message and error count			
				0=disabled	
				1=enabled	
	bit 6	local analog loopback with self test			
				0=disabled	
				1=enabled	
	bit 7	reserved			
S18	0-255	seconds	0	test timer	Widely used, not universal
S21	bit-mapped		0	modem options	Hayes only

continues

TABLE 19.3. Continued

Register	Range	Units	Default	Description	Scope of Application
	bit 0	telco jack used			
				0=RJ-11/ RJ-41S/ RJ-45S	
				1=RJ-12/ RJ-13	
	bit 1	reserved			
	bit 2	RTS/CTS handling			
				0=RTS follows CTS	
				1=CTS always on	
	bit 3, 4	DTR handling			
				0,0=modem ignores DTR	
				0,1=modem to command state when DTR goes off	
				1,0=modem hangs up when DTR goes off	
				1,1=modem initializes when DTR goes off	
	bit 5	DCD handling			
				0=DCD always on	
				1=DCD indicates presence of carrier	
	bit 6	DSR handling			

Register	Range	Units	Default	Description	Scope of Application
				0=DSR always on	
				1=DSR indicates modem is off-hook and in data mode	
	bit 7	long space disconnect			
				0=disabled	
				1=enabled	
S22	bit-mapped		76(Hex)	modem option register	Commonly used
	bit 0,1	speaker volume			
				0,0=low	
				0,1=low	
				1,0=medium	
				1,1=high	
	bit 2,3	speaker control			
				0,0=speaker disabled	
				0,1=speaker on until carrier detected	
				1,0=speaker always on	
				1,1=speaker on on between dialing and carrier detect	
	bit 4,5,6				

continues

TABLE 19.3. Continued

Register	Range	Units	Default	Description	Scope of Application
		result code options			
				0,0,0=300 baud modem result codes only	
				1,0,0=modem does not detect dialtone or busy	
				1,0,1=modem detects dialtone only	
				1,1,0=modem detects busy signal only	
				1,1,1=modem detects dialtone and busy signal	
				other settings undefined	
	bit 7	make/ break pulse dial ratio			
				0=39% make, 61% break	
				1=33% make, 67% break	
S23	bit-mapped		7	modem option register	Commonly used
	bit 0	obey request			

Register	Range	Units	Default	Description	Scope of Application
		from remote modem for remote digital loopback			
				0=disabled	
				1=enabled	
	bit 1,2	communication rate			
				0,0=0 to 300 bps	
				0,1=reserved	
				1,0=1200 bps	
				1,1=2400 bps	
	bit 3	reserved			
	bit 4,5	parity option			
				0,0=even	
				0,1=space	
				1,0=odd	
				1,1=mark/none	
	bit 6,7	guard tones			
				0,0=disabled	
				0,1=550 Hz guard tone	
				1,0=1800 Hz guard tone	
				1,1=reserved	
S27	bit-mapped		40(Hex)	modem options register	Hayes only

continues

TABLE 19.3. Continued

Register	Range	Units	Default	Description	Scope of Application
	bit 0,1	trans-mission mode			
				0,0=asynchronous	
				0,1=synchronous with async call placement	
				1,0=synchronous with stored number dialing	
				1,1=synchronous with manual dialing	
	bit 2	dialup or lease-line operation			
				0=dialup line	
				1=leased-line	
	bit 3	reserved			
	bit 4,5	source of synchronous clock			
				0,0=local modem	
				0,1=host computer or data terminal	
				1,0=derived from received carrier	
				1,1=reserved	

Register	Range	Units	Default	Description	Scope of Application
	bit 6	Bell or CCITT operation			
				0=CCITT v.22 bis/v.22	
				1=Bell 212A	
	bit 7	reserved			

TABLE 19.4. S-register assignments used by representative modem makers

Register	Description	Used by
S0	Number of rings before answering	Most modems
S1	Ring count	Most modems
S2	Code used for Escape character	Most modems
S3	Code used for Return character	Most modems
S4	Code used for line feed character	Most modems
S5	Code used for Backspace character	Most modems
S6	Time to wait for dial tone	Most modems
S7	Time to wait for carrier	Most modems
S8	Length of pause elicited by comma character	Most modems
S9	Response time to carrier detect	Most modems
S10	Time delay before hanging up	Most modems
S11	DTMF duration	Most modems
S12	Escape code dead time	Most modems
S13	Reserved	Hayes, Practical Peripherals
S13	Defines remote configuration escape character	MultiTech

continues

TABLE 19.4. Continued

Register	Description	Used by
S13	Modem options (bit-mapped)	USRobotics
S14	Response codes and duplex operation control; also controls tone/pulse dialing and original/answer modes (bit-mapped)	Hayes
S14	Disconnect upon escape; enable autoretraining (bit-mapped)	USRobotics
S15	Reserved	Hayes, Practical Peripherals
S15	Delay for callback attempts after passwords exchanged	MultiTech
S15	Test register (bit-mapped)	USRobotics
S16	Modem test options (bit-mapped)	Boca, Hayes, USRobotics
S16	Number of callback attempts allowed after password exchange	MultiTech
S17	Reserved	Hayes, Practical Peripherals, USRobotics
S17	Length of break time to PC	MultiTech
S18	Timer for tests	Most modems
S19	Reserved	Hayes, Practical Peripherals
S19	Inactivity timer delay	USRobotics
S20	Reserved	Hayes, Practical Peripherals, USRobotics
S21	V.24 options (bit-mapped)	Boca
S21	Handshake control and jack selection (bit-mapped)	Hayes
S21	Break length in error-control mode	USRobotics
S22	Speaker control and busy detection (bit-mapped)	Most modems

Register	*Description*	*Used by*
S22	Code for XON character	USRobotics
S23	Communications parameters including guard tones, speed, and parity (bit-mapped)	Hayes
S23	Code for XOFF character	USRobotics
S24	Specifies DSR/CTS/CD drop-out time	MultiTech
S24	Time between pulsed DSR signals	USRobotics
S25	Delay before activating DTR	Boca, Hayes, USRobotics
S25	DTR dropout time	MultiTech
S26	RTS to CTS delay	Hayes, USRobotics
S26	Allowed number of password failures	MultiTech
S27	Bit-mapped options	Boca
S27	Synchronous/asynchronous control (bit-mapped)	Hayes
S27	Proprietary bit-mapped options	USRobotics
S28	Bit-mapped options	Boca
S28	V.32 handshake tone duration	USRobotics
S29	Flash-dial modifier time	Boca
S29	Allowed idle time between commands after password	MultiTech
S29	V.21 handshake tone duration	USRobotics
S30	Inactivity time before automatic disconnect	Boca, MultiTech
S31	Bit-mapped options	Boca
S32	Code used for XON character	Boca
S32	Time to wait for a Return during escape sequence	MultiTech
S32	Voice/data switch function	USRobotics
S33	Code used for XOFF character	Boca
S33	Packet size	USRobotics
S34	Reserved	Boca

continues

TABLE 19.4. Continued

Register	Description	Used by
S34	Command string buffer size	MultiTech
S34	V.32 troubleshooting (bit-mapped)	USRobotics
S35	Reserved	Boca
S36	LAPM failure (bit-mapped)	Boca
S37	Desired DTE connection speed	Boca, Practical Peripherals
S38	Delay before hang-up when DTR drops	Boca, Practical Peripherals, USRobotics
S39	Flow control (bit-mapped)	Boca
S39	Reserved	Practical Peripherals
S40	Reserved	Practical Peripherals
S41	Reserved	Practical Peripherals
S41	Number of remote access attempts allowed	USRobotics
S42	Reserved	Boca, Practical Peripherals
S42	Code for remote access escape character	USRobotics
S43	Reserved	Boca
S43	Current DCE speed (read-only)	Practical Peripherals
S43	Guard time for remote access sequence	USRobotics
S44	Reserved	Boca
S44	Delay before attempt to restore lost leased-line connection	USRobotics
S45	Reserved	Boca
S46	Data compression selection	Boca, Practical Peripherals

Register	Description	Used by
S48	V.42 negotiation selection	Boca
S48	Feature negotiation enabled/disabled	Practical Peripherals
S51	MNP/V.42 control	USRobotics
S53	Dial security feature control (bit-mapped)	USRobotics
S54	Used for factory debugging	USRobotics
S55	Used for factory debugging (V.Fast Class)	USRobotics
S56	V.Fast Class modulation options (bit-mapped)	USRobotics
S80	Reserved	Boca
S82	Break handling options	Boca, Practical Peripherals
S83	Reserved	Practical Peripherals
S84	Reserved	Practical Peripherals
S85	Reserved	Practical Peripherals
S86	Call failure responses	Boca, Practical Peripherals
S95	Extended result codes	Boca, Practical Peripherals

Controlling S-register settings is merely a matter of using the S-command family. To set a value in a given S-register, you must specify the register number, an equals sign (=), and the new value to give the register. For example, to set register S10 to value 32, you would send this command to your modem:

    ATS10=32

where AT is the attention command, S indicates you want to change an S-register, 10 is the register number, the = indicates you want to change its value, and the 32 is the new value.

To read the value of an S-register, you use the S command again. After you specify the register number, you only need to append a question mark to make an inquiry. For example, to check the value stored in register S10, you send this command to your modem:

    ATS10?

where AT is the attention command, the S indicates you want to check an S-register, 10 is the register number, and the question mark denotes the command as an inquiry. Your modem would respond 32, providing you had given the previous command to set the register to that value.

Setup Switches

Modems can be programmed to treat their various connections in different ways to match the needs of software. Some programs, for example, require that the modem keep them abreast of the connection through the Carrier Detect signal. Other programs couldn't care less about Carrier Detect but carefully scrutinize Data Set Ready. To accommodate the range of communications applications, most modems have setup switches that determine the handling of their control lines. In one position, a switch may force Carrier Detect to stay on continually, for example. The other setting might cause the status of Carrier Detect to follow the state of the modems' conversations.

These switches take two forms: mechanical and electrical. Mechanical switches are generally of the DIP variety. In the prototypical modem, the original Hayes Smartmodem 1200, these switches are hidden behind the front panel of the modem. (To get to them, carefully pry up the trailing ears of the sides of the bezel, first one side, then the other of the black front panel of the modem. Then pull it forward and off.)

Most commercial modems that use DIP switches are patterned after the Hayes Smartmodem 1200 or its kin. Some of these DIP switch settings are shown in Table 19.5; along with software commands, they control the same functions in other modems.

TABLE 19.5. Hayes Smartmodem DIP Switch and Command Settings

Function	SM 1200	SM 1200B	SM 1200B	SM 2400 V-series
	External	Full-Card	Half-Card	Internal & External
DTR Status	Switch 1	Switch 4	Switch 4	Software
Ignore DTR*	Down	Down	Right	&D0
Follow DTR	Up	Up	Left	&D1,&D2,&D3

Function	*SM 1200*	*SM 1200B*	*SM 1200B*	*SM 2400 V-series*
Result Code Format	Sw2/Software	Software	Software	Software
Numeric	Down/V0	V0	V0	V0
Verbose*	Up/V1	V1	V1	V1
Result Code Display	Sw3/Software	Software	Software	Software
Enabled*	Down/Q0	Q0	Q0	Q0
Disabled	Up/Q1	Q1	Q1	Q1
Software State Echo	SW4/Software	Software	Software	Software
Disabled	Down/E0	E0	E0	E0
Enabled*	Up/E1	E1	E1	E1
Auto-Answer	Sw5/Software	Software	Software	Software
Disabled*	Down/S0=0	S0=0	S0=0	S0=0
Enabled	Up/S0=1	S0=1	S0=1	S0=1
Carrier Detect	Switch 6	Switch 3	Switch 3	Software
Always True*	Down	Up	Left	&C0
Follow DCD	Up	Down	Right	&C1
Telco Jack Type	Switch 7	Switch 2	Switch 2	Software
Single-Line*	Up	Up	Left	&J0
Multi-Line	Down	Down	Right	&J1
Software Dumb Strap	Switch 8	-	-	-

continues

TABLE 19.5. Continued

Function	SM 1200	SM 1200B	SM 1200B	SM 2400 V-series
Enabled*	Down	Preset	Preset	Rightmost pins
Disabled	Up	n/a	n/a	Leftmost pins
1200bps Protocol	Sw9/Software	Sw5/Software	Software	Software
CCITT v.22	Down/B0	Down/B0	B0	B0
BELL 212A*	Up/B1	Up/B1	B1	B1
Response to DTR on/off	Switch 10	-	-	-
Software				
Modem Reset	Down	n/a	n/a	&D3
Go to Command State	n/a	n/a	n/a	&D1
Hang Up	Up	n/a	n/a	&D2
Port Selection	-	Switch 1	Switch 1	External Switch
COM 1*	n/a	Down	Right	Right
COM 2	n/a	Up	Left	Left
Pulse Dial Type	-	Switch 6	-	Software
US*	Preset	Up	Preset	&P0
International	n/a	Down	n/a	&P1

Note: Asterisk indicates the factory default setting.

The other kind of switch is electrical and is used by most current modems. First finding wide application in the Smartmode 2400, this form of electrical setup uses EEPROM memory for non-volatile storage. You change these settings by sending S-register commands to the modem from your computer. Because of their EEPROM nature, they retain their settings even when the modem is turned off or unplugged.

Other modems follow this pattern but use another memory technology—for example, battery backed-up dynamic RAM. A few don't make any effort toward removing the volatility. Such modems require that you reprogram their settings every time you turn them on. Although you cannot do much to make modem memory nonvolatile, you can make life easier using disk memory. Simply add the modem settings you want to enforce to the setup strings that many communications software packages send to the modem before they begin to make a connection.

Response Codes

Commands sent to a Hayes-compatible modem are one-way. Without some means of confirmation, you would never know whether the modem actually received your command, let alone acted on it. Moreover, you also need some means for the modem to tell you what it discovers about your connection to the telephone line. The modem needs to signal you when it detects another modem at the end of the line, for example.

These commands for the Smartmodem 2400, which has no DIP switches, duplicate the functions of the DIP switches of the Smartmodem 1200.

Part of the Hayes command set is a series of response codes that serves that feedback function. When the modem needs to tell you something, it sends code numbers or words to apprise you of the situation via the same connection used to send data between your computer and modem. In the Hayes scheme of things, you can set the modem to send simple numeric codes, consisting solely of codes (which you can then look up in your modem manual, if you have one) or verbose responses, which may be one or more words long in something close to everyday English.

Typical responses include OK to signify that a command has been received and acted on, CONNECT 1200 to indicate that you have linked with a 1200 bits-per-second modem, and RINGING to tell you that the phone at the other end of the connection is ringing. Representative modem response codes are listed in table 19.6. Beyond the basic first ten, manufacturers have set their own result codes independently. Consequently the same number may have different meanings for different modems.

TABLE 19.6. Representative Modem Response Codes

Numeric Code	Verbose Code	Definition
0	OK	Command executed without error
1	CONNECT	Carrier has been detected
2	RING	Phone is ringing
3	NO CARRIER	Carrier lost or never detected

continues

TABLE 19.6. Continued

Numeric Code	Verbose Code	Definition
4	ERROR	Error in command line or line too long
5	CONNECT 1200	Connection established at 1200 bps
6	NO DIALTONE	Dialtone not detected in waiting period
7	BUSY	Modem detected a busy signal
8	NO ANSWER	No silence detected while waiting for a quiet answer
10	CONNECT 2400	Connection established at 2400 bps
11	RINGING	Distant telephone ringing; or 11 CONNECT 4800 Connection established at 4800 bps
12	VOICE	Human being or answering machine detected at other end of the connection
12	CONNECT 9600	Connection established at 9600 bps
13	CONNECT 9600	Connection established at 9600 bps
14	CONNECT 19200	Connection established at 19,200 bps
18	CONNECT 4800	Connection established at 4800 bps
20	CONNECT 7200	Connection established at 7200 bps
21	CONNECT 12000	Connection established at 12000 bps
25	CONNECT 14400	Connection established at 14400 bps
28	CONNECT 38400	Connection established at 38,400 bps
40	CARRIER 300	Carrier detected at 300 bps
46	CARRIER 1200	Carrier detected at 1200 bps
47	CARRIER 2400	Carrier detected at 2400 bps
47	CONNECT 16800	Connection established at 16800 bps
48	CARRIER 4800	Carrier detected at 4800 bps
50	CARRIER 9600	Carrier detected at 9600 bps
66	COMPRESSION: CLASS 5	MNP5 data compression enabled
67	COMPRESSION: V.42BIS	V.42bis compression enabled
69	COMPRESSION: NONE	Data compression diabled
70	PROTOCOL: NONE	Standard asynchronous mode
77	PROTOCOL: V.42/LAPM	V.42 error-correction mode: LAPM

Numeric Code	Verbose Code	Definition
80	PROTOCOL: MNP	Alternate error-correction protocol: MNP
85	CONNECT 19200	Connection established at 19200 bps
91	CONNECT 21600	Connection established at 21600 bps
99	CONNECT 24000	Connection established at 24000 bps
103	CONNECT 26400	Connection established at 26400 bps
107	CONNECT 28800	Connection established at 28800 bps

Note: Duplication in the table entries reflects different code assignments by different manufacturers.

Note that because the response codes flow from your modem to your computer as part of the regular data stream, you may accidentally confuse them with text being received from the far end of your connection.

Setup Strings

Back when modems only had one or two speeds and all communications protocols were handled by your communications software, you usually just gave your modem a command to dial the phone and waited for a connection. Today, however, there are many options for configuring a modem, and they often differ depending on the modem or service with which you communicate. Whereas some modems remember their basic configuration in EEPROM memory so that you can set it once and forget it, others need to be reminded every time you use the modem. Consequently, you may need to change the configuration of your modem every time you start your communications program or even dial the phone.

To set or change the configuration of your modem, your communications program sends a string of commands out your serial port. This often long block of characters is called a setup string. Sending the right setup string is vitally important in assuring that your modem will work with your software and the connection you want to make.

Although the setup string looks as forbidding as a secret code written in Cyrillic characters, you can deconstruct it easily. Each element of the string is drawn from the modem command set and can be interpreted individually.

A setup string (or addition to your modem's dialing command) can be useful in avoiding problems with call waiting on modem lines. The click that warns you of an incoming call while you're using a line plays havoc with modems. Most interpret the click as a loss-of-carrier and automatically disconnect. To avoid the problem, you can use your modem setup string to reprogram the amount of time your modem waits before hanging up when it detects a loss of carrier. Registers S9 and S10 control this delay. The command ATS10=30 (or adding S10=30 to your setup string) will set the delay for three seconds, enough to prevent the automatic hang-up.

Another way to avoid the disconnect problem is to cancel call waiting. In most calling areas dialing *70 on your phone before making a call disables call waiting during the next call. You can add the *70 to your modem's dialing command to automatically defeat call waiting. For example, change your dialing command from ATDT5551212 to ATDT*70,5551212 (the comma adds a pause to give the telephone time to recover).

Dialing and Answering

Nearly all modems today fully automate the process of linking with another modem. Your communications software sends commands to the modem to dial the phone, and the other modem knows what to do when the telephone rings. Early modems, however, were not so capable, and these automatic features had to be explicitly pointed out in modem specifications.

An auto-dial modem has the innate capability to generate pulse-dial or DTMF (dual-tone modulated frequency or touch-tone) dialing signals independent of a telephone set. Upon receiving a dialing command from you or your software, the modem dials the phone and makes a connection. Without auto-dial, you would have to dial the phone yourself, listen for the screech of the remote modem's answer, plug in your modem, and then hang up the phone.

At the other end of the connection, an auto-answer modem can detect the incoming ringing voltage (the low-frequency, high-voltage signal that makes the bell on a telephone ring) and seize the telephone line as if it had been answered by you in person. After seizing the phone line, the auto-answer modem sends a signal to its host computer to tell it that it has answered the phone. The computer then can interact with the caller.

Nearly all modern modems also include automatic speed sensing. This feature allows the modem to automatically adjust its speed to match that of a distant modem, if it can. High-speed modems usually negotiate the highest possible shared speed to operate at using proprietary protocols.

Early modems attempt to adjust to the speed at which you send them data, again if it is within the range of speeds that the modem can handle. Modems with built-in data compression make this option undesirable because you will always want to send data to the modem at the highest speed your serial port will allow and your modem will accept (at least 57,600 bits per second with a V.32 bis/V.42bis modem and 115,200 bits per second with a V.34 modem). The modem that follows these standards will adjust its speed to match whatever it connects with during the process of handshaking.

Handshaking

Once a modem makes a connection, it must negotiate the standard that it and the distant modem will follow. This process of negotiation is termed *modem handshaking*. The sequence involved in the handshake differs with the type of modem and standard, and it can get complicated as speeds go up.

When using the V.22bis standard, for example, the distant modem that detects a ring on the telephone line goes off the hook (picks up the line), then does nothing for at least two seconds. This period of silence, called the billing delay, is required by telephone company rules to give the phone system a chance to determine that the connection has been made and start billing you for it. After the billing delay, the remote modem sends out its answer tone, between 2.6 and 4 seconds of a 2100 Hz tone. The answer tone lets anyone who dials your modem line as a wrong number know that they have not reached their significant other. It also gives people with manual-start modems a chance to put their modems in data mode. It also lets the telephone company know that you have made a data connection so that the phone company can switch off the echo suppressors on the line and let your modems fend for themselves in canceling echoes. The dialing modem doesn't do anything but listen while all of this posturing goes on.

After the answer tone is finished, the distant modem becomes quiet for about 75 milliseconds, marking the end of the answer tone. Then it sends out what you hear as a burst of static. It's actually a 1200 bits-per-second signal (shuffling between 2250 and 2550 Hz) containing an unscrambled binary 1 signal—that is, pulses indicating a logical positive in digital code. After about 155 milliseconds of this noise, the dialing modem remains silent for about 1/2 second, and then sends out its 00 and 11 code patterns at 1200 bits per second for about 100 milliseconds, a signal called S1. Then the dialing modem switches to sending out a "scrambled" binary 1 signal (one that has its power smoothed out across the modem's bandwidth). When the answering modem, which is still sending out an unscrambled binary 1, recognizes the dialing modem's S1 signal, the answering modem begins sending out the S1 for 100 milliseconds. Then it switches to a scrambled binary 1 for 500 milliseconds. Finally, it ups the rate to 2400 bits per second and sends out another 200 milliseconds of binary one. About 600 milliseconds after the dialing modem detects the scrambled binary 1 signal from the answering modem, it too switches to scrambled 1s at 2400 bits per second for 200 milliseconds. This completes the negotiations, and the two modems are ready to transfer information.

The S1 signals let the two modems know that they will communicate using V.22bis rather than slower speed V.22 or Bell 212A. If these signals are not detected, the modems known quickly that they will have to communicate at 1200 bits per second. The two scrambled binary 1 signals assure the two modems that their 2400-bits-per-second exchanges will be successful.

Modem handshaking at higher speeds is even more complicated. In addition to negotiating their own speed, the modems have to measure the characteristics of the telephone line, for instance to calibrate the delays to make their echo cancellers work.

Under V.32, for example, a connection starts out the same as in V.22bis because the billing delay must still be accounted for. But after the delay, the V.32 answering modem sends out a V.25 answer tone that reverses phase every 450 milliseconds to tell the telephone system that the modems will handle the echo cancellation. This signal is the clicking noise you hear at the beginning of a high-speed modem connection.

The dialing modem waits one second after making the connection and sends out an 1800 Hz tone to let the answering modem (which is still sending out the answer tone) that it is a V.32

modem. If the answering modem hears this tone, after it completes its 2.6 to 4.0 second answer tone, it immediately tries to connect. If the answering modem doesn't hear the dialing modem's tone, it first tries to connect as a V.22bis modem (by sending the unscrambled binary 1 signal). If the dialing modem doesn't respond, the answering modem tried to connect as V.32 once again just in case something interfered with the initial attempt.

To make the V.32 connection, the answering modem sends out a combination of 600 and 3000 Hz tones for at least 27 milliseconds, then reverses the phase of the signal. The dialing modem responds to the phase reversal by reversing the phase of its 1800 Hz signal. The answering modem responds to this by reversing the phase of its signal again. These three phase reversals allow the modems to time how long it takes a signal to complete the entire connection, information needed to program the echo cancellation circuitry inside the modems.

Next, the dialing modem sends out a training signal that's from 650 to 3525 milliseconds long so that the answering modem can adjust its phone line equalization. The answering modem waits for the dialing modem to finish, and then sends out its own training signal. When the dialing modem has finished its set up, it signals back to the answering modem. Then both modems exchange scrambled binary 1 signals for at least 53 milliseconds and are ready to pass data. At this point, your modem will signal you CONNECT 9600.

Once the connection is made, the modems will see whether they can use V.42 error-correction or V.42 bit compression. The dialing modem begins the process by sending out a stream of alternating parity XON characters while listening for a response. If the answering modem doesn't respond in 750 milliseconds, the dialing modem assumes that the recipient doesn't understand and tries an alternate protocol (for example MNP). If the answering modem understands the XON characters, it responds by sending the letters EC (for error-correction) 10 times and prepares to use synchronous LAPM protocol. The dialing modem then uses the LAPM protocol to send out an Exchange Identification frame (XID), which codes the details of the error-correction it would like to use. The answering modem responds with its selection of the features desired by the dialing modem that it can use, and those become the basis of the error-correction actually put to work. These include whether to use V.42bis compression. The two modem then exchange signals to enter data-transfer mode.

Caller Identification

Some modems can take advantage of the telephone company's caller identification service to screen calls for security. In areas supporting caller identification service, central office equipment at the telephone company adds a three-part identification signal between the first and second ring of a telephone call. The format of this signal starts with a series of alternating digital 1s and 0s followed by a marking state. The end part of the signal is the actual caller identification data—not just the originating telephone number but also a date and time stamp as well as a checksum. The entire signal lasts 450 milliseconds.

A modem designed for receiving caller identification can check the originating number before connecting with an incoming call. The modem can assure that only calls from approved numbers are accepted and can aid in maintaining a full audit trail of the calls received.

Protocols

Even the best telephone connection sneaks errors into modem communications. When sending text back and forth, the result is only a few garbled characters. But if you try to send an executable program through a modem connection and an error creeps in, the result will be unpredictable. Your system will likely respond oddly or crash when you run the mistransmitted code. Before the world agreed on standards for error-correction in modem connections, a number of different methods called file transfer protocols were developed to help prevent errors when exchanging files.

Xmodem

The first of these protocols was created in 1978 by Ward Christensen and quickly became the de facto standard for error-free file transmission. Called Xmodem or MODEM7, Christensen's technique worked by breaking files into blocks 128 bytes long, transmitting the blocks one at a time, and verifying the accuracy of each. If the receiving system found an error, it requested that the bad block be retransmitted as many times as necessary to get through error free (or until the process automatically times out).

To detect errors, Xmodem uses a checksum byte added to each block which, through application of an algorithm, indicates whether the transmission was successful. When a block is successfully received, the receiving system sends back an ACK byte (ASCII code TK); if unsuccessful, it sends back a NAK (ASCII TK) byte.

Xmodem CRC

Some errors in a block can result in a valid checksum. A more robust form of Xmodem substitutes a Cyclical Redundancy Check for the checksum (stealing another byte). Most systems that use Xmodem try to use the CRC algorithm first (because it is more reliable), but if one of the systems trying to communicate doesn't support CRC, the protocol reverts to ordinary Xmodem.

Xmodem-1K

Another way to avoid the substantial overhead of acknowledging multiple blocks is to use larger blocks. The Xmodem-1K protocol expands the 128-byte block of Xmodem CRC to 1024 bytes. The larger blocks give this protocol a substantial advantage over its predecessor in moving larger files.

WXmodem

One problem with Xmodem is that the sending modem must wait for an acknowledgment between sending blocks. With long delays, this wait can substantially slow transmissions. The WXmodem protocol (which stands for Windowed Xmodem) removes the wait. As with ordinary Xmodem, it uses check-summed 128-byte blocks, but the sending system assumes that every block is properly received and sends all blocks one after another. The receiving modem responds normally with ACK or NAK acknowledgments. Although the sending modem often gets one to four blocks ahead of the receiving modem, it tracks the acknowledgments it receives and can resend the proper block when necessary.

Ymodem

As with Xmodem-1K, Ymodem takes advantage of larger blocks to speed transmissions. It uses 1024-byte blocks and cyclic redundancy checking for error detection. Although sometimes confused with Xmodem-1K, it differs by including a batch mode that allows multiple files to be transferred with a single command. Sometimes it is described as Ymodem Batch.

Ymodem-g

After modems with built-in hardware error-correction became available, a new variant of the Ymodem protocol without software error recovery was developed as Ymodem-g. Although Ymodem-g still breaks files into 1024-byte blocks for transfer, it sends them as a continuous stream. If an error sneaks past the hardware error-detection scheme and is reported back to the sending system, the entire transfer is canceled. It also supports batch transfers.

Zmodem

The principle behind Zmodem is that the only blocks that matter in error-correction are those that are received defectively. As with WXmodem and Ymodem-g, Zmodem blasts out blocks non-stop, and it only acts on the NAKs it gets from the receiving system. Zmodem compromises on block size, using 512-byte blocks. The protocol also has recovery capabilities. If a protocol transfer is interrupted, the system can resume it later without the need to retransmit the blocks already sent.

Kermit

Developed at Columbia University in 1981, Kermit—named after Jim Henson's favorite frog— was designed to ship files between dissimilar computer systems. Unlike Xmodem, however, the way that Kermit moves data is negotiable. Kermit uses blocks (which the protocol calls *packets*) and checksum error detection but adjusts its packet size to accommodate the fixed packet sizes used by some computer system or to work with marginal connections. It also can use 7-bit connections to transfer 8-bit data by specially coding characters when necessary. Kermit also can recover from major line errors by resynchronizing the transmissions of modems after their interruption.

Fax

Nearly every high-speed modem sold today has built-in fax capabilities. This bonus results from the huge demand for fax in the business world coupled with the trivial cost of adding fax capabilities to a modern modem. Everything that's necessary for fax comes built into the same chip sets that make normal high-speed modem communications possible.

Definitions

Fax, short for facsimile transmissions, gives the power of *Star Trek's* transporter system (usually without the aliens and pyrotechnics) to anyone who needs to get a document somewhere else in the world at the speed of light. Although fax doesn't quite dematerialize paper, it does move the images and information a document contains across continents and reconstructs it at the end of its near-instantaneous travels. The recipient gets to hold in his own hands a nearly exact duplicate of the original, the infamous "reasonable facsimile."

From that angle, fax is a telecopier—a Xerox machine with a thousand miles of wire between where you slide the original in and the duplicate falls out. In fact, the now aging telecopiers made by Xerox Corporation were the progenitors of today's fax machines.

Today fax involves the use of a fax modem, a device that converts page scans into a form compatible with the international telephone system. Or you can use a stand-alone fax machine, which combines a fax modem with a scanner, printer, and telephone set. In the PC realm, the term fax modem also refers to adapter boards that slide into expansion slots to give the host computer the capability to send and receive fax transmissions.

In a classic fax system, you start using fax by dialing up a distant fax system using a touch pad on your fax machine, just as you would any other telephone. You slide a sheet of paper into the fax's scanner, and the page curls around a drum in front of a photodetector. Much as a television picture is broken into numerous scan lines, a fax machine scans images as a series of lines, takes them one at a time, and strings all of the lines scanned from a document into a continuous stream of information. The fax machine converts the data stream into a series of modulated tones for transmission over the telephone line. After making a connection at the receiving end, another fax machine converts the data stream into black and white dots representing the original image much as a television set reconstructs a TV image. A printer puts the results on paper using thermal or laser printer technology.

PC fax systems can do away with the paper. PC fax software can take the all-electronic images you draw or paint with your graphics software and convert it into the standard format that's used for fax transmissions. A fax modem in your PC can then send that data to a standard fax machine, which converts the data into hard copy form. Or your PC fax system can receive a transmission from a standard fax machine and capture the image into a graphics file. You then can convert the file into another graphic format using conversion software, edit the image with your favorite painting program, or turn its text contents into ASCII form using OCR software. You even can turn your PC into the equivalent of a standard fax machine by adding a scanner to capture images from paper. Your printer will turn fax reception into hard copy, although at a fraction of the speed of a stand-alone fax machine.

Larger businesses with PC networks incorporate fax servers to allow their employees to share a common facility for sending their PC-based faxes. The fax server eliminates the need for each PC in the network to be equipped with its own fax modem and telephone line.

Reception through fax servers has been problematic, however, because conventional fax messages provide no easy means for electronic routing through a network to the proper recipient. To solve this problem, the fax industry is developing standards for subaddressing capabilities. Subaddresses will be invaluable to businesses with PC networks using fax servers. With current technology, giving each user a private fax mailbox means a separate telephone line for each. Using a subaddress, a single fax server can receive all fax messages and route them to the proper recipient. The fax subaddress will be a mailbox number that's added to your primary telephone number. It will direct the automatic routing of the message through a network fax server to an individual's fax mailbox. The subaddress number will be transmitted during the opening handshake of the fax modems, and it will be independent from the primary telephone number.

PC fax beats stand-alone fax with its management capabilities. PC fax software can broadcast fax messages to as wide a mailing list as you can accommodate on your hard disk, waiting until early morning hours when long-distance rates are cheapest to make the calls. You easily can manage the mailing list as you would any other PC database.

The concept of facsimile transmissions is not new. As early as 1842, Alexander Bain patented an electro-mechanical device that could translate wire-based signals into marks on paper. Newspaper wire photos, which are based on the same principles, have been used for generations.

The widespread use of fax in business is a more recent phenomenon, however, and its growth parallels that of the PC for much the same underlying reason. Desktop computers did not take off until the industry found a standard to follow, the IBM PC. Similarly, the explosive growth of fax began only after the CCITT adopted standards for the transmission of facsimile data.

Analog Standards

The original system, now termed Group 1, was based on analog technology and used frequency shift keying, much as 300 baud modems do, to transmit a page of information in six minutes.

Group 2 improved that analog technology and doubled the speed of transmission, up to three minutes per page.

Group 3

The big break with the past was the CCITT's adoption in 1980 of the Group 3 fax protocol, which is entirely digitally based. Using data compression and modems that operate at up to 14,400 bits per second, full page documents can be transmitted in 20 to 60 seconds using the Group 3 protocol. New transmission standards promise to pump up the basic Group 3 data rate to 28,800 bits per second.

The basic speed of a Group 3 fax transmission depends on the underlying communications standard that the fax product follows. These standards are similar to data modem standards. With the exception of V.34, data and fax modems operate under different standards, even when using the same data rates. Consequently, data and fax modems are not interchangeable, and a modem that provides high-speed fax capabilities (say 9600 bps) may operate more slowly in data mode (say 2400 bps).

Data Rates

The Group 3 protocol does not define a single speed for fax transmissions but allows the use of any of a variety of transmission standards. At data rates of 2400 and 4800 bits per second, fax modems operate under the V.27 ter standard. At 7200 and 9600 bits per second, they follow V.29 (or V.17, which incorporates these V.29 modes). At 12,000 and 14,400 bits per second, fax modems follow V.17. The V.34 standard will take both fax and data modems up to 28,800 bits per second. New standards will allow the use of the Group 3 fax protocol over ISDN and other future digital telephone services.

Fax modems typically are described by the communications standards they support or by the maximum data rate at which they can operate. Most modern fax modems follow the V.17 standard, which incorporates the lower V.29 speeds. Most also will fall back to V.27 ter to accommodate older, slower fax products.

Binary File Transfer

More than just following the same modem standard, the capabilities of fax service is merging with those of standard data communications. New fax modems, for example, incorporate binary file transfer capabilities, which enable them to ship BFT files from one fax system to another as easily as document pages. You could, for example, send a file from your PC to a printer for a remote print out or to a PC where it could be received automatically. The receiving fax modem picks up the line, makes the connection, and records the file as dutifully as it would an ordinary fax page—without anyone standing around to control the modem.

Compression

Data compression makes the true speed of transmitting a page dependent on the amount of detail that it contains. In operation, the data compression algorithm reduces the amount of data that must be transferred by a factor of 5 to 10. On the other hand, a bad phone connection can slow fax transmissions as fax modems automatically fall back to lower speeds to cope with poor line quality.

Group 3 fax products may use any of three levels of data compression designated as MH, MR, and MMR. The typical Group 3 fax product includes only MH compression. The others are optional, and MMR is particularly rare. To be sure that a given fax products uses MR or MMR, you will need to check its specifications.

Every Group 3 fax machine and PC fax modem incorporates a transmission technique called Modified Huffman encoding, which is also known as one-dimensional encoding. In a typical fax machine, you slide a page into the machine, place the call, and the machine calls a distant number. Once the connection is negotiated, the fax machine scans the page with a photodetector inside the machine, which detects the black-and-white patterns on the page one line at a time at a resolution of 200 dots per inch. The result is a series of bits with the digital 1s and 0s corresponding to the black and white samples each 1/200th of an inch. The fax machine compresses this raw data stream with run-length encoding. Instead of individual dots, the pattern is coded as short line segments, and the code indicates the number of dots in each segment. The fax machine sends this run-length coded data to the remote fax machine. Included in the transmitted signal is a rudimentary form of error protection, but missed bits are not reproduced when the receiving fax machine reconstructs the original page.

Modified Huffman encoding was built into the Group 3 standard in 1980 so that a fax machine could send a full page in less than one minute using a standard V.27 ter modem that operated at 4800 bits per second. With 9600 bps modems, that time is cut nearly in half.

Modified read encoding was added as an option shortly after MH encoding was adopted. MR starts with standard MH encoding for the first line of the transmission but then encodes the second line as differences from the first line. Because with fine images, line data changes little between adjacent lines, usually little change information is required. To prevent errors from rippling through an entire document, at the third line MR starts over with a plain MH scan. In other words, odd-numbered scan lines are MH and even lines contain only difference information from the previous line. If a full line is lost in transmission, MR limits the damage to, at most, two lines. Overall, the transmission time savings in advancing from MH to MR amounts to 15 percent to 20 percent, the exact figure depending on message contents.

Modified read encoding foregoes the safety of the MR technique and records the entire page as difference data. Using MMR, the first line serves as a reference and is all white. Every subsequent line is encoded as the difference from the preceding line until the end of a page. However, an error in any one line will repeat in every subsequent line, so losing one line can garble an entire page. To help prevent such problems, MMR can incorporate its own error-correction mode (ECM) through which the receiving fax system can request the retransmission of any lines received in error. Only the bad lines are updated, and the rest of the page is reconstructed from the new data. MMR with ECM is the most efficient scheme used for compressing fax transmissions and can cut the time needed for a page transmission with MH in half.

Under the original Group 3 standard, two degrees of resolution or on-paper sharpness are possible: standard, which allows 1,728 dots horizontally across the page (about 200 dots per inch) and 100 dots per inch vertically; and fine, which doubles the vertical resolution to achieve 200 x 200 dpi and requires about twice the transmission time. Fine resolution also approximately doubles the time required to transmit a fax page because it doubles the data that must be moved.

Revisions to the Group 3 standard have added more possible resolutions. Two new resolutions compensate for the slight elongation that creeps into fax documents when generated and transmitted in purely electronic form. New fax products may optionally send and receive at a resolutions of 204 x 98 pixels per inch in standard mode or 204 x 196 pixels per inch in fine mode. Two new high-resolution modes of 300 x 300 pixels per inch and 400 x 400 pixels per inch were also established. The 300 x 300 mode enables fax machines, laser printers, and scanners to share the same resolution levels for higher quality when transferring images between them. To take advantage of these resolutions, both sending and receiving fax equipment must support the new modes.

Group 4

In 1984 the CCITT approved a super-performance facsimile standard, Group 4, which allows resolutions of up to 400 x 400 dpi as well as higher speed transmissions of lower resolutions. Although not quite typeset quality (phototypesetters are capable of resolutions of about 1,200 dpi), the best of Group 4 is about equal to the resolving capability of the human eye at normal reading distance. However, today's Group 4 fax machines require high-speed, dedicated lines and do not operate as dial-up devices. Group 3 equipment using new, higher resolution standards and coupled to digital services offers a lower cost alternative to Group 4.

Interface Classes

As with data modems, fax modems must link up with your PC and its software. Unlike data modems, which were blessed with a standard since early on (the Hayes command set), fax modems lacked a single standard. In recent years, however, the Electronics Industry Association and the Telecommunications Industry Association have created a standard that is essentially an extension to the Hayes AT command set. The standard embraces two classes.

Class 1 is the earlier standard. Under the Class 1 standard, most of the processing of fax documents is performed by PC software. The resulting fax data is sent to the modem for direct transmission.

Class 2 shifts the work of preparing the fax document for transmission to the fax modem itself. The modem hardware handles the data compression and error control for the transmission. The Class 2 standard also incorporates additional flow-control and station-identification features.

These classes hint at the most significant difference between PC-based fax systems, which is software. Fax modem hardware determines the connections that can be made, but the software determines the ultimate capabilities of the system. A fax modem that adheres to various standards (classes as well as protocols) will open for you the widest selection of software and the widest range of features.

Physical Matters

Nearly every modem made today has all the standard features that you might normally want. After all, once a manufacturer starts integrating features into its circuit chips, adding a few more features is about the equivalent of punching more holes in a sieve. The only time you're likely to run into a modem deficient in today's convenience features is when you try to make do with a modem manufactured to yesterday's standards.

Packaging

Perhaps the biggest choice you have in buying a new modem is whether it is installed inside your PC as an internal modem or connects outside your PC through a cable as an external modem. Internal modems themselves fall into three classes: expansion slot, PCMCIA, and proprietary. Expansion slot modems are like any other expansion cards that plug into a vacant slot inside your PC. PCMCIA modems are about the size of credit cards and fit the standard PC card slots built into most newer notebook computers and low-power desktop PCs. Proprietary internal modems are those designed for a specific model or range of models of notebook PC. External modems are boxes that plug into one of your PC's serial ports and they come in two varieties: full-size and pocket.

For the most part, packaging is a matter of aesthetics and convenience. The same features and performance are available in most packages. (The exception being proprietary modems, which are falling from favor and may not incorporate the latest standards.) Modem makers use exactly the same chip sets for external, expansion board, and PCMCIA modems. The only differences are the manner in which you attach the modem to your PC and the price you pay.

Expansion board modems are the least expensive means of acquiring the technology of a given modem standard. The price represents design simplicity. Most expansion board modems are little more than chip sets soldered to circuit boards. Any circuit board maker can punch them out by the thousandfold. External modems necessarily cost more because of the extra hardware they require: a case, power supply, a serial connector, and convenience features like indicator lights. You will also need a serial cable to connect an external modem—a hidden cost that you should consider in pricing comparisons. Pocket modems and PCMCIA modems are the more expensive because, well, manufacturers charge what the market will bear.

There are a few practical reasons for preferring one style of modem packaging over another. Full-size and pocket external modems offer the advantage of system indifference. You can move your external modem between different computer systems, even those that are not IBM compatible, simply by pulling the plug. Moving an expansion board modem requires popping the lid off of your PC and the recipient and all the folderol that follows. PCMCIA modems promise system indifference in the future. You probably cannot plug one into your desktop machine today, but you can move one from your current notebook PC to the next notebook PC you buy.

External modems are generally more convenient to operate. Full-size external modems have indicators that allow you to directly monitor the status of your modem connection. Internal modems (both expansion board and PCMCIA) have no space for lights. Some allow you to put simulated indicators on your monitor, but these take up display space and may interfere with the operation of your communications programs. Most pocket modems follow the internal modem pattern and lack lights. You can also switch off an external modem independently from your PC if you need a brute-force method of ending a connection or resetting parameters. With an internal modem, you have to switch off your PC to get the same effect.

On the other hand, internal modems are physically more convenient. They take up no extra desk space and you don't have to deal with a tangle of cords, plugs, or transformers vying for the few holes in your wall outlet. There are no extra boxes on your desk or another thing to switch off when you put your system to sleep at night. An internal PCMCIA modem means one less loose package to tuck away in the seat pouch in front of you to forget or otherwise lose in your travels.

Pocket modems tend to be a less expensive alternative to the high price of proprietary internal and PCMCIA modems. Pocket modems can be designed to run either on internal batteries or draw their power from the telephone line itself. If you have ever gotten stuck with a dead battery in an emergency, you already know the advantage of line power. PCMCIA and proprietary modems run off power supplied by your PC, which can shorten the battery run-time of the machine.

Tiny PCMCIA modems present a big problem to modem designers: the PCMCIA card slot is too narrow to accommodate a standard telephone connector. Manufacturers have found three ways of working around the problem. Some use adapter cords that plug into a thin jack on the card to give you a standard phone jack. But you also get another opportunity to lose something that you will have a difficult time finding a replacement for. Another solution is the pop-out phone jack. For traveling, it slides into the modem. When you need to communicate, you pop out a skeletal jack that fits a standard telephone modular connector. The third alternative is the least pleasing. The card modem slides into a standard PCMCIA slot but bulges at the far end to accommodate a modular phone plug. These cards do not fit the PCMCIA standard. They may block an adjacent card slot, and they project from your PC so you can snap them off as you rush from cab to airport.

Connections

Nearly all modems sold for PCs today are direct-connect modems. They plug directly into the electrical wires of the telephone system. They are a tribute to the simplicity of the modular telephone wiring system, but they can be bothersome if you encounter a telephone that lacks modular wiring.

An alternative way to connect a modem without modular worries is an acoustic coupler. The very first modems used acoustic couplers to avoid any electrical contact with telephone lines because years ago hooking your modem directly to the phone line was neither practical nor legal. It wasn't practical because modular jacks weren't available. It wasn't legal because telephone company regulations dating long before the AT&T telephone monopoly was split up did not permit individuals to directly connect modems to their telephone lines. Instead of electrical connections, these vintage modems sent their signals to telephones as sound waves, acoustically, directly into the handset of a standard telephone. An acoustic coupler converts the tone-like analog signals made by the modem into sounds that are then picked up by the microphone in the telephone handset and passed through the telephone network as electrical signals. To make the sound connection a two-way street, the acoustic coupler also incorporated a microphone to pick up the squawks emanating from the ear piece of the telephone handset, convert them into electrical signals, and supply them to the modem for demodulation.

Acoustic couplers are still available and can take many forms. In early equipment, the acoustic coupler was integral to the modem; it was a special cradle in which you lay the telephone handset. Today, you're more likely to see couplers made from two rubber cups designed to engulf the mouthpiece and earpiece of a telephone handset. This latter form of acoustic coupler persists because it allows modems to be readily connected and disconnected from non-modular telephones—those that you cannot unplug to directly attach a modem. This connectability is especially important for roving computers that may be called upon to tie their internal modems into non-modular pay station and hotel room telephones.

Although acoustic couplers were normally used only at low speeds—typically ordinary Bell 103 communications at 300 baud—high-speed acoustic couplers that operate at speeds up to 9600 bits per second are available.

Chapter 20

Networking

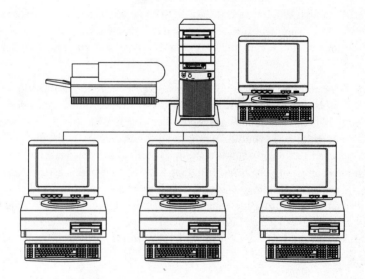

Networks link from two to thousands of PCs together, enabling them to share files and resources. In addition, a network can centralize the management of a huge base of PCs, providing one location for coordinated security, backup, upgrades, and control.

By themselves, PCs might never have usurped the role of the mainframe or other large computer systems. Big systems would hold an important business advantage: they are able to link all the workers at a facility. Because the mainframe holds the data (as well as all the computing power) in one centralized location, its storage is easily shared. All workers can have access to the same information and can even work together on projects, communicating with one another through the central computer.

The network provides connectivity that gives the entire web of PCs collective power far beyond that of the mainframe. Anywhere two or more PCs are present, the features and facilities added by a network can make your using PCs easier, more accommodating, and more powerful.

The challenge you face in linking one PC to others is the same as that faced by a child growing up with siblings—it has to learn to share. When kids share, you get more quiet, greater peace of mind, and less bloodshed. When PCs share, you get the convenience of sharing files and other resources, centralized management (including the capability to back up all PCs from one location or to use one PC to back up others), and improved communication between workers in your business.

The drawback to connectivity is that computer networks are even more difficult to understand and manage than a platoon of teenagers. They have their own rules, their own value system, their own hardware needs, even their own language. Just listening in on a conversation between network pros is enough to make you suspect that an alien invasion from the planet Oxy-10 has succeeded. To get even a glimmer of understanding, you need to know your way around layers of standards, architectures, and protocols. Installing a network operating system can take system managers days; deciphering its idiosyncrasies can keep users and operators puzzled for weeks. Network host adapters often prove incompatible with other PC hardware, their required interrupts and I/O addresses locking horns with SCSI boards, port controllers, and other peripherals. And weaving the wiring for a network is like threading a needle while wearing boxing gloves during a cyclone that has blown out the electricity, the candles, and your last rays of hope.

In fact, no one in his right mind would tangle with a network were the benefits not so great. File sharing across the network alone eliminates a major source of data loss, which is duplication of records and out-of-sync file updates. Better still, a network lets you get organized. You can put all your important files in one central location where they are easier to protect, both from disaster and theft. Instead of worrying about backing up half a dozen PCs individually, you can easily handle the chore with one command. Electronic mail can bring order to the chaos of tracking messages and appointments, even in a small office. With network-based e-mail, you can communicate with your coworkers without scattering memo slips everywhere. Sharing a costly laser printer or large hard disk (with some networks, even modems) can cut your capital cost of a computer's equipment by thousands or tens of thousands of dollars. Instead of buying a flotilla of personal laser printers, for example, you can serve everyone's hard copy needs with just one machine.

OSI Reference Model

The biggest issue in building a network is getting everything to work with everything else—in other words, basic compatibility. By its very nature, a network embraces a more diverse array of species than Noah escorted into his ark. Besides different brands of PCs, networks have to have some provisions to accommodate printers, modems, CD-ROM players, fax systems, computers, and workstations that follow their own standards, access to mainframes and remote data bases, cellular systems, and whatever else anyone might want to plug in. Although some of these devices might naturally communicate, other combinations turn cacophony into chaos. Not only are there enough differences in the hardware interfaces to keep you stripping and soldering cables until the next technology comes home, you need to translate command sets, data formats, and even character codes.

In 1984, the International Standards Organization laid out a blueprint to bring order to the nonsense of networking by publishing the *Open Systems Interconnection Reference Model*. The approach was much like that used for PC intercompatibility: layering. Just as a PC has a software layer (the operating system) and a firmware layer (the BIOS) to link your application software to your underlying hardware (the PC), the ISO built a network compatibility system from seven layers ranging from the connecting wire to software applications. These layers define functions and protocols that enable the wide variety of network hardware and software to work together.

The layering defined by the OSI Reference Model provides insight into how the various elements of a network—from the wire running through your office ceiling to the Windows menu of your mail program—fit together and interact. Although few actual networks or network products exactly fit the model (the ISO is working on a complete set of standards), the layers show how networks must be structured and the problems in building a network. The OSI Reference Model has become the standard framework for describing networks.

Physical

The first layer of the OSI Reference Model is the Physical layer that defines the basic hardware of the network, which is the cable that conducts the flow of information between the devices linked by the network. This layer defines not only the type of wire (for example coaxial cable, twisted-pair wire) but the possible lengths and connections of the wire, the signals on the wire, and the interfaces of the cabling system. This is the level at which the device that connects a PC to the network (the network host adapter) is defined.

Data Link

Layer 2 in a network is called the Data Link layer. It defines how information gains access to the wiring system. The Data Link layer defines the basic protocol used in the local network. This is the method used for deciding which PC can send a message over the cable at any given time, the form of the messages, and the transmission method of those messages.

This level defines the structure of the data that is transferred across the network. All data transmitted under a given protocol takes a common form called the packet or network data frame, each of which is a block of data that is strictly formatted and may include destination and source identification as well as error-correction information. All network data transfers are divided into one or more packets, the length of which is carefully controlled.

Breaking network messages into multiple packets enables the network to be shared without interference and interminable waits for access. If you transferred a large file, say a bitmap, across the network in one piece, you might monopolize the entire network for the duration of the transfer. Everyone would have to wait. By breaking all transfers into manageable pieces, everyone gets access in a relatively brief period, making the network more responsive.

Network

Layer 3 in the OSI Reference Model is the Network layer, which defines how the network moves information from one device to another. This layer corresponds to the hardware-interface function BIOS of an individual PC because it provides a common software interface that hides differences in underlying hardware. Software of higher layers can run on any lower layer hardware because of the compatibility this layer affords. Protocols that enable the exchange of packets between different networks operate at this level.

Transport

Layer 4 is for the control data movement across the network. This Transport layer defines how messages are handled, particularly how the network reacts to packets that become lost or other errors that may occur.

Session

Layer 5 of the OSI Reference Model defines the interaction between applications and hardware much as a PC BIOS provides function calls for programs. By using functions defined at this Session layer, programmers can create software that will operate on any of a wide variety of hardware. In other words, the Session layer provides the interface for applications and the network. Among PCs, the most common of these application interfaces is IBM's Network Basic Input/Output System, or NetBIOS.

Presentation

Layer 6, the Presentation layer, provides the file interface between network devices and the PC software. This layer defines the code and format conversions that must take place, so that applications running under a PC operating system, such as DOS, OS/2, or Macintosh System 7, can understand files stored under the network's native format.

Application

Layer 7 is the part of the network that you deal with personally. This Application layer includes the basic services you expect from any network including the capability to deal with files, send messages to other network users through the mail system, and to control print jobs.

Topologies

The topology of a network is the lay of the cables across the land. Most networks involve cables, lots of them, with at least one leading to every PC. Like the proverbial can of worms, they can crawl off in every direction and create chaos.

If PCs are to talk to one another, however, somehow the cables must come together so that signals can move from one PC to another. Networks operate at high frequencies, and their signals behave like the transmissions of radio stations. The network waves flash down the wires, bounce around, and ricochet from every splice. The waves themselves stretch and bend, losing their shape and their digital purity.

To work reliably, the network cable must be a carefully controlled environment. It must present a constant impedance to the signal, and every connection must be properly made. Any irregularity increases the chance of noise, interference, and error.

Designers have developed several topologies for PC networks. Most can be reduced to one of three basic layouts: linear, ring, and star. The names describe how the cables run throughout an installation.

Linear

The network with linear cabling has a single backbone, one main cable that runs from one end of the system to the other. Along the way, PCs tap into this backbone to send and receive signals. The PCs link to the backbone with a single cable through which they both send and receive. In effect, the network backbone functions as a data bus, and this configuration is often called a bus topology.

In the typical installation, a wire leads from the PC to the backbone, and a T-connector links the two. The network backbone has a definite beginning and end. In most cases, these ends are terminated with a resistor matching the characteristic impedance of the cable in the background. That is, a 61 ohm network cable will have a 61 ohm termination at either end. These terminations prevent signals from reflecting from the ends of the cable, helping ensure signal integrity.

Ring

The ring topology looks like a linear network that's biting its own tail. The backbone is a continuous loop, a ring, with no end. But the ring is not a single, continuous wire. Instead it is made of short segments daisy-chained from one PC to the next, the last connected, in turn, to the first. Each PC thus has two connections. One wire connects a PC to the PC before it in the ring, and a second wire leads to the next PC in the ring. Signals must traverse through one PC to get to the next, and the signals typically are listened to and analyzed along the way.

Star

Both linear and ring topologies sprawl all over creation. The star topology shines a ray of light into tangled installations. Just as rays blast out from the core of a star, in the star topology connecting cables emanate from a centralized location called a hub, and each cable links a single PC into the network. A popular image for star topology is an old-fashioned wagon wheel—the network server is the hub, the cables are the spokes, and the PCs are ignored in the analogy. Try visualizing them as clumps of mud clinging to the rim (which, depending on your particular network situation, may be an apt metaphor).

In the most popular network systems based on the star topology, each cable is actually twofold. Each has two distinct connections, one for sending data from the hub to an individual PC and one for the PC to send data back to the hub. These paired connections are typically packaged into a single cable.

Star-style networks have become popular because their topology matches that of other office wiring. In the typical office building, the most common wiring is used by telephones and telephone wiring converges at the wiring closet, in which is the PBX (Private Branch Exchange, the telephone switching equipment for a business). Star-style topologies require only a single cable and connection for each device to link to the central location where all cables converge into the network hub.

As distinct as these three topologies seem, they are really not so different. Cut the ring, for example, and the result is a linear system. Or shrink the ring down to a single point, and the result is a star. This confluence is hardly coincidental. All networks must perform the same functions, so you should expect all the varieties to be functionally the same.

Hierarchies

Topology describes only one physical aspect of a network. The connections between the various PCs in a network also can fit one of two logical hierarchies. The alternatives form a class system among PCs. Some networks treat all PCs the same; others elevate particular computers to a special, more important role. Although the network serves the same role in either case, these two hierarchical systems enforce a few differences in how the network is used.

Client-Server

Before PC networks, mainframe computers extended their power to individual desks through terminal connections. By necessity, these mainframe systems put all the computer power in one central location that served the needs of everyone using the system. There simply wasn't any other computer power in the system.

In big companies, this kind of computer system organization became an entrenched part of the corporate bureaucracy. Transferring the structure to PCs was natural. At first, the computer managers merely connected PCs to the mainframe as smarter terminals. The connection schemes were called micro-to-mainframe links.

Eventually, however, some managers discovered that PCs provided more power at substantially less cost than the mainframe, and the actual computing was shifted down to the desktop. The powerful mainframe computer was left to do nothing but supply data (and sometimes program) files to the PCs. Managers needed no large amount of enlightenment to see that even a modestly powerful PC could shuffle files around, and the mainframe was replaced by a PC that could manage the shared storage required by the system. Because the special PC served the needs of the other PCs, it was called a *server*. The corresponding term for the desktop PC workstation is *client*, a carryover from the mainframe days. This form of network link is, consequently, called a client-server hierarchy. Note that the special role of the server gives it more importance but also relegates it to the role of a slave that serves the needs of many masters, the clients. The server in a client-server network runs special software (the network operating system).

The server need not be a PC. Sometimes a mainframe still slaves away at the center of a network. Typically, the server is a special PC more powerful than the rest in the network (notwithstanding that the server's work is less computorially intense than that of the clients it serves). Its most important feature is storage. Because its file space is shared by many—perhaps hundreds—of PCs, it requires huge amounts of mass storage. In addition, the server is designed to be more reliable because all the PCs in the network depend on its proper functioning. If it fails, the entire network suffers.

Most modern servers are designed to be fault tolerant. That is, they will continue to run without interruption despite a fault, such as the failure of a hardware subsystem. Most servers also use the most powerful available microprocessors, not from need, but because the price difference is tiny once the additional ruggedness and storage are factored in—and because most managers think that the single most important PC in a network should be the most powerful.

Peer-to-Peer

The client-server is a royalist system, particularly if you view a nation's leader as a servant of the people rather than a profiteer. The opposite is the true democracy in which every PC is equal. PCs share files and other resources (such as printers) among one another. They share equally, each as the peer of the others, so this scheme is called *peer-to-peer networking.*

Peer-to-peer means that there is no dedicated file server as you would find in big, complex networks. All PCs can have their own, local storage, and each PC is (or can be) granted access to the disk drives and printers connected to the others. In most peer-to-peer schemes, the same DOS commands apply to both the drives local to an individual computer and those accessed remotely through the network. Because most people already know enough about DOS to change drive letters, they can put the network to work almost instantly.

Even in peer-to-peer networks, some PCs are likely to be more powerful than others or have larger disk drives or some such distinction. Some PCs may have only floppy disks and depend on the network to supply the equivalent of hard disk storage. In other words, some PCs are created more equal than others. In fact, it's not unusual for a peer-to-peer network to have a single dominant PC that serves most of the needs of the others. Functionally, the client-server and peer-to-peer architectures are not digitally distinct like black and white but shade into one another.

In a peer-to-peer network, no one PC needs to be particularly endowed with overwhelming mass storage or an incomprehensible network operating system. Each computer connects to the network using simple driver software that makes the resources of the other PCs appear as extra disk drives and printers. There's no monstrous network operating system to deal with, only a few extra entries to each PC's CONFIG.SYS or AUTOEXEC.BAT file. Although someone does have to make decisions in setting up the peer-to-peer network (such as which PCs have access to which drives in other PCs), day-to-day operations usually don't require an administrator.

The peer-to-peer scheme has another advantage: you don't need to buy an expensive file server. Not only will that save cash, it can give you the security of redundancy. The failure of a server puts an entire network out of action. The failure of a network peer only eliminates that peer; the rest of the network continues to operate. And if you duplicate vital files on at least two peers, you'll never have to fear losing data from the crash of a single system.

Alternatives

Certainly everyone doesn't have the need for a network. If you have only one PC, you have nothing to connect together. If you have more than one PC, you probably would like to link them together, but you may be afraid of the work involved.

You have good reason. Even companies with their own computer resource departments typically hire consultants when planning a network. The issues are entirely unlike those of managing individual PCs, and most involve the snarl of wire that's the heart—or at least circulatory system—of the network. For example, the network guru has to worry about such things as coaxial cables, terminations, loop resistance, and (probably) the phases of the moon.

Fortunately with 10Base-T, an entire network can be plug-and-play, linked together with cables you can buy directly. For more complex or permanent installations, 10Base-T lets you take advantage of existing telephone wiring to install the network without blasting holes in walls and ceilings.

Other networking systems aspire to be as easy and inexpensive as 10Base-T.

Ethernet

The progenitor of all of today's networks is the Ethernet system originally developed in the 1970s at the Xerox Corporation's Palo Alto Research Center for linking its workstations to laser printers. The invention of Ethernet is usually credited to Robert Metcalf, who later went on to found 3Com Corporation, an early major supplier of PC networking hardware and software. During its first years, Ethernet was proprietary to Xerox, a technology without a purpose, in a world in which the PC had not yet been invented.

In September 1980, however, Xerox joined with minicomputer maker Digital Equipment Corporation and semiconductor manufacturer Intel Corporation to publish the first Ethernet specification, which later became known as E.SPEC VER.1. The original specification was followed in November 1982, by a revision that has become today's widely used standard, E.SPEC VER.2.

This specification is not what most people call Ethernet, however. In January 1985, the Institute of Electrical and Electronic Engineers published a networking system derived from Ethernet but not identical with it. The result was the IEEE 802.3 specification. Ethernet and IEEE 802.3 share many characteristics—physically, they use the same wiring and connection schemes—but each uses its own packet structure. Consequently, although you can plug host adapters for true Ethernet and IEEE 802.3 together in the same cabling system, the two standards will not be able to talk to one another. Some PC host adapters, however, know how to speak both languages and can exchange packets with either standard.

The basis of Ethernet is a clever scheme for arbitrating access to the central bus of the system. The protocol, formally described as Carrier Sensing, Multiple Access with Collision Detection is often described as being like a party line. It's not. It's much more like polite conversation. All the PCs in the network patiently listen to everything that's going on across the network backbone. Only when there is a pause in the conversation will a new PC begin to speak. And if two or more PCs start to talk at the same time, all become quiet. They will wait for a random interval (and because it is random, each will wait a different interval) and, after the wait, attempt to begin speaking again. One will be lucky and win access to the network. The other, unlucky PCs will hear the first PC blabbing away and wait for another pause.

Access to the network line is not guaranteed in any period by the Ethernet protocol. The laws of probability guide the system, and they dictate that eventually every device that desires access will get it. Consequently, Ethernet is described as a probabilistic access system. As a practical matter, when few devices (compared to the bandwidth of the system) attempt to use the Ethernet system, delays are minimal because all of them trying to talk at one time is unlikely. As demand approaches the capacity of the system, however, the efficiency of probability-based protocol plummets. The size limit of an Ethernet system is not set by the number of PCs but by the amount of traffic; the more packets PCs send, the more contention and the more frustrated attempts.

The Ethernet protocol has many physical embodiments. These can embrace any topology, type of cable, or speed. The IEEE 802.3 specification defines several of these, and assigns a code name to each. Today's most popular Ethernet implementations operate at a raw speed of 10 MHz. That is, the clock frequency of the signals on the Ethernet (or IEEE 802.3) wire is 10 MHz. Actual throughput is lower because packets cannot occupy the full bandwidth of the Ethernet system. Moreover, every packet contains formatting and address data that steals space which could be used for data.

Today's three most popular IEEE 802.3 implementations are 10Base-5, 10Base-2, and 10Base-T. Although daunting at first look, you can remember the names as codes: The first number indicates the operating speed of the system in megahertz; the central word "Base" indicates that Ethernet protocol is the basis of the system; and the final character designates the wire used for the system. The final digit (when numerical) refers to the distance in hundreds of feet the network can stretch, but as a practical matter also specifies the type of cable used. Coincidentally, the number also describes the diameter of the cable; under the 10 MHz 802.3 standard, the "5" stands for a thick coaxial cable that's about one-half inch (five-tenths) of an inch in diameter; the "2" refers to a thinner coaxial cable about two-tenths inch in diameter; the "T" indicates twisted-pair wiring like that used by telephone systems.

Other differences besides cable type separate these Ethernet schemes. The 10Base-5 and 10Base-2 use a linear topology; 10Base-T is built in a star configuration. All three IEEE 802.3 systems operate at the same 10 MHz speed using the same Ethernet protocol, so a single network can tie together all three technologies without the need for such complications as protocol converters. In typical complex installations, thick coaxial cable links far-flung workgroups, each of which is tied together locally with a 10Base-T hub. This flexibility makes IEEE 802.3 today's leading networking choice.

StarLAN is the Ethernet derivative developed by AT&T and sanctioned by the IEEE as 1Base-5 in the 802.3 specification. As you would expect from a networking system designed by a telephone company, it was designed to use unshielded twisted-pair wiring with a star configuration (although nodes can also be daisy-chained) that can take advantage of standard office telephone wiring (where all the wires from a given office or floor converge in a wiring closet). The speed of StarLAN was set at 1 MHz to ensure reliable operation over the inexpensive wiring the system used. Because 10Base-T effectively fills the same wiring niche with 10 times the speed, StarLAN has fallen out of favor.

AppleTalk

Apple Computer developed its own networking scheme for its Macintosh computers. Called AppleTalk, the network is built around an Apple-developed hardware implementation that Apple called LocalTalk. In operation, LocalTalk is similar to Ethernet in that it uses probabilistic access with Carrier Sensing, Multiple Access technology. Instead of after-the-fact collision detection, however, LocalTalk uses collision avoidance. Originally designed for shielded twisted-pair cable, many LocalTalk networks use unshielded twisted-pair telephone wiring. The LocalTalk system is slow, however, with a communication speed of 230.4 KHz (that's about one quarter megahertz).

Token Ring

The major alternative protocol to Ethernet is a concept called token-passing. In this scheme, the token is a coded electronic signal used to control network access. IBM originated the most popular form of this protocol, which after further development was sanctioned by the IEEE as its 802.5 standard. Because this standard requires a ring topology, it is commonly called Token Ring networking.

In a token-passing system, all PCs remain silent until given permission to talk on the network line. They get permission by receiving the token. A single token circulates around the entire network, passed from PC to PC in a closed loop that forms a ring topology. If a PC receives the token and has no packets to give to the network to deliver, it simply passes along the token to the next PC in the ring. If, however, the PC has a packet to send, it links the packet to the token along with the address of the destination PC (or server). All the PCs around the ring then pass this token and packet along until it reaches its destination. The receiving PC strips off the data and puts the token back on the network, tagged to indicate that the target PC has received its packet. The remaining PCs in the network pass the token around until it reaches the original sending PC. The originating PC removes the tag and passes the token along the network to enable another PC to send a packet.

This token-passing method offers two chief benefits, reliability and guaranteed access. Because the token circulates back to the sending PC, it gives a confirmation that the packet was properly received by the recipient. The protocol also ensures that the PC next in line after the sending PC will always be the next one to get the token to enable communication. As the token circulates, it allows each PC to use the network. The token must go all the way around the ring—and give every other PC a chance to use the network—before it returns to any given PC to enable it to use the network again. Access to the network is guaranteed even when network traffic is heavy. No PC can get locked out of the network because of a run of bad luck in trying to gain access.

The original Token Ring specification called for operation at 4 MHz. A revision to the standard allows for operation at 16 MHz. The specification originally required the use of a special four-wire shield twisted-pair cabling, but current standards allow for several types of cabling including unshielded twisted-pair wires.

ARCnet

Another token-passing network system, ARCnet, predates IEEE 802.5 Token Ring. ARCnet was developed in 1977 by Datapoint Corporation. In an ARCnet system, each PC is assigned an eight-bit address from 1 to 255. The token is passed from one PC to the next in numerical order. Each PC codes the token signal with the address of the next address in the network, the network automatically configuring itself so that only active address numbers are used. The number is broadcast on the network so that all PCs receive every token, but only the one with the right address can use it. If the PC receiving the token has a packet to send, it is then allowed to send out the packet. When the packet is received, an acknowledgment is sent back to the originating PC. The PC then passes the token to the next highest address. If the PC that receives the token has no packets to send, it simply changes the address in the token to the next higher value and broadcasts the token.

Because the token is broadcast, the ARCnet system does not require a ring. Instead it uses a simple bus topology that includes star-like hubs. ARCnet hubs are either active or passive. Active hubs amplify the ARCnet signal and act as distribution amplifiers to any number of ports (typically eight). Passive hubs act like simple signal splitters and typically connect up to four PCs. The basic ARCnet system uses coaxial cable. Compared to today's Ethernet systems, it is slow, operating at 2.5 megahertz.

FDDI

Although many publications use the acronym FDDI to refer to any network using optical fibers as the transmission medium, it actually refers to an international networking standard sanctioned by the American National Standards Institute and the International Standards Organization. The initials stand for Fiber Distributed Data Interface. The standard is based on a dual counter-rotating, fiber-optic ring topology operating with a 100 MHz data rate. The FDDI standard permits the connection of up to a maximum of 1000 PCs or other nodes with a distance up to 2 to 3 kilometers between PCs and an entire spread up to 100 kilometers.

Zero-Slot LANs

When you need to connect only a few PCs and you don't care about speed, you have an alternative in several proprietary systems that are lumped together as Zero-Slot LANs. These earn their name from their capability to give you a network connection without requiring you to fill an expansion slot in your PC with a network host adapter. Instead of a host adapter, most Zero-Slot LANs use a port already built into most PCs, the serial port.

Protocols and topologies of Zero-Slot LANs vary with each manufacturer's implementation. Some are built as star-like systems with centralized hubs; others are connected as buses. Nearly all use twisted-pair wiring, although some need only three connections and others use up to eight. The former take advantage of a protocol derived from Ethernet; the latter use the handshaking signals in the serial port for hardware arbitration of access to the network.

The one factor shared by all Zero-Slot LANs is low speed. All are constrained by the maximum speed of the basic PC serial port, which is 115,200 bits per second (or about one-tenth mega-hertz). Lower speeds are often necessary with long reaches of cable because Zero-Slot LAN signals are particularly prone to interference. Serial ports provide only single-ended signals, which are not able to cancel induced noise and interference as is possible with balanced signals.

Cabling

One of the biggest problems faced by network system designers is keeping radiation and interference under control. All wires act as antenna, sending and receiving signals. As frequencies increase and wire lengths increase, the radiation increases. The pressure is on network designers to increase both the speed (with higher frequencies) and reach of networks (with longer cables) to keep up with the increasing demands of industry.

Two strategies are commonly used to combat interference from network wiring. One is the coaxial cable, so called because it has a central conductor surrounded by one or more shields that may be a continuous braid or metalized plastic film. Each shield amounts to a long thin tube, and each shares the same longitudinal axis: the central conductor. The surrounding shield typically operates at ground potential, which prevents stray signals from leaking out of the central conductor or noise seeping in. Because of its shielding, coaxial cable is naturally resistant to radiation. As a result, coax was the early choice for network wiring.

Coaxial cables generally use single-ended signals. That is, only a single conductor, the central conductor of the coaxial cable, carries information. The outer conductor operates at ground potential to serve as a shield. Any voltage that might be induced in the central conductor (to become noise or interference) first affects the outer conductor. Because the outer conductor is at ground potential, it shorts out the noise before it can affect the central conductor. (Noise signals are voltages in excess of ground potential; so, forcing the noise to ground potential reduces its value to zero.)

The primary alternative is twisted-pair wiring, which earns its name from being made of two identical insulated conducting wires that are twisted around one another in a loose double-helix. The most common form of twisted-pair wiring lacks the shield of coaxial cable and is often denoted by the acronym UTP, which stands for unshielded twisted pair.

Most UTP wiring is installed in the form of multi-pair cables with up to several hundred pairs inside a single plastic sheath. The most common varieties have 4 to 25 twisted pairs in a single cable. The pairs inside the cable are distinguished from one another by color coding. The body of the wiring is one color alternating with a thinner band of another color. In the two wires of a given pair, the background and banding color are opposites—that is, one wire will have a white background with a blue band and its mate will have a blue background with a white band. Each pair has a different color code (see Table 20.1). The most common type of UTP cable conforms to the AT&T specification for D-Inside Wire (DIW). The same type of wiring also corresponds to IBM's Type 3 cabling specification for Token Ring networking.

TABLE 20.1. Unshielded Twisted-Pair Color Code

Pair Number	Color Code	Pair Number	Color Code
1	White/Blue	12	Black/Orange
2	White/Orange	13	Black/Green
3	White/Green	14	Black/Brown
4	White/Brown	15	Black/Slate
5	White/Slate	16	Yellow/Blue
6	Red/Blue	17	Yellow/Orange
7	Red/Orange	18	Yellow/Green
8	Red/Green	19	Yellow/Brown
9	Red/Brown	20	Yellow/Slate
10	Red/Slate	21	Violet/Blue
11	Black/Blue	22	Violet/Orange

Pair Number	Color Code	Pair Number	Color Code
23	Violet/Green	25	Violet/Slate
24	Violet/Brown		

Key: First color is the body of the wire; second color is the strips. The mate of the wire pair has the color scheme (body/stripe) reversed.

To minimize radiation and interference, most systems that are based on UTP use differential signals. Each conductor carries the same information at different polarities (plus and minus), and the equipment signal subtracts the signal on one conductor from the other before it is amplified (thus finding the difference between the two conductors and the name of the signal type). Because of the polarity difference of the desired signals on the conductors, subtracting them from one another actually doubles the strength of the signal. Noise that is picked up by the wire, however, appears at about equal strength in both wires. The subtraction thus cancels out the noise. Twisting the pair of wires together helps ensure that each conductor picks up the same noise. In addition, any radiation from the wire tends to cancel itself out because the signals radiated from the two conductors are added together. Again, the twist helps ensure that the two signals are equally radiated.

For extra protection, some twisted-pair wiring is available with shielding. As with coaxial cable, the shielding prevents interference from getting to the signal conductors.

In practical application, twisted-pair wiring has several advantages over coaxial cable. It's cheaper to make and sell. It's more flexible and easier to work with. And zillions of miles of twisted-pair wire are installed in offices around the world (it is telephone wire). On the other hand, coaxial cable holds the advantage when it comes to distance. Coaxial cable provides an environment to signals that's more carefully controlled. In general, its shielding and controlled impedance allow for the handling of higher frequencies, which means that network signals are less likely to blur and lose the sharp edges necessary for unambiguous identification as digital values.

Each major wiring standard has its own cabling requirements. Although the limits set by the standard for each cabling scheme seem modest (up to a 100 or so PCs), these limits apply to only a single network cable. You can link multiple cables together using network concentrators, or you can extend the reach of a single cable over a long range using a repeater, which is simply an amplifier for network signals. The repeater boosts the signal on the network cable (and may offer ports to link together several network buses) without changing the data on the bus.

10Base-5

Under the IEEE 802.3 specification, wiring for 10Base-5 networks uses thick coaxial cable with a characteristic impedance of 50 ohms. The standard permits the bus to be up to 500 meters (1,640 feet) long with a 50 ohm terminating resistor at each end. The special cable used for thick-wire networks is covered with a yellow jacket for normal use and an orange jacket for plenum installation (for example, over a suspended ceiling in an airspace that's used as part of the building ventilation system). Because of this coloring, thick wire is often called yellow cable. It is similar to standard RG-8/U coaxial cable (which is generally black) but has somewhat different electrical characteristics.

Each PC is attached to the network bus through a transceiver, which is most often a wire tape that clamps onto the wire and penetrates through the jacket and shield to make its connection without breaking or stripping the bus. Because of the way it clamps onto the bus and sucks out the signal, this kind of transceiver is often called a vampire tap. Linking the transceiver and the PC is another special cable called the Attached Unit Interface cable. The AUI cable can be up to 50 meters (164 feet) long. Under the IEEE 802.3 specification, you can connect up to 100 transceivers to a single 10Base-5 backbone.

10Base-2

In the IEEE 802.3 scheme of things, 10Base-2 is called thin wire or thinnet. It uses a double-shielded 50 ohm coaxial cable similar to but not identical with RG-58/U, another 50 ohm cable used for a variety of applications including Citizens' Band radio. Under the IEEE specification, the 10Base-2 bus cable should not exceed a length of 185 meters (about 600 feet) but some host adapter manufacturers allow runs of up to 300 meters (about 1,000 feet).

Taps into the 10Base-2 bus require transceivers, but 10Base-2 network host adapters incorporate integral transceivers. The cabling then takes the form of a daisy-chain using T-connectors on the host adapter. A T-connector plugs into a single jack on the back of the network host adapter. One cable of the network bus plugs into one leg of the T-connector on the host adapter, and another cable plugs into a second T-connector leg and runs to the next host adapter in the network. The network bus consequently comprises multiple short segments. All connections to it are made using BNC connectors. In place of a network cable at the first and last transceivers in a backbone, you plug in a 50 ohm cable terminator instead. You can connect up to 30 transceivers to a single 10Base-2 backbone.

10Base-T

Because of its star topology, 10Base-T networks use point-to-point wiring. Each network cable stretches from one point (a PC or other node) to another at the hub. The hub has a wiring jack for each network node; each PC host adapter has a single connector.

The basic 10Base-T system uses unshielded twisted-pair cable. In most permanently installed networks, wall jacks that conform to the eight-wire RJ-45 design link to standard D-Inside Wire buried inside walls and above ceilings. To link between the wall jacks and the jacks on 10Base-T host adapters, you should use special round modular cables. Ordinary flat telephone wires do not twist their leads and are not suitable to high-speed network use.

Although 10Base-T uses eight-wire (four-pair cabling) and eight-pin connectors, only four wires actually carry signals. Normally the wires between hub and host adapter use straight-through wiring. The PC transmits on pins 2 and 1 and receives on pins 6 and 3 (the first number being the positive side of the connection). Patching between hubs may require cross-over cables that link pins 1 to 3 and 2 to 6. Figure 20.1 shows the connections for both straight-through and cross-over 10Base-T cables.

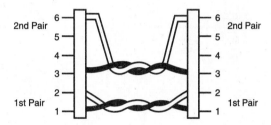

FIGURE 20.1. 10Base-T connections.

The 10Base-T specifications enable the entire cable run between hub and host adapter to be no more than 100 meters (about 325 feet). This distance includes the cable inside the wall as well as the leads between the hub and building wiring and between the node and building wiring. Only one PC or node can be connected to each hub jack, but the number of PCs that can be connected to a single hub is limited only by the number of jacks on the hub. Most 10Base-T hubs provide a thin or thick wire connector for linking to other hubs, concentrators, or repeaters.

Chapter 21
Mass Storage Systems

Mass storage is where you put the data that you need to keep at hand but which will not fit into memory. Designed to hold and retrieve megabytes at a moment's notice, mass storage traditionally has been the realm of magnetic disks, but other technologies and formats now serve specialized purposes and await their chances to move into the mainstream.

The difference between genius and mere intelligence is storage. The quick-witted react fast, but the true genius can call upon memories, experiences, and knowledge to find real answers. PCs are no different. Putting a fast microprocessor in your PC would be meaningless without a means to store programs and data for current and future use. Mass storage is the key to giving your PC the long-term memory that it needs.

Essentially an electronic closet, mass storage is where you put information that you don't want to constantly hold in your hands but that you don't want to throw away, either. As with the straw hats, squash rackets, wallpaper tailings, and all the rest of your dimly remembered possessions that pile up out of sight behind the closet door, retrieving a particular item from mass storage can take longer than when you have what you want at hand.

Personal computers use several varieties of mass storage. In most PCs, the primary mass storage mediums are the hard disk drive and, to a lesser extent, the floppy disk drive—both of which are based on magnetic recording technology. For specialized storage, other technologies also are becoming prominent; primary among them are laser-based optical systems. For the mass storage of data you need, streaming and cassette tape drives are often the leading choices.

All of these media share the defining characteristics of mass storage. They deal with data en masse in that they store thousands and millions of bytes at a time. They also store that information on-line. To earn their huge capacities, the mass storage system moves the data out of the direct control of your PC's microprocessor. Instead of being held in your computer's memory where each byte can be accessed directly by your system's microprocessor, mass storage data requires two steps to use. First, the information must be moved from the mass storage device into your system's memory. Then that information can be accessed by the microprocessor.

Mass storage can be on-line storage, instantly accessible by your microprocessor's commands, or off-line storage, requiring some extra intervention (such as you sliding a cartridge into a drive) for your system to get the bytes that it needs. Sometimes, the term near-line storage is used to refer to systems in which information isn't instantly available but can be put into instant reach by microprocessor command. The jukebox—an automatic mechanism that selects CD-ROM cartridges (sometimes tape cartridges)—is the most common example.

Moving bytes from mass storage to memory determines how quickly stored information can be accessed. In practical on-line systems, the time required for this access ranges from less than 0.01 second in the fastest hard disks to 1000 seconds in some tape systems, spanning a range of 100,000 or five orders of magnitude.

By definition, the best off-line storage systems have substantially longer access times than the quickest on-line systems. Even with fast-access disk cartridges, the minimum access time for off-line data is measured in seconds because of the need to find and load a particular cartridge. The slowest on-line and the fastest off-line storage system speeds, however, may overlap because the time to ready an off-line cartridge can be substantially shorter than the period required to locate needed information written on a long on-line tape.

Various mass storage systems span other ranges as well as speeds. Storage capacity reaches from as little as the 160 kilobytes of the single-sided floppy disk to the multiple gigabytes accommodated by helical tape systems. Costs run from less than $100 to more than $10,000.

The best way to put these huge ranges into perspective is to examine the technologies that underlie them. All mass storage systems are unified by a singular principal—they use some kind of mechanical motion to separate and organize each bit of information they store. To retain each bit, these systems make some kind of physical change to the storage medium—burning holes in it, blasting bits into oblivion, changing its color, or altering a magnetic field.

Magnetic Storage

Magnetic storage media have long been the favored choice for computer mass storage. The primary attraction of magnetic storage is nonvolatility. That is, unlike most electronic or solid-state storage systems, magnetic fields require no periodic addition of energy to maintain their state once they are set.

Magnetism

The issue is permanence. Magnetic fields have the wonderful property of being static and semi-permanent. On their own, they don't move or change. The electricity used by electronic circuits is just the opposite. It is constantly on the go and seeks to dissipate itself as quickly as possible. The difference is fundamental. Magnetic fields are set up by the spins of atoms physically locked in place. Electric charges are carried by mobile particles—mostly electrons—that not only refuse to stay in place but also are individually resistant to predictions of where they are or are going.

Given the right force in the right amount, however, magnetic spins can be upset, twisted from one orientation to another. Because magnetic fields are amenable to change rather than being entirely permanent, magnetism is useful for data storage. After all, if a magnetic field were permanent and unchangeable, it would present no means of recording information. If it couldn't be changed, nothing about it could be altered to reflect the addition of information.

At the elemental particle level, magnetic spins are eternal, but taken collectively, they can be made to come and go. A single spin can be oriented in only one direction, but in virtually any direction. If two adjacent particles spin on opposite directions, they cancel one another out when viewed from a larger, macroscopic perspective.

Altering those spin orientations takes a force of some kind, and that's the key to making magnetic storage work. That force can make an alteration to a magnetic field, and after the field has changed, it will keep its new state until some other force acts upon it.

The force that most readily changes one magnetic field is another magnetic field. (Yes, some permanent magnets can be demagnetized just by heating them sufficiently, but the demagnetization is actually an effect of the interaction of the many minute magnetic fields of the magnetic material.)

Despite their different behavior in electronics and storage systems, magnetism and electricity are manifestations of the same underlying elemental force. Both are electromagnetic phenomena. One result of that commonalty makes magnetic storage particularly desirable to electronics designers—magnetic fields can be created by the flow of electrical energy. Consequently, evanescent electricity can be used to create and alter semipermanent magnetic fields.

When set up, magnetic fields are essentially self-sustaining. They require no energy to maintain, because they are fundamentally a characteristic displayed by the minute particles that make up the entire universe (at least according to current physical theories). On the submicroscopic scale of elemental particles, the spins that form magnetic fields are, for the most part, unchangeable and unchanging. Nothing is normally subtracted from them—they don't give up energy even when they are put to work. They can affect other electromagnetic phenomena, for example, used in mass to divert the flow of electricity. In such a case, however, all the energy in the system comes from the electrical flow—the magnetism is a gate, but the cattle that escape from the corral are solely electrons.

The magnetic fields that are useful in storage systems are those large enough to measure and effect changes on things that we can see. This magnetism is the macroscopic result of the sum of many microscopic magnetic fields, many elemental spins. Magnetism is a characteristic of submicroscopic particles. (Strictly speaking, in modern science magnetism is made from particles itself, but we don't have to be quite so particular for the purpose of understanding magnetic computer storage.)

Magnetic Materials

Three chemical elements are magnetic—iron, nickel, and cobalt. The macroscopic strength as well as other properties of these magnetic materials can be improved by alloying them, together and with nonmagnetic materials, particularly rare earths like samarium.

Many particles at the molecular level have their own intrinsic magnetic fields. At the observable (macroscopic) level, they do not behave like magnets because their constituent particles are organized—or disorganized—randomly so that in bulk, the cumulative effects of all their magnetic fields tend to cancel out. In contrast, the majority of the minute magnetic particles of a permanent magnet are oriented in the same direction. The majority prevails, and the material has a net magnetic field.

Some materials can be magnetized. That is, their constituent microscopic magnetic fields can be realigned so that they reveal a net macroscopic magnetic field. For instance, by subjecting a piece of soft iron to a strong magnetic field, the iron will become magnetized.

Magnetic Storage

If that strong magnetic field is produced by an electromagnet, all the constituents of a magnetic storage system become available. Electrical energy can be use to alter a magnetic field, which can be later detected. Put a lump of soft iron within the confines of an unenergized electromagnet. Any time you return, you can determine whether the electromagnet has been energized in your absence by checking for the presence of a magnetic field in the iron. In effect, you have stored exactly one bit of information.

To store more, you need to be able to organize the information. You need to know the order of the bits. In magnetic storage systems, information is arranged physically by the way data travel serially in time. Instead of being electronic blips that flicker on and off as the milliseconds tick off, magnetic pulses are stored like a row of dots on a piece of paper—a long chain with beginning and end. This physical arrangement can be directly translated to the temporal arrangement of data used in a serial transmission system just by scanning the dots across the paper. The first dot becomes the first pulse in the serial stream, and each subsequent dot follows neatly in the data stream as the paper is scanned.

Instead of paper, magnetic storage systems use one or another form of media—generally a disk or long ribbon of plastic tape—covered with a magnetically reactive mixture. The form of medium directly influences the speed at which information can be retrieved from the system.

Digital Magnetic Systems

Computer mass storage systems differ in principle and operation from tape systems used for audio and video recording. Whereas audio and video cassettes record analog signals on tape; computers use digital signals.

In the next few years, this situation will likely change as digital audio and video tape recorders become increasingly available. Eventually, the analog audio and video tape will become historical footnotes, much as the analog vinyl phonograph record was replaced by the all-digital compact disc.

In analog systems, the strength of the magnetic field written on a tape varies in correspondence with the signal being recorded. The intensity of the recorded field can span a range of more than six orders of magnitude. Digital systems generally use a code that relies on patterns of pulses, and all the pulses have exactly the same intensity.

The technological shift from analog to digital is rooted in some of the characteristics of digital storage that make it the top choice where accuracy is concerned. Digital storage resists the intrusion of noise that inevitably pollutes and degrades analog storage. Every time a copy is made of an analog recording, the noise that accompanies the desired signal essentially doubles because the background noise of the original source is added to the background noise of the new recording medium; however, the desired signal does not change. This addition of noise is necessary to preserve the nuances of the analog recording—every twitch in the analog signal adds information to the whole. The analog system cannot distinguish between noise and nuance. In digital recording, however, there's a sharp line between noise and signal. Noise below the digital threshold can be ignored without losing the nuances of the signal. Consequently, a digital recording system can eliminate the noise built up in making copies. Moreover, noise can creep into analog recordings as the storage medium deteriorates; whereas the digital system can ignore most of the noise added by age. In fact, properly designed digital systems can even correct minor errors that get added to their signals.

Saturation

Digital recordings avoid noise because they ignore all strength variations of the magnetic field except the most dramatic. They just look for the unambiguous "it's either there or not" style of digital pulses of information. Analog systems achieve their varying strengths of field by aligning the tiny molecular magnets in the medium. A stronger electromagnetic field causes a greater percentage of the fields of these molecules to line up with the field, almost in direct proportion to the field strength, to produce an analog recording. Because digital systems need not worry about intermediate levels of signal, they can lay down the strongest possible field that the tape can hold. This level of signal is called saturation because much as a saturated sponge can suck up no more water, the particles on the tape cannot produce a stronger magnetic field.

Although going from no magnetic field to a saturated field would seem to be the widest discrepancy possible in magnetic recording—and therefore the least ambiguous and most suitable for digital information—this contrast is not the greatest possible or easiest to achieve. Magnetic systems attempt to store information as densely as possible, trying to cram the information in so that every magnetic particle holds one data bit. Magnetic particles are extremely difficult to demagnetize—but the polarity of their magnetic orientation is relatively easy to change. Digital magnetic systems exploit this capability to change polarity and record data as it shifts between the orientations of the magnetic fields of the particles on the tape. The difference between the tape being saturated with a field in one direction and the tape being saturated with a field in the opposite direction is the greatest contrast possible in a magnetic system and is exploited by nearly all of today's digital magnetic storage systems.

Coercivity

One word that you may encounter in the description of a magnetic medium is *coercivity*, a term that describes how strongly a magnetic field resists change, which translates into how strong of a magnetic field a particular medium can store. Stronger stored fields are better because the more intense field stands out better against the random background noise that is present in any storage medium. Because a higher coercivity medium resists change better than a low coercivity material, it also is less likely to change or degrade because of the effects of external influences. Of course, a higher coercivity and its greater resistance to change means that a recording system requires a more powerful magnetic field to maximally magnetize the medium. Equipment must be particularly designed to take advantage of high-coercivity materials.

With hard disks, which characteristically mate the medium with the mechanisms for life, matching the coercivity of a medium with the recording equipment is permanently handled by the manufacturer. The two are matched permanently when a drive is made. Removable media devices—floppy disks, tape cartridges, cassettes, etc.—pose more of a problem. If media are interchangeable and have different coercivities, you face the possibility of using the wrong media in a particular drive. Such problems often occur with floppy disks, particularly when you want to skimp and use cheaper double-density media in high-density or extra-density drives.

Moreover, the need for a matching drive and medium makes upgrading a less-than-simple matter. Obtaining optimum performance requires that changes in media be matched by hardware upgrades. Even when better media are developed, they may not deliver better results with existing equipment.

The unit of measurement for coercivity is the Oersted. As storage media have been miniaturized, the coercivity of the magnetic materials as measured in Oersteds has generally increased. The greater intrinsic field strength makes up for the smaller area upon which data are recorded. With higher coercivities, more information can be squeezed into the tighter confines of the newer storage formats. For example, old 5.25-inch floppy disks had a coercivity of 300 Oersteds. Today's high-density 3.5-inch floppies have coercivities of 750 Oersteds. Similarly, the coercivities of the tapes used in today's high-capacity quarter-inch cartridges are greater than that of the last generation. Older standards used 550 Oersted media; data cartridges with capacities in excess of 1.5 gigabytes and minicartridges with capacities beyond 128 megabytes require 900-Oersted tape. Although invisible to you, the coercivities of tiny modern hard disk drives are much higher than big old drives.

Coercivity is a temperature-dependent property. As the temperature of a medium increases, its resistance to magnetic change declines. That's one reason you can demagnetize an otherwise permanent magnet by heating it red hot. Magnetic media dramatically shift from being un-changeable to changeable—meaning a drop in coercivity—at a material-dependent temperature called the *Curie temperature*. Magneto-optical recording systems take advantage of this coercivity shift by using a laser beam to heat a small area of magnetic medium that is under the influence of a magnetic field otherwise not strong enough to affect the medium. At room temperature, the media used by magneto-optical systems have coercivities on the order of 6000 Oersteds; when heated by a laser, that coercivity falls to a few hundred Oersteds. Because of this dramatic change in coercivity, the magnetic field applied to the magneto-optical medium changes only the area heated by the laser above its Curie temperature (rather than the whole area under the magnetic influence). Because a laser can be tightly focused to a much smaller spot than is possible with traditional disk read-write heads, using such a laser-boosted system allows data to be defined by tinier areas of recording medium. A disk of a given size thus can store more data when its magnetic storage is optically assisted. Such media are resistant to the effects of stray magnetic fields (which may change low coercivity fields) as long as they are kept at room temperature.

Retentivity

Another term that appears in the descriptions of magnetic media is retentivity, which measures how well a particular medium retains or remembers the field that it is subjected to. Although magnetic media are sometimes depended upon to last forever—think of the master tapes of phonograph records—the stored magnetic fields begin to degrade as soon as they have been recorded. A higher retentivity ensures a longer life for the signals recorded on the medium.

No practical magnetic material has perfect retentivity; however, the random element of modern physical theories ensures that. Even the best hard disks slowly deteriorate with age, showing an increasing number of errors as time passes after data has been written. To avoid such deterioration of so-called permanent records, many computer professionals believe that magnetically stored recordings should be periodically refreshed. For example, they exercise tapes stored in mainframe computer libraries periodically (in intervals from several months to several years depending on the personal philosophy and paranoia of the person managing the storage). Although noticeable degradation may require several years (perhaps a decade or more), these tape caretakers do not want to stake their data—and their jobs—on media written long ago.

If you're worried about the impermanence of magnetic recording, you can do the same thing the professionals do—refresh your storage. You can back up your data, restore your hard disk, copy floppy disks, or simply make new backup tapes.

Hard disks, the storage medium that most people depend on and worry about, take an extra step to completely refresh. After you back up your hard disk, you should low-level format it, if you have a drive that allows low-level formatting. Only older drives with device-level interfaces, such as ST506 and ESDI, benefit from (and even permit) low-level reformatting. These drives also are the ones most likely to benefit from reformatting.

Modern hard disks that use the system-level AT or SCSI interfaces make the disk formatting inaccessible to PC software. They are permanently low-level formatted during manufacture and have retentivities high enough to maintain their format integrity throughout their useful lives.

If you have an older disk, you need to low-level reformat your older drive instead of issuing a simple DOS FORMAT command, because only low-level formatting writes to the complete disk surface. DOS formatting affects only the data storage areas of a hard disk. The low-level format process writes address marks on the disk that also can deteriorate with age. When one of these sector markings inadvertently changes, you should see a `Sector Not Found` or similar error that makes files impossible to read. Rewriting them with a low-level format can rejuvenate your cantankerous old disk.

After you low-level format your older disk, partition it using DOS's FDISK command. Finally, restore all of your files.

Several hard disk utility packages have special nondestructive, low-level formatting procedures directly aimed at hard disk rejuvenation. These work by copying all the data stored on a disk track to another location on the disk, which low-level reformats the original sector to refresh it (including its sector identification markings) and then rewrites the original data back to the track. The advantage of these systems is convenience. Although they still recommend that you make a full disk backup before running the disk rejuvenation routine, they relieve you of the need to make a full restoration of the backup (unless in the rare case that something goes wrong with the rejuvenation process). As with the manual rejuvenation procedure, these programs usually work only with hard disk drives that use device-level interfaces.

Flux Transitions

The ones and zeroes of digital information are not normally represented by the absolute direction in which the magnetic field is oriented, but by a change from one orientation to another so that they can take advantage of the most easily detected maximal magnetic change—from saturation in one direction to saturation in the other. These dramatic changes are termed flux transitions because the magnetic field or flux makes a transition between each of its two allowed states. In the very simplest magnetic recording systems, the occurrence of a flux transition would be the equivalent of a digital one; no transition would be a digital zero.

The system must know when to expect a flux transition, or it would never know that it had missed one. Somehow the magnetic medium and the recording system must be synchronized with one another so that the system knows the point at which a flux transition should occur or not. Instead of simple bit-for-bit recording, digital magnetic storage requires an elaborate coding system to keep the data straight.

Data Coding

Certainly, assigning a single flux transition the job of storing a digital bit could be made to work, but this obvious solution is hardly the optimal one. For instance, to prevent errors, a direct one-to-one correspondence of flux-to-data would require that the pulse train on the recording medium be exactly synchronized with the expectations of the circuitry reading the data, perhaps by carefully adjusting the speed of the medium to match the expected data rate. A mismatch would result in all of the data read or written being in error. It might take several spins of the disk—each spin lasting more than a dozen milliseconds—to get back in sync.

By including extra flux transitions on the disk to help define the meaning of each flux change on a magnetic medium, you could eliminate the need for exact speed control or other physical means of synchronizing the stored data. All popular magnetic recording systems use this expedient to store data asynchronously. However, all of these asynchronous recording schemes also impose a need for control information to help make sense from the unsynchronized flux transition pulse train.

Single-Density Recording

In one of the earliest magnetic digital recording schemes called Frequency Modulation, or FM recording, the place in which a flux transition containing a digital bit was going to occur was marked by an extra transition called a clock bit. The clock bits form a periodic train of pulses that enables the system to be synchronized. The existence of a flux change between those corresponding to two clock bits indicated a digital 1, and no flux change between clocks indicated a digital 0.

The FM system requires a reasonably loose frequency tolerance. That is, the system could reliably detect the presence or absence of pulse bits between clock bits even if the clock frequency was not precise. In addition, the bandwidth of the system is quite narrow, so circuit tolerances are not critical. The disadvantage of the system is that two flux changes were needed to record each bit of data, the least-dense practical packing of data on disk.

Initial digital magnetic storage devices used the FM technique, and for years it was the prevailing standard. After improvements in data packing were achieved, FM became the point of reference, often termed single-density recording.

Double-Density Recording

Modified Frequency Modulation recording (MFM) or double-density recording was once the most widely used coding system for PC hard disks and is still used by many PC floppy disk drives. Double-density recording eliminates the hard clock bits of single-density to pack information on the magnetic medium twice as densely.

Instead of clock bits, digital 1s are stored as a flux transition and 0s as the lack of a transition within a given period. To prevent flux reversals from occurring too far apart, an extra flux reversal is always added between consecutive 0s.

Group Coded Recording

Even though double-density recording essentially packs every flux transition with a bit of data, it's not the most dense way of packing information on the disk. Other data coding techniques can as much as double the information stored in a given system as compared to double-density recording.

FM and MFM share a common characteristic, a one-to-one correspondence between bits of data and the change recorded on the disk. Although such a correspondence is the obvious way to encode information, it is not the only way. Moreover, the strict correspondence does not always make the most efficient use of the storage medium.

The primary alternative way of encoding data is to map groups of bits to magnetic patterns on the magnetic storage medium. Encoding information in this way is called Group Coded Recording or GCR.

On the surface, group coding appears like a binary cipher. Just as in the secret codes used by simplistic spies in which each letter of the alphabet corresponds to another, group coding reduced to an absurdity would make a pattern like 0101 record on a disk as a pattern of flux transitions like TTNT where T is a transition and N is no transition. Just as simple translations buy the spy little secrecy (such transpositional codes can be broken in minutes by anyone with a rudimentary knowledge of ciphering), they do little for the storage system. Where they become valuable is in using special easy-to-record patterns of flux transitions for each data group, typically with more transitions than there are bits in the data group. This technique succeeds in achieving higher real densities because the real limit on data storage capacity is the spacing of flux transitions in the magnetic medium. The characteristics of the magnetic medium, the speed at which the disk spins, and the design of the disk read-write head together determine the minimum and maximum spacing of the flux changes in the medium. If the flux changes are too close together, the read-write head might not be able to distinguish between them; if they are too far apart, they cannot be reliably detected.

By tinkering with the artificial restraints on data storage, more information can be packed within the limits of flux transition spacing in the medium.

Run Length Limited, or RLL, is one special case of Group Coded Recording designed to use a complex form of data manipulation to fit more information in the storage medium without exceeding the range limits of its capability to handle flux transitions. In the most common form of RLL, termed 2,7, each byte of data is translated into a pattern of 16 flux transitions.

Although this manipulation requires twice the number of flux transition bits to store a given amount of information, it has the virtue that only a tiny fraction of the total number of 16-bit codes is needed to unambiguously store all the possible eight-bit data codes. There are 256 eight-bit codes and 65,536 sixteen-bit codes. Consequently, the engineer designing the system has a great range of 16-bit codes to choose from for each byte of data. If he's particularly astute, he can find patterns of flux translations that are particularly easy to record on the disk. In the 2,7 RLL system, the 16-bit patterns are chosen so that between two and seven digital zeroes are between each set of digital ones in the resulting 16-bit data stream of flux transitions. The 16-bit code patterns that do not enforce the 2,7 rule are made illegal and never appear in the data stream that goes to the magnetic storage device.

Although the coding scheme requires twice as many bits to encode its data, the pulses in the data stream better fit within the flux transition limits of the recording medium. In fact, the 2,7 RLL code ensures that flux transitions will be three times farther apart than in double-density recording, because only the digital ones cause flux changes, and they are always spaced at least three binary places apart. Although there are twice as many code bits in the data stream because of the 8-to-16 bit translation, their corresponding flux transitions will be three times closer together on the magnetic medium while still maintaining the same spacing as would be produced by MFM. The overall gain in storage density achieved by 2,7 RLL over MFM is 50 percent.

The disadvantage of the greater recording density is that much more complex control electronics and wider bandwidth electronics in the storage device are required to handle the higher data throughput.

Advanced RLL

A more advanced RLL coding system improves not only the storage density that can be achieved on a disk but also is more tolerate of old-fashioned disks. This newer system differs from 2,7 RLL in that it uses a different code that changes the bit pattern so that the number of sequential zeros is between three and nine. This system, known for obvious reasons as 3,9 RLL or Advanced RLL still uses an 8- to 16-bit code translation, but it ensures that digital ones will never be closer than every four bits. As a result, it allows data to be packed into flux transitions four times denser. The net gain, allowing for the loss in data translation, amounts to 100 percent. Information can be stored about twice as densely with 3,9 RLL as ordinary double-density recording techniques.

This seemingly extraordinary data packing capability is a result of the various artificial limits enforced in most data storage systems. Until recently, most storage devices were designed for double-density recording, and they followed tightly defined interface standards for the connections between themselves and their control electronics. However, new interfacing schemes for hard disks isolate the data coding from the stream of data sent to the computer host. Drive manufacturers are thus free to use whatever form of data coding they like, and neither you nor your PC ever know the difference. Consequently, with modern hard disk drives, the form of data coding used is rarely revealed (unless you take a critical look at the manufacturer's specification sheet). The information is irrelevant when you use an advanced disk interface.

Data Compression

In group coding, the correspondence between each bit pattern in the input data and the flux transitions represented by it is independent of all the other bit patterns in the data stream. Each pattern directly corresponds to its own pattern of flux transitions. The group coding system can mindlessly match bit pattern for flux pattern to achieve the optimal storage density of each byte of data.

But group coding does not represent the most efficient way of squeezing information into a storage medium. Many of the bytes in a stream of data are redundant. Their information content could be represented in some other manner using many fewer bytes. Group coding seeks to represent the stream of individual bytes without regard to content, simply ensuring each pattern can be faithfully reproduced. It does nothing to guarantee the actual information is encoded in the data stream as efficiently as possible.

In contrast to the local view taken by the group-coding mechanism, data compression systems take a global view. By examining the patterns of bytes rather than the bit patterns inside each byte, the compression system seeks to find patterns that can be more efficiently represented. The goal of the data compression system is to eliminate redundancy, separating the bulk from the content. In effect, the compression system squeezes the air out of the data stream. Data compression can reduce fat files into their slimmest possible representation which can later, through a decompression process, be reconstituted into their original form.

Most compression systems work by reducing recurrent patterns in the data stream into short tokens. For example, the two-byte pattern "at" could be coded as a single byte such as "@," cutting the storage requirement in half. Most compression systems don't permanently assign tokens to bit patterns but instead make the assignments on the fly. They work on individual blocks of data one at a time, starting afresh with each block. Consequently, the patterns stored by the tokens of one block may be entirely different from those used in the next block. The key to decoding the patterns from the tokens is included as part of the data stream.

Disk compression systems put data compression technology to work by increasing the apparent capacity of your disk drives. Generally, they work by creating a virtual drive with expanded capacity, which you can access as though it were a normal (but larger) disk drive. The compression system automatically takes care of compressing and decompressing your data as you work with it. The information is stored in compressed form on your physical disk drive, which is hidden from you.

The compression ratio compares the resultant storage requirements to those required by the uncompressed data. For example, a compression ratio of 90 percent would reduce storage requirements by 90 percent. The compressed data could be stored in 10 percent of the space required by its original form. Most data compression systems achieve about a 50 percent compression ratio on the mix of data found that most people use.

Because the compression ratio varies with the kind of data you store, the ultimate capacity of a disk that uses compression is impossible to predict. The available capacity reported by DOS on a compressed drive is only an estimate based on the assumed compression ratio of the system. You can change this assumption to increase the reported remaining capacity of your disk drive, but the actual remaining capacity (which depends on the data you store, not the assumption) will not change.

Compression Implementations

Compression is a data transformation much like all the other manipulations made by a microprocessor. Consequently, an ordinary software program can convert your PC's microprocessor into an excellent data compressor.

Such software-only compression systems like that built into MS DOS Versions 6.0 and later (and upgrade PC DOS Versions 6.1 and later) can be used to increase disk or tape capacity. Some software compression systems work as software drivers. They intercept the data stream headed for your hard disk, reroute it through a compression algorithm run by your PC's microprocessor, and pass the result to your disk instead of the original data. When the compressed data is later read, the compressed data stream is captured, its bytes processed by a complementary decompression algorithm, and the results passed to your application software.

With older commercial software-only disk compression systems, these software drivers loaded through your system's CONFIG.SYS and AUTOEXEC.BAT files. This arrangement made the operation of the compression system and your PC confusing. The designers of the compression systems tried to make their disk compression invisible. Because of the way that DOS was designed, the only way the disk compression device driver could create a compressed drive was to give it a new name (drive letter). The disk compression software automatically switched the letter of the compressed drive with the letter assigned to your physical boot drive. The larger capacity compressed drive thus appeared to be drive C: (your boot drive), but your boot drive was actually hidden under some other name. Your CONFIG.SYS and AUTOEXEC.BAT files had to remain uncompressed for DOS to read and load them so that it could load the drivers to read the compressed parts of your disk drives. Although you expected to find these files on your boot drive (nominally drive C:), the files were really on the hidden physical drive.

The real solution was to change the structure of DOS, which Microsoft did with Version 6.0. Before MS DOS 6.0 reads your PC's CONFIG.SYS file, it checks for another configuration file, RVSPACE.BIN, which holds the disk compression driver. If present, this driver gets loaded first, so the compression system is operational even before DOS reads your CONFIG.SYS file. As a result, your CONFIG.SYS is stored on the virtual compressed drive in compressed format, and you access it the same way you would any file. (Your physical drive is still renamed something else, usually Drive H:, but you never need to access it.)

The advantage of software-only compression is that you pay for nothing other than the program—nothing if you rely on a recent version of DOS—yet you almost miraculously get two times more storage space. As with any software, however, software-only disk compression imposes additional system overhead. In older PCs with 386 and earlier microprocessors, this overhead can be sufficient to slow disk response. You can take a load off your older microprocessor hardware-based compression using a compression coprocessor board. The coprocessor substitutes its power for that of your microprocessor in compression operations, eliminating the performance handicap of software compression.

Some hard disk manufacturers have incorporated device-level compression into some of their products. This technology moves the compression coprocessor from an expansion board to the disk drive. Such disks can store more information than their resources would otherwise allow. Because the compression circuitry is part of the drive and automatically fits in the middle of the data stream, there's no need for software drivers to make this form of compression work. Unlike ordinary software or hardware compression that requires driver software limiting its use to a specific operating system, device-level compression will work with any operating system. All it requires is basic hardware compatibility: an interface into which you can plug in the drive.

Software, coprocessor (hardware), and device-level compression use essentially the same compression methods. As a result, using more than one of these methods is counterproductive. After you have compressed data, you cannot squeeze it again (at least using the same algorithm).

Compression has proven to be such a valuable technology that it is used in other ways besides increasing disk storage. For example, advanced modem protocols often include data compression to increase throughput levels. In addition, file archiving software also takes advantage of compression to more effectively use your disk's space.

File archiving software differs from ordinary disk compression in several ways. It is not automatic; you manually select the files you want to archive and compress. The archiving software does not work on the fly but instead executes upon your command. It compresses files individually but can package several files together into a single archive file. Archive files are stored as ordinary DOS files but can be read or executed only after they have been uncompressed.

Because these archiving systems do not compress on the fly, they can spend extra time to optimize their compression—for example trying several compression algorithms to find the most successful one. They can often achieve higher compression ratios than standard disk compression software. (Because they are time insensitive, these programs can try more complex compression methods and avoid the rule that a compressed file can be compressed no further.)

Lossless Versus Lossy Compression

Most compression systems assume that you want to get back every byte and every bit that you store. You don't want numbers disappearing from your spreadsheets or commands from your programs. You assume that decompressing the compressed data will yield everything you started with—without losing a bit. The processes that deliver that result are called lossless compression systems.

Sometimes, however, your data may contain more detail than you need. For example, you might scan a photo with a true-color 24-bit scanner and display it on an ordinary VGA system with a color range of only 256 hues. All the precise color information in your scan is wasted on your display, and the substantial disk space you use for storing it could be put to better use.

Analog images converted to digital form and analog audio recordings digitized often contain subtle nuances beyond the perception of most people. Some data reduction schemes called lossy compression systems ignore these fine nuances. The reconstituted data does not exactly replicate the original. For viewing or listening, the restored data is often good enough. Because lossy compression systems work faster than lossless schemes and because their resulting compression ratios are higher, they are often used in time- and space-sensitive applications—digital image and sound storage.

Sequential and Random Access Media

The original electronic mass storage system was magnetic tape—actually a thin strip of paper upon which a thin layer of refined rust had been glued. Later, the paper gave way to plastic, and the iron oxide coating gave way to a number of improved magnetic particles, based on iron, chrome dioxide, and various mixtures of similar compounds.

Tape Recording

The machine that recorded upon these ribbons was the Magnetophone, the first practical tape recorder, made by the German company Telefunken. From this World War II vintage device, able to capture only analog sounds, tape recording gradually gained the capability to record video and digital data. Today, both data cassettes and streaming tape system are based on the direct offspring of the first tape recorder.

These tape media have a very straightforward design. The tape moves from left to right past a stationary read-write head. When a current is passed through an electromagnetic coil in this head, it creates the magnetic field needed to write data onto the tape.

When the tape is later passed in front of this head, the moving magnetic field generated by the magnetized particles on the tape induces a minuscule current in the head. This current is then amplified and converted into digital data. The write current used in putting data on the tape overpowers whatever fields already exist on the tape, both erasing them and imposing a new magnetic orientation to the particles representing the information to be recorded.

Sequential Media

A fundamental characteristic of tape recording is that information is stored on tape one-dimensionally—in a straight line across the length of the tape. This form of storage is called sequential because all of the bits of data are organized one after another in a strict sequence, like those paper-based dots. In digital systems, one bit follows after the other for the full length of the tape. Although the width of the tape may be put to use in multitrack, and the helical recording may be used by video systems, conceptually these, too, store information in one dimension only.

In the Newtonian universe (the only one that appears to make sense to the normal human mind), the shortest distance between two points is always a straight line. Alas, in magnetic tape systems, the shortest distance between two bits of data on a tape may also be a long time. To read two widely separated bits on a tape, all the tape between them must be passed over. Although all the bits in between are not to be used, they must be scanned in the journey from the first to second bits. If you want to retrieve information not stored in order on a tape, the tape must shuttle back and forth to find the data in the order that you want it. All that tape movement to find data means wasted time.

In theory, there's nothing wrong with sequential storage schemes—depending on the storage medium that's used, they can be very fast. For example, one form of solid-state computer memory, the all-electronic shift register, moves data sequentially at nearly the speed of light.

The sequential mass storage systems of today's computers are not so blessed with speed, however. Because of their mechanical foundations, most tape systems operate somewhat slower than the speed of light. For example, although light can zip across the vacuum of the universe at 186,000 miles per second (or so), cassette tape crawls along at one and seven-eighths inches per second. Although light can get from here to the moon and back in a few seconds, moving a cassette tape that distance would take about 10 billion times longer, several thousand years.

Although no tape stretches as long as the 238,000 mile distance to the moon, sequential data access can be irritatingly slow. Instead of delivering the near-instant response most of today's impatient power users demand, picking a file from a tape can take as long as 10 minutes. Even the best of today's tape systems require 30 seconds or more to find a file. If you had to load all your programs and data files from tape, you might as well take up crocheting to tide you through the times you're forced to wait.

Most sequential systems store data in blocks, sometimes called exactly that, sometimes called records. The storage system defines the structure and content of each block. Typically, each block includes identifying information (such as a block number) and error-control information in addition to the actual data. Blocks are stored in order on tape. In some systems, they lay end to end while others separate them with blank areas called Inter-Record Gaps.

Most tape systems use multiple tracks to increase their storage (some systems spread as many as 144 tracks across tape just one-quarter inch wide). The otherwise stationary read-write head in the tape machine moves up and down to select the correct track.

Some tape standards put a directory on the tape that holds the location of information on the tape. By consulting the directory, the drive can determine which track holds the information you want. Instead of scanning across hundreds of megabytes to find what you need, the tape drive can zero in on the correct track, substantially trimming the response time of the tape system.

Random Access Media

On floppy and most hard computer disks, the recorded data are organized to take advantage of the two-dimensional aspect of the flat, wide disk surface to give even faster access than is possible with the directory system on tape. Instead of being arranged in a single straight line, disk-based data are spread across several concentric circles like lanes in a circular race track or the pattern of waves rolling away from a splash. Some optical drives follow this system, but many other optical systems modify this arrangement, changing the concentric circles into one tightly packed spiral that continuously winds from edge to the center of the disk. But even these continuous-data systems behave much as if they had concentric circles of information.

Tracks

The mechanism for making this arrangement is quite elementary. The disk moves in one dimension under the read-write head, which scans the tape in a circle as it spins and defines a track, which runs across the surface of the disk much like one of the lanes of a racetrack. In most disk systems the head, too, can move—else the read-write head would be stuck forever hovering over the same track and the same stored data, making it a sequential storage system that wastes most of the usable storage surface of the disk.

In most of today's disks systems, the read-write moves across a radius of the disk, perpendicular to a tangent of the tracks. The read-write head can quickly move between the different tracks on the disk. Although the shortest distance between two points (or two bytes) remains a straight line, to get from one byte to another, the read-write head can take short cuts across the lanes of the racetrack. After the head reaches the correct track, it still must wait for the desired bit of information to cycle around under it. However, disks spin relatively quickly—300 revolutions per minute for most floppy disks and 3600 rpm for most hard disks—so you need to wait only a fraction of a second for the right byte to reach your system.

Because the head can jump from byte to byte at widely separated locations on the disk surface and because data can be read and retrieved in any order or at random in the two-dimensional disk system, disk storage systems are often called random access devices, even though they fall a bit short of the mark with their need to wait while hovering over a track.

The random access capability of magnetic disk systems makes the combination much faster than sequential tape media for the mass storage of data. Disks are so superior and so much more convenient than tapes that tape is almost never used as a primary mass storage system. Usually, tape plays only a secondary role as a backup system. Disks are used to store programs and files that need to be loaded on a moment's notice.

In optical systems with a single continuous track spiral, the read-write head still must move radially across the disk if just to follow the long spiral. Because it still can leap from one part of the continuous track to another, the moving head also endows these systems with fast random access speeds. Because the head can follow the track inward without jogging and briefly skipping over an unreadable disk area, these continuous track systems can smoothly read long blocks of data at high speeds. Consequently, they offer excellent random-access speeds and high continuous data transfer rates.

In modern hard disks, the actual physical track arrangement has become irrelevant. Using special electronics, disk designers are able to mask the physical characteristics of the drive and to make it respond as though it has some other geometry. Using such a masking process, engineers can make otherwise incompatible drives function in PCs. For example, neither DOS nor most BIOSs allows the use of more than 1024 tracks (or cylinders) on a hard disk. Using this masking technique, the logical disk geometry your PC sees can be kept within this limit even if the drive actually has 2048 tracks.

Sectors

Tracks are usually broken down into smaller segments called sectors. The number of sectors on each track varies from eight on some floppy disks to 51 or more on some modern, high-capacity drives. On disks that use device-level interfaces, the number of sectors is the same on all tracks, even though information has to be squeezed in more tightly on the tracks nearer the center of the disk because the track diameter is smaller. Normally, the sector size is 512 bytes in the IBM scheme of things.

Each sector is unambiguously identified with special magnetic markings on the disk. These sector identifications are part of the format of the disk. Figure 21.1 shows the contents of a typical sector identification.

Zoned Recording

An increasing number of drives use tricks to pack more sectors on the longer tracks nearer the outer edge of disk platters. Special electronics hide these odd sector arrangements from your computer, disguising the sector arrangement so that it looks as if all tracks are equally endowed with sectors.

The technology behind squeezing in more sectors is complex. Normally, hard disks spin at a constant rate. If they alter their speed so that they spin faster when the read-write head is over the longer outer tracks to pack in more data, access time would suffer. Although the head could dash about quickly, the system would have to wait while the disk spun up or down to the appropriate speed for reading or writing.

Using a technique called Multiple-Zone Recording solves this problem. Instead of changing disk speed, MZR drives alter the frequency at which their electronics operate depending on the zones (a contiguous group of tracks) that the head hovers over. The different frequencies result in different data densities.

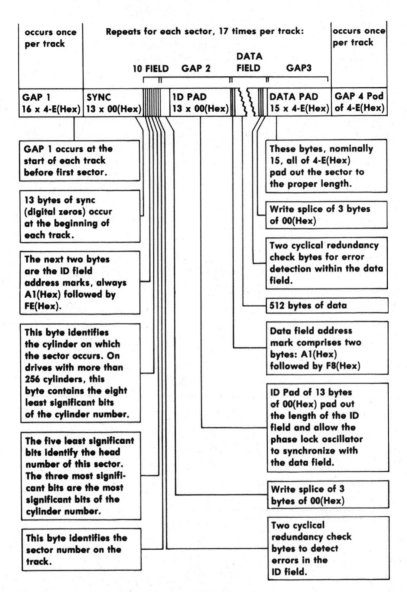

Figure 21.1. Typical sector ID markings (ST5061412).

Conventional disks that use constant frequencies end up recording at lesser densities on the outer tracks of disk platters because more of the medium spins under the head in a given period. Multiple-zone recording allows maintaining a nearly constant data density across the disk. Using higher frequencies at the outer tracks of a disk increases their data density to that of the inner tracks. This, in turn, can substantially increase overall disk capacity without compromising reliability.

Sometimes MZR technology is described as Zoned Constant Angular Velocity (ZCAV) recording, a term which confirms that the spin rate remains the same (constant angular velocity), but the platter is divided into areas with different recording densities (zones). Seagate Technologies uses a proprietary form of MZR called Zone-Bit Recording—different name, same effect.

The MZR drive must somehow mask its actual physical characteristics so that it looks to your PC as if it has a standard geometry, such as tracks of 17 sectors, each sector storing 512 data bytes. DOS can't deal with disks that magically change from having 17 sectors per track one minute to 23 sectors, then to 31. This masking process is simplified by using a system-level interface.

Sector Translation

The number of heads, tracks, and sectors are important when configuring your PC. These values determine the signals the drive controller must send to your drive to find a given byte of data. Normally, you indicate these values when you run your PC's setup procedure. The masking techniques used to hide the actual number of tracks and sectors mean that you configure your system to the logical track and sector arrangement created by the drive electronics rather than the actual physical configuration of the drive. This conversion of the physical arrangement of sectors on the drive to a logical configuration more compatible with its software is called *sector translation*.

Some state-of-the-art drives go further. They not only mask their physical characteristics but also have enough intelligence so that the drive can sense what parameters (the number of heads, cylinders, and sectors) your PC expects. The drive then automatically matches those parameters. This feature is called translation mode.

A drive that supports translation mode will accept any drive parameters you choose with your PC's setup procedure, providing you don't specify more capacity than the drive is capable of supplying. For example, you could buy an 80-megabyte drive that supports translation mode, and it will automatically adapt to emulate whatever number of heads and cylinders you have entered into your setup program.

Translation mode has one drawback, however. After you format a drive with translation mode, its logical configuration is set and cannot be changed without reformatting the drive. Although the drive can still automatically adapt, your data cannot.

A problem arises if the CMOS configuration memory of your PC is corrupted. For example, if you replace the battery in your PC and have to reconfigure your system, you have to remember the old drive parameters you had set to recover the data you stored. If you want to transfer a drive and its data between different systems, you have to be sure to use the same setup parameters in each system.

Unfortunately, a translation-mode drive offers no help as to what parameters to use other than telling you its capacity. Consequently, as a future reference, you should label your hard disk with the parameters (or drive type) you had set when you format it.

Clusters

The operating system used by your PC doesn't deal directly in clusters. Old friend DOS instead allocates disk storage into handy groups of sectors called clusters, sometimes called allocation units. Each cluster is an interchangeable unit of a standard size that can vary from 512 to 8096 bytes depending on disk type, its format, and the operating system that you use.

Control Electronics

Mass storage system usually consists of three parts, which are sometimes combined together. The actual drive or transport (complete with its own internal electronics) handles the medium, spooling the tape or spinning the disk. The controller electronics generate the signals that control the transport from commands given by the host computer system. The host adapter converts the signals generated by the host computer—for our purposes, the signals that travel on the ISA, EISA, Micro Channel, or local bus—into those that are compatible with the controller.

Primeval Controllers

Before the appearance of the IBM XT, most controllers for mass storage devices were most often free-standing circuit boards that were installed in the same housing as the hard disk drive itself. A separate host adapter card would convert the signals of the host computer to those of the standard favored by the controller. The host adapter and controller were linked by a kind of glorified parallel port. Control functions were distributed in three places—the host adapter inside the computer; the controller, which was typically mated in the cabinet with the mass storage device; and the transport electronics that were part of the mass storage device.

Many early add-ons for PCs, such as hard disks and tape backup systems, used this separate controller-adapter disk drive system. The manufacturers of these products had good reason to do this. This design allowed mass storage equipment to mate with virtually any computer system simply by substituting a different host adapter. Off-the-shelf controllers could be designed so that they could be matched to any computer system, giving them the widest possible market. After all, before the PC, there was no such thing as a truly universal bus standard. When incompatible computers of unlike designs were sold in quantities of dozens and hundreds (unlike the millions of standardized IBM-style machines sold today), this technique opened large enough markets to make the manufacture of mass storage systems economically feasible.

Moreover, there was a good, practical reason for separating the host adapter and controller. The combination of controller and host adapter circuitry would likely consume more board space than would fit into an ordinary PC expansion slot.

Combined Host Adapter-and-Controller

Although neither the PC bus nor the Micro Channel qualify as universal standards, their huge user bases easily justify the manufacture of products designed exclusively for them. As the success of the first IBM Personal Computer began to prove such acceptance was coming, controller manufacturers began to integrate the host adapter and storage system controller electronics onto a single expansion board. Today, most mass storage systems use this approach, mating with the storage device on one end and the PC's expansion bus (whatever standard it might follow) on the other. This single board is also called a controller because that is its primary function, and its combination nature is taken for granted.

The IBM XT hard disk subsystem heralded the change from the host adapter-controller system. The XT controller unified the host adapter and controller functions on a single, dense circuit board. This pioneering controller, initially made for IBM by Xebec Corporation, set the pattern for the next generation of devices. The great majority of hard disk controllers follow this two-in-one pattern. The AT followed this scheme, using a controlled developed by Western Digital Corporation, specifically model WD1002. Because software was written to take advantage of the features of this specific controller, it set the trend for all designs that followed. Nearly all hard disk controllers used in PCs to this day emulate the features of the WD1002.

Embedded Controllers

The next logical step in controller design is to move the circuitry out of the expansion slot and put it on the drive. This change is called integrating or embedding the controller function in their storage devices. This technology is technically termed Integrated Drive Electronics, although in general use the abbreviation IDE often refers to a specific kind of disk interface, one that uses the AT expansion bus for its connections, which is formally (and correctly) termed the AT Attachment, the ATA interface, or the AT interface.

The Small Computer System Interface or SCSI represents one of the fullest implementations of an embedded disk controller. SCSI, discussed in detail later in this chapter, operates as a fully arbitrated expansion bus and allows device-independent interchanges of data at high speeds.

Integrated Hard Disk Cards

The alternate strategy to putting the expansion board-based electronics on the hard disk is to put the hard disk on the expansion board. This also integrates the drive electronics, and in fact, the first true embedded interfaces were used on hard disk cards, which put all three essential functions (host adapter, controller, and storage device) together on a single board-like assembly that would slide into a standard expansion slot. Of course, this strategy is only effective when you don't require access to the medium used by the mass storage device, characteristic only of hard disks. Miniaturization and standardization have made embedded control electronics on conventionally mounted drives the preferred interface choice.

Device-Level Interfaces

The whole purpose of the controller is to link a disk or tape drive with its computer host. So that the widest variety of devices can be connected to a controller, the signals in this connection have been standardized.

The interface can appear at one of two levels. A device-level interface is designed to link a particular kind of device to its host. The interface is particular to the signals developed by that device and will generally work with no other. A system-level interface connects at a higher level, after all the signals from the device have been converted to the kind used by the host computer system. The signals used by a system-level interface are not specific to any single kind of device. For example, tape drives, hard disks, floppy disks, and even scanners and printers can use the same system-level interface. Each would require its own specific device-level interface.

Three device-level interfaces are regularly used in PC-based mass storage systems including the floppy disk interface and two hard disk interfaces, ST506 and the Enhanced Small Device Interface or ESDI. Although nearly all PCs still use the floppy disk interface, device-level hard disk interfaces are rarely used in modern PCs. Their only current application is to accommodate old-technology hard disks.

Floppy Disk Interface

The floppy disk interface connection scheme is also used by a number of inexpensive tape backup systems. In operation, it's much like a glorified serial port that's had a few new command lines added to it to handle the particular functions associated with the floppy disk drive. Only a few signals are required to control the two floppy disk drives normally attached by a single cable to the controller.

Two Drive Select signals are used to individually select either the first or second drive, A or B. (In four-drive systems, the signals for A in the second cable control drive C, and those of B control D.) If the signal assigned to a particular drive is not present, all the other input and output circuits of the drive are deactivated, except for those that control the drive motor. In this way, two drives can share the bulk of the wires in the controller cable without interference.

However, this control scheme also means that only one drive in a pair can be active at a time. You can write to drive B at the same time as you read from drive A. That's why you must transfer the data held on a disk (or file) from one drive into memory before you can copy it to another drive.

One wire is used for each drive to switch its spindle motor on and off. These are called, individually, Drive Select A and Drive Select B. Although it is possible to make both motors spin simultaneously, rules laid down by IBM admonish against activating these two lines to make both floppy disk drive motors run at the same time (this saves power in the severely constrained PC system and is a moot issue in the single-drive XT system). The two drives in your PC may run simultaneously for brief periods due to a delay built into most drives that keeps their motors running for a few seconds after the Motor Enable signal stops.

Two signals in the floppy disk interface control the head position of each of the attached drives. One, Step Pulse, merely tells the stepper motor on the drive with its Drive Select active to move one step—that's exactly one track—toward or away from the center of the disk. The Direction signal controls which way the pulses move the head. If this signal is active, the head moves toward the center.

To determine which of the two sides of a double-sided disk to read, one signal, called Write Select, is used. When this signal is active, it tells the disk drive to use the upper head. When no signal is present, the disk drive automatically uses the default (lower) head.

Writing to disk requires two signals on the interface. Write Data contains the information that's actually to be written magnetically onto the disk. It consists of nothing but a series of pulses corresponding exactly to the flux transitions that are to be made on the disk. The read-write head merely echoes these signals magnetically. As a fail-safe that precludes the possibility of accidentally writing over valuable data, a second signal called Write Enable is used. No write current is sent to the read-write head unless this signal is active.

Four signals are passed back from the floppy disk drive to the controller through the interface. Two of these help the controller determine where the head is located. Track 0 indicates to the controller when the head is above the outermost track on the disk so that the controller knows from where to start counting head-moving pulses. Index helps the drive determine the location of each bit on a disk track. One pulse is generated on the Index line for each revolution of the disk. The controller can time the distance between ensuing data pulses based on the reference provided by the Index signal.

In addition, the Write Protect signal is derived from the sensor that detects the existence or absence of a write-protect tab on a diskette. If a tab is present, this signal is active. The Read Data signal comprises a series of electrical pulses that exactly matches the train of flux transition on the floppy disk.

Controllers

The basic purpose of the floppy disk controller is to convert the requests from the BIOS or direct hardware commands that are couched in terms of track and sector numbers into the pulses that move the head to the proper location on the disk. For the most efficient operation, the controller must also remember where the head is located, index the head as necessary, and report errors when they occur.

In its translation function, the floppy disk controller must make sense from the stream of unformatted pulses delivered from the drive. It first must find the beginning of each track from the Index pulse and then mark out each sector from the information embedded in the data stream. When it identifies a requested sector, it must then read the information it contains and convert that information from serial to parallel form so that it can be sent through the PC bus. In writing, the controller must first identify the proper sector to write to—which is a read operation—and then switch on the write current to put data into that sector before the next sector on the disk begins.

Most of the hard work of the controller is handled by a single integrated circuit, the 765 controller chip. The 765 works much like a microprocessor, carrying out certain operations in response to commands that it receives through registers connected to your computer's I/O ports. This programmability makes the 765 and the floppy disk controllers made from it extremely versatile—able to adapt to changes in media and storage format as the PC industry has evolved. None of the essential floppy disk drive parameters are cast in stone or the silicon on the controller. The number of heads, tracks, and sectors on a disk are set by loading numbers into the registers of the 765. The values that the controller will use are normally loaded into the controller when you boot up your computer. You ordinarily don't have to worry about them after that. With the right on-board support circuitry and BIOS code, the same controller can often handle floppy disks ranging from ancient eight-inch monsters to the latest extra-density (2.88MB) 3.5-inch pocket-liners. Because older designs could not foresee the potential of future floppy disk formats, however, not all controllers are compatible with all floppy disk formats. To get full use of more recent floppy configurations, you'll need a version of DOS or other operating system designed to accommodate them. (See Chapter 24.)

Special software can reprogram your controller to make it read, write, and format floppy disks that differ from the IBM standard. Two types of software perform this reprogramming. Copy-protection schemes may alter vital drive parameters by misnumbering sectors, adding extra sectors, or executing a similar operation that cannot be duplicated using normal IBM parameters. Disk compatibility software alters the controller programming to make the floppy disk drives in your system act like those used by other computers such as those that use the CP/M operating system. Note, however, that although the IBM system is flexible, it cannot handle all possibilities, such as Commodore or Apple disks. Those computers used entirely different drive-control hardware that the 765 cannot mimic.

Over the last decade, the floppy disk controller has evolved from an entity of its own to a few circuits on the system board. The original design that IBM plugged into its first PC was also adopted by the XT and Portable PC was a separate board. With the AT, the floppy disk circuitry was packaged with the hard disk control circuitry on the system's hard disk controller, saving an expansion slot. With the advent of the PS/2 series, the floppy disk controller was trivialized onto the system board.

Modern PC-compatible computers can use any of these three designs. All work equally well. The main design considerations are slot usage and cost. Some clone-makers find it less expensive to slide in an expansion board than to build floppy disk circuitry on the system board. Although these designs may waste an expansion slot, that's rarely a consideration for a company trying to package PCs as cheaply as possible. For you, as a PC purchaser, the chief floppy-controller issue arises when you upgrade; if you install a new hard disk controller, replacing one that incorporated floppy disk circuitry, you need to replicate your old floppy disk circuitry in your upgrade.

Connectors

The floppy disk interface has changed subtly over the years. The original PC and XT floppy-disk controller used an edge connector to attach to the floppy-disk cable. AT and more recent controllers generally use pin connectors. In either case, the same signals appear at the same pins. Table 21.1 gives a pin-out for the standard PC floppy disk interface connector. Similarly, the connectors on floppy disks are changing as well. Nearly all 5 1/4-inch drives use edge connectors; most 3 1/2-inch drives use pin connectors.

TABLE 21.1. Pin-out for Floppy Disk Interface

Disk Drive Connector (A Drive) 34-Pin Connector	Disk Drive Connector (B Drive) 34-Pin Connector	Host Adapter Connector 34-Pin Internal	Host Adapter Connector 37-Pin (XT) External	Function
1	1	1	20	Ground
2	2	2	1	Unused
3	3	3	21	Ground
4	4	4	2	Unused
5	5	5	22	Ground
6	6	6	3	Unused

continues

TABLE 21.1. Continued

Disk Drive Connector (A Drive) 34-Pin Connector	Disk Drive Connector (B Drive) 34-Pin Connector	Host Adapter Connector 34-Pin Internal	Host Adapter Connector 37-Pin (XT) External	Function
7	7	7	23	Ground
8	8	8	6	Index
9	9	9	24	Ground
16	10	10	NC	Motor Enable A
15	11	11	25	Ground
14	12	12	NC	Drive Select B
13	13	13	26	Ground
12	14	14	NC	Drive Select A
11	15	15	27	Ground
10	16	16	NC	Motor Enable B
17	17	17	28	Ground
18	18	18	11	Direction (Stepper Motor)
19	19	19	29	Ground
20	20	20	12	Step Pulse
21	21	21	30	Ground
22	22	22	18	Write Data
23	23	23	31	Ground
24	24	24	14	Write Enable
25	25	25	32	Ground
26	26	26	15	Track 0
27	27	27	33	Ground

Disk Drive Connector (A Drive) 34-Pin Connector	Disk Drive Connector (B Drive) 34-Pin Connector	Host Adapter Connector 34-Pin Internal	Host Adapter Connector 37-Pin (XT) External	Function
28	28	28	16	Write Protect
29	29	29	34	Ground
30	30	30	17	Read Data
31	31	31	35	Ground
32	32	32	13	Select Head 1
33	33	33	36	Ground
34	34	34	4	Unused
NC	NC	NC	5	Unused
NC	NC	NC	7	Motor Enable C
NC	NC	NC	8	Drive Select D
NC	NC	NC	9	Drive Select C
NC	NC	NC	10	Motor Enable D
NC	NC	NC	37	Ground

In addition to the edge connector on the card, PC and XT controllers provide a second 37-pin connector on the card option retaining bracket. All the signals necessary for running a third and a fourth floppy disk are available there. Most newer floppy disk controllers only provide for two drives, although a few four-drive controllers are available from third-party manufacturers. Chapter 23 details the floppy disk cabling scheme.

ST506/412

The original hard disk interface used in the IBM XT, AT, and some models of PS/2 computers followed an industry standard device-level interface called ST506/412. Unlike the names of other interfaces that are acronyms, the ST506 name has little significance. The initials stand for Shugart Technology, the company that originated the interface, and the numbers just distinguish this design from others much like the model number of automobiles or cameras.

As with the floppy disk interface, ST506 transfers data to and from the disk drive in serial form. Bits are read as flux transitions off the disk and delivered in original form to the controller through a single data wire. The data separator in the controller then figures out which bits are meaningful data and which are formatting or sector identification information.

The stream of actual data bits then goes to a deserializer circuit that converts the serial train of bits into parallel data compatible with the bus of the host computer. At the same time, the data is checked for errors, and most of the errors are corrected.

The ST506 standard does not specify the data-coding method of the signal recorded on disk or passed through the interface. It only provides a serial channel between drive and controller. Consequently, ST506 accommodates MFM, RLL, and Advanced RLL coding methods. However, drives must be able to deal with the higher frequencies of advanced modulation methods. The disk controllers determine the modulation method and data coding, so the choice of controller determines what is recorded on disk. Unlike the floppy disk interface, the ST506 interface uses two cables—a wide control cable with 34 connections, and a smaller data cable with 20 connections. Table 21.2 shows the functions assigned to each of these connections.

TABLE 21.2. ST506 cable pin-out

Control Cable

Host Adapter Pin	Function (on host adapter)	Drive C Pin	Drive D Pin
1	Ground	1	1
2	Reduced write current (HS3)	2	2
3	Ground	3	3
4	Reserved (Head select 2)	4	4
5	Ground	5	5
6	Write gate	6	6
7	Ground	7	7
8	Seek complete	8	8

Host Adapter Pin	Function (on host adapter)	Drive C Pin	Drive D Pin
9	Ground	9	9
10	Track 0	10	10
11	Ground	11	11
12	Write fault	12	12
13	Ground	13	13
14	Head select 0	14	14
15	Key	15	15
16	Reserved	16	16
17	Ground	17	17
18	Head select 1	18	18
19	Ground	19	19
20	Index	20	20
21	Ground	21	21
22	Ready	22	22
23	Ground	23	23
24	Step	24	24
25	Ground	29	25
26	Drive select 0	28	26
27	Ground	27	27
28	Drive select 1	26	28
29	Ground	25	29
30	Reserved (Drive select 2)	30	30
31	Ground	31	31
32	Reserved (Drive select 3)	32	32
33	Ground	33	33
34	Direction in	34	34

continues

TABLE 21.2. Continued

Data Cable

Pin	Function (on host adapter)	Pin	Pin
1	Drive select	1	1
2	Ground	2	2
3	Reserved	3	3
4	Ground	4	4
5	Reserved	5	5
6	Ground	6	6
7	Reserved	7	7
8	Ground	8	8
9	Reserved	9	9
10	Reserved	10	10
11	Ground	11	11
12	Ground	12	12
13	MFM write data +	13	13
14	MFM write data -	14	14
15	Ground	15	15
16	Ground	16	16
17	MFM read data +	17	17
18	MFM read data -	18	18
19	Ground	19	19
20	Ground	20	20

In new PCs, the ST506 interface is essentially obsolete. Hard-disk makers long ago stopped designing new drives using the interface, and few new drives using it are available. The interface's primary defect was speed. ST506 was designed in the days when PC performance was 50 or more times slower than today's best machines. Back then, it moved data faster than any PC could possibly absorb it. Today, PCs far outclass ST506 drives.

The ST506 interface was not suitable for upgrading. Because it is a device-level interface, the timing of its signals is directly matched to physical attributes of the drives using it. That is, its operating frequencies are forever tied to a transfer rate governed by the spin of the disk. None of these values can be changed without altering the others. Faster disks thus required a new, faster interface.

Cabling

The ST506 interface requires you to connect three cables to each disk drive: a data cable, a control cable, and a power cable. Only the data and control cables originate in the disk controller; the power cable comes directly from the power supply. Just to make things interesting, each drive gets its own data cable but shares a single data cable.

The Data Cable

In the ST506 environment, the data cable for the interface is quite straightforward. Usually a ribbon cable, it comprises 20 conductors. On the disk drive end, the cable terminates in a female edge connector. To provide the keying that prevents inadvertent reversal, a plastic insert often is placed between the second and third rows of pins in this edge connector, and the mating circuit board edge on the disk drive is slotted between the matching contacts.

Because ribbon cables are polarized and generally marked with a colored leader corresponding to the number 1 conductor, you should have no problem properly orienting a hard disk data cable even if the plastic key is absent. The colored leader on the edge of the cable that indicates the location of conductor 1 always goes to the side of the hard disk contact (see fig. 21.2)—the edge of which is closest to the keying slot.

The other end of the cable generally features a header connector that slips over the golden pins of a circuit board header. This end of the cable usually is not keyed—although sometimes a header pin is removed and the corresponding hole in the connector is plugged. Usually the circuit board on which the header is mounted is stenciled with a legend identifying a few pin numbers. The keying stripe on the cable is always oriented toward pin 1 or pin 2, away from pins 19 and 20.

Most hard-disk controllers provide headers for plugging in two data cables—one for each disk drive that the controller is capable of operating. Usually, these headers are labeled as J3 and J4, and the lower number jack is meant for the first hard disk.

Plugging the data cable into the wrong disk drive controller header is not a fatal error. Although the disk drive system will not operate properly, no damage is likely to result. The drive may seem to operate properly, rattle its head around, and light its activity indicator (because the control cable in the proper position ensures that the drive does what it is supposed to do). Error messages, however, will appear on-screen (because the controller is not receiving data on the pins that it expects to). Moving the cable to the correct header brings the disk drive to life, assuming that you don't run across additional problems.

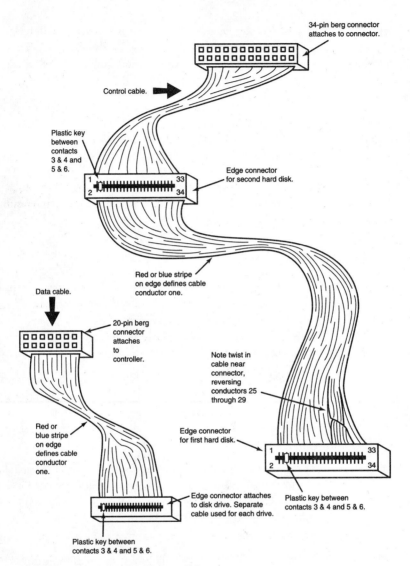

34-pin berg connector
attaches to connector.

Control cable.

Plastic key
between
contacts
3 & 4 and
5 & 6.

Edge connector
for second hard disk.

Red or blue stripe
on edge defines cable
conductor one.

Data cable.

20-pin berg
connector
attaches
to
controller.

Note twist in
cable near
connector,
reversing
conductors 25
through 29

Red or
blue stripe
on edge
defines cable
conductor
one.

Edge connector
for first hard disk.

Edge connector attaches
to disk drive. Separate
cable used for each drive.

Plastic key between
contacts 3 & 4 and 5 & 6.

Plastic key between
contacts 3 & 4 and 5 & 6.

Figure 21.2. Edge connector, header, and keying.

Control Cable

The signals from the controller that specify what the hard disk drive is supposed to do are relayed through a 34-conductor cable. Much like floppy disk cables, the hard disk control cable is designed to daisy-chain two devices—one end of the cable plugs into the controller, and two connectors are provided for attaching to individual disk drives.

The PC's hard disk daisy-chain scheme is reminiscent of that used by floppy disks, and the hard disk control cable is very similar to the floppy disk control-and-data cable. Both cables, for example, may have several conductors twisted near the first disk drive connector (the connector that is plugged into what DOS recognizes as drive C). The connector in the middle of the cable—without the twist—gets plugged into drive D.

Despite the similarity of the cable twist, hard disk control cables and floppy disk control-and-data cables are not the same. Each of these two species of disk drive cables twists different conductors in the ribbon cable. Substituting one for the other will not be successful.

If you have a number of loose, uninstalled floppy control-and-data hard disk control cables, to avoid confusion you should plainly identify the nature of each cable. One good strategy is to use an indelible ink marker to label the drive connectors with the proper identifying letters—A and B for floppy cables, for example, and C and D for hard disk cables. Or mark on the ribbon cable itself floppy or hard disk.

Drive Select Jumpers

Every hard disk must be uniquely definable by the system in which it resides. Although DOS uses drive letters such as the familiar C, the drive letter is only a logical identification. The hardware of your system also requires a unique physical identification for each drive. Every ST506 hard disk is thus assigned a device number or a drive select number, much as floppy disks are. Device numbers generally are selected by jumpers or DIP switches located on the hard disk.

Special Concerns

No matter what drive letter DOS assigns to a hard disk, the IBM ST506 hard disk scheme requires that each hard disk be set up as the second hard disk drive. For hard disks that start numbering with device 1, a PC hard disk must be number 2. For those that start numbering with 0, a PC hard disk must be set as number 1.

Both drives in a system are thus set with the same device number. The control cable takes care of distinguishing one drive from another. The twist in the cable makes the drive plugged into the connector at the end of the cable appear to the system as the first drive. The other disk, set up as the second drive and connected by a length of cable without twists, appears exactly as it should, as the second drive.

No hard and fast rule says you must obey the PC scheme. As long as you know what you're doing, you can use a straight-through or twisted cable. The secret to success is knowing how to set the drive-select jumpers on your hard disk for your particular configuration.

To use a straight-through control cable to connect a single hard disk to your ST506 standard controller, you must set the drive-select jumper on the disk drive to reflect it being the first drive in your system. To daisy-chain two hard disks on a single control cable that does not have a twist before the last connector on the cable, set the drive you want to be recognized as C as the lowest drive select number in your system and the drive to be recognized as D as the second-lowest drive select.

Most ST506 and hard disks support drive-select values in excess of two. The PC cabling scheme never uses these settings. Instead, the system favored by most PC makers uses separate disk-drive controllers for each pair of hard disks.

Drive-letter assignments are actually issued by DOS. DOS follows a strict order in assigning drive letters, starting by giving the letter C to the first hard disk (or other device) it finds in its logical search. This search begins with reading through the system BIOS and then progresses through the device drivers in the system's CONFIG.SYS file.

The BIOS search involves not just the firmware contained in the system or planar board ROM but also the code in add-in peripheral expansion boards, including any hard-disk controllers.

The general rule is that drive-select jumpers (and cable twists) distinguish the hard disks attached to a given controller, and base-memory addresses distinguish controllers.

ESDI

When the ST506 interface proved to be too slow, drive maker Maxtor developed its own improved version, which, like its predecessor, was embraced by the drive industry as a standard. Known as the Enhanced Small Device Interface, the new scheme upped the performance of ST506. It used essentially the same control and data signals but pushed them to higher speeds and also added a handful of new features. Initial drives doubled the transfer of ST506 without changing the basic drive mechanism—the drive just packed twice as much data (in twice as many sectors) on each track. Doubling the data per track and disk spin meant doubling the transfer rate—to 10 MHz.

True to its origins, ESDI uses similar connections to those of the ST506 interface, including the same two-cable system. You need to connect three cables to each drive (power, data, and control). As with ST506, you also need to properly set the drive select jumpers on an ESDI drive and to terminate the last drive connected to the control cable.

Despite these physical similarities, the two interfaces are not electrically compatible. As a result, you cannot plug an ESDI drive into an ST506 interface and expect the system to work. Nor will an ST506 drive work through an ESDI connection. The pin-out of the ESDI connection scheme is shown in Table 21.3.

TABLE 21.3. ESDI Cable Pinout

Control Cable

Host Adapter Pin	Function	Drive C Pin	Drive D Pin
1	Ground	1	1
2	Head select 3	2	2
3	Ground	3	3
4	Head select 2	4	4
5	Ground	5	5
6	Write gate	6	6
7	Ground	7	7
8	Config/Status data	8	8
9	Ground	9	9
10	Transfer Acknowledge	10	10
11	Ground	11	11
12	Attention	12	12
13	Ground	13	13
14	Head select 0	14	14
15	Key	15	15
16	Sector/Addr mark found	16	16
17	Ground	17	17
18	Head select 1	18	18
19	Ground	19	19
20	Index	20	20
21	Ground	21	21
22	Ready	22	22
23	Ground	23	23
24	Tranfer request	24	24
25	Ground	29	25

continues

TABLE 21.3. Continued

Control Cable

Host Adapter Pin	Function	Drive C Pin	Drive D Pin
26	Drive select 0	28	26
27	Ground	27	27
28	Drive select 1	26	28
29	Ground	25	29
30	Drive select 2	30	30
31	Ground	31	31
32	Read gate	32	32
33	Ground	33	33
34	Command data	34	34

Data cable

Pin	Function	Pin	Pin
1	Drive selected	1	1
2	Sector/Address mark found	2	2
3	Seek complete	3	3
4	Address mark enable	4	4
5	Reserved for step mode	5	5
6	Ground	6	6
7	Write clock +	7	7
8	Write clock -	8	8
9	Cartridge changed	9	9
10	Read reference clock +	10	10
11	Read reference clock -	11	11
12	Ground	12	12

Data cable

Host Adapter Pin	Function	Drive C Pin	Drive D Pin
13	NRZ write data +	13	13
14	NRZ write data -	14	14
15	Ground	15	15
16	Ground	16	16
17	NRZ read data +	17	17
18	NRZ read data -	18	18
19	Ground	19	19
20	Index	20	20

As with the ST506 standard, the ESDI is a device-level interface. Its connections are fundamentally made directly to the device that's to be connected to the system. In the case of hard disks, ESDI goes beyond ST506 by allowing configuration and bad-track information to be stored on the drive. Instead of requiring the host computer to know what kind of disk drive is connected through the interface, each ESDI drive can tell its controller how many tracks, cylinders, and such it has. Instead of requiring that you test for and type all the bad tracks on the drive, it enables the manufacturer to test the disk, flag the bad tracks, and store that information on the disk in a standardized form that the controller can access directly. Unfortunately, virtually no PCs ever took advantage of this information; nearly all ESDI-based systems required you to configure their CMOS memory for vital drive parameters exactly as you would have with ST506 drives.

The biggest virtue of ESDI has proven to be its similarity to ST506 coupled with higher speed. Installing an ESDI drive system hardly differs from installing an ST506 drive, yet you get higher performance. From its beginnings as a 10 MHz interface, ESDI evolved into higher speed versions. The interface specification allowed for slower and faster speeds—late high-performance ESDI drives were able to achieve peak transfer rates as high as 25 MHz. ESDI also was designed with the idea of adapting the interface to tape systems, although it has not won wide acceptance for that application. After a brief moment in the sun, however, ESDI has fallen from favor. Its split drive/controller design no longer makes sense for PC or drive designers, and it is running into a performance roadblock. Its serial data channel is reaching its upper speed limit. Disk interfaces allowing parallel transfers are taking its place. By late 1991, most hard disk manufacturers had spurned ESDI for new drive development, instead turning exclusively to system-level interfaces.

System-Level Interfaces

In contrast to device-level interfaces, system-level interfaces give the mass storage designer a great deal of freedom. The inner workings of the storage device are hidden from the interface—all that comes out is formatted data compatible with the host computer. Although conventional device-level designs push the raw data stream from the disk or other device through the interface (with the data goes device formatting information such as sector identifications), system-level interfaces transfer only active data. The system level passes along only an executive summary of the device's information; device-level interfaces must include the footnotes, page numbers, and irrelevant digressions. Without all the chaff, the system-level interface can move more data even when operating at exactly the same clock rate as a device-level interface.

Moreover, today's system-level interfaces are not constrained by the serial limitations of the popular device-level interfaces. The AT Attachment interface pass data 8 or 16 bits at a time; the latest SCSI connections support transfers up to 32 bits wide. Although the system-level interfaces aren't clocked as fast as the quickest device-level interfaces, they deliver greater throughput. In fact, the lowest clocks of the system-level interfaces is an advantage that reduces design and radiation problems.

In addition, because the actual device is hidden from the interface signals, the system-level design allows technical innovation without altering compatibility. New technologies for higher capacities, greater security, or even faster throughput can be accommodated without violating the standard. Because all the essential circuitry of each device's controller is built into any system-level interface device, you don't need to carefully match an AT interface hard disk to a controller, for example, to get a working system. You don't have to worry whether a particular drive can handle RLL data coding or what its ESDI transfer rate may be. The manufacturer has already done that for you. These advantages—and many more—have made system-level interfaces the designs of choice for today's PC peripherals.

AT Attachment

The dominant hard disk interface for the PC has become the AT Attachment design—a natural outcome considering that the interface is based on the ISA expansion bus, which is the most widely used computer bus. The performance of this system-level interface outclasses every device-level interface by a wide margin and is second only to the latest incarnations of the SCSI design.

Although the AT interface began as a design chosen for its low cost for small capacity drives, it has grown up. The trend to the AT interface has dramatically accelerated over the last few years for three very good reasons. The interface holds distinct advantages for disk-drive makers, computer makers, and computer buyers.

First, the most important. You, as a computer buyer and user, gain a great deal of convenience from AT interface drives. Connecting them is easy—they require only two cables: a signal cable and a power cable. Most of the worries in connecting a traditional hard disk are absent. You have no need to fret about proper terminations or where and which drive gets plugged into the daisy-chain cable.

In the AT-interface scheme, the drives and not the cable determine what drive letter is assigned to each drive. Moreover, you don't have to worry about such things as RLL data coding or modulation technique. In fact, most of the latest ATA drives make the system setup procedure easier than ever, tolerating a wide range of setup parameters.

AT interface connections also offer some of the highest data-transfer rates of any hard disk interfacing scheme for personal computers. AT interface data-transfer speeds can be as much as two to three times higher than the old performance leader, ESDI. Moreover, the AT interface promises to put more megabytes in your PC for a lower price than the more conventional hard disk interfaces.

Computer makers benefit from AT-interface technology because they don't need to put separate hard disk controllers in their products. That is an immediate cost benefit—the manufacturer doesn't have to pay for the unneeded controller and can pass along the lower price to you. In addition, AT interface drives can lower assembly cost because there's one less cable and one less expansion board to install in the system.

Of course, building a special AT interface connector to a system board adds to the manufacturer's cost of making a system. But today's latest chipsets that form the basis for system board designs have internal AT interface support, giving the system manufacturers a hard disk interface at essentially no charge. The added system board connector may be the only cost added by including an AT interface for hard disks and other peripherals.

Integrating control electronics on the drive to make an AT interface may not at first seem to benefit the hard disk maker. After all, the integration makes a more complex product that should be more expensive to manufacture. But other benefits won by IDE and improvements in other areas of disk design have made the integration of control electronics a big plus for hard-disk and other device manufacturers.

As with all electronics, the trend for the control circuitry on hard-disk drives has been toward large-scale integration, combining all the needed functions into one large chip (or a small set of larger chips). Although engineering functions onto a VLSI chip is expensive, manufacturing is less so, and assembly can be cheaper; VLSI means fewer components so there is not as much to install. There's also less to fail, so AT interface drives can cost less to warrant and maintain.

For disk manufacturers, the best part of any AT interface is the freedom it gives hard-disk designers in getting the most capacity possible from a given mechanism. All the vital details of disk design and operation are effectively hidden from the host computer by the AT-interface connection. AT-interface drives can break traditional rules and limits with impunity. Your system never knows the difference. You get the gain without conventional hard disk pains.

History

The idea for using an ordinary AT interface for linking hard disks to PCs goes back to the primeval days when Compaq Computer Corporation was developing its long-discontinued Portable II computer. Work on designing the new interface started in 1985 as a means to minimize the number of slots required to integrate a hard drive into the computer. The Portable II would be short of slots, and eliminating a slot-mounted hard-disk controller would free up one more slot. In this first design, the controller was still a separate board built by Western Digital Corporation to Compaq specifications but coupled directly to the drive.

The term Integrated Drive Electronics first appeared in early 1986, when Compaq worked with Western Digital and the Magnetic Peripherals division of Control Data Corporation (the division is now part of Seagate) to integrate the WD controller chip onto a CDC half-height, 5 1/4-inch, 40M hard disk drive. In this implementation, the controller was grafted onto the hard disk assembly, but its circuitry was identifiable by a controller separate from the rest of the drive's electronics. This drive was first used in the Deskpro 386, in which it connected to a multifunction board in one of the machine's expansion slots. At this time, the specification was first expanded to handle two drives through one connection.

In the middle of 1986, in parallel with the CDC effort, Compaq and Conner Peripherals started a joint development effort to emulate what was then called the IDE interface with a gate array that was integrated with the rest of the control electronics of the hard disk. At this point, the controller had truly become integrated in an effort to reduce the cost and complexity of the hard disk system while improving its reliability. The AT interface connector was first moved to the system board with Compaq's Portable III.

After the benefits of the AT-bus connection were proved, other disk makers adopted the standard. But because no official standard or even unofficial guidelines had been declared, each drive maker added its own nuances and variations to the interface. Consequently, early drives based on the AT interface from different manufacturers may suffer compatibility problems, principally when you try to connect two drives of different makes to a single AT interface connector.

An industry group called the Common Access Method (CAM) Committee, was formed in October 1988 from companies that make and use hard-disk drives to develop in AT interface standard. The group formalized the specifications for the AT Attachment interface in March 1989, and in November 1990 submitted them as a proposed standard to the American National Standards Institute in November 1990. In 1991, a standard was finally and formally approved, and the CAM Committee disbanded shortly thereafter. Other organizations (principally the Small Form Factor Committee) now work on revising and expanding the original specification.

Implementation

In purest form, an AT interface drive would be one you could slide directly into an expansion slot inside your PC—a hard disk card. The drive would use exactly the same signals as any other expansion board and exactly the same connector. After all, the expansion bus is the real AT interface.

True AT interface drives are different. Contrary to what you would expect from the interface name, drives that use the AT interface specification do not use a direct connection to the standard ISA expansion bus. Instead, they attach to a special connector with signals somewhat different from those floating around on the ISA bus.

One reason for this difference is that the expansion buses inside computers are not designed to have cables plugged into them. Their circuitry is not optimized for transmitting signals beyond the backplane of the system board. Moreover, you wouldn't want to plug a full-height 5 1/4-inch hard disk directly into an expansion slot—at least if you wanted any hope of further expanding your system. The drive would be just too big and clumsy.

The AT drive interface instead uses a special connector on the system board of PCs compatible with the standard. Alternately, a small host adapter board (which should never be called a controller card because the control electronics are on the drive) can be used to adapt a PC using the ISA or EISA expansion bus to accept an AT interface drive. Micro Channel and local bus signals differ substantially from those used by the AT interface, so those buses are not directly compatible with AT interface drives. However, because of the popularity of drives using the AT interface, some board makers have made conversion products that enable you to connect AT interface drives to Micro Channel systems or local bus slots.

The AT interface for hard disks doesn't aim for full-plug compatibility with the ISA bus. Instead, it modifies the bus signals somewhat to give it more reach and less complexity. You simply don't need all 98 connections of the ISA expansion bus to run a hard disk drive. Hard disk drives are not normally memory-mapped devices, for example, so there's no need to give a hard disk control of all 24 addressing lines of the AT bus.

Instead of direct access to bus addressing, in the AT interface design, the cable going to the hard disk is connected to address-decoding logic circuitry. Thanks to this circuitry, only the signals sent to the addresses used in controlling the hard disk are sent to the drive. The address lines become superfluous. The actual addresses used by the AT interface connection are not part of the specification but are determined by the circuitry and BIOS of the host computer.

In addition to address-decoding logic, the AT interface design adds buffering circuits to enable the connection to safely transverse the length of cable running to the disk drive. Because of the relatively high speed of these signals(corresponding to the 8 MHz bus clock of the ISA expansion bus), the length of this connecting cable is severely constrained. Under the AT interface specifications, signal cables are limited to 18 inches.

The initial AT interface specification reduced the 98 pins used by the two ISA bus connectors to a single 40-pin connector. In addition to the 16 bits of data (some AT interface drives and host adapter implementation may use just 8 bits exactly as some expansion boards have only 8-bit connectors), a variety of control signals are provided for. These signals manage the functions of the AT interface drive through input/output registers in the control circuitry on the drive. Among these control signals are those to request reading or writing data, to make DMA transfers, to check the results of running diagnostics, and to indicate which of the two drives that can be connected to an AT interface port is to perform a given function. The interface also provides a "spindle sync" signal so that two drives can spin synchronously, as is required for some implementations of drive array.

The 40 connections of the AT interface are made using a pin connector rather than the edge connector used for expansion boards. A pin connector (often called a header) comprises two rows of square, gold-plated pins spaced 1/10 inch apart in both directions.

To prevent you from hooking up the ATA signal cable improperly, these AT interface connectors are keyed. That is, of the 40 pins in two rows that make up the host connector, pin 20 is not present (it may be literally clipped off). The corresponding hole on the cable connector is plugged. If you try to plug in the connector upside down (or backward, depending on your point of view about these things), the plug will hit a pin rather than the pin 20 space it expects, thus preventing you from plugging in the connector.

Seven of the connections of the AT Attachment interface (numbers 2, 19, 22, 24, 26, 30, and 40) are grounds, scattered among the signals to provide some degree of isolation from one another. Sixteen pins (3 through 18) are devoted to data, although the specification allows for 8-bit connections using only the odd numbered 8 pins in the sequence. The remaining 16 pins are assigned various signal control functions such as those to manage reading or writing data, make DMA transfers, and coordinate the operation of two drives.

The AT Attachment signals primarily concerned with controlling the transfer of data across the interface are given their own dedicated connections. Commands to the drives and the responses from the drives (including error indications) are passed through 17 8-bit registers.

The two drives permitted under the AT Attachment standard share the connection and receive all signals across the interface indiscriminately. To signal which drive should act on a given command, the AT Attachment uses a special control register. The same register also determines the head, track, and sector that is to be used at any given time.

Seven signals are used to select among the registers. The registers are divided into two groups: Control Block Registers and Command Registers, indicated by two interface signals. Activating the Drive Chip Select 0 signal (pin 37) selects the Control Block registers. Activating the Drive Chip Select 1 signal (pin 38) selects the Command Block Registers. When the Drive I/O Write signal (pin 23) is active, the registers that accept commands from the host are accessible through the interface data lines. When the Drive I/O Read signal (pin 25) is active, the registers indicate drive status through the data lines.

Drive Address Bus 0 through 2 and located on pins 35, 33, and 36 (with the other signals) control which register is currently selected and accessible through the data lines. The AT Attachment standard defines two read and one write control-block register as well as seven read and seven write command-block registers. Of these, one write command-block register selects the active drive and head (up to 16 heads are allowed). Two registers select the drive track (allowing up to 65,536 tracks on a single drive), another register selects the sector to start reading from or writing to, and another register selects the number of the track to be read or written. The read registers indicate which drive and head is active, and which track and head are being scanned. Other registers provide status information and define errors that occur during drive operation.

The number of register bits available sets the logical limits on device size: up to 16 heads, 65,536 tracks and 256 sectors per track. Because many PCs are incapable of handling more than 1,024 tracks, the maximum practical capacity of an AT Attachment drive is 2,147,483,648 bytes (2 gigabytes).

During active data transfers, separate signals are used as strobes to indicate that the data going to or coming from the drive or values in the control registers is valid and can be used. The falling edge of the Drive I/O Read signal (pin 25) indicates to the host that valid data read from the disk is on the bus. The falling edge of the Drive I/O Write signal (pin 23) indicates that data on the bus to be written on disk is valid.

The Drive 16-bit I/O signal (pin 32) indicates whether the read or write transfer comprises 8 or 16 bits. The signal is active to indicate 16-bit transfers.

Normally, AT Attachment transfers are accomplished through programmed I/O, the standard mode of operation using the standard AT hard disk BIOS. However, the AT Attachment standard optionally supports Direct Memory Access transfers. Two signals control handshaking during DMA data moves. The drive signals that it is ready to read data and transfer it in DMA mode by asserting the DMA Request signal (pin 21). The computer host acknowledges that it is ready to accept that data with the DMA Acknowledge signal (pin 29). If the host cannot accept all the data at the same time, it removes the DMA Acknowledge signal until it is ready to receive more.

In DMA write operations, the host PC uses DMA Acknowledge to indicate that it has data available, and the active drive uses DMA Request for handshaking to control the flow of data. The Drive I/O Read and Write signals indicate in which direction the data should flow (as a disk read or write).

An AT Attachment disk drive can interrupt the host computer to gain immediate attention by activating the Drive Interrupt signal (pin 31). On programmed I/O transfers, the drive generates an interrupt at the beginning of each block of data (typically a sector) to be transferred. On DMA transfers, the interrupt is used to indicate that only the command has been completed. (The interrupt used is determined by the host's circuitry.)

A drive can signal to the host computer that it is not ready to process a read or write request using the I/O Channel Ready signal (pin 27). Normally, this signal is activated; the drive switches it off when it cannot immediately respond to a request to transfer data.

The Drive Reset signal (pin 1) causes the drive to return to its normal power-on state, ignoring transfers in progress and losing the contents of its registers (returning them to their default values). Normally, the drive is activated briefly (for at least 25 microseconds) when the host computer is turned on so that it will initialize itself. Activating this signal thereafter will cancel the command in progress and reinitialize the drive.

The Passed Diagnostics signal (pin 34) is used by the slave drive to indicate to its host that it is running its diagnostics. The passed in the name does not mean that the diagnostics are completed successfully but that the results are ready to be passed along to the host system. Actual results (and the command to actually execute diagnostics) is given through the AT Attachment registers.

The Spindle Sync/Cable Select signal (pin 28) can be used at the drive manu-facturer's option to make the drives spin synchronously (as is required by some drive-array technologies) or to set drive identification as master or slave by the cable rather than using a jumper or switch on the drive. When used as a spindle-synchronizing signal, the master drive generates a periodic pulse (typically once each revolution of the disk although the actual timing is left to the drive manu-facturer), and the slave uses this signal to lock its spin to the master. When this connection is used as a cable-select signal, supplying a ground on pin 28 causes a drive to function as the master (drive 0); leaving the connection open causes the connected drive to act as the slave (drive 1).

A single signal, termed Drive Active/Drive 1 Present located on pin 39, indicates that one of the drives is active (for example, to illuminate the drive activity indicator on the system front panel). The same pin is used by the host signal to determine whether one or two AT Attachment drives are installed when the power is switched on. The drive assigned as the slave is given a 400-millisecond period during system startup to put a signal on this pin to indicate its availability; after waiting 450 milliseconds to give the slave drive time to signal, the master drive puts its signal on the pin to indicate its presence to the host computer. It switches its signal off and converts the function of the signal to drive activity when the drive accepts its first command from the host computer or after waiting 31 seconds, whichever comes first.

As comprehensive as the AT Attachment standard is, it doesn't define everything. Most impor-tantly, it governs only the connection between the PC and drive. Everything upstream—that is, inside the computer—is left to the designer of the host PC. AT Attachment does not indicate the logical location of its control registers. The decoding logic that determines those values is part of the host adapter circuitry of the PC. The system BIOS (or add-in BIOS) provides the needed information for establishing the link.

The system BIOS is thus critical to getting AT Attachment drives to operate properly. Some older BIOSes may not be able to properly control AT Attachment drives. In particular, AMI

BIOSes dated before 9 April 1990 were not completely compatible. To use an AT Attachment drive in a system with one of these older BIOSes, you must replace the BIOS.

Without a doubt, AT Attachment will continue to grow and flourish because it brings two worlds together—not just the disk and PC, but you and drive makers. AT Attachment gives you the easiest and most worry-free of all interfaces to install. Drive manufacturers get the potential for more speed and capacity. And both you and the manufacturers win with lower prices.

Cabling

The AT Attachment scheme simplifies cabling in other ways. All the signals in the cable are extended to each of the two drives that potentially can be attached to a single host connector. Both drives that can be connected to a host AT Attachment port through the cable receive exactly the same signals on the same pins. No weird twists in the ribbon cable are used to distinguish the drives from one another, as is required in IBM's ST506 and ESDI connection arrangements. Instead, the signals to and from individual AT Attachment-interfaced drives are distinguished by control signals and timing. Table 21.4 shows the basic AT Attachment cable.

TABLE 21.4. AT Attachment (IDE) Pin-Out

Pin	Function	Pin	Function
A	Vendor Unique	B	Vendor Unique
C	Vendor Unique	D	Vendor Unique
E	(keypin)	F	(keypin)
1	RESET-	2	Ground
3	Data line 7	4	Data line 8
5	Data line 6	6	Data line 9
7	Data line 5	8	Data line 10
9	Data line 4	10	Data line 11
11	Data line 3	12	Data line 12
13	Data line 2	14	Data line 13
15	Data line 1	16	Data line 14
17	Data line 0	18	Data line 15
19	Ground	20	(keypin)
21	DMARQ	22	Ground
23	DIOW-	24	Ground
25	DIOR-	26	Ground

continues

TABLE 21.4. Continued

Pin	Function	Pin	Function
27	IORDY	28	PSYNC:CSEL
29	DMACK-	30	Ground
31	INTRQ	32	IOCS16-
33	DA1	34	PDIAG-
35	DAO	36	DA2
37	CS1FX-	38	CS3FX-
39	DASP-	40	Ground
41	+5V (Logic)	42	+5V (Motor)
43	Ground (Return)	44	Type- (0=ATA)

Multiple Drives

When two drives are connected to a single AT Attachment port, they do not behave as equals. One drive is designated as the master, and the other is the slave. However, the master is master only in nomenclature. The master drive does not control the slave. Its only superior function is to perform signal decoding for both drives in the two-drive system.

All AT Attachment drives have the potential for being masters or slaves. The function of each drive is determined by jumper settings on the drive. With a jumper in one position, a drive will act as the master. In another position, it will be a slave.

Only one master and one slave are permitted in a single AT Attachment connection, so each of the two drives in a single AT Attachment chain must have its master/slave jumpers properly set for the system to work. Most drives are shipped jumpered for operation as the master, so you only have to adjust the second AT Attachment drive you add to the short chain.

Some AT interface host adapters enable you to connect more than two drives. They add their own extra BIOS code to the system so that your PC can recognize more than two drives. Electrically, these host adapters provide two isolated AT interface drive systems, each with its own master and slave drives. No formal standard exists for this kind of extended AT interface configuration, but ATA-2 will add its own means for increasing the number of drives you can install in a single PC.

Terminations

AT Attachment drives do not normally require you to adjust terminations when you install them as you need to with ST506 or ESDI drives. In the AT Attachment design, terminations are unnecessary. Exactly like plugging expansion cards into an expansion bus, the AT Attachment bus is designed to be properly loaded with any of its possible loads—zero, one, or two drives. Essentially, then, AT Attachment installation means that you plug in your hard disks. That's about all.

Performance

Speed is the most promising aspect of the AT interface, but early drives didn't deliver on that promise. Through the end of 1991, most AT interface drives were merely modifications of older products and designs with the necessary control electronics grafted on. Consequently, these drives were held back by issues related to the performance constraints of old interfaces such as drive rotation rate and data density. New drive designs aimed specifically at system-level interfaces are pushing the AT interface ahead.

The potential of the AT interface is great: because it's based on the AT bus, it should be able to deliver throughput that exactly matches the host computer's bus. No additional limits need to be imposed by other standard interfaces that the signal must traverse through. The ST506 and ESDI interfaces, on the other hand, force information going to and from the disk to slow to a single-file serial rate from one-third to one-twelfth the potential of the ISA bus.

The potential throughput of the AT interface connection is exactly the same as the ISA bus. At a nominal 8 MHz clock rate, an 8-bit AT interface connection can move data as quickly as 4M per second (each transfer requires two bus cycles, so the interface moves each byte at half the bus's clock rate). In 16-bit form, potential throughput doubles to 8M per second.

These speeds represent theoretical maxima. Your actual performance will differ because real-world throughput is limited by the mechanical speed of the drive. However, AT interface devices can approach the speed limit of the interface if they use large on-board buffers and those buffers are full of the data requested from the computer hosts. This design isolates the data request from the mechanical delays of operating the drive.

ATA Packet Interface

CD-ROM is rapidly moving from optional to mandatory in most PCs. The easy exchangeability of hundreds of megabytes is welcome not just for multimedia systems but also anytime you need a great deal of files and information—anything from new operating systems to dictionaries. Many new PCs are making CD-ROMs standard equipment.

Most CD-ROM players use SCSI interfaces, which means that the computer maker must add yet another connector and its associated circuitry to its basic PC. As manufacturers plumb the lowest ranges of prices that they can offer their PCs, they've eyed the AT interface connector greedily. If the AT interface will handle two drives, and most PCs need only one hard disk, why can't they plug the CD-ROM player there, too?

The answer is as simple as ATA and SCSI not matching—different connectors—but it goes deeper. The AT interface lacks the facilities to control everything that a CD-ROM player needs to do. Hard disks merely absorb and disgorge data. When it comes to ordinary data, however, CD-ROMs are simpler still—they only discharge data. They also usher audio around, though. The AT interface provides no means of linking audio to your PC, nor does it give any means of controlling the audio signals or several other aspects of normal CD-ROM operation.

The connection problem is easily solved. SCSI has no audio connection, either, but relies on an extra jack or two. Control is another matter—one for which the Small Form Factor Committee offers a solution: the ATA Packet Interface. An enhancement to the ordinary AT interface, ATAPI gives the system a means of sending packets of commands to CD-ROM players. The commands exactly match those used by SCSI, making the translation of SCSI CD-ROM products to the new system easier. The hardware side of the ATAPI enhancement is nothing more than the standard 40-pin ATA connector augmented by two jacks for audio signals (one serial digital, one two-channel analog). The ATAPI specification is designed to be completely compatible with existing ATA hardware and drivers. It changes nothing on the computer side of the AT connection, and it does not affect the design or operation of ATA hard disk drives. It just gives the makers of CD-ROM players and programmers guidance as to how to link their products to PCs in a standard way.

Under ATAPI, a CD-ROM player can replace the slave AT interface drive in your PC. But the specification requires that CD-ROM players be configurable as master or slave so that you can connect two CD-ROM drives to a single ATA cable.

Normally, an ATA hard disk gets its commands through eight registers called the Task File, which passes along all the commands and parameters needed to operate the disk. Unfortunately, these eight registers are not sufficient for the needed CD-ROM control. ATAPI adds one new command: the Packet Command that initiates a mode in which multiple writes to the Task File will send packets of commands to the CD-ROM player. Most ATAPI command packets contain 12 bytes, although the standard also defines 16-byte packets for compatibility with future devices.

Although ATAPI uses many of the same block and command definitions described by SCSI, it does not use many of the other features of SCSI protocol such as messaging, bus sharing with multiple computers, disconnect/reconnect, and linking and queuing of commands.

The first of the 12 bytes in the ATAPI Command Packet (byte 0) is an operation code that defines the command itself. The initial ATAPI specification defined 29 operation codes, two of which are reserved for CD-ROM XT systems. The third through sixth byte (bytes 2-5) of each packet hold the logical block address of the data to be used if the command involves the use of data. The CD-ROM logical addresses start with zero as the first block and increase sequentially up to the last block. The eight and ninth bytes (bytes 7 and 8) of the packet define the length of the transfer, parameter list, or allocation involved in the command. Special extended commands add an extra byte for indicating this length. The remaining bytes in the packet are not defined by the specification but are reserved for future implementations.

ATA-2

The ATA Packet Interface is one part of a larger effort to enlarge and revise the AT Attachment specification. The goal, which some manufacturers term Enhanced ATA and others call ATA-2, is to increase the capabilities of the AT interface to handle all the basic needs of a PC, including the higher data-transfer rates expected from new products.

There's no sign of when an ATA-2 standard will be adopted. In fact, no one even knows what organization will put its official imprimatur on such a specification. In the interim, however, two manufacturers are working toward their own visions of what the next generation of ATA will be. Since 1993, Western Digital Corporation has been promoting a set of improved ATA features that it collectively calls *Enhanced IDE*. At the same time, Seagate Technology has proposed a more modest alternative, which it calls *Fast ATA*.

Enhanced IDE

According to Western Digital, four features define Enhanced IDE: breaking the 528M capacity barrier; increasing data throughput; increasing the number of drives per system beyond two; and allowing devices other than hard disks to share the ATA connection. The Enhanced IDE program unites four individual strategies to bring these features to life.

To overcome the inherent drive size limitation of 528M caused by the interaction of the ATA specification and BIOS disk parameter constraints, Enhanced IDE requires a rewritten BIOS that addresses the disk drive in terms of a 28-bit *Logical Block Addresses (or LBA)* instead of cylinders, heads, and sectors. Each sector on the drive would be assigned a unique address, so the maximum capacity of the drive would be constrained only by the BIOS sector limit—that's 63 sectors per track, 1024 tracks, and 255 heads or a total capacity of 8.4GB.

The Enhanced IDE design also designates a flag bit in one of the drive's registers (specifically bit 6 of the drive's SDH register) to indicate whether the drive uses cylinder-head-sector addressing or LBA addressing. The penalty of the Enhanced IDE system is that it requires the Interrupt 13 firmware code of the host computer to be rewritten to accommodate the new addressing scheme. In other words, getting full capacity from an Enhanced IDE drive will require either a new PC with a BIOS that specifically supports Enhanced IDE (several are already available) or an add-in host adapter card that has its own compatible BIOS.

The transfer speed limitations of the ATA system are primarily a result of the AT interface inherent in the original design. Advanced expansion buses like VL Bus or PCI don't help because of the integrated AT bus, which limits peak transfer rate to two to three megabytes per second. Enhanced IDE takes two approaches to bursting through this barrier.

Most PCs use programmed input/output (PIO) techniques for transferring data from the disk to the host computer. The host microprocessor handles each step of the transfer of information into memory. In a system using the standard AT interface for its hard disk, the host microprocessor functions as a master controlling the drive as a slave. The master issues commands to transfer data and blindly hopes that the slave can carry them out expeditiously. Unfortunately, the drive has to behave as if it is using an ISA expansion bus (the AT interface) even if it is connected using a higher-speed advanced bus, so any advantage of the advanced bus is lost.

Enhanced IDE shifts control to the hard disk drive. The drive uses the I/O Channel Ready signal on the bus to take command and regulate the flow of data. The drive can then optimize its transfers for the available bandwidth of the bus. According to Western Digital, this design extended the transfer rate of the IDE system to about 11 megabytes per second (using standard 180 nanosecond bus PIO cycle times).

The downside of this design is that it requires a redesign of the host system to allow the drive to take control. Some systems already have been designed to allow flow control using the I/O Channel Ready signal, and application-specific integrated circuits and chipsets that support this ability are now available to PC makers. To allow Enhanced IDE drives to work (although at the lower, standard ATA rate) in older systems, Enhanced IDE drives default to operation using the older, slower method. To enable the high-speed PIO transfer mode, the host computer must send a Set Features command to properly configure the drive.

For even faster transfers, Enhanced IDE envisions using Direct Memory Access techniques for transferring data from drives to memory without host microprocessor intervention. In conjunction with a new advanced transfer DMA mode of the PCI expansion bus (Type F MDA), peak transfer rates of up to 8.33 megabytes per second are possible. A proposal to reduce the cycle time of multi-word drive transfers to 150 nanoseconds would increase the peak transfer rate to 13 megabytes per second.

Taking advantage of these faster DMA modes will also require a rewritten BIOS and new device drivers. You'll also want a PCI-based system to achieve maximum transfer rate—which means you'll need a new PC.

To increase the number of drives that can be installed in a single PC, the Enhanced IDE proposal imagines stepping back to the old ST506 expedient: primary and secondary host adapters or controllers in a PC. Enhanced IDE will simply put a second AT-interface system (which inherently supports two drives) in a PC. The second AT-interface system will move the base address of its BIOS code and use a separate hardware interrupt (interrupt 15) than the primary drive system. The secondary drive system will have its own ATA cable connector and cable. Two drives will daisy-chain to it just as they would in an ordinary two-drive ATA system.

Again, this Enhanced IDE innovation requires an alternation to the host system's BIOS so that all four drives can be identified. It also requires a second ATA connector. Western Digital imagines that adding the capability of two more drives will add about one dollar to the price of a PC.

On the software side, few operating system changes would be required. Versions of DOS since 3.0 have allowed for seven hard disks in a single system without special drivers. OS/2 versions since 1.31 have allowed for four drives. Novell NetWare makes provisions for up to eight ATA drives. Because Windows 3.1 accesses system disk drives through the Interrupt 13 function of the BIOS, the basic BIOS changes will automatically add Windows support.

The Enhanced IDE design requires absolutely no changes to the drives themselves. Even current drives will plug in and be properly recognized without a problem.

To allow devices other than hard disk drives to share a single connection, Enhanced IDE incorporates the ATAPI design, discussed previously.

Fast ATA

Seagate Technology believes that Enhanced IDE requires too many system changes to be a viable solution for a more immediate need: faster disk transfer rates. To help drives keep up with overall PC performance technology, Seagate developed and is promoting Fast ATA.

Stripped to its essence, Fast ATA is little more than the performance improvements envisioned by Enhanced IDE. It pushes PIO transfers up to 11 megabytes per second using the I/O Channel Ready signal for control. Fast DMA cycles on advanced expansion buses using multiword transfers push the peak transfer rate to 13.3 megabytes per second.

According to Seagate, Fast ATA requires virtually no changes in its PC host. It can be made to work with standard host adapters, standard BIOSs, and standard operating systems. Most PCs already incorporate the setup options required to configure a Fast ATA drive (says Seagate), and newer BIOS versions will be able to automatically configure systems for the fastest possible disk transfers.

People in the disk-drive industry expect the submission for standardization of a complete ATA-2 specification that essentially follows the Enhanced IDE design in late 1994. Fast ATA is essentially a subset of Enhanced IDE and represent an interim (but effective) solution.

ATA-3

Work is progressing to push the AT Attachment standard beyond the limits envisioned in its next version. Work already has begun on an ATA-3 standard. Unlike ATA-2, the later incarnation probably will make dramatic changes in the interface—requiring changes to drivers, cables, and termination requirements. What will not change will be the registers used, the commands, and protocols so that new drives will require new connections but will work with existing software (operating systems and applications). The benefit of these changes will be higher speed. Designers look forward to a data-transfer rate of about 20M per second using programmed input/output and even higher speeds using multiword (wide-bus) direct memory access control.

ATA-3 also will change the form of the ATA specification, breaking the single standard into multiple documents, and the specification will become a multilayer architecture. The ATAPI will divide into both a CD-ROM command set and a tape drive command set, which together will parallel the hard disk drive command set. Support for other removable media devices (for example, cartridge hard disks and magneto-optical drives) also will be incorporated. The standard will include a transport level—that is, a signalling scheme—and a physical level that defines the connections and form of the new electronic interface.

All of the details of ATA-3 probably will not be formalized until 1995 or later.

SCSI

Pronounced "scuzzy" by much of the computer industry (but sometimes "sexy" by its most fervent advocates), SCSI is a system-level interfaces that provides what is essentially a complete expansion bus into which to plug peripherals. SCSI isn't simply a connection that links a device or two to your PC. Rather, it functions like a sub-bus. SCSI devices can exchange data among themselves without the intervention of the host computer's microprocessor. In fact, they can act across the SCSI bus even while other transfers are shifting across the host computer's normal expansion bus.

The original SCSI standard evolved from another interface called SASI, the Shugart Associates Standard Interface. This interface was developed in 1981 by hard-disk pioneer Shugart Associates with NCR Corporation as an 8-bit parallel connection between host computers and disk drives. Later that year, the X3T9 committee of the American National Standards Institute used the SASI specification as the foundation for its work on a parallel interface standard. That standard, now known as SCSI, was formally approved in 1986.

As with any expansion bus, any of a variety of device types can be connected to the SCSI bus almost indiscriminately, all communicating to your PC through a single-port connection. Up to seven SCSI devices can be daisy-chained to one SCSI port. All the devices function independently, under the control of the host system through the SCSI port.

As with the AT interface, SCSI provides a parallel connection between its devices and the SCSI adapter. In most SCSI systems, only a single cable—albeit one with a wealth of conductors—is needed for a SCSI linkup.

Under the original SCSI specification, SCSI operated at a speed of 5 MHz. Its 8-bit parallel interface (with one additional bit for parity) allowed for a peak data transfer rate of 5M per second.

SCSI-2

In 1991, a revision of SCSI was introduced to help fix some of the problems in mating SCSI devices, as well as to increase the speed of SCSI transfers. Referred to as SCSI 2, the new standard integrated a complete software-control system called the Common Command Set with several optional hardware enhancements. These included the broadening of the 8-bit SCSI data bus to wide SCSI, which can use 16 or 32 data lines. These would double the effective peak transfer rate of the interface to 10M or 20M per second. In addition, the top speed of SCSI transfers was doubled with the addition of fast SCSI. With an 8-bit bus width, fast SCSI pushed transfer rates up to 10M per second; wide and fast SCSI could peak at 20M to 40M per second.

SCSI-3

Almost immediately after the SCSI-2 standard was approved, the industry began work on its successor. The proposed SCSI-3 further refines the standard. In a dramatic backward shift, SCSI-3 again separates the software from the hardware, making the CCS independent of the underlying hardware. In addition, SCSI-3 provides mechanisms for using the CCS across several hardware-connection schemes. In addition to Parallel SCSI, essentially what we know as SCSI-2 today—the new standard will support Serial SCSI based on the P1394 standard (see Chapter 19, Serial Ports), a fiber optical connection, and several others. Moreover, Parallel SCSI is enhanced into 16-bit SCSI, which increases the device total that can be connected to a single SCSI bus to 16. SCSI-3 also takes care of some of the details, officially standardizing the P-connector used in most wide SCSI-2 implementations.

The speed of SCSI-3 depends on its hardware implementation. The cabling methods and speed of SCSI-2 are still allowed, but new transmission systems allow transfer rates in excess of 100M per second.

Operation and Arbitration

All devices connected to a single SCSI bus function independently, under the control of the host system through the SCSI adapter. Rather than just using signals on dedicated conductors on the bus that can be understood by devices as dumb as a light bulb, SCSI presupposes a high degree of intelligence in the devices it connects and provides its own command set—essentially, its own computer language—for controlling the devices.

Not only is SCSI more like an expansion bus of a computer than a traditional hard disk interface, but it also resembles today's more advanced Micro Channel and NuBus designs. Like the latest computer buses, SCSI provides an arbitration scheme. Arbitration enables the devices connected to the bus to determine which of them can send data across the bus at a given time. Instead of being controlled by the host computer and suffering delays while its microprocessor does other things, the arbitration of the SCSI bus is distributed among all the devices on the bus.

Arbitration on the SCSI bus is handled by hardware. Each of the up to seven SCSI devices is assigned a unique identifying number, usually by setting jumpers or DIP switches on the drive in a manner similar to the Drive Select jumpers on an ST506 device.

When a device, called the Initiator, wants to access the SCSI bus, it waits until the bus is free and then identifies itself by sending a signal down one of the SCSI data lines. At the same time, it transmits a signal down another SCSI data line corresponding to the other SCSI device, called the target, that it wants to interact with. The eight data lines in the SCSI connection allow the unique identification of seven SCSI devices and one host.

Note that SCSI devices can initiate arbitration on their own, independent of the host. Two SCSI devices also can transfer information between one another without host intervention. A SCSI hard disk, for example, may back itself up to a SCSI tape drive without requiring the attention of (and robbing performance from) its host computer. Better than background operation, this form of backup represents true parallel processing in the computer system.

In addition, SCSI provides for reselecting. That is, a device that temporarily does not need bus access can release the bus, carry out another operation, and then resume control. You can command a disk drive to format, and it can carry out that operation without tying up the bus, for example. The net result is, again, true parallel processing.

Because SCSI is a high-level interface, it also isolates the computer from the inner workings of the peripherals connected to it. The SCSI standard allows hard disks to monitor their own bad tracks independently from the computer host. The disk drive reassigns bad tracks and reports back to its computer host as if it were a perfect disk. In addition, hard disk drives can be designed to automatically detect sectors that are going bad and to reassign the data they contain elsewhere, all without the host computer or the user ever being aware of any problems.

Hardware

The basic SCSI hardware interface is a parallel 8-bit bus with a ninth parity bit for error detection. As a bus, all devices are simultaneously connected and receive all transmissions (commands and data). Commands are routed to individual SCSI devices by identifying them by their SCSI address. SCSI uses a 3-bit addressing scheme, allowing 8 unambiguous addresses, which usually are given in standard Arabic numerals as SCSI ID Numbers 0 through 7. One of these, 7, is reserved for the SCSI host adapter. The other addresses, 0 through 6, can be assigned to any device connected anywhere in the SCSI chain. Each address is assigned a priority to the device using it with 7 (the host adapter) having the top priority and 0 having the lowest priority.

Except for the arbitrary address of 7 assigned to the host adapter, you assign the addresses that each SCSI device uses. You set the addresses on most SCSI devices by switch or jumper. Most external SCSI devices are assigned their ID number by a pushbutton or rotary switch on the rear panel of the equipment. Internal SCSI devices such as hard disks typically have several jumpers or switches on each device that sets its SCSI ID. The most basic rule is simple: SCSI ID number must be unique, so never assign to two or more devices in the same SCSI chain the same ID number.

In general, you can assign any number to any device, as long as you configure your software properly. A SCSI driver may require that you indicate the SCSI address that you assign to your CD-ROM player, for example. In some cases, programmers steal your freedom in assigning SCSI identification numbers. The software for the CD-ROM player may demand that you assign a particular address to the player in order for it to work. One exception to this rule is that most SCSI host adapters that emulate the Western Digital WD1002 controller require that any SCSI drive meant to boot your PC use the ID number 0 (zero).

The original SCSI specifications allowed for two types of SCSI buses: single-ended and differential. Single-ended SCSI uses an unbalanced or single-ended electrical signal—a single wire for each signal, with all signals in the bus using a single common ground return. Differential SCSI uses balanced or differential signals. Each signal on the SCSI bus has its own return line that is isolated from the reference ground. Differential SCSI signals use twisted-pair wiring. Most SCSI implementations have been single-ended because they require half the pins, cheaper wire, and simpler electronics than do differential SCSI implementations.

As with all single-ended electrical systems, single-ended SCSI is more prone to picking up noise and interference than differential SCSI. As a result, the specifications for SCSI systems that use single-ended signals limit cable lengths to no more than 6 meters (just under 20 feet). Differential SCSI allows for bus lengths up to 25 meters (about 82 feet). You must have at least one-third meter (about 12 inches) of cable between SCSI devices, so the shortest possible SCSI cable is that length. External SCSI cables should be shielded.

SCSI devices can use asynchronous or synchronous transfer protocols when communicating. Asynchronous SCSI transmissions are slower because they require more overhead—a handshake signal for every byte transferred. Synchronous SCSI transfers require less overhead. You can mix both asynchronous and synchronous devices in a single SCSI system.

SCSI Cabling

Because SCSI is a bus, you connect devices together by daisy-chaining. You run a straight cable (no twists or crossovers) from the host adapter to each SCSI device.

Internal SCSI devices like hard disks use a simple flat ribbon cable with multiple connectors attached to it. All connectors have identical signals, so you can use any convenient connector for any SCSI device. The devices and host adapter use SCSI ID numbers to sort out which commands and data go where.

External SCSI cabling is somewhat different. You run a cable from the host adapter to the first device in the external SCSI chain. For the next device, you plug another cable into the first device, and then plug the other end of the cable into a second device. Just continue in the same manner adding another cable for each additional device.

Most external SCSI devices have two SCSI connectors to facilitate such daisy-chaining. It doesn't matter which of the two connectors on the SCSI device you use to attach each cable. Functionally, both connectors are the same; each is equally adept at handling incoming and outgoing signals.

The standard SCSI connector has 50 pins arranged in two rows of 25 and looks like an enlarged Centronics printer connector. This connector is standardized by the SCSI specifications and is termed the A Connector (See Table 21.5). A few host adapters and some external SCSI devices use 25-pin, D-shell connectors (like the parallel ports on the back of your PC),which were popularized by Apple Computer for its Macintosh equipment. The 25-pin connectors can handle only single-ended signals because they don't have enough connections for differential signals. You need an adapter cable to match these devices. It's best to put any 25-pin SCSI device at the end of the SCSI daisy-chain. Table 21.6 shows the signal assignment on these connectors.

TABLE 21.5. SCSI A-Cable

Pin	Function	Pin	Function
1	GROUND	26	Data bit 0
2	GROUND	27	Data bit 1
3	GROUND	28	Data bit 2
4	GROUND	29	Data bit 3
5	GROUND	30	Data bit 4
6	GROUND	31	Data bit 5
7	GROUND	32	Data bit 6
8	GROUND	33	Data bit 7
9	GROUND	34	Parity bit
10	GROUND	35	GROUND
11	5V/3.3V GROUND	36	5V/3.3V (Motor)
12	12V/5V GROUND	37	12V/5V
13	TERMPWR	38	TERMPWR
14	12V/5V	39	12V/5V GROUND
15	5V/3.3V (Logic)	40	5V/3.3V (Return)
16	-ADDR #1/GROUND	41	-ATN
17	GROUND	42	SYNC
18	GROUND	43	-BSY
19	GROUND	44	-ACK
20	GROUND	45	-RST
21	-ADDR #2/GROUND	46	-MSG
22	GROUND	47	-SEL
23	-ADDR #3/GROUND	48	-C/D
24	GROUND	49	-REQ
25	VU/GROUND	50	-I/O

TABLE 21.6. 25-Pin D-Shell SCSI Implementation (for example, Apple)

Pin	Function	Corresponding 50-pin assignment
1	-REQ	49
2	-MSG	46
3	-I/O	50
4	-RST	45
5	-ACK	44
6	-BSY	43
7	Ground	16,18,19
8	Data bit 0	26
9	Ground	20,21,22
10	Data bit 3	29
11	Data bit 5	31
12	Data bit 6	32
13	Data bit 7	33
14	Ground	1,2,3
15	-C/D	48
16	Ground	4,5,6
17	-ATN	41
18	Ground	7,8,9
19	-SEL	47
20	Parity bit	34
21	Data bit 1	27
22	Data bit 2	28
23	Data bit 4	30
24	Ground	23,24,25
25	Termination power	38

Wide SCSI requires more connections than are possible with the A cable alone. Although the SCSI-2 specifications indicate the use of a second, B cable to provide a path for these additional signals, most developers use a similar cable called the P cable instead. Both the B and P cables use high-density, 68-pin, SCSI-2 connectors consisting of two rows of 34 male contacts on 0.050-inch x 0.100-inch centers. Only the pin assignment of the connector differs. Under the SCSI-3 proposal, bus widths up 16 bits use the P cable (called the primary cable); wider buses require a secondary cable with the same connector but different signals and pinouts (see Table 21.7).

TABLE 21.7. SCSI P-Cable; Single-Ended Primary Bus

Pin	Function	Pin	Function
1	Ground	35	Data bit 12
2	Ground	36	Data bit 13
3	Ground	37	Data bit 14
4	Ground	38	Data bit 15
5	Ground	39	Parity bit 1
6	Ground	40	Data bit 0
7	Ground	41	Data bit 1
8	Ground	42	Data bit 2
9	Ground	43	Data bit 3
10	Ground	44	Data bit 4
11	Ground	45	Data bit 5
12	Ground	46	Data bit 6
13	Ground	47	Data bit 7
14	Ground	48	Parity bit 0
15	Ground	49	Ground
16	Ground	50	Ground
17	Termination Power	51	Termination Power
18	Termination Power	52	Termination Power
19	Reserved	53	Reserved
20	Ground	54	Ground
21	Ground	55	-ATN
22	Ground	56	Ground
23	Ground	57	-BSY
24	Ground	58	-ACK
25	Ground	59	-RST
26	Ground	60	-MSG
27	Ground	61	-SEL
28	Ground	62	-C/D
29	Ground	63	-REQ
30	Ground	64	-I/O
31	Ground	65	Data bit 8

Pin	Function	Pin	Function
32	Ground	66	Data bit 9
33	Ground	67	Data bit 10
34	Ground	68	Data bit 11

Source: ISO X3T9.2 855D

SCSI P-Cable; Single-Ended Secondary Bus

Pin	Function	Pin	Function
1	Ground	35	Data bit 28
2	Ground	36	Data bit 29
3	Ground	37	Data bit 30
4	Ground	38	Data bit 31
5	Ground	39	Parity bit 3
6	Ground	40	Data bit 16
7	Ground	41	Data bit 17
8	Ground	42	Data bit 18
9	Ground	43	Data bit 19
10	Ground	44	Data bit 20
11	Ground	45	Data bit 21
12	Ground	46	Data bit 22
13	Ground	47	Data bit 23
14	Ground	48	Parity bit 2
15	Ground	49	Ground
16	Ground	50	Ground
17	Termination Power	51	Termination Power
18	Termination Power	52	Termination Power
19	Reserved	53	Reserved
20	Ground	54	Ground
21	Ground	55	Terminated
22	Ground	56	Ground
23	Ground	57	Terminated
24	Ground	58	-ACKQ
25	Ground	59	Terminated

continues

TABLE 21.7. Continued

SCSI P-Cable; Single-Ended Secondary Bus

Pin	Function	Pin	Function
26	Ground	60	Terminated
27	Ground	61	Terminated
28	Ground	62	Terminated
29	Ground	63	-REQQ
30	Ground	64	Terminated
31	Ground	65	Data bit 24
32	Ground	66	Data bit 25
33	Ground	67	Data bit 26
34	Ground	68	Data bit 27

Source: ISO X3T9.2 855D

SCSI P-Cable; Differential Primary Bus

Pin	Function	Pin	Function
1	Data bit 12 +	35	Data bit 12 -
2	Data bit 13 +	36	Data bit 13 -
3	Data bit 14 +	37	Data bit 14 -
4	Data bit 15 +	38	Data bit 15 -
5	Parity bit 1 +	39	Parity bit 1 -
6	Ground	40	Ground
7	Data bit 0 +	41	Data bit 0 -
8	Data bit 1 +	42	Data bit 1 -
9	Data bit 2 +	43	Data bit 2 -
10	Data bit 3 +	44	Data bit 3 -
11	Data bit 4 +	45	Data bit 4 -
12	Data bit 5 +	46	Data bit 5 -
13	Data bit 6 +	47	Data bit 6 -
14	Data bit 7 +	48	Data bit 7 -
15	Parity bit 0 +	49	Parity bit 0 -
16	Differential sensing	50	Ground
17	Termination Power	51	Termination Power
18	Termination Power	52	Termination Power

SCSI P-Cable; Differential Primary Bus

Pin	Function	Pin	Function
19	Reserved	53	Reserved
20	+ATN	54	-ATN
21	Ground	55	Ground
22	+BSY	56	-BSY
23	+ACK	57	-ACK
24	+RST	58	-RST
25	+MSG	59	-MSG
26	+SEL	60	-SEL
27	+C/D	61	-C/D
28	+REQ	62	-REQ
29	+I/O	63	-I/O
30	Ground	64	Ground
31	Data bit 8 +	65	Data bit 8 -
32	Data bit 9 +	66	Data bit 9 -
33	Data bit 10 +	67	Data bit 10 -
34	Data bit 11 +	68	Data bit 11 -

SCSI P-Cable; Differential Secondary Bus

Pin	Function	Pin	Function
1	Data bit 28 +	35	Data bit 28
2	Data bit 29 +	36	Data bit 29
3	Data bit 30 +	37	Data bit 30
4	Data bit 31 +	38	Data bit 31
5	Parity bit 3 +	39	Parity bit 3
6	Ground	40	Ground
7	Data bit 16 +	41	Data bit 16
8	Data bit 17 +	42	Data bit 17
9	Data bit 18 +	43	Data bit 18
10	Data bit 19 +	44	Data bit 19
11	Data bit 20 +	45	Data bit 20
12	Data bit 21 +	46	Data bit 21
13	Data bit 22 +	47	Data bit 22

continues

TABLE 21.7. Continued

SCSI P-Cable; Differential Secondary Bus

Pin	Function	Pin	Function
14	Data bit 23 +	48	Data bit 23
15	Parity bit 2 +	49	Parity bit 2
16	Differential sensing	50	Ground
17	Termination Power	51	Termination
18	Termination Power	52	Termination
19	Reserved	53	Reserved
20	Terminated	54	Terminated
21	Ground	55	Ground
22	Terminated	56	Terminated
23	+ACKQ	57	-ACKQ
24	Terminated	58	Terminated
25	Terminated	59	Terminated
26	Terminated	60	Terminated
27	Terminated	61	Terminated
28	+REQQ	62	-REQQ
29	Terminated	63	Terminated
30	Ground	64	Ground
31	Data bit 24 +	65	Data bit 24
32	Data bit 25 +	66	Data bit 25
33	Data bit 26 +	67	Data bit 26
34	Data bit 27 +	68	Data bit 27

Source: ISO X3T9.2 855D

After you finish connecting your SCSI cables and terminating your daisy-chain, be sure to snap in place the retaining clips or wires on each SCSI connector to be sure that each connector is held securely in place. This mechanical locking is particularly important with SCSI connections because the wiring works like old-fashioned Christmas lights—if one goes out, they all go out. Not only will whatever SCSI device that has a loose connector be out of touch, all other devices after the loose connector in the chain also will lose communication. Moreover, because the chain will no longer be terminated properly, even the devices earlier in the chain may not work reliably. Locking the wire on each SCSI connector will help ensure that none of the connectors accidentally gets loosened.

SCSI Terminations

Eventually your SCSI daisy-chain will come to an end. You will have one last device to which you have no more peripherals to connect. To prevent spurious signals from bouncing back and forth across the SCSI cable chain, the SCSI standard requires that you properly terminate the entire SCSI system. The SCSI-2 standard allows for two methods of terminating SCSI buses.

Alternative 1 is the old-fashioned (original SCSI) method of passive terminations using only resistors. Electrically, the terminator is the equivalent of a voltage source of three volts in series with a 132-ohm resistor. This value is achieved by connecting a single-ended signal through a 220-ohm resistor to the TERMPWR line and through a 330-ohm resistor to ground. All signals on the SCSI bus (except those labeled Ground, TERMPWR, or Reserved by the standard) require this kind of termination at each end of the bus. Alternative 1 terminations work well when four or fewer devices are connected to the SCSI bus.

Alternative 2 uses active terminations. The terminator uses a voltage regulator to source a 2.85 VDC level in series with a 110-ohm resistor. This active termination reduces the susceptibility of the bus to noise, particularly when cables are long or when many devices are connected to the bus.

Differential signals use a different termination method. All signals are terminated at each end of the cable with a network having two 330-ohm resistors and a 150-ohm resistor arranged to provide the equivalent of a 122-ohm impedance. The TERMPWR line connects to the negative signal line through a 330-ohm resistor; the negative signal line is connected to the positive through the 150-ohm resistor; and the positive signal line is connected to the ground through the second 330-ohm resistor (see fig. 21.3).

SCSI initiators supply the termination power to their TERMPWR connections through diodes to prevent termination power from other devices from flowing back into the device. Although target devices do not need to supply terminator power, any SCSI device is permitted to supply terminator power.

A third form of termination called Forced Perfect Termination is rarely used. FPT uses diodes to regulate the power on the SCSI bus.

In classic SCSI implementations, the three most popular physical means of providing a SCSI termination are internally with resistor packs, externally with dummy termination plugs, and using switches as shown in figure 21.4. SCSI-2 systems with active terminations usually use switches.

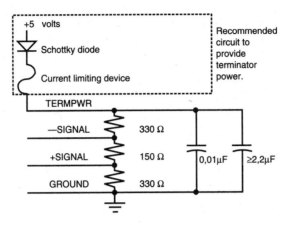

Figure 21.3. SCSI active termination schematic.

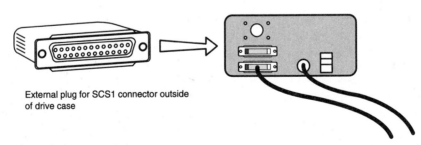

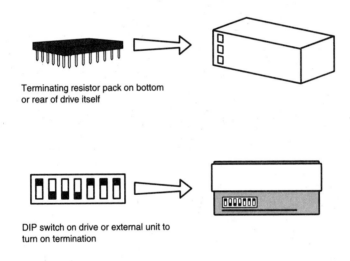

Figure 21.4. Classic SCSI termination methods.

Resistor packs are components attached directly to circuit boards. Unlike the other interfaces, SCSI devices typically use three (instead of one) resistor packs for their terminations. Most PC-based SCSI host adapters and hard disks come with termination resistors already installed on them.

You easily can identify terminating resistors as three identical components about an inch long and one-quarter to three-eighths inches high and hardly an eighth inch thick. Most commonly, these resistor packs are red, brownish yellow, or black and shiny, and they are located adjacent to the SCSI connector on the SCSI device or host adapter. When necessary, you remove these terminations simply by pulling them out of their sockets on the circuit board.

External SCSI terminators are plugs that look like short extensions to the SCSI jacks on the back of SCSI devices. One end of the terminator plugs into one of the SCSI device's jacks, and the other end of the dummy plug yields another jack that can be attached to another SCSI cable. Some external terminators, however, lack the second jack on the back. Generally, the absence of a second connector is no problem because the dummy plug should be attached only to the last device in the SCSI chain.

Switches, the third variety of termination, may be found on both external and internal drives. Sometimes a single switch handles the entire termination, but occasionally a SCSI drive will have three banks of DIP switches that all must be flipped to the same position to select whether the termination is active. These switches are sometimes found on the SCSI device or on the case of an external unit.

A few external SCSI devices rely on the terminators on the drive inside their cases for their terminations. For these, you must take apart the device to adjust the terminators.

According to the SCSI specification, the first and last device in a SCSI chain must be terminated. The first device is almost always the SCSI host adapter in your PC. If you install a single internal hard disk to the host adapter, the hard disk becomes the other end of the chain and requires termination. Similarly, a single external hard disk also requires termination.

With multiple devices connected to a single host adapter, the termination issue becomes complex. Generally, the host adapter will be one end of the SCSI chain except when you have both internal and external devices connected to it. Then, and only then, should you remove the terminations from your host adapter. In that case, the device nearest the end of the internal SCSI cable should be terminated as should the external device at the end of the daisy-chain of cables— the only external device that likely has a connector without a cable plugged into it. Remove or switch off the terminators on all other devices.

Compatibility

SCSI hard disks entirely isolate the host computer from concerns about disk sector and tracks. The SCSI system deals with data at a higher level, as blocks, so any block-oriented device can take advantage of the connection scheme. This arrangement works well in the Macintosh environment because the Mac operating system has built-in provisions for dealing with SCSI. PC DOS and MS DOS lack such provisions, however, so SCSI host adapters for IBM-standard systems must convert sector and track requests into their SCSI equivalent. As a result, the system gets, at best, an indirect look at the disk drive. At worst, the overhead required for the address conversions can considerably slow the performance of an IBM-based SCSI system. This symptom was particularly noticeable in the first generation of SCSI devices and host adapters. Drive and host adapter manufacturers have learned to glean more of SCSI's speed, but you still find a wide variance in the throughputs of the SCSI host adapters on the market. The quickest approach the performance potential of the interface; the worst drag speed down to the level of the ancient interfaces.

The Apple Macintosh implementation of SCSI has been criticized for being at variance from the otherwise accepted industry standard, but the only place it varies is with the connector choice. The standard SCSI hook-up uses a single special 50-pin connector. In the existing asynchronous implementation of SCSI, more than half the wires in the connectors are used as grounds (redundant signal return lines). The Macintosh uses a 25-pin miniature D-shell connector much like that used by serial ports and does away with many of the redundant ground connections. The more compact size of this connector was probably one reason for its choice. It also makes cabling easier and more convenient.

A bigger compatibility issue arises when trying to take advantage of SCSI's capability to link multiple devices to one host adapter. Some devices just will not work with others. The incompatibilities arise out of the flexibility of the SCSI standard. Although the specification strictly defines all hardware parameters, it is much more loose when it comes to software features. Much of the SCSI command set is optional—devices only have to implement the features that they will use. Moreover, the SCSI specification provides no standard means of the host computer controlling SCSI devices through the interface. That is left up to the system designer.

Although this approach works well in the environment that SCSI was originally designed for— minicomputers—and in which the device maker also configures the host adapter to match a particular computer system, it fails in the multisplendored DOS world. Four methods have been used for logically linking SCSI to PCs: ASPI, CAM, Int 4Ah, and LADDR.

Int 4Ah and LADDR have found limited support. When IBM integrated SCSI support into its PS/2 series of computers, it used a system interrupt, number 04A(Hex), to command the SCSI system. As with other aspects of PS/2s, few other manufacturers have copied this feature. LADDR stands for Layered Device Driver Architecture and was Microsoft's first stab at linking to SCSI. Although aimed at making SCSI easier to use with multitasking and built into OS/2 Version 2.1, few makers of SCSI equipment provide drivers to accommodate LADDR.

The Common Access Method or CAM Committee—the same group that helped to develop the AT Attachment standard—has developed its own implementation of the SCSI standard that allows access to SCSI devices directly through your PC's operating system. Although as this is written, a CAM standard was not formally adopted by any standard-setting organization, but the specification has been around long enough that many manufacturers use it for their products. Such CAM-compliant SCSI host adapters have onboard BIOSes that will link with your operating system. Programs written to take advantage of CAM then can make requests to your operating system and have them carried out by the appropriate SCSI device.Unfortunately, DOS is not currently CAM-compliant, although OS/2 versions since 2.0 are CAM-compliant.

The Advanced SCSI Programming Interface or ASPI is an alternate SCSI control system that originally was developed by host adapter-maker Adaptec (the A in ASPI originally stood for Adaptec, but the company yielded to change to broaden the appeal of the standard) and is now widely used in the PC industry. Adaptec calls it a defacto standard. ASPI uses a layered approach to the software interface using driver software. Programs communicate and send commands to SCSI devices through an individual software driver for each device. An overall ASPI driver links the individual device drivers to the SCSI system hardware.

The BIOS on an ASPI-compliant host adapter merely provides fundamental services that establish the link with the ASPI driver. In general, the ASPI BIOS provides WD1002 emulation. It enables you to connect one or two SCSI hard disks to the host adapter and have them mimic a Western Digital WD1002 ST506-style hard-disk controller and its associated disks. Without further ado or drivers, the first SCSI disk is able to boot your system as drive C and the second serve as drive D. That's as far as the BIOS support goes, however. Without the loading software drivers, your ASPI-based system cannot recognize further hard disks or other SCSI devices.

To completely set up an ASPI system, you must install all the required device drivers in your PC's CONFIG.SYS file. You have to install the ASPI driver when you install your host adapter and install a driver for each SCSI device you connect (except the first two hard disks). Because the device-specific software drivers need the ASPI driver to link to the SCSI system, you should ensure that the ASPI driver entry precedes that of other SCSI device drivers in your PC's CONFIG.SYS file.

One problem you may encounter when getting your ASPI system to work may have its roots in impatience. If you bought your SCSI host adapter along with a hard disk and were anxious to get things running, you simply may have connected everything as if it were an IDE AT-interface or ESDI hard disk. The hard disk probably would have worked just fine (thanks to the WD1002 emulation of the BIOS), but when you later try to install a CD-ROM player, its driver will not be able to find the ASPI driver you failed to install. You will see an obscure error message about the lack of an ASPI driver that probably will make you scratch your head for hours. The solution to this problem is to fetch the disk that came with your SCSI host adapter and install the ASPI driver.

Most software drivers search for their target devices when they are booted into your system. Consequently, all your external SCSI devices should be running when you switch on your PC. Turn on your SCSI devices before you switch on your PC or use a power director (outlet box) that ensures that your entire computer system—PC and SCSI peripherals—switch on simultaneously.

Power Cables

All drives require power to run their motors and their control electronics, and most drives regardless of size or interface use the same kind of power connection. The primary exceptions are the 3 1/2-inch hard disks meant for installation in IBM's PS/2 internal drive bays which have their power and signal connectors integrated into a single plug-in unit. With other drives, the power connection is a standard device power plug—a nylon connector that accommodates four separate wires, one of which is redundant. Note that the AT Attachment standard also recognizes a miniaturized power connector like that used by some 3 1/2-inch floppy disk drives. Power connectors and power requirements are discussed in Chapter 9, "The Power Supply."

Caching

All mass storage devices—be they magnetic hard disks, floppies, or optical—face two primary performance constraints: access speed and transfer rate. Access speed is the inevitable delay between the instant your computer requests a particular byte or block of information from the disk drive and when that information is located on the disk. In specifications, access speed is represented by a number termed average access time, which describes the mean time (in milliseconds) required for the read-write head of a drive to move between disk tracks. Transfer rate describes the speed at which the information stored on the disk can be moved into the working memory of your PC. It is usually measured in megabytes per second.

Access speed and transfer rate are issues of design, but their ultimate limits arise from mechanical issues. Access speed is determined principally by the speed at which the disk mechanism can fling its head about. Smaller heads, having less inertia, generally can be snapped into place more quickly, although a more robust mechanism can bestow a measure of snap to heavier head assemblies. Transfer rate limitations arise mostly from the combination of the rotational rate of the disk and the density at which information is stored on each track. The faster the disk spins and the closer that the data bits fit together on the disk, the more bits will spin by the head in a given period, producing a quicker flow of information.

Because of the mechanical nature of these speed limits, any miraculous improvement in disk performance is impossible. Because laws of motion involving inertia and other principles that scientists hold dear preclude instantaneous acceleration, access delays can never be eliminated from mechanical systems. More to the point, practical mechanisms can never lower the delays to the point that some people—likely including yourself—won't be bothered by them. Similarly, the rotation rates of disks are limited by such issues as mechanical integrity (spin a disk too fast and centrifugal force will tear it apart) and the fact that the packing of data is constrained by the capability of the read-write technology to resolve individual bits on the disk surface.

The big problem with these mechanical limits is that they are orders of magnitude lower than the electronic and logic limits of computers. A computer thinks in nanoseconds and microseconds but has to wait milliseconds when it needs data from a disk. The computer may need to wait longer when it needs to transfer a large block of information from a mass storage device.

The best way to hurdle these mechanical barriers is with caching. A suitable device cache enables required information to be retrieved at near electronic speeds. The optional High Performance File System used by OS/2 incorporates its own cache, as does the similar file system used by Windows NT.

In DOS-based systems, the cache brings an additional benefit. DOS is essentially a single-threaded operating system. DOS steps through each of its functions one at a time, waiting for the last to complete before it advances to the next. In writing to a disk, for example, DOS waits until the write operation is completed before it returns control back to you.

DOS doesn't have to work that way. Caches can add a degree of concurrence to the operating system by returning control of your system to you while the disk write operations finish. This simple expedience can be sufficient to cut in half the time required to write to your disk system.

Hardware Versus Software Caches

Caching is generally classified into two types—hardware and software—depending on the type of memory used to build the cache, but it is better distinguished by where in the system it takes place. The hardware/software line is drawn in implementation. The hardware-based cache requires that you add some kind of additional memory to your system to use for caching. Software-based caches use part of the RAM in your PC to build the cache. As with data compression, there are three potential logical locations for a mass storage cache: on the device, in its controller or host adapter, or in your PC's RAM.

Although a lot has been written about the advantage of hardware versus software caching, the issues all boil down to one: cost. To add hardware caching to a PC means to install additional memory. During the DRAM shortage a couple of years ago, the cost of memory imposed a severe penalty. Today, the RAM for a reasonable cache (1M) is almost trivial. However, the difference in cost between a cached disk controller or host adapter and one without is much more substantial—a cached controller may cost three to five times more.

A software cache generally requires no additional memory in your system, instead taking advantage of whatever leftover RAM you want to assign to disk acceleration. If you have no spare RAM, you can add extra megabytes for no more than the cost of SIMMs (single in-line memory modules).

The logical location of the cache determines the ultimate performance advantage it can add to your system. Although every kind of cache helps minimize the slowdowns imposed by the mechanical nature of disk storage, some help to sidestep system bottlenecks better than others. At the same time, some caches are easier to deal with and offer fewer compatibility problems than others.

Device-Mounted Caches

The straightforward place to put a hardware cache is on the disk drive itself. That way, the cache can be added to the system invisibly and at no cost for extra memory or software. The drive simply appears faster to you and your software.

The disk-based cache has three primary shortcomings. It's not entirely adaptable to all kinds of hard disks. It works best with disks that use system-level interfaces such as SCSI (the Small Computer System Interface) and AT interface, which separate the actual data stored on the disk from housekeeping information (sector identifications) in the disk's electronics. Moreover, the on-disk cache does nothing to improve the performance of other parts of the disk system that hinder performance such as the interface and the expansion bus. Finally, disk-based caching cannot do anything to improve the performance of an existing disk system. To gain its benefits, you must slide in a new disk drive.

Controller-Based Caches

The next logical place to put a cache is on the disk controller or host adapter. This location adds the flexibility of endowing any disk, old or new, with a cache. It also can overcome some of the limits imposed by the disk interface. When the data you need is in the cache, it can be sent to your system as fast as the expansion bus can carry it without concern for the transfer rate through the disk interface. But that still leaves a bottleneck in many systems—the bus itself. Expansion buses operate at a fraction of the speed that quicker microprocessors can handle data, so the bus connection can lead to a substantial slowdown in even cached disk performance. And because controller-based caches require extra hardware, they add to the cost of your mass storage system.

Software Caches

The final place to put a cache is in your system's own memory using a software-mediated product. Because such a location is downstream from the expansion bus, it can not only acceler-ate the mechanical aspects of disk performance but it also can break through the bus bottleneck. The memory used in the software cache is the fastest RAM in your system, as it is directly connected to your PC's microprocessor.

The drawbacks of the downstream software cache are several. The cache steals away RAM that could be otherwise used by programs. Because most caches operate as software drivers, they may be invisible to programs that direct control of disk hardware, resulting in conflicts that can corrupt disk data. And because the software cache must be controlled and maintained by your PC's main microprocessor, your system may slow down somewhat.

The first and last of these problems should be no cause for worry. Any cache will need additional memory, and the downstream software cache uses the least expensive RAM available—simple memory expansion for your system board without the necessity for outboard hardware control-lers. Moreover, better software caches minimize their memory impact.

The microprocessor overhead extracted by a software cache should, for the most part, be invisible to you. Few if any software caches run continually in the background, sapping clock cycles from your system's microprocessor. Most instead swing into action only when your PC is accessing its disk subsystem. With reasonable sizes of cache, the acceleration gained overwhelms the microprocessor overhead. Cache overhead may shave off 2 percent of your microprocessor's power during disk activity while improving disk performance by 50 percent or more, for example. The net gain, 48 percent—or more—more than makes up for the overhead.

Compatibility problems are more difficult to eliminate because they result from fundamental mismatches between utility software and the cache-driver software. Fortunately, these days only one very specific variety of software is likely to crash into a cache: hard disk utilities and specialty disk drivers such as Disk Manager (from On-Track Computer Systems) and SpeedStor (Storage Dimensions) that are used to match nonstandard hard disks to PCs. With the latest releases of cache software and these utilities, most of the problems have been worked out. Earlier program versions may have problems, however. Any software that chooses to directly access the registers of a hard disk controller (for whatever purpose) may subvert the cache and cause data to disappear.

If you run into such difficulties, you have an easy solution—simply switch off the cache while you take advantage of the disk utility. Because most such programs are used only occasionally (for example, file recovery or disk optimization), the time and trouble required to switch off the cache will not amount to much.

Cache Operation

Commercial disk-caching programs differ in three principal ways: how they handle read operations, how (and whether) they cache disk-write operations, and their usage and management of system memory. Getting the right cache for your PC and the way you work requires investigating all three methods.

Read Buffering

The fundamental function of a disk cache is buffering read operations. The cache software fills its memory with what data anticipates your system and software will need and supplies that information from its buffers on request at RAM speed when there is a cache hit. If there is a miss, the cache directs the software to retrieve data from disk at disk speed.

The design issues control how efficient that read cache operates—and thus how often it speeds up disk operations. These issues include how the memory of the cache is filled with data, how the contents of memory are updated, and how the cache recognizes whether needed information is contained in its memory.

The first issue appears simple. After all, before you can expect to read anything in a cache, there must be something there. But filling a cache is a task akin to seeing an omen; the cache-control software must make a stab at predicting your system's needs. Most caches take a straightforward approach, reading somewhat more disk than your application software requests of a given disk track or (less commonly) file. The underlying assumption is that you'll need more of what you're already looking at.

After a few read requests, the cache memory will fill up, and the control software is faced with the problem of what to save and what to discard to make room for new data. Several different algorithms are used by the writers of software caches. Most are variations of Least Frequently Used (LFU) and Least Recently Used (LRU) designs, in that order of popularity. The former discards the data in the cache that your system has asked least often. The latter throws away the data that was requested the longest time previously. The LFU technique is more complex and demands more from system resources, so LRU often performs better. Even so, in typical systems, the gain performance in using the two techniques falls within about eight percent of one another, close enough to be a draw.

Keeping track of the data in the cache is a matter of minimizing the time required to determine whether needed data is held within the cache. In general, cache programs assign tags to associate data in memory with data on the disk. The exact handling of this information, like the other details of caching algorithms used by specific products, is a matter of great secrecy among most commercial cache publishers. For the most part, publishers treat their technology as if it were black magic—but even more mysterious.

Despite such proprietary miracles, even cache publishers admit that read performance differs little among commercial software disk caches. You probably will not see a difference whether you use a costly third-party cache or one that comes free with your PC or operating system when all you do is read from your hard disk.

Accelerating write operations is another matter entirely. Some caches (generally the free ones) ignore write operations entirely, forcing direct disk access—and the resultant delays—when your software wants to store or change data in mass storage. The underlying philosophy is to be safe although slow.

Write Buffering

The reason for this conservative approach is that caching write operations is fraught with dangers. Overcoming these problems takes a lot of development time, making a cache with write buffering more expensive to create.

The biggest worry comes with delayed writing, caused by the cache accumulating data to be written to disk for a preset period or waiting for a time when your system is no longer busy. The cache then can write the data to disk without slowing anything down. In addition, the cache can reorganize the data to optimize the head movement of the drive and to eliminate multiple, sequential changes to a disk sector by writing only the last of the changes to disk.

While the cache is collecting and holding information, your system reacts as if the disk has been written to at RAM speed. Press the Save button, and you immediately get control of your system so that you can go on to something else.

To gain this responsiveness, however, you put your data at risk. Between the time your software thinks it has written to disk and when the data actually is stored, it is vulnerable to accidental or intentional power failure. You may think that an important file has been written and switch off your PC, and whatever data was held in the write cache would evaporate with the flow of electricity through your machine. Moreover, the damage can be worse than just losing a file. Some operating systems and operating environments are designed to automatically recover when a power failure terminates their operation midstream. But this software may expect to have its disk changes written in a particular order that the write cache may violate for sake of speed. The operating system thus may be thwarted in its efforts to recover and rebuild itself. Even worse, the system may rebuild itself incorrectly and become a disaster waiting to happen.

To avoid such problems, many disk caches avoid caching writes entirely or do not use delayed-writing techniques. Caches that do allow delayed writings typically make it an optional feature that can be defeated by those who are especially concerned about data integrity. The caches also may allow you to set the maximum allowable writing delay—the shorter the delay, the less data will be at risk (but the less performance improvement you can expect). Write-caching programs also may intercept warm boot commands (the Ctrl-Alt-Del keystroke sequence) and force the flushing of the cache—writing all of its contents to disk—immediately before allowing the reboot to occur. Of course, this strategy does no good with a cold (power off) boot.

An alternative write-caching technology eliminates delayed writing and instead relies on operating your disk drive concurrently with other operations to give an apparent performance increase. The technique is simple in concept—the cache accepts data from your application and immediately begins writing it to disk. However, instead of holding back your system while the data is doled out through the drive interface and drive mechanism, you get control of your software as soon as the information has been written into the cache memory. The actual writing to disk continues for some time afterward, concurrent with the continuation of normal operation of your PC.

Such concurrent writing technology is not risk-free. Switching off your PC immediately after control returns to a program after a disk write can result in lost data because everything may not have been spooled off to disk. However, there will be no unpredictable period of vulnerability as is the case with delayed writing systems. As soon as the drive-activity indicator extinguishes, you're safe to switch off or reboot your PC.

The time saved by concurrent writing approaches that of delayed writing with a properly designed caching program. Both techniques require the same time to transfer information into the cache, and both return control of your system immediately thereafter. Although delayed writing may minimize the time actually spent in writing to disk, these savings probably will be invisible to you.

Memory Usage

Memory marks another major difference between software-caching programs. Certainly all respectable commercial caching products now can use all principal PC memory types—conventional (DOS), expanded (EMS), and extended (XMS) memory—but these products differ substantially in how efficiently the memory needs of the cache can be shared with other system resources.

Nearly every software-based, speed-up technology that can be applied to a PC requires some memory usage, but caches and print spoolers are notorious for their needs for huge blocks of RAM. The more memory devoted to such speed-up technologies, the greater the performance gain. But the memory used for these functions must be drawn from somewhere, and that increasingly means away from the resources that could be used for executing programs. Every megabyte devoted to your disk cache is one less megabyte usable by Windows or the applications running under Windows.

Most of the time, you are left to allocate the memory between the various functions of your PC. After all, every computer setup is unique, and your needs may be quite different from those of someone else—you may want a huge cache while others may want the greatest possible program space. Allocating memory yourself requires carefully examining the needs of your software. With print spoolers, for example, you must devote enough memory to handle the worst-case print job, or your gain may be for nothing—you will still be stuck waiting for your printer when the spooler fills up. The memory that you allocate to the spooler for this worst-case scenario is then forever drawn away from the reach of your software.

A trend among caching programs is to make memory allocation dynamic, taking memory away from your system only when you need it or sharing memory with other functions.

Caches differ substantially in their capabilities to share. Many simply don't. After all, at $30-$50 per megabyte, adding more RAM to accommodate the cache is not an overwhelming expenditure. Some caches, however, dynamically allocate memory among themselves and other functions like RAM disks and print spoolers. With these caches you need to devote less RAM to gain the same level of performance improvement from all memory-hogging functions.

Using a Cache

After you elect to install a software cache in your system, you have a number of decisions to make. Among the first is whether to take advantage of write caching or to rely solely on speeding up read operations. The decision hinges on two factors: how you work and your willingness to take a risk.

If you use your PC only casually, you don't want to bother thinking about managing your system, or you don't think you can remember to pause a few seconds to flush the cache before rebooting or switching off your system, you may want to avoid write caching. If you experience one instance of brain fade, turning off the power switch before the cache has finished writing to your disk, you will ever afterward curse caching.

Even if you're careful, write caching imposes a risk—an extended risk of power failure and software crashes. Realistically, the risk is very small. You're no more likely to lose data in your write cache from such causes as you would any other information. But you are adding slightly to a period of great vulnerability. If you want to eke out the most possible acceleration from a disk cache, you will want a product that handles write caching in some manner. The decision between delayed writing or concurrent writing depends on your personal assessment of the risk involved.

After you choose a product, you need to install it. In doing so, you are faced with the toughest decision of all—how much of your system's RAM to devote to the cache. The basic rule is that the more memory you devote to caching, the more you will enhance the performance of your disk drive. Software caches smaller than 64K may not be large enough to overcome the handicaps of their own operating overhead. Most cache publishers recommend that a minimum of 256K to 384K be devoted to a software cache and prefer 512K to 1M. At that level, you can expect a hit ratio approaching 90 percent with normal disk usage.

What kind of memory to use is another issue. Among the basic choices—DOS, extended, or expanded—the worst choice is DOS. Every byte you steal from DOS memory is one that cannot be used by your software. Moreover, you simply cannot make a large cache from DOS memory because, by definition, there is not a lot of DOS memory.

In 8088-based computers (XT-class), your best choice is expanded memory. Of course, getting expanded memory for a cache involves adding an expanded memory board. You may find that the cost of a memory board and that of a hardware disk-caching controller are quite similar. In this case, there is little reason to prefer one over the other because XT systems face no bus bottleneck—the entire system is equally slow.

With 286-based, AT-class systems operating at 10 MHz or less, you have your choice of extended or expanded memory, most of which must be installed in expansion slots. Your choice between the two memory types does not matter—both types will deliver approximately equal performance. Moreover, a hardware cache may have a speed advantage because of its lack of software overhead. The bus bottleneck will be the same for memory boards or hardware caches.

As the system-clock speeds rise above 10 MHz and race ahead of the bus clock, performance issues begin to favor software over hardware caching, assuming that the memory used for the software cache is system-board memory. A memory board installed in an expansion slot will suffer the bus bottleneck and be unable to deliver performance better than a hardware cache.

In these faster systems, extended memory should be preferred for your software cache. Even when expanded memory is emulated by fast system-board RAM, it cannot quite keep up with plain extended memory. Expanded memory requires additional system-management overhead which is not required by extended memory.

Chapter 22

Hard Disks

In most PCs, the hard disk is the principal mass storage system. It holds all of your programs and data files and must deliver them to your system at an instant's notice. Hard disks differ by technology, interface, speed, and capacity—all of which are interrelated.

A PC without a hard disk demonstrates solid-state senility—all that's left of long-term memory are the brief flashbacks that can be loaded (with great effort and glacial speed) from floppy disks. What's left is a curiosity to be nursed along until death overtakes it—probably your own— because a PC without a hard disk will make you wish you were dead.

The hard disk is the premiere mass storage device for today's PCs. No other peripheral can approach the usefulness of the hard disk's combination of speed, capacity, and straightforward user installation. In fact, without today's big, fast disks you probably wouldn't even consider a quick 32- or 64-bit microprocessor. You couldn't keep enough data in your system to make the fast chip useful.

The hard disk puts the bulk of your programs and data at your fingertips, ready for instant access. It can speed up everyday work by loading programs in a fraction of the time required by floppy disks. By storing and sorting through data very quickly, it makes many of your programs seem to run faster. The hard disk even makes the rest of your computer system seem more responsive.

The hard disk deals in megabytes, hundreds of them. In one second, the disk has to be able to remember or disgorge the information equivalent of the entire contents of a physics textbook or novel. And it must be equally capable of casting aside its memories and replacing them with revised versions to keep your system up to date. That's a big challenge, particularly for a device that may be no larger than a deck of playing cards and uses less power than a nightlight.

In the first decade of PCs, hard disks evolved from high-priced luxuries to simple necessities. In fact, the evolution of the PC echoes and emphasizes the changed perception of the hard disk. The first PC made no provision for a hard disk. The XT brought hard disk capabilities. The AT put the emphasis on hard disk performance. No respectable computer with a 286 microprocessor, let alone a 386 or newer chip could deliver on its performance potential without the speed and capacity of a hard disk drive. Windows and OS/2 make mandatory a hard disk with a hundred megabytes or more of capacity.

Depending on your needs and demands, hard disks can be expensive or cheap. Like tires, power tools, and companions, they come in various sizes and speed ratings. You can scrounge through ads and find decade-old hard disk drives that will still plug into your PC at prices that will make Scrooge smile—and you weep while you wait and wait for its ancient technology to catch up with the demands of a modern microprocessor.

In truth, today's hard disk drives have little in common with their forebears of as few as five years ago. Modern hard disks take up less space, respond faster, have several times the capacity, last several times as long, and have nowhere near the failure potential of older drives. A modern drive won't even plug into your PC the same way early hard disks did. New and constantly evolving interfaces promise to keep pushing up speeds while making installation easier.

Although the standards of speed and quality among hard disks have never been higher, sorting among your options has never been tougher. As the range of available products grows wider, the differences between the competition at each level have narrowed. Finding the one right hard disk now more than ever requires understanding what's inside a drive, what the different mechanisms and technology are, and what best mates with a modern machine.

Naming Conventions

The place to begin any discussion is getting a handle on what you're talking about. The name hard disk seems straightforward enough, distinguishing such products from the other familiar mass storage device, the floppy disk. Although the floppy disk is based on a flexible carrier for its magnetic medium, the hard disk uses a rigid—or hard—substrate called a platter (which, of course, has a disk shape). The name is descriptive but hardly exhaustive or universal. Hard disk drives wear several other monikers, some apt and accurate, others not.

IBM, credited with inventing the technology, has favored the term fixed disk to hard disk. The reasoning is that the platter in a hard disk is fixed inside the drive, rather than being removable like a floppy disk. Of course, some hard disk drives use removable media, destroying the "fixed" distinction. At least that turn of phrase is better than Direct Access Storage Device (or DASD) the company's moniker for the technology when used among mainframes.

The better name for the hard disk drive is magnetic disk storage. Other technologies, such as optical-based CD ROMs, also use hard disks.

Winchester Disk Drives

Perhaps the most familiar synonym for "hard disk drive" is Winchester disk drive, often clipped simply to Winchester by those in the know—or who think they are. In truth, few of today's hard disks have the right to wear the label "Winchester." And that's good.

Winchester refers to the underlying technology used by the read-write head in the disk drive. The head in a Winchester drive is attached to a slight airfoil like an airplane wing and operates as a flying read-write head, floating a few microinches (millionth of an inch) above the surface of the disk. Unlike the airplane wing that moves through the air to gain the lift that levitates it, the air moves and the read-write head stands still (at least in the direction of the airflow). The spinning of the disk in the drive itself stirs up the air to raise the head. The advantage of this design is that the head does not touch the disk—at least when the disk is spinning—so there's no rubbing or wearing of the disk surface. At the same time, the read-write head is close enough (six to twelve microinches in a modern drive) that the magnetic fields of the medium and head don't spread too far.

The way that the name "Winchester" got associated with this technology has become part of computer folklore. The first drive to use this technology was developed by IBM Corporation at its Hursley Laboratory, which happens to be located near Winchester, England. But that felicitous location has nothing to do with the drive's epithet. Rather, the name resulted from a bit of word association, according to IBM. The original IBM disk drive that used this technology was code-named "3030" because it had two sides, each of which could store 30 megabytes. To some people, this designation recalled the famous Winchester 3030 repeating rifle that, according to legend, won the West. The name "Winchester" was subsequently transferred to the like-numbered disk drive. The multi-syllabic moniker not only stuck but was generalized to the flying head technology upon which the drive was based. For example, a new head technology, called Whitney, results in much smaller, faster, and sturdier assemblies that have replaced the original Winchester head design in many if not most products. Coming hard disk drives may abandon the flying head for one that swims in a thick liquid. Likely, however, the Winchester name will persist in general use for all hard disk drives.

Bernoulli Technology

Iomega Corporation turned flying head technology upside down to create one of the best-known alternatives to the hard disk, the Bernoulli Box. The medium in an Iomega drive is actually a floppy disk, and the unique Bernoulli technology allows the flexible medium to spin at speeds approaching those of modern hard disk drives. Instead of using the airflow generated by the spinning disk to lift the head above a rigid disk, these drives use a flexible disk that spins near a rigid surface called a Bernoulli plate. Air pressure differences caused by the spinning medium suck the disk close to the Bernoulli plate but prevent the disk and plate from touching. As a result, the spinning flexible disk is stabilized. Without the Bernoulli plate, the disk would wrinkle and fold as its speed increased. The flexible medium bends around the head without touching it under the force of the air pressure. The advantage of using a flexible disk instead of a rigid one is that the former has much lower mass, which helps to limit damage during head crashes. The disadvantage is that the medium is constantly flexed and eventually wears out.

The name is drawn from the Bernoulli theorem or principle, first propounded by the 18th Century Swiss mathematician and physicist Daniel Bernoulli. His principle states that the total energy at any point in a fluid system is constant; thus faster moving fluids exert less pressure. The faster air flows over a surface, the lower the pressure. The speedy airflow between the Bernoulli plate and disk lowers the air pressure between them, and the disk gets sucked close to the plate.

Magneto-Optical Storage

Another kind of magnetic storage uses laser optics to pack more bytes in a given space. Called magneto-optical storage, it is currently the most widely used rewritable optical data recording technology. At its heart, however, the medium is essentially magnetic. To your PC, drives that use the technology—called magneto-optical or MO drives—work exactly like other random-access storage devices. Many do their best to emulate ordinary hard disks.

The magneto-optical name describes the principle used in these products. The recording medium in each disk is fundamentally a magnetic material (but one unlike anything you'll find on hard disks and floppies) that relies on magnetic fields to store information. The optical part is used only to assist the magnetic mechanism, to refine its perceptions. A tightly focused laser beam points out where the magnetic mechanism is to write data onto the disk and prepares the medium to make it recordable. In reading, however, MO drives are purely optical. The laser by itself reads the magnetically stored data from the disk.

The combination of optical and magnetic technologies results from necessity. The principal problem is not making the medium rewritable but maintaining rewritability over many write operations. Materials that are physically altered in recording suffer fatigue, which limits their life. Other rewritable optical media—phase-change and dye-polymer recording—alters the disk to such an extent that erasing and rewriting is possible only a limited number of times. The medium simply wears out. The magnetic materials used by MO drives don't physically change during the recording process. Only the fields of the particles of magnetic medium are altered. The particles themselves don't change. Because MO drives are based on this well-understood principle, they are generally considered to be capable of an unlimited number of write-rewrite cycles. There's no worry about stress, fatigue, failure, and data loss.

Hard Disk Technology

No matter the terminology—hard disk, Winchester, or fixed disk—or the variation used in the recording process—Bernoulli or magneto-optical—the underlying principles are the same in high-speed magnetic mass storage systems—as are your concerns in installing, using, and taking advantage of one.

Not all hard disks are created equal. Different hard disk models are made from different materials using different technologies and under different standards. As a result, the performance, capacities, and prices of hard disks cover a wide range—from a few hundred dollars to tens of thousands. Understanding these differences will help you better judge the quality and value available in any disk product. You'll also better understand what you need to do to get one running and keep it that way.

The hard disk is actually a combination device, a chimera that's part electronic and part mechanical. Electronically, the hard disk performs the noble function of turning evanescent pulses of electronic digital data into more permanent magnetic fields. As with other magnetic recording devices—from cassette recorders to floppy disks—the hard disk accomplishes its end using an electromagnet, its read-write head, to align the polarities of magnetic particles on the hard disks themselves. Other electronics in the hard disk system control the mechanical half of the drive and help it properly arrange the magnetic storage and locate the information that is stored on the disk.

Drive Mechanism

The mechanism of the typical hard disk is actually rather simple, comprising fewer moving parts than such exotic devices as the electric razor and pencil sharpener. The basic elements of the system include a stack of one or more platters—the actual hard disks themselves. Each of these platters serves as a substrate upon which is laid a magnetic medium in which data can be recorded. Together the platters rotate as a unit on a shaft, called the spindle. Typically, the shaft connects directly to a spindle motor that spins the entire assembly (see fig. 22.1).

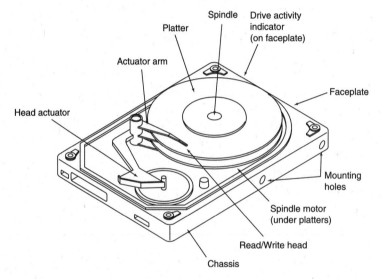

FIGURE 22.1. Hard-disk nomenclature.

The first disk drives (back in the era of the original IBM Winchester) used synchronous motors. That is, the motor was designed to lock its rotation rate to the frequency of the AC power line supplying the disk drive. As a result, most motors of early hard disk drives spun the disk at the same rate as the power line frequency, 3600 revolutions per minute, which equals the 60 cycles per second of commercial power in the United States.

Synchronous motors are typically big, heavy, and expensive. They also run on normal line voltage—117 volts AC—which is not desirable to have floating around inside computer equipment where a couple of errant volts can cause a system crash. As hard disks were miniaturized, disk makers adopted a new technology—the servo-controlled DC motor—that eliminated these problems. A servo-controlled motor uses feedback to maintain a constant and accurate rotation rate. That is, a sensor in the disk drive constantly monitors how fast the drive spins and adjusts the spin rate should the disk vary from its design specifications.

Because servo motor technology does not depend on the power line frequency, manufacturers are free to use any rotation rate they want for drives that use it. Early hard disks with servo motors stuck with the standard 3600 RPM spin to match their signal interfaces designed around that rotation rate. When interface standards shifted from the device level to the system level, however, matching rotation speed to data rate became irrelevant. With system-level interfaces, the raw data is already separated, deserialized, and buffered on the drive itself. The data speeds inside the drive are entirely independent from those outside. With this design, engineers have a strong incentive for increasing the spin rate of the disk platter: The faster the drive rotates, the shorter the time that passes between the scan of any two points on the surface of the disk. A faster spinning platter makes a faster responding drive and one that can transfer information more quickly. With the design freedom afforded by modern disk interfaces, disk designers can choose any spin speed without worrying about signal compatibility. As a result, the highest performing hard disks have spins substantially higher than the old standard—some rotate as quickly as 5400 or 7200 RPM.

Note that disk rotation speed cannot be increased indefinitely. Centrifugal force tends to tear apart anything that spins at high rates, and hard disks are no exception. Disk designers must balance achieving better performance with the self-destructive tendencies of rapidly spinning mechanisms. Moreover, overhead in PC disk systems tends to overwhelm the speed increases won by quickening disk spin. Raising speed results in diminishing returns. According to some developers, the optimum rotation rate (the best trade-off between cost and performance) for hard disks is between 4500 and 5400 RPM.

Constant Spin

Unlike floppy disk drives, most hard disk platters are kept constantly spinning (at least while the disk drive is powered up) because achieving a stable spin of the massive stack of platters at their relatively high speeds may require 10 to 30 seconds for a 5.25-inch disk drive; half that time or less for 3.5-inch and smaller drives because there's less inertia to overcome. The constant spin earns the hard disk one of its two biggest benefits—the data recorded on it is nearly instantly accessible. Floppies, on the other hand, require you to wait a half-second or so until they get spinning up to speed.

In some applications, particularly notebook computers, the constantly spinning hard disk takes a toll. Keeping the disk rotating means constant consumption of power by the spindle motor, which means shorter battery life. Consequently, some hard disks aimed at portable computers are designed to be able to cease spinning when they are not needed. Typically, the support electronics in the host computer determine when the disk should stop spinning. In most machines that means if you don't access the hard disk for a while, the computer assumes that you've fallen asleep, died, or had your body occupied by aliens and won't be needing to use the disk for a while. When you do send out a command to read or write the disk, you then will have to wait while it spins back up to speed—possibly as long as several seconds. Subsequent accesses then occur at high hard disk speeds until the drive thinks you've died again and shuts itself down.

Latency

Despite the quick and constant rotation rate of a hard disk, it cannot deliver information instantly on request. There's always a slight delay that's called latency. This term describes how long after you issue a command to read to or write from a hard disk that the disk rotates to the proper angular position to locate the specific data needed. For example, if a program requests a byte from a hard disk and that byte has just passed under the read-write head, the disk must spin one full turn before that byte can be read from the disk and sent to the program. If read and write requests occur at essentially random times in regard to the spin of the disk (as they do) on the average the disk has to make half a spin before the read-write head is properly positioned to read or write the required data. Normal latency at 3600 RPM means that the quickest you can expect your hard disk—on the average—to find the information you want is 8.33 milliseconds. For a computer that operates with nanosecond timing, that's a long wait, indeed.

The newer hard disks with higher spin speeds cut latency. The relationship between rotation and latency is linear, so each percentage increase in spin pushes down latency by the same factor. A modern drive with a 5400 RPM spin achieves a latency of 5.6 milliseconds.

Data Transfer Rate

The speed of the spin of a hard disk also influences how quickly data can be continuously read from a drive. At a given storage density (which disk designers try to make as high as possible to pack as much information in as small a package as possible), the quicker a disk spins, the faster information can be read from it. As spin rates increase, more bits on the surface of the disk pass beneath the read-write head in a given period. This increase directly translates into a faster flow of data—more bits per second.

The speed at which information is moved from the disk to its control electronics (or its PC host) is termed the data transfer rate of the drive. Data transfer rate is measured in megabits per second, megahertz (typically these two take the same numeric value) or megabytes per second (one-eighth the megabit per second rate). Higher is better.

The data transfer rates quoted for most hard disks are computed values rather than the speeds you should expect in using a hard disk drive in the real world. A number of factors drive down the actual rate at which information can be transferred from a disk drive.

Every disk interface has overhead. Early disk interfaces (see ST506 and ESDI, following) measured transfer rate as the speed at which they could push raw data between the drive and its controller—everything on the disk was shoved across the interface. Along with the data you wanted came a flood of formatting details that would be stripped out. Modern interfaces don't deal in raw data, so they don't suffer this limitation. But they still are slowed by the time and overhead needed to negotiate each data transfer.

The measure of the actual amount of useful information that moves between a disk drive and your PC is called the throughput. It is always lower—substantially lower—than the disk's data transfer rate. The actual throughput achieved by a drive system varies with where the measurement is made because each step along the way imposes overhead. The throughput between your drive and controller is higher than between drive and memory. And the actual throughput to your programs—which must be managed by your operating system—is slower still. Throughput to DOS on the order of a few hundred kilobytes per second is not unusual for hard disk drives that have quoted transfer rates in excess of five megabytes per second.

The Disk Within

The disk spinning inside the hard disk drive is central to the drive—in more ways than one. The diameter of this platter determines how physically large a drive mechanism must be. In fact, most hard disk drives are measured by the size of their platters. When the PC first burst upon the world, hard disk makers were making valiant attempts at hard disk platter miniaturization, moving from those eight inches in diameter (so-called eight-inch disks) to 5.25-inch platters. Today, the trend is to ever-smaller platters. Most large-capacity drives bound for desktop computer systems now use 3.5-inch platters. Those meant for PCs in which weight and size must be minimized (which means, of course, notebook and smaller PCs) have platters measuring 2.5, 1.8, or 1.3 inches (currently the smallest) in diameter. (See Chapter 10, "Cases," for form-factor details.)

Magneto-optical drives appeared on the scene later, and they mimicked the magnetic drives that were available. The first magneto-optical drives used disks measuring a nominal 5.25 inches across. Smaller, lower-capacity drives use 3.5-inch disks.

To increase storage capacity in conventional magnetic hard disk storage systems, both sides of a platter are used for storing information, each surface with its own read-write head. (One head is on the bottom where it must fly below the platter.) In addition, manufacturers often put several platters on a single spindle, making a taller package with the same diameter as a single platter. The number of platters inside a hard disk also influences the speed at which data stored on the hard disk can be found. The more platters a given disk drive uses, the greater the probability that one of the heads associated with one of those platters will be above the byte that's being searched for. Consequently, the time to find information is reduced.

Adding platters has drawbacks besides increasing the height of a drive. More platters means greater mass so their greater inertia requires longer to spin up to speed. This is not a problem for desktop machines—power-on memory checks typically take longer than even the most laggardly hard disk requires to spin up. But an additional wait is annoying in laptop and notebook computers that slow down and stop their hard disks to save battery energy. Additionally, because each surface of each platter in a hard disk has its own head, the head actuator mechanism inevitably gets larger and more complex as the number of platters increases. Inertia again takes its toll, slowing down the movement of the heads and increasing the access time of the drive. Of course, drive makers can compensate for the increased head actuator mass with more powerful actuators, but that adds to the size and cost of the drive.

Platter Composition

The platters of a conventional magnetic hard disk are precisely machined to an extremely fine tolerance measured in microinches. They have to be—remember, the read-write head flies just a few microinches above each platter. If the disk juts up, the result is akin to a DC-10 encountering Pike's Peak, a crash that's good for neither airplane nor hard disk. Consequently, disk makers try to ensure that platters are as flat and smooth as possible.

The most common substrate material is aluminum, which has several virtues: it's easy to machine to a relatively smooth surface; it's generally inert, so it won't react with the material covering it; it's non-magnetic so it won't affect the recording process; it's been used for a long while (since the first disk drives) and is consequently a familiar material. And above all, it's cheap.

A newer alternative is commonly called the glass platter, although the actual material used can range from ordinary window glass to advanced ceramic compounds akin to Space Shuttle skin. Glass platters excel at exactly the same qualities as do aluminum platters. On the positive side, they hold the advantage of being able to be made smoother and allowing read-write heads to fly lower. But because glass is newer, it's less familiar to work with. Consequently, glass-plattered drives are moving slowly into the product mainstream.

Areal Density

The smoothness of the substrate affects how tightly information can be packed on the surface of a platter. The term used to describe this characteristic is areal density, that is, the amount of data that can be packed onto a given area of the platter surface. The most common unit for measuring areal density is megabits per square inch. The higher the areal density, the more information can be stored on a single platter. Smaller hard disks require greater areal densities to achieve the same capacities as larger units.

Areal density is generally measured in megabytes per square inch of disk surface, and current products achieve values on the order of 100 to 200M per square inch.

A number of factors influence the areal density that can be achieved by a given hard disk drive. The key factor is the size of the magnetic domain that encodes each bit of data, which is controlled in turn by several factors. These include the height at which the read-write head flies and the particle (grain) size of the medium.

Manufacturers make read-write heads smaller to generate smaller fields and fly them as closely to the platter as possible without risking the head running into the jagged peaks of surface roughness. The smoothness of the medium limits the lowest possible flying height—a head can fly closer to a smoother surface.

The size of magnetic domains on a disk is also limited by the size of the magnetic particles themselves. A domain cannot be smaller than the particle that stores it. At one time, ball mills ground a magnetic oxide medium until the particle size was small enough for the desired application. Platters were coated with a slurry of the resulting magnetic material. Modern magnetic materials minimize grain size by electroplating the platters.

Oxide Media

The first magnetic medium used in hard disks was made from the same materials used in conventional audio recording tapes, ferric or ferrous oxide compounds—essentially fine grains of rather exotic rust. As with recording tape, the oxide particles are milled in a mixture of other compounds including a glue-like binder and often a lubricant. The binder also serves to isolate individual oxide particles from one another. This mud-like mixture is then coated onto the platters.

The technology of oxide coatings is old and well developed. The process has been evolving for more than 50 years and now rates as a well-understood, familiar—and obsolete—technology. New hard disk designs have abandoned oxide media and with several good reasons. Oxide particles are not the best storers of magnetic information, however. Oxides tend to have lower coercivities, and their grains tend to be large when compared to other, newer media technologies. Both of these factors tend to limit the areal density available with oxide media. The slight surface roughness of the oxide medium compounds that of the platter surface, requiring the hard disk read-write head to fly farther away from it than other media, which also reduces maximum storage density. In addition, oxide coatings are generally soft and are more prone to getting damaged when the head skids to a stop, when the disk ceases its spin, or when a shock to the drive causes the head to skitter across the platter surface, potentially strafing your data as effectively as an attack by the Red Baron.

Thin Film Media

In nearly all current hard disk drives, oxide coatings have been replaced by thin-film magnetic media. As the name implies, a thin-film disk has a microscopically skinny layer of a pure metal, or mixture of metals, mechanically bound to its surface. These thin-films can be applied either by plating the platter much the way chrome is applied to automobile bumpers, or by sputtering, a form of vapor plating in which metal is ejected off a hot electrode in a vacuum and electrically attracted to the disk platter.

Thin-film media hold several special advantages over oxide technology. The very thinness of thin-film media allows higher areal densities because the magnetic field has less thickness in which to spread out. Because the thin-film surface is smoother, it allows heads to fly closer. Thin-film media also has higher coercivities, which allows smaller areas to produce the strong magnetic pulses needed for error-free reading of the data on the disk.

One reason that thin-film can be so thin and support high areal densities is that, as with chrome-plated automobile bumpers and faucets, plated and sputtered media require no binders to hold their magnetic layers in place. Moreover, as with chrome plating, the thin-films on hard disk platters are genuinely hard, many times tougher than oxide coatings. That makes them less susceptible to most forms of head crashing—the head merely bounces off the thin-film platter just as it would your car's bumpers.

Contamination

Besides shock, head crashes also can result from contaminants such as dust or air pollution particles on the media surface that can strike the head and upset its flight. The head touching the disk surface may result in a nick to the media which not only destroys the storage capability of the media in the area struck by the head but also can loosen particles of media that can, in turn, cause further contamination and crashing.

Fortunately, the almost universal use of thin-film media and more robust drive mechanisms has made head crashes things of the past. Although you should still be careful with your hard disk (no sense tempting fate or your service contract), in normal use you need not worry about crashes. Most of today's hard disk drives are designed for the rigors of portable computers—that means, the computer moving during operation, say when the aircraft hits a pocket of turbulence—so a nudge now and again won't destroy the disk.

To be on the safe side, and to help guard against contamination of the platter surface with dust, hair, and other floating gunk, most hard disks keep all their vulnerable parts in a protective chamber. In fact, this need to avoid contamination is why nearly all PC hard disks use nonremovable media, sealed out of harm's way.

The disk chamber is not completely air tight. Usually, a small vent is designed into the system to allow the air pressure inside the disk drive to adjust to changes in environmental air pressure. Although this air exchange is minimal, a filter in this vent system traps particles before they can enter the drive. Microscopic pollutants, such as corrosive molecules in the air, can seep through the filter, however, potentially damaging the disk surface. Although the influx of such pollutant is small—the hard disk vent does not foster airflow, only pressure equalization—it is best not to operate a hard disk in a polluted environment. You wouldn't want to be there to use it, anyhow.

Removable Media Drives

So-called removable hard disks put the hard disk platter (or platters) in a plastic cartridge that can be withdrawn from the disk drive mechanism and separately stored. Other platters can be inserted in the drive and interchanged, much like floppy disks.

Sealing these removable platters from the atmosphere is practically impossible. As a consequence, removable media drive manufacturers often use tough-plated media in their products to make them more resistant to head crash damage. Usually, they suck the air—and, they hope, the contaminants—out of the cartridge before they allow the platters to begin to spin.

In addition, the head actuator of the removable media drive must be toughened up and some means must be found to move the head from a great distance from the platters (so that the platters can be safely removed or inserted into the drive) to a tiny distance (so they can fly the proper distance from the platter). These robust mechanisms are inherently slower than the fastest hard disks, imposing a penalty on the average access times of such products.

To circumvent such difficulties, a new product area puts the entire drive mechanism in a removable cartridge form—motor, platter, head, actuator, and protective chamber are fashioned into one removable unit. Such removable drives have all the security advantages of other removable media devices. In addition, they can be built more like hard disks, with fewer contamination and crash worries and greater speed. Currently, their sole drawback is a higher price.

A new alternative is the hard disk carrier, which turns any 3.5-inch drive into a removable unit. The carrier has two parts: a mounting assembly that installs permanently inside a drive bay in your PC, and the carrier itself into which you bolt a disk drive. The carrier then slides in and out of the mounting assembly. You plug in the drive before you boot up and pull it out at the end of the day to lock it in your safe or put it under your pillow.

Magneto-Optical Media

The medium used by magneto-optical disks differs substantially from their magnetic siblings. Moreover, all magneto-optical systems use cartridges. The MO medium is suited to cartridge design because it is relatively invulnerable to the environmental dangers that can damage magnetic media. Moreover, the storage densities of MO storage allow a single platter cartridge to hold useful amounts of data.

Despite their common name, 5.25-inch MO cartridges are filled with optical disk platters that actually measure 130 millimeters (5.12 inches) in diameter. The cartridges themselves measure 0.43 by 5.31 by 6.02 inches (HWD) and somewhat resemble 3.5-inch floppy disks in that the disk itself is protected by a sliding metal shutter. So-called 3.5-inch magneto-optical disks have platters that are actually 90 millimeters across in a cartridge shell, about the same size and appearance as a 3.5-inch floppy disk—only the MO disks are thicker. Figures 22.2, 22.3, and 22.4 illustrate the two sizes of MO cartridges.

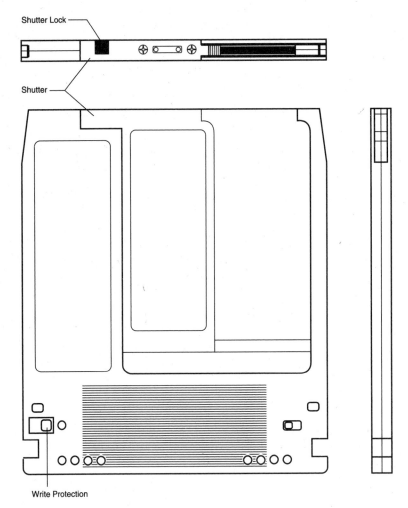

FIGURE 22.2. MO cartridge layout.

The magnetic medium on an MO disk is constructed from several layers. First, the plastic substrate of the disk is isolated with a dielectric coating. The actual magneto-optical compound—an alloy of terbium (a rare-earth element), iron, and cobalt—comes next, protected by another dielectric coating. A layer of aluminum atop this provides a reflective surface for the tracking mechanism. This sandwich is then covered by 0.30 millimeters of transparent plastic. Disks are made single-sided; then two are glued together back-to-back to produce two-sided media.

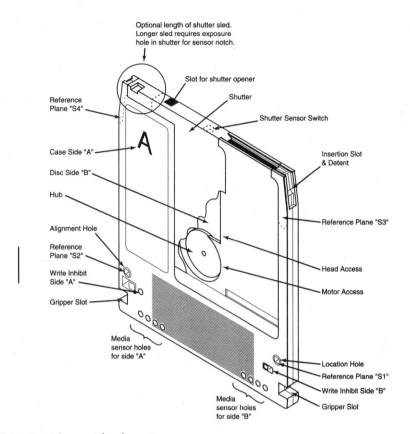

FIGURE 22.3. MO cartridge layout.

Unlike conventional Winchester disks that store data on a number of concentric tracks or cylinders, under the ISO standard, MO drives use a single, continuous spiral track much like the groove on an old vinyl phonograph record. The spiral optimizes the data transfer of the drive because the read-write head does not need to be moved between tracks during extended data transfers. It scans smoothly across the disk instead.

Capacity is an oft-cited advantage of optical media generally and MO products specifically. But the capacities of MO systems are not that much larger than what purely magnetic drives offer. In fact, 3.5-inch magneto-optical drives offer less capacity than today's state-of-the art 3.5-inch magnetic hard disks. Even 5.25-inch magneto-optical drives do not outshine the capacities of magnetic drives, despite their greater storage densities.

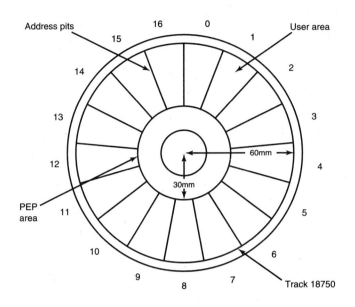

Viewed from lens

FIGURE 22.4. MO cartridge layout.

But direct comparisons between Winchester and MO capacities are misleading. The quoted capacities of both types of drives are in roughly the same ballpark, but the technologies are playing different games. Drives using 5.25-inch disks may quote roughly similar capacities for either technology, a maximum of about a gigabyte. But Winchester drives might use up to eight internal disks or platters (15 recordable surfaces) to achieve that capacity while the higher data packing density of MO drives allows them to reach the same figure with a single platter locked inside a removable cartridge.

The capacities quoted for MO cartridges don't take into account how much storage is actually on-line. Although 5.25-inch MO drives are quoted with capacities in the range 600 to 1000 megabytes, only half of the figure that manufacturers commonly quote is actually available at any one time. The disks in today's cartridges array their storage across two sides, and current MO drives have a single read-write head, so only one side of a cartridge can be read from or written to at a time. To access the other side, you have to physically remove the cartridge from the drive, flip it over, and slide it back in. Consequently, only half of the total capacity of the cartridge is actually on-line at a time.

On the other hand, while MO drives are usually rated with capacities per cartridge, a single drive has an effectively unlimited capacity. Run out of space, and you need only to slide in a new cartridge or flip over the one that's in the drive. You can stock up on as many cartridges as you can afford (the price per cartridge currently is about $250). Of course, only about 300 megabytes of that unlimited total can be accessed at a time.

Read-Write Heads

Besides the platters, the only other moving part in most hard disk drives is the head system. In nearly all drives, one read-write head is associated with each side of each platter and flies just above or below its surface. Each of these read-write heads is flexibly connected to a more rigid arm which supports the flying assembly. Usually several of these arms are linked together to form a single moving (usually pivoting) unit.

Altitude Effects

The height at which the read-write head of a hard disk flies is one factor in determining the ultimate storage capacity of the drive. Magnetic fields spread out with distance, so the farther the head is from the disk, the larger the apparent size of the field is generated by a flux transition on the disk. Moving the head closer shrinks the apparent size of the flux transitions, allowing them to be packed closer together on the disk surface and increasing the capacity of the disk. The typical first-generation hard disk head flew about 10 to 12 microinches—millionth of an inch—above the surface of the platter. Modern disk drive heads fly closer, on the order of five microinches. These lower heights are possible thanks to smoother platters and smooth thin-film media.

Head distance is not an issue with magneto-optical media because the focus of the laser beam (which can be controlled for various distances) rather than the size of the write head's magnetic field determines the areal storage density.

Contact Heads

Magnetic fields spread out with distance, so the closer the read-write head flies to the platter surface, the more focused its fields and the smaller the area it can write to and read from. Lowering the flying height of a hard disk head therefore increases its potential storage capacity.

The limiting case is flying at zero altitude. Flying at such a low height is fraught with danger. Just as trees, barns, and other obstacles loom in the way of low-flying aircraft, surface imperfections of hard disks can have similar deleterious consequences on a low-flying head. When the head has no ground clearance, it runs into a further problem—friction. The head constantly rubbing against the disk surface will soon wear something out. It doesn't matter whether the platter or the head succumbs, the result is the same—a dysfunctional disk.

Nevertheless, the optimum flying height for a hard disk head is zero. Drive makers have found a way around the problem of friction—constant lubrication for the head in the form of a viscous liquid. In effect, the head swims instead of flies, and the liquid prevents both from wearing out. In coming years, expect to see these contact-disks as an alternative to flying head designs.

Head Actuators

Each read-write head scans the hard disk for information. Were the head nothing more than that, fixed in position as is the head of a tape recorder, it would only be able to read a narrow section of the disk. The head and the entire assembly to which it is attached must be able to move in order to take advantage of all the recordable area on the hard disk. The mechanism that moves the head assembly is called the head actuator. Usually, the head assembly is pivoted and is swung across the disk by a special head actuator solenoid or motor.

Modern head actuator designs also help increase hard disk capacity. This increase is achieved by precision. One of the most important limits on the density of data storage in a disk system is the capability of the mechanism to exactly and repeatably locate a specific location on the disk surface that stores a bit of information. The more precise the mechanism, the tighter it can pack data. The better actuators (along with the dimensional stability of the rigid platters themselves) are used in the hard disk for a more stable, more precise storage environment that can reliably pack information at a greater density.

The head actuator is part of an electro-mechanical system which also includes the electronics that control the movement of the head. Two distinct types of electronic systems are commonly used in hard disk designs, open-loop actuators and closed-loop actuators. Open-loop systems are essentially obsolete in modern hard disk drives. They played an important role, however, in the development of the hard disk drive—the disks used in the XT and AT were based on open-loop systems.

Specific types of hard disk mechanisms are associated with these open-loop and closed-loop design techniques. Most open-loop systems used band-stepper technology. Today's closed-loop hard disks almost universally use servo-voice coil actuators.

Whether the "loop" is open or closed merely indicates whether direct feedback about the head position is used in controlling the actuator. An open-loop system gets no direct feedback; it moves the head and hopes that it gets to the right place. Closed-loop systems give the drive feedback about the location of the read-write head over the platters. Consequently, closed-loop drives can have higher storage densities because the head can be more precisely placed when it knows its exact location above the disk platters.

Band-Stepper Actuators

The band-stepper actuator is in principle the same mechanism used to move floppy disk heads. Typically, the band-stepper actuator uses a stepping motor to generate the force to move the head. A stepping motor is a special direct current motor that turns in discrete increments in response to electrical pulses from the control electronics instead of spinning. The electronics of the band-stepper system send out a given number of pulses and assume the stepper motor rotates that number of steps. The band of the band-stepper is simply a thin strip of metal that couples the rotating shaft of the motor to the linear travel of the head. Each pulse from the control electronics thus moves the head across one track of the hard disk. The speed at which this form of actuator can operate is limited by the rate at which pulses can reliably be sent to the motor.

The advantages of the band-stepper design are its electrical simplicity and the capability to use all platter surfaces for storing data. On the downside, practical stepper motor designs limit the number of tracks (one track per step, remember) and the speed at which the head can move (and your data found) because each pulse must be individually recognizable by the actuator with some error margin allowed for. Modern microelectronics have eliminated electrical simplicity as an issue, and higher areal densities achievable by other designs permit larger storage even if one of the platter surfaces in the drive cannot be used for storage. As a result, band-stepper hard disks are obsolete, and no current products from the major disk vendors use this technology.

Servo-Voice Coil Actuators

The closed-loop system gets a constant stream of information regarding the head position from the disk, so it always knows exactly where the head is. The system determines the location of the head by constantly reading from a special, dedicated side of one platter—the servo surface—which stores a special magnetic pattern that allows the drive mechanism to identify each storage location on the disk. Some more recent magnetic hard disks put the servo information on the same recording surface as the stored data. This combined data-and-servo system is called embedded servo technology.

The most common of the closed-loop actuator systems uses a voice coil mechanism that operates like the voice coil in a loudspeaker and is therefore called a servo-voice coil actuator. In this design, a magnetic field is generated on a coil of wire (a solenoid) by the controlling electronics, and this field pulls the head mechanism against the force of a spring. By varying the current in the coil, the head mechanism is drawn farther from its anchoring spring, and the head moves across the disk. The voice coil mechanism connects directly to a pivoting arm that also supports the read-write head above the platter. The varying force of the voice coil swings the head radially in an arc across the platter surface.

Because of its closed-loop nature, the servo-voice coil system doesn't have to count out each step to the disk location it needs to travel to. It can quickly move to approximately the correct place, and in milliseconds, fine tune its location based on the servo information. This speed, and the tight track spacing afforded by closed-loop positioning, has made servo-voice coil hard disks the current choice of all major hard disk manufacturers.

Magneto-optical drives use an embedded servo system for locating tracks but fail to deliver the high speeds of magnetic servo-based systems because the optical head mechanism is substantially more massive than the diminuitive magnetic head.

Dual-Actuator Drives

Even the servo-voice coil mechanism has to obey the laws of physics. It cannot move the head instantly from one track to another, so there is always a slight delay when the head has to search out a particular byte. One of the principal goals in improving hard disk performance is minimizing this delay. Drive-makers have squeezed about all they can get out of traditional mechanisms by reducing the mass (and thus inertia) of the head assembly. Dramatic speed improvements require a radical change.

One such departure from traditional design first developed by Conner Peripherals is the dual-actuator hard disk. Instead of a single head per platter, the Conner design uses two, each attached to its own independent actuator. Either head can scan across the entire surface of the platter. With properly designed electronics, this mechanism can cut latency in half on isolated disk operations and eliminate the delays imposed by head movement on back-to-back read or write requests.

Latency can be trimmed by installing the two head actuators at diametrically opposed positions across the disk. The drive electronics can determine which head is nearest the desired data and use it for the read or write operation. Because one of the heads has to be within half a revolution of the desired data, the rotational latency is one-half the time it takes the platter to make a complete spin.

When read and write requests are stacked, this two-head system can effectively eliminate track access delays. One head can seek while the other is reading or writing and thus be ready for the next drive operation. This technique does not work with current versions of DOS, however, because DOS requires one disk operation to be completed before requesting another one. More advanced operating systems take full advantage of this design.

Landing Zone

Hard disks are most vulnerable to head crash damage when they are turned off. As soon as you flick the off switch on your computer, the platters of its hard disk must stop spinning, and the airflow that keeps the heads flying stops. Generally, the airflow decreases gradually, and the head slowly progresses downward, eventually landing like an airplane on the disk media.

In truth, however, any head landing is more of a controlled crash and holds the potential for disk damage. Consequently, most hard disks—even those with thin-film media—have a dedicated landing zone reserved in their media in which no data can be recorded. This landing zone is usually at one edge of the actual data storage area.

Park-and-Lock

Usually a software command is necessary to bring the head to the landing zone and hold it there while the disk spins down. This process is called head parking. Some drives are designed so that whenever their power is switched off, the head automatically retracts to the landing zone before the disk spins down. Such drives are termed automatic head parking.

Even when the read-write head touches down in the proper landing zone when the power to the disk drive is turned off, potential problems can still arise. An impact or other shock to the system can jar the head out of the landing zone, in the process bouncing it across the vulnerable medium. To guard against such disasters, a growing number of hard disks lock their read-write heads in place at the landing zone when power is removed. This feature is generally termed automatic park-and-lock. Nearly all modern hard disk drives have park-and-lock.

Disk Geometry

A combination of the hard disk mechanism, its controller, and the software operating it all dictates the manner in which data is arranged on the platter. Unlike floppy disks, which are often interchanged, hard disks need not fit any particular standard because their media are never at large; they are always sealed inside the drive mechanism. Because platters cannot be removed from drives (providing you don't take matters into your own hands with a can opener and crowbar) they have no need of interchangability. The physical layout of the data on disk is thus left to the imagination of the disk's designer.

The disk designer is not given free rein, however, because of one overriding necessity—compatibility with DOS and the IBM hardware standard. Certain disk parameters must arbitrarily be set at values that true compatibility requires. Of course, where there's a roadblock, there's an engineer with a pocket calculator figuring out exactly how much effort sidestepping it will take. Today's advanced drive electronics allow the designers the widest possible latitude in selecting hard disk parameters—whatever doesn't match the PC standard, the electronics fake so that your PC doesn't know about the rules violations. Consequently, what your PC sees follows the PC standard to the letter, but what goes on inside the drive is the engineer's business.

To understand this parameter monkey business, you first need to know a bit of hard disk geography—where the drive puts your bytes. The storage arrangement is called the drive's geometry and it determines the setup parameters of the drive used in its installation. Figure 22.5 graphically illustrates hard disk geometry.

Tracks

No matter the type of magnetic media or style of head actuator used by a disk, the read-write head must stop its lateral motion across the disk whenever it reads or writes data. While it is stationary, the platter spins underneath it. Each time the platter completes one spin, the head traces a full circle across its surface. This circle is called a track.

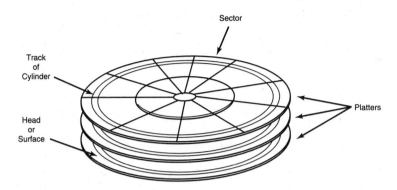

FIGURE 22.5. Hard disk geometry.

Cylinders

Each head traces out a separate track across its associated platter. Because the combination of all the tracks traced out at a given head actuator position forms the outline of a solid cylinder, such a vertical stack of tracks is often termed exactly that: a cylinder.

The number of cylinders is permanently determined when the drive is manufactured by the magnetic pattern written on the servo surface (which you cannot alter) of the drive. Typical PC hard disks have between 312 and 2048 cylinders (or tracks per platter), although a number of constraints limit many hard disks to only 1024 useful cylinders.

Sectors

Most hard disk systems further divide each track into short arcs termed sectors, and the sector is the basic storage unit of the drive. Some operating systems use the sector as their basic storage unit as does, for example, the High Performance File System of OS/2. DOS, however, gathers together several sectors to make its basic unit of storage for disk files, the cluster.

Sectors can be soft, marked magnetically with bit patterns embedded in the data on the track itself, or hard, set by the drive mechanism itself. Soft sectors are demarcated using a low-level format program, and their number can vary almost arbitrarily, depending on the formatting software and the interface used for connecting the disk. Disks with device-level interfaces are essentially soft-sectored. For all practical purposes, disks with system-level interfaces are hard-sectored because their sector size is set by the servo information encoded on the drive platters which cannot be changed after the drive leaves the factory. Magneto-optical cartridges are hard-sectored by an embedded optical format pre-recorded on the medium.

In the PC hard disk industry, the size of a sector is almost universally 512 bytes. (Magneto-optical cartridges are available with either 512-byte or 1024-byte sectors.) Modern hard disks with system-level AT Attachment and SCSI interfaces may have almost any number of sectors per track. They may even put differing numbers of sectors on inner and outer tracks. Data transfer rate standards fixed the sector counts of old drives using device-level interfaces. Drives using the ST506 interface and MFM data coding almost invariably had 17 on each track. Shifting to RLL upped the sector count to 25 or 26. ESDI drives usually have about 34 sectors per track.

The sector count on any given track of a traditional hard disk is the same as every other track because hard disks once almost invariably used constant angular velocity recording. This technology sets the speed of the disk's spin at a constant rate so that in any given period over any given track, the drive's read-write head hangs over the same length arc (measured in degrees) of the disk. The actual length of the arc, measured linearly (in inches or centimeters) varies depending on the radial position of the head. Sectors on tracks farther from the center of the disk are longer. Despite their greater length, however, the outer-track sectors hold the same data as the shorter inner sectors. Constant angular velocity equipment is easy to build because the disk spins at a constant number of RPM. Old vinyl phonograph records are the best example of constant angular velocity recording—the black platters spun at an invariate 33, 45, or 78 RPM. Nearly all hard disks and all ISO standard magneto-optical drives use constant angular velocity recording.

A more efficient technology, called constant linear velocity recording, alters the spin speed of the disk depending on how near the center tracks the read-write head lies so that in any given period the same length of track passes below the head. When the head is above the outer tracks of the disk, where the circumference is greater, the slower spin allows more data to be packed into each track. Using this technology, more sectors could be packed onto the longer outer tracks. Constant linear velocity recording therefore permits more information to be packed on a disk. For this reason, constant linear velocity recording is used for high-capacity media such as audio Compact Discs. Some non-standard MO systems (such as Maxtor's Tahiti drives) also use constant linear velocity recording to pack more data onto their disks.

But constant linear velocity recording is ill-suited to hard disks. For the disk platter to be properly read or written, it must be spinning at the proper rate. Hard disk heads regularly bounce from the outer tracks to the inner tracks as your software requests them to read or write data. Slowing or speeding up the platter to the proper speed would require a lengthy wait, perhaps seconds because of inertia, which would shoot the average access time of the drive through the roof.

Zoned recording is the compromise, allowing nearly uniform storage densities as with constant linear velocity densities, while maintaining an unchanging spin rate as with constant angular velocity recording.

Write Precompensation

Constant angular velocity recording has another drawback. The shorter sectors closer to the spindle require data to be packed into them more tightly, squeezing the magnetic flux reversals in the recording medium ever closer together. The capability of many magnetic media to hold flux transitions falls off as the transitions are packed more tightly—pinched together, they produce a feebler field and induce a lower current in the read-write head.

One way of dealing with this problem is to write on the disk with a stronger magnetic field as the sectors get closer to the spindle. By increasing the current in the read-write head when it writes nearer the center of the disk, the on-disk flux transitions can be made stronger. They then can induce stronger currents in the read-write head when that area of the disk is read.

This process is called write precompensation because the increased writing current compensates for the fall off in disk responses nearer its center at a place logically before the information is stored on the disk. Drives with system-level interfaces automatically make the necessary compensation. Your PC must instruct older device-level interfaced drives when to add the necessary write precompensation. Some drives, particularly older models, require that you indicate the write precompensation cylinder when you set up your system. Modern drives do not. When you don't need write precompensation, you should specify either cylinder 0 or 65535, depending on your PC's BIOS, to indicate not to apply write precompensation.

Capacity Limits

Disk designers are not free to use any geometry for their products. A number of design aspects of PCs and their operating systems constrain them. Many of these limits date back to the dark days when IBM originally engineered its systems (which the rest of the PC industry dutifully copied—limits and all—for compatibility's sake). For example, IBM's engineers severely constrained the size and number of File Allocation Table entries and limited the number of cylinders that its hardware and software could reach.

For personal computer models up to the first generation of ATs and their compatibles, the maximum possible cylinder count for a hard disk totaled 1024. This limit was enforced throughout the hardware and software of the system—and survives in both the DOS partition table and many systems' BIOSs. Although you could plug a hard disk with a larger cylinder count into most PCs, many systems allow you to access only the first 1024 cylinders because neither DOS nor the controller can count higher.

This low cylinder count can be a severe limitation because the current trend in hard disk design is toward shorter drives, 3.5-inch drives that stand one inch tall being some of the tallest of current models. The low headroom means that fewer platters can be stacked in the drive. The only way to fill the smaller housing with more data is to pack it more densely on each platter—which means adding more cylinders.

Translation Mode

Drive makers have found a better way around the problem, sector translation or translation mode. Essentially, the hard disk translates its own geometry from one arrangement to another.

For example, while a drive might have 2048 cylinders and three heads, the drive electronics are designed to respond as if the drive was actually built with only 1024 cylinders and six heads, sneaking under the limit. Because the translation occurs in the drive hardware itself, neither you nor your system has to worry what the actual physical cylinder and head arrangement might be. Sector translation works most effectively on embedded interface drives—AT Attachment and SCSI—which give the disk designer full control over all aspects of the disk controller hardware.

A few manufacturers take this translation one step further. Not only can some of their drives make the translation, the final arrangement is flexible, and the drive itself can determine what's best. For example, some Seagate AT Attachment drives check your system to see what drive geometry it expects; then the drive changes like a chameleon to that configuration.

The 32-Megabyte Addressing Limit

DOS versions before 4.0 limited the maximum size of disk addressable as a single unit to 32 megabytes. For compatibility with older software (particularly hard disk utilities), many people still stick with this limit and partition their hard disks into a number of 32-megabyte volumes.

The limit arose from a combination of factors: the space IBM and Microsoft allowed for the file allocation table and the number of sectors that were assigned to each cluster. DOS normally divides files into clusters of four sectors. It keeps track of which clusters are part of which file using the File Allocation Table. The number of clusters that DOS can address is limited by the overall size of the File Allocation Table and the size of each entry in the table.

In versions of DOS before 3.0, each entry in the File Allocation Table was a byte and a half— that is, 12 bits—allowing a maximum of 4096 clusters to be identified. In these early version of DOS, clusters were made from eight sectors, totaling 4096 bytes each. Under this scheme, the maximum size for a standard DOS volume would be 16 megabytes.

Starting with DOS version 3.0, each File Allocation Table entry was allowed to be either 12 or 16 bits, depending on disk capacity. For disks smaller than about 16 megabytes, 12-bit allocation units are used. Larger disks get the 16-bit File Allocation Table entries, permitting a total of 65,536 entries. With the larger number of allocation table entries, cluster size was reduced to four sectors, or 2048 bytes.

Not all of those entries are useful, however, because versions of DOS from 3.0 to 3.32 (and, for compatibility reasons, OS/2 version 1.0) limit the size of the File Allocation Table itself to 16,384 entries. That number of entries coupled to the cluster size of four sectors results in the 32-megabyte addressing limit of DOS. Larger disks are not possible using this scheme because no space is available for recording more than 16,384 File Allocation Table entries.

DOS 4.0 first broke the 32-megabyte limit by allocating the 65,536 bytes to the File Allocation Table. This change alone effectively quadrupled the maximum hard disk capacity to 128 megabytes. This limit is, of course, also imposed by the 16-bit size of File Allocation Table entries as well.

DOS versions 5.0 and later allow you to take a step beyond this 128-megabyte partition limit by altering the size of each cluster. For example, doubling the size of each cluster from four to eight sectors (2048 to 4096 bytes each) effectively double the maximum disk size without changing the the size of FAT entries. In fact, even before DOS 5.0, some hard-disk management programs resorted to this technique to break the old 32- and 128-megabyte limits. DOS 5.0 allows a cluster to be made from up to 16 sectors (8192 bytes).

As clever as it is, this technique has its drawback. It can be wasteful. Disk space is divvied up in units of a cluster. No matter how small a file (or a subdirectory, which is simply a special kind of file) may be, it occupies at minimum one cluster of disk space. Larger files take up entire clusters, but any fractional cluster of space that's left over requires another cluster. On average, each file on the disk wastes half a cluster of space. The more files, the more waste. The larger the clusters, the more waste. Unless you work exclusively with massive files, increasing cluster size to increase disk capacity is a technique to avoid whenever possible.

DOS 5 and 6 also are designed to use the smallest cluster size possible for a given disk capacity. Consequently, disks with capacities up to 134,217,728 bytes could be addressed as a single unit with 2048-byte clusters. With 8192-byte clusters, the maximum size of a single unit or disk partition is 536,870,912 bytes. Both DOS 5 and 6 handle larger disks but require partitioning them into these half-gigabyte chunks.

Other Constraints

Other standards conspire to limit the maximum capacity of hard disk drives. The conventional system BIOS defines the functions of hardware interrupt 013(Hex) for controlling the hard disk drive. By itself, this BIOS limit is not much of a limit at all—it limits disks to a maximum of 63 sectors per track, 255 heads, and 1024 cylinders. That's a potential total capacity of 8.4 gigabytes. The ATA interface specification, however, limits disks to 255 sectors per track, 16 heads, and 65,536 cylinders—potentially 136.9 gigabytes per disk. Together, however, the BIOS and ATA constraints limit disks to no more than 63 sectors per track (the BIOS limit), 16 heads (the ATA limit), and 1024 tracks (the BIOS limit again). The result is that many ATA disks were constrained to capacities of 528M or less.

Because of the needs for ever-greater capacities with today's PCs, drive and BIOS makers have developed a system that sidesteps the ATA parameter limits. Instead of addressing the disk by cylinder, head, and sector, these new systems use logical addressing blocks under the ATA-2 scheme. Taking advantage of this newer addressing method requires a BIOS that supports the feature, which means either having a new PC with explicit support or adding an ATA host adapter which has a built-in BIOS that provides such support.

Most systems ATA disks are constrained to capacities of 528 MB or less. Larger ATA disks are possible, but most systems cannot ordinarily address their full storage range. SCSI drives, on the other hand, do not suffer the ATA-imposed limit and are not as constrained in maximum capacity.

Disk Parameters

Taken together, the number of platters (or heads), the number of cylinders, and the point at which write precompensation begins make up the set of disk parameters. With drives that use device-level interfaces and older ATA drives, these three numbers are required by the disk drive controller to properly operate a disk drive.

In early model computers, such as the IBM XT and early add-on disk subsystems, the disk parameters were permanently encoded into the ROM firmware of the disk controller itself. Using this technique, every controller had to be matched to the disk drive model that it was to operate.

A few aftermarket suppliers had a better idea. They recorded the disk parameters on the disk itself in a place that would be reachable in the same way across many different models of disk drive. As part of the boot-up process, the disk drive would be commanded to read back its identifying information, loading it into the controller. Thereafter, the controller could properly run the drive.

With the IBM AT, a new method of getting disk parameters to the controller was developed. The parameters were stored in the CMOS setup memory of the computer. The controller read the parameters from the CMOS and then could properly run the drive. This same technique is used by the PS/2 series of computers.

ESDI, SCSI, and most ATA drives permit the drive parameters to be embedded in the system. For instance, ESDI drives can record their parameters on the disk itself because the location and means of accessing this information is standardized. Unfortunately, the BIOSs of most PCs do not know how to access the formatting information encoded on ESDI and ATA disks, so you have to enter the parameters manually when you set up your PC. With a modern hard disk using the AT Attachment interface and automatic translation mode, you don't have to worry about exactly matching these parameters. As long as you set your system with any parameters that yield the proper drive capacity, the disk itself makes the right parameter match. ATA systems that use logical block addressing also have no need for setting drive parameters.

Modern SCSI host adapters use their own BIOSs and operate independently from your PC's setup parameters. (Some AT Attachment host adapters have their own BIOSs and therefore do not require parameter settings, either.) When you connect a SCSI drive alone, you should usually set up your system as if it has no hard disks. The SCSI host adapter takes care of the details, reading the drive parameters from the drive itself and relaying the setup information to your PC.

Table 22.1 lists the essential drive parameters of most of the commonly available hard disks that require the setup with today's PCs.

TABLE 22.1. Parameters for Common Hard Disks

Alps	Model	Interface	Capacity	Cylinders	Heads	Sectors
	DRND-10A	MFM	10	615	2	17
	DRND-20A	MFM	20	615	4	17
	DRPO-20D	MFM/RLL	20	615	2	26
	RPO-20A	MFM/RLL	20	615	2	26
Ampex	Model	Interface	Capacity	Cylinders	Heads	Sectors
	PYXIS-13	MFM	10	320	4	17
	PYXIS-20	MFM	15	320	6	17
	PYXIS-27	MFM	20	320	8	17
	PYXIS-7	MFM	5	320	2	17
Areal	Model	Interface	Capacity	Cylinders	Heads	Sectors
	A120	ATA	124	1024	4	60
	A180	ATA	181	1488	4	60
	MD-2060	ATA	61	1024	2	60
	MD-2080	ATA	80	1323	2	60
Atasi	Model	Interface	Capacity	Cylinders	Heads	Sectors
	#AT-6120	ESDI	1051	1925	15	71
	AT-3020	MFM	17	645	3	17
	AT-3033	MFM	28	645	5	17
	AT-3046	MFM	39	645	7	17
	AT-3051	MFM	43	704	7	17
	AT-3051+	MFM	44	733	7	17
	AT-3053	MFM	44	733	7	17
	AT-3075	MFM	67	1024	8	17
	AT-3085	MFM/RLL	71	1024	8	26
	AT-3128	MFM	109	1024	8	26
	AT-676	ESDI	765	1632	15	54
BASF	Model	Interface	Capacity	Cylinders	Heads	Sectors
	6185	MFM	23	440	6	17
	6186	MFM	15	440	4	17
	6187	MFM	8	440	2	17
	6188-R1	MFM	10	612	2	17
	6188-R3	MFM	21	612	4	17

Bull	Model	Interface	Capacity	Cylinders	Heads	Sectors
	D-530	MFM	26	987	3	17
	D-550	MFM	43	97	5	17
	D-570	MFM	60	987	7	17
	D-585	MFM	71	1166	7	17
C. Itoh	Model	Interface	Capacity	Cylinders	Heads	Sectors
	YD-3042	MFM/RLL	44	788	4	26
	YD-3082	MFM/RLL	87	788	8	26
	YD-3530	MFM	32	731	5	17
	YD-3540	MFM	45	731	7	17
Century Data	Model	Interface	Capacity	Cylinders	Heads	Sectors
	CAST 10203E	ESDI	55	1050	3	35
	CAST 10203S	SCSI	55	1050	3	35
	CAST 10304E	ESDI	75	1050	4	35
	CAST 10304S	SCSI	75	1050	4	35
	CAST 10305E	ESDI	94	1050	5	35
	CAST 10305S	SCSI	94	1050	5	35
	CAST 14404E	ESDI	114	1590	4	35
	CAST 14404S	SCSI	114	1590	4	35
	CAST 14405E	ESDI	140	1590	5	35
	CAST 14405S	SCSI	140	1590	5	35
	CAST 14406E	ESDI	170	1590	6	35
	CAST 14406S	SCSI	170	1590	6	35
	CAST 24509E	ESDI	258	1599	9	35
	CAST 24509S	SCSI	258	1599	9	35
	CAST 24611E	ESDI	315	1599	11	35
	CAST 24611S	SCSI	315	1599	11	35
	CAST 24713E	ESDI	372	1599	13	35
	CAST 24713S	SCSI	372	1599	13	35
CMI	Model	Interface	Capacity	Cylinders	Heads	Sectors
	#CM5205	MFM	4	256	2	17
	CM3206	MFM	10	306	4	17

continues

TABLE 22.1. Continued

CMI	Model	Interface	Capacity	Cylinders	Heads	Sectors
	CM3426	MFM	20	615	4	17
	CM5206	MFM	5	306	2	17
	CM5410	MFM	8	256	4	17
	CM5412	MFM	10	306	4	17
	CM5616	MFM	13	256	6	17
	CM5619	MFM	15	306	6	17
	CM5826	MFM	21	306	8	17
	CM6213	MFM	11	640	2	17
	CM6426	MFM	21	615	4	17
	CM6426S	MFM	22	640	4	17
	CM6640	MFM	33	640	6	17
	CM7660	MFM	50	960	6	17
	CM7880	MFM	67	960	8	17
Cognito	Model	Interface	Capacity	Cylinders	Heads	Sectors
	CG-906	MFM	5	306	2	17
	CG-912	MFM	11	306	4	17
	CG-925	MFM	21	612	4	17
	PT-912	MFM	11	612	2	17
	PT-925	MFM	21	612	4	17
Conner	Model	Interface	Capacity	Cylinders	Heads	Sectors
	#CP-4044	ATA	43	1104	2	38
	CP-2020	SCSI	21	642	2	32
	CP-2024	ATA	21	653	2	32
	CP-2034	ATA	32	823	2	38
	CP-2064	ATA	64	823	4	38
	CP-2084	ATA	85	548	8	38
	CP-2304	ATA	209	1348	8	39
	CP-3000	ATA	43	976	5	17
	CP-30060	SCSI	61	1524	2	39
	CP-30064	ATA	61	762	4	39

Conner	Model	Interface	Capacity	Cylinders	Heads	Sectors
	CP-30080	SCSI	84	1053	4	39
	CP-30084	ATA	84	526	8	39
	CP-30084E	ATA	85	905	4	46
	CP-30100	SCSI	120	1522	4	39
	CP-30104	ATA	120	1522	4	39
	CP-30174E	ATA	170	903	8	46
	CP-3020	SCSI	21	622	2	33
	CP-30200	SCSI	213	2119	4	49
	CP-30204	ATA	213	683	16	38
	CP-3022	ATA	21	622	2	33
	CP-3024	ATA	22	636	2	33
	CP-3040	SCSI	42	1026	2	40
	CP-3044	ATA	43	1047	2	40
	CP-3100	SCSI	105	776	8	33
	CP-3102	ATA	104	776	8	33
	CP-3104	ATA	105	776	8	33
	CP-3111	ATA	112	832	8	33
	CP-3114	ATA	112	832	8	33
	CP-3180	SCSI	84	832	6	33
	CP-3184	ATA	84	832	6	33
	CP-3200/F	SCSI	213	1366	8	38
	CP-3204/F	ATA	213	683	16	38
	CP-3304	ATA	340	659	16	63
	CP-3364	ATA	362	702	16	63
	CP-340	SCSI	42	788	4	26
	CP-342	ATA	40	805	4	26
	CP-344	ATA	43	788	4	26
	CP-3504	ATA	509	987	16	63
	CP-3554	ATA	544	1054	16	63
	CP-4024	ATA	22	627	2	34

continues

TABLE 22.1. Continued

Control Data	Model	Interface	Capacity	Cylinders	Heads	Sectors
	#94155-86	MFM	72	925	9	17
	#94208-75	ATA	60	969	5	26
	#94351-126	SCSI	111	1068	7	29
	24221-125M	SCSI	110	1024	3	36
	24221-209M	SCSI	183	1024	5	36
	94155-120	MFM/RLL	102	960	8	26
	94155-135	MFM	115	960	9	26
	94155-19	MFM	18	697	3	17
	94155-21	MFM	18	697	3	17
	94155-25	MFM	24	697	4	17
	94155-28	MFM	24	697	4	17
	94155-36	MFM	30	697	5	17
	94155-38	MFM	31	733	5	17
	94155-48	MFM	40	925	5	17
	94155-51	MFM	43	989	5	17
	94155-57	MFM	48	925	6	17
	94155-67	MFM	58	925	7	17
	94155-77	MFM	64	925	8	17
	94155-85	MFM	71	1024	8	17
	94155-96	MFM	80	1024	9	17
	94156-48	ESDI	40	925	5	17
	94156-67	ESDI	56	925	7	17
	94156-86	ESDI	72	925	9	17
	94161-101	SCSI	86	969	5	26
	94161-121	SCSI	120	969	7	26
	94161-141	SCSI	140	969	7	26
	94161-155	SCSI	150	969	9	36
	94161-182	SCSI	155	969	9	36
	94166-101	ESDI	84	969	5	34
	94166-141	ESDI	118	969	7	34
	94166-182	ESDI	152	969	9	34

Control Data	Model	Interface	Capacity	Cylinders	Heads	Sectors
	94171-300	SCSI	288	1365	9	36
	94171-344	SCSI	335	1549	9	36
	94171-350	SCSI	300	1412	9	46
	94171-375	SCSI	375	1549	9	35
	94171-376	SCSI	330	1546	9	45
	94181-385D	SCSI	337	791	15	36
	94181-385H	SCSI	330	791	15	55
	94181-574	SCSI	574	1549	15	36
	94181-702	SCSI	601	1546	15	54
	94181-702M	SCSI	613	1549	15	54
	94186-265	ESDI	221	1412	9	34
	94186-324	ESDI	270	1412	11	34
	94186-383	ESDI	319	1412	13	34
	94186-383H	ESDI	319	1224	15	34
	94186-383S	ESDI	338	1412	13	36
	94186-442	ESDI	368	1412	15	34
	94186-442H	ESDI	368	1412	15	34
	94191-766	SCSI	676	1632	15	54
	94191-766M	SCSI	676	1632	15	54
	94196-383	ESDI	338	1412	13	34
	94196-766	ESDI	664	1632	15	54
	94204-65	ATA	65	948	5	26
	94204-71	ATA	71	1032	5	26
	94204-74	ATA	65	948	5	26
	94204-81	ATA	71	1032	5	26
	94205-30	MFM	25	989	3	17
	94205-41	MFM/RLL	38	989	3	26
	94205-51	MFM/RLL	43	989	3	26
	94205-77	MFM/RLL	65	989	5	26
	94211-106	ESDI	89	1024	5	34
	94211-106	SCSI	91	1022	5	26
	94211-209	SCSI	142	1547	5	36

continues

TABLE 22.1. Continued

Control Data	Model	Interface	Capacity	Cylinders	Heads	Sectors
	94211-91	SCSI	91	969	5	36
	94221-125	SCSI	107	1544	3	36
	94221-190	SCSI	190	1547	5	36
	94221-209	SCSI	183	1544	5	36
	94241-383	SCSI	338	1261	7	36
	94241-502	SCSI	435	1755	7	69
	94244-219	ATA	191	1747	4	54
	94244-274	ATA	241	1747	5	54
	94244-383	ATA	338	1747	7	54
	94246-182	ESDI	160	1453	4	36
	94246-182	ATA	160	1453	4	36
	94246-383	ESDI	338	1747	7	54
	94246-383	ATA	338	1747	7	54
	94314-136	ATA	120	1068	5	36
	94316-111	ESDI	98	1072	5	36
	94316-136	ESDI	120	1268	5	36
	94316-155	ESDI	138	1072	7	36
	94316-200	ESDI	177	1072	9	36
	94335-100	MFM	83	1072	9	17
	94335-150	MFM/RLL	128	1072	9	26
	94335-55	MFM	46	1072	5	17
	94351-111	SCSI	98	1068	5	36
	94351-128	SCSI	111	1068	7	36
	94351-133	SCSI	116	1268	7	36
	94351-133S	SCSI-2	116	1268	7	36
	94351-134	SCSI	117	1068	7	36
	94351-155	SCSI	138	1068	7	36
	94351-155S	SCSI-2	138	1068	7	36
	94351-160	SCSI	142	1068	9	29
	94351-172	SCSI	150	1068	9	36
	94351-186S	SCSI-2	163	1268	7	36

Control Data	Model	Interface	Capacity	Cylinders	Heads	Sectors
	94351-200	SCSI	177	1068	9	36
	94351-200	SCSI-2	177	1068	9	36
	94351-230	SCSI	210	1272	9	36
	94351-90	SCSI	79	1068	5	29
	94354-111	ATA	98	1072	5	36
	94354-126	ATA	111	1072	7	29
	94354-133	ATA	117	1272	5	36
	94354-135	ATA	119	1072	9	29
	94354-155	ATA	138	1072	7	36
	94354-160	ATA	143	1072	9	29
	94354-172	ATA	157	1072	9	36
	94354-186	ATA	164	1272	7	36
	94354-200	ATA	177	1072	9	36
	94354-230	ATA	211	1272	9	36
	94354-90	ATA	79	1072	5	29
	94356-111	ESDI	98	1072	5	36
	94356-155	ESDI	138	1072	7	36
	94356-200	ESDI	177	1072	9	36
	94601-767H	SCSI-2	665	1356	15	64
	94601-767M	SCSI	676	1508	15	54
Disctec	*Model*	*Interface*	*Capacity*	*Cylinders*	*Heads*	*Sectors*
	RHD-20	ATA	21	615	2	34
	RHD-60	ATA	63	1024	2	60
Disctron	*Model*	*Interface*	*Capacity*	*Cylinders*	*Heads*	*Sectors*
	D-503	MFM	3	153	2	17
	D-504	MFM	4	215	2	17
	D-506	MFM	5	153	4	17
	D-507	MFM	5	306	2	17
	D-509	MFM	8	215	4	17
	D-512	MFM	11	153	8	17
	D-513	MFM	11	215	6	17

continues

TABLE 22.1. Continued

Disktron	Model	Interface	Capacity	Cylinders	Heads	Sectors
	D-514	MFM	11	306	4	17
	D-518	MFM	15	215	8	17
	D-519	MFM	16	306	6	17
	D-526	MFM	21	306	8	17
Epson	Model	Interface	Capacity	Cylinders	Heads	Sectors
	HD850	MFM	11	306	4	17
	HD860	MFM	21	612	4	17
Fuju	Model	Interface	Capacity	Cylinders	Heads	Sectors
	FK301-13	MFM	10	306	4	17
	FK302-13	MFM	10	612	2	17
	FK302-26	MFM	21	612	4	17
	FK302-39	MFM	32	612	6	17
	FK303-52	MFM	40	615	8	17
	FK305-26	MFM	21	615	4	17
	FK305-39	MFM	32	615	6	17
	FK305-39R	MFM/RLL	32	615	4	26
	FK305-58R	MFM/RLL	49	615	6	26
	FK308S-39R	SCSI	31	615	4	26
	FK308S-58R	SCSI	45	615	6	26
	FK309-26	MFM	20	615	4	17
	FK309-39	MFM	32	615	6	17
	FK309-39R	MFM/RLL	30	615	4	26
	FK309S-50R	SCSI	41	615	4	26
Fujitsu	Model	Interface	Capacity	Cylinders	Heads	Sectors
	#M2234AS	MFM	16	320	6	17
	#M2249SB	SCSI	343	1243	15	19
	M2225D	MFM	21	615	4	17
	M2225DR	MFM/RLL	32	615	4	26
	M2226D	MFM	30	615	6	17
	M2226DR	MFM/RLL	49	615	6	26

Fujitsu	Model	Interface	Capacity	Cylinders	Heads	Sectors
	M2227D	MFM	40	615	8	17
	M2227DR	MFM	65	615	8	26
	M2230AS	MFM	5	320	2	17
	M2230AT	MFM	5	320	2	17
	M2231	MFM	5	306	2	17
	M2233AS	MFM	11	320	4	17
	M2233AT	MFM	11	320	4	17
	M2235AS	MFM	22	320	8	17
	M2241AS	MFM	25	754	4	17
	M2242AS	MFM	43	754	7	17
	M2243AS	MFM	68	754	11	17
	M2243R	MFM/RLL	110	1186	7	26
	M2243T	MFM	68	1186	7	17
	M2245SA	SCSI	148	823	10	35
	M2246E	ESDI	172	823	10	35
	M2247E	ESDI	143	1243	7	64
	M2247S	SCSI	138	1243	7	65
	M2247SA	SCSI	149	1243	7	36
	M2247SB	SCSI	160	1243	7	19
	M2248E	ESDI	224	1243	11	64
	M2248S	SCSI	221	1243	11	65
	M2248SA	SCSI	238	1243	11	36
	M2248SB	SCSI	252	1243	11	19
	M2249E	ESDI	305	1243	15	64
	M2249S	SCSI	303	1243	15	65
	M2249SA	SCSI	324	1243	15	36
	M2261E	ESDI	326	1658	8	53
	M2262E	ESDI	448	1658	11	48
	M2263E	ESDI	675	1658	15	53
	M2263HA	SCSI	672	1658	15	53
	M2266HA	SCSI	1079	1658	15	85

continues

TABLE 22.1. Continued

Fujitsu	Model	Interface	Capacity	Cylinders	Heads	Sectors
	M2611SA	SCSI	45	1334	2	34
	M2611T	ATA	45	1334	3	33
	M2612SA	SCSI	90	1334	4	34
	M2612T	ATA	90	1334	4	33
	M2613SA	SCSI	136	1334	6	34
	M2613T	ATA	135	1334	6	33
	M2614SA	SCSI	182	1334	8	34
	M2614T	ATA	180	1334	8	33
	M2622SA	SCSI	330	1435	8	56
	M2622T	ATA	330	1435	8	56
	M2623SA	SCSI	425	1435	10	56
	M2623T	ATA	425	1435	10	56
	M2624SA	SCSI	520	1435	12	56
	M2624T	ATA	520	1435	12	56
	M2631T	ATA	45	916	2	48
Hewlett-Packard	Model	Interface	Capacity	Cylinders	Heads	Sectors
	HP-97544E	ESDI	340	1457	8	57
	HP-97544S	SCSI	331	1447	8	56
	HP-97544T	SCSI-2	331	1447	8	56
	HP-97548E	ESDI	680	1457	16	57
	HP-97548S	SCSI	663	1447	16	56
	HP-97548T	SCSI-2	663	1447	16	56
	HP-97549T	SCSI-2	1000	1911	16	64
	HP-97556E	ESDI	681	1680	11	72
	HP-97556T	SCSI-2	673	1670	11	72
	HP-97558E	ESDI	1084	1962	15	72
	HP-97558T	SCSI-2	1075	1952	15	72
	HP-97560E	ESDI	1374	1962	19	72
	HP-97560T	SCSI-2	1363	1952	19	72
	HP-C2233S	SCSI-2	238	1511	5	49

Hewlett-Packard	Model	Interface	Capacity	Cylinders	Heads	Sectors
	HP-C2234S	SCSI-2	334	1511	7	61
	HP-C2235S	SCSI-2	429	1511	9	73
	HP-D1660A	ESDI	333	1457	8	73
	HP-D1661A	ESDI	667	1457	16	57
Hitachi	Model	Interface	Capacity	Cylinders	Heads	Sectors
	DK511-8	MFM	67	823	10	17
	DK301-1	MFM	10	306	4	17
	DK301-2	MFM	15	306	6	17
	DK502-2	MFM	21	615	4	17
	DK511-3	MFM	30	699	5	17
	DK511-5	MFM	42	699	7	17
	DK512-12	ESDI	94	823	7	34
	DK512-17	ESDI	134	823	10	34
	DK512-8	ESDI	67	823	5	34
	DK512c-12	SCSI	94	823	7	34
	DK512c-17	SCSI	134	819	10	34
	DK512c-8	SCSI	67	823	5	34
	DK514-38	ESDI	330	903	14	51
	DK514C-38	SCSI	321	903	14	51
	DK515-78	ESDI	673	1361	14	69
	DK515C-78	SCSI	661	1261	14	69
	DK512-5	MFM	42	823	6	17
	DK522-10	ESDI	103	823	6	36
	DK522C-10	SCSI	88	819	6	35
IMI	Model	Interface	Capacity	Cylinders	Heads	Sectors
	5006	MFM	5	306	2	17
	5007	MFM	5	312	2	17
	5012	MFM	10	306	4	17
	5018	MFM	15	306	6	17
	7720	MFM	21	310	4	17
	7740	MFM	43	315	8	17

continues

TABLE 22.1. Continued

Kalok	Model	Interface	Capacity	Cylinders	Heads	Sectors
	KL3100	ATA	105	820	6	35
	KL3120	ATA	120	820	6	40
	KL320	MFM	21	615	4	17
	KL330	MFM/RLL	32	615	4	26
	KL341	SCSI	40	644	4	26
	KL343	ATA	42	676	4	31
	P5-125	ATA	125	2048	2	80
	P5-250	ATA	251	2048	4	80
Kyocera	Model	Interface	Capacity	Cylinders	Heads	Sectors
	KC20	MFM	21	615	4	17
	KC30	MFM/RLL	32	615	4	26
	KC40GA	ATA	41	1075	2	26
	KC80C	SCSI	87	787	8	28
Lapine	Model	Interface	Capacity	Cylinders	Heads	Sectors
	3522	MFM	10	306	4	17
	Titan 20	MFM	21	615	4	17
	LT10	MFM	10	615	2	17
	LT20	MFM	20	615	4	17
	LT200	MFM	20	614	4	17
	LT2000	MFM	20	614	4	17
	LT300	MFM/RLL	32	614	4	26
	Titan 30	MFM/RLL	32	615	4	26
	Titan 3532	MFM/RLL	32	615	4	26
Maxtor	Model	Interface	Capacity	Cylinders	Heads	Sectors
	7040A	ATA	41	1170	2	36
	7040S	SCSI	40	1155	2	36
	7080A	ATA	81	1170	4	36
	LXT-100S	SCSI	96	73	8	32

Maxtor	Model	Interface	Capacity	Cylinders	Heads	Sectors
	LXT-200A	ATA	207	1320	7	45
	LXT-200S	SCSI	191	1320	7	33
	LXT-213A	ATA	213	1320	7	55
	LXT-213S	SCSI	200	1320	7	55
	LXT-340A	ATA	340	1560	7	47
	LXT-340S	SCSI	340	1560	7	47
	LXT-50S	SCSI	48	733	4	32
	P0-12S	SCSI	1027	1632	15	72
	P1-08E	ESDI	969	1778	9	72
	P1-08S	SCSI	696	1778	9	72
	P1-12E	ESDI	1051	1778	15	72
	P1-12S	SCSI	1005	1216	19	72
	P1-13E	ESDI	1160	1778	15	72
	P1-16E	ESDI	1331	1778	19	72
	P1-17E	ESDI	1470	1778	19	72
	P1-17S	SCSI	1470	1778	19	72
	XT1050	MFM	38	902	5	17
	XT1065	MFM	52	918	7	17
	XT1085	MFM	68	1024	8	17
	XT1105	MFM	82	918	11	17
	XT1120R	MFM/RLL	104	1024	8	26
	XT1140	MFM	116	918	15	17
	XT2085	MFM	72	1224	7	17
	XT2140	MFM	113	1224	11	17
	XT2190	MFM	159	1224	15	17
	XT4170E	ESDI	157	1224	7	35
	XT4170S	SCSI	157	1224	7	36
	XT4175E	ESDI	149	1224	7	34
	XT4179E	ESDI	158	1224	7	36
	XT4230E	ESDI	203	1224	9	35
	XT4280E	ESDI	234	1224	11	34

continues

TABLE 22.1. Continued

Maxtor	Model	Interface	Capacity	Cylinders	Heads	Sectors
	XT4280S	SCSI	241	1224	11	36
	XT4380E	ESDI	338	1224	15	35
	XT4380S	SCSI	337	1224	15	36
	XT81000E	ESDI	889	1632	15	54
	XT8380E	ESDI	360	1632	8	54
	XT8380S	SCSI	360	1632	8	54
	XT8610E	ESDI	541	1632	12	54
	XT8702S	SCSI	616	1490	15	54
	XT8760S	SCSI	675	1632	15	54
	XT880E	ESDI	694	1274	15	7117

Memorex	Model	Interface	Capacity	Cylinders	Heads	Sectors
	310	MFM	2	118	2	17
	321	MFM	5	320	2	17
	322	MFM	10	320	4	17
	323	MFM	15	320	6	17
	324	MFM	20	320	8	17
	450	MFM	10	612	2	17
	512	MFM	25	961	3	17
	513	MFM	41	961	5	17
	670	SCSI-2	667		15	
	1030	SCSI-2	1030		15	
	1548	Fast SCSI-2	1748		15	
	1302	MFM	20	830	3	17
	1303	MFM	34	830	5	17
	1304	MFM	41	830	6	17
	1323	MFM	35	1024	4	17
	1324	MFM	53	1024	6	17
	1325	MFM	71	1024	8	17
	1333	MFM	34	1024	4	17
	1334	MFM	53	1024	6	17

Memorex	Model	Interface	Capacity	Cylinders	Heads	Sectors
	1335	MFM	71	1024	8	17
	1352	ESDI	30	1024	2	36
	1353	ESDI	75	1024	4	36
	1354	ESDI	113	1024	6	36
	1355	ESDI	151	1024	8	36
	1373	SCSI	73	1024	4	36
	1374	SCSI	109	1024	6	36
	1375	SCSI	146	1024	8	36
	1551	ESDI	149	1224	7	34
	1624	Fast SCSI-2	667		7	
	1908	Fast SCSI-2	1381		15	
	1924	Fast SCSI-2	2100		21	
	2105	Fast SCSI-2 Variable	648	1745	8	
	2112	Fast SCSI-2 Variable	1214	1745	15	
	2112A	ATA	1214	2034	16	63
	1323A	MFM	44	1024	5	17
	1324A	MFM	62	1024	7	17
	1333A	MFM	44	1024	5	17
	1334A	MFM	62	1024	7	17
	1352A	ESDI	41	1024	3	36
	1353A	ESDI	94	1024	5	36
	1354A	ESDI	132	1024	7	36
	1372A	SCSI	91	1024	5	36
	1374A	SCSI	127	1024	7	36
	1488-15	SCSI	675	1628	15	54
	1516-10S	ESDI	678	1840	10	72
	1517-13	ESDI	922	1925	13	72
	1518-14	ESDI	993	1925	14	72
	1518-15	ESDI	1064	1925	15	72
	1528-15	SCSI-2	1341	2106	15	84

continues

TABLE 22.1. Continued

Micropolis	Model	Interface	Capacity	Cylinders	Heads	Sectors
	1538-15	ESDI	872	1925	15	71
	1554-11	ESDI	234	1224	11	34
	1554-7	ESDI	158	1224	7	36
	1555-12	ESDI	255	1224	12	34
	1555-8	ESDI	180	1224	8	36
	1555-9	ESDI	203	1224	9	36
	1556-10	ESDI	226	1224	10	36
	1556-11	ESDI	248	1224	11	36
	1556-13	ESDI	276	1224	13	34
	1557-12	ESDI	270	1224	12	36
	1557-13	ESDI	293	124	13	36
	1557-14	ESDI	315	1224	14	36
	1557-14	ESDI	315	1224	14	36
	1557-15	ESDI	338	1224	15	36
	1557-15	ESDI	338	1224	15	36
	1558-14	ESDI	315	1224	14	36
	1558-15	ESDI	338	1224	15	36
	1566-11	ESDI	496	1632	11	54
	1567-12	ESDI	541	1632	12	54
	1567-13	ESDI	586	1632	13	54
	1568-14	ESDI	631	1632	14	54
	1568-15	ESDI	676	1632	15	54
	1576-11	SCSI	243	1224	11	36
	1577-12	SCSI	266	1224	12	36
	1577-13	SCSI	287	1224	13	36
	1578-14	SCSI	310	1224	14	36
	1578-15	SCSI	332	1224	15	36
	1586-11	SCSI	490	1632	11	54
	1587-12	SCSI	535	1632	12	54
	1587-13	SCSI	579	1632	13	54

Micropolis	Model	Interface	Capacity	Cylinders	Heads	Sectors
	1588-14	SCSI	624	1632	14	54
	1588-15	SCSI	668	1632	15	54
	1590-15	SCSI	1049	1919	15	71
	1596-10S	SCSI	668	1834	10	72
	1597-13	SCSI	909	1919	13	72
	1598-14	SCSI	979	1919	14	72
	1652-4	ESDI	92	1249	4	36
	1653-5	ESDI	115	1249	5	36
	1654-6	ESDI	138	1249	6	36
	1654-7	ESDI	161	1249	7	36
	1663-4	ESDI	197	1780	4	36
	1663-5	ESDI	246	1780	5	36
	1664-6	ESDI	295	1780	6	54
	1664-7	ESDI	345	1780	7	54
	1673-4	SCSI	90	1249	4	36
	1673-5	SCSI	112	1249	5	36
	1674-6	SCSI	135	1249	6	36
	1674-7	SCSI	158	1249	7	36
	1683-4	SCSI	193	1776	4	54
	1683-5	SCSI	242	1776	5	54
	1684-6	SCSI	291	1776	6	54
	1684-7	SCSI	340	1776	7	54
	1743-5	ATA	112	1140	5	28
	1744-6	ATA	135	1140	6	28
	1744-7	ATA	157	1140	7	28
	1745-8	ATA	180	1140	8	28
	1745-9	ATA	202	1140	9	28
	1773-5	SCSI	112	1140	5	28
	1774-6	SCSI	135	1140	6	28
	1774-7	SCSI	157	1140	7	28
	1775-8	SCSI	180	1140	8	28
	1775-9	SCSI	202	1140	9	28

continues

TABLE 22.1. Continued

Micropolis	Model	Interface	Capacity	Cylinders	Heads	Sectors
	2105A	ATA	648	1255	16	63
Microscience	Model	Interface	Capacity	Cylinders	Heads	Sectors
	4050	MFM	45	1024	5	17
	4060	MFM/RLL	68	1024	5	26
	4070	MFM	62	1024	7	17
	4090	MFM/RLL	95	1024	7	26
	5040	ESDI	46	855	3	35
	5070	ESDI	77	855	5	35
	5100	ESDI	107	855	7	35
	5160	ESDI	159	1271	7	35
	6100	SCSI	110	855	7	36
	7040	ATA	47	855	3	36
	7100	ATA	107	855	7	35
	7200	ATA	201	1277	7	44
	7400	ATA	420	1904	8	39
	8040	ATA	43	1047	2	40
	8080	ATA	85	1768	2	47
	8200	ATA	210	1904	4	39
	5070-20	SDI	86	960	5	35
	5100-20	ESDI	120	960	7	35
	7070-20	ATA	86	960	5	35
	7100-20	ATA	120	960	7	35
	7100-2	ATA	121	1077	5	44
	8040/MLC	ATA	42	1024	2	40
	FH21200	ESDI	1062	1921	15	72
	FH21600	ESDI	1418	2147	15	86
	FH2414	ESDI	367	1658	8	54
	FH2777	ESDI	688	1658	15	54
	FH31200	SCSI	1062	1921	15	72
	FH31600	SCSI	1418	2147	15	86
	FH3414	SCSI	367	1658	8	54

Microscience	Model	Interface	Capacity	Cylinders	Heads	Sectors
	FH3777	SCSI	688	1658	15	54
	HH1050	MFM	45	1024	5	17
	HH1060	MFM/RLL	66	1024	5	26
	HH1075	MFM	62	1024	7	17
	HH1080	MFM/RLL	95	1024	7	26
	HH1090	MFM	80	1314	7	17
	HH1095	MFM/RLL	95	1024	7	26
	HH1120	MFM	122	1314	7	26
	HH2012	MFM	10	306	4	17
	HH2120	ESDI	128	1024	7	35
	HH2160	ESDI	160	1276	7	35
	HH312	MFM	10	306	4	17
	HH3120	SCSI	121	1314	5	36
	HH315	MFM	21	612	4	17
	HH3160	SCSI	169	1314	7	36
	HH330 (RLL)	MFM	33	612	4	26
	HH612	MFM	10	62	2	17
	HH712A	MFM	10	612	2	17
	HH725	MFM	21	612	4	17
	HH738	MFM/RLL	33	612	4	26
	HH825	MFM	21	612	4	17
	HH830	MFM	33	612	4	26
Miniscribe	Model	Interface	Capacity	Cylinders	Heads	Sectors
	1006	MFM	5	206	2	17
	1012	MFM	10	306	4	17
	2006	MFM	5	306	2	17
	2012	MFM	10	306	4	17
	3006	MFM	5	306	2	17
	3012	MFM	10	612	2	17
	3053	MFM	44	1024	5	17
	3085	MFM	71	1170	7	17

continues

TABLE 22.1. Continued

Miniscribe	Model	Interface	Capacity	Cylinders	Heads	Sectors
	3212	MFM	10	612	2	17
	3412	MFM	21	615	4	17
	3425	MFM	21	615	4	17
	3438	MFM/RLL	32	615	4	26
	3650	MFM	42	809	6	17
	3675	MFM/RLL	63	809	6	26
	4010	MFM	8	480	2	17
	4020	MFM	17	480	4	17
	5330	MFM	25	480	6	17
	5338	MFM	32	612	6	17
	5440	MFM	32	480	8	17
	5451	MFM	43	612	8	17
	6032	MFM	26	1024	3	17
	6053	MFM	44	1024	5	17
	6074	MFM	62	1024	7	17
	6079	MFM/RLL	68	1024	5	26
	6085	MFM	71	1024	8	17
	6128	MFM/RLL	110	1024	8	26
	6212	MFM	10	612	2	17
	7426	MFM	21	612	4	17
	8225	MFM/RLL	20	771	2	26
	8412	MFM	10	306	4	17
	8425	MFM	21	615	4	17
	8438	MFM/RLL	32	615	4	26
	8450	MFM/RLL	41	771	4	26
	97803	ESDI	676	1661	15	54
	3085E	ESDI	72	1270	3	36
	3085S	SCSI	72	1255	3	36
	3130E	ESDI	112	1250	5	36
	3130S	SCSI	115	1255	5	36
	3180E	ESDI	157	1250	7	36

Miniscribe	Model	Interface	Capacity	Cylinders	Heads	Sectors
	3180S	SCSI	153	1255	7	36
	6170E	ESDI	130	1024	8	36
	7040A	ATA	36	980	2	36
	7080A	ATA	72	980	4	36
	7080S	SCSI	81	1155	4	36
	8051A	ATA	43	745	4	28
	8051S	SCSI	45	793	4	28
	8255AT	ATA	21	745	2	28
	8255C	MFM	21	798	2	26
	8255S	SCSI	21	804	2	26
	8434F	MFM/RLL	32	615	4	26
	8438XT	ATA	32	615	4	26
	8450AT	ATA	42	745	4	28
	8450C	MFM	40	748	4	26
	8450XT	ATA	42	805	4	26
	9000E	ESDI	338	1224	15	36
	9000S	SCSI	347	1220	15	36
	9230E	ESDI	203	1224	9	36
	9230S	SCSI	203	1224	9	36
	9380E	ESDI	338	1224	15	36
	9380S	SCSI	347	1224	15	36
	9424E	ESDI	360	1661	8	54
	9424S	SCSI	355	1661	8	54
	9780S	SCSI	668	1661	15	54
Mitsubishi	Model	Interface	Capacity	Cylinders	Heads	Sectors
	MR521	MFM	10	612	2	17
	MR522	MFM	20	612	4	17
	MR5301E	ESDI	65	977	5	26
	MR533	MFM	25	971	3	17
	MR535	MFM	42	977	5	17
	MR535R	MFM/RLL	65	977	5	17

continues

TABLE 22.1. Continued

Mitsubishi	Model	Interface	Capacity	Cylinders	Heads	Sectors
	MR535S	SCSI	65	977	5	26
	MR537S	SCSI	65	977	5	26
MMI	Model	Interface	Capacity	Cylinders	Heads	Sectors
	M106	MFM	5	306	2	17
	M112	MFM	10	306	4	17
	M125	MFM	20	306	8	17
	M212	MFM	10	306	4	17
	M225	MFM	20	306	8	17
	M306	MFM	5	306	2	17
	M312	MFM	10	306	4	17
	M325	MFM	20	306	8	17
	M5012	MFM	10	306	4	17
NEC	Model	Interface	Capacity	Cylinders	Heads	Sectors
	D3126	MFM	20	615	4	17
	D3142	MFM	42	642	8	17
	D3146H	MFM	40	615	8	17
	D3661	ESDI	118	915	7	36
	D3735	ATA	56	1084	2	41
	D3755	ATA	105	1250	4	41
	D3761	ATA	114	915	7	35
	D3835	SCSI	45	1084	2	41
	D3855	SCSI	105	1250	4	41
	D3861	SCSI	114	915	7	35
	D5114	MFM	5	306	2	17
	D5124	MFM	10	309	4	17
	D5126	MFM	20	612	4	17
	D5127H	MFM/RLL	32	612	4	26
	D5146	MFM	40	615	8	17
	D5147H	MFM/RLL	65	615	8	26
	D5452	MFM	71	823	10	17

NEC	Model	Interface	Capacity	Cylinders	Heads	Sectors
	D5652	ESDI	143	823	10	34
	D5655	ESDI	153	1224	7	35
	D5662	ESDI	319	1224	15	34
	D5681	ESDI	664	1633	15	53
	D5882	SCSI	665	1633	15	53
	D5892	SCSI	1404	1678	19	86
Newbuty Data	Model	Interface	Capacity	Cylinders	Heads	Sectors
	NDR1065	MFM	55	918	7	17
	NDR1085	MFM	71	125	8	17
	NDR1105	MFM	87	918	11	17
	NDR1140	MFM	119	918	15	17
	NDR2085	MFM	74	1224	7	17
	NDR2140	MFM	117	1224	11	17
	NDR2190	MFM	160	1224	15	17
	NDR3170S	SCSI	146	1224	9	26
	NDR320	MFM	21	615	4	17
	NDR3280S	SCSI	244	1224	15	26
	NDR340	MFM	42	615	8	17
	NDR360	MFM/RLL	65	15	8	26
	NDR4170	ESDI	149	1224	7	34
	NDR4175	ESDI	157	1224	7	36
	NDR4380	ESDI	338	1224	15	36
	NDR4380S	SCSI	319	124	15	34
Okidata	Model	Interface	Capacity	Cylinders	Heads	Sectors
	OD526	MFM/RLL	31	612	4	26
	OD540	MFM/RLL	47	612	6	26
Olivetti	Model	Interface	Capacity	Cylinders	Heads	Sectors
	HD661/11	MFM	10	612	2	17
	HD662/12	MFM	20	612	4	17
	XM5210	MFM	10	612	4	17
Otari	Model	Interface	Capacity	Cylinders	Heads	Sectors
	C214	MFM	10	306	4	17

continues

TABLE 22.1. Continued

Otari	Model	Interface	Capacity	Cylinders	Heads	Sectors
	C507	MFM	5	306	2	17
	C514	MFM	10	306	4	17
	C519	MFM	15	306	6	17
	C526	MFM	10	306	8	17
Panasonic	Model	Interface	Capacity	Cylinders	Heads	Sectors
	JU-116	MFM	20	615	4	17
	JU-128	MFM	42	733	7	17
Pairietek	Model	Interface	Capacity	Cylinders	Heads	Sectors
	120	ATA	21	615	2	34
	240	ATA	42	615	4	34
Priam	Model	Interface	Capacity	Cylinders	Heads	Sectors
	502	MFM	46	755	7	17
	504	MFM	46	755	7	17
	514	MFM	117	1224	11	17
	519	MFM	160	1224	15	17
	617	ESDI	153	1225	7	36
	623	ESDI	196	752	15	34
	628	ESDI	241	1225	11	36
	630	ESDI	319	1224	15	34
	638	ESDI	329	1225	15	36
	717	SCSI	153	1225	7	36
	728	SCSI	241	1225	11	36
	738	SCSI	329	1225	15	36
	3504	MFM	44	771	5	17
	ID100	MFM/RLL	103	1166		25
	ID120	ESDI	121	1024	7	33
	ID130	MFM	132	1224	15	17
	ID150	ESDI	159	1276	7	35
	ID160	ESDI	158	1225	7	36
	ID20	MFM	26	987	3	17

Priam	Model	Interface	Capacity	Cylinders	Heads	Sectors
	ID230	MFM/RLL	233	1224	15	25
	ID250	ESDI	248	1225	11	36
	ID330	ESDI	338	1225	15	36
	ID330E	ESDi	336	1218	15	36
	ID330S	SCSI	338	1218	15	36
	ID40	MFM	43	981	5	17
	ID45	MFM	50	1166	5	17
	ID45H	MFM	44	1024	5	17
	ID60	MFM	59	981	7	17
	ID62	MFM	62	1166	7	17
	ID75	MFM/RLL	73	1166		25
	V130R	MFM/RLL	39	987	3	26
	V150	MFM	42	987	5	17
	V160	MFM	50	1166	5	17
	V170	MFM	60	987	7	17
	V170R	MFM/RLL	91	987	7	26
	V185	MFM	71	1166	7	17
	V519	MFM	159	1224	15	17
Quantum	Model	Interface	Capacity	Cylinders	Heads	Sectors
	PRO 120AT	ATA	120	814	9	32
	PRO 120S	SCSI	120	814	9	32
	PRO 210AT	ATA	209	873	13	36
	PRO 210S	SCSI	209	873	13	36
	PRO 40AT	ATA	42	965	5	17
	PRO 40S	SCSI	42	965	5	17
	PRO 80AT	ATA	84	965	10	17
	PRO 80S	SCSI	84	965	10	17
	PRO LPS105AT	ATA	105	755	16	17
	PRO LPS105S	SCSI	105	755	16	17
	PRO LPS240AT	ATA	235	723	13	51
	PRO LPS240S	SCSI	235	723	13	51

continues

TABLE 22.1. Continued

Quantum	Model	Interface	Capacity	Cylinders	Heads	Sectors
	PRO LPS52AT	ATA	52	751	8	17
	PRO LPS52S	SCSI	52	751	8	17
	PRO LPS80AT	ATA	86	616	16	17
	PRO LPS80S	SCSI	86	616	16	17
	Q160	SCSI	200	971	12	36
	Q250	SCSI	53	823	4	36
	Q280	SCSI	80	823	6	36
	Q510	MFM	8	512	2	17
	Q520	MFM	18	512	4	17
	Q530	MFM	27	512	6	17
	Q540	MFM	36	512	8	17
Rodime	Model	Interface	Capacity	Cylinders	Heads	Sectors
	R0103	MFM	9	192	6	17
	R05065	MFM	53	1224	5	17
	R0101	MFM	3	192	2	17
	R0102	MFM	6	192	4	17
	R0104	MFM	12	192	8	17
	R0201	MFM	5	321	2	17
	R0201E	MFM	11	640	2	17
	R0202	MFM	11	321	4	17
	R0202E	MFM	22	640	4	17
	R0203	MFM	16	321	6	17
	R0203E	MFM	33	640	6	17
	R0204	MFM	22	320	8	17
	R0204E	MFM	44	640	8	17
	R0251	MFM	5	306	2	17
	R0252	MFM	10	306	4	17
	R03045	MFM	37	872	5	17
	R03055	MFM	45	872	6	17
	R0355T	SCSI	45	1053	3	28

Rodime	Model	Interface	Capacity	Cylinders	Heads	Sectors
	R03057S	SCSI	45	680	5	26
	R03058A	ATA	45	868	3	34
	R03058T	SCSI	45	868	3	34
	R03060R	MFM/RLL	49	750	5	26
	R03065	MFM	53	872	7	17
	R03075R	MFM/RLL	59	750	6	26
	R03085R	MFM/RLL	69	750	7	26
	R03085S	SCSI	70	750	7	26
	R03088T	SCSI	76	868	5	34
	R03090T	SCSI	75	1053	5	28
	R03095A	ATA	80	923	5	34
	R03099AP	ATA	80	1030	4	28
	R03121A	ATA	122	1207	4	53
	R03128A	ATA	105	868	7	34
	R03128T	SCSI	105	868	7	34
	R03129TS	SCSI	105	1091	5	41
	R03130T	SCSI	105	1053	7	28
	R03135A	ATA	112	923	7	34
	R03139A	ATA	112	523	15	28
	R03139TP	SCSI	112	1148	5	42
	R03199AP	ATA	112	1168	5	28
	R03199TS	SCSI	163	1216	7	41
	R03209A	ATA	163	759	15	28
	R03259A	ATA	213	990	15	28
	R03259AP	ATA	213	1235	9	28
	R03259T	SCSI	210	1216	9	41
	R03259TP	SCSI	210	1189	9	42
	R03259TS	SCSI	210	1216	9	41
	R05075E	ESDI	65	1224	3	35
	R05075S	SCSI	61	1219	3	33
	R05078S	SCSI	61	1219	3	33
	R05090	MFM	74	1224	7	17

continues

TABLE 22.1. Continued

Rodime	Model	Interface	Capacity	Cylinders	Heads	Sectors
	R05125E	ESDI	109	1224	5	35
	R05125S	SCSI	103	1219	5	33
	R05130R	MFM/RLL	114	1224	7	26
	R05178S	SCSI	144	1219	7	33
	R05180E	ESDI	153	1224	7	35
	R05180S	SCSI	144	1219	7	33
	R0652A	SCSI	20	306	4	33
	R0652B	SCSI	20	306	4	33
	R0752A	SCSI	20	306	4	33
Samsung	Model	Interface	Capacity	Cylinders	Heads	Sectors
	SHD-3101A	ATA	105	1282	4	40
	SHD-3201S	SCSI	211	1376	7	43
Seagate	Model	Interface	Capacity	Cylinders	Heads	Sectors
	AT1480N	SCSI-2	426	1476	9	62
	ST1057A	ATA	53	1024	6	17
	ST1090A	ATA	79	1072	5	29
	ST1090N	SCSI	79	1068	5	29
	ST1096N	SCSI	80	906	7	26
	ST1100	MFM	83	1072	9	17
	ST1102A	ATA	89	1024	10	17
	ST1106R	MFM/RLL	91	977	7	26
	ST1111A	ATA	98	1072	5	36
	ST1111E	ESDI	98	1072	5	36
	ST1111N	SCSI	98	1068	5	36
	ST1126A	ATA	111	1072	7	29
	ST1126N	SCSI	111	1068	7	29
	ST1133A	ATA	117	1272	5	36
	ST1133NS	SCSI-2	116	1268	5	36
	ST1144A	ATA	130	1001	15	17
	ST1150R	MFM/RLL	128	1072	9	26

Seagate	Model	Interface	Capacity	Cylinders	Heads	Sectors
	ST1156A	ATA	138	1072	7	36
	ST1156E	ESDI	138	1072	7	36
	ST1156N	SCSI	138	1068	7	36
	ST1156NS	SCSI-2	138	1068	7	36
	ST1162N	SCSI	142	1068	9	29
	ST1186A	ATA	164	1272	7	36
	ST1186NS	SCSI-2	163	1268	7	36
	ST1201A	ATA	177	1072	9	36
	ST1201E	ESDI	177	1072	9	36
	ST1201N	SCSI	177	1068	9	36
	ST1201NS	SCSI-2	177	1068	9	36
	ST1239A	ATA	211	1272	9	36
	ST1239NS	SCSI-2	210	1268	9	36
	ST124	MFM	21	615	4	17
	ST125	MFM	21	615	4	17
	ST125A	ATA	21	404	4	26
	ST125N	SCSI	21	407	4	26
	ST138	MFM	32	615	6	17
	ST138A	ATA	32	604	4	26
	ST138N	SCSI	32	615	4	26
	ST138R	MFM/RLL	33	615	4	26
	ST1400N	SCSI-2	331	1476	7	62
	ST1480A	ATA	426	1474	9	62
	ST151	MFM	43	977	5	17
	ST157A	ATA	45	560	6	26
	ST157N	SCSI	49	615	6	26
	ST157R	MFM/RLL	49	615	6	26
	ST177N	SCSI	61	921	5	26
	ST206	MFM	5	306	2	17
	ST2106E	ESDI	92	1024	5	36
	ST2106N	SCSI	91	1022	5	36

continues

TABLE 22.1. Continued

Seagate	Model	Interface	Capacity	Cylinders	Heads	Sectors
	ST212	MFM	10	306	4	17
	ST2125N	SCSI	107	1544	3	45
	ST213	MFM	10	615	2	17
	ST2182E	ESDI	160	1452	4	54
	ST2209N	SCSI	179	1544	5	45
	ST225	MFM	21	615	4	17
	ST225N	SCSI	21	615	4	17
	ST225R	MFM/RLL	21	667	2	31
	ST2274A	ATA	241	1747	5	54
	ST2383A	ATA	338	1747	7	54
	ST2383E	ESDI	337	1747	7	54
	ST2383N	SCSI	337	1261	7	74
	ST238R	MFM/RLL	32	615	4	26
	ST2502N	SCSI	435	1755	7	69
	ST250R	MFM/RLL	42	667	4	31
	ST251	MFM	43	820	6	17
	ST251N	SCSI	43	820	4	26
	ST251N-1	SCSI	43	630	4	34
	ST252	MFM	43	820	6	17
	ST253	MFM	43	989	5	17
	ST274A	ATA	65	948	5	26
	ST277N	SCSI	65	820	6	26
	ST277N-1	SCSI	65	630	6	34
	ST277R	MFM/RLL	65	820	6	26
	ST278R	MFM/RLL	65	820	6	26
	ST279R	MFM/RLL	65	989	5	26
	ST280A	ATA	71	1032	5	27
	ST296N	SCSI	80	820	6	34
	ST3051A	ATA	43	820	6	17
	ST3096A	ATA	89	1024	10	17

Seagate	Model	Interface	Capacity	Cylinders	Heads	Sectors
	ST3120A	ATA	107	1024	12	17
	ST3144A	ATA	131	1001	15	17
	ST325A	ATA	21	615	4	17
	ST351A	ATA	43	820	6	17
	ST4026	MFM	21	615	4	17
	ST4038	MFM	31	733	5	17
	ST4051	MFM	42	977	5	17
	ST406	MFM	5	306	2	17
	ST4085	MFM	71	1024	8	17
	ST4086	MFM	72	925	9	17
	ST4096	MFM	80	1024	9	17
	ST4097	MFM	80	1024	9	17
	ST412	MFM	10	306	4	17
	ST41200N	SCSI	1037	1931	15	71
	ST4135R	MFM/RLL	115	960	9	26
	ST4144R	MFM/RLL	123	1024	9	26
	ST41520N	SCSI-2	1352	2102	17	ZBR
	ST41600N	SCSI-2	1352	2101	17	75
	ST41650N	SCSI-2	1415	2107	15	87
	ST41651N	SCSI-2	1415	2107	15	ZBR
	ST4182E	ESDI	160	969	9	36
	ST4182N	SCSI	155	969	9	35
	ST419	MFM	15	306	6	17
	ST4250N	SCSI	300	1412	9	46
	ST4376N	SCSI	330	1546	9	45
	ST4383E	ESDI	338	1412	12	36
	ST4384E	ESDI	338	1224	15	36
	ST4385N	SCSI	330	791	15	55
	ST4442E	ESDI	390	1412	15	36
	ST4702N	SCSI	601	1546	15	50
	ST4766E	ESDI	676	1032	15	54
	ST4766N	SCSI	676	1632	15	54

continues

TABLE 22.1. Continued

Seagate	Model	Interface	Capacity	Cylinders	Heads	Sectors
	ST4767E	ESDI	676	1399	15	63
	ST4767N	SCSI-2	665	1356	15	64
	ST4769E	ESDI	691	1552	15	53
	ST506	MFM	5	153	4	17
Selmen's	Model	Interface	Capacity	Cylinders	Heads	Sectors
	1200	ESDI	174	1216	8	35
	1300	ESDI	261	1216	12	35
	2200	SCSI	174	1216	8	35
	2300	SCSI	261	1216	12	35
	4410	ESDI	322	1100	11	52
	4420	SCSI	334	1100	11	54
	5710	ESDI	655	1224	15	48
	5720	SCSI	655	1224	15	48
	5810	ESDI	688	1658	15	54
	5820	SCSI	688	1658	15	54
	6200	SCSI	1062	1921	15	72
Shugart	Model	Interface	Capacity	Cylinders	Heads	Sectors
	SA604	MFM	5	160	4	17
	SA606	MFM	7	160	6	17
	SA607	MFM	5	306	4	17
	SA612	MFM	10	306	4	17
	SA706	MFM	6	320	2	17
	SA712	MFM	10	320	4	17
Syquest	Model	Interface	Capacity	Cylinders	Heads	Sectors
	SQ225F	MFM	20	615	4	17
	SQ306F	MFM	5	306	2	17
	SQ306R	MFM	5	306	2	17
	SQ306RD	MFM	5	306	2	17
	SQ312	MFM	10	615	2	17
	SQ312F	MFM	20	612	4	17

Syquest	Model	Interface	Capacity	Cylinders	Heads	Sectors
	SQ312RD	MFM	10	615	2	17
	SQ319	MFM	10	612	2	17
	SQ325	MFM	20	612	4	17
	SQ325F	MFM	20	615	4	17
	SQ338F	MFM	30	615	6	17
	SQ340AF	MFM	38	649	6	17
Tandon	Model	Interface	Capacity	Cylinders	Heads	Sectors
	TM703	MFM	10	733	5	17
	TM2085	SCSI	74	1004	9	36
	TM2128	SCSI	115	1004	9	36
	TM2170	SCSI	154	1344	9	36
	TM24	MFM/RL	41	782	4	26
	TM246	MFM/RLL	62	782	6	26
	TM251	MFM	5	306	2	17
	TM252	MFM	10	306	4	17
	TM261	MFM	10	615	2	17
	TM262	MFM	21	615	4	17
	TM262R	MFM/RLL	20	782	2	26
	TM264	MFM/RLL	41	782	4	26
	TM3085	MFM	71	1024	8	17
	TM3085R	MFM/RLL	104	1024	8	26
	TM344	MFM/RLL	41	782	4	26
	TM346	MFM/RLL	62	782	6	26
	TM361	MFM	10	615	2	17
	TM362	MFM	21	615	4	17
	TM362R	MFM/RLL	20	782	2	26
	TM364	MFM/RLL	41	782	4	26
	TM501	MFM	5	306	2	17
	TM502	MFM	10	306	4	17
	TM503	MFM	15	306	6	17
	TM602S	MFM	5	153	4	17
	TM603S	MFM	10	153	6	17

continues

TABLE 22.1. Continued

Tandon	Model	Interface	Capacity	Cylinders	Heads	Sectors
	TM603SE	MFM	21	230	6	17
	TM702	MFM/RLL	20	615	4	26
	TM702AT	MFM	8	615	4	17
	TM703AT	MFM	31	733	5	17
	TM705	MFM	41	962	5	17
	TM755	MFM	43	981	5	17
Teac	Model	Interface	Capacity	Cylinders	Heads	Sectors
	SD150	MFM	10	306	4	17
	SD340-A	ATA	43	1050	2	40
	SD340S	SCSI	43	1050	2	40
	SD380	ATA	86	1050	4	40
	SD380-S	SCSI	86	1050	4	40
	SD510	MFM	10	306	4	17
	SD520	MFM	20	615	4	17
Toshiba	Model	Interface	Capacity	Cylinders	Heads	Sectors
	MK134FA	MFM	44	733	7	17
	MK153FA	ESDI	74	830	5	35
	MK153FB	SCSI	74	830	5	35
	MK154FA	ESDI	104	830	7	35
	MK154FB	SCSI	104	830	7	35
	MK156FA	ESDI	148	830	10	35
	MK156FB	SCSI	148	830	10	35
	MK232FB	SCSI	45	845	3	35
	MK233FB	SCSI	76	845	5	35
	MK234FB	SCSI	106	845	7	35
	MK234FC	ATA	106	845	7	35
	MK250FA	ESDI	382	1224	10	35
	MK250FB	SCSI	382	1224	10	35
	MK355FA	ESDI	459	1632	9	53
	MK355FB	SCSI	459	1632	9	53

Toshiba	Model	Interface	Capacity	Cylinders	Heads	Sectors
	MK358FA	ESDI	765	1632	15	53
	MK358FB	SCSI	765	1632	15	53
	MK53FA/B	MFM	43	830	5	17
	MK53FA/B	MFM/RLL	64	830	5	26
	MK54FA/B	MFM	60	830	7	17
	MK54FA/B	MFM/RLL	90	830	7	26
	MK556FA	ESDI	152	830	10	35
	MK56FA/B	MFM	86	830	10	17
	MK56FA/B	MFM/RLL	129	830	10	26
Tulin	Model	Interface	Capacity	Cylinders	Heads	Sectors
	TL213	MFM	10	640	2	17
	TL226	MFM	22	640	4	17
	TL238	MFM	22	640	4	17
	TL240	MFM	33	640	6	17
	TL258	MFM	33	640	6	17
	TL326	MFM	22	640	4	17
	TL340	MFM	33	640	6	17
Vertex	Model	Interface	Capacity	Cylinders	Heads	Sectors
	V130	MFM	26	987	3	17
	V150	MFM	43	987	5	17
	V170	MFM	60	987	7	17
Western	Model	Interface	Capacity	Cylinders	Heads	Sectors
	WD AB130	ATA	32	733	5	17
	WD AC140	ATA	42	980	5	17
	WD AC160	ATA	62	1024	7	17
	WD AC280	ATA	85	980	10	17
	WD AH260	ATA	63	1024	7	17
	WD262	MFM	20	615	4	17
	WD344R	MFM/RLL	40	782	4	26
	WD362	MFM	20	615	4	17
	WD382R	MFM/RLL	20	782	2	26

continues

TABLE 22.1. Continued

Western	Model	Interface	Capacity	Cylinders	Heads	Sectors
	WD383R	MFM/RLL	30	615	4	26
	WD384R	MFM/RLL	40	782	4	26
	WD544R	MFM/RLL	40	782	4	26
	WD582R	MFM/RLL	20	782	2	26
	WD583R	MFM/RLL	30	615	4	26
	WD584R	MFM/RLL	49	782	4	26
	WD93024	ATA	20	782	2	27
	WD93028	ATA	20	782	2	27
	WD93034	ATA	30	782	3	27
	WD93038	ATA	30	782	3	27
	WD93044	ATA	40	782	4	27
	WD93048	ATA	40	782	4	27
	WD95024	ATA	20	782	2	27
	WD95028	ATA	20	782	2	27
	WD95034	ATA	30	782	3	27
	WD95044	ATA	40	782	4	27
	WD95058	ATA	40	782	4	27
	Model	*Interface*	*Capacity*	*Cylinders*	*Heads*	*Sectors*
	ZM3540	ATA	518	2142	6	60 to 96
	ZM3540	Fast SCSI-2	518	2142	6	60 to 96
	ZM3272	ATA	260	2076	4	55

Performance Issues

When shopping for hard disks, many people become preoccupied with disk performance. They believe that some drives find and transfer information faster than others. They're right. But the differences between state-of-the-art hard disk drives are much smaller than they used to be, and in a properly set up system the remaining differences can be almost completely equalized.

The performance of a hard disk is directly related to design choices in making the mechanism. The head actuator has the greatest effect on the speed at which data can be retrieved from the disk, the number of platters exerting a smaller effect. Because the head actuator designs used by hard disk makers have converged, as have the number of platters per drive because of height restrictions of modern form factors, the performance of various products has also converged.

Clearly, however, all hard disks don't deliver the same performance. The differences are particularly obvious when you compare a drive that's a few years old with a current product. Understanding the issues involved in hard disk performance will help you better appreciate the strides made by the industry in the last few years and show you what improvements may still lie ahead.

Average Access Time

You've already encountered the term latency, which indicates the average delay in finding a given bit of data imposed because of the spin of the disk. Another factor also influences how long elapses between the moment the disk drive receives a request to reveal what's stored at a given place on the disk and when the drive is actually ready to read or write at that place—the speed at which the read-write head can move radially from one cylinder to another. This speed is expressed in a number of ways, often as a seek time. Track-to-track seek time indicates the period required to move the head from one track to the next. More important, however, is the average access time (sometimes rendered as average seek time), which specifies how long it takes the read-write head to move on the average to any cylinder (or radial position). Lower average access times, expressed in milliseconds, are better.

The type of head actuator technology, the mass of the actuator assembly, the physical power of the actuator itself, and the width of the data area on the disk all influence average access time. Voice-coil actuators are quicker than stepper designs. Lighter actuators have less inertia and can accelerate and settle down faster. A more powerful actuator mechanism can knock around the head assembly with greater alacrity. And the narrower the band on the disk holding information, the shorter the distance the head must travel between tracks.

Real world access times vary by more than a factor of ten. Old technology drives responded with average access times as long as 150 milliseconds. The newest drives are closer to 10 milliseconds. Dual-actuator drives can virtually eliminate the access time required on consecutive read or write requests.

How low an average access time you need depends mostly on your impatience. Quicker is always better. In the past it cost more. Today, however, the differences are smaller and almost inconsequential. The only accepted guidelines are the IBM specifications for its various products. The first hard disk installed in an IBM personal computer resided in the XT and had a specified average access time of 85 milliseconds. The next generation IBM personal computer, the AT, required a drive with an average access time of 40 milliseconds.

With 386 and more recent computers, however, the IBM guidance falls by the wayside. The company has installed drives with various access times in different computer models, so no one figure can offer real guidance. The next performance level for the AT drive is about 28 milliseconds, which serves the first generation of 386-based PCs quite well. Fast 386 machines (25 MHz and above) and 486SX machines are better served by drives operating in the vicinity of 20 milliseconds. Machines based on the 486DX and better microprocessors can benefit from drives with average access times of 15 milliseconds or better.

Advanced disk controllers, particularly those used in disk arrays, are able to minimize the delays cause by head seeks using a technique called elevator seeking. When confronted with several read or write requests for different disk tracks, the controller organizes the requests in the way that moves the head the least between seeks. Like an elevator, it courses through the seek requests from the lower numbered tracks to the higher numbered tracks and then goes back on the next requests first taking care of the higher numbered tracks and working its way back to the lower numbered tracks. The data gathered for each individual request is stored in the controller and doled out at the proper time.

Elevator seeking improves performance in drive systems that receive multiple requests for data nearly simultaneously. DOS, as a single-threaded operating system, cannot take advantage of this access-acceleration technique. DOS requires that each seek request be fulfilled before it sends the next to the disk. In network systems, however, multiple seek requests can and do occur simultaneously. Elevator seeking can substantially cut the disk access time in such systems.

Data Transfer Rate

After a byte or record is found on the disk, it must be transferred to the host computer. Another disk system specification, the data transfer rate, reflects how fast bytes are batted back and forth, affecting how quickly information can shuttle between microprocessor and hard disk. The transfer rate of a disk is controlled by a number of design factors completely separate from those of the average access time.

Through the years, the factor constraining the transfer rate of particular computer systems has shifted from the host microprocessor, to the disk interface, to the bus, and the disk drive. For example, the limit on the transfer rate of the original IBM Personal Computer XT was the 8088 microprocessor itself, which was unable to process information as quickly as even the laggardly ST506 interface. PCs based on the 386 microprocessor finally raced ahead of disk and interface performance, so drive manufacturers have begun to concentrate on improving the throughput of these aspects of disk systems.

One limit in transfer rate that cannot be exceeded is the data transfer rate of the interface connecting a hard disk to its host computer. A drive cannot move information faster than the interface allows. The old ST506 interface is the slowest currently in use. Although RLL, Advanced RLL, and ESDI help speed it up, AT Attachment (and particularly ATA updates) and SCSI hold greater potential.

The transfer rate of a hard disk is expressed in megahertz (MHz) or megabytes per second (or MB/sec, which is one-eighth the megahertz rate). The old ST506 standard specified a peak transfer rate of 0.625 MB/sec. Using RLL coding boosts the ST506 interface to 0.9375 MB/sec.

As originally propounded, ESDI delivered a 1.25 MB/sec transfer rate, but more advanced products have pushed that value to 3.125 MB/sec. With an eight-bit connection, the AT Attachment interface permits a transfer rate of 4 MB/sec; with a 16-bit connection, about 8 MB/sec. ATA-2 proposals push the rate up to 11 MB/sec using programmed input/output and 13.3 MB/sec using DMA control. The original SCSI connection permitted a 5 MB/sec transfer rate; Fast SCSI 2 boosts that to 10 MB/sec. Sixteen-bit wide SCSI 2 matches that figure; 32-bit wide SCSI 2 doubles it to 20 MB/sec; and 32-bit wide SCSI 2 coupled with Fast SCSI 2 pushes it all the way to 40 MB/sec.

Remember, of course, that because ST506 and ESDI are device-level interfaces, actual throughput of drives using them falls to lower values because transfer overhead must be deducted from the raw rates given here (see Chapter 21).

Another interface issue may limit transfer rates below the highest of these values: the host computer bus. The ISA bus has a maximum effective transfer rate of 8 MB/sec and constrains faster SCSI links. EISA connections can be as high as 33 MB/sec; Micro Channel as low as 10 MB/sec (16-bit bus operating at 10 MHz), although a 32-bit Micro Channel connection starts at 20 MHz and may offer rates as high as 40 MB/sec in advanced transfer modes. All local bus links exceed basic disk interface transfer rates.

Note that all of these rates are peak values that cannot be sustained for long periods, so effective transfer rates through bus connections will necessarily be lower than the preceding values (see Chapter 6).

Today's disk and bus interfaces are rarely the bottlenecks constricting disk transfer rates. Physical factors in the construction of the drive nearly always constrain the transfer rate to a lower value. The primary constraint results from the combination of the speed of a disk's spin and its track density—that is, the number of 512-byte sectors in each track. The faster the platter spins and the denser the data on each track, the more information that passes under the read-write head in a given period. With device-level interfaces, this raw stream of data is what is passed through the interface—the product of spin speed and the capacity of each track yields the raw data rate. Most system-level interfaced drives made through about 1991 were based on the same mechanisms used for the device-level drives and so achieved the same actual throughputs despite the greater potential of their interfaces. The situation was the equivalent of having a 16-lane interstate highway with only three licensed cars on the road. As manufacturers have turned away from device-level interfaces and concentrated on improving system-level interfaced drives with new designs (such as faster rotation rates, zone-bit recording, and on-disk caching), actual throughputs are rising. The high transfer rates of the most advanced interfaces give engineers substantial growing room, however.

If you check the specifications of many SCSI hard disk drives and host adapters, you'll likely see several figures given for transfer rates. For example, a SCSI host adapter may specify the disk-to-adapter transfer rate (5 MB/sec) and an adpter-to-host transfer rate (20 MB/sec or even 33 MB/sec). Without some performance-enhancing feature on the host adapter, the lower figure would be the more accurate representation of the speed you could expect from such a system. However, disk caching on the host adapter allows such a host adapter to operate near the higher adapter-to-host transfer rate.

Sector Interleave

Back in the days when microprocessors lagged hard disk performance, system engineers worried about adequately slowing drive performance to achieve an optimum match with the host PC. Sector interleaving was the primary method of achieving the happiest marriage. Interleave is no longer an issue with most modern hard disks.

The sector interleave of a hard disk refers to the relationship of the logical arrangement of sectors in a track to their actual physical arrangement. For example, sectors might be numbered 1 through 17 and data stored sequentially in them. But on the disk, consecutively numbered sectors need not be laid next to each other. The actual order is not important to the disk controller because it reads the sector identification (essentially the number assigned the sector) rather than checking the sector position on the disk when it needs to find a particular sector. This mapping between the logical and physical sector locations is determined by the low-level format of the hard disk.

Sector interleaving works by forcing the disk drive to skip a given number of sectors when DOS tells it to read consecutive sectors. For instance, DOS may instruct the drive to read sectors one and two. The hard disk system reads sector one; then the arrangement of sectors causes it to skip the next six sectors before reading the sector bearing the number two identification. The time that elapses while the six unread sectors pass by gives the host computer a chance to catch up with the disk.

The ratio of the length of a sector to the distance between the start of two logically consecutive sectors is termed the interleave factor. Because the length used for measuring interleave is one sector, often only the righthand factor in the ratio is used to describe the interleave. Thus, a disk in which no sectors are skipped would be said to have an interleave factor of 1:1, or simply one. If five sectors are skipped between each one that's used, the interleave factor would be 1:6, or six.

Although interleaving would appear to invariably slow the transfer rate of a disk system, the optimum interleave actually helps improve performance. Higher or lower interleave values impair performance—and setting an interleave too low has the most dramatic and deleterious effect. Consider, for example, what happens when a PC is not ready for the next sector being read from the disk—the disk must complete an entire spin before the sector can be read again, typically a delay of about 17 milliseconds (at 3600 RPM). If skipping one sector is sufficient to give the PC time to catch up, the added delay is only one millisecond (assuming 17 sectors per track). In this case, the proper interleave makes the disk system 17 times faster than not inter-leaving, a compelling argument for achieving the optimum interleave.

Note that erring on the high side yields less of a penalty than too low of an interleave. Skipping an extra sector delays the next sector read by only one millisecond, compared to the 17 milliseconds imposed by erring on the low side.

Because of the tremendous penalty for setting interleave factors too low, IBM was perhaps overly conservative in specifying interleave factors for the XT and AT hard disks. The XT used an interleave of six; the AT, three. These systems often achieve somewhat better disk performance with lower transfer rates. Specialty programs such as SpinRite (from Gibson Research) allow you to determine the optimum interleave for the hard disk in your system. Note that while a 1:1 interleave might appear optimum, it rarely is. Most AT and better computers that use hard disks without track buffering typically work best with an interleave factor of two.

Interleave is not an issue with hard disks that have track buffers, which includes essentially all modern disks with system-level interfaces (AT Attachment and SCSI) and even many ESDI drives.

Cylinder Skewing

Although a 1:1 interleave factor sounds like the most desirable, it is not without its own problems. After the disk drive head finishes reading one track, it must be repositioned slightly to read the next. As with any mechanical movement, repositioning the head requires a slight time. Although brief, this repositioning period is long enough that should the head try moving from the end of one track to the beginning of another, it gets there too late. Consequently, you have to wait while the whole track passes below the head until it is ready to read the beginning of the second track.

This problem is easily solved by the simple expedient of not aligning the starting points of all tracks along the same radial line. By offsetting the beginning of each track slightly from the end of the preceding track, the travel time of the head can be compensated for. Because the beginning of the first sector of each track and cylinder do not line up but are somewhat skewed, this technique is called track skewing or cylinder skewing.

Track Buffering

With modern hard disks and controllers, interleave has become irrelevant. Control electronics (either on an expansion board or embedded in the drive) use track buffering on-disk buffer memory that stores the contents of an entire track—to better match the information needs of the host computer. When you send a read request to a controller with a track buffer, it reads the entire disk track no matter how much information you actually need. If you need information from two consecutive sectors, they are read from the controller's buffer independently of the spin of the disk. Disks in track-buffered systems operate best with a 1:1 interleave. Nearly all but the oldest ESDI drives are designed to work with track-buffered controllers, have built-in track buffers, or use some even more advanced transfer optimizing methods.

Disk Caching

The ultimate means of isolating your PC from the mechanical vagaries of hard disk seeking is disk caching. Caching eliminates the delays involved in seeking when a read request (or write request in a system that supports write caching) involves data already stored in the cache—the information is retrieved at RAM speed. Similarly, the cache pushes the transfer rate of data stored in the cache up to the ceiling imposed by the slowest interface between the cache and host microprocessor. With an on-disk cache, the drive interface will likely be the primary constraint; with a hardware cache in the disk controller or host adapter, the bus interface is the limit; with a software cache, microprocessor and memory access speed are the only constraints.

Magneto-Optical Technology

Although magneto-optical drives function much like standard hard disks—both have spinning platters, magnetic recording media, and radially moving heads—many aspects of their operation differ substantially from more conventional drives. Although MO drives store information magnetically, they read the data from disk optically and require a special thermal boost—also achieved optically—to write data.

Write Operation

The writing process for an MO system relies on the combined effects of magnetic fields and laser-beam optics. The drives use a conventional magnetic field, called the bias field, to write data onto the disk. Of course, the nature of the field is limited by the same factors in Winchester disks—the size of the magnetic domains that are written is limited by the distance between the read-write head and the medium and is, at any practical distance, much larger than the size of a spot created by a focused laser.

To get the size of a magnetic domain down to truly minuscule size, MO drives use the laser beam to assist magnetic writing. In effect, the laser illuminates a tiny area within a larger magnetic field, and only this area is affected by the field.

This optical-assist in magnetic recording works because of the particular magnetic medium chosen for use in MO disks. This medium differs from that of ordinary Winchester drives in having a higher coercivity, a resistance to changing its magnetic orientation. In fact, the coercivity of an MO disk is about an order of magnitude higher than the 600 or so Oersteds of coercivity of the typical Winchester disk.

This high coercivity alone gives MO disks one of their biggest advantages over traditional Winchesters—they are virtually immune to self-erasure. All magnetic media tend to self-erase, that is, with passing time their magnetic fields lose intensity because of the combined effects of all external and internal magnetic fields upon them. The fields just get weaker. The higher the coercivity, the better a medium resists self-erasure. Consequently, MO disks with their high coercivities are able to maintain data more reliably over a longer period than Winchester disks.

The quoted lifetime for MO disks is 10 to 15 years. Although that's difficult to prove because MO drives have not even existed for 10 years, many people in the industry view that claimed lifetime as conservative. Traditional magnetic media requires refreshing every few years to guarantee the integrity of their contents. Mainframe computer data tapes are typically refreshed every two years. MO media promises to substantially extend the time between refreshes, if not eliminating the need for refreshing entirely.

The high coercivity of MO media also makes the disks resistant to the effects of stray magnetic fields. Although a refrigerator magnet means death to the data stored on a floppy disk, it would likely have no effect on an MO disk (but you still wouldn't want to clamp your MO disks to your system unit with refrigerator magnets). This resistance to stray fields means that you have to worry less about where and how you store MO cartridges.

Along with such benefits, the higher coercivity of MO media brings another challenge: obtaining a high enough magnetic flux to change the magnetic orientation of the media while keeping the size of recorded domains small. Reducing this high coercivity is how the laser assists the bias magnet in an MO drive.

The coercivity of the magnetic medium used by MO disks, as with virtually all magnetic materials, decreases as its temperature increases and becomes zero at the media-dependent Curie temperature. By warming the MO disk medium sufficiently close to the Curie temperature, the necessary field strength to initiate a change can be reduced to a practical level. The magnetic medium used by MO disks is specifically engineered for a low Curie temperature, about 150 degrees Celsius.

The same laser that's used for reading the MO disk can simply be increased in intensity to heat up the recording medium to its Curie temperature. This laser beam can be tightly focused to achieve a tiny spot size. Although the magnetic field acting on the medium may cover a wide area, only the tiny spot heated by the laser actually changes its magnetic orientation because only that tiny spot is heated high enough to have a sufficiently low coercivity.

Practical mechanisms based on this design have one intrinsic drawback. The bias magnetic field must remain oriented in a single direction during the process of writing a large swath of a disk, a full sector or track. The field cannot change quickly because the high inductance of the electro-magnet that forms the field prevents the rapid switching of the magnet's polarities. The field must be far larger and stronger than those of Winchester disks because the magneto-optical head is substantially farther from the disk—it doesn't fly but rides on a track.

Because of the inability of the magnetic field to change rapidly, the bias magnet in today's MO drives can align magnetic fields in a given area of a disk track only one direction each time that portion of a track passes beneath the read-write head. For example, when the bias field is polarized in the upward direction, it can change downward-oriented fields on the disk to upward polarity, but it cannot alter upward-oriented fields to the downward direction.

Practical MO systems today therefore require a two-step rewriting process. Before an area can be rewritten on the disk, all fields in that area must be oriented in a single direction. In other words, a given disk area must be separately erased before it can be recorded. In conventional MO drive designs, this erasure process requires a separate pass under the bias magnet with the polarity of the magnet temporarily reversed. After one pass for erasing previously written material, the field of the magnetic head is reversed again to the writing orientation. The actual information is written to disk on a second pass under the head. The only areas that change magnetic polarity are those struck with and heated by the laser beam.

The penalty for this two-step process is an apparent increase in the average access time of MO drives when writing data. The extra time for a second pass is substantial. Although speeds vary, many MO drives spin their disks at a leisurely 2400 revolutions per minute, roughly a third slower than Winchester disks (which typically operate at about 3600 RPM). Each turn of such an MO disk therefore requires 25 milliseconds. Even discounting head movement, the average access time for writing to an MO drive cannot possibly be faster than 37.5 milliseconds. (On the average, the data to be erased will be half a spin away from the read-write head, 12.5 milliseconds, and a second spin to write the data will take an additional 25 milliseconds.) Understandably most manufacturers are working on "one-pass" MO drives and are speeding the spins of their disks. Some drives now spin faster, at the same 3600 RPM rate as hard disks. The 3.5-inch MO drives typically operate at 3000 RPM.

The MO drive also suffers another performance handicap. Although Winchester read-write heads are typically flyweight mechanisms weighing a fraction of a gram, the read-write heads of MO drives are massive assemblies of magnetic and optical parts. Typically this MO head mounts on a sled that slides on parallel steel tubes that act as a track. Moving that massive head requires a robust mechanism and, thanks to the principal of inertia, takes substantially longer to speed up, slow down, and settle as compared to a Winchester head. In fact, when it comes to average access time, there is almost no comparison between Winchesters, which now can write data as quickly as 15 milliseconds between random bytes, and MO drives which, at their current best, are no faster than 60 ms.—not counting the twice-around write penalty.

The optical sled used by MO drives isn't without its redeeming qualities, however. Unlike the Winchester drive head, which must fly micro-inches above the media surface to pack data tightly on the disk, optical heads can work at a distance. The guide rods absolutely fix the distance between the head and the disk that's truly huge compared to Winchesters—and with that distance comes safety. Head crashes are impossible on MO drives because the head is restrained from moving close to the media. In fact, only the laser beam ever touches the disk surface (or should—keep your fingers out of the protective door in the MO cartridge!).

As with CDs, the optically active surface of an MO disk is sealed beneath a tough layer of transparent plastic, again minimizing damage. The laser beam focuses through the clear covering. Because the beam is out of focus at the surface of the disk and only converges to a spot underneath the clear surface layer, the effect of imperfections such as scratches or dust on the top of the disk have relatively little effect on the accuracy of disk reading or writing. Of course, MO drives also incorporate error-correction to minimize the appearance of errors in the stream of stored data.

Read Operation

At the field strengths common to electronic gear, light beams are generally unreactive with magnetic fields. Fiber optic cables, for example, are impervious to the effects of normal electro-magnetic noise that would pollute ordinary wires. Consequently, getting a laser to read the miniscule magnetic fields on an MO disk is a challenge.

The trick used in MO technology is polarization. The MO disk is read by a laser beam that is reflected from the disk surface as in other technologies, but in the MO drive, the laser beam is polarized. That is, the plane of orientation of its photons in the laser beam are all aligned in one direction.

When the polarized beam strikes the magnetically aligned particles of the disk, the magnetic field of the media particles causes the plane of polarization of the light beam to rotate slightly, a phenomenon called the Kerr effect. While small, as little as a 1-percent shift in early MO media but now reportedly up to 7 percent, this change in polarization can be detected as reliably as the direct magnetic reading of a Winchester disk. A polarized beam passing through a second polarizing material diminishes in intensity depending on how closely the polarity of the beam is aligned with that of the second material. In effect, the polarity change becomes a readily detected intensity change.

Standards

Even with MO drives, data exchange depends on standardization. The cartridges written on one machine must be readable by others. From diverse beginnings, MO products have gone a long way to achieve the necessary standardization to the extent that the International Standards Organization (ISO) has propounded a set of specifications for 5.25-inch and 3.5-inch MO cartridges. The ISO standard guarantees that any ISO-standard cartridge can be used in any drive supporting the ISO standard. Although that sounds like a straightforward statement, it has its complexities.

For 5.25-inch MO disks, the ISO standard is actually a dual standard. It allows cartridges of two types: those that store data in 1024-byte sectors and those that store data in 512-byte sectors. Because larger sectors mean less overhead—among other things, fewer sector identification markers are required—1024-byte per sector cartridges can store more data, about 650 megabytes per cartridge (about 325 per side) versus 594 (often rounded to 600) megabytes for 512-byte per sector cartridges (about 297 megabytes per side). The actual capacity of each cartridge varies and is inevitably smaller than these figures because, as with hard disks, magneto-optical cartridges may have bad sectors that cannot be used for data storage. The smaller, 3.5-inch cartridges store about 128MB using 512 bytes per sector, 25 sectors per track, and 10,000 tracks on a cartridge.

Under the ISO standard, a 5.25-inch drive must be able to read and write both 512- and 1024-byte-per-sector cartridges. Drives produced before the standard was adopted (or by companies not recognizing the standard) may be limited to one or the other size. Some manufacturers offer drives that support not only ISO cartridge standards but also their own, proprietary storage formats. For example, the Tahiti drive produced by Maxtor augments its ISO capabilities with a special format and data storage method that packs up to 1 gigabyte per cartridge. Using constant linear velocity recording, it fills the longer, outer tracks of each disk with more sectors full of data. In contrast, the ISO standards call for constant angular velocity recording (meaning the disk spins at a constant rate) which puts the same number of sectors—and the same amount of data—on every disk track.

The strongest point of the ISO standard is that it strictly defines the MO cartridge and the media it contains. Not only does this aspect of the standard ensure physical compatibility of cartridges, but it also ensures that multiple sources of supply are available, potentially making media less expensive.

As with all too many personal computer "standards," however, the ISO standard is not a panacea that guarantees cartridges written in one MO drive are readable by another. Although the ISO standard does specify the physical format in which data is stored on the disk, it does not indicate the logical format. Different system integrators may opt for their own disk partitioning schemes, and the software drivers used by one MO system vendor may not recognize the partitioning used by another maker.

Performance

Besides the issue of average access time and the spin speed of the disks (which determines data transfer rate), the format of an MO cartridge can determine the overall performance of the MO system. The way the capacity of an MO cartridge is carved up (as well as the disk's formatting and even the number of bytes per sector) affects the data throughput performance of a drive. A cartridge partitioned for standard 32-megabyte DOS volumes may deliver half the effective throughput of a drive using a proprietary partitioning scheme that allows the entire capacity of one cartridge side to be addressed as a single volume. This performance effect arises because of larger volumes on MO cartridges resulting in larger DOS storage clusters, and larger clusters reduce the overhead involved in extended data transfers.

Performance of MO drives also varies more widely than conventional hard disks because the ISO standard specifies that MO drives use the Small Computer System Interface (SCSI) to connect to their hosts. Although this interface choice has its advantage in flexibility (for example, up to seven SCSI devices can be connected to a single host adapter), SCSI also can be a handicap for

DOS users. ISO magneto-optical drives, like all SCSI devices in DOS-based computers, can be severely constrained by performance of the SCSI host adapter used. A good SCSI host adapter allows an MO drive to transfer data at the speed at which data can be recovered from the spinning disk, a rate on par with a today's best Winchester hard disks. A poor SCSI adapter may limit mass storage throughput to 10 percent of its possible peak rate and may make the overall system look painfully slow.

Applications

The spiral tracks of MO cartridges demonstrate that designers of the drives recognize that the technology is not at its best when randomly accessing data but rather favors large sequential transfers. Consequently, current MO drive systems are not aimed at universally replacing Winchester hard disks as primary mass storage media. Their role today is seen as secondary mass storage—the uncharted territory that lies between hard disks and streaming tape.

In other words, MO drives are not for every application, but they have significant strengths that make a particularly good choice when a safe, secure means of storing hundreds of megabytes is required. Graphics and audio/visual systems are particular candidates because MO cartridges provide the capacity needed for the easy exchange of extremely large files. Engineers, for example, can put huge CAD files on disks to archive them.

MO drives also can make an excellent backup medium, particularly for network applications. A single cartridge can back up all but the largest hard disks. Moreover, the ability to rewrite cartridges allows them to fit into backup arrangements in which backup media are routinely recycled. Compared to tape media, restoration of files from MO disks is fast and easy. MO cartridges, however, are substantially more expensive than open-reel or cartridge tapes of the same capacity by a factor of at least two.

MO disks also can serve as an excellent archival medium. Cartridges are compact enough to carry several in a briefcase or to lock securely in a safe. Data stored on them is safe for long-term storage because MO media are virtually free from self-erasure and resist external magnetic perils, thanks to their high coercivity.

In some systems, MO drives could replace hard disks as the primary mass storage system. With suitable caching software, the apparent performance of MO disks can be hoisted nearly to the level of a conventional hard disk. The lag in access time is still apparent during cache misses, however.

Writing an obituary for hard disks is probably premature. Rewritable magneto-optical disks probably won't displace Winchester technology soon. Like most new technologies, MO will likely achieve its greatest success in a new role, one that it will likely define itself. As it stands now, MO technology is both useful and available. And it affords possibilities that may change the way you use your PC.

Drive Arrays

When you need more capacity than a single hard disk can provide, you have two choices: trim your needs or plug in more disks. But changing your needs means changing your lifestyle—foregoing instant access to all of your files by deleting some from your disk, switching to data compression, or keeping a tighter watch on backup files and intermediary versions of projects under development. Of course, changing your lifestyle is about as easy as teaching an old dog to change its spots. The one application with storage needs likely to exceed that capacity of today's individual hard disks—1.5 gigabyte and climbing—is a network server, and a total lifestyle change for a network server is about as probable as getting a platoon of toddlers to clean up a playroom littered with a near-infinite collection of toys.

Consequently, when the bytes run really low, you're left with the need for multiple disks. In most single-user PCs, each of these multiple drives acts independently and appears as a separate drive letter (or group of drive letters) under DOS. Through software, such multiple drive systems can even be made to emulate one large disk with a total storage capacity equal to that of its constituent drives. Since DOS only does one thing at a time, such a solution is satisfactory, but it's hardly the optimum arrangement in which reliability and providing dozens of users instant access is concerned. Instead of operating each disk independently, you can gain higher speeds, greater resistance to errors, and improved reliability by linking the drives through hardware to make a drive array—what has come to be known as a Redundant Array of Inexpensive Disks or RAID.

The premise of the drive array is elementary—combine a number of individual hard disks to create a massive virtual system. But a drive array is more than several hard disks connected to a single controller. In an array, the drives are coordinated, and the controller specially allocates information between them using a program called Array Management Software. The AMS controls all the physical hard disks in the array and makes them appear to your PC as if they were one logical drive. For example, in some drive arrays, the AMS ensures that the spin of each drive is synchronized and that divides up blocks of data to spread among several physical hard disks.

The obvious benefit of the drive array is the same as any multiple disk installation—capacity. Two disks can hold more than one, and four more than two. But drive array technology also can accelerate mass store performance and can increase reliability.

Data Striping

The secret to both of these innovations is the way the various hard disks in the drive array are combined. They are not arranged in a serial list where the second drive takes over once the capacity of the first is completely used up. Instead, data is split between drives at the bit, byte, or block level. For example, in a four-drive system, two bits of every byte might come from the first hard disk, the next two bits from the second drive, and so on. The four drives then could pour a single byte into the data stream four times faster—moving all the information in the byte would take only as long as it would for a single drive to move two bits. Alternately, a four-byte storage cluster could be made from a sector from each of the four drives. This technique of splitting data between several drives is called data striping.

At this primitive level, data striping has a severe disadvantage: the failure of any drive in the system results in the complete failure of the entire system. The reliability of the entire array can be no greater than that of the least reliable drive in the array. The speed and capacity of such a system are greater but so are the risks involved in using it.

Redundancy and Reliability

By sacrificing part of its potential capacity, an array of drives can yield a more reliable, even fault-tolerant, storage system. The key is redundancy. Instead of a straight division of the bits, bytes, and blocks each drive in the array stores, the information split between the drives can overlap.

For example, in the four-drive system instead of each drive getting two bits of each byte, each drive might store four. The first drive would take the first four bits of a given byte, the second drive the third, fourth, fifth, and sixth bits; the third, the fifth, sixth, seventh, and eighth; the fourth, the seventh, eighth, first, and second. This digital overlap allows the correct information to be pulled from another drive when one encounters an error. Better yet, if any single hard disk should fail, all of the data it stored could be reconstituted from the other drives.

This kind of system is said to be fault-tolerant. That is, a single fault—the failure of one hard disk—will be tolerated, meaning that the system operates without the loss of any vital function. Fault tolerance is extremely valuable in network applications because the crash of a single hard disk does not bring down the network. A massive equipment failure therefore becomes a bother rather than a disaster.

The example array represents the most primitive of drive array implementations, one that is particularly wasteful of the available storage resources. Advanced information coding methods allow higher efficiencies in storage, so a strict duplication of every bit is not required. Moreover, advanced drive arrays even allow a failed drive to be replaced and the data that was stored upon it reconstructed without interrupting the normal operation of the array. A network server with such a drive array wouldn't have to be shut down even for disk repairs.

RAID Implementations

Just connecting four drives to a SCSI controller won't create a drive array. An array requires special electronics to handle the digital coding and control of the individual drives. The electronics of these systems are proprietary to their manufacturers. The array controller then connects to your PC through a proprietary or standard interface. SCSI is becoming the top choice. Currently, most drive arrays are assembled by computer manufacturers for their own systems, but a growing number are becoming available as plug-in additions to PCs.

In 1988 three researchers at the University of California at Berkeley—David A. Patterson, Garth Gibson, and Randy H. Katz—first outlined five disk array models in a paper entitled A Case for Redundant Arrays of Inexpensive Disks. They called their models RAID Levels and labeled them as RAID 1 through 5, appropriately enough. Their numerical designations were arbitrary and were not meant to indicate that RAID 1 is better or worse than RAID 5. The numbers simply provide a label for each technology that can be readily understood by the cognoscenti.

In 1993, these levels were formalized in the first edition of the RAIDBook, published by the RAID Advisory Board, an association of suppliers and consumers of RAID-related mass storage products. The book is part of one of the RAID Advisory Board's principal objectives, the standardization of the terminology of RAID-related technology. Although the board does not officially set standards, it does prepare them for submission to the recognized standards organizations. The board also tests the function and performance of RAID products and verifies that they perform a basic set of functions correctly.

The RAID Advisory Board currently recognizes nine RAID implementation levels. Five of these conform to the original Berkeley RAID definintions. Beyond the five array levels described by the Berkeley group, several other RAID terms are used and acknowledged by the RAID Advisory Board. These include RAID Level 0, RAID Level 6, RAID Level 10, and RAID Level 53.

RAID Level 1

The simplest of drive arrays, RAID Level 1, consists of two equal-capacity disks that mirror one another. One disk duplicates all the files of the other, essentially serving as a backup copy. Should one of the drives fail, the other can serve in its stead.

This reliability is the chief advantage of RAID Level 1 technology. The entire system has the same capacity as one of its drives alone. In other words, the RAID Level 1 system yields only 50 percent of its potential storage capacity, making it the most expensive array implementation. Performance depends on the sophistication of the array controller. Simple systems deliver exactly the performance of one of the drives in the array. A more sophisticated controller could potentially double data throughput by simultaneously reading alternate sectors from both drives. Upon the failure of one of the drives, performance reverts to that of a single drive, but no information (and no network time) is lost.

RAID Level 2

The next step up in array sophistication is RAID Level 2, which interleaves bits or blocks of data as explained earlier in the description of drive arrays. The individual drives in the array operate in parallel, typically with their spindles synchronized.

To improve reliability, RAID Level 2 systems use redundant disks to correct single-bit errors and detect double-bit errors. The number of extra disks needed depends on the error-correction algorithm used. For example, an array of eight data drives may use three error correction drives. High-end arrays with 32 data drives may use seven error correction drives. The data, complete with error-detection code, is delivered directly to the array controller. The controller can instantly recognize and correct for errors as they occur, without slowing the speed in which information is read and transferred to the host computer.

The RAID Level 2 design anticipates that disk errors occur often, almost regularly. At one time, mass storage devices might have been error-prone, but no longer. Consequently, RAID Level 2 can be overkill except in the most critical of circumstances.

The principal benefit of RAID Level 2 is performance—because of their pure parallel nature it and RAID Level 3 are the best-performing array technologies, at least in systems that require a single, high-speed stream of data. In other words, it yields a high data transfer rate. Depending on the number of drives in the array, an entire byte or even 32-bit double-word could be read in the same period it would take a single drive to read one bit. Normal single-bit disk errors don't hinder this performance in any way because of RAID Level 2's on-the-fly error-correction.

The primary defect in the RAID Level 2 design arises from its basic storage unit being multiple sectors. As with any hard disk, the smallest unit each drive in the array can store is one sector. File sizes must increase in units of multiple sectors—one drawn from each drive. In a ten drive array, for example, even the tiniest two-byte file would steal ten sectors (5120 bytes) of disk space. (Under DOS, which uses clusters of four sectors, the two-byte file would take a total of 20480 bytes!) In actual applications, this drawback is not severe because systems that need the single-stream speed and instant error-correction of RAID Level 2 also tend to be those using large files, for example, mainframes.

RAID Level 3

This level is one step down from RAID Level 2. Although RAID Level 3 still uses multiple drives operating in parallel interleaving bits or blocks of data, instead of full error correction, it allows only for parity checking. That is, errors can be detected but without the guarantee of recovery.

Parity checking requires fewer extra drives in the array—typically only one per array—making it a less expensive alternative. When a parity error is detected, the RAID Level 3 controller reads the entire array again to get it right. This re-reading imposes a substantial performance penalty—the disks must spin entirely around again, yielding a 17 millisecond delay in reading the data. Of course, the delay appears only when disk errors are detected. Modern hard disks offer such high reliability that the delays are rare. In effect, RAID Level 3 compared to RAID Level 2 trades off fewer drives for a slight performance penalty that occurs only rarely.

RAID Level 4

This level interleaves not bits nor blocks but sectors. The sectors are read serially, as if the drives in the array were functionally one large drive with more heads and platters. (Of course, for higher performance a controller with adequate buffering could read two or more sectors at the same time, storing the later sectors in fast RAM and delivering them immediately after the preceding sector has been sent to the computer host.) For reliability, one drive in the array is dedicated to parity checking. RAID Level 4 earns favor because it permits small arrays of as few as two drives, although larger arrays make more efficient use of the available disk storage.

The dedicated parity drive is the biggest weakness of the RAID Level 4 scheme. In writing, RAID Level 4 maintains the parity drive by reading the data drives, updating the parity information, and then writing the update to the parity drive. This read-update-write cycle adds a performance penalty to every write, although read operations are unhindered.

RAID Level 4 offers an extra benefit for operating systems that can process multiple data requests simultaneously. An intelligent RAID Level 4 controller can process multiple input/output requests, reorganize them, and read its drives in the most efficient manner, perhaps even in parallel. For example, while a sector from one file is being read from one drive, a sector from another file can read from another drive. This parallel operation can improve the effective throughput of such operating systems.

RAID Level 5

This level eliminates the dedicated parity drive from the RAID Level 4 array and allows the parity-check function to rotate through the various drives in the array. Error checking is thus distributed across all disks in the array. In properly designed implementations, enough redundancy can be built in to make the system fault tolerant.

RAID Level 5 is probably the most popular drive-array technology currently in use because it works with almost any number of drives, including arrays as small as two, yet permits redundancy and fault tolerance to be built in.

RAID Level 0

Early workers used the term RAID Level 0 to refer to the absence of any array technology. According to the RAID Advisory Board, however, the term refers to an array that simply uses data striping to distribute data across several physical disks. Although this RAID Level 0 offers no greater reliability than the worst of the physical drives making up the array, it can improve the performance of the overall storage system.

RAID Level 6

To further improve the fault tolerance of RAID Level 5, the same Berkeley researchers who developed the initial five RAID levels proposed one more, now known as RAID Level 6. This level adds a second parity drive to the RAID level 5 array. The chief benefit is that any two drives in the array can fail without the loss of data. This enables an array to remain in active service while an individual physical drive is being repaired yet still remain fault tolerant. In effect, a RAID Level 6 array with a single failed physical disk becomes a RAID Level 5 array. The drawback of the RAID Level 6 design is that it requires two parity blocks to be written during every write operation. Its write performance is extremely low, although read performance can achieve levels on par with RAID Level 5.

RAID Level 10

Some arrays employ multiple RAID technologies. RAID Level 10 represents a layering of RAID Levels 0 and 1 to combine the benefits of each. (Sometimes RAID Level 10 is called RAID Level 0&1 to more specifically point at its origins.) To improve input/output performance, RAID Level 10 employs data striping, splitting data blocks between multiple drives. Moreover, the Array Management Software can further speed read operations by filling multiple operations simultaneously from the two mirrored arrays (at times when both halves of the mirror are functional, of course.) To improve reliability, the RAID level uses mirroring so that the striped arrays are exactly duplicated. This technology achieves the benefits of both of its individual layers. Its chief drawback is cost. As with simple mirroring, it doubles the amount of physical storage needed for a given amount of logical storage.

RAID Level 53

This level represents a layering of RAID Level 0 and RAID Level 3—the incoming data is striped between two RAID Level 3 arrays. The capacity of the RAID Level 53 array is the total of the capacity of the individual underlying RAID Level 3 arrays. Input/output performance is enhanced by the striping between multiple arrays. Throughput is improved by the underlying RAID Level 3 arrays. Because the simple striping of the top RAID Level 0 layer adds no redundant data, reliability falls. RAID Level 3 arrays, however, are inherently so fault tolerant that the overall reliability of the RAID Level 53 array far exceeds that of an individual hard disk drive. As with a RAID Level 3 array, the failure of a single drive will not adversely affect data integrity.

Figures 22.6 through 22.14 show graphically how these RAID implementations differ. Which implementation is best depends on what you most want to achieve with a drive array: efficient use of drive capacity, fewest number of drives, greatest reliability, or quickest performance. For example, RAID 1 provides the greatest redundancy (thus reliability), and RAID 2 the best performance (followed closely by RAID 3).

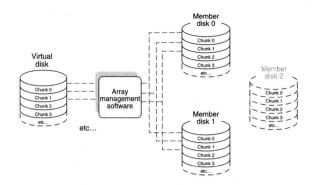

FIGURE 22.6. Data mapping for a RAID Level 1 Array.

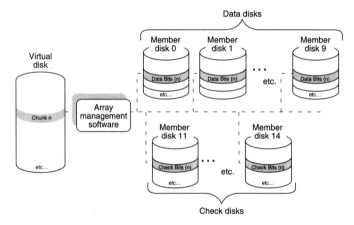

FIGURE 22.7. Data mapping for a RAID Level 2 Array.

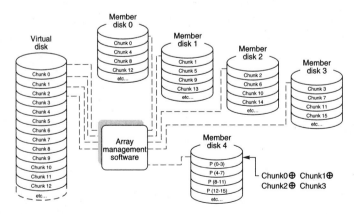

FIGURE 22.8. Data mapping for a RAID Level 3 Array.

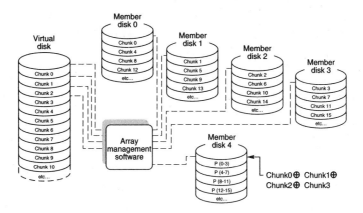

FIGURE 22.9. Data mapping for a RAID Level 4 Array.

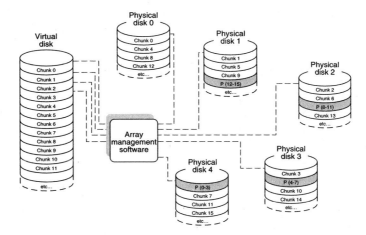

FIGURE 22.10. Data mapping for a RAID Level 5 Array.

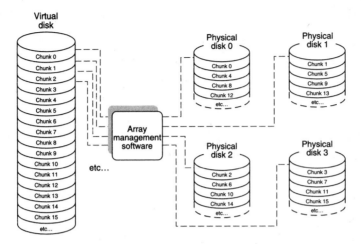

FIGURE 22.11. Data mapping for a RAID Level 0 Array.

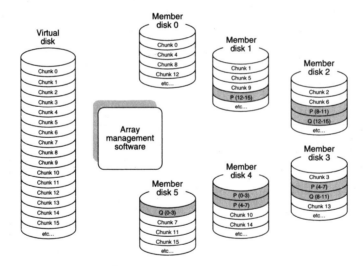

FIGURE 22.12. More RAID implementations.

Parallel Access Arrays

In Parallel Access Arrays, all of the individual physical drives in the array participate in every input and output operation of the array. In other words, all of the drives operate in unison. Systems that correspond to the RAID 2 or RAID 3 design fit this definition. The drives in

Independent Access Arrays can operate independently. In advanced arrays, several individual drives may perform different input and output operations simultaneously, filling multiple input and output requests at the same time. Systems that follow the RAID 4 or RAID 5 designs fit this definition. Although RAID 1 drives may operate either as parallel access or independent access arrays, most practical systems operate RAID 1 drives independently.

The RAID Advisory Board can be reached at the following address:

> RAID Advisory Board
> 6931 Glenview Lane
> Lino Lakes, Minnesota 55014-1296

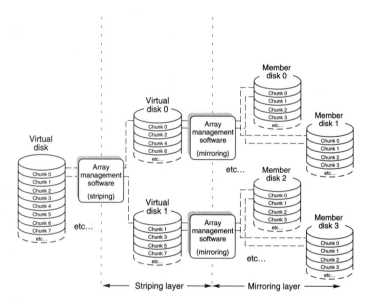

FIGURE 22.13. Data mapping in a RAID Level 10 Array

Drive Packaging

You don't have to be a hardware wizard to figure out that a hard disk has to fit where you want to install it. As drive form factors shrink, however, you'd think that these concerns would go away. This issue becomes one of making a tiny drive big enough to bolt into yesterday's giant-size drive bays. But physical drive installation isn't so simple. Today, you're more likely than ever to try to squeeze a second (third or whatever) drive into the confines of a fully-expanded PC. Moreover, matching drive and bay size isn't enough. You've also got to pack in a controller or host adapter and wring out enough juice to power the drive product you choose.

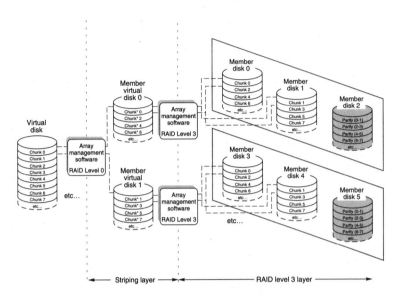

FIGURE 22.14. Data mapping in a RAID Level 53 Array.

Internal Installation

It should be obvious that your drive must fit where you want to put it. It must have a form factor that matches one of the available drive bays in your computer or, if it's smaller, you need an adapter kit to fit it in.

Mounting a hard disk is much the same as installing a floppy disk drive. Unlike floppy disk drives, however, hard disks have no controls, knobs, or removable media that require user attention. Consequently, hard disks do not require front panel access and can therefore be buried inside your computer without sacrificing anything other than a glance at the drive activity indicator LED on the front of most hard disks. Many small footprint desktop computers do exactly that—space for an inch-high 3.5-inch hard disk drive may be nothing but a bay bent from a slice of sheet steel appended in some opportune place inside the system. Without an instruction manual or vivid imagination, you'd never find where they've tucked away a tiny hard disk drive. Drives now consume so little power that proper cooling no longer dictates mounting position.

Most systems still provide half-height 5.25-inch bays for hard disk storage. With a modern 3.5-inch hard disk drive, your only concern is that you get a mounting kit to match the drive to the larger bay—or be sure that your system provides some way of installing a small disk in a larger bay. For example, the trays that ALR tower-style computers use for both hard and floppy disk drives easily accommodate either 5.25-inch or 3.5-inch drives without adapters. In general, AT-style cases that use rails to mount drives require adapters. Systems in which drives directly screw in generally accept a small drive in a large bay if you're willing to forego the sturdiness of screwing in both sides of the drive. Systems designed from the start with 3.5-inch bays pose no installation problems—unless you want to cram in an ancient 5.25-inch drive (in which case your best option may be to take a circular saw to the drive—shave a few inches off, and the drive will fit without a problem, although this technique will compromise the access time of the drive, stretching it from milliseconds to millennia).

Hard Disk Cards

In 1985, the hard disk makers at Quantum Corporation hit upon an idea with so much promise that they created a new company to develop and promote it. The company was Plus Development Corporation; the idea, the Hardcard, was essentially a hard disk on a standard-size PC expansion card. Since then, Plus Development has gone on to develop other products—and to be absorbed back into Quantum. Nevertheless, the original idea must still be regarded as inspired. The all-in-one HardCard package eliminated all the hardware worries of installing a hard disk. It required no cables, no bloody knuckles, and no worries about an errant touch on a delicate circuit causing a $100 per hour repair job. In addition, the Hardcard was a perfect fit for systems that had no drive bays available for adding another disk.

The original Hardcard used a proprietary disk controller and a special low-power, low-profile disk drive, all manufactured by Japan electronics giant, Matsushita Industrial Corporation. In effect, it was the first integrated drive electronics (IDE) product for PCs sold in the consumer market.

The first HardCard was a modest device. Its capacity was 10 megabytes, its performance on par only with the ordinary XT hard disk. And it was expensive, priced at about three times the level of do-it-yourself hard disk systems of equivalent performance and capacity. Since then, Plus has developed the product to capacities beyond 100 megabytes with performance on par with separate hard disk drives. Modern HardCards also use the same 16-bit bus interface as other hard disk host adapters and controllers. To date, however, no Micro Channel hard disk cards have been developed.

Even the low-capacity original HardCard was enough to prove the viability of the combined hard disk on an expansion board idea, now generally termed the hard disk card. Several manufacturers followed suit, often simply bolting a short disk controller to a small-format hard disk. Most of these have disappeared from the market as a result of Plus aggressively protecting its patents on the card-in-a-slot concept. In that nearly all new PCs come with a hard disk as standard equipment and most people have now worked up the courage to tackle normal drive installation, the HardCard's particular product niche is becoming small indeed. Quantum no longer manufactures the HardCard, citing that the reduced pricing of IDE drives no longer makes the HardCard a profitable item.

HardCards still have their value. They make an ideal supplement to standard equipment drives, one that can be installed even by folks whose manual dexterity is rivaled only by their ability to fly through the air unassisted. They also serve as a convenient way of setting up multiple PCs in a corporation. You can write all the files you want to install on several PCs onto a single HardCard and transfer all the files (even the file structure) to the native hard disk in each machine. Just plug the master HardCard into each machine in turn and issue a single XCOPY command.

Hard Disk Power

Power is a problem with every hard disk—including the tiniest hard card—that's installed in factory issue IBM PCs. The constant spin of the hard disk platters that gives near-instant response extracts one penalty—the drive must continually draw power to keep up the spin even when your PC is doing something that doesn't involve the disk.

Older hard disks, for instance, the behemoth full-height 5.25-inch drives of the AT age, have electrical requirements that could strain computers with smaller power supplies such as the 63.5 watt original PC and 100-watt clone machines. You can work around such problems by installing a larger power supply in computers that are deficient in wattage.

On the other hand, modern 3.5-inch drives draw a fraction of the power of the dinosaurs (most are under 10 watts, many under five), so power issues rarely arise. Moreover, any PC with a 135-watt or larger power supply should have enough reserves for at least one hard disk drive no matter the vintage of the disk. Stick with modern desktop PCs—most of which have 200-watt power supplies—and a modern hard disk, and drive power is not a problem.

The power difficulty you'll likely encounter is finding a connector to plug into the drive. Many systems provide too few drive power connectors for full expansion. Check your PC before you order a new hard disk to ensure that a power connector is available for the new drive. If not, add a wye cable to your shopping list.

A wye cable is designed to intercept the power connector meant for one drive and split it two ways. This cable has one male drive power connector (like the power jacks on the backs of most disk drives) and two female connectors (matching the one you remove from the power jack on the back of a drive). Plug the connector you remove from the drive jack into the male plug, and you're left with two female plugs that accommodate two disk drives. Figure 22.15 shows a typical Y cable.

Host Adapters

Any hard disk you install also must electronically match the computer in which it is to be used. You need a spare connection from your existing hard disk controller or host adapter or you need to install a second controller/adapter.

Some early PCs pose particular problems. For example, while the controller of an XT can handle a second disk drive, both drives must have the same hardware parameters (including use of the old ST506 interface). You cannot mix MFM and RLL drives on one controller—even though both drive types use the ST506 interface, RLL controller can provide only RLL signals.

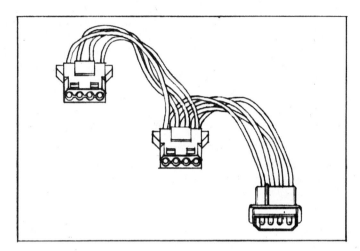

FIGURE 22.15. A typical Y cable.

Modern PCs and drive interfaces allow you more freedom. ESDI permits you to use two drives (with that interface, of course) of any capacity. AT Attachment host adapters are equally flexible. SCSI host adapters allow up to seven drives to be connected, and all seven can have different setup parameters.

If you want to install a hard disk in a system that has not had a hard disk before (for example, because you're building it from scratch) or if you want to change interfaces (for example, to replace an aged ST506 drive with one with a low-cost AT Attachment unit), you'll need a new controller or host adapter. Don't forget that many systems combine the hard disk and floppy disk control functions in one PC expansion board. If you replace such a controller to move to a new interface, don't forget to get a new host adapter with floppy disk circuitry or a separate floppy disk controller board.

External Installation

External chassis units were once—and briefly—the only hard disks that you could attach to your PC. They simultaneously solved two problems with the first PC, inadequate space and inadequate power. Another advantage often cited by the manufacturers of these devices was that they added no heat inside your PC. The external chassis also allows you to use very large drives—eight-inch and larger disks—with your PC.

None of these arguments make sense in an age of gigabyte drives only slightly larger than a deck of playing cards. But external drives still thrive for several reasons: The advent of drive arrays, the versatility of plugging in and moving between systems, and laptop computers with no other provisions for hard disk expansion. Moreover, there's nothing inherently evil about external drive installation. The only real drawbacks are the additional costs involved—not just the dollars required to pay for an extra box and power supply.

Most often external drives are assembled by system houses, companies that buy raw disk drives, controller electronics, and the other hardware needed to make a complete system and put everything together into one no-hassles package. Although the system integrator is one level removed from the original disk drive manufacturer who adds their own profit to the price you have to pay, the bargain is not necessarily bad. The system integrator not only assembles the complete unit, saving you the trouble, but also the integrator usually tests the finished product, adding one degree of quality control and eliminating a degree of worry.

Where still available, the external chassis hard disk subsystem comprises a complete mass storage subsystem, one that includes the disk drive proper, a case with built-in power supply, and a host adapter card. Ancient external drives packaged the actual drive controller in the external chassis and used a simple host adapter in your PC. For a while, external drives put the controller inside your PC. Modern units have gone back to the old-fashioned design with the actual controller in the external box. Actually, the controller is an embedded interface built into the hard disk itself, and the board in your PC is simply an ordinary AT Attachment or SCSI host adapter.

In any case, the external chassis must be connected to your computer by a cable of some kind. The FCC provides a tremendous incentive for manufacturers to make these connecting cables as short as possible—shorter cables are less likely to radiate interference, so getting FCC certification for external drives with shorter cables is easier. But short cables can severely restrict your flexibility in positioning the drive where you want it. You might be forced to put the unit to the left of your computer and rearrange your desk around the needs of the disk drive.

No matter the length of the cable, it's also one more thing to get in the way. And it's one more thing to go wrong. Connectors are the most troublesome part of any circuit and one of the elements most likely to fail.

On the other hand, external drives can be somewhat easier to install. For the most part, you won't have to deal with nuts, bolts, and screws because the external chassis is usually supplied to you completely assembled. Instead, you only need to plug the host adapter into an expansion slot inside your computer and then link the external chassis and the adapter with the cable supplied by the manufacturer.

Reliability

You trust your valuable data to your hard disk. You naturally expect to be able to find what you want when you want it. You don't want to see such ominous messages as General Disk Failure when you're preparing next year's budget (or explaining what went awry with last year's). You want your drive to be as reliable as, say, a brick.

Unfortunately, judging the reliability of the average hard disk these days by just looking at it is about as worthwhile as looking at a brick. Little of the electronics are visible and even less of the mechanism. For all intents, purposes, and assessments, the hard disk is a sealed black box that won't reveal its secrets without the aid of a can-opener. And should you use such means to investigate a disk in the store, your salesperson will be happy to present you with a bill for your subject drive after he recovers from his myocardial infarction.

MTBF

Your alternative is taking the salesperson's word, and at best he'll quote whatever lies the drive maker tells him. Most of these lies are numeric, the most commonly quoted being the Mean Time Between Failures or MTBF.

The MTBF of a hard disk should give you a general indication of its reliability, but today the figures are almost ridiculous. Where drives were once rated at about 25,000 hours, most are now rated in the range 100,000 to 160,000 hours—that's 11 to 18 years. Some manufacturers now list their MTBF figures as 300,000 or more hours—34 years. Your PC (or you, for that matter) should last as long. A long MTBF is an assurance of a long-lasting drive. But you'll also want to consider how the manufacturer backs up its MTBF claim. A 500,000 hour MTBF is meaningless if the manufacturer gives you only a 90-day warranty.

Warranty

Rather than taking the manufacturer's word, you may want to see how the manufacturer backs up what it says. That is, check the warranty. Hard disk drives may be warranted by the vendor or the manufacturer. You'll probably depend more on the vendor's warranty, so that should be your first concern.

The easy-to-quantify issue is the length of the warranty. A hard disk warranty should extend for at least 90 days. You'll find that better products—and better vendors— offer hard disk warranties measured in years.

How that warranty is honored is important. Because you have no control over what happens to a drive that you return for repair, you should prefer a warranty that gives you a replacement drive (at least if the product dies in its first few weeks of life) rather than risking getting your old drive back as a time-bomb, waiting to go off the second the warranty expires.

Manufacturers' warranties are trickier to get a handle on. In general, the warranty period starts when the product is sold to your vendor, not to you, so it may expire sooner than you think. Worse, a manufacturer may choose not to recognize its warranty if you don't buy from an authorized dealer. So it's important to clarify whether you get a manufacturer's warranty when you buy your drive.

At least the drive manufacturer has the facilities for properly handling repairs and a reputation to uphold, so you shouldn't worry about having your drive repaired rather than replaced by the manufacturer.

Support

Of course, the warranty does you no good if the drive works in the abstract but not inside your PC. Depending on the manufacturer of the hard disk, you may have one or two avenues of support for the drive you buy to help overcome such problems. In most cases, the preferred first choice for support is the vendor who sold you the drive. You'll want to check out what the drive vendor offers.

Before you buy, ask the salesman about his company's support policy. Check to see whether the vendor even has a support number. Because you'll probably install your drive in the evening, you'll want to be sure that the number is staffed at any conceivable hour you might call (say around the clock). Check whether the support line is toll-free and that there are enough people to answer your questions immediately. You don't want to have to wait—perhaps forever—for someone to call you back.

Some vendors depend solely on the drive manufacturer's support staff. Drive makers run a wide range in the support they offer end users. Some won't even talk to you. They deal only with vendors, not with the real users of their products. Others prefer that you start with your dealer but will help in a pinch. Some have consumer support lines, and a few are even toll-free.

Setup and Operation

After a drive is physically installed and cabled in place inside your PC, you must let your computer know what you've done. With PCs, XTs, and third-party systems with disk parameters encoded into firmware, you needn't do anything. The firmware sends the proper message to the system and lets it know what's going on. With ATs and later computers, however, you must take positive steps to setup your system for a new hard disk.

Starting with the AT (and the XT Model 286), IBM set the pattern for the PC industry by allowing you to set drive parameters through sofware. This ability increased your hard disk choices because the disk configuration information was no longer hard-coded into BIOS firmware. Fifteen configurations are built into the hard disk BIOS, and half of a byte of CMOS storage is used as a pointer to indicate which set of parameters your system would use. These configurations are in the same form as disk parameters, and they should match the parameters of the disk that you choose to use.

When you run your PC's setup program, you're inserting the proper information for the disk drive you have into this special memory location. Each of the two drives that the standard setup BIOS allows can be any of the drive types in the list. Mixing drive types is permitted, today taken for granted, although it was once a luxury.

More recent PCs have expanded the number of different configurations that are predefined in the memory of the controller and have necessarily expanded the CMOS pointer storage to a full byte. These systems, too, allow you to connect two different drive types to a single controller.

IBM is generally consistent about what numbers it assigns to each drive type. The first 15 types used by the AT retain their numbers even in the wider collections available in later machines. The IBM drive number assignments for different hard disk configurations are given in Table 22.2.

TABLE 22.2. IBM drive number assignments

AT supports types 1-15
XAT Model 286 supports types 1-24
PS/2s support types 1-32

Type	Cylinders	Heads	Write Precomp	Landing Zone	Capacity (MB)
1	306	4	128	305	10
2	615	4	300	615	21
3	615	6	300	615	32
4	940	8	512	940	65
5	940	6	512	940	49
6	615	4	None	615	21
7	462	8	256	511	32
8	733	5	None	733	32
9	900	15	None	901	117
10	820	3	None	820	21
11	855	5	None	855	37
12	855	7	None	855	52
13	306	8	128	319	21
14	733	7	None	733	44
15	0	0	None	0	0
16	612	4	All	663	21
17	977	5	300	977	42
18	977	7	None	977	59
19	1024	7	512	1023	62
20	733	5	300	732	32
21	733	7	300	732	44

continues

TABLE 22.2. Continued

Type	Cylinders	Heads	Write Precomp	Landing Zone	Capacity (MB)
22	733	5	300	733	32
23	306	4	None	336	10
24	612	4	305	663	21
25	306	4	None	340	10
26	612	4	None	670	21
27	698	7	300	732	85 [ESDI]
28	976	5	488	977	85 [ESDI]
29	306	4	All	340	10
30	611	4	306	663	42 [ESDI]
31	732	7	300	732	89 [ESDI]
32	1023	5	None	1023	89 [ESDI]

Note: Capacities based on an ESDI drive having 34 sectors per cylinder; other drives assumed to have 17 sectors per cylinder.

Although compatible computer manufacturers usually copied IBM for the first 15 drive type choices, many makers went in their own directions for the later extrapolations. Indeed, many began to offer a wider choice of hard disk types even before IBM. The parameters are specific to each BIOS incarnation and vary among manufacturers and sometimes among system models. In general, you can check your various drive options by running the setup program provided with your PC, either on a setup disk or built into its BIOS.

Unsupported Drives

You can work a lack of support for the drive you want to add in several ways. The easiest is to use a drive with automatic sector translation, which makes the best match possible as long as you set your system up for the correct capacity. Otherwise matching an unsupported drive requires extra software or foregoing some of the capacity of your drive.

Special drive installation software such as On-Track Computer System's Disk Manager and Storage Dimension's SpeedStor set up software drivers to match unsupported disks to your system. Run the installation software, select the proper disk model from a menu, and the match is automatically made. The only shortcoming to this software setup system is that it works only with DOS.

If you can come close to matching your drive's parameters, however, you can generally get a specific hard disk to work by matching the drive type number of a unit with fewer cylinders than the drive you have. For instance, if you have a drive with 1224 cylinders, choose a drive type with the same number of heads as your new drive but 1024 cylinders. The penalty for this expedient is a loss of capacity: other 200 cylinders will not be accessible on your system. Similarly, you can specify fewer heads than your system actually has, but in such a case you're likely to give up much more capacity to make a match. Do this only as a last resort.

Most modern BIOSs make provisions for you to accommodate nearly every drive by allowing you to indicate the parameters of any hard disk. For example, the AMI BIOS reserves drive type 47 for you to type the heads, cylinders, sectors, write precompensation needs, and landing zone of whatever drive you have.

Drive Activity Indicator

Nearly all hard disks have a drive activity indicator—a small red or green LED that illuminates when the drive is being accessed by your system. If you're installing a new hard disk into some systems, however, you may notice that this LED lights as soon as you switch on the power to your system and stays on all the time. Most of the time this constant glow is not an indication of a problem. Rather, it results from the IBM AT hard disk design.

All IBM computers with internal hard disk mounting allow for a front panel drive activity indicator. In every case, the signal that controls this indicator is derived from the hard disk controller and not the disk drive itself, so it reflects what the controller tells the drive to do and not what the drive is actually doing. The controller makes the drive think that it's constantly selected and active, causing the constant glow of its light. If a red light inside your computer bothers you, you can often disconnect the LED on the drive or clip one of its leads.

Data Structures

A new hard disk is like a newborn baby: although some capabilities are built-in, its mind and memory are essentially blank. It has to learn about the world before it can do what it was designed for. For example, many drives must construct the individual sectors that they use for storage from the undifferentiated lengths of individual tracks.

Much like floppy disk drives, the organization of a hard disk drive is called its format. Hard disks differ from floppies in that two levels of organization wear the same title—the low-level format and the DOS format. Both are necessary to use a given disk under DOS, but each has its own role and requires it own procedure to set up.

Low-Level Formatting

All drives must have their sectors individually defined on each track. Hard disks with device-level interfaces typically came with their tracks and cylinders predefined—either by the steps of its stepper motor head actuator or by the servo tracks on the servo platter of a voice-coil actuated drive—but the sectors were nowhere to be seen or sensed. Before data can be written on such a disk, the sectors have to be marked to serve as guidepost markers so that the information can later be found and retrieved. The process by which sectors are defined on the hard disk is called low-level formatting because it occurs at a control level below the reaches of normal DOS commands.

Creating a low-level format requires running a low-level formatting program. Some versions of DOS shipped with IBM-compatible computers include such a program under a name like LLFORMAT or HDPREP. Most disk diagnostic programs also include low-level formatting routines. Low-level formatters for pre-1987 IBM Personal Computers were included with the Advanced Diagnostics programs that IBM sold to accompany its PC and AT systems. The low-level formatting program for PS/2-series machines is included on the reference disk that accompanies each computer, but it is hidden. To use this low-level formatting program, boot up your PS/2 from its Reference Diskette. At the first screen, where you are asked to type Enter to continue, press the Enter key. You should then see the Main Menu, which offers you seven menu selections that you can do with the program. Ignore them. Instead, press the Ctrl and letter A keys (Ctrl-A) simultaneously. Your machine then loads its Advanced Diagnostics. You can choose the low-level format routine from its two-selection menu.

Many of the manufacturers of aftermarket ST506 and ESDI hard disk controllers include the necessary program for low-level formatting a hard disk connected to their product in the controller's ROM firmware. These routines are normally executed through the GO command of the DOS DEBUG program. For instance, a number of these routines are accessed by typing the following instruction at the DEBUG hyphen prompt:

```
G=C800:5
```

If you try this with your controller and it doesn't work, you'll likely lock up your system. If it works, you'll be prompted on the screen. The built-in low-level formatting routines of some vary a few bytes in position in their add-in BIOSs. You may want to try starting execution at C800:6 or C800:8 if the first example does not work. Other than locking up your computer, you won't do any damage to anything. In particular, you won't hurt any data on a new hard disk because there's nothing there to begin with!

Most hard disk drives with system-level interfaces (which means most hard disks) now come with their low-level formats already in place. Some don't even permit low-level formatting. For example, AT Attachment drives that may use sector translation make the actual geometry of the drive indecipherable by your PC. The manufacturers of these drives assure their customers that once the hard disk is formatted at the factory, it never needs to be formatted again.

As noted in Chapter 20, all magnetic media tend to deteriorate with age. That is, the flux transitions in the hard disk medium tend to get weaker as time passes. As soon as a flux transition is written, it gradually loses strength. Eventually, it can become weak enough to be ambiguous and result in an error when it is read. The flux transitions in the data areas of your hard disk get rejuvenated every time you write to them, starting their long trek to deterioration all over again. The low-level format information is written once and never gets rejuvenated, at least if you don't low-level format your disk again.

Some people believe that low-level formatting their disk periodically increases its reliability and helps forestall disk errors. In fact, with older drives that permit it, a low-level format can eliminate disk errors. Backing up such a drive and running its low-level format program once every couple of years is an excellent idea—even if it doesn't prolong the life of the disk, the backup you make may become valuable should disaster strike your system.

Newer drives use higher coercivity media and are more resistant to age deterioration. Most disk makers believe that low-level format rejuvenation is no longer necessary with their current products.

Bad Tracks and Sectors

In the manufacturing of hard disk platters, defects occasionally occur in the magnetic medium. These defects will not properly record data. Sectors in which these defects occur are called bad sectors; the tracks containing the sectors are called bad tracks.

Your computer can deal with bad sectors by locking them out of normal use. During the low-level formatting process, the sectors that do not work properly are recorded, and your system is prevented from using them. The only ill effect of reserving these bad sectors is that the available capacity of your hard disk may diminish by a small amount.

Some low-level formatting programs require that you enter bad sector data before you begin the formatting process. Although this seems redundant—the format program checks for them anyhow—it's not. Factory checks for bad sectors are more rigorous than the format routine. This close scrutiny helps minimize future failure. Tedious as it is, you should enter the bad sector data when the low-level format program calls for it. The listing of bad sectors is usually on a sheet of paper accompanying the disk drive or on a label affixed to the drive itself.

The only time that a bad sector is an evil thing is when it occurs on the first track of the disk. The first track (Track 0) is used to hold partition and booting data. This information must be located on the first track of the disk. If it cannot be written there, the disk won't work.

Should you get a hard disk with Track 0 bad, return it to the dealer from whom you bought it. If you reformat a disk after a head crash and discover Track 0 bad during the format process, you need a new disk.

Partitioning

When the low-level format is in place on a hard disk, you must partition it. Partitioning is a function of the operating system. It sets up the logical structure of the hard disk to a form that is compatible with the operating system.

The program for partitioning your hard disk goes under various guises. In some versions of DOS it is called FDISK; others use HDPREP; others may use another name. No matter the nomenclature, you must run this program for low-level formatting of your disk for your PC to recognize the disk. If you don't, you'll get an error message when you boot up your system.

In general, partitioning is a way that you divide your physical hard disk into the equivalent of several logical disk drives. Each behaves as if it were a separate hard disk. The purpose of partitioning is threefold: it helps organize your disk; it allows you to take advantage of larger disks than the logical structure of DOS can handle; and it allows you to keep several separate operating systems and file systems on one disk drive.

As the partitioning scheme was originally envisioned for PCs, each partition would use a different operating systems. Your PC treated these individual partitions as truly isolated disks—when you used one, you could not reach the data or programs on another. The different operating systems simply did not know how to access files used by other operating systems. The operating system that you booted in could recognize only its own files.

Newer operating systems are enlightened enough to know how to read files used by other operating systems, so in some cases they can invade the partitions also used by other operating systems. Although these operating systems can dig into the files of the other system, they cannot directly run programs for a foreign operating system without emulating the other operating system. This sharing of data often is a one-way street because ancient operating systems are unaware (or uncaring) that you might want to share files. For example, OS/2 easily peers into DOS files, but DOS is normally forbidden from dabbling in the High Performance File System that you can use under OS/2.

In versions of DOS before 3.3, the operating system could recognize only one partition. DOS 3.3 added extended DOS partitions that allowed DOS to recognize two partitions—the first or primary DOS partition and the extended DOS partition. This scheme allowed you to sidestep the 32 MB addressing limit built into early versions of DOS without radically altering the structure of DOS. The primary partition was limited to 32 MB by the structure of the file allocation table (see below). The extended DOS partition faced no such limit. To make it compatible with DOS, however, the extended partition had to be divided into 32 MB volumes. DOS treats each volume as an individual logical hard disk and identifies each with its own drive letter.

Current versions of DOS (through DOS 6) allow all partitions to accommodate up to 512 MB. They also enable you to set up one primary DOS partition and use the other three available partitions as extended DOS partitions, any of which you can split into individual volumes.

Your PC keeps track of disk partitions using a master partition table located in the first physical sector of a hard disk. It is offset from the start of the disk—that is sector 00(Hex), cylinder 00(Hex), head 00(Hex)—by 364 bytes. In other words, the master partition table is at offset 01BE(Hex) from the beginning of your hard disk. The master partition table consists of 64 bytes, which is subdivided into four 16-byte entries to accommodate the four possible partitions.

Extended DOS partitions each have their own partition tables to store the values needed to define their logical volumes (known as extended volumes). Each of these extended volumes starts with its own extended partition table that uses a format identical to the master partition table. If a disk has more than one extended volume, the extended partition table of the first points to the next volume, so the partition tables form a chain.

The first byte in the master partition table is a boot flag; it indicates whether the partition is bootable. A bootable partition has a value of 80(Hex) here (and has the necessary code to boot the system in its first sector). Non-bootable partitions are marked with the value 00(Hex). Of DOS partitions, only the primary partition is bootable.

The partition table defines the size of a partition by its starting and ending sectors. The three bytes starting at offset 01(Hex) encode the starting head, sector, and cylinder numbers. The three bytes starting at 05(Hex) encode the ending head, sector, and cylinder numbers. In both cases, the head number is a full byte value; the sector number is coded as the lower six bits of the second byte; and the cylinder number takes the upper two bits of this byte and all eight bits of the next byte. Together these values define the maximum disk geometry that this partitioning scheme can accommodate: 256 heads (eight bits); 64 sectors (six bits); and 1024 cylinders (10 bits).

The byte trapped between the starting and ending sector data at offset 04(Hex) is the System Indicator Byte which defines the file system used inside the partition. Table 22.3 lists the defined values for this byte.

TABLE 22.3. Defined values for system indicator byte

Offset 04(Hex) in each 16-byte partition table record

00(Hex)	Unused partition
01(Hex)	Primary DOS partition, 12-bit FAT entries
04(Hex)	Primary DOS partition, 16-bit FAT entries
05(Hex)	Extended DOS partition, 16-bit FAT entries
06(Hex)	Huge partition (>32MB under DOS 4 or OS/2)
07(Hex)	HPFS partition

A double word (four bytes) at offset 08(Hex) stores the starting sector number relative to the first sector on the disk. Another double word at 0C(Hex) stores the length of the partition in sectors.

When your PC boots up, your PC normally scans through the partition table to find the boot partition. As the boot process unfolds, DOS assigns logical drive letters to each volume that it sets up. First it searches through all of the physical hard disks in your system that contain primary DOS partitions and assigns them identifying letters in sequence starting with C: for the boot drive. After all primary partitions have been identified, DOS continues to assign drive letters to volumes in extended partitions, dealing with all the volumes of one physical hard disk before going on to the next.

DOS Formatting

The final step in preparing a disk for use is formatting it with the operating system you intend to use. With DOS, that means running the FORMAT program. The current DOS FORMAT program does not overwrite the data areas of a hard disk (which means it won't rejuvenate them). It simply refreshes the file allocation table. (That's why you can unformat disks—by storing a copy of the FAT elsewhere on the disk the unformatting program can reconstruct the FAT to find all the files hidden by the DOS formatting operation.)

Note that IBM operating systems are backwardly compatible but not forwardly compatible. If you format a hard disk under DOS 5.0 or if you boot from a floppy with DOS 3.3 on it, you may not be able to read your hard disk. You will either get an error message or see strange things on your screen—such as file names consisting of odd combinations of numbers and smiley faces. Never write to a hard disk using a version of DOS from a previous generation to the format that's on the disk. If you do, the disk will be irreparably damaged.

Operation

To store a file on disk, DOS breaks it down into a group of clusters, perhaps hundreds of them. Each cluster can be drawn from anywhere on the disk. Sequential pieces of a file do not necessarily have to be stored in clusters that are physically adjacent.

The earliest—and now obsolete—versions of DOS follow a simple rule in picking which clusters are assigned to each file. The first available cluster, the one nearest the beginning of the disk, is always the next one used. Therefore, on a new disk, clusters are picked one after another, and all the clusters in a file are contiguous.

When a file is erased, its clusters are freed for reuse. These newly freed clusters, being closer to the beginning of the disk, are the first ones chosen when the next file is written to disk. In effect, DOS first fills in the holes left by the erased file. As a result, the clusters of new files may be scattered all over the disk.

The earliest versions of DOS use this strange strategy because they were written at a time when capacity was more important than speed. The goal was to pack files on the disk as stingily as possible.

Starting with version 3.0, DOS doesn't immediately try to use the first available cluster closest to the beginning of the disk. Instead, it attempts to write on never-before-used clusters before filling in any erased clusters. This helps ensure that the clusters of a file are closer to one another, a technique that improves the speed of reading a file from the disk.

File Allocation Table

To keep track of which cluster belongs in which file, DOS uses a File Allocation Table or FAT, essentially a map of the clusters on the disk. When you read to a file, DOS automatically and invisibly checks the FAT to find all the clusters of the file; when you write to the disk, it checks the FAT for available clusters. No matter how scattered over your disk the individual clusters of a file may be, you—and your software—only see a single file.

It's important to keep cluster size small because clusters are the smallest possible storage unit on a disk. Consequently, the smallest batch file you create steals at least one cluster of disk space—a ten-byte batch file could occupy 8192 bytes on the disk. On the average, every file larger than one cluster also wastes half a cluster worth of disk space. Moreover, every directory, even those not containing files, also steals at least one cluster from a disk. Consequently, the smaller the cluster size, the less disk space wasted on unused storage.

DOS versions through 3.3 used FATs with 12-bit entries cluster numbers, allowing a total of 4096 uniquely named clusters. With 8192 byte clusters, the maximum possible disk (or partition size) was 33,554,432—the infamous old DOS 32MB limit. DOS 4.0 and later allow 16-bit FAT entries, which allow a total of 65,536 uniquely named clusters. With cluster size kept at a space-saving 2048 bytes, the maximum permissible possible disk size is 134,217,728 (or 128MB). Larger disks or partitions—up to 512MB—are accommodated by increasing cluster size, stepwise, through 4096 to 8192 bytes. DOS 5.0 can handle even larger disks by dividing them into multiple partitions, each kept within the limits imposed by the combination of cluster and FAT entry size.

Compression

Disk compression, as used in DOS 6.0 and 6.2, imposes additional structure on the FAT system. To store the compressed file data, DOS creates a virtual disk drive and stores its data in a single file called the compressed volume file. This file has a structure that mimics an ordinary disk drive using a file allocation table.

DOS works with individual sectors instead of clusters when storing compressed data in the compressed volume file. DOS takes uncompressed data one cluster at a time and maps it in compressed form into sectors in the compressed volume file. To locate which sector belongs to each file, it used a special FAT called the MDFAT (Microsoft DoubleSpace FAT) that encodes the first sector used for storing a given cluster, the number of sectors required for coding the cluster, and the number of the cluster in the uncompressed volume that's stored in those sectors.

When DOS needs the data for a file, it first searches for the clusters it needs in the main disk FAT, then looks up the corresponding starting and length values from the MDFAT. With that information, DOS locates the data, uncompresses it, and passes it along to your applications.

To speed up operations when writing compressed data to disk, DOS uses a second kind of FAT in the compressed volume file. Called the BitFAT, this structure reports which sectors reserved in the compressed volume file hold active data and which are empty. The BitFAT uses only one bit for each sector as a flag to indicate whether a sector is occupied.

Because disk compression is imposed on the underlying operating system, its storage suffers the limitations imposed on by that operating system. In the case of DOS, individual uncompressed volumes can be no larger than 512MB, which limits the compressed volume file to that size. At nominal two-to-one compression, that constrains a compressed DOS volume to about one gigabyte.

High Performance File System

The High Performance File System used by OS/2 uses an entirely different storage scheme from DOS. The basic unit of storage used by the HPFS scheme is the sector. Sectors are identified by Relative Sector Numbers, each of which is 32-bits long—sufficient to encode 4,294,967,296 sectors or a total disk space of 2048 gigabytes. Sectors are numbered sequentially, starting with the first one in the HPFS partition. Files are allocated in multiples of single sectors; directories, however, are made from one or more blocks of four sectors.

Each file or directory on the disk is identified by its File NODE, which stores descriptive data about the file or directory. This information includes file attributes, creation date, modification dates, access dates, sizes, and a pointer that indicate in which sector the data in the file is stored. Each File NODE is one sector (512 bytes) long. Up to 254 bytes of the File NODE of a disk file store an extended file name, which can include upper and lowercase characters, some punctuation (for example, periods), and spaces.

As with a DOS file system, an HPFS disk organizes its storage from a root directory. In an HPFS system, however, the root directory does not have a fixed location or size. Instead, the root directory is identified by reference to the disk Super Block, which is a special sector that is always kept as the sixteenth sector from the beginning of the HPFS partition. The twelfth and thirteenth bytes—that is, at an offset of 0C(Hex) from the start of the block—of the Super Block points to the location of the root direcotry File NODE. Free space on the disk is identified by a bit-mapped table.

As with other FNODEs, a pointer in the root directory FNODE stores the location of the first block of four sectors assigned to the root directory. The root directory is identical to the other directories in the HPFS hierarchy, and like them it can expand or shrink as the number of files it contains changes. If the root directory needs to expand beyond its initial four sectors, it splits into a tree-like structure. The File Node of the root directory then points to the base File Node of the tree, and each pointer in the tree points to one directory entry and possibly a pointer to another directory node that may in turn point to entries whose names are sorted before the pointer entry. This structure provides a quick path for finding a particular entry, along with a simple method of scanning all entries.

The HPFS shares with DOS the capability to accommodate any length file (that will fit in the partition, of course) by assigning multiple allocation units (sectors in the case of the HPFS) that need not be contiguous. The HPFS, however, pre-allocates sectors to a file at the time it is opened, so a file may be assigned sectors that do not contain active data. The File Node of the file maintains an accurate total of the sectors that are actually used for storing information. This pre-allocation scheme helps prevent files from becoming fragmented. Normally, the block of sectors assigned to a file will be contiguous, and the file will not become fragmented until all the contiguous sectors have been used up.

Two types of sectors are used to track the sectors assigned a given file. For files that have few fragments, the File Node maintains a list of all the Relative Sector Numbers of the first sector in a block of sectors used by the file as well as the total number of sectors in the file before those of each block. To capture all the data in a file, OS/2 finds the Relative Sector Number of the first block of sectors used by the file and the total number of sectors in the block. It then checks the next Relative Sector Number and keeps counting with a running total of sectors in the file.

If a file has many fragments, it uses a tree-style table of pointers to indicate the location of each block of sectors. The entry in the file's File Node table then stores pointers to the sectors, which themselves store pointer, to the data. Each of these sectors identifies itself as to whether it points to data, or more pointers, with a special flag.

Besides its huge capacity, the HPFS has significant advantages when dealing with large hierarchies of directories, directories containing large numbers of files, and large files. Although both the HPFS and DOS use tree-structured directory systems, the directories in the HPFS are not arranged like a tree. Each directory is stored in a tree-like structure that, coupled with the presorting of entries automatically performed by the HPFS, allows faster searches of large directories. The HPFS also arranges directories on the disk to reduce the time required to access them—instead of starting at the edge of the disk, they fan out from the center.

Chapter 23
Floppy Disks

The floppy disk is the premiere data-exchange medium for PCs and the most popular backup system. Except for a few notebook computers, all PCs come with at least one floppy disk drive as standard equipment. Although floppy disk drives come in a variety of sizes and capacities (disks measure from 2 1/2 to 8 inches in diameter and store from 160K up to 2.88M each), all work in essentially the same way.

Since the first PC booted up, the floppy disk has been a blessing and a curse, subject of the same old saw usually reserved for kids, spouses, and governments—"You can't live with them, and you can't live without them."

You can't live without floppy disks because they provide the one universal means of information interchange, data storage, and file archiving used by PCs. They're convenient—you can stuff half a dozen 3 1/2-inch floppy disks into a shirt pocket—and easy to use. Slide a disk into a slot, press a button or close a door, and you've got another megabyte or so online.

But most people have a hard time living with floppy disks because of their frustration factor. Floppy disks are simply slow and small. No matter how much a floppy disk holds, it will be a few kilobytes shy of what you need. Moreover, floppy disks are plagued by problems. Subtle magnetic differences between disks often have no apparent effect until months after you've trusted your important data to a disk that can no longer be read. A profusion of standards means you need to carefully match disks to drives, drive to controllers, and the whole kaboodle to DOS. You never seem to have the right drive to match the disk that came in the box of software—or enough space for all the drives you need to match the proliferating floppy disk standards. Indeed, floppies are like taxes—something that everyone lives with and no one likes.

The floppy disk itself is only part of a system. Just as a nail is worthless in the abstract (without the hammer to drive it in place and the arm to swing the hammer), so is a floppy disk, unless you have all the other parts of the system. These include the floppy disks themselves, called the media, the floppy disk drive mechanism, the floppy disk drive controller, and the disk operating system software. All four elements are essential for the proper (and useful) operation of the system.

Media

The floppy disk provides a recording medium that has several positive qualities. The flat disk surface allows an approximation of random access. As with hard disks, data is arranged in tracks and sectors. The disk rotates the sectors under a read/write head, which travels radially across the disk to mark off tracks. More important, the floppy disk is a removable medium. You can shuffle dozens of floppies in and out of drives to extend your storage capacity. The floppy disk in the drive provides online storage. Off-line, you can keep as many floppy disks as you want.

The term floppy disk is one of those amazingly descriptive terms that abound in this age of genericisms. Inside its protective shell, the floppy disk medium is both floppy, (flexible), and a wide, flat disk. The disks are stamped out from wide rolls of the magnetic medium like cutting cookies from dough.

The wide rolls look like hyperpituitary audio or video tape, and that's no coincidence. Its composition is the same as for recording tape—a polyester substrate on which a magnetic oxide is bound. Unlike tape, however, all floppy disks are coated with magnetic material on both sides. The substrate is thicker than tape, too, about three mils.

Single-Sided Disks

Even though all floppy disks have an oxide coating on both sides, many disks are sold as single-sided. Rather than restricting the coating to one side, the manufacturer of single-sided floppy disks restricts its testing to one side. Only one side of a single-sided disk is certified for recording. That is, the manufacturer of the disk only guarantees that one side works properly. By convention, the bottom surface of the disk is used in single-sided floppy disk drives.

The actual testing of the floppy disk is one of the most costly parts of the manufacturing process. Testing two sides takes more time and inevitably results in more rejected disks. Two sides simply provide more space in which problems can occur. Both single-sided and double-sided floppy disks may be made from exactly the same batch of magnetic medium.

Many people cut the price they pay for floppy disks by substituting their own testing (during the floppy disk format process) for that ordinarily performed by the manufacturer. They buy single-sided disks and format them as double-sided. This process shifts the cost of the rejected disks (which still should be usable as single-sided media if you want to hand a copy of one of your data files to a friend, for example) from manufacturer to user.

Disk makers will tell you that their testing is more thorough and critical than what you can accomplish with your disk drives, and they are right. But your application may not be crucial enough to require the absolute (or nearly so) certainty of factory testing.

High-Density Disks

Not all magnetic media are the same. Different manufacturers have their own secret formula for the right magnetic coating to spread on the disk. One of the differences is the size of magnetic particles that actually remember the data. So-called high-density disks use a magnetic medium with a notably finer grain, allowing the disk to pack more information into a smaller space. These floppy disks have higher coercivities than normal density floppies.

All floppy disk drives use MFM recording that produces double-density recording. Both normal and high-density disks, therefore, are double-density, even though many manufacturers reserve the double-density term for lower capacity 5 1/4-inch floppy disks. Some computers used floppies termed quad-density with capacities in between those of normal and high-density floppies (720K on a 5 1/4-inch disk), but this format was never adopted as an IBM or DOS standard.

You often can format a normal density disk as if it were a high-density floppy, particularly with 5 1/4-inch disks because most floppy disk drives of that size cannot tell the difference between the media. Although you will sometimes get a large number of errors, many normal density floppy disks format just fine at high density. Only with the passing of time does the difference in coercivities take its toll. As these wrongly formatted disks age, they develop read errors much more quickly than properly formatted disks. Consequently, your seemingly secure storage becomes unreliable. Lose enough files (and one should be enough) and you will not want to experiment in such short-sighted penny-savings.

Extra-High Density Disks

The latest incarnation of the floppy disk pushes the storage capacity of a single disk to a new high, 4M each, about 2.88M with standard DOS formatting. Although the same size and shape as their predecessor normal and high-density floppy disks, these extra-high-density floppy disks use an entirely different magnetic material (barium-ferrite) with a substantially higher coercivity than even high-density disks. Moreover, the magnetic particles of this medium are aligned vertically (perpendicular to the disk surface) rather than laterally like other floppy disks. Consequently, extra-high density floppy disks are so different that they require a new kind of drive mechanism. Normal and high-density floppy disks cannot be used for extra-high density recording (although the extra-high density drives are backwardly compatible with older media used at the rated capacity of each medium).

Disk Sizes

Floppy disks have been made in sizes from 12 inches down to 2 inches with untold variety between. Only three of these have acquired any degree of acceptance in the PC community: 8-inch, 5 1/4-inch, and 3 1/2-inch diameters. Disks with a 2 1/2-inch diameter were used for a brief period by one notebook computer. The numbers describe the diameter of the disk coated with magnetic medium itself. All disks are covered with a plastic sheath or shell that extends their dimensions.

The biggest floppies came first. Introduced in 1971, the 8-inch floppy disk had become a standard among small computer systems before the first IBM PC was introduced. These large floppies had a number of features going for them. They were compact (at least compared to the ream of paper that could hold the same amount of information), convenient, and standardized.

Above all, these disks were inexpensive to produce and reliable enough to depend on. From the computer hobbyists' standpoint, their random access capability made them a godsend for good performance, at least when compared to the only affordable alternative, the cassette tape.

By the time IBM introduced its first PC, other computer makers had moved to the 5 1/4-inch floppy, a size that was introduced in 1976. IBM simply followed the trend and adopted the size. Because these were smaller than the older 8-inch variety, these 5 1/4-inch floppies were called diskettes by some people. The name later spread to even smaller sizes.

When the PC rolled out, each computer manufacturer had its own data storage format (and capacity) for the small disks. More than 50 data formats were used by various manufacturers at one time or another. The prestige of the IBM name and the success of PC sales made the IBM format the first true standard for 5 1/4-inch floppy disks.

The primary advantage of the 5 1/4-inch floppy was its compact size. It made desktop computers possible. On the downside, the smaller size meant smaller capacities. The first IBM-standard 5 1/4-inch floppy disks stored only 160K compared to the megabyte capacity of the 8-inch disk.

Portable laptop computers forced the issue of still smaller disks on the world even before the introduction of the PS/2 series made them standard across the IBM product line. Besides being compact, the 3 1/2-inch floppy medium also boasts more storage capacity (owing to oxide advances and a precision design) and greater ruggedness (because of the tough plastic shell).

5 1/4-Inch Floppies

The 5 1/4-inch disk is a sandwich in which the bologna is the disk itself. Appropriately named, the disk is 5 1/4 inches across; the shell it fits in extends to a full 5 1/2 inches square. The layout of a 5 1/4-inch floppy disk is shown in figure 23.1.

The shell is folded from a tough, flexible plastic and sonically welded together. Inside the shell is a layer of nonwoven cloth, the liner, that serves to reduce the friction of the disk spinning against the shell and to sweep contaminants off the disk.

The large hole in the center of the shell allows the drive hub of the disk drive to fit through. The hole cut out in the outer shell of the disk enables the drive mechanism to clamp onto the disk and spin it without slippage. The liberal lateral and longitudinal play of the disk in its shell allows it to be precisely centered on the hub.

The hub clamp is shaped like a truncated cone. The narrower portion slips into the hub hole of the disk and as it is forced down against the drive hub itself to clamp the disk, its increasing diameter forces the disk into the proper position. The clamp holds the disk against the hub by pressing down against a narrow (about 1/16th inch) circle of disk around the hub hole.

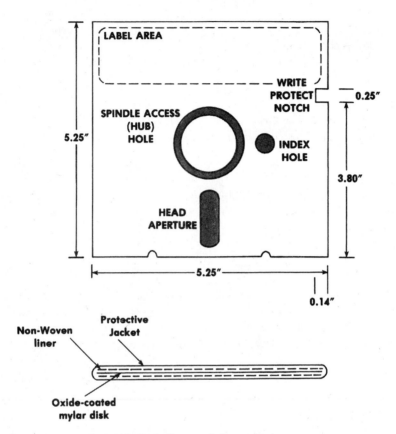

FIGURE 23.1. Layout of a 5 1/4-inch floppy disk.

This area of the disk is the most prone to wear and damage. Centering can warp and tear it; the disk spinning before clamping can wear at it. To forestall damage, many disks are equipped with protective hub rings that reinforce this vital center area of the disk. Some disks have rings on both sides; other disks have a ring on one side only (which should be on the bottom, where the most wear takes place). Some disks (primarily high-density floppies) don't have any rings. The hub rings are one more thing to get out of alignment on the disk. The tighter tolerances of high-density recording make alignments more critical.

Index Hole

A smaller hole in the floppy shell not far from the hub hole is designed to allow mechanical indexing of the disk. If you rotate a 5 1/4-inch disk inside its shell (spread your fingers inside the hub hole to rotate it without touching the magnetic surface), eventually you can make a small hole in the disk line up with the one in the disk shell. This is the index hole.

The original concept behind the index hole was that a light shining against the disk could detect the hole and thus precisely determine the radial position of the disk. Detection of the hole provided an absolute marker of where the disk was in its rotation.

Some disks had multiple holes. Some floppy disk drives used these holes to mark the beginning of each sector of storage. Because of the absolute marking method that was fixed by the disk hardware itself, these floppy disks were called hard-sectored.

The floppy disk drives used in ordinary PCs don't use the hole in the floppy for any purpose whatsoever. It's just an artifact from previous designs. PC floppy disk drives mark off their sectors magnetically. Because the position of each sector can be changed by software—the operating system that controls the drive—such floppy disks are said to be soft-sectored.

Ignoring holes is a lot easier than making do without them, so disk drives based on soft-sectoring can use disks designed for hard- or soft-sectoring. Systems designed for hard-sectoring cannot use soft-sectored disks, however. If you have such a machine left over from the dark ages of desktop computing, you might want to think about hoarding floppies—if you can find a source of supply.

Sector Count

The actual format of data on soft-sectored floppy disks varies under the control of the software that you use. IBM's original DOS 1.0 knew only one floppy disk format that put 40 tracks on one side of a 5 1/4-inch floppy disk only, each track divided into eight sectors. The total capacity of such a disk was 160K. When double-sided disk drives and a new version of DOS became available, the capacity of each disk doubled.

DOS 2.0 brought additional formats. The operating system was adjusted to put nine sectors on each of 40 tracks. This version of DOS was backwardly compatible with the earlier versions and would let any double-sided drive read, write, or format disks with one or two sides and eight or nine sectors per track.

The high-density disks introduced with the AT and DOS 3.0 gained their extra storage space by increasing the density of data in both directions. Under the new DOS with high-density floppy disks and matching drives, 80 tracks were laid on each side of the disk with 15 sectors per track.

The 5 1/4-inch, high-density drive also rotates at 360 RPM, which is unlike the double-density drive, which rotates at 300 RPM. To lay down the bits on a diskette surface in a compatible manner with double-density format, the data rate is increased from 250 KBS to 300 KBS.

The extra-high-density magnetic medium has not been used for 5 1/4-inch floppies.

Track Width

To achieve that greater number of tracks, the read/write head of high-density floppy disk drives was made narrower. The result of this change is a backward incompatibility in writing and formatting double-density disks. Although a high-density drive can read, write, and format any

IBM 5 1/4-inch floppy disk format, the disks it makes may not be readable on a double-density drive. The narrow head doesn't fill the entire track with magnetic data, and whatever magnetic fields are left outside the range of the narrow head may confuse the wider head of a double-density drive (see fig. 23.2).

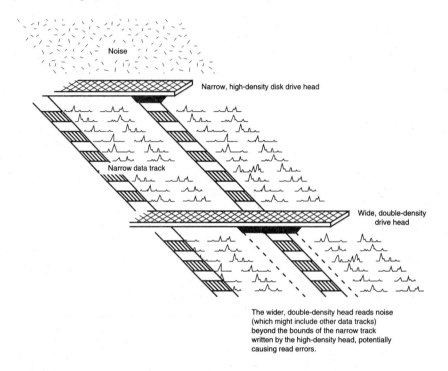

FIGURE 23.2. Double- versus high-density floppy disk heads.

In general, if you format a double-density disk in a double-density drive, the data that a high-density drive puts on that disk also will be readable by the double-density drive. If, however, you write anything on a disk with a double-density drive and write over it using a high-density drive, that disk likely will be unreadable by a double-density drive (although the high-density drive may have no trouble reading back what it has written).

Head Access Aperture

The large oval hole or slot—it's shaped sort of like an elongated racetrack—in both sides of the disk shell enables the read/write head(s) of the floppy disk drive to contact the disk surface. Two rules govern this slot, termed the head access aperture: the end of the disk closest to this hole goes into the disk drive first, and never touches the disk surface itself, which can be seen through this hole. Those two rules are about all you need to know to operate a floppy disk drive successfully.

Write-Protect Notch

The shell surrounding a 5 1/4-inch disk is generally square, except for a notch near one corner. Called the write-protect notch, this cutout is sensed by a switch inside the disk drive. If the slot is found, then you have write access to the disk, enabling you to read, write, or format the disk. If the notch is covered with a write-protect tab or a piece of tape, the disk drive sensor will not find it. The drive then reports to your computer that the disk is write-protected, and you will not be able to write to or format the disk.

Eight-inch disks also have write-protect notches, but they work just the opposite. The absence of a notch indicates to the drive that you can write on the disk. Uncovering the notch write protects the disk.

The scheme used by 5 1/4-inch disks has several advantages. If you insert a disk upside down, the write-protect notch is in the wrong place, and the drive will not be able to find it. It effectively prevents you from trying to write to an upside down disk, possibly destroying valuable data. Special disks without notches can be made that can never be written to (disk-duplicating machinery does not have to obey the notch rule). With these special notchless disks, distribution copies of software can be protected from accidental erasures or alterations.

You cannot override the physical write-protection afforded by the notch through software. Even though you may get the message `Abort, Retry, Ignore?` (or, with newer versions of DOS, `Abort, Retry, Fail?`) after a write-protect error, telling the system to Ignore will not override the protection. You can, however, remove the write-protect tab or carefully cut the disk shell to make your own notch.

If you like to live dangerously, you also can cut the wire from the switch that senses the write-protect notch in the disk drive. Shortly thereafter, when you make your first mistake and destroy your only copy of a program or data file, you'll discover how valuable hardware write protection can be.

3 1/2-Inch Floppies

Portable computers and downsized machines like Apple's Macintosh drove the need for still smaller floppy disks. A variety of abortive attempts, including a miniaturized 5 1/4-inch system that had two inches of diameter lopped off, finally led to the near-universal acceptance of the demonstrably superior 3 1/2-inch system originally promulgated by Sony. In their favor, 3 1/2-inch disks are convenient critters, exactly shirt pocket size, and they are tough and reliable enough to be tossed around with impunity. The layout of a 3 1/2-inch floppy disk is shown in figure 23.3.

Shell

The 3 1/2-inch system embodies several improvements over the veteran 5 1/4-inch design. Most notable is its hard shell, tough and only slightly flexible. The hard shell protects the fragile disk while allowing you the freedom of carrying out such crimes, forbidden with 5 1/4-inch disks, of writing on an already-applied disk label with a ballpoint pen. Unlike the bigger disks, which leave a large head-access swath of the disk vulnerable to dirt, dust, and fingerprints, the 3 1/2-inch design covers the vulnerable access area with a spring-loaded sliding metal shield or shutter. It opens automatically only when you insert a disk into a drive. This protection means that 3 1/2-inch disks don't need the protection of a sleeve or shuck.

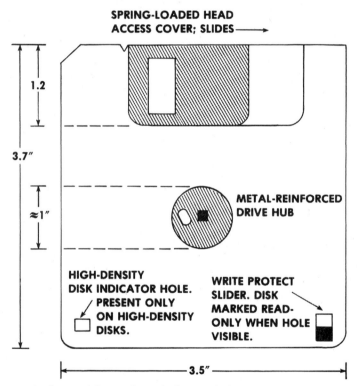

FIGURE 23.3. The layout of a 3 1/2-inch floppy disk.

Insertion Key

Unlike 5 1/4-inch disks, the 3 1/2-inch disk is designed to prevent improper insertion. One corner is truncated so that a disk only fully engages in a disk drive when correctly oriented.

Write-Protection

Instead of a write-protect notch and tap, the 3 1/2-inch design uses a hole and a plastic slider. When the slider blocks the hole, you can read, write, and format the disk. When the slider is moved back to reveal the hole (or is entirely absent, as it is on many software distribution disks) the disk is write-protected.

Tracks

The storage capacity of the 3 1/2-inch disk proves that less can be more. Although less than half the surface area of a 5 1/4-inch disk is available for recording on a 3 1/2-inch disk, the standard format of the little disk can actually pack in more data—up to 720K at normal density, and 1.44M at high density. The larger capacities result from the use of a more finely grained medium with better magnetic properties and greater precision. The old problem of disk centering is reduced by the 3 1/2-inch disk's metal hub, which allows easier, more positive mechanical action with less chance of damage or wear. Instead of 48 or 96 tracks per inch, the 3 1/2-inch design squeezes in 135 tracks per inch. Because of the cramped quarters, however, only 80 of these narrow tracks fit on a disk.

Sector Count

The lower capacity IBM 3 1/2-inch drives, used in the IBM Convertible and some compatible computers, use the same physical and logical layout as ordinary double-sided, double-density disks—512-byte sectors arranged nine per track—and increase capacity solely by doubling the number of tracks per disk side (up to 80 tracks) to attain 720K per disk. The high density disks used by the PS/2 line and nearly all more recent compatibles double the density of the data in each track (to fit 18 sectors per track) to achieve their 1.44M limit. Single-sided 3 1/2-inch disks are not supported in the IBM universe.

Your disk drive can tell whether you've put a normal density or high density floppy disk into it. An extra high density notch marks the disks with greater capacity.

Extra-high density disks maintain the same number of tracks as their predecessors—80—at the same 135-track-per-inch spacing as high-density floppies but double the number of sectors per track, from 18 to 36. The track width is maintained at the same value as older floppy disk styles. This arrangement allows extra-high density floppy disk drives to read and write both 720K and 1.44M floppies without compatibility problems.

Aberrations

The inexorable march from floppies 8 inches across to today's 3 1/2-inch disks has left several bodies along the wayside. Well-meaning engineers created designs that seemed like good ideas at the time, but earned their demises with their own shortcomings. You may encounter references to these technologies, so for the sake of completeness, here's a tip of the hat for floppies best left forgotten.

Flippy Disks

A nearly forgotten word in the PC lexicon is the flippy disk. This odd beast was a 5 1/4-inch floppy that could be flipped over in a single-sided disk drive so that you could use the other side of the disk. Because the write-protect notch was the only thing that prevented the disk from being flipped, innovative entrepreneurs cut an extra notch in the other side of the disk shell. With that expedient, you could slide the flippy into your floppy either side up.

Flippies were useful only in PCs with single-sided disk drives—which means no modern PC. Worse, the flippy design had a fatal flaw—when a disk is flipped over, it spins in the opposite direction, dislodging the dirt that its liner has swept up, potentially shortening the life of the magnetic coating on the disk.

2 1/2-Inch Floppies

In 1989, Zenith Data System introduced a novel and short-lived 2 1/2-inch floppy disk system patterned after the double-density 3 1/2-inch drive system. The arrangement of tracks and sectors on the drive was the same for the two media, giving both a capacity of 720K, but the 2 1/2-inch drives obviously packed information more tightly. The reason for the smaller size was simply to make floppy disk drives fit into the tiniest possible package—Zenith believing that no one would want a notebook computer that could not use removable media. Unfortunately for Zenith, no one wanted to use a nonstandard floppy disk drive that lacked the primary reason why people insisted on having floppies in their PCs—moving data to the desktop computers by exchanging disks. Although you could back up your files to one of the tiny floppies, you had to connect the Zenith notebook computer to your desktop machine to actually transfer data. After the Zenith experience, no other manufacturer opted for 2 1/2-inch drives.

Floppy Disk Drives

As computer equipment goes, floppy disk drives are simple devices. The essential components are a spindle motor, which spins the disk, and a stepper-motor that drives a metal band in and out to position the read/write heads, an assembly that is collectively called the head actuator. A manual mechanism is provided for lowering a hub clamp to center, locking the disk in place, and pressing the heads against the surface of the disk. In all except the single-sided drives of the original PC, two heads are used that pinch together around the disk to read and write from either side of the medium. The tracks on either side of the disk are interleaved so that one head is slightly offset above the other.

Speed Control

All of the electronics packed onto the one or more circuit boards attached to the drive unit merely control those simple disk drive operations. A servo system keeps the disk spinning at the correct speed. Usually an optical sensor looks at a stroboscopic pattern of black dots on a white disk on the spindle assembly. The electronics count the dots that pass the sensor in a given period to determine the speed at which it turns, adjusting it as necessary. Some drives use similar sensors based on magnetism rather than optics, but they work in essentially the same way—counting the number of passing magnetic pulses in a given period to determine the speed of the drive.

Head Control

Other electronics control the radial position of the head assembly to the disk. The stepper motor that moves the head reacts to voltage pulses by moving one or more discrete steps a few degrees (hence the descriptive name of this type of motor). Signals from the floppy disk controller card in the host computer tell the disk drive which track of the disk to move its head to. The electronics on the drive then send the appropriate number of pulses to the stepper motor to move the head to the designated track.

The basic floppy disk mechanism receives no feedback on where the head is on the disk. It merely assumes that it gets to the right place because of the number of steps the actuator makes. Although the drive does its best to remember the position of the head, hard reality can leave the head other than in its expected place. You can reach in and manually jostle the head mechanism, for example. Or you might switch off your computer with the head halfway across the disk. Once the power is off, all the circuitry forgets, and the location of the head becomes an unknown.

Note that the stepper motors in most double-density floppy disk drives sold today are capable of tracing out all 40 tracks used by the IBM floppy disk format. Some earlier computers did not require all 40 tracks. Consequently, some drives made for these computers—usually those drives closed out at prices that seem too good to be true—may not have a full 40-track range. Caveat emptor!

Head Indexing

So that the head can be put in the right place with assurance, the drive resorts to a process called indexing; it moves the head as far as it will go toward the edge of the disk. Once the head reaches this index position, it can travel no farther, no matter how hard the actuator tries to move it. The drive electronics make sure that the actuator moves the head a sufficient number of steps (a number greater than the width of the disk) to assure that the head will stop at the index position. After the head has reached the index position, the control electronics can move it a given number of actuator steps and know exactly where on the radius of the disk the head is located.

Extra-High Density Drives

To cope with the extra-high density recording medium, extra-high density floppy disk drives required a radical innovation—an extra head for each surface. The extra-high density medium is so difficult to work with that it requires a separate erase head. The extra head is fixed to the same actuator as the read/write head and moves with it track to track. When writing data, the erase head prepares the area for the read/write head by aligning the disk flux transitions in the same direction. The read/write heads then can change their orientation to record data.

DOS Requirements

Functionally, there's no difference between drive heights. Full-, half-, third-, and quarter-height drives can all read and write the same floppy disks (providing the disks are the proper diameter, of course). The only potential incompatibility may appear when archeologists unearth early PCs. Earlier versions of DOS require drive timing which is so critical that only full-height drives were thought to be able to work reliably. When half-height 5.25-inch drives were introduced by IBM in 1984, IBM warned against their use with DOS 2.0 or earlier. Because of the slower mechanism of the smaller drives, IBM increased a few time constants in DOS 2.1, which was made available at the same time as the thinner drives.

Not only do DOS 3.0 and later versions take into account the requirements of half-height drives, these later versions of DOS also support high density (1.2M) 5 1/4-inch drives. You must use DOS 3.0 or later with 1.2M floppy disks. The first DOS version to support 3 1/2-inch drives was DOS 3.2, which supports only the 720K drives used by the PC Convertible. The high-density 3 1/2-inch drives with 1.44M capacity used by the PS/2 series require either DOS 3.3 (or later) or OS/2. Extra-high density floppy disk drives require DOS 5.0 or later.

Controllers

Although operating a floppy disk drive seems simple, it's actually a complex operation with many levels of control. When you press the Save button while running an application program, your button press does not connect directly to the drive. Instead, the keystroke is detected by your computer's hardware and recognized by its BIOS. The BIOS, in turn, sends the appropriate electronic code to your application program. The program then probably makes one or more requests to DOS to write something to disk. DOS sends instructions to the BIOS, and the BIOS sends codes to ports on the disk control hardware. Finally, this hardware tells the drive where to move its head and what to do once the head gets where it's going.

The penultimate piece of hardware in this chain is the floppy disk controller. It has two purposes in operating your system's floppy disks. One is to translate the logical commands from your computer system, which usually are generated by the BIOS, into the exact electrical signals that control the disk drive. The other function is to translate the stream of pulses generated by the floppy disk head into data in the form that your computer can deal with it.

The best way to understand the operation of the floppy disk controller is to examine the signals that control the floppy disk drive and those that the drive sends to its computer host.

Two signals, Drive Select A and Drive Select B are used to individually select the first or second drive, A or B. (In four-drive systems, the signals for A in the second cable control drive C, and those of B control D.) If the signal assigned to a particular drive is not present, all the other input and output circuits of the drive are deactivated, except for those that control the drive motor. In this way, two drives can share the bulk of the wires in the controller cable without interference. However, this control scheme also means that only one drive in a pair can be active at a time. You can write to drive B at the same time you read from drive A. That's why you must transfer the data held on a disk (or file) from one drive into memory before you can copy it to another drive.

One wire is used for each drive to switch its spindle motor on and off. These are called, individually, drive select A and drive select B . Although it is possible to make both motors spin simultaneously, rules laid down by IBM admonish against activating these two lines to make both floppy disk drive motors run at the same time (this saves power in the severely constrained PC system and is a moot issue in the single-drive XT system). Of course, the two drives in your PC may run simultaneously for brief periods due to a delay built into most drives that keeps their motors running for a few seconds after the Motor Enable signal stops.

Two signals control the head position. One, step pulse, merely tells the stepper motor on the drive to move one step (that's exactly one track) toward or away from the center of the disk. The direction signal controls which way the pulses move the head. If this signal is active, the head moves toward the center.

To determine which of the two sides of a double-sided disk to read, one signal, called write select, is used. When this signal is active, it tells the disk drive to use the upper head. When no signal is present, the disk drive automatically uses the default (lower) head.

Writing to disk requires two signals. Write data comprises the information that's actually to be written magnetically onto the disk. It consists of a series of pulses corresponding exactly to the flux transitions that are to be made on the disk. The read/write head merely echoes these signals magnetically. As a fail-safe to preclude the possibility of accidentally writing over valuable data, a second signal called write enable is used. No write current is sent to the read/write head unless this signal is active.

The data rate of the data signal varies with the disk drive type. A normal density floppy accepts and sends data at a rate of 250 kilobits per second. A high-density drive operates at 500 kilobits per second. An extra-high density drive operates at one megabit per second.

The controller receives four signals back from the floppy disk drive.

Two of these help the controller determine where the head is located. Track 0 indicates to the controller when the head is above the outermost track on the disk so the controller knows from where to start counting head-moving pulses. Index helps the drive determine the location of each bit on a disk track. One pulse is generated on the Index line for each revolution of the disk. The controller can time the distance between ensuing data pulses based on the reference provided by the Index signal.

The write protect signal is derived from the sensor that detects the existence or absence of a write-protect tab on a diskette. If a tab is present, this signal is active.

The read data signal comprises a series of electrical pulses that exactly matches the train of flux transition on the floppy disk. The data rates correspond to those used for writing to the disk.

In its control function, the floppy disk controller must convert the requests from the BIOS or direct hardware commands that are couched in terms of track and sector numbers into the pulses that move the head to the proper location on the disk. For the most efficient operation, the controller also must remember where the head is located, index the head as necessary, and report errors when they occur.

In its translation function, the floppy disk controller must make sense from the stream of unformatted pulses delivered from the drive. It first must find the beginning of each track from the Index pulse, then mark out each sector from the information embedded in the data stream. Once it identifies a requested sector, it then must read the information it contains and convert it from serial to parallel form so that it can be sent through the PC bus. In writing, the controller must first identify the proper sector to write to (which is a read operation) and then switch on the write current to put data into that sector before the next sector on the disk begins.

Most of the hard work of the controller is handled by a single integrated circuit, the 765 controller chip. (In contemporary PCs, the function of the 765 often is integrated inside chipsets.) The 765 works much like a microprocessor. It carries out certain operations in response to commands that it receives through registers connected to your computer's I/O ports.

This programmability makes the 765 and the PC-style floppy disk controller extremely versatile. None of the essential floppy disk drive parameters is cast in stone or the silicon on the controller. The numbers of heads, tracks, and sectors on a disk are set by loading numbers into the registers of the 765. Usually, the normal IBM operating values are loaded into the controller when you boot up your computer. You ordinarily don't have to worry about them after that.

Special software can reprogram your controller to make it read, write, and format floppy disks that differ from the PC standard. Two types of software perform this reprogramming. Copy-protection schemes may alter vital drive parameters by misnumbering sectors, adding extra sectors, or a similar operation which cannot be duplicated using normal PC parameters. Disk compatibility software alters the controller programming to make the floppy disk drives in your system act like those used by other computers such as those that use the CP/M operating system. Note, however, that although the PC system is flexible, it cannot handle all possibilities, such as Commodore or Apple disks. Those computers use entirely different drive control hardware that the 765 cannot mimic.

Controller Integration

PC makers have used three distinct styles of floppy disk controller—stand-alone, combined, and integrated. The original design used by IBM in the first PC was also adopted by the XT and Portable PC, and used a stand-alone floppy disk controller. The PCjr used a separate but functionally identical design. The floppy disk controller of the AT and XT Model 286 were combined with the hard disk controller. All PC/2 models have their floppy disk controllers built into their system board circuitry. The extra-density controllers of more recent PS/2s are similarly integrated. Other computer manufacturers have adopted all of these designs.

Format Compatibility

In theory, any PC should be able to use standard double-density, double-sided floppy disk drives. (Although IBM's PS/2s can operate normal density 5 1/4-inch floppy drives, finding matching drives for these machines can be difficult.) Normal-density floppies are thus the only truly universal storage system across the entire PC industry, making their media the one format with the widest range of compatibilities.

High-density 5 1/4-inch drives with 1.2M data capacity are, in general, supported only by PC hardware that post-dates IBM's model AT. The BIOSs of earlier machines (such as IBM's PCs, XTs, Portable PCs, and the PCjr) are unable to handle the larger number of tracks used by these drives. Similarly, 3 1/2-inch drives are not supported by the hardware machines earlier than the PS/2 series because that's when IBM introduced its 3.5-inch implementation, which the rest of the PC industry subsequently followed.

The primary culprit in floppy disk incompatibility with both newer and older generations is generally your system BIOS. The BIOS stores all the instructions your computer knows on its own for matching the 765 to different floppy disk types. If your system BIOS lacks the instructions needed to make a 3 1/2-inch drive work, you cannot plug such a drive into your PC and expect it to play properly, for example.

Determining whether your PC is compatible with a given type of floppy disk drive can be as easy as checking your system's owner's manual or as difficult as trial-and-error experimentation. One place to start is with the date your system was made. Computers designed before the IBM AT was announced in August 1984 are likely to recognize only double-density (360K) 5 1/4-inch floppy disk drives because high-density 5 1/4-inch drives were not introduced until the first AT was. Systems designed before IBM introduced its ill-starred PC Convertible laptop computer are unlikely to use double-density 3 1/2-inch drives because—guess what—IBM introduced the 720K format with that machine. IBM began using high-density 3 1/2-inch drives with the introduction of its PS/2 series in 1987, although a few manufacturers anticipated this format.

If you don't know when your system was designed or introduced (most people don't), you're not out of luck. You can take a quick look at your PC's setup procedure—either the setup procedure you can select from the keyboard when your computer boots or the disk-based setup program that accompanied your computer when you bought it. Check the options that setup gives you for floppy disk drives.

The setup program used by most computers since the introduction of the AT includes a set of choices from which you select the style of floppy disk drive you have installed as drive A and B. Check what your choices are. If the style of floppy disk drive that you want to install is listed in setup, you're home free—your floppy disk upgrade will work with your PC after a simple mechanical installation job.

If your PC does not have a setup program, it was likely designed by the old school—in the days before the AT. Consequently, your system most likely knows only about double-density 5 1/4-inch floppy disk drives.

Laptop computers are an entirely different matter. Most laptop computer manufacturers recognize the problems of media incompatibility and allow for some means of connecting an external 5 1/4-inch floppy disk drive to their products. Most of these add-on drives attach to dedicated proprietary floppy disk ports on the laptop computer. These manufacturers offer their own products (typically expensive) for adding floppy disk drives.

The lack of direct support for a given floppy disk drive type by your PC does not mean that you're forever precluded from adding that variety of floppy disk drive. You just need to take a few extra steps to teach your PC how to handle the renegade drive.

You must use one of three strategies: adding driver software, upgrading your floppy disk controller along with the floppy disk drive, or altering the BIOS of your computer. The first is the universal approach, the least expensive, and the one that requires the least tinkering with the solid-state secrets of your PC. It's also the most limited.

Driver software supplements the code that's contained in your system BIOS with special instructions for handling the new type of floppy disk drive. The drivers load through your system's CONFIG.SYS file just like any other device driver would.

That's the first limitation of using driver software—your system has to boot up before the driver can be read. Consequently, driver software is not an adequate solution for your boot floppy, drive A. It's the classic catch-22—the system cannot boot from the floppy because it has to read the driver first, but to read the driver it first must boot the system.

Moreover, because the driver loads after DOS takes control of your PC, driver software is operating-system specific. You need a different driver for DOS than you will for OS/2 or Unix. In many cases, you may not be able to find driver software for operating systems other than DOS. If you're planning on moving up to a new operating system, you probably will not want to go the driver route.

Some software, such as some disk utilities and backup programs, takes direct hardware control of floppy disk drives, ignoring software drivers. These applications may not work on a floppy disk drive that uses a software driver. Worse, the software may try to work and spin the floppy disk drive into chaotic operation. This, in turn, may destroy the data on floppies you put into the drive.

Software drivers also add a petty irritation. Because DOS brings them to life after all other disk drives in your system have been initialized through your system's BIOS, they take on drive letter identifications further down the line than the last BIOS-based drive. So your new driver-based floppy will likely be recognized as drive D rather than drive B.

All told, software drivers are technically the least desirable way of matching a foreign floppy disk drive to a PC. Unfortunately, they are also the only universal method of doing so, and sometimes the only method permitted by a given PC. Apart from the perfect hardware match, driver software is also the least expensive means of matching a floppy to your PC.

Many floppy disk kits include a software driver to help you upgrade systems that need one. Note that this driver is used in addition to the DRIVER.SYS program that comes with recent versions of DOS. The driver that comes with the floppy disk drive tells your PC how to operate the floppy disk drive; DRIVER.SYS tells your system how to recognize that new floppy disk drive.

In many PCs, you can match an odd floppy disk drive by changing your floppy disk controller. Many—but far from all—modern floppy disk controllers come equipped with an add-on BIOS that adds the necessary instructions to your system's existing BIOS to allow it to control any standard floppy disk drive type. But if you want to add a new floppy disk controller with BIOS support to your PC, you have to be careful. Older controllers and the least expensive recent controllers do not have the necessary BIOS code built in.

To ensure that you get the BIOS you need, you have to ask when you order a particular controller whether it has its own BIOS. Better yet, check when you order a new floppy controller to be sure that it will allow you to use a specific floppy disk drive type with your PC.

Computers that have their floppy disk control circuitry built into their system boards require you to disable the system-board floppy circuitry before you add a new controller card. If you cannot disable the system-board floppy-disk control circuitry of your PC, you will not be able to add a new controller. Micro Channel PS/2s also foreclose on the possibility of controller-based BIOS upgrades because Micro Channel-based floppy controller cards are virtually impossible to find.

The most satisfying solution to the floppy incompatibility problem is adding a new BIOS to your PC so that all the needed floppy disk instructions are built into your computer. This change requires that you remove two (or four) large integrated circuit chips from the system board of your PC and replace the chips with new ones. That part of the job takes only a few minutes (after you open and disassemble your PC).

The more difficult part of the job is finding a BIOS upgrade that will work with your computer. Although several companies manufacture BIOSs, these companies aim their sales efforts at providing chips to computer makers. They don't ordinarily deal in single-piece quantities with individual end-users like you.

Moreover, unless a BIOS upgrade is available from the original maker of your PC, you have no guarantee that the new BIOS actually will work with your computer. In other words, you generally cannot buy a BIOS off the shelf. What you can do is contact the dealer who originally sold you your computer and ask if its manufacturer offers a BIOS upgrade. If such an upgrade is available, your dealer will be the best (and likely only) source of supply.

Drive and Cabling Configuration

The original IBM floppy system is the standard for nearly all floppy disk systems. It was designed so that you can install floppy disk drives with a minimum of thought.

Drive Select Jumpers

The cabling used in a floppy disk subsystem apparently presumes that a drive attached to it already knows whether it is supposed to be drive A or B in your system. However, for compatibility reasons, all floppy disk drives are created equal with a common design for all drive letters. So that a given floppy disk drive can assume the identity of A or B, drive manufacturers equipped their products with DIP switches or jumpers to select the appropriate appellation. Termed *drive select jumpers*, most floppy disk drives allow you to select one of four potential identities.

For reasons related to their functions—they essentially switch some of the connections delivered by the cable—drive select jumpers usually can be found on a drive near the edge connector onto which you attach the cable. Usually you will be faced with an array of jumpers or switches, probably either, each labeled with a not-too-meaningful combination of two or three letters and numbers. The drive select jumpers can be identified (when they are labeled) by their two-character prefix DS. From there, different disk-drive manufacturers go in two directions. Some start numbering the drive-select settings with one and count up to four; others start with one and venture only as far as three.

Drive Select Settings

In the IBM scheme of things, which of these settings applied to drive A or B—or even C or D—has no relevance. All floppy disk drives in an IBM-style computer are set to be the second drive in the system. A special twist to the floppy disk connecting cable sorts out the proper disk-drive identity.

To configure a floppy disk drive for installation in an IBM-style system, you should invariably set it as the second drive, paying no attention to whether it will be A or B. With drives in which the drive select jumpers are numbered starting with 0, all floppy disk drives should be set as 1. With drives in which the number of the drive select jumpers begins with 1, all drives should be set as 2.

Drive Cabling

The special twist that sorts out the drive identities is exactly that—a group of five conductors in the floppy disk cable are twisted in the run to one of its connectors. This twist reverses the drive-select and motor-control signals in the cable as well as rearranges some of the ground wires in the cable (which effectively makes no change. See figure 23.4.).

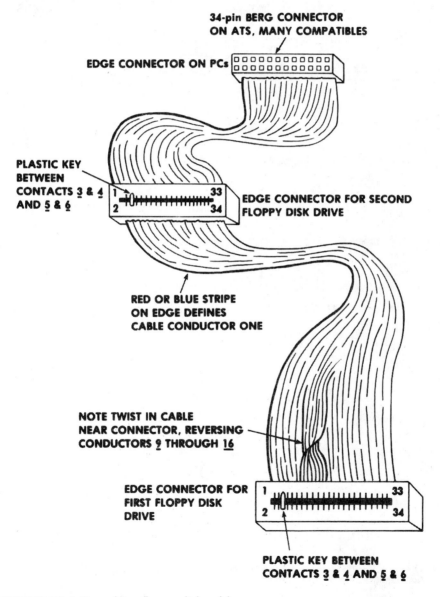

FIGURE 23.4. Two-drive floppy disk cable.

Because all drives are set up as the second drive, this reversal makes the drive attached to the cable after the twist the first drive, drive A. Drive A is attached to the connector at the end of the cable, the one where the wire twist takes place. Drive B is attached to the connector in the middle of the length of the cable. The third connector, at the end of the cable with no twist, goes to the floppy disk controller.

Single-Drive and Straight-Through Cables

With hard disk drives, you can use a straight-through cable (one without the twist near the last connectors) to operate a single disk drive by moving the drive-select jumper of the connected hard disk to the first drive position. This tactic will not work with floppy disk drives. The twisted part of the cable moves not only the drive-select conductor but also the motor-control conductor. You cannot, therefore, use a straight-through cable with a single floppy disk drive in your computer system.

If you make your own floppy disk cable to handle a single drive, you have to abide by the IBM drive-select numbering scheme. You have to make a twist in the conductors, as shown in figure 23.5.

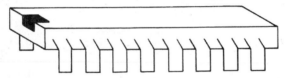

(can be black, blue, or opaque amber)

1. Dual in-line package; usually has eight *pairs* of "legs".

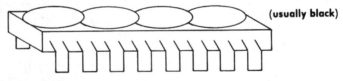

(usually black)

2. Sometimes the dual in-line package appears "lumpy".

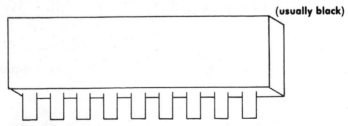

(usually black)

**3. Single in-line package generally has nine "legs".
Sometimes it, too, appears lumpy.**

FIGURE 23.5. Terminating resistors.

Terminating Resistor Networks

In the floppy disk system originally developed by IBM and used by compatible computer makers, there was but one physical difference between drives A and B. Drive A always had a terminating resistor network installed. Drive B always did not. In three or four floppy disk drive systems, drive C always had a terminating resistor. Drive D did not.

That simple rule proved more confusing than most people could deal with. Consequently, modern floppy disk drives often are equipped with a nonremovable terminating resistor pack. Years of experience had proven that an extra terminator in the floppy disk system had little effect on its operation. With the simple expedient of soldering down the terminator, drive manufacturers eliminated all the problems unskilled installers had with floppies and trimmed a few cents in cost by omitting a socket for the resistor network.

Purpose

The terminating resistor network absorbs the excess current that flows through the connection between the floppy disk controller and the drive electronics. The circuits are designed so that a specific current is expected to flow through them. The terminating resistor network forces the proper current to flow so that no excess is left in the system. Without the terminating resistor, the signal going to the floppy disk drive would be mismatched and may bounce back and forth through the circuitry before finally decaying, possibly resulting in errors. By absorbing the excess, the terminating resistor prevents those potential errors. The terminating resistor network is always located on the last drive that's physically connected to the cable because that's where the signal reflections would occur.

Two terminating resistors (for example, leaving the resistor network installed on both disk drives in your system) would in theory cause too much current to flow, and that might lead to the premature failure of the circuits themselves. It does reduce the signal voltage, but lower voltage is less of a problem than too much. That's why manufacturers soldered resistors in the drives rather than omitting them to avoid termination confusion.

Removable terminating resistors are typically rated at 2.2 kilohms (an ohm being the basic unit of electrical resistance; a kilohm being 1000 ohms). Nonremovable terminating resistors are nominally rated at 1 kilohm. Consequently, two drives with nonremovable terminating resistors have approximately the same value as a properly terminated system. If only one drive with a nonremovable resistor is installed in a PC—either alone or with a drive with a 2.2K terminating resistor pack installed—the mismatch is only half of what it would be by breaking the hard-and-fast rule. That's actually close enough to eliminate most problems. If you have a drive with a removable termination, you'll still want to abide by the rules because otherwise the terminating resistance can get too high or low.

Identification

Identifying terminating resistor packs is quite easy. They usually take on one of two forms— either housed in a single in-line package or, more usually, in a dual in-line package that looks like an ordinary integrated circuit (except that it's sometimes blue or amber instead of black and may be shinier). Single in-line packages usually resemble small oblong blocks, about one inch long, 1/8 inch thick, and 1/2 inch high. Nine separate leads, at 1/10-inch spacing, project from the bottom of the network and into a socket or directly through the printed circuit board of the floppy disk drive electronics. Nonremovable terminations usually take the single in-line form.

In most contemporary floppy disk drives, the termination resistor stands out because it's the only socket-mounted device on the circuit board (refer to fig. 23.5).

Location

The terminating resistor network in most floppy disk drives is found adjacent to the edge connector to which you plug in the drive. Because the network must be removed from a generic drive in roughly half its installations, the resistor network is generally accessible near the rear edge of the printed circuit board holding the electronics of the drive. Usually it is near or adjacent to the drive select jumpers or switches.

Removal

For the most part, when you need to make a floppy disk drive with a removable termination either drive B or drive D, you only need pull out the resistor. To remove the common SIP networks, you just grip them with your fingers or pliers and pull them firmly away from their sockets. If you use pliers, grip only tightly enough that the resistor pack doesn't slip out of the plier's jaws. If you squeeze too hard, you can crush the resistor pack. You can pull out DIP networks most easily with a special tool—a chip puller designed for popping out integrated circuits. Or you can pry a DIP network with a small screwdriver, easing up one end first and then the other. If you try to pry out the resistor with one push, you're likely to bend the leads on the terminator pack, making it difficult to plug back in (should you ever need to).

Floptical

Just as magneto-optical hard disk drives interbreed two technologies, so does the floptical disk drive. Where MO drives seek to pry marketshare away from traditional hard disks, floptical diskettes aim at the old-fashioned floppy disk.

The primary lure of the floptical diskette is capacity. Where conventional 3 1/2-inch floppy disks now hold up to about 2.88M, the current implementations of floptical drives store 21M of formatted data (25M unformatted) in exactly the same size package.

Not only are floptical diskettes identical in size to 3 1/2-inch floppies, the old-technology floppies will slide into a floptical disk drive. The drives are backwardly compatible with 1.44M and 720K (but not 2.88M) floppy disks. The new drives read and write conventional magnetic diskettes.

This compatibility is possible because floptical technology is a magnetic recording process. Your data never spurts through a light beam or laser. By using special high-density recording media and special heads, the storage density is increased above that of floppy disks.

Medium

The principal problem with ordinary floppy disks is entirely different from that faced by the high-capacity magnetic storage leader, the hard disk. Hard disks are limited in the density of data they can store by the distance the read/write head flies above the media. Floppies put their heads in contact with the drive, so they can in theory (and all else being equal) exceed the storage densities of hard disks.

The problem with floppies is that they are, well, floppy. Because the medium is not dimensionally stable—after all, floppies flop—reliably recovering data on narrow, closely spaced tracks is difficult if not impossible. The disk expands and contracts with temperature changes and deforms as it spins around inside its shell.

Floptical drives use an optical servo track to solve the problem. A special optical servomechanism keeps the magnetic read/write head in position to properly write and read the disk. The optical servo information is embedded in the disk during its manufacture and cannot be altered by the recording process. In fact, it cannot be erased by normal means. You can run a floptical disk under a bulk degausser and it will not lose its servo information.

Flopticals achieve their high storage capacity by increasing the track count compared to conventional floppy disks. Where standard 3 1/2-inch floppies have 80 tracks, flopticals have 755 tracks. Each of these tracks is formatted with 27 sectors, each of which holds the standard 512 bytes. This geometry yields exactly 10,437,120 bytes per side or a total disk capacity of 20,874,240 bytes. Floptical drives spin their disks at 720 revolutions per minute, a rate which enables them to read and transfer 165,888 bits per second.

The magnetic medium of a floptical disk is the same barium-ferrite material used in other modern storage systems. To achieve higher head-positioning accuracy to put more tracks on a disk, floptical disks are etched servo tracks on one side (the bottom). The circular servo tracks, spaced 20.4 microns apart, form a pattern of tiny regular indentations. The servo information can be individually etched with a high-power laser beam or mechanically stamped into the disk.

Interface

Floptical drives look much like ordinary 3 1/2-inch floppy disk drives. The chief difference is that flopticals have a laser built in to help follow the precise tracks on the disks. Disks slide into the drive the same as ordinary floppies. On the outside, only the capacity appears different.

Electrically, however, the floptical drive faces a problem. An ordinary 765 chip will not do, so the drive has its own, built-in control electronics. As a result, you cannot plug a flopical drive into an ordinary floppy disk controller.

Floptical drives use either of two interfaces: one proprietary, and one a variation of the SCSI standard. The proprietary interface (used by Iomega Corporation for its Floptical Subsystem) allows you to install the floptical drive by connecting a single cable as with any floppy disk drive. By selecting a jumper on the proprietary Iomega host adapter board, you can configure the floptical as drive A so that it can boot your system from it. Other floptical drives use the SCSI interface with all the attendant concerns of a SCSI connection. In addition, some require a special on-board SCSI BIOS that includes code to let your PC recognize the floptical as an ordinary floppy disk drive.

In either case, you will need additional software to use the floptical drive effectively. Existing versions of DOS do not know about the special requirements of floptical drives, so you need special formatting as well as disk copying and comparing utilities.

Disk Care

The rules governing the care of any size or type of floppy disks are all based on the prevention of damage. Two forces can impair the function of floppies: physical damage and magnetism.

Magnetic Enemies

Magnetic enemies are insidious. Invisible magnetic fields can alter or erase the data you have stored on your floppy disk. If the file allocation table of the disk is damaged, for example, you may never be able to recover information from your disk even though it's still written there.

Sources of potentially damaging magnetism abound in the office. Old-fashioned telephones, the kind your grandmother bought from the phone company when Ma Bell lost her monopoly, had actual ringing bells inside them that were operated by powerful electromagnets. Whenever one of these telephones rang, it set up a magnetic field that could erase disks that were near or under-neath the telephone. This telephone-bell magnetic field was not too strong, however, and keeping your disks a few inches from the phone would have been a sufficient safeguard.

Other common disk-damaging devices include magnetized scissors, those clever little paper-clip holders with ring magnets at the top to hold the clips in readiness, and even the motorized playthings found on some executives' desks. Even some monitors may exude magnetic fields from their power supplies or degaussing coils.

You can probably find a magnetic field seeping out of something in your office if you look diligently enough. Maintaining just a slight separation between potential degausses and your floppy disks is a wise practice.

Physical Dangers

Physical damage includes anything that may alter the surface or substrate of the floppy disk. Any alteration—be it a coating of dust, oily fingerprints, or a physical tear or crease—is enough to interfere with the proper operation of the disk.

Writing on a disk table with ballpoint pen, a commonly cited problem, can crease a 5 1/4-inch disk. When the head scrapes over the disk, the crease causes a slight, temporary loss of contact with the disk. The data that might be read during that period is lost, resulting in a disk error. Folding or creasing the disk, even within its protective shuck, causes the same problem.

Dirt and fingerprints are cumulative and work slowly, wearing out the disk and your disk-drive mechanism. They can combine to literally gum up the works. Loose labels and write-protect tabs can come free and also damage your disk or drive mechanism.

As mentioned earlier, 3 1/2-inch disks are more resistant to damage. Loose labels can still cause problems, however, and the write-protect tabs can, occasionally, get caught in the drive.

Care Recommendations

The best way to prevent disk problems is to take good care of your disks. Always keep them in their protective sleeves when they are not being actively used. Before you switch off your computer, remove the disk from the drive and put it away. Although there is little risk of IBM computers damaging a disk when the computer is powered down, even inside the machine a disk can collect potentially destructive dust on its surface. It's much less likely to accumulate dust inside its sleeve.

Keep your disks organized in a disk file cabinet. Although most are made from plastic and thus offer no magnetic shielding, they put your disks far enough away from most magnetic sources that magnetic damage is minimized. Just don't put your magnetized scissors inside with the disks. The file cabinet also protects the disks from physical damage, besides keeping you organized.

Radical Recovery

The protective (generally black) plastic shell of the 5 1/4-inch floppy disk deflects most woes that might afflict your data. Sometimes, however, it becomes the problem rather than the solution. When one of your floppy disks suffers some tremendous indignity—say from being trod upon by the local high school cross-country team wearing their cleats—the damage done to the shell may be all that stands between you and reading your data from the disk. The shell might get so bent that it no longer will fit into the drive slot or so corrugated that the disk will not turn inside it. If you have data on such a disk, all is not lost—at least not yet.

Radical surgery can give you a chance to see what's left on the disk. Using the medical recovery technique, you may be able to save your data, although your disk has met its end. (The harder shell of 3 1/2-inch floppies normally prevents the problems afflicting 5 1/4-inch floppies that are amenable to radical repair.)

Radical recovery merely means separating the disk from its shell for one last spin in your disk drive. To get the disk out of its shell, you can either break the sonic welds holding the shell closed (more difficult than it sounds) or slice off one edge of the shell with a (unmagnetized) pair of scissors or paper cutter. If you need to open the shell of a 3 1/2-inch floppy, it is fairly simple to pry off the protective door and then pry the two halves of the disk apart. Of course, if the hardshell of your 3 1/2-inch disk has somehow been mangled, the odds are that the data inside is fairly mangled as well.

After you open the shell of your 5 1/4-inch disk, carefully slide the disk out, touching its surface as little as possible. With most disk drives, you can gently insert this naked disk right into the slot, watching carefully as you operate the level to lower the head so that the centering hub actually engages the center hole of the vulnerable disk.

Some floppy disk drives have an antihead crash lock that prevents you from lowering the head without a disk in its shell being present in the drive. If that's the case for yours, you'll have to sacrifice a second, good quality disk. Slice the new disk open, pull out the disk, and reinsert the disk from the corrupted shell.

After you have your bad floppy in a disk drive, copy its contents to a new disk to substitute it for the old. You should be able to get more than a few spins from your disk. You stand a good, though hardly perfect, chance of recovering the information stored on it.

Chapter 24
Compact Discs

From a simple stereo component, the Compact Disc has blossomed into today's premiere digital exchange medium. A single disk can slip up to 680 megabytes of information into your PC. In coming years, the CD will become a mandatory part of all PCs, just as it is required in all multimedia systems. But the CD is not a singular thing—nearly every application has its own standards and requirements.

For the distribution of digital information—music or data—the Compact Disc is typically the most affordable alternative for moving hundreds of megabytes to thousands of locations. This low cost makes the CD-ROM the premiere digital publishing medium. Already hundreds of CD-ROM titles are available, each one holding an encyclopedia of data.

The CD-ROM system just doesn't make sense without the availability of disks with data already stored on them. Because you can't write to a CD-ROM, you can't do anything with the drive unless you have something to read. In other words, a CD-ROM player is not something to buy in the abstract—you must have some software in mind that you want to slide into it. After all, if nothing but Hawaiian music were available on audio CD, who but the most dedicated listeners would buy a player?

A wide variety of CD-ROM disks are available, though not yet for everyone's tastes. There is great potential for the growth of the CD-ROM market because of their inexpensiveness and the ease of duplicating them.

Developed by the joint efforts of Philips and Sony Corporation in the early 1980's, when the digital age was taking over the stereo industry, the Compact Disc was first and foremost a high-fidelity delivery medium. Initially released in the United States in 1983, within five years it had replaced the vinyl phonograph record as the premiere stereophonic medium because of its wide-range, lack of noise, invulnerability to damage, and long projected life.

The 70 or so minutes of music that was one of the core specifications in designing the Compact Disc system—enough to hold Beethoven's Ninth Symphony—was a lot of data, more than 600 megabytes worth. With a covetous gleam, computer engineers eyed the shiny medium and discovered that data is data (okay, data are data) and the Compact Disc could be a repository for more megabytes than anyone had reason to use. (Remember, these were the days when the pot at the end of the rainbow held a 20 or 30 megabyte hard disk.) When someone got the idea that a plastic puck that cost a buck to make and retailed for $16.99 could be filled with last year's statistics and markets for $249, the rush was on. The Compact Disc became the CD-ROM (which stands for Compact Disc, Read-Only Memory), and megabytes came to the masses—at a price.

Soon sound became only one of the applications of the Compact Disc medium. The original name had to be extended to distinguish musical CDs from all the others. To computer people, the CD of the stereo system became the CD-DA, Compact Disc, Digital Audio.

Cheap and easy duplication make CD-ROM an ideal distribution medium. Its versatility (the same basic technology stores data, sound, and video) came about because all engineers eagerly search for big, cheap storage. The Compact Disc has both of those virtues by design. Hardly coincidentally, the same stuff that the Compact Disc stores so well is the core of multimedia. Quite naturally, those little silver discs are the enabling factor behind the multimedia explosion in PCs. Moreover, the Compact Disc is central to the digitalization and computerization of photography, or at least photographic storage. The PhotoCD system promises to hold your images longer and more compactly than long familiar photographic film. Within the next few years, the CD-ROM will likely become as mandatory in your next PC as the hard disk is today.

Technology

One of the great virtues of the Compact Disc is storage density—little discs mean a lot of megabytes. The enabling technology behind that high density is optics. Unlike virtually all other PC storage media, the Compact Disc and CD-ROM use light waves instead of magnetic fields to encode information.

The virtues of light for storage are numerous. Using lenses, you can focus a beam of light— particularly coherent laser light—to a tiny spot smaller than the most diminutive magnetic domain writeable on a hard disk drive. Unlike the restricted magnetic fields of hard disks that have to be used within a range of a few millionths of an inch, light travels distance with ease. Leaping along some 5.9 trillion miles in a year, some beams have been traveling since almost the beginning of the universe 10 to 15 billion years ago. The equipment that generates the beam of light that writes or reads optical storage need not be anywhere near the medium itself, which gives equipment designers more freedom than they possibly deserve.

Optical technology underlies the CD-ROM. The basic idea is that you can encode binary data as a pattern of black and white splotches just as on and off electrical signals can. You can make your mark in a variety of ways. The old reliable method is plain, ordinary ink on paper. The bar codes found universally on supermarket products do exactly that.

Reading the patterns of light and dark takes only a photodetector, an electrical component that reacts to different brightness levels by changing its resistance. Light simply lets electricity flow through the photodetector more easily. Aim the photodetector at the bar code, and it can judge the difference between the bars and background as you move it along (or move the product along in front of it). The lasers that read in the check-out quicken the scan. The photodetector watches the reflections of the red laser beam and patiently waits until a recognizable pattern—the bar code as the laser scans across it—emerges from the noise.

You could store the data of a computer file in one gigantic bar code and bring back paper tape as a storage medium. Even if you were willing to risk your important data to a medium that turns yellow and flakes apart under the unblinking eye of the sun like a beach bum with a bad complexion, you'd still have all the joy of dealing with a sequential storage medium. That means renew your subscription to your favorite magazines because you'll have a lot of waiting to do.

The disk, with its random access abilities, is better suited as a storage system. That choice was obvious even to the audio-oriented engineers who put the first Compact Disc systems together. They had a successful pattern to follow: the old black vinyl phonograph record. The ability to drop a needle on any track of a record had become ingrained in the hearts and minds of music lovers for more than 100 years. Any new music storage system needed equally fast and easy access to any selection. The same fast and easy access suits computer storage equally well.

Media

The heart of the CD-ROM system is the disk itself. After you've stepped past the obvious decision to choose the disk for its random-access abilities, you face many pragmatic decisions: What size disk? What should it be made from? How fast should it spin? What's the best way to put the optical pattern on the disk? What's the cheapest way to duplicate a million copies when the album goes platinum? Audio engineers made pragmatic choices about all of these factors long before the idea of CD-ROM had even been conceived.

Size is related to playing time. The bigger the disk, the more data it holds, all else being equal. But a platter the size of a wading pool would win favor with no one but plastics manufacturers. Shrinking the size of every splotch of the recorded digital code increases the storage capacity of any size disk, but technology and manufacturing tolerances limit the minimum size of the storage splotch. Given the maximum storage density that a workable optical technology would allow (about 150 megabytes per square inch), the total amount of storage dictates the size of the disk. With the "Ode to Joy" as a design goal and the optical technology of 1980 to take them there, engineers found a 4.6-inch platter their ideal compromise. A nice, round 100 millimeters was just too small for Beethoven.

The form of the code was another pragmatic choice. For a successful optical music storage system, normal printing and duplication methods all had their drawbacks. Printing the disk with ink was out of the question because no printing process can reliably re-create detail as fine as was necessary. Photography could keep all the detail—an early optical storage system prototype was based on photo technology—but photographic images are not readily made in million-lot quantities.

Besides printing, the one reproduction process that was successfully used to make millions was the stamping of ordinary photograph records, essentially a precision molding process. Mechanical molding and precision optical recording don't seem a very good match. But engineers found a way. By altering the texture of a surface mechanically, they could change its reflectivity. A coarse surface doesn't reflect light as well as a smooth one; a dark pit doesn't reflect light as well as a highly polished mirror. That was the breakthrough: the optical storage disk would be a reflective mirror that would be dotted with dark pits to encode data. A laser beam could blast pits into the disk. Then the pits, a mechanical feature, could be duplicated with stamping equipment similar to that used in manufacturing ordinary phonograph records.

Those concepts underlie the process of manufacturing Compact Discs. First a disk master is recorded on a special machine with a high-powered laser that blasts the pits into a blank recording master making a mechanical recording. Then, the master is made into a mold. One master can make many duplicate molds, each which is then mounted in a stamping machine. The machine heats the mold and injects a glob of plastic into it. After giving the plastic a chance to cool, the stamping machine ejects the disk and takes another gulp of plastic.

Another machine takes the newly stamped disc and aluminizes it so that it has a shiny, mirror-like finish. (Some discs, notably those used by Kodak for its PhotoCD system, get a gold coating.) To protect the shine, the disk is laminated with a clear plastic cover that guards the mechanical pattern from chemical and physical abuse (oxidation and scratches).

This process is much like the manufacture of vinyl records. The principal differences are that the CD has only one recorded side, its details are finer, and it gets an after-treatment of plating and laminating. The finishing steps add to the cost of the Compact Disc, but most of the cost in making a disc is attributable to the cost of the data it stores—either royalties to a recording act or the people who create, compile, or confuse the information that's to be distributed.

CD-ROM disks themselves store information exactly the same way it's stored on the CDs in your stereo system, only instead of getting up to 75 minutes of music, a CD-ROM disk holds about 680 megabytes of data. That data can be anything from simple text to SuperVGA images, programs, and the full circle back to music for multimedia systems.

Compared to vinyl phonograph records or magnetic disks, Compact Discs offer a storage medium that is long-lived and immune to most abuse. The protective clear plastic layer resists physical tortures (in fact, Compact Discs are more vulnerable to scratches on their label side than the side that is scanned with the playback laser). The data pits are sealed within layers of the disk itself and are never touched by anything other than a light beam—they never wear out and acquire errors only when you abuse the disks purposely or carelessly (for example, by scratching them against one another when not storing them in their plastic jewel boxes). Although error correction prevents errors from showing up in the data, a bad scratch can prevent a disk from being read.

Compact Discs show their phonograph heritage in another way. Instead of using a series of concentric tracks as with magnetic computer storage systems, the data track on the CD is one long, continuous spiral much like the single groove on a phonograph record. The CD player scans the track from near the center of the disk to the outer rim.

To maximize the storage available on a disc, the CD system uses constant linear velocity recording. The disc spins faster for its inner tracks than it does for the outer tracks so that the same length of track appears under the read/write head every second. The spin varies from about 300 RPM at the inner diameter to 100 RPM at the outside edge.

Format

As with other disk media, the CD divides its capacity into short segments called sectors. In the CD-ROM realm, however, these sectors are also called large frames and are the basic unit of addressing. Because of the long spiral track, the number of sectors or large frames per track is meaningless—it's simply the total number of sectors on the drive. The number varies but can reach about 315,000 (for example, for 70 minutes of music).

Large frames define the physical format of a Compact Disc and are defined by the CD-ROM media standards to contain 2352 bytes. (Other configurations can put 2048, 2052, 2056, 2324, 2332, 2340, or 2352 bytes in a large frame.) The CD-ROM media standards allow for several data formats within each large frame, dependent on the application for which the CD-ROM is meant. In simple data storage applications, data mode one, 2048 bytes in a 2352-byte large frame actually store data. The remaining 304 bytes are divided among a synchronization field (12 bytes), sector address tag field (4 bytes), and an auxiliary field (288 bytes). In data mode two, which was designed for less critical applications not requiring heavy-duty error-correction, some of the bytes in the auxiliary field may also be used for data storage, providing 2336 bytes of useful storage in each large frame. Other storage systems allocate storage bytes differently but in the same large frame structure.

The four bytes of sector address tag field identify each large frame unambiguously. The identification method hints at the musical origins of the CD-ROM system—each large frame bears an identification by minute, second, and frame which corresponds to the playing time of a musical disc. One byte each is provided for storing the minute count, second count, and frame count in binary coded decimal form. BCD storage allows up to 100 values per byte, more than enough to encode 75 frames per second, 60 seconds per minute, and the 70 minute maximum playing time of a Compact Disc (as audio storage). The fourth byte is a flag that indicates the data storage mode of frame.

In data mode one, the auxiliary field is used for error detection and correction. The first four bytes of the field store a primary error-detection code, and are followed by eight bytes of zeros. The last 276 hold a layered error-correction code. This layered code is sufficient for detecting and repairing multiple-bit errors in the data field.

Extended architecture rearranges the byte assignment of these data modes to suit multi-session applications. In XA Mode 2 Form 1, the twelve bytes of sync and four of header are followed by an eight-byte subheader that helps identify the contents of the data bytes, 2048 of which follow. The frame ends with an auxiliary field storing four bytes of error detection and 276 bytes of error correction code. In XA Mode 2 Form 2, the auxiliary field shrinks to four bytes; the leftover bytes extending the data contents to 2324 bytes.

Data Coding

The bytes of the large frame do not directly correspond to the bit pattern of pits that are blasted into the surface of the CD-ROM. Much as hard disks use different forms of modulation to optimize both the capacity and integrity of their storage, the Compact Disc uses a special data-to-optical translation code. Circuitry inside the Compact Disc system converts the data stream of a large frame into a bit pattern made from 98 small frames.

Each small frame stores 24 bytes of data (thus 98 of them equal a 2352-byte large frame) but consists of 588 optical bits. Besides the main data channel, each small frame includes an invisible data byte called the subchannel and its own error-correction code. Each byte of this information is translated into 14 bits of optical code. To these 14 bits, the signal processing circuitry adds three merging bits, the values of which are chosen to minimize the low frequency content of the signal and optimize the performance of the phase-lock loop circuit used in recovering data from the disk.

The optical bits of a small frame are functionally divided into four sections. The first 27 bits comprise a synchronization pattern. They are followed by the byte of subchannel data, which is translated into 17 bits (14-bit data code plus three merging bits). Next comes the 24 data bytes, (translated in 408 bits), followed by eight bytes of error correction code (translated into 136 bits).

The subchannel byte actually encodes eight separate subchannels, designated with letters from P through W. Each bit has its own function. For example, the P subchannel is a flag used to control audio muting. The Q subchannel is used to identify large frames in audio recording.

As with a hard disk, this deep structure is hidden from your normal application software. The only concern of your applications is to determine how the 2048 (or so) bytes of active storage in each large frame are divided up and used. The CD-ROM drive translates the block requests made by the SCSI (or other interface) into the correct values in the synchronization field to find data.

Addressing

The basic addressing scheme of the Compact Disc is the track, but CD tracks are not the same as hard disk tracks. Instead of indicating a head position or cylinder, the track on a CD is a logical structure akin to the individual tracks or cuts on a phonograph record.

A single Compact Disc is organized as one up to 99 tracks. Although a single CD can accommodate a mix of audio, video, and digital data, each track must be purely one of the three. Consequently, a disc mixing audio, video, and data would need to have at least three tracks.

The tracks on a disc are contiguous and sequentially numbered, although the first track containing information may have a value greater than one. Each track consists of at least 300 large frames (that's four seconds of audio playing time). Part of each track is a transition area called pre-gap and post-gap areas (for data discs) or pause areas (for audio disks).

Each disk has a lead-in area and a lead-out area corresponding to the lead-in and lead-out of phonograph records. The lead-in area is designated track zero, and the lead-out area is track 0AA(Hex). Neither is reported as part of the capacity of the disk, although the subchannel of the lead-in contains the table of contents of the disc. The table of contents lists every track and its address (given in the format of minutes, seconds, and frames).

Tracks are subdivided into up to 99 indices by values encoded in the subchannel byte of nine out of ten small frames. An index is a point of reference that's internal to the track. The number and location of each index are not stored in the table of contents. The pre-gap area is assigned an index value of zero.

Standards

The Compact Disc medium has proven so compelling that everyone wants to use it. Unfortunately, everyone wants to use it in his own way. And everyone wants to have his own standards. Not quite everyone gets his own standards, but nearly every application does. Moreover, as with other systems of PC mass storage, the standardization of CD-ROM occurs at several levels—hardware and software.

At the hardware level, Compact Disc systems are governed by several different standards that depend on what the system will be used for. The industry standards are commonly known by the color of the cover of the book that governs them. These include (in spectral order):

Red Book

Red Book describes CD-DA, the original Compact Disk application, which stores audio information in digital form. The name Red Book refers to the international standard (ISO 10149) which was published as a book with a red cover and specifies the digitization and sampling rate details including the data-transfer rate and the exact type of pulse code modulation used.

Green Book

Green Book governs CD-I, Compact Disc-Interactive, developed by Philips as a hardware and software standard for bringing together text, sound, and video on a single disk. Under the Green Book standard, CD-I uses Adaptive Delta Pulse Code Modulation to squeeze more audio on every disk (up to two full hours of full-quality stereo or 20 hours of monaural voice-quality sound). CD-I allows the audio, video, and data tracks to be interleaved on the disc so that they can be combined by your PC into an approximation of a multimedia extravaganza.

Orange Book

Orange Book is the official tome that describes the needs and standards for recordable Compact Disc systems. It turns the otherwise read-only medium into a write-once medium so you can make your own CDs (on expensive equipment).

Yellow Book

Yellow Book describes the data format standards for CD-ROM disks and includes CD-XA, which adds compressed audio information to other CD-ROM data.

Proprietary Standards

In addition, several manufacturers have tried to take the Compact Disc medium in their own directions and have developed what are still proprietary standards which they hope will someday sweep through the industry (along with their products). Among these are:

➤ Video Interactive System, developed by Microsoft and Tandy Corporation

➤ CD-TV, a proprietary video storage standard developed by Commodore International

➤ MMCD, a multimedia standard for hand-held Compact Disc players developed by Sony Corporation

➤ PhotoCD, a standard for storing high-quality photographic images developed by Eastman Kodak Company

Although these hardware standards define Compact Disc formatting and data storage methods, they do not specify how your operating systems and applications will use the disk-based storage. They are like the low-level format of a hard disk. In dedicated hardware applications—like audio Compact Disc systems—that level of standardization is sufficient. Your PC, however, needs some means of finding files equivalent to the FAT and directory structure of other ordinary disk systems.

CD-DA

Developed jointly by Philips and Sony Corporation, the CD-Digital Audio system was first introduced in the United States in 1983. The standard CD-DA disc holds up to about 70 minutes of stereo music with a range equivalent to today's FM radio stations—the high end goes just beyond 15 KHz; the low end, nearly to DC. The system stores audio data with a resolution of 16 bits, so each analog audio level is quantified as one of 65,536 levels. With linear encoding, that's sufficient for a dynamic range of 96 decibels, that is $20\log(16^2)$. To accommodate an upper frequency limit of 15 KHz with adequate roll-off for practical anti-aliasing filters, the system uses a sampling rate of 44.1 KHz.

Under the Red Book standard, this digital data is restructured into 24-byte blocks, arranged as six samples of each of a pair of stereophonic channels (each of which has a depth of 16 bits). These 24 bytes are encoded along with control and subchannel information into the 588 optical bits of a small frame, each of which stores about 136 microseconds of music. Ninety-eight of these small frames are grouped together in a large frame, and 75 large frames make one second of recorded sound.

In CD-DA systems, the large frame lacks the sync field, header, and error correction code used in CD-ROM storage. Instead, the error-correction and control information is encoded in the small frames. The necessary information to identify each large frame is spread through all 98 bits of subchannel Q in a given large frame. One bit of the subchannel Q data is drawn from each small frame.

From the subchannel Q data, a sector is identified by its ordinary playing time location (in minutes, seconds, and frame from the beginning of the disk). The 98 bits of the subchannel Q signal spread across the large frame are structured into nine separate parts: a two-bit synchronization field; a four-bit address field to identify the format of the subchannel Q data; a four-bit control field with more data about the format; an eight-bit track number; an eight-bit index number; a 24-bit address counting up from the beginning of the track (counting down from the beginning of the track in the pre-gap area); eight reserved bits; a 24-bit absolute address from the start of the disk; and 16 bits of error correction code. At least nine of ten consecutive large frames must have their subchannel Q signals in this format.

In the remaining large sectors, two more subchannel Q formats are optional. If used, they must occur in at least one out of 100 consecutive large frames. One is a disc catalog number which remains unchanged for the duration of the disk; the other is a special recording code that is specific and unchanging to each track.

PhotoCD

Fall asleep at the wheel and have your car plunge down a cliff as a bright orange fireball, and you're unlikely to do it again. Somehow the world's largest maker of photosensitive films managed to snooze as the home movie market abandoned chemical-based photography and embraced the magnetic marvel of the videocassette. In a decade eight-millimeter film virtually disappeared and eight-millimeter magnetic tape (sans the Kodak label) is one of the hottest formats around.

Fast forward a few years, and it's not hard to imagine the world of the electronic image completely eclipsing chemical-based still photography. With such less-than-delightful prospects on the horizon, Kodak made a move to try to control at least part of the electronic imaging revolution: the PhotoCD. The company created a way of combining traditional photography with electronic viewing. Take pictures with your Nikon or Minolta, send the film to Kodak, and see the results on your television set.

Compared to lugging out the old slide projector, yanking out a reluctant screen, squaring things up, pulling the shades to make the room almost dark enough, and then having your last projector bulb flash out two seconds into the slide show, the PhotoCD sounds like a compelling idea. Video similarly simplifies soporific home-movie viewing. But you don't have to process videocassettes, and you can recycle them. Moreover, PhotoCD targeted the slide-projection market—one dying its own ignoble death for other reasons. Its impact on the snapshot market proved negligible—after all, you can't put a CD or television screen in your wallet.

But PhotoCD has proven successful as something else: a catalog, exchange, and storage system for visual images. Professional photographers have embraced PhotoCD for distributing portfolios and preserving images without the worries of shifting and fading colors. Graphic artists have found that the commercial PhotoCD system is a fast, inexpensive way of scanning photographs into a format compatible with their visual editing systems.

Kodak's choice of Compact Discs for image storage was natural. They could capitalize on the familiarity, capacity, and longevity of the medium. But the PhotoCD system was not designed for mass production but for the writing of individual disks. Instead of requiring mastering at some stamping plant, Kodak envisioned ordinary photofinishers writing PhotoCD discs. Consequently, PhotoCD is based on recordable CD technology.

At the hardware level, the PhotoCD system follows the Green Book standard of the Compact Disc-Interactive system. At the software level, however, it required bending the normal standards. The most important change required by the PhotoCD system is that the disc medium be capable of storing multiple sessions. That is, instead of the entirety of the disk being mastered all at once, you can add images to a partly used CD. This multi-session use frustrates the standard CD-DA system of encoding a catalog on the lead-in track because the track would have to be changed to reflect the additions to the disc—an impossibility with a write-once medium.

Color

Because Kodak envisioned standard television sets as the primary playback medium for the PhotoCD system, the company optimized the on-disc image format for television compatibility. Instead of breaking the image into red, green, and blue components, it is stored in luminance/chrominance form with one primary channel corresponding to brightness (Y) and two color signals (C^1 and C^2). This YCC format also makes image compression easier.

The PhotoCD process begins with the scanning of the original photographic images, positive (slides) or negative. The Kodak system uses a 36-bit scanning system that devotes a full 12 bits of resolution to each primary color. At this step, image processing standardizes basic color characteristics so that the image, no matter its origins, reproduces properly on a standard television set (specifically, a screen that conforms to the recommendation for high-definition TV, CCIR 709). Because every film has its own spectral characteristics, the scanning system compensates using a Scene Balancing Algorithm—essentially a color look-up table—specific to each film type.

Instead of directly translating the brightness into digital values, the Kodak system uses a nonlinear transformation to optimize the range of brightness levels the system can accommodate. Table 24.1 shows the relationship between the reflectance of the original image (as revealed in the density of the film being scanned) to the encoded brightness level that's recorded.

TABLE 24.1. Scanned Reflectance and Coded Brightness Values for the PhotoCD System

% Reflectance (Brightness)	Y code value (PhotoCD Code Value)
1	8
2	16
5	34
10	53
15	67
20	79
30	98
40	114
50	128
60	141
70	152
80	163
90	173
100	182
107	188
120	199
140	215
160	229
180	243
200	255

So that specular highlights (bright reflections) and fluorescent colors in the original image reproduce properly, the PhotoCD system encodes brightness values as high as 200% of white, defined by Kodak as "a perfect, non-fluorescent white-reflecting diffuser in the original scene." Photographic materials are designed to capture this brighter-than-white information, up to about 200% of the reference white point. In addition, this extended range also allows balance adjustments and other manipulations during the encoding process.

The math in the conversion from primary colors (red, green, and blue) signals to the luminance/chrominance format results (the equations are shown in Table 24.2) in values that exceed the dynamic range of the brightness encoding, so the PhotoCD system uses a more refined mapping which compresses the brightness levels in excess of 100%. The playback system compensates for this compression of brightness values so that the levels reproduce properly.

TABLE 24.2. RGB/YCC Conversion Algorithms of PhotoCD System

$$Y' = 1.3584 * Y$$
$$C1' = 2.2179 * (C1-156)$$
$$C2' = 1.8215 * (C2-137)$$
$$R = Y' + C2'$$
$$G = Y' - 0.194 * C1' - 0.509 * C2'$$
$$B = Y' + C1'$$

(Conversions based on SMPTE 240M, the digital specifications for broadcast TV.)

Resolution

The PhotoCD system originally was designed to be hardware-specific. Consumers would buy a special PhotoCD player to connect to their television sets. To ease the price burden somewhat, PhotoCD players could also play back audio discs.

Compared to a modern PC, dedicated PhotoCD players are dumb. After all, if they were smarter, they would be computers. PhotoCD players are designed like audio machines—not to manipulate images but simply to reproduce them. The most advanced controls allow lingering on one or another image or jogging across a disk to find a view you like. Consequently, the PhotoCD player has no complex image manipulation circuitry. However, Kodak wanted to provide the PhotoCD system with a way to quickly review a catalog of thumbnail images, producing TV quality images, storing high-resolution photographic quality images, and not waste time converting from one resolution to another. The logical solution was to put multiple copies of each image on a disc at different resolutions. The system need only recall the image of the required resolution without wasting time converting it or even reading through a larger data file. Compared to the needs of high-resolution images, the additional storage requirements of low-resolution pictures is minimal. The convenience gained and cost saved are tremendous.

For consumer-quality PhotoCDs, the highest resolution of any image is 3072 by 2048 pixels, which translates to just under 100 lines per millimeter resolution across a 35 millimeter slide.

Because the PhotoCD system was designed primarily for playback through television sets, the resolution for this level—768 by 512 pixels—is classed as its base image. Higher and lower resolution formats on the disc are classed by the amount of information they contain. These include 4Base with resolution of 1536 by 1024 pixels and 16Base with photo-quality resolution of 3072 by 2048 pixels. Base/4 images have 384 by 256-pixel resolution, and Base/16 images have 192 by 128-pixel resolution. Professional PhotoCDs include an additional resolution mode to accommodate the potentials of medium and large format film, 64Base with 6144 by 4096-pixel resolution.

Image Compression

The data of each of these images is grouped together into an Image Pac, which corresponds to a separate file on the disc. The five separate images in each Image Pac would require 25,264,128 bytes without compression. Kodak uses a successive-difference system to compress the image with minimal information loss. In effect, the original is first scanned at maximum resolution (16Base), then scanned at the next lower resolution (4Base). The lower resolution is extrapolated up to the higher resolution, the differences (called residuals) noted and recorded using a lossless Huffman code. This compression is repeated down to the Base image, which is stored at uncompressed, as the lower resolution Base/4 and Base/16 images. This compression reduces the space needed for each Image Pac down to 3 to 6.5 megabytes. The data for the high-resolution image for the Professional PhotoCD system is stored in the form of residuals in a separate file called the Image Pac Extension.

Every PhotoCD includes an on-disc image catalog stored in a file called OVERVIEW.PCD as a collection of the Base/16 images on the disk. Each disc also includes a digital data directory in the lead-in track. When you use a disc for multiple sessions, the OVERVIEW.PCD file gets updated by building a new one on the disc. Kodak has not revealed the inner structure of the files used for the PhotoCD system.

CD-ROM

As its name implies, CD-Read Only Memory is fundamentally an adaptation of the Compact Disc to storing digital information—rock-and-roll comes to computer storage. Contrary to the implications of the name, however, you can write to CD-ROM discs with your PC, providing you buy the right (which means expensive) equipment. For most applications, however, the CD-ROM is true to its designation—it delivers data from elsewhere into your PC. Once a CD-ROM disk is pressed, the data it holds cannot be altered. Its pits are present for eternity.

In the beginning, CD-ROM was an entity unto itself, a storage medium that mimicked other mass storage devices. It used its own storage format. The kind of data that the CD-ROM lent itself to was unlike that of other storage systems, however. The CD-ROM supplied an excellent means for distributing sounds and images for multimedia systems, consequently engineers adapted its storage format to better suit a mixture of data types. The original CD-ROM format was extended to cover these additional kinds of data with its Extended Architecture. The result was the Yellow Book standard.

Format

The Yellow Book describes how to put information on a CD-ROM disk. It does not, however, define how to organize that data into files. In the DOS world, two file standards have been popular. The first was called High Sierra format. Later this format was upgraded to the current standard, the ISO 9660 specification.

The only practical difference between these two standards is that the driver software supplied with some CD-ROM players, particularly older ones, meant for use with High Sierra formatted disks may not recognize ISO 9660 disks. You're likely to get an error message that says something like "Disc not High Sierra." The problem is that the old version of the Microsoft CD-ROM extensions—the driver that adapts your CD-ROM player to work with DOS—cannot recognize ISO 9660 disks.

To meld CD-ROM technology with DOS, Microsoft Corporation created a standard bit of operating code to add onto DOS to make the players work. These are called the DOS CD-ROM extensions, and several versions have been written. The CD-ROM extensions before Version 2.0 exhibit the incompatibility problem between High Sierra and ISO 9660 noted above. The solution is to buy a software upgrade to the CD-ROM extensions that came with your CD-ROM player from the vendor who sold you the equipment. A better solution is to avoid the problem and ensure any CD-ROM player you purchase comes with version 2.0 or later of the Microsoft CD-ROM extensions.

ISO 9660 embraces all forms of data you're likely to use with your PC. Compatible disks can hold files for data as well as audio and video information.

Players

In that a computer CD-ROM player has the same basic job as a CD-Digital Audio machine in your home stereo, you'd expect the technology inside each to be about the same. In fact, all have similar mechanisms.

CD-ROM players tend to be more expensive than stereo models because retrieving computer data is more demanding. A tiny musical flaw that may pass unnoticed even by trained ears could have disastrous consequences in a data stream. Misreading a decimal point as a number, even zero, can result in error-laden calculations. To minimize, if not eliminate, such problems, computer CD-ROM players require different error correction circuitry than is built into stereo equipment that uses much more powerful algorithms. CD-DA errors are corrected at the small frame level, 24 bytes at a time. CD-ROM data errors are corrected at the large frame level, 2048 or more bytes at a time.

CD-ROM players also require more intimate control and faster access times. The toughest job a digital audio player faces is moving from track to track when you press a button. A CD-ROM player must skate between tracks as quickly as possible—in milliseconds if your human expectations are to be fulfilled.

Even the link between your PC and CD-ROM player complicates the drive and makes it more expensive. By itself a CD-ROM player does nothing but spin its disk. Your computer must tell the player what information to look for and read out. And your computer is needed to display—visually and aurally—the information the CD-ROM player finds, be it text, a graphic image, or a musical selection. Sending those commands requires an interface of some kind, in most cases either SCSI or ATAPI. Neither is needed in a digital audio player.

Transfer Rate

Unlike music and video systems, which require real-time playback of their data (unless you prefer to watch the recorded world race by as if overdosed on adrenalin), digital data is not ordinarily locked to a specific time frame. In fact, most people would rather have information shipped as quickly as possible from disc to memory.

For real-time playback, the original CD-Digital Audio system required a 150 kilobyte per second data transfer rate. In the data domain, however, that's mighty slow—one-quarter to one-tenth the throughput of a modern hard disk even after you account for all overhead. Raw hard disk transfer rates exceed 50 times the CD-DA rate.

The transfer rate of a Compact Disc system is a direct function of the speed at which the disc itself spins. Increasing the data transfer rate requires higher rotation speeds. Consequently, today's CD-ROM players operate at multiples of the standard CD-DA spin rate. Double-speed drives spin twice as fast to deliver 300 KB/sec transfer rates; triple-speed drives, 450 KB/sec; and quadruple-speed drives, 600 KB/sec.

For the time being, the higher of these speeds is sufficient for most applications. Even many 486-based PCs cannot handle CD-ROM data at the rate that triple-speed drives deliver it because of software overhead.

High-speed drives can retain their compatibility with Red Book audio by buffering. They read the audio data at their higher rate and pump it into their buffer. Then they unload the buffer at the real-time rate.

Access Time

Compared to magnetic hard disks, CD-ROM players are laggardly beasts. Mass is the reason. The optical head of the CD system is substantially more massive than the flyweight mechanisms of hard disks. Instead of a delicate read/write head, the CD-ROM player has a large optical assembly that typically moves on a track. The assembly has more mass to move, which translates into a longer wait for the head to settle into place.

Besides the mass of the head, the constant linear velocity recording system of CD-ROMs slows the access speed. Because the spin rate of the disk platter varies depending on how far the read/write head is located from the center of the disk, as the head moves from track to track, the spin rate of the disk changes. With music, which is normally played sequentially, that's no problem. The speed difference between tracks is tiny, and the drive can quickly adjust for it. Make the CD system into a random-access mechanism, and suddenly speed changes become a big issue. The drive may need to move its head from the innermost to outermost track, requiring a drastic speed change. The inertia of the disk spin guarantees a wait while the disk spins up or down.

Some old CD-ROM players required nearly one second to find and read a given large frame of data. Modern designs cut that time to 100 to 200 milliseconds, still about ten times longer than the typical hard disk drive.

Mechanism

Nearly all CD-ROM players fit a standard half-height 5.25-inch drive bay for one very practical reason: a 4.6-inch disc simply won't fit into a 3.5-inch drive slot.

How you get a disc into a CD-ROM player varies with the design of the machine. Some mechanisms incorporate a sliding drawer much like that on most audio CD systems. The drawer slides out either at the control of a micromotor or spring. You simply drop the disk in and slide the drawer closed.

Some CD-ROM players make the job even easier—and safer—for your discs. You load your discs into a special carrier that resembles the plastic jewel-box case that most commercial music CDs come in. When you want to load a disk into the CD-ROM player, you slide the whole carrier into a waiting slot. Most people buy a carrier for each CD-ROM disk they have because of this convenience and the extra protection the carrier affords the disk—no scratches and no fingerprints, guaranteed! CD-ROM changers use multiple-disk cartridges exactly like those used by audio CD changers.

Interface

The connection between CD-ROM players and your PC also has been, for the most part, standardized. The majority of CD-ROM players that you can buy today use the Small Computer Systems Interface or SCSI to link with your computer. A few ancient CD-ROM players connect through a serial or parallel port. A few others use proprietary connections, which are primarily based on the AT Attachment interface. The next generation of CD-ROM drives will likely opt for an ATAPI connection, a standardized AT Attachment interface system. ATAPI promises to be lower in cost and confusion when compared to SCSI systems.

Drivers

As with other peripherals, a hardware connection is not enough to bring a CD-ROM drive to life. It must be recognized by your software. While some operating systems naturally know how to work with SCSI ports and CD-ROM drives, others may require special driver software. DOS requires drivers. You may need two drivers: one to match the SCSI port to your PC and a separate driver to match the drive to your operating system. For DOS, this drive will likely be MSCDEX.EXE.

Although loading these drivers is enough to gain access to the CD-ROM drive, it may not enable you to use the data that it contains. Most CD-ROMs contain their own searching or operating software that you must run to read the data stored on them. This software may run from the DOS prompt, or (as is more likely with modern multimedia software) from within Windows or OS/2. Each CD-ROM disk you have will likely require its own data access software. If you acquire a lot of CD-ROM disks, you may overpopulate your Presentation Manager with a multitude of odd little icons, most of which won't work because you'll have the wrong disc in your drive.

MPC

The most popular application for CD-ROMs today is multimedia. It is also the most demanding application. Although any PC is sufficient for finding a word in a CD-ROM-based dictionary, spinning tales with images and stereo sound takes a special machine. To ensure that you won't be disappointed in the performance of multimedia software on your PC, the Multimedia PC Marketing Council published a standard in 1992 that described the minimum equipment configuration of a Multimedia PC. The requirements include a PC equipped with at least a 16MHz 386SX microprocessor, 4MB of RAM, a 40MB hard disk, a color VGA system, a mouse, and a CD-ROM player capable of a 150 KB/sec transfer rate. The council declares systems and products fully ready for multimedia (and that pay a hefty licensing fee) Multi-Media PC-compatible or MPC-compatible. All but the lowest-end PCs sold in the last couple of years meet or exceed that standard.

In 1993, however, the Multimedia PC Marketing Council took note that technology has enabled authors to create more demanding multimedia applications that required a new standard of performance. Consequently, the council published revised specifications in 1993 as MPC-2. To reach this level of performance, your PC needs at least a 486SX microprocessor operating at 25MHz, 8MB of RAM, a VGA display, a mouse, and a double-speed CD-ROM drive (one capable of a transfer rate of 300 KB/sec or better).

Of course, you'll want this level of performance just to keep up with the majority of systems sold today. And that's to be expected because multimedia is now the mainstream.

Chapter 25
Tape

Tape is for backup—your insurance that a disaster doesn't erase every last vestige of your valuable data. You also can use some of the standardized tape systems as exchange media—the floppy disk for the age of megabytes. Tape systems come in a number of formats with different capacities, speeds, and levels of convenience. The best, however, is the one that's easiest to use.

Faith is trusting your most valuable possessions—purportedly to protect them—to a sealed black box filled with fragile machinery you don't understand honed to split-hair tolerances and vulnerable to a multitude of ills—electroshock, impact, even old age. One misstep, and your treasures can be destroyed.

Such groundless, even misguided, trust has no place in business and definitely no role in the rigorous world of personal computers, but that's exactly what you do every time you save a file to your hard disk drive. You send data to a complex, sealed black box with the hope of someday retrieving it. Technology has given us this faith, but just in case the faith is misused, technology has also bequeathed us the tape to use for backup systems.

With tape, you can quickly make a copy of your most valuable data on a movable medium that you can take to preserve somewhere safe. When disaster strikes—as it inevitably does—you always have your tape copy as a backup ready to replace the original. The concept is simple but far from perfect. You have a variety of tape systems to choose from, and all share one undesirable quality—you have to pay for them.

The price is more than monetary. Making a tape backup also extracts a toll in convenience. Far from a miracle or wonder drug, tape backup is more like castor oil for your computer: it's unpalatable and has little perceived value in the abstract, no matter what you have to pay for it. You put up with it because you've been told it's good for you in some way that you hope to never test. No matter how much sugar is mixed in with it, you still wish it (and the need for it) would go away. It won't, so you might as well swallow hard and take advantage of the protection tape offers you and your PC.

Background

Tape was the first magnetic mass storage system, harking back to the last days of World War II. Although first used for voice and music, tape soon invaded the computer world, first as a convenient alternative to punched cards and punched paper tape—the primary storage system used by mainframe computers. Later, information transfer became an important use for tape. Databases could be moved between systems as easily as carting around one or more spools of tape. After magnetic disks assumed the lead in primary storage, tape systems were adapted to backing them up.

Personal computers benefited from the evolution of tape in the mainframe environment. Never considered as primary storage—except in the nightmares of the first PC's original designers who thoughtfully included a cassette port on the machine for its millions of users to ignore—tape started life in the PC workplace in the same role it serves today, as a backup medium. Although some software vendors viewed the huge, cheap storage of tape cartridges as a file interchange medium, the attempts at establishing it as a standard for such purposes have been but flirtations. For years, it has beckoned, but it's never taken itself seriously enough to maintain a long-lasting relationship.

As a physical entity, tape is both straightforward and esoteric. It is straightforward in design, providing the perfect sequential medium—a long, thin ribbon that can hold orderly sequences of information. The esoteric part involves the materials used in its construction.

Operation

Tape drives are often described by how they work as well as by the packaging of the medium they use. Most different technologies span many media; all influence how quickly the tape system operates and how convenient it is to use.

Start-Stop Tape

The fundamental difference between tape drives is how they move the tape. Early drives operated in start-stop mode; they handled data one block (ranging from 128 bytes to a few kilobytes) at a time and wrote it to tape as it was received. Between blocks of data, the drive stopped moving the tape and awaited the next block. The drive had to prepare the tape for each block, identifying the block so that the data could be properly recovered. The start-stop operation was necessary with early PCs for another reason; most computers were so slow that they could not move data to the drive as fast as the drive could write it to tape.

Streaming Tape

When computer speeds caught up to tape speeds, tape drives could write data continuously to tape without pausing between records. Data flowed from computer to tape in an unbroken stream, hence engineers called this mode of operation *streaming tape.*

Drives using streaming tape technology can accept data and write it to tape at a rate limited only by the speed the medium moves and the density at which bits are packed—the linear density of the data on the tape. Because the tape does not have to stop between blocks, the drive wastes no time. The streaming design also lowers the cost of tape drives because the drives do not have to accelerate the tape quickly or brake the motion of the tape spools, allowing a lighter weight mechanism to be used. Nearly all PC tape drives are now capable of streaming data to tape.

Parallel Recording

The first tape machines used with computer systems were multi-track drives. They recorded nine separate data channels called tracks across the width of the tape. The first of these machines used parallel recording in which they spread each byte across their tracks, one bit per track with one track for parity. A tape was good for only one pass across the read/write head, after which the tape needed to be rewound for storage. Newer tape systems elaborate on this design by laying 18 or 36 tracks across a tape, corresponding to a digital word or double word.

Parallel recording provides a high transfer rate for a given tape speed but makes data retrieval time-consuming—finding a given byte might require fast forwarding across an entire tape.

Serpentine Recording

Most PC tape systems use multi-track drives but do not write tracks in parallel. Instead, they convert the incoming data into serial form and write that to the tape. Serial recording across multiple tracks results in a recording method called *serpentine recording*.

Serpentine cartridge drives write data bits sequentially across the tape in one direction on one track at a time continuing for the length of the tape. When the drive reaches the end of the tape, it reverses the direction the tape travels and cogs its read/write head down one step to the next track. At the end of that pass, the drive repeats the process until it runs out of data or fills all the tracks. A serpentine tape system can access data relatively quickly by jogging its head between tracks because it needs to scan only a fraction of the data on the tape for what you want.

Medium

The tape used by any system consists of two essential layers—the backing and the coating. The backing provides the support strength needed to hold the tape together while it is flung back-and-forth across the transport. Progress in the quality of the backing material mirrors developments in the plastics industry. The first tape was based on paper. Shortly after the introduction of commercial tape recorders at the beginning of the 1950s, cellulose acetate (the same plastic used in safety film in photography for three decades previously) was adopted. The state-of-the-art plastic is polyester, of double-knit leisure-suit fame. In tape, polyester has a timeless style of its own—flexible and long-wearing with a bit of stretch. It needs all those qualities to withstand the twists and turns of today's torturous mechanisms, fast shuttle speeds, and abrupt changes of direction.

Coatings also evolved over the decades, as they have for all magnetic media. Although most tapes are coated with doped magnetic oxides, coatings of pure metal particles in binders and even vapor-plated metal films have been used for tape. Tape coatings are governed by the same principles as other magnetic media; the form is different, but the composition remains the same.

In backup systems, the packaging of the tape is as important as its composition. The form the tape package takes determines the mechanism required for writing to and reading from it.

Formats

In general, the trend has been to package tape in an ever-more convenient form. Tape started out as loose spools that required threading as elaborate as threading a vintage 16mm film projector. Clever engineers got the idea of putting both the supply and take-up reels (or spools) in a single cartridge so that threading was minimized. After the cartridges were standardized, the tape engineers concentrated on cramming more data into the cartridges.

The result of these efforts is the diversity of tape systems now available for plugging into your PC. Four major types of tape systems (as well as a few out-of-the-mainstream technologies) are sometimes used in personal computer systems, all of which were originally designed for other purposes. These include open-reel tape, cassettes, quarter-inch cartridges, and helical-scan tape.

Open-Reel Tape

The classic computer tape medium uses individual tape spools termed open-reel tape because the spools are not kept inside protective shells, as are other computer tape formats. All the Big-Brother-style computer films of the 1950s and early 1960s used the jerky, back-and-forth movement of big open reel tape transports that are a symbol of the vast computer power of the age. At the time, the big reels of tape were the primary storage systems of those computers, and the back-and-forth rocking of the tape was the machine's quest to find a given record. As you can imagine, put to such purposes, the average access time of the tapes was measured in seconds and could stretch for an eternity—particularly when the right tape was not mounted on the transport.

From a diversity of formats, one standard quickly evolved in open-reel tape. The tape, nominally one-half inch wide, is split into nine parallel tracks, each running the full length of the tape. One track is used for each bit of a byte of data, the ninth track containing parity-checking information. Every byte is recorded in parallel—a lateral slice across the tape. Because of these physical characteristics of the medium, open-reel tape is often termed half-inch or nine-track tape.

Individual reels of tape can be almost any diameter larger than the three-inch central hole. The most common sizes are seven and ten and one-half inches in diameter. Tape lengths vary with reel size and with the thickness of the tape itself. A 10-inch spool holds 2,500 to 3,600 feet of tape.

As open-reel technology evolved, the distance between each byte was gradually reduced, packing an increasing amount of information on every inch of tape. Originally, open-reel tapes were recorded using FM signals, packing 800 bytes on every linear inch of the tape. Advancing to

MFM doubled the capacity to 1,600 bpi. This density is now the most common in open-reel tape. More exotic transports push data densities up to 3,200 or even 6,250 bpi.

Data is recorded on open-reel tape in distinct blocks, each separated by a stretch of blank tape called the inter-block gap. The length of this gap can vary from a fraction of an inch to several inches, depending on characteristics of the overall system (involving such factors as how quickly the host computer can send and receive information from the tape subsystem). Together, the tape length, data density, and inter-block gap determine the capacity of a single reel of tape. The common 1,600 bpi density and a reasonable inter-block gap can put about 40 megabytes on a ten-inch reel.

Although once considered great, that 40-megabytes isn't much by today's PC storage standards. It takes awfully large reels to pack a workable amount of information, and that's the chief disadvantage of open-reel tape. Tape reels are big and clumsy, and the drives match. When a single reel is more than ten inches across, fitting a drive to handle it inside a 5-1/4-inch drive is more than difficult. Ten-inch reels themselves are massive; spinning (and stopping) them requires a great deal of torque, which means large, powerful motors—again something incompatible with the compact necessities of the PC. In fact, most open-reel tape transports dwarf the typical PC; some look more like small refrigerators.

Open-reel drives also tend to be expensive because they are essentially low-volume yet precision machinery. Price increases as storage density increases. Today, low-density, 1,600 bpi drives are available in the PC price range; one vendor sells a unit for under $1,000. But high-density open-reel systems still cost more than a good, high-speed PC—$3,000 and up. Unlike other PC peripherals, the price of open-reel tape has been stable for years. No breakthrough technologies are on the horizon to revolutionize nine-track tape and its pricing.

On the positive side, age and mass can be virtues when it comes to system and data integrity. Because of the low density used in recording, each flux transition on an open reel tape involves a greater number of oxide particles, making it potentially more resistant to degradation (all other oxide characteristics being equal). The big, heavyweight drives are generally sturdy, designed for industrial use, and should last nearly forever when attached to a PC.

As a backup system alone, open reel tape is not much of a bargain, however. Other tape systems, particularly the various cartridge formats, are less expensive and—according to their design specifications—as reliable or even more reliable. For most people, cartridges also are easier to use.

Open-reel tape excels as a data-interchange medium, however. Almost any 1,600 bpi tape is readable on almost any open-reel transport. Although block lengths and inter-block gaps may vary, these differences are relatively easy to compensate for. Consequently, open-reel remains the medium of choice for shifting information between mainframe and minicomputers. For example, most mailing lists are delivered on open-reel tapes. An open-reel transport opens this world to the personal computer, allowing the interchange of megabytes of information with virtually any other system. Although most open-reel systems for PCs concentrate on the inter-changeability of the tapes, they also include provisions for making open-reel backups. Think of the backup capability as a bonus rather than the reason for buying an open-reel system.

3480 Cartridges

Mainframe computer operators endured the inconveniences of open-reel tape for more than 20 years before an accepted successor appeared on the scene. A new tape system that's essentially a cross between cartridges and open-reel is replacing old-fashioned open-reel tapes in the role of backup storage. Because of its newness, however, the system has not yet proven a successor to open-reel tape as an interchange medium.

Termed 3480 after the model number of the first IBM machine that used the new media, the system is based on cartridges that are little more than open-reel tapes stuffed into a protective shell. The tape is still half an inch wide, and it runs through the drive much like open-reel tapes. The drive mechanism pulls the tape out of the cartridge, winds it onto a tape up spool, shuttles it back and forth to find and write data, and rewinds it back into the cartridge when it is done. In effect, the cartridge is just an oddly shaped all-enclosing reel that doesn't itself rotate. Not only can people more easily slide tapes into drives, but automatic mechanisms can locate and load tapes. Such mechanisms are often called juke boxes because they work like the classic 1950's Wurlitzers that gave three plays for a quarter, selecting the songs to play from an internal array of disks—complete with big windows so that you could stare in amazement at the mechanical wonder.

The 3480 system holds a bigger advantage over open-reel than just convenience in mounting tapes, however. The upgrade to 3480 also brings double the number of tracks, and a once or twice more doubling is promised in the future by IBM. In IBM's current implementation, these eighteen tracks are written in two parallel sets of nine tracks simultaneously, which doubles the data transfer speed and throughput of the system. In addition, the recording density is higher than open-reel tapes, increasing both capacity and the data speed of the system. The result of this redesign is that a cartridge with less than a quarter the volume of an open-reel tape (3480 cartridges measure 4-3/4 x 4-1/4 x 3/4 inches) can hold much more data— hundreds of mega-bytes.

The disadvantage of these innovations is the price. All 3480 tape transports currently available are big ticket ($20,000-plus) products designed for the mainframe market.

Several companies worked at adapting the 3480-style cartridge into systems practical (and affordable) for PC applications. These systems shared only the medium with the mainframe technology, using different data formats from the true IBM 3480 tape drive. From the PC perspective, these systems faded into obscurity, probably because they lacked the big advantage of open-reel tape. They were not capable of exchanging information with mainframes.

Cassette Tape

Introduced originally as a dictation medium, cassettes grew up—into a stereophonic music recording medium that spawned a market for equipment sometimes costing thousands of dollars—and down—into the realm of cheap, portable recorders costing $10-20. These low-end machines represent the cheapest way ever created to magnetically record information. Cassettes use modem-like methods to record digital signals modulated onto audible tones. Low prices and ready accessibility made cassettes the choice of early computer hobbyists for recording data and pushed cassettes into the commercial market as a distribution medium for computer software, mostly for inexpensive home-style computers.

When the PC first came on the market, the cassette was seen as a viable storage alternative, at least among the home and hobbyist computer markets, by industry watchers with eyeglasses as thick as bathyscaph portholes. Even IBM caught cassette mania and elected to build a port for attaching a cassette machine into every PC. (See Appendix D, "Ancient History.")

Little more than a year later the marketplace myopia improved, and the storage needs of the PC showed the shortcomings of audio cassette technology adapted to data: slow speed and sequential access. The modulation-audio method of recording yielded a data rate about equivalent to a 1,200 bits per second modem, and finding data on a tape took a long time or much guessing with your finger on the fast-forward button. These practical matters led to the cassette port being dropped from the XT and all subsequent IBM computers. Among PCs, the cassette as a primary data storage device is mostly of historical interest.

In the last few years, the cassette mechanism has proven a compelling platform, however. Teac developed a new, high-speed cassette transport aimed particularly at data storage. It abandoned the audio cassette standard used by earlier systems and pegged its performance on par with higher priced cartridge-based backup systems using a digital recording system. The result was called the digital cassette or D/CAS for short. These data-only cassettes now represent a viable secondary storage technology. (Note that D/CAS is entirely different from the Digital Compact Cassette, DCC, stereo audio medium; while both systems are digital, both the equipment and tapes are substantially different.)

Developed—and patented—by the Dutch Philips conglomerate, the audio cassette was just one of many attempts to sidestep the biggest complaint against open-reel tape systems: the tapes were difficult to handle and hard to thread through the recording mechanism. The idea did not originate with Philips. An earlier attempt by RCA, which used a similar but larger cassette package, failed ignobly in the marketplace. The Compact Cassette, as it was labeled by Philips, was successful because it was more convenient and did not aspire so high. It was not designed as a high-fidelity medium, but grew into that market as technology improved its modest quality. While the RCA cartridge was about the size of a thin book, the Compact Cassette fit into a shirt pocket and was quite at home when it was on the go in portable equipment. Size and convenience led to its adoption as the autosound medium of choice and then the general high-fidelity medium of choice. (Even before the introduction of the Compact Disc, cassettes had earned the majority of the music market.)

The basic cassette mechanism takes the two spools of the open-reel tape transport and puts them inside a plastic shell. The shell protects the tape because the tape is always attached to both spools, eliminating the need for threading.

The sides of the cassette shell serve as the sides of the tape reel—holding the tape in place so that the center of the spool doesn't pop out. This function is augmented by a pair of Teflon slip sheets, one on either side of the tape inside the shell, that help to eliminate the friction of the tape against the shell. A clear plastic window in either side of the shell enables you to look at how much tape is on either spool—how much is left to record on or play back.

The reels inside the cassette themselves are merely hubs that the tape can wrap around. A small clip that forms part of the perimeter of the hub holds the end of the tape to the hub. At various points around the inside of the shell, guides are provided to ensure that the tape travels in the correct path.

The shell is thickened at the open edge to allow the record/playback head and the drive puck to be inserted against the tape.

The cassette also incorporates protection against accidental erasure of valuable music or information. On the rear edge of the cassette—away from where the head inserts—are a pair of plastic tabs protecting hole-like depressions in the shell. A finger from the cassette transport attempts to push its way into this hole. If it succeeds, it registers that the cassette is write-protected. Breaking off one of these tabs therefore protects the cassette from accidental erasure. To restore recordability, the hole needs only to be covered up. Cellophane or masking tape—even a Band-Aid or file folder label works for that purpose. Two such tabs exist—one to protect each side of the tape. The tab in the upper left protects the top side of the cassette. (Turn the cassette over, and the other side becomes the top—but the tab that allows recording on this side still appears in the upper left.)

More recent audio cassettes may have additional notches on the rear edge to indicate to the automatic sensing cassette disk the type of tape inside the cassette shell. Audio tape comes in four varieties that require different settings on the cassette recording for optimal operation.

The Teac D/CAS data cassettes add one huge notch on the backbone of the cassette that works as a key to lock out audio cassettes from their digital mechanisms. Even were the notch not there, ordinary audio tapes wouldn't work in the Teac mechanism. The high-speed cassette system requires a special cassette designed to match its magnetic and mechanical requirements.

The first Teac system used two tracks on each cassette, one for recording in each direction. However, the mechanism was bi-directional and automatically used both sides. Not only did you not need to flip over a tape in the Teac system, you were prohibited from doing so. The asymmetrical placement of the identifying notch absolutely precludes the use of the wrong side of a tape.

The first Teac D/CAS system could put a full 60MB on one tape. That was quickly increased to 160MB. In 1991, Teac introduced a new mechanism (their model number MT-2ST/F50) that pushed capacity to 600 MB. Using a standard SCSI-2 interface, it can move information onto tape at a rate of up to 242K per second.

Quarter-Inch Data Cartridges

A few years after the cassette was introduced to take dictation, 3M Company first offered a quarter-inch tape cartridge as a data recording medium. First put on the market in 1972, these initial quarter-inch cartridges were designed for telecommunications and data acquisition applications calling for the storage of serial data, such as programming private business telephone exchanges and recording events. No one imagined that the quarter-inch cartridge would evolve into the premiere personal computer backup medium; no PCs existed at the time.

The initial concept behind the quarter-inch tape cartridge appears to be the same as that of the cassette—put the two spools of tape from the open-reel system into an easy-to-handle plastic box. In function, operation, and construction, the cassette and cartridge are entirely different because the needs of dictation and data storage are entirely different. Compared to the cassette, the tape cartridge requires greater precision and smoother operation. To achieve that end, a new mechanical design was invented by Robert von Behren of the 3M Company, who patented it in 1971—quarter-inch cartridge mechanism.

Instead of using the capstan drive system like cassettes, the quarter-inch cartridge operates with a belt drive system. A thin, isoelastic belt stretches throughout the cartridge mechanism, looping around (and making contact with) both the supply and take-up spools on their outer perimeters. The belt also passes around a rubber drive wheel, which contacts a capstan in the tape drive.

The capstan moves the belt but is cut away with a recess that prevents it from touching the tape. The friction of the belt against the outside of the tape reels drives the tape. This system is gentler to the tape because the driving pressure is spread evenly over a large area of the tape instead of pinching the tape tightly between two rollers. In addition, it provides for smoother tape travel and packing of the tape on the spools. The tape is wound, and the guide and other parts of the mechanism arranged so that the fragile magnetic surface of the tape touches nothing but the read/write head (see fig. 25.1).

For sturdiness, the cartridge is built around an aluminum baseplate. The rest of the cartridge is transparent plastic, allowing the condition of the tape and the mechanism to be readily viewed.

The essence of the design is that the cartridge itself acts as the tape drive. It contains the tape guides, the tape, and the tape moving mechanism. Although that means that the data cartridge is somewhat more expensive to make, drives are less expensive because they essentially need only a motor and a head. The design also ensures the best possible consistency of tape alignment and minimizes the need for adjustments to the drive.

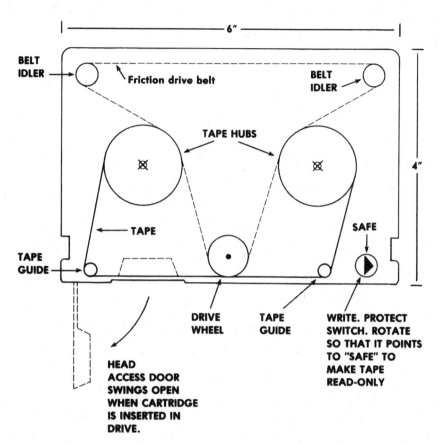

FIGURE 25.1. Quarter-inch cartridge mechanisms (DC-600 style cartridge is shown; the DC2000 is similar but smaller).

Early Systems

The initial cartridge, called the DC300A by 3M Company, held 300 feet of tape in a package almost the size of a paperback book—a full 6 x 4 x 5/8 inches. The cartridge mechanism was designed to operate at a speed of 30 inches per second, using phase encoding (single-density recording) to put a density of 1,600 bits per inch serially (one track at a time) on the tape—a data rate of 48 kilobits per second. Two or four tracks were used one at a time. Drives for this format were made by 3M Company, Kennedy, Qantax, DEI, and, briefly, IBM.

In 1979, DEI quadrupled the speed and capacity of the quarter-inch cartridge by introducing a drive that recorded four tracks in parallel, still at 30 inches per second and 1,600 bits per inch. The new mechanism achieved a 192 kilobits per second data rate using standard DC300A tapes.

Even though these cartridges only held 1.8 megabytes unformatted—one megabyte formatted, the same as an eight-inch floppy disk—using this recording method, the data rate was high enough to interest the computer industry.

A year later, another four-track drive for the DC300A cartridge was introduced. The capacity of the system was increased to about 15 megabytes by shifting to MFM recording and pushing the data density to 6,400 bits per inch. Although the 192 kilobits per second transfer rate and 30 inches per second speed were maintained, data was transferred serially, one track at a time. As late as 1988, this ground-breaking drive was still in production, although it was no longer used in mass market PC products, being superseded in those applications by higher capacity systems.

Since then, tape lengths have again been increased to as much as 900 feet, although the most popular length is the 600 feet contained in the cartridges that were initially designated DC600. Current implementations of cartridge technology use cartridges the same size and shape as the 3M originals. However, capacities have blossomed into the gigabyte range thanks to multitrack heads, high-density recording media, and error correction. Existing standards put up to 13 gigabytes in a single cartridge. The ultimate capacity of the format is believed to be about 100 gigabytes per cartridge.

The DC600 cartridge is now a thing of the past—but in name only. New designations have been added to take into account other media and tape length differences that affect storage capacities. The generic name for a full-size quarter-inch tape cartridge is officially the data cartridge, and commercial products are designated by model numbers reflecting their capacities or, occasionally, the industry standards they abide by. Tapes for earlier cartridge standards follow a regular naming rule. The model number starts with DC (for Data Cartridge); a "6" is carried over from the earlier "600" designation (the length of the tape in the cartridge); and three digits (or so) indicate the tape capacity. Table 25.1 lists the capacities and other characteristics of these DC6000-style and newer cartridges.

TABLE 25.1. Capacities and Characteristics of QIC Cartridges

Cartridge Type	Cartridge Size	Nominal Capacity	Tape Lgth. (Ft.)	Tracks on Tape	Recording Density (flux transitions per inch)	Compatible Systems
DC 100A	1/8-in	67M	140	2	3,200	HP-85
DC 300A	Data	2.9M	300	4	3,200	QIC-11
DC 300XL/P	Data	45M	450	9	3,200-10,000	QIC-11/24
DC 600A	Data	60M	600	9	10,000	QIC-24
DC 600HW	Data	60M	600	11	10,000	Sentinel

Cartridge Type	Cartridge Size	Nominal Capacity	Tape Lgth. (Ft.)	Tracks on Tape	Recording Density (flux transitions per inch)	Compatible Systems
DC 1000	1/8-in	20M	185	12	12,500	Irwin 10/20
DC 2000	Mini	40M	205	20	10,000	QIC-40/100
DC 2080	Mini	80M	205	32	15,000	QIC-80
DC 2120	Mini	120M	307.5	32	15,000	QIC-80/128
DC 2155	Mini	155M	307.5	29	18,000	MT-01N
DC 2255	Mini	255M	295	40	22,125	QIC-3010-MC
DC 2300	Mini	560M	215	40	38,750	Excel 1G
DC 2500	Mini	500M	295	40	44,250	QIC-3020-MC
DC 2555	Mini	555M	295	40	50,800	QIC-3030-MC
DC 2750	Mini	750M	295	40	38,750	EXB-2501
DC 6037	Data	37M	155	18	12,500	WIX-120/150
DC 6150	Data	150M	620	18	12,000	QIC-120/150
DC 615A	Data	15M	150	9	10,000	QIC-24
DC 6250	Data	250M	1020	18	12,500	QIC-120/150
DC 6350	Data	320M	620	26	20,00	QIC-525
DC 6525	Data	525M	1020	26	20,000	QIC-525
Magnus 1.0	Data	1G	760	30	45,000	QIC-1000
Magnus 1.2	Data	1.2G	760	30	45,000	QIC-1000
Magnus 1.35	Data	1.35G	760	30	38,750	QIC-1350
Magnus 1.6	Data	1.6G	950	30	38,750	QIC-1350
Magnus 2.0	Data	2G	950	42	50,800	QIC-2G
Magnus 2.1	Data	2.1G	950	30	50,800	QIC-2100

Source: 3M Company

QIC

Only the media was the same in early products based on quarter-inch cartridges. Each drive manufacturer went in its own direction, not only varying the number of tracks and density of data on the tape, but also how the tape drive connected with its computer host. Every tape system was proprietary, a situation that doesn't give a computer supervisor a feeling of security when a lifetime of data is packed onto cartridges. Proprietary standards mean that whatever is stored on tape is at risk to the whims of the manufacturer. A discontinued product line could render tape unreadable in the future as drives break down. Moreover, the diversity of tape systems meant that each manufacturer essentially had to start from scratch in developing each model.

To try to lessen the chaos in the tape cartridge marketplace, a number of tape drive manufacturers—including DEI, Archive, Cipher Data, and Tandberg—met together at the National Computer Conference in Houston in 1982. They decided to form a committee to develop standards so that a uniform class of products could be introduced. The organization took the name Working Group for Quarter-Inch Cartridge Drive Compatibility, a name often shortened into QIC committee. In November, 1987, the organization was officially incorporated as Quarter-Inch Cartridge Standards, Inc.

The QIC committee was formed primarily of drive manufacturers who did not sell directly to the PC market and initially concerned itself with physical standardization. Data formats were left for system integrators to develop—and, in general, each one designed his own. With time, the committee developed into a trade association, and it recognized the need for format standardization, too. Today, it promulgates standards at all levels of the application of tape. Table 25.2 summarizes the data cartridge standards adopted by QIC to date.

TABLE 25.2. QIC Data Cartridge Standards

Standard	Native Capacity	Tracks	Bits per inch	Tape (inches per sec.)	Tape Speed Coercivity (Oersteds)	Original Adoption Date
QIC-24-DC	60	9	8,000	90	550	22-Apr-83
QIC-120-DC	125M	15	10,000	90	550	30-Oct-85
QIC-150-DC	150/250M	18	10,000	90	550	12-Feb-87
QIC-525-DC	320/525M	26	16,000	90/120	550	24-May-89
QIC-1000-DC	1.2G	30	36,000	53.3/80	550	24-Oct-90
QIC-1350-DC	1.6G	30	51,667	90/120	900	24-May-89
QIC-2GB-DC	2.56	42	40,640	70.9	900	4-Jun-92
QIC-2100-DC	2.6G	30	67,773	91.5/120	900	20-Jun-91
QIC-5GB-DC	5G	44	96,000	90	900	3-Dec-92
QIC-5010-DC	13G	144	67,773	30/60/120	900	27-Feb-92

Source: Quarter-Inch Cartridge Drive Standards, Inc.

The first standard developed by the committee to reach the marketplace in a commercial product was QIC-24, a nine-track version of a DC300 tape drive. The standard was formally approved in April, 1983, and the first commercial units shipped later that year. QIC-24 (now QIC-24-DC, the suffix indicating Data Cartridge, QIC's designation for larger tape cartridges) achieved its 60 MB of storage per tape at a density of 8,000 bits per inch. Using one-track-at-a-time serpentine recording at 90 inches per second, the system sent 720 kilobits of data per second through its QIC-02 interface.

Since then, the story of data cartridges is a continuing increase in capacity won through increasing the density of storage. New standards push up the number of bits per inch storage along the length of the tape and the number of tracks lined with data across the tape.

By slightly increasing the data density to 10,000 bits per inch and squeezing 15 tracks across the quarter-inch width of the tape, the QIC-120-DC standard more than doubles individual cartridge capacity to 125 MB. Adopted in October, 1985, the new QIC-120-DC drives could read (but not write) QIC-24-DC cartridges. Their higher storage density also increased their raw data transfer rate to 900 kilobits per second.

In February, 1987, QIC adopted its QIC-150-DC standard. A slight change in geometry along with longer tapes gave another doubling in capacity. QIC-150-DC put 18 tracks across the tape at the same 10,000 bits per inch density as QIC-125-DC. With shorter tapes (DC6150), the new standard put 150 megabytes in a cartridge; longer DC6250 tapes hold up to 250 megabytes using this format. QIC-150-DC drives can read but not write tapes made under both earlier QIC standards.

The next capacity push came in May, 1989, with the adoption of QIC-525-DC (formerly designated QIC-320). By increasing both linear and densities by 60 percent (to 16,000 bits per inch and 26 tracks), drives abiding this standard packed up to 525 megabytes on DC6525 tapes (320 megabytes on D6320 tapes). In addition, an optional tape speed increase to 120 inches per second allowed the raw transfer rate to climb to 1.92 megabits per second from tape to controller. The standard also allows for a slower, 90 inches per second speed and read compatibility with QIC-120-DC and QIC-150-DC tapes.

In October, 1990, QIC adopted the last standard to use its traditional tape medium—that is, 550 Oersted magnetic tape using group-coded recording—QIC-1000-DC. Packing 30 tracks across the tape and recording with a bit density of 36,000 per inch, the new format fit up to 1.2 gigabytes per tape cartridge. Although the new standard lowered maximum tape speed to 80 inches per second (53.3 inches per second could also be used), the higher density yielded a faster raw transfer rate, about 2.8 megabits per second. QIC-1000-DC drives could read tapes made under all previous QIC data cartridge standards except for QIC-24-DC.

At the same time QIC-525-DC was adopted, however, QIC also pushed data cartridges into the future with new technologies. The QIC-1350-DC standard introduced a new data coding method—1,7 Run Length Limited—and new, higher coercivity (900 Oersted) media. The new tape and coding let manufacturers push data density up to 51,667 bits per inch. Using 30 tracks across the tape, QIC-1350-DC can fit 1.6 gigabytes on a cartridge. At its 120 inches per second top tape speed (90 ips also allowed), the system can achieve a raw transfer rate of about 6.2 megabits per second.

Using longer tapes and a somewhat higher data density (67,773 bits per inch) the QIC-2100-DC standard, adopted in June, 1991, stretched single cartridge capacity to 2.6 gigabytes. QIC-1350-DC drives could also read QIC-525-DC and QIC-1000-DC tapes; QIC-2100-DC drives read these tapes as well as those made under the QIC-1350-DC standard cartridge using nine tracks; QIC-120, 125MB; QIC-150, up to 250MB across 18 tracks. Later standards incorporate the drive capacity as part of the designation.

Challenged by other media with greater per-cartridge storage and high transfer rates (such as eight-millimeter tape), in 1992 QIC developed three new standards to push quarter-inch cartridges into multi-gigabyte territory. QIC-2GB-DC sliced 900 Oersted tape into 42 tracks at a data density of 40,640 bits per inch, cramming 2.5 gigabytes onto a single cartridge. QIC-5GB-DC pushed the bit-density to 96,000 per inch and added two tracks (to 44) to fit up to 5 GB per cartridge. QIC-5010-DC put up to 13 megabytes on a tape by lining up 144 thin tracks across the quarter-inch tape with data at a bit-density of 67,773 per inch. Of these, QIC-5GB-DC reaches the highest raw transfer rate (about 8.6 megabits per second at 90 ips) and the greatest compatibility. DC-5GB-DC drives can read any earlier QIC data cartridge physical format. Table 25.3 summarizes the backward compatibilities of the various QIC data cartridge standards.

TABLE 25.3. QIC Data Cartridge Backward Compatibility

Standard	QIC-24 DC	QIC-120 DC	QIC-150 DC	QIC-525-DC	QIC-1000-DC
QIC-24-DC	YES	NO	NO	NO	NO
QIC-120-DC	YES	YES	NO	NO	NO
QIC-150-DC	YES	YES	YES	NO	NO
QIC-525-DC	NO	YES	YES	YES	NO
QIC-1000-DC	NO	YES	YES	YES	YES
QIC-1350-DC	NO	NO	NO	YES	YES
QIC-2GB-DC	NO	YES	YES	YES	YES
QIC-2100-DC	NO	NO	NO	YES	YES
QIC-5GB-DC	YES	YES	YES	YES	YES
QIC-5010-DC	NO	NO	YES	YES	YES

Source: QIC, 12/10/93

QIC-1350-DC	QIC-2GB-DC	QIC-2100-DC	QIC-5GB-DC	QIC-5010-DC
NO	NO	NO	NO	NO
NO	NO	NO	NO	NO
NO	NO	NO	NO	NO
NO	NO	NO	NO	NO
NO	NO	NO	NO	NO
YES	NO	NO	NO	NO
NO	YES	NO	NO	NO
YES	NO	YES	NO	NO
YES	YES	YES	YES	NO
YES	NO	YES	NO	YES

Minicartridges

If standard quarter-inch cartridges have a drawback, it's their size. Squeezing a drive to handle a six-by-four cartridge into a standard 5.25-inch drive bay is a challenge; fitting one in a modern 3.5-inch bay is an impossibility. Seeking a more compact medium, quarter-inch cartridge makers cut their products down to size, reducing tape capacity while preserving the proven drive mechanism. The result was the minicartridge. The smaller size was adopted by the QIC Committee, which now promulgates a standard for it. Table 25.4 summarizes QIC's minicartridge standards.

TABLE 25.4. QIC Minicartridge Standards

Standard	Native Capacity	Tracks	Bits per inch	Tape (inches per sec.)	Tape Speed Coercivity (Oersteds)	Original Adoption Date
QIC-40-MC	60	20	10,000	25/50	550	4-Jun-86
QIC-80-MC	125M	28	14,700	25/50	550	3-Feb-88
QIC-100-MC	40M	24	10,000	60	550	19-Mar-85
QIC-128-MC	128M	32	16,000	90	550	23-May-89
QIC-3010-MC	255M	40	22,125	22.6	900	10-Jun-93

continues

TABLE 25.4. Continued

Standard	Native Capacity	Tracks	Bits per inch	Tape (inches per sec.)	Tape Speed Coercivity (Oersteds)	Original Adoption Date
QIC-3020-MC	500M	40	44,250	22.6	900	21-Jun-93
QIC-3030-MC	580M	40	40,600	60	900	18-Apr-91
QIC-3040-MC	840M	42/52	40,600	70.9	900	9-Dec-93
QIC-3080-MC	1.6G	60	60,000	30-80	900	30-Jan-94
QIC-3090-MC	2G	48	93,333	56.5	1300	30-Jan-94
QIC-3070-MC	4G	144	67,773	N/A	900	27-Feb-92

Source: Quarter-Inch Cartridge Drive Standards, Inc.

The first minicartridge was introduced by 3M Company with the model designation DC2000, so minicartridges are often called DC2000-style cartridges. As with DC6000-size cartridges, the model designations of most minicartridges encode the cartridge capacity as their last digits. A DC2080 cartridge is designed for 80MB capacity; a DC2120 cartridge is designed for 120MB.

The minicartridge package measures just under 3.25 x 2.5 x 0.625 inches. As originally developed, it held 205 feet of tape with the same nominal quarter-inch width used by larger cartridges, hence the initial "2" in the designation.

One big advantage of the smaller cartridges is that drives for them easily fit into standard 3.5-inch bays. On the other hand, cartridge capacities are necessarily lower than full-size cartridges if just because less room for tape is available inside. From humble beginnings (40 megabytes total capacity), the storage reserves of minicartridges have grown to four gigabytes under current QIC standards. The QIC Committee envisions the small cartridges eventually holding up to 30 gigabytes.

The number of minicartridge tape drive manufacturers is surprisingly small. In 1994, they totaled about seven: Alloy, Braemar, Colorado Memory Systems, Conner (which had acquired Archive, which had acquired Irwin Magnetic), Mountain, 3M Company, and Wangtek. Other names are found on the market, but they are usually affiliates of one of these makers. For example, Maynard is the retail arm of Archive, and Irwin is now a division of Maynard, all of which are owned by Conner. Summit is a spin-off production group for Mountain.

QIC-40-MC

The first major standard used with minicartridges to win wide acceptance was QIC-40-MC. Adopted in June, 1986, the QIC-40-MC standard was originally designed primarily to be a low-cost backup medium for DOS- and OS/2-oriented systems. To keep end-user expenses under control, it was designed to link with PCs using a spare channel in conventional floppy disk controllers. Thanks to this interface, the first QIC-40-MC drives simply plugged into a vacant connector on the PC's floppy disk cable, which had the downside of limiting systems with a minicartridge drive to a single floppy drive. Modern drives link in various ways to allow two floppy drives to be used in the host PC.

Under the QIC-40-MC standard, 20 tracks were arrayed across the width of the tape, each of which held roughly two megabytes of data. Each track was divided into 68 segments of 29 sectors. Each sector stored 1,024 bytes. The standard specifies modified frequency modulation (MFM) recording, the normal output of a floppy disk controller. At standard data rates and tape speeds, information was packed at a density of 10,000 bits per inch. The operating speed of the tape depended on the kind of floppy disk controller that you linked up with. A normal-density controller (one that worked only with 360K floppies) produced a data rate of 250 kilobits per second, resulting in a tape speed of 25 inches per second. High-density controllers, which operate at 500 kilobits per second, yielded a tape speed of 50 inches per second.

QIC-40-MC went beyond earlier QIC standards by specifying the format of data on the tape. The format assigned sectors to files in much the same way as disk space is allocated. Each tape had the equivalent of a file allocation table that listed the bad sectors contained on the tape so that no bytes were risked on bad or marginal media. Data on the tape was specifically structured under the QIC-40-MC format (see fig. 25.2).

One-third of the possible 60-megabyte capacity of a DC2000 tape under the QIC-40-MC format was devoted to identifying the format structure of the tape and to data error-correction. Two methods of error correction were used, cyclical redundancy checking and a Reed Solomon code (an efficient error-correction algorithm used, among other places, in interplanetary communications—really!). The resulting theoretical error rate was extremely low—one in 10^{14}— one bad bit in 100 trillion. Do the math, and that should ensure that less than one tape in two hundred thousand had a single bit error. If achieved, the result would be fewer errors than you might expect with a typical disk drive.

The chief disadvantage of QIC-40-MC was time. Using QIC-40-MC often was an exercise in patience. Because of the use of the floppy disk interface, data transfers were limited to floppy disk speeds. Early QIC-40-MC drives also required as long as half a minute to index their read/write heads to find the edge of the tape before they started a backup session. They had to properly position themselves over the very narrow tracks on the tape. Modern drives eliminated this lengthy wait.

As with floppy disks, however, QIC-40-MC tapes required formatting before they could be used. Because the tapes had much greater capacity than floppy disks, the formatting process took commensurately longer—one full-speed pass across the head for each track. That added up to about an hour for 40 megabytes. To save formatting time, many manufacturers of QIC-40-MC systems allowed partially formatting a tape to a lower capacity, often in two-megabyte increments representing a single track. The better solution now used by most manufacturers of more modern tape formats is the preformatted cartridge. Many media vendors sell minicartridges with the formatting already done at only a slight premium over the price of unformatted tapes.

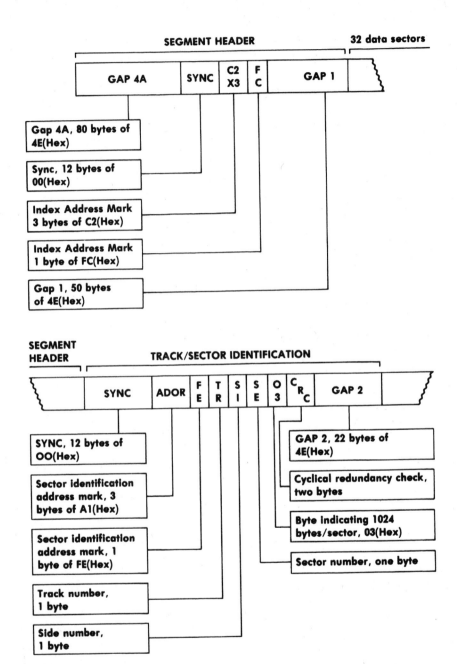

FIGURE 25.2. QIC-40 logical structure, part 1.

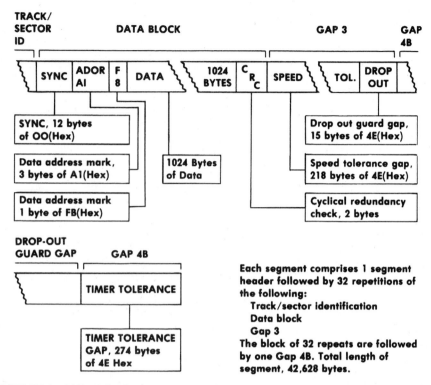

FIGURE 25.2. QIC-40 logical structure, part 2.

The formatting requirement of QIC-40-MC and subsequent minicartridge standards is not all bad. Along with the bother comes a number of benefits. For example, during the format process, bad sectors can be reserved. Because the tape is formatted with a file allocation tape, individual tape sectors can be accessed randomly. Although the tape still must be shuttled to any given spot, the format allows each sector to be unambiguously identified without reference to its neighbors. That means that you don't have to read through the whole tape just to find a single file. As a result, a QIC-40-MC tape can mimic the operation—though not the random-access speed—of a floppy disk. In addition, formatted tapes make appending files to a partially used tape easy because the system can quickly find where it left off writing to the tape.

QIC-80-MC

The next step up from QIC-40-MC is the QIC-80-MC, introduced in February, 1988, which essentially extrapolates on the earlier standard. QIC-80-MC defines not only the physical arrangement of tracks on the tape and data density but also the logical data format on the tape (which, in theory, makes cartridges made on one drive interchangeable with those made on another—a goal finally being achieved); error correction (which theoretically reduces tape error rate below that of the disk being backed up); and the data compression schemes that can optionally be used. Tape drives that follow the QIC-80-MC standard can read but not write cartridges conforming with the older QIC-40-MC standard.

The principal on-tape difference between the older and newer standards is that QIC-80-MC puts more, narrower tracks on a tape—28 rather than 20. In addition, the density of data on each track is increased from 10,000 bits per inch to 14,700. The net difference is an effective doubling of tape data storage capacity to 80 megabytes.

Although QIC-80-MC drives can use floppy disk controllers, they need not. Their interface is based on the 765 floppy disk controller chip or its equivalent, which may be part of a separate host adapter board or a spare channel in your PC's existing floppy disk controller. Which form this circuitry takes determines how easy a specific minicartridge system is to install. Some drives plug directly into any spare floppy disk drive connectors in your system. Others intercept the signals from your floppy disk controller before it goes to your drives, adding a wire and a bit of confusion inside your PC. Still others use extra expansion boards with their own dedicated electronics (which are still based on floppy disk controller chips).

Although the QIC-80-MC interface is based on a traditional floppy disk controller, the standard also supports the higher data rate used by extra-density floppy disk drives, one megabit per second. Extended length tapes that are 50 percent longer can increase the capacity of a QIC-80-MC system to 120 megabytes per cartridge. Most QIC-80-MC systems also offer the option of data compression, which can nominally yet again double cartridge capacity. (As with any data compression system, the compression ratio varies with what's being compressed—whereas programs may compress by only 10 percent, graphic files often can be reduced 90 percent.) Consequently, most makers of QIC-80-MC systems advertise them by their theoretical maximum capacity, 250 megabytes.

QIC-100-MC

The next number up from QIC-80-MC on the standards roster is QIC-100-MC, but the nomenclature is misleading. QIC-100-MC was actually the first minicartridge that QIC adopted, dating from March, 1985. Whereas the QIC-40-MC and QIC-80-MC names hint at the nominal capacities of the systems, QIC-100-MC does not. Under the QIC-100-MC standard, only 40MB can be packed on a tape.

The purpose of the additional 40MB standard was performance. By using its own controller based on the SCSI standard rather than sharing one with floppy disk drives, QIC-100-MC allowed for the option of higher data transfer rates. Of course, the additional cost of the SCSI controller also meant that QIC-100-MC systems were more expensive than floppy based systems. QIC-100-MC proved an aberration and never achieved the mainstream acceptance of QIC-40-MC or QIC-80-MC. Even the QIC Committee describes the QIC-100-MC standard as "aging," the only minicartridge standard with that designation.

QIC-100-MC allowed for serial data writing across 12 or 24 serpentine tracks at a density of 12,000 flux reversals per inch. The standard was looser than QIC-40-MC and did not define a block length. As with QIC-40-MC, QIC-100-MC tapes required formatting prior to their use.

QIC-128-MC

In May, 1989, QIC adopted its last minicartridge standard based on older 550 Oersted media, QIC-128-MC. Essentially an update of QIC-100-MC, the newer format added half again as many tracks to its predecessor (bringing the total to 32) and increased the storage density, and upped the tape speed from 60 to 90 inches per second. These changes boosted the capacity of the system by more than threefold, from 40 to 128 megabytes using DC2165 cartridges. DC-128-MC drives also can use shorter DC2110 tapes but then only deliver 86 megabytes of storage. Drives that follow the QIC-128-MC standard can read tapes made under the QIC-100-MC specification.

QIC-3000-Series

To increase the capacity of minicartridges to keep pace with fast-growing hard disks, the QIC Committee switched to new, higher coercivity media for all its later minicartridge standards. Starting in 1991, all QIC minicartridge standards are based on tape with 900 Oersted or higher coercivities. This break with the past is reflected in a new nomenclature, which no longer corresponds to capacity.

The first of these new standards was adopted in April, 1991, and brought the same high-speed technology used by larger data cartridges to the minicartridge format. Originally designated QIC-470 and QIC-555M but later renamed QIC-3030-MC, the new standard pushed up data density to 40,600 bits per inch while rolling the tape along at 60 inches per second, sufficient to deliver an effective raw transfer rate approaching 2.5 megabits per second. To move this high-speed data stream to your system, QIC endowed the new standard with a SCSI-2 interface. To maximize capacity, the QIC-3030-MC standard specified 40 tracks across the quarter-inch tape width, yielding 580 megabytes on a standard 900 Oersted QIC-143 cartridge. The new design was unlike anything else in the minicartridge arena, so QIC-3030-MC drives were not back-wardly compatible with any previous standard.

A few months later, in June, 1991, QIC adopted another standard in the same capacity range, QIC-3020-MC (previously designated as QIC-385 and QIC-500M), that allowed drives to read QIC-40-MC and QIC-80-MC cartridges. As with those predecessors, QIC designed this new format to use floppy disk or AT Attachment (IDE) interfaces. To accommodate these interfaces, QIC lowered the tape speed to 22.6 inches per second while maintaining a high data density (44,250 bits per inch). As with QIC-3030-MC, QIC-3020-MC put 40 tracks across the tape, allowing the two standards to share the same physical mechanism with only a firmware change needed to alter the speed and data density. The resulting format packed 500 MB on a standard QIC-143 minicartridge.

To counter the threat from helical media, in February, 1992, QIC introduced a refined version of QIC-3030-MC that could pack up to four gigabytes of uncompressed data on a single minicartridge. Achieving that capacity required slicing the tracks thinly—144 of them across the tape—and increasing linear density up to 67,773 bits per inch. Drives complying with the resulting standard, designated QIC-3070-MC, also can read QIC-3030MC tapes.

In June, 1993, QIC adopted a lower capacity version of QIC-(e)3020-MC as QIC-3010-MC. By halving the data density, the new standard halved the capacity of the tape with all other vital parameters unchanged. The resulting standard is less demanding on equipment and results in less dense storage, which should be more reliable. Because of its heritage, QIC-3010-MC drives can read QIC-40-MC and QIC-80-MC tapes. Moreover, QIC-3030-MC drives can read QIC-3010-MC tapes, but lower capacity drives cannot read the tapes made on higher capacity mechanisms.

Competing directly with Digital Audio Tape (discussed later) in the low-gigabyte backup range are two standards adopted by QIC in January, 1994. QIC-3080-MC puts up to 1.6 gigabytes on a now-standard 900 Oersted minicartridge by laying 60 tracks across the tape with a linear data density of 60,000 bits per inch with a tape speed of 30 to 80 inches per second. QIC-3090-MC increases per-cartridge storage with higher data densities made possible by 1300 Oersted tape. A single QIC-3090-MC holds up to two gigabytes spread across 48 tracks at a linear density of 93.333 bits per inch. In the QIC-3090-MC system, the tape travels at 56.5 inches per second.

The largest capacity format for minicartridges approved by QIC packs up to four gigabytes per tape. QIC-3070-MC, adopted February, 1992, specifies laying 144 tracks across a 900 Oersted quarter-inch tape at a linear density of 67,773 bits per inch. The drives use special cartridges (QIC-138) but can read tapes made under the QIC-3030-MC standard as well as its own.

Data Compression

You can nominally double the capacity of any tape backup using data compression software. In fact, QIC standards cover two compression algorithms. QIC-122 is based on the same algorithm used by Stac Electronics commercial Stacker software. QIC-130 is a compression standard developed by Hewlett-Packard Company that uses an algorithm called DCLZ, which stands for Data Compression according to Lempel and Ziv. Both QIC compression methods rely on the same underlying compression principle: they reduce repetitive data to a short token that refers to a longer block of data kept in a dictionary. They work by checking the incoming data stream for sequences recorded in the dictionary, replacing each one it finds with the corresponding token. Either algorithm provides a data-dependent apparent increase in cartridge capacity averaging around a factor of two.

With the exception of the three earlier data cartridge standards (QIC-24-DC, QIC-120-DC, and QIC-150-DC), QIC standards allow manufacturers to optionally choose either variety of compression for their products. Minicartridge manufacturers have the same choice except under the QIC-100-MC and QIC-128-MC standards (for which no compression standard has been adopted), and QIC-3010-MC and QIC-3020-MC (for which QIC has adopted only the QIC-122 compression standard).

Cartridge Compatibility

Compatibility remains a thorny issue with quarter-inch tape cartridges. Tapes of the same physical size fit into drives regardless of format, but to operate properly they must be matched to the mechanism because of differing coercivities. With the few exceptions already noted, tapes made under one standard are unreadable by drives following another standard. The exceptions, however, enable you to install a new drive without the need to update and replace all your backup tapes.

Compatibility concerns run deeper, however. Even if two drives follow a given QIC standard, they may not produce tapes that are interchangeable between them. Some QIC standards define only the physical format of data on the tape—that is, the number of tracks and bits per inch. Individual managers are left to decide how that storage should be managed, for example by dividing it into blocks or sectors. Some QIC standards do define a logical format for tape-based data, but they fall short of actually specifying the exact arrangement of the tape file structure. That's left to the individual software developer who makes the backup program to run the tape system. As a result, although tapes are interchangeable between different drives and can be read without regard to the equipment used, your backup software might not be able to make sense of the results. Because there's no compatibility of file structure, you can read every byte on a tape in any system, but all you might end up with is a big pile of data—files can run into one another and even intermingle.

Some QIC standards are designed to permit interchangeability. In fact, two QIC standards (QIC-140 and QIC-141) specify read-only minicartridges and data cartridges designed for distributing software. The use of cartridge tape has not, however, won wide acceptance for program distribution. The cost of mass producing CD-ROMs is much less, although tape can be competitive with recordable Compact Discs when distribution requires only a few copies.

Helical-Scan Systems

The basic principle of all the preceding tape systems is that the tape moves past a stationary head. The speed the tape moves and the density of data on the tape together determine how fast information can be read or written, just as the data density and rotation rate of disks control data rate. Back in the 50s, however, data rate was already an issue when engineers tried to put television pictures on ordinary recording tape. They had the equivalent of megabytes to move every second, and most ordinary tape systems topped out in the thousands. The inspired idea that made video recording possible was to make the head move as well as the tape to increase the relative speed of the two.

Obviously, the head could not move parallel to the tape. The first videotape machines made the head move nearly perpendicular to the tape movement. Through decades of development, however, rotating a head at a slight angle to the tape so that the head traces out a section of a helix against the tape has proven to be the most practical system. The resulting process is called helical scan recording. Today, two helical-scan systems are popular, eight-millimeter and Digital Audio Tape (DAT).

In a helical scan recording system, the rotating heads are mounted on a drum. The tape wraps around the drum outside its protective cartridge. Two arms pull the tape out of the cartridge and wrap it about halfway around the drum. (Some systems, like unlamented Betamax, wrap tape nearly all the way around the drum.) So that the heads travel at an angle across the tape, the drum is canted at a slight angle, about five degrees for eight-millimeter drives and about six degrees for DAT.

Helical scan recording can take advantage of the entire tape surface. Conventional stationary-head recording systems must leave blank areas—*guard bands*—between the tracks containing data. Helical systems can and do overlap tracks. Although current eight-millimeter systems use guard bands, DAT writes the edges of tracks over one another.

This overlapping works because the rotating head drum actually has two (or more) heads on it, and each head writes data at a different angular relationship (called the *azimuth*) to the tracks on the tape. In reading data, the head responds strongly to the data written at the same azimuth as the head and weakly at the other azimuth. In DAT machines, one head is skewed 20 degrees forward from perpendicular to its track; the other head is skewed backward an equal amount.

Eight Millimeter

Probably the most familiar incarnation of eight-millimeter tape is in miniaturized camcorders. Sony pioneered the medium as a compact, high-quality video recording system. The same tapes were later adapted to data recording by Exabyte Corporation and first released on the PC market in 1987. The Exabyte remains the sole supplier of eight millimeter digital tape drives.

Video recorders have in the past been used as the basis of tape backup systems. However, these relied on converting digital computer signals into an analog format that could be recorded on tape as if it were a video signal. Alpha Microsystems used this approach in a product the company calls *Videotrax*, which used a single expansion card in the host computer converts hard disk or other system data into NTSC (National Television Standards Committee) video signals. The resulting signals were then stored on a conventional videocassette recorder.

The eight-millimeter helical system created by Exabyte, on the other hand, records digital data in a digital format without conversion. In fact, the Exabyte system shares only the cassette with the eight-millimeter video recording system. The signals and equipment are entirely different.

The eight-millimeter cassette resembles an audio cassette because it has two hubs within its plastic shell, but the tape is much wider (eight millimeters, of course, that's 0.315 inch compared to 0.150 inch for cassette tape) and a hinged door on the cassette protects the tape from physical damage. The cassette itself measures 3.75-inch by 2.5-inch and about half an inch thick.

In the original Exabyte eight-millimeter digital recording system, the head drum rotated at 1,800 revolutions per minute while the tape traveled past it at 10.89 millimeters per second to achieve a track density of 819 per inch and a flux density of 54 kilobits per inch—enough to squeeze 2.5 megabytes on a single cartridge. Improvements extended the capacity to five megabytes without compression and up to 10GB with compression. The tape can be rapidly shuttled forward and backward to find any given location (and block of data) within about 15 seconds.

Eight millimeter drives tend to be quite expensive. Complete systems cost thousands of dollars. A raw drive alone starts at over one thousand dollars. Its primary market is backing up file servers, machines that can benefit from its huge capacity.

Digital Audio Tape

Developed originally as a means to record music, Digital Audio Tape was first released as a computer storage medium in 1989. Using a tape four millimeters wide (and sometimes called four millimeter tape), DAT uses tiny cartridges to store huge amounts of data. The first DAT system could pack 1.3 gigabytes into a cassette measuring only 0.4 x 2.9 x 2.1 inches (HWD). The result is the most dense storage of any current computer tape medium, 114 megabits per square inch on special 1450 Oersted metal particle tape (the same material as used by eight millimeter digital tape systems). A cassette holds either 60 or 90 meters of this tape. The shorter tapes store 1.3GB; the longer tapes store 2.0GB.

In a DAT drive, the tape barely creeps along, requiring about three seconds to move an inch—a tape speed of eight millimeters per second. The head drum, however, spins rapidly at 2,000 revolutions per minute, putting down 1,869 tracks across a linear inch of tape with flux transitions packed 61 kilobits per inch.

DAT technology has two important strengths: access speed and capacity. In the audio realm, the DAT medium was designed for rapid access to information—finding a musical selection. Consequently, when translated into the computer realm, DAT could locate a file in about 15 seconds. Although access speed is of little importance for backups, quick times make for easy file restorations.

Nonstandard Tape Systems

A number of tape systems have been developed by clever engineers, which, while often brilliant, failed to ignite the market. Typically, these nonstandard systems excelled in one or more characteristics (such as price, performance, capacity, or convenience), but never yielded an overall package that bettered the established formats. Most disappeared quietly into the ages—and usually with good reason. You might still encounter some of these technologies as close-outs and, increasingly, in museums (or in PCs that should be in museums). Among these forgotten and forgettable formats are DC1000 cartridges, servo-formatted tapes, and spooled tape.

DC1000 Cartridges

About the same length and width as DC2000s but thinner, DC1000 cartridges used 150 mil (thousandths of an inch) wide tape—the same width as audio cassette tape—and held 10 to 20 megabytes. In a world in which 200-megabyte hard disks are becoming the norm, the fate of such a small capacity system is not hard to predict.

Tape systems based on the DC1000 cartridge at one time proved popular mostly because of their low price. In fact, when interfaced through a floppy disk controller, DC1000 systems were among the least expensive tape systems available for small computer systems. Irwin Magnetic (absorbed by Conner Peripherals) dominated the industry and essentially set its own standard for such products.

The DC1000 had no inherent flaw but low capacity. The format could not keep up with the fast growth in hard disk capacities. Moreover, the prices of DC2000 systems fell while the QIC Committee was able to wring ever larger capacities from the tapes. The marketplace simply outgrew DC1000.

Servo-Formatted Minicartridges

For a period, DC1000 was successful, so Irwin Magnetic adapted some of its technology to the larger DC2000 cartridges. Instead of using the standard QIC-40-MC or QIC-80-MC format on DC2000 tapes, Irwin developed its own proprietary (and QIC-incompatible) embedded-servo tape format. The servo data on the tape helps positively position the read/write head in relation to the thin track on the tape, allowing the use of a less precise, lower cost tape drive.

Again, nothing was inherently wrong with the technology. In fact, future high-capacity QIC formats would use a variation on the same scheme. The system worked so well that at one time Irwin Magnetic had about half the market for minicartridge tape drives. However, other companies pushed the prices of their QIC-80-MC products below that of the Irwin drives, and the company lost market share. Although the drives are still available, the company was acquired by Archive Corporation and later folded into the company's other operations.

Spooled Tape

For a brief while one company, Interdyne, offered what could be viewed as a cross between quarter-inch cartridges and open reel tape—or even 3480 cartridges with narrower tape and without the cartridge. The design was called spooled tape. That is, you slid a plastic-cased spool of quarter-inch tape into a drive that automatically threaded it onto an integral tape-up spool. As with many tape backup systems, the Interdyne spooled tape drive used a floppy disk controller. In theory, the cartridgeless cartridges were cheaper than other designs, but the Interdyne design failed to catch on.

Other Issues

When buying a tape drive or its media, you confront other issues besides the tape format. Among these are the way the drive installs in (or out) of your PC and the media that you slide into the drive.

Internal and External Drives

Internal and external units are generally much the same—the only effective difference is that you need a free drive bay to install an internal system. External systems tend to be costlier because they require a case and a connecting cable. However, they offer the advantage that you can shuttle a single backup drive between several PCs (providing that you equip each with the necessary host adapter).

Better still are external drives that link to PCs through standard bi-directional parallel ports. Because nearly every PC has a parallel port built in, you can shuttle one of these machines around without the worry of adding host adapters. Using conventional parallel ports, such drives can attain the speeds of other units that use floppy disk interfaces. Linked with Enhanced Parallel Ports, they can rival backup systems with SCSI connections. If you have a number of PCs to regularly back up, a single external tape drive can do the job.

Internal drives are the choice when you don't want clutter or want to save the cost the drive manufacturer charges for packaging and powering an external unit. As with other peripherals you install internally, you must have a free bay for an internal tape drive, and the bay requires front panel access. Nearly all internal tape drives require the power as used by disk drives—positive five volts DC for their logic, twelve volts for their drive motors—and they link to your PC's power supply with a standard drive power connector.

Media Matching

As with other removable media drives, cartridges (or whatever) serve as the raw material that a tape drive works upon. Although most tape media are entirely different from tape cartridges used in audio and video products, some data tape cartridges are physically similar to their other worldly counterparts—D/CAS, eight millimeter, and DAT cassettes. Considering the premium prices charged for data-certified media, substituting audio or video cassettes can be tempting indeed. Even within the realm of computer products, it is sometimes tempting to substitute a cheaper minicartridge for those officially sanctioned for a tape drive.

Unfortunately, data tapes are engineered with different characteristics such as coercivity and retentivity. Mismatches between the needs of a machine and the characteristics of the media result in poor performance—even unusable backups. In some cases, designers have tried to prevent you from sliding the wrong media into a drive. For exampe, audio cassettes do not fit a D/CAS machine because of the coding notch in the backbone of the latter. Audio and video helical scan cassettes, however, do fit computer drives. Because computer systems put much more stringent requirements on their media, you should not attempt to substitute one for another. Although a drop-out on an audio tape likely is undetectable (powerful error-correction circuitry ensures that), the same tape flaw can result in an error and loss of data in a computer system. With eight millimeter tape, matching the right medium is more critical because eight millimeter video tapes are designed for analog recording, while computer systems put digital data recorded into saturation onto their tapes.

Much as metal tape does not sound very good when used in a stereo that is not "metal ready," the wrong tape in a data system can result in an unacceptably high error rate. If you value your data, do not attempt to use a tape not certified for the data density your system uses.

Backup Software

The tape drive is only part of a true backup system. Just as important is the software that runs the system. The software determines what you can do with a tape drive and how you do it.

Almost universally, today's backup software gives you (or should give you) menu control and some means of automating your regular backup procedure—for example, a batch mode or command-driven option. If you only make occasional backups, you probably do not want to spend the time learning an elaborate command structure, so these menu-controlled systems are often best. However, if you want to automate the backup process and make untended backups, you'll either want software that can be run in command mode or a program that has provisions to automatically swing into action while you count sheep, worrying whether it will actually work and whether you've left your PC switched on.

In general, the following two backup techniques have evolved—image and file-by-file backups—with manufacturers each developing their own format standard for their own tapes.

> *Image backups.* The image backup is a bit-for-bit copy of the original disk. Bytes are merely read from the disk and copied on tape without a glance to their content or structure. Because little processing overhead is involved, these image backups can be fast.

The problem with image backups is that they typically require restoring to exactly the same drive as was backed up because they read the bad tracks with the good and unused disk areas with those that are used. Obviously, this technique is not very versatile if you want to exchange data between systems—or if your hard disk crashes and must be replaced. One solution to this problem is adding intelligence to the restoration program so that it can add the needed structure when moving files back to disk from tape.

Another image problem is that the image backup is an all-or-nothing process. Although it may be the fastest way of moving all the information from a disk to tape, it fails when it comes to backing up a single file. Along with that file, the rest of the entire disk contents must be backed up—a big waste of time.

File-by-file backups. File-by-file backups add structure to the information as it is backed up. Although processing overhead tends to slow down file-by-file systems, finding files within the structure (and hence, individual file restoration) is easier.

The problem with file-by-file backups is the time required to process the file structure data. In the past, this processing time slowed most systems so severely they could not supply data to tape drives fast enough to keep the tape streaming. When the drive reverted to start-stop recording, backup times skyrocketed.

More powerful PCs and better backup software changed this situation. Most PCs are powerful enough to read disk data, process it, and send it to a tape drive fast enough to keep the drive streaming. File-by-file backups are more efficient because they back up only the data you need to backup, but they can take a performance lead over image backups. Consequently, file-by-file backing up has almost completely replaced the image backup process today.

File-by-file backup systems afford several methods of selecting files to be written to tape. You can specify files by typing a file name or some identifying characteristic or tag files by choosing them from a menu-like display.

Several identifying characteristics help you select files. The most popular of these, which should be expected as normal file selection options, include archive bits, which indicate whether a file has been previously backed up; date stamps, which enable you to backup files changed after a given date; and subdirectory searches, which include all files in the daughter directories of the one being backed up. Some software also enables you to specifically exclude files from a backup session, either by name or tagging.

Most tape systems enable you to give a name to every backup session that can later be read to identify a tape if, for example, you neglect to put a physical label on it. Many backup systems also enable you to embed a password so that the secrecy of your data is not compromised if a tape is lost or stolen.

Cost Issues

For most people, the most important factor guiding their backup choice is cost. In general, more buys more—speed, capacity, compatibility, and convenience.

The most expensive systems for PCs today are those that use nine-track open-reel tapes. They earn their keep by giving your data the utmost security as well as providing a portal through which you can access and exchange data with other computer systems. Next in the price spectrum are the helical scan systems. You pay for their prodigious capacities and advanced spinning-head technology.

In quarter-inch cartridges, larger DC6000-style systems are the most expensive, but are also fastest and have the larger capacity.

Tape Requirements

With any removable media system, the cost of the medium can quickly eclipse the price of the hardware. Consequently, you will be tempted to limit the number of tapes in which you invest.

For most backup scenarios, you will want sufficient media capacity to hold a minimum of three complete backups. For greater peace of mind or more elaborate backup rituals—such as keeping a separate backup for each day of the week—your media needs increase. Most people actively use between six and ten tapes in their regular backup routine.

You also should figure in the cost of periodically replacing any media that can wear out. All tape media and all disks except for cartridge hard disks eventually wear out.

The exact amount of life to expect from a particular medium depends on your own personal paranoia. According to one major media manufacturer, DEI, DC600-style cartridges should last for 5,000 to 6,000 passes across the read/write head. On the other hand, cautious mainframe managers may routinely replace open reel tapes after they've been used as few as 50 times. A good compromise, according to DEI, is annual replacement of your backup tapes.

When you look beyond backing up, other considerations can overrule the price differences between systems. For instance, when you absolutely need access to mainframe tapes or want to interchange information, you'll have to bite the bullet and budget for an open-reel tape drive.

Backup Strategy

The best backup system is the one that you are most likely to use—and use routinely. No matter how good or expensive it is, a backup system is worthless if you never bother to put it to work. The easiest and most convenient backup system to operate is the one least likely to be ignored—

and the one most likely to help when disaster strikes.

No matter what backup hardware you choose, you still need a backup system. That system requires more than just hardware, even more than software. To make it work, you must adhere to a strict backup routine after you make one overall backup of all the files on your hard disk.

If you plan on overseeing all your backups as they happen, the fastest backup system is always the more endurable. If your time is valuable and if you don't mind leaving your PC running overnight (and have the faith that it will, indeed, continue to run overnight), taking advantage of automatic backup programs makes the time spent backing up meaningless. If you don't have to wait, it doesn't matter how long it takes.

Even a slow backup system is better than none, and even an occasional backup beats not having any. All it takes is one disk crash, however, for you to learn how important it is to take the time—no matter how long—to keep your backups current.

The best backup system is the one that enforces the routine you are most likely to follow—the one that ensures that you have protection when the worst does happen. A backup system that does not get used (or used often) is not a backup system at all.

Appendix A
Regulations

Radio Frequency Emission

You may not think of your PC as a radio transmitter, but it is. As with all electrical devices, a computer radiates electromagnetic fields. The frequencies at which your PC operates puts these fields in the range that a radio or television set may pick up. Of course, these radio emissions are not intentional. They are an unwanted byproduct of a simple physical principle. Any moving electronic current, including the minuscule logic signals inside your PC, creates an electromagnetic field. If the current flow starts and stops or changes direction, it induces an electromagnetic field that causes radio waves to radiate into space. (Unchanging current flows produce steady-state or static fields.)

The unintentional nature of these signals does not matter to the FCC (Federal Communications Commission). Almost anything that gets into the airwaves is within the jurisdiction of the Commission. In fact, its oversight of signals starts at frequencies that you could hear if they were sound waves—9,000 Hertz—and keeps going almost to frequencies you could see as light waves—300 billion Hz.

The Commission created a body of rules and regulations that cover signals akin to those emitted by your computer, and it has Congressional authority to enforce its rules. It can, in fact, determine which computers can be sold and when—and which will haunt their designers as costly yet stillborn, unmarketable products. Every personal computer and most computer peripherals sold in the United States must comply with these rules and regulations.

Nevertheless, few people (including the makers of many PCs and peripheral products) know what those rules govern, what they are meant to achieve, and why anyone should care. In ignorance or in defiance of the FCC's authority, many computer manufacturers offer PCs for sale without regard to these rules. Selling such computers is illegal in the United States.

For the computer designer who is aware of and obedient to the FCC rules, complying with them is that last hoop to be leapt through, the final test before his life's work can nestle on your dealer's shelf. The need for certification affects you, too. Because of this need for certification, your access to new technology is considerably slowed. Any computer product must be ready to be sold before it can be certified, and certification can take six to eight weeks. Automatically, the latest gear faces a month and a half or longer delay getting to market.

On the other hand, the good side of certification may seem slight. For example, FCC certification does not guarantee that a computer product is safe. Health and safety are not the concern of the FCC; a product that meets FCC standards could nevertheless radiate harmful signals or contaminate your office with arcane poisons. The FCC rules also do not guarantee that a given computer product absolutely won't interfere with your radio or television reception. (That's why instructions for eliminating interference caused by a computer are included in the manual of properly certified equipment.) All FCC certification shows is that a particular product does not exceed a given level of interference with broadcast services, such as television and radio transmissions (including cellular phones, emergency radio services, and the radio-navigation equipment used by airplanes). Even though it doesn't seem like much, achieving this level of protection is something for which you and your neighbors should be thankful—even if it is often a big headache for computer manufacturers.

Interference

Interference is one of the most important reasons underlying the FCC's very existence. The Commission was created in 1934 primarily (but not exclusively) to sort out the mess made by early broadcasters who, in the 1920s, transmitted signals whenever, wherever, and however they wanted. As a result, in some places the airwaves became a thick goulash from which no radio could successfully sort a single program. The FCC was created to bring order to that chaos, and to do so it created strict rules to prevent interference between radio stations. As other services began to use the airwaves, the FCC set rules for them, too, always with the same purpose, to prevent signals from interfering with one another—not to limit what you can hear but to ensure that you can clearly hear what is there.

Although at first the FCC was interested only in signals meant to be broadcast, the advent of modern computer equipment operating at high frequencies created a new source of radio interference. The clock frequencies of computers currently sit in the middle of communications frequencies and are edging up on the television and FM broadcast bands. (A few older computers operate at frequencies within the AM broadcast band, but IBM-standard PCs have never stooped so low.)

Potential radio and television interference doesn't seem like a cause for concern. Compared to the quality of network television programming, interference can be an improvement. When the FCC took control and created the computer emission standards, however, the situation was more serious. At the time (the late 1970s), emissions from computer-like equipment were already proving to be a dangerous if not life-threatening problem. For example, according to the FCC, the police departments of several Western states reported their radios were receiving interference from coin-operated video games based on computer-style circuitry. At an East Coast airport, interference in aeronautical communications was traced to the computer-like electronic cash register at a drug store a mile away. Hobbyist-style computers and hand-held calculators were already on the market and were known to generate spurious radio signals. The Radio Shack TRS-80 was notorious for the television interference it generated. Even though the personal computer boom of the 1980s could not have been foreseen, the increased use of high-frequency digital logic circuitry promised that the situation could only become worse.

In a first attempt to regulate the emissions of personal computers, the FCC developed a special set of rules for them, enacted in October 1979, as the infamous Subpart J of Part 15 emblazoned on the certification stickers on millions of PCs sold through 1989. In March of that year, the rules were rewritten to bring together computers and other equipment that generated similar interference in a rewritten Part 15 as Subpart B. The new rules apply to all electronic equipment that inadvertently creates radio signals. The FCC calls this equipment unintentional radiators, as opposed to devices that intentionally create radio signals for communications or related purposes. Of course, intentional radiators from television stations to garage door openers also are governed by the FCC rules.

Scope of Regulation

The new FCC rules specifically cover personal computers as well as other larger and smaller computer systems—from mainframes to pocket calculators. In addition, personal computer peripherals also are included. In fact, most peripherals must undergo the same certification process as computer systems. The rules explicitly define which peripherals require certification and which do not.

Peripherals, according to the FCC, include both internal and external devices used to enhance a personal computer. External devices connected to a PC require their own certification unless they are sold together with the computer, in which case the PC and peripheral must be certified together. Internal peripherals need not be certified only if they do not affect the speed or performance of the computer and do not connect with external cables.

A serial communications board or a graphics board needs to be certified because it has a connector for external devices. A turbo upgrade board requires certification because it increases the speed and radiation potential of the computer. A memory-only expansion board or a hard disk controller does not require certification.

Computer components ordinarily used only in making a computer at the factory are considered to be subassemblies and as such do not require certification. When subassemblies are united to make a personal computer that will be sold to end users, the entire computer must be certified.

Cases, motherboards, and power supplies are specifically designated as subassemblies and need not—and cannot—be FCC certified. As things stand now, a computer motherboard does not require certification, but when that motherboard is installed in a case with a power supply sold as a personal computer, the entire assembly must be certified. Several organizations, including IBM, have lobbied to get motherboards separately certified, but as of this writing the efforts have not been successful.

The rules recognize that the testing apparatus required for compliance with verification is beyond the reach of the average computer hobbyist—and, implicitly, that the hobbyist may be beyond the reach of the FCC if just because the effects of his efforts are so minor. Consequently, the FCC rules allow a specific exception to the need for certification for homemade personal computers. For this exception to apply, the homebuilt PC must meet all three of the following criteria: one, it must not be marketed or offered for sale; two, it must not be made from a kit; and three, it must be made in quantities of five or fewer solely for personal use. Commercial computer kits, on the other hand, must be certified by the FCC.

Some kinds of commercial personal computer equipment also are specifically excluded from the need for certification under the FCC rules. Low-power devices are unlikely to radiate substantial interference, so equipment that uses less than six nanowatts (billionths of a watt) in its high-frequency circuits are specifically excluded. All current microprocessors use far more power than this. For example, a 50 MHz 486 microprocessor uses about nine watts, about a billion times too much energy to sneak through the lower barrier of the requirements.

Equipment that operates at very low frequencies does not have to comply with the FCC rules that cover certification. A frequency of nine kilohertz is the minimum cut-off for the FCC definition of digital device, so slower (more correctly, glacial) systems need not worry. The effective limit is actually much higher—devices operating at speeds lower than 1.705MHz that do not use AC power also are excluded.

Mice and joysticks are explicitly excluded from the need for certification because they contain no high-frequency circuits and use no high-frequency signals. However, a smart mouse with its own internal microprocessor requires certification.

FCC Classes

By now, only the dead and the demented are unaware that the FCC divides digital devices into two classes, A and B, with entirely different standards for allowable emissions and testing. The division is made on the basis of where the equipment is likely to be used. Class A digital devices are those suited only to business, commercial, and industrial applications. Class B applies to digital devices likely to be used in the home.

The FCC rules explicitly define personal computers—all personal computers—as Class B equipment. The rules also define the specific term "personal computer" so that just about anything you may think of laying your hands on qualifies. What was classed as a "home" computer years ago—for example, the Commodore 64—is specifically included because the FCC included any computer that uses a television set as its display device in its personal computer definition. The rules go even farther. Computers with dedicated display systems, such as the PC that's probably sitting on your desk, meet the FCC definition as a personal computer if it has the following three characteristics:

1. It was marketed through a retail dealer or direct mail outlet.
2. Advertisements of the equipment are directed toward the general public rather than restricted to commercial users.
3. The computer operates on battery or 120-volt AC electrical power.

Note that how a particular computer actually is sold does not matter. As long as a particular model has been offered for sale through a dealer or direct mail outlet, it meets the first requirement.

The definition of Class A equipment implicitly covers mainframe and minicomputers, most of which use industrial-strength 230 volt power. According to the rules, however, the most important distinguishing characteristic is that Class A devices are of such nature or cost that they would or could not be used at home by individuals. Here the FCC gives manufacturers an out.

Manufacturers or importers can apply to the FCC to have specific personal computers treated as Class A devices providing the computer is of such a nature—priced too high or delivers performance too high—that it is not suitable for residential or hobbyist use.

No hard and fast rule covers what is too powerful or too expensive to be a computer suitable for use in the home. One general (but not absolute) guideline used by the FCC is that a base retail price higher than $5,000 makes a computer more likely to be used in a business setting. Currently, computers based on Pentium or more powerful microprocessors may be powerful enough to likely earn the FCC's approval to be rated as Class A devices. As the power of PCs increases, prices plummet, and the expectations of home users skyrocket, this guideline likely will shift.

Note manufacturers cannot simply declare that a given computer is a Class A device. They must apply to the FCC for such a classification—and they must be able to support their claims. The FCC confirms its classification with a letter of notification.

All portable personal computers are considered to be Class B devices because their very portability makes them likely to be used in a residential setting. Although Class A portable computers are theoretically conceivable—for example, a machine dedicated to taking seismological measurements in oil prospecting—general purpose portable PCs cannot qualify as Class A devices. In other words, any portable computer from the smallest palmtop to an arm-stretching old lunchbox offered to you for sale as a Class A device violates the FCC rules. Legally, such a computer cannot be sold in the United States.

A substantial incentive exists for manufacturers to want their products treated as Class A devices. Not only are the emission requirements more lax for Class A devices, but in addition, a personal computer rated Class A does not require the lengthy FCC certification process. Instead, a Class A device only needs to be *verified* by its maker to comply with the FCC rules. In other words, while Class B equipment must be certified by the FCC, a process which involves the FCC or, more usually, a special lab actually testing the equipment. The results of the tests are filed with the FCC, and the FCC then issues the certification. A Class A device is tested and verified to comply with the FCC rules by its manufacturer, and the manufacturer simply files the results. The latter process is admittedly quicker. It also offers the potential for creative interpretation of the rules. For example, a manufacturer might succumb to marketing pressure and say equipment is verified before it actually is. However, the FCC can double-check Class A verified equipment and prohibit its sale if it doesn't in fact meet the standard and punish those who fraudulently claim to have verified equipment.

Radiation Limits

The justification of the distinction between Class A and B devices may seem nebulous, and the different forms of test procedures insupportable, but there's good reason behind both.

The emission limits for a Class B device are not arbitrary or capricious. They represent a value believed by the FCC to be low enough that they do not cause interference to radio or television reception when more than one wall and 30 feet separate the computer and the television set or radio. That 30 feet and one wall is a reasonable description of the distance between one household and another (at least it's reasonable to the FCC). In other words, the standard is designed so that if Class B equipment causes interference at all, it is only a bother in the home of the person owning the computer. The neighbors shouldn't have anything to worry about.

Class A equipment, on the other hand, may produce interference in equipment nearly ten times farther away. The higher tolerance for interference is based on the assumption that most residential areas are substantially more than 30 feet from industrial or commercial buildings. This greater separation means that even with greater emissions, Class A devices should not bother the neighbors. However, in a residential neighborhood, a Class A device may cause interference to neighbors' radio and television reception.

Two kinds of emissions are covered by the limits in the FCC rules: conductive emissions, those conducted through the wires in the power cord; and radiation, the signals broadcast as radio signals from the computer into space. The maximum strength of the emissions varies with frequency. Table A.1 lists the limits for the two classes of equipment.

TABLE A.1. Emission Limits for Class A and Class B Digital Devices

Conducted Limits

Frequency of Emission (MHz)	Conductive Limit (millivolts)	
	Class A	Class B
0.45 to 1.705	1000	250
1.705 to 30.0	3000	250

Radiated LimitsClass A

Frequency of Emission (MHz)	Maximum Field Strength (microvolts per meter) measured at ten meters
30 to 88	90
88 to 216	150
216 to 960	210
960 and above	300

Class B

Frequency of Emission (MHz)	Maximum Field Strength (microvolts per meter) measured at three meters
30 to 88	100
88 to 216	150
216 to 960	200
960 and above	500

The different testing arrangements—verification versus certification—for Class A and B equipment reflect some of the realities the FCC envisioned in the two types of computer equipment with which the rules are concerned. Class B products are those mass produced in the thousands or millions. Sending a sample to a lab should be no hardship (except for the delay imposed in the certification process). Class A equipment may likely be unique, for example a custom-installed mainframe in an environmentally-controlled computer room. Sending a one-of-a-kind mainframe computer to the FCC testing lab would be impractical at best. Moreover, because more Class B than Class A devices are likely to be unleashed on the public, a higher degree of assurance against interference from the more popular equipment seems warranted.

Under the FCC rules, commercial or industrial equipment can be sent to the FCC to be certified as Class B equipment, and Class B equipment can be used in business locations. The opposite is not true, however. Class A equipment should not be used in residential areas.

Enforcement

The law doesn't say that you can't use a Class A device in your home, nor will the Radio Police bust down your door if you do. The FCC rules implicitly allow you to get away with using a Class A device in your home—as long as no one notices. If, however, your computer causes interference to someone's radio or television reception—no matter whether your PC is a Class A or Class B device—you are responsible for eliminating the interference. If you don't, the FCC can order you to stop using your computer until you fix the interference problem, and if you don't obey the order, you may be fined or imprisoned. That threat alone should be sufficient to make you think twice about using a Class A device at home.

If that policy seems to incorporate more than a bit of Big Brother, you should be aware that the FCC also has the authority to demand to see your personal computer almost whenever they want. The FCC rules require that the owner of any Class A or B device (or any equipment subject to the FCC rules) make the equipment and any accompanying certification available for inspection upon request at any reasonable time (generally, that means 9 AM to 5 PM on workdays). You also must "promptly furnish" any FCC representative that calls upon you with such information as may be requested concerning the operation of your personal computer.

You needn't watch warily out your windows for big vans slowly driving down your street with dish antennae pointed in your general direction, however. Those vans are things of cheap spy novels and cheaper movies. In reality, the FCC uses ordinary-looking cars that may not even have an evident antenna. Moreover, the FCC doesn't arbitrarily go out looking for people holding Class A computers in their homes. The interference-locating equipment goes out in response to complaints, so odds are you'll hear from your neighbors before the FCC knocks.

The bigger concern of the FCC is that interference-causing equipment is not sold in the first place so you do not get a chance to put wavy lines through all your neighbors' favorite television shows. To that end, the FCC rules prohibit Class B equipment from being sold or offered for sale.

Class B personal computers not FCC certified cannot legally be advertised for sale, although ads announcing products with a disclaimer noting that the device is not certified (and thus, not available for sale) are permitted. If a company markets a computer that has neither been approved by the FCC as a Class A device nor certified as complying as a Class B device, the company may be ordered to stop selling the equipment and fined. If the company continues to flaunt the rules, company officials could be jailed. According to the FCC, most companies get into compliance right away.

Before a Class B device is certified, it can be displayed at shows and demonstrated with the appropriate disclaimer attached. The primary prohibition is against sales of non-certified equipment. For example, demonstration units could be distributed, but "demo" models could not be sold to computer dealers for display.

Verification and Certification

If after testing a given device qualifies for certification, the FCC certifies the unit and issues a certification number, which may be an alphanumeric set of characters. (Manufacturers often select their own numbers.)

Every model of personal computer that differs as to case, power supply, or motherboard must be separately certified. If a manufacturer offers two case styles—desktop and floor-standing—and three system boards—386SX, 386DX, and 486DX—each of the six configurations needs to be separately certified.

Computers from different vendors can share the same FCC number, providing they are identical units made by a single manufacturer differing only cosmetically—for example, in label or color. In the past, the FCC required that it be notified about different trade names used on certified products, but this requirement was relaxed with the new (1989) rules. Computers with different packaging, processors, or power supplies cannot share an FCC certification number, even if they are made by the same manufacturer.

A personal computer need not be recertified if it differs from a certified model only in the addition of a certified peripheral. For example, a manufacturer could create a separate model by installing an extra FCC-certified serial board, and that new model would be covered by the certification of the old one.

A claim sometimes made by small computer makers—that a product is made only from FCC-certified subassemblies and thus does not require FCC certification itself—is simply impossible. A PC cannot be built without a power supply, case, or motherboard, and these three subassemblies cannot be FCC certified. Any computer manufactured from subassemblies must be FCC certified as a completed unit.

All these rules seem to make FCC certification important only to computer manufacturers. After all, you are still liable for clearing up the interference generated by your PC no matter whether it's Class A or B. But FCC certification should be important to you.

Equipment Design

Achieving Class B certification takes a better design and better workmanship. Although a certification sticker is no guarantee that a particular product is well-made, that sticker does show that the PC or peripheral to which it is attached meets an important technical standard that uncertified equipment does not. Although you should not rely entirely on FCC certification when buying a PC, it does give you one more piece of evidence about the quality of your prospective purchase.

Manufacturers use a number of different strategies to minimize radiation. As speeds increase, they must be increasingly diligent.

The heavy steel case of the typical PC, XT, AT, or compatible computer does a reasonable job of limiting RFI. Plastic cases require special treatments to minimize radiation. The treatment of choice is a conductive paint, often rich with silver, which shields the computer much like the full metal jacket of other computers.

As PC operating frequencies increase, the spurious radiation becomes more pernicious. Any crack in the case may allow too much radio energy to leak out. If different parts of the chassis and the lid of the case are not electrically connected, RFI can leak out. In addition, any cable attached to the computer potentially can act as an antenna, sending out signals as effectively as a radio station.

A number of design elements help reduce RFI. Special metal fingers on the edge of the case and its lid ensure that the two pieces are in good electrical contact. Cables can be shielded. RFI absorbing ferrite beads can be wrapped around wires before they leave the chassis to suck up excess energy before it leaks out. Each of these cures adds a bit to the cost of the computer, both for the materials and for their fabrication and installation. Moreover, it can take a substantial time to track down all the leaks and plug them.

Interference also can be minimized at the point of its origin. For example, IBM designed its PS/2s from the ground up to be inherently low in radio frequency emissions. Their system boards and the Micro Channel are designed in such a way that spurious radiation is at a minimum. The outer layers of the planar boards consist primarily of ground layers, which shield the high frequency signals within the inner layers of the circuit board. Ground wires alternate with every few active conductors on the Micro Channel to partially shield the bus.

The bottom line is that a Class B device must be designed to be less likely to cause interference than a Class A computer. Not only does that mean you are less likely to get involved in an imbroglio with your neighbors about their television reception, it also means that a Class B computer may be built better with more attention to detail. In addition, lower emissions at radio frequencies generally go hand-in-hand with lower emissions at lower frequencies. That can be comforting should you worry about the health effects of low-frequency radiation.

ELF and VLF Radiation

At the bottom of the electromagnetic spectrum is Extremely Low Frequency (ELF) radiation. Strictly defined, ELF comprises the frequency range from 3 to 30 Hertz, but in common usage the term is extended to any frequency below 30,000 Hertz. As with all frequencies below 450 KHz, ELF is ignored in the FCC certification process. ELF has long been thought innocuous, but a number of newspaper and magazine articles have raised doubts about its safety.

Strictly speaking, the ELF of concern is not radiation but captive electric and magnetic fields generated by strong electric currents in power systems, appliances, and other electrical equipment (which includes computers and their peripherals). The two types of fields—electrical and magnetic—are related and arise from the same phenomena, but have individual distinguishing characteristics. Electric fields generate a potential (a voltage), are measured in millivolts or volts per meter, and are relatively easily shielded against using a conductive material. Magnetic fields generate a current (amperage), are measured in milliamps per meter or sometimes in related units of gauss, and are difficult to shield against.

While older monitors emitted copious magnetic and electric fields—mostly above and from the left side of the sets—most manufacturers are designing new products to meet a stringent radiation standard adopted in Sweden by the Swedish Board for Measurement and Testing, internationally known by its Swedish initials, MPR.

MPR Standards

The Swedish safety standard pertains to a number of aspects of monitor emissions, including x-radiation, static electrical fields, low-frequency electrical fields, and low-frequency magnetic fields. Actually, two Swedish standards exist, an old one (now termed MPR I); and a new one (MPR II), published in December, 1990. Whereas MPR I focused solely on alternating magnetic fields with frequencies between 1 KHz and 400 KHz, MPR II extended the standard to both electrical and magnetic fields and lowered the reach of the standard to 5 Hz. This revision has important implications for you and monitor makers. Some manufacturers claim their products meet the Swedish standard even when they only comply with MPR I. But MPR I covers only one aspect of monitor emissions—basically horizontal scanning frequencies. MPR II extends to the vertical frequency range as well as covering power line frequencies.

The MPR II standard requires particular measurements of electrical and magnetic fields to be made at various points around the monitor under carefully controlled conditions. Both types of fields are measured in two bands (5 Hz to 2 KHz and 2 KHz to 400 KHz) at distances approximating normal working distance at dozens of positions around the monitor. Electrical fields must be less than 25 volts per meter in the lower band and 2.5 volts per meter in the upper band; magnetic fields, below 250 nanoteslas (2.5 milligauss) in the lower band and below 25 nanoteslas in the upper band.

TCO Limits

The Swedish white-collar labor union known as TCO promulgates its own standards even tougher than those of MPR II. The chief difference between MPR II and TCO is the distance at which measurements are made. Whereas MPR II specifies measurements to be made at 50 centimeters from the monitor screen, TCO makes the same measurements at 30 centimeters. In effect, TCO requires monitor emissions to be roughly half that permitted by MPR II. Consequently, TCO is currently the strictest standard to be applied to monitor emissions.

The Swedish standards are the toughest in the world, so compliance with them is the best assurance that a monitor is as safe as possible. However, neither MPR nor TCO compliance is a complete assurance of safety. Safe and unsafe levels of these low-frequency fields have yet to be confidently determined. Some research actually suggests biological activity at field strengths permitted under the Swedish standards.

Underwriters Laboratories Listing

When you switch on your desktop PC, you probably don't expect the electricity inside to jolt out and send you corkscrewing, dropping you to the floor—your heart in fibrillation, your soul in limbo, and your coworkers gathered around wondering who will get your window office they've all lusted after for years. Nor do you think of your workstation as a potential flame-thrower, a time-release modern Molotov that gives nightmares to fire marshals and Smokey the Bear. You have faith in the safety of your PC and the rest of your array of office equipment. But nothing about modern electronics makes equipment built from them inherently safe. Quite to the contrary, all electrical devices have some shock potential. Voltages inside your PC's power supply are quite sufficient to electrocute you or to kindle your office aflame.

Worse, your shields against such prospective disasters may not be as impregnable as you think. For example, insurance kicks in only after the fact—little solace when you've been thrown onto your back, legs twitching. Government regulatory agencies react with enforced recalls and product bans even more slowly, only after a string of catastrophes hints that something not-so-subtle infects a certain product line. Anyone with memories of color televisions igniting apartments faster than you can say "instant on" knows that sometimes even companies with excellent reputations accidentally release potentially dangerous products.

Several testing and certification organizations do offer you the assurance that the equipment you trust your livelihood and life to is safe. Among these are the Canada Standards Association, Underwriters Laboratories Inc., and Verband Deutscher Elektrotechniker. The most familiar is Underwriters Laboratories because the organization has been active in the United States for about a century. The CSA is the Canadian equivalent; the VDE, German.

The trademarked stylized "UL" inside a circle means that independent safety engineers at Underwriters Laboratories have examined the design and a sample unit of the product and found it to meet their stringent safety standards. In addition, to assure you that the initial safety of your PC wasn't shortchanged later in production, other UL engineers occasionally spot check the manufacturer and random products off the assembly line.

Underwriters Laboratories is not a government agency; nor is it the child of some Sixties-vintage publicity-minded consumer-safety promoter. Rather, Underwriters Laboratories is an independent, non-profit organization that functions both as a safety engineering consultant and certification organization. It's a commercial business that earns its livelihood from manufacturers who pay for its services in detecting what's wrong with their products before they are put on the market.

Instead of governmental authority, the power of the UL arises from it standards and reputation—a particularly long reputation. The organization dates from almost as far back as commercial electrical power—well before the age of government regulations, consumer organizations, or even Upton Sinclair's exposes.

Founded in 1894 by William Henry Merrill, the UL was first known as the Underwriters' Electrical Bureau and primarily concerned itself with safety testing the products of the fledgling electrical industry. At the time, the entire organization comprised three people—Merrill, Edward Teall, and W. S. Boyd—and was appropriately housed above a fire station in Chicago. Since then, the company has expanded in employment (the roster now totals thousands); offices (four, one each in Northbrook, Illinois; Melville, New York; Research Triangle Park, North Carolina; and Santa Clara, California); and other areas. It now sets standards and tests nearly any product about which there may be safety concerns, from PCs to space heaters and, appropriately, fire extinguishers. The organization was formally incorporated as Underwriters Laboratory Inc. in 1901.

Although they are the product of a private business, Underwriters Laboratories' standards can have legal significance. The standards developed by the UL can and have been incorporated into statutes and ordinances.

A particularly relevant example pertains in part to PCs. The National Electrical Code, which is incorporated into the laws of numerous municipalities, specifies that as of July 1, 1991, any equipment intended to be electrically connected to a telecommunications network must be listed for that purpose (National Electrical Code, Article 800-51, subparagraph i). In communities enforcing the national code, then, your PC must be listed if you have a modem in it that you intend on connecting to a telephone line. A UL label on you PC constitutes the required listing.

Because Underwriters Laboratories is not an arm of the government, it cannot arbitrarily force a company to follow its standards. It relies instead on cooperation and contract. To use the UL logo, a company must enter into a contract with Underwriters Laboratories. In effect, it licenses the use of the trademarked symbol.

Underwriters Laboratories does not just grant a license for the payment of a fee. To earn the right to use the logo, a company must agree to follow the appropriate UL standards. More importantly, the company must submit a sample of the equipment to Underwriters Laboratories so that it can be tested and certified to conform with the standard. The contract also imposes a continuing duty on the manufacturer to conform with the appropriate standard and gives the UL the right to check compliance. The UL can award its symbol to the products it chooses or withhold it and enforce its conditions on the use of its symbol under federal law. The UL symbol can appear on any or all products in their class. It indicates compliance with safety rather than performance standards, and it implies no relative measure of quality.

Computer Safety Standards

Computers, even electrical devices in general, are not the only or even primary concern of Underwriters Laboratories. The organization develops standards for and tests everything from building materials to fire alarm systems. Today PCs must conform primarily with but one of hundreds of Underwriters Laboratory standards, designated as UL 1950.

The UL 1950 standard applies to all information technology equipment. First published on March 15, 1989, it became effective March 15, 1992, meaning equipment must meet the standard to be sold wearing the UL logo after that date. Computer equipment now being made is now tested for conformance with the UL 1950 specifications.

In the 10 or 15 years before 1989, other standards applied to data processing equipment: UL 478 for information-processing and business equipment; and UL 114 for office appliances and business equipment. UL 1950 replaces both.

The new standard was not arbitrarily created, but represents an attempt to unite various standards in use around the world by the unaffiliated CSA, VDE, and others. Manufacturers can follow the guidance of one standard rather than several perhaps conflicting standards for equipment to be used in Europe, Canada, and the United States.

UL 1950 covers everything from ordinary desktop PCs and their peripherals (disk drives to printers) to mainframe computers to simple desktop calculators to typewriters. Special standards with different requirements cover industrial computer devices that may have to work in severe environments, such as those with explosive fumes.

The inch-thick document covers nearly all aspects of equipment design and construction and outlines the testing procedure that Underwriters Laboratories applies. These range from insulation and wiring to mechanical strength and resistance to fire. Even relevant markings and identifications on the product are covered. If you are interested, the complete, copyrighted publication can be ordered directly from Underwriters Laboratories.

UL Recognition Versus UL Listing

In granting its approval to electrical devices, Underwriters Laboratories uses three strictly defined terms: listing, recognition, and classification. These terms are not interchangeable; the standards for each are different and even apply to different kinds of devices.

Recognition is an approval granted to electrical components, products not complete in themselves but used in making a complete product. Light switches and computer power supplies are typical of equipment that earns UL recognition. UL-recognized devices are entitled to wear a special symbol—a slanted combination of the letter U and a backward R (for recognition) combined together.

Listing applies to complete products that you can buy—an entire appliance, monitor, or computer system unit. Listed products are allowed to wear the familiar UL trademark, the circle with the letters "UL" within it (see fig. A.1).

FIGURE A.1. The Underwriter's Laboratories logo.

A UL-listed product is often made from UL-recognized components, but doesn't have to be; nor does the use of UL-recognized components automatically confer a UL listing on the finished product. Rather, using UL-recognized components helps the manufacturer more easily achieve a listing.

A UL listing means that a product is safe for use in the form in which it is delivered to you. A UL-recognized product is safe when installed and used properly. The listing lifts the responsibility from you.

Although a UL-recognized component might be safe in itself, the possibility always exists that it could be installed in a product in such a way to make it dangerous. For example, a heat-generating power supply could be shoehorned into a tight case that lacks adequate ventilation, leading to overheating and fire potential. Although the power supply was UL-recognized, such a dangerous complete assembly could not be UL listed.

Any company that tells you that its PC is UL recognized is mistaken; it cannot be. The UL does not give recognition to complete computer systems. Manufacturers may rightly claim that a computer doesn't need to be listed because it is built from UL-recognized components; and because a listing is voluntary, and a computer legally need not be UL listed at all. The statement, while technically accurate, is misleading.

The operative words in such a statement are that the computer is not UL listed, so it gives you no assurance that the completed system complies with UL design and manufacturing standards. In other words, if you ask a PC maker whether its product is UL listed, and the response is that the system is made from UL-recognized components, the answer is probably an evasion of the word "no."

UL classification generally applies only to commercial or industrial products that the UL tests for conformance with specific published standards or regulatory codes, or that have been evaluated with respect to certain hazards or to perform under specific conditions. A UL-classified device bears no specific symbol, but instead is marked with the UL's name and a statement indicating the extent of the product's classification. For the most part, UL classification has no relevance to commercial PCs.

The Approval Process

Getting a product UL listed, recognized, or classified is a multi-step process. It all begins when the manufacturer voluntarily contacts Underwriters Laboratories. This first step can be a simple letter or phone call. The manufacturer then follows up by submitting a formal request for testing along with a product description, photos, instructions, brochures, and whatever else might be helpful in showing the UL exactly what the equipment is.

From the information provided, Underwriters Laboratories then determines what standards the product must meet, and what tests are necessary to ensure compliance with them. It then notifies the manufacturer of the testing requirements, including the number of samples required and the cost.

If the manufacturer agrees, it sends an application form, deposit, and the requested samples to UL; and UL examines and tests the product.

Should the product pass scrutiny, Underwriters Laboratories issues a final report and sends the manufacturer notice of the listing of its product. Arrangements are made for follow-up procedures, including spot-checking of production. The manufacturer then is authorized to use the UL mark on its product and in brochures and advertisements for the product.

If the product fails UL testing, UL notifies the manufacturer of the results and suggests changes necessary for passing the tests. The manufacturer then can make design corrections and resubmit the product.

Underwriters Laboratories approaches each product to be tested in a methodical way. In general, the testing procedure begins at the outside and works its way in.

The starting point is the power cord. UL engineers make sure that the power cord itself is suitable to the application—that it can carry enough current without overheating and is tough enough to withstand being trod upon.

From there, the UL safety engineers turn their attention to the case itself. Plastic cases are especially rigorously checked. They must be strong enough to withstand normal abuse such as impacts and hot environments. After all, if the case breaks, you could injure yourself on the pieces or by accidentally touching the circuitry inside.

Flammability is another concern. Plastic cases must not contribute to the propagation of fires. Nor should it give off toxic fumes. These tests involve the classic trial-by-fire, in effect setting a torch to the PC being evaluated.

Even the ventilation holes in the case are checked. Here the engineer has several concerns. Ventilation slots must be large enough to allow airflow sufficient that the device doesn't become overheated, but the holes must also be small enough so that a user (or the child of a user) cannot poke a finger through and get a shock. They must also be located in such a way that something cannot fall inside and create a short circuit or fire.

Inside the case, the primary (utility) power is the principal concern. The UL engineers check the voltages present not only with everything operating normally, but also under faulty conditions. Isolation between power and logic circuits is verified to be certain, for example, when you grab the connector to unplug your printer and you are not surprised with a shockingly high voltage.

Equipment also is tested under operation to determine how hot it becomes under worst-case conditions. In the case of a PC, all its expansion slots and drive bays are filled so that the maximum load is put on the power supply and cooling systems. The PC (or other device) is then run until its temperature stabilizes, and the internal temperatures are measured. The primary concern is that excess heat does not cause degradation of components that can lead to fire or shock.

The amount of current the equipment actually draws is measured so that you know for sure what your electrical outlets will be called upon to supply. The UL also performs a leakage current test, so that you can be sure that when you lean against the case of a PC with your feet in a puddle, there's not enough current to give you a shock. In addition, a dielectric voltage test is performed to ensure that the insulation on the equipment is sufficient to protect you from electrical dangers.

The UL engineers even verify the printed ratings of the device—both those on the back of the equipment and those in the instruction manual—to be sure that they properly reflect the type of power the device may be plugged into, and the amount of current it draws. They ensure that the information provided is adequate—at least about the electrical nature of the device—for you to properly use the equipment.

The UL doesn't stop with testing the single unit that the manufacturer first submits for evaluation. After all, a nefarious manufacturer might be tempted to build a super-rugged prototype, send it in for evaluation, and then build the units it sells from the cheapest, flimsiest parts available. Consequently, to keep the UL mark on their equipment, manufacturers must agree to follow-up tests on all their products that come down the assembly line.

The follow-up tests the manufacturer must make on each unit produced include a production-line dielectric voltage test and an earthing continuity test. For the former, a voltage is applied between the two electrical contacts of the unit's plug (the flat blades) and the ground connection (the round pin). Passing this test ensures that nothing in the manufacturing process damages any wiring in the unit that could cause a short circuit, leading to shock potential from touching the unit's case. The earthing continuity test ensures that the ground pin on the power cord actually is connected to all user-accessible parts of the case. It ensures that the case of every unit made is properly grounded.

Under terms of the contract with Underwriters Laboratories, the manufacturer opens its production facilities to random UL spot checks four times a year. Without notice, a UL engineer may knock on the door and ask to see the equipment being made and test units off the assembly line.

A UL listing often sets apart the computers made by major manufacturers—the so-called first and second tiers of the industry—from the low-margin, low-cost makers that recently moved from garages into industrial parks. Computers from larger manufacturers like Compaq and IBM all wear UL listings. Many mail-order systems do not.

One reason for this separation is that old-line manufacturers know that the major businesses that are their principal customers often require the assurance of UL listing on the products they buy. Another reason is that many smaller companies may not know what UL approval is all about or how to achieve it. Perhaps the most compelling reason you don't see the UL label on bottom-of-the-barrel PCs is that getting a UL listing can be expensive.

The computer maker must bear the entire cost of the UL approval process. Essentially, that means contracting with Underwriters Laboratories for the supply of safety engineering expertise.

Underwriters Laboratories charges for the time of its engineers who disassemble the computer to see how it is made and how its construction affects its safety. The manufacturer also must pay for the costs of testing the computer system. In addition to the time of the engineer, part of the cost of running the entire Underwriters Laboratories worldwide operation must be factored into the cost of achieving a listing—as well as the cost for follow-up inspections. In other words, getting a listing is not cheap.

The exact charge by the UL for sending a product through the listing process varies with what the product is and, like any contract, is subject to negotiation. According to UL publications, identical charge schedules apply to all investigations. Some products, however, may require more UL involvement and consulting work. One peripheral manufacturer reported that its average cost of submitting a product for UL evaluation ran between $3,000 and $5,000.

That's just the starting point, however. Those charges assume a perfect product that's completely safe from an engineering standpoint. Underwriters Laboratories, after inspecting and testing the product, may make suggestions about improving the product's safety—suggestions the manufacturer must abide to gain a listing. Each of those improvements adds to the development cost of the product.

Moreover, the manufacturer must submit the equipment to Underwriters Laboratories to be evaluated by testing that at times verges on the destructive. For example, handheld devices must undergo drop tests from one meter high onto a hardwood floor. After the test, the product must remain safe—but it need not remain operable. Other tests involve simulating faults, heating, and even applying flames to the equipment. Even if the evaluation sample comes back in a single piece after testing, it still may not be salable.

One company that manufacturers UL-listed peripherals writes off the cost of the evaluation sample as part of the UL approval process. For a small company making 586-based PCs, that's hardly a trivial expense.

All told, the cost of achieving a UL listing for a complete computer system starts at about $10,000 and can spiral upward if the original design was particularly inept from the standpoint of safety, according to companies contacted by PC Magazine. Some small system vendors may have invested far less than that much capital in the entire design of their products. It may represent the complete profits from months of production in today's highly competitive low-end of the PC market.

For many manufacturers, the cost of a UL listing is not a consideration. It's as much a necessity as a microprocessor in a PC. The UL labels broadens the market for the product. And although it doesn't ensure against product liability lawsuits, a UL listing is evidence that the product design did meet recognized safety standards.

Whether to buy a product lacking a UL listing is a personal decision. Certainly equipment lacking a UL listing can be just as safe as listed devices. But the UL logo gives you the assurance that the product wearing it has been independently tested for safety. It's one of the few forms of peace of mind you can buy.

Appendix B
Health Issues

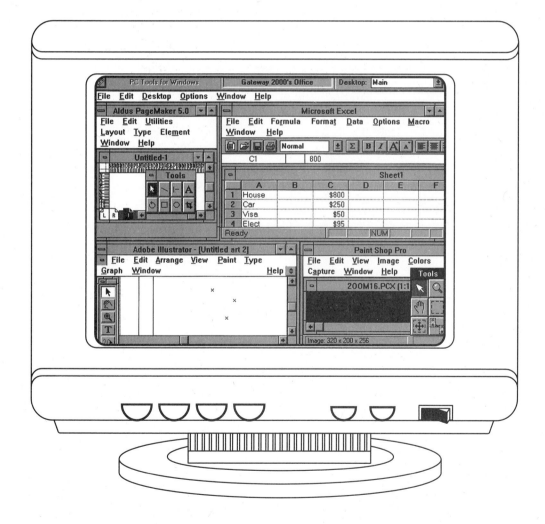

Repetitive Strain Injury

The hand-to-keyboard relationship can be very straining when you are working on a PC. No one wants to type, even though it's probably the fastest available means of entering information into your PC. But typing is more than a bother. It also can cause permanent damage to your hands and wrists. Although it may sound odd, the health problem of most concern in regard to keyboard use is the same ailment suffered by chicken pluckers and meat packers. Once you understand the cause, however, the association is obvious.

The primary health issue associated with keyboards is *repetitive strain injury* or *RSI*, a painful, often debilitating disorder that develops when people must execute the same manual task over and over again. If you don't take the proper precautions, typing can cause permanent damage to your hands and wrists.

The risks of RSI are real. In a study conducted by the South Australian Health Commission in 1984, it was found that 56 percent of keyboard operators had recurring symptoms of keyboard-caused injury, 8 percent of them serious enough to contact a health-care provider.

With keyboarding, the most common manifestation of RSI is carpal tunnel syndrome. A similar ailment, wrist tendonitis, also has been associated with keyboard use.

The carpal tunnel is a narrow passageway in your wrist through which the median nerve passes, carrying sensations for your entire hand. The finger flexor tendons link your fingers to the muscles in your lower arm. The tunnel is formed by walls of solid bone on three sides with the bottom enclosed by transverse carpal ligament—a tough, inelastic cartilage.

Carpal tunnel syndrome is caused by the tendons protecting themselves from overuse. Each tendon is surrounded by a thin, fluid-filled sack called a synovid sheath, which swells with extra fluid to protect the tendon. Scientifically, this swelling is called tendonitis. When these sacks swell in the carpal tunnel, they can pinch the median nerve against the bones or the carpal ligament. The result can be loss of sensation in the hand and debilitating pain.

The prognosis is not good. Treatment may involve an enforced vacation or medical leave of absence during which no typing is permitted. Physical therapy, cortisone injections, and even surgery sometimes are necessary.

Although the problem develops over a period of years, the onset of pain caused by carpal tunnel syndrome often appears suddenly. Some sufferers have no symptoms one night and wake up the next morning in excruciating pain, unable to work for months. In most cases, those afflicted with carpal tunnel syndrome have ignored the warning signs of the problem: a minor pain in the wrist after a day of typing, and numbness in the thumb or fingers.

People have been typing for more than 100 years, yet carpal tunnel syndrome appears to be a recent phenomenon. The diagnosis is not new—nor is the condition caused by a recently evolved virus or bacterium. Rather, typing habits have, in general, changed.

Today, a typist's fingers stay as close to the home row on the keyboard as possible. A simple press of the pinkie is all that's needed for a carriage return. Old typewriters required a definite change of position and a resounding right hook to send the carriage back to the left after each page, and the typist had to extract one sheet and roll a new one into the typewriter. All of these simple, necessary acts added variation to the typing process. Moreover, computers encourage extended use.

This difference between old-fashioned typing and keyboarding hints at one way of avoiding carpal tunnel syndrome—take a break. Remove your fingers from the home row and wrap them around a coffee cup. Do something different for a while. As you will see in the next section, it's better still to get up from your chair and take a walk or otherwise temporarily divorce yourself from your workplace.

Sources agree that keyboarding with your wrists in the wrong position aggravates your wrists and may cause carpal tunnel syndrome. The wrong position is anything but the naturally straight position your wrists take on in relation to your arm when you stand relaxed with your arms dangling at your side. You should adjust the angle of your keyboard to keep your wrists straight (if you can).

A number of innovative and odd redesigns of the computer keyboard have been developed by ambitious inventors, most based on sound theory and an optimistic view of reality. No matter how beneficial, it's unlikely that bent, oddly shaped, or vertical keyboards will catch on. But keyboards with widened wrist-rests and add-on accessories that provide wrist support may be useful in helping you keep your hands in the proper typing position.

Back Problems

People whose jobs involve sitting in one place all day often complain of health problems be they hemorrhoids, obesity, or an aching back. Putting a PC in front of you will not change the complaints or make the PC the cause of your problems.

The human body was not designed for the couch-potato lifestyle. Proper circulation depends on moving your legs to push venous blood back to your heart. Immobilize yourself in front of a PC, and you will pay for it in aches and pains—and worse. Studies have shown that the feet of office workers who spend the day at their desks swell by four to six percent by the end of the day. Another study suggested that prolonged, quiet sitting may lead to a gradual increase in cardiovascular strain.

In a survey of 852 video data terminal (VDT) users at New York State government offices in 1985, one-third of the female operators experienced frequent or daily neck pain. One-fourth reported back or shoulder pain. For unknown reasons, males reported problems 10 to 20 percent less often than females. Most studies attribute these pains to poor posture caused by nonoptimal seating.

At one time, nearly every source recommended the same posture for working at a PC—back straight, feet firmly flat against the floor, arms at your sides, a 90-degree bend at the elbow, and your wrists straight at the keyboard. Only Marines and debutantes are likely to sit this way. One reason is office furniture. Except for specially designed, ergonomic computer chairs, standard office equipment is typically not designed to adjust to the full range of settings required to accommodate the diversity of human beings. The range is a wide one. A 1982 study reported in the *Journal of Ergology* showed that preferred keyboard height varied from 28 to 34.25 inches; the preferred screen height ranged from 36.25 to 45.5 inches.

Moreover, there is substantial doubt that the classic recommendation for seating posture is best for computer users. The New York study showed a preference among VDT workers to lean back so that their bodies were at angles between 97 and 121 degrees. A report published by the Swedish National Board of Safety and Health in 1986 noted that the generally accepted "correct" sitting posture—back straight—is not supported by any scientific evidence. In fact, relieving pressure on the knees caused by this posture recommendation has resulted in a reduction of the height of furniture of about four inches in the twentieth century, even though most people are about four inches taller. Raising both tables and chairs by about three inches resulted in reduced back pain and a reduction in leg swelling among workers.

Other studies show that when people are instructed on how to adjust furniture and then left to their own devices, they rarely assume the textbook-perfect posture. They lean back at up to 31 degrees from the vertical and relax their way through the workday. And they feel better about it.

But even adjustable furniture is problematic. First, it's worthless unless someone shows you how to adjust it—the process can be complex because some chairs alone have 15 separate adjustments! Second, one study seemed to show that it takes about one week to get close to an optimum adjustment of your computer furniture. Third, current advice is against becoming too comfortable. If you settle so perfectly into your chair that you don't want to move, you're likely to develop the sedentary problems you wanted to avoid. You may want to adjust your chair periodically throughout the day, just as you adjust your driving position periodically on long trips.

Monitor Safety

Typists of 100 years ago didn't experience carpal tunnel syndrome, and they certainly didn't need to worry about health issues related to monitors! However, as the computer age progresses, all kinds of health issues are surfacing: eyestrain, radiation effects, and pregnancy concerns.

Eyestrain

Today there is a general consensus that staring at a monitor screen all day in and of itself does not cause permanent damage. This research-based conclusion contradicts earlier speculation that long-term computer use does cause such vision problems as myopia (near-sightedness) and cataracts.

The research has been extensive and convincing. Studies conducted over a number of years in Canada (five years) and Holland (2.5 years) found no deterioration in vision from computer use that could not be attributed to normal aging. A report on ophthalmological examinations comparing VDT users and non-users among members of the Newspaper Guild in 1985 found just one difference between the two groups: a tendency of VDT users to become slightly cross-eyed (esophoric). Admittedly, severe esophoria can be a problem, but the likely cause was how the VDTs were used, not some intrinsic property of the equipment. In fact, a statement made on behalf of the American Academy of Ophthalmology in 1984 concluded that existing evidence indicated that VDTs were safe for normal use and present no hazard to vision. There was no indication that VDT use could harm normal eyes or worsen existing pathologic eye conditions.

But that's far from giving monitors a clean bill of health. Over the short term, visual problems do arise among VDT users. In a 1988 study, 26.3 percent of the participants developed significant temporary myopia (nearsightedness) after VDT work and another 42.1 percent showed changes bordering on significant. A 1984 study showed that after working on a VDT, the time required to shift focus between near and far objects increased. And a 1981 study showed an increased incidence of eye fatigue and irritation among VDT users as compared to other office workers, although eye examinations showed the same level of eye problems in both groups. The eye irritation found in this study often persisted well beyond the period in which the VDT was used, often through the next morning.

Scientists have sought the cause of these irritations, and most research points in one direction: not to the VDTs themselves, but to how, where, and under what conditions the computer equipment was used. A 1988 study reported in the *New York State Journal of Medicine* attributed the eye irritations complained of by VDT workers to ergonomic considerations such as glare, improper lighting, improperly corrected vision, and poor arrangement of work materials. A Swedish study in 1986 found that glare was significantly correlated with eye fatigue (as was the need to decipher handwriting).

Eliminating eyestrain, irritation, and fatigue means removing the source of the problems—the shortcomings in the work environment. For the most part, that means changing the lighting in the room containing your PC to reduce glare and equalize the illumination on your work, moving your monitor to a more comfortable viewing position to lighten the burden on the muscles that shift your gaze, and, if all else fails, adding a glare shield or buying a new monitor.

According to most experts, the amount of lighting required varies with the job that you do. If you're working on watches or other delicate, detailed work, you will want your workplace as bright as 3500 to 5000 lux (lux is a unit of measurement of illumination; bright sunlight is 100,000 lux; a moonlit night, 0.1 lux). Normal office work falls into the range of 100 to 500 lux. In general, VDT users prefer lighting on the dark side to offer better screen contrast. On the other hand, dealing with paperwork requires light on the brighter side. You will need to find a happy medium. In most cases, that means reducing overall lighting with a task light—an adjustable lamp that can be arranged to shine on your reading materials but not on your monitor screen.

The biggest nemesis when it comes to illumination is glare, reflections of bright light sources off the glass surface of your monitor screen. To reduce glare, many people recommend diffuse overhead lighting supplemented by localized task lights. If you have a window in your workplace, you should align your monitor screen at right angles to the window to minimize reflections.

Substantial debate surrounds the issue of antiglare treatments on monitor screens. The treatments soften the image, putting it slightly out of focus, and decrease contrast. Of course, antiglare treatment would not be necessary if the monitor were used under optimum viewing conditions. Because few displays are used in optimum conditions, most monitor manufacturers install glare-reducing picture tubes.

Many equipment makers recommend against using an add-on antiglare screen in front of your monitor unless you have no other means of reducing glare. All such screens reduce image sharpness, which can be a source of eye fatigue.

In fact, fatigue is one area in which computer equipment itself may be an issue. Some studies have correlated poor-quality displays with increased eye fatigue.

If you decide to replace your monitor, examine those with flatter screens, which are less prone to glare. Curved monitor screens act like the convex mirrors that stores use to catch shoplifters and see other goings-on in the aisles. The face of the tube reflects light sources over a wide angle, invariably catching a lamp, overhead light, or a window. A flat or nearly flat screen is less likely to include extraneous light sources in its view.

Your monitor should be equipped with a tilt-swivel stand. Most health and safety recommendations mandate a tilt-swivel base.

The obvious adjustment is to align your monitor to minimize glare. If glare is not a problem, IBM recommends that the face of the monitor be aligned so that the top of the screen is set back 10 to 15 degrees from the vertical part of the screen.

Another step to combat eye fatigue is to sharpen up your screen by chasing away dust. Monitor screens naturally attract dust because the high voltage used by their electron beams builds up a static charge on the face of the tube. This charge collects dust the same way that balloons stick to a wool sweater. Most sources recommend using a damp—not dripping wet—rag to gently wipe the dust off the screen. Be careful not to get the screen really wet, because any liquid that runs down the screen can drip inside and damage the monitor's circuitry.

Research indicates that your eyes will become less fatigued if you don't have to look up at your monitor. Consequently, most experts agree that the optimum height for your monitor screen is such that the top of the screen is at eye level. That way you never have to look up to see what's on-screen. If you slouch in your chair (which may not be such a bad posture after all—see the section on back pain), you may not want to stack your monitor on top of your system unit.

You should have some kind of stand or holder for your references when you type. To minimize eye fatigue, experts recommend that you keep your drafts, notes, or whatever you're typing from at the same distance from your eyes as the monitor screen. That way you will not have to shift focus every time you check your notes. Less shifting of focus is believed to minimize fatigue.

Periodically, however, you should take a break and shift your focus. Look around the office, out the window, or count the holes in the acoustical tile. Anything to change your focus and relax your eyes. To minimize eyestrain, fatigue, and irritation, the idea is to moderate your eye work—don't shift your focus dozens of times a minute or lock your eyes at a consistent distance for hours on end.

A number of studies have shown that the people most likely to suffer from vision-related problems when working on PCs are those who have uncorrected vision deficiencies. Although you may be able to read your monitor screen even if you are slightly nearsighted or anastigmatic (and refuse to wear glasses or contacts), you're more likely to develop headaches and other symptoms of eye strain and fatigue from your work. In addition, some bifocals are not suited to computer work because their change in correction is too low.

You should have your eyes checked periodically (some sources say twice a year) if you work regularly on a PC or VDT. In some cases, you may want special corrective lenses to use only while working on your PC. Be sure to let your optometrist or ophthalmalogist know that you perform substantial work on a PC.

Radiation

Monitors are thought by many people to pose dangers beyond eyestrain. Monitors operate at frequencies that may have some health effects and may generate forms of radiation that have been proven harmful. The health effects of these emissions are not completely understood.

Although dedicated monitors for PCs are relatively new, they share many common characteristics with VDTs that have been in use for nearly 40 years and about which a substantial body of health-related data has been generated. Both monitor and VDT technologies use signals of approximately the same frequencies. Both generate many of the same EMR components.

Even with VDTs, however, the issue of health effects remains unresolved after decades of study. No true consensus on the safety of VDTs—or personal computer monitors—has emerged. The conflicting results of studies have lined up two opposing parties unlikely to be swayed by the arguments of the other. On one side are the makers of electronic equipment and the organizations that employ the people who use them. They believe that the equipment is safe. The other side, the people who actually must work at VDTs and personal computers all day long have their doubts. It's the classic employer-employee struggle, with a technological twist.

The employee viewpoint is buttressed by a variety of studies that show biological effects of electromagnetic radiation and an association between VDT use and health problems. The most infamous of these problems is the increased risk of miscarriage. A famous study conducted for Kaiser Permanente in California (published in 1988) showed that among 1,583 pregnant women, those who used VDTs for more than 20 hours per week had a significantly elevated rate of miscarriage.

On the other hand, VDT makers and employers rally a whole range of other studies (many of which they have funded) that have failed to find any such risk to VDT users. A 1989 University of Toronto study of 800 pregnant mice subjected to electromagnetic fields of the kind given off by VDTs suggested that there is no relationship between spontaneous abortion and VDT electromagnetic fields.

Although that may be good news if you're a pregnant mouse, pregnant human workers may not be reassured. And that's the problem. As in any scientific discipline, the VDT studies are subject to interpretation. Moreover, the human VDT studies are correlational rather than causal—they associate a problem with VDT use but cannot prove a true cause-and-effect relationship. The EMR from the computer terminals could be causing miscarriages, or some other factor related to the terminal could be the cause. The way in which a study was conducted could even show that some type of relationship exists. The Kaiser study itself admits that its results may have been confounded by unmeasured workplace factors such as poor ergonomics and job-related stress. Stress rather than radiation is, in fact, a prime contender for the cause of health effects associated with VDT use.

On the other hand, a growing number of studies have found cause-and-effect relationships between EMR and biological changes in tissues grown under laboratory conditions. Some of these effects occurred when the tissues were subjected to electromagnetic fields of the same nature as those created by personal computers and VDTs.

The radiation emitted by monitors and VDTs falls into several distinct bands, some with known health effects and some in which health effects are less defined. Among the most important of these frequency ranges are X-radiation, ultraviolet radiation, microwave radiation, very low frequency radiation, and extremely low frequency radiation.

X-Radiation

Perhaps the most publicized danger involved with equipment based on cathode-ray technology—things like television picture tubes, oscilloscopes, radar screens, and computer monitors—is X-radiation.

X-rays are known to cause cancer, and the mechanism is well understood. X-rays are ionizing radiation. The photons making up the X-ray signal contain sufficient energy to break up the chemical bonds in molecules, including the DNA in chromosomes. After the DNA in a cell has been changed, the genetic code of the cell is altered. The cell mutates, perhaps dying immediately or just subtly changing its activity. After the DNA of a cell is changed and the cell replicates, the changes are passed on to its progeny. One potential is for the growth-control mechanism of the cell to change. As a result, the cell and its offspring may multiply rapidly and uncontrollably as cancer.

The chances that any one cell will react with X-rays in such a way as to cause cancer are minuscule. If enough rays react with a sufficient number of cells, the cancer potential becomes real and worrisome.

X-radiation is associated with color television screens—and, thus, with color computer monitors. This association is based on the scare stories of the early 1960s when early color television sets did, indeed, produce prodigious amounts of X-radiation.

One of the many ways that X-rays can be produced is through the rapid deceleration of electrons. As the electrons slow down, they have to give up energy. Depending on the momentum of the electron, some of this energy is given off as X-rays.

X-rays are classified as two types: low-energy or soft X-rays with wavelengths from one-tenth to one nanometer, and high-energy or hard X-rays with wavelengths shorter than one-tenth of a nanometer. Because of their low energy, soft X-rays have little penetrating power. Hard X-rays can pass through and interact with the human body. Medical X-rays are hard. They can cause cell damage, and consequently, the government has placed strict limits on exposure to them.

Early television sets used a vacuum tube high-voltage rectifier, a small tube that generated the current to drive the electron beam in the display tube. These rectifiers were essentially miniature X-ray tubes. They functioned by passing a huge electron flux through the tube, from cathode to anode, and the electrons were rapidly decelerated at the anode. X-rays were emitted in the process.

The X-ray excitement that ultimately caused the federal government to issue strict regulations on the X-radiation emitted by television sets (as well as computer terminals) was real. Certain television sets emitted X-rays of such strength that you could make a radiograph of the bones in your hand using the television as an X-ray source.

Not all televisions were so dangerous, however. In fact, the culprits were proved to be defectively manufactured shunt regulator tubes that did not properly shield their anodes. The result was the emission of a concentrated, pencil-like beam of electrons through the bottom of the television set. Unless you had the television resting on your stomach—unlikely in those days of 100-pound monster TVs—you would have been safe from its effects.

Moreover, vacuum tube high-voltage rectifiers and shunt regulators are obsolete. They have been replaced by solid-state silicon diodes that use no X-radiation—electrons go through no rapid deceleration in silicon diodes. No known PC monitor uses vacuum tube rectifiers, so the X-radiation problem in PCs from that source should be nonexistent.

However, all CRT-based devices have another potential source of X-ray emissions. Every CRT creates its image by shooting a ray of electrons at the phosphors that coat the inner face of the screen. When they strike the phosphors, these electrons also rapidly decelerate. Most of the energy from the electron beam goes to excite the phosphors, which in turn emit the visible light of the image. Some of it, however, can generate X-rays. The higher the voltage inside the tube, the larger the X-ray flux. Color tubes, which operate at potentials as high as 30 kilovolts, produce thousands of times more X-radiation than do monochrome tubes, which operate below 20 kilovolts. (X-ray emissions increase by about a factor of 10 for every 1 kilovolt increase.)

But it's unlikely that much X-radiation leaks out of any computer monitor. The electron beams inside their CRTs have little energy and produce only soft X-rays. This radiation is effectively absorbed by the special face glass of the CRT.

Although the CRT looks like a simple thing in itself—hardly more than an oddly shaped glass bottle with some metal pins sticking out of its narrow end—it's a complex creation, believed to be the most complicated consumer product made before the advent of the microprocessor. Rather than one uniform kind of glass, the tube is crafted from several varieties, each tailored to a specific purpose. The wide face of the tube is thick, sometimes as much as one-half inch. It's made from glasses rich in strontium and lead, which block the X-ray emissions from the beam within the tube.

Regulations by the Food and Drug Administration set a maximum limit of X-ray emissions from televisions and terminals alike at 0.5 milliroentgens per hour at a distance of five centimeters from the screen—that's about two inches, close watching indeed. Devices with greater emissions are not permitted to be sold in this country. Moreover, the measurement of X-radiation under this standard must be made under worst-case conditions. Not only must all controls on a set being measured be advanced to the position maximizing X-radiation (settings at which the set is unlikely to be operated) but also failure conditions that would result in the worst-possible X-ray emissions must be simulated. (The failure of a voltage regulator that would increase the potential of the CRT electron beam is an example. These simulations often result in the catastrophic failure of the equipment during the test.)

Compliance testing by the FDA has turned up X-ray emissions from computer terminals. For example, a 1981 study found that roughly 1 out of 12 VDTs evaluated emitted X-radiation above the 0.5 milliroentgen per hour limit. The problems were confined to 8 units (out of 91), which represented three different models. The out-of-compliance models were either recalled to be modified to comply with emissions requirements or were not permitted to be sold on the U.S. market.

The vast majority of computer monitors emit virtually no X-rays. In fact, their thick, lead-enriched glass screens actually can shield you from background X-radiation.

Ultraviolet Radiation

Ultraviolet (UV) radiation is part of sunlight— a growing part owing to the diminishing ozone layer in the stratosphere. Its name describes it—ultraviolet is the invisible component of sunlight beyond the violet end of the spectrum. It has shorter waves (180 to 400 nanometers) and higher frequencies than visible light. Physically, that means that ultraviolet photons are more energetic than those of visible light. In fact, the ultraviolet spectrum spans the transitionary range between ionizing and non-ionizing radiation. UV photons can be so energetic that they cause chromosomal damage. UV has been implicated in causing cancer. It also can burn the skin. UV also triggers the skin's protective tanning reaction.

Unlike X-rays, however, ultraviolet rays are not penetrating. The thick atmospheric blanket of ozone stops them well; a thick blanket of cotton, or even a thin shirt, does quite a good job. Consequently, the effects of ultraviolet rays on the human body are limited to the places that sunlight can reach—the skin and the eyes. Today, it is generally agreed that exposure to ultraviolet radiation can cause skin cancer, cataracts, conjunctivitis (irritation of the lining of the eye), keratitis (inflammation of the cornea), pain, and light intolerance.

Current evidence indicates that UV exposure is cumulative. That is, the longer you bathe in its rays over your lifetime and the stronger the rays, the greater the chances of unfavorable consequences. It also is believed that exposure early in life has a greater effect than later exposure.

All computer monitors emit some UV rays along with the visible light of their images. However, the most energetic and thus the most dangerous wavelengths cannot escape the CRT. Ordinary glass strongly absorbs ultraviolet radiation with wavelengths shorter than about 350 nanometers. The only part of the UV spectrum that may be present in CRT emissions is, therefore, the range of 350 to 400 nanometers. (Some sources list the beginning of UV radiation at 380 nanometers.)

Ultraviolet emissions are present to some extent from monitors, but the emission level declines with decreasing wavelength and is virtually absent in most cases at wavelengths higher than about 350 nanometers. Because most color monitors use phosphors of the same family (P22), all have similar UV emission characteristics. Invariably, however, monitor ultraviolet emissions are less than visible radiation—typically no more than 5 percent of the level of the maximum emission in the visible spectrum. In contrast, a "deluxe cool white" fluorescent tube, the kind often used in office lighting, puts out UV rays at a level of about 20 percent of its maximum visible emissions. Based on typical monitor brightness levels and office lighting levels mandated by OSHA, CRT emissions of UV would be a fraction (in the range of one-quarter) of the level reflected from a white sheet of paper on a desktop when the monitor is operated under the test conditions (brightness and contrast advanced fully, screen fully lit). In normal operation, UV emissions from a monitor would be substantially less. In other words, although monitors do emit measurable amounts of UV radiation, fluorescent lighting poses many times the danger of the typical computer monitor. Sunlight is substantially more dangerous.

Microwave Radiation

Microwave energy—the stuff that cooks in microwave ovens and blasts radar beams over the horizon—has well-documented effects on living cells. Like a potato in the microwave oven, this energy cooks. The mechanism is well understood. The energy of the microwave signal excites water and fat molecules, transferring to them as thermal energy (heat). Food is cooked by microwaves because the heat induced in them accumulates faster than it radiates away, raising the temperature. Cell proteins break down as temperature increases. Cells die. The food is cooked.

Microwaves penetrate moderate distances through living tissue. Consequently, organs inside a body can be heated (potentially killed) by microwave beams. The thermal energy of microwaves also is known to cause cataracts.

Wavelengths longer than microwaves (those typical of VHF television, FM, and standard broadcast radio signals) also cause thermal effects by transferring energy to materials, but they are not as reactive with biological tissue. They tend to penetrate without being absorbed.

Outside of the thermal effects, microwave and other radiation in the radio spectrum (that is, higher in frequency than about 30 kilohertz) is thought not to pose other health hazards. Some studies have implicated microwaves in causing cataracts, although most of these have been at intensities that cause thermal effects. Cataracts caused by nonthermal microwaves have been reported, although the preponderance of studies have found to the contrary.

Microwave and other radio-frequency heating requires very strong signals. Microwave ovens operate at levels of hundreds of watts. Computer monitors don't even draw hundreds of watts from wall outlets. Although they may emit some microwaves, the amounts are small. In fact, the government ensures that such emissions are well below the levels associated with heating effects. All computer equipment must be certified to abide by subpart B (formerly subpart J) of part 15 of the Federal Communications Commission (FCC) rules and regulations, which sets interference standards that are well below (by orders of magnitude) the radiation levels necessary for thermal effects. Whereas health standards deal in volts per meter, the FCC interference standard limits emissions to microvolts per meter (the exact value depends on frequency).

Moreover, PCs do not directly create microwave energy. Although microwaves theoretically are created as harmonics of the signals generated inside the computer, the levels of the microwave signals are essentially unmeasurable.

A possibility exists that there are nonthermal microwave effects that may be active at lower signal levels. If these effects are real, they are believed to be a result of the low-frequency modulation of microwaves. These modulation effects would be similar to the effects of direct radiation at lower frequencies.

Low-Frequency Radiation

A number of studies have correlated the strong ELF fields associated with power lines and electrical distribution systems with increased cancer risk. Electric blankets and waterbed heaters also have been implicated. ELF fields similar to those generated by some computer equipment have demonstrated biological effects in the laboratory. These effects include changes in cell membrane permeability, altered prenatal development, and the promotion of the growth of cancerous cells.

ELF research has been of two types: laboratory studies on cell cultures and animal tissues, and epidemiological studies—research that starts with sick people and attempts to find a common link between their backgrounds.

The epidemiological studies of power distribution systems have mostly taken the form of correlating illnesses with the exposure to ELF fields. To date, the results of these studies have been mixed. The most recent studies, however, have been aimed at answering the criticisms of previous studies that found a positive correlation between the presence of ELF fields (the fields themselves were not measured) and childhood cancer. In the United States and Sweden, correlations between cancer and strong ELF fields associated with electrical distribution systems have been found, although other contradictory studies also have been published.

In the laboratory, the potential biological effects of ELF at levels below those which would cause the heating of tissue have been extensively investigated for about the last decade. The results of that research are beginning to show that far from being innocuous and noninteractive with biological tissue, ELF electrical and magnetic fields can be subtly active with both beneficial and harmful effects. On the positive side, ELF fields are used in treating bone fractures. The fields apparently promote bone growth and hasten healing. On the downside, ELF fields have demonstrated effects on calcium channel permeability of cell membranes, which can affect a variety of cell functions, including the transmission of electrical signals in nerve tissue. The fields also have been shown to affect protein synthesis and alter circadian rhythms. ELF fields also appear to promote the growth of cancerous cells. Research has further demonstrated that developing nervous systems may be particularly susceptible to ELF fields, and that these effects may be latent, showing up only in specific situations or at later times.

Of course, not all of these dire studies stand up to scrutiny. The results of some have failed attempts at replication. And, of course, since these lab studies were carried out in vitro, there is no guarantee that the effects on human beings will be identical. A consensus is, however, emerging that ELF fields can be biologically active at levels lower than were once thought possible.

One of the discoveries about ELF fields is that they do not behave like ionizing radiation. The fields are not energetic enough at the molecular level to change or destroy the chemical bonds in cells. They don't damage chromosomes. Instead, the ELF fields seem to mimic the electrical changes that normally occur in living cells in the body. By changing the calcium permeability of cells, ELF fields can change the response of a nerve cell to stimulation. This mimicking of normal cellular processes may be the root of the cancer-promoting potential of ELF. The membrane sites at which some ELF reaction occurs appears to act as receptors for cancer-promoting chemicals. ELF fields appear to increase the chemical activity of a compound, ornithine decarboxylase. This effect has been associated with cancer promotion. ELF fields also disrupt the functions of cell gap junctions, another effect associated with cancer growth.

Some studies have found ELF fields to have an odd aspect that complicates research. Chemical carcinogens and ionizing radiation are believed to behave in a linear fashion—the dangers of each increase as the exposure level increases. While some ELF effects show a similar relationship to intensity, some studies have found "window" effects—biological effects that occur only with certain field strengths (or certain frequencies) of ELF and not at higher or lower values. In addition, the window effects of ELF also appear to depend on the presence and orientation of static fields, like the Earth's magnetic field. One study on chick brain tissue showed changes in calcium ion flux with 60 Hz ELF fields with strengths of 35, 40, and 42.5 volts per meter, while fields of 25, 30, and 45 volts per meter showed no effect.

For health scientists, just the possibility of window effects is worrisome. If these effects are real (doubts persist that they are), they would preclude the development of exposure standards. The effects of ELF fields would vary with the individual experiencing them because the size and shape of one's body affects the strength of voltages and currents induced inside it by the ELF fields.

To complicate matters further, the waveform associated with ELF fields appears to affect their biological activity. Least active appear to be the sinusoidal waves that are characteristic of utility-supplied electricity. The most active appear to be pulsed fields like those generated by radar and fields with sawtooth waveforms, which are characteristically generated by the sweep circuitry in televisions and monitors.

Because of the potential harm that may be caused by these emissions, most monitor manufacturers now offer products that conform with the Swedish safety standards MPR and TCO. Monitors that meet these standards have essentially no measurable emissions—the standards themselves represent the limits of measurement.

If you have an older monitor that does not conform to these standards and you believe that ELF fields are dangerous, you can take steps to minimize your exposure to them. Sit in front of your computer where the ELF fields are the weakest. Avoid sitting near the sides of nearby computer monitors, particularly the left side. Because both the magnetic and electric ELF fields generated by computer equipment fall off quickly with increased distance, you can minimize your exposure by working as far from your computer and its display as is consistent with good ergonomics. In other words, don't back off so far that you have to squint or strain to reach what you need to get at.

Monitors emit more ELF than do computer systems, and this radiation appears to be related to the scanning signals used by their CRTs. You can avoid the fields associated with scanning signals (which may be more dangerous than the more pervasive sinusoidal waveforms) by using a display based on an alternative technology, such as an LCD display.

It's unlikely that your computer monitor will kill you. Even if the worst of the effects attributed to ELF prove true, you will likely face greater risks to your health from other forms of pollution, such as the cigarette smoke you inhale (either your own or that of coworkers), the cholesterol in your bloodstream, and the peanut butter you spread on your noontime sandwich.

Pregnancy

Those nefarious types who use scare tactics that capitalize on the fears of expectant families to sell computer-safety equipment usually cite one particular study that linked VDT usage with miscarriages. Rarely do they go into detail about the study they use to support their dire warnings. The study, reported in 1988 in the *American Journal of Industrial Medicine*, was conducted among 1,583 women who used obstetricians and gynecological clinics affiliated with the Kaiser Permanent Medical Care Program in the San Francisco Bay area. The study's goal was to determine the effect of the insecticide Malathion on early pregnancy. The scientists conducting the study were very thorough and presented participants with a lengthy questionnaire. After crunching the statistics to find correlations, only one result popped out. A higher rate of miscarriage was correlated with women who used VDTs more than 20 hours per week. The researchers noted that the VDTs were not the cause of the miscarriages but attributed it to "an occupational effect not related to VDTs" such as stress or working conditions. Recent studies tend to reinforce this conclusion, including a tightly controlled 1989 report published in the *International Journal of Epidemiology*.

Another worrisome development that some health mongers cite is the appearance of clusters of miscarriages among VDT workers. Among workers in the Dallas computer center of a large retailer, 8 out of 12 pregnancies in which conception occurred between May 1979 and June 1980 resulted in spontaneous abortion or neonatal death. To anyone in the group, these occurrences would seem dire. The National Centers for Disease Control investigated, however, and determined that the problem was not related to proximity to VDTs or the time spent working on them.

In perspective, these clusters don't even rise to the status of statistical aberrations. Remember, there are thousands, if not hundreds of thousands of similar groups that work on PCs. A gaussian distribution of miscarriages among groups would imply that a few groups would have an abnormally high number of miscarriages and a few abnormally low. No one notices the low end because (nearly) everyone expects to have a problem-free pregnancy and a perfect child. Moreover, another factor could be at work—such as a boss with a bullwhip who has elevated workplace stress to an art form.

The conclusion is not that you have nothing to worry about if you are pregnant and working on a PC. Some sources indicate that up to 20 percent of all pregnancies end in miscarriage, PC present or not. Your job that involves working on a PC may cause stress that can lead to health and pregnancy problems. If you have suitable working conditions and you take care of yourself, however, you can rest easy knowing that you will not be causing your child-to-be any hardship.

Appendix C

Serial Communications Troubleshooting

Because of all the variations in serial port connection and operation, you're apt to run into a configuration that doesn't work properly. The results of a serial mismatch range from slow or no data flow to strange characters appearing in text to serial data simply disappearing into the ether.

Sorting out such difficulties causes serial port experts to turn to their best friend—the break-out box. This glorified double serial connector plugs into your PC's serial port, and your serial cable plugs into it. Then lights on the break-out box indicate which signals are active on the serial port. Jumpers in the break-out box let you play the equivalent of musical chairs with the serial wiring until you get a combination that lights the right lights and starts the connection properly cooing.

But you don't need a break-out box to do basic troubleshooting. If you carefully observe the symptoms and think about how serial ports work—and what can go wrong—you often can get a recalcitrant serial connection talking. What follows is a troubleshooting guide set up as the questions you should ask yourself as you work your way through your serial problems.

Does the Port Hardware Work?

All too often we blame problems on the wrong party. What may seem to be a serial port problem could be a device disaster or cabling catastrophe. The first step in diagnosing any serial communication problem is to zero in on the area of trouble.

The chore is made easier if you already have one serial circuit that works properly. You can switch ports and see whether the problem stays with the device you are trying to use or moves with the port assignment. Check for this by moving the connection of a working serial device over to the reluctant port by moving the cable connector that's directly plugged into the port (not the one plugged into the serial device). If, after you alter the software to address the port being used, the serial device that you have moved works with the otherwise unwilling port, odds are that your serial port is working just fine, but you have a problem with the cabling or device attached to it.

Another preliminary check to make is whether the serial device you want to use is designed to operate as a DCE or DTE device. The cable you use depends on the device type. When connected to an IBM-compatible computer, a DCE device should work with a straight-through cable. A DTE device connected to a PC or PS/2 requires a special cable of some kind. If the cable and device type don't match, no data can flow. If the lack of alignment of sending and receiving signals doesn't let it get lost, the lack of handshaking prevents either device from transmitting so much as a bit.

Can You Get Anything To Work?

When you don't have the luxury of having a serial port and accessory that have been proven to work, you'll need to resort to more exhaustive and exhausting testing. You can check the port by trying a known-to-be-functional serial device with it.

The best piece of test equipment is probably a Hayes-compatible modem and a straight-through (not cross-over) connecting cable that you know is good. Plug the modem into the port and see whether it works. If it does, you've narrowed down the problem areas to the other serial device and its cabling. If the modem doesn't work, perhaps because it was the device you were originally trying to connect to the recalcitrant circuitry, you need to dig deeper.

If you don't have a serial device that you know is good or the one that you have fails to work, the next step is to examine in what manner the port has failed. Actually, you've already done this in discovering that the port doesn't work. But instead of throwing up your hands in disgust, note how the failure occurred and the condition the failure left your system.

The most common problem encountered with serial ports is that they don't work. Trying to send data to a serial port results in nothing happening and perhaps the loss of the control of your computer, with rebooting the only medicine that can bring it back to life.

The most basic problem is that you may not have a serial port even though you think you do. You've plugged in what you think is a serial card, and it isn't. Or it is a serial card, but it doesn't work.

The first step is to make certain that your system recognizes the serial port. You can do so by checking the port assignments in memory using the DOS diagnostic Debug. The Dump command (simply the letter D) in Debug displays on the screen data that is stored in memory. The particular locations of interest are those beginning at absolute address 400(hex). In PCs, XTs, and ATs, the first four bytes at 400(hex) store the port assignments of the two serial ports that these computers support. PS/2 and most modern computers use the first eight bytes to store the four port assignments that the PS/2 supports. As with most PC-based data, these port assignments are stored by the least significant byte first.

To display the serial port assignments of your system, run Debug, then at the hyphen prompt enter the following command:

```
-d 40:0
```

(which means to dump to the display the 128 bytes starting at absolute memory location 400[hex]).

For instance, if your system has one serial port, you should get a display such as this:

```
.OR80
-d 40:0

0040:0000 F8 03 00 00 00 00 00 00-78 03 00 00 00 00 00 00   ........x.......
0040:0010 63 42 F0 C0 02 00 00 80-00 00 2A 00 2A 00 20 39   cB........*.*. 9
0040:0020 34 05 30 0B 3A 27 30 0B-0D 1C 09 0F 0B 25 66 21   4.0.:'0......%f!
0040:0030 64 20 65 12 62 30 75 16-67 22 0D 1C 64 20 01 80   d e.b0u.g"..d ..
0040:0040 4E 00 00 00 00 00 00 09-02 03 50 00 00 10 00 00   N.........P.....
0040:0050 00 18 00 00 00 00 00 00-00 00 00 00 00 00 00 00   ................
0040:0060 07 06 00 D4 03 29 30 98-00 B3 09 04 F3 5F 0B 00   .....)0......_..
0040:0070 00 00 00 00 00 01 00 00-14 14 14 14 01 01 01 01   ................

.OR60
```

The first two bytes indicate that this system has a single serial port assigned at port number 03F8(hex), exactly where it belongs.

Is There a Port Resource Conflict?

If you do have the luxury of more than one port but you also have the pain that none of them work or that they don't work in pairs, the problem could be a conflict in their port assignments. You may have two ports that are both trying to be COM1, for instance. With two different pieces of hardware responding to each of your computer's commands, neither you nor your software has any idea which of the pair is responding when. Your system may behave intermittently or not at all.

You can easily walk into the dual port trap when your system comes equipped with a standard equipment serial output built into its system board, and you add an internal modem, multifunction board, or some mouse adapters. Because neither the computer nor the add-in product has made you specifically tangle with a serial port, you can easily forget about one of them. If it happens (as it usually does) that serial systems have chosen the same port assignment, confusion reigns until you sort it out.

The first step in analyzing any serial problem is counting the number of ports in your system. Add-in serial boards, multifunction products with built-in ports, internal modems, standard-equipment system board serial ports, and mouse adapter boards that use a serial connection all count.

If you count more than two and have a PC, XT, or AT, you'll need to do some thinking. If one of them is an internal modem, odds are you can assign it as "COM3," which is the proper thing to do. Many communication packages—presumably including the one that may have been included with the internal modem—recognize this COM3 as a legitimate port assignment. DOS versions before 5.0 and your PC may not recognize this port, so you won't be able to use the DOS Mode command to make it accessible as a printer port. Because you're unlikely to manipulate your modem directly through DOS, you probably won't miss it.

Similarly, the driver software that accompanies the mouse-and-adapter board combination should allow you to assign the mouse interface to a series of ports that won't collide with your regular serial communications.

Are Interrupts Properly Assigned?

Some serial boards force you to assign serial ports and the interrupts that service them separately, perhaps through moving separate jumpers. If you receive the board with the port assignment for COM1 but its interrupt is set for COM2, the serial port may work intermittently or not at all.

Other peripherals also may attempt to use one of the interrupts that should be assigned to your serial port. For instance, a tape backup system or a bus mouse that purports not to use a serial port may try to steal interrupt three from your COM2 serial port.

One prime symptom of this condition is sporadic operation of the port. Sometimes it works and sometimes it doesn't, depending on what other accessories you're using. Of course, another device may totally preempt the serial port and prevent its operation at all.

The obvious solution to this sort of problem is to ensure that every port has its own interrupt and reassign those that are in conflict—if you can. The PC and XT are notoriously short of hardware interrupts to assign to peripherals.

Remember, COM1 and COM3, and COM2 and COM4 share interrupts (see Chapter 19), and devices using the shared interrupt may collide and crash your system.

Do You Have Handshaking?

If your serial port suffers no interrupt or address port conflicts and otherwise seems operable but fails to work with a specific serial device, the likely cause is a lack of handshaking. This problem is most likely when your serial port failure does not totally lock up your system but instead allows you to abort whatever you were trying to do with the serial port, perhaps by pressing Ctrl-Break or Ctrl-C. The likely cause is that the handshake wiring of this serial circuit is not arranged properly.

Remember, unless you have software that specifically nullifies the need, every PC, XT, AT, or PS/2 requires that its handshaking demands be met before a byte leaves any serial port. In addition, mismatching DCE and DTE devices and their cables invariably guarantees a failure of handshaking.

You can verify handshaking in two ways—testing and the empirical approach.

Testing requires a Volt-Ohm Meter (or VOM) or a digital logic probe. Simply dig into the connector attached to the serial port in question and measure the voltages or logic states at the DSR, CTS, and CD pins. If handshaking signals are present, you should measure a positive voltage, usually in excess of five volts, when you touch each of the three pins. The indicator of the logic probe should glow when touched to these pins.

Empirically, you can connect the DSR, CTS, and CD pins directly to the DTR to ensure that handshaking is present at least at the PC-end of the circuit. You can either solder the necessary wires in place (a messy solution, but one that works) or invest in a break-out box that allows you to experiment. If after making this adjustment your PC acts differently, as if it has sent at least some characters to the serial device, you experienced a handshaking problem. (If your PC acts like it has sent out data and if the serial device—such as a printer—acts as if it has received nothing, odds are your TXD and RXD lines need to be crossed, and what you thought was a DCE was a DTE device.)

Are Characters Disappearing?

If your serial device seems to work OK but loses characters from whatever is sent to it, the likely cause is a flow control problem. Typically, a serial printer rattles out characters that appear just fine until you try to read them. Characters, words, sentences, and whole paragraphs may disappear. Lines may ignore margin settings because carriage-return and line-feed characters get lost on their way from computer to printer, too.

The problem is caused by handshaking working too well. Instead of the handshake signal being interrupted when the receiving device has no buffer room to work with incoming characters, the handshake signals are locked on. To your computer, your printer always looks as if it wants more, more, more, even though it is choking on what it has already received.

Check the connection used for flow control—it may be CTS or something totally unrelated (such as DEC and NEC's pin 19)—and ensure that it is connected to DSR or CTS on your PC. In addition, verify that both devices in your serial system are using the same flow control protocol. If your computer is dumping characters under hardware control, your printer may be desperately sending XOFF after XOFF, trying to stave off the flow. If protocols don't match, you'll likely lose characters.

Are Print Jobs Truncated?

If your serial print jobs finish before you think they should, for instance before the last page is printed, or if your serial print jobs suddenly stop with an error message like `Device Timeout Error`, the cause is that you forgot to add the P parameter to the end of the Mode command you used to set up your computer's serial port parameters. The printer does not respond fast enough to satisfy your computer, so it thinks something is wrong.

Do You Get Gibberish?

If your serial system gives every indication of working except all that it produces is gibberish, you probably have not properly matched serial port parameters at the two ends of the connection. Your computer is sending characters at one bit rate, and the serial device is expecting to receive them at another. Similarly, you may have your computer set for odd parity when the other end of the connection is expecting even. The two devices are not speaking the same language, so it's natural that they would get confused. The solution to the problem is simply to match the communications parameters at both ends of the connection.

Appendix D

Ancient History

 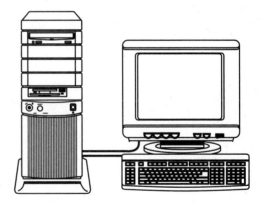

No other field in history has changed as fast as personal computing. What once was technology's greatest invention is relegated to the top shelf in a forgotten closet a few years later. After a decade, much equipment can be forgotten without regret—unless, of course, you're one of those who has made an investment in it and has faithfully nursed it along. Even the most ancient PC can serve a vital purpose, be it simply capturing characters as a word processor, managing your modem while your main PC does other things, or taking messages while you are out.

In the first edition of this book, the original IBM Personal Computer family was covered in depth because a good percentage of people with PCs used those wearing the IBM label. Through the years, this percentage has fallen, and even those original PCs have fallen by the wayside. But these ancient machines haven't been forgotten. They can still do useful work, be it helping with homework or answering the phone. This appendix covers topics once part of the PC mainstream but now relevant only to those harboring vintage equipment.

PC BIOS Upgrades

The watershed difference between the first IBM PC, the machine with a maximum memory capacity of 64K on its system board, and the PC2, which has a system board with 256K capacity, is the BIOS. The original IBM PC BIOS was written before such things as hard disks were to become an expected part of a personal computer system. No provisions were made in the BIOS for automatically adding extra code to it. It was nonextensible.

The PC2 BIOS (and that of the XT, released at the same time, as well as all later IBM and compatible computers) solved the problem by adding special code to the BIOS routines which makes the machine, as the last step of the boot-up process, look for extra pieces of BIOS code.

The line of demarcation between the two versions of the PC BIOS is October 27, 1982. A BIOS dated earlier is not extensible. If you want to add a VGA board, a hard disk that can boot the system, or any of the numerous options available today that require an extensible BIOS, you'll need to replace the chips in these older PCs. While IBM at one time offered BIOS upgrades for these machines, the chips have been discontinued and are no longer available from IBM. Third-party BIOS vendors may offer upgrade chips for these machines, but third-party BIOSs can convert such a PC into a PC-compatible that will not be able to run IBM Advanced BASIC.

Considering the value of these machines is now about the same or less than a BIOS upgrade, you may want to consider keeping such a PC as a collector's item and not worry about BIOS issues.

Power Issues in Early PCs

In 1981, the Personal Computer was one of the best examples of the miniaturization possible with microelectronics. What were room-size computers fit on desktops. This miniaturization has continued at a rapid pace. Not only have PCs and peripherals become smaller, they have become more fuel efficient. That is, they use less power (which, in turn, lets them be made even smaller).

The energy budget of a laptop computer can be as little as five watts, less than half what it takes to spin a single floppy disk drive in the original PC.

With today's typical power supply averaging about 200 watts, power is not an issue in a desktop computer. But this profusion of power was not always the rule. The first IBM PC was sorely ill equipped to supply electricity to its peripherals.

PC Power Inadequacies

Although it's hard to peg exactly how much power any particular computer might require, one generalization can be made reliably—the 63.5 watts of the original PC-series is clearly inadequate for a contemporary personal computer. A workable rule of thumb is that a 63.5-watt PC has enough expansion power for running two of the three following internal peripherals: a multi-function card, a PC-vintage internal modem, and a hard disk card. Any additional expansion cards (not counting the floppy disk controller) further reduce the chances of successfully operating a hard disk card. However, if you're careful about the products you choose, you may be able to squeak by with all three. For instance, select a low-power consumption hard disk card (the now discontinued 5-watt, 10-megabyte Western Digital FileCard or an 8-watt Plus Development HardCard) and a modern day single-chip modem, and you can stock all the memory a PC can handle—640K.

The best strategy is not to try to sneak by because insufficient power inevitably results in the system crashing—irrevocably locking up—either when you first turn it on or unexpectedly any time thereafter. The crash wipes out all your current work, and, should it happen at a particularly inauspicious time, it may scramble the file allocation table of the hard disk and make all the data you have stored inaccessible and unusable.

The best way to avoid such problems is to ensure your system has an adequate power supply. If you have a 63.5-watt PC, you should replace the power supply with one that has more oomph, or you can opt for an external disk with its own source of power.

The 135-watt power supply of the XT and the larger power supplies of later IBM computers should handle most hard disks. Most compatible computers are rated at greater than 130 watts because the power deficiencies of the PC became known early, while compatible designs were still on the drawing board. A few ancient compatibles came equipped with 100-watt supplies, however, and these may not be able to power older, faster hard disks.

Zenith Power Supply Problems

Most modern PCs have no problem continuing to operate during the short transfer times occurring when a standby power system shifts to battery power during an outage. However, one model of IBM XT is known to have difficulties continuing to run during even the quickest transfers. The machines in question are IBM XTs equipped with a power supply made in Mexico by Zenith Electronics. These are early XTs, made between the introduction of the XT in 1982 and 1985. Although most personal computers operate unflinchingly through power failure or switching time 20-40 milliseconds long, these Zenith-equipped XTs may shut down (losing all data in memory) during power outages as short as a few milliseconds.

The underlying problem is the Power-Good connection. The actual DC output from all PC power supplies (including the Zenith) continues for about 30-45 milliseconds after utility-supplied electricity fails because of the filtering circuitry inside the power supply. With all PCs other than Zenith-equipped XTs, the Power-Good line remains valid for 10-15 milliseconds after line voltage fails, so shorter interruptions won't affect the computer. The Power-Good line in Zenith power supplies almost immediately becomes invalid. As a result, the computer quickly shuts down even though power still may be available inside the power supply.

Because of this inordinate sensitivity, most standby power systems cannot protect a Zenith-equipped XT. If you have such a computer, you have three options in ensuring blackout protection—buying an uninterruptible power system instead of a standby power system (which is very costly); buying one of the few standby supplies that switch fast enough for the XT (which involves carefully checking the specification and believing what the manufacturer lists there); or installing a new power supply into the XT without the Power-Good problem. This last option is the least expensive and often the easiest.

According to American Power Conversion Corporation, which makes a special standby power supply model to handle the needs of more temperamental XTs, Zenith power supplies can be identified in two ways. By looking slightly upward through the ventilation slots in the rear of the computer, a small white sticker that says "Made in Mexico" can be seen in the Zenith supplies. In addition, the receptacle for the power line cord on Zenith power supplies is held in place by black rivets. On Astec power supplies, silver or green rivets are used.

Locating Defective Memory Chips

All current PCs now use memory modules, which makes finding defective memory a trivial, trial-and-error task that takes a few minutes. Older PCs, however, used discrete chips, often as many as 36 of them, which were much more delicate and time-consuming to remove and insert. Trial-and-error replacement of individual chips is impractical. Fortunately, the built-in diagnostics of most PCs allow you to zero in on a bad chip. All you need to do is write down the error code display on the screen so that you can decipher which chip is bad.

With PC/2s and XTs, the left digit of the error code, should it be from 0 to 3, indicates which system board bank contains the bad chip. Banks are numbered starting with bank zero, which is the rearmost of the four on the system board (see fig. D.1).

PC1s require examination of the left two digits. 00 indicates a failure in the first bank (the rearmost), 04 the second bank, 08 the third bank, and 0C the bank nearest the front panel of the machine (see fig. D.2).

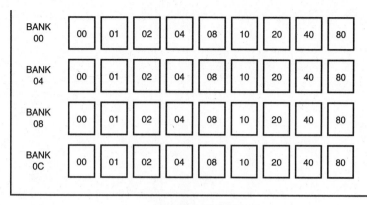

FRONT OF CHASSIS

Figure D.1. Bank designations on PC/2s and XTs.

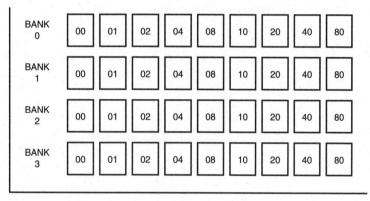

FRONT OF CHASSIS

Figure D.2. Bank designations on PC1s.

In ATs, take the left two digits of the error code. A number from 00 to 03 indicates the failure was in system board bank zero; from 04 to 07 indicates an error in bank one. Each bank comprises two rows of nine chips, starting with bank zero at the front of the machine. In ATs, the lower numbered chips also are toward the front of the machine (see fig. D.3).

Expansion boards in either kind of system complicate matters, but a little math helps sort things out. In any style system, the first two digits indicate the bad bank by its memory address. You must convert these hexadecimal numbers into a memory address and then multiply by an appropriate factor. The bad bank begins with the address corresponding to that number of kilobytes. For eight-bit PCs, the multiplication factor is four; for 16-bit machines, the factor is 64.

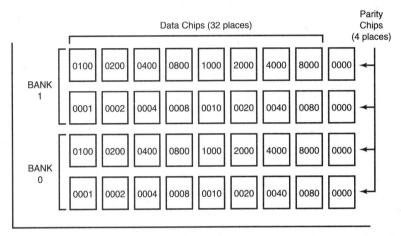

Figure D.3. Chip designation in ATs.

For example, to determine the bad bank in an XT that produced the error code beginning with the digits 18, first convert the hexadecimal 18 into decimal (16+8=24) and then multiply by 4. The result is 64K, indicating that the error is in the second bank (which starts at 64K because each bank contains 64K).

In eight-bit PCs, the last two digits code the bad chip or chips. To find it, convert the last two digits displayed by the error code from hexadecimal into binary notation. The location of the 1s in the resulting number indicates the position of the bad chip. The complication is that you start counting from right to left on the system board.

Another complication: converting two digits of hexadecimal into binary results in eight digits. There are nine chips in a bank. The first chip (the one on the left) on eight-bit system boards is the parity check chip. It's not included in the position-indicating error code. If the parity check chip is bad, the last two digits of the error code are 0s.

For instance, if you get an error code of 0420, convert the last two digits (20) into the binary equivalent (00100000), so you count three chips over from the right to find the bad chip.

If after you make the hexadecimal to binary conversion, you get more than a single 1 in the resulting binary code, both indicated chips should be replaced.

In 16-bit PCs, the last four digits represent the chip code. Convert these from hexadecimal to binary, and you have a display of two eight-bit rows of chips with the bad one indicated by the 1 or 1s that appear in the number.

On AT system boards, the map is backward just as for PC and XTs. In addition, of the two eight-digit binary pairs you get from converting the four hexadecimal digits, the last indicates the chip row toward the front of the computer. However, the chips on the far right (rather than the left) are the parity chips and are skipped in the counting.

The two parity check chips in each bank are not distinguished from one another in this scheme. If the last four hexadecimal digits of the AT error code come up all 0s, either parity chip in that bank could be bad. You'll need to replace them both.

For Micro Channel PS/2s, the pragmatic approach can be much quicker than tangling with math. With the Model 50 in which you have two memory modules and you know you need to replace one, why not just pop in the replacement? If it fixes the problem, you've avoided the brain strain. If it doesn't work, switch the module you've pulled out with the one you haven't changed, and your problem should go away. The Model 60 and others with four system board banks slightly complicate things with four modules.

Cassette Data Storage

The first PC made a floppy disk drive (and a single-sided, 160K unit at that) entirely optional. Without one, the only mass storage available to the PC was a cassette drive.

The software required for using a cassette system is built into the ROM BIOS that is part of every PC. Cassettes could be used without DOS or any other program. Turn on an original PC without a DOS disk in its floppy drive, and the system boots up in BASIC, ready to read and write to cassette.

The only things you need to add are the cassette deck and a connecting cable, neither of which is available from IBM.

The cassette deck is the easy part. Almost any remote-controllable cassette drive works. Battery-powered portables are most easily adapted.

The only remote-control facility required is a motor on/off switch. Most portable cassette decks provide this facility as a small jack on the machine, usually appropriately labeled as "Remote." The cheap external microphones most often used with these units often include a switch that closes these contacts to allow you to control the cassette recorder from the microphone. The PC duplicates the function of this switch, turning on the cassette drive motor as it is needed to copy files to tape.

Note that the computer has only this on/off power. It cannot change the operating mode of the cassette. Before you give the computer control, you must press the Play button on the recorder and set the tape to the spot at which you want to begin.

The cassette recorder also requires a signal connection with your PC—actually, two of them: one for the output from the computer to be recorded and one from the recorder to the computer so that tapes can be read back. The recorder-to-PC connection plugs into the recorder's headphone jack. The PC-to-recorder signal often gives you a choice of two connections—the Mic or microphone input (nominally 75 millivolts) or a line-level input (nominally 680 millivolts). The difference between these two is critical. A line-level signal can overload a microphone input causing distortion and errors in the data stream. A microphone connected to a line input is not powerful enough to affect a good recording.

IBM allowed for both types of cassette inputs. A jumper on the system board selects the output level of the signal bound for the cassette recorder through the jack on the rear panel of the PC. You only need to adjust this jumper to reflect the sort of cassette input you want to use. For microphone inputs, use the "M" position (for Microphone), which bridges the two jumper pins on the left. For high-level inputs, use the "A" position (for Auxiliary) by moving the jumper to the pair of pins on the right (see fig. D.4). If one setting doesn't work, try the other.

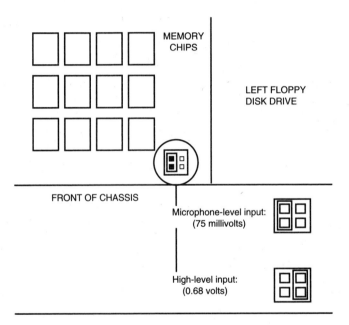

Figure D.4. PC cassette jumper positions.

The required cable is available from Radio Shack. It's the same as those used by the Tandy Model 100-200 line and a number of other Tandy computers. Or you can make your own cable, as shown in figure D.5. Data from the computer to the cassette recorder travels on Pin 4; from the cassette to the computer, it uses Pin 5. Pins 1 and 3 provide a normally open relay circuit to control the cassette motor—the relay closes to complete the circuit and to run the cassette motor. This contact is rated at 1 amp, 6 volts, and Pin 3 is considered the switched contact. Pin 2 is grounded.

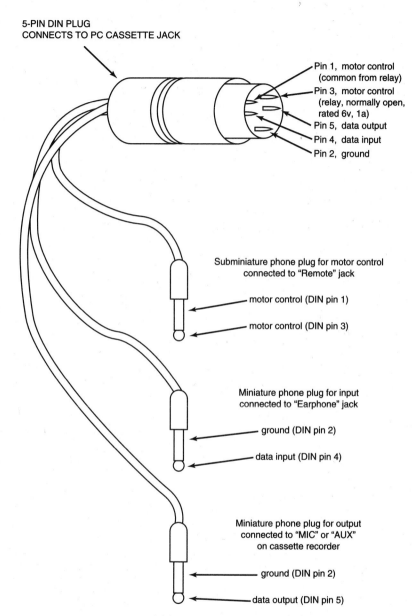

5-PIN DIN PLUG CONNECTS TO PC CASSETTE JACK

Pin 1, motor control (common from relay)

Pin 3, motor control (relay, normally open, rated 6v, 1a)

Pin 5, data output

Pin 4, data input

Pin 2, ground

Subminiature phone plug for motor control connected to "Remote" jack

motor control (DIN pin 1)

motor control (DIN pin 3)

Miniature phone plug for input connected to "Earphone" jack

ground (DIN pin 2)

data input (DIN pin 4)

Miniature phone plug for output connected to "MIC" or "AUX" on cassette recorder

ground (DIN pin 2)

data output (DIN pin 5)

Figure D.5. A PC-to-cassette cable.

Display Adapter Setup

Today's VGA systems make any sort of adjustment to your PC's motherboard unnecessary. For example, the VGA system allows your PC to detect whether a color or monochrome monitor is attached. In the original IBM video design, however, no feedback of this sort was provided from display to the host computer. Many programs needed to know what kind of display and adapter were connected to the system, if just to know the correct block of memory to which to write display information.

PC and XT Switch Settings

To let the host computer know what sort of displays and adapters are connected to it, the original PC and XT require that you set a pair of DIP switches. The switch setting determines where the computer will send video information. Have the switches set improperly and the computer boots up with an invisible error message—you get an error because the switch settings are improper but you won't be able to see it because the computer doesn't know the correct base address for the display adapter. All you see is a cursor slowly flashing on the screen (because the cursor is generated by the display adapter independent of the rest of the computer).

The same switches also determine whether systems equipped with color displays boot up in 40-column mode or 80-column mode. Another setting is used if an EGA or VGA board is used with the computer. The settings of the PC and XT display switches are shown in figure D.6.

Primary and Secondary Displays

In the original PC and XT scheme of things, you can connect either or both an MDA or CGA adapter and matching monitor. If you connected one of each kind of adapter, the one for which the DIP switches were set would be the primary display. The boot message and most of the other images would appear on that display. You could switch between displays using the MODE utility supplied with DOS.

AT Monitor Switch

By the time IBM had introduced the AT, the DIP switches used for setting up the computer had been simplified and repackaged as the Setup program that accompanied the system. One problem remained, however. If the computer did not know what kind of display was attached, it might use the wrong memory area when attempting to run the Setup program.

To let the AT know what kind of display is connected to the system—or which of the displays is primary—IBM incorporated a single slide switch on the AT system board to select monitor type. Figure D.7 shows the proper positions of the switch for use with color and monochrome displays.

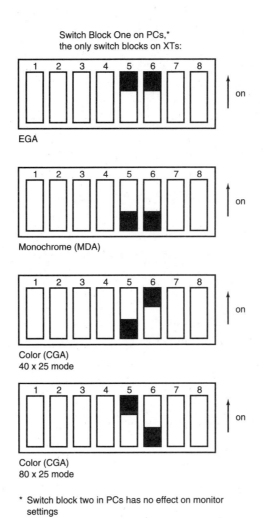

Figure D.6. PC and XT display switch settings.

EGA Switches

The BIOS of the EGA takes over the video sections of the BIOS of the PC, XT, and other computers in which the board is installed. It has the capability of operating either monochrome or color displays. Although sync polarity coding allows the EGA to handle CGA- and EGA-style displays with impunity, its switches must be set to reflect color or monochrome operation. The reason is simple—every color monitor expects display memory in the same place, but the monochome area is different.

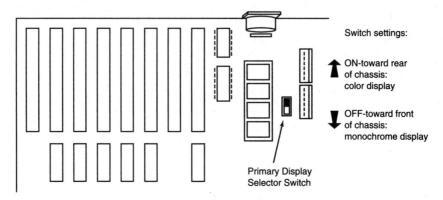

Figure D.7. Switch positions for color and monochrome monitors.

Because the EGA can be set up as either a color or monochrome display adapter, it is possible to install it in conjunction with other video adapters. When the EGA is in its color mode, it co-resides with an MDA; when the EGA is in monochrome mode, it co-resides with a CGA.

The switches on the rear, accessible through the cutout in the EGA retaining bracket, must be set properly to reflect the type of monitor to which the adapter connected and whether it is co-residing with another display adapter. Table D.1 shows the settings of these switches.

TABLE D.1. Display switch settings

EGA Operating Mode	Other Display Adapter	Sw1	Sw2	Sw3	Sw4

To use the monitor connected to the EGA adapter as the primary display:

EGA Operating Mode	Other Display Adapter	Sw1	Sw2	Sw3	Sw4
40 x 25 Color	Monochrome (MDA)	On	Off	Off	On
80 x 25 Color	Monochrome (MDA)	On	Off	Off	Off
EGA Emulation*	Monochrome (MDA)	Off	On	On	On
High Res. EGA	Monochrome (MDA)	Off	On	On	Off
Monochrome	CGA 40 x 25	Off	On	Off	On
Monochrome	CGA 80 x 25	Off	On	Off	Off

EGA Operating Mode	Other Display Adapter	Sw1	Sw2	Sw3	Sw4

To use a monitor connected to the EGA as the secondary display:

EGA Operating Mode	Other Display Adapter	Sw1	Sw2	Sw3	Sw4
40 x 25 Color	Monochrome (MDA)	On	On	On	On
80 x 25 Color	Monochrome (MDA)	On	On	On	Off
EGA Emulation*	Monochrome (MDA)	On	On	Off	On
High Res. EGA	Monochrome (MDA)	On	On	Off	Off

EGA Operating Mode	Other Display Adapter	Sw1	Sw2	Sw3	Sw4
Monochrome	CGA 40 x 25	On	Off	On	On
Monochrome	CGA 80 x 25	On	Off	On	Off

*EGA emulation mode means the EGA maps 5 x 7 (in 8 x 8 box) CGA characters to 7 x 9 (in 8 x 14 box) EGA characters.

Most third-party EGA adapters use a similar switch scheme. Those that have but four setup switches usually use exactly the same settings as the IBM EGA. Those with a greater number of DIP switches usually use a superset of the IBM settings.

VGA Setup

By the time IBM released the VGA system, DIP switches were a thing of the past. IBM's VGA adapter—and most of those that are hardware compatible with it—uses no switches. It automatically configures itself for a color or monochrome display. The host system is prepared for a VGA adapter the same as it would be for an EGA.

Note that only one VGA board can be used in a system and that it cannot co-reside with other video adapters, so settings for such operations are not needed. The 8514/A does co-reside with a VGA adapter, but provisions for cooperative operation are built into the 8514/A.

WORM (Write-Once, Read-Many)

WORM stands for Write-Once, Read-Multiple times (or Many times), and that's exactly what the system does. WORM drives give your PC the capability to write data into high-density optical storage. Like stone tablets carved for the ages, the WORM can never change. What you write becomes a permanent record, your mark for posterity. If you need to keep archives or to make an unalterable audit trial, no medium keeps you as honest as WORM.

As with other optical technologies, WORM is based on lasers and spinning disks. Inside the WORM drive a laser beam reacts with the inner medium of an optical disk and blasts dark spots on it, forever changing the disk. The pattern of light and dark spots made by the laser correspond to bits of data stored.

WORM drives store data as permanent physical changes in the disk surface that alter the disk's reflectivity. But the WORM drive can't dig pits to master disks as can a CD-ROM master recorder. The WORM media is already safely encapsulated in plastic when you receive it, so pit-blasting in the CD-ROM sense won't work. Instead of digging, WORMs work by chemically darkening or evaporating the reflective medium inside their disks.

The already encapsulated form of WORM disks has another ramification—WORM disks are not easily duplicated by stamping as are CD-ROMs. The surface of the WORM disk is always smooth, no matter what happens inside. Consequently, every WORM disk must be written individually. Each disk is either an original—or that wonderful oxymoron, an original copy. Duplicating a disk means reading the data from one and streaming it over to another—that's a transfer of hundreds of megabytes at optical rates. If there ever were a million-selling prerecorded WORM disk, you wouldn't want to be responsible for pressing the buttons to make the copies.

As a result of these issues, WORM technology fits a very limited, very specialized niche— actually, three of them: data acquisition, archival backup storage, and data retrieval systems. In data acquisition, you need a permanent record of the measurement you've made of other data. A WORM drive accommodates megabytes of information and keeps you honest by not permitting you to doctor the data later. As a backup system, WORM drives offer moderate speed, large capacity, the capability to interchange cartridges, and (again) permanence. Data retrieval systems, where megabytes are put on-line for reference, benefit from the capacity of WORM, its capability to create and store megabytes rather than just read them like CD-ROM, and (yet again) permanence.

WORM disks are no more indestructible than any computer medium you can throw in the fireplace. Compared to other forms of computer storage, however, WORM comes off well. While common phenomena like the magnetic fields of telephone bells and the aurora borealis conspire against all forms of magnetic storage, today's optical WORM disks are safe from just about everything except acetone rains. Magnets—no matter how strong—won't alter the data. Even the current corroding atmosphere can't get through the tough plastic coating of the disks.

The claimed life for WORM optical cartridges is 10 years, versus three years for magnetic media. Barring cataclysm, the data on WORM cartridges can endure longer than the expected life of the host computer.

Standards

Because WORM is a specialized, niche technology, the range of available products is small. But a small range doesn't mean a lack of variety, particularly when it comes to standardization.

Although more than a dozen companies manufacture WORM drives, two firms dominate the industry—Literal (formerly Information Storage, Inc.) and Panasonic. Most of the available WORM products follow one of three standards, two of which are defined by standard-setting organizations, one of which is proprietary.

Both the International Standards Organization (ISO) and the American National Standards Institute (ANSI) have created specifications outlining WORM storage systems. The two systems are physically incompatible. A cartridge for a drive that follows one standard won't work in a drive designed to match the other. The differences aren't little, easily resolvable things like sector size or the color of the cartridges. The standards vary by such indisputable differences as the size of the cartridge, the capacity of the cartridge, and the data storage format on the cartridge.

Although most WORM cartridges use disks measuring about 5.25 inches in diameter, the protective shell wrapped around these disks varies in thickness and mechanical accoutrements, rendering different manufacturers' products noninterchangeable. You can't even slide a cartridge meant for one drive into a drive made under another WORM standard.

The digital contents of the cartridges also vary. The ISO standard allows for a total cartridge capacity of about 650 megabytes. Manufacturers such as Pioneer, Laser Magnetic Storage, and Hitachi make drives that conform to ISO specifications.

The ANSI standard allows for capacities of about double that sanctioned by the ISO, 1.2 gigabytes per disk. ISO cartridges are somewhat thicker than ANSI cartridges. Literal makes drives that conform to the ANSI standard. Literal also makes another half-breed product; it's a thick shell like that of the ISO standard but the 5.25-inch disk inside stores as much data as an ANSI disk—1.2 gigabytes.

Panasonic follows the beat of its own drummer and is able to fit about 940 megabytes into its proprietary cartridge. Contrary to what you may expect, the Panasonic proprietary standard yields the lowest cost per megabyte of WORM systems.

Besides the 5.25-inch WORM drives most often used by personal computers, larger systems also are available for applications that are even more specialized. Among the most popular of these are 12-inch disks that provide the basis for immense digital libraries and information retrieval systems. A single 12-inch cartridge can hold six gigabytes—3.2 per side. Those prodigious amounts are multiplied by jukeboxes, WORM cartridge changers that automatically select and load cartridges when the data stored on them is required. The leading manufacturer of 12-inch WORM systems is Sony.

Media

In general, the various cartridges used by personal computer WORM standards consist of a thin metalized film medium encapsulated in a clear polycarbonate plastic disk. The actual disk is further protected by a high-impact plastic shell with a sliding metal door that allows access for the optical read/write head of the drive.

WORM disks are sold with the optical equivalent of a low-level format already in place. Some of the first WORM drives formatted their cartridges with grooves that the laser beam tracked to write and read information. This style of formatting has been superseded in nearly all existing drives by flat disks on which servo information is blasted onto (and through) the disk with a laser during manufacture.

As with floppy disks, WORM disks can be either single-sided or double-sided. But unlike magnetic media, however, WORM cartridges must be physically flipped over to access the second side, exactly as you would do with an old-fashioned vinyl phonograph record.

Drives

The one-way data flow means that WORM drives are necessarily more expensive than playback-only systems (like CD-ROM) because they need recording circuitry. The lasers in WORM drives require higher power to do their recording, as well. Moreover, the smaller market for WORM technology means that the drives don't benefit so handsomely from the economies of scale. In fact, WORM drives often cost 10 times as much as CD-ROM players.

WORM drives are not a degraded form of rewritable optical technology. The two systems use quite different technologies. Although both systems are based on laser beams, their operating principles are quite unalike. Most rewritable disks rely on a special optically bi-stable medium that can be shifted between two states of reflectivity (which may differ only by a few percent) under the joint influence of the laser and a magnetic field. Hence, they are magneto-optical systems. The WORM drive uses a laser to ablate a hole in a thin metal film (actually, the laser only pokes a tiny hole in the medium; surface tension enlarges it to its final form).

WORM drives themselves conform to the 5.25-inch form factor used by older hard disks (except, of course, those that use 12-inch and other size cartridges!). Nearly all available WORM drives require a full-height drive bay, although a half-height model is available from Ricoh. While at one time all WORM drives used proprietary interfaces, the SCSI connection is now dominant in the field. Nearly any WORM drive that you can buy today will have a SCSI interface.

With the development of rewritable optical disks, many people consider WORM technology to be an orphan, or worse, a retiree—still around after all these years but with no purpose left in life. Actually, orphan is closer to the truth. Unlike other products that disappear in the dust riled up by onrushing technology, WORM drives have hung on, always on the periphery of the consciousness of the computer industry, just like orphans and other social problems that always lurk in the background. Like orphans, WORM drives hold great promise, at least if you take your time to investigate their potentials.

WORM drives are orphans, too, because they have no close kin—cousins, maybe, but no real brothers and sisters, no parents (of course), and likely no offspring. If you have an application that requires large capacities and unalterable permanence, WORM may be your only choice—now and for a long time.

Index

B